Footprint

South American Handbook 2004

Ben Box

South America is a place I love, and I think, if you take it right through from Darién to Fuego, it's the grandest, richest most wonderful bit of earth upon this planet.

Sir Arthur Conan Doyle, *The Lost World*

80th edition

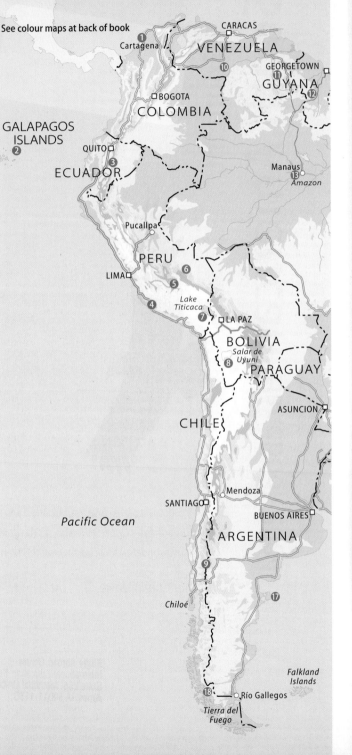

South American Highlights

See colour maps at back of book

1 Cartagena
Beautiful colonial city, with a dark history and sparkling beaches

2 The Galápagos Islands
The greatest wildlife show on earth

3 Cotopaxi
Herds of wild horses and llamas beneath a perfect, snow-capped volcano

4 The Nasca Lines
Giant whales, spiders and hummingbirds, mysteriously etched in the desert

5 Machu Picchu and the Sacred Valley of the Incas
South America's top archaeological attraction, with the gringo capital, Cusco, close by

6 Manu National Park
Home to giant otters and jaguars

7 Lake Titicaca
The world's highest navigable lake, with reed boats, island communities and incomparable light

8 Salar de Uyuni
Blinding white salt flats, red and green lakes, flamingos and volcanoes

9 The Lake District
Beautiful sheets of water overlooked by forests and volcanoes for climbing and skiing

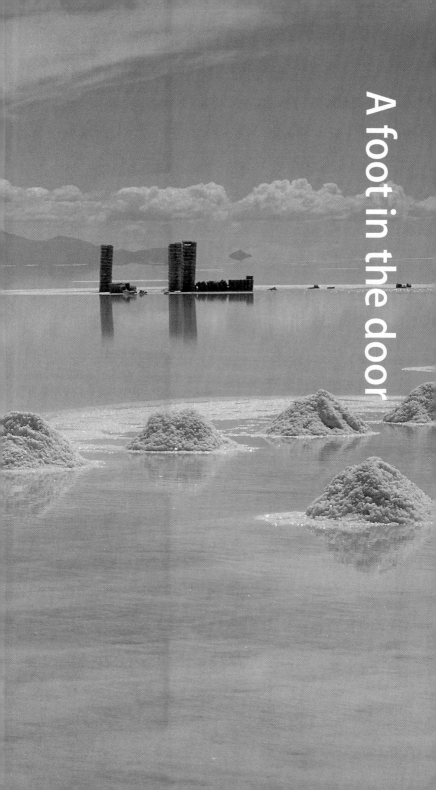

A foot in the door

La Vida Boca (right) You can have any colour you choose, as long as it's not the same as the neighbours', in La Boca, Buenos Aires
The big waters (below) Iguazú Falls on the Argentina/Brazil border are the mightiest on the continent
Worth its salt (previous pages) Land and sky are one on the Salar de Uyuni, Bolivia, the largest salt flat in the world

Do the strand (above) Revellers taking part in Bahia beach carnival, Salvador, Brazil
Serene moments (right) Fishing boats at anchor before the next foray into the Pacific, La Serena, Chile.

Introducing South America

In 1924, when this Handbook began chronicling the ways of South America, the voyage out was by sea. You can still sail down to Rio or Valparaíso, but today it's more usual to take a jet and travel advice has moved on from shipboard etiquette to which cliffs have the best hang-gliding.

If your system is jaded, South America will uplift your senses with the tropical sun rising over a rainforest river, the bracing wind blowing off the southern ice fields, the smell of ripe guava in the countryside, the fire of chili from that innocent-looking bottle on the table. Frigate birds soar over Caribbean beaches, while penguins congregate in the lee of glaciers. Condors patrol the thermals over vast Andean canyons, while tiny tamarins skitter through the remnants of coastal forests in Brazil. And in between are plateaux, wetlands and the Amazon Basin, the earth's greatest jungle, where the immensity of the trees and the tiny details of the wildlife are truly amazing.

South American societies embrace the indigenous and the multicultural. One day you can be in a village where time moves without the complications of schedules or internet, the next you're in an air-conditioned mall surrounded by all the top designer labels, or out on the town, partying till the small hours. We cannot do without the medicines derived from rainforest plants, nor many of the continent's commodities. The rhythms of its music fill our sound systems; its artists influence our fashions. Even the top footballers are exported to the European leagues.

There are all the adventure sports you can imagine, from high altitude to the depths of the sea. If pumping adrenaline is not your thing, there is ample scope for volunteering. Or enter the spirit world with a shaman, explore the past, from the great prehispanic civilizations, through colonial times to now, or investigate the gastronomy, from the humble potato in its umpteen varieties to the most sophisticated of wines. After 80 Handbook years, the essential message remains unchanged: despite having two of the world's great oceans to east and west, South America knows no boundaries.

South American beauty

The Andes   Running the length of the western side of the continent is the Andean mountain chain. Avenues of volcanoes stride across the Equator and, in southern Peru, look down upon canyons deeper than any others on earth. Bleak high altitude plains, some blinding white with salt, gleam under a crystal-clear sky. This is a landscape of geysers and strata of rocks in colours you never knew existed in stone. Condors soar in the mountains, waterfowl dabble in the marshes and flamingos fly over red and green lakes. There is also the lush Andes, where the slopes dive down to the Amazon basin. Agricultural terraces cling to impossibly steep hillsides and there are acres of flowers, coffee, coca and corn. In this unstable but beautiful environment, minerals such as silver, gold, copper and nitrates have brought great riches and led to much exploitation. Lake Titicaca, the highest navigable lake in the world, was the cradle of the Inca civilization and the Inca himself held court in Cusco. His royal roadways radiated to the four corners of the world. The descendants of the Incas and other cultures now keep traditions alive, mingling them with the beliefs of the Spanish conquistadors and the pressures of the global market.

The Lakes   The Andes head south, leaving giants like Aconcagua (the highest peak in the Americas) behind. On either side of the Cordillera beautiful lakes with strange names shelter beneath snow-capped peaks: Nahuel Huapi, Futalaufquen, Calafquen, Panguipulli. On their shores are resorts for summer water sports, fishing and winter skiing. National parks protect evocative-sounding trees, like the *alerce*, the *arrayán*, the *lenca* and the *araucaria*, the famous monkey puzzle tree. Take Lake Llanquihue in Chile, for example, with three volcanoes in full view, pretty Germanic towns, an annual classical music festival, trekking, riding, biking, rafting – who could ask for more?

Patagonia   On the Argentine side of the mountains, the beech forests and lakes of the foothills give way to a treeless plateau, scoured by dust-laden winds for much of the year. Sheep farms huddle in valleys where there is water. Scattered communities established themselves in the 19th century, most notably the Welsh towns, where you can find tea and cakes as if brought to you straight from the Valleys of Wales. On the Pacific side, Chilean Patagonia is wet and windy, a confusion of fjords and channels, with ancient woodlands and glaciers tumbling into the sea. The pioneering Carretera Austral runs through this stunning scenery, until the land puts a halt to any more roads. Before the mountains disappear into the uttermost reaches of the Pacific Ocean, the Andes have a final, dramatic display. The peaks of the Chaitén Massif and the Torres del Paine National Park are a fabulous world of towers, spires, lakes and forests, a paradise for trekkers and birdwatchers.

Atlantic South America   On the Península Valdés, on the Atlantic coast of Argentine Patagonia, Southern right whales and elephant seals come to breed in the sheltered bays. Further south, penguins, orcas, dolphins and sea lions flourish in these waters. Travelling north towards Buenos Aires and Uruguay, the sea becomes warmer, the climate mild enough for resorts such as Mar del Plata and Punta del Este to burst at the seams each summer. The coast of Brazil, all 7,408 km of it, is an endless succession of beaches, in wooded coves, dotted with islands in the south, palm tree and dune-fringed in the north. You can surf, dance, dune-buggy to exhaustion, or find a secluded cove to while away the hours. Great historical ports like Rio de Janeiro, Salvador and Belém have become major tourist destinations, epitomising the Brazilian mix of music, carnival and the colonial and modern.

Homeward bound (left) On our way home at the village of Horto in Ceará, Northeast Brazil
Artistic nature (below) The Arbol de Piedra – a tree carved in stone by the harsh elements of the Bolivian altiplano – looks like it belongs on a Dalí canvas

Mask no questions (left) Dancer from La Diablada festival, Oruro (Bolivia)
Icing on the lake (above) Although the Perito Moreno glacier in Argentine Patagonia has stopped advancing, it is still an icy marvel

View from above (right) The winged Virgin of Quito gazes benignly from Cerro Panecillo over the capital of Ecuador

Beach ball (below) Summer playground for Argentines and Brazilians, Punta del Este, Uruguay, is one of the foremost beach resorts in South America

Senior señoras (Previous page) Two elderly ladies buying soft drinks from a street vendor at the Huata fiesta in the Cordillera Negra, Peru

Looking on the bright side
(above) Guambiano Indians share a joke at Silvia market, southern Colombia

Lost in space (right) A lone vicuña stands alert in the stark, ashy emptiness of the Lauca National Park, northern Chile

Paradise found

East of the Andes, the highlands fall away to jungle and plains. Roads to the lowlands struggle over ridges and down through steep gorges to hot and humid forests. If you fly, the greenness of the Amazon Basin stretches ahead of you with no end in sight. On the Amazon's perimeter are the *llanos* of the Orinoco and the Pantanal, both of which flood seasonally and where cattle and cowboys share the land with wild birds and animals. Mysterious ecosystems hide on table-top mountains on the Venezuela/Brazil border and in Bolivia, so unlike anything else on earth that the only fitting analogy is Conan Doyle's Lost World. On a tributary of the great Paraná river, blazing rainbows glitter in the mists which hang over Iguazú, where 275 waterfalls cascade into a great gorge on the Argentina/Brazil border. South of the jungle and the wetlands is yet more cowboy territory, the Argentine *pampas*, a vast but fertile emptiness where the *gaucho* rides. *Estancias* with ancient trees and antique furnishings wait to welcome visitors. Windpumps raise water to the surface and the oven bird builds its nest, six times its own size, on the fence and telegraph posts.

The heart of the continent

North of the fertile heartlands of Chile, the Pacific coast rapidly turns to desert as sea currents and mountains drive the rain far inland. The occasional shower will transform what looks like utter barrenness into a riot of colour as dormant flowers seize the moment to bloom. Some places receive no rain at all, ever. Others are covered in mist for over half the year. It sounds uninhabitable, yet prehispanic cultures thrived here. They left their monuments in sculptures etched into the surface of the desert, most famously at Nasca in Peru. Pyramid builders welcomed gods from the sea and irrigated the soil to feed great cities of adobe bricks. Irrigation today produces olives, asparagus, flowers and sugar and there is rich offshore fishing for man and seabirds. At islands such as the Ballestas (Peru) and Isla de la Plata (Ecuador) you can see much marine life, but the destination *par excellence* is the Galápagos. On the peaks of massive volcanoes, which jut into the ocean, albatross, boobies, giant tortoises and iguanas have evolved with little instinctive fear of man, a paradise for naturalists.

The Pacific deserts

North of the Amazon delta, Guyane, Suriname and Guyana are classed as Caribbean states, despite having many South American features: thick rainforest, ancient mountains and bronze-tinted rivers. Culturally, though, with their mixture of African, Amerindian, Hindu, Indonesian and European, they stand apart. North and west of the Orinoco in Venezuela, where the mainland almost touches Trinidad, is where the Caribbean truly begins, the land where Columbus made his first South American landfall. There is African influence here: listen to the drumming in some of Venezuela's coastal festivals. Colombia's Caribbean, which stretches to the Panamanian isthmus, is the inspiration for Gabriel García Márquez' world of magic realism, it is the land of banana plantations, accordian-led *vallenato* music and the secretive Indians of the Guajira Peninsula and the Sierra Nevada de Santa Marta. Its history of slavery and pirates can be seen in the fortifications of the beautiful city of Cartagena (Colombia), where today pelicans and frigate birds share the beaches with holiday-makers.

The Caribbean

Natural born thriller

The Amazon When the Spaniard, Francisco de Orellana, floated across the South American continent via the Amazon in 1542, he and his crew brought back tales of royal highways, grand cities and ferocious women warriors (their resemblance to the Amazons of Greek myth gave the river its name). The highways and cities were probably mirages brought on by hunger and the sun on the water; the female warriors melted into the forest never to be seen again. Soon European explorers were seeking the fabulous El Dorado in what they called the 'Green Hell', but the myths gradually evaporated as scientists began to uncover the Amazon's mysteries. The Indian cultures who survive in this vast tissue of waterways have a knowledge of the environment unmatched by science. But it is under threat from road building, tree-felling and burning for unsustainable agriculture, gold prospecting and mining. Among the fears is that, before this immense plant repository is fully understood, it will have disappeared.

The Amazon can only be described with superlatives: the largest watershed in the world, the greatest area of tropical rainforest (6 million square km), the greatest volume of water flowing into the ocean, more tributaries than any other river. No bridge crosses the main course for its entire length.

The Amazon Basin contains 20% of the world's plant and bird species, 10% of the mammals and an inestimable number of insects. In the waters live some 2,000 species of fish, from the three-metre long *arapaima*, to the voracious *piranha*. Also in the waters are shy giant otters, caiman and two species of freshwater dolphin, the pink and the grey. There are trees that strangle their neighbours, palms with a million thorns, plants that heal and vines that will blow your mind. Canopy walkways strung high-up in the trees reveal a lifestyle which never touches ground, while stalking in the undergrowth is the mythical jaguar, whose influence has spread through almost every religion that has come into contact with the rainforest.

Senses working overtime In South America senses struggle to acclimatize. Volcanoes come to life and threaten cities in Ecuador (as well as creating a new tourist attraction); earth tremors are a fact of life in Santiago de Chile; rivers cascade down mountain sides, off plateaux, or meander through swamps and forest; glaciers creak and break into lakes and bays in Patagonia. Pelicans plunge into the tropical seas, only to be harried by frigate birds for their catch. Penguins and seals do their fishing in the colder waters of the southern latitudes. On salt licks in the forest a procession of parrots and macaws take turns for their mineral breakfast. The quickfire movement of a hummingbird's wings contrast sharply with the slow, hundred-year growth of the puya raimondii flower.

When the Spanish and Portuguese arrived here over 500 years ago, many civilizations had risen and fallen. The Incas were at the height of their powers, but were soon overthrown. Nomadic and forest Indians were (and still are in a few rare cases) living an existence that had sustained them for centuries. European dominance has altered every aspect of the continent. But traditions have survived, by adapting old ideas to new settings as communities are invaded by outsiders, people are displaced by natural or political pressures and as successive waves of tourists come to share their culture. The best way to see these processes at work is in the countless festivals, where Christian and indigenous religious symbols merge, brass bands blare, masqueraders represent mythical and real figures and the age-old desire to have a good time is taken to its limit. South America continues to enchant, thrill and frustrate in equal measure. Its appeal will endure for another eighty years and beyond.

15

The road is long (left) a herder drives his cattle through the Cuchilla Grande hills, central Uruguay
Another brick in the wall (below) The prehispanic walled city of Kuelap in northern Peru contains three times more stones than The Great Pyramid at Giza
Icon see clearly now (next page) Christ the Saviour and other religious paraphernalia for sale outside San Francisco church, Quito – but who is the chap in the red tie?

Blue Monday (left) Street corner conversation in Tabay, Venezuela
Jungle look (above) Rising straight up from the river, Amazonian rainforest in Peru hides untold mysteries of plant and animal life

Contents

Map symbols

Administration
- -- - International border
- ⌇⌇⌇ State/province border
- □ Capital city
- ○ Other city/town

Roads and travel
- ═══ National highway (including Pan-American Highway)
- ━━ Paved road
- ━━ Unpaved all-weather road (including unpaved sections of Pan-American Highway)
- - - - Seasonal unpaved road/track
- ······ Footpath
- ⊢■ Railway with station

Water features
- ∼∼ River
- ⬭ Lake
- ⋎ Marshland
- ▦ Beach
- ≋ Ocean
- 🌊 Waterfall
- ∼∼ Reef
- ⛴ Ferry

Cities and towns
- ◻ Sight
- ▇ Sleeping
- ● Eating
- ▦ Building
- ▤ Main through route
- ▤ Main street
- ▤ Minor street
- ▦ Pedestrianized street
- Σ 工 Tunnel
- → One way street
- ⋈ Bridge
- ⁞⁞⁞⁞ Steps
- ▦ Park, garden, stadium

- ▰▰▰ Fortified wall
- ✈ Airport
- ⑤ Bank
- 🚌 Bus station
- Ⓜ Metro station
- ✚ Hospital
- 🏪 Market
- 🏛 Museum
- Ⓟ Police
- ✉ Post office
- 🄸 Tourist office
- ✝ Cathedral, church
- ✡ Synagogue
- ☪ Mosque
- 🛢 Petrol
- @ Internet
- ♪ Telephone office
- ⛳ Golf
- Ⓟ Parking
- Ⓐ Detail map
- ◁Ⓐ Related map

Topographical features
- ◎ Contours (approx), rock outcrop
- ⛰ Mountain
- 🌋 Volcano
- ⌐ Mountain pass
- ⌣⌣ Escarpment
- ▦ Gorge
- ▦ Glacier
- ▦ Salt flat

Other symbols
- ⁖ Archaeological site
- ◆ National park/wildlife reserve
- ⚘ Viewing point
- ▲ Camp site
- ⌂ Refuge
- 🌴🌴 Deciduous/palm trees
- 🌲 Mangrove

Planning your trip

First-time travel guide

Detailed planning information is given for each country in the relevant chapter

South America is a magnificently varied part of the world and tremendously hospitable. It is a tantalizing mixture of enticing images and ambiguous press reports, inspiring an air of mystery and a certain amount of trepidation. In common with many other parts of the world, South America suffers from meteorological, geological and social uncertainties. Within that context you will find some of the most dramatic landscapes on earth, biological diversity in a range of habitats, historical monuments of strength and elegance and a deep cultural resilience.

South America is a big place, so it's important not to be too ambitious on a first visit. Decide what type of holiday you want and research which countries offer what you are interested in. Then work out an itinerary in which the places you want to see and the distance between them coincides with the amount of time you have available. Over the years a Gringo Trail became firmly established, a network of places to which foreigners tended to gravitate for reasons of shared interests, lower prices, safety in numbers and so on. Some of these places have passed into legend, others are still going strong. New places are added as fashions change, or transport links are opened.

Getting around By plane you can visit many places and airpasses, both regional and domestic, will reduce the cost of flying, but if your travel budget does not stretch to air tickets, bus is the only economical alternative. Making long, or mountainous journeys by bus takes many hours, so you should build this factor into your itinerary. Trains are now few and far between and certainly cannot be relied upon as main means of transport. Car hire is expensive and tiring, but those who like driving can do well and many travellers take their own cars or motorcycles. Cycling is also popular.

When to go It all depends on latitude: eg the far south of Argentina and Chile is busiest in the southern hemisphere summer, December-February; in winter, June-August, it is cold and snow and rain can disrupt transport. The further north you go the more the seasons fall into wet and dry. The Peruvian and Bolivian Andes are dry (and very cold at night) April-October, the rest of the year is rainy. The Sierras of Ecuador and Colombia are wet February-May and October-November. East of the Andes is wet November-April, wettest March-May in the Amazon Basin. Each chapter describes the intricacies of the weather, but changes in world climate and periodic phenomena such as El Niño can play havoc with the general rules.

Language The main language of the continent is Spanish, except Portuguese in Brazil, English in Guyana, Dutch in Suriname and French in Guiane. If you have no Spanish or Portuguese, learn some, either before you go, or on a course when you get there.

Money Take a credit or debit card, and US dollars in cash or travellers' cheques for those occasions when the ATM network isn't available (either because of remoteness or because of system failure).

Documents Visa requirements vary a lot. Check with a consulate before you leave. Not every country has full South American representation, nor is every country represented in South America.

Health risks The main health risks involve mosquitos (which transmit malaria and dengue fever); altitude sickness; tropical diseases and parasites which adequate precautions and information can help to prevent; stomach bugs; and overexposure to the sun.

Safety No entire country is a must to avoid. Colombia has most areas which should be treated with caution, but also has parts which can be visited in safety. Also to be treated with respect are some isolated bits of Peru and sensitive border areas. Big cities are more dangerous than the countryside and in busy places like bus stations and markets you need to keep your wits about you.

Where to stay & what to eat There are hotels throughout the price range. The most variety will be found in cities and main tourist centres. Youth hostels may be affiliated internationally or nationally, or not at all. Availability of campsites varies from country to country. Living with families is possible, especially if you are on a language course.

Cost of travelling

◀

The cost in US$, per person per day, for two people travelling together on an economy, but not the most basic, budget is approximately:

Argentina	20	**Chile**	25-40
Paraguay	40	**Uruguay**	15-25
Bolivia	25-30	**Colombia**	25
Peru	25-35	**Venezuela**	25
Brazil	25	**Ecuador**	15-40

*In the Guianas, allow perhaps US$25 per person per day for Guyana but this will substantially increase if you venture into the interior. Suriname is impossible to estimate given the problems of its exchange rate. Guyane is French and expensive. **NB** More than one price indicates seasonal variations in prices (eg high season in southern Chile), or including expensive areas such as jungle trips.*

Local food is generally good, with lots of regional specialities, even within countries. Stick to what is local wherever you are, you'll do much better than trying to find international food. Vegetarians are best served in tourist areas, although many cities have "healthy eating" outlets.

Internet Access to the internet gets better all the time and prices in cyber cafés are often very low. Many hotels now have email for bookings.

Getting there The easiest way to get to South America is by air (but not always by direct flight). From the USA you can get there by road, but you have to transport your vehicle around the Darien Gap between Panama and Colombia.

Best value How much money you need to take varies from country to country. You can get by on US$15 a day in several countries, but US$25 is the norm for good value, low (but not basic) travel. To make your money go further, ask for hotel rooms without TV (and without a bath if privacy is not an issue). Look for hostels that let you use the kitchen. Eat the *menú del día* (dish of the day, with different names in different countries), usually served at lunchtime. Investigate city bus routes, but use taxis when you have all your luggage with you or where they are the only safe option. Avoid high season or holidays, when prices rise.

Adventure Hiking, trekking, climbing, white water rafting, you name it, you can do it and, compared with *See page 58 for* other parts of the world, at competitive prices. Anywhere in the Andes is good for this type of *more details on* adventure, but some places like the Inca Trail (Peru) or Torres del Paine (Chile) are expensive *adventure sports* because of demand. If paying for guides and equipment, remember that you get what you pay for. The same applies to mountain biking, for which there are ample opportunities. Some other ideas: surfing (Peru, Brazil); skiing (Argentina. Chile); diving (Colombia, Brazil), off-roading (Argentina), parapenting and hang gliding (anywhere there is a cliff to throw yourself off – Peru, Brazil, Argentina, Venezuela).

Gap year & South America has always been popular for gap years and career breaks and there are many **volunteering** options for volunteering, eg on environmental projects in Ecuador, working with street kids in any big city, or teaching.

Historical Peru's archaeological sites rival those of anywhere on earth. Colombia, Ecuador and Bolivia **tourism** also have important sites. Machu Picchu (Peru) stands out as a destination – and worth every penny of the entry price – but its builders, the Incas, were the last in a long line of cultures that left great monuments. Every country except the Guianas has fine examples of colonial art and architecture, either isolated, or concentrations such as in Minas Gerais or North East Brazil.

Nature There are natural features worth seeing, often protected as national parks, round every corner. In many places, nature tourism and adventure are related (eg Peru's Cordillera Blanca, Argentina's Fitzroy Massif), but for more peaceful occupations there's fabulous wildlife watching everywhere. For low-cost jungle trips, try Bolivia; but the infrastructure is better in Peru, Brazil and Ecuador.

Partying & chilling
If you want to party, head for Cusco or the Lima suburb of Barranco (Peru); Buenos Aires, especially for tango; or Brazil: Rio de Janeiro, São Paulo, the beach bars in Salvador or Ceará. Most capital cities have good nightlife and there are fiestas all year round, especially at Carnival time. Beaches can be deserted, as are many in Brazil, or major resorts like Viña del Mar, Punta del Este, Mar del Plata or Cartagena. Estancias (farms) are good places to relax, but tend not to be cheap: best are in Argentina, Uruguay, Paraguay, or the coffee farms in Colombia. In Peru shamen can guide you down mystical paths, usually with the aid of mind-altering potions. For the more conservative, go wine-tasting in Argentina and Chile.

Shopping
Handicrafts are sold everywhere, most notably Andean textiles, ceramics, woodwork, leather and jewellery. In many markets bargaining is expected. Take essentials from home, pariculary specialist items (eg for sports, or health).

Twenty-one ways to get off the beaten track

Tired of fighting your way through rush hour crowds? In the vastness of South America, escape from the Gringo Trail is never more than a stone's throw away. On the practical side, many of the continent's seldom-visited areas can be reached economically: all you need is curiosity and the desire to pack your bags and go. Listening to the shriek of macaws echoing through the stillness of the forest or the howl of the glacial wind over the high mountain passes, you'll wonder if the office ever really existed.

Mountains
Extending from the Caribbean coast to the glaciers of Patagonia, the Andes encompass a breathtaking range of mountain environments and experiences. Unlike many of the world's mountain regions, parts of the Andes have scarcely seen a goretex boot.

The remote and little-visited **Cordillera Apolobamba** in Bolivia offer sanctuary for traditional cultures and rare Andean fauna. These mountains possess some of the best climbing and trekking in the Andes, with condors circling the peaks and the rare spectacled bear clinging to existence on the range's forested eastern slopes.

The **Nevado Sajama and Lauca National Park**, on the Bolivia-Chile border offer awesome opportunities for climbing Bolivia's highest peak, chilling out and wrinkling the skin in hot springs, or exploring the park's pristine mountain habitats.

Three towering volcanic peaks and extensive tracts of untamed wilderness in between, **Sangay National Park** in Ecuador is the Andes at its most elemental. Anyone wishing to scale the shuddering flanks of Sangay itself should come prepared with a bin-lid shield as protection against molten rocks ejected from the crater. Tungurahua, once a sleeping giant, is waking, it's summit glows fiery red in the night sky, threatening the resort of Baños.

The spectacular **Sierra Nevada de Cocuy** in Colombia offer tremendous views cross Los Llanos, the great plains of the Orinoco. Treacherous weather and guerrilla-dodging add to the fun.

Wildlife
The Amazon Rainforest, covering some 6 million sq km and spilling across the borders of nine countries, is arguably the world's greatest remaining wilderness. Huge areas of the Amazon remain unexplored, but in South America, still a continent dominated by the forces of nature, there is even more, from the sweeping plains of Los Llanos in Venezuela and Colombia to the temperate rainforests of Chilean Patagonia.

Guyana is one of the final frontiers of Latin America, with few visitors. The Iwokrama Rainforest Program is a pioneering project for research and sustainable development, one of the best places to catch a glimpse of the elusive jaguar. Alternatively there's the Rupununi Savanna for cowboy fantasies and wildlife watching. Imagine a tropical version of the American Wild West and add the chance to meet some of South America's few remaining giant otters and harpy eagles.

Jewel of Brazil's endangered *cerrado* ecosystem, **Emas National Park** presents excellent wildlife viewing opportunities and remains a stronghold of the seldom seen maned wolf and giant anteater. Emas possesses the greatest concentration of termite mounds on the planet, which is paradise if you're an anteater! At the beginning of the rainy season (September-October) the termite larvae glow and the night time savanna lights up with it's own bioluminescent response to the Manhattan skyline.

Recently created and largely unexplored, the **Central Suriname Game Reserve** covers 10% of Suriname, deep in the country's green heart. If your ambition is to discover an unknown species or ten, this could be the place.

Ilha do Bananal is one of the world's greatest river islands. In this transition zone between Amazonian forests and the *cerrado* of Central Brazil, ecotourism opportunities abound and sport fishing ranks among the best in South America.

In **Noel Kempff Mercado National Park**, Bolivia's northeastern wilderness, waterfalls cascade from the cliffs of the ancient Huanchaca Plateau. This could have been Conan Doyle's 'Lost World' and even today reaching Noel Kempff is an adventure. Inaccessibility has preserved some of South America's rarest and most impressive flora and fauna, truly, the land that time forgot.

Esteros do Iberá, Argentina's little known rival to the Pantanal, is a wildlife haven of marshes, forests and palm savanna providing nature's antidote to the turbulence of Buenos Aires.

With thousands of kilometres of unspoiled coastline, South America is the ideal place to find an untouched patch of sand – a far cry from Rio's Copacabana.

Islands & beaches

Good diving and beautiful beaches divided by rocky headlands, **Tayrona National Park** is little visited in troubled Colombia. This is what the Americas looked like when Columbus first gazed upon its shores – give or take the occasional hammock.

A far-flung Colombian Caribbean island, **Providencia** boasts gorgeous coral reefs and a distinctive English-speaking Caribbean culture. On this former hideaway of pirate Henry Morgan, who knows, you could even come upon some buried treasure!

On the coast of **Rio Grande de Norte and Ceará**, in Brazil, you can blast along hundreds of kilometres of undeveloped beaches in an open-topped buggy, explore the region's giant sand dunes that rise above an emerald ocean, and absorb the traditional Afro-Brazilian culture of the tiny fishing villages that dot the coastline.

South America's human history began thousands of years before Pizarro crushed the Inca Empire with horses and Spanish steel. The remains of hundreds of pre-Inca cultures litter the continent.

Lost worlds & ancient cultures

San Agustín, set in flowering valleys and canyons of the upper Río Magdalena in Colombia, was once home to a great, but enigmatic civilization. Their legacy, painted burial tombs and hundreds of intricately carved statues of men and beasts, lie scattered throughout the region and can be reached on foot, horseback, or by jeep.

The **Vilcabamba Mountains** of Peru were the last refuge of Manco Inca's rebellion against the Conquistadors, Vilcabamba's frozen peaks and jungled river canyons are still shrouded in mystery.

The **Jesuit Missions Circuit** in Bolivia is a reminder of an idealistic past. The ornate decoration of the Mission churches stands in vivid contrast to the empty landscape that surrounds them.

Planning your trip

Millions of years before the first humans stepped onto the South American continent, the earth trembled under the weight of very different masters. The **Argentine badlands** contain some the richest dinosaur fossil deposits on the planet – with a bit of patience the next earthshaking discovery could be yours.

Rivers/white water

South American rivers provide some of the world's finest white water and often give access to regions inaccessible on foot.

The **Río Tuichi** in Bolivia combines jungle exploration with some adrenaline pumping white water on this, a roller-coaster ride from Andes to Amazon. The upper Tuichi takes you to an area few westerners have ever seen and descends through some of the planet's most bio-diverse rainforests.

The **Río Cotahuasi** has carved a canyon over 3-km deep through the arid mountains of southern Peru. A descent of the Cotahuasi is truly one of the world's great white water experiences, passing through an area of traditional villages and rich pre-Columbian history. The inexperienced should not apply.

Roads to nowhere

South America is the land of the road (or river!) less travelled, a continent where opportunity beckons at every turn. Here are a couple to whet your appetite.

The **Carreterra Austral** in Chile is the South's wild road, passing snow capped volcanoes, raging rivers, glacial fjords and isolated communities. Take a step off the road and there's all the windswept isolation you can handle.

One of the least travelled roads into Bolivia is the route across the **Gran Chaco** in Paraguay. This peculiar area of marshland and thorn scrub has only 100,000 inhabitants in an area of 24 million ha. When it's hot, it's very hot (temperatures can reach 45º C) and when it's wet is impassable. But the bus will get through, somehow.

Finding out more

Travel and safety information: **South American Explorer's** is a non-profit educational organization staffed by volunteers, widely recognized as the best place to go for information on South America. Highly recommended as a source for specialized information, member-written trip reports, maps, lectures, library resources. SAE publishes a 64-page quarterly journal, helps members plan trips and expeditions, stores gear, holds post, hosts book exchanges, provides expert travel advice, etc. Annual membership fee US$50

individual (US$80 couple) plus US$10 for overseas postage of its *quarterly* journal, *The South American Explorer*. The SAE membership card is good for many discounts throughout Ecuador and Peru. The Clubhouses, in Quito, Lima and Cusco, are attractive and friendly; it is not necessary to 'explore' to feel at home there. SAE will sell used equipment on consignment (donations of used equipment, unused medicines, etc are welcome). The SAE Headquarters are located in the USA: 126 Indian Creek Rd, Ithaca, NY, 14850, T607 277 0488, F607-277 6122, ithacaclub@saexplorers.org For information and travel tips on-line: www.saexplorers.org Official representatives in UK: Bradt Publications, 19 High Street, Chalfont St Peters, Bucks, SL9 9QE, T01753-893444, Info@bradt-travelguides.com If signing up in UK please allow 4-6 weeks for receipt of membership card.

The Latin American Travel Advisor: This web site (**www.amerispan.com/lata/**) contains a varied collection of articles offering practical advice for travellers to South and Central America.

See also Ron Mader's website **www.planeta.com**, which contains masses of useful information on ecotourism, conservation, travel, news, links, language schools and articles.

It is better to seek advice on security before you leave from your own consulate than from travel agencies. Before you travel you can contact: **British Foreign & Commonwealth Office**, Travel Advice Unit, T0117 9169000. *Footprint* is a partner in the Foreign and

Planning your trip

Commonwealth Office's *Know before you go* campaign www.fco.gov.uk/knowbeforeyougo US State Department's **Bureau of Consular Affairs**, Overseas Citizens Services, T202-647 4225, F202-647 3000, travel.state.gov/travel_warnings.html Australian **Department of Foreign Affairs**, T06-6261 3305, www.dfat.gov.au/consular/advice.html

Useful websites   Website addresses for individual countries are given in the relevant chapters, in Essentials and throughout the text. The following is a miscellaneous selection of sites, which may be of interest:
www.bootsnall.om/cgi-bin/gt/samericatravelguides/index.shtml On-line travel guides for the whole region, updated monthly.
gibbons.best.vwh.net Cultures of the Andes and Quechua.
http://gosouthamerica.about.com/ South America for Visitors: plenty of articles and links on sights, planning, countries, culture, gay and lesbian travel.
www.gsmp.org The Guiana Shield Media Project site with information on environmental issues for nothern South America.
www.lanic.utexas.edu The Latin American Network Information Center: loads of information on everything.
www.lata.org Lists tour operators, hotels, airlines etc.
www.latinsynergy.org Ecotourism website with articles, travel tips, statistics, maps and links.
www.latinworld.com/sur Links to individual Latin American countries.
www.oanda.com Currency converter and for all your financial needs.
www.oas.org The Organization of American States site, with its magazine *Americas*.
www.politicalresources.net/s_america.htm If you are into politics, this is the portal for you, with links to political parties, governments and related matters.
www.southamericadaily.com From the World News Network, links to newspapers, plus environment, health, business and travel sites.
www.virtualtourist.com/f/4/ South America travel forum, which can take you down some interesting alleyways, lots of links, trips, etc; good exploring here.
For the lowdown on the latest Latin sounds contact *Putumayo*, www.putumayo.com

Language
See page for a full list of Spanish words and phrases   Without some knowledge of Spanish (or Portuguese) you will become very frustrated and feel helpless in many situations. English, or any other language, is absolutely useless off the beaten track. Some initial study, to get you up to a basic vocabulary of 500 words or so, and a pocket dictionary and phrase-book, are most strongly recommended: your pleasure will be doubled if you can talk to the locals. Not all the locals speak Spanish, of course; apart from Brazil's Portuguese, you will find that some Indians in the more remote highland parts of Bolivia and Peru, and lowland Indians in Amazonia, speak only their indigenous languages, though there will usually be at least one person in each village who can speak Spanish (or Portuguese).

The basic Spanish of Hispanic America is that of southwestern Spain, with soft 'c's' and 'z's' pronounced as 's', and not as 'th' as in the other parts of Spain. There are several regional variations in pronunciation, particularly in the River Plate countries, which are noted in the Argentine section Essentials. Differences in vocabulary also exist, both between peninsular Spanish and Latin American Spanish, and between the usages of the different countries.

If you are going to Brazil, you should learn some Portuguese. Spanish is not adequate: you may be understood but you will probably not be able to understand the answers. Language classes are available at low cost in a number of centres in South America, for instance Quito. See the text for details, under Language Courses.

AmeriSpan, PO Box 40007, Philadelphia, PA 19106-0007, T215-751 1100 (worldwide), T1-800-879 6640 (USA, Canada), F215-751 1986, www.amerispan.com, offers Spanish immersion programmes, educational tours, volunteer and internship positions throughout Latin America. Language programmes are offered in Buenos Aires, Córdoba, Sucre, Santiago, Cuenca, Quito, Cusco, Montevideo, Caracas, Mérida and Puerto La Cruz. Portuguese courses can also be arranged in Maceió and Rio de Janeiro. In Ecuador, they also offer a discount card for use in hotels, restaurants and shops. *LanguagesAbroad.com*, 317 Adelaide St West, Suite 900, Toronto, Ontario, Canada, M5V 1P9, T416-925 2112, toll free 1-800-219 9924, F416-925 5990, www.languagesabroad.com, offers Spanish and Portuguese programmes in every South American country except Colombia and Paraguay. They also have language immersion

▶ *Spanish and Portuguese pronounciation*

Spanish

The stress in a Spanish word conforms to one of three rules: 1) if the word ends in a vowel, or in **n** or **s**, the accent falls on the penultimate syllable (ventana, ventanas); 2) if the word ends in a consonant other than **n** or **s**, the accent falls on the last syllable (hablar); 3) if the word is to be stressed on a syllable contrary to either of the above rules, the acute accent on the relevant vowel indicates where the stress is to be placed (pantal**ó**n, met**á**fora). Note that adverbs such as cuando, 'when', take an accent when used interrogatively: ¿cuándo?, 'when?'

Vowels: *a*, short as in English 'cat'; *e* as in English 'pay', but shorter in a syllable ending in a consonant; *i* as in English 'seek'; *o* as in English 'cot' (North American ` caught'), but more like 'pope' when the vowel ends a syllable; *u* as in English 'food'; after 'q' and in 'gue', 'gui', u is unpronounced; in 'güe' and 'güi' it is pronounced; *y* when a vowel, pronounced like 'i'; when a semiconsonant or consonant, it is pronounced like English 'yes'; *ai*, *ay* as in English 'write'; *ei*, *ey* as in English 'eight'; *oi*, *oy* as in English 'voice'

Unless listed below **consonants** can be pronounced in Spanish as they are in English. *b*, *v* their sound is interchangeable and is a cross between the English 'b' and 'v', except at the beginning of a word or after 'm' or 'n' when it is like English 'b'; *c* like English 'k', except before 'e' or 'i' when it is as the 's' in English 'sip'; *g* before 'e' and 'i' it is the same as j; *h* when on its own, never pronounced; *j* as the 'ch' in the Scottish 'loch'; *ll* as the 'g' in English 'beige'; sometimes as the 'lli' in 'million'; *ñ* as the 'ni' in English 'onion'; *rr* trilled much more strongly than in English;

x depending on its location, pronounced as in English 'fox', or 'sip', or like 'gs'; *z* as the 's' in English 'sip'.

Portuguese

There is no standard Portuguese and there are many differences between the Portuguese of Portugal and the Portuguese of Brazil. If learning Portuguese before you go, get lessons with a Brazilian, or from a language course which teaches Brazilian Portuguese. Within Brazil itself, there are variations in pronunciation, intonation, phraseology and slang. This makes for great richness and for the possibility of great enjoyment in the language. Describing the complex Portuguese vocalic system is best left to the experts; it would take up too much space here. A couple of points which the newcomer to the language will spot immediately however are: the use of the til (~) over *a* and *o*. This makes the vowel a nasal vowel. Vowels also become nasal when a word ends in *m* or *ns*, when a vowel is followed by *m* + consonant, or by *n* + consonant. Another important point of spelling is that words ending in *i* or *u* are accented on the last syllable, though unlike Spanish no accent is used there. This is especially important in place names: Buriti, Guarapari, Caxambu, Iguaçu. Note also the use of *ç*, which changes the pronunciation of *c* from hard [k] to soft [s].

NB In conversation, most people refer to *you* as "você", although in the south and in Pará "tu" is more common. To be more polite, use "O senhor/A Senhora". For *us*, "a gente" (people, folks) is very common when it includes *you* too.

courses throughout the world. Similarly, *Cactus*, 4 Clarence House, 3031 North St, Brighton BN1 1EB, T0845-130 4775, www.cactuslanguage.com For a list of Spanish schools, see www.planeta.com/ecotravel/schools/schoollist.html

Working in South America If you are seeking more than casual work in any South American country, there will be income tax implications which you should research at the relevant consulate before leaving home. **Voluntary work** falls generally into three main categories: community projects, conservation and teaching. A number of organizations can arrange a 'voluntourism' package for you, in which you will probably have to pay for your airfare and raise money before you go. You will probably be working at grass-roots level and conditions may be harsh. But at the same time you will be contributing to the local community or its environment and gaining a new perspective on travelling.

There is some overlap between volunteering and gap year or career break tourism as many people who make this type of trip are going to do some form of work . There is an increasing amount of help for students on a gap year and, in the UK at least, a well-planned and productive gap year can be a positive advantage when it comes to university and job application. The career-break market is growing fast and there is help on-line to guide you. Some organizations guide you all the way throught the planning and finding something to do; others a quite specific in the type of project or country in which they operate. Here is a list of ideas: **www.gapyear.com**, **www.gap.org.uk** and **www.yearoutgroup.org** for that year away. For range of options, try **www.gvi.co.uk** (Global Vision International), or **www.i-to- i.com**. More specific (but not limited to South America) are **www.raleigh.org.uk** (Raleigh International), **www.com cat.org** (Catalytic Comminities, projects in Brazil), **www.mad venturer.com** and **www.thepodsite.co.uk** (Personal Overseas Development), with projects only in Peru, **www.out reachinternational.co.uk** (Outreach), with projects in Ecuador, www.teaching-abroad.co.uk (Teaching and Projects Abroad), for more than teaching, in Bolivia, Chile and Peru, and **www.vso.org.uk** (Voluntary Service Overseas), working in the Guianas, **Colombia and Venezuela. Also contact** *South American Explorers*, see above. If looking for a paying job, visit the *International Career and Employment Center*, www.internationaljobs.org Another resource is www.vacationwork.co.uk, the site of Vacation Work, who publish a number of books, including Susan Griffith's *Work your Way around the World*, now in its 11th edition.

Festival guide

End February: Fiesta de la Vendimia, **Mendoza** (Mendoza), grape harvest and wine festival.
15 August: El Toreo de la Vincha, **Casabindo** (Jujuy), celebration of Nuestra Señora del Rosario with the last remaining bullfight in Argentina.
15 September: El Cristo del Milagro, **Salta** (Salta), procession of the Lord and the Virgin of the Miracles to commemorate the cessation of earthquakes in 1692.
10 November: Día de la Tradición, **throughout Argentina**, gaucho parades, with traditional music, on the days leading up to the day itself.

Argentina
*www.whatsonwhen. com, and
www.national-holiday s.com
for worldwide information on festivals and events*

24 January to first week in February: Alacitas Fair, **La Paz**, a celebration of Ekeko, the household god of good fortune and plenty.
2 February: La Virgen de la Candelaria, **Copacabana**, processions, fireworks, dancing and bullfights on the shores of Lake Titicaca (also celebrated in many rural communities).
February/March: La Diablada, **Oruro**, celebrations in the high Andes with tremendous masked dancers and displays. Carnival is also worth seeing in the lowland city of **Santa Cruz de la Sierra**.
Mid-March: Phujllay, **Tarabuco** (Sucre), a joint celebration of carnival and the Battle of Jumbate (12 March 1816), with music and dancing.
May/June: Festividad del Señor del Gran Poder, **La Paz**, thousands of dancers in procession through the centre of the city.
June-August (movable): Masked and costumed dances are the highlight of the four-day Fiesta de la Virgen de Urkupiña in **Quillacolla**, near Cochabamba.

Bolivia

February/March: Carnaval, **throughout Brazil**, but the most famous are **Rio de Janeiro, Salvador de Bahia, São Paulo** and **Pernambuco (Recife/Olinda)**, parades (sometimes competitive, as in Rio), dancing, music, balls and general revelry.
June: Festas Juninhas, **throughout Brazil**, to celebrate various saints days in the month; also Bumba-meu-boi, in **Maranhão state**, drummers and dancers in a festival which mixes Portuguese, African and indigenous traditions; last three days of June, Festa do Boi, **Parintins** (Amazonas), another festival based on the bull, whose main event is the competition between two rival groups of dancers.
The weekend after 15 August: Festa da Boa Morte, **Cachoeira** (Bahia), the processions of the Sisterhood of Good Death; also in August (third week) is the Festa do Peão Boiadeiro, **Barretos** (São Paulo), the largest rodeo in the world.
October: Oktoberfest, **Blumenau**, modelled on the famous festival of Munich, with German

Brazil

beer, music and traditions, all in the context of German immigration to this part of Brazil. Also in this month is Círio, **Belém** (Pará), the festival of candles for Nossa Senhora de Nazaré.

31 December: Reveillon, on **many beaches in Brazil**, especially **Rio de Janeiro**, a massive party to celebrate New Year. Principally at this time, but also on other dates, a number of places hold the more solemn festival of flowers, boats and candles in honour of Yemenjá, the Afro-Brazilian goddess of the sea.

Chile **End-January to early February**: Semanas Musicales, **Frutillar**, 10 days of classical music on the shores of beautiful Lago Llanquihue.

January-February: Muestra Cultural Mapuche, **Villarrica**, a celebration of the Mapuche culture, with music, singing, dancing and handicrafts. Also in February in this region there are various sports events.

Mid-February: Semana Valdiviana, **Valdivia**, a festival of various events, including the arts, culminating in a grand carnival on the river, with a procession of boats, fireworks and the election of a beauty queen.

End-March: National Rodeo Championships, **Rancagua**, the climax of a series of popular events throughout the summer, with competitions, dancing and displays of *huaso* (cowboy) culture.

12-18 July: La Virgen del Carmen, **La Tirana** (Iquique), one of Chile's most famous religious festivals which draws thousands of pilgrims. Also celebrated in **Santiago** at the Templo Votivo de Maipú on 16 July.

Colombia **February/March**: Carnaval, **Barranquilla**, one of the best carnivals in South America, with parades of masked dancers, floats, street dancing and beauty contests. It is less commercialized than some of the Brazilian events.

March: Caribbean Music Festival, **Cartagena**, groups from all over the Caribbean region attend. Also in March or April, Cartagena holds a film festival. The city's other great festival is Independence, in the second week of November, which can be pretty riotous.

March/April: Semana Santa, **Popayán**, throughout Easter week, there are spectacular processions and, in the following week, child processions. There is also a major festival of religious music in Holy Week.

April: Festival de la Leyenda Vallenata, **Valledupar** (César), thousands attend the festival of accordian-based *vallenato* music.

First week of August: Fiesta de las Flores y Desfile de Silleteros, **Medellín**, a great flower fair with parades and music.

Ecuador **February**: Fiesta de las Frutas y las Flores, **Ambato**, a carnival with parades, festivities and bullfights; unlike other Andean carnivals, the throwing of water and other messy stuff is banned.

June: Los San Juanes, the combined festivals of, 21st: Inti Raymi, 24th: San Juan Bautista, and 29th: San Pedro y San Pablo, **Otavalo and Imbabura province**, mostly indigenous celebrations of the summer solstice and saints' days, music, dancing, bullfights, regattas on Laguna San Pablo.

Second week of September: Yamor and Colla Raimi, **Otavalo**, lots of festivities and events to celebrate the equinox and the festival of the moon.

6 December: Día de Quito, **Quito**, commemorating the founding of the city with parades, bullfights, shows and music. The city is busy right through Christmas up to the 31st, *Años Viejos*, the New Year celebrations which take place all over the country.

Christmas-time: **Cuenca**, many parades, the highlight being the *Pase del Niño Viajero*, the finest Christmas parade in the country.

Paraguay **February/March**: Carnaval, **throughout the country**.

8 December: La Inmaculada Concepción, **Caacupé**, Paraguay's main religious festival at the shrine of Nuestra Señora de los Milagros, attended by people from Paraguay, Argentina and Brazil, processions, fireworks and displays by bottle-dancers.

Peru **First two weeks of February**: La Virgen de la Candelaria, **Puno** and the shores of Lake Titicaca, masked dancers and bands compete in a famous festival in which local legends and characters are represented.

March/April: Semana Santa, **Arequipa** and **Ayacucho**, both cities celebrate Holy Week with fine processions, but each has its unique elements: the burning of an effigy of Judas in Arequipa and beautiful floral 'paintings' in Ayacucho, where Easter celebrations are among the world's finest.

June: Semana de Andinismo, **Huaraz**, international climbing and skiing week. In late June in this region also, San Juan and San Pedro are celebrated.

June: there are several major festivals in and around **Cusco**: Corpus Christi, on the Thursday after Trinity; mid-June, Q'Olloriti, the ice festival at 4,700 m on a glacier; 24th, Inti Raymi, the Inca festival of the winter solstice at Sacsayhuaman (this is preceded by a beer festival and, one week later, the Ollanta-Raymi in Ollantaytambo). Also in mid-June is the Huiracocha dance festival at Raqchi.

Last week of September: Festival de la Primavera, **Trujillo**, with beauty pageant, Caballos de Paso horse shows and cultural events.

February/March: Carnaval, **Montevideo**, notable for its *camdombe* drummers. Uruguay

March/April: Semana Santa, **throughout the country** Holy Week is celebrated, but especially in **Montevideo** where it coincides with the Semana Criolla, a traditional gaucho festival.

February: week preceding Ash Wednesday: Feria del Sol, **Mérida**, a festival in this Andean city. Venezuela

February/March: Carnaval, **throughout the country**, but most famous is the traditional pre-Lenten carnival in **Carúpano**, the last of its kind in the country, with costumed dancers, masked women, drinking, etc.

Early June, Corpus Christi: Diablos Danzantes, **San Francisco de Yare** (Miranda), dancers in red devil-masks parade with their drums and rattles.

24 June: San Juan Bautista, Bailes de Tambor: **Barlovento Coast** in villages such as Chua, Cata and Ocumare de la Costa, a magnificent celebration of drumming. The drums can also be heard on 29 June (San Pedro) and at Christmas.

Planning your trip

Guyana   **23 February**: Mashramani/Republic Day, **Georgetown**, a week-long carnival including this date, with steel band competitions, calypso, dances with masquerade characters and sporting events.
March/April: **Phagwah**, the Hindu Spring festival.
March/April: Easter, **Georgetown**, as well as the Christian ceremony, Easter marks the start of the kite-flying season.
November (usually): **Deepavali** (Divali), the Hindu festival of light.

Suriname   **Phagwah** and **Divali** are celebrated as in Guyana.
March/April: Easter celebrations include parades in **Paramaribo**.
End-December-early-January: Surifesta, **Paramaribo**, cultural shows, street parties, flower and art markets, New Year celebrations.

Guyane   **February/March**: Carnaval, celebrations begin in January, leading up to the four days preceding Ash Wednesday, each of which has a specific theme, with parades, dancing and music.

Disabled travellers

In most of South America, facilities for the disabled are severely lacking. For those in wheelchairs, ramps and toilet access are limited to some of the more upmarket, or most recently-built hotels. Pavements are often in a poor state of repair or crowded with street vendors. Most archaeological sites, even Machu Picchu, have little or no wheelchair access. Visually or hearing-impaired travellers are similarly poorly catered for, but there are experienced guides in some places who can provide individual attention. There are also travel companies outside South America who specialize in holidays which are tailor-made for the individual's level of disability. Some moves are being made to improve the situation. In Chile all new public buildings are supposed to provide access for the disabled by law; *PromPerú* has initiated a programme to provide facilities at airports, tourist sites, etc; Quito's trolley buses are supposed to have wheelchair access, but they are often too crowded to make this practical. While disabled South Americans have to rely on others to get around, foreigners will find that people are generally very helpful. A useful website is **Global Access - Disabled Travel Network**, www.geocities.com/Paris/1502 Another informative site, with lots of advice on how to travel with specific disabilities, plus listings and links belongs to the Society for Accessible Travel and Hospitality, **www.sath.org** You might want to read *Nothing Ventured*, edited by Alison Walsh (Harper Collins), which gives personal accounts of worldwide journeys by disabled travellers, plus advice and listings.

Gay and lesbian travellers

Much of Latin America is quite intolerant of homosexuality. Rural areas tend to be more conservative in these matters than cities. It is therefore wise to respect this and avoid provoking a reaction. For the gay or lesbian traveller, however, certain cities have active communities and there are local and international organizations which can provide information. The best centres are Buenos Aires (Argentina), Santiago (Chile), Rio de Janeiro and other cities in Brazil, Lima (Peru) and Quito (Ecuador). Helpful websites include, **general**: www.bluway.com www.gayscape.com www.outandabout.com **Argentina**: www.mundogay.com (in Spanish) **Brazil**: riogayguide.com (lots of information) **Chile**: www.gaychile.com (very useful, in Spanish, English, French and German) **Ecuador**: www.quitogay.net (in Spanish and English) **Peru**: gaylimape.tripod.com (good site, in English, lots of links and information) www.deambiente.com and www.gayperu.com/gp.htm (both in Spanish).

Student travellers

Student cards must carry a photograph if they are to be of any use in Latin America for discounts. If you are in full-time education you will be entitled to an International Student Identity Card, which is distributed by student travel offices and travel agencies in 77 countries. The ISIC gives you special prices on all forms of transport such as air, sea, rail, and access to a variety of other concessions and services. If you need to find the location of your nearest ISIC office contact: The **ISIC Association**, Herengracht 479, 1017 BS Amsterdam, Holland T+31-20-421 2800, F+31-20-421 2810, www.istc.org

Travelling with children

Travel with children can bring you into closer contact with South American families and, generally, presents no special problems – in fact the path is often smoother for family groups. Officials tend to be more amenable where children are concerned and they are pleased if your child knows a little Spanish or Portuguese. Moreover, thieves and pickpockets seem to have some traditional respect for families, and may leave you alone because of it!

For health matters, see page 60. Visit www.babygoes2.com

People contemplating overland travel in South America with children should remember that a lot of time can be spent waiting for public transport. On bus journeys, if the children are good at amusing themselves, or can readily sleep while travelling, the problems can be considerably lessened. If your child is of an early reading age, take reading material with you as it is difficult, and expensive to find. A bag of, say 30 pieces, of *Duplo* or *Lego* can keep young children occupied for hours, while a *GameBoy* is ideal for older children. Travel on trains, while not as fast or at times as comfortable as buses, allows more scope for moving about. Some trains provide tables between seats, so that games can be played. Beware of doors left open for ventilation especially if air-conditioning is not working. If hiring a car, check that it has rear seat belts.

Buy nappies/diapers at every available opportunity, in case of short supply later on

On all long-distance buses you pay for each seat, and there are no half-fares if the children occupy a seat each. For shorter trips it is cheaper, if less comfortable, to seat small children on your knee. Often there are spare seats which children can occupy after tickets have been collected. In city and local excursion buses, small children generally do not pay a fare, but are not entitled to a seat when paying customers are standing. On sightseeing tours you should *always* bargain for a family rate – often children can go free. (In trains, reductions for children are general, but not universal.) All civil airlines charge half for children under 12, but some military services don't have half-fares, or have younger age limits. Children's fares on Lloyd Aéreo Boliviano are considerably more than half, and there is only a 7 kg baggage allowance. (LAB also checks children's ages on passports.) Note that a child travelling free on a long excursion is not always covered by the operator's travel insurance; it is advisable to pay a small premium to arrange cover.

Food can be a problem if the children are not adaptable. It is easier to take food such as biscuits, drinks and bread with you on longer trips than to rely on meal stops where the food may not be to taste. Avocados are safe and nutritious; they can be fed to babies as young as six months and most older children like them. A small immersion heater and jug for making hot drinks is invaluable, but remember that electric current varies. Try and get a dual-voltage one (110v and 220v).

In all **hotels**, try to negotiate family rates. If charges are per person, always insist that two children will occupy one bed only, therefore counting as one tariff. If rates are per bed, the same applies. In either case you can almost always get a reduced rate at cheaper hotels. Occasionally when travelling with a child you will be refused a room in a hotel that is 'unsuitable'. On river boat trips, unless you have very large hammocks, it may be more comfortable and cost effective to hire a two-berth cabin for two adults and a child. (In restaurants, you can normally buy children's helpings, or divide one full-size helping between two children.)

Women travellers

Many women travel alone or in pairs in South America without undue difficulty. Attitudes and courtesy towards western women, especially those on their own, vary from country to country. The following hints have mainly been supplied by women, but most apply to any

Planning your trip

single traveller. First time exposure to countries where sections of the population live in extreme poverty or squalor and may even be starving can cause odd psychological reactions in visitors. So can the exceptional curiosity extended to visitors, especially women. Simply be prepared for this and try not to over-react. When you set out, err on the side of caution until your instincts have adjusted to the customs of a new culture. If, as a single woman, you can befriend a local woman, you will learn much more about the country you are visiting. Unless actively avoiding foreigners like yourself, don't go too far from the beaten track; there is a very definite 'gringo trail' which you can join, or follow, if seeking company. This can be helpful when looking for safe accommodation, especially if arriving after dark (which is best avoided). Remember that for a single woman a taxi at night can be as dangerous as wandering around on her own. At borders dress as smartly as possible. Travelling by train is a good way to meet locals, but buses are much easier for a person alone; on major routes your seat is often reserved and your luggage can usually be locked in the hold. It is easier for men to take the friendliness of locals at face value; women may be subject to much unwanted attention. To help minimize this, do not wear suggestive clothing and do not flirt. By wearing a wedding ring, carrying a photograph of your 'husband' and 'children', and saying that your 'husband' is close at hand, you may dissuade an aspiring suitor. When asked how long you are travelling, say only for a short time because a long journey may give the impression that you are wealthy (even if you are not). If politeness fails, do not feel bad about showing offence and departing. When accepting a social invitation, make sure that someone knows the address and the time you left. Ask if you can bring a friend (even if you do not intend to do so). A good rule is always to act with confidence, as though you know where you are going, even if you do not. Someone who looks lost is more likely to attract unwanted attention. Do not disclose to strangers where you are staying.

Essentials

Before you travel

Getting in
*See the Essentials
section of each country
for particular details*

Documents Passports: Latin Americans, especially officials, are very document-minded. You should always carry your passport in a safe place about your person, or if not going far, leave it in the hotel safe. If staying in a country for several weeks, it is worth while registering at your embassy or consulate. Then, if your passport is stolen, the process of replacing it is simplified and speeded up. Keeping photocopies of essential documents, including your flight ticket, and some additional passport-sized photographs, is recommended. An alternative, if you have an email account, is to send yourself before you leave home a message containing all important details, addresses, etc which you can access in an emergency.

It is your responsibility to ensure that your passport is stamped in and out when you cross borders. The absence of entry and exit stamps can cause serious difficulties: seek out the proper immigration offices if the stamping process is not carried out as you cross. Also, do not lose your entry card; replacing one causes a lot of trouble, and possibly expense. Citizens of countries which oblige visitors to have a visa can expect more delays and problems at border crossings. If planning to study in Latin America for a long period, make every effort to get a student visa in advance.

Identity and Membership Cards Membership cards of British, European and US motoring organizations can be useful for discounts off items such as hotel charges, car rentals, maps and towing charges. Business people should carry a good supply of visiting cards, which are essential for good business relations in Latin America. Identity, membership or business cards in Spanish or Portuguese (or a translation) and an official letter of introduction in Spanish or Portuguese are also useful. See above for Student cards.

What to take
*A good principle is
to take half the
clothes, and twice
the money, that you
think you will need*

*Always take out a
good travel insurance
policy, see Health
section, page 60*

Everybody has their own preferences, but listed here are those most often mentioned. These include an inflatable travel pillow for neck support and strong shoes (remember that footwear over 9½ English size, or 42 European size, is difficult to find in South America). You should also take waterproof clothing and waterproof treatment for leather footwear and wax earplugs, which are vital for those long bus trips or in noisy hotels. Also important are rubber-thong Japanese-type sandals, which can be worn in showers to avoid athlete's foot, and a sheet sleeping-bag to avoid sleeping on filthy sheets in cheap hotels. Other useful things to take with you include: a clothes line, a nailbrush, a vacuum flask, a water bottle, a universal bath- and basin-plug of the flanged type that will fit any waste-pipe (or improvise one from a sheet of thick rubber), string, electrical insulating tape, a Swiss Army knife, an alarm clock for those early-morning bus departures, candles (for frequent power cuts), a torch/flashlight, pocket mirror, pocket calculator, an adaptor, a padlock for the doors of the cheapest hotels (or for tent zip if camping), a small first aid kit, sun hat, contraceptives, and a small sewing kit. The most security-conscious may also wish to include a length of chain and padlock for securing luggage to bed or bus/train seat, and a lockable canvas cover for your rucksack.

A list of useful medicines and health-related items is given in the Health section. To these might be added some lip salve with sun protection, waterless soap and pre-moistened wipes (such as *Wet Ones*). Always carry toilet paper, which is especially important on long bus trips. Contact lens wearers: should note that lens solution can be difficult to find in Bolivia and Peru. Ask for it in a chemist/pharmacy, rather than an optician's.

Money

Cash
*See each country's
Money section in
Essentials for
exchange rates as at
July 2003*

The three main ways of keeping in funds while travelling are with US dollars cash, US dollars travellers' cheques (TCs), or credit cards/current account cards.

Sterling and other currencies are not recommended. Though the risk of loss is greater, the chief benefit of US dollar notes is that better rates and lower commissions can usually be obtained for them. In many countries, US dollar notes are only accepted if they are in excellent, if not perfect condition (likewise, do not accept local currency notes in poor condition). Low-value US dollar bills should be carried for changing into local currency if arriving in a country when banks or *casas de cambio* are closed (US$5 or US$10 bills). They are very useful for shopping: shopkeepers and exchange shops (*casas de cambio*) tend to give better exchange rates than hotels or banks (but see below). The better hotels will normally change travellers' cheques for their guests (often at a rather poor rate), but if you are travelling on the cheap it is essential to keep in funds; at weekends and on public holidays never run out of local currency. Take plenty of local currency, in small denominations, when making trips off the beaten track.

It is straightfoward to obtain a cash advance against a credit card and, in the text, we give the names of banks that do this. There are two international **ATM** (automatic telling machine) acceptance systems, Plus and Cirrus. Many issuers of debit and credit cards are linked to one, or both. Many banks are linked usually to one, but coverage is not uniform throughout the continent (eg Cirrus is less common in Brazil than Plus) so it may be wise to take two types of cards. Frequently, the rates of exchange on ATM withdrawals are the best available. Find out before you leave what ATM coverage there is in the countries you will visit and what international 'functionality' your card has. Check if your bank or credit card company imposes handling charges. Obviously you must ensure that the account to which your **debit card** refers contains sufficient funds. A suggestion: before travelling, set up two bank accounts. One has all your funds but no debit card. The other has no funds but does have a debit card. As you travel, use the internet to transfer money from the full account to the empty account when you need it and withdraw cash from an ATM. That way, if your debit card is stolen, you won't be at risk of losing all your capital.

By using a debit card rather than a credit card you incur fewer bank charges, although a credit card is needed as well for some purchases. With a **credit card**, obtain a credit limit sufficient for your needs, or pay money in to put the account in credit. If travelling for a long time, consider a direct debit to clear your account regularly. Do not rely on one card, in case of loss. If you do lose a card, immediately contact the 24-hour helpline of the issuer in your home country (keep this number in a safe place).

For purchases, credit cards of the Visa and MasterCard (Eurocard, Access) groups, American Express (Amex), Carte Blanche and Diners Club can be used. Credit card transactions are normally at an officially recognized rate of exchange; they are often subject to tax. For credit card security, insist that imprints are made in your presence and that any imprints incorrectly completed should be torn into tiny pieces. Also destroy the carbon papers after the form is completed (signatures can be copied from them).

Money can be transferred between banks. A recommended method is, before leaving, to find out which local bank is correspondent to your bank at home, then when you need funds, telex your own bank and ask them to telex the money to the local bank (confirming by fax). Give exact information to your bank of the routing number of the receiving bank. Cash in dollars, local currency depending on the country, can be received within 48 banking hours. Visa ATM locations: www.visalatam.com; MasterCard: www.mastercard.com; for American Express information: www.americanexpress.com; for Western Union agents: www.westernunion.com

Plastic

Emergency contact numbers for credit card loss or theft are given in the relevant country's Essentials section

Essentials

Traveller's cheques These are convenient but they attract thieves (though refunds can of course be arranged) and you will find that they are more difficult than dollar bills to change in small towns (denominations of US$50 and US$100 are preferable, though one does need a few of US$20). American Express, Visa or Thomas Cook US$ traveller's cheques are recommended, but less commission is often charged on Citibank traveller's cheques, if they are cashed at Latin American branches of that bank. It is a good idea to take two kinds of cheque: if large numbers of one kind have recently been forged or stolen, making people suspicious, it is unlikely to have happened simultaneously with the other kind. Several banks charge a high fixed commission for changing traveller's cheques because they don't really want to be bothered. Exchange houses (*casas de cambio*) are usually much better for this service. Some establishments may ask to see the customer's record of purchase before accepting.

Exchange Most of the countries described in this book have freedom of exchange between US dollars and the local currency (in Ecuador the local currency is the US dollar). A few have a parallel rate of exchange, which is not always better than the official rate. Local conditions are described in the relevant chapters. Changing money on the street: if possible, do not do so alone. If unsure of the currency of the country you are about to enter, check rates with more than one changer at the border, or ask locals or departing travellers.

If departing by air, do not leave yourself too little money to pay the airport departure tax, which is never waived

Whenever you leave a country, sell any local currency before leaving, because the further away you get, the less the value of a country's money.

Americans should know that if they run out of funds they can usually expect no help from the US Embassy or Consul other than a referral to some welfare organization. Find out before you go precisely what services and assistance your embassy or consulate can provide if you find yourself in difficulties.

Cost of travelling A limited budget will restrict how much ground you can cover because, even if you eke our your céntimos, you will not be able to go too far because of the costs of getting back to where your

homeward flight leaves from. Also bear in mind that the cost of living varies from country to country. Your dollars will go further in Ecuador or Bolivia than in Brazil, Paraguay or Uruguay. These cheaper countries are therefore good places to end your journey as lower prices will be better suited to dwindling travel funds. An economy-budget traveller can expect to spend US$25-40 per day (see box on page 23). If you are happy to count every penny every night and pay as you go, your funds will last longer than if you indulge in the occasional night of luxury, or wish to spend a few days in a jungle lodge. Prebooking, including over the internet, often means you will spend more because the security of knowing you have a bed reserved for the night must be weighed against the freedom to shop around. Usually, you do not have to book ahead (although it is comforting to have your night of arrival in the country arranged), except at major holiday times in popular resorts or for important festivals. It is wise to reserve flights in advance at all times (and reconfirm bookings) and to reserve bus seats in advance when a festival is in the offing. Also allow for price increases in high season (each chapter indicates when this may be) and around public holidays.

Getting there

All the main airlines flying to each country are given in the 'Essentials' sections. There is no standard baggage allowance to Latin America. If you fly via the USA you are allowed two pieces of luggage up to 32 kg per case. Brazil has adopted this system, but it is not uniformly applied by all airlines. On flights from Europe there is a weight allowance of 20 or 23 kg, although some carriers out of Europe use the two-piece system, but may not apply it in both directions. The two-piece system is gaining wider acceptance, but it is always best to check in advance. Excess baggage charges can be high. The weight limits for internal flights are often lower; best to enquire beforehand.

Air

Prices & discounts It is possible to fly to most South American countries direct from France, Spain or UK. Main US gateways (also for connections from Europe) are Miami, Houston, Dallas, Atlanta and New York. On the west coast, Los Angeles has flights to several South American cities. If buying airline tickets routed through the USA, check that US taxes are included in the price. From the UK flights to Bogotá, Buenos Aires, Caracas, Rio and São Paulo start at between US$640-715 (in low season). Lima is more expensive (US$900), higher still in July and at Christmas. From the USA, Lima, Caracas and Bogotá are generally the cheapest destinations (around US$250-450). From Australia, Buenos Aires offers the best value all year (US$1,050-1,180).

Most airlines offer discounted fares on scheduled flights through agencies who specialize in this type of fare. For a list of these agencies see box page 43. The busy seasons are 7 December-15 January and 10 July-10 September. If you intend travelling during those times, book as far ahead as possible. Between February- May and September-November special offers may be available.

Other fares on scheduled services fall into three groups: **a)** **Excursion (return) fares** with restricted validity. Some carriers permit a change of dates on payment of a fee. **b)** **Yearly fares** These may be bought on a one-way or return basis. Some airlines require a specified return date, changeable upon payment of a fee. To leave the return completely open is possible for an extra fee. **c)** **Student (or under 26) fares** Do not assume that student tickets are the cheapest; though they are often very flexible, they are usually more expensive than a) or b) above. Some airlines are flexible on the age limit, others strict. One way and returns available. For people intending to travel a linear route and return from a different point from that at which they entered, there are 'Open Jaws' fares, which are available on student, yearly, or excursion fares.

If you buy discounted air tickets *always* check the reservation with the airline concerned to make sure the flight still exists. Also remember the IATA airlines' schedules change in March and October each year, so if you're going to be away a long time it's best to leave return flight coupons open. In addition, check whether you are entitled to any refund or re-issued ticket if you lose, or have stolen, a discounted air ticket. Some airlines require the repurchase of a

Discount flight agents

In the UK and Ireland: *STA Travel*, 86 Old Brompton Road, London SW7 3LQ, T0870 160 0599, www.statravel.co.uk They have other branches in London, as well as in Brighton, Bristol, Cambridge, Leeds, Manchester, Newcastle-Upon-Tyne and Oxford and on many University campuses. Specialists in low-cost student/youth flights and tours, also good for student IDs and insurance. *Trailfinders*, 194 Kensington High Street, London W8 7RG, T020-7938-3939. They also have other branches in London, as well as in Birmingham, Bristol, Cambridge, Glasgow, Leeds, Manchester, Newcastle, Oxford, Dublin and Belfast.

In North America: *Air Brokers International*, 323 Geary Street, Suite 411, San Francisco, CA94102, T01-800-883-3273, www.airbrokers.com Consolidator and specialist on RTW and Circle Pacific tickets. A student/ budget agency with branches in many other US cities. **Discount Airfares Worldwide On-Line**, www.etn.nl/discount.htm A hub of consolidator and discount agent links. **International Travel Network/Airlines of the Web**, www.itn.net/airlines Online air travel information and reservations. *STA Travel*, T1-800-836-4115, www.statravel.com With branches all over the US. *Travel CUTS*, 187 College Street, Toronto, ON M5T 1P7, T1-866-246-9762, www.travelcuts.com Specialist in student discount fares, IDs and other travel services. Branches in other Canadian cities as well as California, USA. **Travelocity**, www.travelocity.com Online consolidator.

In Australia and New Zealand: *Flight Centre*, with offices throughout Australia and other countries. In Australia call T133-133 or log on to www.flightcentre.com.au *STA Travel*, www.statravel.com.au 260 Hoddle Street, Abbotsford, Victoria 3067, T03-8417 6911. In NZ: Level 8, 229 Queen Street, Auckland, T09-309 9723. Also in major towns and university campuses. **Travel.com.au**, 80 Clarence Street, Sydney NSW Australia, T02-9249-5444, outside Sydney: T1300-130-482, www.travel.com.au

NB Using the web for booking flights, hotels and other services directly is becoming an increasingly popular way of making holiday reservations. You can make some good deals this way. Be aware, though, that cutting out the travel agents is denying yourself the experience that they can give, not just in terms of the best flights to suit your itinerary, but also advice on documents, insurance and other matters before you set out, safety, routes, lodging and times of year to travel. A reputable agent will also be bonded to give you some protection if arrangements collapse while you are travelling.

Essentials

ticket before you can apply for a refund, which will not be given until after the validity of the original ticket has expired. The *Iberia* group and *Air France*, for example, operate this costly system. Travel insurance in some cases covers lost tickets.

The *Mercosur Airpass* which applies to Brazil, Argentina, Chile, Uruguay and Paraguay, using several local carriers, is available to any passenger with a return ticket to a participating country. It must be bought in conjunction with an international flight; minimum stay is seven days, maximum 30, at least two countries must be visited. Maximum number of coupons is eight, the maximum number of stops per country is two. Fares are calculated on a mileage basis and range from US$225 to US$870. The All America Airpass, a multi-carrier, multi-country facility put together by Hahn Air of Germany, is built up from individual sectors at specially negotiated rates which can be bought just as a single journey, or a multi-sector trip, as required and according to cost. It is valid for 90 days from the use of the first coupon. *Grupo Taca* and *Copa* both offer airpasses linking South, Central and North America and have an attractive programme of sector fares. See the respective country sections for airpasses operated by national airlines. **Air passes**

Travelling as a passenger on a cargo ship to South America is not a cheap way to go, but if you have the time and want a bit of luxury, it makes a great alternative to flying. There has also been an upsurge of interest after 11 September 2001. There are sailings from Europe to the Caribbean, east and west coasts of South America. Likewise, you can sail from US ports to east and west coast South America. In the main, passage is round trip only. **Sea**

▶ *Specialist tour operators*

4starSouth America, T1-800-887 5686 (USA), T0871-711 5370 (UK), www.4starSouthAmerica.com (tours), www.4starFlights.com (flights)

Austral Tours, 20 Upper Tachbrook Street, London SW1V 1SH, T020-7233 5384, F020-7233 5385, www.latinamerica.co.uk

Condor Journeys & Adventures, 2 Ferry Bank, Colintrave, Argyll PA22 3ar, T1700-841318, www.condorjourneys-adventures.com

Discover Chile Tours, Discover Peru Tours, Discover Argentina Tours, 5775 Blue Lagoon Drive, suite 190, Miami, FL 33126, T305-266 5827, T1-800 826 4845, www.discoverchile.com

Dragoman, Camp Green, Debenham, Suffolk IP14 6LA, T01728-861133, www.dragoman.co.uk

eXito, 108 Rutgers Street, Fort Collins, CO 80525, T1-800-655 4053, T970-482 3019 (worldwide), www.exito-travel.com

Exodus Travels, Grange Mills, 9 Weir Road, London SW12 ONE, T020-8675 5550, www.exodus.co.uk

ExpeditionTrips.com, 6553 California Ave SW, Seattle, WA 98136, T206-547 0700, F206-634 9104, www.ExpeditionTrips.com

GAP Adventures, 19 Duncan Street, Toronto, Ontario M5H 3H1, T1-800-465 5600, www.gap.ca

Geodyssey, 116 Tollington Park, London N4 3RB, T020-7281 7788, www.geodyssey.co.uk

Go Latin Tours, 9300 South Dixie Highway, Suite 200, Miami, Florida 33156, T1-800-254 7378 (toll free), www.2000latintours.com

Guerba Adventure & Discovery Holidays, Wessex House, 40 Station Rd, Westbury, Wilts, BA13 3JN, T0845-1309770, info@guerba.co.uk

Journey Latin America, 12-13 Heathfield Terrace, Chiswick, London W4 4JE, T020-8747 8315, and 12 St Ann's Square, 2nd floor, Manchester M2 7HW, T0161-832 1441, F0161-832 1551,

www.journeylatinamerica.co.uk

Ladatco, 3006 Aviation Ave #4C, Coconut Grove, FL 33133, T800-327 6162, www.ladatco.com

Last Frontiers, Fleet Marston Farm, Aylesbury HP18 0QT, T01296-653000, www.lastfrontiers.co.uk

MILA Tours, 100 S Greenleaf, Gurnee IL 60031, T1-800-367 7378, www.milatours.com

Myths and Mountains, 976 Tee Court, Incline Village, NV 89451, USA, T800- 670 myth, 775-832 5454, F775-832 4454, www.mythsandmountains.com

Reef and Rainforest Tours Ltd, 1 The Plains, Totnes, Devon TQ9 5DR, T01803-866965, F01803-865916, www.reefrainforest.co.uk

South American Experience, 47 Causton Street, London SW1P 4AT, T020-7976 5511, www.southamericanexperience.co.uk

South American Tours, Hanauer Landstrasse 208-216, D-60314, Germany, T+49-69-405 8970, F+49–69-440432, www.southamericatours.de

Southtrip, Sarmiento 347, 4th floor, of 19, Buenos Aires, Argentina, T+54-11-4328 7075, www.southtrip.com

STA Travel, see Discount flight agents.

Steppes Latin America, 51 Castle Street, Cirencester, Glos GL7 1QD, T01285 885333, www.steppeslatinamerica.co.uk

Trailfinders, see Discount flight agents.

Travelbag, 3-5 High Street, Alton, Hampshire, GU34 1TL, T0870 890 1456, www.travelbag.co.uk

Trips Worldwide, 14 Frederick Place, Clifton, Bristol BS8 1AS, T0117-311 4400, www.tripsworldwide.co.uk

Tucan, with affiliated travel agencies worldwide, www.tucantravel.com

Veloso Tours, 33-34 Warple Way, London W3 0RG, T020-8762 0616, F020-8762 0716, www.veloso.com

World Expeditions, T020-8870 2600, www.worldexpeditions.co.uk

Useful contacts for advice and tickets: Andy Whitehouse at *Strand Voyages*, Charing Cross Shopping Concourse, The Strand, London WC2N 4HZ, T020-7836 6363, F020-7497 0078, www.strandtravel.co.uk *Strand Voyages* are booking agents for all routes. *Cargo Ship Voyages Ltd*, Hemley, Woodbridge, Suffolk IP12 4QF, T/F01473-736265, cargovoyager@btconnect.com *The Cruise People*, 88 York Street, London W1H 1QT, T020-7723 2450 (reservations 0800-526313), www.cruisepeople.co.uk In Europe, *SGV Reisezentrum Weggis* (Mr Urs Steiner), Seestrasse 7, CH-6353, Weggis, Switzerland, T041-390 1133, www.frachtschiffreisen.ch In the USA, *Travltips Cruise and Freighter Travel Association*, PO Box 580188, Flushing, NY

11358, T800-8728584, www.travltips.com On the web the *Internet Guide to Freighter Travel*, www.geocities.com/freighterman.geo/mainmenu.html Do not try to get a passage on a non-passenger carrying cargo ship to South America from a European port; it is not possible.

Touching down

Appearance There is a natural prejudice in all countries against travellers who ignore personal hygiene and have a generally dirty and unkempt appearance. Most Latin Americans, if they can afford it, devote great care to their clothes and appearance; it is appreciated if visitors do likewise. Buying clothing locally can help you to look less like a tourist.

Local customs
& laws

Essentials

Courtesy Remember that politeness – even a little ceremoniousness – is much appreciated. Men should always remove any headgear and say "con permiso" ("com licença" in Brazil) when entering offices, and be prepared to shake hands (this is much more common in Latin America than in Europe or North America); always say "Buenos días" (until midday) or "Buenas tardes" ("Bom dia" or "Boa tarde" in Brazil) and wait for a reply before proceeding further. Always remember that the traveller from abroad has enjoyed greater advantages in life than most Latin American minor officials and should be friendly and courteous in consequence. Never be impatient. Do not criticize situations in public: the officials may know more English than you think and they can certainly interpret gestures and facial expressions. Be judicious about discussing politics with strangers. Politeness can be a liability, however, in some situations; most Latin Americans are disorderly queuers. In commercial transactions (such as buying a meal and goods in a shop), politeness should be accompanied by firmness, and always ask the price first (arguing about money in a foreign language can be very difficult).

Politeness should also be extended to street traders; saying "No, gracias" or "Não, obrigado/a" with a smile is better than an arrogant dismissal. Whether you give money to beggars is a personal matter, but your decision should be influenced by whether a person is

Essentials

begging out of need or trying to cash in on the tourist trail. In the former case, local people giving may provide an indication. Giving money to children is a separate issue, upon which most agree: don't do it. There are occasions where giving food in a restaurant may be appropriate, but first inform yourself of local practice.

Moira Chubb, from New Zealand, suggests that if you are a guest and are offered food that arouses your suspicions, the only courteous way out is to feign an allergy or a stomach ailment. If worried about the purity of ice for drinks, ask for a beer.

Always ask people before taking pics or videos

Photography Pre-paid Kodak slide film cannot be developed in South America; it is also very hard to find. Kodachrome is almost impossible to buy. Some travellers (but not all) have advised against mailing exposed films home; either take them with you, or have them developed, but not printed, once you have checked the laboratory's quality. Note that postal authorities may use less sensitive equipment for X-ray screening than the airports do. Modern controlled X-ray machines are supposed to be safe for any speed of film, but it is worth trying to avoid X-ray as the doses are cumulative. Many airport officials will allow film to be passed outside X-ray arches; they may also hand-check a suitcase with a large quantity of film if asked politely. Western camera shops sell double lead-lined bags which will protect new and used film from x-rays. Black and white is a problem. Often it is shoddily machine-processed and the negatives are ruined. Ask the store if you can see an example of their laboratory's work and if they hand-develop.

Exposed film can be protected in humid areas by putting it in a balloon and tying a knot. Similarly keeping your camera in a plastic bag may reduce the effects of humidity. Humidity absorbing sachets can also be bought.

Responsible tourism
Spend money on locally produced goods and use common sense when bargaining – your few dollars saved may be a week's salary to others. Protect wildlife and other natural resources – don't buy souvenirs or goods made from wildlife unless they are clearly sustainably produced and are not protected under CITES legislation (CITES controls trade in endangered species)

Travel to the furthest corners of the globe is now commonplace and the mass movement of people for leisure and business is a major source of foreign exchange and economic development in many parts of South America. In some regions (eg the Galápagos Islands and Machu Picchu) it is probably the most significant economic activity.

The benefits of international travel are self-evident for both hosts and travellers: employment, increased understanding of different cultures, business and leisure opportunities. At the same time there is clearly a downside to the industry. Where visitor pressure is high and/or poorly regulated, adverse impacts to society and the natural environment may be apparent. Paradoxically, this is as true in undeveloped and pristine areas (where culture and the natural environment are less 'prepared' for even small numbers of visitors) as in major resort destinations.

The travel industry is growing rapidly and increasingly the impacts of this supposedly 'smokeless' industry are becoming apparent. These impacts can seem remote and unrelated to an individual trip or holiday (eg air travel is clearly implicated in global warming and damage to the ozone layer, resort location and construction can destroy natural habitats and restrict traditional rights and activities) but, individual choice and awareness can make a difference in many instances, and collectively, travellers are having a significant effect in shaping a more responsible and sustainable industry.

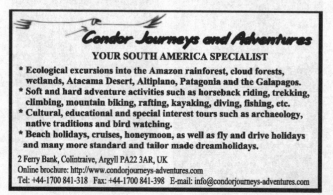

▶ *Carnet de passages*

*There are two recognized documents for taking a vehicle through customs in South America: a carnet de passages issued jointly by the **Fedération Internationale de l'Automobile** (FIA – Paris) and the **Alliance Internationale de Tourisme** (AIT-Geneva), and the Libreta de Pasos por Aduana issued by the **Federación Interamericana de Touring y Automóvil Clubs** (FITAC). The libreta, a 10-page book of three-part passes for customs, should be available from any South American automobile club member of FITAC. In practice it is only available to non-residents from the **Touring y Automóvil Club de Venezuela** and, at US$400, is not worth the effort or expense. If you purchase one of these documents, get a carnet de passages, issued in the country where the vehicle is registered. In the UK it costs £75 for 25 pages, available from the **RAC** or the **AA**. In Canada the fee is $450 CDN, but in all cases you have to add on deposits and insurance premiums, which can take the cost into the thousands, depending on the value of the car. The carnet is valid 12 months. In the USA the **AAA** does not issue the carnet, although the HQ in Washington DC may give advice. It is available from the **Canadian Automobile Association**, 1145 Hunt Club Road, suite 200, Ottawa, K1V 0Y3, T613-247 0118, www.caa.ca who can give full details. Ask the motoring organization in your home country about availability of the carnet.*

The carnet de passages is recognized by all South American customs authorities and, in theory, required by all except Bolivia. While entry to most countries may be possible without this document (and may not even be asked for), passage through customs should be much quicker and easier with it.

Of course travel can have beneficial impacts and this is something to which every traveller can contribute. Many National Parks are part funded by receipts from visitors. Similarly, travellers can promote patronage and protection of important archaeological sites and heritage through their interest and contributions via entrance and performance fees. They can also support small-scale enterprises by staying in locally run hotels and hostels, eating in local restaurants and by purchasing local goods, supplies and arts and crafts. In fact, since the Responsible Travel section was first introduced in the South American Handbook in 1992 there has been a phenomenal growth in *tourism that promotes and supports the conservation of natural environments and is also fair and equitable to local communities*. This "ecotourism" segment is probably the fastest growing sector of the travel industry and provides a vast and growing range of destinations and activities in South America.

While the authenticity of some ecotourism operators' claims need to be interpreted with care, there is clearly both a huge demand for this type of activity and also significant opportunities to support worthwhile conservation and social development initiatives. Organizations such as **Conservation International** (T001-202-912 1000, www.ecotour.org), the **Eco-Tourism society** (T001-802-651 9818, ecotourism.org), **Planeta** (www.planeta.com) and **Tourism Concern** (T44-20-7753 3330, www.tourism concern.org.uk) have begun to develop and/or promote ecotourism projects and destinations and their web sites are an excellent source of information and details for sites and initiatives throughout South America. Additionally, organizations such as, **Earthwatch** T44-1865-318838 or in the US 978-461 0881, www.earthwatch.org) and **Discovery Initiatives** (T44-1285-643333, www.discoveryinitiatives.com) offer opportunities to participate directly in scientific research and development projects throughout the region.

South America offers unique and unforgettable experiences – often based on the natural environment, cultural heritage and local society. These are the reasons many of us choose to travel and why many more will want to do so in the future. Shouldn't we provide an opportunity for future travellers and hosts to enjoy the quality of experience and interaction that we take for granted?

Safety **Drugs** Users of drugs, even of soft ones, without medical prescription should be particularly careful, as some countries impose heavy penalties – up to 10 years' imprisonment – for even the simple possession of such substances. In this connection, the planting of drugs on travellers, by traffickers or the police, is not unknown. If offered drugs on the street, make no response at all and keep walking. Note that people who roll their own cigarettes are often suspected of carrying drugs and subjected to intensive searches. Advisable to stick to commercial brands of cigarettes.

Keeping safe Generally speaking, most places in South America are no more dangerous than any major city in Europe or North America. In provincial towns, main places of interest, on day time buses and in ordinary restaurants the visitor should be quite safe. Nevertheless, in large cities (particularly in crowded places, eg bus stations, markets), crime exists, most of which is opportunistic. If you are aware of the dangers, act confidently and use your common sense, you will lessen many of the risks. The following tips are all endorsed by travellers. Keep all documents secure; hide your main cash supply in different places or under your clothes: extra pockets sewn inside shirts and trousers, pockets closed with a zip or safety pin, moneybelts (best worn under rather than outside your clothes at the waist), neck or leg pouches, a thin chain for attaching a purse to your bag or under your clothes and elasticated support bandages for keeping money and cheques above the elbow or below the knee have been repeatedly recommended. Keep cameras in bags; take spare spectacles (eyeglasses); don't wear expensive wrist-watches or jewellery. If you wear a shoulder-bag in a market, carry it in front of you.

For specific local problems, see under the individual countries in the text

Ignore mustard smearers and paint or shampoo sprayers, and strangers' remarks like "what's that on your shoulder?" or "have you seen that dirt on your shoe?" Furthermore, don't bend over to pick up money or other items in the street. These are all ruses intended to distract your attention and make you easy prey for an accomplice to steal from. Take local advice about being out at night and, if walking after dark, walk in the road, not on the pavement/sidewalk.

Ruses involving `plainclothes policemen' are infrequent, but it is worth knowing that the real police only have the right to see your passport (not your money, tickets or hotel room). Before handing anything over, ask why they need to see it and make sure you understand the reason. Insist on seeing identification and on going to the police station by main roads. On no account take them directly back to your lodgings. Be even more suspicious if he seeks confirmation of his status from a passer-by. A related scam is for a 'tourist' to gain your confidence, then accomplices create a reason to check your documents. If someone tries to bribe you, insist on a receipt. If attacked, remember your assailants may well be armed, and try not to resist.

Leave any valuables you don't need in safe-deposit in your hotel when sightseeing locally. Always keep an inventory of what you have deposited. If there is no safe, lock your bags and secure them in your room (some people take eyelet-screws for padlocking cupboards or drawers). If you lose valuables, always report to the police and note details of the report – for insurance purposes.

When you have all your luggage with you, be careful. From airports take official taxis or special airport buses. Take a taxi between bus station/railway station and hotel. Keep your bags with you in the taxi and pay only when you and your luggage are safely out of the vehicle. Make sure the taxi has inner door handles and do not share the ride with a stranger. Avoid night buses; never arrive at night; and watch your belongings whether they are stowed inside or outside the cabin (roof top luggage racks create extra problems, which are sometimes unavoidable – make sure your bag is waterproof). Major bus lines often issue a luggage ticket when bags are stored in the hold of the bus. Finally, never accept food, drink, sweets or cigarettes from unknown fellow-travellers on buses or trains. They may be drugged, and you would wake up hours later without your belongings.

Rape This can happen anywhere. If you are the victim of a sexual assault, you are advised in the first instance to contact a doctor (this can be your home doctor if you prefer). You will need tests to determine whether you have contracted any sexually-transmitted diseases; you may also need advice on post-coital contraception. You should also contact your embassy, where consular staff are very willing to help in such cases.

Police Whereas in Europe and North America we are accustomed to law enforcement on a systematic basis, in general, enforcement in Latin America is achieved by periodic campaigns.

The most typical is a round-up of criminals in the cities just before Christmas. In December, therefore, you may well be asked for identification at any time, and if you cannot produce it, you will be jailed. If a visitor is jailed his or her friends should provide food every day. This is especially important for people on a diet, such as diabetics. In the event of a vehicle accident in which anyone is injured, all drivers involved are automatically detained until blame has been established, and this does not usually take less than two weeks.

Never offer a bribe unless you are fully conversant with the customs of the country. (In Chile, for instance, it would land you in serious trouble if you tried to bribe a *carabinero*.) Wait until the official makes the suggestion, or offer money in some form which is apparently not bribery, for example "In our country we have a system of on-the-spot fines (*multas de inmediato*). Is there a similar system here?" Do not assume that an official who accepts a bribe is prepared to do anything else that is illegal. You bribe him to persuade him to do his job, or to persuade him not to do it, or to do it more quickly, or more slowly. You do not bribe him to do something which is against the law. The mere suggestion would make him very upset. If an official suggests that a bribe must be paid before you can proceed on your way, be patient (assuming you have the time) and he may relent.

Where to stay

Hotels
See inside front cover for our hotel grade price guide. Unless otherwise stated, it is assumed that hotels listed are clean and friendly and that rooms have shower and toilet. In any class, hotel rooms facing the street may be noisy always ask for the best, quietest room

For about US$10, a cheap but not bad hotel room can be found in most countries, although in some of the Andean countries you may not have to pay that much. For those on a really tight budget, it is a good idea to ask for a boarding house – *casa de huéspedes, hospedaje, pensión, casa familial* or *residencial*, according to country – they are normally to be found in abundance near bus and railway stations and markets. Good value hotels can also be found near truckers' stops/service stations; they are usually secure. There are often great seasonal variations in hotel prices in resorts. Remember, cheaper hotels don't always supply soap, towels and toilet paper; in colder (higher) regions they may not supply enough blankets, so take your own or a sleeping bag. To avoid price hikes for gringos, ask if there is a cheaper room.

Experiment in International Living Ltd, 287 Worcester Rd, Malvern, Worcestershire WR14 1AB, T0800-018 4015 or 01684-562577, F562212, and offices worldwide, www.eiluk.org Can arrange stays with families from one to four weeks in Argentina, Chile, Ecuador and Brazil. This has been recommended as an excellent way to meet people and learn the language. They also offer gap year opportunities.

NB The electric showers used in innumerable hotels should be checked for obvious flaws in the wiring; try not to touch the rose while it is producing hot water.

Cockroaches These are ubiquitous and unpleasant, but not dangerous. Take some insecticide powder if staying in cheap hotels; *Baygon* (Bayer) has been recommended. Stuff toilet paper in any holes in walls that you may suspect of being parts of cockroach runs.

Toilets
Many hotels, restaurants and bars have inadequate water supplies. **Almost without exception used toilet paper should not be flushed down the pan, but placed in the receptacle provided**. This applies even in quite expensive hotels. Failing to observe this custom will block the pan or drain, a considerable health risk. It is quite common for people to stand on the toilet seat (facing the wall – easier to balance).

Youth hostels
Organizations affiliated to the Youth Hostels movement exist in Argentina, Brazil, Colombia, Chile, Peru and Uruguay. There is an associate organization in Ecuador. More information in the country sections and from *Hostelling International* (was the International Youth Hostel Federation). An independent site on hostelling is the *Internet Guide to Hostelling*, www.hostels.com

Camping
Organized campsites are referred to in the text immediately below hotel lists, under each town. If there is no organized site in town, a football pitch or gravel pit might serve. Obey the following rules for 'wild' camping: (1) arrive in daylight and pitch your tent as it gets dark; (2) ask permission to camp from the parish priest, or the fire chief, or the police, or a farmer regarding his own property; (3) never ask a group of people – especially young people; (4) never camp on a beach (because of sandflies and thieves). If you can't get information from anyone, camp in a

spot where you can't be seen from the nearest inhabited place, or road, and make sure no one saw you go there. In Argentina and Brazil, it is common to camp at gas/petrol stations. As Béatrice Völkle of Gampelen, Switzerland, adds, camping wild may be preferable to those organized sites which are treated as discos, with only the afternoon reserved for sleeping.

If taking a cooker, the most frequent recommendation is a multifuel stove (eg MSR International, Coleman Peak 1), which will burn unleaded petrol or, if that is not available, kerosene, *benzina blanca*, etc. Alcohol-burning stoves are simple, reliable, but slow and you have to carry a lot of fuel: for a methylated spirit-burning stove, the following fuels apply, *alcohol desnaturalizado, alcohol metílico, alcohol puro (de caña)* or *alcohol para quemar*. Ask for 95%, but 70% will suffice. In all countries fuel can usually be found in chemists/pharmacies. Gas cylinders and bottles are usually exchangeable, but if not can be recharged; specify whether you use butane or propane. Gas canisters are not always available. The Camping Clube do Brasil gives 50% discounts to holders of international campers' cards.

Getting around

The continent has an extensive road system with frequent bus services. The buses are often comfortable; the difficulties of Andean terrain affect the quality of vehicles. In mountainous country do not expect buses to get to their destination after long journeys anywhere near on time. Do not turn up for a bus at the last minute; if it is full it may depart early. Tall travellers are advised to take aisle rather than window seats on long journeys as this allows more leg room. When the journey takes more than three or four hours, meal stops at country inns or bars, good and bad, are the rule. Usually, no announcement is made on the duration of a stop: ask the driver and follow him, if he eats, eat. See what the locals are eating – and buy likewise, or make sure you're stocked up well on food and drink at the start. For drinks, stick to bottled water or soft drinks or coffee (black). The food sold by vendors at bus stops may be all right: watch if locals are buying, though unpeeled fruit is of course reliable.

Buses & trains
See Getting there for details of air transport including air passes

Where they still run, trains are slower than buses. They tend to provide finer scenery and you can normally see much more wildlife than from the road – it is less disturbed by one or two trains a day than by the more frequent road traffic.

The machine A normal car will reach most places of interest, but high ground clearance is useful for badly surfaced or unsurfaced roads and for fording rivers. Four-wheel drive vehicles are recommended for greater flexibility in mountain and jungle territory. In Patagonia, main roads are gravel rather than paved: perfectly passable without 4WD, just rough and dusty. Consider fitting wire guards for headlamps, and for windscreens too. Wherever you travel you should expect from time to time to find roads that are badly maintained, damaged or closed during the wet season, and delays because of floods, landslides and huge potholes. Diesel cars are much cheaper to run than petrol ones and the fuel is easily available, although in Venezuela you may have to look hard for it outside Caracas. Most towns can supply a mechanic of sorts and probably parts for Bosch fuel injection equipment. Watch the

Car

mechanics like a hawk, since there's always a brisk market in spares. That apart, they enjoy a challenge, and can fix most things, eventually. Standard European and Japanese cars run on fuel with a higher octane rating than is commonly available in North, South or Central America, and in Brazil petrol (gasolina) is in fact gasohol, with a 12% admixture of alcohol. A high compression fuel injection engine will not like this.

Security Spare no ingenuity in making your car secure. Anything less than the Brink's armoured van can be broken into and unsecured parts on the exterior (wing mirrors, spot lamps, even wheels without locking nuts) are likely to be stolen too. Try never to leave the car unattended except in a locked garage or guarded parking space. Lock the clutch or accelerator to the steering wheel with a heavy, obvious chain or lock. Street children will generally protect your car fiercely in exchange for a tip.

Documents To drive your own vehicle in South America, you must have an international driver's licence. You must also have the vehicle's registration document in the name of the driver, or, in the case of a car registered in someone else's name, a notarized letter of authorization. Most countries give a limited period of stay, but allow an extension if requested in advance. Be very careful to keep **all** the papers you are given when you enter, to produce when you leave (see box, *Carnet de passages*).

Insurance Insurance for the vehicle against accident, damage or theft is best arranged in the country of origin. In Latin American countries it is very expensive to insure against accident and theft, especially as you should take into account the value of the car increased by duties calculated in real (ie non devaluing) terms. If the car is stolen or written off you will be required to pay very high import duty on its value. A few countries insist on compulsory third party insurance, to be bought at the border: in other countries it's technically required, but not checked up on (Venezuela seems to be the only country where it is easy to obtain). Get the legally required minimum cover, not expensive, as soon as you can, because if you should be involved in an accident and are uninsured, your car could be confiscated. If anyone is hurt, do not pick them up (you may become liable). Seek assistance from the nearest police station or hospital if you are able to do so.

Car hire The main international car hire companies operate in all countries, but they do tend to be very expensive, reflecting the high costs and accident rates. Hotels and tourist agencies will tell you where to find cheaper rates, but you will need to check that you have such basics as spare wheel, toolkit and functioning lights etc. You'll probably have more fun if you drive yourself, although it's always possible to hire a car with driver. If you plan to do a lot of driving and will have time at the end to dispose of it, investigate the possibility of buying a second hand car locally: since hiring is so expensive it may well work out cheaper and will probably do you just as well. Car rental websites: *Avis* www.avis.com (in all countries except Bolivia, Colombia, Guyana, Paraguay); *Budget* www.budget.com (in all countries except Bolivia, Paraguay, Suriname); *Hertz* www.hertz.com (in all countries except Guyana); *Localiza* www.localiza.com.br (Argentina, Bolivia, Brazil, Ecuador, Paraguay, Peru, Uruguay); *National* www.nationalcar.com (Chile, Colombia, Paraguay, Peru). **Car Hire Insurance** Check exactly what the hirer's insurance policy covers. In many cases it will only protect you against minor bumps and scrapes, not major accidents, nor 'natural' damage (eg flooding). Ask if extra cover is available. Also find out, if using a credit card, whether the card automatically includes insurance. Beware of being billed for scratches which were on the vehicle before you hired it. This includes checking the windscreen and what procedures are involved if a new one is needed.

Shipping a vehicle From Europe or the USA you can go to Panama and shop around for the best value sailing to whichever port best suits your travelling plans. It is also possible to ship a vehicle from Costa Rica. Alternatively you can ship a vehicle direct from Europe or the USA.

A book containing much practical information on South American motoring conditions and requirements is *Driving to Heaven*, by Derek Stansfield (available from the author, Ropley, Broad Oak, Sturminster Newton, Dorset DT10 2HG, UK, T/F01258-472534, £4.95 plus postage, if outside the UK, or from www.amazon.co.uk).

Essentials

Motorcycling
People are generally very amicable to motorcyclists

The motorcycle The bike should be off road capable. Buying a bike in the States and driving down works out cheaper than buying one in the UK. Get to know the bike before you go, ask the dealers in your country what goes wrong with it and arrange a link whereby you can get parts flown out to you.

Security Try not to leave a fully laden bike on its own. An Abus D or chain will keep the bike secure. A cheap alarm gives you peace of mind if you leave the bike outside a hotel at night. Most hotels will allow you to bring the bike inside. Look for hotels that have a courtyard or more secure parking and never leave luggage on the bike overnight or while it is unattended. Also take a cover for the bike.

Documents A passport, International Driving Licence and bike registration document are necessary. Riders fare much better with a *carnet de passages* than without it.

Shipping Bikes may be sent from Panama to Colombia by cargo flight (eg *Girag Ltda Colombia*, offices at Tocumen airport – Panama, Bogotá and Barranquilla), or from Miami to Caracas. From South America to Europe, check all possibilities as it can be cheaper to fly a bike home than to ship it.

Border crossings If you do not have a *carnet*, do not try to cross borders on a Sunday or a holiday anywhere as a charge is levied on the usually free borders in South America. South American customs and immigration inspectors are mostly friendly, polite and efficient. If in doubt ask to see the boss and/or the rule book.

Cycling
Pace yourself; do not be too ambitious at the start of the journey and plan ahead for the type of terrain that you will covering each day

Unless you are planning a journey almost exclusively on paved roads – when a high quality touring bike such as a Dawes Super Galaxy would suffice – a mountain bike is strongly recommended. The good quality ones (and the cast iron rule is **never** to skimp on quality), are incredibly tough and rugged, with low gear ratios for difficult terrain, wide tyres with plenty of tread for good road-holding, V brakes, sealed hubs and bottom bracket and a low centre of gravity for improved stability. A chrome-alloy frame is a desirable choice over aluminium as it can be welded if necessary. Although touring bikes, and to a lesser extent

mountain bikes and spares are available in the larger Latin American cities, remember that in the developing world most indigenous manufactured goods are shoddy and rarely last. If your bike is shock suspension equipped, take your own replacement parts and know how to overhaul them. In some countries, such as Chile and Uruguay, imported components can be found but they tend to be extremely expensive. (Shimano parts are generally the easiest to find.) Buy everything you possibly can before you leave home. *Richard's New Bicycle Book* (Pan, £12.99) makes useful reading for even the most mechanically minded.

Useful tips Wind, not hills is the enemy of the cyclist. Try to make the best use of the times of day when there is little; mornings tend to be best but there is no steadfast rule. In parts of Patagonia there can be gusting winds of 80 kph around the clock at some times of year, whereas in other areas there can be none. Take care to avoid dehydration, by drinking regularly. In hot, dry areas with limited supplies of water, be sure to carry an ample supply. Take an effective water filtration pump (eg Pur Explorer). For food, carry the staples (such as sugar, salt, dried milk, tea, coffee, porridge oats, raisins and dried soups) and supplement these with whatever local foods can be found in the markets. Give your bicycle a thorough daily check for loose nuts or bolts or bearings. See that all parts run smoothly. A good chain should last 5,000 miles, 8,000 km or more, but be sure to keep it as clean as possible – an old toothbrush is good for this – and to oil it lightly from time to time. Carry 'zap-straps' to fasten components together quickly and securely when disassembling your bike for bus or train transport. Remember that thieves are attracted to towns and cities, so when sightseeing, try to leave your bicycle with someone such as a café owner or a priest. Country people tend to be more honest and are usually friendly and very inquisitive. However, don't take unnecessary risks; always see that your bicycle is secure (most hotels will allow bikes to be kept in rooms). In more remote regions dogs can be vicious; carry a stick or some small stones, or use your water bottle as a spray to frighten them off. Traffic on main roads can be a nightmare; it is usually far more rewarding to keep to the smaller roads or to paths if they exist. Most cyclists agree that the main danger comes from other traffic. Dismount and move off the road when two large vehicles are passing you on a narrow, shoulderless road. You will be heartily thanked with honks and waves, even a free meal at times. A rearview mirror has been frequently recommended to forewarn you of vehicles which are too close behind. You also need to watch out for hazards such as oncoming, overtaking vehicles, unstable loads on trucks and protruding loads. Make yourself conspicuous by wearing bright clothing and a helmet. Most towns have a bicycle shop of some description, but it is best to do your own repairs and adjustments whenever possible. If undertaking your own maintenance, make sure you know how to do it. Knowing how to do simple overhauls, and carrying extra bearings for bottom bracket and hub repairs for local bikes (usually BMX styles), will earn you much gratitude, especially in isolated villages.

Many cycle tourists are opting for rugged trailers as opposed to the old rack and pannier system. The end product may look a little unwieldy but little time is necessary to get used to the new feeling. The biggest advantage is that you still have a bike, instantly, not an over laden tank on two wheels. It would be a shame to miss out on the amazing trail riding that exists all over the continent. Trailers are also much more rugged than racks, which constantly break, and are much easier to weld.

The **Expedition Advisory Centre**, administered by the Royal Geographical Society, 1, Kensington Gore, London SW7 2AR, T020-7591 3008, www.rgs.org, has published a useful monograph entitled *Bicycle Expeditions*, by **Paul Vickers**. Published in March 1990, can be downloaded from the RGS's website. Useful websites are *Bike South America*, www.e-ddws.com/bsa/ and the cycling portal www.cyclery.com Also recommended is *Cyclo Accueil Cyclo*, 3 rue Limouzin, 42160 Andrézieux, France, cacoadou@netcourier.com This is an organization of long-haul tourers who open their homes for free to passing cyclists.

Because expanding air services have captured the lucrative end of the passenger market, passenger services on the rivers are in decline. Worst hit have been the upper reaches; rivers like the Ucayali in Peru, but the trend is apparent throughout the region. The situation has been aggravated for the casual traveller by a new generation of purpose-built tugs (all engine-room and bridge), that can handle up to a dozen freight barges but have no

Remember that you can always stick your bike on a bus, canoe or plane to get yourself nearer to the heart of where you want your wheels to take you. This is especially useful when there are long stretches of major road ahead, where all that stretches before you are hours of turbulence as the constant stream of heavy trucks and long-haul buses zoom by

In almost any country it is possible to rent a bike for a few days, or join an organized tour for riding in the mountains. You should check, however, that the machine you are hiring is up to the conditions you will be encountering, or that the tour company is not a fly-by-night outfit without back-up, good bikes or maintenance

Essentials

Boat

passenger accommodation. In Peru passenger boats must now supplement incomes by carrying cargo, and this lengthens their journey cycle. In the face of long delays, travellers might consider shorter 'legs' involving more frequent changes of boat; though the more local the service, the slower and more uncomfortable it will be.

Hammocks, mosquito nets (not always good quality), plastic containers for water storage, kettles and cooking utensils can be purchased in any sizeable riverside town, as well as tinned food. Fresh bread, cake, eggs and fruit are available in most villages. Cabin bunks are provided with thin mattresses but these are often foul. Replacements can be bought locally but rolls of plastic foam that can be cut to size are also available and much cheaper. Eye-screws for securing washing lines and mosquito nets are useful, and tall passengers who are not taking a hammock and who may find insufficient headroom on some boats should consider a camp-chair.

In Venezuelan Amazonas hitching rides on boats is possible if you camp at the harbour or police post where all boats must register. Take any boat going in your direction as long as it reaches the next police post. See the special section on the Brazilian Amazon, page 525.

Maps & guide books Those from the *Institutos Geográficos Militares* in the capitals are often the only good maps available in Latin America. It is therefore wise to get as many as possible in your home country before leaving, especially if travelling by land. A recommended series of general maps is that published by **International Travel Maps** (ITM), 345 West Broadway, Vancouver BC, V5Y 1P8, Canada, T604-879 3621, F604-879 4521, www.itmb.com, several compiled with historical notes, by the late Kevin Healey. Available (among others) are South America South, North East and North West (1:4M), Ecuador (1:1M), The Galapagos Islands (1:500,000), Easter Island (1:30,000), Argentina (1:4M), The Amazon (1:4M), Uruguay (1:800,000), Venezuela (1:1.75M), Guyana (1:850,000) and Surinam (1:750,000). Another map series that has been mentioned is that of **New World Edition**, Bertelsmann, Neumarkter Strasse 18, 81673 München, Germany, *Mittelamerika, Südamerika Nord, Südamerika Sud, Brasilien* (all 1:4M). London's **Stanfords**, 12-14 Long Acre, Covent Garden, WC2E 9LP, T020-7836 1321, www.stanfords.co.uk, also sells a wide variety of guides and maps. Branches in Bristol and Manchester.

Keeping in touch

Internet Email is common and public access to the internet is becoming widespread with cybercafés opening in both large and small towns. In large cities an hour in a cyber café will cost between US$0.50-2, with some variation between busy and quiet times. Speed varies enormously, from city to city, café to café. Away from population centres service is slower and more expensive. Remember that for many South Americans cyber cafés provide their only access to a computer, so it can be a very busy place and providers can get overloaded. We list some cybercafés in the text. Two websites which give information on cybercafés are: www.netcafeguide.com and www.netcafes.com

Postal services vary in efficiency from country to country and prices are quite high; pilfering is   **Post**
frequent. All mail, especially packages, should be registered. Check before leaving home if your
embassy will hold mail, and for how long, in preference to the Poste Restante/General Delivery
(*Lista de Correos*) department of a country's Post Office. (Cardholders can use American Express
agencies.) If there seems to be no mail at the Lista under the initial letter of your surname, ask
them to look under the initial of your forename or your middle name. Remember that there is
no W in Spanish; look under V, or ask. For the smallest risk of misunderstanding, use title, initial
and surname only. If having items sent to you by courier (such as DHL), do not use poste
restante, but an address such as a hotel: a signature is required on receipt.

AT&T's 'USA Direct', *Sprint* and *MCI* are all available for calls to the USA. It is much cheaper than   **Telephone**
operator-assisted calls. Details given under individual countries. Other countries such as the UK
and Canada have similar systems; obtain details before leaving home. With privatization, more
and more companies are coming onto the market; check prices carefully. Many places with
public fax machines (post offices, telephone companies or shops) will receive messages as well
as send. Fax machines are often switched off; you may have to phone to confirm receipt.

South America has more local and community radio stations than practically anywhere else   **World Band**
in the world; a shortwave (world band) radio offers a practical means to brush up on the   **Radio**
language, sample popular culture and absorb some of the richly varied regional music.
International broadcasters such as the *BBC World Service*, the *Voice of America*, Boston
(Mass)-based *Monitor Radio International* (operated by *Christian Science Monitor*) and the
Quito-based Evangelical station, *HCJB*, keep the traveller abreast of news and events, in both
English and Spanish.

Compact or miniature portables are recommended, with digital tuning and a full range of
shortwave bands, as well as FM, long and medium wave. Detailed advice on radio models
(£150 for a decent one) and wavelengths can be found in the annual publication, ***Passport to
World Band Radio*** (Box 300, Penn's Park, PA 18943, USA, £15.50). Details of local stations is
listed in ***World Radio and TV Handbook*** (WTRH), PO Box 9027, 1006 AA Amsterdam, The
Netherlands, £15.80 (www.amazon.co.uk, prices). Both of these, free wavelength guides and
selected radio sets are available from the BBC World Service Bookshop, Bush House Arcade,
Bush House, Strand, London WC2B 4PH, UK, T020-7557 2576.

Food and drink

Food in South America is enticingly varied and regionally-based. Within one country you
cannot guarantee that what you enjoyed on the coast will be available in the Sierras. It is
impossible to list here what is on offer and there is a paragraph on each nation's food and
drink under 'Essentials'. Here are a few tasters, though: fish from Amazonian rivers, from
Chilean Pacific waters, and fresh from Andean lakes; or try *ceviche*, raw fish marinated in
lemon juice and chili (best in Peru and Ecuador). If meat is your thing, go to an Argentine or
Uruguayan *parrillada* (barbecue), or a Brazilian *churrascaria* - at the *rodizio* restaurants, they
will bring the meat until you can eat no more. Also in Brazil, there's the traditional *feijoada*
(meat and beans, with a lot more besides) and the African-style food of Bahia. An Andean
speciality is *cuy*, guinea pig and don't forget that the potato is native to the Andes, with more
varieties than you've had fish and chips. Chicken is the basis of many dishes, such as *ajiaco* in
Colombia. Corn (maize) and yucca are staples and in many places starchy vegetables are the
main form of carbohydrate. Chinese restaurants tend to offer good value and where there are
large immigrant communities you'll find excellent Japanese or Italian restaurants. Pizza is
pretty ubiquitous, sometimes genuine, sometimes anything but. Then there's fruit, fruit and
more fruit in all the tropical regions, eaten fresh or as ice cream, or drunk as juice.

In all countries except Brazil and Chile (where cold meats, cheese, eggs, fruit etc generally
figure) breakfast usually means coffee or tea with rolls and butter, and anything more is
charged extra. In Colombia and Ecuador breakfast usually means eggs, a roll, fruit juice and a
mug of milk with coffee; say "breakfast without eggs" if you do not want that much.
Vegetarians should be able to list all the foods they cannot eat; saying "Soy vegetariano/a"

Essentials

(I'm a vegetarian) or "no como carne" (I don't eat meat) is often not enough. Most restaurants serve a daily special meal, usually at lunchtime, which is cheap and good. Other than that you can expect to pay from US$7 in Peru, Ecuador or Bolivia, to US$15 in Uruguay on breakfast and dinner per day.

Shopping

You can also ship items home

Handicrafts, like food, enjoy regional distinctiveness, especially in items such as textiles. Each region, village even, has its own characteristic pattern or style of cloth, so the choice is enormous. Throughout the Andes, weaving has spiritual significance as well as a practical side. Reproductions of pre-Columbian designs can be found in pottery and jewellery and many crafts people throughout the continent make delightful items in gold and silver. Gemstones are good in Brazil. Leather goods are best in the cattle countries, Argentina, Uruguay, Brazil and Colombia, while Peru is now marketing native cotton. Musical instruments (eg from Bolivia), gaucho wear, the mate drinking gourd and silver straw (*bombilla*), soapstone carvings and all manner of ceramics, from useful pots to figurines are just some of the things you can bring home with you. Remember that handicrafts can almost invariably be bought more cheaply away from the capital, though the choice may be less wide. Bargaining seems to be the general rule in most countries' street markets, but don't make a fool of yourself by bargaining over what, to you, is a small amount of money.

If British travellers have no space in their luggage, they might like to remember *Tumi*, the Latin American Craft Centre, who specialize in Mexican and Andean products and who produce cultural and educational videos for schools: at 8/9 New Bond St Place, Bath BA1 1BH (T01225-480470, www.tumicrafts.com). *Tumi* (Music) Ltd specializes in different rhythms of Latin America. See *Arts and Crafts of South America*, by **Lucy Davies** and **Mo Fini**, published by Tumi (1994), for a fine introduction to the subject. There are similar shops in the USA.

Sport and activities

Hiking & trekking

A network of paths and tracks covers much of South America and is in constant use by the local people. In countries with a large Indian population – Ecuador, Peru and Bolivia, for instance – you can walk just about anywhere, but in the more European countries, such as Venezuela, Chile, and Argentina, you must usually limit yourself to the many excellent national parks with hiking trails.

Hiking and backpacking should not be approached casually. Even if you only plan to be out a couple of hours you should have comfortable, safe footwear (which can cope with the wet) and a daypack to carry your sweater and waterproof (which must be more than showerproof). At high altitudes the difference in temperature between sun and shade is remarkable. Longer trips require basic backpacking equipment. Essential items are: backpack with frame, sleeping bag, closed cell foam mat for insulation, stove, tent or tarpaulin, dried food (not tins), water bottle, compass. Some, but not all of these things, are available locally.

When planning treks in the Andes you should be aware of the effects and dangers of acute mountain sickness, and cerebral and pulmonary oedema (see Health, page 64). These can be avoided by spending a few days acclimatizing to the altitude before starting your walk, and by climbing slowly. Otherwise there are fewer dangers than in most cities. Hikers have little to fear from the animal kingdom apart from insects (although it's best to avoid actually stepping on a snake), and robbery and assault are rare. You are much more of a threat to the environment than vice versa. Leave no evidence of your passing; don't litter and don't give gratuitous presents of sweets or money to rural villagers. Respect their system of reciprocity; if they give you hospitality or food, then is the time to reciprocate with presents.

For trekking in mountain areas, where the weather can deteriorate rapidly (eg in Torres del Paine), trekkers should consider taking the following equipment (list supplied by Andrew Dobbie of Swansea, who adds that it "is in no way finite"): **Clothing**: warm hat (wool or man-made fibre), thermal underwear, T-shirts/shirts, trousers (quick-drying and preferably windproof, never jeans), warm (wool or fleece) jumper/jacket (preferably two), gloves, waterproof jacket and over trousers (preferably Gore-Tex), shorts, walking boots and socks, change of footwear or flip-flops. Camping Gear: tent (capable of withstanding high winds), sleeping mat (closed cell – Karrimat – or inflatable – Thermarest), sleeping bag (three-season minimum rating), sleeping bag liner, stove and spare parts, fuel, matches and lighter, cooking and eating utensils, pan scrubber, survival bag. **Food**: very much personal preference but at least two days' more supplies than you plan to use; tea, coffee, sugar, dried milk; porridge, dried fruit, honey; soup, pasta, rice, soya (TVP); fresh fruit and vegetables; bread, cheese, crackers; biscuits, chocolate; salt, pepper, other herbs and spices, cooking oil. **Miscellaneous**: map and compass, torch and spare batteries, trowel for burying excreta (which can be done after toilet paper has been burnt in the excavated hole – but take care fire doesn't spread), pen and notebook, Swiss army knife, sunglasses, sun cream, lip salve and insect repellent, first aid kit, water bottle, toiletries and towel.

Other sports

In Peru, Ecuador and Bolivia, **mountain biking** is relatively new, so there are routes to discover and little in the way of guide books to follow. Having said that there are companies specializing in biking, many of the `gravity-assisted' type, with good equipment and back-up. Colombia is a cycling nation and there are some great rides in Argentina and Chile (the Carretera Austral, for instance).

Whitewater is rapidly taking off as a sport, but standards of safety and experience vary quite a lot. Anywhere where rivers cascade off the Andes (Argentina, Chile, Peru, Bolivia, Ecuador, Venezuela) has ample opportunities, but beginners need not be alarmed as there are gentler rivers on which to learn the art (eg the Urubamba in Peru). Talking of falling off mountains, **parapenting** and **hang gliding** can be taken to extreme limits, such as at the Angel Falls in Venezuela, or again practised at beginner level in many places. Tandem jumps are hugely popular in Rio de Janeiro, and the views are unmatched. Other major sports are **diving** in the oceans off Colombia, the Galápagos and Brazil; **surfing**, at many spots on the Pacific coast and in Brazil; and **skiing**, most developed in Argentina and Chile, but with some low-infrastructure, high adventure areas in Peru. But don't just limit yourself to the obvious, take advantage of whatever is on offer wherever you are: sandboarding or buggy-riding down giant sand dunes, riding with gauchos, bungee jumping, playing golf on the highest course in the world (La Paz).

Adventure Highs in South America

Reach the top of the highest peak in the Americas and travel down in the company of condors. **Paragliding** from the summit of Aconcagua (6,959m) in **Argentina** accords the ultimate in South American views, with the Andean chain stretching far into the distance.

Jutting out from the high plateau of **Venezuela's** Gran Sabana, Mount Roraima (2,810m) is the highest of the table-top mountain *tepuis*, and a challenging wilderness **hike**. A contender for Conan Doyle's "Lost World", its strange rock formations and dense jungle seem to be from another planet.

The **Cordilleras Blanca** and **Huayhuash** in Peru are popular with **climbers and trekkers** alike, but hold many other possibilities. The spectacular mountains offer many new routes for ski mountaineering and the chance to bag a first descent. **Ski and climbing** experience essential - ask locally for information on snow conditions and possible routes.

Kayak the emerald waters of one of the continents top rivers. The **Futaleufú** cascades through lush, largely untouched forest on its way through Chilean Patagonia, providing some of the most exhilarating stretches of white water in the Southern Hemisphere. Rafting is another option, for those who prefer not to go solo.

Canter across the Chilean páramo and explore Patagonia **riding** with gauchos through **Chile's** Torres del Paine National Park. Huge granite towers, open pampas and lakes dotted with icebergs are home to a vast amount of wildlife, and travelling on horseback allows access to remote and scarcely visited areas.

Take to two wheels for thrilling descents of some of the world's highest mountains. Chimborazo (6,310m) and Cotopaxi (5,897m) are part of **Ecuador's** avenue of volcanoes and the near-perfect cones are ideal for **mountain biking**. Beautiful views and adrenalin rush are guaranteed.

Essentials

Explore the Macanao Peninsula on Venezuela's **Isla Margarita** on **horseback**. Undeveloped hidden beaches and stretches of cactus forest make enjoyable riding country. Later take to the water and try the fast and furious sport of kite surfing. The world's fastest growing sport certainly makes for more than your average beach holiday.

Spending several days **mountain biking** through the **Urubamba Valley** in the popular Cusco region of Peru will get you away from the crowds. Cycle down to the valley through the Maras salt pans – still in use today – and visit the Inca sites of Ollantaytambo and Pisac. The ride from Pisac to the pass of Tres Cruces, gateway from Andes to Amazon, is sure to leave you breathless with incredible sunset views.

Exploring the reefs and inquisitive sea life of the **Galápagos Islands** from underwater is a truly memorable experience. **Snorkelling and diving** around the islands is strictly controlled for minimum impact on wildlife, although sea lions, turtles, dolphins and numerous sea bird species seem impervious to the potential threat of man.

Head to the southern seas and explore the fjords of **Patagonia** and the Chiloé archipelago by **sea kayak**. Visit isolated communities dotted over the emerald islands or paddle the glassy waters of the fjords, where towering peaks plunge directly into the sea. The numerous albatross, penguin and petrel that patrol the waters are sometimes joined by pods of killer whales.

Diving in the waters of Fernando de Noronha Islands, **Brazil** you may be accompanied by spinner dolphins, but very few tourists. Access to the islands is restricted and their waters are a protected nature reserve. Afterwards, back on the mainland, join the local party and celebrate carnival in the colonial town of Olinda.

For a close-up view of South America's fauna, try **camping** in the Pantanal wetlands of **Brazil**. This vast area is home to many spectacular birds and mammals, including macaw, jabiru stork, anteater and puma. Nearby Bonito offers excellent **snorkelling** in beautiful underground caverns and crystal clear rivers alive with fish. Both areas should only be visited accompanied by a guide, and arriving in the Pantanal before the end of the wet season could involve wading across anaconda-inhabited marshes.

Experience a close encounter with the largest mammals on the planet, **whale watching** off Argentina's **Valdés Peninsular**. Southern Right whales breed in the Patagonian waters every year, and the almost uninhabited area is home to a host of other wildlife. You may be able to get closer still – wildife census are carried out by willing participants using sea kayaks to collect information.

The Auracaria forests of Conguillio National Park, **Chile** are deserted in winter, and the slopes of Llaima and Lonquimay volcanoes provide perfect terrain for **ski touring**. Make fresh tracks amongst monkey puzzle trees, and carve turns through lava flows in landscapes that date from prehistoric times.

Go **trekking** in the Gran Vilaya region of northern **Peru** and you may stumble on an ancient city from the Chachapoyas culture. Large areas of the forested mountains remain unexplored, and several extensive archeological finds have been uncovered in the last few years. The cloud forest is dense and overgrown paths are difficult to find. The area is one of the remaining habitats of the Andean bear.

Brazil's **Chapada Diamantina** National Park has some beautiful **trekking** possibilities and the park is rich in its biodiversity. Waterfalls, hidden caves and table-top mountains abound in the extensive area. The nearby colonial town of Lençóis, established for diamond exploitation in the mid 1800s, is the perfect place to relax after several days hiking.

The bizarre scenery of the Salar de Uyuni can be explored on four-day **jeep trips** from Uyuni, **Bolivia**. The dazzling expanse of the world's largest salt flat and the surrounding desert are full of weird and wonderful scenery: lunar landscapes and cactus-covered islands. It's also possible by **bike**, but expert assistance is advised - losing your sense of direction is easy when crossing the salt.

Health

Local populations in South America are exposed to a range of health risks not encountered in the western world. Many of the diseases are major problems for the local poor and destitute. The risk to travellers is more remote but cannot be ignored. Obviously five-star travel is going to carry less risk than back-packing on a minimal budget. The health care in the region is varied. There are many excellent private and government clinics/hospitals. As with all medical care, first impressions count. If a facility is grubby, staff wear grey coats instead of white ones then be wary of the general standard of medicine and hygiene. A good tip is to contact the embassy or consulate on arrival and ask where the recommended clinics (those used by diplomats) are. Diseases you may be exposed to are caused by viruses, bacteria and parasites. Tropical South America (Bolivia, Brazil, Colombia, Ecuador, French Guiana, Guyana, Paraguay, Peru, Suriname and Venezuela) poses a greater disease risk than Temperate South America (Argentina, Chile, Falkland Islands (Malvinas), and Uruguay). Other health problems, such as altitude sickness, may affect you along the entire length of the Andes.

Disease risks

The greatest disease risk in Tropical South America is caused by the greater volume of insect disease carriers in the shape of mosquitoes and sandflies. The parasitic diseases are many but the two key ones are **malaria** and South American trypanosomiasis (known as **Chagas Disease**). The key viral disease is **Dengue fever**, which is transmitted by a mosquito that bites in the day, see page 64. Bacterial diseases include tuberculosis (**TB**) and some causes of traveller's **diarrhoea**.

Before you go
For travel insurance check out Direct Line, www.directline.com

Ideally see your GP or travel clinic at least six weeks before departure for general advice on travel risks, malaria and **vaccinations**. Make sure you have **travel insurance**, get a **dental check**, know your own **blood group** and if you suffer a long-term condition such as diabetes or epilepsy make sure someone knows or that you have a Medic Alert bracelet/necklace with this information.

Vaccinations for your South American trip

Polio Recommended if nil in last 10 years.
Tetanus Recommended if nil in last 10 years (but after 5 doses you have had enough for life).
Typhoid Recommended if nil in last 3 years.
Yellow Fever Obligatory for most areas except Chile, Paraguay, Argentina and Uruguay. However, if you are travelling around South America it is best to get this vaccine since you will need it for the northern areas.
Rabies Recommended if going to jungle and/or remote areas.
Hepatitis A Recommended – the disease can be caught easily from food/water.

Further Information

When you arrive in each country let the Embassy or Consulate know. The information can be useful if a friend/relative gets ill at home and there is a desperate search for you around the globe. You can also ask them about locally recommended medical facilities and do's and don'ts.

Organizations & websites

Foreign and Commonwealth Office (FCO)
This is a key travel advice site, with useful information on the country, people, climate and lists the UK embassies/consulates. The site also promotes the concept of 'Know Before You Go'. And encourages travel insurance and appropriate travel health advice. It has links to the

Department of Health travel advice site, listed below. **www.fco.gov.uk**

Department of Health Travel Advice

This excellent site is also available as a free booklet, the **T6**, from Post offices. It lists the vaccine advice requirements for each country. **www.doh.gov.uk/traveladvice**

Medic Alert

This is the website of the foundation that produces bracelets and necklaces for those with existing medical problems. Once you have ordered your bracelet/necklace you write your key medical details on paper inside it, so that if you collapse, a medical person can identify you as someone with epilepsy or allergy to peanuts etc. **www.medicalalert.co.uk**

Blood Care Foundation

The Blood Care Foundation is a Kent based charity 'dedicated to the provision of screened blood and resuscitation fluids in countries where these are not readily available.' It will dispatch certified non-infected blood of the right type to your hospital/clinic. The blood is flown in from various centres around the world. **www.bloodcare.org.uk**

Public Health Laboratory Service (has malaria guidelines)

This site has the malaria advice guidelines for travel around the world. It gives specific advice about the right drugs for each location. It also has useful information for those who are pregnant, suffering from epilepsy or planning to travel with children. www.phls.org.uk

Centers for Disease Control and Prevention (USA)

This site from the US Government gives excellent advice on travel health, has useful disease maps and has details of disease outbreaks. **www.cdc.gov**

World Health Organization

The WHO site has links to the WHO Blue Book on travel advice. This lists the diseases in different regions of the world. It describes vaccination schedules and makes clear which countries have Yellow Fever Vaccination certificate requirements. www.who.int

Tropical Medicine Bureau

This Irish based site has a good collection of general travel health information and disease risks. **www.tmb.ie**

Fit for Travel

This site from Scotland provides a quick A-Z of vaccine and travel health advice requirements for each country. **www.fitfortravel.scot.nhs.uk**

British Travel Health Association

This is the official website of an organization of travel health professionals. **www.btha.org**

NetDoctor

This general health advice site has a useful section on travel and has an ask the expert, interactive chat forum. **www.Netdoctor.co.uk**

Travel Screening Services

This is the author's website. A private clinic dedicated to integrated travel health. The clinic gives vaccine, travel health advice, email and SMS text vaccine reminders and screens returned travellers for tropical diseases. **www.travelscreening.co.uk**

Books & leaflets   *The Travellers Good Health Guide* by **Dr Ted Lankester.**(ISBN 0-85969-827-0)

Expedition Medicine (The Royal Geographic Society) Editors **David Warrell** and **Sarah Anderson**. (ISBN 1 86197 040-4)

International Travel and Health, World Health Organisation, Geneva (ISBN 92 4 158026 7)

The World's Most Dangerous Places by **Robert Young Pelton**, **Coskun Aral** and **Wink Dulles.** (ISBN 1-566952-140-9)

The Travellers Guide to Health (T6) can be obtained by calling the Health Literature Line on 0800 555 777

Advice for travellers on avoiding the risks of HIV and AIDS (Travel Safe) available from Department of Health, PO Box 777, London SE1 6XH.

The Blood Care Foundation. Order from PO Box 7, Sevenoaks, Kent, TN13 2SZ, T 01732 742 427.

What to take   **Mosquito repellents** Remember that DEET (Di-ethyltoluamide) is the gold standard. Apply the repellent every 4-6 hours but more often if you are sweating heavily. If a non-DEET product is used check who tested it. Validated products (tested at the London School of

Hygiene and Tropical Medicine) include *Mosiguard*, Non-DEET *Jungle formula* and non-DEET *Autan*. If you want to use citronella remember that it must be applied very frequently (ie hourly to be effective)

Anti-malarials Specialist advice is required as to which type to take. General principles are that all except *Malarone* should be continued for four weeks after leaving the malarious area. *Malarone* needs to be continued for only seven days afterwards (if a tablet is missed or vomited seek specialist advice). The start times for the anti-malarials vary in that if you have never taken *Lariam* (Mefloquine) before it is advised to start it at least 2-3 weeks before the entry to a malarial zone (this is to help identify serious side-effects early). *Chloroquine* and *Paludrine* are often started a week before the trip to establish a pattern but *Doxycycline* and *Malarone* can be started only 1-2 days before entry to the malarial area. It is risky to buy medicinal tablets abroad because doses may differ and there may be a trade in false drugs.

Insect bite relief If you are prone to insects' bites or develop lumps quite soon after being bitten, carry an Aspivenin kit. This syringe suction device is available from *Boots Chemists* and draws out some of the allergic materials and provides quick relief.

Painkillers Paracetomol or a suitable painkiller can have multiple uses for symptoms but remember that more than eight paracetmol a day can lead to liver failure.

Antibiotics Ciproxin (*Ciprofloxacin*) is a useful antibiotic for traveller's diarrhoea (which can affect up to 70% of travellers). It can be obtained by private prescription in the UK which is expensive or bought over the counter in South American pharmacies, but if you do this check that the pills are in date. You take one 500 mg tablet when the diarrhoea starts and if you do not feel better in 24 hours the diarrhoea is likely to have a non-bacterial cause and may be viral. Viral causes of diarrhoea will settle on their own. However, with all diarrhoeas try to keep hydrated by taking the right mixture of salt and water. This is available as Rehydration Salts in ready made sachets or can be made up by adding a teaspoon of sugar and a half teaspoon of salt to a litre of clean water. Flat carbonated drinks can also be used.

Diarrhoea treatment *Immodium* is a great standby for those diarrhoeas that occur at awkward times ie before a long coach/train journey or on a trek. It helps stop the flow of diarrhoea and in the author's view is of more benefit than harm. It was believed that letting the bacteria or viruses flow out had to be more beneficial. However, with *Immodium* they still come out but in a more solid form. *Pepto-Bismol* is used a lot by the Americans for diarrhoea. It certainly relieves symptoms but like *Immodium* it is not a cure for underlying disease. Be aware that it turns the stool black as well as making it more solid.

Sun block the Australian's have a great campaign, which has reduced skin cancer. It is called Slip, Slap, Slop. Slip on a shirt, Slap on a hat, slop on sun screen. SPF stands for Sunscreen Protection Factor. It is measured by determining how long a given person takes to "burn" with and without the sunscreen product on. If it takes 10 times longer with the sunscreen product then that product has an SPF of 10. If it only takes twice as long then that product has an SPF of 2. In reality, the testing labs don't really burn the test subjects. They give them just enough UVR to cause the skin to turn barely red. This minimum dose is called the MED (minimal erythemal dose). The higher the SPF the greater the protection. However, do not just use higher factors just to stay out in the sun longer. 'Flash frying' (desperate bursts of excessive exposure), as it is called, is known to increase the risks of skin cancer.

MedicAlert These simple bracelets, or an equivalent, should be carried or worn by anyone with a significant medical condition.

Washing Biodegradable soap for jungle areas or ordinary soap for emergencies. Handwashing is the safest way of preventing unwanted muck to mouth transmission before you eat.

For longer trips involving jungle treks take a clean needle pack, clean dental pack and water filtration device.

Travel With Care, Homeway, Amesbury, Wiltshire, SP4 7BH, T0870 7459261, www.travelwithcare.co.uk provides a large range of products for sale.

An A-Z of health risks

Air pollution

Many large Latin American cities are notorious for their poor air quality. Expect sore throats and itchy eyes. Sufferers from asthma or bronchitis may have to increase their regular maintenance treatment.

Altitude sickness

Symptoms: This can creep up on you as just a mild headache with nausea or lethargy. The more serious disease is caused by fluid collecting in the brain in the enclosed space of the skull and can lead to coma and death. A lung disease with breathlessness and fluid infiltration of the lungs is also recognised.

Cures: The best cure is to descend as soon as possible.

Prevention: Get acclimatized. Do not try to reach the highest levels on your first few days of arrival. Try to avoid flying directly into the cities of highest altitude such as La Paz. Climbers like to take treatment drugs as protective measures but this can lead to macho idiocy and death. The peaks are still there and so are the trails, whether it takes you personally a bit longer than someone else does not matter as long as you come back down alive.

Chagas Disease

Symptoms: The disease occurs throughout South America, affects locals more than travellers, but travellers can be exposed by sleeping in mud-constructed huts where the bug that carries the parasite bites and defaecates on an exposed part of skin. You may notice nothing at all or a local swelling, with fever, tiredness and enlargement of lymph glands, spleen and liver. The seriousness of the parasite infection is caused by the long-term effects which include gross enlargement of the heart and/or guts.

Cures: Early treatment is required with toxic drugs.

Prevention: Sleep under a permethrin treated bed net and use insect repellents.

Dengue Fever

Symptoms: This disease can be contracted throughout South America. In travellers this can cause a severe flu like illness with fever, lethargy, enlarged lymph glands and muscle pains. It starts suddenly, lasts for 2-3 days, seems to get better for 2-3 days and then kicks in again for another 2-3 days. It is usually all over in an unpleasant week. The local children are prone to the much nastier haemorrhagic form of the disease, which causes them to bleed from internal organs, mucous membranes and often leads to their death.

Cures: The traveller's disease is self limiting and forces rest and recuperation on the sufferer.

Prevention: The mosquitoes that carry the Dengue virus bite during the day unlike the malaria mosquitoes. Sadly this means that repellent and covered limbs are a 24 hr issue. Check your accommodation for flower pots and shallow pools of water since these are where the Dengue-carrying mosquitoes breed.

Diarrhoea/ intestinal upset

This is almost inevitable. One study showed that up to 70% of all travellers may suffer during their trip.

Symptoms: Diarrhoea can refer either to loose stools or an increased frequency; both of these can be a nuisance. It should be short lasting. Persistence beyond two weeks, with blood or pain, require specialist medical attention.

Cures: *Ciproxin* will cure many of the bacterial causes but none of the viral ones. Immodium and *Pepto-Bismol* provide symptomatic relief. Dehydration can be a key problem especially in hot climates and is best avoided by the early start of Oral Rehydration Salts (at least one large cup of drink for each loose stool).

Prevention: The standard advice is to be careful with water and ice for drinking. Ask yourself where the water came from. If you have any doubts then boil it or filter and treat it. There are many filter/treatment devices now available on the market. Food can also transmit disease. Be wary of salads (what were they washed in? who handled them?), re-heated foods or food that has been left out in the sun having been cooked earlier in the day. There is a simple adage that says 'wash it, peel it, boil it or forget it'. Also be wary of unpasteurised dairy products these can transmit a range of diseases from brucellosis (fevers and constipation), to listeria (meningitis) and tuberculosis of the gut (obstruction, constipation, fevers and weight loss).

Some forest and riverine rodents carry hanta virus, epidemics of which have occurred in Argentina and Chile, but do occur worldwide. Symptoms are a flu-like illness which can lead to complications. Try as far as possible to avoid rodent-infested areas, especially close contact with rodent droppings. Campers and parents with small children should be especially careful. **Hanta virus**

Symptoms: Hepatitis means inflammation of the liver. Viral causes of Hepatitis can be acquired anywhere in South America. The most obvious sign is if your skin or the whites of your eyes become yellow. However, prior to this all that you may notice is itching and tiredness.
Cures: Early on, depending on the type of Hepatitis, a vaccine or immunoglobulin may reduce the duration of the illness.
Prevention: Pre-travel Hepatitis A vaccine is the best bet. Hepatitis B is spread by a different route by blood and unprotected sexual intercourse, both of which can be avoided. Unfortunately there is no vaccine for Hepatitis C or the increasing alphabetical list of other Hepatitis viruses. **Hepatitis**

Symptoms: A skin form of this disease occurs in all countries of South America except Chile and Uruguay. The main disease areas are in Bolivia, Brazil and Peru. If infected, you may notice a raised lump, which leads to a purplish discoloration on white skin and a possible ulcer. The parasite is transmitted by the bite of a sandfly. Sandflies do not fly very far and the greatest risk is at ground levels, so if you can avoid sleeping on the jungle floor do so. Seek advice for any persistent skin lesion or nasal symptom.
Cures: Several weeks treatment is required under specialist supervision. The drugs themselves are toxic but if not taken in sufficient amounts recurrence of the disease is more likely.
Prevention: Sleep above ground, under a permethrin treated net, use insect repellent and get a specialist opinion on any unusual skin lesions soon after return. **Leishmaniasis**

Various forms of leptospirosis occur throughout Latin America, transmitted by a bacterium which is excreted in rodent urine. Fresh water and moist soil harbour the organisms, which enter the body through cuts and scratches. If you suffer from any form of prolonged fever consult a doctor. **Leptospirosis**

Malaria can cause death within 24 hrs. It can start as something just resembling an attack of flu. You may feel tired, lethargic, headachy or worse, develop fits, coma and then death. You should have a low index of suspicion because it is very easy to write off vague symptoms, which may actually be malaria. Whilst abroad and on return get tested as soon as possible, the test could save your life.
Cures: Treatment is with drugs and may be oral or into a vein depending on the seriousness of the infection.
Prevention: This is best summarised by the B and C of the ABCD, see below: Bite avoidance and Chemoprophylaxis. Some would prefer to take test kits for malaria with them and have standby treatment available. However, the field test of the blood kits has had poor results. When you have malaria you do not perform well enough to do the tests correctly to make the right diagnosis. Standby treatment (treatment that you carry and take yourself for malaria) should still ideally be supervised by a doctor since the drugs themselves can be toxic if taken incorrectly. The Royal Homeopathic Hospital in the UK does not advocate homeopathic options for malaria prevention or treatment. **Malaria**

A for Awareness
Tropical South America: Malaria exists in all 10 areas of Tropical South America. Although some areas have a low risk of the disease, Paraguay is the only country, which has the less **deadly vivax** form of malaria. The other nine have areas with a risk of the deadly **falciparum** malaria.
Temperate South America: Malaria is only of concern in some parts of north-western Argentina. Always check with your doctor or travel clinic for the most up to date advice.
B for Bite Avoidance
Wear clothes that cover arms and legs and use effective insect repellents in areas with known risks of insect-spread disease. Use a mosquito net dipped in permethrin as both a physical and chemical barrier at night in the same areas. **Malaria precautions for your South American trip**

Essentials

Essentials

C for Chemoprophylaxis
Depending on the type of malaria and your previous medical condition/psychological profile take the right drug before, during and after your trip. Always check with your doctor or travel clinic for the most up to date advice.

D for Diagnosis
Remember that up to a year after your return an illness could be caused by malaria. Be forceful about asking for a malaria test, even if the doctor says it is 'only flu.' The symptoms of malaria are wide ranging from fever, lethargy, headache, muscle pains, flu-like illness, to diarrhoea and convulsions. Malaria can lead to coma and death.

Marine bites & stings   Certain tropical sea fish when trodden upon inject venom into bathers' feet. This can be exceptionally painful. Wear plastic shoes if such creatures are reported. The pain can be relieved by immersing the foot in extremely hot water for as long as the pain persists.

Prickly heat   A very common intensely itchy rash is avoided by frequent washing and by wearing loose clothing. It is cured by allowing skin to dry off (through use of powder and spending two nights in an air-conditioned hotel!).

Rabies   Remember that rabies is endemic throughout Latin America, so avoid dogs that are behaving strangely and cover your toes at night from the vampire bats, which also carry the disease. If you are bitten by a domestic or wild animal, do not leave things to chance: scrub the wound with soap and water and/or disinfectant, try to at least determine the animal's ownership, where possible, and seek medical assistance at once. The course of treatment depends on whether you have already been satisfactorily vaccinated against rabies. If you have (this is worthwhile if you are spending lengths of time in developing countries) then some further doses of vaccine are all that is required. Human diploid vaccine is the best, but expensive: other, older kinds of vaccine, such as that derived from duck embryos may be the only types available. These are effective, much cheaper and interchangeable generally with the human derived types. If not already vaccinated then anti rabies serum (immunoglobulin) may be required in addition. It is important to finish the course of treatment.

Schistosomiasis (bilharzia)   Symptoms: The *mansoni* form of this flat worm occurs in Suriname and Venezuela. The form that penetrates the skin after you have swum or waded through snail infested water can cause a local itch soon after, fever after a few weeks and much later diarrhoea, abdominal pain and spleen or liver enlargement.
Cures: A single drug cures this disease.
Prevention: Avoid infected waters, check the CDC, WHO websites and a travel clinic specialist for up to date information.

Sexual health   Unprotected sex can spread HIV, Hepatitis B and C, Gonorrhea (green discharge), chlamydia (nothing to see but may cause painful urination and later female infertility), painful recurrent herpes, syphilis and warts, just to name a few. You can cut down on the risks by using condoms, a femidom or if you want to be completely safe, by avoiding sex altogether.

Snake bite & other animal bites & stings   It is a very rare event indeed for travellers, but if you are unlucky (or careless) enough to be bitten by a venomous snake, spider, scorpion or sea creature, try to identify the creature, without putting yourself in further danger. Snake bites in particular are very frightening, but in fact rarely poisonous – even venomous snakes bite without injecting venom. Victims should be taken to a hospital or a doctor without delay. Commercial snake bite and scorpion kits are available, but are usually only useful for the specific types of snake or scorpion. Most serum has to be given intravenously so it is not much good equipping yourself with it unless you are used to making injections into veins. It is best to rely on local practice in these cases, because the particular creatures will be known about locally and appropriate treatment can be given.
    Treatment of snake bite: Reassure and comfort the victim frequently. Immobilize the limb by a bandage or a splint and get the person to lie still. Do not slash the bite area and try to suck out the poison because this sort of heroism does more harm than good. If you know

how to use a tourniquet in these circumstances, you will not need this advice. If you are not experienced, do not apply a tourniquet. What you might expect if bitten are: fright, swelling, pain and bruising around the bite and soreness of the regional lymph glands, perhaps nausea, vomiting and a fever. Symptoms of serious poisoning would be: numbness and tingling of the face, muscular spasms, convulsions, shortness of breath or a failure of the blood to clot, causing generalized bleeding.

Precautions: Do not walk in snake territory in bare feet or sandals – wear proper shoes or boots. If you encounter a snake stay put until it slithers away and do not investigate a wounded snake. Spiders and scorpions may be found in the more basic hotels, especially in the Andean countries. If stung, rest and take plenty of fluids and call a doctor. The best precaution is to keep beds away from the walls and look inside your shoes and under the toilet seat every morning.

Other tropical diseases and problems found in jungle areas: These are usually transmitted by biting insects. They are often related to African diseases and were probably introduced by the slave labour trade. Onchocerciasis (river blindness) carried by blackflies is found in parts of Venezuela. Wearing long trousers and a long sleeved shirt in infected areas protects against these flies. DEET is also effective. Epidemics of meningitis occur from time-to-time. Be careful about swimming in piranha or caribe infested rivers. It is a good idea not to swim naked: the Candiru fish can follow urine currents and become lodged in body orifices. Swimwear offers some protection.

Symptoms: People with white skin are notorious for becoming red in hot countries because they like to stay out longer than everyone else and do not use adequate skin protection factors. This can lead to sunburn, which is painful, followed by flaking of skin. Aloe vera gel is a good pain reliever for sunburn. Long-term sun damage leads to a loss of elasticity of skin and the development of pre-cancerous lesions. Many years later a mild or a very malignant form of cancer may develop. The milder basal cell carcinoma, if detected early, can be treated by cutting it out or freezing it. The much nastier malignant melanoma may have already spread to bone and brain at the time that it is first noticed.
Prevention: Follow the Australians with their Slip, Slap, Slop campaign.

Acquired through eating the cysts of the worm in undercooked beef or pork. Humans can also get the cystic stage of the pork tape worm (cysticercosis) through food or water contaminated by human faeces. The cysts get into the muscle and brain, and cause fits months or years later.

Ticks usually attach themselves to the lower parts of the body often after walking in areas where cattle have grazed. They take a while to attach themselves strongly, but swell up as they start to suck blood. The important thing is to remove them gently, so that they do not leave their head parts in your skin because this can cause a nasty allergic reaction some days later. Do not use petrol, vaseline, lighted cigarettes etc to remove the tick, but, with a pair of tweezers remove the beast gently by gripping it at the attached (head) end and rock it out in very much the same way that a tooth is extracted. Certain tropical flies which lay their eggs under the skin of sheep and cattle also occasionally do the same thing to humans with the unpleasant result that a maggot grows under the skin and pops up as a boil or pimple. The best way to remove these is to cover the boil with oil, vaseline or nail varnish so as to stop the maggot breathing, then to squeeze it out gently the next day.

Symptoms: TB can cause fever, night sweats and a chronic cough. Some people cough up blood. You may not know you have it but your friends will remark on your gradual weight loss and lack of energy. The lung type of TB is spread by coughs. Sometimes TB causes swelling of the lymph glands. TB can be spread by dairy products. Gut or pelvic TB can cause abdominal lumps, gut obstruction and even infertility. All parts of the body can be affected by TB.
Cures: After diagnosis at least 6 months continuous treatment with several drugs is required.
Prevention: Unfortunately BCG vaccine may not protect against lung TB. The best you can do is avoid unpasteurised dairy products and do not let anyone cough or splutter all over you.

Sun protection

Tapeworms

Ticks

Tuberculosis (TB)

Typhoid fever Symptoms This a gut infection which can spread to the blood stream. You get it from someone else's muck getting into your mouth. A classic example would be the waiter who fails to wash his hands and then serves you a salad. The fever is an obvious feature, occasionally there is a mild red rash on the stomach and often you have a headache. Constipation or diarrhoea can occur. Gut pain and hearing problems may also feature. Deaths occur from a hole 'punched' straight through the gut.

Cures: Antibiotics are required and you are probably best managed in hospital.

Prevention: The vaccine is very effective and is best boosted every 3 years. Watch what you eat and the hygiene of the place or those serving your food.

Typhus This can still occur and is carried by ticks. There is usually a reaction at the site of the bite and a fever. Seek medical advice.

Underwater Health If you go diving make sure that you are fit do so. The **British Scuba Association** (BSAC, Telford's Quay, South Pier Road, Ellesmere Port, Cheshire CH65 4FL, UK, T0151 350 6200, F0151 350 6215, www.bsac.com) can put you in touch with doctors who do medical examinations. Protect your feet from cuts, beach dog parasites (larva migrans) and sea urchins. The latter are almost impossible to remove but can be dissolved with lime or vinegar.

Cures: Antibiotics for secondary infections. Serious diving injuries may need time in a Decompression Chamber.

Prevention: Check that the dive company knows what it is doing, has appropriate certification from BSAC or PADI, the **Professional Association of Diving Instructors**, (www.padi.com) and that the equipment is well maintained.

Water There are a number of ways of purifying water. Dirty water should first be strained through a filter bag and then boiled or treated. Bringing water to a rolling boil at sea level is sufficient to make the water safe for drinking, but at higher altitudes you have to boil the water for a few minutes longer to ensure all microbes are killed. There are sterilizing methods that can be used and there are proprietary preparations containing chlorine (eg *Puritabs*) or iodine (eg *Pota Aqua*) compounds. Chlorine compounds generally do not kill protozoa (eg Giardia). There are a number of water filters now on the market available in personal and expedition size. They work either on mechanical or chemical principles, or may do both. Make sure you take the spare parts or spare chemicals with you and do not believe everything the manufacturers say.

Argentina

Argentina

Argentina is back on the map - not that the thrills of this hugely varied country ever went away. One of the few bonuses of recent economic problems is that Argentina is affordable for tourists again and there is so much to enjoy - from nights tangoing in the chic quarters of Buenos Aires to long days riding with gauchos in the grasslands of the pampas. You can climb to the roof of the Americas, raft Andean rivers or ski with celebrities. You can visit the birthplace of revolutionary Che Guevara and the resting place of a dinosaur known to have been bigger than T Rex. One train climbs from colonial Salta to the clouds, another chuffs through the emptiness of Patagonia. On the Patagonian coast, at Península Valdés, Southern right whales and elephant seals come to breed in the sheltered bays, while estuaries are home to colonies of penguins and pods of dolphin. Lonely roads cross the vast, empty plateau inland, leading to the petrified remains of giant forests and a cave with 10,000 year-old paintings of hands and animals. The Andean mountain chain ends in a jagged finale at the peaks of the Chaitén Massif, with some of the best trekking on the continent. At the northern border with Brazil, 275 waterfalls cascade into a great gorge at Iguazú. Swifts dart behind the torrents of water and birds and butterflies are easy to see in the surrounding forest. This is a must on anyone's itinerary. Endangered mammals, giant storks and anacondas live side-by-side in the Iberá marshes. In the dried-up river beds of San Juan, there are exotic, eroded rockforms at Talampaya and Ischigualasto. To set the taste buds tingling, the vineyards of Mendoza and the traditional Welsh tearooms of the Chubut valley hang out the welcome sign. And (vegetarians look away), don't forget the meat, barbecued on an open wood fire at the end of the day.

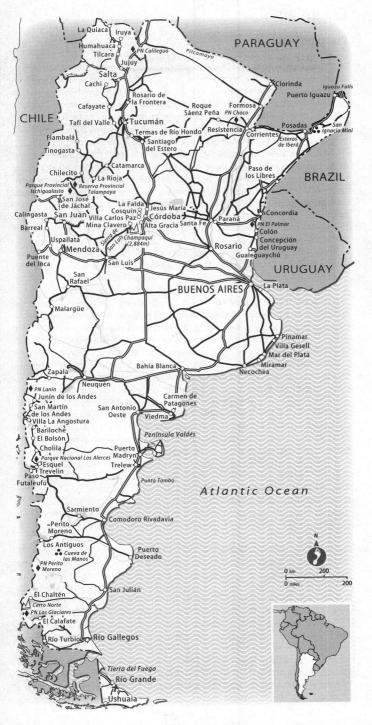

Argentina

PARAGUAY

La Quiaca Iruya
Humahuaca
Tilcara
Jujuy *PN Calilegua* *Pilcomayo*
Salta
Cachi
Cafayate Rosario de
la Frontera Roque Formosa Clorinda
Sáenz Peña *PN Chaco* *Iguazu Falls*
Puerto Iguazú
CHILE Tafí del Valle Tucumán Termas de Río Hondo Resistencia Corrientes Posadas
Fiambalá Santiago San
del Estero Ignacio Mini
Tinogasta *Esteros*
de Iberá
Catamarca
Chilecito La Rioja Paso de
Parque Provincial *Reserva Provincial* los Libres BRAZIL
Ischigualasto *Talampaya*
San José La Falda Jesús María
de Jáchal Cosquín Córdoba Concordia
Calingasta San Juan Villa Carlos Paz Paraná *PN El Palmar*
Barreal Mina Clavero Alta Gracia Santa Fe Colón
Uspallata *Sierra de* Concepción
Mendoza *San Luis Champaquí* Rosario del Uruguay
(2,884m) Gualeguaychú
Puente
del Inca San Luis URUGUAY
San
Rafael BUENOS AIRES La Plata

Malargüe

Pinamar
Villa Gesell
Mar del Plata
Zapala Bahía Blanca Miramar
PN Lanín Neuquén Necochea
Junín de los Andes
San Martín San Antonio Carmen de
de los Andes Oeste Patagones
Villa La Angostura Viedma
Bariloche *Península Valdés*
El Bolsón
Cholila Puerto
Parque Nacional Los Alerces Madryn
Esquel Trelew
Trevelin
Paso *Punta Tombo*
Futaleufú *Atlantic Ocean*

Sarmiento

Perito Comodoro Rivadavia
Moreno
Los Antiguos
Cueva de Puerto
las Manos Deseado
PN Perito
Moreno
El Chaltén
Cerro Norte San Julián
PN Los Glaciares
El Calafate
Río Turbio Río Gallegos

Tierra del Fuego
Río Grande

Ushuaia

0 km   200
0 miles   200

N

Essentials

Planning your trip

Where to go   The capital, **Buenos Aires**, has a distinctly European feel, its architecture mostly 20th-century, though earlier buildings can be found in San Telmo district. The central docklands have been reclaimed as an upmarket restaurant zone and the Palermo district, with its large parks, is becoming increasingly popular for eating out. Across the Río de la Plata is Uruguay; just west is Tigre, on the Paraná delta, a popular spot for escaping the city; to the east are coastal resorts which lead round to the most famous, Mar del Plata. West and south of Buenos Aires stretch the grasslands of the pampas, home of the *gaucho* (cowboy) and large *estancias*.

Through **Northwest Argentina** a string of cities gives access to the Andean foothills and the higher peaks. On the way to the mountains are Córdoba, an important industrial centre close to resorts in the Sierras de Córdoba, and Santiago del Estero, Argentina's oldest city. From Tucumán, in view of the Andes, there is a beautiful route through desert foothills around Cafayate and the Valles Calchaquíes to the fine city and tourist hub of Salta. It is the departure point for the Tren a Las Nubes (the Train to the Clouds), which climbs to 4,475 m on a railway to high altitude mining communities. From Salta there are routes to Bolivia, through an area of isolated villages, and to Paraguay across the Chaco. There are also bus services to Chile.

In the **Northeast**, the wetlands of Mesopotamia have some interesting wildlife zones, such as the Iberá Marshes, and in Misiones province, sandwiched between Brazil and Paraguay, are ruined Jesuit missions, principally San Ignacio Miní. The highlight of this region are the magnificent Iguazú Falls, usually included on any itinerary to the country.

Back in the Northwest, **Ruta 40** starts its long, frequently remote journey beside the Andes to the far south. Among the many attractions it passes are the city of Mendoza, on the main Buenos Aires-Santiago road, with its vineyards, climbing and skiing centres, and the strange lunar landscapes of San Juan province. It traverses the **Lake District**, renowned for its lovely scenery and good fishing. The main centres are San Martín de los Andes and Bariloche, but there are many smaller places to visit, like Esquel, the terminus of the Old Patagonian Express. From Bariloche, and a number of other points, there are crossings to Chile. Ruta 40 continues south to the stunning peaks and glaciers of Los Glaciares national park.

On the Atlantic side of **Patagonia**, a good place to break the journey is Puerto Madryn and the Península Valdés. Here you can see whales, elephant seals, guanaco and other wildlife at close quarters (but check on the best times to view the animals). Just south of here are the Welsh communities of the Chubut Valley and, south again, three areas of petrified forest. Río Gallegos is the most southerly town of any size on the mainland. One road goes west to the most visited part of Los Glaciares, El Calafate, near where the Perito Moreno glacier tumbles into Lago Argentino. Just north of here, El Chaltén at the foot of the jagged FitzRoy massif has some of the most spectacular trekking in the country. This increasingly popular area now forms part of the circuit which includes the Torres del Paine national park in Chile. Beyond Río Gallegos is Tierra del Fuego, shared with Chile; on the Argentine side is what claims to be the southernmost town in the world, Ushuaia, on the shores of the Beagle Channel.

When to go   Climate ranges from sub-tropical in the north to cold temperate in Tierra del Fuego. It is temperate and quite healthy in the densely populated central zone. From mid-December to the end of February Buenos Aires can be oppressively hot and humid, with temperatures ranging from 27°C (80°F) to 35°C (95°F) and an average humidity of 70%. The city is half-closed in late December and early January as many people escape on holiday. Autumn can be a good time to visit and spring in Buenos Aires (September-October) is often very pleasant indeed.

The Northeast is best visited in Argentine winter when it is cooler and drier. Corrientes and Misiones provinces are wet in August and especially September. The winter is also a good time to visit the Northwest, but routes to Chile across the Andes may be closed by snow at this time and spring and autumn may be better: summer rains, especially in Jujuy, can make roads impassable. In the winter months of June, July and August establishments may close in the far south, transport can be restricted and routes across the Andes to Chile may be blocked by snow. Spring and autumn are the best seasons for visiting the Lake District. Ideally

Argentine embassies and consulates

Australia *John McEwen House, 7 National Circuit, 2nd floor, Barton, ACT 2006, T6273 9111, F6273 0500, www.argentina.org.au*
Belgium *225 Avenue Louise B.3, 1050 Brussels, T2-647 7812, F2-647 9319, info@embargentina.be*
Canada *90 Sparks Street, Suite 910, Ottawa KIP 5B4, T613-236 2351, F613-235 2659, www.argentina-canada.net*
Denmark *Borgergade 16, 1st floor, 13000 Copenhagen, T3315 8082, F3315 5574, embardin@cybercity.vip.dk*
France *6 rue Cimarosa, 75116 Paris, T44052700, F4553 4633, argentine-en-france@noos.fr*
Germany *Dorotheestrasse 89, floor 3, 10117 Berlin, T30-226 6890, F30-229 1400, www.argentinische-botschaft.de*
Israel *Herzliya Business Park, Medinat Hayeudim 85, 3rd floor, Herzliya Pituah 46120, T9970 2743, F9970 2748, embarg@netvision.net.il*
Italy *Piazza dell'Esquilino 2, 00185 Rome, T474 2551, F481 9787, www.ambasciata-argentina.com*
Japan *Moto Azabu 2-14-14, Minato Ku, 1060046 Tokyo, T3-5420 7101, F3-5420 7109, www.embargentina.or.jp*

Netherlands *Javastraat 20, 2585 AN The Hague, T70-365 4836, F70-392 4900, fepbaj@mrecic.gov.ar*
New Zealand *142 Lambton Quay, 14th floor, Wellington, T4-472 8330, F4-472 8331, www.arg.org.nz*
Spain *C Pedro de Valdivia 21, 28006 Madrid, T562 2800, F563 5185, www.portalargentino.net*
Sweden *Grevgatan 5-2 TR, S-104 40 Stockholm, T663 1965, F661 0009, secom@argemb.se*
Switzerland *Jungfraustrasse 1, 3005 Bern, T31-352 3565, F31-352 0519, resembar@freesurf.ch*
UK *65 Brooke Street, London W1K 4AH, T202-7318 1300, F020-7318 1301, www.argentine-embassy-uk.org*
Consulate: *27 Three Kings Yard, London W1Y 1FL, T020-7318 1340, F020-7318 1349*
USA *1600 New Hampshire Avenue, NW Washington DC, 20009, T202-238 6400, F202-332 3171, www.embajadaargentina-usa.org*
Consulates: *12 West 56th Street, New York, NY100019, T212-6030400, F212-3973523; 800 Brickell Avenue, PH1, Miami, FL33131, T305-358 0530, F305-371 7108, cmiam@earthlink.net*

Patagonia should be visited in December or February/March, avoiding the winter months when the weather is cold and many services are closed. January is best avoided as this is the Argentine summer holiday period and some destinations, notably in Patagonia, are very crowded. There are also school holidays in July and some facilities such as youth hostels may be heavily booked in this period. Note that Bariloche is a very popular destination for school groups in July and December/early January.

Finding out more

The national office of the **Secretaría de Turismo** is at Santa Fe 883, Buenos Aires, T4312 2232, www.turismo.gov.ar Addresses of other tourist offices in the country are given in the text. For tourist information abroad, contact Argentine embassies and consulates (see box), or **Argentina National Tourist Office**, 12 West 56th Street, New York, HY 10019, USA, T212-603 0443, F212-315 5545.

Each province has a tourist office, *Casa de Provincia*, in Buenos Aires, worth visiting if planning to travel around the country, with helpful tourist information (open Monday-Friday usually, 1000-1630/1730, depending on office): *Buenos Aires Province*, Av Callao 237, T4371 7045/7. Others on Calle Callao are *Córdoba* No 332, T4371 1668. *Chaco* No 328, T4372 3045. *Mendoza* No 445, T4371 7301. *La Rioja* No 745, T4815 1929. **Others: Catamarca**, Córdoba 2080, T/F4374 6891. *Chubut*, Sarmiento 1172, T4382 2009, www.chubutour.com.ar *Corrientes*, San Martín 333, p 4, T/F4394 2808, www.corrientes.com.ar *Entre Ríos*, Suipacha 846, T4326 2573. *Formosa*, H Yrigoyen 1429, T4381 2037. *Jujuy*, Santa Fe 967, T4394 2295. *La Pampa*, Suipacha 346, T/F4326 0511. *Mar del Plata*, Corrientes 1660, local 16, in La Plaza complex, T4384 5658, www.mardelplata.gov.ar *Misiones*, Santa Fe 989, T4322 0686.

See www.turismo. gov.ar also in English. See also www.buenos aires.gov.ar

Argentina

Municipalidad de la Costa, B Mitre 1135, T4381 0764, www.lacostaturismo.com.ar *Neuquén*, Perón 687, T4327 2454. *Pinamar*, Florida 930 p 5, T4311 0693, www.pinamar.gov.ar *Río Negro*, Tucumán 1916, T4371 7078, www.rionegro.gov.ar *Salta*, Diagonal Norte 933, T4326 2456, F4326 0110. *San Juan*, Sarmiento 1251, T4382 9241, F4382 9465. *San Luis*, Azcuénaga 1083, T4822 0426, F4823 9413, www.turismoensanluis.gov.ar *Santa Cruz*, Suipacha 1120, T4325 3102. *Santa Fe*, Montevideo 373, p 2, T/F4375 4570, www.ellitoral.com.ar www.santafe.gov.ar *Santiago del Estero*, Florida 274, T4326 9418, F4326 5915. *Tierra del Fuego*, Marcelo T de Alvear 790, T4311 0233, www.tierradelfuego.gov.ar *Tucumán*, Suipacha 140, T4322 0564, www.tucumanturismo.com *Villa Gesell*, B Mitre 1702, T4374 5098, F4374 5099. For tourist information on Patagonia and bookings for cheap accommodation and youth hostels, contact *Asatej*, see Useful addresses on page 111.

Websites   A site with tourist information for the whole country is **www.liveargentina.com** In Spanish, English, Portuguese, French, Italian and German. Argentine search engines are **http://ar.yahoo.com** and **www.grippo.com/** For news, entertainment, weather, tourism, channels and phone directory, see **www.terra.com.ar** (in Spanish). **www.expatvillage.com** has information on life in Buenos Aires and useful travel information. **www.mercotour.com** contains information on travel and other matters in Argentina, Uruguay, Chile and Brazil, in Spanish, English and Portuguese. For a list of newspapers, see below.

Language   Spanish, with variant words and pronunciation. English comes second; French and Italian (especially in Patagonia) may be useful. The chief variant pronunciations are the replacement of the 'll' and 'y' sounds by a soft 'j' sound, as in 'azure' (though note that this is not done in Mendoza, Santiago del Estero and several other northern provinces), the omission of the 'd' sound in words ending in '-ado' (generally considered uncultured), the omission of final 's' sounds, the pronunciation of 's' before a consonant as a Scottish or German 'ch', and the substitution in the north and west of the normal rolled 'r' sound by a hybrid 'rj'. In grammar the Spanish 'tú' is replaced by 'vos' and the second person singular conjugation of verbs has the accent on the last syllable eg *vos tenés, podés*, etc. In the north and northwest, though, the Spanish is more akin to that spoken in the rest of Latin America. *Amerispan Unlimited*, PO Box 58129, Philadelphia, PA 19102-8129, T(215)751-1100 worldwide, T(800)879-6640 North America, www.amerispan.com Specialize in Spanish immersion, volunteer and eduactional programmes throughout South America.

Before you travel

Visas &   Check visa requirements in advance. Passports are not required by citizens of neighbouring
immigration   countries who hold identity cards issued by their own governments. No visa is necessary for US citizens, British citizens and nationals of other western European countries, Canada, Bolivia, Brazil, Chile, Panama, Paraguay, Uruguay, Venezuela, Mexico, El Salvador, Guatemala, Nicaragua, Honduras, Costa Rica, Colombia, Ecuador, Peru, Dominican Republic, Haiti, Barbados, Jamaica, St

Lucia, Trinidad and Tobago, Hong Kong, Malaysia, Israel, Czech Republic, Slovak Republic, Hungary, Poland, Turkey, Croatia, Slovenia, Serbia and Montenegro, South Africa, Australia, New Zealand, Singapore and Japan, who are given a tourist card on entry and may stay for three months, a period which can be renewed for another three months (fee US$100) at the **National Directorate of Migration**, Antártida Argentina 1335/55, edificios 3 y 4, Buenos Aires, T4317 0200, F4317 0282, open 0800-1300. For all others there are three forms of visa: a business 'temporary' visa (£32.45, valid one year), a tourist visa (US$19.50 approximately, fees change monthly), and a transit visa. **Tourist visas** are usually valid for three months and multiple entry. If leaving Argentina on a short trip, check on re-entry that border officials look at the correct expiry date on your visa, otherwise they will give only 30 days. Renewing a visa is difficult and can only be done for 30-day periods. Visitors should carry passports at all times; backpackers are particular targets for thorough searches – just stay calm; it is illegal not to have identification handy. When crossing land borders, remember that though the migration and customs officials are generally friendly, helpful and efficient, the police at the control posts a little further into Argentina tend to be extremely bureaucratic.

At land borders, 90 days' permission to stay is usually given without proof of transportation out of Argentina. Make sure you are given a tourist card, otherwise you will have to obtain one before leaving the country. If you need a 90-day extension for your stay then leave the country (eg at Iguazú), and 90 further days will be given on return. Visa extensions may also be obtained from the address above, ask for 'Prorrogas de Permanencia': fee US$100. No renewals are given after the expiry date. To authorize an exit stamp if your visa or tourist stamp has expired, go to Yrigoyen 952 where a 10-day authorization will be given for US$50. Alternatively, you can forego all the paperwork by paying a US$50 fine at a border immigration post (queues are shorter than in Buenos Aires, but still allow 30 minutes).

NB At Argentine/Uruguayan borders one immigration official will stamp passports for both countries. Argentine immigration and customs officials wear civilian dress. The border patrol, *gendarmería*, in green combat fatigues, operates some borders.

Duty-free allowance No duties are charged on clothing, personal effects, toilet necessities, etc. Cameras, typewriters, binoculars, radios and other things which a tourist normally carries are duty-free if they have been used and only one of each article is carried. This is also true of scientific and professional instruments for personal use. Travellers may only bring in new personal goods up to a value of US$300 (US$100 from neighbouring countries); the amount of duty and tax payable amounts to 50% of the item's cost. Baggage claim tags are inspected at the exit from the customs inspection area.

Customs

Two litres of alcoholic drinks, 400 cigarettes and 50 cigars are also allowed in duty-free; for tourists originating from neighbouring countries the respective quantities allowed are one litre, 200 and 20. You can buy duty-free goods on arrival at Ezeiza airport.

If having packages sent to Argentina, do not use the green customs label unless the contents are of real value and you expect to pay duty. For such things as books or samples use the white label if available. A heavy tax is imposed on packages sent to Argentina by courier.

Money

The peso is divided into 100 centavos. Peso notes in circulation: 2, 5, 10, 20, 50 and 100. Coins in circulation: 1, 5, 10, 25 and 50 centavos and 1 peso. Foreigners are advised to use credit cards to withdraw cash, where possible, and for making payments. If paying in cash, do so in pesos because, away from the capital especially, dollars are often not accepted for fear of forgeries. Also be aware of any changes to foreign exchange regulations.

Currency
Argentine peso exchange rate with US$: 2.89

Because of provincial government debt and, since January 2002, the country's financial crisis, a wide variety of bonds have been issued in lieu of pesos. In 2003 the expectation was that these bonds would be phased out, but the process may take a year. Travellers are advised to avoid provincial currency. Bonds are only valid in the province in which they are issued, except those called 'Lecop', which are issued by the central government. Only use pesos (or dollars if allowed to do so) and try to give the exact amount. There seems to be an unwritten rule that if you pay in pesos, you will get change in pesos.

Argentina

ATMs (known as Cajeros Automáticos) can be found everywhere throughout the country except small towns. They are usually *Banelco* or *Link*, accepting international cards. Until the banking system has been stabilized, using ATMs is far better than over-the-counter transactions. When crossing a land border into Argentina, make sure you have some Argentine currency as there are normally no facilities at the border.

Credit cards American Express, Diners Club, Visa and MasterCard cards are all widely accepted in the major cities and provincial capitals, though less so outside these. There is a high surcharge on credit card transactions in many establishments; many hotels offer reductions for cash. Credit cards are readily accepted in all main towns, even in the south, but outside main towns their use is limited. Many service stations accept credit cards **Automóvil Club Argentino** (ACA) stations only take cards from members; YPF accepts Visa. All shops, hotels and places showing *Argencard* signs will accept Eurocard and Access, but you must state that these cards are affiliated to MasterCard. *Argencard* will not permit cash advances on these cards in outlying regions, and is itself very slow in advancing cash. Mastercard emergency number T011-4340 5700, Visa 011-4379 3333.

Cost of travelling In 2002, devaluation of the peso made Argentina, formerly the most expensive country in South America, considerably cheaper for the foreign visitor. Budget travellers should allow about US$20 a day for food, accommodation and travel. This takes into account spending time in Patagonia, which is more expensive than the centre and north, and having to stay in hotels on those occasions where there is no hostel. Hotel prices in 2003 started at about US$7-10 pp in uncategorized establishments (US$5-6 pp in a double room), with many good rooms available from US$15-40. Breakfast will cost about US$1.75-3.50, while cheap meals range from US$4-7.50 (US$2-3 for sandwich or pizza). **Value-added tax** VAT is not levied on most medicines and some foodstuffs but on all other products and services at 21%.

Getting there

Air **From Europe** There are flights to Buenos Aires from London, Barcelona, Madrid, Frankfurt, Paris, Milan, Rome, Zurich with European carriers, plus *Aerolíneas Argentinas* from London, Madrid and Rome. **From North America** AR and/or other South American and North American airlines fly from Miami, New York, Los Angeles, San Francisco, Washington, Dallas and Chicago. **From Australasia and South Africa** *Aerolíneas Argentinas/Qantas* fly from Sydney, Australia, via Auckland, New Zealand, four times a week. *Malaysia Airlines* fly from Kuala Lumpur via Johannesburg and Cape Town. **From Latin America** AR and other national carriers fly between Buenos Aires and all the South American capitals, plus Santa Cruz and Cochabamba in Bolivia. Several flights between Buenos Aires and Rio de Janeiro and São Paulo stop over in Porto Alegre. There are also flights from Salvador. See under Brazil for the *Mercosur* Air Pass. There are also flights from Havana and Mexico City.

Road Tourists can take into Argentina their own cars, and vehicles bought or hired in neighbouring countries for up to eight months under international documentation. In practice, no papers other than the car's title document is asked for, except at remote crossings where a *libreta de pasos por aduana* may be required. No specific papers are usually required to take a Brazilian registered car into Argentina.

Touching down

Airport information Do not send unaccompanied luggage to Argentina; it can take up to three days of form-filling to retrieve it from the airport. Paying overweight, though expensive, saves time.

Airport tax US$31 for all international flights, except to Montevideo from Aeroparque, which is subject to US$16.50 tax; and Punta del Este from Aeroparque, which is US$20.50. Tax on domestic flights is US$7.25. All taxes are payable only in pesos. These taxes include security, immigration and customs charges; check with the agent selling your flight ticket if these charges have been

Touching down

Business hours Banks, government offices, insurance offices and business houses are not open on Saturday; normal office hours are 0900-1200, 1400-1900. **Banks**: 1000-1500 but time varies according to the city, and sometimes according to the season. (See under names of cities in text.) **Government** Offices: 1230-1930 (winter) and 0730-1300 (summer). **Post Offices**: stamps on sale during working days 0800-2000 but 0800-1400 on Saturday. **Shops** 0900-2000, though many close at 1300 on Saturday. Outside the main cities many close for the daily afternoon siesta, reopening at about 1700. 24-hour opening is allowed except on Monday; this applies mainly to restaurants, foodshops, barbers, newspaper shops, art, book and record stores.

IDD 54 When ringing: equal tones with long pauses. If engaged equal tones with equal pauses.

Official time Three hours behind GMT.

Voltage 220 volts (and 110 too in some hotels), 50 cycles, AC, European Continental-type plugs in old buildings, Australian three-pin flat-type in the new. Adaptors can be purchased locally for either type (ie from new three-pin to old two-pin and vice-versa).

Weights and measures The metric system is used.

---

included in the price. When in transit from one international flight to another, you may be obliged to pass through immigration and customs, have your passport stamped and be made to pay an airport tax on departure. There is a 5% tax on the purchase of air tickets. Airport tax can be prepaid.

Clothing Shorts are worn in Buenos Aires and residential suburbs in spring, summer and autumn, but their use is not common outside the capital. In general, dress tends to be formal (unless casual wear is specified on an invitation) in Buenos Aires and for evening outings to shows, etc. Men wearing earrings can expect comments, even hostility, in the provinces.

Local customs & laws

Generally, Argentina is one of the safest countries in South America but the change in economic fortunes has forced many Argentines into poverty and desperation. In Buenos Aires and, to a lesser extent, in other major cities, opportunistic crime is on the increase. Most obvious is the old trick of spraying mustard, ketchup or some other substance on you and then getting an accomplice to clean you off (and remove your wallet). If you are sprayed, walk straight on. There are many other scams, even assaults. Be alert; avoid marginal areas, lonely streets at night and crowded places. In the capital take taxis, preferably radio taxis, for safety. Highways may be blocked by road pickets (often the unemployed). There is usually no threat to travellers, just hours of inconvenience.

Safety
Never carry weapons, or drugs without prescriptions

Where to stay

In the beach and inland resorts there are many good hotels and *pensiones*; names are therefore not always given. Bed and breakfast accommodation throughout Argentina can be booked via www.argentinabandb.com.ar, in English, Spanish and French. Look out for special accommodation deals, such as weekend packages, three nights for the price of two, etc. **Hotel bills**: four- and five-star hotels normally add 21% VAT to the bill. Mid-range hoteliers will probably ask you "¿necesita factura?", do you need a bill? And, by implication, do you want to help me avoid taxes? If you say no, I don't want a bill, you will probably get a lower rate. If you say yes, you'll get the officially-posted rate, the *factura* and a look of disappointment. Cheapest places don't usually ask if you need a bill and don't offer one. It is often the case that you will pay less by booking a room at reception, rather than over the internet, where higher prices apply.

Hotels
See inside the front cover for our hotel grade price guide

Camping is very popular in Argentina (except in Buenos Aires) and there are sites with services, both municipal, free, and paying private campsites in most tourist centres. Most are very noisy and many are closed off-season. The average price throughout the country is US$1.50-2 pp if you have your own tent, plus a charge for the site. Camping is allowed at the

Camping

side of major highways and in all national parks (except at Iguazú Falls). Wild camping in deserted areas is possible, but note that in Patagonia strong winds make camping very difficult. Many *ACA* and *YPF* service stations have a site where one can camp (usually free) and in general service station owners are very friendly to campers, but ask first. Service stations usually have hot showers. A list of camping sites is available from *ACA* (labelled for members, but should be easily available) and from the national tourist information office in Buenos Aires, which has a free booklet, *1ra Guía Argentina de Campamentos.*

Regular (blue bottle) Camping Gaz International is available in Buenos Aires. White gas (*bencina blanca*) is readily available in hardware shops (*ferreterías*) but may not be known by that name; if not, try asking for *solvente.*

Youth hostels *Hostelling International Argentina,* or *Red Argentina de Alojamiento para Jóvenes (RAAJ)*, Florida 835 p 3, of 319B, Buenos Aires, T4511 8712, F4312 0089, www.hostelslatinamerica.org bOffers 10% discount to card-holders at their hostels throughout Argentina. **NB** A HI card in Argentina costs US$14, ISIC cards also sold. In Buenos Aires there are many hostels, with new ones opening all the time. Outside the capital youth hostels are spreading (some open only February to March). ***Argentina Hostels Club (AHC)*** is a network of 25 independent hostels throughout the country: www.argentinahostels.com Some towns offer free accommodation to young travellers in the holiday season, on floors of schools or church halls; some fire stations will let you sleep on the floor for free (sometimes men only).

Getting around

Air

All local flights are fully booked way in advance for travel in Dec For airline information, www.aeropuertos arg.com.ar

Internal air services are run by *Aerolíneas Argentinas* (AR – www.aerolineas.com.ar), *Austral* (part of AR), *Aerovip*, *American Falcon* (www.americanfalcon.com.ar), *Southern Winds* (www.sw.com.ar) and the army airline *LADE* (in Patagonia – www.lade.com.ar), which provides a good extended schedule with new Fokker F-28 jets. Two other airlines, *Lapa* and *Dinar* ceased operating in April 2003, but rescue packages were being mounted for both. Their services are not included in the text below. Some airlines operate during the high season, or are air taxis on a semi-regular schedule. All airlines operate standby systems, at half regular price, buy ticket 2-3 hrs before flight. It is only worth doing this off season. Children under three travel free. *LADE* also operates discount tickets: spouse (65%) and children (35%). Check in 2 hrs before flight to avoid being 'bumped off' from overbooking. Meals are rarely served on internal flights.

Visit Argentina fare *Aerolíneas Argentinas* sell a **Visit Argentina ticket**: three flight coupons costing US$300, with US$125 for each extra coupon (no maximum limit). It is valid for 90 days and must be purchased outside Argentina and in conjunction with a Transatlantic *AR* flight ticket. (If you fly on a different carrier the airpass costs US$450 and each extra coupon US$185.) Note that for children under two years *Visit Argentina* fare is 10%. The airpass is valid on *Austral*. Routing must be booked when the coupons are issued: subsequent changes cost US$25, but changes of date are free. One stop only is permitted per town; this includes making a connection (as many flights radiate from Buenos Aires, journeys to and from the capital count as legs on the airpass, so a four-coupon pass might not get you very far). If you start your journey outside Buenos Aires on a Sunday, when *Aerolíneas Argentinas* offices are closed, you may have difficulty getting vouchers issued at the airport. If you wish to visit Tierra del Fuego and Lago Argentino it is better to fly on the *Visit Argentina* pass to Río Grande or Ushuaia and travel around by bus or *LADE* from there than to stop off in El Calafate, fly to Ushuaia and thence back to Buenos Aires, which will use three coupons. It is unwise to set up too tight a schedule because of delays which may be caused by bad weather. Flights between Buenos Aires and El Calafate or Río Gallegos are often fully booked two to three weeks ahead, and there may be similar difficulties on the routes to Bariloche and Iguazú. If you are 'wait-listed' they cannot ensure a seat. Reconfirmation at least 24 hours ahead of a flight is important and it is essential to make it at the point of departure. Extra charges are made for reconfirming *LADE* flights but they are not high.

All motorists are required to carry two warning triangles, a fire-extinguisher, a rigid tow bar, a first aid kit, full car documentation together with international driving licence (for non-residents, but see Car hire below), and the handbrake must be fully operative. Safety belts must be worn if fitted. Although few checks are made in most of the country, with the notable exceptions of roads into Rosario and Buenos Aires, checks have been reported on cars entering the country. Parking restrictions are strictly enforced: a tow truck tours the towns; the cost of recovery is US$75. You may not export fuel from Argentina, so use up fuel in spare jerry cans while you are in the country. Always fill up when you can in less developed areas like Chaco and Formosa and in parts of Patagonia as filling stations are infrequent. Petrol/gasoline costs on average US$0.70 per litre and diesel US$0.50. There is a 40% discount on fuel in the provinces of Chubut, Santa Cruz and Tierra del Fierro and in the towns of Sierra Grande and El Bolsón in Río Grande. Octane rating for gasoline ('*nafta*') is as follows: regular gasoline 83; super 93. Unleaded fuel is widely available in 93, 95 and 97 octane. *ACA* sells petrol vouchers (*vales de nafta*) for use in *ACA* stations. Shell and Esso stations are slightly more expensive.

Car
*Most of Argentina
is served by about
215,578 km of road,
but only 29% are
paved and a further
17% improved*

To obtain documents for a resident (holder of resident visa, staying at least six months in the country) to take a car out of Argentina, you can go to *ACA* in Buenos Aires for advice and paperwork. **NB** Non-residents may buy a car in Argentina but are in no circumstances allowed to take it out of the country; it must be resold in Argentina, preferably in the province where it was purchased. Non-residents who take cars into Argentina are not allowed to sell them and will encounter problems trying to leave the country without the vehicle. Third party insurance is obligatory; best obtained from the *ACA*, for members only.

Most main roads are paved, if rather narrow (road maps are a good indication of quality), and roadside services are good. Road surface conditions vary once you leave main towns. On the gravel (called *ripio* on maps) and dirt roads, to avoid flying stones don't follow trucks too closely, overtake with plenty of room and pull well over and slow down for oncoming vehicles. Most main roads now have private tolls, ranging from US$1 to US$5; tolls are spaced about every 100 km. Secondary roads (which have not been privatized) are generally in poor condition. Sometimes you may not be allowed to reach a border if you do not intend to cross it, stopping, eg 20 km from the border.

Automóvil Club Argentino (*ACA*), Av Libertador Gen San Martín 1850, 1st floor, T4802 6061, www.aca.org.ar open 1000-1800, has a travel documents service, complete car service facilities, insurance facilities, hotel lists, camping information, road information, road charts (*hojas de ruta*, about US$1.20 each to members), and maps (of whole country, showing service stations and *hosterías*, US$2 to members, US$4.75 to non-members, and of each province). A tourist guide book is for sale at a discount to members and members of recognized foreign motoring organizations. Foreign automobile clubs with reciprocity with *ACA* are allowed to use *ACA* facilities and benefit from discounts (you must present a membership card). Non-members will not receive any help if in trouble. *ACA* membership is US$10 per month, permitting payment with Eurocard (Argencard) for fuel in its service stations, 20% discount on hotel rooms and maps, and discounts at associated hotels, campsites and 10% discount on meals. *ACA* accommodation comes in four types: *Motel*, *Hostería*, *Hotel*, and *Unidad Turística*, and they also organize campsites. A *motel* may have as few as three rooms, and only one night's stay is permitted. *Hosterías* have very attractive buildings and are very friendly. *Hoteles* are smarter and more impersonal. All have meal facilities of some kind. Anyone, motorist or not, can get in touch with the organization to find out about accommodation or road conditions. **Touring Club Argentino**, Esmeralda 605, T4322 7994, touringclubargentino@hotmail.com Has similar travel services but no service stations.

Minimum age for renting is 25 (private arrangements may be possible). A credit card is useful. Highest prices are in Patagonia. Discounts are available for weekly rental. Check the insurance details carefully, especially the excess clause. You must ensure that the renting agency gives you ownership papers of the vehicle, which have to be shown at police and military checks. At tourist centres such as Salta, Posadas, Bariloche or Mendoza it may be more economical to hire a taxi with driver, which includes the guide, the fuel, the insurance and the mechanic. *Avis* offers an efficient service with the possibility of complete insurance and unlimited mileage for rentals of seven days or more, but you should prebook from abroad. No one-way fee if returned to

Car hire
*See car rental
web addresses
on page 52*

Argentina

another *Avis* office, but the car may not be taken out of the country. **Localiza**, a Brazilian company, accepts drivers aged at least 21 (according to Brazilian rules, but higher insurance). It also offers four-wheel drive vehicles, though only from Buenos Aires. Taking a rented car out of Argentina is difficult with any company.

Bus Express buses between cities are dearer than the *comunes*, but well worth the extra money for the fewer stops. When buying tickets at a bus office, don't assume you've been automatically allotted a seat: make sure you have one. Buses have strong a/c, even more so in summer; take a sweater for night journeys. Note that luggage is handled by *maleteros*, who expect payment (theoretically US$0.50, but in practice you can offer less) though many Argentines refuse to pay.

Hitchhiking Argentina is getting increasingly difficult and much less safe for this. Traffic can be sparse, especially at distances from the main towns, and in Patagonia.

Internal checkpoints There are checkpoints to prevent food, vegetable and meat products entering Patagonia, the Western provinces of Mendoza and San Juan, and the Northwestern provinces of Catamarca, Tucumán, Salta and Jujuy. All vehicles and passengers entering these areas are searched and prohibited products are confiscated.

Taxis Licensed taxis known as *Radio Taxi* can be hired on the street, or can be called in advance and are safer. There is also a system known as *Remise*, where car and driver are booked from an office and operate with a fixed fare (more than a regular taxi).

Train Trains only run on 22,000 of its 42,000 km of track and most of its is used only by freight services. There are few passenger services outside the Buenos Aires area.

Maps Several series of road maps are available including those of the *ACA*, *YPF* (the oil company) and the *Automapas* published by **Línea Azul** (regional maps, Michelin-style, high quality). Topographical maps are issued by the **Instituto Geográfico Militar**, Cabildo 301, Casilla 1426, Buenos Aires (one block from Subte Ministro Carranza, Line D, or take bus 152). 1:500,000 sheets cost US$3 each and are 'years old'; better coverage of 1:100,000 and 1:250,000, but no general physical maps of the whole country or city plans. Helpful staff, sales office accessible from street, no passport required, map series indices on counter, open Mon-Fri, 0800-1300. *ITMB* publishes a 1:4,000,000 map of Argentina.

Keeping in touch

Internet Use of email is widespread and access to the internet is easy to find in cities and most towns. Most phone offices (*locutorios*) have email facilities.

Post Letters from Argentina take 10-14 days to get to the UK and the USA. For assured delivery, register everything. Small parcels only of 1 kg at post offices; larger parcels from Encomiendas Internacionales, **Centro Postal Internacional**, Av Comodoro Py y Antártida Argentina, near Retiro Station, Buenos Aires, and in main provincial cities. Larger parcels must first be examined, before final packing, by Customs, then wrapped (up to 2 kg, brown paper; over 2 kg must be sewn in linen cloth), then sealed by Customs, then taken to Encomiendas Internacionales for posting. Cheap packing service available. Customs usually open in the morning only. All incoming packages are opened by customs. *Poste restante* is available in every town's main post office, fee US$0.50.

Telephone Two private companies operate telephone services, **Telecom** in the north and **Telefónica Argentina** in the south. Buenos Aires Federal District and the country as a whole are split roughly in two halves. For the user there is no difference and the two companies' phone cards are interchangeable. For domestic calls public phones operate on phone cards of various values, which are more convenient than *cospeles* (tokens), which can be purchased at news stands

Argentina

(different tokens for local and inland calls). Domestic phone calls are priced at three rates: normal 0800-1000, 1300-2200, Sat 0800-1300; peak 1000-1300, Mon-Fri; night rate 2200-0800, Sat 1300-2400 and all day Sun and holidays. Peak is most expensive; night rate is cheapest and at this time also international calls are reduced by 20%. Both companies also have fax and, often, internet services. There are also privately-run *locutorios* (phone offices), offering a good telephone, fax and internet service. International public phones display the DDI sign (Discado Directo Internacional). DDN (Discado Directo Nacional) is for phone calls within Argentina. Provide yourself with enough phone cards (or tokens) in Buenos Aires because in the regions many phone booths exist, but the cards and tokens are harder to find. Most telephone company offices in principal cities have a phone for *USA Direct*; if they do not, they can direct you to one. *BT* Chargecard can be used to the UK via the operator (T0800-54401).

Media

Newspapers Buenos Aires dailies: *La Nación* (www.lanacion.com.ar), *La Prensa* (www.laprensa.com.ar), *Clarín* (www.clarin.com.ar), *La Razón* (www.larazon.com.ar). Evening paper: *Crónica* (www2.cronica.com.ar). The daily, *Página Doce* (www.pagina12.com.ar), is popular among intellectuals. English language daily: *Buenos Aires Herald,* www.buenosaires herald.com **Magazines**: *Noticias* (www.noticias.uolsinectis.com.ar), *Gente* (www.gente.com.ar) German-language weekly, *Argentinisches Tageblatt*, available everywhere, very informative.

Radio English language radio broadcasts can be heard daily on short wave: 0100-0130 on 6060 KHz 49m, 0230-0300 on 11710 KHz 25m, 0430-0500 and 2230-2300 on 15345 KHz 19m; *Radiodifusión Argentina al Exterior*, Casilla de Correo 555, 1000, Buenos Aires. This is a government station and broadcasts also in Japanese, Arabic, German, French, Italian and Portuguese. Foreign radio stations (including the BBC) are receivable on short wave.

Food and drink

Food

National dishes are based in the main upon plentiful supplies of beef. Many dishes are distinctive and excellent; the *asado*, a roast cooked on an open fire or grill; *puchero*, a stew, very good indeed; *bife a caballo*, steak topped with a fried egg; the *carbonada* (onions, tomatoes, minced beef), particularly good in Buenos Aires; *churrasco*, a thick grilled steak; *parrillada*, a mixed grill, mainly roast meat, offal, and sausages, *chorizos* (including *morcilla*, black pudding to the British, or blood sausage), though do not confuse this with *bife de chorizo*, which is a rump steak (*bife de lomo* is fillet steak). A *choripán* is a roll with a *chorizo* inside. *Arroz con pollo* is a delicious combination of rice, chicken, eggs, vegetables and strong sauce. *Puchero de gallina* is chicken, sausage, maize, potatoes and squash cooked together. *Empanada* is a tasty meat pie; *empanadas de humita* are filled with a thick paste of cooked corn/maize, onions, cheese and flour *Milanesa de pollo* (breaded, boneless chicken) is usually good value. Also popular is *milanesa*, a breaded veal cutlet. *Ñoquis* (gnocchi), potato dumplings normally served with meat and tomato sauce, are tasty and often the cheapest item on the menu; they are also a good vegetarian option when served with either *al tuco* or Argentine roquefort (note that a few places only serve them on the 29th of the month, when you should put a coin under your plate for luck). *Locro* is a thick stew made of maize, white beans, beef, sausages, pumpkin and herbs. Pizzas come in all sorts of exotic flavours, both savoury and sweet. **NB** Extras such as chips, *puré* (mashed potato), etc are ordered and served separately, and are not cheap. Almost uniquely in Latin America, salads are quite safe. A popular sweet is *dulce de leche* (especially from Chascomús), milk and sugar evaporated to a pale, soft fudge. Other popular desserts are *almendrado* (ice cream rolled in crushed almonds), *dulce de batata* (sweet potato preserve), *dulce de membrillo* (quince preserve), *dulce de zapallo* (pumpkin in syrup); these *dulces* are often eaten with cheese. *Postre Balcarce*, a cream and meringue cake and *alfajores*, maize-flour biscuits filled with *dulce de leche* or apricot jam, are also very popular. Note that *al natural* in reference to fruit means canned without sugar (fresh fruit is *al fresco*) Croissants (known as *media lunas*) come in two varieties: *de grasa* (dry) and *de mantequilla* (rich and fluffy). Sweets: the Havana brands have been particularly recommended. Excellent Italian-style ice cream with exotic flavours. For local recipes (in Spanish) *Las comidas de mi pueblo*, by Margarita Palacios, is recommended.

Offices close for 2-2½ hrs for lunch between 1200 and 1500. Around 1700, many people go to a *confitería* for tea, sandwiches and cakes. Dinner often begins at 2200 or 2230; it is, in the main, a repetition of lunch. The cheapest option is always to have the set lunch as a main meal of the day and then find cheap, wholesome snacks for breakfast and supper. Also good value are *tenedor libre* restaurants – eat all you want for a fixed price. Those wishing to prepare their own food will find supermarkets fairly cheap for basics.

Drink   Argentine wines (including champagnes, both charmat and champenoise) are sound throughout the price range. The ordinary *vinos de la casa*, or *comunes* are wholesome and relatively cheap; the reds are better than the whites. The local beers, mainly lager-type, are quite acceptable. In restaurants wines are quite expensive. Hard liquor is relatively cheap, except for imported whisky. *Clericó* is a white-wine *sangría* drunk in summer. It is best not to drink the tap water; in the main cities it is often heavily chlorinated. It is usual to drink soda or mineral water at restaurants, and many Argentines mix it with their cheaper wine and with ice, as a refreshing drink in summer.

Shopping

Local leather goods in Buenos Aires, eg coats (leather or suede), handbags and shoes. **NB** Leather from the *carpincho* is from the capybara and should not be purchased. A gourd for drinking *yerba mate* and the silver *bombilla* which goes with it, perhaps a pair of *gaucho* trousers, the *bombachas*. Ponchos (red and black for men, all colours for women). Articles of onyx, especially in Salta. Silver handicrafts. Woollens, especially in Bariloche and Mar del Plata.

Sport and activities

Birdwatching   At least 980 of the 2,926 species of birds registered in South America exist in Argentina, in places with easy access. Enthusiasts head for Península Valdés, Patagonia, the subtropical forests in the northwest, or the Iberá Marshes and Chaco savanna in the northeast. The pampas, too, have rich birdlife: flamingoes rise in a pink and white cloud, egrets gleam white against the blue sky, pink spoonbills dig in the mud and rheas stalk in the distance. Most fascinating are the oven birds, *horneros*, which build oven-shaped nests six times as big as themselves on the top of telegraph and fence posts. Details are available from **Asociación Ornitológica del Plata** (address under Buenos Aires).

Climbing   The Andes offer great climbing opportunities. Among the most popular peaks are Aconcagua, in Mendoza province, Pissis in Catamarca, and Lanín and Tronador, reached from the Lake District. The northern part of Los Glaciares national park, around El Chaltén, has some spectacular peaks with very difficult mountaineering. Climbing clubs (**Club Andino**) can be found in Mendoza, Bariloche, Esquel, Junín de los Andes, Ushuaia and other cities and in some places equipment can be hired.

Estancia tourism   An *estancia* is, generally speaking, a farm, but the term covers a wide variety of establishments and many have opened their doors to visitors. In the pampas, *estancias* tend to be cattle ranches extending for thousands of hectares; in the west they often have vineyards; northeastern *estancias* border swamps; those in Patagonia are sheep farms at the foot of the mountains or beside lakes. Wherever you choose, be it to relax, or observe the workings of the place, you will gain an insight into aspects of the culture and economy of Argentina. Many offer horse riding and other options such as fishing, canoeing, walking and birdwatching.

Fishing   The three main areas for fishing are the Northern Zone, around Junín de los Andes, extending south to Bariloche; the Central Zone around Esquel; the Southern Zone around Río Gallegos and Río Grande. The first two of these areas are in the lake district. Among the best lakes are: Lagos Traful, Gutiérrez, Mascardi, Futalaufquen (in Los Alerces National Park), Meliquina, Falkner, Villarino, Nuevo, Lacar, Lolog, Currruhué, Chico, Huechulafquen, Paimún, Epulafquen, Tromen (all in Lanín National Park), and, in the far north, Quillén. The Río Limay has good trout fishing, as do the rivers further north, the Quilquihue, Malle, Chimehuín, Collón-Curá, Hermoso, Meliquina and Caleufú. The southern fishing zone includes the Ríos Gallegos, Chico, Grande, Fuego, Ewan, San Pablo and Lago Fagnano near Ushuaia. It is famous for runs of sea trout. All rivers are 'catch and release'. The best time for fishing is at the beginning of the season, that is, in November and December (the season runs from early November to the end of March). To fish anywhere in Argentina you need a permit, which costs US$5 per day, US$15 per week, US$50 per year. In the Northern Zone forestry commission inspectors are very diligent.

Fossil hunting

There are areas of fascinating rock formations, different coloured strata and strange landscapes, especially in the northwest. San Juan province has some of the most spectacular examples. A large number of dinosaur fossils have been discovered in various locations (Neuquén, La Rioja, Chubut and other parts of Patagonia) and there are museums displaying the finds (eg Plaza Huincul and Rincón de los Sauces, Neuquén; Trelew, Chubut).

Off-roading

Large areas of Argentina are ideal for offroading since there are wide expanses of flat land or gently rolling hills with no woods, snow or ice. The vegetation is sparse and there are few animals or people. Patagonia, with is endless steppes interrupted only by rivers, gorges and gullies, is recommended, but some of the Andean valleys of the west and northwest are worth exploring. There are also some rough roads in the Andes, such as San Antonio de los Cobres to Catamarca via Antofagasta de la Sierra and the Laguna Brava area in La Rioja that make for adventurous driving. Note that hiring four-wheel drive vehicles is easier in provincial cities than in Buenos Aires, but is certainly not cheap. Also, avoid the wettest and coldest months: October-November (spring) and April-May (autumn) are best.

Skiing

The season is roughly from May to October, depending on the weather and resort. Las Leñas, south of Mendoza, is of international standard. Major resorts exist on Cerro Catedral and Cerro Otto near Bariloche and Chapelco near San Martín de los Andes. Smaller resorts, with fewer facilities, can be found near Mendoza (Los Penitentes, Vallecitos and Manantiales), in the Lake District (Caviahue, Cerro Bayo; La Hoya – near Esquel) and near Ushuaia (Cerro Martial, Wallner).

Trekking

There is ample scope for short- and long-distance trekking, on foot and on horseback. The best locations are in the foothills and higher up in the Andes. Some suggestions are the valleys around Salta, San Juan and La Rioja, Mendoza and Malargüe, in the national parks of the Lake District, and around El Chaltén in Los Glaciares national park.

Watersports

Surfing, windsurfing and waterskiing are practised along the Atlantic coast south of Buenos Aires. There are some good whitewater rafting runs in Mendoza province, near the provincial capital and near San Rafael and Malargüe. In the Lake District there are possibilities in the Lanín, Nahuel Huapi and Los Alerces national parks.

Wine tasting

Good wine is made in Argentina and vineyards can be visited in Mendoza province and Cafayate (in the south of Salta province).

Holidays and festivals

No work may be done on the national holidays (1 January, Good Friday, 1 May, 25 May, 10 June, 20 June, 9 July, 17 August, 12 October and 25 December) except where specifically established by law. There are limited bus services on 25 and 31 December. On Holy Thursday and 8 December employers are left free to decide whether their employees should work, but banks and public offices are closed. Banks are also closed on 31 December. There are gaucho parades throughout Argentina, with traditional music, on the days leading up to the *Día de la Tradición*, 10 November. On 30 December (not 31 because so many offices in the centre are closed) there is a ticker-tape tradition in downtown Buenos Aires: it snows paper and the crowds stuff passing cars and buses with long streamers.

Health

See also the Health
section in Essentials
at the beginning of
the book, page 60

Argentina is generally a healthy country to visit, with good sanitary services. In Buenos Aires and in some provinces, like Neuquén and Salta, medical assistance, including operations, X-ray and medication, is free in provincial hospitals, even for foreigners. Sometimes, though, you must pay for materials. All private clinics, on the other hand, charge. Medicines are more expensive than in Europe. Smallpox vaccination is no longer required to enter Argentina. If intending to visit the low-lying tropical areas, it is advisable to take precautions against malaria. Chagas' disease is found in northwest Argentina. To counter the effects of altitude in the northwest, chew coca leaves or take *te de coca* (use of coca is legal, its trade is not). In the south take plenty of sunscreen to prevent burning owing to the thinning of the ozone layer. Certain shellfish from the Atlantic coast are affected once or twice a year by red tide (*Marea Roja*), an algae poisonous to humans, at which time the public is warned not to eat the shellfish. Buy seafood, if self-catering, from fishmongers with fridge or freezer. To be certain, soak fish for 30 minutes in water with a little vinegar.

Buenos Aires

With its elegant architecture and fashion-conscious inhabitants, Buenos Aires is often seen as more European than South American. Among its fine boulevards, neat plazas, parks, museums and theatres, there are chic shops and superb restaurants. However, the enormous steaks and the passionate tango are distinctly Argentine, and to really understand the country, you have to know its capital.

*Phone code: 011
Colour map 8, grid B5
Population:
capital 2.78 million
Gran Buenos Aires
12.05 million*

*Extreme humidity and
unusual pollen
conditions may affect
asthma sufferers*

Buenos Aires lies on the Río de la Plata, or River Plate, not a river but an estuary or great basin, 300 km long and from 37 to 200 km wide, into which flow the Ríos Paraná and Uruguay and their tributaries. It is muddy and shallow and the passage of ocean vessels is only made possible by continuous dredging. The capital has been virtually rebuilt since the beginning of the 20th-century and its oldest buildings mostly date from the early 1900s, with some elegant examples from the 1920s and 30s. The centre has maintained the original lay-out since its foundation and so the streets are often narrow and mostly one-way. Its original name, 'Santa María del Buen Ayre' was a recognition of the good winds which brought sailors across the ocean.

Ins & outs

For more detailed
information, see
Transport, page 104

Getting there Buenos Aires has 2 airports, Ezeiza, for international flights, and Aeroparque, for domestic flights, some services to Uruguay and to other neighbouring countries. Ezeiza is 35 km southwest of the centre by a good dual carriageway which links with the General Paz highway which circles the city. The safest way between airport and city is by an airport bus service run by **Manuel Tienda León**, which has convenient offices and charges US$5 one way. Taxis charge US$8 (plus US$1 toll), but do not have a good reputation for security. *Remise* taxis (booked in advance) charge US$14 (including toll for a return journey) airport to town. Aeroparque is 4 km north of the city centre on the riverside; *Manuel Tienda León* has buses between the airports and also runs from Aeroparque to the centre for US$2. Remises charge US$3.50 and ordinary taxis US$2.50. *Transfer Express* operates on-request *remise* taxis, vans and minibuses from both airports to any point in town and between them; convenient for large groups. As well as by air, travellers from Uruguay arrive by ferry (fast catamaran or slower vessels), docking in the port in the heart of the city, or by bus. All international and interprovincial buses use the Retiro bus terminal at Ramos Mejía y Antártida Argentina, which is next to the Retiro railway station. Both are served by city buses, taxis and Line C of the Subte (metro). Other train services, to the province of Buenos Aires and the suburbs use Constitución, Once and Federico Lacroze stations, all served by bus, taxi and Subte.

Getting around The commercial heart of the city, from Retiro station and Plaza San Martín through Plaza de Mayo to San Telmo, east of Avenida 9 de Julio, can be explored on foot, but you'll probably want to take a couple of days to explore its many museums, shops and markets. Many places of interest lie outside this zone, so you will need to use public transport at some stage. City **buses** (*colectivos*) are plentiful, see below for city guides. The fare is US$0.25. The **metro**, or Subte, has five lines; a single fare is US$0.20. Yellow and black **taxis** should not be hailed on the street; for security, book a radio taxi by phone (and make sure the meter is set when you get in). *Remise* taxis, booked only through an office, cost more but are usually more reliable. See Transport, below, for full details. Street numbers start from the dock side rising from east to west, but north/south streets are numbered from Av Rivadavia, 1 block north of Av de Mayo rising in both directions. Calle Juan D Perón used to be called Cangallo, and Scalabrini Ortiz used to be Canning (the old names are still referred to). Av Roque Sáenz Peña and Av Julio A Roca are commonly referred to as Diagonal Norte and Diagonal Sur respectively.

Tourist offices National office at Santa Fe 883 with maps and literature covering the whole country. Open Mon-Fri 0900-1700, T4312 2232/5550, info@turismo.gov.ar There are kiosks at Aeroparque (*Aerolíneas Argentinas* section), and at Ezeiza Airport, daily 0900-2000. There are city-run tourist kiosks open 1200-2000 on Florida, junction with Roque Sáenz Peña, at Abasto Shopping Mall (Av Corrientes 3200), in Recoleta (on Av Quintana, junction with Ortiz), in Puerto Madero, Dock 4, and at Retiro Bus Station (ground floor). City information T4313 0187, 1000-1800, municipal website www.buenosaires.gov.ar (go to 'bue' page), in Spanish, English and Portuguese. Tango information centre at Sarmiento 1551, T4373 2823, www.tangodata.com.ar Free guided tours are usually organized by the city authorities: free leaflet from city-run offices. Privately run tourist office (very helpful) in the basement at Galerías Pacíficos, on Florida. For free tourist information anywhere in the country T0800-555 0016 (0800-2000). Those overcharged or cheated can go to any tourist office or to **Casa del Consumidor**, Esmeralda 340, T4326 4540 (Mon-Fri 0900-1700).

Federal District of Buenos Aires

Detail maps
A Buenos Aires centre, page 90
B Recoleta & Palermo, page 92
C San Telmo, page 93

Tourist information Good guides to bus and subway routes are *Guía T, Lumi, Peuser* and *Filcar* (usually covering the city and Greater Buenos Aires in two separate editions), US$1-4 available at news stands. Also handy is Auto Mapa's pocket-size *Plano guía* of the Federal Capital, available at news stands, US$2.70. *Buenos Aires Day & Night* is a free bi-monthly tourist magazine with useful information and a downtown map available together with similar publications at tourist kiosks and hotels. *La Nación* has a Sun tourism section (very informative) and a *Vía Libre* entertainments section on Fri. Also on Fri, the youth section of *Clarín* (*Sí*) lists free entertainments. *Clarín* runs an up-to-date website on entertainment, www.laguia.clarin.com; *Página 12* has a youth supplement on Thu called *NO*. The *Buenos Aires Herald* publishes *Get Out* on Fri, listing entertainments. Information on what's on at www.buenosairesherald.com

Sights

Around the Plaza de Mayo

The heart of the city is the **Plaza de Mayo**. The **Casa de Gobierno** on the east side of the Plaza, and called the *Casa Rosada* because it is pink, contains the offices of the President of the Republic. It is notable for its statuary and the rich furnishing of its halls. ■ *Tours: Mon-Fri 1500, 1700, free (from Hipólito Yrigoyen 219; passport is required), T4344 3804.* The **Museo de los Presidentes** (in the basement) has historical memorabilia. ■ *Mon-Fri 1000-1800, T4344 3804. Guided visits at 1100 and 1600, free.* Behind the building, in the semicircular Parque Colón, is a large statue of Columbus. **Antiguo Congreso Nacional** (Old Congress Hall, 1864-1905) on the south of the Plaza, Balcarce 139, is a National Monument. ■ *Thu, 1500-1700, closed Jan, free.* The **Cathedral**, Rivadavia 437, on the north of Plaza, stands on the site of the first church in Buenos Aires. The current structure dates from 1758-1807, but the 18th-century towers were never rebuilt, so that the architectural proportions have suffered. The imposing tomb (1880) of the Liberator, Gen José de San Martín, is guarded by soldiers in fancy uniforms. ■ *Masses: Mon-Fri 0900, 1100, 1230, 1800, Sat 1100, 1800, Sun 1100, 1200, 1300, 1800. Visiting hours Mon-Fri 0800-1900, Sat-Sun 0900-1930. For guided visits, T4331 2845.* **Museo del Cabildo y la Revolución de Mayo** is in the old Cabildo where the movement for independence from Spain was first planned. It's worth a visit, especially for the paintings of old Buenos Aires, the documents and maps recording the May 1810 revolution, and memorabilia of the 1806 British attack; also Jesuit art. In the patio is a café and stalls selling handicrafts (Thu-Fri 1100-1800). ■ *Museum open Wed-Fri 1130-1800, Sat-Sun 1300-1800, T4334 1782.* Also on the Plaza is the Palacio de Gobierno de la Ciudad (City Hall). Within a few blocks north of the Plaza are the main banks and business houses.

On the Plaza de Mayo, the **Mothers of the Plaza de Mayo** march in remembrance of their children who disappeared during the 'dirty war' of the 1970s (their addresses are H Yrigoyen 1582 and Piedras 730). The Mothers march anti-clockwise round the central monument every Thursday at 1530, with photos of their disappeared loved-ones pinned to their chests.

West of the Plaza de Mayo

Running west from the Plaza, the Av de Mayo leads 1½ km to the **Palacio del Congreso** (Congress Hall) in the Plaza del Congreso. This huge Greco-Roman building houses the seat of the legislature. ■ *Free access for public at sittings from Hipólito Yrigoyen 1849 (to check T6310 7100 or 4959 3000); passport essential. Guided tour from same address on Mon-Fri at 1000, 1100, 1600 and 1700, when Congress is not sitting (tours at 1100 and 1600 are in English).* Avenida de Mayo crosses the **Avenida 9 de Julio**, one of the widest avenues in the world, which consists of three major carriageways with heavy traffic, separated in some parts by wide grass borders. Five blocks north of Avenida de Mayo the great **Plaza de la República**, with a 67 m obelisk commemorating the 400th anniversary of the city's founding, is at the junction of Avenida 9 de Julio with Avenidas Roque Sáenz Peña and Corrientes. **Teatro Colón**, overlooking Avenida 9 de Julio with its main entrance on Libertad, between Tucumán and Viamonte, is one of the world's great opera houses. The Colón's interior is resplendent with red plush and gilt; the stage is huge, and salons, dressing rooms and banquet halls are equally sumptuous. The season runs from March to early December and there are concert performances most days. ■ *Guided tours including* **Museo del Teatro Colón** *from entrance at Toscanini 1168 (on C Viamonte side) or from Tucumán 1171 Mon-Sat 1100, 1200, 1300, 1430, 1500, 1600, Sun 1100, 1300, 1500 (Jan-Feb: Tue-Sat hourly 1000-1700, Sun hourly 1100-1500), in Spanish, French (on request) and English. Recommended. US$3 (children or ISIC card US$1.50) T4378 7132/33, visitas@teatrocolon.org.ar Tickets sold 2 days before performance, from the C Tucumán side of the theatre, Tue-Sat 1000-2000, Sun 1000-1700, Mon only for same day events. The cheapest seat is US$0.30 (available even on the same day) and 'El Paraíso' tickets are available for standing room in The Gods – queue for a good spot. There are free concerts at Salón Dorado daily 1730, except Mon; visit www.teatrocolon.org.ar*

Close by is the **Museo del Teatro Nacional Cervantes**, Córdoba 1199, with history of the theatre in Argentina. ■ *Mon-Fri 1000-1700. The theatre also stages performances. T4815 8881 in advance.* **Museo Judío**, Libertad 769, has religious objects relating to Jewish presence in Argentina in a 19th-century synagogue. ■ *Tue and Thu 1500-1800; take identification. T4372 0014.* **La Chacarita**, Guzmán 670, a well known cemetery, has the much-visited, lovingly tended tombs of Juan Perón and Carlos Gardel, the tango singer. ■ *Daily 0700-1800, take Subte Line B to the Federico Lacroze station.*

North of the Plaza de Mayo

The city's traditional shopping centre, Calle Florida, is reserved for pedestrians, with clothes and souvenir shops, restaurants and the elegant Galerías Pacífico. More shops are to be found on Avenida Santa Fe, which crosses Florida at Plaza San Martín. Avenida Corrientes, a street of theatres, bookshops, restaurants and cafés, and nearby Calle Lavalle (partly reserved for pedestrians), used to be the entertainment centre, but both are now regarded as faded. Recoleta, Palermo and Puerto Madero have become much more fashionable (see below). The **Basílica Nuesta Señora de La Merced**, J D Perón y Reconquista 207, built in 1783, is a beautiful colonial church. Next door is the **Convento San Ramón**, founded in 1604, with a restaurant. On Calle San Martín, **Museo Numismático Dr José Evaristo Uriburu**, in the **Banco Central** library, No 216, 1st floor, is fascinating and overlooks a central foyer, ask guard for directions. ■ *Mon-Fri 1000-1500, free, T4348 3882.* **Museo y Biblioteca Mitre**, No 336, preserves intact the household of President Bartolomé Mitre; has a coin and map collection and historical archives. ■ *Mon-Fri 1300-1830, US$0.30, T4394 8240.*

The **Plaza San Martín** has a monument to San Martín in the centre and, at the north end, a memorial with an eternal flame to those who fell in the Falklands/Malvinas War of 1982. On the plaza, **Palacio San Martín**, Arenales 761, built 1905-09, is three houses linked together, with free guided tours. ■ *Thu 1100, Fri 1500,1600,1700 (Fri tours in Spanish and English), free, T4819 8092.* **Museo de Armas**, Av Santa Fe 702 y Maipú, has all kinds of weaponry related to Argentine history, including the 1982 Falklands/Malvinas War, plus Oriental weapons. ■ *Tue-Fri 1430-1930, closed 15 Dec-15 Mar, US$0.60, T4311 1071.*

Plaza Fuerza Aérea Argentina (formerly Plaza Británica) has the clock tower presented by British and Anglo-Argentine residents (open Wed-Sat 1200-1900, free), while in the **Plaza Canadá** (in front of the Retiro Station) there is a Pacific Northwest Indian totem pole, donated by the Canadian government. Behind Retiro station **Museo Nacional Ferroviario**, Avenida del Libertador 405, is for railway fans: locomotives, machinery, documents of the Argentine system's history (building in very poor condition). ■ *Mon-Fri 1000-1600. Archives 1000-1400, free, T4318 3343.* In a warehouse beside is the workshop of the sculptor Carlos Regazzoni who recycles refuse material from railways. ■ *Ring the bell, US$1.*

---

66 99 *The South American Handbook 1924*

On Buenos Aires *The capital of Argentina, the largest city south of the Equator and the largest Spanish-speaking city in the world, it is one of the world's handsomest and wealthiest cities.*

Avenida 9 de Julio meets Avenida del Libertador, the principal way out of the city to the north and west, between Retiro and La Recoleta. One of the city's best museums, **Museo de Arte Hispanoamericano Isaac Fernández Blanco**, Suipacha 1422 (three blocks west of Retiro), contains a fascinating collection of colonial art, especially paintings and silver, in a beautiful neocolonial mansion (Palacio Noel, 1920s) with Spanish gardens; free weekend concerts and regular tango lessons on Monday and Thursday. ■ *Tue-Sun, 1400-1900, Thu free; US$0.30. For guided visits in English or French contact Lía Guerrico at T4327 0228/0272. Guided tours in Spanish Sat, Sun 1600.*

Recoleta & Palermo

Nuestra Señora del Pilar, Junín 1898, is a jewel of colonial architecture dating from 1732 (renovated in later centuries), facing onto the public gardens of Recoleta. A fine wooden image of San Pedro de Alcántara, attributed to the famous 17th-century Spanish sculptor Alonso Cano, is preserved in a side chapel on the left, and there are stunning gold altars. Downstairs is an interesting museum of religious art.

Next to it, the **Cemetery of the Recoleta** is one of the sights of Buenos Aires, entrance at Junín 1790, not far from Museo de Bellas Artes (see below). With its streets and alleys separating family mausoleums built in every imaginable architectural style, La Recoleta is often compared to a miniature city. Among the famous names from Argentine history is Evita Perón who lies in the Duarte family mausoleum: to find it from the entrance go to the first tree-filled plaza; turn left and where this avenue meets a main avenue (go just beyond the Turriaca tomb), turn right; then take the third passage on the left. ■ *0700-1745. Tours last Sun of month (not in summer), 1430, T4803 1594.* On Saturday and Sunday there is a good craft market near the entrance (1100-1800), with street artists and performers. The **Centro Cultural Recoleta**, next to the cemetery, specializes in contemporary local art. ■ *Mon-Fri 1400-2100, Sat, Sun, holidays 1000-2100, T4803 9744.* Also the Buenos Aires Design Centre, with good design and handicraft shops and many restaurants. Several buses: 110, 102, 17, 60 (walk from corner of Las Heras y Junín, two blocks); from downtown, eg Correo Central, 61/62, 93, 130 to Avenida del Libertador y Avenida Pueyrredón.

Another excellent museum, **Museo de Bellas Artes** (National Gallery), Avenida del Libertador 1473, gives a taste of Argentine art, in addition to a fine collection of European works, particularly post-Impressionist. Superb Argentine 19th and 20th-century paintings, sculpture and wooden carvings. Film shows on Friday 1830; classical music concerts on Sunday 1730. ■ *Tue-Fri 1230-1930, Sat-Sun 0930-1930. Guided tours Tue-Sun 1700 for Argentine art, 1800 for European art, tours for children Sat 1500, free, T4801 3390. Warmly recommended.* The **Museo Nacional de Arte Decorativo**, Avenida del Libertador 1902, contains collections of painting, furniture, porcelain, crystal, sculpture. ■ *Daily 1400-1900. Guided visits Wed, Thu and Fri 1630, US$0.60, half-price to ISIC holders, T4802 6606.* The building is shared with the **Museo Nacional de Arte Oriental**; permanent exhibition of Chinese, Japanese, Hindu and Islamic art. ■ *Temporarily closed.* **Biblioteca Nacional** (The National Library) is housed in a modern building at Avenida del Libertador 1600 y Agüero 2502, where only a fraction of the extensive stock can be seen. Art gallery, periodical and journal archives; cultural events held here. ■ *Mon-Fri 0900-2100, Sat and Sun 1200-1900, closed Jan. Guided tours in Spanish daily 1600, T4806 6155.*

Museo de Motivos Populares Argentinos José Hernández, Avenida Libertador 2373, widest collection of Argentine folkloric art, with rooms dedicated to indigenous, colonial and Gaucho artefacts; handicraft shop and library. ■ *Wed-Sun 1300-1900, US$0.30, free Sun, T4802 7294/9967.* The city's third unmissable museum, **Museo de Arte Latinoamericano (MALBA)**, houses renowned Latin American artists' works: powerful, moving and highly recommended. It's not a vast collection, but representative of the best from the continent. Good library, cinema, seminars and shop ■ *Daily 1200-2000 (Wed free till 2100; Tue closed), US$1.30 (free for ISIC holders). T4808 6500, Av Figueroa Alcorta 3415, www.malba.org.ar Guided tours in English can be booked a week in advance, T4808 6556. Good restaurant.*

The fine **Palermo Parks**, officially known as the Parque Tres de Febrero, are famous for their extensive rose garden, Andalusian Patio, and delightful **Jardín Japonés** (with café). ■ *Daily 1000-1800, US$1, T4804 4922.* Close by is the **Hipódromo Argentino** (Palermo racecourse) (■ *Races 10 days per month, US$0.30-3, T4777 9001*). Opposite the parks are the Botanical and Zoological Gardens. At the entrance to the **Planetarium** (just off Belisario Roldán, in Palermo Park) are several large meteorites from Campo del Cielo. ■ *Shows at weekends US$1.30; small museum, , T4771 9393.* **Museo de Artes Plásticas Eduardo Sívori**, Avenida Infanta Isabel 555 (Parque Tres de Febrero). Emphasis on 19th and 20th-century Argentine art, sculpture and tapestry. ■ *Tue-Fri 1200-2000, Sat and Sun 1000-2000 (1800 in winter), US$0.30, Wed free, T4774 9452.* The **Show Grounds** of the Argentine Rural Society, next to Palermo Park, entrance on Plaza Italia, stage the Annual Livestock Exhibition, known as Exposición Rural, in July. The **Botanical Gardens**, Santa Fe 3951, entrance from Plaza Italia (take Subte, line D) or from Calle República Arabe Siria, contain characteristic specimens of the world's vegetation. The trees native to the different provinces of Argentina are brought together in one section. ■ *The Gardens, daily 0800-1800, contain the Museo del Jardín Botánico, T4831 2951, whose collection of Argentine Flora is open Mon-Fri 0800-1500.*

There are three important museums in Belgrano: **Museo Histórico Sarmiento**, Juramento 2180 (Belgrano), the National Congress and presidential offices in 1880; documents and personal effects of the former president; library of his work. ■ *Tue-Fri 1400-1900, Sun 1500-1900, US$0.30, Thu free, guided visits Sun 1600, T4783 7555, museosarmiento@fibertel.com.ar* **Museo de Arte Español Enrique Larreta**, Juramento 2291, Belgrano. The home of the writer Larreta, with paintings and religious art from the 14th to the 20th century. ■ *Daily 1400-2000, Tue closed, guided visits Sun 1500,1700, T4783 2640 for guided tour in language other than Spanish. US$0.30, Thu free.* **Museo Casa Yrurtia**, O'Higgins 2390, esq Blanco Encalada (Belgrano), an old house crammed with sculpture, paintings, furniture and the collections of artist Rogelio Yrurtia and his wife; peaceful garden. ■ *Tue-Fri 1300-1900, Sun 1500-1900, US$0.30, Tue free, guided visits Sun 1700, T/F4781 0385.*

The church of **San Ignacio de Loyola**, begun 1664, is the oldest colonial building in Buenos Aires (renovated in 18th and 19th centuries). It stands in a block of Jesuit origin, called the **Manzana de las Luces** (Enlightenment Square – Moreno, Alsina, Perú and Bolívar). Also in this block are the Colegio Nacional de Buenos Aires, formerly the Jesuits' Colegio Máximo (18th century), the Procuraduría de las Misiones and 18th-century tunnels. For centuries the whole block was the centre of intellectual activity, though little remains today. Church and School on Calle Bolívar. Guided tours, from Perú 272, sadly do not explore the tunnels. ■ *Mon-Fri 1500, Sat and Sun 1500, 1630, 1800 (Mon 1300 free tour from Alsina y Perú) in Spanish (in English by prior arrangement), arrive 15 mins before tour, US$1.30, T4342 4655.* **Museo de la Ciudad**, Alsina 412. Permanent exhibition covering social history and popular culture, special exhibitions on daily life in Buenos Aires changed every two months, and a reference library open to the public. ■ *Mon-Fri, 1100-1900, Sun, 1500-1900, US$0.30, free on Wed, T4343 2123.* **San Francisco**, Alsina y Defensa, run by the Franciscan Order, was built 1730-1754 and given a new façade in 1911.

Santo Domingo, Defensa y Belgrano, was founded in 1751. During the British attack on Buenos Aires in 1806 some of Whitelocke's soldiers took refuge in the church. The local forces bombarded it, the British capitulated and their regimental colours were preserved in the church. General Belgrano is buried here. There are occasional concerts in the church.

Museo Etnográfico JB Ambrosetti, Moreno 350, has anthropological and ethnographic collections from around the world, including Bolivian and Mapuche silverwork. ■ *Daily 1400-1900 (in summer 1600-2000), US$0.30, T4345 8196.*

South of Plaza de Mayo

Argentina

Buenos Aires centre

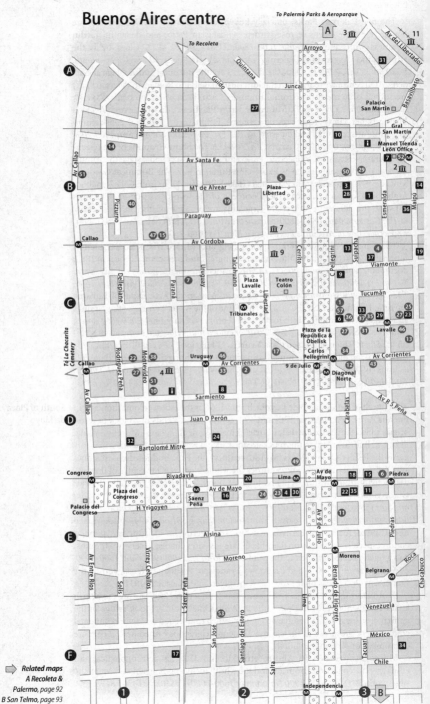

Argentina

Related maps
A Recoleta &
Palermo, page 92
B San Telmo, page 93

Argentina

■ Sleeping
1 Aspen Towers *B3*
2 Avenida *D4*
3 Bisonte Palace *B3*
4 Castelar *E2*
5 Claridge *C4*
6 Colón *C3*
7 Crillon *B3*
8 Dido *C2*
9 El Cachafaz *C3*
10 Embajador *B3*
11 España *E3*
12 Frossard *C4*
13 Goya *C3*
14 Gran Dorá *B3*
15 Gran Hispano *D3*
16 Gran Vedra *E2*
17 La Casa de Etty *F1*
18 La Giralda *D3*
19 Maipú *C3*
20 Marbella *E2*
21 Marriott Plaza *B4*
22 Milhouse *E3*
23 O'Rei *C3*
24 Orense *D2*
25 Orly *B4*
26 Principado *B4*
27 Recoleta Hostel *A2*
28 Regente Palace *B3*
29 Regis *C3*
30 Reyna *E2*
31 Sofitel Buenos Aires *A3*
32 St Nicholas *D1*
33 Suipacha Inn *C3*
34 Tango City Hostel Inn *F3*
35 Uruguay *E3*
36 Victory *B3*
37 V&S *C3*
38 Waldorf *B4*

● Eating
1 9 de Julio *C3*
2 Banchero *D2*
3 Bolsa de Comercio *D5*
4 Broccolino *C3*
5 Café de la Biblioteca *B2*
6 Café Tortoni *D3*
7 Casa China *C2*
8 Catalinas *B4*
9 Chino Central *D4*
10 Chiquilín *D1*
11 Club Español *E3*
12 Confitería Ideal *D3*
13 Criollo *C3*
14 Cumaná *B1*
15 Dietética Córdoba *B1*
16 Dora *B4*
17 Edelweiss *C2*
18 El Bar de Boca *D4*
19 El Cuartito *B2*
20 El Establo *B4*
21 El Figón de Bonilla *C5*
22 El Gato Negro *C1*
23 El Globo *E2*
24 El Imparcial *E2*
25 El Mundo *C3*
26 El Navegante *C5*

27 El Palacio de la Papa
   Frita *C3/D1*
28 El Querandí *E4*
29 El Yatasto *B3*
30 Empire *B4*
31 Florida Garden *B4*
32 Granix *D4*
33 Güerrín *D2*
34 Il Gatto *C3*
35 La Casona del
   Nonno *C3*
36 La Estancia *C3*
37 La Huerta *C3*
38 La Paz *C1*
39 La Pipeta *C4*
40 La Porcherie *B1*
41 La Posada de 1820 *C4*
42 La Puerto Rico *E4*
43 Las Cuartetas *D3*
44 Las Nazarenas *A4*
45 La Ventana *E4*
46 Los Inmortales *C2/C3*
47 Lotos *B1*
48 Morizono *B4*
49 Museo del Jamón *D2*
50 Natacha *B3*
51 Pepito & Pippo *B1/D1*
52 Petit París *B3*
53 Plaza Mayor *F2*
54 Richmond *C4*
55 Sabot *B4*
56 Status *E1*
57 Tomo Uno *B4*
58 Tulasi *B4*

🏛 Museums
1 Casa de Gobierno
   (Casa Rosada) &
   Museo de los
   Presidentes *D5*
2 Museo de Armas *B3*
3 Museo de Arte
   Hispanoamericano
   Isaac Fernández
   Blanco *A3*
4 Museo de Arte
   Moderno & Teatro
   General San
   Martín *D1*
5 Museo de la
   Ciudad *E4*
6 Museo del Cabildo
   y la Revolución
   de Mayo *E4*
7 Museo del Teatro
   Nacional Cervantes *B2*
8 Museo Etnográfico
   JB Ambrosetti *E4*
9 Museo Judío *C2*
10 Museo y Biblioteca
   Mitre *D4*
11 Museo Nacional
   Ferroviario at Retiro
   Station *A3*
12 Museo Numismático
   Dr José Evaristo
   Uriburu *D4*

Argentina

San Telmo
& La Boca
One of the few places which still has late colonial and Rosista buildings is the *barrio* of **San Telmo**, south of Plaza de Mayo, around Plaza Dorrego. It's an atmospheric place, with lots of cafés, antique shops and little art galleries. On Sundays especially, it has a great atmosphere, with an antiques market at the Plaza Dorrego (see page 103), free tango shows and live music. The 29 bus connects La Boca with San Telmo. **Museo de Arte Moderno**, San Juan 350, with a salon at Avenida Corrientes 1530, 9th floor: international exhibitions and a permanent collection of 20th-century art in an old tobacco warehouse. ■ *Tue-Fri 1000-2000, Sat, Sun and holidays 1100-2000. Guided tours Tue-Sun 1700. US$0.30, Wed free, T4361 1121.* **Museo del**

Recoleta & Palermo

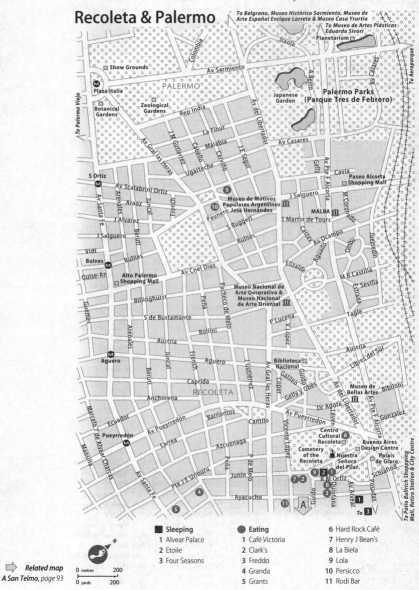

Sleeping
1 Alvear Palace
2 Etoile
3 Four Seasons

Eating
1 Café Victoria
2 Clark's
3 Freddo
4 Granda
5 Grants

6 Hard Rock Café
7 Henry J Bean's
8 La Biela
9 Lola
10 Persico
11 Rodi Bar

Related map
A San Telmo, page 93

0 metres   200
0 yards   200

Cine Pablo Ducros Hicken, Defensa 1220, dedicated to the history of Argentine cinema, with a library of over 600 sound films and newsreels from four decades. ■ *Mon-Fri 1100-1900, Sat-Sun 1130-1830, US$0.30, free on Wed. Film exhibitions on Wed and Sun 1600, US$0.30, T4361 2462.*

Parque Lezama, Defensa y Brasil, originally one of the most beautiful in the city, now rather run down, has an imposing statue of Pedro de Mendoza, who (according to tradition) founded the original city in 1536 on this spot. In the park is the **Museo Histórico Nacional**, Defensa 1600. Argentine history, San Martín's uniforms and the original furniture and door of the house in which he died at Boulogne. ■ *Tue - Sun 1300-1800, US$0.30, guided tours Sat and Sun 1530, T4307 1182.*

East of the Plaza de Mayo, behind the Casa Rosada, a broad avenue, Paseo Colón, runs south towards San Telmo and the old port district of **La Boca**, where the Riachuelo flows into the Plata. (La Boca is reached by bus 152 from Avenida Santa Fe, or Alem, or bus 29 from Plaza de Mayo, US$0.25.) The area's distinctive brightly painted tin and wooden houses can be seen along El Caminito, the little pedestrian street used as a theatre and art market. Visit the **Museo de Bellas Artes Benito Quinquela**, Pedro de Mendoza 1835, with more than 1,000 works by Argentine artists, particularly Benito Quinquela Martín (1890-1977), who painted La Boca port life. Also sculptures and figureheads rescued from ships. ■ *Tue-Fri 1000-1730, Sat-Sun 1100-1730, closed Jan, US$0.30, T4301 1080.* La Boca is the poorest and roughest area within central Buenos Aires and tourists are, unfortunately, targets for crime. Don't go alone and stay within the cleaned-up, touristy part of El Caminito and along the quay only as far as the Avellaneda bridge. Avoid the area at night. The area is especially rowdy when the Boca Juniors football club is playing at home. **Museo de la Pasión Boquense**, Brandsen 805, T4362 1100. For Boca Juniors and football fans. ■ *Tue-Sun 1000-1800, tickets available for a museum visit together with a stadium seat for a match on the same day, US$2.50.*

Fragata Presidente Sarmiento, dock 3, next to Avenida Alicia Moreau de Justo y Perón, Puerto Madero, a sailing ship used as a naval training ship until 1961; now a

Docks & Costanera Sur

San Telmo

Sleeping	Eating	Bars & clubs
1 Buenos Ayres Hostel	1 El Desnivel	3 Bar Sur
2 Hostal de San Telmo	2 La Casa de Esteban de Luca	4 El Balcón
3 Hostel-Inn	6 Sandanzas	5 El Viejo Almacén
4 La Casita de San Telmo	7 Victoria	6 Mr Mate
5 Oxford		

Related map A Recoleta & Palermo, *page 92*

Argentina

museum. ■ *Daily 0900-2200, US$0.60, T4334 9386.* Nearby, in dock 4, is the **Corbeta Uruguay**, the sailing ship which rescued Otto Nordenskjold's Antarctic expedition in 1903. ■ *Daily 0900-2100 all year, US$0.30, T4314 1090.* The **Puerto Madero** dock area has been renovated, the 19th-century warehouses being turned into restaurants and bars, an attractive place for a stroll and popular nightspot. East of San Telmo on the far side of the docks, the Avenida Costanera runs as a long, spacious boulevard. A stretch of marshland reclaimed from the river forms the interesting **Costanera Sur Wildlife Reserve**, where there are more than 200 species of birds, including the curve-billed reed hunter. ■ *Tue-Sun 0800-1900 (in winter, closes at 1800). The entrance is at Av Tristán Achával Rodríguez 1550, T4315 1320; for pedestrians and bikers only. Free, guided tours available at weekends, but much can be seen from the road before then (binoculars useful). It is 30 minutes walk from the entrance to the river shore, taking about 3 hrs to walk the whole perimeter. In summer it is very hot with little shade. For details (birdwatching, in particular) contact Aves Argentinas/AOP (see page 111). Take bus 4 or 2.*

Essentials

Sleeping
■ *on maps*

Rates given below are generally the minimum rates. Room tax (VAT/IVA) is 21% and is not always included in the price. Air conditioning (a/c) is a must in high summer. Many of the cheaper hotels in the central area give large reductions on the daily rate for long stays. Hotels with red-green lights, or marked *Albergue Transitorio,* are hotels for homeless lovers (for stays of 1½-2 hrs).

More expensive hotels can often be booked more cheaply through Buenos Aires travel agencies. Most hotels will give a discount for cash

In the centre LL*Hilton*, Av Macacha Güemes 351, Puerto Madero, T4891 0000, reservations ba@hilton.com A few blocks from banking district and located next to Costanera Sur, *El Faro* restaurant, health club and pool. LL *Marriott Plaza*, Florida 1005, T4318 3000, www.marriotthotels.com On Plaza San Martín, one of the most traditional hotels in town, opened in 1908. L *Claridge*, Tucumán 535, T4314 7700, www.claridge-hotel.com.ar Highly recommended. L *Aspen Towers*, Paraguay 857, T4313 1919, www.aspentowers.com.ar Small, spacious rooms, good breakfast. A *Colón*, Carlos Pellegrini 507, T4320 3500, www.colon-hotel.com.ar Overlooking Av 9 de Julio and Teatro Colón, excellent, charming bedrooms, comfortable, pool, gym, great breakfasts, perfect service. Highly recommended. A *Crillon*, Santa Fe 796, T4312 8181, www.hotelcrillon.com.ar Comfortable, good breakfast. A *Regente Palace*, Suipacha 964, T4328 6800, www.regente.com Very good, central, English spoken, buffet breakfast, sports facilities, stores luggage.

B *Bisonte Palace*, MT de Alvear 910, T4328 4751, www.hotelbisonte.com Very good, welcoming. B *Castelar*, Av de Mayo 1152, T4383 5001, www.castelarhotel.com.ar Elegant and attractive 1920s hotel, Turkish baths, good. B *Principado*, Paraguay 481, T4313 3022, hotel@principado.com.ar With breakfast, central, helpful. C *Gran Hotal Dorá*, Maipú 963, T4312 7391, www.dorahotel.com.ar Charming, old fashioned, comfortable rooms, good service, attractive lounge with paintings, recommended. C *Embajador*, Carlos Pellegrini 1185, T4326 5302, www.embajadohotel.com.ar Good value and service, with breakfast. C *Orly*, Paraguay 474, T/F4312 5344, www.orly.com.ar Good location, old fashioned, helpful, good lunches, English spoken, holds mail for guests, arranges tours and taxis, a/c. C *Regis*, Lavalle 813, T/F4327 2605, regisventas@orho-hoteles.com.ar Good value, nice atmosphere, with breakfast. C *Victory*, Maipú 880, T4314 5440, www.victoryhotel.com.ar A/c, modern, heating, TV, comfortable, luggage store. C *Waldorf*, Paraguay 450, T4312 2071, www.waldorf-hotel.com.ar Comfortable, rooms of varying standards, garage, a/c. C *Frossard*, Tucumán 686, T4322 1811, www.hotelfrossard.com.ar Renovated, comfortable, cable TV, convenient, good.

D *Avenida*, Av de Mayo 623, T4342 5664, F4343 7951. With breakfast, a/c, heating, simple but elegant, comfortable, bar. D *Goya*, Suipacha 748, T4322 9269, www.goyahotel.com.ar A/c, quiet, **B** for luxurious double rooms. D *Gran Hotel Hispano*, Av de Mayo 861, T4342 3472, hhispano@hhispano.com.ar Breakfast extra, some a/c, spacious, pleasant patio, stores luggage, helpful. D *Gran Hotel Vedra*, Av de Mayo 1350, T4383 0584, ghvedra@argentina.com Cheaper rooms with fan, stores luggage, small restaurant, English spoken. Recommended. D *Marbella*, Av de Mayo 1261, T/F4383 3573, info@hotelmarbella.com.ar Modernized, quiet, breakfast, a/c, free internet, English, French, Italian, Portuguese and German spoken, cheap restaurant. Highly recommended. **D** *Orense*, B Mitre 1359, T4372 4441, informes@hotelorense.com.ar With breakfast, a/c (**E** with fan), TV, laundry facilities. Recommended. **D** *Suipacha Inn*, Suipacha 515, T4322 0099, www.full men.com.ar Good value, neat small rooms with a/c, basic breakfast. **E** *La Giralda*, Tacuarí 17, T4345 3917, F4342 2142. Student discounts and for long stays. Recommended. **E** *Maipú*, Maipú 735, T4322 5142. Popular, hot water, basic, cheaper without bath, stores luggage, laundry facilities. **E** *O'Rei*, Lavalle 733, T4394 7112, hotelorei@yahoo.com.ar **F** without bath, central, simple but comfortable, spotless, laundry facilities, helpful. **E** *Reyna*, Av de Mayo 1120, T4381 2496. Old fashioned, helpful, cheaper without bath, warm, noisy, ask for discounts. **E** *Tandil*, Av de Mayo 890, T4343 2597, supertandil2@hotmail.com Comfortable new hotel, rooms with bath, cable TV, kitchen and laundry facilities. **E** *Uruguay*, Tacuarí 83, T4334 3456. Central, good value. Recommended (opposite is **D** *España*, T4343 5541, full of character).

   Recoleta and Palermo LL *Alvear Palace*, Alvear 1891, T/F4808 2100, www.alvea rpalace.com Older-style, roof garden, shopping gallery, elegant, extremely good. **LL** *Four Seasons*, Posadas 1086, T4321 1200, www.fourseasons.com/buenosaires Modern tower, pool, restaurant, including 7 suites at luxurious La Mansión residence. **LL** *Sofitel Buenos Aires*, Arroyo 841-49, T4131 0000. Opened in 2002 in a renovated 1920s building, has become one of the finest hotels in the city. **AL** *Etoile*, R Ortiz 1835, T4805 2626, www.etoile.com.ar Outstanding location, rooftop pool, rooms with kitchenette.

San Telmo D *La Casita de San Telmo* Cochabamba 286 T/F4307 5073/8796, guimbo@ pinos.com 6 rooms in restored colonial house, rooms rented by day, week or month. **E** *Victoria*, Chacabuco 726, T/F4361 2135. With bath, fan, kitchen and laundry facilities, popular with tango dancers, good meeting place. **F** pp *Oxford*, Chacabuco 719, T4361 8581. With breakfast, spacious rooms with bath, fan, good value, safe.

Take care around San Telmo at night: do not walk alone, take Radio Taxis

Argentina

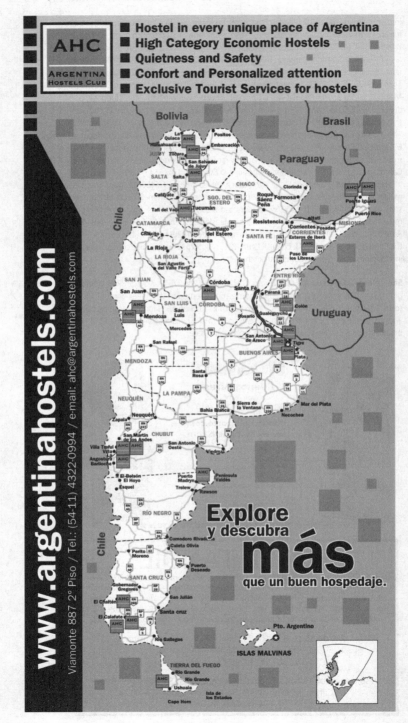

Youth hostels **E** pp *Buenos Ayres*, Pasaje San Lorenzo 320, San Telmo, T4361 0694, www.buenosayreshostel.com New, with breakfast, also rooms with bath, hot water, kitchen, laundry, internet access. **E** pp and up *Milhouse Hostel*, Hipolito Yrigoyen 959, T/F4345 9604, www.milhousehostel.com In 1890 house, lovely rooms and dorms, central, comfortable, free breakfast, cooking facilities, laundry, internet, tango lessons. Discounts for HI members. Recommended.

E pp *Recoleta Hostel*, Libertad 1216 (no sign), T4812 4419, F4815 6622, www.trhostel.com.ar Shared and **D** double rooms, with breakfast, cooking facilities, TV. **E** pp *St Nicholas*, B Mitre 1691 y Rodríguez Peña, T4373 5920/8841, www.snhostel.com Beautifully restored old house, spotless, cooking facilities, large roof terrace, luggage store; also **D** double rooms. Discounts for HI members. Recommended. **E-F** pp *Sandanzas*, Balcarce 1351, T4300 7375, www.sandanzas.com.ar Original and welcoming, small but airy, internet, kitchen, breakfast included. **E** *The Tango City Hostel Inn*, Piedras 680, T4300 5764. A converted old house, large basement with bar, kitchen and pool tables, cramped rooms with a/c, functional bathrooms, lively atmosphere, free pick up from airport and free internet access, breakfast included. **F** pp *Che Lagarto*, Av San Juan 1836, T4304 7618 (subte line E to Entre Ríos; buses 37, 53, 126), www.chelagarto.com Backpackers' hostel with special events to involve guests in local culture, including tango classes, lively atmosphere, breakfast (**D** double rooms), pool, internet access, self-catering, free airport pick up. **F** pp *El Cachafaz*, Viamonte 982, T4328 1445, www.elcachafaz.com.ar Shared rooms, with breakfast, internet access, laundry facilities. Worldwide chain *Hostel-Inn* has opened **F** pp *Hostel Inn*, Humberto I 820, T4300 7992 (toll free 0800-666HOSTEL), www.hostel-inn.com **E** pp in double room, free internet, with breakfast, gym, a/c, shows, airport and bus station transfers. Recommended. **F** pp *Hostal de San Telmo*, Carlos Calvo 614, T4300 6899, www.elhostaldesantelmo.com Dormitories, small

Argentina

double rooms, breakfast, kitchen, internet access, luggage store, English spoken (bus 126, 9, 70 or 45 from bus terminal, 86 from airport). **F** pp *Lime House*, Lima 11, T4383 4561, www.limehouseargentina.com Great views of Av 9 de Julio, welcoming, run by young owners, spacious communal rooms, home-brewed beer, cooking and laundry facilities, free internet, also **D** double rooms. **F** pp *Mandinka*, Cochabamba 554, T4361 2255. Helpful, lots of information, free internet, with breakfast. **F** pp *Urbano Hostel*, Av de Mayo 1385, p 6, T/F 4372 5494, www.urbanohostel.com.ar Smart, new hostel, 40 beds in dorms of 4 and 6, laundry, internet, cafeteria, brekafast included, good views. **F** pp *V&S*, Viamonte 887, T4322 0994, www.hostelclub.com **D** in double room with bath, central, lively atmosphere, kitchen and laundry facilities, lounge, bar, luggage storage, internet access. **G** pp *Del Aguila*, Espinosa 1628, T4581 6663, www.delaguilahostel.com Hot water, cooking and laundry facilities, large roof terrace, free transport to bus terminal and airport, internet access (buses 24, 105, 106, 109, 146). See page 78 *Red Argentina de Alojamiento para Jóvenes* and *Argentina Hostels Club*.

Student residences F pp *Dido*, Sarmiento 1343 T4373 5349, hosteldido@bigfoot.com www.residenciasuniversitarias.8m.com With kitchen, TV, roof terrace, single or shared rooms, monthly and ISIC discounts. Recommended. Accommodation for students and tourists with host families is arranged by *Argentina B&B*, run by Silvia Demetilla, www.argentinabandb.com.ar Reliable and cheap accommodation in Buenos Aires and in other towns; recommended. Many hosts speak English, others will give you a chance to practise your Spanish. Also *La Casa de Etty*, Luis Sáenz Peña 617, T4384 6378. Run by Esther Corcias, who also runs *Organización Coret* (host families), coret@ ciudad.com.ar *Rolando Lucini*, T4601 9926, www.livebuenosaires.com.ar Offers home stay (**C** pp) including lodging and walking and car tours for 3 days, excellent attention, free pick-up from airport or stations.

Apartments/self catering *BUENOSAIRESFLATRENTAL*, Luis Sáenz Peña 277 p 5, T4372 5422, T155 183 5367, www.rioflatrental.com *ByT Argentina*, T4804 1783, www.bytargentina.com Accommodation in residences and host families; also furnished flats. *Jorge A Gibbons*, T4542 1768, fgibbons@infovia.com.ar Speaks English, finds flats.

Eating
● *on maps*

Get the tourist office's Funny Resto Map; useful starting point for the centre.

The Buenos Aires Herald publishes a handy Guide to Good Eating in Buenos Aires with a guide to local wines by Dereck Foster

Eating out in Buenos Aires is great, with a huge variety of restaurants from the chic to the cheap. If in doubt, head for **Puerto Madero**, where there are lots of good mid range places. **NB** In many mid to upper range restaurants, lunch is far cheaper than dinner. A portion at a *comidas para llevar* (take away) place costs US$1.50-2.50. Many cheaper restaurants are *tenedor libre*, eat as much as you like for a fixed price. The following list gives only those restaurants easily accessible for people staying in the city centre.

In the centre: **Expensive**: *Catalinas*, Reconquista 850. Seafood. *Chiquilín*, Sarmiento 1599. Pasta and meat, good value. *Dora*, Alem 1016. Huge steaks, get there early to beat the queue. *Edelweiss*, Libertad 431. Tuna steaks, pasta, grill, expensive and famous. *El Establo*, Paraguay 489, good *parrilla*, for eating at any time. *La Porcherie*, Montevideo 966. Wide selection, good food and prices. *Las Nazarenas*, Reconquista 1132. Good for beef, expensive. *Morizono*, Paraguay 3521 and Paraguay y Reconquista. Japanese, very good. *Museo del Jamón*, Cerrito y Rivadavia. Good for tapas, seafood dishes and ham. *9 de Julio*, C Pellegrini 587. Very good value. *Plaza Mayor*, Venezuela 1399. Seafood, very popular. *Tomo Uno*, Carlos Pellegrini 521 (*Hotel Panamericano*). Trout, mignon, shrimp, home-made pasta, closed Sun.

Mid-range: *Bolsa de Comercio*, 25 de Mayo 359. Downstairs at the Stock Exchange, good, lunch only. *Broccolino*, Esmeralda 776. Excellent Italian, very popular, try *pechuguitas*. *Casa China*, Viamonte 1476. *Chino Central*, Rivadavia 656. *Club Español*, B de Irigoyen 180 (on Av 9 de Julio, near Av de Mayo). Luxurious ambience, fine building, quiet, very good food. Good value *parrilla* at *Criollo*, Maipú 442. *Cumaná*, Rodríguez Peña 1149. *Empanadas, tamales, humitas*, etc, also pizzas, good value. *El Figón de Bonilla*, Alem 673. Rustic style, good. *El Imparcial*, H Yrigoyen 1201, and opposite, *El Globo*, No 1199. Both recommended. *El Mundo*, Maipú 550. Good. *El Navegante*, Viamonte 154. Fish and seafood. *El Palacio de la Papa Frita*, Lavalle 735 and 954, Corrientes 1620. 10% ISIC discount. *El Yatasto*, Suipacha 1015. Small, open till late, popular. *Empire*, Pasaje Tres Sargentos 427. Good Thai food and atmosphere, open for lunch and dinner Mon-Fri, dinner only Sat, closed Sun. *Il Gatto*, Corrientes 959. Popular Italian. *Juana M*, Carlos Pellegrini 1535. Offers very good dishes in a spacious basement. *La Casona del Nonno*, Lavalle 827. Popular, *parrilla* and pasta. *La Estancia*, Lavalle 941. Popular with business people, excellent grills and service. *La Panadería*, Medrano 1502. Lively atmosphere with music at weekends. *La Pipeta*, San Martín 498, downstairs. Serving for 40 years, good, noisy, closed Sun. *La Posada de 1820*, Tucumán 501. Good value, steak and chips etc. *Natacha*, M T de Alvear 901. Steaks and wine good value. *Pepito*, Montevideo 383. Very good. *Petit París*, Av Santa Fe 774. Popular with locals, good lunch. *Pippo*, Montevideo 341 (entrance also from Paraná 356) and at Av Callao 1077. Large pasta house, simple food, very popular. *Sabot*, 25 de Mayo 756. Very good business lunches. *Status*, Virrey Cevallos e H Yrigoyen. Peruvian dishes. *Tulasi*, MT de Alvear 628. Indian and vegetarian, good.

Cheap: *El Cuartito*, Talcahuano 937, a traditional and good *pizzería*. *Los Inmortales*, Lavalle 746. Specializes in pizza, good, 10% ISIC discount. There are other locations: some serve *à la carte* dishes which are plentiful, and are open also from 1500-2000 when most other restaurants are closed. 4 famous cheap *pizzerías* in the centre are on Corrientes: *Banchero*, No 1300; *Las Cuartetas*, No 838, *Güerrín*, No 1368 (fabulous atmospheric place, stand at the zinc bar, an institution) and *Los Inmortales*, No 1369, same chain as above. *Angelín*, Córdoba 5270. Popular pizzería, take away and eat in.

Vegetarian Mid-range: *Dietética Córdoba*, Córdoba 1557. Also shop, open Mon-Fri 1200-2000, Sat 0900-1500. *Granix*, Florida 165, p 1. *Tenedor libre*, bland but filling, lunchtime Mon-Fri. *Lotos*, Córdoba 1577. Open 1130-1800. *El Rincón Orgánico*, Gurruchaga 1001, T4777 5082. **Cheap**: *La Ciboulette* Sarmiento 1810. Excellent value, *tenedor libre*, friendly staff. *La Huerta*, Lavalle 895, p 1. *Tenedor libre*, reasonable.

Recoleta and Palermo In Recolata: **Expensive**: *Clark's* Junín 1777, T4801 9502. English atmosphere, excellent service. Recommended. *Granda*, Junín 1281. French bistro, good. *Lola*, Roberto M Ortiz 1805. Good pasta, lamb and fish. **Mid-range**: *Rodi Bar*, Vicente López 1900. Excellent *bife* and other dishes. *Sirop*, Pasaje del Correo, Vte Lopez 1661, T4813 5900. Delightful chic design, delicious French-inspired food, superb patisserie too. Highly recommended. **Cheap**: *Grants*, Junín 1155. *Tenedor libre*, mainly Chinese, also barbecued meats, pasta, seafood, go with an appetite, other locations. *La Madeleine*, Av Santa Fe 1726, Great for delicious pastas, bright cheerful place, open 24 hrs. Recommended.

Recoleta Village on Vicente López for good night-time atmosphere

In Palermo Expensive: *Christophe*, Fitz Roy 1994. French. *Olsen*, Gorriti 5870. Scandinavian dishes; cheaper set lunch. **Mid-range**: *Cangas de Narcea*, Godoy Cruz 3108. Good local restaurant, steak, pasta. *La Cupertina*, Cabrera 5300 y Godoy Cruz. Small, good value regional dishes, homemade desserts, also take-away. *Luciana*, Amenabar 1202, T4788 4999. Lively trattoria with excellent Italian food. *Te Mataré Ramírez*, Paraguay 4062, T4831 9156. `Aphrodisiac' food, excellent, sensuous atmosphere, mellow live jazz, fabulous chocolate desserts, deserves its reputation. **Cheap**: *Grant's*, Scalabrini Ortiz 3170, see above.

Las Cañitas district has become popular and fashionable for a wide range of interesting restaurants. **Mid-range**: *Campo Bravo*, Baez 292. Elegant *parrilla*, superb trout and vegetables, cool atmosphere. *Morelia*, Baez 260. Fine pizzas on the *parrilla* or in wood ovens, attractive roof terrace. **Palermo Viejo** is a great place for lunch, with cobbled streets, and 1900's buildings, now housing avant-garde shops. Lots of restaurants around the Plaza.

San Telmo Expensive: *La Casa de Esteban de Luca*, Defensa 1000. Very good food and wines. **Mid-range**: *El Desnivel*, Defensa 855. Popular, good atmosphere. For ice cream, *Sumo*, Independencia y Piedras.

The **Costanera Rafael Obligado** along the river front (far end of Aeroparque) is lined with eating places: try **Expensive**: *Morena Beach*. Fish and seafood (good river views at Club Náutico Puerto Norte). *Happening* and *Clo Clo*, La Pampa y Costanera, T4788 0488. Good value for lunch, reservation required. Typical *parrilla* at *Rodizio*, Costanera Norte, opposite *Balneario Coconor*. Self-service and waiter service, other branches, for example Av Callao y Juncal, good value, popular. **Mid-range**: *Siga la Vaca* is a good *parrilla* and the cheapest option in the area.

Take taxi, or colectivo 45 from Plaza Constitución, Plaza San Martín or Retiro to Ciudad Universitaria

In **Puerto Madero**, along Av Alicia Moreau de Justo (from north to south), are **Expensive**: *Katrine*, No 138. Pasta and fish. *Xcaret* No 164. *Bice*, No 192, mostly Italian, good. *Las Lilas*, No 516. Excellent *parrilla*. Similar is *La Caballeriza* at No 580. Good service. *La Parolaccia*, Nos 1052 and 1160. Pasta and seafood, does bargain executive lunch for US$ 4 Mon-Fri only. Branches of *Rodizio* and *Happening*. Many others. **Mid-range**: Av Alicia Moreau de Justo: *El Mirasol del Puerto*, No 202. *Bahía Madero*, No 430. Highly recommended.

La Boca La Boca is famous for its cheap cantinas, visited in huge groups. Do not walk in La Boca at night: take a Radio Taxi directly to the restaurant. **Mid-range**: *El Obrero*, Caffarena 64 y Av Pedro de Mendoza. For pasta. *El Puentecito*, Vieytes 1895. Cheap Argentine dishes.

Cafés *Richmond*, Florida 468 between Lavalle and Corrientes. Genteel (chess played between 1200-2400). Well-known are the *Florida Garden*, Florida y Paraguay. Good coffee and cakes and the *Confitería Ideal*, Suipacha 384. Old, faded, good service, cakes and snacks. Recommended. Also *Aroma*, Florida y Alvear, a great place to relax, with huge space upstairs, sofas by big windows onto Florida, read the papers, and watch the world go by. The *Damiani* chain, eg Florida 825, is good for coffee and apple pie. *Café Verdi*, Esmeralda 758. Salads, other dishes, bakery. Many on Av del Libertador in the Palermo area. *El Querandí*, Perú y Moreno. Popular with intellectuals and students, good atmosphere, well known for its Gin Fizz. On Corrientes: *La Paz*, No 1593 (for drinks, not food). *El Gato Negro*, No 1669. Old pharmacy, wide choice of coffees and teas, good cakes. *Clásica y Moderna*, Callao 892. Bookshop at back, great atmosphere, good for breakfast through to drinks at night, live music Thu-Sat. Highly recommended. *Café de la Biblioteca*, M T de Alvear 1155 (Asociación Biblioteca de Mujeres). Coffee and light snacks, books. *Freddo*, Pacheco de Melo y Callao, Ayacucho y Quintana, Santa Fe y Callao and at shopping malls, 'the city's best ice cream'. Grandsons of Freddo´s founders offer excellent ice creams at *Persicco*, Salguero y Cabello, Maure y Migueletes and Av Rivadavia on 4900 block. Other good ice cream parlours: *Saverio*, Av San Juan 2816, *La Veneciana*, basement of Galerías Pacíficas, *Via Flaminia*, Florida 121. At Av Quintana 596 (Recoleta) is café *La Biela*, restaurant and *whiskería*, elegant. Also in Recoleta: *Café Victoria*, Roberto M Ortiz 1865, *sandwichería*. Popular, refined, great cakes. Recommended. *Hard Rock Café*, in Paseo del Pilar, Av Pueyrredón y Av Del Libertador, ISIC 15% discount. *Henry J Bean's*, Junín 1749 and Arce 907 (Las Cañitas), ISIC 10% discount. *Café Tortoni*, Av de Mayo 825-9. An important Buenos Aires landmark, the elegant haunt of artists and writers for over 100 years old, with interesting *peña* evenings of poetry and music, see also Jazz and Tango, below. Delicious cakes and coffee, but pricey. *La Puerto Rico*, Alsina 420 One of the oldest *confiterías* in town. Another traditional place is *Las Violetas*, Av Rivadavia y Medrano.

Bars & clubs

Generally it is not worth going to clubs before 0230 at weekends. Dress is usually smart

Bars *Boquitas Pintadas*, Estados Unidos 1393, T4381 6064. Bar and hotel, German-run. *El Bar de Boca*, Sarmiento 667. For light meals and beer and Boca football club merchandise. Most cafés serve tea or coffee plus *facturas*, or pastries, for breakfast, US$ 0.80-1.20 (bakery shops sell 10 *facturas* for US$1). **Brew pubs**: *Buller Brewing Company*, Roberto M Ortiz 1827 (Recoleta). Happy hour till 2100. *Brewhouse Club*, Estados Unidos 745 (SanTelmo). **Irish Pubs**: *The Kilkenny*, MT de Alvear 399 esq Reconquista. Open 1730-0600 (Sat opens at 2000), happy hour 1730-2100, very popular. *The Shamrock*, Rodríguez Peña 1220. Irish-run, popular, expensive Guinness, happy hour for ISIC card holders. Also *Druid Inn*, Reconquista 1040. Live music weekly, English spoken. Next door is *Porto Pirata*. *Celta Bar*, Rodríguez Peña y Sarmiento. *The Temple Bar*, MT de Alvear 945.

There are good bars in San Telmo around Plaza Dorrego, for example *El Balcón*, and on Humberto I. *Mr Mate*, Estados Unidos 523. The only place dedicated to the national drink. *Enoteka*, Defensa 891. Tue-Sun 1100-2300, a wine bar charging from US$1.30 for a glass, wide selection. Also bars and restaurants in Palermo Viejo and Las Cañitas districts, with live music (usually beginning 2330-2400). Also at *El Samovar de Rasputín*, Del Valle Iberlucea 1251, Caminito, T4302 3190. Good blues and rock, dinner and/or show, Fri, Sat, Sun. Good and popular are *Club del Vino*, Cabrera 4737, T4833 8300, live music, various styles including tango, *Niceto*, Niceto Vega 5510 (Palermo Hollywood district) and *La Cigale*, 25 de Mayo 722, T4312 8275.

The latest trend is the supper club, a fashionable restaurant serving dinner around 2200, which clears the table at 0100 for all-night dancing, eg *El Living*, M T de Alvear 1540, T4811

4730, *La Diosa*, Av Costanera Rafael Obligado 3731 (Costa Salguero), T4806 1079, for young people, and *Moliere*, Balcarce y Chile, T4343 2623. Very popular, cheap beer. *Cemento*, Estados Unidos 1234. Club with live shows. Also *New York City*, Alvarez Thomas 1391, T4552 4141. Chic. *Mitos Argentinos*, Humberto I 489, near Plaza Dorrego, T4362 7810. Dancing to 'rock national' music, in the daytime has tango and lunch with live music and audience participation. *El Dorado*, H Yrigoyen y 9 de Julio. Interesting, different. *Pacha*, Av Costanera Rafael Obligado y Pampa, T4788 4280. Electronic music. *El Divino*, Cecilia Grierson 225 (Puerto Madero, on dock 4), T4316 8400. *Buenos Aires News*, Paseo de la Infanta Isabel s/n, T4778 1500 *Luna Morena*, Av Chiclana 4118, T4925 7478.

Jazz clubs *Café Tortoni*, Av de Mayo 825, T4342 4328 www.cafetortoni.com.ar Features the Creole Jazz Band (Dixieland), Fri 2100, also tango (see below). Recommended. *Notorious*, Av Callao 966, T4813 6888. Live jazz at a music shop, Mon-Sat 2100. Live jazz and tango also at *La Revuelta* , Alvarez Thomas 1368, T4553 5530; *Thelonious*, Salguero 1884, T4829 1562.

Salsa clubs *La Salsera*, Yatay 961. Highly regarded. *Kiko Salsa*, Alvarez Thomas 1166, T4551 6551. Popular Fri and Sat late night. *Azúcar*, Av Corrientes 3330, T4865 3103. Clubs with 'tropical' music or *bailanta* on Plaza Once, near Av Rivadavia y Av Pueyrredón, *El Reventón* and *Fantástico Bailable*. Salsa classes at *La Trastienda*, Balcarce 460, Wed 2030, US$0.50, also some jazz shows.

Gay clubs *Amerika*, Gascón 1040, www.ameri-k.com.ar Most gay discos charge US$2-3 entry on door. *Sitges*, Av Córdoba 4119. Gay and lesbian bar, near *Amerika*.

Cinemas The selection of films is excellent, ranging from new Hollywood releases to Argentine and world cinema; details are listed daily in all main newspapers. Films are shown uncensored and most foreign films are subtitled. Tickets best booked early afternoon to ensure good seats (average price US$3, with discount Wed and for first show daily; other discounts depending on cinema). Tickets obtainable, sometimes cheaper, from ticket agencies (*carteleras*), such as *Vea Más*, Paseo La Plaza, Corrientes 1660, local 2, T6320 5319 (the cheapest), *Cartelera*, Lavalle 742, T4322 1559, *Cartelera Baires*, Corrientes 1382, local 24, T4372 5058, and *Entradas con Descuento*, Lavalle 835, local 27, T4322 9263. Seats can also be booked by phone with credit card in shopping centres for US$0.30 each ticket. Many cinemas in shopping malls, in Puerto Madero (Dock 1) and in Belgrano (Av Cabildo and environs). On Fri and Sat nights many central cinemas have *trasnoches*, late shows starting at 0100. At *Village Recoleta* (Vicente López y Junín) there is a cinema complex with *trasnoche* programmes on Wed, Fri and Sat. Independent foreign and national films are shown during the *Festival de Cine Independiente*, held every Apr.

Entertainment
Details of most events are given in Espectáculos section of main newspapers, Buenos Aires Herald (English) on Fri and www.laguia.clarin.com

Cultural events The *Luna Park* stadium holds pop/jazz concerts, sports events, ballet and musicals, at Bouchard 465, near Correo Central, T4312 2135, www.lunapark.com.ar *Tango Week*, leading up to National Tango Day (11 Dec), has free events all over the city, details posted around the city and at tourist offices. *Teatro Gral San Martín*, Corrientes 1530, T4371 0111/8 or 0800-333 5254, www.teatrosanmartin.com.ar Organizes many cultural activities, many free, including concerts, 50% ISIC discount for Thu, Fri and Sun events (only in advance at 4th floor, Mon-Fri). The theatre's Sala Leopoldo Lugones shows international classic films, daily, US$1. *Centro Cultural Borges*, Galerías Pacífico, Viamonte y San Martín, p 1, T5555 5450/5449. Music and dance concerts, special exhibitions upstairs, some shows with discounts for students. *Centro Cultural Recoleta*, Junín 1930, next to the Recoleta cemetery. Has many free activities. *Palais de Glace*, Posadas 1725, T4804 1163/4805 4354. Temporary art exhibitions and other cultural events. *Fundación Proa*, Av Pedro de Mendoza 1929, T4303 0909. Contemporary art in La Boca.

Tango shows: *La Ventana*, Balcarce 431, T4331 0217. Daily dinner from 2000 (dinner and show US$33) or show with 2 drinks, 2200, US$25, very touristy but very good. *El Viejo Almacén*, Independencia y Balcarce, T4307 7388. Daily, dinner from 2000, show 2200, US$50 with all drinks, dinner and show, also touristy but recommended. *El Querandí*, Perú 302, T5199 1770. Tango show restaurant, daily show (2215) US$24 dinner (2030), and show US$36 including drink. In San Telmo: *La Cumparsita*, Chile 302, T4302 3387. Authentic, US$10 including

Tango shows are mostly overpriced and tourist-oriented; they usually have touts inviting tourists in. Mix with locals at milongas

drink and some food, 2230-0400. *Bar Sur*, Estados Unidos 299, T4362 6086. 2030-0300, US$15 including all-you-can-eat pizza, drinks extra. *Señor Tango* Vieytes 1655, Barracas, T4303 0231. Spectacular show with dancers, horses etc, US$27, starts 2200.*Café Tortoni*, address above, daily evening tango shows, US$4 (a US$2 min expenditure at the bar is requested).

Tango information desk at Centro Cultural San Martín, Sarmiento 1551, T4373 2823, 1000-2000, www.tangodata. com.ar Also www.elfueytango. com.ar

Milongas are increasingly popular events among young dancers, where tango and milonga are played (the latter having more cheerful music, looser steps) and take place in several locations. Lessons are usually followed by dancing; live orchestras occasionally (US$1.70): *La Viruta*, Armenia 1366, T4774 6357, www.lavirutatango.com Very popular. Wed,Sun 2300, Fri, Sat 2400; *El Viejo Correo*, Díaz Vélez 4820 (Parque Centenario), T4862 0520, Fri-Sun; *Dandi*, Piedras 936, T4307 7623; *Salón Canning*, Scalabrini Ortiz 1331, T4832 6753; *Gricel*, La Rioja 1180, T4957 7157; *Confitería Ideal* (address above) T4605 8234. Lessons Mon-Fri from 1500 (from 2100 Fri), not Tue or Sat, dancing afterwards, class US$1; *El Beso*, Riobamba 416, T15-4195 5221; *La Catedral*, Sarmiento 4006, T15-5325 1630; *La Calesita*, Comodoro Rivadavia 1350, T4744 5187, only Sat 2130; *Centro Cultural Torquato Tasso*, Defensa 1575, T4307 6506, www.tangotasso.com Fri-Sat 2230 with live orchestra, English spoken. *Tango Discovery*, www.tangodiscovery.com Offers non-conventional tango lessons Thu 2200 at Boedo 722, T4523 9756 or 15-4051 1562.

Tickets are much cheaper if bought from bars around Santa Fe y Pueyrredón from 0100

Theatre About 20 commercial theatres play all year round. There are many amateur theatres. You are advised to book as early as possible for a seat at a concert, ballet, or opera. Tickets for most popular shows (including rock and pop concerts) are sold also through *Ticketek*, T5237 7200, *Entrada Plus*, T4324 1010 or *Ticketmaster*, T4321 9700, www.tm.com.ar For other ticket agencies, see Cinemas, above.

Shopping
Most shops close lunchtime on Sat. The main, fashionable shopping streets are Florida and Santa Fe (especially between 1,000 and 2,000 blocks)

Kelly's, Paraguay 431. A very large selection of reasonably priced Argentine handicrafts in wool, leather, wood, etc. *Regionales La Rueda*, Paraguay 728. Gaucho artefacts, woollen goods, silver, leather, good prices. *Plata Nativa*, Galería del Sol, Florida 860, local 41. For Latin American folk handicrafts. *Martín Fierro*, Santa Fe 992. Good handicrafts, stonework etc. Recommended. Very good aboriginal-style crafts at *Arte y Esperanza*, Balcarce 234, *Alhué*, Juncal 1625 and *Artesanías Argentinas*, Montevideo 1386. *Campanera Dalla Fontana*, Reconquista 735. Leather factory, fast, efficient and reasonably priced for made-to-measure clothes. Quality, inexpensive leather goods at *All Horses*, Suipacha 1350. *Aida*, Galería de la Flor, local 30, Florida 670. Can make a leather jacket to measure in the same day. *Galería del Caminante*, Florida 844. Has a variety of good shops with leather goods, arts and crafts, souvenirs, etc. *XL*, in Paseo Alcorta, Alto Palermo, Unicenter, Abasto and Alto Avellaneda shopping malls. *Marcelo Loeb*, *galería* at Maipú 466. For antique postcards from all over the world, not cheap, same *galería* has several philatelic and numismatic shops. C Defensa in San Telmo is good for antique shops. *Pasaje de la Defensa*, Defensa 1179. A beautifully restored colonial house containing small shops. *Casa Piscitelli*, San Martín 450. Has a large selection of tapes and CDs, no rock or pop music.

Foreign books are now hard to find and prices are very high. For foreign newspapers try news stands on Florida, in Recoleta district and kiosk at Corrientes y Maipú

Bookshops *ABC*, Av Córdoba 685 and Rawson 2105 in Martínez suburb, www.libreriasabc.com.ar Good selection of English and German books, expensive, also sells *Footprint Handbooks*. *Distal*, Corrientes 913 (sells *Footprint*) with branches at Florida 528 and 738. *Joyce Proust & Co*, Tucumán 1545, p 1. Paperbacks in English, Portuguese, French, Italian; classics, language texts, etc, good prices. *Librería Rodríguez*, Sarmiento 835. Good selection of English books and magazines upstairs, has another branch at Florida 377. *Yenny*, at main shopping malls and airports, stocks *Footprint*, good selection of English classics. French bookshop at *Oficina del Libro Francés*, Esmeralda 861. *Librería Ensayo*, Lavalle 528. Good selection of English and German books. Italian books at *Asociación Dante Alighieri*, Tucumán 1646. *Asatej Bookshop*, see Useful addresses on page 111. *El Ateneo*, Florida 340, basement. Has good selection of English books, other branches including Av Santa Fe 1860 (in a former sumptuous cinema) and Av Callao 1380, www.tematika.com *Kel Ediciones*, MT de Alvear 1369 and Conde 1990 (Belgrano). Good stock of English books. *Acme Agency*, Suipacha 245, p 1. For imported English books, also Arenales 885. *Lola*, Viamonte 976, 2 p, T4322 3920. Mon-Fri 1200-1830, the only specialist in Latin American Natural History, birdwatching, most books in English. *El Viajero* Carlos Pellegrini 1233, T4394 7941, www.elviajero.com Large stock of travel books, library, information service, good place to research travel plans.

For used and rare books *The Antique Bookshop*, Libertad 1236. Recommended. Second-hand English language books from *British and American Benevolent Society* (*BABS Bookstore*), Av Santa Fe 512, Acassuso, T4747 3492 (take train from Retiro), Mon-Wed 0900-1800, Sat 1000-1230 (in summer, Wed mornings only). *Aquilanti*, Rincón 79, T4952 4546, for Latin American history. *Entrelibros*, Av Cabildo 2280 and Santa Fe 2450, local 7, expensive. *L'Amateur*, Esmeralda 882. For antique maps and prints. Several good used books shops at *Galería Buenos Aires*, Florida 835 (basement; eg *Helena de Buenos Aires*, local 32, good stock of Patagonia books. Every Apr the Feria del Libro is held at the Rural Society grounds, on Plaza Italia; exhibitions, shows and books for sale in all languages.

Camping equipment Good equipment from *Buenos Aires Sports*, Panamericana y Paraná, Martínez (Shopping Unicenter, 2nd level). *Eurocamping*, Paraná 761. *Fugate* (no sign), Gascón 238 (off Rivadavia 4000 block), T4982 0203. Also repairs equipment. *Outside Mountain Equipment*, Plaza Este 3671 (estación Saavedra), T4541 2084. *Ski Center*, Esmeralda 346, T4326 1207. Good camping stores also at Guatemala 5451. Camping gas available at *Britam*, B Mitre 1111, *Todo Gas*, Sarmiento 1540, and *El Pescador*, Paraguay y Libertad. *Cacique Camping*, Esteban Echeverría 3360, Munro, T4762 4475. Manufactured clothing and equipment. *Ecrin*, Mendoza 1679, T4784 4799, info@escalada.com Imported climbing equipment.

Markets For souvenirs, antiques, etc, *Plaza Dorrego*, San Telmo. With free tango performances and live music, Sun 1000-1700, atmospheric, and interesting array of 'antiques'. *Feria Hippie*, in Recoleta, near cemetery. Big craft and jewellery market, Sat and Sun, good street atmosphere, expensive. *Feria de Las Artes* (Fri, 1200-1700) on Defensa y Alsina. Sat craft, jewellery, etc market, at *Plaza Belgrano*, near Belgrano Barrancas station on Juramento, between Cuba y Obligado, 1000-2000. Handicraft market at weekends at *Parque Lezama*, San Telmo. *Plaza Italia*, Santa Fe y Uriarte (Palermo). Second hand textbooks and magazines (daily), handicrafts market on Sat 1200-2000, Sun 1000-2000. Plastic arts and expensive, imported Peruvian and Ecuadorean goods in the *Caminito*, Vuelta de Rocha (Boca), 1000-2000 summer, 0900-1900 winter. At *Parque Rivadavia*, Rivadavia 4900. Books and magazines (daily), records, toys, stamps and coins, Sun 0900-1300. Sat market in *Parque Centenario*, Díaz Vélez y L Marechal, on weekends. Local crafts, good, cheap hand-made clothes. *Feria de Mataderos*, Lisandro de la Torre y Av de los Corrales, subte E to end of line then taxi (US$2.50), or buses 36, 92, 97, 126, 141. Long way but worth it: few tourists, fair of Argentine handicrafts and traditions, music and dance festivals, gaucho horsemanship skills, every Sun and holidays from 1100 (Sat 1800-2400 in summer); nearby *Museo de los Corrales*, Av de los Corrales 6436, T4687 1949, Mon-Fri 1030-1930, Sat 1400-2000, Sun 1200-1800. *Mercado de las Luces*, Perú y Alsina, Mon-Fri 1100-1900, Sun 1400-1900. Handicrafts. *Casi nuevo*, Av Santa Fe 512, Acassuso (train from Retiro). Thrift shop, Mon-Wed 0900-1800, Sat 1000-1230.

Shopping malls *Patio Bullrich*, Av Del Libertador 750 and Posadas 1245, chic clothes, and boutiques selling high quality leather goods. *Alto Palermo*, Col Díaz y Santa Fe, good clothes shops. *Paseo La Plaza*, at Corrientes 1660, also has theatres and a few restaurants. *Paseo Alcorta*, Salguero y Figueroa Alcorta, 4 levels, cinemas, supermarket, stores, many cheap restaurants (take colectivo 130 from Correo Central). *Galerías Pacífico*, on Florida, between Córdoba and Viamonte (open 1000-2100), is a beautiful mall with fine murals and architecture, many exclusive shops, cinemas and good food mall with wide choice and low prices in basement. Also good set-price restaurant on 2nd floor (lunches only) and free tango sessions on lower-ground floor (Fri-Sat 2000). Free guided visits from desk on main floor. *Abasto de Buenos Aires*, Av Corrientes 3247, T4959 3400. In the former city's fruit and vegetable market building: cheaper clothes, good choice.

Rugby and football: are both played to a very high standard. Soccer fans should see Boca Juniors, matches Sun 1500-1900; also sometimes on Fri or Sat (depending on time of year),

Sport & activities

Argentina

cheapest entry US$3-5 (stadium La Bombonera, Brandsen 700, La Boca, T4309 4700, www.bocajuniors.com.ar open weekdays for visits – see the murals; buses 29, 33, 53, 64, 86, 152), or their arch-rivals, River Plate (to stadium take bus 29 from centre going north). Soccer season Mar-Jun, Aug-Dec. Rugby season Apr-Oct/Nov. **Cricket**: is played at 4 clubs in Greater Buenos Aires between Nov and Mar. More information at **Asociación de Cricket Argentino**, T4806 7306. **Golf**: visitors wishing to play at the leading private golf clubs should bring handicap certificate and make telephone booking. There are about a dozen such clubs. Weekend play is possible only with a member. Good hotels may be able to make special arrangements. *Campo de Golf de la Ciudad* in Palermo, open to anyone at any time, US$7. For information, **Asociación Argentina de Golf**, T4325 1113. **Horse racing**: at Hipódromo Argentino de Palermo, a large, modern racecourse, popular throughout the year, and at San Isidro. Riding schools at both courses. **Motor racing**: There are stock racing and Formula 3 competitions, mostly from Mar to mid-Dec and drag racing all year round, Fri evenings, from US$1 at the **Oscar Alfredo Gálvez Autodrome**, Av Coronel Roca y Av General Paz, T4605 3333. **Polo**: the high handicap season is Sep to Dec, but it is played all year round (low season Mar-May). Argentina has the top polo players in the world. A visit to the national finals at Palermo in Nov and Dec is recommended. For information, **Asociación Argentina de Polo**, T4342 8321. **Swimming**: public baths near Aeroparque, *Punta Carrasco* (best, most expensive, also tennis courts), *Costa Salguero* and *Parque Norte*, both popular. At *Club de Amigos*, Av Figueroa Alcorta y Av Sarmiento, T4801 1213, US$6.50 (including entrance), open all year round.

Tour operators
English is widely spoken

An excellent way of seeing Buenos Aires and its surroundings is by 3-hr tour, especially for those travelling alone, or concerned about security. Longer tours include dinner and a tango show, or a gaucho *fiesta* at a ranch (excellent food and dancing). Bookable through most travel agents. *Autobuses Sudamericanos*, B de Irigoyen 1370, local 12, T4300 0528/4648 0031, autobusessudamericana@yahoo.com City tour US$6, also longer tours, international buses, sells AmerbusPass. *BAT, Buenos Aires Tur*, Lavalle 1444, T4371 2304, city tours (US$6) twice daily; Tigre and Delta, daily, 5hrs (US$13). *Buenos Aires Vision*, Esmeralda 356 p 8, T4394 4682. City tours, Tigre and Delta, Tango (US$33, cheaper without dinner) and *Fiesta Gaucha* (US$27). *Eternautas*, Arcos 2514, T4781 8868, www.eternautas.com Historical, cultural and artistic tours of the city and Pampas guided by university historians in English, French or Spanish, flexible, also Tue and Sat walking tours from steps of Banco de la Nación, Rivadavia y 25 de Mayo, 1000 and 1700, 2 hrs. *Tripping*, Marcos Dartiguelongue and Leonardo Kawakami, T4791 6769, T15-4993 3848 (mob), trippingbsas@hotmail.com Tours to dance clubs, football matches, parachute jumps, horseback trips and city bike tours. Four-hour cycle tours with *Urban biking*, Sarmiento 212, p 12, T4371 1338, www.urbanbiking.com US$18, meal included, also night and day tours to Tigre.

Among the recommended travel agents are: *ATI*, Esmeralda 567, T4329 9000. Mainly group travel, very efficient, many branches. *Eves Turismo*, Tucumán 702, T4393 6151. Helpful and efficient, recommended for flights. *Exprinter*, San Martín 170, T4341 6600, Galería Güemes, info@exprinter-viajes.com.ar (especially their 5-day, 4-night tour to Iguazú and San Ignacio Miní). *Turismo Feeling*, San Martín 969, p 9, T4313 5533. Excellent and reliable horseback trips and adventure tourism. *Flyer*, Reconquista 617, p 8, T4313 8224, www.flyer-de.de English, Dutch, German spoken, repeatedly recommended, especially for *estancias*, fishing, polo, motorhome rental. *Say Huque*, Viamonte 749, p 6, T5199 2517, sayhuque@arnet.com.ar Good value for tours in Argentina. *Southdoors Group*, MT de Alvear 776, p 4, office 41, T4313 9093, www.southdoors.com Very helpful for *estancia* visits. *Tangol*, Florida 971, p 1, T4312 7276, www.tangol.com Specializes in football and tango programmes in town, English spoken.

Transport
Colectivos cover a very wide radius and are clean, frequent, efficient and very fast (hang on tight)

Local Buses: the basic fare for *colectivos* (city buses) is US$0.25, US$0.40 to the suburbs. Have coins ready for ticket machine as drivers do not sell tickets, but may give change. **NB** The bus number is not always sufficient indication of destination, as each number has a variety of routes, but bus stops display routes of buses stopping there and little plaques are displayed in the driver's window.

Car hire: driving in Buenos Aires is no problem, provided you have eyes in the back of your head and good nerves. Note that traffic fines are high and police increasingly on the lookout for drivers without the correct papers. See also Essentials, page 52 for international rental agencies. *Europcar*, Maipú 965, T4311 1000, aireservas@arnet.com.ar There are several national rental agencies, eg *Express*, C Pellegrini 1576, T4326 0338 or T0800-999 8234, express-rentacar@ grupoexpress.com.ar or *Unirent*, Av LN Alem 699, T/F 4315 0777 **Motoring Associations**: see page 79 for details of service.

Metro ('Subte') 5 lines link the outer parts of the city to the centre. Line 'A' runs under C Rivadavia, from Plaza de Mayo to Primera Junta. Line 'B' from central Post Office, on Av L N Alem, under Av Corrientes to Federico Lacroze railway station at Chacarita. Line 'C' links Plaza Constitución with the Retiro railway station, and provides connections with all the other lines. Line 'D' runs from Plaza de Mayo (Catedral), under Sáenz Peña (Diagonal Norte), Córdoba, Santa Fe and Palermo to Congreso de Tucumán (Belgrano). Line 'E' runs from Plaza de Mayo (Cabildo, on C Bolívar) through San Juan to Plaza de los Virreyes (connection to Premetro train service to the southwest end of the city). Note that 3 stations, 9 de Julio (Line 'D'), Diagonal Norte (Line 'C') and Carlos Pellegrini (Line 'B') are linked by pedestrian tunnels. The fare is US$0.20, the same for any direct trip or combination between lines; magnetic cards (for 1, 2, 5, 10 or 30 journeys) must be bought at the station before boarding; dollars not accepted. Trains are operated by *Metrovías*, T4555 1616 or T0800-555 1616. System operates 0500-2250 (Sun 0800-2200). Line A, the oldest was built in 1913, the earliest in South America. Backpacks and luggage allowed. Free map (if available) from stations and tourist office.

Many of the stations in the centre, especially on Line 'E', have fine tile-work designs and pictures

Taxis are painted yellow and black, and carry Taxi flags. Fares are shown in pesos. The meter starts at US$0.35 when the flag goes down; make sure it isn't running when you get in. A fixed rate of US$0.04 for every 200 m or 1-min wait is charged thereafter. A charge is sometimes made for each piece of hand baggage (ask first). **Security** Always phone a radio taxi. Taxis from a registered company are safer, and some 'Radio Taxis' you see on the street are false. Check that the driver's licence is displayed. Lock doors on the inside. Four common taxi driver tricks are 1) to take you on a longer than necessary ride; 2) to switch low-denomination notes for higher ones preferred by the passenger (don't back down, demand to go to the police station); 3) to grab the passenger's baggage and prevent him/her from leaving the taxi (scream for help); 4) to quote 'old' prices for new, eg 'quince' (15) for 1.50 pesos, 'veinte y seis' (26) for 2.60 pesos, etc. If the driver says he has a puncture or mechanical problem, get out at once (unless you are in the middle of nowhere) and try to keep your luggage with you. Worst places are the two airports and Retiro; make sure you know roughly what the fare should be before the journey: eg from Aeroparque to: Ezeiza US$8 (plus toll), Congreso US$2.70, Plaza de Mayo US$2.70, Retiro US$2.30, La Boca US$3.50. In theory fares double for journeys outside city limits (Gen Paz circular highway), but you can often negotiate. **Radio Taxis** (same colours and fares) are managed by several different companies (eg *Del Plata*, T4504 7776; *Pídalo*, T4956 1200; *Llámenos*, T4815 3333) and are recommended as a safer alternative.

Phone a radio taxi from a phone box or locutorio, giving the address of where you are, and you'll usually be collected within 5 mins

Remise taxis operate all over the city, run from an office and have no meter. The companies are identified by signs on the pavement. Fares, which are fixed and can be cheaper than regular taxis, can be verified by phoning the office, and items left in the car can easily be reclaimed. Good companies are *Le Coq*, T4963 9391/2, 4963 8532, and *Intercar*, T4867 2100, good airport service.

About 10% tip expected

Tram: Old-fashioned street cars operate Mar-Nov on Sat and holidays 1600-1930 and Sun 1000-1300, 1600-1930 and Dec-Feb on Sat and holidays 1700-2030, Sun 1000-1300, 1700-2030, free, on a circular route along the streets of Caballito district, from C Emilio Mitre 500, Subte Primera Junta (Line A) or Emilio Mitre (Line E), no stops en route. Operated by *Asociación de los Amigos del Tranvía*, T4431 1073.

Long distance Air: Ezeiza (officially Ministro Pistarini, T5480 6111), the international airport, is 35 km southwest of the centre by a good dual carriageway, which links with the General Paz circular Highway round the city. The airport has two terminals: 'A' for all airlines except *Aerolíneas Argentinas*, which uses 'B'. 'A' has a very modern check-in hall. There are duty free shops (expensive), exchange facilities (*Banco de la Nación*; *Banco Piano*; *Global Exchange*) and ATMs (Visa and MasterCard), post office (open 0800-2000) and a left luggage

Argentina

office (US$3 per piece). No hotels nearby. There is a *Devolución IVA/Tax Free* desk (return of VAT) for purchases such as leather goods. Reports of pilfering from luggage. To discourage this have your bags sealed after inspection by Secure Bags, US$5 per piece. Hotel booking service at Tourist Information desk – helpful, but prices are higher if booked in this way. A display in immigration shows choices and prices of transport into the city.

Airport buses: special buses to/from the centre are run by *Manuel Tienda León* (office in front of you as you arrive), company office at Santa Fe 790 (T4314 3636) next to *Hotel Crillon*, near Plaza San Martín. To **Ezeiza**: 0400, 0500, then every 30 mins till 2030 and 2130; from Ezeiza: 0600-0045 regular buses, then also for night arrivals, US$5 (US$10 return; half fare for ISIC holders), 40-min journey, credit cards accepted. *Manuel Tienda León* will also collect passengers from addresses in centre for no extra charge, book the previous day. Services on request with *Transfer Express*, T0800-444 4872, reservas@transferexpress.com.ar, airport office in front of you as you arrive. **Local buses**: No 86 (white and blue, *Empresa Duvi*, T4302 6067) runs to the centre from outside the airport terminal to the left as you leave the building, 2 hrs, US$0.45, coins only, runs all day, every 14 mins during the day. To travel to Ezeiza, catch the bus at Av de Mayo y Perú, 1 block from Plaza de Mayo (many other stops, but this is central) – make sure it has 'Aeropuerto' red sign in the window as many 86s stop short of Ezeiza. **Taxis**: from centre to Ezeiza US$8 (plus US$1 toll) but bargain. Fixed-price *remise taxis* for up to 4 passengers can be booked from the *Manuel Tienda León* or *Transfer Express* counter at Ezeiza, US$14 (plus US$1 toll) from airport to town. **NB** Avoid unmarked cars at Ezeiza no matter how attractive the fare may sound; drivers are adept at separating you from far more money than you can possibly owe them. Always ask to see the taxi driver's licence. If you take an ordinary taxi the Policía Aeronáutica on duty notes down the car's licence and time of departure. There have been recent reports of taxi drivers taking Ezeiza airport-bound passengers to remote places, stealing all their luggage and leaving them there. If in doubt, take a *remise* or airport bus.

Aeroparque (Jorge Newbery Airport), 4 km north of the centre, T5480 6111, handles all internal flights, services to **Punta del Este** and **Montevideo** and a few flights to other neighbouring countries. The terminal is divided into 3 sections, 'A' for *AR, Austral* check-in desks and international arrivals, 'B' for *Aerovip, Pluna* and *American Falcon* check-in desks, 'C' for *Southern Winds* and *LADE* check-in desks and *Aerovip, Southern Winds* and *LADE* arrivals. On the 1st floor there is a *patio de comidas*, many shops and the airport tax counter. At the airport also tourist information, car rental, bus companies, bank, ATMs, exchange facilities, post office, public phones and luggage deposit (between sections A-B at the information point), US$1.30 per piece a day. **Buses** *Manuel Tienda León* buses to Aeroparque (see above for address), 0640-0125, every 30 to 45 mins; from Aeroparque (departs from sector C, stops at *AR*), 0815-1945 every 30 mins and 2045, 20-min journey, US$2. *Transfer Express* services available also to/from Aeroparque. Local buses 33 and 45 run from outside the airport to the Retiro railway station, then to **La Boca** and **Constitución** respectively. No 37 goes to **Palermo** and **Recoleta** and No 160 to **Palermo** and **Almagro**. If going to the airport, make sure it goes to Aeroparque by asking the driver, US$0.25. **Remise taxis**: are operated by *Transfer Express* and *Manuel Tienda León*, US$3.50 to centre, US$15 to Ezeiza. Ordinary taxi to centre US$2.50. *Manuel Tienda León* operates buses between Ezeiza and Aeroparque airports, stopping in city centre, US$7. *Aerolíneas Argentinas, Aerovip, Austral* and *Southern Winds* offer daily flights to the main cities, for details see text under intended destination, see also page 78 for the Visit Argentina fare. *LADE* offers weekly flights to **Trelew** and **Bariloche** with several stops in Patagonia.

Taxis from official rank in bus terminal are registered with police and safe. For extra security, take a taxi booked from a booth on the bus platform itself, more expensive but very secure

Bus Long distance bus terminal at Ramos Mejía y Antártida Argentina (Subte Line C), behind Retiro station, for information T4310 0700. Information desk is at the top of long ramp to your left. All ticket offices are upstairs, even numbers to the left, foreign companies at the very end (full list at the top of the escalator). Buenos Aires city information desk on ground floor. At the basement level there are left-luggage lockers, US$0.60 for 1 day (with two 1 peso coins); *Guard pack* charges US$0.60-1 per day (US$1.60 for a bike); companies also store luggage only up to 2 hrs before departures, at the basement level. Fares vary according to time of year and comfort: advance booking is essential Dec-Mar, Easter, Jul and long weekends. *Coche cama* is advisable for overnight journeys: seats fully recline and food is served for just a few pesos more. Travellers have reported getting student discounts without showing evidence of status, so it's always worth asking. For further details of bus services and fares, look under proposed destinations. There are no direct buses to either of the airports.

International buses International services are run by both local and foreign companies. Direct buses to **Santiago** (Chile), 1,400 km, 20-22 hrs, US$33-42; also to **Arica** with *CATA* and *Ahumada/Fénix*, 50 hrs, US$90-100. To **Bolivia**: buses from both countries only reach the international border, then a new ticket must be bought. Several companies go from Retiro to **La Quiaca** (US$33-36) and to **Pocitos** (US$32-38). Cheapest route to Pocitos is by bus to **Tucumán**, then re-book for Pocitos. To **Asunción** (Paraguay), 1,370 km via Clorinda (toll bridge): about 15 bus companies, all close to each other at the Retiro bus terminal. You have choice between executive (luxury service, 16 hrs, US$36), *diferencial* (with food, drinks, 17-18 hrs, US$25-30) and *común* (without food, but a/c, toilet, 17-18 hrs, US$20-23). Also to **Ciudad del Este** (18 hrs, US$23), **Encarnación** (12 hrs, US$18-20) and minor destinations in Paraguay. Tickets can be bought up to 30 days in advance. To **Peru** *Ormeño* (T4313 2259) and *El Rápido Internacional* (T4393 5057), direct service to **Lima** (only stops for meals), Mon, Wed, Sat 1800 or Tue, Fri, Sun 1800 respectively, 3 days, US$116, including all meals (if you need a visa for Chile, get one before travelling), the route is: Mendoza, Coquimbo, Arica, Tacna, Nasca, Ica, Lima. Direct buses to **Brazil** via Paso de los Libres by *Pluma*: **São Paulo**, 38 hrs, US$74, **Rio de Janeiro**, 45 hrs, US$82, **Porto Alegre**, 20 hrs, US$50-70, **Curitiba**, 30 hrs, US$65, **Florianópolis**, 24 hrs, US$60-83, **Foz do Iguaçu**, 18 hrs, US$20. *Crucero del Norte* also goes to **Foz do Iguaçu**, US$23; *Flecha Bus* goes to **Porto Alegre** (US$54-70) and **Florianópolis** (US$64-81). To **Rio de Janeiro**, changing buses at Posadas and Foz do Iguaçu is almost half price, 50 hrs. A third route across the Río de la Plata and through Uruguay is a bit cheaper, not as long and offers a variety of transport and journey breaks. Tickets from *Pluma*, Córdoba 461, T4311 4871.

To Uruguay Direct **road** connections by means of 2 bridges over the Río Uruguay between Colón and Paysandú and between Puerto Unzué and Fray Bentos (much slower than the air or sea routes). Bus to **Montevideo**: *Bus de la Carrera*, 1000, 2200 and 2300 daily, 8 hrs, with a *dormibus* at 2230 (US$23), via Zárate-Gualeguaychú-Puerto Unzué-Fray Bentos-Mercedes. *CAUVI* goes also to Montevideo and to **Punta del Este** (10 hrs, US$28-30). *Boats and buses heavily booked Dec-Mar, especially at weekends*

Boat connections: **1)** Direct to **Montevideo**, *Buquebus*, Terminal de Aliscafos, Av Córdoba y Madero and in Patio Bullrich shopping centre, p 1, loc 231, T4316 6500, www.buquebus.com, twice a day, 2½-3 hrs, US$52 tourist class, US$63 1st class one way, vehicles US$57-70, motorcycles US$44, bus connection to Punta del Este, US$8.50. **2)** To **Colonia**, services by 2 companies: *Buquebus*: 2 ferry services a day, 2 hrs 40 mins, US$16 tourist class, US$22 1st class one way, with bus connection to Montevideo (US$6 extra), and to Punta del Este (US$12). Motorcycles US$15, cars, US$23-30. *Ferrylíneas Sea Cat*, operates a fast service to Colonia from same terminal, 2 to 3 daily, 50 mins, US$28 tourist class, US$34 1st class one way, vehicles US$39-44, motorcycles US$21. **3)** To **Piriápolis**, *Buquebus*, weekly, 3 hrs 15 mins, tourist class US$60, 1st class US$75, vehicles US$84-102, motorcycles US$54. **4)** From Tigre to Carmelo, boats are operated by *Cacciola* at 0830, 1630, 3 hrs, US$9 (£18 return) to Carmelo, and US$14 to Montevideo. *Cacciola* office: Florida 520, p 1, oficina 113, T4393 6100 and international terminal, Lavalle 520, Tigre, T4749 0329, www.cacciolaviajes.com, credit cards accepted. It is advisable to book in advance; connecting bus from offices to port and from Carmelo to Montevideo. **5)** From Tigre to Nueva Palmira, *Líneas Delta Argentina*, from Tigre 0745, also 1700 Fri 3 hrs, US$16 round trip, bus connections to Colonia (US$17 round trip from Tigre), T4749 0537, information T4731 1236. **NB** No money changing facilities in Tigre, and poor elsewhere.

Beware of overcharging by taxis from the harbour to the centre of Buenos Aires. US$1 port tax is charged on all services from Tigre, US$0.50 port tax in Buenos Aires to Colonia (US$1 port tax to Montevideo). *Do not buy Uruguayan bus tickets in Buenos Aires; wait till you get to Colonia*

To Colonia by **air** from Jorge Newbery Airport (Aeroparque) 15 mins with *Air Class* (check-in desk at section B, T4393 0792). Buy tickets in advance especially at weekends when flights are fully booked. Continue by bus to Montevideo. Also from Jorge Newbery, *AR*, *Pluma* and *Aerovip* fly to Montevideo and Punta del Este with several daily flights in high season.

Argentina

Trains There are 4 main terminals: **Retiro** (3 lines: **Mitre, Belgrano, San Martín** in separate buildings): Mitre line (run by *TBA*, T4317 4407, www.tbanet.com.ar Urban and suburban services: to **Belgrano, Mitre** (connection to Tren de la Costa, see below), **Olivos, San Isidro, Tigre** (see below), **Capilla del Señor** (connection at Victoria, US$0.90), **Escobar** and **Zárate** (connection at Villa Ballester, US$0.90); long distance services: to **Rosario Norte**, one weekly on Fri evening, 6 hrs, US$3.50, to **Tucumán** via Rosario, Mon and Fri, 2100, returning Mon and Thu 1000, 26 hrs, US$20 sleeper, US$16 pullman, US$13 1st (service run by *NOA Ferrocarriles*, T4893 2244). Belgrano line run by *Ferrovías*, T4511 8833. San Martín line run by *Metropolitano*, T4018 0700, www.tms.com.ar Urban and suburban services: to **Palermo, Chacarita, Devoto**, Hurlingham and Pilar. Long distance services: to Junín, daily, 5hrs, US$4. **Constitución**: Roca line (run by *Metropolitano*, see above). Urban and suburban services to La Plata (US$ 0.50), Ezeiza (US$0.35), Ranelagh (US$0.27) and Quilmes (US$0.20). Long distance services (run by *Ferrobaires*, T4304 0028/3165): Bahía Blanca, 5 weekly, 12½ hrs, US$7-13, food mediocre; to Mar del Plata daily, US$7-13, 5 hrs; to Pinamar, 2 weekly, US$7-13, 6 hrs; to Miramar, in summer only, daily, 7 hrs, US$7-13; to Tandil, US$7-13, weekly, 7½ hrs; to Quequén, 2 weekly, 12 hrs, US$7-13, and to Bolívar. **Federico Lacroze** Urquiza line and Metro headquarters (run by *Metrovías*, T4555 1616, www.metrovias.com.ar). Suburban services: to General Lemos. **Once**: Sarmiento line (run by *TBA*, see above). Urban and suburban services: to Caballito, Flores, Merlo, Luján (connection at Moreno, US$0.60), Mercedes (US$1) and Lobos. A fast service runs daily between Puerto Madero (station at Av Alicia Moreau de Justo y Perón) and Castelar. Tickets checked before boarding and on train and collected at the end of the journey; urban and suburban fares are charged according different sections of each line).

Directory **Airline offices** *Aerolíneas Argentinas* (*AR*) and *Austral*, Perú y Rivadavia, Av LN Alem 1134 and Av Cabildo 2900, T0810-2228 6527, www.aerolineas.com.ar *Aerovip*, Cerrito 1318, T0810-444 2376. *Air Canada*, Av Córdoba 656, T4327 3640.*Air France*, San Martín 344 p 23, T4317 4700 or T0800-222 2600.*Alitalia*, Av Santa Fe 887, T4310 9910. *American Airlines*, Av Santa Fe 881, T4318 1000, Av Pueyrredón 1889 and branches in Belgrano and Acassuso. *Avianca*, Carlos Pellegrini 1163 p 4, T4394 5990. *British Airways*, Carlos Pellegrini 1163, p 10, T4320 6600. *Cubana*, Sarmiento 552 p 11, T4326 5291. *Iberia*, Carlos Pellegrini, 1161 p 1, T4131 1000. *KLM*, Suipacha 268 p 9, T4326 8422. *LAB*, Carlos Pellegrini 141, T4323 1900. *Lan Chile*, Cerrito y Paraguay, T4378 2200, www.lanchile.com *Líneas Aéreas del Estado* (*LADE*), Perú 710, T5129 9000, Aeroparque T4514 1524, reservas@lade.com.ar *Lufthansa*, M T Alvear 636, T4319 0610, www.lufthansa-argentina.com *Mexicana*, Av Córdoba 755 p 1, T4312 6152 *Pluma* and *Varig*, Florida 1, T4329 9211, www.com.uy/plunaargentina, www.varig.com.br *Qantas*, Av Córdoba 673 p 13, T4514 4726, www.qantasargentina.com.ar *Southern Winds*, Av Santa Fe 784, T0810-777 7979, www.sw.com.ar *Swiss International Airlines*, Santa Fe 846 p 1, T4319 0000. *Taca*, Carlos Pellegrini 1275, T4325 8222. *TAM*, Cerrito 1030, T4819 4800 or T0810 333 3333. *United*, Av Madero 900, T0810-777 8648.

ATMs are widespread, use credit cards for withdrawing cash. For lost or stolen cards: Mastercard T4340 5700, Visa T4379 3333

Banks Practices are constantly changing while the economy is still in upheaval, and using credit cards in ATMs is both easier and safer than carrying TCs. Most banks charge commission especially on TCs (as much as US$10). US dollar bills are often scanned electronically for forgeries, while TCs are sometimes very difficult to change and you may be asked for proof of purchase. Banks open Mon-Fri 1000-1500, be prepared for long delays. *Lloyds TSB Bank*, Florida 999, T0810-555 6937, Visa cash advances. Many branches in the city. *Citibank*, B Mitre 502, T0810-444 2484, changes only Citicorps TCs cheques, no commission, also Visa, MasterCard; branch at Florida 199. *HSBC*, 25 de Mayo 258, also at Florida 229, changes Thomas Cook TCs with US$10 commission. *American Express* offices are at Arenales 707 y Maipú, by Plaza San Martín, T4311 1906, where you can apply for a card, get financial services and change Amex TCs (1000-1500 only, no commission into US$ or pesos). Visa and MasterCard ATMs at branches of *Banco de la Nación Argentina, ABN Amro Bank, BNP* and others. MasterCard/Cirrus also at *Argencard* offices. *Casas de cambio* include *Banco Piano*, San Martín 345, T4322 0768 (has 24-hr exchange facility at Ezeiza airport), www.bancopiano.com.ar *Forex*, MT de Alvear 540, opposite *Marriott Plaza Hotel*. *Eves*, Tucumán 702. Major credit cards usually accepted but check for surcharges. General *MasterCard* office at Perú 151, T4348 7070, open 0930-1800. *Visa*, Corrientes 1437, p 2, T4379 3333. Other South American currencies can only be exchanged in *casas de cambio*. *Western Union*, branches in several Correo Argentino post offices and at Av Córdoba 975; check for other branches, T0800-800 3030.

Communications **Internet**: Prices range from US$0.30 to US$0.65 per hr, shop around. Many *locutorios* (phone offices) have internet access. *De la City*, Lavalle 491. *Cyberbar*, Av de Mayo 933,

US$0.40 per hr. *Cybercafé*, Maure 1886, Belgrano. *Sudat.com*, Maipú 486 (basement). Several PCs, good 24-hr service. *Comunicar*, Lavalle y Cerrito, US$0.26 per hr at weekends. **General Post Office:** Correo Central, *Correos Argentinos*, Sarmiento y Alem, Mon-Fri, 0800-2000, Sat 0900-1300. *Poste Restante* on ground floor (US$0.50 per letter). Philatelic section open Mon-Fri 0900-1900. **Centro Postal Internacional**, for all parcels over 2 kg for mailing abroad, at Av Comodoro Py y Antártida Argentina, near Retiro station, helpful, many languages spoken, packaging materials available, open Mon-Fri 1000 to 1700 (see page 80.) Check both Correo Central and Centro Postal Internacional for *poste restante*. Post office without queues at Montevideo 1408 near Plaza V López, friendly staff, Spanish only. Also at Santa Fe 945. *UPS*, Bernardo de Irigoyen 974, T4339 2877. **Telephone:** the city is split into 2 telephone zones, owned by *Telecom* and *Telefónica Argentina*. Corrientes 705 (open Mon-Fri 0730-2300, Sat, Sun 0900-2300) for international phone calls, fax and internet access. International and local calls as well as fax also from phone offices (*locutorios* or *telecentros*), of which there are many in the city centre. Public telephone boxes operate with coins (US$0.08 min charge for local calls) and cards (available at *kioskos*). These cards are protected by a sealed wrapper: don't accept cards without a wrapper or with a broken seal. International telephone calls from hotels may incur a 40-50% commission in addition to government tax of about the same amount.

Cultural centres **British Council**, M T de Alvear 590, p 4, T4311 9814, F4311 7747 (Mon-Thu 1100-1500). **British Arts Centre** (BAC), Suipacha 1333, T4393 6941, www.britishartscentre.org.ar English plays and films, music concerts, photography exhibitions (closed Jan). **Goethe Institut**, Corrientes 319, T4311 5338/8964, German library (Mon,Tue,Thu 1230-1930, Fri 1230-1600) and newspapers, free German films shown, cultural programmes, German language courses. In the same building, upstairs, is the German Club, Corrientes 327. **Alliance Française**, Córdoba 946, T4322 0068. French library, temporary film and art exhibitions. **Instituto Cultural Argentino Norteamericano (ICANA)**, Maipú 686, T5382 1500. **Biblioteca Centro Lincoln**, Maipú 686, T5382 1536, open Mon- Fri 1000-1800, library (borrowing for members only), English/US newspapers.

Embassies and consulates All open Mon-Fri unless stated otherwise. **Australia**, Villanueva y Zabala, T4779 3500, www.argentina.embassy.gov.au 0830-1100, ticket queuing system; take bus 29 along Av Luis María Campos to Zabala. **Austria**, French 3671, T4802 1400, www.austria.org.ar Mon-Thu 0900-1200. **Belgium**, Defensa 113 p 8, T4331 0066, 0800-1300. **Bolivian Consulate**, Belgrano 1670, p 1, T4381 4171, 0900-1400, visa while you wait or a month wait (depending on the country of origin), tourist bureau. **Brazilian Consulate**, C Pellegrini 1363, p 5, T4515 6500, www.conbrasil.org.ar 1000-1300, tourist visa takes at least 48 hrs, US$25-120. **Canada**, Tagle 2828, T4808 1000, www.dfait-maeci.gc.ca/bairs Mon-Thu 1400-1600, tourist visa Mon-Thu 0845-1130 **Chilean Consulate**, San Martín 439, p 9, T4394 6582, 0900-1300. **Denmark**, Alem 1074, p 9, T4312 6901/6935, ambadane@ambadane.org.ar Mon-Thu 0930-1200. **France**, Santa Fe 846, p 3, T4312 2409, 0900-1200. **Germany**, Villanueva 1055, T4778 2500, www.embalemana.com.ar 0830-1100. **Greece**, Arenales 1658, T4811 4811, 1000-1300. **Ireland**, Av Del Libertador 1068 p 6, T4325 8588, info@irlanda.org.ar 0900-1300, 1400-1530. **Israel**, Av de Mayo 701, p 10, T4338 2500, Mon-Thu 0900-1200, Fri 0900-1100. **Italy**, consulate at M T de Alvear 1125, T4816 6133/36, 0900-1300. **Japanese Consulate**, Bouchard 547 p 15, T4318 8200, 0915-1230, 1430-1630. **Netherlands**, Olga Cossentini 831 p 3, Puerto Madero, T4338 0050, www.embajadaholanda.int.ar **New Zealand**, C Pellegrini 1427 p 5, T4328 0301, kiwiargentina@datamarket.com.ar Mon-Thu 0900-1300, 1400-1730, Fri 0900-1300. **Norway**, Esmeralda 909, p 3 B, T4312 1904, 0900-1400. **Paraguayan Consulate**, Viamonte 1851, T4814 4803, 0800-1400. **Portugal**, Maipú 942 p 17, T4515 0520, 0900-1230. **Spain**, Guido 1760, T4811 0070, 0830-1400. **Sweden**, Tacuarí 147 p 6, T4342 1422, 1000-1200. **Switzerland**, Santa Fe 846, p10, T4311 6491, open 0900-1200. **UK**, Luis Agote 2412/52 (near corner Pueyrredón y Guido), T4576 2222, F4808 2274, www.britain.org.ar 0900-1200. **Uruguay**, Av Las Heras 1915, consulate T4807 3040, www.embajadauruguay.com.ar Open 0930- 1530, visa takes up to 72 hrs. **US Embassy and Consulate General**, Colombia 4300, T5777 4533/34 or T4514 1830, 0900-1800.

Language schools *Argentina I.L.E.E*, Av Callao 339, p 3, T4782 7173, www.argentinailee.com Recommended by individuals and organizations alike. *Programa Tango* adds tango lessons to Spanish. Accommodation arranged. *Cedic*, Reconquista 715, p 11 E, T/F4315 1156. Recommended. Spanish classes at *Instituto del Sur*, Bernardo de Irigoyen 668, p 1, T4334 1487, www.delsur.com.ar Individual and groups, cheap. *Oh Español*, Scalabrini Ortiz 2395, p 6 M, T/F4832 7794, www.oh-escuela.com.ar *PLS*, Carabelas 241 p 1, T4394 0543, F4394 0635, www.pls.com.ar Recommended for travellers and executives and their families; also translation and interpreting services. *Universidad de Buenos Aires*, 25 de Mayo 221, T4334 7512 or T4343 1196, idlab@filo.uba.ar Offers cheap, coherent courses, including summer intensive courses. For other schools teaching Spanish, and for private tutors look in *Buenos Aires Herald* in the classified advertisements. Enquire also at *Asatej* (see Useful addresses). **Schools which teach English to Argentines include:** *International House*, Pacheco de Melo 2555, T4805 6393, www.international-house.com.ar British-owned and run. *Berlitz*, Av de Mayo 847, T4342 0202, several branches. There are many others. Vacancies are advertised in the *Buenos Aires Herald* or search on www.inglesnet.com Before being allowed to teach, you must officially have a work permit (difficult to obtain) but schools may offer casual employment without one (particularly to people searching for longer-term employment). If unsure of your papers, ask at Migraciones (address below). A degree in education or TEFL/TESL is often required. 'Coordinadoras', usually women, who do not have an institute but run English 'schools' out of their homes, hire native English-speakers and send them out on jobs. Pay varies between US$3 and 7 per hour. Adverts occasionally appear in the *Herald*, but most contacts are by word of mouth.

For doctors and dentists, contact your consulate or the tourist office for recommendations

Medical services **Urgent medical service:** for free municipal ambulance service to an emergency hospital department (day and night) **Casualty ward,** *Sala de guardia*, T107 or T4923 1051/58 (SAME). **Inoculations: Hospital Rivadavia,** Sánchez de Bustamante 2531 y Av Las Heras 2670, T4809 2000, Mon-Fri, 0800-1200 (bus 37, 38, 59, 60, 92, 93 or 102 from Plaza Constitución), or **Dirección de Sanidad de Fronteras y Terminales de Transporte,** Ing Huergo 690, T4343 1190, Mon 1400-1500, Tue 1100-1200, Wed 1300-1400, Thu and Fri 1500-1600, bus 20 from Retiro, no appointment required (yellow fever only; take passport). If not provided, buy the vaccines in *Laboratorio Biol*, Uriburu 153, T4953 7215, or in larger chemists. Many chemists have signs indicating that they give injections. Any hospital with an infectology department will give hepatitis A. *Travel Medicine Service (Centros Médicos Stamboulian)*, 25 de Mayo 575, T4311 3000, French 3085, T4802 7772, www.viajeros.cei.com.ar Private health advice for travellers and inoculations centre. **Public Hospitals: Hospital Argerich,** Almte Brown esq Pi y Margall 750, T4362 5555/5811. **Hospital Juan A Fernández,** Cerviño y Bulnes, T4808 2600, good medical attention. If affected by pollen, asthma sufferers can get treatment at the **Hospital de Clínicas José de San Martín,** Av Córdoba 2351, T5950 8000, cheap treatment. **Children's Hospitals** (Ricardo Gutiérrez), Gallo 1330, T4962 9264/65, www.guti.gov.ar (Garrahan), Combate de los Pozos 1881, T4308 4300. **British Hospital,** Perdriel 74, T4309 6400, www.hospitalbritanico.org.ar US$12 a visit. Dental treatment at Solís 2180, T4305 2530/2110. **German Hospital,** Av Pueyrredón 1640, between Beruti and Juncal, T4821 1700 or T4827 7000, www.hospitalaleman.com.ar Both maintain first-aid centres (*centros asistenciales*) as do the other main hospitals. **French Hospital,** La Rioja 951, T4866 2546/60, www.cefran.com/site/hospital.htm **Dental Hospital,** M T de Alvear 2142, T4964 1259. **Eye Hospital,** Av San Juan 2021, T4941 5555. Fire accidents: **Hospital de Quemados,** Av Pedro Goyena 369, T4923 4082/3022. For poison emergencies call T4658 7777, T4654 6648, T4962 6666, or go to Sánchez de Bustamante 1390.

If robbed or attacked, call the tourist police, Comisaría del Turista, Av Corrientes 436, T4346 5748 (24 hrs), English spoken. Keep this number on you

Security Buenos Aires has lost its reputation as a safe city. Street crime is on the rise, especially in tourist areas. Be particularly careful when boarding buses, and near the Retiro train and bus stations. Beware of bag-snatching gangs in parks and markets, especially on Sun, and do not go to La Boca alone. There are allegedly more uniformed police on the streets, but be alert at all times. See also Safety, page 77, on mustard-spraying gangs; these operate in main squares and tourist areas. Beware other distractions such as people asking directions. Do not change money on the street. If your passport is stolen, call your embassy for emergency help, and remember to get a new 'entrada' stamp at the **Dirección Nacional de Migraciones**.

Useful addresses **Migraciones:** (Immigration), Antártida Argentina 1335/55, edificios 3 y 4 (visas extended mornings only), T4317 0200, F4317 0282, 0800-1300 (see also Documents in Essentials). **Central Police Station:** Moreno 1550, Virrey Cevallos 362, T4370 5911/5800 (emergency, T101 from any phone, free). **Comisión Nacional de Museos y Monumentos y Lugares Históricos:** Av de Mayo 556, T4343 5835, heritage preservation official agency. **Administración de Parques Nacionales,** Santa Fe 690, opposite Plaza San Martín, T4311 0303, Mon-Fri 1000-1700, has leaflets on national parks. Also library (*Biblioteca Perito Moreno*), open to public Tue-Fri 1000-1300, 1400-1700. **Aves Argentinas/AOP** (a BirdLife International partner), 25 de Mayo 749 p 2, T4312 8958, for information on birdwatching and specialist tours, good library open Wed and Fri 1400-2000 (closed Jan). **Student organizations:** *Asatej*: Helpful Argentine Youth and Student Travel Organization, runs a Student Flight Centre, Florida 835, p 3, oficina 320, T4114 7500, F4311 6158, www.asatej.com Offering booking for flights (student discounts) including cheap one-way flights (long waiting lists), hotels and travel; information for all South America, noticeboard for travellers, ISIC cards sold (giving extensive discounts; Argentine ISIC guide available here), English and French spoken; also runs: *Red Argentino de Alojamiento Para Jovenes* (affiliated to HI), see page ; *Asatej Travel Store*, at the same office, selling wide range of travel goods. *Oviajes*, Uruguay 385, p 6, T4371 6137 also at Echeverría 2498 p 1, T4785 7840/7884, and at Sarmiento 667, p 3, T5199 0830, www.oviajes.com.ar Offers travel facilities, ticket sales, information, and issues HI and Hostels of Europe, ISIC, ITIC and G0 25 cards, aimed at students, teachers and independent travellers. Cheap fares also at *TIJE*, San Martín 674 p 3, T4326 2036 or branches at Paraguay 1178, T5218 2800 and Zabala 1736, p 1, www.tije.com **YMCA:** (Central), Reconquista 439, T4311 4785. **YWCA:** Tucumán 844, T4322 1550.

Around Buenos Aires

This touristy little town is a popular weekend destination lying on the lush jungly banks of the Río Luján, with a fun fair and an excellent fruit and handicrafts market at nearby Canal San Fernando daily 1100-2000 on Calle Sarmiento. North of the town is the delta of the Río Paraná: innumerable canals and rivulets, with holiday homes and restaurants on the banks and a fruit-growing centre. The fishing is excellent and the

Tigre
Population: 40,000
29 km NW of
Buenos Aires

peace is only disturbed by motor-boats at weekends. Regattas are held in November and March. Take a trip on one of the regular launch services (*lanchas colectivas*) which run to all parts of the delta, including taxi launches – watch prices for these – from the wharf (*Estación Fluvial*). Tourist catamarans, five services daily, 1 to 2-hour trips, US$2.50-3.50, run by *Interisleña* (on Río Tigre, T4731 0261/63) and *Río Tur* (Puerto de Frutos, T4731 0280). Longer trips (4½ hrs) to the open Río de la Plata estuary are available only with *Catamarán Libertad* from Puerto de Olivos at weekends.

The **Museo Naval**, Paseo Victorica 602, is worth a visit. ■ *Mon-Fri 0830-1730, Sat, Sun 1030-1830, US$0.60, 50% ISIC discount, T4749 0608*. Covers origins and development of Argentine navy. There are also relics of the 1982 Falklands/Malvinas War on display outside. The **Museo de la Reconquista**, Avenida Liniers 818 (y Padre Castañeda), near the location of Liniers' landing in 1806, celebrates the reconquest of Buenos Aires by the Argentines from the British in 1806-07. ■ *Wed-Sun 1000-1800, free, closed Jan, T4512 4496*. **Tourist office** at Estación Fluvial, T4512 4497, 0900-1700, www.tigre.gov.ar *Centro de Guías de Tigre y Delta*, T4749 0543, www.guiasdelta.com.ar For guided walks and launch trips.

Sleeping and eating There are no good hotels in Tigre itself. On the islands of the Delta: **C** pp *El Tropezón*, T4728 1012. An old inn on the Río Paraná de las Palmas island, including meals, formerly a haunt of Hemingway, now frequented by affluent *porteños*. Highly recommended despite the mosquitoes. **D** pp *I'Marangatú*, on Río San Antonio, T4728 0752. Includes breakfast and dinner, pool, sports facilities. **A** *Los Pecanes*, 90 mins by launch from Tigre, T4728 1932. Price is for a weekend for 2, rooms have fan, mosquito nets (20% discount on weekdays); Anglo-Argentine owners, meals extra, home-grown vegetables, good *asados*. Day visits for US$8 pp including meals. **C** *Delta Youth Hostel*, at Río Luján y Abra Vieja, T4728 0396/4717 4648 Clean, 3 ha park, hot showers, double rooms with bath, including breakfast, table tennis, volleyball, canoes, restaurant, basic cooking facilities. Restaurants on the waterfront in Tigre across the Río Tigre from railway line; cheaper places on Italia and Cazón on the near side. There are also restaurants on islands in the delta to which excursions run.

Transport Trains: Take train from Retiro station (FC Mitre section) to Tigre or to Bartolomé Mitre and change to the Maipú station (the stations are linked) for the **Tren de la Costa**, T4002 6000, US$0.60 one way (US$0.50 Mon-Fri, nonstop ticket), every 10 mins Mon-Thu 0710-2300, Fri 0710-2400, Sat-Sun 0830-0010, 25 mins journey. (Buses to Tren de la Costa are 60 from Constitución, 19 or 71 from Once, 152 from centre.) Several stations on this line have shopping centres (eg San Isidro), and the terminus, Estación Delta, has the huge fun fair, *El Parque de la Costa*, and a casino. You can get off the train as many times as you want on the same ticket. **Buses** Take No 60 from Constitución: the 60 'bajo' takes a little longer than the 60 'alto' but is more interesting for sightseeing. **Ferries** To **Carmelo** (Uruguay) leave from *Cacciola* dock (see page 107). Overnight trips to Carmelo (from US$35 including accommodation) and bus connections to **Montevideo** (6 hrs from Tigre, US$28 return plus port tax) are also available from *Cacciola*.

Isla Martín García
45 km N of Buenos Aires

This island in the Río de la Plata (Juan Díaz de Solís' landfall in 1516) used to be a military base. Now it is an ecological/historical centre and an ideal excursion from the capital, with many trails through the cane brakes, trees and rocky outcrops – interesting birds and flowers. Boat trips: four weekly from Tigre at 0900, returning 2030, 3 hours journey, US$16 including light lunch, *asado* and guide (US$33 pp including weekend overnight at inn, full board). Reservations can be made through *Cacciola* (address under Ferries to Uruguay, below), who also handle bookings for the inn and restaurant on the island. There is also a campsite.

Luján
Phone code: 02323
Population: 65,000
66 km W of Buenos Aires

This is a place of pilgrimage for devout Catholics throughout Argentina. In 1630 an image of the Virgin brought by ship from Brazil was being transported to its new owner in Santiago del Estero by ox cart, when the cart got stuck, despite strenuous efforts by men and oxen to move it. This was taken as a sign that the Virgin willed she should stay there, A chapel was built for the image, and around it grew Luján. The chapel has long since been superseded by an impressive neo-Gothic basilica and the Virgin now stands on the High Altar. Each arch of the church is dedicated to an Argentine province, and the transepts to Uruguay, Paraguay and Ireland. Behind the Cabildo is the river, with river walks, cruises and restaurants (an excellent one is *L'Eau Vive* on the road to Buenos Aires at Constitución 2112, run by nuns, pleasant surroundings). Luján is a very popular spot at weekends, and there are huge pilgrimages on 5 October, 8 May and 8 December, when the town is completely packed.

Museo Histórico Colonial, in the old Cabildo building, is one of the most interesting museums in the country. Exhibits illustrate its historical and political development. General Beresford, the commander of the British troops which seized Buenos Aires in 1806, was a prisoner here, as were Generals Mitre, Paz and Belgrano in later years. ■ *Wed-Fri 1215-1800, Sat, Sun 1015-1800, closed Jan. US$0.30.* Next to it are museums devoted to transport and to motor vehicles and there is also a poor **Museo de Bellas Artes**. Wonderful **horse riding** at *Las Patronas* stables, near Mercedes, T02324-430421, laspatronas@yahoo.com.ar US$35 for a complete day in the ranch with horse riding and lunch. Recommended.

Transport Buses from Buenos Aires (Plaza Once) Bus 52 and (Plaza Italia at Palermo) bus 57, frequent, 1 hr 50 mins with direct service, US$1.50. To **San Antonio de Areco**, 3 a day, US$1.20, Empresa Argentina, 1 hr. Train to Once station, US$0.60 (change at Moreno).

San Antonio de Areco is a completely authentic, late 19th-century town, with crumbling single-storey buildings around a plaza filled with palms and plane trees, streets lined with orange trees, and an attractive *costanera* along the river bank. There are several *estancias* nearby and the town itself has historical *boliches* (combined bar and provisions store). The gaucho traditions are maintained in silver, textiles and leather handicrafts of the highest quality, as well as frequent gaucho activities, the most important of which is the **Day of Tradition** in the second week of February (book accommodation ahead), with traditional parades, gaucho games, events on horseback, music and dance. **Museo Gauchesco Ricardo Güiraldes**, on Camino Güiraldes, is a replica of a typical *estancia* of the late 19th century, with impressive *gaucho* artefacts and displays on the life of Güiraldes, the writer whose best-known book, *Don Segundo Sombra*, celebrates the gaucho. ■ *Daily except Tue, 1100-1700, US$0.70.* Superb gaucho **silverwork** for sale at the workshop and museum of *Juan José Draghi*. ■ *Alvear 345, T454219.* Excellent **chocolates** at *La Olla de Cobre*, Matheu 433, T453105, with a charming little café for drinking chocolate and the most amazing home-made *alfajores.* There is a large park spanning the river near the **tourist information centre** at Zerboni y Arellano, T453165, www.sanantoniodeareco.com The **Centro Cultural y Museo Usina Vieja**, Alsina 66, is the city museum ■ *Tue-Fri 0800-1400, Sat, Sun, holidays 1100-1700, free.* There are ATMs on the plaza.

Sleeping C *Hostal Draghi*, San Martín 477, T454515, draghi@arecoonline.com.ar Charming, traditional style, very comfortable, with kitchen and bathroom. Also recommended: **D** *Hostal de Areco*, Zapiola 25, T456118, **D** *Posada del Ceibo*, Irigoyen y Smith, T454614, and especially **D** *Los Abuelos*, Zerboni y Zapiola T456390. All in renovated 1900s houses, breakfast included. **E** *Res San Cayetano* (and *San Antonio* next door), Segundo Sombra 515, T456393. Basic but pleasant rooms, with breakfast. **Camping** 3 sites in the park by the river: best is *Club River Plate*, Av del Valle y Alvear, T452744, US$3 per tent, sports club, shady sites with all facilities, pool. Also *Auto-camping La Porteña*, a beautiful spot 12 km from town on the Güiraldes *estancia.*

Estancias Some of the province's finest *estancias* are within easy reach for day visits, offering horse riding, an *asado* lunch, and other activities. Better still, stay overnight to really appreciate the peace and beauty of these historical places. **L** *La Bamba*, T456293, T011-4732 1269, www.la-bamba.com.ar Dating from 1830, in grand parkland, charming rooms, English-speaking owners who have lived here for generations, superb meals.

Argentina

San Antonio de Areco
Phone code: 02326
Colour map 8, grid B5
112 km NW of
Buenos Aires

Look at estancias online: www.vivalas pampas.com.ar, www.turismo.gov.ar/ active tourism

AL *El Ombú*, T492080, T011-4710 2795, www.estanciaelombu.com Fine house with magnificent terrace dating from 1890, comfortable rooms, horse riding, English-speaking owners. **AL** *La Porteña*, T453770, www.estancialaportenia.com.ar House dates from 1823, where Güiraldes lived and wrote, simple spacious rooms, terrace with views of the polo pitch. All three recommended. *La Cinacina*, T452045/452773, www.lacinacina.com.ar A day *estancia*, US$10pp for a visit, with music and *asado*.

Eating Many *parrillas* on the bank of the Río Areco. *La Filomena*, Vieytes 395. Elegant, modern, delicious food, with live music at weekends. *El Almacén*, Bolivar 66. Original 1900s store and place to eat. *La Costa Reyes*, Zerboni y Belgrano, on the *costanera* near the park. Delicious *parrilla*. *Ramos Generales*. Perfect place to try regional dishes such. *La Vuelta del Gato* opposite the park. Good pizzas and local salami, with traditional *patero* wine. **Nightlife**: *Pulpería Las Ganas*, Vieytes y Pellegrini. Evening drinks in an authentic traditional bar, music at weekends from 2200.

Transport Buses from Buenos Aires (Retiro bus terminal), 2 hrs, US$3.60, every hour with Chevallier or Pullman General Belgrano.

South of Buenos Aires

South of Buenos Aires, the rich farming lands of the pampa húmeda stretch seemingly without end, punctuated by quiet pioneer towns, like Chascomús, and the houses of grand estancias. Argentina's former wealth lay in these splendid places, where you can stay as a guest, go horse riding, and get a great insight into the country's history and gaucho culture. The pampas are fringed by the great curve of Atlantic coast with a fine array of beach resorts, from chic Cariló to laid-back Villa Gesell, and the famous Mar del Plata, with unspoilt tranquil places in between. Two mountain ranges pop up from the pampas, at Tandil and Sierra de la Ventana, both offering great walking and marvellous views. Though not tourist attractions, the university city of La Plata and quieter Bahía Blanca are both good places to stop along the way south.

La Plata

Phone code: 0221
Colour map 8, grid B5
Population: 545,000
56 km SE of
Buenos Aires

La Plata, on the Río de la Plata, was founded in 1882 as capital of Buenos Aires province and is now an important administrative centre, with an excellent university. It's a well-planned city, reminiscent of Paris in places, with the French-style **legislature** and the elegant **Casa de Gobierno** on **Plaza San Martín**, central in a series of plazas along the spine of the city. On **Plaza Moreno** to the south there's an impressive Italianate palace housing the **Municipalidad**, and the **Cathedral,** a striking neo-Gothic brick construction. North of Plaza San Martín is La Plata's splendid park, the **Paseo del Bosque**, with mature trees, a boating lake and the **Museo de La Plata**, which houses an outstanding collection of stuffed animals, wonderful dinosaur skeletons and artefacts from pre-Columbian peoples throughout the Americas. ■ *Daily 1000-1800, closed 1 Jan, 1 May, 25 Dec, US$1.50, free guided tours, weekdays 1400, 1600, Sat-Sun hourly, in Spanish and in English (phone first), T425 7744, www.fcnym.unlp.edu.ar Highly recommended.* 8 km northwest of the city the **República de los Niños** is Eva Peron's legacy, a delightful children's village with scaled-down castles, oriental palaces, a train, boat lake and restaurant. Fun for a picnic. ■ *Col Gral Belgrano y Calle 501, take a train from La Plata or Buenos Aires to Gonnet station. US$0.30, or bus 338, children free, car park US$1. Open daily 1000-2200.* The **Parque Ecológico** is another good place for families, with native forest and llamas, armadillos and ñandú roaming around. ■ *Camino Centenario y San Luis. Villa Elisa. T473-2449 Open 0900-1930. Free. Take bus 273 D or E.*

There's a small municipal **tourist office** at Pasaje Dardo Rocha, an Italianate palace which also houses a gallery of contemporary Latin American art, Calle 50 entre 6 y 7, T427 1843. ■ *Gallery open 1000-1300, 1500-1800, weekends 1500-1800, free. www.cultura.laplata.gov.ar/ Tourist office T427 1535, Mon-Fri 1000-1700, and long weekends only.*

There are few reasonable mid-price hotels: **B** *Hotel Corregidor*, Calle 6 No 1026, T425 6800. Upmarket, modern business hotel, well furnished, pleasant public rooms. **B** *Hotel Argentino*, Calle 46 No. 536, T423 4111. Good value. **D** *Catedral*, Calle 49 No.965, T483 0091. Modest but welcoming, modern, with fan, breakfast included. **D** *La Plata Hotel*, Av 51 No 783, T/F422 9090. Modern, well furnished, comfortable, spacious bathrooms. **Estancia**: **A** *Casa de Campo La China*, 60 km from La Plata on Ruta 11, T0221-421 2931, mceciliagargia2002@yahoo.com.ar A charming 1930´s adobe house set in eucalyptus woods, with beautifully decorated spacious rooms off an open gallery, with open views, day visits (US$25) to ride horses, or in carriages, eat *asado*, or stay the night, guests of charming Cecilia and Marcelo, who speak perfect English. Delicious food. Highly recommended.

Eating:*Don Quijote*, Plaza Paso. Delicious food in lovely surroundings, well known. The oldest restaurant in town is *La Aguada*, C 50 entre 7 y 8. More for *minutas* (light meals) than big dinners, but famous for its *papas fritas* (chips - the chip soufflé is amazing). *El Gran Chaparral*, C 60 y C 117 (Paseo del Bosque). Good *parrilla* in the park, great steaks. *El Modelo*, C 54 y C5. Traditional *cervecería*, with good menu and great beer. *Confitería París*, C 7 y 49. The best croissants, and a lovely place for coffee.

Trains To/from **Buenos Aires** (Constitución), frequent, US$0.75, 1 hr 10 mins (ticket office hidden behind shops opposite platform 6). **Buses** Terminal at Calle 4 and Diagonal 74. Information T427 3186/427 3198. To **Buenos Aires**, 1½ hrs, US$2, every 30 mins, all through the night from Retiro terminal, daytime only from Plaza Constitución. To **San Clemente del Tuyú**, US$5.

Sleeping & eating
The streets have numbers, rather than names, but watch out for the confusing diagonals

Transport

Pampas towns and estancias

To get to the heart of the pampas, stay in one of many estancias scattered over the plains. There are several accessible from the main roads to the coast, fast Ruta 2 (be prepared for tolls) and Ruta 11, near two well-preserved historic towns, Chasomús and Dolores. At Punta Indio,165 km from Buenos Aires, is 1920's Tudor style **Estancia Juan Gerónimo**, set on the coast in a beautiful nature reserve which protects a huge variety of fauna. You can walk and ride horses in the 4,000-ha estate enjoying total peace, simple and elegant accommodation, exquisite food. ■ *T011-493 74326, www.tierrabuena.com.ar/juangeronimo. US$15pp for the day, L full board, all activities included. English and French spoken.*

Look up estancias on the province's website: www.vivalaspampas. com, and www.caminodel gaucho.com.ar T0221 425 7482

A beautifully preserved town from the 1900's, with a rather Wild West feel to it, Chasmús is a lively place built on a huge lake, perfect for fishing and water sports. There's a great little museum **Museo Pampeano**, Muñoz y Lastra, with gaucho artefacts. The **tourist office** is at Libres del Sur 242,1st floor, or on the laguna. T430405, 0900-19000 daily, www.chascomus.com.ar

Chascomús
Phone code: 02241

Sleeping **E** *Laguna*, Libres del Sur y Maipú, T426113. The town's best, good value, pleasant quiet rooms. More classy accommodation in apart-hotels and *cabañas*, **A** *La Posada*, Costanera España, T423503, on the laguna, delightful, very comfortable. **A** *Torre Azul*, Mercedes y Tandil, T422984, torre_azul@topmail.com.ar pool and spa. Great food, and very cheap, at the traditional *parrilla El Colonial*, Lastra y Belgrano, or for fish at *El Viejo Lobo*, Mitre y Dolores. **Estancias**: **LL** *Haras La Viviana*, 45 km from Chascomús, T011-4791 2406, www.laviviana.com Perfect for horse riding, since fine polo ponies are bred here. Tiny cabins in gardens by a huge laguna where you can kayak or fish, very peaceful, good service, lady novelist owner is quite a character, fluent English spoken. **AL** full board *La Horqueta*, 3 km from Chascomús on Ruta 20, T011-4813 1910, www.lahorqueta.com 1898 Tudor style mansion in lovely grounds with laguna for fishing, horse riding, bikes to borrow, English-speaking hosts, safe gardens especially good for children, plain food. Both *estancias* will collect you from Chascomús.

Transport Frequent **buses** to Buenos Aires, La Plata, Mar del Plata, and daily to Bahía Blanca, Tandil and Villa Gesell; terminal T422595. **Trains** daily to Buenos Aires, Tandil and Mar del Plata.

Dolores
Phone code: 02245

A delightful small town, like stepping back in time to the 1900's, very tranquil. **Museo Libres del Sur**, open daily 1000-1700, US$0.30, is an old house, full of gaucho silver, plaited leather *tablero*, branding irons, and a huge cart from 1868.

Sleeping The most beautiful *estancia* in the pampas, and one of the oldest, is **L** *Dos Talas*, 10 km away, T443020, 155 13282, www.dostalas.com.ar An elegant house in grand parkland designed by Charles Thays, with fascinating history, visible in all the family photos, artefacts and the vast library. This is one of the few *estancias* where you are truly the owners' guests. The rooms and the service are impeccable, the food exquisite; stay for days, completely relax. Pool, riding, English spoken. Highly recommended.

Tandil
Phone code: 02293

The **Sierras de Tandil** are 2,000 million years old, among the world's oldest mountains, beautiful curved hills of granite and basalt, offering wonderful walking and riding. Tandil itself is an attractive, breezy town, a good base for exploring the sierras, with a couple of marvellous *estancias* close by. There's a park **Parque Independencia**, with great views from the hill with its Moorish-style castle, and an amphitheatre, where there's a famous community theatre event throughout Easter week (book accommodation ahead). The nearest peak, 5 km away, **Cerro El Centinela**, offers wild countryside for riding, climbing, walking, ascent by cable car, and regional delicacies at the restaurants. Very helpful **Tourist information** at 9 de Julio 555, T432073, or at the bus terminal. www.tandil.gov.ar www.tandilturismo.com

Sleeping **B** *Las Acacias*, Av Brasil 642, T423373, www.posadalasacacias.com.ar Attractive modern hostería in traditional-style house, good service, Italian and English spoken. **B** *Cabañas Brisas Serranas*, Scavini y Los Corales, T423111. Very comfortable, pool. **C** *Hotel Hermitage*, Av Avellaneda y Rondeau, T423987. Good value, quiet, next to park, good service. **D** *Bed and Breakfast Belgrano 39*, Belgrano 39, T426989, www.cybertandi.com.ar/byb One of the best places to stay, comfortable, in an idyllic walled garden with small pool, charming English hosts. Recommended. The real experience of Tandil lies in the beauty of its surroundings, best explored by staying in an *estancia*. **A** *Ave María*, 16 km from Tandil, past Cerro El Centinela, T422843, www.avemariatandil.com.ar In beautiful gardens overlooking the rocky summits of the sierras. You're encouraged to feel at home and relax, swim in the pool or walk in the grounds, hills and woodland. Impeccable rooms, superb food and discreet staff who speak English. Highly recommended. Alternatively, 45 km southwest with the most magnificent setting in the sierras, **L** *Siempre Verde*, T02292-498555, lasiempreverde@dilhard.com.ar A 1900's house with traditional-style rooms, good views. The owners, descendants of one of Argentina's most important families, are very hospitable and helpful. Wonderful horse riding and walking among the sierras, fishing, *asados* on the hillside, camping. Highly recommended.

Eating *Epoca de Quesos*, San Martín y 14 de Julio, T448750. Atmospheric, delicious local produce, wines and *picadas*. For *parrilla*, try **La Tranquera**, Falucho y Nicaragua. *El Molino*, Juncal 936. Broad menu of delicious food. *Parador del Sol* in the *balneario* by Lago del Fuerte, Zarini s/n, T435697. Great pastas and salads. A couple of km from the centre, *Un Lugar*, Av San Gabriel 2380, T155 07895 (call for directions) is recommended for excellent food in lovely surroundings, closed Monday. **Cheap**: *Tenedor libre* at **La Amistad** Pinto 736. Plenty of *pizzerías*. **Bar**: Trendy crowd at *Bar Tolomé*, Rodríguez y Mitre. *Liverpool*, 9 de Julio y San Martín. Beatles style, very relaxed. **Cafés**: Many along 9 de Julio, but *Golden Bar* serves good coffee and sandwiches, and *Trocadero* is a lively meeting place.

Sport and activities Trekking: Contact an approved guide who will take you to otherwise inaccessible privately owned land for trekking. *Eco de las Sierras*, T442741, 156 21083, Lucrecia Ballesteros, highly recommended guide, young, friendly and knowledgeable. *Horizonte Vertical*, T432762, mountain climbing and walking, *Tandil Aventuro*, T421836, trekking and mountain biking. **Horseriding**: *Cabalgatas Autóctono*, T427725.

Transport Frequent buses from Buenos Aires, Bahía Blanca, Mar del Plata, Necochea. Bus terminal Av Buzón 650, travel information T432092. Also trains from Buenos Aires and Bahía Blanca, station T423002.

The Atlantic Coast

Among the 500 km of resorts stretching from to San Clemente de Tuyú to Monte Hermoso, the most attractive is upmarket Pinamar, with the chic Cariló next door. Villa Gesell is relaxed and friendly, while, next to it are the quiet, beautiful Mar Azul and Mar de las Pampas. Mar del Plata, Argentina's most famous resort, is a huge city with packed beaches, popular for its lively nightlife and casino; much more appealing in winter. Next to it, tranquil Miramar is great for young families, and Necochea has wild expanses of dunes to explore. Since accommodation is plentiful all along the coast, only a small selection is listed here; there are well-organized tourist offices in all resorts with complete lists. Avoid January when the whole stretch is packed out.

Most resorts have balnearios, private beaches, where you pay US$3-7 per day for use of a sunshade or beach hut, showers, toilets and restaurants

San Clemente del Tuyú is closest to the capital, the first of a string of identical small resorts known as **Partido de la Costa**, not worth a detour unless you're keen on fishing. They're old-fashioned towns, cheaper than the more popular resorts further southwest, but rather run down. There's excellent sea fishing, for shark, *pejerrey* and *brotola* from pier or boats, and fish can often be bought on the beach from local fishermen, but since the Río de la Plata flows here, the water is poor for bathing. San Clemente's main attraction is *Mundo Marino*, a sea life centre with performing seals and dolphins, fun, perhaps, for small children. ■ *US$5, signposted from road into town, T430300, www.mundomarino.com.ar* Buses to Mar del Plata (and to resorts in between) are frequent, *Rápido del Sud*, *El Rápido Argentino*, US$5, 5 hours. To Buenos Aires, several companies, US$4-7. **Tourist information** at Mar del Tuyú, T02246-433035, www.lacostaturismo.com.ar Plenty of small hotels and campsites. At **Punta Rasa**, 9 km north, there is a lighthouse and a nature reserve, which, in summer, is home to thousands of migratory birds from the northern hemisphere. www.vidasilvestre.org.ar There's a beautiful stretch of empty beach 15 km south of **Mar de Ajó,** the southernmost of these resorts, which belongs to one of the few *estancias* to offer horse riding on the sands, *Palantelén*, T02257-420983, www.palantelen.com.ar A peaceful place to walk and relax, delightful house, private tango lessons, charming English-speaking hosts. Highly recommended.

The two most desirable resorts on the coast are next to each other, with the quiet old fashioned Belgian pioneer town Ostende in between. **Pinamar** is great for young people and families, with smart *balnearios* ranging from chic, quiet places with superb restaurants, to very trendy spots with loud music, beach parties and live bands at night. There are golf courses and tennis courts, and fine hotels and smart restaurants all along the main street, Avenida Bunge, running perpendicular to the sea. It's a stylish and well-maintained resort, slightly pricey. Explore the dunes at **Reserva Dunícola**, 13 km north, by horse or 4WD. **Tourist office** at Avenida. Bunge 654, T491680, www.pinamar.gov.ar www.pinamarturismo.com.ar English spoken, helpful, will arrange accommodation. **Cariló**, the most exclusive resort of all, has a huge area of mature woodland, where its luxury apart-hotels and *cabañas* are all tastefully concealed. The *balnearios* are neat and exclusive – of which *Hemingway* is *the* place, full of wealthy Porteños – and there are good restaurants and shops around the tiny centre, Cerezo and Carpintero.

Pinamar & Cariló
Phone code: 02254
340km from Buenos Aires, via Ruta 11

Argentina

There are 120 hotels in Pinamar, of a high standard, all 4 stars have a pool. Book ahead in Jan and Feb

Sleeping and Eating Pinamar (all recommended): **A-B** *Ramada Resort*, Av del Mar y de las Gaviotas, T480900, www.ramadapinamar.com.ar Everything you'd expect from the international chain with a prime position on the beach, very comfortable. **A-B** *Del Bosque*, Av Bunge 1550, T482480, elbosque@telpin.com.ar Very attractive, though not on the beach, a smart 4 star with good service. **A-B** *Reviens*, Burriquetas 79, T497010, www.hotelreviens.com Modern, luxurious, international style, with beach access. **B** *Las Araucarias*, Av Bunge 1411, T480812, www.pinamarturismo.com.ar Attractive, smaller hotel with gardens. **B** *Playas*, Av Bunge 140, T482236, www.pinamarsa.com.ar A lovely setting with stylishly decorated rooms, and comfortable lounge, small pool, good service. **C** *Soleado Hotel*, Sarmiento y Nuestras Malvinas, T490304, www.pinamarturismo.com.ar Bright, beachfront hotel with cosy rooms. **D** *La Posada*, Del Odiseo 324, T482267, www.oinamar.com.ar/ Iaposada Good value, more old-fashioned style, comfortable. Recommended as the best **restaurants**: *Tante,* De las Artes 35, T482735. *La Carreta*, De las Artes 153, T484950. **Balnearios**: *UFO* and *El Signo*, for teenagers, *CR* and *Mama Concert* for dinner and live music (*CR* with pool during the day). **Youth hostel** Mitre 149, T482908. **Camping** Several well equipped sites (US$5-8 per day), all near the beach at Ostende. **Cariló**: **AL** *Marcin*, Laurel y el Mar, T570888,www.hotelmarcin.com.ar Modern and luxurious, on the beach. Most of the apart-hotels are luxurious, have pool. **AL** *Cariló Village*, Carpintero y Divisadero, T470244, www.carilovillage.com.ar Well designed, cottagey, has spa. **B-C** *La Posta de Cariló*, Avurtada y Cerezo, T470796. Apart-hotel, recommended.

Transport Bus terminal 4 blocks north of main plaza at Av Bunge e Intermédanos, T403500. To **Buenos Aires**, US$12, 4-5hrs, several companies. For trains, see page 112.

Villa Gesell

Phone code: 02255
Population: 40,000
22 km south
of Pinamar

In contrast to the rather elite Cariló, Villa Gesell is warm, welcoming and very laid-back. Set amid thousands of trees planted by its German founder, it has grown in recent years into a thriving tourist town, but retains its village feel. The beaches are safe and there's plenty of nightlife. In January, it's overrun by Argentine youth, far quieter in late Febraury and March. Next to it are the two of the most tranquil and charming beach retreats: idyllic and wooded **Mar de las Pampas** and **Mar Azul** are both still underdeveloped, with fine *cabañas* to choose from. Get a map from the tourist office in Villa Gesell, or as you enter Mar de las Pampas. There's no grid system and it can be tricky finding your way around. Villa Gesell's main street is Avenida 3, pedestrianized in the evenings, full of cafés, restaurants and bars. Main **tourist office** at the bus terminal, T477253, or on the right as you drive into town, Avenida de los Pioneros, 1921, T458118, open 0800-2200 daily in summer. Very helpful, English spoken. www.villagesell.gov.ar

Sleeping AL *Terrazas Club*, Av 2 entre 104 y 105, T462181, www.terrazasclubhotel.com.ar The smartest in town, great service, huge breakfasts, pool and access to the *Azulmarina* Spa, T450545, www.spaazulmarina.com.ar **A** *Delfin Azul*, Paseos 104 No 459, T462521, www.ghoteldelfinazul.com.ar Cosy and comfortable, with sauna. **C** *Playa*, Alameda 205 y C 303, T458027. The first ever hotel, in the wooded old part of town, renovated, comfortable. **D** *Hostería Gran Chalet*, Paseo 105 No 447 y Av 4-5, T462913. Warm welcome, comfortable rooms, good breakfast. Recommended. **E** pp *Hospedaje Aguas Verdes*, Av 5, entre 104 y 105, T462040, clo@terra.com.ar Airy, with a little garden, rooms for 2-6, some English spoken. **Camping**: Many sites between Villa Gesell and Mar de las Pampas.
     Mar del las Pampas: **A** *Posada Piñen*, Juan de Garay al 600 y R Payró, T479974, www.posadapinen.rtu.com.ar Very comfortable, close to sea. Many attractive well-equipped *cabañas*, including *Arco Iris*, Victoria Ocampo s/n, T011-4775 8536, www.arcoiris.com.ar 2 wonderful tea rooms in the woods: *Lupita!*, Cruz del Sur y Los Incas, T479699, and *Viejos Tiempos*, Leonicio Paiva e Cruz del Sur, T479524.

Transport To **Villa Gesell**, regular flights (in summer) from Buenos Aires to airport, 5 km away, taxi US$3, usually minibuses meet each flight. Several companies, book in advance at weekends. Buses direct to **Buenos Aires**, 5 hrs, US$12. To **Mar del Plata** 2 hrs, US$3.30. Also buses from Mendoza, Córdoba, etc. Terminal at Av 3 y Paseo 140.

Mar del Plata

The oldest and most famous Argentine resort has lost much of its charm since it was built in 1874. It's now a huge city offering great nightlife in summer, but if you like some space on the beach, it's best to go elsewhere. The are hundreds of hotels, all busy (and double the price) in January-February; winter can be pleasantly warm, and much quieter.

Phone code: 0223
Colour map 8, grid C5
Population: 560,000
400 km from
Buenos Aires

The city centre is around **Playa Bristol**, with the huge casino, and **Plaza San Martín**, with pedestrian streets Rivadavia and San Martín full of shops and restaurants. 10 blocks southwest, the area of Los Troncos contains some remarkable mansions dating from Mar del Plata's heyday, from mock Tudor **Villa Blaquier** to **Villa Ortiz Basualdo** (1909), inspired by Loire chateaux, now the **Museo Municipal de Arte**, Avenida Colón 1189, with rooms furnished in period style. ■ *Daily in summer 1700-2200, US$1, including guided tour.* Nearby is the splendid **Museo del Mar**, Avenida Colón 1114, T451 3553, www.museodelmar.org with its vast collection of 30,000 sea shells, café and roof terrace. ■ *From 0800-2000, 2400 on Sat. US$1.50.* The **Centro Cultural Victoria Ocampo**, Matheu 1851, T4920569, is a beautiful 1900's wooden house in lovely gardens, where the famous author entertained illustrious literary figures. ■ *Daily in summer; ring to check current opening times. US$1.* Nearby is the **Villa Mitre**, Lamadrid 3870, owned by a descendent of Bartolomé Mitre; with a collection of artefacts. ■ *Mon-Fri 0900-2000 Sat/Sun 1600-2000, in summer. US$0.70.*

Beaches include fashionable **Playa Grande**, where the best hotels and shops are, as well as the famous golf course, with private *balnearios* for wealthy *porteños*, a small area open to the public; **Playa La Perla**, now packed and pretty grim, but **Playa Punta Mogotes**, further west, is by far the most appealing. The **port area**, south of Playa Grande, is interesting when the old orange fishing boats come in, and at night, for its wonderful seafood restaurants. A sealion colony basks on rusting wrecks by the Escollera Sur (southern breakwater) and fishing is good all along the coast, where *pejerrey*, *corvina* and *pescadilla* abound. Lots of theatres, cinemas, and the **Casino**. ■ *Open Dec to end-Apr, 1600-0330; 1600-0400 on Sat. Winter opening, May-Dec, Mon-Fri 1500-0230; weekends 1500-0300. Free; minimum bet US$0.50.* Lively festivals are 17 November, Day of Tradition, with gaucho-related events, the national fishing festival in late January, and the international film festival in mid-March.

Beaches are filled with hundreds of tiny beach huts, carpas, rented by the day for US$5-7, entitling you to use the balneario's showers, toilets, restaurants

Sleeping

Busy traffic makes it impossible to move along the coast in summer: choose a hotel near the beach you want

L *Costa Galana*, Bv Marítimo 5725, T486 0000, reservas@hotelcostagalana.com.ar The best by far, stylish, 5 star, at Playa Grandet. **A** *Hermitage*, Bv Marítimo 2657, T451 9081, www.lacapital.net.com.ar/hermitag Charming old-fashioned 4 star on the seafront. **B** *Spa República*, Córdoba 1968, T492 1142, hosparep@statics.com.ar Modern, with pool and spa, good restaurant. Highly recommended. **C** *Argentino*, Belgrano 2225 y Entre Ríos, T493 2223, www.argentinohotel-mdp.com.ar Modern rooms in this traditional 4 star in the city, also apartments, good value. Recommended. **C** *Sasso*, Av Martínez de Hoz 3545, T484 2500. Comfortable rooms and pool, older style, near Playa Punta Mogotes. **D** *Selent*, Arenales 2347, T494 0878, www.hotelselent.com.ar Quiet with neat rooms. Recommended. **D** *Los Troncos*, Rodríguez Peña 156, T451 8882. Small, chalet-style, handy for Güemes, with garden. **E** *Costa Mogotes*, Martínez de Hoz 2401, T484 2337. Tidy, modern, with airy confitería, near Playa Punta Mogotes. **Camping** Many on the road south of the city, but far better sites at Villa Gesell. **Apartment rental** Monthly rent for flats US$100-180, chalets (sleeping 4-6) US$170-400.

Eating

Two areas have become popular for smaller shops bars and restaurants: around C Güemes: *Tisiano*, San Lorenzo 1332, good pasta restaurant, and *La Bodeguita*, Castelli 1252, Cuban bar with food. *El Condal*, *picadas* and drinks. Around Alem, next to cemetery, lots of pubs and bars. Traditional favourites: *Parrilla Trenelauken*, Mitre 2807. *Confitería Manolo*, famous for *churros*. Seafood restaurants in the Centro Comercial Puerto, many brightly lit and not atmospheric: best is *El Viejo Pop*, T480 1632. Candlelit, superb paella. *Taberna Baska*, 12 de Octubre 3301. Good seafood. *Dalmacio*, Almte Brown 1958. A la carte, good quality and value. *Tenedor libre* restaurants of all kinds along San Martín, and cheap restaurants along Rivadavia.

Argentina

Bars & clubs   Most nightclubs are on Av Constitución, and start at around 0200: *Chocolate*, No 4471, big and chic, under 25s, *Sobremonte*, No 6690, huge complex of bars and dancefloors (it's fine to be over 25 here!).

Transport   **Air** Camet airport, T478 3990, 10 km north of town. Several flights daily to **Buenos Aires**, *LADE* (T493 8220), *AR/Austral* (T496 0101). *LADE* also to many Patagonian towns once a week. *Remise* taxi from airport to town, mini bus US$2. **Trains** To **Buenos Aires** (Constitución) from Estación Norte, Luro 4599, T475 6076, about 13 blocks from the centre. Buses to/from centre 511, 512, 512B, 541. Daily services at 0745 and 2845, 5½ hrs, US$10 pullman to US$6 for tourist. Also services to Miramar. **Boat** Boat trips visiting Isla de los Lobos, Playa Grande, Cabo Corrientes and Playa Bristol leave from the harbour, US$2, 40 mins, summer and weekends in winter. Longer cruises on the *Anamora*, 1130, 1400, 1600, 1800, from Dársena B, Muelle de Guardacostas in the port, US$5, T489 0310. **Buses** For information T451 5406. The bus terminal, in a former railway station, is central at Alberti y Las Heras, but short on services. Not a place to hang around at night. *El Rápido*, T451 0600, *Flecha bus*, T486 0512, *TAC*, T451 0014, *Chevalier*, T451 8447. *La Estrella*, T486 0915. To **Buenos Aires**, 6 hrs, US$13 , many companies; *Chevalier* , and *Costera Criolla*, also have *coche cama*. To **La Plata**, 6 hrs, US$12. *El Cóndor* and *Rápido Argentino*. To **San Clemente del Tuyú**, *Empresa Costamar*, frequent, 5 hrs, US$8. To **Miramar** hourly, 45 mins, US$1.30. To **Bahía Blanca**, only *Pampa*, 6 daily, US$11, 5½ hrs. Change there for buses to Bariloche and Puerto Madryn.

Directory   **Banks** *Lloyds TSB Bank*, Luro 3101, open 1000-1600, cash advances on Visa. *Casas de Cambio Jonestur*, San Martín 2574. *Amex*, at *Oti Internacional*, San Luis 1630, T494 5414. *La Moneta*, Rivadavia 2615. **Communications** **Telephone** many *locutorios* around the town, and broadband internet everywhere. **Cultural centres** Cultural events: reduced price tickets are often available from *Cartelera Baires*, Santa Fe 1844, local 33, or from *Galería de los Teatros*, Santa Fe 1751. Asociación Argentina de Cultura Inglesa, San Luis 2498, friendly, extensive library. **Tourist offices** Belgrano 2740, T495 1777, 0800-1500, or, more conveniently, next to ex-Hotel Provincial, 0800-2000, www.mardelplata.gov.ar English spoken, good leaflets on daily events with bus routes. Also lists of hotels and apartment/chalet letting agents. The province's office is on the ground floor of the Hotel Provincial, Blvd Marítimo 2500 y Peralta Rammos, T495 5340, www.vivalaspampas.com.ar **Useful addresses** Immigration Office: Rivadavia 3820, T492 4271, open morning.

Inland, 68 km west of Mar de la Plata is the town of **Balcarce** with some splendid art deco buildings and a leafy central plaza. You're most likely to visit the **Museo Juan Manuel Fangio.** Argentina's best-loved racing driver was born here, and the Municipalidad on the plaza has been turned into a great museum, housing all his trophies, and many of the racing cars he drove. Recommended. The **Laguna Brava**, 38 km away, at the foot of the Balcarce hills, offers *pejerrey* fishing, and plentiful birdlife in lovely wooded surroundings. Visit **Estancia Laguna Brava**, RN 226 Km 37.5, T(0223) 460 8002, for horse riding, trekking, mountain biking and water sports on the lake with fine views of Sierra Brava. Frequent buses from Mar de la Plata. D *Balcarce*, C 16 y 17, T422055, good. Also plentiful **campsites:** *Complejo Polideportivo*, Route 55, Km 63.5, T420251, with pools and good facilities, all kinds of sports too. *Club de Pesca de Villa Laguna Brava* RN 226, Km 38.5, well organized site, with all facilities, and good fishing. Excellent *parrillas* on the outskirts. **Tourist information** Calle 17 No 671, T02266-425758, www.balcarce.mun.gba.gov.ar

Mar del Plata to Bahia Blanca

Miramar
Phone code: 02291
Colour map 8, grid C5
Population: 22,000
53 km SW of Mar del Plata, along coast road

Miramar is a charming small resort, known as the 'city of bicycles', and oriented towards families with small children. It has a big leafy plaza at its centre, a good stretch of beach with soft sand, and a very pleasant relaxed atmosphere; a quieter, low-key alternative to Mar del Plata. The most attractive area of the town is away from the high rise buildings on the sea front, at the **Vivero Dunícola Florentino Ameghino**, a 502 ha forest park on the beach, with lots of walks, restaurants and picnic places for *asado* among the mature trees. The **tourist office** is on the central plaza, Calle 28 No 1086, T02291-420190, www.miramar-digital.com Helpful, accommodation lists and maps. ■ *0700-2100 Mon-Fri, and weekends 0900-2100*. Lots of restaurants along Calle 21, and good cafés at *balnearios* on the sea front.

Sleeping One of the most attractive places is **C** *América*, Diag Rosende Mitre 1114, T420847. Spanish colonial style, surrounded by trees, lots of games for children, bikes for hire, lovely gardens. **C** *Gran Rex*, Av Mitre 805, T420783. Rather austere modern block, but comfortable rooms and good bathrooms. **D** *Brisas del Mar*, C 29 No 557, T420334. Sea front, family-run, neat rooms, cheery restaurant, attentive, good value. **Camping** Lots of sites including **F** pp *El Durazno*, 2 km from town, with good facilities, shops, restaurant and *cabañas*, take bus 501 marked 'Playas'.

Transport In summer only, there is a Ferrobaires **train** daily except Sun to Mar del Plata. Station at C 40 y 13, T420657. **Bus**: 8 daily to Buenos Aires, many companies, US$10. To Mar del Plata, US$1.40, *Rápido del Sur*, from C 23 y 24, T423359. To Necochea, *El Rápido*, US$3.

Necochea is a well-established resort, famous for its long stretch of beach, and while the central area is built up and busy in summer months, further west there are beautiful empty beaches and high sand dunes. There's also a fine golf club and rafting nearby on the river Quequén. **Tourist office** on the beach front at Av 79 y Av 2, T425983/430158, www.necocheanatural.com English spoken, it has a list of apartments for rent. Also upstairs at the **municipalidad**, Calle 56 No 2956, T422631. There are banks with ATMs and *locutorios* along the pedestrianised C 83.

The **Parque Miguel Lillo** (named after the Argentine botanist) starts three blocks west of Plaza San Martín and stretches along the seafront, a wonderful dense forest of over 600 ha. There are lovely walks along paths, many campsites and picnic spots, a swan lake with paddle boats, an amphitheatre, lots of restaurants, and places to practise various sports. West of Necochea, there's a natural arch of rock at the **Cueva del Tigre**, and beyond it stretches a vast empty beach, separated from the land by sand dunes up to 100 m high, the **Médano Blanco**. This is an exhilarating area for walking or horse riding and the dunes are popular for 4WD riding. Vehicles and buses stop where the road ends at Parador Médano Blanco (a good place for lunch) where you can rent 4WDs for US$30, T155 68931.

Sleeping The best and newest is **C** *Ñikén*, C 87 No 335, T432323, 2 blocks from the sea. Very comfortable, 4 star, pool, good facilities, good restaurant, excellent service. **C** *Presidente*, C 4 No 4040, T423800. Also 4 star and recommended for excellent service, comfortable rooms and pool. **C** *Bahía*, Diagonal San Martín 731, T42353. Really kind owners, comfortable rooms. And **C** *España*, C 89 No 215, T422896, (ACA affiliated). More modern, well suited to families, attentive staff. Both recommended. Close together, 2 blocks from the sea, and open all year are: **C** *San Miguel*, C 85 No 301, T/F425155 (ACA). Good service, comfortable, good value. **C** *San Martín*, C 6 No 4198, T/F437000. With a good restaurant. **D** *Hostería del Bosque*, C 89 No 350, T/F420002. 5 blocks from beach, quiet, comfortable, great restaurant. Recommended. **D** *Marino*, Av 79 No 253, T524140, open summer only. One of the first hotels, with a wonderful staircase and patios, faded grandeur, but full of character. **Camping** Recommended: *Camping UATRE*, Av 10 y 187, T438278, the best site, a few km west of town towards Médano Blanco, great facilities, beautifully situated *cabañas* too. US$1pp per day. *Río Quequén*, C 22 y Ribera Río Quequén, T422145/428051. Campsites on beach US$1 pp in season.

Eating There are some excellent seafood restaurants, of which most famous is *Cantina Venezia*, near the port at Av 59 No 259, delicious fish. Also try *El Rincón de López*, Av 10 No 3288. For *parrilla*, *Chimichurri*, C 83 No 345, is recommended. And the classic *Parrilla El Loco*, Av 10 y 65, deservedly popular for superb steaks. There's also a superb little campsite restaurant, *Río Piedra*, C 22 at the river bank, T154 64873, gorgeous surroundings.

Transport Buses Terminal at Av 58 y Jesuita Cardiel, T422470, 3 km from the beach area; bus 513, 517 from outside the terminal to the beach. Taxi to beach area US$1. To **Buenos**

[margin right]

Argentina

Necochea
Phone code: 02262
Colour map 8, grid C5
Population: 65,000

Most hotels are in the seafront area just north of Av 2. There are at least 100 within 700 m of the beach

Aires, US$15 , *La Estrella*, *El Cóndor* and few others. To Mar del Plata, *El Rápido*, US$3. To Bahía Blanca, *El Rápido* US$10. For **trains**, see under Buenos Aires.

Bahía Blanca

Phone code: 0291
Colour map 8, grid C4
Population: 300,000

The province's most important port and naval base, Bahía Blanca is a quiet, attractive city. It's a good starting point for exploring **Sierra de la Ventana**, 100 km north, or relaxing on beaches an hour to the east. The architecture is remarkable with many fine buildings especially around the central **Plaza Rivadavia**, notably the ornate, Italianate **Municipalidad** of 1904 and the French-style **Banco de la Nación** (1927). Three blocks north on the main shopping street, Alsina, there's the classical **Teatro Colón** (1922). Northwest of the plaza, there's the attractive **Parque de Mayo** with a fine golf course and sports centre nearby. The **Museo Histórico**, at the side of the Teatro Municipal, Dorrego 116, has sections on the pre-Hispanic period and interesting photos of early Bahía Blanca. ■ *Open 1500-2000*. Not to be missed, though, is the **Museo del Puerto**, Torres y Carrega, 7 km away in the port area at **Ingeniero White**, with entertaining and imaginative displays on immigrant life in the early 20th century, and a quaint *confitería* on Sunday. ■ *Open weekends, 1730-2030 summer, 1500-2000 winter. Bus 500A or 504 from plaza. Taxi US$3.*

There's a smart modern shopping mall 2 km north of town on Sarmiento, with cheap food hall, cinema (T453 5844) and supermarket. Also supermarket *Cooperativa* on Donado.

Sleeping   **B** *Argos*, España 149, T455 0404, www.hotelargos.com.ar 3 blocks from plaza, smart 4-star business hotel, comfortable rooms, good breakfast, restaurant. **B** *Austral*, Colón 159, T456 1700, www.hoteles-austral.com.ar Friendlier 4-star with plain rooms, good views, attentive service, and decent restaurant. **C** *Bahía*, Chiclana 251, T455 0601, www.bahia-hotel.com.ar New business hotel, good value, well-equipped comfortable rooms, bright bar and *confitería*. Recommended. **C** *Italia*, Brown 181, T456 2700. 1920's building, in need of a face lift, ask to see a few rooms before deciding, good *confitería*, central. **D** *Barne*, H Yrigoyen 270, T T453 0294. Family-run, good value, welcoming. Near railway station: **D** *Res Roma*, Cerri 759, T453 8500, clean, though some rooms without windows, quiet area – take care here at nights. **Camping** A couple of options in town, but far better to head for Pehuen Có or Monte Hermoso, see Excursions, above.

Eating   The port also has a superb chic fish restaurant, *Micho*, Guillermo Torres 3875, T457 0346 (but go there by taxi at night, as it's in an insalubrious area). Take bus 500 or 501. *Lola Mora*, Av Alem y Sarmiento. Sophisticated, delicious Mediterranean food, in an elegant colonial-style house, US$8 for 3 courses and wine. *La Negra*, Av Alem 59. Great Italian food, excellent pastas and fish, lively atmosphere, arrive early (2100). *Santino*, Dorrego 38. Italian-influenced, quiet sophisticated atmosphere, good value and a welcoming glass of champagne. US$6 for 2 courses and wine. Recommended. *El Mundo de la Pizza*, Dorrego 53. Fabulous pizzas, lots of choice, the city's favourite. *For You*, Belgrano 69. Cheap *tenedor libre parrilla* and Chinese food, as much as you can eat for US$3. **Cafés**: *La Piazza*, on the corner of the plaza at O'Higgins y Chiclana. Great coffee, buzzing atmosphere, good salads, and cakes too. *Muñoz*, O'Higgins y Drago. Sophisticated café. *El Cofre*, Dorrego 2 e Yrigoyen. Laid back, good for a coffee during the day with internet access, drink and live music at weekends with a young crowd. **Nightlife**: Lots of discos on Fuerte Argentino (along the stream leading to the park) mainly catering for under 25's: *Chocolate*, *Bonito*. Best place for anyone over 25 is *La Barraca*.

Transport   **Local bus**: US$0.40, but you need to buy *tarjetas* (cards) from kiosks for 1, 2, 4 or 10 journeys. **Air** Airport Comandante Espora, lies 11 km northeast of centre, US$3 in a taxi. Airport information T486 1456. Daily flights to **Buenos Aires** with *AR/Austral* (T456 0561/0810-2228 6527) and *LADE* (T452 1063). *LADE* has weekly flights to **Bariloche, Mar del Plata, Neuquén, Puerto Madryn, San Antonio Oeste, San Martín de los Andes** (may involve changes). **Trains** Station at Av Gral Cerri 750, T452 9196. To **Buenos Aires** 3 weekly, 12½ hrs, pullman

US$13, 1st US$9, tourist US$7. **Buses** Terminal in old railway station 18 blocks from centre, at Estados Unidos y Brown, T481 9615, connected by buses 512, 514, or taxi US$2, no hotels nearby. To **Buenos Aires** frequent, several companies, 8½ hrs, US$10-15, shop around. Most comfortable by far is *Plusmar* suite bus, US$20 (T456 0616). To **Mar del Plata**, *El Rápido*, US$10, 7 hrs. To **Córdoba**, US$18, 12 hrs. To **Neuquén**, 6 a day, 8 hrs, US$10. To **Necochea**, *El Rápido*, 5 hrs, US$ 8. To **Viedma** *Ceferino*, *Plusmar* and *Río Paraná* (to Carmen de Patagones), 4 hrs, US$5-6. To **Trelew**, *Don Otto* and others, US$28, 10 ½ hrs. To **Río Gallegos**, *Don Otto* US$34. To **Tornquist**, US$2, *Río Paraná* and *La Estrella/El Cóndor*, 1 hr 20 min; to **Sierra de la Ventana** (town) *La Estrella/El Cóndor* and *Expreso Cabildo*, US$. Also *combi* (Minibus service like a shared taxi) with *Geotur* T450 1190, terminal at San Martín 455.

Banks Many ATMs on plaza for all major cards. *Lloyds TSB Bank*, Chiclana 299, T455 3263. *Citibank*, Chiclana 232. *Casas de Cambio*: *Pullman*, San Martín 171. **Communications** Internet: Many places along Zelarrayan and Estomba near plaza. **Post Office:** Moreno 34. **Telephone:** Big *locutorio* at Alsina 108, also internet. **Tourist office** In the Municipalidad on the main plaza, Alsina 65 (small door outside to the right), T459 4007, www.bahiablanca.gov.ar Very helpful. Mon-Fri 0730-1900, sat 1000-1300.

Directory

At **Pehuén-Có**, 84 km east of Bahía Blanca, there's a long stretch of sandy beaches, with dunes, relatively empty and unspoilt (beware of jellyfish when wind is in the south), signposted from the main road 24 km from Bahía Blanca. It has a wild and untouristy feel, with a single hotel, several campsites well shaded, and a couple of places to eat. ■ *Combis Ariber minibus taxi service, ring to be collected from anywhere in town, T4565523, Combibus, T155-700400.* There's a more established resort at **Monte Hermoso**, 106 km east, with more hotels and a better organized campsite, but quiet, with a family feel, and wonderful beaches. One of the few places on the coast where the sun rises and sets over the sea. ■ *Combis Ariber and Combibus as above.*

Trips from Bahía Blanca

Sleeping and eating B *La Goleta*, Av Pte Perón y C 10, T481142, modern, upmarket, lovely rooms with seaviews. **D** *Petit Hotel*, Av Argentina 244, T491818, simple, modernised 1940's style, family-run, on the beach, cheap restaurant, *El Faro*, on the beach (breakfast extra). Recommended. **Camping**: *Americano*, T481149 signposted from main road 5 km before town (bus or taxi from town). Lovely shady site by beach, US$11 per group of 4 per day, hot showers, pool, restaurant, food shop, *locutorio*. Recommended. Many others, most with good facilities. *Marfil*, Valle Encantado 91, the smartest, delicious fish and pastas. Also *Pizza Jet*, Valle Encantado e Int Majluf. Hugely popular for all kinds of food, arrive before 2130.

The magnificent **Sierra de la Ventana**, the highest range of hills in the pampas, lie within easy reach of Bahía for a day or weekend visit. They're as old as those in Tandil, but much more accessible for long hikes, with stunning views from their craggy peaks. There are daily buses and *combis* from Bahía Blanca, but you could stop at **Tornquist**, 70 km north of Bahía Blanca by Ruta 33, a small quaint place, with an attractive park in the huge central plaza. **E** *San José*, Güemes 138, T0291-494 0152, small, quiet, modern; **G Camping** at *Parque Norte*, a popular lakeside park to bathe and picnic, just north on Ruta 76, T494 0661.

Sierra de la Ventana
Phone code 0291
100 km north of
Bahía Blanca

The sierras are accessed within the **Parque Provincial Ernesto Tornquist**, 25 km northeast of Tornquist on Ruta 76. The entrance is signposted after the massive ornate gates from the Tornquist family home. Nearby is *Campamento Base*, T0291-491 0067, camping, basic dormitory, hot showers. At the entrance to the park itself, there's a car park and interpretation centre with *guardeparques*, who can advise on walks. From here it's a three-hour walk to the summit of **Cerro de la Ventana**, which has fantastic views from the 'window' (which gives the range its name), in the summit ridge. 5 km further along Ruta 76 is the forestry station and a visitors' centre, T0291-491 0039, with audio-visual display, from where a guided visit (only with own vehicle, 4-5 hours) is organized to natural caves (one with petroglyphs). Also from here, a 2-hour trail goes to Cerro Bahía Blanca. **Villa Ventana**, 10 km further, is a pretty, wooded settlement with excellent teashop, *Casa de Heidi*, and good food at *Las Golondrinas*. Lots of accommodation in *cabañas*;

municipal campsite by river with all facilities. **C** *Hotel El Mirador*, before you reach the Villa, right underneath Cerro de la Ventana, T494 1338, comfortable rooms, some with tremendous views, very peaceful, and good restaurant. Helpful **tourist office** at entrance to village, T491 0095, www.sierradelaventana.org.ar

The town of **Sierra de la Ventana**, further east, is a good centre for exploring the hills, with a greater choice of hotels than Villa Ventana, and wonderful open landscapes all around. There is a 18-hole golf course, and good trout fishing in the Río Sauce Grande. Excellent **tourist information** at office on Avenida Roca, just before railway track, T491 5303 (website above). *Geotur*, San Martín 193, T0291-491 5355, for minibus transport from Bahía (dropping you off at the entrance to the park for walking), organizing guided trekking, mountain biking and horseback excursions.

Sleeping A *Estancia Cerro de la Cruz*, just outside Sierra town (phone for directions) T156-486957. Luxurious *estancia* with beautiful views, charming hosts. Recommended. **C-D** *Las Vertientes*, signposted to the left just before the turning to Sierra de la Ventana town, T491 0064, lasvertientes@ba.net Very welcoming ranch, relaxing, horse riding, also day visits, US$10pp. **D** *Alihuen*, Frontini, near Río Sauce Grande, T491 5074. Delightful. Recommended. **D** *Provincial*, Drago y Malvinas, T491 5025. Old 1940's place, quaint, fabulous views, restaurant, pool, good value. **D** *Cabañas La Caledonia* in **Villa Arcadia**, a couple of blocks over the railway track, T156-462003. Well equipped in pretty gardens. Next door, and not to be missed, is tea under the walnut trees at the old tea room, *La Angelita*, fresh scones, delicious cakes, roquefort pancakes. Highly recommended. **Camping**: *Sierra Aventura*, Av San Martín y Camino a la Hoya, T452 4787 pretty site with eucalyptus trees, hot showers.

Córdoba, Central Sierras and San Luis

Córdoba, the second city in the country, has some fine historic buildings and a lively university population. It is also an important route centre. The Sierras de Córdoba contain many pleasant, small resorts in the hills.

Córdoba

Capital of Córdoba Province, the city was founded in 1573. The site of the first university in the country, established in 1613 by the Jesuits, it now has two universities. It is an important industrial centre, the home of Argentina's motor industry, and a busy modern city with a flourishing shopping centre.

Ins & outs
Phone code: 0351
Colour map 8, grid A3
Population: 1.4 million
Altitude: 440 m

Getting there Pajas Blancas **airport**, 13 km north of city, T475 0392, has shops, post office, a good restaurant and a *casa de cambio* (open Mon-Fri 1000-1500). The bus service (US$0.30) can be unreliable; a regular or *remise* taxi charges around US$3-5. **Bus terminal** at Blvd Perón 250, T434 1700. Left luggage lockers, US$0.65 per day, *remise* taxi desk, ATM, tourist office at the lower level, where the ticket offices are. Taxi US$0.65 to Plaza San Martín. Minibuses, *diferenciales*, have better services to the sierras and depart from nearby platform; tickets on bus or from offices at terminal, 1st floor

Tourist offices Municipal tourist office in the old Cabildo, Deán Funes 15, T428 5856. Also at Centro Obispo Mercadillo (on plaza), Rosario de Santa Fe 39, T428 5600, or Patio Olmos Shopping Mall, Av San Juan y Vélez Sarsfield, T420 4100, as well as at the bus terminal and at the airport. All open early morning to late at night, with useful city maps and information on guided walks and cycle tours. For provincial tourist information T434 8260. See also the websites: www.cordobatrip.com and www.cordoba.net Both in Spanish.

At the city's heart is **Plaza San Martín**, with a statue of the Liberator. On the west side is the old **Cabildo**, Independencia 30, built around two internal patios. It now houses the tourist office, a small gallery, a restaurant and a bookshop. ■ *Free, except for entry to exhibitions. 0900-2100 (Mon 1400-2100).* Next to it stands the **Cathedral**, the oldest in Argentina (begun 1640, consecrated 1671), with attractive stained glass windows and a richly-decorated ceiling. Look out for statues of angels resembling native Americans. ■ *0800-1200, 1630-2000.* Behind the cathedral is the pleasant **Plaza del Fundador**, with a statue to the city founder Jerónimo Luis de Cabrera. One of the features of this part of the city is its old churches. Near Plaza San Martín at Independencia 122 is the 16th-century **Carmelo Convent** and chapel of **Santa Teresa**, whose rooms and beautiful patio form the **Museo de Arte Religioso Juan de Tejeda**. This houses one of the finest collections of religious art in the country. ■ *Wed-Sat 0930-1230, US$0.35. Guided visits also in English and French.* The **Manzana Jesuítica**, contained within Av Vélez Sarsfield, Caseros, Duarte Quirós and Obispo Trejo, has been declared a world heritage site by Unesco. **La Compañía** (Obispo Trejo y Caseros, built between 1640 and 1676) has a vaulted ceiling reminiscent of a ship's hull. Behind it, on Caseros, is the beautiful **Capilla Doméstica**, a private 17th century Jesuit chapel (guided visits only), next to which are two former Jesuit institutions, the main building of the **Universidad Nacional de Córdoba** and the **Colegio Nacional de Montserrat**. ■ *Tue-Sun 0900-1300, 1600-2000, US$1, T4332075. All guided visits (available in English) leave from Obispo Trejo 242, Tue-Sun 1000, 1100, 1700, 1800.* **La Merced** at 25 de Mayo 83, was built in the early 19th century, though its fine gilt wooden pulpit dates from the colonial period. On its exterior, overlooking Rivadavia, are fine murals in ceramic by local artist Armando Sica. Further east, at Blvd J D Perón, is the magnificent late 19th-century **Mitre railway station**, now closed, though its beautiful tiled *confitería* is still in use.

Museo Marqués de Sobremonte, in the only surviving colonial family residence in the city, was the house of Rafael Núñez, governor of Córdoba: 18th and 19th provincial history. ■ *Tue-Sat 1000-1600 (in summer Mon-Fri 0900-1500), US$0.35, T4331661. Rosario de Santa Fe 218, 1 block east of San Martin. Texts in English and German.* **Museo Municipal de Bellas Artes** has a permanent collection of contemporary art by celebrated Argentine artists in an early 20th-century mansion. ■ *Tue-Sun 0900-2100, US$0.35, T433 1512. Av General Paz 33.*

Sights
The municipality runs good, daily city tours leaving from the Centro Obispo Mercadillo. See Tourist offices, below

Argentina

A *NH Panorama*, Alvear 251, T410 3900, www.nh-hoteles.com Comfortable, functional, small pool, restaurant. A *Windsor*, Buenos Aires 214, T422 4012, www.windsortower.com Small, smart, warm, large breakfast. C *Cristal*, Entre Ríos 58, T424 5000, www.hotelcristal.com.ar Good, comfortable, a/c, large breakfast. C *Sussex*, San Jerónimo 125, T422 9070, hotelsussex@arnet.com A/c, with breakfast, well kept, small pool. D *Del Sol*, Balcarce 144, T423 3961. Decent value, recently renovated rooms, a/c and breakfast. D *Heydi*, Bv Illia 615, T421 8906, www.hotelheydi.com.ar Best value in town, quiet, 3 star, pleasant rooms, breakfast included. E *Alto Paraná*, Paraná 230, T428 1625, hotelaltoparana@arnet.com.ar Close to bus terminal, hot shower, TV, with breakfast, good value. E *Entre Ríos*, Entre Ríos 567, T/F 423 0311. Basic, welcoming staff, some rooms have a/c, includes breakfast (1 room adapted for wheelchairs), 10% discount for ISIC members. E *Harbor*, Paraná 126, T421 7300, www.hotelharbor.com.ar Cramped rooms but very clean with welcoming staff. E *Martins*, San Jerónimo 339, T421 2319, martinshotel@yahoo.com.ar Funny mix of styles, but plain rooms are OK, small bathrooms. E *Quetzal*, San Jerónimo 579, T/F 422 9106. Recently refurbished, good value, breakfast extra. F pp *Córdoba Hostel*, Ituzaingó 1070, T468 7359, www.cordobahostel.com.ar In Nueva Córdoba district, only hostel accommodation of the city, rather small but has decent facilities for sleeping, cooking and relaxing with private lockers in rooms and large breakfasts. Small discount for IH members. F *Helvetia*, San Jerónimo 479, T421 7297. Renovated rooms with fan, but basic and dirty, nice patio. F pp *Mi Valle*, Corrientes 586, 5 mins from the bus terminal. Fan, small, nice, family-run.

Sleeping
■ *on map*

Argentina

Eating
● *on map*
Numerous grills of all kinds on city outskirts, especially in the Cerro de las Rosas district, for outdoor meals when the weather is suitable

Mid-range: *Betos*, San Juan 450. Best *lomitos* in town, *parrilla*. Recommended. *L'América*, Caseros 67, T4271734. Small imaginative menu, from traditional to sushi to French, large selection of wines, homemade bread, excellent service, also cheap set menus. *La Cocina de Osés*, Independencia 512. Nicely decorated if rather formal, good for fish, meat dishes and homemade pastas. *Las Rías de Galicia*, Montevideo 271. For seafood. *La Vieja Casa del Francés*, Independencia 508. Delicious grills, inviting atmosphere, French owners. *Novecento*, at the Cabildo. Smart and lively, superb Mediterranean-style cooking, excellent service. Lunch only, bar open 0800-2000. *Upacanejo*, San Jerónimo 171. Based on a popular comic character (staff dressed accordingly), *parrilla* serving excellent beef and chicken.

Cheap: *Alfonsina*, Duarte Quirós 66. Rural style in an old house, simple meals or breakfasts with homemade bread, also piano and guitar music (play if you wish). **Cafés**: *El Ruedo*, Obispo Trejo y 27 de Abril. A lively *confitería*, also serving light meals. *Ignatius*, Buenos Aires y Entre Ríos. Tasty *facturas*, croissants and good music. *Puerto Illia*, Bv Illia 555. By bus terminal, and open 24 hrs for breakfasts and simple meals - great if you arrive at night. *Sorocabana*, Buenos Aires y San Jerónimo. Great cheap breakfasts, popular, good views on the Plaza.

Bars & clubs
Northwest of town **Cerro Las Rosas**, locally referred just as *Cerro*, has a lively area of bars and clubs (US$3.50 pp) along Av Rafael Núñez, such as the bar *Arcimboldo*, No 4567 and *Factory*, No 3964, popular club with electronic and Latin dance music. More rock and roll *Villa Agur*, José Roque Funes y Tristán Malbrán, food and live music. Another popular area is further northwest in **Chateau Carreras**: most popular club is *Carreras*, on Av Ramón J Cárcano. For a lower budgets, **El Abasto** district, on the river (about 8 blocks north of Plaza San Martín)

Córdoba

2 Córdoba Hostel *A2*	9 Mi Valle *B3*
3 Cristal *B3*	10 NH Panorama *A1*
4 Del Sol *B3*	11 Quetzal *B3*
5 Entre Ríos *B3*	12 Sussex *A2*
6 Harbor *B3*	13 Windsor *B2*
7 Helvetia *B3*	
8 Heydi *B2*	

■ Sleeping
1 Alto Paraná *B3*

● Eating
1 Alfonsina *B2*

2 Betos *B1*	8 Las Rías de Galicia *B1*
3 El Arrabal *B2*	9 Piccadilly *C2*
4 El Ruedo *A2*	10 Puerto Illia *B3*
5 Ignatius *B2*	11 Reina Alba *C1*
6 L'América *A2*	12 Rock & Feller's *C1*
7 La Cocina de Osés & La Vieja Casa del Francés *B3*	13 Sorocabana *B3*
	14 Upacanejo *A2*

0 metres 100
0 yards 100

has several good places like the very popular *Casa Babylon*, Bv Las Heras 48, disco night Fri, rock Sat. Before 1900, taste the wines at *Dvino*, Pasaje Agustín Pérez 32 (behind Puente Alvear). There are plenty of affordable options around Bv San Juan and Av Vélez Sarsfield, along La Cañada or south of Bv Illia at Nueva Córdoba district. *Reina Alba*, Obispo Trejo y F Rivera, is a redesigned old house open after sunset, chic bar. *Rita*, Independencia 1162, is another refurbished old house with a trendy clientele. Student bars along Rondeau between Av H Yrigoyen and Chacabuco. Less noisy are *Rock&Feller's*, Av H Yrigoyen 320, bar and res-taurant, and *Picadilly*, No 464, live jazz, blues and bossa nova after midnight. *Cuarteto* music, definitively a Cordobés invention and tropically-inspired, is hugely popular.

Cinema Many cinemas including *Cineclub Municipal*, Bv Illia 49, and *Teatro Córdoba*, 27 de Abril 275, Both showing old, independent and foreign language films. **Theatre** The Festival of Latinamerican Theatre is held every Oct. *Teatro del Libertador*, Av Vélez Sarsfield 367, T433 2312, is traditional and sumptuous, with a rich history. **Tango** *Confitería Mitre*, Bv Perón 101 (in the railway station), tango class before *milonga* (public place to dance) begins, US$1.30. The patio at the Cabildo on Fri has tango lessons and dance. *El Arrabal*, Belgrano y Fructuoso Rivera, restaurant with a tango show after midnight, Fri and Sat, US$1.70 extra.

Entertainment
See free listings magazines La Cova and Ocio en Córdoba, local newspaper La Voz del Interior, and www.cordoba.net for events

Bookshops *Librería Blackpool*, Deán Funes 395, for imported English books. *Yenny-El Ateneo*, Av Gral Paz 180. Has some English titles. **Handicraft market** in *Paseo de las Artes*, Achával Rodríguez y La Cañada, Sat-Sun 1600-2200 (in summer 1800-2300), ceramics, leather, wood and metalware. Also *Unión de Artesanos*, San Martín 42 (Galería San Martín, local 22) and *Mundo Aborigen*, Rivadavia 155. **Shopping malls**: *Córdoba Shopping*, José de Goyechea 2851 (Villa Cabrera), *Nuevocentro*, Av Duarte Quirós 1400, and the central *Patio Olmos*, Av Vélez Sarsfield y Bv San Juan.

Shopping
Main shopping area, with many galerías, is north of Plaza San Martín

Local Bus: Municipal buses and electric buses (trolleys) do not accept cash. You have to buy tokens (*cospeles*) or cards from kiosks, normal US$0.30.

Transport

Long distance Air*AR/Austral* run a daily shuttle service to/from **Buenos Aires**, about 1 hr. Most major Argentine cities are served by *AR* and *Southern Winds* usually via BsAs. Interna-tional flights to **Bolivia** (Santa Cruz), **Brazil** and **Chile** direct, others via BsAs.

Buses To **Buenos Aires**, several companies, 9-11 hrs, US$12 *común*, US$17 *coche cama*. To **Salta**, 12 hrs, US$12-14. To **Jujuy**, US$15, , 12 hrs. To **Mendoza**, 10-12 hrs, frequent, US$10-12. To **La Rioja**, 6-7 hrs, US$7. To **Catamarca**, 5-7 hrs, US$7. To **San Luis**, *Andesmar, Autotransportes San Juan-Mar del Plata, TAC*, 7 hrs, US$6-8. *TAC* and *Andesmar* have con-necting services to several destinations in **Patagonia**. See towns below for buses to the Sierras de Córdoba.

International services: To **Santiago** (Chile), US$20, 17-19 hrs, *CATA, TAC*. To **Bolivia** take *Balut* or *Andesmar* services to the border at La Quiaca (19 hrs, US$20) or Pocitos (17 hrs, US$20-23).

Airline offices *Aerolíneas Argentinas/Austral*, Colón 520, T410 7676. *LAB*, Colón 166, T421 6458. *Lan Chile*, Figueroa Alcorta 206, T475 9555. *Southern Winds*, Figueroa Alcorta 192, T0810-7777979. **Banks** Open in the morning. LECOP bonds are in circulation together with pesos, but a discount is applied when changing into pesos. There are *Link* and *Banelco* ATMs at many locations. All ATMs take international credit cards. **Citibank**, Ituzaingó 238, changes Citicorp and Visa TCs (no commission). *Exprinter*, Rivadavia 47. Cash and Amex TCs (low commission). *Barujel*, Rivadavia y 25 de Mayo. Cash, Amex TCs (15% commission), Visa TCs; also Western Union branch. **Communications** Internet: Many places charging US$0.35 per hr. *Mega Cyber*, Marcelo T de Alvear 229, is open till 0500. **Post Office:** Colón 210, parcel service on the ground floor beside the customs office. **Telephone:** There are hundreds of *locutorios* throughout the city, many with a post office and internet access. **Cultural centres** Asociación Argentina de Cultura Británica, Av H Yrigoyen 496, T468 1995. Good library with books, magazines, newspapers, English teaching materials, videos and a small reading room, open Mon-Fri 0900-2000. **Consulates** Bolivia, Av Rafael Núñez 3788, T481 7381. **Chile**, Crisol 280, T469 0432. **Language schools** ILEE, T4824829, www.ilee.com.ar Spanish courses and accommodation arranged. **Medical services** Medical emergencies, T107. **Hospital Córdoba**, Av

Directory

Argentina

Patria 656, T434 9000. **Hospital Clínicas**, Santa Rosa 1564, T433 7010. **Useful addresses** *Dirección Nacional de Migraciones*, Caseros 676, T422 2740. *Police*, T101. Fire department, T100.

Sierras de Córdoba

The Sierras de Córdoba offer beautiful mountain landscapes with many rivers and streams, plus the advantage of good infrastructure and accessibility. Popular for tourism among the upper classes in the late 19th century, the area was opened up for mass tourism in the 1940's with the building of lots of hotels. More recently, adventure tourism has taken off, so there's something for everyone in the hills and valleys. The most visited sights lie along the valleys of **Punilla**, **Traslasierra** and **Calamuchita**, and on the east side of the **Sierra Chica**, north of Córdoba, all forming itineraries of about 70 km long each. There's a useful network of dirt roads (usually used for rally competitions!). Summer rainstorms may cause sudden floods along riversides. Beware when choosing a campsite.

Villa Carlos Paz
Phone code: 03541
Population: 56,000
Altitude: 642 m
36 km W of Córdoba
Tourist information at www.sierras cordobesas.com.ar

In the Punilla Valley is this large modern town on an artificial lake Lago San Roque. It is the nearest resort to Córdoba and is therefore often crowded. Trips on the lake are offered in all kinds of water-vehicles, from amphibious trucks to catamarans (stalls along Avenida San Martín, opposite bus station, US$3.30). A chair-lift runs from the Complejo Aerosilla to the summit of the Cerro de la Cruz, which offers splendid views (US$3.30). **Tourist offices** at San Martín 400 and No 1000, T0810-888 2729 or 421624, open 0700-2100. North of Villa Carlos Paz, on Ruta 38, a road branches west to Tanti from where local buses go to **Los Gigantes**, a paradise for climbers, two-day treks possible (entry US$1). Club Andino has several *refugios*; contact *Club Andino Córdoba*, T0351-480 5126.

Plenty of hotels, in all price categories most with pools and parking

Sleeping C *Florida*, Belgrano 45, T421905, floridahotel@arnet.com.ar Opposite bus station, 3 star, comfortable, a/c, with breakfast, pool. Another good value place next to the bus station is D *Los Sauces*, Av San Martín 510, T421807, www.hotellossauces.com.ar Recently refurbished, good service, pool and restaurant, breakfast included, English spoken. **Camping** *ACA* site, Av San Martín y Nahuel Huapi, T422132. Many others.

Transport Buses: Villa Carlos Paz is a transport hub and there are frequent buses to **Buenos Aires** and other main destinations, as well as to the towns in the Punilla and Traslasierra valleys. To the **Calamuchita valley** the only option is *Sarmiento* bus to Alta Gracia, 1 hr, US$0.85, several daily. To/from **Córdoba**, *Ciudad de Córdoba*, also *Car-Cor* and *El Serra* minibus services , 45 mins, US$0.80.

Cosquín
Phone code: 03541
Population: 18,800
Altitude: 708 m
26 km N of Villa Carlos Paz

Situated on the banks of the Río Cosquín, it is the site of the most important **folklore festival**, in the last two weeks in January. A popular rock festival is held in early February so that accommodation is almost impossible to find between 10 January and 10 February. **Museo Camín Cosquín** at Km 760, out of town, minerals, fossils and archaeology, recommended. ■ *0900-1230, 1400-1800 (closing later in summer), US$0.65, T451184*. There is a tourist office on Plaza Próspero Molino, T453701. Take a *remise* taxi from the town centre, US$5 (or walk 2 hrs) to the Pan de Azúcar hill (1,260 m), from where there is a good view over the Punilla valley. Chairlift to top (all year round). *La Calera*, *TAC* and *Ciudad de Córdoba* run frequent buses along the Punilla valley and to Córdoba.

Sleeping C (half board) *La Puerta del Sol*, Perón 820, T452045, lapuertadelsol@hotmail.com Good reputation, a decent choice, pool, car hire. E *Ale*, Tucumán 809, T450232. Basic but clean, with bath, but no breakfast. E *Siempreverde*, Santa Fe 525 (behind Plaza Molina), T450093, siempreverdehosteria@hotmail.com Spotless, with breakfast, welcoming and very informative owner María Cristina, some rooms small, comfortable, gorgeous garden with a huge tree. Several campsites.

La Falda is a good base for walking, if not an attractive town. The tourist office is at Avenida España 50 (at the former railway station), T423007. Visit the **Trenshow**, model railway museum at Las Murallas 200. ■ *0930-2000, US$2, T423041.* **Camino de El Cuadrado** crosses the sierras eastward to Río Ceballos, passing an excellent vantage point at *Balcón de las Nubes* and the 18th-century *Estancia El Silencio*, 11 km of La Falda, where is a small museum and outdoor activities are organized. To the west, an 80-km rough winding road goes to La Higuera, across the Cumbres de Gaspar. It crosses the vast **Pampa de Olaén**, a 1,100-m high grass-covered plateau with the tiny, 18th-century chapel of **Santa Bárbara** (20 km of La Falda) and the **Cascadas de Olaén**, with three waterfalls, 2 km south of the chapel.

La Falda
Phone code: 03548
Population: 15,000
Altitude: 934 m
82 km N of Córdoba

Sleeping and eating D *La Asturiana*, Av Edén 835, T422923, hotellaasturiana@yahoo.com.ar Simple, comfortable rooms, pool, superb breakfast. **D** *L'Hirondelle*, Av Edén 861, T422825. Welcoming, large garden with pool, restaurant. **D** *Old Garden*, Capital Federal 28, T422842. More central, quiet and homely, large pool, breakfast. **E** *El Colonial*, 9 de Julio 491, T421831. Early 50s décor in the reception and dining room, large pool. **Camping** *Balneario 7 Cascadas*, next to the dam and the seven falls (west of town), T425808. Hot showers, electricity and a food shop, US$1.30 a day pp. *Remise* taxi charges US$1.70. *El Cristal*, San Lorenzo 39, very good cooking, where the locals eat. *Pachamama*, Av Edén 127. Health food shop with cheap organic vegetable pies, or wholemeal pizzas and *empanadas*.

All 80 hotels are full in Dec-Feb

Sports For paragliding, contact tourist office where there is a list of instructors; US$23 per jump with instructor. Mountain bike hire: *Club Edén 201*, Av Edén 201, US$3.50 per day. **Tour operators** *Turismo Talampaya*, T470412 or 15630384, turismotalampaya@yahoo.com.ar 4WD full-day trips to the Pampa de Olaén and Jesuit Estancia La Candelaria for US$15 pp. *VH*, T424831 or 15562740, vhcabalgatas@hotmail.com Horse rides to nearby hills from US$5/hr pp.

Transport Buses to Córdoba from La Falda US$1.70-2, La Calera and Ciudad de Córdoba, also minibuses. Daily buses to Buenos Aires and other national destinations.

North from Córdoba

Capilla del Monte (*Phone code*: 03458; *Altitude*: 979 m), 106 km north of Córdoba and set in the heart of the Sierras, is a good centre for trekking, paragliding and exploring this area. Excursions in the hills, particularly to Cerro Uritorco, 1,979 m, 4 hrs via La Toma where there are medicinal waters and from where there are further walking opportunities (US$1.50). There is horse riding and tours to meditation and 'energy' centres: the location of many sightings of UFOs, the area is popular for 'mystical tourism'. Tourist office in the old railway station. ■ *Open daily 0830-2030, some English spoken, T481903.*

Sleeping and transport D *La Casona*, Pueyrredón 774, T482679, silviadon48@hotmail.com 19th century villa on a hill, surrounded by palm trees, pool, homemade meals, English spoken. **D** *Petit Sierras*, Pueyrredón y Salta, T481667, petitsierras@capilladelmonte.com.ar Renovated hotel with comfortable rooms. The owners run the restaurant *A Fuego Lento*, at the access of town (discounts and free transport for guests). **Camping** Municipal site *Calabalumba*, 600 m north of the centre, T481903, **G** pp , shady with pool, hot water, also *cabañas* for 4 to 6 people. **Buses** to Córdoba, 3 hrs, US$3; to **Buenos Aires**, many companies daily.

Estancia de Jesús María, dating from the 17th century, has the remains of its once famous winery; in the cloister is an excellent **Museo Jesuítico**, where Cusco-style paintings, religious objects and a curious collection of plates are exhibited. ■ *Mon-Fri 0800-1900, Sat-Sun 1000-1200, 1400-1800 (1500-1900 in summer and spring), US$0.65, Mon free, T420126. Easy 15-min walk from bus station: take Av Juan B Justo, north, turn left at Av Cleto Peña, cross bridge on river and follow a dirt*

Jesús María
Colour map 8, grid A3
Population: 27,000
Altitude: 533 m
51 km N of Córdoba
on Ruta 9
(several hotels)

Argentina

Argentina

road right about 300 m. **Estancia de Caroya**, a rather more humble place, is in the southern suburbs. Also from the 17th century, it is a large white building around a lovely patio, with a quaint stone chapel beside it. ■ *Daily 0900-1300, 1400-1800 (1500-1900 in summer and spring), US$0.35, T426701. It is a 20-min walk from bus station.* **Estancia de Santa Catalina** remains in private hands, beautifully located in the countryside northwest of Jesús María; no public transport. This is the largest of the *estancias* and has the most splendid buildings. ■ *Tue-Sun 1000-1800 (1100-1900 in summer), free, T421600. From the bus station, remise taxis charge US$8-10 return including 2 hrs stay.* Each January there is a gaucho and folklore festival, lasting 10 nights from 2nd week; very popular. Some 4 km north of Jesús María is **Sinsacate**, a fine colonial posting inn, now a museum, with chapel attached.

At Rayo Cortado, 114 km north of Jesús María, a turning leads west to **Cerro Colorado**, 160 km north of Córdoba, the former home of the late Argentine folklore singer and composer Atahualpa Yupanqui. His house is a museum, ask in the village for the curator. There are about 35,000 rock paintings by the indigenous Comechingones in the nearby **Cerro Colorado** archaeological park and a small archaeological museum. ■ *0800-1800, US$0.35, only with guide, 1-1½ hrs tour. There is a cheap hostería, T03522-422180, and campsite. An unpaved road, 12 km, branches off Ruta 9 at Santa Elena, 104 km north of Jesús María. Buses: Ciudad de Córdoba goes to/from Córdoba 3 times weekly, 4½ hrs, US$5.*

Southwest of Córdoba

A scenic road southwest from Villa Carlos Paz passes **Icho Cruz**, before climbing into the Sierra Grande and crossing the Pampa de Achala, a huge granite plateau at 2,000 m. At La Pampilla, 55 km from Villa Carlos Paz, is the entrance to the **Parque Nacional Quebrada del Condorito**, covering 40,000 ha of the Pampa de Achala and surrounding slopes. This is the easternmost habitat of the condor and an ideal flying school for the younger birds. Sightings are not guaranteed (Balcón Sur is a likely spot), but there's great trekking on the *pastizal de altura* (sierran grassland). ■ *Several camping places. Tours from Villa Carlos Paz. If you go with your own vehicle, park it at the NGO Fundación Cóndor (9 km before La Pampilla), beside a handicraft shop (1 km before La Pampilla) or at El Cóndor (7 km after La Pampilla). Ciudad de Córdoba and TAC buses both can stop at La Pampilla on their way to Mina Clavero (from Villa Carlos Paz: 1 hr, US$1.90). National Park administration at Sabattini 33, T433371, Villa Carlos Paz, www.carlospaz.gov.ar/pncondorito*

Mina Clavero
Colour map 8, grid A3
Phone code: 03544
Population: 6,800
Altitude: 915 m
40 km W of Córdoba

This is a good centre for exploring the high *sierra* and the Traslasierra Valley. There is an intriguing museum, **Museo Rocsen**, 13 km south and about 5 km from the village of Nono; the personal collection of Sr Bouchón, it includes furniture, minerals, instruments, animals ('by far the best natural history and cultural museum, a whole day is needed to visit', Federico Kirbus). ■ *Daily 0900 till sunset, US$1, T498218, www.museorocsen.org Taxi, US$1.30.* The large **tourist office** with an ATM is next to the intersection of Avenida San Martín and Avenida Mitre, T470171, mclavero. turismo@traslasierra.com Open at 0900 till very late. There are many hotels, *hosterías, hospedajes*, campsites and restaurants around Mina Clavero; others at Cura Brochero and Nono. Buses from Mina Clavero to Córdoba, US$4-6 depending on route 3-6 hours; to Buenos Aires, TAC, US$17, 12 hours; to Mendoza, 9 hours, US$11.

South from Córdoba

Alta Gracia
Phone code: 03547
Colour map 8, grid A3
Population: 42,600
Altitude: 580 m
39 km SW of Córdoba

Alta Gracia, beside Lago Tajamar, has an interesting Jesuit *estancia* (a UNESCO World Heritage Site). The major buildings of the *estancia* are situated around the plaza. The church, completed in 1762, with a baroque façade but no tower, is open for services only. To the north of the church is the former Residence, built round a cloister and housing the **Museo del Virrey Liniers**. ■ *Tue-Fri 0900-1300, 1500-*

1900, Sat, Sun 0930-1230, 1530-1830 (in summer Tue-Fri 0900-2000, Sat-Sun 0930-1230, 1700-2000), US$0.65 (Wed free), frequent free guided visits in Spanish, also in English Tue-Sun 1000-1200, 1700-1900, T421303. The **Museo Manuel de Falla**, C Pellegrini 1100, is where the Spanish composer spent his last years. ■ *0900-1900, free.* Beautiful views from the Gruta de la Virgen de Lourdes, 3 km west of town. Tourist offices inside clock tower by Lago Tajamar, T428128. ■ *Buses to Córdoba, US$0.70, every 15 mins, 1 hr. Campsite at Alta Gracia.*

The **Bosque Alegre and Observatory**, 21 km northwest, afford good views over Córdoba, Alta Gracia and the Sierra Grande. ■ *Fri-Sun 1000-1300, 1500-1800 (Tue-Sun, same times, in summer).* Che Guevara grew up in Alta Gracia after his parents left Rosario to live in the more refreshing environment in the foothills of the Andes. He had started to suffer from asthma, which would plague him for the rest of his life. See page 174. **Museo Casa de Ernesto Che Guevara**, is in Villa Nydia, Avellaneda 501, where he lived between 1935-1937 and 1939-1943 before going to Córdoba: plenty of personal belongings from his childhood and youth, also the letter addressed to Fidel Castro where Che resigns from his position in Cuba. Texts in Spanish, but staff will translate into English, if asked. ■ *0900-1850, US$0.65, T428579. From the Sierras Hotel, go north along C Vélez Sarsfield -Quintana and turn left on C Avellaneda.*

Sleeping and eating D*Hispania*, Vélez Sarsfield 57, T426555. Very comfortable, with breakfast, fine view of the sierras. Recommended. The owners also run restaurant *Hispania*, Urquiza 90, an excellent and moderately priced place serving fish and seafood. *Morena*, Av Sarmiento 413, good food in nice old house. **Camping** *Los Sauces* in Parque Federico Garcia Lorca, northwest of town, T420349.

Villa General Belgrano

Phone code: 03546
85 km S of Córdoba

This completely German town was founded by the surviving interned seamen from the *Graf Spee*, some of whom still live here. It is a good centre for excursions in the surrounding mountains. Genuine German cakes and smoked sausages are sold, there is an Oktoberfest, a *Fiesta de la Masa Vienesa* in Easter week, for lovers of pastries, and the *Fiesta del Chocolate Alpino* during July holidays. The **tourist office** is at Avenida Roca 168, T461215 (or free T125), www.elsitiodelavilla.com Daily 0800-2000; climb its tower for panoramic views. Excursions can be made to **La Cumbrecita**, a charming German village 30 km west, from where Champaquí can be climbed (detailed map essential).

South of La Cumbrecita is **Villa Alpina**, a remote resort set in the forested upper valley of Río de los Reartes, 38 km west, along a poor gravel road. This is the best base for a 2-day trek to the **Cerro Champaquí** (2,790 m), 19 km from the village, a rewarding hike not only for the superb mountainous scenery, but also for the chance to meet local inhabitants at the several *puestos* on the way to the summit. Expect to meet many other trekkers too in high season. Go with a local guide to avoid getting lost: information at Villa General Belgrano tourist office.

Sleeping

D *Alpino*, Av Roca y 25 de Mayo, T461355. Decent rooms, cooking facilities, pleasant garden. Next to the bus station is **D** *Berna*, Vélez Sarsfield 86, T/F461097, berna@tecomnet.com.ar Swiss owners, good rooms with breakfast, large garden with pool (rates 50% higher in high season). **D** *La Posada de Akasha*, Los Manantiales 60, T462440. Comfortable, pool, welcoming (low season rates). **G** pp *El Rincón*, T461323, rincon@calamuchitanet.com.ar The only hostel in town is beautifully set in dense forests and green clearings. Dormitories, double or single rooms with bath (US$4 pp) and camping (US$1.30 pp). US$1 extra for either bed linen or superb breakfasts. Meals for US$2.30 on request. 20% ISIC and HI discounts available, half price for children under 16. In high season rates are 25% higher and the hostel is usually full. 10 min-walk from terminal. Recommended. **Camping** *La Florida*, Ruta 5, laflorida@calamuchitanet.com.ar Open all year, US$2 pp, hot showers, pool, also *cabañas*, tours, restaurant, German owners. **La Cumbrecita** has various hotels (**B-D**) and *hospedajes* in the **E** pp range.

Argentina

| Transport | **Buses** To/from **Córdoba**, 1½-2 hrs, US$3. To **Buenos Aires**, 11-12 hrs, US$16. To **La Cumbrecita** with *Pájaro Blanco*, Av San Martín 105, T461709, every 2 to 4 hrs, 1 hr 20 mins, US$5.50 return. |

San Luis Province

Phone code: 02652
Colour map 8, grid B2
Population: 150,000
Altitude: 765 m
791 km W of
Buenos Aires
412 km SW
of Córdoba

The provincial capital, founded by Martín de Loyola, the governor of Chile, in 1596, **San Luis** stands at the south end of the Punta de los Venados hills. The area is rich in minerals including onyx. Visit the **Centro Artesanal San Martín de Porras**, run by the Dominican fathers, on Plaza Independencia, where rugs are woven. ■ *0700-1300 excluding Sat and Sun*. There is an excellent **tourist office** at Junín y San Martín and the Subsecretaría de Turismo is at 9 de Julio 934, T433853, www.sanluis.gov.ar

Sleeping & eating
Most restaurants close at weekends. Hotel restaurants close Sun

Several on Pres Illia A *Quintana*, No 546, T/F438400. 4-star, best, without breakfast, large rooms, restaurant, parking. **C** *Gran San Luis*, No 470, T425049, F430148. With breakfast, restaurant (closed weekends), pool, parking. **C** *Grand Palace*, Rivadavia 657, T422059. With breakfast, parking, central, spacious, good lunches. **D** *Aiello*, No 431, T425609, F425694. With breakfast, a/c, spacious, garage, restaurant open weekdays. Recommended. **D** *Intihuasi*, La Pampa 815 (behind Casa de Cultura). Spotless, TV, lounge. Highly recommended. **E** *San Antonio*, Ejército de los Andes 1602, T422717. Without breakfast, restaurant. **Camping** Río Volcán, 4 km from town.

El Cantón de Neuchatel, San Martín 745, opposite Cathedral on main plaza. Open Sun, modest. *Michel*, Lafinur 1361. Good food and service. *Rotisería La Porteña*, Junín y Gral Paz. Good food, reasonable prices. Many on Av del Fundador, including *Gustoso, Saborido y Cia*, No 1100, "amazingly good".

Transport
Bus terminal at Vía España between San Martín y Rivadavia. To **Buenos Aires**, US$21-27. To **Mendoza**, US$9, 3 hrs.

The Sierras de San Luis
Northeast of the city are several ranges of hills, which are becoming more accessible with the building of paved roads. The western edge of the sierras can be visited by taking Ruta 9 northeast from San Luis via El Trapiche (bus from San Luis, US$4 return) to **Carolina**, where a disused goldmine can be seen. A statue of a gold miner overlooks the main plaza. There is *Hostería Las Verbenas*, T424425. Four-wheel drive vehicles can drive up Tomolasta mountain (2,000 m). From this road the Cuesta Larga descends to San Francisco del Monte de Oro, from where it is possible to follow Ruta 146 to Mina Clavero in Córdoba province.

The central part of the Sierras is best reached by Ruta 20 to **La Toma**, 70 km east of San Luís, the cheapest place to buy green onyx (**D** *Italia*, Belgrano 644, T421295, hot showers). North of La Toma a paved road runs as far as Libertador General San Martín (known as San Martín), 75 km, a good centre for exploring the rolling hills of the northern sierras (**E** *Hostería San Martín*, with bath and breakfast, meals served, good value, recommended).

Merlo (*Altitude*: 700 m. *Phone code*: 02656), almost at the San Luis-Córdoba border, is a small town on the western slopes of the Sierra de Comechingones. It enjoys a fresher climate than the pampas in summer, and the area is being promoted for its rich wildlife, particularly birds. There are many walks and excursions to *balnearios*, waterfalls and other attractions. Mountain biking, trekking, horse riding, fishing and jeep tours are all possible. *Valle del Sol*, T476109, has tours to Sierra de las Quijadas, minimum 6. The tourist office is at Mercau 605, T476078. There are many hotels, *hosterías* and *residenciales* both in the town and nearby. Most in Merlo are along Av del Sol. **A** *Altos del Rincón*, Av de los Césares 2977, T476333, very welcoming, nice rooms. Bus terminal 3 blocks from plaza. Frequent services to San Luis; to Buenos Aires, *TAC*, *Sierras Cordobesas* and *Chevallier*, US$21, 12 hrs; to Córdoba, *TAC*, 7 hours.

The Northwest

This area includes routes to the fine colonial city of Salta, a good base for exploring the Andean regions, the Quebrada de Humahuaca north of Jujuy and Cachi in the Calchaquí valleys to the south. With extremely varied landscapes, the area is rich in both contemporary and ancient culture, with prehispanic ruins at Quilmes, Tilcara and Santa Rosa de Tastil.

Buenos Aires

Founded in 1553 by conquistadores pushing south from Peru, this is the oldest Argentine city, though little of its history is visible today. It's slightly run down, but the people are relaxed and welcoming. On the **Plaza Libertad** stand the **Municipalidad** and the **Cathedral** (the fifth on the site), with the Cabildo-like Prefectura of Police. The fine **Casa de Gobierno** is on Plaza San Martín, three blocks north . In the convent of **Santo Domingo**, Urquiza y 25 de Mayo, is one of two copies of the 'Turin Shroud', given by Philip II to his 'beloved colonies of America'. On Plaza Lugones is the church of **San Francisco**, the oldest surviving church in the city, founded in 1565, with the cell of San Francisco Solano, patron saint of Tucumán, who stayed here in 1593. Beyond it is the pleasant **Parque Francisco de Aguirre**. A highly recommended museum, **Museo de Ciencias Antropológicas**, , Avellaneda 353, has a breathtaking collection of prehispanic artefacts, exquisitely painted funerary urns, flattened skulls, anthropomorphic ceramics and musical instruments. ■ *Mon-Fri 0730-1330, 1400-2000, Sat-Sun 1000-1200. Free.* Also interesting is the **Museo Histórico Provincial**, Urquiza 354, in a 200-year old mansion, contains a wide variety of 18th- and 19th-century artefacts from wealthy local families. ■ *Mon-Fri 0700-1300, 1400-2000, Sat-Sun 1000-1200, free.* **Carnival** is celebrated in February. The **tourist office** is on Plaza Libertad, T422 6777.

Santiago del Estero
Phone code: 0385
Colour map 6,
grid C4
Population: 212,000
Altitude: 200 m
395 km N of Córdoba
159 km SE of Tucumán

Sleeping and eating C *Libertador*, Catamarca 47, T421 9252, www.hotellibertador.com.ar Smart and relaxing, spacious lounge, plain rooms, patio with pool (summer only), elegant restaurant, 5 blocks south of the plaza in the better-off part of town. C *Carlos V*, Independencia 110, T424 0303, hotelcarlosv@arnet.com.ar Cheaper and more luxurious, on the corner of the plaza, pool, good restaurant. D *del Centro*, 9 de Julio 131, T422 4350. Very comfortable with nicely decorated rooms. Recommended. E *Savoy*, Peatonal Tucumán 39, T421 2344. Good budget option, full of character and faded art nouveau grandeur, large rooms, very simple.**Camping** *Las Casuarinas*, Parque Aguirre. *Mia Mamma*, on the main plaza at 24 de Septiembre 15. A cheery place for *parrilla* and tasty pastas, with good salad starters. *Periko's* on the plaza, lively, popular, for *lomitos* and pizzas. *Cantina China*, Mitre and 24 de Septiembre. Very cheap Chinese *tenedor libre.*

Transport Air *AR* to Buenos Aires. **Buses** Terminal has toilets, a *locutorio*, basic café and kiosks, as well as stalls selling food. Taxi US$0.30 into town, or 8 blocks' walk. **Córdoba**, 6 hrs, US$5-7; **Jujuy**, 7 hrs, US$7; **Salta**, 6 hrs, US$11; **Tucumán**, 2 hrs, US$3. To **Catamarca**, 1 daily at 1600, 7 hrs, US$5, otherwise go via Tucuman.

Bus information
T421 3746

Some 65 km north of Santiago del Estero is **Termas de Río Hondo** (phone code: 03858), Argentina's most popular spa town which has its warm mineral-laden waters piped into every hotel in the city (160 of them), making it a mecca (or Lourdes?) for older visitors with arthritic or skin conditions in July and August, when you'll need to book in advance. The hotels aside, the town is mostly run down, with a cream-coloured casino dominating the scruffy plaza and scores of *alfajores* shops. The **tourist office**, though, is helpful for accommodation advice: Caseros 132, T422143, or www.LasTermasDeRioHondo.com C *Termal Río Hondo*, T421455, www.hoteltermalriohondo.com.ar Most comfortable, modern rooms, medical services, pool, good restaurant. C *De los Pinos*, Caseros y Maipú, T421043.

Next best, attractive Spanish style, a little removed from the centre. For dinner, try *parrilla* at *San Cayetano*, or homely *Renacimiento*, both on Sarmiento (main street), reasonably priced. Cheaper still, on Alberdi y Sarmiento is *El Chorizo Loco*, a lively pizzería. The bus terminal is 8 blocks from the centre, but buses will stop at the plaza, opposite the casino, if asked. There are shops and banks all around the plaza. **Camping** Two sites near river: *Del Río*, Av Yrigoyen y Ruta 9; *La Olla*, Av Yrigoyen y Lascano. Also *ACA*, on access to Dique Frontal (4 km from town), T421648; *El Mirador*, Ruta 9 y Urquiza. All charge about US$2 pp. **Buses** to Santiago del Estero, 1 hour, US$2 and to Tucumán, 2 hours, US$2.

Tucumán

Phone code: 0381
Colour map 6, grid C4
Population: 700,000
Altitude: 450 m
Siesta from 1230-1630
is strictly observed

San Miguel de Tucumán was founded by Spaniards coming south from Peru in 1565. Capital of a province rich in sugar, tobacco and citrus fruits, it is the biggest and busiest city in the north. It stands on a plain and is sweltering hot in summer, when you might prefer to retreat to the cooler mountain town of **Tafí del Valle** in the Sierra de Aconquija to the west. On the west side of the main Plaza Independencia is the **Casa Padilla (Museo de la Ciudad)**, with a small collection of art and antiques in a historical house. ■ *Mon-Sat 0900-1230, 1600-1900 (in summer, mornings only).* Also on this side is the ornate **Casa de Gobierno** and, nearby, the church of **San Francisco**, with a picturesque façade. One block north, the **Museo Arqueológico**, 25 de Mayo 265 in University building, has a fine collection. ■ *Mon-Fri 0800-1200.* On the south side of Plaza Independencia is the **Cathedral** and, two blocks south, the interesting **Casa Histórica** where, in 1816, the country's Declaration of Independence was drawn up. ■ *Daily 0900-1300,1500-1900, US$1; son et lumière programme in garden nightly (not Thu, except in Jul) at 2030, adults US$2, children US$1, tickets also from tourist office on Plaza Independencia, no seats.*

East of the centre is the **Parque de Julio**, one of the finest urban parks in Argentina. Extending over 400 ha, it contains a wide range of sub-tropical trees as well as a

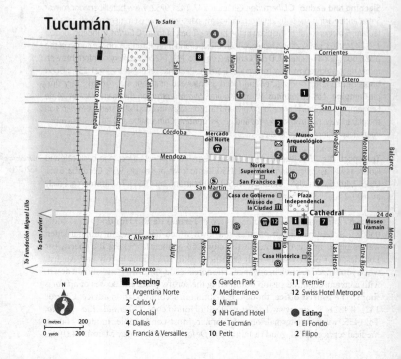

Tucumán

■ Sleeping	6 Garden Park	11 Premier
1 Argentina Norte	7 Mediterráneo	12 Swiss Hotel Metropol
2 Carlos V	8 Miami	
3 Colonial	9 NH Grand Hotel	● Eating
4 Dallas	de Tucumán	1 El Fondo
5 Francia & Versailles	10 Petit	2 Filipo

Argentina

lake and sports facilities. The **Museo de la Industria Azucarera** traces the development of the local sugar industry. ■ *Daily 0900-1800, free.* There are good views over the city from **Cerro San Javier**, 27 km west of the city (*Empresa Ber Bus*, US$1.50 from bus terminal).

Argentina

Sleeping
■ *on map*
All hotels listed include breakfast and have fans or a/c

B *NH Grand Hotel del Tucumán*, Av Soldati 380, T450 2250, www.grandhotel.com.ar Good value, luxurious, minimalist hotel, overlooking Parque 9 de Julio, outstanding food and service, pool (open to non-residents, only in high season), sauna, gym. Highly recommended. **B** *Suites Garden Park*, Av Soldati 330, T431 0700, www.gardenparkhotel.com.ar Smart, welcoming 4-star, views over Parque 9 de Julio, pool, gym, sauna, restaurant. Also apartments. **C** *Carlos V*, 25 de Mayo 330, T431 1666, www.redcarlosv.com.ar Central, good service, with elegant restaurant. **C** *Colonial*, San Martín 35, T431 1523. Near terminal on busy street, interior rooms quiet and comfortable, though dark. Minimal breakfast. **C** *Dallas*, Corrientes 985, T421 8500. Very welcoming, nicely furnished rooms, good bathrooms. Recommended. **C** *Premier*, Crisóstomo Alvarez 510, T/F431 0381, info@redcarlosv.com.ar Spacious comfortable rooms, modern bathrooms. Recommended. **C** *Mediterráneo*, 24 de Septiembre 364, T431 0025, www.hotelmediterraneo.com.ar Good rooms, TV, a/c. **C** *Swiss Hotel Metropol*, 24 de Septiembre 524, T431 1180, www.swisshotelmetropol.com With breakfast, large rooms, restaurant, parking, pool, very nice. **D** *Francia*, Crisóstomo Alvarez 467, T/F431 0781. Cheap apartments for 5, plain but comfortable high-ceilinged rooms, central, good budget option. **D** *Versailles*, Crisóstomo Alvarez 481, T422 9760, F422 9763. A touch of class, comfortable beds, and good service. Recommended. **E** *Miami*, Junín 580, T431 0265, F 422 2405. Good modern hostel with discounts for HI members, pool, a/c, TV. **E** *Petit*, Crisóstomo Alvarez 765, T421 3902. Spacious old house with patio, quiet, cheaper without bath or fan. **G** pp *Argentina Norte*, Laprida 456, T430 2716, www.argentinanorte.com/hostel Youth hostel in restored house, well-equipped kitchen, internet, English spoken, new, good.

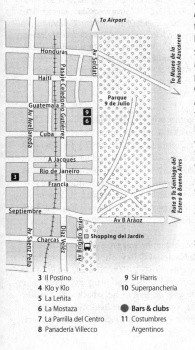

3 Il Postino
4 Klo y Klo
5 La Leñita
6 La Mostaza
7 La Parrilla del Centro
8 Panadería Villecco
9 Sir Harris
10 Superpanchería

● **Bars & clubs**
11 Costumbres Argentinos

Eating
● *on map*
Many popular restaurants and cafés along 25 de Mayo, north from Plaza Independencia, and on Plaza Hipólito Yrigoyen

Mid-range: *El Fondo*, San Martín 848, T422 2161. Superb renowned steak house. *Klo y Klo*, Junín 663. Delightful, good range of seafood and pastas. *La Leñita*, 25 de Mayo 377. Recommended for excellent *parrilla*, and superb salads. *La Parrilla del Centro*, San Martín 391. Excellent steak, reasonable prices. **Cheap**: *Il Postino*, 25 de Mayo y Córdoba. Attractive buzzing pizza place. *Sir Harris*, Laprida y Mendoza. A Tucumán institution, good quality *tenedor libre* in cosy pub-like place. Recommended. **Cafés**: *Superpanchería*, 25 de Mayo, huge range of salads and toppings in this bright busy hot dog place. Good coffee at *Filipo*, Mendoza y 25 de Mayo, a popular smart cafe, with a good atmosphere. *La Mostaza*, San Martín 742. Lively and trendy café, cheap breakfasts. *Panadería Villecco*, Corrientes 751. Exceptional bread, also wholemeal (*integral*). **Bar**: *Costumbres Argentinos*, San Juan 666 y Maipú. Good atmosphere, intimate, for late drinks.

Festivals

9 Jul, *Independence Day* and **24 Sep**, *Battle of Tucumán*, are both celebrated with huge processions and partying.

Argentina

Shopping   *Mercado Artesanal*, 24 de Septiembre 565. Small, but nice selection of lace, wood and leather work. Daily 0800-1300, 1700-2200 (in summer, mornings only). *Regionales del Jardín*, Congreso 18. Good selection of local jams, *alfajores* etc. *Norte* supermarket, Muñecas 137.

Transport   **Local Buses** operate on *cospeles*, US$0.35, which you have to buy in advance in kiosks. **Car hire**: *Avis*, at airport, T426 7777, avis@tucuman.com *Donde Rent a Car*, Gob Gutiérrez 1384, T428 3626. *Movil Renta*, San Lorenzo 370, T431 0550, www.movilrenta.com.ar and at airport.

Long distance Air: Airport at Benjamín Matienzo, 10 km east of town. Bus No 120 from terminal (*cospeles*, US$0.70, required). Taxi US$4. *Cielos del Norte*, T426 5555, minibuses to/from airport to/from any place in town, US$1.50. To **Buenos Aires**, *AR/Austral* (T431 1030) and *Southern Winds* (T422 5554), also to **Salta** and **Córdoba**.

Bus terminal has 70 ticket offices best to ask information kiosk opposite Disco T430 4696/422 2221   **Buses** Modern terminal 6 blocks east of Plaza Independencia on Av Brigido Terán, with huge shopping complex, left luggage lockers (US$1), tourist information office (by *boletería* 1), lots of *locutorios*, toilets and banks. Bus 3 from outside terminal to San Lorenzo y 9 de Julio in centre. Taxi to centre US$0.50-1. To **Buenos Aires**, many companies, 16 hrs, US$20-25. To **Tafí del Valle**, 2½ hrs, US$3. To **Salta** direct (not via Cafayate), 4½ hrs, several companies US$7. To **Cafayate**, 5hrs, US$7. To **Posadas**, *La Nueva Estrella, Autotransportes Mendoza*, 16 hrs, US$18-21. To **Mendoza**, 13 hrs, US$12, via Catamarca, La Rioja, and San Juan. To **Catamarca**, *Aconquija* and other companies, 4 hrs, US$4. To **Tinogasta**, via **Andalgalá** and **Belén**, *Gutiérrez*, 3 a week, daily in high season. To **Córdoba**, 8 hrs, US$7. To **Santiago del Estero**, 2 hrs, US$3. To **La Quiaca** (border with Bolivia), *Balut*, 10 hrs, US$12. To **Santiago** (Chile) via Mendoza, *Andesmar* and *El Rápido Internacional*, daily, 24 hrs, US$18-23 . To **Lima** (Perú), *El Rápido Internacional*, 3 a week, via Mendoza, US$80.

Trains Service to **Buenos Aires** via Rosario run by *NOA Ferrocarriles*, T422 0861, more information given under Buenos Aires.

Directory   **Banks** Most banks along San Martín especially 700 block between Junín and Maipú. *Maguitur*, San Martín 765, T431 0032, accepts TCs. *Maxicambio*, San Martín 779, T422 5399. **Communications** Internet: *Cyber Noa*, 9 de Julio y San Lorenzo and *Centro Digital*, Chacabuco 32. **Post Office**: Córdoba y 25 de Mayo, open Mon-Fri 0800-2000. **Telephone:** Lots of *locutorios* including *Telecentros*, at 24 de Septiembre 612, Buenos Aires y Lavalle, San Lorenzo 704, offering internet access, US$0.40 per hr. **Cultural centres** *Alliance Française*, Laprida 456, T421 9651, free events in French. **Tourist office** On the plaza at 24 de Septiembre 484, T430 3644, www.turismoentucuman.com Open 0800-2200. Also in the bus terminal and airport.

Tucumán to Salta

Via Rosario de la Frontera   There are two routes to Salta, the more beautiful is via Tafí del Valle, Cafayate and the Quebrada de las Conchas. However, it's quicker to go via Rosario de la Frontera and Güemes. **Rosario de la Frontera** (*Altitude*: 769 m; *Phone code*: 03876), 130 km north of Tucumán, is a convenient place for a stop, with thermal springs 8 km away. . **B** *Termas*, Route 34 (6 km from bus station), T481004, hoteltermas@hotmail.com A rambling place, with good food, and thermal swimming pool, horse riding, and golf. Baths US$2. About 1 km from *Hotel Termas* is the more comfortable **C** *ACA hostería*, T481143. About 20 km north is the historical post house, **Posta de Yatasto**, with museum, 2 km east of the main road; campsite.

Parque Nacional El Rey   *There is no public transport to the park; it's best to go on an organised expedition*   About 70 km north of Rosario de la Frontera, at Lumbreras, a road branches off Route 9 and runs 90 km northeast to the **Parque Nacional El Rey**, one of three cloudforest parks in the northwest. Stretching from heights of over 2,300m through jungle to the flat arid Chaco in the east, it contains a variety of animal and plant life. There's free camping and marked trails, but accessible only on foot or horseback with a guide; insects are a problem. ■ *Park office in Salta, España 366, T4312683. Although drier in winter, the access road is poor, not recommended for ordinary vehicles.* Federico Norte,

Norte Trekking, T0387-436 11844, www.nortetrekking.com runs the best expeditions, US$60 pp per day, all inclusive, camping, trekking, rafting, 4WD.

To reach Cafayate, first go south on RN38, until 46 km south of Tucumán, Route **Via Cafayate**
307 branches northwest, through a gorge with sub-tropical vegetation to Tafí del
Valle. Often wisps of cloud formed by warm air moving up from the lowlands rise
like smoke over the artificial Embalse La Angostura. At Km 27 on this road is a statue
to El Indio, with picnic area.

A small town and popular weekend retreat from the heat of Tucuman in the summer, **Tafí del Valle**
Tafí del Valle has a cool microclimate, and makes a good base for walking, with several *Phone code: 03867*
peaks of the Sierra de Aconquija providing satisfying day-hikes. There's some excel- *Population: 7,000*
lent, if pricey, accommodation. The **Capilla Jesuítica y Museo de La Banda**, an *106km from Tucumán*
18th-century chapel and 19th-century *estancia* (with museum of archaeology and *Altitude: 1,976 m*
religious art) can be visited. ■ *Mon-Sat 0900-1900, Sun 0900-1600 (closing early off* *Not to be confused*
season), US$0.50, includes a guided visit. **Museo Los Tesoros de Tafí**, at La Banda, *with Tafí Viejo which is*
T421563, small archaeological museum. Juan Carlos Yapura, owner, guides day walks *10 km N of the city*
to aboriginal sites in nearby mountains. Tourist information to the south of semi-cir-
cular plaza, 0800-1800 daily, no phone. Map US$1. ATM at Banco de Tucumán,
Miguel Critto 311, T421033, all cards.

Some 10 km south is the **Parque de los Menhires**, a collection of 129 engraved
granite monoliths standing to the south of a reservoir, the Dique la Angostura. Particularly atmospheric in the mornings, the stones are engraved with designs of
unknown significance, moved here from various sites in 1977. ■ *Buses from Tafí,*
US$1. Tucumán-Cafayate buses stop on request. 5km further west, **El Mollar** is
another weekend village with campsites and *cabañas*, and popular with teenagers.

Sleeping C *Mirador del Tafí*, T/F421219, www.miradordeltafi.com.ar Warm attractive *Many places, including*
rooms and spacious lounge, superb restaurant, excellent views. Highly recommended. *hotels, close off season*
C *Hostería Tafí del Valle* , Av San Martín y Gdor Campero, T421027. New ACA hotel, right at the
top of the town, with splendid views, good restaurant, luxurious small rooms, pool.
C *Lunahuana*, Av Critto 540, T421330, www. lunahuana.com.ar Stylish comfortable rooms,
and spacious duplexes for families, also with good views. **C** *La Rosada*, Belgrano 322,
T421323/146, miguel_torres@sinectis.com.ar Spacious rooms, well decorated, lots of expeditions on offer and free use of cycles. **D** *Hostería Los Cuartos*, Av Juan Calchaquí s/n, T/F421444
or Tucumán (0381)-15587 4230, www.turismoentucuman.com/loscuartos
Wonderful old *estancia*, rooms full of character, charming hosts. Recommended. Also offer a
day at the *estancia*, lunch, horse riding. Delicious *té criollo*, and farm cheese can be bought here
or at cheese shop on Av Miguel Critto. **F** *Hospedaje El Valle*, above the big souvenir emporium
at Perón 56, T421641. Basic but clean, some rooms with bath. Much more welcoming, **F** pp
La Cumbre, Av Perón 120, T421768. Recently refurbished, rooms for 2 to 5, bar, cooking facilities, good atmosphere. Helpful owner is a tour operator. **Camping** *Los Sauzales*. Run down,
US$2 pp plus tent. Better sites at El Mollar, among them *La Mutual*.

Eating Many places along Av Perón including: *El Rancho de Félix*, recommended; *There is a cheese*
Parador Tafinisto, *parrilla*; *El Portal de Tafí*, very good food, excellent *empanadas*. Cheap *festival in early Feb,*
pastas at *El Paballón*. Good breakfasts at *Panadería El Sol*, Av Critto y Av Perón, local bread *with live music*
and cheese shops further down Av Critto.

Tour operators *La Cumbre*, Av Perón 120 T421768, www.turismoentucuman.com/
lacumbre Energetic and helpful company, offering full day walks to nearby peaks, waterfalls
and ruins, or to Cerro Muñoz, with an *asado* at the summit.

Transport Buses Smart new terminal on Av Critto, with café, toilets, helpful information,
T421031. To/from **Tucumán**, *Aconquija*, T421025, 8 daily, 2½ hrs, US$4. To **Cafayate** 6 a
day, 1½-2½ hrs, US$6 (via Santa María, US$7). To **Salta**, 6 daily, 8 hrs, US$4.

Santa María and Quilmes

From Tafí the road runs 56 km northwest over the 3,040 m Infiernillo Pass (Km 85) with spectacular views and through grand arid landscape to sunny **Amaichá del Valle** (Museo de Piedra, T421004, highly recommended, with overview of the Calchaquí culture, geology, tapestry by Héctor Cruz for sale, US$1.20). From Amaichá the paved road continues north 15 km to the junction with Route 40. **Santa María** (*Population*: 10,000), 22 km south of Amaichá by paved road, is a delightful, untouristy small town with an interesting archaeology museum on the plaza, pleasant hotels and a municipal campsite. Also a *locutorio*, and the only ATM for miles. Tourist information: T421083. (South of Santa María, Route 40 goes to Belén, see page 170.)

35 km north, the striking ruins of **Quilmes**, can be found 5 km off the main road. The setting is amazing, an intricate web of walls built into the mountain side, where 5,000 members of a Diaguita tribe lived, resisting Inca, and then Spanish domination, before being marched off to Córdoba and to the Quilmes in Buenos Aires where the beer comes from. ■ *0800-1800, US$1, includes guide and museum. Café.* **C** *Parador Ruinas de Quilmes*, T03892-421075. Peaceful, very comfortable, boldly designed with weavings and ceramics, great views of Quilmes, good restaurant, and free camping. Recommended. ■ *For a day's visit take 0600* Aconquija *bus from Cafayate to Santa María, alight at stop 5 km from site, or take 0700 bus from Santa María; take 1130 bus back to Cafayate, US$2.*

Cafayate

Phone code: 03868
Colour map 6, grid C3
Population: 8,432
Altitude: 1,660 m

Cafayate is a popular town for daytrippers and tourists, attracted by its dry sunny climate, its picturesque setting against the backdrop of the Andes and its excellent wines, of which the fruity white *torrontés* is unique to Argentina. **Cerro San Isidro** (5 hours return) gives you a view of the Aconquija chain in the south and Nevado de Cachi in the north. Six **bodegas** can be visited, including: *Bodega La Rosa*, owned by Michel Torino, highly recommended, with superb wines and a splendid setting. ■ *At the junction of Rutas 68 and 40, T421201, www.micheltorino.com.ar Hourly visits, also accommodation (see below). Etchart*, more modest but also famous for good wine. Ask to visit their boutique bodega, *San Pedro de Yacochuya*. ■ *2 km south on Ruta 40, T421310. Offers tours daily, but ring first to book.* Also at Yacochuya, *La Finca Domingo*, with handicrafts and ruins as well as the bodega, and lovely views. Smaller, but worth exploring: *Vasija Secreta* (on outskirts, next to *ACA hostería*), T421503, the oldest in the valley, English spoken.

The modest **Museo de la Vid y El Vino** on Güemes Sur tells the history of wine through old wine-making equipment. ■ *Daily 0800-2000.* The tiny **Museo Arqueológico Rodolfo I Bravo**, Calchaquí y Colón, has beautiful funerary urns, worth seeing if you haven't come across them elsewhere. ■ *Open on request, US$0.50, T421054.* ATMs at *Banco de la Nación* (but no TCs), Toscano y NS del Rosario. Also at *Banco Salta*, Mitre y San Martin. **Tourist office** is in a kiosk on the main plaza. ■ *Daily 0800-2200, T421125.*

Sleeping
Accommodation is hard to find at holiday periods. Off season, prices are much lower

A *Bodega La Rosa*, Rutas 68 y 40, T421201, www.micheltorino.com.ar Luxurious, quiet retreat with fine food and excellent wines, set in gorgeous gardens. Highly recommended. **C** *Los Sauces*, Calchaquí 62, T421158, directly behind the cathedral. Small tasteful rooms, breakfast included. **D** *Asembal*, Güemes Norte y Almagro, T421065. Attractive rooms, good restaurant, parking, good value and welcoming. **D** *Briones*, Toscano 80, on the main plaza, T421270. Elegant colonial style place, open in high season only. **D** *Hostería Cafayate* (ACA), T421296. Comfortable rooms around a leafy colonial-style patio, restaurant and pool (summer only). Highly recommended. **D** *Tinkunaku*, Diego de Almagro 12, 1 block from plaza, T421148. Pleasant spacious rooms, with weavings on the walls. Recommended. **E** pp *Hostal del Valle*, San Martín 243, T421039, www.NorteVirtual.com Well kept big rooms around leafy patio, charming owner. Highly recommended. **E** *Confort*, Güemes Norte 232, T421091. Slightly kitsch but simple, hospitable staff. **F** *Hostería Docente*, Güemes Norte 160, T421810. Light simple rooms, welcoming and central. **F** pp *El Hospedaje*, de Niño y Salta, T421680.

Simple but pleasant rooms, good value. **F** pp *Cafayate Youth Hostel*, Güemes Norte 441, on the left as you enter the town, T421440. Small, friendly, dorms and 2 doubles, shared bathrooms, English and Italian spoken, trekking organized.

Campsite Municipal site *Lorohuasi* on RN40(S), T421051, US$2 pp plus tent. Hot water, pool, well maintained. Better still, *Luz y Fuerza*, T15639034, on RN40(S), quiet, good value, US$2 pp.

La Carreta de Don Olegario, Güemes Norte y Quintana. Huge and brightly lit, good set menus. *El Rancho*, Toscano 3. Attractive traditional *parrilla*, good regional dishes. **Cheap**: *El Rincón del Amigo*, San Martín 25. For great set menus and *empanadas*. *Las Dos Marías* next door. Small, serves excellent food. *Confitería Bar Las Vinas*, Güemes Sur 58. Open all day, breakfasts and cheap *lomitos*. *El Comedor Criollo*, Güemes Norte 254. A small *parrilla*. Recommended. *El Sol*, on the plaza. Good for snacks and sandwiches. *Helados Miranda*, Güemes Norte 170. Fabulous home made ice cream, including delicious wine flavour.

Eating
Many large restaurants cater for coach parties

Handicrafts Apart from the rather general souvenir shops, there are some fine handicrafts. Visit Calchaquí tapestry exhibition of *Miguel Nanni* on the main plaza, silver work at *Jorge Barraco*, Colón 157, T421244. Paintings by *Calixto Mamaní*, Rivadavia 452. Local pottery is sold in the *Mercado Municipal de Artesanía* on the plaza (pricey).

Shopping

Calchaquí, de Niño 59, T15638185, jmdoratti@hotmail.com Good range of tours, horses, and bike hire. *Metropolitan Tours*, Av Güemes (N) 128, T422130, metropolitannoa@ infovia.com.ar Good variety of trekking, horse riding and bike trips, expert bilingual guides. Also along Quebrada de las Conchas, Quilmes.

Tour operators

Local **Rentals** **Cycle hire**: many places, consult tourist office. *Metropolitan Tours*, see Tour operators, is reliable. **Horses**: can be hired from *La Florida*, Bodega Etchart, 2 km south of Cafayate. **Buses** Two bus terminals: With *El Indio* on Belgrano, ½ block from plaza, to **Salta** via the Quebrada de Cafayate, 3 or 4 daily, US$6 (travel in daylight). To **Angastaco**, daily, 2½ hrs, US$4. To **Santa María** (for Quilmes), daily. For **Tucumán**, go to *Aconquija* at Mitre y Rivadavia, 3 daily, 5 hrs, US$7.

Transport

Route 68 goes northeast from Cafayate to Salta through the dramatic gorge of the Río de las Conchas (also known as the **Quebrada de Cafayate**) with fascinating rock formations of differing colours, all signposted. The road goes through wild and semi-arid landscapes. The vegetation becomes gradually denser as you near Salta, a pretty river winding by your side with tempting picnic spots. Alternatively, take the RN40 north of Cafayate through the stunningly varied landscape of the Valles Calchaquíes to Cachi. The mainly *ripio* road (difficult after rain) winds from the spectacular rock formations of the arid **Quebrada de las Flechas** up through Andean-foothills with lush little oases and tiny unspoilt villages at **San Carlos, Angastaco** and **Molinos** (all with hotels, and limited bus services).

Quebrada de las Conchas

Cachi is a beautiful town, in a valley made fertile by pre-Inca irrigation, set against a backdrop of arid mountains and the majestic Nevado del Cachi (6,380 m). Its rich Diaguita history, starting long before the Incas arrived in 1450, is well presented in the **Museo Arqueológico**, with painted funerary urns and intriguing petroglyphs. ■ *Mon-Fri 0830-1930, Sat-Sun 1000-1300, US$0.30*. The simple church next door has a roof and lecterns made of cactus wood. There are panoramic views from the hill-top cemetery, 20 minutes' walk from the plaza, and satisfying walks to **La Aguada** (6 km away), or to the ruins at **Las Pailas**, 18 km west of Cachi, barely excavated. The view is breathtaking, with huge cacti set against snow-topped Andean peaks. ATM on the plaza at Güemes and Ruiz de los Llanos. ■ *Walking 4 hrs each way, bus from Cachi: get directions from tourist office on the plaza: T491053, helpful, leaflet and map, open daily 0900-1300, 1500-2000. Also excellent handicrafts shop for weavings.*

Cachi
Phone code: 03868
Colour map 6, grid C3
Population: 7,200
Altitude: 2,280 m

Argentina

Sleeping **A** *El Molino de Cachi Adentro*, T491094, www.elmolinodecachi.com 4km on the road to La Aguada, in restored mill, exquisite in every way. **C** *El Cortijo*, opposite the ACA hotel, on Av Automóvil Club s/n, T491034, www.hostalelcortijo.com.ar Lovely peaceful rooms, warm hospitality. Highly recommended. **C** *ACA Hostería Cachi*, at the top of Juan Manuel Castilla, T491904, www.hosteriacachi.com.ar Smart modern rooms, great views, pool, good restaurant, non-residents can use the pool if they eat lunch. **C** *Hostería Llaq'ta Mawka*, Cnel Ruiz de los Llanos s/n (20 m from the plaza), T491016, or 0387-4232832, hostal_llaqta_mawka@hotmail.com One of Cachi's oldest buildings, beautifully renovated, comfortable rooms, pool, helpful local owners who give tourist information and arrange collection from Salta, trekking and horse riding. Recommended. **E** *Hospedaje Don Arturo*, Bustamante s/n, T491087. Homely, small rooms on a quiet old street. **G** *Hospedaje El Nevado de Cachi*, Ruiz de los Llanos y F Suárez, T491063. Impeccable small rooms around a central courtyard. Recommended. The municipal **campsite** is at Av Travella s/n, T491053, with pool and sports complex, also *cabañas* and *albergue*. **Eating**: Apart from the ACA, *Oliver Café* and *Confitería El Sol* on the plaza, are both good for cheap regional food.

Transport Buses To *Salta*, *Marcos Rueda*, T491063, daily, 4 hrs, US$6. To **Molinos** daily. To **Cafayate** *El Indio* Thu morning only, returning Thu afternoon.

Cachi to Salta   Follow Ruta 40 for 11 km north to Payogasta (*Hostería*), then turn right to Ruta 33. This *ripio* road climbs continuously up the Cuesta del Obispo passing a dead-straight stretch of 14 km known as La Recta del Tin-Tin through the magnificent **Los Cardones National Park**, with huge candelabra cacti, up to 6 m in height. The road reaches the summit at Piedra de Molino (3,347 m) after 43 km. Then it plunges down through the Quebrada de Escoipe, a breathtaking valley between olive green mountains, one of Argentina's great routes. The road rejoins Ruta 68 at El Carril, from where it is 37 km back to Salta.

Salta

Phone code: 0387
Colour map 6, grid C3
Population: 400,000
Altitude: 1,190 m
1,600 km N of B Aires

Founded in 1582, Salta is an atmospheric city, with many fine colonial buildings, tall palm trees waving in elegant plazas, stirring folkloric music and fabulous food. It lies in the broad Lerma valley, surrounded by steep and forested mountains, and is the base for exploring the subtropical rainforest, the wide open puna and the stark splendour of the Quebrada de Humahuaca.

Ins & outs
For more detailed information see Transport, page 144

Getting there There are regular flights to Salta: the airport is 11 km southwest, a US$1 shuttle bus ride to town (taxi US$3). The bus terminal is eight blocks east of the centre. **Getting around** A fascinating city to explore on foot; in a couple of hours you can get a feel for its wonderful architecture. Good maps are available from the tourist office and many hotels are in or near the centre. Local buses in the city charge US$0.25. **Tourist offices** Provincial **Tourist Office**, Buenos Aires 93 (1 block from main plaza), T431 0950/0640, www.turismosalta.com Open weekdays 0800-2100, weekends 0900-2000. Very helpful, gives free maps, arranges accommodation in private houses in high season (Jul), only when hotels are fully booked. Other websites: www.turismoensalta.com (Cámara de Turismo, Alvarado 455, p 1, T401 1002); www.iruya.com and www.redsalta.com

Sights

Many museums are closed in the afternoons in summer; check museum opening times at tourist office

The heart of the city is **Plaza 9 de Julio**, planted with tall palms and surrounded by colonial buildings. The **Cabildo**, 1783, one of the few to be found intact in the country, houses the impressive **Museo Histórico del Norte** (Caseros 549), with displays on pre-Columbian and colonial history, independence wars, and a fine 18th-century pulpit. Recommended. ■ *Tue-Sat 0930-1330, 1530-2030 (Sat 1630–2000). Sun 0930-1300, US$0.80.* A block southwest is the **Museo de la Ciudad 'Casa de**

Hernández', Florida 97, T4373352, a fine 18th century mansion: furniture and dull portraits, but a marvellous painting of Güemes. ■ *Mon-Sat 0900-1300, Mon-Fri 1530 - 2000, closed Sun.* Opposite the Cabildo, the 19th-century **Cathedral** (open mornings and evenings) contains a huge late baroque altar and the much venerated images of the Virgin Mary and of the Cristo del Milagro, sent from Spain in 1592. The miracle was the sudden cessation of a terrifying series of earthquakes when the images were paraded through the streets on 15 September 1692. They still are, each September. The magnificent façade of **San Francisco** church (on Caseros) rises above the skyline with its splendid tower, ornately decorated in plum red and gold. ■ *0700-1200, 1730-2100, Free guided visits in Spanish.* Further along Caseros, the Convent of **San Bernardo**, rebuilt in colonial style in the mid-19th century, has a beautifully carved wooden portal of 1762, but is not open to visitors.

At the end of Caseros is the **Cerro San Bernardo** (1,458 m), accessible by cable car (*teleférico* from Parque San Martín), daily 1000-1930, US$2 return, children

Argentina

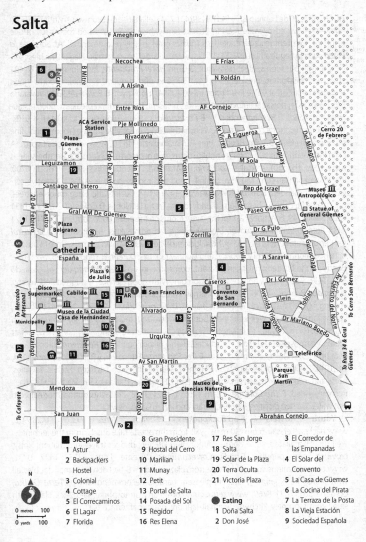

Sleeping	8 Gran Presidente	17 Res San Jorge	3 El Corredor de
1 Astur	9 Hostal del Cerro	18 Salta	las Empanadas
2 Backpackers	10 Marilian	19 Solar de la Plaza	4 El Solar del
Hostel	11 Munay	20 Terra Oculta	Convento
3 Colonial	12 Petit	21 Victoria Plaza	5 La Casa de Güemes
4 Cottage	13 Portal de Salta		6 La Cocina del Pirata
5 El Correcaminos	14 Posada del Sol	**Eating**	7 La Terraza de la Posta
6 El Lagar	15 Regidor	1 Doña Salta	8 La Vieja Estación
7 Florida	16 Res Elena	2 Don José	9 Sociedad Española

US\$1.50, fine views. 30 minutes' walk to return. The park is open and spacious, with a lake where rowing boats can be hired. Further along Avenida H Yrigoyen is an impressive **statue to General Güemes**, whose *gaucho* troops repelled seven powerful Spanish invasions from Bolivia between 1814 and 1821.

The city's best museum is up beyond the Güemes statue, **Museo Antropológico**, Paseo Güemes, with fascinating displays on pre-Inca cultures: painted urns, intriguing board-flattened skulls (meant to confer superiority), a mummy discovered high in the Andes and many objects from Tastil (see page 145). ■ *Mon-Fri 0800-1830, Sat 0900-1300, 1500-1800. Helpful and knowledgeable staff. US\$0.70.* www.antropologico.gov.ar **Museo de Ciencias Naturales**, in Parque San Martín, displays a bewildering number of stuffed animals and birds; the armadillo collection is interesting. ■ *Tue-Sun 1400-1800, US\$0.30.*

Essentials

Sleeping
■ *on map*
Book ahead in Jul holidays and around 10-16 Sep during celebrations of Cristo del Milagro

AL *El Lagar*, 20 de Febrero 877, T431 9439/421 7943, ellagar@arnet.com.ar An intimate boutique hotel owned by wine-making Etchart family, beautifully furnished rooms full of fine paintings, excellent restaurant, gardens (guests only). Highly recommended. **AL** *Solar de la Plaza*, Juan M Leguizamon 669, T431 5111, www.solardelaplaza.com.ar Elegant, faultless service, sumptuous rooms, great restaurant. **B** *Gran Hotel Presidente*, Av Belgrano 353, T/F431 2022, reservas@grhotelpresidente.com.ar Chic and ultra-modern, very plush rooms, good restaurant with great value fixed price menu (US\$4), pool, gym. **B** *Portal de Salta*, Alvarado 341, T431 3674, porsalta@infovia.com.ar A/c, pleasant, helpful, good breakfast, pool, restaurant, parking. Recommended. **B** *Portezuelo*, Av Turística 1, T431 0104, www.portezuelohotel.com Good views over the city, comfortable modern rooms, pool, fine restaurant, parking. **B** *Salta*, Buenos Aires 1, in main plaza, T431 0740, www.hotelsalta.com A Salta institution with neo-colonial public rooms, but bedrooms don't match up (the suite is marvellous though), popular *confitería*. **C** *Marilian*, Buenos Aires 176, T/F421 6700, www.hotelmarilian.com Modern, central, good bathrooms, huge breakfasts, attentive service. Recommended. **D** *Astur*, Rivadavia 752, T421 2107. Quaint little place on quiet street, good value for couples, basic rooms, handy for the Tren a las Nubes. **D** *Colonial*, Zuviría 6, T431 0805, F431 4249. Functional, ask for the larger rooms on the plaza. **D** *Florida*, Urquiza 718, T421 2133, hotelflorida@salnet.com.ar Stores luggage, fan, no breakfast. Recommended. **D** *Hostal del Cerro*, Santa Fe 456, T431 8572, hostaldelcerro@hotmail.com On the park, close to bus terminal, comfortable, with TV, cooking and laundry facilities. **D** *Petit*, H Yrigoyen 225, T4213012. Handy for the bus terminal, plain pleasant rooms around a patio. **D** *Posada del Sol*, Alvarado 646, T431 7300, www.hotelposadadelsol.com With good service though dated rooms. **D** *Regidor*, Buenos Aires 8, T431 1305. Smart wood panelling everywhere, small rooms, welcoming, good restaurant, excellent value. **D** *Victoria Plaza*, Zuviría 16, T431 8500 , vplaza@arnet.com.ar Well-equipped but unmodernized rooms, *confitería*. **E** *Munay*, San Martín 656, T4224936, munayhotel@hotmail.com Excellent budget option, new, smart rooms, warm welcome, breakfast included. Highly recommended. **E** *Res Elena*, Buenos Aires 256, T421 1529. Quiet, `charming', safe. **E** *Res San Jorge*, Esteco 244 y Ruiz de los Llanos 1164, T4210443, hotelsanjorge@arnet.com Homely, with laundry and limited kitchen facilities, horse and trekking excursions (take buses 3 and 10 from bus station to San Martín y Malvinas). Recommended. **F** *The Cottage*, Juramento 54, T421 3668, hostalthecottage@hotmail.com Hot water, kitchen facilities, internet, library and information, new.

Youth hostels **F** pp *Backpackers*, Buenos Aires 930, T4235910, www.backpackerssalta.com 30 mins' walk from the plaza - take Bus 12 from the terminal – well-run, HI affiliated, small dorms, laundry and kitchen, budget travel information. Noisy, crowded and popular. **F** pp *El Correcaminos*, Vicente López 353, T422 0731, www.correcamminos.com.ar 4 blocks from plaza, modern 8-bed dorms, 2 small doubles, all with shared bath, laundry, kitchen, pleasant garden. Recommended. **F** pp *Terra Oculta*, Córdoba 361, T421 8769, www.terraoculta.com Party atmosphere, laid back place with small dorms, homely, kitchen, TV, email, laundry, great roof terrace bar.

Outside Salta At San Lorenzo, 11 km northwest of the centre, **B** *Hostal Selva Montana*, C Alfonsina Storni 2315, T492 1184, www.iruya.com/ent/selvamontana Extremely comfortable and relaxing modern hotel in traditional style, in forested hills, pool, good service. Highly recommended. Hourly bus service from Salta terminal, *Empresa Chávez*, platform 15, 30 mins, US$0.30. Last bus back about 2330. **B** *Finca Los Los*, 40km from Salta at the entrance to the Valles Calchaquíes, T431 7258, www.redsalta.com/loslos Open Mar to Dec. Fabulous hilltop views, charming rooms, beautiful gardens, pool, unforgettable horse riding to *asados* in the forested mountains. Handy for the airport and Cachi. Highly recommended. **A** *Finca San Antonio*, Route 68 Km146, El Carril, T/F0387-490 2457, rcornejo@salnet.com.ar 17th- century farm, pool, horse riding, farming activities. **A** pp *Finca El Manantial*, 25 km from Salta, T439 5506 or T156-858480, elmanantial@arnet.com.ar Formal style, beautiful views, lovely rooms, marvellous food, swimming, farming activities. **C** *Hostería de Chicoana*, in Chicoana, 47 km south, T490 7009, martinpek@salnet.com.ar Bohemian colonial style, English and German spoken, adventure excursions and horses for hire. Recommended. **Camping** See Campo Quijano, under **Salta to Chile**, below. **Camping shops** *HR Maluf*, San Martín y Buenos Aires, and one at La Rioja 995. Also *Canigó*, Caseros 727 and *Status*, Zuviría 201.

Among Salta's most desirable places to stay are its colonial-style estancias, known locally as fincas

Mid-range/cheap: *El Solar del Convento*, Caseros 444, half a block from plaza. Elegant and not expensive, champagne when you arrive, delicious steaks. Recommended. *La Terraza de la Posta*, España 456. Huge menu, but great for steak and *empanadas*. Cheap menus. Recommended. *La Casa de Güemes*, España 730. Popular, local dishes and *parrilla*, traditionally cooked in the house where Güemes lived. *El Corredor de las Empanadas*, Caseros 117. Delicious *empanadas* and tasty local dishes in airy surroundings. *Doña Salta*, Córdoba 46 (opposite San Francisco church). Excellent regional dishes and atmosphere, good value. *Don José*, Urquiza 484. Good *parrilla*. *Sociedad Española*, Balcarce 653. Excellent. *La Cocina del Pirata*, Balcarce, serves delicious regional food. *Café del Paseo* at *Hotel Colonial*, Zuviría 6. Open 24 hrs, superb breakfast, good value. *Plaza Café* next to *Hotel Salta* is more popular with Salteños, good for coffee or breakfast. **Seriously cheap**: The **Mercado Municipal** at San Martín y Florida is unbeatable and atmospheric. Lots of good places around the Plaza 9 de Julio for *empanadas*.

Eating
● *on map*
Salta has delicious and distinctive cuisine: try the Locro, Humitas and Tamales

Music Many bars, called *peñas*, with excellent live bands on Balcarce towards railway station. *Balderrama* is much touted but touristy. Head instead for *La Vieja Estación*, Balcarce 885, T421 7727. Great atmosphere, good food. *La Casona del Molino*, Caseros 2600, T155-015934. Most authentic, in a crumbling old colonial house, good food and drink. *Gauchos de Güemes*, Uruguay 750, T492 1621, popular, delicious regional food.

Entertainment
Visit a peña to hear Salta's passionate folklore music live

15 Sep, *Cristo del Milagro* (see above); **24 Sep**, *Battles of Tucumán and Salta*. On **16-17 Jun**, folk music in evening and *gaucho* parade in morning around the Güemes statue. Salta celebrates *Carnival* with processions on the **4 weekends before Ash Wednesday** at 2200 in Ciudad de Salta Stadium, 4 km south of town (US$0.50); also *Mardi Gras* (**Shrove Tuesday**) with a procession of decorated floats and dancers with intricate masks of feathers and mirrors. Water is squirted at passers-by and *bombas de agua* (small balloons to be filled with water) are sold for dropping from balconies.

Local festivals

Mercado Municipal, San Martín y Florida, for meat, fish, vegetables, *empanadas*, *humitas* and other produce and handicrafts, closed 1300-1700 and Sun. *Mercado Artesanal* on the western outskirts, at San Martín 2555, T434 2808, daily 0900-2100, take bus 2, 3, or 7 from Av San Martín in centre and get off as bus crosses the railway line. Excellent range and high quality. *Siwok Crafts*, Zuviría 30. Quality wood carvings by the Wichi indigenous people, and typical *yika* woven bags. Leather boots are made at *Torcivia*, Vicente López 1046. *Feria del Libro*, Buenos Aires 83. *Librería Rayuela*, Alvarado 570. Foreign-language books. *Plural Libros*, Buenos Aires 220. Helpful. Good supermarkets: *Disco*, Florida y Caseros and Mitre y Leguizamon; *Norte*, 20 de Febrero y Caseros. 24-hr pharmacy, *San Francisco*, Deán Funes 596, T421 2984.

Shopping
Arts and handicrafts are often cheaper in surrounding villages

Argentina

Tour operators

Out of season, tours often run only if there is sufficient demand; check carefully that tour will run on the day you want

All agencies charge similar prices for tours (though some charge extra for credit card payments): Salta city US$10; Quebrada del Toro US$30; Cachi US$25; Humahuaca US$30; San Antonio de las Cobres US$30; Cafayate (1 day) US$25; 2-day tour to Cafayate, Angastaco, Molinos, Cachi, US$45. *Andino Travesías*, España 202, p 2, T422 5333, www.andinosalta.com Adventurous trips combining horses, bikes and trekking. *Bici tours*, T4394887, 156838067. Biker_s_2000@yaho.com Specialists in cycle tours. *Hernán Uriburu*, Leguizamon 446, T431 0605, www.nortetrekking.com/hru.htm Well known and highly regarded for his horse- or mule-riding expeditions to the mountains, sleeping at locals' houses, highly professional. *Movitrack*, Buenos Aires 28, T431 6749, www.movitrack.com.ar The great alternative to Tren a las Nubes: entertaining safaris in a 4WD truck, to San Antonio de los Cobres, Humahuaca, Cafayate and Iruya, also over Paso de Sico to Chile, German, English spoken, very professional. Recommended. *Norte Trekking*, Av del Libertador 1151, Barrio Grand Bourg, T436 1844, www.nortetrekking.com Excellent tours all over Salta and Jujuy, to Iruya, over Jama Pass to San Pedro de Atacama, hiking, horse riding, excursions to El Rey national park with experienced guide Federico Norte, knowledgeable, speaks English. Tailors tours to your interest and budget. Highly recommended. *Puna Expediciones*, Agustín Usandivaras 230, T434 1875 or T154-030263, www.punaexpeditions.com Well qualified and experienced guide Luis H Aguilar organizes treks in remote areas of Salta and Jujuy. Highly recommended. *Ricardo Clark Expeditions*, Caseros 121, T/F421 5390, www.clarkexpediciones.com Specialist tours for bird watchers, English spoken. *Saltur*, Caseros 485, T421 2012, F432 1111, saltursalta@arnet.com.ar 4WD expeditions to national parks, Calchaquí valley, horsriding. *Turismo del Altiplano*, Buenos Aires 68, T422 2394, laltiplano@hotmail.com Conventional and adventure tourism, English spoken. *Turismo San Lorenzo*, Dávalos 960, San Lorenzo. T492 1757, www.1 turismosanlorenzo.com For horse riding and adventure tourism, well run. *La Veloz Turismo*, Buenos Aires 44, T401 2000, www.lavelozturismo.com Tren a las Nubes. English spoken.

Transport

Local Car hire: *Avis*, at the airport, Ruta 51, T424 2289, salta@avis.com.ar Efficient and very helpful, recommended. *Europe Rent A Car*, Buenos Aires 186, T422 3609. *Ruiz Moreno*, Buenos Aires 1, T431 8049, in *Hotel Salta*, helpful. *Semisa Renta Truck 4x4*, Buenos Aires 1, Local 6, T423 6295, febearzi@salnet.com.ar *Integral*, Buenos Aires 189, T155-016451.

Long distance Air: *LAB* to Santa Cruz (Bolivia). *AR* flies to Bs As (2 hrs). *AR, LAB* to Córdoba. Bus 22 to access to airport from San Martín, US$0.35; don't be fooled by taxi touts who tell you there is no bus. Taxi from airport to bus station US$4.

Buses: Terminal (being rebuilt, 2003) is 8 blocks east of the main plaza, T401 1143 for information. Toilets, *locutorio*, café, *panadería*, kiosks. To **Buenos Aires**, several daily, US$30 *semicama*, 20-22 hrs (*TAC* - T431 6600), *Panamericano, Brown, Chevallier* - T431 2819, *La Internacional* and others). To **Córdoba**, several daily, 12 hrs, US$12-14, *Panamericano* (T401 1118), twice daily, *Veloz del Norte*. To **Santiago del Estero**, 6 hrs, US$11. To **Tucumán**, 4½ hrs, several firms (*La Veloz del Norte* recommended), US$7. To **Mendoza** via Tucumán, several companies, daily, US$25 17-20 hrs. To **Jujuy**, *Balut* , *La Veloz del Norte*, *Atahualpa* and others, hourly between 0600 and 2200, 'directo', US$2.50, 2 hrs. To **La Rioja**, US$11, 10 hrs. To **Puerto Iguazú**, US$35 , 24 hrs, daily. To **Cafayate**, US$6, 3½ hrs, 2-4 daily, to **Santa María**, US$13, daily, to **Angastaco**, twice a week, US$10, (*Marcos Rueda*, T421 4447), to **Belén**, weekly (*El Indio*, T431 9389*)*. To **Cachi**, daily, 4 hrs, US$6, to **Molinos**, 4 a week, US$9 and to **La Poma**, US$8, 6½ hrs, 3 weekly, *Marcos Rueda*. To **Rosario de la Frontera**, US$2.50, 2½ hrs. To **San Antonio de Los Cobres**, 5 hrs, *El Quebradeño*, daily, US$5.50.

International: To Paraguay: *La Nueva Estrella*, T422 4048, runs 3 services weekly to Clorinda (at the border), US$29, 17 hrs; buses or taxis will take you from there to Paraguay for a small fee. Alternatively travel to **Resistencia**, daily, US$18 with *La Veloz del Norte, Flecha Bus, La Nueva Estrella, Autotransportes Mendoza* or to **Formosa**, with *La Nueva Estrella*, US$25, 15 hrs, changing then, to a direct bus to Asunción. For description of border, see page . To **Chile**: Services to **Calama, San Pedro de Atacama, Antofagasta, Iquique** and **Arica** with *Géminis*, via Jujuy and the Jama Pass, twice a week, US$35 to **San Pedro** and **Calama**, US$43, 18 hrs to Antofagasta. Tour operators charge US$50 to San Pedro. To **Bolivia**: To **La Quiaca**, on Bolivian border, *Balut* and others, 7 hrs, US$7-10. To **Orán**, daily, 6 hrs, US$6, and **Aguas**

Cloud line

One of the great railway journeys of South America is the Tren a las Nubes (Train to the Clouds). Engineered by Richard Maury, of Pennsylvania (who is commemorated by the station at Km 78 which bears his name) this remarkable project was built in stages between 1921 and 1948, by which time developments in road and air transport had already reduced its importance. The line includes 21 tunnels, 13 viaducts, 31 bridges, 2 loops and 2 zig-zags. From Salta the line climbs gently to Campo Quijano (Km 40, 1,520 m), where it enters the Quebrada del Toro, an impressive rock-strewn gorge. At El Alisal (Km 50) and Chorrillos (Km 66) there are zig-zags as the line climbs the side of the gorge before turning north into the valley of the Río Rosario near Puerto Tastil (Km 101, 2,675 m), missing the archaeological areas around Santa Rosa de Tastil. At Km 122 and Km 129 the line goes into 360° loops before reaching Diego de Almagro (3,304 m). At Abra Muñano (3,952 m) the road to San Antonio can be seen zig-zagging its way up the end-wall of the Quebrada del Toro below. From Muñano (3,936 m) the line drops slightly to San Antonio, Km 196. The spectacular viaduct at La Polvorilla is 21 km further at 4,190 m, just beyond the branch line to the mines at La Concordia. The highest point on the line is reached at Abra Chorrillos (4,475 m, Km 231). From here the line runs on another 335 km across a rocky barren plateau 3,500-4,300 m above sea level before reaching Socompa (3,865 m).

Argentina

Blancas with **Balut** and **La Veloz del Norte**, US$8, daily for Bermejo, Bolivia; thence road connection to **Tarija**. To **Yacuiba**, via **Pocitos** (Bolivian border, see page 152), for **Santa Cruz**, US$7-12 with several companies to **Pocitos**, 7-10 hrs, very full, road paved.

Trains Station at 20 de February y Ameghino, 9 blocks north of Plaza 9 de Julio, taxi US$1.

Airline offices *AR*, Caseros 475, T431 1331/0862. *Southern Winds*, Caseros 434, T422 5555. **Banks** Banks, open 0730-1300, all have ATMs (many on España). *Banco de la Nación*, Mitre y Belgrano. *Banco de Salta*, España 550 on main plaza. Cashes TCs. *Amex, Chicoana Turismo*, Zuviría 255, changes TCs. *Dinar*, Mitre 101/109. **Communications** Internet: Many fast and cheap places. *Intercafé*, Alvarado 537. *Cibercom*, Buenos Aires 97. **Post Office:** Deán Funes 160, between España and Belgrano. **Telephone:** Several *locutorios* in town, some offer internet access. **Cultural centres** Alliance Française, Santa Fe 20, T421 0827. **Embassies and Consulates** Bolivia, Mariano Boedo 34, T421 1040, open Mon-Fri, 0900-1400 (unhelpful, better to go to Jujuy). Chile, Santiago del Estero 965, T431 1857. Spain, República de Israel 137, T431 2296, F431 0206. Italy, Santiago del Estero 497, T432 1532. France, Santa Fe 156, T431 2403. Germany, Urquiza 409, T421 6525, F431 1772, consul Juan C Kühl, helpful. **Immigration**: Maipú 35, 0730-1230.

Directory

From Salta to Chile

The famous **Tren a las Nubes** is a 900 km, narrow gauge railway running from Salta through the town of San Antonio de los Cobres to Antofagasta, in northern Chile. San Antonio can also be reached by Ruta 51 from Salta, which is being upgraded. At Campo Quijano: **C** *Hostería Punta Callejas*, T0387-490 4086, with bath, comfortable, a/c, pool, tennis, riding, excursions; **D** *Hostería Finca Río Blanco*, T0387-431 4314; *Municipal Campsite*, at the entrance to Quebrada del Toro gorge, lovely spot with good facilities, hot showers, bungalows. From here the road runs along the floor of the Quebrada del Toro before climbing to Alto Blanco (paved section).

Sitting in the vast emptiness of the puna, San Antonio de los Cobres is a simple, remote mining town of adobe houses with a friendly Coya community. Ruta 51 leads to La Polvorilla railway viaduct (see below), 20 km, ask in town for details and beware sudden changes in the weather. At **Santa Rosa de Tastil** there are important prehispanic ruins and a small museum (US$0.30), recommended. Basic accommodation next door to the museum, no electricity or heating, take food, water and candles. Take El Quebradeño bus (see below), a tour from Salta, or share a taxi.

San Antonio de los Cobres
Phone code: 0387
Population: 4,000
Altitude: 3,775 m
196 km by rail
163 km by road
from Salta

C *Hostería de las Nubes*, edge of San Antonio on Salta road (T0387-490 9059), includes breakfast, comfortable, modern and spacious, recommended. **E** *Hospedaje Belgrano*, T4.90 9025, welcoming, hot showers unreliable, evening meals.

F pp *Hostería Inti Huasi*, opposite the Aduana, T490 9041, restaurant. Try the *quesillo de cabra* (goat's cheese) from Estancia Las Cuevas. Good restaurant, *Huaira Huasi*, used by tour groups, good menu.

On all train journeys on this line beware of altitude sickness: do not eat or drink to excess

Transport   The Tren a las Nubes (Train to the Clouds) runs between Salta and La Polvorilla viaduct (400 km round trip). The service operates from Apr to Nov, weather permitting, several times each month with most in the high season (Jul-Sep), depart 0700, return to Salta by 2200, US$70, meals US$8, credit cards not accepted. The train is well-equipped with oxygen facilities and medical staff as well as a restaurant car and snack bar. There is almost constant commentary and entertainment, and English translation can be provided. This service is operated privately and can only be booked in advance through certain travel agents, such as *La Veloz Turismo* or *TEA*, in **Salta**; in Buenos Aires, *La Veloz Turismo*, Esmeralda 320 4th floor, T4326 0126, F4326 0852, trenubes@arnet.com.ar, or *Dinar*, Av Roque Sáenz Peña 933, T4327 8000, F4326 0134, www.trenubes.com.ar **To Socompa** (Chilean border): a cargo train with 2 passenger carriages leaves Salta Wed about 0900 (in theory), ticket office opens 0800 (queue from 0600), US$5 one way to San Antonio, US$8 one way to Socompa, 27 hrs one way via San Antonio (14 hrs). There is a dining car and a bar. Long delays are common on this route and you may do most of the journey in the dark. Take water and warm clothing. Beyond Socompa there are irregular freight trains into Chile (Augusta Victoria, Baquedano or Antofagasta): officially the Chilean railway authorities do not permit passengers to travel on this line, and it's hard to get information about departures. To travel on by train or truck may involve a wait of several days. There are only 4 buildings in Socompa: no food or accommodation, but try the Chilean customs building. **Buses** From San Antonio de los Cobres to Salta, *El Quebradeño*, Mon-Sat 0900, Sun 1000, 5 hrs, US$5.50; stops at Santa Rosa de Tastil (book at *Telefónica* office).

Because of snowfalls, this route may be closed 2-3 times a year, for two or three days each time

Ruta 51 from San Antonio de los Cobres to **San Pedro de Atacama**, Chile uses the **Sico** Pass (4,079 m). It's a spectacular route, crossing white salt lakes dotted with flamingoes and vast expanses of desert. It is more popular with heavy traffic than private vehicles; some 60% of it is unpaved to the border. There is a customs post at Paso Sico (you may be allowed to spend the night here), hours 0900-1900: check first in San Antonio de los Cobres if it is open. Police in San Antonio may be able to advise about road conditions but truck drivers using the route are more reliable. The road on the Argentine side is very good (police checkpoint beyond Catúa). On the Chilean side continue via Mina Laco and Socaire to Toconao (road may be bad between these two points). Customs and immigration are in San Pedro de Atacama. Note that fruit, vegetables and dairy products may not be taken into Chile (search 20 km after Paso Sico). Gasoline is available in San Pedro and Calama. Obtain sufficient drinking water for the trip in San Antonio and do not underestimate the effects of altitude.

Jujuy

Phone code: 0388
Colour map 6, grid C4
Population: 237,000
Altitude: 1,260 m

San Salvador de Jujuy (pronounced Choo-Chooey, with *ch* as in Scottish loch) often referred to by locals as San Salvador, is the capital of Jujuy province and sits in a bowl of lushly wooded mountains. The city was finally established in 1593, after earlier attempts met resistance from local indigenous groups, but the city was plagued by earthquakes, sacking and the Calchaquíes Wars for the next 200 years. It struggled to prosper, then in August 1812 Gen Belgrano, commanding the republican troops, ordered the city to be evacuated and destroyed before the advancing Spanish army. This extraordinary sacrifice is marked on 23-24 August by festivities known as El Exodo Jujeño with gaucho processions and military parades. Though it lacks Salta's elegance, since there are few colonial buildings remaining, it is the starting point for some of the country's most spectacular scenery and its distinctly Andean culture is evident in its food and music.

Away from the busy shopping streets, in the eastern part of the city, is the **Plaza Belgrano**, a wide square planted with tall palms and orange trees. It's lined with impressive buildings, including the elaborate French baroque-style **Casa de Gobierno**, containing the famous flag Belgrano presented to the city. ■ *Daily 0900-2100.* On the west side is the late 19th-century **Cathedral** (the original, 1598-1653, was destroyed by earthquake in 1843) containing one of Argentina's finest colonial treasures: a gold-plated wooden pulpit, carved by Indians in the Jesuit missions, depicting gilded angels mounting the stairs. The modern church of **San Francisco**, Belgrano y Lavalle, contains another fine gilded colonial pulpit, with ceramic angels around it, like that at Yavi. The **Museo Histórico Franciscano**, at the church, includes 17th-century paintings and other artefacts from Cuzco. ■ *Daily 0900-1300, 1600-2100.* There are several other museums, but most worth seeing is the **Museo Arqueológico Provincial**, Lavalle 434, with beautiful ceramics from the Yavi and Humahuaca cultures, haphazardly displayed, a mummified infant, and a 2500-year old sculpture of a goddess giving birth. ■ *Daily 0900-1200, 1500-2100.*

There are hot springs 19 km west at **Termas de Reyes**. This resort (*Hotel Termas de Reyes*, T0388-492 2522, info@termasdereyes.com.ar) is set among magnificent mountains, one hour by bus *Empresa 19 de Abril (línea 14)* from bus terminal, hourly, US$0.50. Municipal baths US$0.50 and pool US$1; also cabins with thermal water.

B *Jujuy Palace*, Belgrano 1060, T/F423 0433, jpalace@imagine.com.ar Conference hotel, well-equipped bedrooms, restaurant has a good reputation. **C** *Panorama*, Belgrano 1295, T423 2533, hotelpanorama@mail.com.ar Another business hotel, but more appealing, better value with stylish rooms. **D** *Fenicia*, 19 de Abril 427, T/F423 1800. A welcoming place, 1980's chic, spacious rooms (ask for the ones with swish bathrooms), some with great views. Recommended. **D** *Internacional*, Belgrano 501 (Plaza Belgrano), T423 1599, interjujuy@imagine.com.ar On north west corner of the Plaza, quiet, smart, good value. Great views over city. Recommended. **D** *Sumay*, Otero 232, T423 5065. Rather dark, but clean, very central, helpful staff. **E** *Huaico*, Av Bolivia 3901, T423 5186, hotelhuaicojujuy@hotmail.com 1½ km from the centre, near the park, useful if you're heading north, with special rates for students. **Near the bus terminal:** there are a number of cheap places, of which the following are safe and comfortable: **E** *Res San Carlos*, República de Siria 459, T422 2286. Shared bath, no TV, but nicely maintained. **E** *Rany's*, Dorrego 327, T423 0042, right next door. Cheaper rooms without TV, pretty basic, but the lady owner is very kind, no breakfast, but loads of cafés around. **F** *San Antonio*, Lisandro de la Torre T422 5998, opposite terminal. Basic, but recently painted, looked after by three sisters and the whole family is kind. Recommended.

Outside the city A-B *Hostería Posta de Lozano*, Ruta 9, Km 18 north, T498 0050, posta@imagine.com.ar Good restaurant, pools with fresh mountain water. Closer to Jujuy, *Finca Don Gustavo*, RN9 Km 7 Los Alisos, T424 0784, www.dongustavo.jujuy.com Rustic accommodation, regional cooking, ranch life.

Camping *El Refugio* is closest, at Yala, Km 14 (see Excursions, above).

Sleeping
Breakfast is included unless stated otherwise

Cheap: *Manos Jujeños*, Sen Pérez 222. For regional specialities, the best *humitas*, charming, recommended for the *folclore* music at weekends. *Ruta 9*, Lavalle 287. Another great place, slightly cheaper, for *locro* and *tamales*. Following Lavalle across the bridge to the bus terminal (where it becomes Dorrego) there are lots of cheap *empanada* places. *Chung King* (where the accommodation upstairs can't be recommended), Alvear 627, is an atmospheric place for regional food. Sister restaurant next door, for '50 kinds of pizza'. Two recommended *parrillas*: *Krysys*, Balcarce 272, popular bistro-style, excellent steaks. *La Candelaria* Alvear 1346, a little further out of town. Good service. For **vegetarians** (or for a break from all the meat), *Madre Tierra*, Belgrano 619, behind the wholemeal bakery of same name. Delicious food (open 0700-1430, 1600-2130). Several good **cafés**, all on the same block of Belgrano between Lavalle and Necochea. *Pingüino* is the best *heladería* in town. *Confitería La Royal* Belgrano 770. A classic café, coffee and pastries. Opposite is *Color Esperanza*. A bright new café serving cheap *lomitos* and hamburgers. *Tía Bigote*, Pérez y Belgrano. Popular café and pizzería. *Sociedad Española*, opposite on the same corner. Serves good cheap set menus with a Spanish flavour.

Eating

Shopping **Handicrafts**: stalls near the cathedral and from the rather limited *Paseo de las Artesanías* on the west side of the plaza. Also *Centro de Arte y Artesanías*, Balcarce 427. **Maps and travel guides**:*Librería Rayuela*, Belgrano 636. *Librería Belgrano*, Belgrano 602. English language magazines and some books. **Markets**: For food, you can't beat the Municipal market at Dorrego y Alem, near the bus terminal. Outside, women sell home-baked *empanadas* and *tamales*, and delicious goat's cheese, and all kinds of herbal cures. **Supermarkets**: *Norte*, Belgrano 825 and a bigger branch at 19 de Abril y Necochea.

Tour operators *De Bor Turismo*, Lavalle 295, T402 0241. 10% discount for ISIC and youth card holders on local excursions. *Horus Turismo*, Belgrano 722, T422 7247, horus@imgine.com.ar *NASA*, Senador Pérez 154, T422 3938. Guided tour to Quebrada de Humahuaca (US$30 pp, min 4 people); 4WD for rent. For information on bird watching, contact Mario Daniel Cheronaza, Peatonal 38, No 848-830, Viviendas 'El Arenal', Jujuy.

Transport

Airport at El Cadillal, 32 km SE
Bus terminal at Iguazú y Dorrego, 6 blocks S of centre, Information T4222134

Air Airport T491 1101. Minibus to town US$2.50; taxi, US$13. Flights to **Buenos Aires**, **Córdoba**, **Tucumán** and **Salta** with *AR*, T423 7100. **Buses** To **Buenos Aires**, 20-24 hrs, US$22 *semi cama*, several daily with *TAC, La Estrella, Panamericano*, and others. Via Tucumán to Córdoba, *Panamericano* and *La Veloz del Norte*, daily to **Tucumán**, 5 hrs, US$7, and **Córdoba**, 14 hrs US$15. To **Salta** hourly, 2 hrs, US$2.50. To **La Quiaca**, 4-6 hrs, US$6, *Panamericano*, *Balut*, *El Quiaqueño*. Several rigorous luggage checks en route for drugs, including coca leaves. To **Humahuaca**, *Evelia* and others, US$2, 3 hrs, several daily, via **Tilcara** 2 hrs, US$2.50. To **Orán** and **Aguas Blancas** (border with Bolivia), daily with *Balut* and *Brown*, via San Pedro and Ledesma. To **Purmamarca**, take buses to Susques or to Humahuaca (those calling at Purmamarca village). To **Susques**, *Purmamarca* and *Andes Bus*, US$ 5, 4-6½ hrs, daily (except Mon). To **Calilegua**: various companies to Libertador Gral San Martín almost every hour, eg *Balut*, from there take a minibus, or taxi for US$1.50. All Pocitos buses pass through Libertador San Martín, eg *Panamericano, Estrella, El Rápido*.

To Chile: via the **Jama** pass (4,200 m), the route taken by most traffic, including trucks, crossing to northern Chile; hours 0900-1900. In this region, the only accommodation is at **Susques**: E pp *Hostal Las Vicuñitas*, T02887-490207, opposite the outstanding church, without bath, hot water, breakfast, 105 km north of San Antonio de los Cobres on a road through utter desert. *Géminis* bus tickets sold at *Ortiz Viajes*, L N Alem 917, ortizviajes@latinmail.com

Directory **Banks** ATMs at: *Banco de Jujuy*, Balcarce y Belgrano, changes dollars. TCs can be changed at tour operators, *De Bor* and *Horus*, addresses above. *Citibank*, Güemes y Balcarce; *Bank Boston*, Alvear 802, *Banco Francés*, Alvear y Lamadrid; *Banco Salta*, San Martín 785.. **Communications** Internet: *Cyber Explora*, Güemes 1049; *Ciber Nob*, Otero 317; *HVA*, Lavalle 390 (all US$0.50 per hour). *Telecom* centres at Alvear 870, Belgrano 730 and elsewhere. **Post Office:** at Independencia and Lamadrid. **Consulates:** Bolivia, Senador Pérez e Independencia, T424 0501, 0900-1300. **Tourist office**: on the plaza at Gorriti y Belgrano. Open Mon-Fri 0700-2100, Sat-Sun 0800-1400, 1500-2100, accommodation leaflet and map. Also at bus terminal 0700-2100. www.jujuy.gov.ar **Useful addresses**: Immigration: 19 de Abril 1057, T422 2638.

North from Jujuy to La Quiaca

For drivers heading off main roads in this area, note that service stations are far apart: at Jujuy, Tilcara, Humahuaca, Abra Pampa and La Quiaca Spare fuel and water must be carried

Ruta 9, the Pan-American Highway, runs through the beautiful **Quebrada de Humahuaca**, a vast gorge of vividly coloured rock, with giant cacti in the higher parts, and emerald green oasis villages on the river below. (January-March ask highway police about flooding on the roads.) The whole area is very rich culturally: there area pre-Inca ruins at Tilcara, and throughout the Quebrada there are fine 16th-century churches and riotous pre-Lent carnival celebrations. In Tilcara, pictures of the Passion are made of flowers and seeds at Easter and a traditional procession on Holy Thursday at night is joined by thousands of pan-pipe musicians.

Beyond Tumbaya, where there's a restored 17th-century chuch, a road runs 3 km west to **Purmamarca**, a quiet, picturesque village, much visited for its spectacular mountain of seven colours, striped strata from terracotta to green (best seen in the morning), a lovely church with remarkable paintings and a good handicrafts market.

Sleeping A *El Manantial del Silencio*, Route 52 Km 3.5, T0388-490 8080, elsilencio@cootepal.com.ar Signposted from the road into Purmamarca. Luxurious rooms, wonderful views, and charming bilingual hosts, riding, pool. **D** *La Posta*, T/F490 8040. Beautiful elevated setting against the mountain, 4 blocks up from the plaza, comfortable rooms with triple single beds only. Its restaurant on the plaza serves delicious local dishes. Both highly recommended. **E** *El Viejo Algarrobo*, also known as *Hospedaje Bebo Vilte*, T/F490 8038, just behind the church. Small but pleasant rooms, cooking facilities, camping in garden. Recommended. More accommodation, maps and bus tickets from the tiny, helpful tourist office on the plaza. (Buses to Susques, 5 weekly, and to Humahuaca, several daily.)

It's worth staying the night in Purmamarca to appreciate the town's quiet rhythm

From Purmamarca a *ripio* road leads through another *quebrada* over the 4,164 m Abra Potrerillos to the **Salinas Grandes** salt flats at about 3,400 m on the Altiplano (fantastic views especially at sunset). From here roads lead southwest past spectacular rock formations along the east side of the salt flats to San Antonio de los Cobres, and west across the salt flats via Susques to the Paso de Jama and Chile. About 7 km north of the Purmamarca turning is **La Posta de Hornillos**, a museum in a restored colonial posting house where Belgrano stayed, also the scene of several battles. ■ *Open, in theory, Wed-Mon 0900-1800, free.* About 2 km further is **Maimará** with its brightly striped rock, known as the 'Artist's Palette', and huge cemetery, decorated with flowers at Easter. (**C** *Posta del Sol*, Martín Rodríguez y San Martín, T499 7156, posta_del_sol@hotmail.com Comfortable, with restaurant, owner is tourist guide and has helpful information.)

Tilcara lies 22 km north of Purmamarca. It's the liveliest Quebrada village, the best base for exploring the area. It has an excellent handicrafts market around its pleasant plaza and plenty of places to stay and to eat. Visit the Pucará, a restored prehispanic hilltop settlement, with panoramic views of the gorge, and the superb **Museo Arqueológico**, with a fine collection of pre-Columbian ceramics, masks and mummies. ■ *Daily 0900-1230, 1400-1800, US$1 for both.* There are four art museums in town and good walks in all directions. Recommended guide for informative trips to the puna, Iruya, Salinas Grandes and archaeological sites, is historian Ariel Mosca, T495 5119, arielpuna@hotmail.com English spoken. There are fiestas at weekends in January, carnival and Holy Week. The tiny **tourist office** is on Belgrano, next to *Hotel de Turismo.* ■ *Open daily 0900-1200, 1500-2100 (closed Sun afternoon). No phone. www.tilcarajujuy.com* There's an ATM on the plaza, taking most international cards.

Tilcara
Phone code: 0388
Colour map 6, grid C3
Population: 3,500
Altitude: 2,460 m

Sleeping C *Posada con los Angeles*, Gorriti s/n (signposted from plaza), T495 5153, www.tilcarajujuy.com.ar/posadaconlosangeles Charming individually designed rooms, garden with views of mountains, relaxed atmosphere, excursions organized. Recommended. **C** *Villar del Ala*, Padilla 100, T495 5100, adriantilcara@hotmail.com Very comfortable 1930's rooms, quiet garden with great views, pool, good food. **D** *Los Establos*, Gorrito s/n (next to *con los Angeles*), T495 5379. Pretty, rustic rooms and well equipped *cabañas* for 2-6 people. **D** *Malka*, San Martín s/n, 5 blocks from plaza up steep hill, T495 5197, www.tilcarajujuy.com.ar/malka Beautifully located *cabañas*, and an outstanding hostel, **F** pp, very comfortable rustic dorms, all with kitchen and laundry facilities, HI affiliated. Owner and guide Juan organizes a great range of trips, including several days' trek to Calilegua, horse riding and bike hire. Highly recommended. **D** *Quinta La Paceña*, Padilla y Ambosetti, T495 5098, quintalapacena@yahoo.com.ar Peaceful, architect-designed traditional adobe house, with stylish rooms for 2-4, gorgeous. **F** pp *La Morada*, Debenedetti s/n, T/F495 5118. Good rooms for 2 to 5 people with cooking facilities. **F** pp *Wiphala*, Jujuy 549, T495 5015, www.wiphala.com.ar Small, warm atmosphere, kitchen. **Camping** *Camping El Jardín*, access on Belgrano, T495 5128, US$2, hot showers, also **F** pp basic hostel accommodation. At **Huacalera**, Km 90, is **D** *Hostal La Granja*, T0388-426 1766, a lovely rustic place with pool, outstanding food and service, a good base for exploring the region. At **Uquía** is a fine church with extraordinary Cuzqueño paintings of angels in 17th-century battle dress. Comfortable **C** *Hostería de Uquía* next door, T03387-490523, also dinner.

Book ahead in carnival and around Easter when Tilcara is very busy

Eating: *Bar del Centro* Belgrano 547. Best in town, delicious inexpensive local dishes, and often live music too, in a beautiful interior. 3 course dinner US$3. Recommended. *El Patio Comidas* Lavalle 352. Great range, lovely patio at the back. *Pachamama*, Belgrano 590, next to *Hotel de Turismo* on the road into Tilcara. Pleasant, airy restuarant and cafe serving regional dishes, plus salads and pastas, reliable, popular with groups. Also lots of cheap places on the Plaza: *El Rincón del Indio Chanampa*, a more basic joint serving *sandwiches de parrilla*, good snacks, live music at weekends. For a taste of Tilcara's culture, don't miss: *El Cafecito* on the plaza. Good coffee and locally-grown herbal teas, live music at weekends from celebrated local musicians. *La Peña de Carlitos*, with music from the charismatic and delightful Carlitos, also *empanadas*, and drinks.

Argentina

Humahuaca

Phone code: 03887
Colour map 6, grid B3
Population: 8,700
Altitude: 2,940 m
129 km N of Jujuy

Although Humahuaca dates from 1594, it was almost entirely rebuilt in the mid-19th century. Now it is visited by daily coach trips. It still has a distinctive culture of its own, though, and is a useful stopping point for travelling north up to the puna, or to Iruya. On 2 February is *La Candelaria* festival. *Jueves de Comadres, Festival de las Coplas y de la Chicha*, at the beginning of carnival is famously lively. Book accommodation ahead. **Tourist information** available from the town hall, office hours. ATM at *Banco de Jujuy* on main plaza, all major credit cards. On the little plaza is the church, **La Candelaria**, originally of 1631, rebuilt 1873-80, containing gaudy gold retables and 12 fine Cuzqueño paintings. Also on the plaza, tourists gather to watch a mechanical figure of San Francisco Solano blessing the town from **El Cabildo**, the neo-colonial town hall, at 1200 daily. Overlooking the town is the massive **Monumento a la Independencia Argentina**, commemorating the heaviest fighting in the country during the Wars of Independence. At **Coctaca**, 10 km northeast, there is an impressive and extensive (40 ha) series of pre-colonial agricultural terraces. To Iruya (see below).

Accommodation is generally basic. Most restaurants open only during the day, but hunt around at night for small cafés where locals eat

Sleeping and Eating C *Camino del Inca*, on the other side of the river, T421136, tito@imagine.com.ar Smart, well built modern place with restaurant (set menu US$4), pool, excursions. Two very simple *residenciales*: **D** *Res Humahuaca*, Córdoba y Corrientes, T421141, 1 block from bus terminal. **E** *Res Colonial*, Entre Ríos 110, T421007. **F** pp *Cabaña El Cardón*, T156-29072, www.elcardon.8K.com Rural *cabaña* for 2-5 with all facilities, also regional foods, excursions and riding, charming family. **F** pp *Posada El Sol*, over bridge from terminal, then 520 m, follow signs, T421466, elsolposada@imagine.com.ar Quiet rural area, rooms for 2-4 in a warm welcoming place, kitchen, also laundry, horse riding, owner will collect from bus station if called in advance. **F** pp *Res El Portillo*, Tucumán 69, T421288, www.epassaporte.com Cramped dormitories and **E** rooms, shared bath, simple bar/restaurant. **Camping** Across bridge by railway station, small charge for use of facilities.

Eating *La Cacharpaya*, Jujuy 295. Good and lively, often filled with parties at lunch time, Andean music. Recommended. *Humahuaca Colonial*, Tucumán 16. Good cheap regional cooking, again, coach parties at midday. *El Rancho*, Belgrano 478, just around the corner from market, tasty local dishes and *pastas caseras*, where the locals eat, set menu US$1.50. *El Pinocho*, Buenos Aires 452, clean family restaurant, cheap local dishes, set menu US$1.50. *Peña de Fortunato*, Jujuy y San Luis. Famous for great atmosphere and music.

Transport Buses to all places along the Quebrada from the terminal (toilets, *confitería*, fruit and sandwich sellers outside), to **Iruya** (see below) and to **La Quiaca**, with *Balut* and *La Quiaqueña* (more comfortable), several daily, 3 hrs, US$4. Rigorous police checks for drugs can cause delays on buses to La Quiaca. Keep passport with you.

Iruya

Colour map 6, grid B3
Altitude: 2,600 m
66 km from Humahuaca

A rough *ripio* road 25 km north of Humahuaca runs northeast from the Panamericana (RN9) 8 km to Iturbe (also called Hipólito Irigoyen), and then up over the 4,000 m Abra del Cóndor before dropping steeply, around many hairpin bends, into the Quebrada de Iruya. The road is very rough and unsuited to small hire cars, but is one of Argentina's most amazing drives. Iruya is a beautiful hamlet wedged on a hillside, like a hide-away. Its warm, friendly inhabitants hold a colourful Rosario festival on first Sunday in October and at Easter. It is worth spending a few days here to go horse riding or walking: the hike (7 hours return) to the remote **San Isidro** is unforgettable. At Titiconte 4 km away, there are unrestored pre-Inca ruins (take guide). Iruya has no ATM or tourist information, but one public phone, and food shops.

Sleeping In Iruya: C *Hostería de Iruya*, T03887-156 29152, a special place, extremely comfortable, with good food, and great views from the top of the village. Highly recommended. **E** pp *Hostal Federico Tercero*, at *Café de Hostal*, bottom of the steep main street, T03887-156 30727, owned by the delightful singer Jesús, with simple rooms, good food from breakfast to dinner, and frequent live music. **F** pp *Hosp Tacacho*, on the Plaza. Family welcome, with simple rooms, tremendous views, *comedor*.

Transport Daily bus service from Humahuaca *Empresa Mendoza* (T03887-421016), 1030 daily, 3 hrs, US$3, returning 1515. Also excursions of several days organized by tour operators.

Some 62 km north of Humahuaca on the Panamericana is Tres Cruces, where customs searches are made on vehicles from Bolivia. **Abra Pampa** (*Population*: 6,000), 91 km north of Humahuaca, is a mining town. **F** *Residencial El Norte*, Sarmiento 530, shared room, hot water, good food. *Res y restaurante Cesarito*, one block from main plaza. At 15 km southwest of Abra Pampa is the vicuña farm at **Miraflores**, the largest in Argentina. Information offered, photography permitted; buses go morning Monday-Saturday Abra Pampa-Miraflores.

Tres Cruces & Abra Pampa

Laguna de los Pozuelos (*Altitude*: 3,650 m), 50 km northwest of Abra Pampa, is a nature reserve with, at its centre, a lake visited by huge colonies of flamingoes. Park office in Abra Pampa, T03887-491048. There are no visitor services and no bus transport, so it's best to go with a guide. By car or bike, the Laguna is 5 km from the road; walk last 800 m to reach the edge of the lagoon. Temperatures can drop to −25°C in winter. *Diego Bach* leads excellent, well-informed excursions, including panning for gold as the Jesuits did. Also five-day treks on horseback to the pristine cloudforest of **Parque Nacional El Baritú**. Highly recommended, T03885-422797, punatours@hotmail.com

From a point 4 km north of Abra Pampa roads branch west to Cochinoca (25 km) and southwest to **Casabindo** (62 km). On 15 August at Casabindo, the local saint's day, the last and only *corrida de toros* (running with bulls) in Argentina is held, amidst a colourful popular celebration. *El Toreo de la Vincha* takes place in front of the church, where a bull defies onlookers to take a ribbon and medal which it carries. The church itself is a magnificent building, with twin bell towers, and inside a superb series of 16th century angels in armour paintings. **F** pp *Albergue*, T03887-491129. Buses to Casabindo from Abra Pampa.

Situated on the border with Bolivia, a concrete bridge links this typical border town with Villazón on the Bolivian side. Warm clothing is essential particularly in winter when temperatures can drop to −15°C, though care should be taken against sunburn during the day. On the third Sunday in October, villagers from the far reaches of the remote *altiplano* come to sell ceramic pots, sheepskins and vegetables, in the colourful three-day *Fiesta de la Olla*. Two ATMs, but no facilities for changing TCs. *Farmacia Nueva*, half a block from Church, has remedies for altitude sickness. **Yavi** is 16 km east of La Quiaca. Its church of San Francisco (1690), one of Argentina's treasures, has a magnificent gold retable and pulpit and windows of onyx. Caretaker Lydia lives opposite the police station and will show you round the church. ■ *Tue-Sun 0900-1200 and Tue-Fri 1500-1800*. Opposite the church is the 18th-century house of the Marqués Campero y Tojo, empty, but for a small selection of handicrafts. **C** *Hostal de Yavi*, T03887-490523, elportillo@cootepal.com.ar Simple rooms but cosy sitting room, good food, relaxed atmosphere. **F** *La Casona 'Jatum Huasi'*, Sen Pérez y San Martín, T03885-422316, mccalizaya@laquiaca.com.ar Welcoming. ■ *Bus 4 times a day from La Quiaca, US$0.50. Taxi available – US$9 return, including one hour wait.*

La Quiaca & Yavi
Phone code: 03885
Altitude: 3,442 m
Colour map 6, grid B3
292 km N of Jujuy

Argentina

Sleeping and eating In Yavi: D *Hostería Munay*, Belgrano 51, T423924, www.muna hotel.jujuy.com Very pleasant, with comfortable rooms. D *Turismo*, Siria y San Martín, T422243, intenmun@laquiaca.com.ar The best place to stay: modern, comfortable rooms with TV, pool, restaurant. E pp *La Frontera* hotel and restaurant, Belgrano y Siria, downhill from *Atahualpa* bus stop, T422269. Good cheap food, basic but decent rooms, hospitable owner. F *Cristal*, Sarmiento 539, T422255. Basic functional rooms, shared bath.

Transport Bus terminal, España y Belgrano, luggage storage. 6-8 buses a day to **Salta** (US$7-10) with *Balut* (7½ hrs), *Atahualpa* and others. Several daily to **Humahuaca**, US$4, 3 hrs, and to **Jujuy**, US$6, 5-6½ hrs. Take own food, as sometimes long delays. Buses are stopped for routine border police controls and searched for coca leaves. **NB** Buses from Jujuy may arrive in the early morning when no restaurants are open and it is freezing cold outside.

Border with Bolivia
Argentine time is 1 hr later than Bolivia

The border bridge is 10 blocks from La Quiaca bus terminal, 15 minutes walk (taxi US$1). Argentine office open 0700-2400; on Saturday, Sunday, and holidays there is a special fee of US$1.50 which may or may not be charged. If leaving Argentina for a short stroll into Villazón, show your passport, but do not let it be stamped by Migración, otherwise you will have to wait 24 hours before being allowed back into Argentina. Formalities on entering Argentina are usually very brief at the border but thorough customs searches are made 100 km south at Tres Cruces. Travellers who need a visa to enter Bolivia are advised to get it before arriving in La Quiaca.

Parque Nacional Calilegua
Colour map 6, grid C3
A huge variety of wildlife is protected here, including 260 species of bird and 60 species of mammals you may spot tapirs, pumas, tarucas, Andean deer and even jaguars

Libertador Gen San Martín, a sugar town 113 km northeast of Jujuy on Ruta 34 to southeastern Bolivia, is the closest base for exploring the **Parque Nacional Calilegua**, an area of peaks over 3,000 m and deep valleys covered in cloud forest, reached by Ruta 83 from just north of the town. In El Libertador there are several hotels, from luxurious C *Posada del Sol*, Los Ceibo y Pucará, T03886-424900, posadadelsol@cooperlib.com.ar, with pool, parking and restaurant (in different building), to the basic D *Artaza*, Victoria 891, T03886-423214, with breakfast. There is a tourist office at the bus terminal. There are six marked trails of various lengths. The best trek is to the summit of Cerro Amarillo (3,720 m), five days round trip from Aguas Negras. There are rangers' houses at Aguas Negras (Guillermo Nicolossi), with camping; drinking water from river nearby, and some cooking facilities and tables, and at Mesada de las Colmenas, 13 km further along the trail (Walter Maciel). Best time for visiting is November-March. Park office at San Lorenzo s/n, Calilegua, T03886-422046, pncalilegua@cooperlib.com.ar ■ *The park entrance is 10 km along the dirt road (hitching from Libertador possible), which climbs through the park and beyond to Valle Grande (basic accommodation and food supplies from shops), 90 km from Libertador.*

Transport Two bus companies leave Libertador daily at 0800 (except Wed) going across the park to **Valle Grande** (US$3, 6 hrs), returning the same day. *Remise* charges about US$2 from Libertador to Park entrance.

Routes to Bolivia

From Libertador, Route 34 runs northeast 244 km, to the Bolivian border at Pocitos (also called Salvador Mazza) and Yacuiba (see Eastern Bolivia, page 336). It passes through **Embarcación** and **Tartagal** (good regional museum, director Ramón Ramos very informative). In **Pocitos**, the border town, is F *Hotel Buen Gusto*, just tolerable. There are no *casas de cambio* here. From Yacuiba, across the border, buses go to Santa Cruz de la Sierra. Customs at Pocitos is not to be trusted (theft reported) and overcharging for 'excess baggage' on buses occurs. ■ *Several bus companies including Atahualpa have services from the border to Salta, Tucumán and other cities.*

An alternative route is via Aguas Blancas. At Pichanal, 85 km northeast of Libertador, Route 50 heads north via **Orán**, an uninteresting place (*Population*: 60,000). C *Alto Verde*, Pellegrini 671, T421214, parking, pool, a/c. D *Res Crisol*, López y Planes, hot water. Recommended.

Aguas Blancas on the border is 53 km from Orán (restaurants, shops, but no accommodation, nowhere to change money and Bolivianos are not accepted south of Aguas Blancas). The passport office is open from 0700 to 1200 and 1500 to 1900. Insist on getting an exit stamp. Buses run from Bermejo, across the river (ferry US$0.50), to Tarija. Northwest of Aguas Blancas is the **Parque Nacional Baritú**, see above, under Abra Pampa. There are no facilities.

Buses Between Aguas Blancas and Orán buses run every 45 mins, US$1, luggage checks on bus. Direct buses to **Güemes**, 8 a day, US$5; through buses to **Salta**, *La Veloz del Norte*, *Panamericano* and *Atahualpa*, several daily, US$8, 7-10 hrs. To **Tucumán**, *La Veloz del Norte*, *Panamericano* and *La Estrella*, 1 a day each company. To **Jujuy** with *Balut* and *Brown*, 3 daily. To **Embarcación**, US$2; some services from Salta and Jujuy call at **Orán** en route to **Tartagal** and **Pocitos**. Note that buses are subject to slow searches for drugs and contraband.

The West

From the flat arid Pampa to the heights of Aconcagua and fertile valleys stretching along the length of the precordillera, the provinces of Mendoza, San Juan, La Rioja and Catamarca cover extreme contrasts. Mendoza is popular for its excellent wines, climbing and superb ski resorts, but the other provinces offer good hiking country and extraordinary landscapes in the national parks of Ichigualasto and Talampaya.

Mendoza

Situated at the foot of the Andes, **Mendoza** is a dynamic and attractive city, surrounded by vineyards and *bodegas*. The city was colonized from Chile in 1561 and it played an important role in gaining independence from Spain when the Liberator José de San Martín set out to cross the Andes from here, to help in the liberation of Chile. Mendoza was completely destroyed by fire and earthquake in 1861, so today it is essentially a modern city of low buildings and wide avenues (as a precaution against earthquakes), thickly planted with trees and gardens.

Phone code: 0261
Colour map 8, grid B2
Population: city 148,000 (with suburbs, 600,000)
Altitude: 756 m

Getting there El Plumerillo **airport**, 8 km north of centre, T430 7837, has a bank, tourist information, a few shops, restaurant and *locutorio*, but no left luggage. Reached from the centre by bus No 60 (subnumber 68) from Alem y Salta, every hr at 35 mins past the hr, 40 mins journey; make sure there is an 'Aeropuerto' sign on the driver's window. Taxi to/from centre US$5. There's a huge modern **bus terminal** on east side of Av Videla, 15 mins walk from centre (go via Av Alem, which has pedestrian tunnel), with shops, post office, *locutorio*, tourist information and supermarket (open till 2130), a good café, left luggage lockers and toilets (between platforms 38 and 39).

Ins & outs
*www.turismo.
mendoza.gov.ar
www.mendoza.gov.ar*

Tourist offices Main office at San Martín, opposite Peatonal Sarmiento, T420 1333, very helpful, English and French spoken. At airport, T448 0017; at bus station, T431 3001. The provincial office is at San Martín 1143, T420-2800. All open 0900-2100. Very helpful office at the entrance to Parque San Martín, open Mon-Fri 0800-1300, 1600-2000, Sat 0900-1300. All hand out maps and accommodation lists, with economical apartments for short lets, private lodgings in high season, also lists of bodegas and advice on buses. Aconcagua information and permits, see Sports, **Climbing**, above. **Useful addresses** *ACA*, Av San Martín 985, T420 2900, and Av Bandera de los Andes y Gdor Videla, T431 3510. **Migraciones**, San Martín 1859, T424 3512.

In the centre of the city is the **Plaza Independencia**, in the middle of which is the small **Museo Municipal de Arte Moderno** and on the east side, leafy streets lined with cafés. Among the other pleasant squares nearby is the **Plaza España**, attractively tiled and with a mural illustrating the epic gaucho poem, *Martín Fierro*. **Plaza**

Sights

Argentina

Buenos
Aires

Pellegrini (Avenida Alem y Av San Juan) is a beautiful small square where wedding photos are taken on Friday and Saturday nights, and a small antiques market.

On the west side of the city is the great **Parque San Martín**, beautifully designed, with a famous zoo, many areas for sports and picnics, and a large lake, where regattas are held. There is also a good restaurant. The **Museo de Ciencias Naturales** has an ancient female mummy among its fossils and stuffed animals. ■ *Open Tue-Sun 0830-1300, Tue-Fri 1400-1900, weekends 1500-1900. T428 7666.* There are views of the Andes rising in a blue-black perpendicular wall, topped off in winter with dazzling snow, into a china-blue sky. ■ *Park open 0900-0200 daily. The entrance is 10 blocks west of the Plaza Independencia, reached by bus 110 'Zoo' from the centre, or the trolley from Sarmiento y 9 de Julio.* On a hill above the park is the Cerro de la Gloria, crowned by an astonishing monument to San Martín, with bas-reliefs depicting various episodes in the equipping of the Army of the Andes and the actual crossing. ■ *An hourly bus ('Oro Negro') runs to the top of the Cerro de la Gloria from the information office at the entrance, US$1 – it's a long walk (45 mins).*

Mendoza's interesting history can be traced through two good museums: **Museo del Pasado Cuyano**, Montevideo 544, housed in a beautiful 1873 mansion, with lots

Mendoza

0 metres 200
0 yards 200

■ Sleeping
1 Campo Base *B1*
2 Carollo & Gran
   Princess *B1*
3 Churrasqueras del
   Parque *A1*
4 Crillon *B1*
5 Damajuana *C1*
6 Dam-sire *B3*
7 Escorial *A3*
8 Gran Balbi *A1*
9 Gran Mendoza *B2*
10 Gran Ritz *B1*
11 Hostal Internacional
   Mendoza *C2*
12 Imperial & Soppelsa *A2*
13 Internacional *B1*
14 Monterrey *A2*
15 Necochea *A1*
16 Nutibara *B1*
17 Palace *A2*
18 Park Hyatt *B1*
19 RJ del Sol *A2*
20 San Remo *A1*

● Eating
1 Aranjuez *A2*
2 Boccaduro *A1*
3 De un Rincón
   de la Boca *A1*
4 Don Otto *A2*
5 Estancia la Florencia *B1*
6 Facundo *B1*
7 La Chacra *B2*
8 La Naturata *C2*
9 Mambrú *A1*
10 Marchigiani *A2*
11 Mesón Español *C2*
12 Montecatini *A1*
13 Mr Dog *A2*
14 Nuevo Mundo *B2*
15 Sr Cheff *B2*
16 Vía Civit Café *B1*

of San Martín memorabilia and an exquisite Spanish 15th-century carved altarpiece. ■ *Mon-Fri 0900-1230. US$0.50, T4236031.* Also recommended is **Museo del Area Fundacional**, Alberdi y Videla Castillo, the city pre-earthquake, with original foundations revealed, and the ruins of Jesuit church **San Francisco** opposite.■ *Tue-Sat 0800-2000, Sun 1500-2000 US$0.50, children under 6 free. T425 6927. Buses 10, 60, 80, 110.* The small **Acuario Municipal** (aquarium), underground at Buenos Aires e Ituzaingó, is fun for kids. ■ *Daily 0900-1230, 1500-2030, US$0.50.*

In the nearby suburb of Luján de Cuyo, there's a small collection of Argentine paintings in the house where Fernando Fader painted decorative murals, at the **Museo Provincial de Bellas Artes**, **Casa de Fader**, Carril San Martín 3671, Mayor Drummond. In the gardens are sculptures. ■ *Tue-Fri 0900-1800, Sat-Sun 1400-1830. US$0.50. T496 0224. Bus 200, 40 mins.*

A few recommended trips are to the pretty village of **Cacheuta**, 29 km west, with thermal springs, to **Potrerillos**, 6 km beyond, for walking, rafting, horse riding, and to **Villavicencio**, 47 km north, good walks and a restaurant in the mountains, and to the mountain pass to Chile (see below) with **Puenta del Inca**, and **Los Penintentes**.

Many bodegas welcome visitors and offer tastings without pressure to buy (grape harvesting season March/April). If you've only time for one, make it **Bodega La Rural (San Felipe)** at Montecaseros 2625, Coquimbito, Maipú. Small, traditional with a marvellous **Museo del Vino**. ■ *T497 2013, US$0.30. Tours Mon-Sat 1000-1630, Sun 1000-1300. Bus 170 (subnumber 173) from La Rioja y Garibaldi.* (In Maipú itself, 15 km south of Mendoza, see the lovely plaza and eat good simple food at the Club Social.) Beautiful **Bodegas Escorihuela** has an excellent restaurant run by renowned Francis Mallman. ■ *Tours Mon-Fri 0930, 1030, 1130, 1230, 1430, 1530. T4242744. Bus 'T' G Cruz from centre 9 de Julio, Godoy Cruz, or bus 170 subnumbers 174, 200, from Rioja, or 40 from the Plaza.* **Norton**, Ruta 15, Km 23.5, Perdriel, Luján, excellent tasting. ■ *Tours on the hour 0900-1200, 1400-1700. T488 0480, www.norton.com.ar Bus 380 from the terminal.* **Pequeña Bodega**, Ugarte 978, La Puntilla, Luján de Cuyo, with a small museum. ■ *Mon-Fri 0900-1300, 1600-2000, T439 2094, take bus 10 (Ugarte) on 25 de Mayo.* **Chandon**, further south on RN40, Km 29, an impressive modern bodega, famous wines. ■ *T4909966. Call for information on tour times. Bus Mitre (no 380) from the terminal, platform 53 /54.* Finally, **Nieto Senetiner**, Guardia Vieja s/n, Vistalaba, wines, lunch (reserve ahead) some accommodation. ■ *Tours Mon-Fri 1000-1600, Sat 0930-1100. T498 0315.* Ask agencies for tours to micro-bodegas, which usually include three wineries, such as *Domaine San Diego*, *Cabrini* and *Dolium*, with a choice of tasting, explanations and extras like local olives and walnuts.

Bodegas

Easiest to get to bodegas by car: buses are erratic, and organized tours are rapid with scanty tastings – only cheaper wines, usually in plastic cups

Sleeping

■ *on map*
Breakfast is included, unless specified otherwise. Larger hotels all have car parking

AL *Park Hyatt*, Chile 1124 on main plaza, T441 1234, www.mendoza.park.hyatt.com Elegant, very comfortable, affordable (if expensive) restaurant, *Bistro M*, with imaginative menu, pool, spa and casino. **B** *Gran Hotel Balbi*, Las Heras 340, T423 3500, F438 0626. Splendid entrance, spacious rooms, small pool and terrace. **B** *Nutibara*, Mitre 867, T429 5428. Welcoming, eclectic décor, pool in a leafy patio, comfortable rooms, quiet and central. Recommended. **B** *Gran Hotel Mendoza*, España 1210 y Espejo, T425 2000, www.hotelmendoza.com Spacious rooms, stylish décor, central, family rooms too. **C** *Carollo*, 25 de Mayo 1184, T423 5666. Slightly old-fashioned but hospitable, this hotel shares its pool and facilities with *Gran Princess* next door. **C** *Crillon*, Perú 1065, T429 5161, F423 9658. Good modernized rooms, pool, warm welcome, slightly overpriced. **C** *Gran Hotel Ritz*, Perú 1008, T423 5115, aristo@infovia.com.ar Very comfortable, reliable, central but quiet location, excellent service. Highly recommended. **C** *Internacional*, Sarmiento 720, T425 5600, www.pro-mendoza.com/hi Reliable and comfortable, spacious rooms, nice pool. **C** *Palace*, Las Heras 70, T/F423 4200. A lovely quiet place, modern rooms, good value. **D** *Monterrey*, Patricias Mendocinas 1532, T438 0901, hoteles@ciudad.com.ar Great value, stylish, spacious, nice modern rooms. **D** *Necochea*, Necochea 541, T425 3501. Pleasant, cheerful, very reasonable and central. **D** *RJ Hotel Del Sol*, Las Heras 212, T438 0218. Big comfortable rooms, central. Highly recommended.

E *San Remo*, Godoy Cruz 477, T423 4068. Quiet, small rooms, TV, rooftop terrace, secure parking. Recommended. **E** *Imperial*, Las Heras 88, T15-414 4680. Old fashioned, plain but comfortable and quiet rooms, good value. **F** pp *Dam-sire*, Viamonte 410, San José Guaymallén, T431 5142, 5 mins from terminal. Family run, includes breakfast, spotless. **Youth hostels** A great new hostel, **D-F** *Damajuana*, Arístides Villanueva 282, T425 5858, www.damajuanahostel.com.ar Very comfortable stylish dorms and double rooms, central, pool in lovely garden. **E** *Hostel Internacional Mendoza*, España 343, T424 0018, www.hostelmendoza.net The most comfortable, a short walk south of the plaza, small rooms with bath, warm atmosphere, great food in the evenings, huge range of excursions. Warmly recommended. **F** *Campo Base*, Mitre 946, T429 0707, www.campo-base.com.ar A livelier place, cramped rooms, but lots of parties and barbecues. Expert guide Roger Cangiani leads very professional Aconcagua expeditions, and gives advice on permits. See helpful site www.cerroaconcagua.com

Camping *Churrasqueras del Parque* in centre of Parque General San Martin, at Bajada del Cerro, T452 6016, 155-123124. There are 2 other sites at El Challao, 6 km west of the city centre, reached by Bus 110 (El Challao) leaving hourly from C Rioja. *Camping Suizo*, Av Champagnat, 9½ km from city, T444 1991, modern, with pool, barbecues, hot showers. Recommended. At Guaymallén, 9 km east, *Saucelandia*, Tirasso s/n, T451 1409. Take insect repellent.

Eating
● *on map*
C Arístides Villanueva, the extension of Colón heading west, has many excellent restaurants and bars

There are lots of open-air cafés for lunch on Peatonal Sarmiento and restaurants around Las Heras. **Mid-range Central**: *La Chacra*, Sarmiento 55. Good set menu lunches, traditional *Mendocino* steaks. Recommended. *Estancia La Florencia*, Sarmiento 698. Excellent modern *parrilla*. *Facundo*, Sarmiento 641. Modern *parrilla*, good salad bar. *Boccaduro*, Mitre 1976. *Parrilla*, popular with locals. *Marchigiani*, Av España 1619, T423 0751. Deservedly popular, wonderful Italian food in traditional style, charming service. Recommended. *Mesón Español*, Montevideo 244. Spanish food, live music at weekends. Cheap lunch menus. *Montecatini* Gral Paz 370. Good Italian food and *parrilla*, more tourist oriented. *Sr Cheff*, Primitivo de la Reta 1071. Long-established, good *parrilla* and fish. *Azafrán*, Arístides Villanueva 287. Wine lover's heaven, excellent *bodegas*, expert advice, superb *picadas*. *Mal de Amores*, Arístides Villanueva 303. Imaginative Mediterranean food, warm and stylish atmosphere. Highly recommended. *Por Acá*, Arístides Villanueva 557. Cosy bohemian living room for pizzas and drinks till late. **Cheap Central**: *La Naturata*, Plaza Pellegrini. Delicious vegetarian food, cheap *tenedor libre*. Highly recommended. *Don Otto*, Las Heras 242. Cheap and cheerful deals. *Mambrú*, Las Heras 554 y Chile. Excellent busy *tenedor libre*. *Nuevo Mundo*, Lavalle 126. Chinese, Italian, *parrilla*, good *tenedor libre*. The atmospheric indoor market on Las Heras has cheap and delicious pizza, *parrilla* and pasta. Open late. *De un Rincón de la Boca*, Las Heras 485. Cheerful *pizzería* with a good range. *Aranjuez*, Lavalle y San Martín. Nice café, good meeting place. Also popular is the chain *Mr Dog*, better than average fast food. Ice cream at *Soppelsa*, Las Heras y España. Recommended. *3 90 (Tres con Noventa)*, Arístides Villanueva 451. Delicious pastas, incredibly cheap, warm cosy atmosphere. Highly recommended. *Guevar*, Arístides Villanueva y Huarpes. Eggs with everything, a fun atmosphere. *Nativa*, No 650. Huge sandwiches.

Bars & clubs
Blues Bar, No 687, popular, reservations for eating T429 0240. Nearby, *Soul Café*, San Juan 456. Popular pub with jazz, lambada, blues, theatre performances, T432 0828. *Vía Civit*, Emilio Civit 277. Superb stylish café on the way to park, exquisite pastries. The Chacras de Coria district has lots of good places to eat and go dancing. Recommended clubs are: *Aloha!*, *El Desert*, *Runner* and *Olimpo*. The most popular place for the young crowd is *La Chimère*, on the road to the airport.

Festivals
The riotous wine harvesting festival, *Fiesta de la Vendimia*, is held in the amphitheatre of the Parque San Martín **first weekend in March**. Hotels fill up fast and prices rise; also in Jul (the ski season) and around **21 Sep** (*the spring festival*).

Shopping
The main shopping area is along San Martín and Las Heras, with good clothes, souvenir, leather and handicraft shops. *Mercado Artesanal*, San Martín 1133, 0830-1930 daily, for traditional leather, baskets, weaving; also weekend market on Plaza Independencia. Cheap: *El*

Turista, Las Heras 351, and *Las Vi*ñas Las Heras 399. Higher quality, *Raíces*, España 1092, just off Peatonal Sarmiento. Good choice of wines at *Vinoteca*, Alem 97, T4203924. **Supermarkets**: *Super Vea*, San Martín y Santiago del Estero, *Metro*, Colón 324.

Bike rental: *Piré*, Las Heras 615, T425 7699, US$4 per day. Also at *Campo Base*, see **Youth hostels** above. **Climbing**: information from Tourist Office. Aconcagua permits from the Cuba building, Parque San Martín (aconcagua@mendoza.gov.ar), in summer, and directly from the park itself at Horcones, Puente del Inca, in winter. *Club Andinista*, F L Beltrán 357, Gillén, T431 9870. See also page 159 for Aconcagua. **Whitewater rafting** is popular on the Río Mendoza; ask agencies for details.

Sport & activities

Lots, especially on Paseo Sarmiento. *Asatej*, San Martín 1360 (at back of shopping arcade), T429 0029, mendoza@asatej.com.ar Very helpful, trips, cheap travel deals. *Huentata*, Las Heras 680, T425 7444. Conventional tours, plus Villavicencio, Cañon del Atuel, horse riding. *Mendoza Viajes* Peatonal Sarmiento 129, T438 0480. Comfortable coaches, professional, cheap deals. *Inca Expedición*, Juan B Justo 343, Ciudad 5500, T429 8494, www.aconcagua.org.ar Private and programmed climbing expeditions, including Aconcagua. *Casa Orviz*, Juan B Justo 536, T425 1281, www.orviz.com Guides, mules, transportation and hire of mountain trekking equipment for Aconcagua. *Campo Base* youth hostel (see above) runs good expeditions, and has a helpful website in English: www.cerroaconcagua.com *Trekking Travel*, Adolfo Calle 4171, VN Gllen, T421 0450, www.clubtrekkingtravel.com.ar Club de Montaña, riding, excursions organized.

Tour operators
Many agencies run trekking, riding and rafting expeditions, as well as traditional tours to Alta Montaña and bodegas

Local Buses: most services have 2 numbers, a general number and a 'subnumber' in brackets which indicates the specific route. To travel on buses within and near the city, it's cheaper with prepaid card which you put into a machine on the bus, sold in shops, the bus terminal and *Mendobus* ticket offices everywhere. US$0.30 two trips, US$1.75 ten. There are 2 trolley bus routes, red and blue, US$0.25. **Car hire**: See **Essentials**, page 52 for international agencies' websites. *Avis* is reliable and efficient. *Dollar* De la Reta 936, T429 9939. *Herbst* at the airport, T4482327.

Transport

Long distance Air: to Buenos Aires: 1 hr 50 mins, *AR only*. LanChile to Santiago, daily.

 Buses: To Buenos Aires, 15 hrs, US$19-27, many companies including *TAC*, *Andesmar*, *La Estrella*. To Bariloche, *Andesmar* daily, US$17, 22 hrs, book well ahead (alternative is *TAC* to Neuquén and change). To Córdoba, *TAC*, 11hrs, US$10. To San Rafael, many daily 3½ hrs, US$4. To San Juan, *TAC*, frequent, *Andesmar*, US$5, 2 hrs. To Tucumán, US$12, *Andesmar*, *Autotransportes Mendoza*, *TAC*, all via San Juan, La Rioja (US$10-12), 10 hrs, and Catamarca 12 hrs, US$9-13. To Salta, *Andesmar*, *América* (via San Juan, La Rioja and Catamarca), 20 hrs, US$25. To Uspallata, 5 a day with *Expreso Uspallata*, US$4, 2¼ hrs. To Potrerillos, 1 hr, US$1.30. No buses to Villavicencio or Vallecitos.

 Transport to Santiago, Chile: Minibuses (US$10, 6 hrs) run by *Chi-Ar* and *Nevada* daily leave when they have 10 passengers. When booking, ensure that the receipt states that you will be picked up and dropped at your hotel; if not you will be dropped at the bus station. Buses to Santiago daily, 10 companies, *Chile Bus, Cata, Tur Bus, Tas Choapa* and *TAC* have been recommended, *Ahumada* has a *coche cama* at 0845; mixed reports on other companies. Most buses are comfortable, 6½-8 hrs, US$8, those with a/c and hostess service (includes breakfast) charge more, worth it when crossing the border as waiting time can be several hours. These companies also daily to Viña del Mar and Valparaíso, US$10. Information at Mendoza bus terminal: shop around. Children under 8 pay 60% of adult fare, but no seat; book at least 1 day ahead. Passport required, tourist cards given on bus. The ride is spectacular. If you want to return, it's cheaper to buy an undated return ticket Santiago-Mendoza. For Chilean side, see under Santiago.

 Other International buses: to La Serena, *Covalle, Cata* and others. To Lima, 3-4 a week, *El Rápido*, and *Ormeño*, T431 4913, 56 hrs, US$34.

Directory **Airline offices** *Aerolíneas Argentinas/Austral*, Peatonal Sarmiento 82, T420 4100. *Varig*, Av España 1002 y Rivadavia, T423 1000. *Southern Winds*, España 943, T429 7788. *LanChile*, Rivadavia 135, T425 7900. **Banks** Many ATMs along San Martín taking all cards. Many *casas de cambio* along San Martín, including *Santiago*, San Martín 1199, T420 0277, *Maguitur*, San Martín 1203, T423 3202. Most open till 2000 Mon-Fri, and some open Sat morning. **Communications** Internet: Several internet cafés in the centre and a number of *locutorios*: a huge one on San Martín y Garibaldi, with internet. *Arlink*, San Martín 928, *Spacenet*, Rivadavia 424, *Telecentro Reydiphone*, San Martín 940. **Cultural centres** *Alianza Francesa*, Chile 1754. *Instituto Dante Alighieri* (Italy), Espejo 638. *Instituto Cultural Argentino-Norteamericano*, Chile 985. *Instituto Cuyano de Cultura Hispánica* (Spain), Villanueva 389. *Goethe Institut*, Morón 265, Mon-Fri, 0800-1200, 1600-2230, German newspapers, Spanish classes, very good. **Medical facilities** Central hospital near bus terminal at Alem y Salta, T420 0600. **Lagomaggiore**, public general hospital (with good reputation) at Timoteo Gordillo s/n, T425 9700. **Hosptal Materno y Infantil Humberto Notti**, Bandera de los Andes 2683, T445 0045. Medical emergencies T428 0000.

Ski resorts
For Las Leñas, see South of Mendoza, below

Vallecitos (season July-September) is a tiny ski resort 21 km from Potrerillos (see below) along a winding *ripio* road. It has a basic ski-lodge, ski school and snack bar. www.skivallecitos.com *Refugio San Bernado*, T154-183857, cosy place run by mountain guides.

Los Penitentes is a much better ski resort, 165 km west of Mendoza, on the road to Chile, named after its majestic mass of pinnacled rocks, looking like a horde of cowled monks. Good skiing on 28 pistes, very reasonably priced, with few people on slopes.

Sleeping **B** *Ayelén*, in middle of village,T420299. Convenient but overpriced, poor restaurant. **C** *Hostería Penitentes*, Villa Los Penitentes T155-090432, penitentehosteria@hotmail.com Cheery place near slopes, good café, cheaper for several nights. Recommended. **E** pp*Hostel Refugio Penitentes*, T0261-429 0707, www.cerroaconcagua.com Welcoming, warm and popular. Also Aconcagua services. For **Puente del Inca** see below.

Mendoza to Chile

The route to Chile is sometimes blocked by snow in winter: if travelling by car in June-October enquire about road conditions from *ACA* in Mendoza (T431 3510). Officially, driving without snow chains and a shovel is prohibited between Uspallata and the border, but this can be resolved in a friendly way with border police. Both *ACA* and Chilean Automobile Club sell, but do not rent, chains.

Uspallata
Phone code: 02624
Colour map 8, grid A1

Ruta 7 is the only route for motorists to the Chilean border, via **Potrerillos** and **Uspallata**. Leave the city south by Avenida J Vicente Zapata, Access Ruta 7, leading to Ruta 40. Follow signs to Potrerillos, Uspallata and Chile. From Mendoza to the Chilean border is 204 km. The construction of a dam has forced a detour around **Cacheuta**, though it's worth a side trip for its relaxing hot springs, and very comfortable hotel, **B** *Termas Cacheuta*, Ruta 82, Km 38, www.termascacheuta.com Warm and inviting rustic-style rooms, lovely spa for day visits too. Recommended.

Potrerillos is a pretty village for horse riding, walking and rafting: *Argentina Rafting* organizes good trips with kayaking T02624-155 691700, www.argentinarafting.com In summer you can hike from Potrerillos to Vallecitos over two days, passing from desert steppe to scenic peaks. Another recommended stopping point is the picturesque village of **Uspallata**, 52 km from Potrerillos. From here you can explore the mysterious Las Bóvedas (5 km on RN39 north) built by the Huarpe Indians under the Jesuits to melt silver, where there is a small, interesting museum. The RN39 leads north to Barreal and Calingasta (see page 164), unpaved for its first part, rough and tricky when the snow melts and floods it in summer. The tourist office in Uspallata keeps unreliable hours. There are two food shops, bakeries, a post office and a YPF station with motel, restaurant, shop and *locutorio* open 0900-2200. *Desnivel Turismo Aventura*, Galería Comercial local 7, T420275, desnivelturismoaventura@yahoo.com.ar Offers rafting, riding, mountain biking, trekking, climbing, skiing.

Sleeping In Potrerillos: **C** *Gran Hotel Potrerillos*, Ruta Nacional 7, Km 50, T02624-482010, with breakfast, faded resort hotel, nice location, pool, or the excellent *ACA* campsite, T482013, well shaded, with pool, clean. **In Uspallata**: **B** *Valle Andino*, Ruta 7, T420033, modern airy place with good rooms, pool and restaurant, breakfast included. **C** *Hotel Uspallata*, on RN 7 towards Chile, T420066, lovely location, spacious modernized place in big gardens away from the centre with pool, good value, comfortable rooms, cheap restaurant. **D** *Los Cóndores*, T420002, www.hostalloscondores.com.ar Great value, bright neat rooms, good restaurant with tasty pasta and cheap set menu. Recommended. **E** pp *Viena*, Las Heras 240, T420046, small family-run place with good little rooms, breakfast included. **Camping** Very basic municipal site, US$2 per tent, hot water but dirty showers and toilets, poor. Cheap, excellent food at *La Estancia de Elias*, Km 1146, good restaurant opposite YPF station. *Pub Tibet*, bar with photos from '7 years in Tibet', shot here. *Bodega del Gato*, in the centre, is a good *parrilla*.

Puente del Inca
Colour map 8, grid B2
Altitude: 2,718 m
72 km W of Uspallata

The road that leads from Uspallata to cross the border to Chile is one of the most dramatic in Argentina, climbing through a gorge of richly coloured rock. Surrounded by mountains of great grandeur, Puente del Inca is a good base for trekking or exploring on horseback. The natural bridge after which the place is named is one of the wonders of South America. Bright ochre yellow, it crosses the Río Mendoza at a height of 19 m, has a span of 21 m, and is 27 m wide, and seems to have been formed by sulphur-bearing hot springs. Watch your footing on the steps; extremely slippery. There are hot thermal baths at the river just under the bridge, a bit dilapidated, but decent temperature (the guard may charge to enter). Horse treks go to Los Penitentes. Los Horcones, the Argentine customs post, is 1 km east: from here you can visit the green lake of Laguna los Horcones: follow signs to **Parque Provincial Aconcagua**, 2 km, where there is a Ranger station, excellent views of Aconcagua, especially morning; free camping, open climbing season only. From here a trail continues to the Plaza de Mulas base camp.

Sleeping C *Hostería Puente del Inca*, RN7, Km 175, T420266, www.www.aymara.com.ar Doubles and rooms for 4-8, huge cosy dining room, advice on Aconcagua from helpful owners, good atmosphere. Warmly recommended. NB more expensive if booked in Mendoza. **F** pp *Hostel La Vieja Estación*, 100 m off the road, next to the Puente, T0261-155 631664. Basic but cheery hostel, cheap meals provided, use of kitchen. **F** *Refugio de Montaña*, small dormitories in the army barracks, helpful. **Camping** Possible next to the church, if your equipment can withstand the winds, also at Lago Horcones inside the park.

Transport Buses: *Expreso Uspallata* from Mendoza for **Uspallata** and **Puente del Inca**, US$4, 3½ hrs, 2 a day in the morning, returning from Puente del Inca in the afternoon. Uspallata-Puente del Inca US$1.50. Local buses also go on from Puente del Inca to **Las Cuevas**, *Expreso Uspallata*, US$4 return (**NB** take passport). You can go to Chile from Puente del Inca with *Tur Bus* at 1000 and 1400, US$10, but be sure to ask for an international ticket.

Aconcagua
Colour map 8, grid B2
Altitude: 6,959 m
The highest peak in the Americas
See www.cerroa concagua.com for information in English

West of Puente del Inca on the right, there is a good view of Aconcagua, sharply silhouetted against the blue sky. In 1985, a complete Inca mummy was discovered at 5,300 m on the mountain. The best time for climbing Aconcagua is from end-December to February. For trekking or climbing it is first necessary to obtain a **permit**: These vary in price for high, mid or low season, and depending on the number of days. In high season (15 December to 31 January), a permit to climb Aconcagua (lasting 21 days) costs US$200, for short trekking US$20. Permits must be bought, in person only, in summer (15 November to 15 March) at *Dirección de Recursos Naturales Renovables*, T425 2090, The Cuba Building, Av Los Robles y Rotonda de Rosedal in the Parque San Martín in Mendoza. ■ *Open Mon-Fri 0800-1800, weekends and holidays 0900-1300*. In winter permits are bought directly from the *guardería* at Laguna Horcones, at the entrance to PN Aconcagua itself.

There are two access routes: Río Horcones and Río Vacas, which lead to the two main base camps, Plaza de Mulas and Plaza Argentina respectively. Río Horcones

Argentina

Argentina

starts a few kilometres from Puente del Inca, at the Horcones ranger station. About 80% of climbers use this route. From here you can go to Plaza de Mulas (4,370 m) for the North Face, or Plaza Francia (4,200 m) for the South Face. The intermediate camp for either is Confluencia (3,300 m), four hours from Horcones. Río Vacas is the access for those wishing to climb the Polish Glacier. The Plaza Argentina base camp (200 m) is three hours from Horcones and the intermediate camps are Pampa de Leñas and Casa de Piedra. From Puente del Inca, mules are available (list at the *Dirección de Recursos Naturales Renovables*, Parque Gral San Martín, Mendoza, about US$80-100 per day for 60 kg of gear). This only takes you to Plaza de Mulas, near which is the highest hotel in the world (see below) and an accident prevention and medical assistance service (climbing season only); crowded in summer. The same service is offered at Plaza Argentina in high season. Climbers should make use of this service to check for early symptoms of mountain sickness and oedema. Take a tent able to withstand 100 mph/160 kph winds, and clothing and sleeping gear for temperatures below –40° C. Allow at least one week for acclimatization at lower altitudes before attempting the summit (four days from Plaza de Mulas). Hotel *Plaza de Mulas*, **AL** pp full board, **C** without meals, good food, information, medical treatment, recommended, also camping area; closed in winter.

In Mendoza you can book *refugio* reservations and programmes which include trekking, or climbing to the summit, with all equipment and accommodation or camping included (see Tour operators, above). Try to agree all contract terms in advance, such as the number of members of a group, so that they aren't changed before your expedition leaves. Treks and climbs are also organized by *Sr Fernando Grajales*, the famous climber, at Moreno 898, 5500 Mendoza, T493830, expediciones@grajales.net (or T421 4330 and ask for *Eduardo Ibarra* at *Hotel Plaza de Mulas* for further information), and by *Roger Cangiani* at *Campo Base* in Mendoza, T429 0707, www.campo-base.com.ar Near the Cementerio is *Los Puquios*, T461-317603, camping, mules, guides. Further information from *Dirección de Recursos Naturales Renovables* (see also under Mendoza, www.mendoza.gov.ar).

Border with Chile

If you need a visa to enter Chile, they are not available at the border: consult consulate in Mendoza

The road to the Chilean border, fully paved, goes through the 3.2-km Cristo Redentor toll road tunnel to Chile (open 24 hours; US$1 for cars, cyclists are not allowed to ride through, ask the officials to help you get a lift). The last settlement before the tunnel is tiny forlorn **Las Cuevas**, 16 km from Puente del Inca, with no accommodation but a basic café and a *kiosko*. In summer you can take the old road over La Cumbre pass to the statue of El Cristo Redentor (Christ the Redeemer), an 8 m statue erected jointly by Chile and Argentina in 1904 to celebrate the settlement of their boundary dispute. Take an all day excursion from Mendoza, drive in a 4WD, after snow has melted, or walk from Las Cuevas (4½ hrs up, 2 hrs down – only to be attempted by the fit, in good weather). *Expreso Uspallata* runs buses to Mendoza.

The Chilean border is beyond Las Cuevas, but all Argentine entry and exit formalities for cars and buses are dealt with at the Argentine customs post, Ingeniero Roque Carranza at Laguna Los Horcones, near Las Cuevas. Customs are open 0730-2300. Car drivers can undertake all formalities in advance at *migraciones* in Mendoza, or Uspallata while refuelling. You can hitchhike, or possibly bargain with bus drivers for a seat, from Los Horcones to Santiago, but if you are dropped at the entrance to the tunnel, you cannot walk through. Customs officers may help by asking motorists to take hitchhikers through to Chile.

South of Mendoza

San Rafael

Phone code: 02627
Colour map 8, grid B2
Population: 107,000
236 km S of Mendoza

San Rafael is a tranquil, leafy small town in the heart of fertile land which is irrigated by snow melt from the Andes to produce fine wines and fruit. A road runs west over El Pehuenche pass to Talca (Chile). Several bodegas can be visited: the impressive champagnerie at *Bianchi*, T422 046 informes@vbianchi.com 5km west on Hpólito Yrigoyen, is the more intimate *Jean Rivier*, H Yrigoyen 2385, T432675, bodega@jrivier.com Excellent wine. The **tourist office** is at Av H Yrigoyen y Balloffet, T437860. A small but interesting natural history museum is 6 km south-east of town at Isla Río Diamante ■ *Tue-Sun 0800-2000, free;* Iselin *bus along Av JA Balloffet.* Lots of appealing small hotels, best is **C** *Kalton*, Yrigoyen 120, T430047, kalton@satlink.com Charming, comfortable, long-established hotel, excellent service, parking. Highly recommended. **Youth hostel E** *Puesta del Sol*, Deán Funes 998, 3 km, T434881, puestadelsol@infovia.com.ar 20 blocks from centre, a popular place with doubles and dorms, good facilities. **Campsites** Site at Isla Río Diamante park, 15 km southeast. A good value *parrilla* is La Fusta, Yrigoyen 538. ■ *Buses to Mendoza, US$4; to Neuquén, US$10, 9 hrs.*

Southwest of San Rafael is the **Cañon de Atuel**, a spectacular gorge 20 km long with strange polychrome rock formations. It is famous as a rafting centre. Daily buses, *Iselin*, go to the Valle Grande dam at the near end of the canyon, returning in the evening, US$2.) Here there is plenty of accommodation, campsites, river rafting and horse riding. San Rafael tour operators run all-day tours. *Raffeish*, T436996, www.raffeish.com.ar Recommended as most professional rafting company. There is no public transport through the gorge to El Nihuel.

www.msanrafael.
com.ar,
www.sanrafael-
tour.com

Argentina

At 182 km southwest of San Rafael, RN40 heads west into the Andes, and from it the road to the famous international ski resort of Las Leñas. It passes **Los Molles**, at Km 30, where there is simple accommodation: best is **C** *Hotel Termas Lahuen-Có*, T499700, 1930's with thermal baths, full board possible. Further along the Las Leñas road is the **Pozo de las Animas**, two natural pits filled with water where the wind makes a ghostly wail, hence the name (Well of the Spirits). At the end of Valle Los Molles is **Las Leñas**, in a spectacular setting with excellent skiing over 7 km on 41 pistes, with a maximum drop of 1,200 m. Beyond Las Leñas the road continues into Valle Hermoso, accessible December-March only. There are several plush hotels, **L** (T for all 471100) and a disco, shop renting equipment and several restaurant. For cheaper accommodation stay in Los Molles or Malargüe. ■ *Buses from San Rafael US$3.75, colectivo US$12.*

Las Leñas
Altitude: 2,250 m
An internationally
renowned chic
ski resort.
Season: mid-Jun to
end-Oct
www.laslenas.com

Further south on Ruta 40, Malargüe is developing as a centre for hiking and horse riding in stunning open landscape nearby. Most remarkable, the **La Payunia** reserve, 208 km south, has vast grasslands and stark volcanoes where thousands of guanacos roam in untouched land, best enjoyed on horseback. The **Laguna Llancanelo**, 75 km southeast, is filled with a great variety of birdlife in spring, when Chilean flamingoes, among others, come to nest. In addition, **Caverna de las Brujas** has extraordinary underground cave formations. There's a helpful tourist office on the main street (right hand side as you drive in from north), next to conference centre (open 0800-2300), T471659, www.malargue.net Weekly flights Buenos Aires to Malargüe airport, more charter flights in the skiing season. Daily buses from Mendoza with *TAC*, minibuses with *Transporte Viento Sur*, both 4 hours, U$7 Several a day from San Rafael. Daily buses in ski season to Las Leñas.

Malargüe
Phone code: 02627
Colour map 8, grid B2
Population: 8,600

Sleeping Accommodation is generally not of a high standard, with some very poor *cabañas*. **B** *Río Grande* , Ruta 40 Norte, T471589, hotelriogrande@slatinos.com.ar The best, with some smart very comfortable 'VIP' rooms, others, **D**, are old and a bit dark. The best restaurant is here, dinner US$4, tasty trout. **C** *La Posta* , Av Roca 374, T471306. Welcoming wood-lined place, also has *parrilla*. **D** *Hotel del Turismo*, San Martín 224, T/F471042. Drab rooms, but good cheap restaurant, *Puli Huén*. There's an impressive conference centre with an attractive bar.

*Hotels issue guests
with a voucher for
50% discount on
Las Leñas lift pass*

Tour operators The tourist office can arrange for you to visit Llancanelo and La Payunia independently. Otherwise, good tours are run by *Karen Travel*, San Martín 1056, T470342, www.karentravel.com.ar Also Cueva de las Brujas, palaeontological site Manqui Malal, and horse riding trips.

San Juan, La Rioja and Catamarca

The oases of San Juan and La Rioja lie between the arid plains and the Andes, with attractive villages in fertile valleys to the west of San Juan. Interesting anthropomorphic rock formations and petroglyphs can be seen in this stark landscape, especially in Parque Nacional Talampaya and Valle de la Luna, where the skeletons of the oldest known dinosaurs on the planet were found.

San Juan

Phone code: 02646
Colour map 8, grid A2
Population: 122,000
Altitude: 650 m
177 km N of Mendoza

San Juan was founded in 1562 and is capital of its namesake province. Nearly destroyed by a 1944 earthquake, the modern centre is well-laid out, but lacks Mendoza's charm and sophistication. You're most likely to visit on the way to the national parks further north, but there are some *bodegas* worth visiting. One of the country's largest wine producers, *Bodegas Bragagnolo*, is on the outskirts of town at Ruta 40 y Avenida Benavídez, Chimbas (bus 20 from terminal; guided tours daily 0830-1330, 1530-1930, not Sunday). The most interesting of the museums, **Museo de Ciencias Naturales**, Predio Ferial, Avenida España y Maipú, includes fossils from Ischigualasto Provincial Park (see below). ■ *Mon-Fri 0900-1400, US$0.50.* **Museo Casa Natal de Sarmiento**, Sarmiento Sur 21, is the birthplace of Domingo Sarmiento (President of the Republic, 1868-1874, also a historian/educator). ■ *Tue-Fri and Sun 0830-1330, 1500-2000, Mon and Sat 0830-1330, US$1, free Sun.* **Museo Histórico Celda de San Martín**, Laprida 57 Este, including the restored cloisters and two cells of the Convent of Santo Domingo. San Martín slept in one of these cells on his way to lead the crossing of the Andes. ■ *Mon-Sat 0900-1400, US$1.*

The **Museo Arqueológico** of the University of San Juan at La Laja, 20 km north, contains an outstanding collection of prehispanic indigenous artefacts, including several well-preserved mummies. Inexpensive thermal baths nearby. ■ *Daily 0930-1700, US$2. Bus 20 from San Juan, 2 a day: take the first (at 0830) to give time to return.* For **Parque Ischigualasto**, see below. **Vallecito**, 64 km east, has a famous shrine to the **Difunta Correa**, Argentina's most loved pagan saint whose infant,

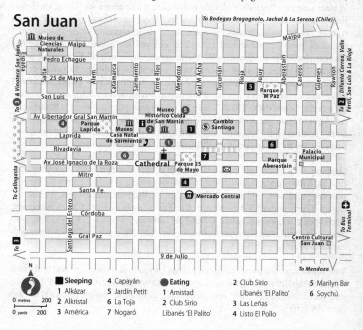

San Juan

To Bodegas Bragagnolo, Jachal & La Serena (Chile)

0 metres 200
0 yards 200

■ Sleeping	4 Capayán	● Eating	2 Club Sirio	5 Marilyn Bar
1 Alkázar	5 Jardín Petit	1 Amistad	Libanés 'El Palito'	6 Soychú
2 Alkristal	6 La Toja	2 Club Sirio	3 Las Leñas	
3 América	7 Nogaró	Libanés 'El Palito'	4 Listo El Pollo	

Argentina

according to legend, survived at her breast even after the mother's death from thirst in the desert. At roadsides everywhere you'll see mounds of plastic bottles left as offerings to ask for safe journeys, and during Holy Week 100,000 pilgrims visit the site. See the remarkable collection of personal items left in tribute in several elaborate shrines, including number plates from all over the world: photographs, stuffed animals, tea sets, hair (in plaits), plastic flowers, trophies, tennis rackets and guitars. There are cafés, toilets and souvenir stalls. Bizarre and fascinating.

Sleeping

■ *on map*
Hotels in A-C range all include breakfast and parking

B *América*, 9 de Julio 1052 Oeste, T421 4514, www.hotel-america.com.ar Modern, very comfortable, good service, tours arranged. Recommended. B *Alkázar*, Laprida 82 Este, T421 4965, www.alkazarhotel.com.ar Comfortable rooms, pool and gym, well run, central. C *Alkristal*, Av de Circunvalacíon 1055 Sur, T425 4145. Very comfortable, well equipped rooms, modern, on outskirts, poor breakfast, but otherwise recommended, good value. Also smart apartments, very cheap for groups. C *Nogaró*, de la Roza 132 Este, T422 7501/5, hotel@nogarosanjuan.com.ar Big, central business hotel with smart bedrooms, pool, and good restaurant. D *Capayán*, Mitre 31 Este, T421 4222, hcapayan@infovia.com.ar Next to cinema on plaza, welcoming place with comfy rooms and good service, restaurant. D *Jardín Petit*, 25 de Mayo 345 Este, T421 1825. Stylish entrance and plain rooms, but warm welcome. Recommended. E *La Toja*, Rivadavia 494 Este, T422 2584. Simple spartan rooms, but decent enough. **Camping** At Chimbas, 7 km north.

Eating

● *on map*

Remolacha, Rivadavia y San Martín. Stylish, warm atmosphere, superb Italian-inspired menu, delicious steaks and pastas. Recommended. *Soychú*, de la Roza 223 Oeste. Excellent vegetarian food. Highly recommended. *Club Sirio Libanés 'El Palito'*, Entre Ríos 33 Sur. Pleasant decor, good tasty food. *Las Leñas*, San Martín 1670 Oeste. Huge atmospheric and popular *parrilla*. *Listo El Pollo*, Av San Martín y Santiago del Estero. Very good, reasonably cheap. *Amistad*, Rivadavia 47 Oeste. Chinese, good value, lots of choice. Many *pizzerías*, *confiterías*, and cafés. *Marilyn Bar*, San Martín y Mendoza. Late night drinks.

Shopping

San Juan is known for its fine bedspreads, blankets, saddle cloths and other items made from sheep, llama and guanaco wool, fine leather, wooden plates and mortars and, of course, its wines. *Mercado Artesanal* at España y San Luis is worth a visit. *Vinoteca San Juan*, Av San Martín 2154 Oeste. Good selection of wines, champagnes and olives.

Tour operators

Turismo Vittorio, Sarmiento 174 Sur, T420 4000, www.turismo-vittorio.com.ar Wide range of conventional and adventure tours, 4WD trips and car hire. *Nerja Tours*, Entre Ríos 178 Sur, T421 5214, www.nerja-tours.com.ar Also good for local trips and adventure tourism.

Transport

Bus terminal information, T422 1604

Long distance Air: Chacritas Airport, 14 km southeast. From **Buenos Aires** with *AR/Austral* (Av San Martín 215 Oeste, T0810-2228 6527, or 425 0487), also to Mendoza. **Buses**: Terminal at Estados Unidos y Santa Fe, 9 blocks east of centre (buses 33 and 35 go through the centre). To **La Rioja**, 6 hrs, US$6.50-8, 4 companies. **Catamarca**, 4 companies, US$11. **Tucumán**, 5 companies, US$12. **Córdoba**, *Socasa, 20 de Julio, Autotransportes San Juan* (T422 1870), 9 hrs, US$8 *coche cama*. **Buenos Aires**, 11 hrs, US$20 *semi cama*, US$30 *coche cama*). To **San Agustín** with *Vallecito*, 3 a day, US$5. Hourly departures to and from **Mendoza** with *TAC* and *Media Agua* and others, 2 hrs, US$5. Also services to **Barreal** and **Calingasta** with *El Triunfo*, T421 4532.

Directory

Banks open 0700-1200

Banks Many *Banelco* and *Link* ATMs accepting international credit cards in centre. *Cambio Santiago*, Gen Acha 52 Sur, T421 2332, weekdays until 2100, Sat until 1300. **Communications Internet:** Several *locutorios* have internet, those at Rivadavia y Acha, on the plaza, and Mendoza 139 Sur are open on Sun. Also *Cyber Café*, Rivadavia 12 Este. *Interredes*, Laprida 362 Este. *IAC*, Acha 142 Norte. **Tourist office** Sarmiento Sur 24 y San Martín, T422 2431, F422 5778, www.ischigualasto.com Open (in theory) Mon-Fri, 0730-2030, Sat-Sun 0900-2000. **Useful addresses** ACA, 9 de Julio y Rawson, T421 4205, information on routes, helpful.

Argentina

West of San Juan

Ruta 12 from San Juan along the canyon of the Río San Juan has been disrupted by work on two dams and is only open after 2000 and Sunday (one-way system as above). When the lakes are full of water, this road will be permanently closed

Calingasta (Phone code: 02648), 135 km west of San Juan along scenic provincial Ruta 12 (open westbound mornings, eastbound afternoons), is an idyllic, secluded village in a green valley with stunning striped rocks (annual cider festival in April). **D** *Hotel de Campo Calingasta*, T421220, restored old colonial-style building, pool, lovely views, very tranquil. **D** *La Capilla*, T421033, includes breakfast, basic but very clean, family-run, the family also sells the *TAC* bus tickets, and has the only public telephone in the village. **Tourist information** at the Municipalidad, Lavalle y Sarmiento, T421066. A good new road connects Pachaco with Talacasto, well-maintained broad *ripio*. To San Juan from Calingasta, take RN12, open currently only as far as Pachaco, and cross river for Talacasto. Road follows course of meandering Río San Juan, through lovely gorge. Cyclists in this area should note that there is very little shade on any of these roads, fill up with water at every opportunity. The police should be consulted before cycling from Calingasta to San Juan.

40 km S of Calingasta on the road to Uspallata Phone code 02648

Barreal A tranquil place between the Andes and the precordillera, with great horse riding in the mountains, trekking to Cerro Mercedaria, and wind-car racing. At **El Leoncito** (2,348 m), 26 km from Barreal there are two observatories (US$3, no public transport; tours can be arranged from San Juan, or at *Hotel Barreal*) and a nature reserve with a semi-arid environment and interesting wildlife, ranger post at entrance, no facilities. For mountain expeditions, Sr Ramón Luís Ossa, highly recommended. He runs mule treks into the Andes, crossing the foothills in summer, from 10 to 21 days between November and April; he can be reached at *Cabañas Doña Pipa*, Mariano Moreno s/n, T441004, www.ossaexpedicion.com The attractive *cabañas* sleep 6-8, well-equipped, breakfast included, open all year, pool, great views. For **tourist information**, T02648-441066.

Sleeping and eating C *Posada San Eduardo*, Av San Martín s/n. A charming colonial-style house, rooms around a courtyard, very pleasant and relaxing. **D** *Hotel Turismo Barreal*, San Martín s/n, T441090, hotelbarreal@yahoo.com.ar Nicely refurbished 1940's place, slightly spartan rooms, and some hostel space, but good restaurant, pool, riding. **Camping** Municipal site, T441241, is shady and well maintained with pool, open all year. Good food at *El Alero* and *Mama Rosa*.

Transport Buses from San Juan daily at 1900, **El Triunfo**, 5 hrs, US$4. Returning to San Juan at 2100. Also minibus run by José Luís Sosa, T441095.

North of San Juan

Ruta 40, the principal tourist route on the east Andean slope, heads north toward Cafayate and Salta, via San José de Jachal. At Talacasto, 55 km from San Juan, Ruta 436 branches toward Las Flores (Km 180) and the Chilean border at Agua Negra pass (4,600 m; open only January to early April), immigration, customs and ACA at Los Flores). **San José de Jachal**, 99 km north of Talacasto is a wine and olive-growing centre with many adobe buildings. From here, the undulating Ruta 40, paved but for the first 25 km to the La Rioja border, crosses dozens of dry watercourses. It continues to Villa Unión (see below), paved but for the last 15 km. ■ *The town has hotels, a campsite behind the ACA station and places to eat.* Expreso Argentino *bus from San Juan at 0730 arrives at 0940.*

The parks of Ischigualasto & Talampaya
Phone code: 02646 Colour map 8, grid A2

Ruta 141 runs across the south of the province towards La Rioja province and Córdoba. Just after Marayes (133 km), paved Ruta 510 (poor in parts) goes north 135 km to **San Agustín del Valle Fértil**, the best base for exploring Ischigualasto. **C** *Hostería Valle Fértil*, Rivadavia s/n, T420015, www.alkazarhotel.com.ar Good, a/c, smart, very comfortable, with fine views, also has *cabañas* and good restaurant. *Hospedajes* include **F** pp *Los Olivos*, Santa Fe y Tucumán, T420115, excellent value, with restaurant, and **F** pp *Ischigualasto*, Mitre y Aberstein, T420146, both with bath and fan; families provide lodging; Several campsites: *La Majadita*. Lovely campsite on river, with hot showers and great views. Municipal campsite by Dique San Agustín.

Tourist information on plaza, T420104. *Empresa Mendoza* bus from Mendoza arrives 0200, better go from San Juan, *Vallecito*, 0700, 1900, four hours, a/c, US$5.

North of San Agustín, at a police checkpoint, 56 km by paved road, a side road goes northwest for 17 km to the 62,000 ha **Parque Provincial Ischigualasto** (a UNESCO World Heritage Site), also known as **Valle de la Luna** for its bizarre sculptural desert landforms. Here the skeletons of the oldest known dinosaurs have been found (230 million years), though you'll have to visit the museum at San Juan to see their bones and fossils (US$2). **Tours and access**: There is one tour route, lasting 2½ hours, visiting only a part of the park but encompassing the most interesting sites. You have to go with a ranger in your own vehicle and it can be crowded at holiday times. Tours from San Juan, US$20 (including breakfast, lunch and tour), 14 hrs; from San Agustín US$10 for a guide (in both towns, ask at tourist office). Taxi to park US$7 from San Agustín (recommended if there are 4 - 5 people), more expensive out of season. You can camp opposite the ranger station, which has a small museum, but bring all food and water; expensive confitería next to ranger station.

Bizarre lunar landscape where the skeletons of the oldest known dinosaurs on earth were found

Just beyond the police checkpoint, near Los Baldecitos, paved Ruta 150 heads east to Patquía and then to La Rioja or Chilecito. From the junction provincial Ruta 76 heads north to Villa Unión. 61 km north of Los Baldecitos a paved road goes 14 km east to the 215,000-ha **Parque Nacional Talampaya**, another collection of spectacular desert landforms and a UNESCO World Heritage Site. The park occupies the site of an ancient lake, where sediments have been eroded by water and wind for some 200 million years, forming a dramatic landscape of pale red hills. Numerous fossils have been found and some 600 year-old petroglyphs can be seen not far from the access to the gorge. Along the *cañón* of the Río Talapmapya, extraordinary structures have been given popular names such as 'the balconies', 'the lift', 'the crib' or 'the owl'. At one point, the gorge narrows to 80 m and rises to 143 m. A refreshing leafy spot in the centre of the gorge, 'the botanical garden', has amazing diverse plants and trees. The end of the *cañón* is marked by the imposing cliffs of 'the cathedral' and the curious 'king on a camel'. 'The chessboard' and 'the monk', 53 m high, lie not far beyond the gorge, marking the end of the so-called **Circuito El Monje**. Only accessible with 4WD vehicles, **Circuito Los Cajones** continues in the same direction up to '*los pizarrones*', an enormous wall of rock, covered with petroglyphs, and then to '*los cajones*', a narrow pass between rock walls. **Circuito Ciudad Perdida** is another possible excursion in the park, southeast of the gorge, accessible only with 4WD vehicles, leading to an area of high cliffs and a large number of breathtaking rock formations. ■*Open 0800- 1700 (summer), 0900-1700 (rest of year). Entry US$2 for Argentines, US$4 for foreigners. T03825-470397.* **Tours and access**: tour operators from La Rioja and Chilecito sometimes combine a visit with nearby Ischigualasto, otherwise access is difficult (check that entrance and guide's fee are included). Independent access is possible, since buses or combis linking La Rioja and Villa Unión stop at the park entrance (a long walk to the *administración*), or better, at Pagancillo (village 30 km north), since most of the park wardens live there and will offer free transfer to the park early the following morning (contact Adolfo Páez). Excursions arranged at the *administración*: guided walks (5 hrs, US$5 pp); guided bike rides (2½ hrs, US$4 pp, cycle and helmet provided). Vehicle guided visits (prices are for the whole group of up to 8 people) for Circuito El Monje (1½ hrs, US$20), Circuito Los Cajones (3 hrs, US$40) and Circuito Ciudad Perdida (6 hrs, US$50); access with own 4WD vehicle is allowed with a guide (US$5, US$10 or US$13 per vehicle for respective itineraries). Best time to visit is in the morning, for best natural light and avoiding strong afternoon winds. *Administración* has small restaurant, toilets, public telephones.

Sleeping Basic campsite next to *administración*, US$1 pp. In Pagancillo, **F** *Hotel Pagancillo*, T03825-156 66828 (shared bath, no breakfast, comfortable) or at *Bar Jatel*.

La Rioja

Argentina

Phone code: 03822
Colour map 8, grid A2
Population: 147,000
Avoid arriving on Sat
night as most things
are shut on Sun

Founded 1591, at the edge of the plains, with views of Sierra de Velasco, La Rioja can be oppressively hot from November to March. But the town comes alive after the daily siesta and during the annual carnival, *Chaya* (in February), and the *Tinkunaco* festival (beginning on New Year's Eve and lasting 4 days). The city's main buildings and plazas date from the late 19th century, while the recent government of Carlos Menem, born in a little town 90 km north, has left a certain affluence. The **Church and Convent of San Francisco**, 25 de Mayo y Bazán y Bustos, contains the Niño Alcalde, a remarkable image of the infant Jesus. You can also see the cell (*celda*) in which San Francisco Solano lived and the orange tree, now dead, which he planted in 1592 (25 de Mayo 218). ■ *Tue-Sun 0900-1200, 1830-2100, free.* San Francisco helped to bring peace between the Spaniards and the indigenous people in 1593, an event celebrated at Tinkunaco. The **Convent of Santo Domingo**, Luna y Lamadrid, dates from 1623, said to be the oldest surviving church in Argentina. **Museo Arqueológico Inca Huasi**, Alberdi 650, owned by the Franciscan Order, contains a huge collection of fine Diaguita Indian ceramics. ■ *Tue-Sat, 0900-1200, US$0.50.* The **Mercado Artesanal**, Luna 790, has rather expensive handicrafts. ■ *Tue-Fri 0800-1200, 1600-2000, Sat-Sun 0900-1300.* In the same building, is the small **Museo de Arte Sacro**, with 18th and 19th century images and Cusqueña school paintings. ■ *Tue-Sat 0800-1200.* In a beautiful and well kept house at the opposite corner, the **Museo Folklórico**, Luna 811, gives a fascinating insight into traditional La Rioja life, with a superb collection of native deities, rustic wine-making machinery and delicate silver *mates*. Well worth a visit too for its leafy patio. ■ *Tue-Sun 0900-1200, 1600-2000 (Tue-Sat 0900-1200 in summer), US$0.35, free guided visits, T428500.* There are good views of La Rioja from Cerro de la Cruz (1,648 m), 23 km west, now a centre for hang-gliding.

Sleeping
A/c or fan are essential
for summer nights

High season is during
Jul winter holidays

B *King's*, Av Quiroga 1070, T422122. 4-star, buffet breakfast included, a/c gym, pool and fine rooms, also car rental. **C** *Plaza*, San Nicolás de Bari y 9 de Julio (on Plaza 25 de Mayo), T425215, www.plazahotel-larioja.com.ar Functional 4-star, pool on top floor, breakfast included, a/c. **D** *Libertador*, Buenos Aires 253, T427794, www.libertadorhotel-lar.com.ar Comfortable, decent rooms, a/c, with breakfast. **D** *Savoy*, San Nicolás de Bari y Roque A Luna, T426894, hotelsavoy@infovia.com.ar In a quiet residential area, tidy, comfortable, with breakfast and a/c, second floor best. **D** *Vincent Apart Hotel*, Santiago del Estero y San Nicolás de Bari, T432326. New flats for up to 4, a/c, with dining room, kitchen and fridge, breakfast included, excellent value for a group of 3 or 4. Recommended. **E** *Mirasol*, Rivadavia 941, T420760. Quiet, comfortable, homely, though the windows look onto a corridor, breakfast extra. **E** *Pensión 9 de Julio*, Copiapó 197 (on Plaza 9 de Julio), T426955. Attractive front patio, with breakfast, hot water, cheaper with shared bath, not very friendly. **Camping** At Balneario Los Sauces, 13 km west on Ruta 75, *Camping de la Sociedad Sirio Libanesa*, hot showers, swimming-pool.

Eating
Mid-range: *Cavadini*, Av Quiroga 1145. Good *parrilla*, informal. *El Corral*, Av Quiroga y Rivadavia. Traditional rustic fare and good local wines. *Los Palotes*, H Yrigoyen 128. Varied menu, including salmon, trout, seafood and Mexican, pleasant atmosphere. *La Vieja Casona*, Rivadavia 427. Popular, smart *parrilla*. **Cheap**: *Alike*, Vélez Sarsfield e H Irigoyen. *Tenedor libre*, wide choice. *La Aldea de la Virgen de Luján*, Rivadavia 756. Lively atmosphere. **Cafés and bars**: *Café de la Plaza* , Rivadavia e H Irigoyen. Modern, popular. *Café del Paseo*, 25 de Mayo y Luna. On main plaza in a small shopping area. *Confitería El Ciervo*, C Joaquín V González opposite main plaza. In the arcade of the Club Social. *El Cielo*, San Nicolás de Bari y Güemes. Popular bar with pool table, open at night. More fun at *El Infierno*, Santa Fe e H Yrigoyen.

Tour operators
For excursions to Talampaya, Valle de la Luna, Laguna Brava and Corona del Inca crater (high season only), city tours and horse riding in Velasco mountains: *Aguada*, T433695 or 15-675699, talampaya_aguada@ciudad.com.ar Helpful agency with good tours. *Corona del Inca*, Luna 914, T450054 or 15-663811, www.coronadelinca.com.ar *Néstor Pantaleo*, Ecuador 813, T422103. Experienced photographer, runs 4WD trips, several languages spoken.

Air To/from **Buenos Aires**, *AR*, T426307, flights usually stop at Catamarca or Córdoba. **Transport**
Buses Terminal 7 blocks south of the Cathedral at Artigas y España (T425453). To **Buenos** *Airport T439211*
Aires, *Gen Urquiza* and *Chevallier* US$18-25, 15-17 hrs. To **Mendoza** (US$10-12) and **San**
Juan (US$6.50-8), 6 hrs. To **Tinogasta**, daily, US$4-5. To **Tucumán** (US$5.50-7), several
companies. To **Salta**, *Andesmar*, 10 hrs, US$11. Also provincial services.

Banks LECOP bonds and provincial bonds with the face of Evita are in circulation and changed 1 to 1 **Directory**
into pesos within the province. US$ cash changed at *Banco de Galicia*, Buenos Aires y San Nicolás de
Bari, and at *Daniel*, exchange facilities at Rivadavia 525. **Communications** Internet:*Cool.com*, Luna
684, US$0.65 per hr.*Cyber Hall*, Rivadavia 763. Good service with webcams, US$0.65 per hr.*Cyber más*,
Rivadavia 909. Open 24 hrs, US$0.35 per hr. **Post Office:** Perón 258. **Telephone:** Several *locutorios* in
the centre and at Av Quiroga e Hipólito Yrigoyen, with internet access (US$0.60/hr) near bus terminal.
Tourist office Luna 345, T453982, www.larioja.gov.ar

Chilecito

Chilecito, 129 km northwest of Patquía, is La Rioja province's second town. Founded *Phone code: 03825*
in 1715, it has good views of Sierra de Famatina, especially from the top of El *Colour map 8, grid A2*
Portezuelo, an easy climb from the end of Calle El Maestro. The region is famous for its *Population: 25,000*
wines, olives and walnuts. **Samay Huasi**, 3 km south of town, was the house of
Joaquín V González, founder of La Plata University. He designed the gardens with
native trees and strange stone monoliths expressing his love of ancient cultures; there's
also a small natural history museum. It's an attractive place for a relaxing day; staying
guests also welcome (**F** pp, **E** pp full board, reserve in advance). ■ *Mon-Fri*
0800-1300, 1330-1930, Sat-Sun 0800-1200, 1500-1900 (closed 22 Dec-6 Jan),
US$0.35. T422629. **Molino San Francisco y Museo de Chilecito**, at J de Ocampo 50,
has archaeological, historical and artistic exhibits. ■ *Mon-Fri 0800-1200, 1600-2100,*
Sat-Sun 0830-1230, 1530-2000, US$0.35. At the **Cooperativa La Riojana**, La Plata
646, you can watch local grapes being processed to make a wide variety of wines. Free
guided visits (45 minutes) and a smart wine shop. ■ *Mon-Fri 0800, 1000, 1200; shop*
open 0600-1400. At **Santa Florentina** (8 km northwest), there are the impressive
remains of a huge early 20th century foundry, linked to Chilecito and La Mejicana
mine by cable car. Tourist office at bus station (no phone). ■ *Daily 0800-1230,*
1530-2100. For more tourist information and pictures visit www.chilecitotour.com or
www.chilecito.net There are a couple of internet places.

D *Chilecito (ACA)*, T Gordillo y A G Ocampo, T422201, 156-66358. A/c, quite comfortable, **Sleeping**
with breakfast, safe parking, pool, restaurant has cheap set menus. **D** *Hostal Mary Pérez*,
Florencio Dávila 280, T/F423156, hostal_mp@hotmail.com Best value, comfortable, welcoming atmosphere, good breakfast. Recommended. **E** *Bellia*, El Maestro 188, T422181.
Rooms open onto a nice garden. Breakfast included, good place for relaxing. **F** pp *Finca del*
Paimán, Mariano Moreno y Santa Rosa (San Miguel, 3 km southeast of town), T/F425102,
www.fincadelpaiman.8m.com Owner, Alejo Piehl, has opened his delightful 4½-ha farm to
guests, spacious rooms, kitchen, breakfast and transport to/from Chilecito included. You can
help with fruit harvesting or jam cooking! Warmly recommended, book in advance.
Camping 3 sites at Santa Florentina and Las Talas, 8 km northwest (remise taxi US$2-2.50).

Mid range *Club Arabe*, 25 de Mayo entre Zelada y Dávila and Famatina. Middle eastern food **Eating**
on request, otherwise the usual dishes served under grapevines. *El Rancho de Ferrito*, Luna
647. Popular *parrilla*, with local wines. *La Rosa*, Ocampo 149, T424693. Relaxing atmosphere,
huge variety of pizzas, more extensive menu Fri and Sat. *El Pelado*, Ocampo 15. For take
away meals when all else closed. *Chloé*, El Maestro y 9 de Julio. Basic meals at café on Plaza (3
others). *Yop´s*, on C Dávila (half block from plaza) attracts a more bohemian crowd.

Chilecito is an excellent base for amazing treks in the Famatina mountains and 1-day trips to **Tour operators**
Talampaya and Valle de la Luna. *Alejo Piehl*, T/F425102, 15672612, www.

Argentina

Argentina

talampaya-turismo.8k.com Experienced guide (see also **Sleeping**, above), all inclusive 1-day tours to Talampaya and Valle de la Luna, US$30 pp, and a variety of unforgettable 1- or 2-day treks (US$35 pp) to Famatina, visiting abandoned cable car stations on the way to the summit. Occasional 4WD trips. Recommended. *Inka Ñan*, T425975, 156-71933. Leopoldo Badoul organises excursions to the province's main attractions. *Asociación Riojana de Turismo Rural*, Av Perón 668, T422828. Guided visits to local farms, very cheap. For **paragliding**, contact Camel Waidatt, T424874, www.cuestavieja.com

Transport   **Buses**   To **San Juan** and Mendoza with *Vallecito*, US$9-10; to **La Rioja**, several times daily, US$3. To **Córdoba**, US$8 and **Buenos Aires**, US$20, *El Práctico, General Urquiza*.

At Nonogasta 16 km south of Chilecito, the partly paved Ruta 40 heads west climbing through a deep narrow canyon in a series of hairpins to the Cuesta de Miranda (2,020 m). After the Cuesta is **Villa Unión**, 92 km from Nonogasta, *Hotel Centro*, on main plaza, has a restaurant. D *Hotel Pircas Negras*, on Ruta 76, T03825-470611. E *Hotel Noryanepat*, JVGonzález 150, T03825-470372, small rooms with a/c, good. From Villa Unión, excursions can be made by four-wheel drive vehicle to the **Reserva Natural Laguna Brava**, 150 km north. The road goes through Vinchina (several basic *hospedajes* and new D *Hotel Corona del Inca*, T03825-494004, hotelcoronadelinca@ciudad.com.ar) and Jagüe (basic facilities). Further on, as you climb the Portezuelo del Peñón, the salt lake of Laguna Brava becomes visible with some of the mightiest volcanoes on earth in the background. From the left these are the perfect cone Veladero (6,436 m), Reclus (6,335 m), Los Gemelos (6,130 m), Pissis (6,882 m) the highest volcano in the world, though inactive, and Bonete (6,759 m) which is visible from Villa Unión and Talampaya. For tours in this area see under Chilecito and La Rioja. **Access**: From Jagüe 4WD and going with two vehicles are essential. Summer rainfalls and winter snow may limit the access to only a short period in the year; usually in April or early May is best. Entry US$5.

Catamarca

Phone code: 03833
Colour map 8, grid A2
Population: 130,000
Altitude: 490 m
153 km NE of La Rioja
240 km S of Tucumán

The Zonda, a strong dry mountain wind, can cause dramatic temperature increases

Officially San Fernando del Valle de Catamarca, the city is capital of its province, on the Río del Valle, between the slopes of the Sierra de Ambato (to the west) and Ancasti (to the east). Now a rather run-down place, Catamarca is most famous for its textiles, and unless you're here for the poncho festival in the second fortnight in July (*feria* with high quality handicrafts, food and live music), there's little to draw you to the city. Summers are unbearably hot with temperatures up to 45° C. 37km north is the much more appealing and prettier weekend retreat of **El Rodeo** with its cooler microclimate, good walks and charming *hosterías*; tourist information T490043 (D *Hostería El Rodeo*, T490296, www.hotelguia.com/elrodeo daily minibus from centre). In the vast open puna to the northwest, there are traces of sophisticated ancient civilizations, and the finest of the city's six museums has an outstanding collection of indigenous artefacts. **Museo Arqueológico Adán Quiroga**, Sarmiento 450. ■ *Mon-Fri 0700-1300, 1430-2000, Sat-Sun 1200-1900, US$0.40. T437413.*

Sleeping
Hotels are mostly unmodernized and overpriced, for businessmen rather than tourists

C *Casino Catamarca*, Pasaje César Carman s/n (behind the ACA service station), T432928, inforcentral@hotelcasinocatamarca.com The smartest place to stay, modern and bright, well decorated rooms, discreetly hidden casino, large pool. D *Arenales*, Sarmiento 542, T431329, www.hotel-arenales.com Comfortable plain rooms, good bathrooms, restaurant. D *El Gran Hotel* Camilo Melet 41, T426715. Delightful, helpful owners, simple spacious rooms. Recommended. D *El Leo III*, Sarmiento 727, T432080. Central, more comfortable than most if nothing special, good value. North of the city towards **Las Juntas**, C *Estancia Los Timones* at Las Piedras Blancas, T425230/156-93193. Recommended. *Los Hermanos Vergara* run buses from Catamarca Terminal Mon to Sat, 0800 and 2000. **Camping** Municipal site 5 km from centre on road to El Rodeo/Las Juntas, US$1.50, clean, friendly, hot showers.

Limited choice: the best is *La Tinaja*, Sarmiento 533. Delicious *parrilla* and excellent pastas, worth the price. *Salsa Criolla*, República 546 on the plaza. Traditional popular *parrilla*, sloppy service, but the beef is good. *Trattoria Montecarlo*, next door, same owner, Italian style. *Family Pizzería* on the plaza. Cheap pizzas, popular. *Richmond* is the most appealing café on the plaza, stylish. *Sociedad Española*, Virgen del Valle 725. Recommended for quality and variety, paella and other Spanish specialities, friendly service; worth the 5 block walk from the plaza.

Eating

Catamarca specialities from: *Cuesta del Portezuelo*, Sarmiento 571 and *Valdez*, Sarmiento 578. You can see carpets being woven at *Mercado Artesanal*, Virgen del Valle 945, wide range of handicrafts, daily 0800-1330, 1500-2100; carpet factory Mon-Fri 0800-1200. **Supermarkets**: *Norte* , Rivadavia 945, in the main pedestrian shopping street.

Shopping

Mountain bikes can be hired from *Club Mountain Bike*, www.mtbcat.com.ar Mountaineering through *Agrupación Calchaqui*, Tourism block, Gral Roca, T436368. Walking expeditions in Antofagasta de la Sierra by *Aníbal Vázquez*, T03835-471001, and paragliding through *Eduardo Bonutto*, T156-88513. Swimming pool at Junín 348, T438802.

Tour operators

Air Airport T430080. *AR/Austral* (Sarmiento 589, T424450) to/from **Buenos Aires**. **Buses** Terminal 5 blocks southeast of plaza at Güemes y Tucumán T437578. Taxi to/from Plaza 25 de Mayo US$0.50. To **Tucumán**, several companies, 3½-4hrs, US$3-5. To **Buenos Aires**, 4 companies daily, 15 hrs, US$20. To **Córdoba**, 4 companies daily, 6 hrs, US$7. To **Santiago del Estero**, *Mendoza*, *La Estrella*, 4 hrs, US$5. To **Mendoza**, several companies, daily, 10 hrs, US$9-13. To **La Rioja**, several companies, US$3, 2 hrs. To **Tinogasta**, 3 companies, US$4. To **Belén** via Aimogasta and Londres, several companies, 5 hrs, US$5-7; *Marín* (via Aconquija).

Transport

Banks Many ATMs for all major cards, along Rivadavia and at bus terminal, *BBVA Banco Francés*, Rivadavia 520. *Banco de la Nación* San Martín 632. **Communications** Internet: *Cedecc*, Esquiú 414. *Taraj Net*, San Martín y Ayacucho. **Telephone:** most *telecentros* around Plaza 25 de Mayo, also at República 845 and Rivadavia 758, open 0700-2400, daily. **Post Office:** San Martín 753, slow, open 0800-1300, 1600-2000. **Tourist office** South side of the plaza next to the cinema, T437791, 0810-7774321, www.catamarca.com www.catamarca.gov.ar 0900-2100, daily. Helpful leaflets on local places of interest, ecotourism etc, bus times and prices.

Directory

Puna west of Catamarca

The high altitude desert of the puna is spectacular, with a distinct culture and remote untouristy towns. It's most easily reached by the paved road to **Aimogasta** and on to the small settlements of Tinogasta and Fiambalá, useful staging posts if taking the Paso San Fransisco to Chile, or north to Andagalá, or to Belén, where the rough road to Antofagasta de la Sierra begins.

Tinogasta (*Phone code: 03837*) is in an oasis of vineyards, olive groves, and poplars. **D** *Viñas del Sol*, Perón 231, T420028. **D** *Hostería Novel*, Córdoba 200, T420009, near airport, friendly. **E** *Res Don Alberto*, A del Pino y Rivadavia, T420323. *Restaurant Casa Grande*, Constitución y Moreno, good meals, try local wines. Buses to Tucumán, *Empresa Gutiérrez*, 3 weekly (daily in high season). To Catamarca, *Empresa Gutiérrez* (connection to Buenos Aires), *Robledo* and *Rubimar*, US$6; to La Rioja, El *Cóndor*, US$4. Tinogasta is the starting point for expeditions to **Pissis** the second highest mountain in South America, 6,882 m. To get there, take Ruta 60 which crosses Tinogasta in the direction of the San Francisco pass. You have to register at the police station outside Fiambalá, take passport. Expeditions organized and horse riding with Omar Monuey, La Espiga de Oro, 25 de Mayo 436 or *Varela Viajes*, T420428. At Fiambalá, contact Jonson and Ruth Reynoso, T496214.

    Fiambalá is 49 km north of Tinogasta, a peaceful place in a vine-filled valley, with **Termas de Fiambalá**, situated hot springs, 14 km east (take a taxi; make sure fare includes wait and return). **D** *Hostería Municipal*, Almagro s/n, T03837-496016, good

Tinogasta & Fiambalá
This is one of the few regions in Argentina where the water is notoriously bad: avoid salads and ice, drink mineral water

Argentina

Argentina

value, also restaurant. At the Termas is a *Complejo Turístico* with cabins (**E** pp), T496016; also camping. *Empresa Gutiérrez* to Catamarca via Tinogasta. For connections to Belén, change bus at Aimogasta. 4WD vehicles may be hired for approaching the Pissis-Ojos region; ask at the Intendencia.

Border with Chile – Paso San Francisco

Fiambalá is the starting-point for the crossing to Chile via Paso San Francisco (4,726 m), 203 km northwest along a paved road. The border is open 0830-1930, T498001. On the Chilean side roads run to El Salvador and Copiapó. This route is closed by snow between June and October; take enough fuel for at least 400 km as there are no service stations from Fiambalá to just before Copiapó.

Belén

Phone code 03835
Colour map 6, grid C3
Population: 8,800
Altitude 1,000m

A quiet intimate little town, Belén is famous for its ponchos, saddlebags and rugs, which you can see being woven in various workshops. The archaeological museum, **Cóndor Huasi** (San Martín y Belgrano, 1st floor, open daily), contains fascinating Diaguita artefacts, and you can walk up C Gral Roca to the statue of Virgin of Belén, high above the town, for good views. Important festival: Nuestra Señora de Belén, 24 December-6 January. **Tourist information** at the bus terminal a block from the plaza. T461539, alpamicuna@cotelbelen.com.ar **C** *Belén*, Belgrano y Cubas, T461501, www.belencat.com.ar Recently refurbished and comfortable, also tour operator. **D** *Samai*, Urquiza 349, T461320, old fashioned but welcoming. *El Unico*, the best *parrilla*, *Bar El Seminario* great for beer and sandwiches, fills the plaza at weekends.

South of Belén, Ruta 40 is paved to Chilecito via **Londres**, a quiet, pretty village. North of Belén Ruta 40 runs another 176 km, largely unpaved, to Santa María at the provincial border with Tucumán (see page 138), and on to Cafayate (page 138), or 260 km north to tiny remote **Antofagasta de la Sierra** and onwards to San Antonio de los Cobres in Salta. East of Belén, a rough and sandy road goes to **Andalgalá**, a former copper-mining town with two archaeological museums, a handicraft market, and a decent hotel **D** *Aquasol*. For excursions and tourist information contact *Andalgalá Turismo*, T03835-422405, turandalgala@cotelbelen.com.ar Very helpful.

Transport Buses from Belén to **Santa María**, **San Cayetano** and **Parra** (connection there with other companies to Cafayate and Salta), daily, 5 hrs, US$4 . To **Tinogasta**, **Robledo**, 3 weekly, 3 hrs, US$4. To **Antofagasta de la Sierra**, *El Antofagasteño*, 3 weekly, 7 hrs, US$12. For more frequent services to **Catamarca** or **La Rioja**, take bus to Aimogasta, 1 hr, US$1.50.

The Northeast

The river systems of the Paraná, Paraguay and Uruguay, with hundreds of minor tributaries, small lakes and marshlands, dominate the Northeast. Between the Paraná and Uruguay rivers is Argentine Mesopotamia containing the provinces of Entre Ríos, Corrientes and Misiones, this last named after Jesuit foundations, whose red stone ruins have been rescued from the jungle. The great attraction of this region is undoubtedly the Iguazú Falls, which tumble into a gorge on a tributary of the Alto Paraná on the border with Brazil. But the region offers other opportunities for wildlife watching, such as the national parks of the Wet Chaco and the amazing flooded plains of the Esteros del Iberá. This is also the region of mate tea, sentimental chamamé music and tiny chipá bread.

Gualeguaychú

Phone code: 03446
Colour map 8, grid B5
Population: 80,000
220 km N of Buenos Aires

Situated on the Río Gualeguaychú, 19 km above its confluence with the Río Paraná, this is a pleasant town with an attractive *costanera* and a lively pre-Lenten carnival. Some 33 km southeast the Libertador Gral San Martín Bridge (5.4 km long) provides the most southerly route across the Río Uruguay, to Fray Bentos (vehicles US$4; pedestrians and cyclists may cross only on vehicles, officials may arrange lifts). The Uruguayan consulate is at Rivadavia 810, T426168.

The **Casa de Aedo**, San José y Rivadavia (on plaza), in the oldest house in the city, served as Garibaldi's headquarters when he sacked the city in 1845. ■ *Wed-Sat 0900-1145, Fri-Sat also 1600-1845 (in summer afternoon times are 1700-1945)*. An old iron bridge crosses the river to the beautiful, 110-ha **Parque Unzué**. Nice walks can be taken along the *costanera* between the bridge and the small port, from where short boat excursions and city tours leave (also from the *balneario municipal*), T423248, high season only. At G Méndez y Costanera is **El Patio del Mate**, a workshop dedicated to the *mate* gourd, coming in all shapes and prices. ■ *Daily 0800-2100, T424371, www.elpatiodelmate.com.ar* About 200 m south of the port is the Plazoleta de los Artesanos in which is the **tourist office** ■ *0800-2000 (closing later in summer), T423668, www.gualeguaychuturismo.com*

Sleeping C *Puerto Sol*, San Lorenzo 477, T/F434017, www.puerto-sol.com.ar Good rooms, a/c, next to the port, has a small resort on a nearby island (transfer included in room rate) for lazing and having a drink. **C** *Tykuá*, Luis N Palma 150, T422625, hoteltykua@arnet.com.ar New, breakfast included, 3 blocks from the bridge (**D** in low season). **D** *Amalfi*, 25 de Mayo 571, T426818. Pleasant, central, old house, quite comfortable, no breakfast, helpful (**E** in low season). **D** *Brutti*, Bolívar 591, T426048. Kind owners, decent rooms with fan and breakfast (**E** in low season). **E** *Lo de Juan*, Alem y Bolívar, T433661. Behind the shop where Juan sells his handicrafts, good rooms with fan, no breakfast. **Camping** Several sites on riverside, next to the bridge and north of it. *Costa Azul*, 200 m northeast of bridge, T423984. Shady, good location, campsite (US$4 a day), wooden cabins (**D** for 4) and small flats with cooking facilities. *Solar del Este*, east end of C Ituzaingó, T433303, www.solardeleste.com.ar Resort on the río Gualeguaychú, popular (US$3 a day). *El Ñandubaysal*, T423298, www.nandubaysal.com.ar The smartest, on the Río Uruguay, 15 km southeast (US$5.50-7.50 per tent plus access fee).

Accommodation is scarce during carnival. Prices double Dec-Mar, Easter and long weekends. The tourist office has a list of family accommodation. Many restaurants on the Costanera

Transport Bus terminal at Bv Artigas y Bv Jurado, T440688 (30-min walk to centre, *remise* taxi US$1.20). To **Concepción del Uruguay**, 1 hr, US$1.50. To **Fray Bentos**, 1¼ hrs, US$2.30, 2 a day (1 on Sun), arrive 30 mins before departure for immigration. To **Buenos Aires**, US$7-8, 3½ hrs, several daily.

The first Argentine port of any size on the Río Uruguay was founded in 1783. The old town is centred on Plaza Ramírez. Overlooking the main plaza is the church of the Immaculate Conception which contains the remains of Gen Urquiza. **Palacio San José**, Urquiza's former mansion, 32 km west of the town, is now a museum, with artefacts from Urquiza's life and a collection of period furniture, recommended. ■ *Mon-Fri 0830-1230, 1400-1830, Sat-Sun 0900-1745 , US$1, free guided visits 1000, 1100, 1500, 1600, www.palaciosanjose.com* Take Ruta 39 west and turn right after Caseros train station. Buses to Paraná or Rosario del Tala stop at El Cruce or Caseros, 4 or 8 km away respectively, US$0.80 (take *remise* taxi from Caseros). *Remise* taxis charge about US$8 with 1½ hrs wait. Tour operators run *combis* in high season US$5 including entry. The **Museo Casa de Delio Panizza**, Galarza y Supremo Entrerriano, is in a mansion dating from 1793 and contains 19th-century furnishings and artefacts. ■ *0900-1200, 1400-1800 (1800-2100 in summer)*. **Tourist office** is at 9 de Julio 844, T425820. ■ *Mon-Fri 0700-1300, 1400-2000, weekends 0700-2200 in high season. www.concepcionentrerios.com.ar*

Concepción del Uruguay
Phone code: 03442
Colour map 8, grid B5
Population: 65,000
74 km N of Gualeguaychú

Sleeping and eating AL pp *Estancia San Pedro*, T03442-428374/03445-482107, esanpedro@ciudad.com.ar Owned by descendants of Urquiza, old rooms full of antiques, very good. **D** *Grand Hotel*, Eva Perón 114, T422851, www.palaciotexier.com.ar Originally a French-style mansion with adjacent theatre, superior rooms (25% pricier) have a/c and TV but not much difference from standard, both include breakfast, no restaurant. **E** *Centro*, Moreno 130, T427429. Spotless, comfy, older front rooms and newer ones on shady patio, breakfast extra. *El Remanso*, Rocamora y Eva Perón. Popular, moderately priced *parrilla*.

Argentina

Transport Buses Terminal at Rocamora y Los Constituyentes, T422352 (remise, US$0.40). To **Buenos Aires**, frequent, 4 hrs, US$8-9. To **Colón**, 45 mins, US$1.

Colón

Colour map 8, grid A5
Population: 19,200
45 km N of Concepción
del Uruguay

Founded in 1863, Colón has shady streets, an attractive *costanera* and long sandy beaches, with cliffs visible from a considerable distance. A road bridge links Colón and Paysandú, Uruguay. The most attractive part of the town is the **port district**, next to Plaza San Martín. On the plaza and the streets which go down to the riverside are fine old houses, including the former passenger terminal, now housing the **tourist office**, Avenida Costanera Quirós y Gouchón ■ *Mon-Fri 0630-2100, Sat 0700-2100, Sun 0800-2100, T421233, www.colonentrerios.com.ar* At Avenida 12 de Abril y Paso is **La Casona** (1868), with a handicraft exhibition and shop. North of the port, Calle Alejo Peyret gives access to the *balnearios* and Calle Belgrano leads to the **Complejo Termal**, with 10 thermal pools (34º to 40º). ■ *Daily 0900-2100, US$1.30, T424717.*

Sleeping and eating **D** *Holimasú*, Belgrano 28, T421305, www.hotelholimasu.com.ar Nice patio, breakfast included, a/c extra. **D** *Hostería Restaurant del Puerto*, Alejo Peyret 158, T422698, hosteriadelpuerto@ciudad.com.ar Great value, lovely atmosphere in old house, breakfast included. **D** *La Posada de David*, Alejo Peyret 97, T423930. Pleasant family house with garden, welcoming, good rooms with breakfast, one room with cooking facilities. **D** *Vieja Calera*, Bolívar 350, T423761, viejacalera@ar.inter.net Dark corridors lead to decent rooms, breakfast included. **E** *Sweet Rose*, 25 de Mayo 10, T156 43487. Quite comfortable, small bathrooms, breakfast extra. **F** pp *Casamate*, Laprida 128, T422385, www.casamate.com.ar HI affiliated (discount for members and students), renovated old house, young owners provide excellent information, shared baths or **D** with bath, breakfasts are superb (US$1.50 if you add scrambled eggs); other meals on request, cooking and laundry facilities, free use of cycles, tours and activities, German and English spoken. Recommended. Several **campsites** along river bank, most US$3 per day. *Camping Municipal Playa Norte*, T422074, a few blocks north of the port district. *Piedras Coloradas*, T421451, a few hundred m south of Av 12 de Abril. Eating places include *La Cosquilla de Angel*, Alejo Peyret 180. The smartest place in town, varied moderately priced meals, including fish, adequate set menu. *El Viejo Almacén*, Gral Urquiza y Paso. Good fish.

Transport Buses Terminal at Paysandú y Sourigues (10 blocks north of main plaza), T421716. Not all long distance buses enter Colón: at Ubajay (70 km north), Parador Gastiazoro, T0345-4905026, is a busy stop for buses going north. To **Buenos Aires**, US$8-10, 5-6 hrs. To **Mercedes** (for Iberá), several companies, 6-7 hrs, US$6-8. To **Paraná**, 4-5 hrs, US$7. **To Uruguay**: via the Artigas Bridge (US$4 toll) all formalities are dealt with on the Uruguayan side. *Migraciones* officials board the bus, but non-Argentines/Uruguayans should get off bus for stamp. Bus to **Paysandú**, US$2-2.30, 45 mins.

Parque Nacional El Palmar

51 km N of Colón

This park of 8,500 ha is on the Río Uruguay, off Ruta 14. The park contains varied scenery with a mature palm forest, sandy beaches on the Uruguay river, Indian tombs and the remains of an 18th-century quarry and port, a good museum and many rheas and other birds. The Yatay palms grow up to 12 m and some are hundreds of years old. It is best to stay overnight as wildlife is more easily seen in the early morning or at sunset. Very popular at weekends in summer. ■ *US$4 (Argentines US$2).*

Transport Buses from Colón, 1 hr, US$1.50, will drop you at the entrance and it is easy to hitch the last 12 km to the park administration. *Remise* taxis from Colón or Ubajay offer tours, eg from Colón: US$15 for a 4-hr return trip, including tour or waiting time. There are camping facilities (electricity, hot water), with restaurant opposite, and a small shop.

Refugio de Vida Silvestre La Aurora del Palmar is opposite the Parque Nacional El Palmar, 3 km south of Ubajay at Km 202 Ruta 14. A private reserve (free entry) protecting a similar environment to that of its neighbour, La Aurora covers 1,150 ha, of which 200 are covered with a mature palm forest. There are also gallery forests along the streams and patches of *espinal* or scrub. Birds are easily seen, as are capybaras along the streams. The administration centre is only 500 m from Ruta 14 and services are well organized. There are guided excursions on horseback, on foot or canoe, 2 hrs maximum, US$3.35-5. Camping US$1.70-2 pp a day plus US$1.30 per tent, or **G** pp in old railway carriages. Buses from Colón or those coming from the north will drop you at the entrance. Tell the driver you are going to La Aurora del Palmar, to avoid confusion with the national park. *Remise* taxi from Ubajay US$1.70. Book in advance or check availability for excursions. T03447-421549, www.auroradelpalmar.com.ar

Just downriver from Salto, Uruguay, Concordia is a prosperous city. The Río Uruguay is impassable for large vessels beyond the rapids of Salto Chico near the city, and Salto Grande 32 km up-river, where there is a large international hydro electric dam, providing a crossing to Uruguay. Above Salto Grande the river is generally known as the Alto Uruguay. In the streets around the main **Plaza 25 de Mayo** there are some fine public buildings. Tourist office on Plaza 25 de Mayo (open daily 0700-2400). The city has a range of hotels and restaurants

Concordia
Colour map 8, grid A5
Population: 93,800
104 km N of Colón

Transport Buses Terminal at Justo y Yrigoyen, 13 blocks northwest of the Plaza 25 de Mayo (reached by No 2 bus). To **Buenos Aires**, US$11, 6½ hrs. To **Paraná** 5 a day.

To Uruguay Ferry: take No 4 bus from terminal marked 'Puerto', for ferry crossing to Salto US$2, tickets obtainable at a small kiosk, which shuts 15 mins before departure, outside migration in building marked 'Resguardo', 5 departures Mon-Fri, 4 departures Sat, 2 departures (0800 1800) Sun, 20 mins, passengers only. **Bus**: service via Salto Grande dam, *Flecha Bus* and *Chadre*, 2 a day each, not Sun, US$2, all formalities on Argentine side, passports checked on bus. **Bicycles** are not allowed to cross the international bridge but officials will help cyclists find a lift. The **Uruguayan consulate** is at Pellegrini 709, of 1 C, T421 0380.

About 153 km upstream from Concordia is the small port of Monte Caseros, with the Uruguayan town of Bella Unión, on the Brazilian border, almost opposite

Linked to the larger Brazilian town of Uruguaiana by a bridge over the Alto Uruguay, Paso de los Libres was founded in 1843 by General Madariaga. It was here that he crossed the river from Brazil with his 100 men and annexed Corrientes province for Argentina. **B** *Alejandro I*, Col López 502, T424100, pool, cable TV, best. Several in **D** range. The town is not regarded as safe (2003).

Paso de los Libres
Colour map 8, grid A5
Population: 25,000
336 km N of Concordia

Transport Buses: Terminal is 1 km from town centre, near border. **To Brazil**: taxi or bus US$2.50. No bus service on Sun.

Rosario

The largest city in the province of Santa Fe and the third largest city in Argentina, Rosario is a great industrial and export centre on the Río Paraná. It has a lively cultural scene with several theatres and bars where there are daily shows. It is also home of many nationally famous musicians and modern artists. The old city centre is Plaza 25 de Mayo. Around it are the **cathedral**, containing the *Virgen del Rosario*, and the **Palacio Municipal**. On the north side is the **Museo de Arte Decorativo**, Santa Fe 748, a sumptuous former family residence housing a valuable private collection of paintings, furniture, tapestries sculptures and silverwork, brought mainly from Europe. ■ *Thu-Sun 1600-2000, free, T480 2547*. Left of the cathedral, the *Pasaje Juramento* opens the pedestrian way to the imposing **Monumento a la Bandera**. This commemorates the site on which, in 1812, General Belgrano, on his way to fight the Spaniards in Jujuy, raised the Argentine flag for the first time. A tower, 70 m high, has excellent panoramic views. ■ *Mon 1400-1800, Tue-Sun 0900-1800 (in summer till 1900), US$0.35 (tower), free (Salón de las Banderas), T/F480 2238*. In the first half of November in the Parque a la Bandera (opposite the monument) *Fiesta de las Colectividades* lasts 10 nights, with stalls offering typical dishes and a stage for folk

Rosario
Phone code: 0341
Colour map 8, grid B5
Population: 1,159,000
295 km NW of Buenos Aires

music and dances. The main show is on 11 November, Día de la Tradición. From plaza 25 de Mayo, Córdoba leads west towards plaza San Martín and beyond, the Boulevar Oroño. These 14 blocks, of which the first seven are for pedestrians only, is the largest concentration of late 19th- and early 20th- century buildings in the city in what is called the **Paseo del Siglo**. The **Museo de Bellas Artes J B Castagnino**, Avenida Pellegrini 2202, just outside the 126-ha Parque Independencia, has an impressive collection of European paintings, particularly French impressionist, Italian baroque and Flemish works, and one of best collections of Argentine paintings and sculpture. ■ *Wed-Mon 1400-2000, US$0.35, T480 2542.*

Che Guevara was born here in 1928. The large white house at Entre Ríos y Urquiza where he lived for the first two years of his life before his family moved to Alta Gracia, near Córdoba (see page 130), is now an insurance company. There are dozens of riverside resorts on the islands and sandbars opposite Rosario. These have restaurants, bars and all the facilities for a day out, with woods, beaches and lagoons. Some have campsites and cabins for rent. Boats depart daily in summer from *La Fluvial* or from *Costa Alta* to the resorts, each with its own transfer service. Weekend services are run the rest of the year.

Sleeping   **B** *Riviera*, San Lorenzo 1460, T/F424 2058, www.solans.com 4-star, business hotel with good rooms, large breakfast, sauna, gym and restaurant. 3 more hotels in the same chain usually have convenient promotions: **B** *Libertador*, Av Corrientes 752, T/F424 1005; **B** *Presidente*, Av Corrientes 919, T/F 424 2789; **C** *República*, San Lorenzo 955, T/F424 8580. **C** *Plaza del Sol*, San Juan 1055, T/F421 9899, plaza@satlink.com.ar Comfortable, spacious rooms, pool on the 11th floor with splendid views, with large breakfast. **D** *La Paz*, Barón de Maua 36, T/F421 0905. Family-owned, central, small, though a bit run down, reasonable rooms, with breakfast. **D** *Rosario*, Cortada Ricardone 1365 (access from Entre Ríos 900 block), T/F424 2170, hrosario@infovia.com.ar Central, good rooms with a/c and breakfast. Larger **C** rooms in annex. **E** *Savoy*, San Lorenzo 1022, T448 0071. Early 20th-century mansion, once Rosario's best hotel, now with faded grandeur, excellent value, attentive service, breakfast included. **Camping** The nearest site is at Granadero Baigorria, 12 km north of centre, at Av Lisandro de la Torre y El Río, T471 4381. Access to beach, hot showers, sport facilities, US$0.35 a day pp plus US$0.65 per tent and US$0.65 per vehicle.

Eating   **Mid-range**: *Amarra*, Av Belgrano y Buenos Aires. Good food, including fish and seafood, quite
A good listing of   formal, cheap set menus Mon-Fri noon. *Bruno*, Montevideo y Av Ovidio Lagos. Homemade
events is in the daily   pastas. *Club Español*, Rioja 1052. Typical menu with some Iberian touches. *Pampa*, Moreno y
newspaper Rosario 12,   Mendoza. A good *parrilla* with attractive 1940s décor. *Rich*, San Juan 1031. A classic in Rosario,
sold with the national   widely varied menu, convenient set meals including pastas, meats and salads. Recommended.
edition of Página 12.   **Cheap**: *Gigante*, San Martín 946. Large popular restaurant offering generous helpings of good
Visit also www.via   food at incredibly low prices. **Cafés and Bars**: *Albaca*, Italia y Mendoza. Agreeable bar with
rosario.com   live music in the evening. *Café de la Opera*, Mendoza y Laprida (next to *Teatro El Círculo*). Jazz,
for the latest   tango, Russian folk music and food, poetry or story-telling, pretty cafe. *Kaffa*, Córdoba 1473.
events info   Good coffee in *El Ateneo* bookshop. *La Sede*, San Lorenzo y Entre Ríos. Very popular cafe at lunchtime. *La Traición de Rita Hayworth*, Dorrego 1170. A *café concert* named after Manuel Puig's novel, live shows, usually Wed-Sun evenings, US$1-2, good food. *Piluso*, Catamarca y Alvear. A lively meeting place by night, also open during day.

Transport   **Air** Airport at Fisherton, 15 km west of centre, T451 1226. *Remises* charge US$4-5. Transfers also arranged by the airlines. Daily flights to/from Buenos Aires with *AR* and *Aerovip*, 45 mins. **Buses** Terminal at Santa Fe y Cafferata , about 30 blocks west of the *Monumento de la Bandera*, T437 2384. Several bus lines to centre with stops on Córdoba (eg 101, 103, 115), US$0.25; from centre, take buses on Plaza 25 de Mayo, going via C Santa Fe. *Remise* US$1.50 . To **Buenos Aires**, 4 hrs, US$7. To **Córdoba**, 6 hrs, US$7. To **Santa Fe**, 2½ hrs, US$4-5. **Trains** Rosario Norte station, Av del Valle y Av Ovidio Lagos. The Buenos Aires-Tucumán service operated by *TBA*, T0800-333 3822, stops weekly in **Rosario** at very inconvenient times and tickets are sold just before departure at the station. To **Tucumán**, US$12; to **Buenos Aires**, US$3.50.

Airline offices *Aerolíneas Argentinas*, Santa Fe 1410, T424 9517. *Aerovip*, Mitre 830, loc 32, T449 6800. **Banks**   Many banks along C Córdoba, east of plaza San Martín. Money exchange at *Transatlántica*, Mitre y Rioja. TCs exchanged at *Banex*, Mitre y Santa Fe. 2% or US$10 commission. **Communications** Internet: several places in centre, US$0.35 per hr.**Post Office:** Córdoba y Buenos Aires. **Tourist office** Main tourist office with efficient staff on the riverside park next to the Monumento a la Bandera, at Av Belgrano y Buenos Aires, T480 2230, www.rosarioturismo.com   A free tourist card is given for discounts at several hotels, restaurants and other services.

Directory

A new, 60-km road has been built from Rosario to **Victoria**, a pretty town overlooking the islands and canals to the west. Panoramic views from the **Mirador de la Virgen de Fátima**, west of centre (take Calle Laprida). There are many 19th- and early 20th-century buildings, several of which have wonderful ironwork on the windows. **Tourist office** is at the north access to town, 25 de Mayo y Bv Sarmiento ■ *Daily 0800-1900, T421885, www.turismovictoria.com.ar   Ask here for lodging at estancias.* **C** *Casablanca*, on Bv Moreno (by Barrio Quinto Cuartel), T424131, lopezmartin1676@yahoo.com.ar   Breakfast included, pool in large garden, restaurant for guests only. **D** *Plaza*, Congreso 455, T421431. Central, very pleasant, with a/c and breakfast, good value. **E** *Dennisse*, Congreso 682, T421186. Spotless, good, breakfast (US$0.65) can be taken on the veranda. **Buses**: to Buenos Aires, 4½-5 hours, US$10-11. To Paraná, 2-3 hours, US$2.50-3.50.

Rosario to Paraná

Ruta 11 heads north to Paraná, passing the **Parque Nacional Diamante** (or **Predelta**), 2,458 ha of marshland and riverine forest of the upper delta of the Río Paraná. It protects many birds, capybaras, otters and the rare *yacaré ñato* . Access is at La Jaula, where there's a free campsite with hot showers and a 200 m footpath leading to a vantage point. Most of the park is only accessible by boat and excursions leaving from La Jaula should be arranged in advance with a tour operator in the town of Diamante. *Remises* from Diamante charge US$1.50-1.60. Entrance is free. The park administration is at Sarmiento 507 (Diamante), T0343-498 3535, predelta@apn.gov.ar Daily 0800-2000. *Davimar*, 25 de Mayo 390, T0343-498 4104, runs boat excursions in the park for about US$8 pp. Accommodation is available at Diamante.

The capital of Entre Ríos was, from 1854-61, capital of the Republic. The centre is situated on a hill offering views over the Río Paraná and beyond to Santa Fe. There are many fine buildings. In the centre is the **Plaza Primero de Mayo**, around which are the **Municipalidad**, the large **Cathedral** and the **Colegio del Huerto**, seat of the Senate of the Argentine Confederation between 1854 and 1861. The **Casa de Gobierno** at Santa Fe y Laprida has a grand façade. Take pedestrianized San Martín and half block west of the corner with 25 de Junio is the fine **Teatro 3 de Febrero** (1908). Two blocks north is the **Plaza Alvear**; on one of its corners is the **provincial tourist office**, Laprida 5. ■ *Mon-Fri 0700-1230, T420 7989, www.vivientrerios.com*   On the west side is the **Museo de Bellas Artes**, Buenos Aires 355, housing a vast collection of artists. ■ *Tue-Fri 0900-1200, 1600-2100, Sat-Sun 1700-2130, US$0.35, T420 7868.* On the north side is the **Museo de Ciencias Naturales y Antropológicas**, Carlos Gardel 62, with natural history and anthropology sections. ■ *Tue-Fri 0800-1200, 1500-1900, Sat 0830-1230, 1500-1900, Sun 0900-1200, US$0.35, T4208894.*The city's glory is **Parque Urquiza**, along the cliffs above the Río Paraná. It has a statue to Gen Urquiza, and a bas-relief showing the battle of Caseros, at which he finally defeated Rosas.

Paraná
Phone code: 0343
Colour map 8, grid A5
Population: 247,600
30 km SE of Santa
Fe via
Hernandarias tunnel

Sleeping B *Mayorazgo*, Etchevehere y Córdoba, on Costanera Alta, T423 0333, www.mayorazgohotel.com Upmarket, overlooking Parque Urquiza, with 4 room categories, casino, pool, gym, restaurant and fine views of the river. **C** *Gran Hotel Paraná*, Urquiza 976, T422 3900, www.hotelesparana.com.ar Overlooking Plaza Primero de Mayo, 3 room categories (breakfast included), smart restaurant *La Fourchette*, gym, discounts at the Club Atlético Estudiantes. In same chain: **D** *Paraná Plaza Jardín*, 9 de Julio 60, T423 1700. With breakfast, pleasant, roof garden. **D** *San Jorge*, Belgrano 368, T/F422 1685, www.sanjorgehotel.com.ar Renovated house, helpful staff, older rooms are cheaper than the modern ones at the back with TV, light breakfast included, cooking facilities. **Camping** *La Toma*, north end of C Blas Parera (10 km northeast of centre), T433 1721. US$0.35 pp plus US$1.30 per tent, hot showers, pool, shop. Bus 5 or 10 from centre.

Transport Buses Terminal at Av Ramírez 2598 (10 blocks southeast of Plaza Primero de Mayo), T422 1282. Buses 1, 4, 5 or 9 to/from centre, US$0.35. *Remise* US$0.50. East across Entre Ríos to **Colón** on Río Uruguay, 4-5 hrs, US$7. To **Buenos Aires**, 6-7 hrs, US$11-12. **To Santa Fe** The two cities are 25 km apart and are separated by several islands. The road goes under the Río Paraná by the Hernandarias tunnel, toll US$1 per car, and then crosses a number of bridges. Frequent bus service by *Etacer* and *Fluviales*, US$1, 50 mins.

Santa Fe

Phone code: 0342
Colour map 8, grid A4
Population: 451,600
184 km from Rosario
Santa Fe suffered
serious flooding
in mid-2003

Santa Fe is the capital of its province and the centre of a very fertile region. It was founded by settlers from Asunción in 1573, though its present site was not occupied until 1653. The south part of the city, around the **Plaza 25 de Mayo** is the historic centre. On the Plaza itself is the majestic **Casa de Gobierno**, built in 1911-17 in French style on the site of the historic Cabildo, in which the 1853 constitution was drafted. Opposite is the **Cathedral**, with its twin towers capped by blue cupolas. On the east side is the **Colegio de la Inmaculada Concepción**, established by the Jesuits and including the Iglesia de **Nuestra Señora de los Milagros**, dating from 1694, more richly decorated with an ornate dome. One block south of the plaza is the Iglesia y Convento de **San Francisco** built in 1680. **Museo Histórico Provincial**, 3 de Febrero 2553, in a building dating from 1690, one of the oldest surviving civil buildings in the country. ■ *Open all year 0830-1200, afternoon hours change frequently, closed Mon, free. T457 3529.* You can swim in the river at Guadalupe beach, on the Costanera Oeste. The modern **Basílica Nuestra Señora de Guadalupe**, Javier de la Rosa 623, is the site of a popular religious pilgrimage on the third Sunday after Easter. Take bus 16 from the centre to the Costanera.

Sleeping **C** *Riogrande*, San Gerónimo 2580, T450 0700, riogrande@santafe.com.ar Santa Fe's best hotel, very good rooms, includes large breakfast. **D** *Castelar*, 25 de Mayo y Peatonal Falucho, T/F456 0999. On a small plaza, 1930's hotel, good value, comfortable, breakfast included, restaurant. **D** *Hostal Santa Fe de la Veracruz*, San Martín 2954, T/F455 1740, hostal_santafe@ciudad.com.ar Traditional favourite, also has **C** superior rooms, all good value, including large breakfast, restaurant, sauna (extra). **E** *Colón*, San Luis 2862, T452 1586. Welcoming staff but gloomy rooms, OK, breakfast and a/c included. **E** *Emperatriz*, Irigoyen Freyre 2440, T/F453 0061. Attractive Hispanic-style building, plain rooms, spacious, comfortable, breakfast and a/c extra. **E** *Niza*, Rivadavia 2755, T/F452 2047. With fan and breakfast, adequate, a/c extra.

Eating
Many good eating
places, with excellent
meals with good wine.
Many places in centre
closed on Sun

Mid-range: *Baviera San Martín*, San Martín 2941. Traditional, varied menu. *Club Sirio Libanés*, 25 de Mayo 2740. Very good Middle Eastern dishes, popular at Sun lunchtime. *El Brigadier*, San Martín 1670. Colonial style, fish and *parrilla*. *El Quincho de Chiquito*, Av Almirante Brown y Obispo Príncipe, (Costanera Oeste). Classic fish restaurant, excellent and good value. *Rivadavia*, Rivadavia 3299. Traditional *parrilla*. **Cafés and Bars**: Santa Fe has a long brewing tradition and local lagers compete with the national monopoly. *Don Ernesto*, San Martín y General López. A traditional cafe in the civic centre. *Las Delicias*, Hipólito Yrigoyen y San Martín. Café and bakery with beautiful décor, good for coffees and pastries, also fruit juices, sandwiches and alcoholic drinks. *Tokio*, on Rivadavia y Crespo (Plaza España). Another historical café. Many lively bars and nightclubs along the *Costanera Este*, across the bridge on Laguna Setúbal, and the Recoleta district, north of centre.

Transport **Air** Airport at Sauce Viejo, 17 km south. T453 4300. Daily *AR* and *Aerovip* to and from **Buenos Aires**. **Buses** Terminal near the centre, Gen M Belgrano 2910, T457 4124. To **Córdoba**, US$8.50, 5 hrs. Many buses to **Buenos Aires** US$11-13; to **Paraná** frequent service US$1, 50 mins; to **Rosario** very frequent, 2½ hrs, US$4-5.

True brew

*Yerba mate (*ilex paraguayensis*) is made into a tea which is widely drunk in Argentina, Paraguay, Brazil and Uruguay. Traditionally associated with the gauchos, the modern mate paraphernalia is a common sight anywhere: the gourd (un mate) in which the tea leaves are steeped, the straw (usually silver) and a thermos of* *hot water to top up the gourd. It was the Jesuits who first grew yerba mate in plantations, inspiring one of the drink's names: té de jesuitas. Also used has been té de Paraguay, but now just mate or yerba will do. In southern Brazil it is called ximarão; in Paraguay tereré, when drunk cold with digestive herbs.*

Directory

Argentina

Banks Banking district around San Martín y Tucumán. Exchange money and TCs at *Tourfé*, San Martín 2500, or at *Columbia*, San Martín 2275. **Tourist offices** Three very good information points: at the bus terminal, T457 4123, 0700-1300, 1500-2100, at Paseo del Restaurador, Bv Pellegrini y Rivadavia, T457 1881, 0700-1900 and at Boca del Tigre, Av Paso y Zavalía, 0700-1900, www.santafeciudad.gov.ar

Iberá Marshes

The **Reserva Natural del Iberá** protects nearly 13,000 sq km of wetlands known as the **Esteros del Iberá**, similar to the Pantanal in Brazil. Over sixty small lakes, no more than a few metres deep, cover 20-30% of the protected area, which is rich in aquatic plants. Like islands in the *lagunas*, *embalsados* are floating vegetation, thick enough to support large animals and trees. Wildlife includes black caiman, marsh deer, capybara and about 300 species of bird, among them the *yabirú* or *Juan Grande*, the largest stork in the western hemisphere. More difficult to see are the endangered maned wolf), the 3-m long yellow anaconda, the *yacaré ñato* and the river otter. There is a visitors' centre by the bridge at the access to Carlos Pellegrini (see below), open 0730-1800. **Mercedes** (*Population*: 30,900. *Phone code*: 03773), 250 km southeast of Corrientes, gives the best access to the **Esteros**, and is the only point for getting regular transport to Carlos Pellegrini. There is small **tourist office** at the bus station. The surrounding countryside is mostly grassy *pampas*, where rheas can be seen, with rocks emerging from the plains from time to time. **Carlos Pellegrini**, 120 km northeast of Mercedes, stands on beautiful *Laguna Iberá*. A one-day visit allows for a 3-hour boat excursion (US$8-12 pp if not included in hotel rates), but some hotels offer more activities for longer stays, eg horse rides or guided walks.

Sleeping Mercedes: **E** *Sol*, San Martín 519, T420283. An old house with clean rooms and a lovely patio; with breakfast. **E** *World*, Pujol 1162, T422508, 3 blocks from bus station. With fan and breakfast, shared bath, other meals available, Iberá information. **F** pp *Delicias del Iberá*, Pujol 1162, T422508. Next to the *combis* to Pellegrini, excellent, shared bath, breakfast and good meals, garden. **Carlos Pellegrini**: **A** pp *Hostería Ñandé Retá*, T/F03773-499411/ 156-29109, T011-4811 2005 (in Buenos Aires), www.nandereta.com Wooden house in a shady grove, full board, excursions included. **A** pp *Posada Aguapé*, T03773-499412/ 156-29759, T/F011-4742 3015 (Buenos Aires), www.iberaesteros.com.ar On the lake with a garden and pool, comfortable rooms, attractive dining room, rates are for full board and include two excursions **A** pp *Posada de la Laguna*, T03773-499413, F011-4737 7274 (Buenos Aires), www.iberalaguna.8k.com Run by painter Elsa Güiraldes and set on the lake, very comfortable, large neat garden and a swimming pool, full board and all excursions included. **D** pp *Posada Ypa Sapukai*, T03773-420155, www.ypasapukai.com.ar Good value, nice atmosphere, excellent staff, excursion to the *laguna* is very well guided (US$8 pp), full board (**E** pp with breakfast only). Recommended. **F** pp *Hosp Guaraní*, Calle 7 y 27, T156-29762, www.guarani.ibera.net Basic, shared bath, owner Ana María Manzanelli arranges boat trips. **F** pp *San Cayetano*, T03773-156 28763. Very basic, run by local guide Roque Pera.

 Sleeping at estancias **B** pp *San Juan Poriahú*, at Loreto, T03781-156 08674, T011-4791 9511 (Buenos Aires). An old estancia run by Marcos García Rams, at the northwest edge of the Esteros, full board, horse rides and boat trips to see wildlife on a property where there has been no hunting at all. Closed Jan, Feb and Jul. Access from Ruta 12. **B** pp *San*

Lorenzo, at Galarza, T03756-481292, www.iberaargentina.com.ar Next to two lakes on the northeast edge of the region, splendid for wildlife watching, full board, only 3 rooms, horse rides, walks, boat trips all included. Boat excursions by night are charged separately. Access from Gobernador Virasoro (90 km), via routes 37 and 41. Transfer can be arranged to/from Gobernador Virasoro or Posadas for an extra charge. Closed Jan-Feb.

Transport Mercedes to **Carlos Pellegrini**: *Rayo Bus* combis daily 1130 from Pujol 1166, T420184, T156 29598, 3 hrs, US$3.30. Combi spends an hour picking up passengers all around Mercedes after leaving the office. Returns from Pellegrini at 0400, book by 2200 the night before at the local grocery (ask for directions). *Itatí II* bus from bus station daily, except Sun, 1200, US$3.30 (returns 0430). Mercedes to **Buenos Aires**, 9-10 hrs, US$12-14. Mercedes to **Corrientes**, 3 hrs, US$3.30-4. To **Puerto Iguazú**, best to go via Corrientes, otherwise via any important town along route 14, eg Paso de los Libres, 130 km southeast.

Parque Nacional Mburucuyá West of the Esteros del Iberá and 180 km southeast of Corrientes, this park covers 17,660 ha, stretching north from the marshes of the Río Santa Lucía. It includes savanna with *yatay* palms, 'islands' of wet Chaco forest, and *esteros*. The *mburucuyá* or passionflower gives the name to the park. Wildlife is easy to see. Formerly two *estancias*, Santa María and Santa Teresa, the land was donated by their owner, the Danish botanist Troels Pedersen, who identified 1,300 different plants here. Provincial route 86 (unpaved) crosses the park for 18 km leading to the information centre and free campsite (hot water and electricity). ■ *The park is 12 km east of the town of Mburucuyá (2 hotels). Buses San Antonio from Corrientes go daily to Mburucuyá, 2½ hrs, US$2.30. Remises from there to the park, US$5. Free entry, T03782-498022.*

Corrientes

Phone code: 03783
Colour map 6, grid C6
Population: 316,500

Corrientes, founded in 1588 is some 30 km below the confluence of the Ríos Paraguay and Alto Paraná. The 2¾ km General Belgrano bridge across the Río Paraná (toll US$1 per car) links the city with Resistencia (25 km), from where Route 11 goes north to Formosa and Asunción. East of Corrientes, Route 12 follows the Alto Paraná to Posadas and Iguazú. The river can make the air heavy, moist and oppressive, but in winter the climate is pleasant. The city is capital of Corrientes province and the setting for Graham Greene's novel, *The Honorary Consul*.

Sights
Museums include: Histórico Regional, 9 de Julio 1044. Bellas Artes, San Juan 643. Artesanías, Quintana 905

The main **Plaza 25 de Mayo** is one of the best-preserved in Argentina. On the north side is the **Jefatura de Policía** built in 19th-century French style. On the east side is the Italianate **Casa de Gobierno** and on the south is the church of **La Merced**. Two blocks east at Mendoza 450 is the **Convent of San Francisco**, rebuilt in 1861 (the original dated from the early 17th century). Six blocks south of Plaza 25 de Mayo is the leafy Plaza de la Cruz, on which the church of **La Cruz de los Milagros** (1897) houses a cross, the Santo Madero, placed there by the founder of the city, Juan Torres de Vera – Indians who tried to burn it were killed by lightning from a cloudless sky. Near the plaza, the **Museo de Ciencias Naturales 'Amadeo Bonpland'**, San Martín 850, named after the French naturalist who travelled with Alexander von Humboldt, contains botanical, zoological, archaeological and mineralogical collections. ■ *Mon-Sat 0900-1200, 1600-2000.* A beautiful walk eastwards, along the Avenida Costanera, beside the Paraná river leads to **Parque Mitre**, from where there are views of sunset.

Sleeping & eating
No good value, inexpensive accommodation in the city. All those listed have a/c

C *Corrientes Plaza*, Junín 1549, T/F466500, www.hotelplazactes.com.ar Business-oriented, comfortable, gym and a small pool. **C** *Gran Hotel Guaraní*, Mendoza 970, T433800, hguarani@gigared.com 4-star, business-oriented with restaurant, pool and gym, parking, large breakfast included. **D** *Hostal del Río*, Plácido Martínez 1098, T/F436100, hostal_del_rio@infovia.com.ar In apartment tower overlooking the port, fine rooms, pleasantly decorated, pool, restaurant, breakfast included. **D** *Orly*, San Juan 867, T427248, hotelorly@arnet.com.ar Central, recently renovated, but pay 50% more for a better class room, with breakfast. **D** *San Martín*, Santa Fe 955, T/F421061, hsanmartin@impsat1.com.ar Central, lacks character but comfortable nonetheless, with breakfast. **D** *Turismo*, Entre Ríos 650, T/F433174. Riverside location, nice style but a bit outdated, smart restaurant, with breakfast, large pool, adjacent casino. *El Solar*, San Lorenzo 830. Informal, busy at lunchtime, meals by weight. *Las Brasas*, Av Costanera y San Martín (near beach). Traditional mid-range *parrilla*, also local fish. *Martha de Bianchetti*, 9 de Julio y Mendoza. Smart cafe and bakery.

Air Camba Punta Airport, 10 km east of city, T458684. (Minibus picks up passengers from hotels, T450072, US$1.30.) *AR* (T424647) to/from Buenos Aires. **Buses** To **Resistencia** US$0.70, *Chaco-Corrientes*, every 15 mins from Av Costanera y La Rioja at the port, 40 mins, US$0.40 return. Main terminal on Av Maipú, 5 km southeast of centre, bus No 103 (be sure toy ask the driver if goes to terminal as same line has many different routes), 20 mins, US$0.20 To **Posadas** US$6.50, 3½-4 hrs, road paved. To **Buenos Aires**, several companies, 11-12 hrs, US$13-26. To **Asunción** (Paraguay), *Crucero del Norte*, *El Pulqui*, 5 hrs, US$6-7.

Transport

Argentina

Communications Internet: *Brujas*, Mendoza 787, US$0.35/hr. Many others **Post Office:** San Juan y San Martín. **Telephone:** Several *telecentros* in centre. **Tourist offices City tourist office** at Plaza Cabral, good map. Daily 0700-2100. **Provincial tourist office**, 25 de Mayo 1330, province and city information. Mon-Fri 0700-1300, 1500-2100, T427200, www.planetacorrientes.com.ar

Directory

The Chaco

The Chaco has two distinct natural zones. The Wet Chaco spreads along the Ríos Paraná and Paraguay covered mainly by marshlands with savanna and groves of *caranday* palms, where birdwatching is excellent. Further west, as rainfall diminishes, scrubland of *algarrobo*, white *quebracho*, *palo borracho* and various types of cacti characterise the Dry Chaco, where South America's highest temperatures, exceeding 45°C, have been recorded. Winters are mild, with an occasional touch of frost in the south. Though this sprawling alluvial lowland rises gradually from east to west, its rise is so gentle (200 m in 900 km) that the rivers which cross it are slow and meandering. It is mostly cattle country, but agriculture has developed in the central part and the southwest of Chaco province, with cotton, maize, soya, sunflower and sorghum.

Although much of the Chaco is inaccessible because of poor roads (many of them impassable during summer rains) and lack of public transport, it has two attractive national parks which are reachable all year round. Resistencia and Formosa are the main cities at the eastern rim, from where almost straight Rutas 16 and 81 respectively go west across the plains to the hills in Salta province. Buses to Salta take Ruta 16, while Ruta 81 has long unpaved sections west of Las Lomitas, which make for a very hard journey after heavy rains. Presidencia Roque Sáenz Peña, 170 km northwest of Resistencia, is a reasonable place to stop over.

The Chaco is one of the main centres of indigenous population in Argentina: the Toba are settled in towns by the Río Paraná and the Wichi, or Mataco, live in the western region. Less numerous are the Mocoví in Chaco and the Pilagá in central Formosa.

The hot and energetic capital of the Province of Chaco, Resistencia is situated 6½ km up the Barranqueras stream on the west bank of the Paraná. On the Paraná itself is the little port of Barranqueras. Resistencia is known as the 'city of the statues', there being over 200 of these in the streets. Four blocks from the central Plaza 25 de Mayo is the **Fogón de los Arrieros**, Brown 350, (between López y Planes and French), a famous club and informal cultural centre, deserving of a visit. ■ *Open to non-members Mon-Sat 0900-1200, Mon-Fri 2100-2300, US$1.70, T426418.* The **Museo Del Hombre Chaqueño**, Juan B Justo 280, is a small anthropological museum with an exhibition of handicrafts by native Wichi, Toba and Mocoví people. It has a fascinating mythology section in which small statues represent Guaraní beliefs (still found in rural areas). ■ *Mon-Fri 0800-1200, 1600-2000, free.* There are banks and *cambios* in the centre for exchange.

Resistencia
Phone code: 03722
Colour map 6, grid C6
Population: 359,100
544 km N of Santa Fe

Argentina

Isla del Cerrito, an island northeast of Resistencia at the confluence of the Ríos Paraná and Paraguay, is a provincial nature reserve of 12,000 ha, covered mainly with grassland and palm trees. At the eastern end (51 km from Resistencia) is Cerrito, a tourist complex with white sand beaches, a history museum, accommodation and restaurants. Combi *Arco Iris* leaves from Juan B Justo y Av Alberdi at 0600, 1100, 1900 for Cerrito, 1 hour, stopping for 30 minutes there, US$1.20.

Sleeping and eating **C** *Covadonga*, Güemes 200 , T444444, hotelcovadonga@infovia. com.ar The city's top hotel, comfortable, a/c, with breakfast, pool, sauna and gym. **D** *Gran Hotel Royal*, Obligado 211, T443666, www.granhotelroyal.com Good value, comfortable, a/c, breakfast included. **E** *Bariloche*, Obligado 239, T421412, jag@cpsarg.com The best value, welcoming, good rooms with a/c, no breakfast so go to cafe at *Gran Hotel Royal*. **E** *El Hotelito*, Av Alberdi 311, T459699. Acceptable for a night, fair rooms, shared bath, breakfast. Few restaurants: *Kebon*, Don Bosco y Güemes.Mid range. *San José*, Roca y Av Alberdi. A popular cafe and *confitería* on Plaza 25 de Mayo with excellent pastries (try *medialunas*) and ice creams. **Camping** 17 blocks northwest of plaza : *Parque Dos de Febrero*, Av Avalos 1000, T458366. In a neat park by the Río Negro, hot water and electricity, US$0.35 pp plus US$0.65 per tent.

Transport **Air** Airport 8 km west of town (no bus), T446009. *AR* (T445550) to/from Buenos Aires. **Buses** To **Corrientes**, *Chaco-Corrientes* buses stop opposite *Norte* supermarket on Av Alberdi e Illia, 40 mins, US$0.40 return. Modern terminal on west outskirts (bus 3 or 10 to centre, 20 mins, US$0.25; *remise* US$1.70). To **Buenos Aires** 12-13 hrs, US$13-26 several companies. To **Formosa** 2-2½ hrs, US$2.70-3.50. To **Iguazú**, 8-10½ hrs, US$11-12, some require change of bus in **Posadas**, 5½ hrs. To **Salta** (for connections to Bolivia), *FlechaBus*, *La Nueva Estrella* , 12½ hrs, US$17-19. To **Asunción** several companies, 5-5½ hrs, US$5-6.

Directory **Communications**: Internet: *Klap*, Illia 12, US$0.40 per hr, open 24 hrs. **Tourist offices**: **City office** on Plaza 25 de Mayo, Mon-Fri 0800-2000, T458289. **Provincial office**, Santa Fe 178, Mon-Fri 0630-2000, Sat 0800-1200, T423547, www.chaco.gov.ar/turismo

Parque Nacional Chaco
115 km NW of Resistencia
Best visited between Apr-Oct to avoid intense summer heat and voracious mosquitoes

The park extends over 15,000 ha and protects one of the last remaining untouched areas of the Wet Chaco with exceptional *quebracho colorado* trees, *caranday* palms and dense riverine forests with orchids along the banks of the Río Negro. Some 340 species of bird have been sighted in the park. Mammals include *carayá* monkeys and, much harder to see, collared peccary, puma and jaguarundi. 300 m from the entrance is the visitors' centre and a free campsite with hot showers and electricity. There you can hire bicycles or horses for US$1.30 per hour. ■ *Free, open 24 hrs, T03725-496166*. The paved Ruta 16 goes northwest from Resistencia and after about 60 km Ruta 9 branches off, leading north to Colonia Elisa and Capitán Solari, 5 km east of the park entrance, via a dirt road. If in a group, call the park in advance to be picked up at Capitán Solari. *La Estrella* run daily buses Resistencia-Capitán Solari, where *remise* taxis should not charge more than US$1 to the park. Tour operators run day-long excursions to the park from Resistencia.

Formosa
Phone code: 03717
Colour map 6, grid C6
Population: 198,100
186 km above Corrientes

The capital of Formosa Province is the only Argentine port of any note on the Río Paraguay. Oppressively hot from November to March, the city is a good base for exploring the rivers running towards the Río Paraguay during the mild winter. **Tourist office** at José M Uriburu 820 (on Plaza San Martín). ■*Mon-Fri 0700-1300, 1600-2000, T420442, www.formosa.gov.ar* Tourism is not well developed, but ask about guided excursions and accommodation at *estancias*.

Sleeping and eating **B** *Turismo*, San Martín 759, T431122, hoteldeturismoformosa@ arnet.com.ar Large building by the river, good views, pricey rooms with a/c and breakfast. **C** *Casa Grande Apart-Hotel*, Av González Lelong 185, T431573, www.casagrandeapart. com.ar 8 blocks north of Av 25 de Mayo, by river, good 1 and 2-room apartments with kitchenette, a/c and breakfast, gym and pool. **D** *Colón*, Belgrano 1068, T426547. Comfortable, a/c and breakfast . **D** *Plaza*, José M Uriburu 920, T426767. On Plaza, good, pool, with breakfast. **F** *Colonial*, San Martín 879, T426346. Basic, a/c, by the river. Opposite bus terminal is **F** *El Extranjero*, Av Gutnisky 2660, T452276. OK, with a/c. **Camping** *Camping Banco Provincial*, 4 km south on Ruta 11, good facilities including pool, T429877. *Las Arianas*, 10 km south (turn off Route 11 at El Pucu, Km 6), T427640. **Eating**: **Mid-range**: *El Fortín*, Mitre 602. Traditional place, good for local fish. *El Tano Marino*, Av 25 de Mayo 55. Italian, pastas are the speciality. *Yayita*, Belgrano 926. Regional dishes, central.

Festivals The world's longest *Via Crucis* pilgrimage with 14 stops along Ruta 81 (registered in the Guinness Book of Records) takes place every Easter week, starting in Formosa and ending at the border with the province of Salta, 501 km northwest. *Festival de la caña con ruda* is held on the last night of **Jul**, when Paraguayan *caña* flavoured by the *ruda* plant is drunk as a protection against the mid-winter blues. Also a good chance to try regional dishes.

Transport **Air** El Pucu airport, 5 km southwest, T452490; *remise*, US$1.70. **AR** (T429314) to Buenos Aires. **Buses** Terminal on west outskirts, T430817 (*remise* US$0.65). To **Asunción**, 3 hrs, US$5.40. To **Resistencia**, 2½ hrs, US$2.70-3.50; to **Buenos Aires** 15-17 hrs, US$16-28.

There are two routes into Paraguay. The easiest crossing is by road via the Puente Loyola, 4 km north of **Clorinda** (*Phone code*: 03718. *Colour map 6, grid C6*). From Puerto Falcón, at the Paraguayan end of the bridge, the road runs 40 km northeast, crossing the Río Paraguay, before reaching Asunción. **Immigration** formalities for entering Argentina are dealt with at the Argentine end, those for leaving Argentina at the Paraguayan end. Crossing, open 24 hours. **Buses** from Puerto Falcón to Asunción, with *Empresa Falcón* US$0.50, every hour, last bus to the centre of Asunción 1830.

 The other route is by ferry from Puerto Pilcomayo, close to Clorinda, to Itá Enramada (Paraguay), US$0.50, 5 minutes, every 30 minutes. Then take bus 9 to Asunción. Argentine **immigration** is at Puerto Pilcomayo, closed at weekends for tourists. Paraguayan immigration at Itá Enramada.

Border with Paraguay

Some 48,000 ha, 65 km northwest of Clorinda is this national park is recognised as a natural wetland, with lakes, marshes and low-lying parts which flood during the rainy season. The remainder is grassland with caranday palm forests and Chaco woodland. Among the protected species are aguará-guazú, giant anteaters and coatis. Caimans, black howler monkeys, rheas and a variety of birds can also be seen. The park has two entrances leading to different areas. Easiest to reach on foot is Laguna Blanca, where there is an information point and a free campsite with electricity and cold water. From there, a footpath goes to the Laguna Blanca, the biggest lake in the park. A bit further is the second entrance, leading to the area of Estero Poí, with another information point and a campsite without facilities. ■ *Access to the park is free, open 24 hrs, administration centre in Laguna Blanca, Av Pueyrredón y Ruta 86, T03718-470045, Mon-Fri 0700-1430.* Godoy *buses run from Formosa or Resistencia to the small towns of Laguna Naick-Neck, 5 km from the park (for going to Laguna Blanca) and Laguna Blanca, 8 km from the park (for going to Estero Poí). Remise taxis from both towns should charge no more than US$3 for these short journeys.*

Parque Nacional Río Pilcomayo

Posadas

This is the main Argentine port on the south bank of the Alto Paraná and the capital of the province of Misiones. On the opposite bank of the river lies the Paraguayan town of Encarnación, reached by the San Roque bridge. The city's centre is **Plaza 9 de Julio**, on which stand the **Cathedral** and the **Gobernación**, in imitation French style. The riverside and adjacent districts are good for a stroll. Follow Rivadavia or Buenos Aires north to Avenida Andrés Guaçurarí (referred also to as Roque Pérez), a pleasant boulevard, lively at night with several bars. Immediately north of it is the small and hilly **Bajada Vieja** or old port district. There is a good **Museo Regional**

Phone code: 03752
Population: 280,500
377 km above Corrientes

Argentina

Aníbal Cambas at Alberdi 600 in the Parque República del Paraguay, 11 blocks north of Plaza 9 de Julio, with a permanent exhibition of Guaraní artefacts and pieces collected from the nearby Jesuit missions. ■ *Mon-Fri 0700-1900*, *T447539*.

Sleeping   **B** *Julio César*, Entre Ríos 1951, T427930, www.juliocesarhotel.com.ar 4-star hotel with pool and gym, spacious but pricey rooms, some with river views, breakfast included. **C** *Continental*, Bolívar 1879 (on Plaza 9 de Julio), T440990, www.hoteleramisiones.com.ar Comfortable standard rooms and more spacious **B** VIP rooms, some have river views, restaurant on first floor. **C** *Posadas*, Bolívar 1949, T440888, www.hotelposadas.com.ar Business hotel with good standard rooms and bigger *especial* rooms, restaurant, free internet access for guests. **D** *City*, Colón 1754, T439401, citytel@arnet.com.ar Gloomy reception, but very good rooms, some overlooking plaza, with breakfast and a/c, restaurant on first floor, parking. **D** *Colonial*, Barrufaldi 2419, T436149. Warm atmosphere, good value, nice rooms with a/c and breakfast, on a quiet street about 15-min walk from centre. **D** *Le Petit*, Santiago del Estero 1630, T436031, F441101. Also good value, small, a short walk from centre on a quiet street, a/c, with breakfast. **E** *Residencial Misiones*, Félix de Azara 1960, T430133. Very hospitable, good rooms with fan, central, old house with a patio, no breakfast, cooking and laundry facilities, popular with travellers.

Eating   **Expensive** *El Mensú*, Fleming y Coronel Reguera (at Bajada Vieja district). Attractive house
Most places offer   offering a varied menu with fish, pastas and a large selection of wines, closed Mon. *Le*
espeto corrido   *Rendez-vous*, San Martín 1786. Formal, with a French touch. **Mid-range** *Diletto*, Bolívar 1729.
eat as much as you   For fish, such as *surubí*, and, curiously, rabbit as their speciality. *Espeto del Rey*, Ayacucho y
can parrilla with meats   Tucumán. *Parrilla*, good food. Try *mandioca frita* (fried manioc). *Mentecato*, San Lorenzo y La
brought to the table   Rioja (opposite casino). Good, open when many others are closed. *La Querencia*, on Bolívar (on Plaza 9 de Julio). Traditional large restaurant offering *parrilla*, *surubí* and pastas.

Tour operators   *Abra*, Colón 1975, T422221, abramisiones@arnet.com.ar Tours to Jesuit ruins (US$20 pp), also those in Paraguay (US$23 pp) and in Brazil (US$48 pp), plus tours to waterfalls. *Guayrá*, San Lorenzo 2208, T433415, www.guayra.com.ar Tours to Iberá (US$50-65 pp if 4 people), to Saltos del Moconá (US$80 pp if 4 people), both sites in a 5-day excursion for US$240 pp (for 4), also car rental and transfer to Carlos Pellegrini (for Iberá).

Transport   **Air** Gen San Martín Airport, 12 km west, T457413, reached by Bus No 8 or 28 in 40 mins, US$0.25, *remise* US$4. To **Buenos Aires**, *AR* (Ayacucho 1728, T432889), some flights call at Corrientes or Formosa.

   Buses New terminal about 5 km out of the city at Av Santa Catalina y Av Quaranta (T456106), on the road to Corrientes. Buses No 4, 8, 15, 21, to/from centre, 20 mins, US$0.25, *remise* US$2. To **Buenos Aires**, 12-13 hrs, US$17-25. Frequent services to **San Ignacio Miní**, 1 hr, US$1.30, and **Puerto Iguazú**, US$8, 5-6 hrs *expreso*. To **Tucumán**, *La Nueva Estrella*, *Autotransportes Mendoza*, 16-18 hrs, US$18-21. **International**: to **Encarnación** (Paraguay), *Servicio Internacional*, 50 mins, US$0.65, leaving at least every half an hour from platforms 11 and 12 (lower level), tickets on bus.

Directory   **Banks** *Banco de La Nación*, Bolívar 1799. Round corner on Félix de Azara are *Banco Río* and*HSBC*. *Citibank*, San Martín y Colón. *Mazza*, Bolívar 1932. For money exchange, TCs accepted. **Communications** Internet: *Anyway*, Féliz de Azara 2067. US$0.35 per hr evenings/weekends, otherwise US$0.50. *Cyber Nick*, San Luis 1847. US$0.35 before 1700, otherwise US$0.50. *Mateando*, on Félix de Azara, next to San Martín. US$0.35 per hr. *Misiol@n*, San Lorenzo 1681, open 24 hrs, US$0.35 per hr. **Post Office:** Bolívar y Ayacucho. **Consulates** Paraguay, San Lorenzo 179, T423858. Mon-Fri 0730-1400. All visas on the same day. **Tourist office** Colón 1985, T447540, www.conozcamisiones.com Open daily 0800-2000. **Immigration**, *Dirección Nacional de Migraciones*, Buenos Aires 1633, T427414.

Border with   Argentine immigration and customs are on the Argentine side of the bridge to
Paraguay   Encarnación. Buses across the bridge (see above) do not stop for formalities; you
For Paraguayan   must get exit stamps. Get off the bus, keep your ticket and luggage, and catch a later
immigration,   bus. Pedestrians and cyclists are not allowed to cross; cyclists must ask officials for

assistance. Boats cross to Encarnación, 6-8 minutes, almost every hour Mon-Fri 0800-1800, US$1. All formalities and ticket office at main building. Port access from Avenida Costanera y Avenida Andrés Guaçurarí, T425044 (*Prefectura*).

San Ignacio Miní

The site of the most impressive Jesuit ruins in the Misiones region is a good base for visiting the other Jesuit ruins and for walking. The local festival is 30-31 July. San Ignacio was founded on its present site in 1696. The 100 sq-m, grass-covered plaza is flanked north, east and west by 30 parallel blocks of stone buildings with four to 10 small, one-room dwellings in each block. The roofs have gone, but the massive metre-thick walls are still standing except where they have been torn down by the *ibapoi* trees. The public buildings, some of them still 10 m high, are on the south side of the plaza. In the centre are the ruins of a large church finished about 1724. The masonry, sandstone from the Río Paraná, was held together by a sandy mud.

Phone code: 03752
Colour map 7, grid C1
63 km NE of Posadas

Inside the entrance, 200 m from the ruins, is the **Centro de Interpretación Jesuítico-Guaraní**, with representations of the lives of the Guaraníes before the arrival of the Spanish, the work of the Jesuits and the consequences of their expulsion, as well as a fine model of the mission in its heyday. **Museo Provincial** contains a small collection of artefacts from Jesuit reducciones. San Ignacio, together with the nearby missions of Santa Ana and Loreto, is a UNESCO World Heritage Site. There are heavy rains in February. Mosquitoes can be a problem. ■ *0700-1900, US$0.80, US$3.50 with guide, tip appreciated if the guards look after your luggage. Allow about 1½ hrs for a leisurely visit. Go early to avoid crowds and the best light for pictures (also late afternoon); good birdwatching. Son et lumière show at the ruins, daily after sunset, cancelled in wet weather, Spanish only, US$0.80.*

The **Casa de Horacio Quiroga**, a Uruguayan writer who lived part of his tragic life here as a farmer and carpenter between 1910 and 1916 in the 1930s, is worth a visit. Many of his short stories were inspired by the subtropical environment and its inhabitants. ■ *0800-1900, T470124, US$0.65 (includes a 40 min-guided visit; ask in advance for an English guide). Take C San Martín (opposite direction to the ruins) to its end where is Gendarmería headquarters. Turn right and on your right are two attractive wood and stone houses. After 200 m the road turns left and 300 m later, a signposted narrow road branches off.*

The ruins of another Jesuit mission, **Loreto**, can be reached by a 3 km dirt road (signposted) which turns off Ruta 12 10 km south of San Ignacio. Little remains other than a few walls, though excavations are in progress. ■ *0700-1830, US$0.35. No public transport to Loreto, bus drops you off on Ruta 12. Otherwise take a tour from Posadas or remise from nearby towns.* A second ruined mission, **Santa Ana**, 16 km south, was the site of the Jesuit iron foundry. Impressive high walls still stand and beautiful steps lead from the church to the wide open plaza The ruins are 700 m along a path from Ruta 12 (signposted). ■ *0700-1900, US$0.35. Buses stop on Ruta 12.*

E *El Descanso*, Pellegrini 270, T470207. Comfortable small detached house, five blocks southwest of main Av Sarmiento. **E** *San Ignacio*, San Martín 823, T470047. Welcoming and very informative owner Beatriz offers very good rooms with a/c and apartments for 4 and 5 people, breakfast US$1.20, evening meals. **G** pp *El Güembé*, Gendarme Medina 525, T470910. Basic, shared bath, only 100 m from the ruins, German owner Roland rents bicycles for US$3.50 a day next door at *Kiosko Alemán*. **G** pp *La Casa de Inés y Juan*, San Martín 1291 (no sign and no phone). Laid back artist and writer's house, 2 rooms, small library and a back-yard for pitching tents (US$1.30 pp per day), where is also a small but delightful pool and a curious bathroom. Meals on request. Recommended. **G** pp *Salpeterer*, Centenario y Av Sarmiento (follow main Av Sarmiento up to its end and turn right 50 m), T470362. Small, basic, tidy, cooking facilities, fan, shared bath (one **E** room for 4 or more with own bath), no breakfast, camping facilities with electricity and hot water for US$0.65 pp per day. *La Aldea*, Rivadavia y Lanusse. An attractive house serving good and cheap pizzas, *empanadas* or other

Sleeping & eating

Argentina

simple meals. *Los Hermanos*, San Martín y Av Sarmiento. Kind owner, the place to go for breakfast, bread or pastries, opens 0700. Several large restaurants for tourists on the streets bordering the Jesuit site.

Camping Two sites on the river splendidly set and very well-kept on a small sandy bay, reached after 45-min walk from town at the end of the road leading to Quiroga's house. *Playa del Sol*, T470115, US$0.35 pp per day plus US$1 per tent. *Club de Pesca y Deportes Náuticos*, on a hilly ground with lush vegetation, US$0.65 pp per day plus US$1 per tent.

Transport Buses stop in front of the church, leaving almost every hour to **Posadas** (US$1.30) or to **Puerto Iguazú** (US$5-6). Do not rely on bus terminal at the end of Av Sarmiento, only a few stop there. More buses stop on Ruta 12 at the access road (Av Sarmiento).

San Ignacio to Puerto Iguazú Ruta 12 continues northeast, running parallel to Río Alto Paraná, towards Puerto Iguazú. With its bright red soil and lush vegetation, this attractive route is known as the Región de las Flores. You get a good view of the local economy: plantations of *yerba mate*, manioc and citrus fruits, timber yards, manioc mills and *yerba mate* factories. The road passes through several small modern towns including Jardín America, Puerto Rico, Montecarlo and Eldorado, with accommodation, campsites, places to eat and regular bus services. Just outside Eldorado, *Estancia Las Mercedes*, Avenida San Martín Km 4, T03751-431511, www.estancialasmercedes.com.ar is an old *yerba mate* farm with period furnishings, open for day visits with activities like riding, boating, and for overnight stays with full board. **Wanda**, 50 km north of Eldorado, was named after a Polish princess and is famous as the site of open-cast amethyst and quartz mines which sell gems. There are guided tours to two of them, *Tierra Colorada* and *Compañía Minera Wanda*, daily 0700-1900.

Gran Salto del Moconá
These falls are known in Brazil as Yucuma

For 3 km the waters of the Río Uruguay create magnificent falls up to 20 m high in a remote part of Misiones. They are surrounded by dense woodland protected by the Parque Estadual do Turvo (Brazil) and the Parque Provincial Moconá, the Reserva Provincial Esmeralda and the Reserva de la Biósfera Yabotí (Argentina). Moconá has vehicle roads and footpaths, accommodation where outdoor activities can be arranged, such as excursions to the falls, trekking in the forests, kayaking, birdwatching and 4WD exploring. Alternative bases are the small towns of El Soberbio (70 km southwest) or San Pedro (92 km northwest). Roads from both towns to Moconá are impassable for ordinary vehicles after heavy rain. Regular bus services run from Posadas to El Soberbio or San Pedro, and from Puerto Iguazú to San Pedro, but no public transport reaches the falls.

Sleeping and tour operators: At **Moconá E** pp *Refugio Moconá*, 3 km from access to the reserve, 8 km from the falls (or contact at Pasaje Dornelles 450, San Pedro), T03751-470022, www.mocona.com Rooms for 4 to 5 people with shared bath, campsite for US$4.30 a day per tent, tents for rent (US$8.50 a day), meals, boat trips and activities. Transfer with sightseeing to/from San Pedro, 2 hrs, US$85 for up to 8 people. At **El Soberbio D** *Hostería Puesta del Sol*, C Suipacha, T03755-495161 (T4300 1377 in Buenos Aires), turismocona@yahoo.com.ar Great views, pool, restaurant, comfortable, with breakfast, a/c. For full board add US$6.50 pp. Boat excursions arranged to the falls, 7 to 8 hrs, US$20 pp (minimum 4 people). A less tiring journey to the falls is by an easy boat crossing to Brazil, then by vehicle to the Parque do Turvo, 7 hrs, meal included, US$20 pp. Otherwise, a 4WD journey on the Argentine side with more opportunities for trekking also takes 7 hrs, with a meal, US$20 pp.

The Iguazú Falls

Colour map 7, grid C1
The falls are 4 times wider than Niagara

The mighty Iguazú Falls are the most overwhelmingly magnificent in all of South America. So impressive are they that Eleanor Roosevelt remarked "poor Niagara" on witnessing them. The falls, on the Argentina-Brazil border, are 19 km upstream from the confluence of the Río Iguazú with the Río Alto Paraná. The Río Iguazú (*guazú* is

Guaraní for big and *I* is Guaraní for water), which rises in the Brazilian hills near Curitiba, receives the waters of some 30 rivers as it crosses the plateau. Above the main falls, the river, sown with wooded islets, opens out to a width of 4 km. There are rapids for 3½ km above the 74 m precipice over which the water plunges in 275 falls over a frontage of 2,470 m, at a rate of 1,750 cu m a second (rising to 12,750 cu m in the rainy season). Viewed from below, the tumbling water is majestically beautiful in its setting of begonias, orchids, ferns and palms. Toucans, flocks of parrots and cacique birds and great dusky swifts dodge in and out along with myriad butterflies (there are at least 500 different species). Above the impact of the water, upon basalt rock, hovers a perpetual 30 m high cloud of mist in which the sun creates blazing rainbows.

On both sides of the falls there are National Parks. Transport between the two parks is via the Ponte Tancredo Neves as there is no crossing at the falls themselves. The Brazilian park offers a superb panoramic view of the whole falls and is best visited in the morning when the light is better for photography (entry fee payable in reais only). The Argentine park (which requires a day to explore properly) offers closer views of the individual falls in their forest setting with its wildlife and butterflies, though to appreciate these properly you need to go early and get well away from the visitors areas. Busiest times are holiday periods and on Sunday. Both parks have visitors' centres and tourist facilities on both sides are constantly being improved.

> **Around the falls**
> *Between Oct and Feb (daylight saving dates change each year) Brazil is 1 hr ahead of Argentina*

Parque Nacional Iguazú covers an area of 67,620 ha. The fauna includes jaguars, tapirs, brown capuchin monkeys, collared anteaters and coatimundis, but these are rarely seen around the falls. There is a huge variety of birds; among the butterflies are shiny blue morphos and red/black heliconius. From the Visitor Centre a small gas-run train (free), the **Tren de la Selva**, whisks visitors on a 25-minute trip through the jungle to the Estación del Diablo, where it's a 1-km walk along catwalks across the Río Iguazú to the park's centrepiece, the **Garanta del Diablo.** A visit here is particularly recommended in the evening when the light is best and the swifts are returning to roost on the cliffs, some behind the water. Trains leave on the hour and 30 minutes past the hour. However, it's best to see the falls from a distance first, with excellent views from the two well-organized trails along the **Circuito Superior** and **Circuito Inferior**, each taking around an hour and a half. To reach these, get off the train at the **Estación Cataratas** (after 10 minutes' journey) and walk down the **Sendero Verde**. The Circuito Superior is a level path which takes you along the easternmost line of falls, Bossetti, Bernabé Mandez, Mbiguá (Guaraní for cormorant) and San Martín, allowing you to see these falls from above. This path is safe for those with walking difficulties, wheelchairs and pushchairs, though you should wear supportive non-slippery shoes. The Circuito Inferior takes you down to the water's edge via a series of steep stairs and walkways with superb views of both San Martín falls and the Gaganta del Diablo from a distance. Wheelchair users, pram pushers, and those who aren't good with steps should go down by the exit route for a smooth and easy descent. You could then return to the Estación Cataratas to take the train to Estación Garganta, 10 and 40 minutes past the hour, and see the falls close up.

At the very bottom of the Circuito Inferior, a free ferry crosses on demand to the small, hilly **Isla San Martín** where trails lead to *miradores* with good close views of the San Martín falls. The park has two further trails: **Sendero Macuco**, 7 km return, starting from near the Visitor Centre and leading to the river via a natural pool (El Pozón) fed by a slender waterfall, **Salto Arrechea** (a good place for bathing and the only permitted place in the park). **Sendero Yacaratiá** starts from the same place, but reaches the river by a different route, and ends at Puerto Macuco, where you could take the *Jungle Explorer* boat to the see the Falls themselves (see below). This trail is really for vehicles and less pleasant to walk along.

■ *US$10, payable in pesos, reais or dollars (guests at Hotel Sheraton should pay and get tickets stamped at the hotel to avoid paying again). Argentines pay US$4. Entry next day is half price if you present the same ticket. Open daily 0800-1900 (1800 in winter). Visitor Centre includes information and photographs of the flora and fauna, as* *well as books for sale. There are places to eat, toilets, shops and a locutorio in the park. In the rainy season, when water levels are high, waterproof coats or swimming costumes are advisable for some of the lower catwalks and for boat trips. Cameras should be carried in a plastic bag.*

Sleeping & eating See under Puerto Iguazú or Foz do Iguaçu (Brazil). Puerto Iguazú is the quieter, safer of the two towns.

Tours & activities A number of activities are offered by *Jungle Explorer*. On *Paseo Ecológico* you float silently 3 km down the river from Estación Garganta to appreciate the wildlife on its banks, 30 mins, US$5. *Aventura Náutica* is a journey by launch to give you a soaking under the Falls, US$10. *Gran Aventura* combines the Aventura Náutica with a longer boat trip and a jeep trip along the Yacaratiá trail, 1 hr, US$24. Tickets available at all embarcation points or at *Sheraton Hotel*. T421696, www.iguazujunglexplorer.com *Explorador Expediciones* offer 2 small-group tours: *Safari a la Cascada* which takes you by jeep to the Arrechea waterfall, stopping along the way to look at wildlife, with a short walk to the falls, 2 hours, US$12. And *Safari en la Selva*, more in-depth interpretation of the wildlife all around, in open jeeps, 2 hours, US$23. Highly recommended. T421600, T15 673318, www.rainforestevt.com.ar and at the *Sheraton Hotel*. The company is run by expert guide *Daniel Somay*. There are also night-time walking tours to the falls when the moon is full; on clear nights the moon casts a blue halo over the falls. The *Sheraton* also rents mountain bikes for US$2.50 for a couple of hrs. Recommended guide: Miguel Castelino, Apartado Postal 22, Puerto Iguazú (3370), Misiones, T420157, FocusTours@aol.com

Transport *Transportes El Práctico* buses run every 45 mins from Puerto Iguazú bus terminal, stopping at the National Park entrance for the purchase of entry tickets, continuing to the Visitor Centre, US$1. First bus 0630, last 1910, journey time 30 mins. Cars are not allowed beyond Visitor Centre (car entry US$3).

Around the Iguazú Falls

■ Sleeping	**2** Sheraton Internacional
1 Das Cataratas	Iguazú Resort

Puerto Iguazú

This modern town is situated 18 km northwest of the falls high above the river on the Argentine side near the confluence of the Ríos Iguazú and Alto Paraná. It serves mainly as a centre for visitors to the falls. The port lies to the north of the town centre at the foot of a hill: from the port you can follow the Río Iguazú downstream towards HitoTres Fronteras, a *mirador* with views over the point where the Ríos Iguazú and Alto Paraná meet and over neighbouring Brazil and Paraguay. There are souvenir shops, toilets and *La Reserva* and *La Barranca* pubs are here; bus US$0.25. **La Aripuca** is a large wooden structure housing a centre for the appreciation of the native tree species and their environment. ■ *US$1.30. Turn off Ruta 12 just after Hotel Cataratas; T423488, English and German spoken, www.aripuca.com.ar* At **Güira Oga** (Casa de los Pájaros) birds that have been injured are treated and reintroduced to the wild. There is also a trail in the forest and a breeding centre for endangered species. ■ *US$1. Open daily 0830-1800. Turn off Ruta 12 at Hotel Orquídeas Palace; T423980 (mob 156-70684).*

Phone code: 03757
Colour map 7, grid C1
Population: 19,000

Sleeping
■ *on map*

L *Sheraton Internacional Iguazú Resort*, T491800, www.sheraton.com/iguazu Fine position overlooking the falls, rooms with garden views cost less, excellent, good restaurant (buffets US$9-9.50, huge breakfast). Taxi to airport US$12. Recommended. **A** *Saint George*, Córdoba 148, T420633, www.hotelsaintgeorge.com With breakfast, comfortable, attentive service, pool and garden, good restaurant with buffet dinner, close to bus station, parking. Recommended. **C** *Cabañas Pirayú*, Av Tres Fronteras 550, on the way to the Hito, T420393, www.pirayu.com.ar Beautiful complex, comfortable *cabañas*, lovely river views, sports and children's games, pool, entertainment. Recommended **C** *Hostería Casa Blanca*, Guaraní 121, 2 blocks from bus station, T421320. With breakfast, family run, large rooms, pleasant. **C** *Hostería Los Helechos*, Amarante 76, T/F420338, www.hosterialoshelechos.com.ar With breakfast, easy-going, popular, well maintained, pool, good value. **D** *Cabañas Leñador*, Ruta 12 Km 5, T421561. Family-run, pool, a/c, TV, games. Recommended. **D** *El Libertador*, Bompland 110, T/F420570. Central, helpful, large bedrooms, those at back have balconies overlooking garden and swimming pool, parking, outdated. **D** *Res Lilian*, Beltrán 183, T420968. Bright modern rooms, quiet, 2 blocks from bus terminal, with breakfast, helpful owners. Recommended. **D** *Lo de Ana*, San Lorenzo 70, T423415, ana10@arnet.com.ar With breakfast, kitchen, German spoken, quiet, good. **D** *Res Paquita*, Córdoba 731, opposite terminal, T420434. Some rooms with balcony, a/c, a bit old-fashioned but nice setting. **D** *Res San Fernando*, Córdoba y Guaraní, near terminal, T421429. With breakfast, popular, good value. **D** *Tierra Colorada*, Córdoba y El Urú 28, T420572. Quiet and comfortable, good atmosphere, with breakfast, very good. **F** pp *Bompland*, Av Bompland 33, T420965. More with a/c, central, family-run. **F** pp *Noelia*, Fray Luis Beltrán 119, T420729. Not far from bus terminal,neat and tidy, family-run, good value,

Argentina

Argentina

with breakfast. **G** pp *Hosp José Gorgues*, Fray L Beltrán 169, T420641. 5 mins from terminal, family run, quiet, garden, laundry, kitchen, good. **Youth hostels** All **F** pp: *Residencial La Cabaña*, Tres Fronteras 434, T420564, iguazu@hostels.org.ar Well run, attractive, nice spaces to sit and eat, good rooms. Recommended. *Residencial Los Amigos*, Fray L Beltrán 82, T420756. Quiet, well maintained, comfortable. *Albergue Residencial Uno*, Beltrán 116, T420529, albergueuno@iguazunet.com Slightly institutional, but OK, accommodation in rooms for 2 to 8, areas to cook and wash (but no machine), tours and activities arranged. *Correcaminos*, Amarante 48, T420967, www.correcaminos.com.ar New, neat rooms, kitchen, bar, games room, also has doubles **E**.

Camping *El Viejo Americano*, Ruta 12, Km 3.5, T420190, www.viejoamericano.com.ar With 3 pools, nicely wooded gardens, also *cabañas* and a hostel, camping US$1.50 pp, food shop, electricity, games area, barbecue places.

Eating
● *on map*
La Rueda, Córdoba 28. Good food at reasonable prices, fish, steaks and pastas. Recommended. *La Esquina*, Córdoba 148. Extensive buffet, beef, fish, friendly service. *Pizza Color*, Córdoba y Amarante. Popular for piza and *parrilla*. *El Quincho del Tío Querido*, Bompland 110. Recommended for *parrilla* and local fish. **Cheap**: *El Charro*, Córdoba 106. Good food, *parrilla*, popular *Jardín de Iguazú*, Córdoba y Misiones, at bus terminal. Good local and Chinese food, *tenedor libre*. *Panificadora Real*, Córdoba y Guaraní. Good bread, open Sun evening; another branch at Victoria y Brasil in the centre.

Tour operators
For operators within the park, see *Jungle Explorer* and *Explorador Expediciones* above. *Explorador* also run recommended 2-day expeditions in 4WDs to the **Salto de Moconá**. *Turismo Cuenca del Plata*, Amarante 76, T421062, cuencadelplata@cuencadelplata.com Conventional tours to the falls, and a half-day trip to a Guaraní village (touristy). *Aguas Grandes*, Mariano Moreno 58, T421140, www.aguasgrandes.com.ar Tours to both sides

Puerto Iguazú

Sleeping ■		Eating ●
1 Albergue Residencial Uno	5 El Libertador	1 El Charro
2 Bompland	6 Hostería Casa Blanca	2 Fechoría
3 Cabañas Pirayú	7 Hostería Los Helechos	3 Jardín de Iguazú
4 Camping	8 Lo de Ana	4 La Rueda
	9 Noelia	5 Panificadora Real
	10 Residencial La Cabaña	
	11 Res Paquita	
	12 Res San Fernando	
	13 Saint George	
	14 Tierra Colorada	

0 metres 200
0 yards 200

of the falls and further afield, activities in the forest, abseiling down waterfalls, good fun. *Cabalgatas por la Selva*, Ruta 12, just after the Rotonda for the road to the international bridge, T155-42180 (mob). For horse riding, 3-hr trips, US$12. Agencies arrange day tours to the Brazilian side (lunch in Foz), Itaipú and Ciudad del Este, though more time is spent shopping than at the Falls. Some include the new Duty Free mall on the Argentine side (not complete yet – 2003). Also to a gem mine at Wanda,US$10, and the Jesuit ruins at San Ignacio Miní, US$20 (better from Posadas, less driving time).

Local Taxis T420973/421707. Fares: to airport US$10, to Argentine falls US$10, to Brazilian **Transport** falls, US$12, to centre of Foz US$10, to Ciudad del Este US$15, to Tierra Colorada mine near Wanda US$25 with wait.

    Air Airport is 20 km southeast of Puerto Iguazú near the Falls, T422013. A bus service between airport and bus terminal connects with plane arrivals and departures, US$3. *AR/Austral* fly direct to **Buenos Aires**, 1 hr 40 mins.

    Buses The bus terminal, at Av Córdoba y Av Misiones, has a phone office, left luggage, various tour company desks and bus offices. To **Buenos Aires**, 16-18 hrs, *Tigre Iguazú*, *Via Bariloche*, daily, US$25 *semi cama*, US$28 *cama*. To **Posadas**, stopping at San Ignacio Miní, frequent, 5-6 hrs, US$8, *expreso*; to **San Ignacio Miní**, US$5-6. *Agencia de Pasajes Noelia*, local 3, T422722, can book tickets beyond Posadas for other destinations in Argentina, ISIC discounts available.

Airline offices *Aerolíneas Argentinas*, Brasil y Aguirre, T420194/420036. **Banks** ATMs at *Macro* **Directory** *Misiones* and *Banco de la Nación*, Av Aguirre 179. *Sheraton* has an ATM. TCs can only be changed at *Cambio Libre* in the Hito Tres Fronteras, open 0800-2200. **Communications** Internet: Generally expensive, US$1-1.20 per hr. *Intercom Iguazú*, Victoria Aguirre 240, p 2, T/F423180. *Telecom*, Victoria Aguirre y Brasil, has internet. Other internet places around here, opposite tourist office. **Embassies and consulates** Brazil, Av Córdoba 264, T421348. **Tourist office** Aguirre 66, T420382, www.iguazuargentina.com Open 0900-2200.

Crossing via the Puente Tancredo Neves. When leaving Argentina, Argentine **Border with** immigration is at the Brazilian end of the bridge. **Brazil**

Transport Buses leave Puerto Iguazú terminal for Foz do Iguaçu every 20 mins, US$1. The bus stops at both sides of the border for Argentine and Brazilian formalities (if you need a visa for Brazil, officially you must have one even for a day visit – immigration does not always insist).Buses also stop at the Duty Free mall. The bus does not wait for those who need stamps, just catch the next one, of whatever company. **Taxis**: between the border and Puerto Iguazú US$3.

Crossing to Paraguay is via Puente Tancredo Neves to Brazil and then via the Puente **Border with** de la Amistad to Ciudad del Este. Brazilian entry and exit stamps are not required **Paraguay** unless you are stopping in Brazil. The Paraguayan consulate is at Bompland 355.

Transport Direct buses (non-stop in Brazil), leave Puerto Iguazú terminal every 30 mins, US$2.50, 45 mins, liable to delays especially in crossing the bridge to Ciudad del Este.

Buenos
Aires

Argentina

The Lake District

The Lake District contains a series of great lakes strung along the foot of the Andes from above 40°S to below 50°S in the Parque Nacional Los Glaciares area. This section covers the northern lakes; for convenience the southern lakes, including those in the Los Glaciares park area, are described under Patagonia. The area is dramatic, beautiful and unspoilt, offering superb trekking, fishing, watersports, climbing and skiing. The most important centre is the city of Bariloche. Off season, from mid-August to mid-November, many excursions, boat trips etc, run on a limited schedule, if at all. Public transport is also limited. See the Chilean chapter, The Lake District, for map and details of the system of lakes on the far side of the Andes. These can be visited through various passes.

Neuquén

Phone code: 0299
Colour map 8, grid C2
Population: 260,000

Founded in 1904 on the west side of the confluence of the Ríos Limay and Neuquén, Neuquén is a pleasant provincial capital and a major stop en route from the east coast to the northern lakes and Bariloche. It serves both the oilfields to the west and the surrounding fruit orchards. There are also many wine *bodegas* nearby. At the Parque Centenario (be sure *not* to take the bus to Centenario industrial suburb), is a *mirador* with good views of the city and the confluence of the rivers, where they become the Negro. Visit **Museo de la Ciudad Paraje Confluencia**, Independencia y Córdoba, interesting small display on the Campaign of the Desert (colonial annihilation of indigenous groups). Facing Neuquén and connected by bridge is Cipolletti, a prosperous centre of the fruit-growing region.

Sleeping & eating
Do not confuse the streets Félix San Martín and Gral San Martín

AL *del Comahue*, Av Argentina 377, T443 2040, www.hahoteles.com 4-star, extremely comfortable, spa, pool, good restaurant. **A** *Express*, Goya y Costa Rica, T449 0100, www.ehotel express.com Handy for the airport, comfortable, international style, nicely decorated and well-equipped, pool and golf. **D** *Alcorta* , Alcorta 84, T442 2652. With breakfast, TV in rooms, also flats for 4, good value. **D** *Royal*, Av Argentina 145, T448 8902, www.hotelguia.com/ hoteles/royal Smart, modern, parking, breakfast included, good value. **E** *Res Inglés*, Félix San Martín 534, T442 2252. Convenient, without breakfast, good. 13 km south on Zapala road is **A** *Hostal del Caminante*, T444 0118. With pool and garden. **Eating** places include *La Birra*, Santa Fe 23. Lots of choice. *Tutto al Dente*, Alberdi 49, for pasta. *Rincón de Montaña*, 9 de Julio 435. Delicious local specialities. *El Reencuentro*, Alaska 6451. Delicious *parrilla*.

Transport
Air Airport 7 km west of centre, T444 0244. Bus US$0.70, taxi US$4. To **Buenos Aires**, *AR/Austral, LADE* and *Southern Winds*. *Southern* Winds and *LADE* fly to many destinations, the latter to the Lake District and Patagonia. Schedules change frequently. **Buses** Terminal at Mitre 147. About a dozen companies to **Buenos Aires** daily, 12-16 hrs, US$25-35. To **Zapala** daily, 3 hrs, US$4. To **San Martín de los Andes** 6 hrs, US$11. (To **Bariloche**, 7 companies, 5-6 hrs, US$11, sit on left. To **Mendoza**, *Andesmar* and 3 others, daily, 12 hrs, US$14. **To Chile**: services to **Temuco** stop for a couple of hrs at the border, 12-14 hrs, US$20, some companies offer discount for return, departures Mon-Thu and Sat; 7 companies, some continuing to destinations en route to **Puerto Montt**.

Directory
Airline offices *AR/Austral*, Santa Fe 52, T442 2409/0810-2228 6527. **Banks** Lots of ATMs along Av Argentina. *Casas de Cambio*: *Pullman*, Alcorta 144, *Exterior*, San Martín 23. **Communications** Internet: At lots of *locutorios* everywhere in centre. *Telecom*, 25 de Mayo 20, open daily till 0030, and Olascoaga 222, open till 2345. **Post Office**: Rivadavia y Santa Fe. **Tourist office** Félix San Martín 182, T442 4089, www.neuquentur.gov.ar Mon-Fri 0700-2000, Sat-Sun 0800-2000.

El Chocón
The area around El Chocón is rich in dinosaur fossils. Red sedimentary rocks have preserved, in relatively good condition, bones and footprints of the animals which

lived in this region during the Cretaceous period about 100 million years ago. The **Museo Paleontológico Ernesto Bachmann** (open daily 0800-2100, T0299-490 1230) displays the fossils of a giant carnivor (Giganotosaurus carolinii). Two walks beside lake to see the dinosaur footprints, guides in museum give good tours. *Aventura Jurásica*, in El Chocón (Alejandro París, T490 1243) offers guided visits to the museum and the surroundings from US$3 pp not including transfers, 2-3 hours. The tourist office organizes guided tours to the 20-km long, 80-m high Cañón Escondido (or Coria) to see dinosaur footprints, 3 hours, US$5. **A** *La Posada del Dinosaurio*, T0299-490 1200, posadadino@infovia.com.ar With breakfast.

There is an excellent geology museum here, **Museo Mineralógico Professor Olsacher**, Etcheluz 52 (same building as bus terminal). Among the collections of minerals, fossils, shells and rocks, is a complete crocodile jaw, believed to be 80 million years old. ■ *Daily 1000-1400, 1800-2000, weekends and holidays 1800-2100, free.* There is an airport, an *ACA* service station, Km 1399 Ruta 22. **C** *Hue Melén*, Brown 929, T422391, good, restaurant. **D** *Coliqueo*, Etcheluz 159, T421308, opposite bus terminal, good. **D** *Pehuén*, Elena de la Vega y Etcheluz, 1 block from bus terminal, T423135, recommended. **E** *Odetto's Grill*, Ejército Argentino 455, T422176, near bus terminal, OK. There is a municipal camping site. **Tourist information**: Av San Martín s/n, T421132.

Zapala
Phone code: 02942
Colour map 8, grid C2
Population: 35,000
185 km W of Neuquén

Transport Buses 4 companies to **San Martín de los Andes**, 3 hrs, US$8, via Junín de los Andes. To **Bariloche** 3 direct buses daily, *Albus*, *TAC*, *ViaBariloche*, change at San Martín. To **Temuco** (Chile) all year, various companies, 10 hrs, Mon, Wed, Fri, US$17. Buy Chilean currency before leaving.

The unspoilt area of **Pehuenia**, reached by *ripio* Ruta 13, holds the country's unique forests of *pehuén* trees (monkey puzzle or araucaria). These ancient trees create a magical atmosphere, especially around the lakes of Aluminé and Moquehue, where a pair of hamlets provide good accommodation. **Villa Pehuenia** is the more popular of the two, picturesquely set in steep wooded hills on the shore of Lago Aluminé. It has a cluster of comfortable *cabañas* and restaurants. **C** *Cabañas Bahía Radal*, T498057, bahiaradal@hotmail.com Luxurious, lake views. **C** *Las Terrazas*, T498036, lasterrazasvillapehuenhia@yahoo.com.ar Beautifully designed Mapuche style, with views over the lake, with also **D** bed and breakfast. Recommended. There are good local dishes at *Costa Azul* restaurant on the lakeside. There's a small tourist kiosk signposted from the main road, T498027. 4 km further on around the lake, turn left at the *gendarmería* and follow a dirt road across the bridge for fine walks in the araucaria forest, also good camping.

Villa Pehuenia & Moquehue
Phone code: 02942
107 km west of Zapala

Another 10 km on Ruta 13 brings you to **Moquehue**, a wilder, more remote village, famous for its fishing. **C** *Hostería Moquehue*, set high above the lake with panoramic views, T02946-15660301, www.hosteriamoquehue.netfirms.com Stylish rooms and excellent food. There is good trekking here and fine camping spots all around these lakes. To complete the Pehuenia circuit, continue along Ruta 13, 11 km to Lago Ñorquinco, past mighty basalt cliffs with *pehuenes* all around, where there's idyllic camping and one rustic *cabaña* on the lakeside at *Ecocamping Ñorquinco*, with café by the roadside. Three buses weekly to Villa Pehuenia and Moquehue from Neuquén.

Known as the trout capital of Argentina, Junín de los Andes is a relaxed, pretty town on the broad Río Chimehuín, with many trout-filled rivers and lakes nearby, and the best base for trekking in Parque Nacional Lanín (see below). Its museum has a fine collection of Mapuche weavings, and there are impressive sculptures at **Vía Christi** on the hill opposite. **Tourist information** is on the leafy Plaza at Col Suárez y Padre Milanesio, T491160. turismo@jdeandes.com.ar ■ *Open summer 0800-2200, Mar-Nov 0800-2100*. Flotadas Chimehuín, T491313, www.todo-patagonia.com/fchimehuin offers fully inclusive fishing packages with expert bilingual guides.

Junín de los Andes
Phone code: 02972
Colour map 8, grid B4
Population: 9,000
 www.turismo.gov.ar/
pesca for fishing
information (English)

Argentina

Sleeping and eating L *Río Dorado Lodge & Fly shop*, Pedro Illera 448, T491548, www.riodorado.com.ar Comfortable, pricey, great for anglers, good fly shop. **D** *Milla Piuké*, Av los Pehuenes y JA Roca, T492378, millapiuke@jandes.com.ar Absolutely delightful, welcoming, comfortable rooms and apartments for families. Highly recommended. **D** *Hostería Chimehuín*, Col Suárez y 25 de Mayo, T491132. Cosy, quaint old fishing lodge by the river. Recommended. **D** *Posada Pehuén*, Col Suárez 560, T491569, posadapehuen@hotmail.com A peaceful bed and breakfast with comfortable rooms, pretty garden, charming owners, good value. **E** *Res Marisa*, JM de Rosas 360, T491175, www.residencialmarisa.com.ar A simple place with helpful owners, very good value. **Camping**: *Mallín Beata Laura Vicuña*, T491149, and *La Isla*, T492029, both on the river and good. Several campsites in beautiful surroundings on Lagos Huechulafquen and Paimún in Parque Nacional Lanín (see below). Good restaurants include *Ruca Hueney*, Col Suárez y Milanesio, steak, trout and pasta dishes. *Confitería Centro de Turismo* next to the tourist office, café/restaurant, good for coffee and sandwiches. *La Aldea de Pescador* on the main road by YPF station. *Parrilla* and trout.

Transport information
T491038

Transport Air: Chapelco airport between Junín and San Martín, served by *Austral* from Buenos Aires and *LADE* (in bus terminal at Villegas 231, San Martín de los Andes, T427672) from Bahía Blanca, Esquel and Bariloche. **Bus**: terminal at Olavarria y F. San Martín, T492038.

Border with Chile – The Tromen Pass

Formalities are carried out at the Argentine side of the Tromen Pass (Chileans call it Mamuil Malal). This route runs through glorious scenery to Pucón (135 km) on Lago Villarrica (Chile). It is less developed than the Huahum and Samoré (Puyehue) routes further south, and definitely not usable during heavy rain or snow (Jun to mid-Nov). Parts are narrow and steep; it is unsuitable for bicycles. (Details of the Chilean side are given under **Puesco**, **The Lake District**) There is a campsite at Puesto Tromen (though very windy), but take food as there are no shops at the pass. The international bus will officially only pick up people at Tromen but at the discretion of the driver can pick up passengers at Puesco (no hotel) at 0900 and Currarehue stops. Buses to Temuco daily except Sunday, with *San Martín* or *Igi-Llaima*, US$5.

Parque Nacional Lanín
This beautiful, large park has sparkling lakes, wooded mountain valleys and one of Argentina's most striking peaks, the snow capped Lanín Volcano

The lakes of **Huechulafquen** and **Paimún** are unspoilt, beautiful, and easily accessible for superb walking and fishing, with 3 *hosterías* and blissful free camping all along the lakeside. ■ *US$1.50 to enter park. Helpful advice on walks from* guardeparques *at the entrance and at Puerto Canoa. Frequent buses from Junín in season, T491038 for information.* Best hotel: **AL** *Hostería Huechulafquen*, T02972-426075, lafquen@smandes.com.ar Comfortable cabin-like rooms, own stretch of beach, expert fishing guide. Geologically, Lanín Volcano (3,776 m) is one of the youngest of the Andes; it is extinct and one of the world's most beautiful mountains. It's three days' challenging climb, with two *refugios* at 2,400 m, starting from the Argentine customs post at Tromen pass, where you must register with *guardeparques,* who check all climbers' equipment and experience. Crampons and ice-axe are essential, as is protection against strong, cold winds. ■ *Entry US$1.50. Before setting off, seek advice from Lanín National Park office, Frey 749, San Martín, on main plaza, T427233, helpful but maps poor. www.parquesnacionales.gov.ar has helpful information in Spanish.*

San Martín de los Andes

Phone code: 02972
Colour map 8, grid C1
Population: 20,000
40 km SW of Junín

This picturesque and touristy little town, with its chocolate-box, chalet-style architecture, is spectacularly set at the east end of Lago Lacar. Mirador Bandurrias, 6 km from the centre offers good views. There is excellent skiing on Cerro Chapelco, and facilities for water skiing, windsurfing and sailing on Lago Lacar. Surrounded by lakes and mountains to explore, the most popular excursions are south along the **Seven Lakes Drive** (see below), north to the thermal baths at **Termas de Lahuen-Co** (also reached on foot from Lago Huechulafquen) and to **Lagos Lolog** and **Lácar**. There's a *ripio* track along the north side of Lago Lácar with beaches and rafting at **Hua Hum**, and along the south to quieter **Quila Quina**, where a 2-hour walk takes you to a quiet Mapuche community. Both can be reached by boat from San Martín's pier, T428427, 45 minutes, US$5 return to Quila Quina, three daily in season. Cyclists can complete a circuit around Lago Lácar, or take the cable car up to Chapelco and come back down the paths.

L *Las Lengas*, Col Pérez 1175, T427659. Attractive spacious rooms, warm relaxing atmosphere, peaceful part of town. **AL** *La Cheminée*, Gral Roca y Mariano Moreno, T427617, lacheminee@ smandes.com.ar Cosy cottage-like rooms, breakfast included, but no restaurant, overpriced in high season. **AL-A** *Alihuen Lodge*, Ruta 62, Km 5.5 (road to Lake Lolog), T426588, F426045. Includes breakfast, other meals available (very good), lovely location and grounds, very comfortable. **AL-A** *La Masia*, Obeid 811, T427879. Spacious, high-ceilinged chalet-style rooms, cosy bar. **A** *La Raclette*, Pérez 1170, T427664. Delightful rooms in charming old building, excellent restaurant. **B** *Hostal del Esquiador*, Col Rhode 975, T427674. Well decorated rooms, lovely sitting room, good service. Great value low season. **B** *Del Viejo Esquiador*, San Martín 1242, T427690. Very comfortable, good beds, in traditional hunting lodge style, excellent service. Recommended. **B** *Intermonti*, Villegas 717, T427454, hotelintermonti@smandes.com.ar Smart rooms with good beds, well-run. **C** *Casa Alta*, Obeid 659, T427456., The home of charming multilingual owners, 'beyond comparison and fantastic' (closed in low season). Book in advance. **C** *Crismalu* Rudecindo Roca 975, T427283, crismalu@smandes.com.ar With breakfast, attractive chalet-style, good value. **C** *Hostería Las Lucarnas*, Pérez 632, T427085. Central, pretty, simple comfortable rooms, English spoken. **D** *Hosteria Bärenhaus*, Los Alamos 156, Barrio Chapelco (8370), T/F422775, www.baerenhaus.com 5km outside town, free pick-up from bus terminal and airport. Welcoming young owners, excellent breakfast, very comfortable rooms with heating, English and German spoken. Recommended. **D** *Hostal del Lago*, Col Rhode 854, T427598. Relaxed homely place, basic bathrooms, good breakfast included, pretty garden.

   Youth hostel: **F** *Puma*, A Fosbery 535, T422443, www.pumahostel.com.ar Discount for HI and ISIC members, dorms and **C** double room with view, laundry, kitchen facilities, internet access, bikes for hire, very well run by mountain guide owner. Recommended. **F** *Rukalhue*, Juez del Valle 682, T427431, www.rukalhue.com.ar Also high quality with good facilities, comfortable dorms and **D** double, 2 blocks from terminal. **Camping** *ACA Camping*, Av Koessler 2176, T429430, with hot water and laundry facilities, also *cabañas*. *Camping Quila Quina*, T426919, www.quilaquina.alojar.com.ar Lovely site on Lago Lácar, 18 km from San Martín, with beaches, immaculate toilet blocks, restaurant and shop.

Avataras, Tte Ramón 765, T427104. Open only Thu-Sat from 2030, inspired, imaginative menu with cuisine from all over the world, from fondue to satay, elegant surroundings, US$13. An excellent treat. *Pionieri*, General Roca 1108. Excellent Italian meals in a cosy house, good service, English and Italian spoken. Recommended. Same owners run *Los Patos* (next door) for take-away food, T428459. *La Chacha*, Rivadavia y San Martín. Much recommended traditional *parrilla* for excellent steaks, good pasta for vegetarians, with good old-fashioned service. *Pura Vida*, Villegas 745. The only vegetarian restaurant in town, small and welcoming, also fish and chicken dishes. *La Costa del Pueblo*, Costanera opposite pier. Overlooking the lake, huge range of pastas, chicken and trout dishes, cheap (US$4 2 courses), good service. Recommended. *Tío Pico*, San Martín y Capitán Drury. Great bar/café, good for lunch. *Ku*, San Martín 1053. Intimate atmosphere for *parrilla*, pastas and delicious mountain specialities, excellent service and wine list. *El Regional* Villegas 955. Popular for regional specialities – smoked trout, patés and hams, El Bolsón's home-made beer, all in cheerful German-style decor. Opposite, *Delikatesse* is recommended for cheap food in cheerful surroundings, great menu deals for US$3.50. Delicious chocolates at *Mamusia* and *Abuela Goye*, both on San Martín.

Cycling Many places in the centre rent mountain and normal bikes, reasonable prices, maps provided. *HG Rodados*, San Martín 1061. Rents mountain bikes, US$6 per day, also spare parts and expertise. **Fishing** Contact the tourist office or the National Park office. *Orvis* fly shop, Gral Villegas 835, T425892. *Jorge Cardillo Pesca* fly shop, Villegas 1061. Both sell equipment and offer fishing excursions. *Patagonian Anglers*, M Moreno 1193,

Sleeping
Single rooms are scarce. There are 2 high seasons, when rates are much higher: Jan/Feb and Jul There are many excellent cabañas for families on the hill at the top of Perito Moreno. Tourist Office provides a list of private addresses in high season

Eating
Lots of places to eat, few of them cheap

Sport & activities
www.turismo.gov.ar/ pesca for fishing information (English)

Argentina

Argentina

T427376, patagoniananglers@smandes.com.ar **Skiing** Chapelco has 29 km of pistes, many of them challenging, with an overall drop of 730 m. Very good slopes and snow conditions make this a popular resort with foreigners and wealthier Argentines. Bus from San Martín to slopes, US$2 return. *Transportes Chapelco*, T02944-156 18875, or 425808. Details, passes, equipment hire from office at San Martín y Elordi, T427845, www.chapelco.com.ar At the foot of the mountain are a restaurant and base lodge, with 3 more restaurants on the mountain and a small café at the top.

Tour operators *El Claro*, Villegas 977, T428876, www.interpatagonia.com/elclaro *Las Taguas*, Perito Moreno 1035, T427483, www.lastaguas.com For marvellous horse riding trips. *Tiempo Patagónico*, San Martín 950, T427113, www.tiempopatagonico.com Excursions and adventure tourism, including rafting at Hua Hum.

Transport **Air** Chapelco airport, 20 km away. See under Junín de los Andes above. **Buses** Terminal at Villegas 251, T427044. toilet facilities, *kiosko*, no *locutorio*. To **Buenos Aires**, 20 hrs, US$40 *coche cama*, daily, 6 companies. To **Bariloche**, 4 hrs, US$8, *Vía Bariloche*, T425325, *Albus*, T428100, via Traful and La Angostura. *Ko Ko*T427422 daily, fast route via Confluencia, or via the Seven Lakes in summer only.**To Chile**: Temuco via Pucón with *Empresa San Martín*, T427294, Mon, Wed, Fri, *Igi-Llaima*, T427750, Tue, Thu, Sat, US$9, 6-8 hrs (heavily booked in summer, rough journey via Paso Hua Hum – see below, sit on the left).

Directory **Banks** Many ATMs on San Martín. Exchange at *Banco de la Nación*, San Martín 687. *Banco de la Provincia de Neuquén*, Obeid y Belgrano. **Police station** Belgrano 635, T427300. **Tourist office** San Martín y Rosas 790, on main plaza, T427347. Open 0800-2100 all year. English and French spoken. Very busy in summer, advisable to go early. www.smandes.gov.ar

Border with Chile – the Hua Hum Pass
This route is theoretically open all year round
A *ripio* road along the north shore of Lago Lácar through the Lanín National Park crosses the border to Puerto Pirehueico. A weekly bus leaves early morning, 2 hrs, US$4, check terminal for schedule; it connects with boat across Lago Pirhueico. Bikes can be taken. For connections from Puerto Pirehueico to Panguipulli and beyond, see Chile chapter.

San Martín de los Andes to Bariloche

There are two routes south to Bariloche. One is the well-maintained *ripio* road known as the '**Seven Lakes Drive**', via Lago Hermoso and Villa La Angostura, which passes beautiful unspoilt stretches of water, framed by steep, forested mountains. There are several places to stay, open summer only. At **Lago Espejo** is D pp *Hostería Los Siete Lagos*, a charming simple place on the shore of Lago Correntoso, great views. Several free campsites without facilities. The other route, more direct but less scenic is via **Confluencia** on the paved Bariloche highway (ACA service station and a hotel, also motel *El Rancho* just before Confluencia). Round-trip excursions along the Seven Lakes route, 5 hours, are operated by several companies, but it's better in your own transport.

Parque Nacional Nahuel Huapi
This park contains lakes, rivers, glaciers, waterfalls, torrents, rapids, valleys, forest, bare mountains and snow-clad peaks
Covering 750,000 ha and stretching along the Chilean border, this is the oldest National Park in Argentina. Many kinds of wild animals live in the region, including the pudú, the endangered huemul (both deer) as well as river otters, cougars and guanacos. Bird life, particularly swans, geese and ducks, is abundant. The outstanding feature is the splendour of the lakes. The largest is **Lago Nahuel Huapi** (*Altitude*: 767 m), 531 sq km and 460 m deep in places, particularly magnificent to explore by boat since the lake is very irregular in shape and long arms of water, or *brazos*, stretch far into the land. On a peninsula in the lake is exquisite **Parque Nacional Los Arrayanes** (see below). There are many islands: the largest is **Isla Victoria**, with its idyllic hotel. Trout and salmon have been introduced.

North of Villa La Angostura, Lagos Correntoso and Espejo both offer stunning scenery, and tranquil places to stay and walk (see above). Navy blue Lago Traful, a short distance to the northeast, can be reached by a road which follows the Río Limay through the Valle Encantado, with its fantastic rock formations or directly from Villa La Angostura. **Villa Traful** is the perfect place to escape to, with fishing, camping, and walking, and on its lakeside, the charming *Hostería Villa Traful*, T479005, **C** *Cabañas Aiken*, T479048, www.aiken.com.ar and *Nancu Lahuen*, a tea room and restaurant serving local trout. Spectacular mountains surround the city of Bariloche, great trekking and skiing country. The most popular walks are described in Bariloche section. South of Lago Nahuel Huapi, Lagos Mascardi, Guillelmo and Gutiérrez offer horse riding, trekking and rafting along the Río Manso. See page 199 for accommodation along their shores.

This pretty town is a popular holiday resort with wealthier Argentines and there are countless restaurants, hotels and *cabaña* complexes around the centre, **El Cruce** . The picturesque port, known as **La Villa**, is 3 km away at the neck of the Quetrihué Peninsula. At its end is **Parque Nacional Los Arrayanes**, with 300 year old specimens of the rare *arrayán* tree, whose flaky bark is cinnamon coloured. The park can be reached on foot or by bike (12 km each way), or you could take the boat back. Boats run twice daily in summer, US$8 return (reservations at **B** *Hotel Angostura*, T494224, www.hotellaangostura.com.ar Lovely lakeside setting, good restaurant). See below for tours by boat from Bariloche. **Tourist office** opposite bus terminal at Avenida Siete Lagos 93, T494124, www.laangostura.com Good maps with accommodation marked. Open high season 0800-2100, low season 0800-2000.

Villa La Angostura
Phone code 02944
Colour map 8, grid C1
Population: 3,000
90 km NW of Bariloche on Lago Nahuel Huapi

Sleeping A *Hostal Las Nieves*, Av Siete Lagos 980, T494573. Small, good location with garden, very comfortable, English spoken, helpful. **A** *Portal de Piedra*, Ruta 231 y Río Bonito, T494278, www.portaldepiedra.com Small, attractive *hostería* in the woods. **B** *Casa del Bosque*, T595229. Chic *cabañas*, secluded in woodland at Puerto Manzana. **C** *Nahuel*, Ruta 231 y Huiliches, T 494737. Good simple rooms, popular *parrilla*. **C** *Verena's Haus*, Los Taiques 268, T 494467. Adults and non-smokers only, German and English spoken, cosy, garden. Recommended. **F** *Hostel la Angostura*, 300 m up road behind tourist office, T494834, www.hostellaangostura.com.ar A warm, luxurious hostel, all small dorms have bathrooms, young welcoming owners organize trips too. Recommended. **F** pp *Lo de Francés*, Lolog 3057, on shore of Lago Correntoso, T155 64063, www.interpatagonia.com/lodefrances Great lake views from this comfortable hostel with all facilities. Recommended. **Camping** *Osa Mayor*, off main road, close to town, T494304, osamayor@oul.com.ar Well designed leafy site, all facilities, also rustic *cabañas*, helpful owner.

Eating Mid-range: Many on the main drag, Av Arrayanes, eg *Hora Cero*, No 45. Warm atmosphere and live music at weekends, popular, big range of excellent pizzas, *pizza libre* (as much as you can eat for US$2) on Wed and Sat is a great deal. *Nativa Café*, No 198. Relaxed and welcoming, excellent pizzas – try the smoked goat topping – huge salads, good place to hang out. *Rincón Suizo*, No 44. High season only, delicious regional specialities with a Swiss twist. *Los Troncos*, No 67. Great local dishes, eg trout-filled ravioli, fabulous cakes and puddings. **Cheap**: If on a budget, the popular *parrilla El Esquiador*, 2 blocks north of the middle of the main street, has cheap fixed-price 3-course menu. Also try jolly *Gran Nevada* for cheap *parrilla*, and *ñoquis*. Takeaway chicken and pastas from the *rotiserie Las Leñas*.

Transport To/from Bariloche, 1¼ hrs, US$3, several companies. If going on to **Osorno** (Chile), you can arrange for the bus company to pick you up at La Angostura, US$7 to Osorno, road paved. Daily buses to **San Martín de los Andes** with *Ko Ko* and *Albus*.

Bariloche

Phone code: 02944
Colour map 8, grid C1
Population: 77,750

Beautifully situated on the south shore of Lago Nahuel Huapi, at the foot of Cerro Otto, San Carlos de Bariloche is an attractive tourist town and the best centre for exploring the National Park. There are many good hotels, restaurants and chocolate shops among its chalet-style stone and wooden buildings. Others along the lake shore have splendid views. Heaving with visitors in summer months, it's less busy in March-April when the forests are in their glory.

Ins & outs

For more detailed information see Transport, page 201

Getting there The airport is 15 km east of town, the bus and train stations 3 km east. Taxis charge US$5 to the former, US$1.50 to the latter. *Del Lago Turismo*, Villegas 222,T430056, run a bus service to meet each arriving/departing flight. US$1, from Mitre y Villegas outside the door of *Aerolíneas Argentinas* building. If staying on the road to Llao Llao, west of town, expect to pay more for transport to your hotel.

Getting around At peak holiday times (Jul and Dec-Jan), Bariloche is very busy with holidaymakers and secondary school students. The best times to visit are in the spring (Sep-Nov) and autumn (Mar-Apr), or Feb for camping and walking and Aug for skiing.

Tourist office Oficina Municipal de Turismo, in Centro Cívico, T423122, www.bariloche.com.ar Open daily 0900-2100, Sat 0900-1900. Has full list of city buses, and details of hikes and campsites in the area and is helpful in finding accommodation. Obtain maps and information at the Nahuel Huapi National Park *intendencia*, at San Martín 24, T423111, open 0900-1400, www.parquesnacionales.com.ar Also useful for information on hiking is *Club Andino Bariloche (CAB)*, 20 de Febrero 30, T422266/424531, www.clubandino.com.ar Open 0900-1300, plus 1600-2100 high season only.

Sights

In the city At the heart of the city is the **Centro Cívico**, built in 'Bariloche Alpine style' and separated from the lake by Avenida Rosas. It includes the **Museo de La Patagonia** which, apart the region's fauna (stuffed), has indigenous artefacts and material from the lives of the first white settlers. ■ *Tue-Fri 1000-1230, 1400-1900, Mon-Sat 1000-1300, US$1*. Next to it is **Biblioteca Sarmiento**, a library and cultural centre. ■ *Mon-Fri, 1000-2000*. The **cathedral**, built in 1946, lies six blocks east of here, with the main commercial area on Mitre in between. Opposite the main entrance to the cathedral there is a huge rock left in this spot by a glacier during the last glacial period. On the lakeshore at 12 de Octubre y Sarmiento is the **Museo Paleontológico**, which displays fossils mainly from Patagonia, including an ichthyosaur and replicas of a giant spider and shark's jaws.

Outside the city Avenida Bustillo runs parallel to the lakeshore west of Bariloche, with access to the mountains above. At Km 5, a cable car (teleférico) goes up to **Cerro Otto** (1,405 m) with its revolving restaurant and splendid views. Transport and other details under Skiing, below. At Km 17.7 a chairlift goes up to **Cerro Campanario** (1,049 m) with fine views of Isla Victoria and Puerto Pañuelo. ■ *Daily 0900-1200, 1400-1800, US$4*. At Km 18.3 **Circuito Chico** begins - a 60-km circular route around Lago Moreno Oeste, past Punto Panorámico and through Puerto Pañuelo to **Llao Llao**, Argentina's most famous hotel (details on this and others on Avenida Bustillo in Sleeping, below.) ■ *Bus No 20, 45 mins, US$0.70. A half-day drive or tour with agency, or full day's cycle*. You could also extend this circuit, returning via **Colonia Suiza** and **Cerro Catedral** (2,388 m), a major ski resort, both starting points for walks (see below). ■ *Bus 10 to Colonia Suiza, Bus 'Catedral' to Catedral. All buses from big bus stop on Moreno y Rolando; see Skiing, below*. Whole-day trip to **Lagos Gutiérrez** and **Mascardi** and beautiful **Pampa Linda** at the base of mighty **Cerro Tronador** (3,478 m), visiting the strange **Ventisquero Negro** (black glacier), highly recommended. Several companies run 12-hour minibus excursions to San Martín de los Andes along the famous **Seven Lakes Drive**, returning via Paso de Córdoba and the Valle Encantado, but these involve few stops.

Among the many great treks possible here, these are recommended: From **Llao Llao**, delightful easy circuit in Valdivian (temperate) rainforest (2 hours), also climb the small hill for wonderful views. ■ *Bus 20 to Llao Llao*. Up to **Refugio López** (2,076 m), 5 hours return, from southeastern tip of Lago Moreno up Arroyo López, for fabulous views. ■ *Bus 10 to Colonia Suiza and López (check return times)*. From Refugio López, extend this to 3-4 day trek via Refugio Italia to **Laguna Jacob** and **Refugio San Martín** (poorly signposted, need experience). From Cerro Catedral to **Refugio Frey** (1,700 m), beautiful setting on small lake, via Río Pedritas (4 hours each way), or via cable car to *Refugio Lynch* and via Punta Nevada (only experienced walkers). To beautiful **Lago Gutiérrez**, 2 km downhill from Cerro Catedral, along lake shore to the road from El Bolsón and walk back to Bariloche (4 hours), or Bus 50. From **Pampa Linda**, idyllic (*hostería*, campsite - see Sleeping), walk up to Refugio Otto Meiling (5 hours each way), to tranquil Laguna Ilon (5½ hrs each way), or across Paso de las Nubes to **Puerto Frías**, boat back to Bariloche (2 days, check if open: closed when boggy). Bus to Pampa Linda from outside Club Andino Bariloche in summer. *Transitando lo Natural*, T423918, 3½ hours, US$8. Contact *CAB* for maps and to check walks are open. For climbing and skiing on Cerros Catedral and Otto, see **Sports** below.

Walks
There's a network of paths in the mountains, and several refugios allowing for treks over several days

Isla Victoria, a half-day excursion (1300-1830) from Puerto Pañuelo (buses 10, 20, 21 to get there) and on to **Bosque de Arrayanes**, on the Quetrihué Peninsula further north (see Villa La Angostura, above) in a full-day excursion (0900-1830, or 1300 till 2000 in season), US$15, take picnic lunch. All day boat trip to **Puerto Blest**, in native Valdivian rainforest. From Puerto Pañuelo (Km 25.5), sail down to Puerto Blest (*hostería*, restaurant), continuing by short bus ride to Puerto Alegre and again by launch to Puerto Frías. From Puerto Blest, walk through forest to the Cascada de los Cántaros (1 hour), recommended. ■ *0730 bus to Puerto Pañuelo where boat excursion leaves to Puerto Blest*, Catedral *and* Turisur.

Boat trips
Out of season, tour boats only sail if demand is sufficient

If you arrive in the high season without a reservation, consult the listing published by the Tourist Office (address above). There's also a booking service in Buenos Aires, at Florida 520 (Galería), room 116. In Bariloche **L** *Edelweiss*, San Martín 202, T426165, www.edelweiss.com.ar 5-star with real attention to detail, excellent service, spacious comfortable rooms, indoor pool and beauty salon. *La Tavola* restaurant is excellent. Highly recommended. **AL** *Nevada*, Rolando 250, T422778, www.nevada.com.ar Warm and welcoming, nicely furnished rooms, good restaurant, with traditional dishes. **B** *Tres Reyes*, 12 de Octubre 135, T426121, hreyes@bariloche.com.ar Traditional lakeside hotel with spacious rooms, splendid views, cheaper to reserve on the spot than by email. **B** *La Pastorella*, Belgrano 127, T424656, www.lapastorella.com.ar Quaint little hostería, whose hospitable owners speak English. Recommended. **B** *El Cristal* Mitre 355, T422002, hotelcristalres@ciudad.com.ar Central, charming, 60's style, comfortable, with TV and minibar (the superior rooms are best). **C** *La Sureña*, San Martín 432, T422013. Central, cosy, small wood-panelled rooms, old-fashioned feel, with TV. **C** *El Ñire*, O'Connor y O'Connor, T423041. Small, warm and pleasant place, English spoken. **D** *Piuké*, Beschtedt 136, T423044. Delightful, simple, nicely decorated, breakfast included, excellent value, German, Italian spoken. **D** *Premier*, Rolando 263, T426168. www.premierhotel.com.ar Good economical choice, small modern rooms with TV, internet, English spoken. Recommended. **D** *Güemes*, Güemes 715, T424785. Lovely, quiet, lots of space, very pleasant, breakfast included, owner is a fishing expert. **D** *El Radal*, 24 de Septiembre 46, T422551. Small, comfortable, restaurant. **E** *Res No Me Olvides*, Av Los Pioneros Km 1, T429140, 30 mins' walk or Bus 50/51 to corner of C Videla then follow signs. Beautiful house in quiet surroundings, use of kitchen, camping. Recommended. **E** *El Ciervo Rojo*, Elflein 115, T/F435541, www.elciervorojo.com Showers, nice rooms, with breakfast, TV, information about treks. **E** *Res Rosán Arko*, Güemes 691, T423109. English and German spoken, cooking facilities, helpful, good trekking information, beautiful garden, camping. Repeatedly recommended.

Sleeping
■ *on map*
Prices rise in two peak seasons: Jul-Aug for skiing, and mid-Dec-Mar for summer holidays This selection gives lake-view, high-season prices where applicable

Argentina

On the road to Llao Llao (Av Bustillo) LL *Llao-Llao*, Km 25, T448530, www.llaollao.com Deservedly famous, superb location, complete luxury, golf course, pool, spa, water sports, restaurant. A *Tunquelén*, Km 24.5, T448400, www.maresur.com 4-star, quiet comfortable, splendid views, feels more secluded than *Llao-Llao*, restaurant, attentive service. Highly recommended. A *Cabañas Villa Huinid*, Km 2.5, T523523, www.villahuninid.com.ar Luxurious *cabañas* with everything you need. Recommended. B *La Caleta*, Km 1.9, T441837. *Cabañas* sleep 4, open fire, excellent value. C *Katy*, Km 24.3, T448023 adikastelic@yahoo.com Delightful, peaceful, garden full of flowers, charming family, breakfast included. Also offers adventure tourism www.gringospatagonia.com

C *Hostería Santa Rita*, Km 7.2, T/F461028, www.santarita.com.ar Close to the centre, peaceful lakeside views, comfortable, lovely terrace, great service. Warmly recommended. Bus 10, 20, 21, to Km 7.5 for this and also: E pp *Hostel Alaska (Hostelling International)*, Km 7.5, T461564, www.alaska-hostel.com Well run, cosy chalet-style, open all year, with doubles and dorms, kitchen facilities, internet, rafting and riding. Many *cabañas* along lakeshore.

The tourist office keeps a list of family accommodation

Family accommodation Among those recommended are: E pp *Mariana Pirker*, 24 de Septiembre 230, T424873. Flats sleeping 2-3, German and English spoken. F pp *Eloisa Lamunière*, Paso 145 ground floor, T422514. Small but homely modern apartment with kitchen facilities. F pp *Casa Nelly*, Beschtedt 658, T422295. Helpful, hot showers and use of kitchen, also camping.

There are some excellent hostels in Bariloche, making a longer stay viable and comfortable

Youth hostels Recommended are: E pp *Aire Sur*, Elflein 158, T522135, airesur@abari.com.ar Light, airy and peaceful, dorms, one double E, lovely terrace, garden with climbing wall, breakfast extra, internet, laundry, cycle hire, knowledgeable owner also runs mountain bike excursions and kayaking. E pp *La Bolsa* , Palacios 405 y Elflein, T423529, www.labolsadeldeporte.com Relaxed atmosphere, rustic rooms – some with great views, deck to sit out on. E pp *Patagonia Andina*, Morales 564, T421861, www.elpatagoniaandina.com.ar Quiet place with comfortable dorms, and twin rooms with shared bath, small kitchen, TV area, sheets included, breakfast extra, internet, advice on trekking. E pp *Ruca Hueney*, Elflein 396, T433986, rucahueney@bariloche.com.ar Lovely, calm, comfortable beds with duvets, fabulous double room (E) with extra bunk beds, bathroom and great view, spotless kitchen, very kind owners, Spanish school. E pp *Hostel 1004*, Edif

Bariloche

N

0 metres 200
0 yards 200

■ **Sleeping**
1 Aire Sur *B2*
2 Albergue El Gaucho *B1* 3
Albergue Rucalhué *A1*
4 Camping *A1*
5 Casa Nelly *B2*
6 Edelweiss *A1*
7 El Ciervo Rojo *B2*
8 El Cristal *A2*
9 El Ñire *A3*
10 El Radal *B1*
11 Güemes *B1*
12 Hostel 1004 *A1*
13 La Bolsa *B2*
14 La Pastorella *B1*
15 La Sureña *A1*
16 Nevada *A2*
17 Patagonia Andina *B1*
18 Periko's *B1*
19 Piuké *A3*
20 Premier *A2*
21 Res Rosán Arko *B1*
22 Ruca Hueney *B2*
23 Tres Reyes *A2*

● **Eating**
1 El Boliche de Alberto *B1*
2 El Boliche de Alberto
Pastas *B2*
3 El Viejo Munich *A2*
4 Familia Weiss *A2*
5 Friends *A2*
6 Jauja *B2*
7 Kandahar *B1*
8 La Jirafa *A2*
9 La Marmite *A2*
10 Pilgrim *A2*
11 Rock Chicken *A2*
12 Simoca *A2*
13 Vegetariano *B1*

Bariloche Center, San Martín 127, p 10, T432228, 1004hostel@ciudad.com.ar Rooms for 3-4, also floor space **F** pp, kitchen facilities, panoramic views, tourist information, English spoken. Connected with the hostel is **F** pp *La Morada*, Cerro Otto Km 5, T441711, www.lamoradahostel.com Ideal place to chill out, amazing views, doubles and dorms, kitchen, laundry, English spoken. **F** pp *Alaska*, Lilinquen 328 (buses 10, 20, 21, get off at La Florida), T/F461561, www.alaska-hostel.com Shared rooms for 4, all with bath, Also double without bath, rustic rooms, nice garden, washing machine, free internet, organizes horse riding, rents mountain bikes. **F** pp *Albergue El Gaucho*, Belgrano 209, T522464, www.hostelgaucho.com.ar Modern, in quiet part of town, some doubles with own bath (**E** pp), English, German and Italian spoken. **F** *Albergue Rucalhué*, Güemes 762, T430888. Cheaper in loft and in low season, kitchen, helpful, luggage store. **F** pp *Periko's*, Morales 555, T522326, www.perikos.com No breakfast but towels and sheets included, kitchen, washing machine, nice atmosphere, quiet, *asado* every Fri.

Camping List of sites from Tourist Office. These are recommended among the many along Bustillo: *Selva Negra*, Km 2.5, T444013. *El Yeti*, Km 5.6. All facilities, also *cabañas*. *Petunia*, Km 13.5. A lovely shady site going down to lakeside with all facilities. Shops and restaurants on most sites; these are closed outside Jan-Mar.

South of Bariloche **F** pp*Refugio Neumeyer*, 18 km southwest of Bariloche, office at 20 de Junio 728, T428995, www.eco-family.com Comfortable hostel, great family centre for trekking, climbing, mountain biking in summer; cross country skiing in winter. Highly recommended. **AL** *El Retorno*, Villa Los Coihues, on the shore of Lago Gutiérrez, T467333, www.hosteriaelretorno.com Stunning lakeside position, comfortable hunting lodge style, with a beach, tennis, very comfortable rooms (Bus 50, follow signs from the road to El Bolsón).

Along **Lago Mascardi**: **A** pp *Hotel Tronador*, T441062, hoteltronador@ bariloche.com.ar 37km from Bariloche, lakeside paradise, lovely rooms, beautiful gardens, charming owner, also riding, fishing and lake excursions. Also camping *La Querencia*. **B** *Mascardi*, T490518, www.mascardi.com Luxurious hotel with a delightful setting. *Camping Las Carpitas*, Km 3.5, T490527, www.lascarpitas.com Summer only, great location, all facilities, also *cabañas*. *Camping Los Rápidos*, T461861, tascha@bariloche.com.ar All facilities, attractive shaded site going down to lake, *confitería*. **D** *Hostería Pampa Linda*, T442038, www.tronador.com A wonderfully comfortable, peaceful base for climbing Tronador and many other treks (plus horse riding, trekking and climbing courses), simple rooms, all with stunning views, restaurant, full board, packed lunch. Owner Sebastián de la Cruz is experienced mountaineer. Highly recommended. *Camping Pampa Linda*, T424531. Idyllic spacious lakeside site with trees.

On this narrow road there are restricted times for going in each direction: check with tourist office

In Bariloche Mid-range: *El Boliche de Alberto*, Villegas 347, T431433. Very good steak and live music. Also try *El Boliche de Alberto Pastas* Elflein 49. *Chez Philippe*, Primera Junta 1080, T427291. Delicious local delicacies, fine French-influenced cuisine. *Familia Weiss*, Palacios y VA O'Connor. Excellent local specialities, live music. Wild boar particularly recommended. *Friends*, Mitre 302. Good for lunch, convenient, lively, open 24 hrs. *Jauja*, Quaglia 366, T422952. Quiet, recommended for good local dishes, good value (also take-away round the corner at Elflein128). *Kandahar*, 20 de Febrero 698, T424702. Atmospheric, warm and intimate, with exquisite food, run by ski champion Marta Peirono de Barber, superb wines and fabulous pisco sour. Reserve in high season. Highly recommended. *La Marmite*, Mitre 329. Cosy, good service, huge range of fondues, good wild boar, delicious cakes for tea too. Recommended. *Pilgrim*, Palacios 167. Irish pub, serves a good range of beers, reasonable meals too. *Tarquino*, 24 de Septiembre y Saavedra. Good food and service and a fine wine selction. *Vegetariano*, 20 de Febrero 730, T421820. Also fish, excellent food, beautifully served, warm atmosphere. Highly recommended. **Cheap** *La Jirafa*, Palacios 288. Cheery family-run place for good food, good value. *Rock Chicken*, Quaglia y Moreno. Small, busy, good value fast food (also take-away). *Simoca*, Palacios 264. Recommended for delicious and cheap Tucumán specialities, huge empanadas. *Panadería Trevisan*, Moreno y Quaglia, for excellent bread and cakes. *Jauja* next door, for legendary ice creams.

Eating
● *on map*
Many good delicatessens for picnics

On the road to Llao Llao, **Av Bustillo** .*El Patacón*, Km 7, T442898. Good *parrilla* and game, pricey. *Tasca Brava*, Km 7, T462599. On lakeside, intimate atmosphere, Patagonian and superb Spanish cooking. *Cerveceria Blest*, Km 11.6, T461026. Wonderful brewery with delicious beers, serving imaginative local and German dishes and steak and kidney pie. Recommended. *Il Gabbiano*, Km 24.3, T448346. Delicious Italian lunches and dinners. *Bellevue,* Km 24.6, T448389. Exquisite tea rooms, worth a special trip to taste Karin's raspberry cheesecake *sachertorte*, in lovely gardens with incredible views. Open 1600-2000, Wed to Sun. Another tearoom, and bed and breakfast, in a lavender garden and selling sweet-smelling produce, *Meli Hue,* Km 24.7, T448029, is recommended.

Shopping
The main commercial centre is on Mitre between the Centro Cívico and Beschtedt

The local **chocolate** is excellent: several shops on Mitre. You can watch chocolates being made at the touristy *El Turista*, Mitre 252. Better chocolate at *Mamushka*, next block, excellent. Very good chocolate at *Fenoglio*, Mitre 301 y Rolando - also superb chocolate ice cream, and at *Abuela Goye*, Mitre 258. Local wines, from the Alto Río Negro, are also good. *Arbol*, Mitre. Sells good quality outdoor gear, lovely clothes and gifts. Handicraft shops along San Martín. *Feria Artesanal Municipal*, Moreno y Rolando. Uno, Moreno 350, *Todo* supermarket, Moreno 319, good selection, cheap.

Sport & activities
Note that at higher levels, winter snow storms can begin as early as Apr, making climbing dangerous

Climbing: best information from **Club Andino Bariloche**, see Tourist offices, above. The club arranges guides. Its booklet '*Guía de Sendas y Picadas*' gives details of climbs and it provides maps (1:150,000) and details of all campsites, hotels and mountain lodges. *Refugios* are run both privately and by Club Andino Bariloche. In treks to *refugios* remember to add costs of ski lifts, buses, food at *refugios* and lodging (in *Club Andino refugios*: US$3 per night, plus US$1.50 for cooking, or US$2.50 for breakfast, US$4 for dinner). Take a good sleeping bag. **Cycling**: bikes can be hired at many places in high season: *Dirty Bikes*, V O'Connor 681, T425616, www.dirtybikes.com Very helpful for repairs too, pricey. *Bike Way*, VA O'Connor, 867, T424202. See also *Aire Sur* under Youth hostels, US$5 per day. Mountain bike excursions, Diego Rodríguez, www.adventure-tours-south.com **Fishing**: *Asociación de Guías Profesionales de Pesca*, T421515, www.guiaspatagonicos.com/guias Fly fishing shop, *Martín Pescador*, Rolando 257, also in Cerro Catedral in winter, Alvear y Sarmiento, T422275, for fishing, camping and skiing equipment. **Horse riding**: contact *Tom Wesley*, in country ranch by the lake at Km 15.5, T448193. Tuition and full day's riding offered. **Paragliding:***Parapente Bariloche*, T462234, 155 52403, parapente@bariloche.com.ar At Cerro Otto. **Skiing**: see page 202. **Trekking**: Club Andino (see below) has 4 maps of hikes, though none shows contours. More detailed maps available from Buenos Aires IGM. Horseflies (*tábanos*) frequent the lake shores and lower areas in summer. Trekking to Chile across the Andes, via Pampa Linda, Lago Frías, Peulla, with *Andescross.com*, T467502, www.andescross.com Expert guides, all included.

Tour operators
Check what your tour includes; cable cars and chair lifts are usually charged as extras

Tours get very booked up in season. Most travel agencies will pick you up from your hotel, and all charge roughly the same prices: Circuito Chico US$5, Isla Victoria and Bosque de Arrayanes US$20, Tronador, Ventisquero Negro and Pampa Linda US$12, Puerto Blest boat trip US$13, plus US$4 to enter national park, plus US$3 for Lago Frías, Cerro Catedral US$7, El Bolsón US$14.50. Also possible to go on 'la Trochita' from El Maitén, but easier from Esquel. *Aguas Bancas*, Mitre 515, T429940, www.aguasblancas.com.ar Rafting on the Río Manso, all grades, with expert guides, and all equipment provided, also bikes and horse riding, traditional lunches included. *Asatej*, San Martín 127, T/F421314, www.asatej.com Cheap flights, adventure tourism and travel all over Argentina. Recommended. *Catedral Turismo*, Palacios, 263, T426444, www.lakecrossing.cl *Cumbres y Lagos Patagonia*, Villegas 222, T423283, cumbres@bariloche.com.ar For rafting, horse riding, trekking, fishing. *Del Lago Turismo*,Villegas 222, T430056, cordille@bariloche.com.ar Very helpful, staff speak fluent English, all conventional tours, plus horse riding, rafting, trips to Tronador (Pampa Linda) if the regular bus isn't running. Also recommended, a combined trip by boat along Lago Mascardi.*Extremo Sur*, Morales 765, T427301, www.extremosur.com Rafting and kayaking, all levels, full days all inclusive packages offered. *Infinito Sur* (Pere Vilarasau Alsina, no office), T154-11370, www.InfinitoSur.com For climbing, trekking, mountain skiing, rafting, expeditions on the *estepa* in Argentine and Chilean Patagonia (in Aysén, T569-595 8820), highly experienced from Bolivia and all points south. *Pucara*, Mitre22, p 1, T430989. Huge range of local trips and further afield to La Trochita and Esquel as well as the Estepa. *San Carlos Travel*, Mitre 213, p 2, T/F432999, sancartrav@ bariloche.com.ar Birdwatching and other specialist tours. *Hans Schulz*, Casilla 1017, T155 08775. Speaks German and English, arranges tours and guides. *Turisur*, Mitre 219, T426109, www.bariloche.com/turisur Boat trips to Bosque de Arrayanes, Isla Victoria and Puerto Blest. Always reserve one day ahead. *Tronador Turismo*, Quaglia 283, T421104, tronador@bariloche.com.ar Conventional tours, trekking and rafting. Also to Refugio Neumeyer, and to Chilean border. Great adventurous wintersports options. **Guides**: For trekking, biking, kayaking, natural history expeditions: *Angel Fernández*, T524609, 156 09799. Extremely knowledgeable and charming, also speaks English. Recommended. *Daniel Feinstein*, T/F442259. Also speaks English. Both experienced in Argentina and Chile.

Argentina

Local Car hire: Best rates from *Localiza* (San Martín 531, T424767), and *Hertz* (Quaglia 352, T423457), helpful, English spoken. *A1 International*, at airport and in town (San Martín 235, T422582). *Open*, Mitre 382, T/F426325, much cheaper. To enter Chile, a permit is necessary. State when booking car. Free with most agencies, allow 24 hrs. **Taxis**: *Remises Bariloche*, T430222, *Remises Moreno*, T435555. **Long distance Air**: Taxi to airport US$5; *Del Lago Turismo*, see above, runs buses from Mitre y Villegas, outside Aerolíneas Argentinas, to meet every flight, US$1. Book ahead for bikes. Many flights a day to **Buenos Aires**, with *AR/Austral* and *Southern Winds*. *AR* also flies to **El Calafate** and **Ushuaia**. *American Falcon* flies to **Puerto Madryn** and **Montevideo**. *Southern Winds* to **Córdoba**. *LADE* to **Bahía Blanca, Comodoro Rivadavia, Esquel, Mar del Plata, Neuquén, Puerto Madryn, San Martín de los Andes** and **Trelew**.

> **Transport**
> *Airport is 15 km E of town. Train station and bus terminal both 3 km E of centre. For international car rental agencies, see Essentials*

 Buses: toilets, small *confitería, kiosko*, no *locutorio* but public phones. Left luggage US$0.50 per day. Buses 10, 20, 21 frequent service from bus/train station to centre of town, US$0.60. Bus company offices:*Vía Bariloche/El Valle*, Mitre 321, T429012; *Andesmar/Albus*, Mitre 385, T430211; *Chevallier/La Estrella/Ko Ko*, Moreno 105, T425914; *TAC*, Moreno 138, T434727; *Cruz del Sur*, T437699. *Don Otto/Río de La Plata*, 12 de Octubre, T437699. *3 de Mayo*, for local services, Moreno 480, T425648. Prices rise in summer. To **Buenos Aires**, 6 companies daily, 22½ hrs, US$50 *coche cama*. To **Bahía Blanca**, 3 companies, US$30. To **Mendoza**, US$17, *TAC* and *Andesmar*, 19 hrs, via Piedra de Aguila, Neuquén, Cipolleti and San Rafael. To **Esquel**, via El Bolsón, *Don Otto, Mar y Valle, Vía Bariloche, Andesmar*, US$6. To **Puerto Madryn**, 14 hrs, US$25 , 14 hrs with *Mar y Vale* and *Don Otto*. To **San Martín de los Andes**, *Ko Ko*, Mon-Sat 1430, US$8, 4 hrs. No direct bus to **Río Gallegos**; you have to spend a night in **Comodoro Rivadavia** en route: *Don Otto* daily, US$19, 14½ hrs. To **Puerto Montt**, see the route to Chile from Bariloche. To **El Calafate**, ask at youth hostel *Alaska*, or *Periko's* about **Safari Route 40**, a 4-day trip down Ruta 40 to Calafate via the Perito Moreno national park, Cueva de Las Manos and Fitz Roy, staying at *Estancia Melike* and Río Mayo en route. US$95 plus accommodation at US$5 per day. www.OverlandPatagonia.com

> *Bus information at terminal T432860*

 Trains: Booking office at station (T423172) closed 1200-1500 weekdays, Sat afternoon and all Sun. Information from the Tourist Office. Tourist service to Viedma, also with sleeper section, and carries cars.

Airline offices *Aerolíneas Argentinas/Austral*, Quaglia 238, T422425. *LADE*, Quaglia 238, T423562. *Southern Winds*, Quaglia 262, T423704. *American Falcon*, Mitre 159, T425200. **Banks** Banks and exchange shops buy and sell virtually all European and South American currencies, besides US dollars. Best rates from *Sudamérica*, Mitre 63, T434555. ATMs on Mitre at 424, 694, 180, Moreno y Quaglia, San Martín 297 and 332. **Communications** Internet: Several cybercafés and at *locutorios* in the centre, all with similar rates. **Post Office**: Moreno 175, closed Sat afternoon and Sun. **Telephone**: Many *locutorios* in the centre. *Telecom*, Mitre y Rolando, has fast internet. **Embassies and consulates** Chile, JM de Rosas 180, T422842, helpful. **Medical facilities** Emergencies: Dial 107, or San Carlos Emergencias, T430000, **Clinic**: Hospital Zonal Moreno 601, T426100. **Useful addresses Customs**: Bariloche centre T425216, Rincón (Argentina), T425734, Pajarito (Chile) T005664-236284.

> **Directory**
> *Immigration office, Libertad 175*

One of South America's most important ski centres is just a few kilometres from Bariloche, at **Cerro Catedral**, with 70 km of slopes of all grades, allowing a total drop of 1,010 m, and 52 km of cross country skiing routes. There are also snowboarding

> **Ski resorts near Bariloche**

areas and a well-equipped base with hotels, restaurants and equipment hire, ski schools and nursery care for children. Book ski equipment in advance in Bariloche from: *Robles Catedral*, T460062, www.roblescatedral.com or *Xtreme*, T460309, www.skipacks.com

Sleeping and eating L *Pire-Hue*, T011-4807 8200, www.pire-hue.com.ar Exclusive 5-star hotel with beautiful rooms and all facilities. *La Raclette*, highly recommended, family place. *El Viejo Lobo*, family-owned restaurant, and, up the slopes, *Refugio Lynch* has restaurant and *confitería*.Information T460125. Open mid-Jun to end-Aug, busiest from mid-Jul to mid-Aug for school holidays. Ski lifts open 0900-1700. Ski lift pass: adults US$14 per day, ski school, US$30 per hr pp.

Transport Bus run by *3 de Mayo*, 'Catedral', leaves Moreno 480 every 90 mins approximately, T425648, US$1. Cable car for Catedral T460090.

Also skiing at **Cerro Otto**. Cable car passengers can take free bus leaving from hut at Centro Cívico, hourly 1030-1730, returning hourly 1115-1915. Ticket for both costs US$8 pp, T441031. There's a revolving *confitería*, craft shop, great views. Also *Club Andino confitería*, 20 minutes' walk from main *confitería* on summit. Ski gear can also be rented by the day, at US$0.50-1 per item, from *Cebron*, Mitre 171, or *Milenium*, Mitre 125. See also *Martín Pescador*, page 200.

Border with Chile **The Samoré (formerly Puyehue) Pass** A spectacular 6-hour drive. A good broad paved road, RN 231, goes around the east end of Lago Nahuel Huapi, then follows the north side of the lake through Villa La Angostura. It passes the junction with 'Ruta de Los Siete Lagos' for San Martín at Km 94, Argentine customs at Km 109 and the pass at Km 125 at an elevation of about 1,280 m, the road largely *ripio* here. Chilean customs is at Km 146 in the middle of a forest. The border is open from the second Saturday of October to 1 May, 0800-2100, winter 0900-2000 but liable to be closed after snowfalls. Hire cars need special papers: ask when booking (free, but may take 24 hours).

Via Lake Todos Los Santos The route is Bariloche to Puerto Pañuelo by road, Puerto Pañuelo to Puerto Blest by boat (1½ hours), Puerto Blest to Puerto Alegre on Lago Frías by bus, cross the lake to Puerto Frías by boat (20 minutes), then 1½ hours by road to Peulla. Leave for Petrohué in the afternoon by boat (2½ hours), cross Lago Todos Los Santos, passing the Osorno volcano, then by bus to Puerto Montt. This route is beautiful, but the weather is often wet.

The Argentine and Chilean border posts are open every day. The launches (and hence the connecting buses) on the lakes serving the direct route via Puerto Blest to Puerto Montt generally do not operate at weekends; check: T425216. There is an absolute ban in Chile on importing any fresh food – meat, cheese, fruit – from Argentina. Further information on border crossings in the Lake District will be found in the Chile chapter. You are strongly advised to get rid of all your Argentine pesos before leaving Argentina; it is useful to have some Chilean pesos before you cross into Chile from Bariloche. Chilean currency can be bought at Puyehue customs at a reasonable rate.

Transport
Take passport when booking
Five bus companies run daily services from Bariloche to **Osorno** (4-6 hrs, US$9-10) and **Puerto Montt** (7-8 hrs, same fare) via the Samore pass: buses usually leave 0730-0800. Companies include *Río de La Plata*, *Vía Bariloche*, *Cruz del Sur*, and *Andesmar* (addresses under Bariloche). Sit on left side for best views. You can buy a ticket to the Chilean border, then another to Puerto Montt, or pay in stages in Chile, but there is little advantage in doing this.

Turismo Catedral (see Tour operators, above) has the monopoly on the famous Three Lakes Crossing to Puerto Montt in Chile, US$140, plus cost of launch at Peulla (US$20), credit cards accepted. Book in advance during the high season, and beware the hard sell. This excursion does not permit return to Bariloche next day. (1 Sep-30 Apr, take own food, departs 0700). For a 2-day crossing (operates all year round), there is an overnight stop in Peulla. Details about accommodation under Peulla, in Chile. You can do the first section to Puerto Blest and Lago Frías in a regular day trip more cheaply. Other agencies sell such excursions, get information from *Turismo Catedral* which owns the exclusive rights to the excursion via the lakes, using their own boats and bus from Puerto Pañuelo to Puerto Frías (*Andina del Sud* operates with them on the Chilean side).

El Bolsón and around

The paved road from Bariloche to El Bolsón, 126 km south, passes the beautiful lakes Gutiérrez, Mascardi and Guillelmo. From the southern end of Lago Mascardi, 35 km south, a *ripio* road (note one-way system) runs west towards Cerro Tronador and **Pampa Linda**, the starting point for excellent trekking including the two-day walk over Paso de los Nubes to Laguna Frías (see **Walks** and **Sleeping** above). **Río Villegas**, about 80 km south, is very beautiful, with world class rafting on the **Río Manso** (E *Hostería Río Villegas*, pleasant, restaurant, just outside the gates of the national park, by the river).

Phone code: 02944
Colour map 8, grid C1
Population: 8,000

El Bolsón is an attractive town situated in a broad fertile valley, surrounded by the mountains of the cordillera and dominated by the dramatic peak of Cerro Piltriquitrón 2,284 m (hence its name: the big bag). It's a magical setting which attracted thousands of hippies to create an ideological community here in the 1970's; they now produce the handicrafts, beers, fruit and jams, sold at the market on Tuesday, Thursday, Saturday. There are many mountain walks and waterfalls nearby, with swimming at the river just 300 m from the centre and good fishing at Lagos Puelo (see below) and Epuyén (shops and petrol available) - both within easy access. The **tourist office** is on San Martín, opposite bus terminal. ■ *0930-2000 all year, until 2300 in high summer. Extremely helpful with maps and accommodation, English spoken. T492604, www.bolsonturistico.com.ar sec_turismo@elbolson.com*

B *Cordillera*, San Martín 3210, T492235, cordillerahotel@elbolson.com With breakfast, modern, comfortable, TV. **C** *La Casona de Odile*, Barrio Luján, T492753, odile@red42.com.ar Idyllic lavender farm by stream, delicious cooking, reserve ahead. Recommended. **C** *Sukal*, high on a hill in Villa Turismo, T492438, www.sukalelbolson.com Peaceful haven in a garden of flowers, breakfast extra, helpful. Recommended. **D** *La Posada de Hamelin*, Int Granollers 2179, T492030, gcapece@elbolson.com Charming rooms, welcoming atmosphere, huge breakfasts, German spoken. Highly recommended. **D** *Hostería Steiner*, San Martín 670, T492224. Another peaceful place with lovely garden, wood fire, German spoken. **D** *Valle Nuevo*, 25 de Mayo y Belgrano, T156-02325. Small very simple rooms, quiet place, breakfast not included, but good value. At Lago Epuyén, 40 km south of El Bolsón, **D** *Refugio del Lago*, T02944-499025. Relaxed place with breakfast, also good meals, trekking, riding, camping. Recommended. Owners are mountain guides.

Youth hostels E *El Pueblito*, 3 km north in Luján, 1 km off Ruta 258, T493560, elpueblitobolson@hotmail.com Cosy wooden building in open country, cooking and laundry facilities, shop, open fire. **E** *Refugio Patagónico*, Islas Malvinas y Pastorino, T156 35463. High quality, small dorms with bath, in a spacious house in open fields, great views of Piltriquitrón, also camping. Recommended. **E** *Sol del Valle*, 25 de Mayo 2329, T492087. Bright hostel with basic rooms, shared bath, kitchen and eating space for big groups, sheets/towels extra, garden with view of Piltriquitrón. There are many **Cabañas** in picturesque settings with lovely views in the Villa Turística. Try *Las Bandurrias*, Ruta 258, north access, T492819.

Camping *La Chacra*, Belgrano 1128, T492111, 15 mins walk from town, well shaded, good facilities, lively atmosphere in season. *Quem Quem*, on river bank Río Quemquemtreu, T493550. Well kept lovely site with hot showers, good walks, free pickup from town. *Arco Iris*, T155 58330. Blissful wooded setting near Río Azul, helpful owners. *El Bolsón*, T492595, on RN258 1 km north of town, small brewery. Recommended. **F** *Campamento Ecológico*, Pagano y Costa del Río, cannot be recommended.

Sleeping
Difficult to find accommodation in the high season: book ahead

Argentina

Eating *La Calabaza*, San Martín y Hube. Good inexpensive food including vegetarian dishes, relaxed atmosphere. *Cerro Lindo* next door, slightly more elegant, delicious pastas. *Jauja*, San Martín 2867. Great meeting place, delicious fish and pasta, outstanding handmade ice cream, English spoken. Recommended. *Don Diego*, San Martín 3217, Good. *El Viejo Maitén*, Roca 359. Good. *Parrilla Las Brasas*, Sarmiento y P Hube. Good. *Acrimbaldo* , San Martín 2790, Good value *tenedor libre*, smoked fish and draft beer. *Il Rizzo*, San Martín 2500, Good value pizzas and draught beer in a lively relaxed café. *La Tosca*, San Martín y Roca. Café, restaurant in summer, warm atmosphere. *Parrilla Patagonia*, San Martín on plaza, lamb, trout, pizzas, cheap fixed menu US$3.

Tour *Patagonia Adventures*, P Hube 418, T492513, www.argentinachileflyfishing.com
operators Rafting, paragliding, fishing, boat trip on Lago Puelo to remote forest lodge. *Grado 42*, Av. Belgrano 406, T493124, grado42@elbolson.org Tours, including La Trochita, helpful information on buses too.

Transport **Buses** Several daily from **Bariloche** and **Esquel** with *Don Otto*, *Vía Bariloche*. Heavily booked in high season, US$5-6.50, 2 hrs.

Around El There are waterfalls at **Cascada Escondida**, 10 km northwest of town, a good place for
Bolsón a picnic, with a tea room nearby. There fine views from **Cerro Piltriquitrón** - drive or taxi 10 km, then walk 1 hour through the sculptures of the **BosqueTallado** (or 6-7 hour round trip walk), food and shelter at *refugio* (1,400 m). Views of the valley from **Cabeza del Indio**, a good 6 km drive or bike ride from the centre, and a pleasant one hour walk up to **Cerro Amigo**: follow Gral Roca east until it becomes Islas Malvinas and continue up the hill. There are wonderful two-day treks to the mountains west of the town, with *refugios* at Cerro Lindo, Cerro Hielo Azul and Cajón de Azul. Cajón de Azul can also be reached in a fabulous day walk up *Río Azul*. *Nehuén* (Belgrano y Perito Moreno, same office as Andesmar) run a *traffic* minibus to Wharton, leaving at 0900, which collects Río Azul walkers at 2000 the same day.

At **Lago Puelo**, 18 km south in the **Parque Nacional Lago Puelo**, there are gentle walks on marked paths, boat trips across the lake, and canoes for rent. Wardens at the park entrance (free) can advise on these and a 3-day trek through magnificent scenery to Chilean border. Regular buses, US$1.40, from Avenida San Martín y Dorrego in El Bolsón go to the lake via Villa Lago Puelo. *Hostería Enebros*, T499413, and *Posada los Niños*, T499117, both **D**; *Camping La Pasarela*, T499061, also many *cabañas*, shops and fuel. Boats: *Juana de Arco*, T493415. Fishing: *Zona Sur*, T156 15989, November-April, US$100 per day for three people, equipment included. Homemade *alfajores* in fairy tale setting at *La Bolsonera* on old road.

Cholila A peaceful sprawling village with superb views of Lago Cholila, crowned by the
Phone code: 02945 Matterhorn-like mountains of Cerros Dos and Tres Picos. Excellent fishing, canoe-
76 km S of El Bolsón ing and kayaking on rivers nearby. The atmospheric wooden cabins where Butch Cassidy, the Sundance Kid and Etta Place lived between 1901 and 1907 are 13 km north along Ruta 71. ■ *Entry US$3.* Behind the ranch is *Casa de Té Galés*, which is most hospitable.

Sleeping A *La Rinconada*, T498091, larinconada@interlink.com.ar Offers tours, horse riding, kayaking, American-owned. **C** *El Trébol*, T/F498055. With breakfast, comfortable rooms with stoves, meals and half board also available, popular with fishing expeditions, reservations advised, bus stops in village 4 km away. *Cabañas Cerro La Momia*, Villa Lago Rivadavia, T0297-446 1796, www.cabanascerrolamomia.com.ar Good setting, basic *cabañas*. **Camping F** *Autocamping Carlos Pelligrini*, next to El Trébol. Free camping in El Morro park. *Camping El Abuelo*, 13 km south. *Butch Cassidy Teahouse* has photos about Butch and co and the owner is well informed about local history.

Esquel

Esquel was originally an offshoot of the Welsh colony at Chubut, 650 km to the east, and still has a pioneer feel. A breezy open town in a fertile valley, with a backdrop of mountains, Esquel is the base for visiting the Parque Nacional Los Alerces and for skiing at **La Hoya** in winter. Good walks from the town to Laguna La Zeta, 5 km, and to Cerro La Cruz, two hours. It's also the departure point for the famous narrow gauge railway, **La Trochita** (see box). The very basic tourist office is at Alvear y Sarmiento, T451927, www.esquel.gov.ar ■ *Open daily 0800-2000, summer 0730-2200. Closed weekends off-season.*

Phone code: 02945
Colour map 9, grid A1
Population: 30,000
272 km S of Bariloche

Argentina

Sleeping

Hotels are often full in Jan-Feb
Ask at tourist office for lodgings in private houses

A *Cumbres Blancas*, Ameghino 1683, T/F455100, www.cpatagonia.com/esq/cblancas Attractive modern building, a little out of centre, very comfortable, airy restaurant, dinner US$7. **B** *Tehuelche*, 9 de Julio 825, T452420, tehuelche@ar.inter.net Comfortable, with breakfast, good restaurant with cheap set menu. **B** *Angelina*, Alvear 758, T452763. Open high season only. Good food, warm, welcoming, Italian spoken. **B** *Canela*, C Los Notros, Villa Ayelén, on road to Trevelin, T/F453890, www.canela-patagonia.com Bed and breakfast and tearoom, English spoken, knowledgeable about Patagonia. **C** *La Tour D'Argent*, San Martín 1063, T454612, www.cpatagonia.com/esq/latour With breakfast, bright, comfortable, good value, popular restaurant. **D** *La Chacra*, Km 4 on Ruta 259 towards Trevelin, T452471. Relaxing, spacious rooms, huge breakfast, Welsh and English spoken. **D** *La Posada*, Chacabuco 905, T454095, laposada@art.inter.ar Tasteful, in quiet part of town, lovely lounge, spacious rooms, breakfast included, excellent value. Recommended. **D** *Hostería Los Tulipanes*, Fontana 365, T452748. Ample breakfast, small rooms, smokers welcome. **E** *Res El Cisne*, Chacabuco 778, T452256. With cooking facilities, quiet, well kept, good value. **G** pp *Mrs Elvey Rowlands' guesthouse*, behind Rivadavia 330, T452578. Warm family welcome, Welsh spoken, with breakfast, basic rooms with shared bath. **F** *Casa Emma Cleri*, Alvear 1021, T452083, T156-87128 (mob). Helpful and hospitable.

Youth hostel E pp *Albergue El Batxoky*, San Martín 661, T450581, www.epaadventure.com.ar Smallish rooms but good atmosphere, kitchen, laundry. **E** *Lago Verde*, Volta 1081, T454396, patagverde@teletel.com.ar Breakfast extra, modern, comfortable, run by tour guides, rooms for 2, kitchen, laundry, near bus terminal, 2 blocks from La Trochita. Recommended.

Camping *El Hogar del Mochilero*, Roca 1028, T452166. Summer only, laundry facilities, 24-hr hot water, friendly owner, internet, free firewood. *Millalen*, Ameghino 2063, T456164, good services. Campsite at Laguna Zeta *La Colina*, Darwin 1400, T454962, US$1.75 pp, hot showers, kitchen facilities, lounge, log fire, also rooms **G** pp. Recommended. *La Rural*, 1km on road to Trevelin, T452580, well organized and shady site with facilities.

Eating

Don Chiquino, behind Av Ameghino 1649. Fun atmosphere with magician owner, games, pastas and pizzas. *Pizzería Don Pipo*, Fontana 649. Good pizzas and *empanadas*. *La Española*, Rivadavia 740. Excellent beef, salad bar, tasty pastas. Recommended. *Los Nietos*, 9 de Julio 910. Good cheap pizzas to take away. *Shangai*, 25 de Mayo 485. Chinese and everything else *tenedor libre*. *Tango Gourmet*, Alvear 949, Restaurant/bar with tango shows and lessons, open 1100-2400. *LaTour d'Argent*, San Martín 1063. Delicious local specialities, good value. *Vascongada*, 9 de Julio y Mitre. Trout and other local specialities. **Cafés**: *María Castaña*, Rivadavia y 25 de Mayo. Popular, good coffee.

Shopping

Casa de Esquel (Robert Müller), 25 de Mayo 415. Wide range of new and second hand books on Patagonia, also local crafts.

Sport & activities

Fishing: tourist office has advice. **Skiing**: One of Argentina's cheapest, with laid back family atmosphere, **La Hoya**, 15 km north, has 22 km of pistes, 7 ski-lifts. For skiing information ask at **Club Andino Esquel**, Volta 649, T453248; bus to La Hoya from Esquel, 3 a day, US$5 return, ski pass US$7. Equipment hire US$4 a day.

▶ *The Old Patagonian Express*

Esquel is the terminus of a 402-km branch-line from Ingeniero Jacobacci, a junction on the old Buenos Aires-Bariloche mainline, 194 km east of Bariloche. This narrow-gauge line (0.75 m wide) took 23 years to build, being finally opened in 1945. It was made famous outside Argentina by Paul Theroux who described it in his book The Old Patagonian Express. The 1922 Henschel and Baldwin steam locomotives (from Germany and USA respectively) are powered by fuel oil and use 100 litres of water every km. Water has to be taken on at least every 40 km along the route. Most of the coaches are Belgian and also date from 1922. If you want to see the engines you need to go to El Maitén where the workshops are.

Until the Argentine government handed responsibility for railways over to the provincial governments in 1994, regular services ran the length of the line. Since then, services have been maintained between Esquel and El Maitén by the provincial government of Chubut.

Tour operators *Esquel Expeditions*, T451763, moranjack@ciudad.com.ar Bespoke adventure trips, trekking and canoeing in the national park, to the gold mine, up Río Futaleufú to Chile, walking in Valdivian rainforest, with experienced mountain guide Jack Moran. *Patagonia Verde*, 9 de Julio 926, T454396. Local tours, Los Alerces, boat trip across Lagos Menéndez and Cisnes, La Trochita. Also adventure excursions, horse riding, rafting, fishing. English spoken.

Transport **Long distance Air** Airport, 20 km east of Esquel, by paved road, US$9 by taxi, US$1.50 by bus. To **Buenos Aires** with *AR. LADE* (Alvear 1085, F452124) to **Bahía Blanca, Bariloche, Comodoro Rivadavia, El Bolsón, El Maitén, Mar del Plata** and **Neuquén**. **Trains** La Trochita (see box above) – the Old Patagonian Express – normally runs from El Maitén on Wed at 1400, 6¼ hrs, US$6.50 (under 6s free), with dining car. Tourist services: Esquel to Nahuel Pan (19 km) Mon, Wed, Sat 1000 (more in high season – Jan and Feb), 2½ hrs, US$4; El Maitén to Desvío Thomae, Sat 1500, 2½ hrs, US$4. Information in El Maitén, T02945-495190, in Esquel T451403. www.latrochita.com.ar has information in English and schedules. Spanish commentary. Tickets from tour operators, or from Esquel station office

Buses Smart terminal at Alvear 1871, T451566, has toilets, *kiosko, locutorio,* left luggage; also for taxis. From Buenos Aires travel via **Bariloche**: *Andesmar* (T450143) can be booked Esquel-Buenos Aires, including change in Bariloche, 24 hrs, *semi cama* US$50. To **Comodoro Rivadavia**, 9 hrs, US$13, *Don Otto* (T453012), 4 times a week (but usually arrives from Bariloche full in season). To **Bariloche**, 4-5hrs, US$6, *Don Otto, Andesmar, Mar y Valle* (T453712), *Vía Bariloche* (T453528). To **El Bolsón**, 2 hrs, US$3, on bus to Bariloche, or via **Los Alerces national park**, Lagos Puelo and Epuyen with *Transportes Esquel*, T453529, daily. To **Trelew**, 9 hrs, US$11. *Mar y Valle, Emp Chubut – Don Otto* daily. To **Trevelin**, *Vía Trevelin* (T455222), Mon-Fri, hourly 0700-2100, every 2 hrs weekends, US$1.05.

Directory **Banks** *Banco de la Nación* Alvear y Roca, open 0730-1300. ATM accepts all cards. ATMs also at*Banco Patagonia*, 25 de Mayo 739, *Bansud*, 25 de Mayo 752. **Communications** **Internet**: Café in Shell station, Alvear y 25 de Mayo, open 24 hrs. *Cyberplanet*, San Martín 994. **Post office** at Av Alvear 1192. **Telephone**: Many *locutorios* in centre, including *Unitel*, 25 de Mayo 528.

Trevelin An offshoot of the Welsh Chubut colony (see box in Patagonia section), where
Colour map 9, grid A1 Welsh is still spoken, the pretty village of Trevelin has a Welsh chapel (built 1910,
Population: 5,000 closed) and tea rooms. The **Museo Regional**, in the old mill (1918) includes
22 km SW of Esquel artefacts from the Welsh colony. ■ *US$1.* The **Hogar de Mi Abuelo** is a private park and museum (*El Malacara*, named after Evans' horse), dedicated to John Evans, one of the first settlers, whose granddaughter acts as a guide. ■ *US$1.* The **Nant-y-fall Falls**, 17 km southwest on the road to the border, are a series of impressive cascades in lovely forest. ■ *US$0.25 pp including guide to all seven falls (1½-hr walk).* There's a helpful **tourist office** in the central plaza, T480120, www.trevelin.org Maps, accommodation, English spoken.

D-E *Casa Verde Hostal*, Los Alerces s/n, T/F48009, casaverdehostel@ciudad.com.ar 'The best hostel in Argentina', by many reckonings. Charming owners Bibiana and Charley, spacious log cabin, comfortable dorms with bathroom, kitchen facilities, laundry, HI member, meals available. Also excursions into Los Alerces. Recommended. **D** *Pezzi*, Sarmiento 353, T480146. Jan-Mar, English spoken, garden. Recommended. Many *cabañas*: tourist office has full list. **Eating**: *Patagonia Celta*, 25 de Mayo s/n. Delicious local specialities, trout and vegetarian dishes, reasonably priced, best in town. Recommended. Large meals at *Parrilla Oregon*, Av San Martín y Laprida. *Parrilla Ruca Laufquen*, Av San Martín y Libertad. Delicious *parrilla* and home-made pasta. The best tea room, offering *té galés* and *torta negra* is *Nain Maggie*, P Moreno 179. Municipal **campsite** near centre. On the road to Esquel 3 km from Trevelin, signposted on the righthand side, is **C** *La Granja Trevelin*, T480096. Macrobiotic meals and good Italian cooking, sells milk, cheese and onions, all facilities, bungalows; excellent horses for hire.

Sleeping & eating

One of the most appealing and untouched expanses of the Andes region, this national park has several lakes including **Lago Futalaufquen**, with some of the best fishing in the area, **Lago Menéndez** which can be crossed by boat to visit rare and impressive *alerce* trees over 2000 years old, and the green waters of **Lago Verde**. Relatively undeveloped, access is possible only to the east side of the park, via a *ripio* road with many camping spots and *hosterías*. ■ *US$2*. Helpful *guardeparques* give out maps and advice on walks at the visitor centre (T471020) in Villa Futalaufquen (southern end of Lago Futulaufquen); also a service station, two food shops, and a restaurant *El Abuelo Monje*. Fishing licences from food shops, the *kiosko* or *Hostería Cume Hué*.

Parque Nacional Los Alerces
Colour map 9, grid A1
60 km W of Esquel

Argentina

Trekking and tours The west half of the park is inaccessible, but there are splendid places to walk all along the eastern shore of Lago Futalaufquen. At its southern end, close to the park headquarters, there are gentle strolls to see waterfalls. At its northern end, walk across the bridge over Río Arrayanes to Lago Verde. A longer trek to **Cerro Dedal** takes 8 hours return, with a steep climb from road to Puerto Limonao, giving wonderful views. Register first with *guardeparques*, and get detailed directions. Start before 1000 and carry plenty of water. Also a two-day hike though *coihue* forest to the tip of **Lago Krügger**; *refugio* open only January/February, where you an take a boat back to Puerto Limonao. **Boat trips**: Across Lago Futalaufquen along the pea-green Río Arrayanes, lined with the extraordinary cinnamon-barked trees. Better still, the unforgettable trip from Puerto Chucao across Lago Menéndez to see the majestic 2600-year old alerce trees, walking to silent Lago Cisne, past the white waters of Río Cisne. ■ *All boat trips run frequently in high season. Book through* Patagonia Verde *in Esquel, T454396, or* Safari Lacustre, www.brazosur.com *US$16-25.*

Sleeping On the east side of Lago Futalaufquen: **AL** *Cume Hué*, T453639, overpriced lodge with basic rooms, but great for fishing. **A** *Hostería Quimé Quipan*, T471021. Comfortable rooms with lake views, dinner included. Recommended. **C** *Bahía Rosales*, T471044. Spacious *cabañas*, *refugio* (**F** pp), camping in open ground, restaurant, all recommended. **D** *Pucón Pai*, T471010. Slightly spartan rooms, but good restaurant, recommended for fishing (holds a fishing festival to open the season); campsite with hot showers, US$2 pp. Next door **D** *Cabañas Tejas Negras*, T471046. Comfortable *cabañas* and good facilities for camping.
  On the west side **L** *Hostería Futalaufquen* just north of Puerto Limonao, T471008, www.brazosur.com Idyllic lakeside setting and splendid architecture, but lacking a warm welcome. Very expensive for tea. **Camping**: *Los Maitenes*, Villa Futalaufquen, excellent, US$1.50 pp plus US$2 per tent. Several campsites at Lagos Rivadavia, Verde and Río Arrayanes, from free to US$3 depending on facilities.

Transport From Esquel Bus (*Transportes Esquel*, T453529) runs daily at 0800 from Esquel along the east side of Lago Futalaufquen, passing Villa Futalaufquen 0915, Lago Verde 1030, Lago Rivadavia 1120, and will drop you at your accommodation, US$3. Returning from Lago Rivadavia at.1830, Lago Verde 1845 and Villa Futalaufquen 2000, back in Esquel 2115. In Jan-Feb and on Sat and Sun it continues to **Cholila**, **El Bolsón** and **Lago Puelo**.

Argentina

Border with Chile – Paso Futaleufú
Colour map 9, grid A1
70 km SW of Esquel via Trevelin

There is a campsite (Camping Río Grande) on the Argentine side of river. Cross the border river by the bridge after passing Argentine customs; Chilean customs is 1 km on the other side of river (one hour for all formalities). Buses From Esquel to Paso Futaleufú, 0800 daily January-February, otherwise Monday, Friday, sometimes Wednesday. *Jacobsen*, US$3. Connecting with bus Futuleufú to Chaitén, Transportes Cordillera, T258633 and *Ebenezer*, between them 4 times a week, and daily January-February. Very little traffic for hitching. From Esquel to the Palena border crossing, bus Sunday, Monday, Wednesday 1700, Friday 0900, return departures Monday, Tuesday, Thursday 0700, Friday 1700.

South of Esquel, Ruta 40 is paved through the towns of **Tecka** and **Gobernador Costa** (E *Hotels Jair*, good value, and *Vega*; municipal campsite with all services, US$1) in Chubut province. At 34 km south of Gobernador Costa, gravelled Ruta 40 forks southwest through the town of Alto Río Senguer, while provincial Ruta 20 heads almost directly south for 81 km, before turning east towards Sarmiento and Comodoro Rivadavia. At La Puerta del Diablo, in the valley of the lower Río Senguer, Ruta 20 intersects provincial Ruta 22, which joins with Ruta 40 at the town of Río Mayo (see page 218). This latter route is completely paved and preferable to Ruta 40 for long-distance motorists; good informal campsites on the west side of the bridge across the Río Senguer.

Patagonia

Patagonia is the vast, windy, mostly treeless plateau covering all of southern Argentina south of the Río Colorado. The Atlantic coast is rich in marine life; penguins, whales and seals can all be seen around Puerto Madryn. The far south offers spectacular scenery in the Parque Nacional de los Glaciares, with the mighty Moreno and Upsalla glaciers, as well as challenging trekking around Mount Fitz Roy. The contrasts are extreme: thousands of handprints can be found in the Cueva de las Manos, but in most of Patagonia there's less than one person to the sq km; far from the densely wooded Andes, there are petrified forests in the deserts; and the legacy of brave early pioneers is the over-abundance of tea and cakes served up by Argentina's Welsh community in the Chubut valley.

Patagonia's appeal lies in its emptiness. Vegetation is sparse, since a relentless dry wind blows continually from the west, raising a haze of dust in summer, which can turn to mud in winter. Rainfall is high only in the foothills of the Andes, where dense virgin beech forests run from Neuquén to Tierra del Fuego. During a brief period in spring, after the snow melt, there is grass on the plateau, but in the desert-like expanses of eastern Patagonia, water can be pumped only in the deep crevices which intersect the land from west to east. This is where the great sheep estancias lie, sheltered from the wind. There is little agriculture except in the north, in the valleys of the Colorado and Negro rivers, where alfalfa is grown and cattle are raised. Centres of population are tiny and most of the towns are small ports on the Atlantic coast. Only Comodoro Rivadavia has a population over 100,000, thanks to its oil industry. Patagonia has attracted many generations of people getting away from it all, from Welsh religious pioneers to Butch Cassidy and the Sundance Kid, and tourism is an increasingly important source of income.

Ins and outs

Getting there
www.lade.com.ar T51 29-9000, ext 35147

Air There are flights to many towns throughout Patagonia; most are to or from Buenos Aires. Main air services are given in the text below. Bear in mind that it's usually cheaper to buy internal flights in Argentina. Prepare for delays in bad weather. Many Air Force *LADE* flights in the region south of Bariloche must be booked in advance from the flight's departure point. The baggage allowance is 15 kg. Flights are often heavily booked ahead, but always check again on the day of the flight if you are told before that it is sold out. *LADE* tickets are much cheaper for a long flight with stops than buying separate segments. *LADE*'s computer reservation system is linked to *Aerolíneas Argentinas*, so flight connections are possible between these airlines.

Road   The principal roads in Patagonia are the Ruta 3, which runs down the Atlantic coast, and the Ruta 40 on the west. One of Argentina's main arteries, Ruta 3 runs from Buenos Aires to Ushuaia, interrupted by the car ferry crossing through Chilean territory across the Magellan Straits to Tierra del Fuego. It is mostly paved, except between Río Gallegos and San Sebastián (80 km north of Río Grande) and for 65 km south of Tolhuin. Regular buses run along the whole stretch, more frequently between Oct and Apr, and there are towns with services and accommodation every few hundred km. However, Ruta 40 is a wide unpaved *ripio* track which zigzags across the moors from Zapala to Lago Argentino, near El Calafate. It's by far the more interesting road, lonely and bleak, with little traffic even in the tourist summer season, offering fine views of the Andes and plenty of wildlife as well as the Alerces and Glaciares National Parks. The east-west road across Patagonia, from south of Esquel in the Lake District to Comodoro Rivadavia, is paved, and there's a good paved highway running from Bariloche through Neuquén to San Antonio Oeste.

Many of the roads in southern Argentina are *ripio* – gravelled – limiting maximum speeds to 60 km per hour, or less where surfaces are poor. Strong winds can also be a hazard. Windscreen and headlight protection is a good idea (expensive to buy, but can be improvised with wire mesh for windscreen, strips cut from plastic bottles for lights). There are cattle grids (*guardaganados*), even on main highways, usually signposted; cross them very slowly. Always carry plenty of fuel, as service stations may be as much as 300 km apart and as a precaution in case of a breakdown, carry warm clothing and make sure your car has anti-freeze. Fuel prices throughout Patagonia are about half the price of the rest of the country.

There are good hotels at Esquel, Perito Moreno and El Calafate, and basic accommodation at Gobernador Gregores and Río Mayo. In summer hotel prices are very high, especially in El Calafate and El Chaltén. In some places there may not be enough hotel beds to meet demand. Camping is increasingly popular and *estancias* may be hospitable to travellers who are stuck for a bed. Many *estancias*, especially in Santa Cruz province, offer transport, excursions and food as well as accommodation: see www.estanciasdesantacruz.com *ACA* establishments, which charge roughly the same prices all over Argentina, are a bargain in Patagonia. As very few hotels and restaurants have a/c or even fans, it can get uncomfortably hot in January.

Sleeping

Wildlife and nature reserves

With **elephant seal** and **sea lion** colonies at the base of chalky cliffs, breeding grounds for **Southern right whales** in the sheltered Golfo Nuevo and the Golfo San José, and **guanacos**, **rheas**, **patagonian hares** and **armadillos** everywhere on land, this is a spectacular region for wildlife. Whales can be seen from June to mid December, particularly interesting with their young September-October. The sea lion breeding season runs from late December to late January, but visiting is good up to late April. Bull elephant seals begin to claim their territory in the first half of August and the breeding season is late September/early October. Orcas can be seen attacking seals at Punta Norte in February/March. Conservation officials can be found at the main viewpoints, informative but only Spanish spoken. The *EcoCentro* in Puerto Madryn, studies the marine ecosystems. The **Punta Loma** sea lion reserve is 15 km southeast of Puerto Madryn, and sea lions can even be seen in Puerto Madryn harbour. ■ *0900-1200, 1430-1730; US$2.50 (free with Península Valdés ticket), information and video. Many companies offer tours, taxi US$10.*

Península Valdés   The Golfos Nuevo and San José are separated by the Istmo Carlos Ameghino, which leads to Península Valdés, a bleak, but beautiful treeless splay of land. In depressions in the heart of the peninsula are large salt flats; Salina Grande is 42 m below sea level. At the entrance to the peninsula, on the isthmus, there is an interesting Visitors' Centre with wonderful whale skeleton. ■ *Entry US$2.* Near the entrance, Isla de los Pájaros can be seen in Golfo San José, though its seabirds can only

See also Puerto Deseado, page 220 and Punta Tombo, page 216

Argentina

Argentina

be viewed through fixed telescopes (at 400 m distance); best time is September-April. The main tourist centre of the Peninsula is **Puerto Pirámide** (*Population*: 100), 90 km east of Puerto Madryn, where boat trips leave to see the whales in season (sailings controlled by Prefectura, according to weather conditions). There's plentiful accommodation and eating places here. Tourist information T495084, aldeaturistica@infovia.com

Punta Norte (176 km) at the north end of the Valdés Peninsula, isn't usually included in tours, but has elephant seals and penguins (September-March) below its high, white cliffs, best seen at low tide. There's a reasonably priced restaurant. At **Caleta Valdés**, 45 km north of Punta Norte, you can see elephant seals at close quarters, and there are three marked walks. At **Punta Delgada** (at the south of the peninsula) elephant seals and other wildlife can be seen. The beach on the entire coast is out of bounds; this is strictly enforced. ■*The best way to see the wildlife is by car. See Puerto Madryn for car hire; fuel will cost about US$10 for the return trip. A taxi costs US$70 per vehicle for the day. Take your time, roads are all unpaved except the road from Puerto Madryn to Puerto Pirámide. In summer there are several well-stocked shops, but take sun protection and drinking water. 28 de Julio bus company from Puerto Madryn to Puerto Pirámide, daily at 1000, returns 1800, US$2 each way, 1 hr.*

Sleeping and eating At Puerto Pirámide: B *ACA Motel*, T495004. Poor restaurant, camping. There is also an *ACA* service station (open daily) with good café and shop. B *Estancia El Sol*, T495007, with restaurant. B *Paradise Pub*, T495030. Helpful, good value food and beer, good atmosphere. Recommended. C *Cabañas en el Mar*, T495049, www.piramides.net Recommended. D *Español*, T495031. Basic but pleasant. Municipal campsite by the black sand beach, T495000, US$2.50 pp (free out of season), hot showers US$0.50, good, get there early to secure a place. Do not camp on the beach: people have been swept away by the incoming tide.

Staying at estancias on the peninsula is a great way to appreciate the wildlife

Punta Delgada A *Faro Punta Delgada*, T15 406304, www.puntadelagada.com In a lighthouse, half and full board, excellent food. Recommended. **Punta Norte** *San Lorenzo*, T456888, www.puntanorte.com See penguins close up. **Punta Cantor** *La Elvira*, T15 668107, www.laelvira.com Traditional Patagonian dishes and comfortable accommodation.

Tour operators Full-day tours take in Puerto Pirámide (with whale-watching in season), plus some, but not necessarily all, of the other wildlife viewing points. Prices are US$ 14 pp, in some cases including the entry to the national park; boat trip to see whales US$12 if not included in tour price. On all excursions take drink, food if you don't want to eat in the expensive restaurants, and binoculars. Most tour companies stay about 1 hr on location. *Tito Bottazzi*, T495050, recommended. *Hydrosport* near the ACA, T495065, hysport@infovia.com.ar Rents scuba equipment and boats, and organizes land and sea wildlife tours to see whales and dolphins. Tours do not run after heavy rain in the low season.

Viedma & Carmen de Patagones
Phone code 02920
Colour map 8, grid C4

These two pleasant towns lie on opposite banks of the Río Negro, about 27 km from its mouth and 250 km south of Bahía Blanca. Patagones is older (1820's) and charming, but most services are in **Viedma** (*Population*: 26,000), on the south bank, the capital of Río Negro Province. A quiet place, its main attraction is the perfect bathing area along the shaded south bank of the river.

Sleeping C *Nijar*, Mitre 490, T422833, most comfortable, smart, modern, good service. C *Austral*, 25 de Mayo y Villarino, T422615, viedma@hoteles-austral.com.ar Also modern. D *Peumayen*, Buenos Aires 334, T425222, old-fashioned friendly place on the plaza. E *Spa Inside*, 25 de Mayo 174, T430459, great value, lovely and quiet, with steam baths. Good municipal campsite near the river, US$2 per person, all facilities including hot showers. Best restaurant is the inexpensive *La Balsa* on the river at Colón y Villarino, delicious seafood. **Estancias**: AL *La Luisa* and *San Juan*, both 40 km away in wilder country, T02920-463725, eleri@viedma.com.ar Traditional Patagonia *estancias* with English speaking owners, riding, cattle mustering, good hospitality, open December to March. Highly recommended.

El Cóndor is a beautiful beach 30 km south of Viedma, three buses a day from Viedma in summer, with hotels open January-February, restaurants and shops, free camping on beach 2 km south. And 45 km further south is the sealion colony, **Lobería Punta Bermeja**, daily bus in summer from Viedma; hitching easy in summer.

Carmen de Patagones (*Population:* 16,000) was founded in 1779 and many early pioneer buildings remain in the pretty streets winding down to the river. There's a fascinating museum, **Museo Histórico**. ■ *JJ Biedma 64, T462729, open daily 0930-1230, 1900-2100, Sun afternoon only.* The two towns are linked by two bridges and a 4-minute frequent ferry crossing. Helpful **tourist office** at Bynon 186, T462054. www.vivalaspampas.com

7 March: Battle of Patagones (1827) is celebrated in a week-long colourful fiesta of horse displays and fine food

Bahía San Blas is an attractive small resort and renowned shark fishing area, 100 km from Patagones. Lots of accommodation, including *Resort Tiburón*, T02920-499202, www.tiburonresort.freeservers.com More information at www.bahiasanblas.com

Transport Air *LADE* (Saavedra 403, T/F424420) fly to **Buenos Aires**, **Mar del Plata**, **Bahía Blanca**, **Neuquén**, **San Martín de Los Andes**, **San Antonio Oeste**, **Puerto Madryn**, **Trelew** and **Comodoro Rivadavia**. **Buses** Terminal in Viedma at Av Pte Perón y Guido, 15 blocks from plaza; taxi US$1. To/from **Buenos Aires** 14 hrs, 3 daily, US$20 , *Don Otto/La Estrella/Cóndor*. To **San Antonio Oeste**, 2½ hrs, several daily, US$4, *Don Otto*. To **Bahía Blanca**, 4 hrs, 4 daily, US$5.

Almost due west and 180 km along the coast, on the Gulf of San Matías, is **San Antonio Oeste** (*Phone code:* 02934. *Population:* 10,000), and 17 km south, the popular beach resort, **Las Grutas**. The caves themselves are not really worth visiting; but the water is famously warm. Las Grutas is closed in the winter, but very crowded in the summer; accessible by bus from San Antonio hourly US$1. San Antonio is on the bus routes north to Bahía Blanca and south as far as Río Gallegos and Punta Arenas.

Puerto Madryn and Península Valdés

Puerto Madryn is a pleasant, breezy seaside town. It stands on the wide bay of Golfo Nuevo, the perfect base for the Península Valdés and its extraordinary array of wildlife, just 70 km east. It was the site of the first Welsh landing in 1865 and is named after the Welsh home of the colonist, Jones Parry. Popular for skin diving and the nature reserves, the town's main industries are a huge aluminium plant and fish processing plants. You can often spot whales directly from the coast at the long beach of **Playa El Doradillo**, 16 km northeast (October-December). **EcoCentro**, Julio Verne 784, is an inspired interactive sea life information centre, art gallery and café, perched on a cliff at the south end of town ■ *1000-1800 daily (but check with tourist office as times change)*, T457470. *US$2.50, reductions for students*. www.ecocentro.org.ar **Museo de Ciencias Naturales y Oceanográfico**, Domecq García y J Menéndez, is informative and worth a visit. ■ *Mon-Fri 0900-1200, 1430-1900, Sat 1430-1900, entry US$1.*

Phone code: 02965 Colour map 9, grid A3 Population: 50,000 250 km S of San Antonio Oeste

AL *Tolosa*, Roque Sáenz Peña 253, T471850, tolosa@hoteltolosa.com.ar Extremely comfortable, modern, great breakfasts. Disabled access. Recommended. **A** *Bahía Nueva*, Av Roca 67, T451677, www.bahianueva.com.ar One of the best sea front hotels, quite small but comfortable rooms, professional staff, cheaper in low season. **A** *Península Valdés*, Av Roca 155, T471292, F452584, www.hotel-peninsula-valdes.com Luxurious minimalist sea front hotel with great views, spa, sauna and gym (bookings from outside Argentina 30% extra). **B-C** *Villa Pirén*, Av Roca 439, T/F456272, www.piren.com.ar Excellent modern rooms and apartments in smart seafront place. **C** *Marina*, Av Roca 7, T/F454915, teokou@ infovia.com.ar Great value little seafront apartments for up to 5 people, book ahead. **C** *Playa*, Av Roca 187, T451446, www.playahotel.com.ar Good sea front location, the slightly pricier more modern rooms are worth it. **C** *Santa Rita*, Gob Maiz 370, T471050.

Sleeping
■ *on map*
Book ahead in summer, and whale season. Note that non-Argentines will often be charged more in the pricier hotels

Welcoming, comfy, wash basins in rooms, good value with dinner included, also kitchen facilities. Often recommended. **D** *Hostería Torremolinos* , Marcos A Zar 64, T453215. Nice, modern, simple, well decorated rooms. **D** *Muelle Viejo*, H Yrigoyen 38, T471284. Ask for the comfortable modernised rooms in this funny old place. Rooms for 4 are excellent value, kitchen facilities. **D-E** *La Posta*, Roca 33, T472422. Residenciallaposta@infovia.com.ar Small rooms, welcoming, with breakfast, on the sea front, also apartments, popular in high season. **E** *Residencial J'Os*, Bolívar 75, T471433. Nice little place, breakfast included.

Youth hostels E *Puerto Madryn Hostelling International*, 25 de Mayo 1136, T/F474426, madryn@hostels.org.ar 10 blocks from the centre of town, modern house, garden, laundry, kitchen facilities, bike rental, double rooms too, English and French spoken. **F** *El Gaulicho* , Marcos A Zar 480, T454163, www.elgaulichohostel.com.ar Best budget option, new, nicely designed, enthusiastic owner, free pick up from bus terminal, *parrilla*, garden, some double rooms, bikes for hire. Highly recommended. **F** pp *Youth hostel Huefur*, Estivariz 245, T453926, huefur245@hotmail.com Rooms for 12 and 4, kitchen, laundry facilities, garden, *parrilla*, with breakfast.

Camping All closed out of season. *ACA*, Boulevard Brown, 3.5 km south of town at Punta Cuevas, T452952, open Sep-Apr, hot showers, café, shop, no kitchen facilities, shady trees, close to the sea. Many people camp on the beach, though there is a municipal site *El Golfito* Camping y Albergue, at Ribera Sur, 1 km before *ACA* site on same road along beach (gives student discount) T454544. All facilities, very crowded, US$2 pp and US$2 per tent for 1st day. Also room with bunkbeds, **F** pp. Bus from town stops 100 m before entrance.

Puerto Madryn

■ Sleeping	6 Muelle Viejo	● Eating	7 La Vaca y
1 Bahía Nueva	7 Península Valdés	1 Antigua Patagonia	El Pollito
& La Posta	8 Playa	2 Centro de Difusión de	8 Lizard Café
2 Camping	9 Santa Rita	la Pescada Artesanal	9 Margarita
3 El Gualicho	10 Tolosa	3 Halloween	10 Mitos
4 Hostería	11 Villa Pirén	4 Havanna	11 Placido
Torremolinos	12 Youth Hostel	5 La Casona de Golfo	12 Taska Beltza
5 Marina	Huefur	6 La Estela	13 Yoaquina

You should try at least one plate of *arroz con mariscos* (rice with a whole selection of squid, prawns, mussels and clams). **Expensive**: *Taska Beltza*, 9 de Julio 345, T15 668085, Without doubt, the best in town, chef 'El Negro' cooks superb paella - book ahead, closed Mon. *Placido*, Av Roca 508. On the beach, stylish, intimate, excellent service, seafood and vegetarian. **Mid-range**: *Antigua Patagonia*, Mitre y RS Pena. Large *parilla* and seafood restaurant, warm atmosphere, good value set menu. *Centro de Difusión de la Pescada Artesanal*, Brown, 7th roundabout, T15 538085. Authentic cantina, where the fishermen's families cook meals with their catch, go early. *La Estela*, Sáenz Peña 27. *La Vaca y el Pollito* , Av Roca y A Storni. Built into the wooden hull of a boat, cosy, *parrilla*, seafood and pastas. *Yoaquina*, Blvd Brown between 1st and 2nd roundabouts, T456058. Relaxed. Beachfront, eat outside in summer, good seafood, open from breakfast to after dinner, cheap lunch menu. **Cheap**: *La Casona de Golfo*, Av Roca 349. Good value *tenedor libre parrilla*, seafood, and 'helados libre'. *Halloween*, Av Roca 1355 Takeaway pizzas and *empanadas*. *Mitos*, 28 de Julio 64. Stylish café with good atmosphere. Recommended. Cheap takeaway food at supermarket *Norte*, 28 de Julio 136, *empanadas*, vegetable tortillas, chicken. **Cafés and Bars**: *Havanna*, Av Roca y 28 de Julio. Smart and buzzing. *Lizard Café*, Av Roca y Av Gales, T458333. Lively, cheap, pizzas. *Margarita*, next to *Ambigu*, RS Peña y Av Roca. Late night drinks and live music.

Eating
● *on map*
Excellent fish
restaurants, but pricier
than in the rest of
Argentina

Diving Puerto Madryn is a diving centre, with several shipwrecked boats in the Golfo Nuevo. A first dive ('bautismo') for beginners costs about US$30 pp. *Safari Submarino*, Blvd Brown 1070, T474110;*Ocean Divers*, Blvd Brown (between 1st and 2nd roundabout), T472569; advanced courses (PADI) and courses on video, photography and underwater communication.

Sport & activities

Many agencies do similar 12-hr tours to the Península Valdés, about US$17, plus US$2 entrance to the Peninsula. They include the interpretation centre, Puerto Pirámides (the whales boat trip is US$12 extra), Punta Delgada and Caleta Valdés. Take water and lunch, and shop around to find out how long you'll spend at each place, how big the group is, and if your guide speaks English. Tours to see the penguins at Punta Tombo and Welsh villages are better from Trelew. Recommended for Península Valdés: *Tito Botazzi*, Blvd Brown 1070, T474110, www.titobottazzi.com Small groups and good bilingual guides. *Argentina Visión*, Av Roca 536, T451427, www.argentinavision.com Also 4WD adventure trips and *estancia* accommodation at Punta Delgada, English and French spoken. *Cuyun Có*, Av Roca 165, T451845, www.cuyunco.com.ar Friendly, also guided nature walks, and *estancia* accommodation.

Tour operators
Many along Av. Roca

Local Car hire: expensive, and note large excess for turning car over. Drive slowly on unpaved *ripio* roads! *Puerto Madryn Turismo*, Roca 624, T452355. *Localiza* has an office (see Car Hire in Essentials). **Mountain bike hire**: *Future Bike*, Juan B Justo 683, T15 665108, *Na Praia*, on the beach at Blvd Brown and Perlotti, T473715, and *XT Mountain Bike*, Av Roca 742, T472232.

Long distance Air: Airport 10 km west; *LADE* to **Buenos Aires**, **Bahía Blanca**, **Viedma**, **Trelew**, **Comodoro Rivadavia** and other Patagonian airports. More flights to **Bariloche**, Buenos Aires, and El Calafate from Trelew. Buses to Trelew stop at entrance to airport if asked. Taxi US$20. Direct bus to Trelew airport, *Puma*, US$3.50, leaves 1½ hrs before flight and takes arriving passengers back to Puerto Madryn

Buses: New terminal at Irigoyen y San Martín (behind old railway station), T451789. To **Buenos Aires**, 18 hrs US$17-20, several companies, *Andesmar* recommended. To **Río Gallegos**, 18 hrs; US$18, *El Pingüino* (connecting to El Calafate, Punta Arenas, Puerto Natales), *Andesmar, TAC, Don Otto*. To **Trelew**, 1 hr, every hr, US$2 with *28 de Julio, Mar y Valle*. To **Bariloche**, 15 hrs, US$25, daily, except Weds, *Mar y Valle*. **Taxis**: outside bus terminal T452966/ 474177and on main plaza.

Transport

Airline offices *Aerolíneas Argentinas*, Roca 303, T421257. *LADE*, Roca 117, T451256. **Banks** Lots of ATMs at the following:*Banco Nación*, 9 de Julio 117. *Banco del Chubut*, 25 de Mayo 154 and *Río*, Mitre 102. **Communications** Internet: *Internet Centro Madryn*, 25 de Mayo y Belgrano. US$0.60 per hour. *Re Creo*, Roque Sáenz Peña 101. **Post Office**, Belgrano y Maiz, 0900-1200, 1500-1900. **Telephone**, many *locutorios* in the centre. **Medical services** For emergencies call 107 or 451240. **Tourist office** Av Roca 223, T/F453504, www.madryn.gov.ar Open Mon-Fri 0700-2100, Sat-Sun 0830-1330, 1530-2030, helpful.

Directory

Argentina

Argentina

Trelew

Phone code: 02965
Colour map 9, grid A3
Population: 61,000

Pronounced 'Trel-ay-Oo', Trelew is a busy town, with an excellent musuem and a shady plaza, which hosts a small handicraft market at weekends. Evidence of Welsh settlement remains only in a few brick buildings: the 1889 **Capilla Tabernacl**, on Belgrano, between San Martín and 25 de Mayo, and the **Salón San David**, a 1913 Welsh meeting hall. On the road to Rawson, 3 km south, is one of the oldest standing Welsh chapels, **Capilla Moriah**, from 1880, with a simple interior and graves of many original settlers in the cemetery. The excellent **Museo Paleontológico Egidio Feruglio**, Fontana 140, presents the origins of life, dynamically poised dinosaur skeletons, with free tours in English, German and Italian. Also café and shop. Highly recommended. ■ *US$2.50. Mon-Fri 1000-2000 spring and summer, 1000-1800 rest of year, Sat-Sun 1000-2000, T432100, www.mef.org.ar* Also information about **Parque Paleontológico Bryn-Gwyn**, 8 km from Gaiman (see below). The **Museo Regional Pueblo de Luis**, Fontana y 9 de Julio, in the old 1889 railway station, with displays on indigenous societies, failed Spanish attempts at settlement and on Welsh colonization. ■ *Mon-Fri 0800-2000, Sat closed. Sun 1700-2000.*

Sleeping
■ *on map*

B *Rayentray*, San Martín y Belgrano, T434702, rcvcentral@ar.inter.net Large, modernized, comfortable rooms, professional staff, breakfast included, pool. **C** *Libertador*, Rivadavia 31, T/F420220, www.hotellibertador.com.ar Modern, highly recommended for service and comfortable rooms, breakfast included. **E** *Touring Club*, Fontana 240, T/F425790, htouring@ar.inter.net Gorgeous 1920's bar, faded elegance, simple rooms, great value, breakfast extra. Open from breakfast to the small hours for sandwiches and drinks. Recommended. **E** *Galicia*, 9 de Julio 214, T433802, www.sipatagonia.com/hotelgalicia Central, grand entrance, comfortable rooms, good value. **F** pp *Rivadavia*, Rivadavia 55, T434172. Simple rooms with TV, breakfast extra, the cheapest recommendable place.

Eating
● *on map*

El Viejo Molino Gales 250, T428019. Open 1130-0030 (closed Mon), best in town, in renovated 1886 flour mill, for Patagonian lamb, pastas, good value set menu with wine included. *La Bodeguita*, Belgrano 374. Delicious pastas and pizzas, with interesting art on the walls.

Trelew

0 metres 100
0 yards 100

■ **Sleeping**		● **Eating**	
1 Galicia	3 Rayentray	1 Delicatesse	3 El Viejo Molino
2 Libertador	4 Rivadavia	2 El Quijote	4 La Bodeguita
	5 Touring Club		5 Mi Ciudad

Keeping up with the Joneses

On 28 July 1865, 153 Welsh immigrants landed at Puerto Madryn, then a deserted beach deep in Indian country. After three weeks they pushed, on foot, across the parched pampa and into the Chubut river valley, where there is flat cultivable land along the riverside for a distance of 80 kilometres upstream. Here, maintained in part by the Argentine Government, they settled, but it was three years before they realized the land was barren unless watered. They drew water from the river, which is higher than the surrounding flats, and later built a fine system of irrigation canals. The colony, reinforced later by immigrants from Wales and from the United States, prospered, but in 1899 a great flood drowned the valley and some of the immigrants left for Canada. The last Welsh contingent arrived in 1911. The object of the colony had been to create a `Little Wales beyond Wales', and for four generations they kept the Welsh language alive. The language is, however, dying out in the fifth generation. There is an offshoot of the colony of Chubut at Trevelin, at the foot of the Andes nearly 650 km to the west, settled in 1888 (see page 206). It is interesting that this distant land gave to the Welsh language one of its most endearing classics: Dringo'r Andes (Climbing the Andes), written by one of the early women settlers.

Argentina

Delicatesse, Belgrano y San Martin. Best pizzas in town, cheery place, popular with families. *El Quijote*, Rivadavia 463. Recommended *parrilla*, popular with locals. *Mi Cuidad*, Belgrano y San Martin. Smart café serving great coffee; read the papers here. Also cheap takeaway food at supermarket *Norte*, Soberanía y Belgrano.

Tour operators Agencies run tours to Punta Tombo, US$18, Chubut Valley (half-day), US$10, both as full day US$22. Tours to Península Valdés are best done from Puerto Madryn. *Nieve y Mar*, Italia 20, T434114, www.nievmartours.com.ar Punta Tombo and Valdés, bilingual guides (reserve ahead), organized and efficient. *Patagonia Grandes Espacios*, Belgrano 338, T435161, www.surturismo.com.ar Good excursions to Punta Tombo and Gaiman, but also paleontological trips, staying in chacras, whale watching. Recommended.

Transport **Car hire**: expensive. Airport desks are staffed only at flight arrival times and cars are snapped up quickly. All have offices in town. See Essentials at front of book for international agencies. **Air** *AR* have flights to/from **Buenos Aires**, **El Calafate** and **Ushuaia**. *LADE* flies to Patagonian airports from **Viedma** to **Comodoro Rivadavia**, as well as **Bariloche**. Airport 5 km north of centre; taxis about US$6-8 . Local buses to/from Puerto Madryn stop at the airport entrance if asked, turning is 10 mins walk, US$3.50; *AR* runs special bus service to connect with its flights. **Buses** Terminal on Plaza del Centenario, T420121. **Long distance**: To **Buenos Aires**, 20 hrs; US$20, several companies go daily, including *TAC, El Pingüino, Que Bus, Don Otto, Andesmar, El Cóndor*. To **Comodoro Rivadavia**, 5 hrs, US$8, many companies, to **Río Gallegos**, 17 hrs; US$20, many companies. To **Esquel**, 10hrs, US$11. **Local**: *Mar y Valle* and *28 de Julio* both go frequently to **Gaiman**, 30 mins; US$1, and **Dolavon** 1 hr, US$1.50, to **Puerto Madryn**, 1 hr, US$2, to **Puerto Pirámide**, 2½ hrs; US$5. **Companies** : *Andesmar*, T433535; *El Pingüino*, T427400; *Don Otto*, T432434; *TAC*, T431452; *El Cóndor*, T433748; *28 de Julio/Mar y Valle*, T432429; *Que Bus*, T422760.

Directory **Airline offices** *Aerolineas Argentinas*, 25 de Mayo 33, T420170. *LADE*, Terminal de Omnibus, offices 12 /13, T435925. **Banks** Open Mon-Fri 0830-1300. *Banco de la Nación*, 25 de Mayo y Fontana. *Banco del Sud*, 9 de Julio 320, cash advance on Visa. **Communications** **Internet**: 25 de Mayo y Rivadavia. **Post Office**: 25 de Mayo and Mitre. **Telephone**: *Telefónica*, Roca y Pje Tucumán, and several *locutorios* in the centre. **Tourist office** On the plaza at Mitre 387, T420139. Open Mon-Fri 0800-1400, 1500-2100, Sat/Sun 0900-1300, 1500-2000. www.turismotrelew.gov.ar.

Gaiman A small pretty place with old brick houses retaining the Welsh pioneer feel, Gaiman hosts the annual Eisteddfod (Welsh festival of arts) in October. It's renowned for delicious, and excessive 'traditional' Welsh teas and its fascinating, miniscule museum,

Colour map 9, grid A3
Population: 4,400
18 km W of Trelew

Museo Histórico Regional Galés, Sarmiento y 28 de Julio, revealing the spartan lives of the idealistic Welsh pioneers. ■ *US$0.50 Tue-Sun 1500-1900. Curator Mrs Roberts is very knowledgeable.* **Parque Paleontológico Bryn Gwyn**, 8 km south of town, fossil beds 40 million years old, tour and visitors' centre ■*Open 1000-1900, end Sep to end Mar, daily. US$1.80. T432100, www.mef.org.ar Taxi from Gaiman US$1.70.* **El Desafío**, two blocks west of the plaza, is a quaint private theme-park with pergolas and dinosaurs made of rubbish.■ *US$2.50, tickets valid 2 months.*

Most facilities are closed out of season

Sleeping and eating **C** *Ty Gwyn*, 9 de Julio 111, T491009, tygwyn@cpsarg.com Very neat and comfortable, with TV, excellent. **D** *Plas y Coed*, Jones 123, T491133. Marta Rees' delightful tea room has rooms in an annex next door, includes breakfast. Highly recommended. **D** pp *Gwesty Tywi*, Jones 342, T491292, gwestywi@infovia.com.ar Pretty, well-kept bed and breakfast. Small municipal **campsite** beyond Casa de Té Gaiman, poor, no facilities. *El Angel*, Jones 850. Stylish small restaurant serving excellent food. *La Colonia*, quality *panadería* on the main street. *Tavern Las*, small pub at Tello y Miguel Jones. *Siop Bara* sells cakes and ice creams. Welsh teas are served from about 1500 (US$5) by several **Tea Rooms**. The best, and oldest, is *Plas Y Coed* (see above). Marta Rees is a wonderful raconteur and fabulous cook. *Ty Gwyn*, 9 de Julio 111, is larger, more modern and welcoming; generous teas. *Ty Nain*, on Yrigoyen 283, the prettiest house and full of history, owned by Mirna Jones.

Dolavon, founded in 1919, is a quiet settlement, with a few buildings reminiscent of the Welsh past. The main street, Avenida Roca, runs parallel to the irrigation canal built by the settlers, where willow trees now trail into the water, and there's a Welsh chapel, **Capilla Carmel** at one end. The old flour mill at Maipú y Roca dates from 1927 and can be visited - the key is kept in the Municipalidad, Roca 188 (next to *Banco Provincial del Chubut*). There's *Autoserivicio Belgrano* at the far end of San Martin, for food supplies, but no tea rooms, and nowhere to stay. The **municipal campsite**, 2 blocks north of the river, is free, with good facilities.

In the irrigated valley between Dolavon and Gaiman, you'll see more Welsh chapels tucked away among fringes of tall *alamo* (poplar) trees and silver birches (best if you're in your own transport). The **San David chapel** (1917) is a beautifully preserved brick construction, with an elegant bell tower, and sturdy oak-studded door, in a quiet spot surrounded by birches.

Paved Ruta 25 runs from Dolavon west to the upper Chubut Valley, passing near the **Florentino Ameghino** dam, a good leafy spot for a picnic. From Ameghino to Tecka on Route 40 (south of Trevelin) is one of the most beautiful routes across Patagonia from the coast to the Andes, lots of wildlife to be seen. It goes through Las Plumas (mind the bridge if driving), Los Altares, which has camping, fuel and some shops, and Paso de Los Indios.

Punta Tombo

The largest breeding ground for Magellanic penguins in Patagonia

This nature reserve is 107 km south of Trelew, open from September, when huge numbers of Magellanic penguins come here to breed. Chicks can be seen from mid November; they take to the water January-February. It's fascinating to see these creatures up close, but noisy colonies of tourists dominate in the morning; it's quieter in the afternoon. You'll see guanacos, hares and rheas on the way. ■ *Park entrance US$4 . Tours from Trelew and Puerto Madryn, US$17; 45 mins at the site, where there's a café and toilets. Access from Ruta 1, a ripio road between Trelew and Camarones. Closed after Mar.*

Another large **penguin colony** - with lots of other marine life - is at Cabo Dos Bahías, easily reached from the small town of **Camarones** 275 km north of Comodoro Rivadavia. ■ *Open all year, US$5.Taxi from Camarones US$10.* The Guarda Fauna is 25 km from town. ■ *There are buses Mon, Wed, Fri 0800 from Trelew to Camarones,* El Nañdú, *T427499, US$6.50, 3 hrs, returns same day 1600.*

Comodoro Rivadavia

The largest city in the province of Chubut, oil was discovered here in 1907. It looks rather unkempt, reflecting changing fortunes in the oil industry, the history of which is described at the **Museo del Petroleo**, 3km north, San Lorenzo 250. ■ *Tue-Fri 0900-1800, Sat-Sun 1500-1800. T455 9558. Taxi US$4.* There's a beach at Rada Tilly, 8 km south (buses every 30 minutes); walk along beach at low tide to see sea lions.

Phone code: 0297
Colour map 9, grid A2
Population: 145,000
387 km S of Trelew

Sleeping & eating

B *Lucania Palazzo*, Moreno 676, T449 9338, www.lucania-palazzo.com Most luxurious, superb rooms, sea views, good value, huge American breakfast, sauna and gym included. Recommended. **C** *Comodoro*, 9 de Julio 770, T447 2300, info@comodorohotel.com.ar Buffet breakfast included, pay extra for larger rooms. **D** *Azul*, Sarmiento 724, T447 4628, Breakfast extra, quiet old place with lovely bright rooms, kind, great views from the *confitería*. **D** *Rua Marina*, Belgrano 738, T447 6877. With TV and breakfast, good budget choice. **E***Hospedaje Cari Hué*, Belgrano 563, T447 2946. Best budget choice, breakfast extra, shared bath, nice owners who like backpackers! *Cayo Coco*, Rivadavia 102. Excellent pizzas, good service. *La Nueva Rosada*, Belgrano 861. Good for beef or chicken. *Peperoni*, Rivadavia 348. Cheerful, modern, pastas. *Dionisius*, 9 de Julio y Rivadavia. Elegant *parrilla*, set menu US$5. *La Barra*, San Martín 686. For breakfast, coffee or lunch. *La Barca*, Belgrano 935. Good *tenedor libre*. *Café El Sol*, Av Rivadavia y 25 de Mayo. Good café to hang out in. Also cheap food in *Superquick* in *La Anónima* supermarket, San Martín y Güemes.

Transport

Air Airport, 13 km north. Bus No 6 to airport from bus terminal, hourly (45 mins), US$0.25. Taxi to airport, US$4.50. To **Buenos Aires**, *AR/Austral*. *LADE* flies to all Patagonian destinations once or twice a week, plus **Bariloche**, **El Bolsón** and **Esquel**.

Buses Terminal in centre at Pellegrini 730, T446 7305; has luggage store, good *confitería* upstairs, toilets, excellent tourist information office 0800-2100, some kiosks. Services to **Buenos Aires** 2 daily, 28 hrs, US$45. To **Bariloche**, 14½ hrs, US$19, *Don Otto*. To **Esquel** (paved road) 8 hrs direct with *ETAP* and *Don Otto*, US$13. In summer buses usually arrive full; book ahead. To **Río Gallegos**, *Don Otto*, *Pingüino* and *TAC* daily, 11 hrs, US$13. To **Puerto Madryn**, US$10-12, and **Trelew**, US$8, several companies. *La Unión* to **Caleta Olivia**, hourly, US$1.70. To **Sarmiento**, US$5, 2½ hrs at 0800, 1300, 1900. To **Coyhaique** (Chile), *Giobbi*, US$15, 12 hrs, twice a week.

Directory

Airline offices *Aerolineas Argentinas*, 9 de Julio 870, T444 0050. *LADE*, Rivadavia 360, T447 6565. **Banks** Many ATMs and major banks along San Martín. Change money at *Thaler*, San Martín 270, Mon-Sat 1000-1300, or at weekends *ETAP* in bus terminal. **Communications** Post Office: San Martín y Moreno. **Tourist office** Rivadavia 430, T446 2376, Mon-Fri 0900-1400, English spoken. Also in bus terminal. www.comodoro.gov.ar

From Comodoro Rivadavia to Chile

If you're keen to explore the petrified forests south of Sarmiento and the Cueva de las Manos near Perito Moreno, take the road to Chile running west from Comodoro Rivadavia. It's 156 km to Colonia Sarmiento (known as Sarmiento), a quiet relaxed place, sitting just south of two large lakes, Musters and Colhué Huapi. This is the best base for seeing the 70 million-year old **petrified forests** of fallen araucaria trees, nearly 3 m round and 15-20 m long: a remarkable sight. Most accessible is the **Bosque Petrificado José Ormachea**, 32 km south of Sarmiento on a *ripio* road, entry US$2.50, warden T4898047. Less easy to reach is the bleaker **Víctor Szlapelis** petrified forest, some 40 km further southwest along the same road (follow signposts, road from Sarmiento in good condition). From December to March a *combi* service runs twice daily: contact Sarmiento tourist office. Taxi Sarmiento to forests, US$16 (3 passengers), including 1 hour wait. Contact Sr Juan José Valero, the park ranger, for guided tours, Uruguay 43, T0297-489 8407 (see also the Monumento Natural Bosques Petrificados). The **tourist office** is on Avenida San Martín casi Alberdi, T489

Sarmiento
Colour map 9, grid A2
Population: 7,000
Phone code 0297

Argentina

Argentina

8220, helpful, has map of town. Frequent buses to Comodoro Rivadavia. To Chile via Río Mayo, *Giobbi*, 0200, twice weekly; seats are scarce in Río Mayo. From Sarmiento you can reach Esquel (448 km north along Rutas 20 and 40); overnight buses on Sunday stop at Río Mayo, take food for journey.

Sleeping **C** *Hostería Los Lagos*, Roca y Alberdi, T493046. Good, heating, restaurant. 10 km from Sarmiento is **C** *Chacra Labrador*, T0297-489 3329, agna@coopsar.com.ar Excellent small *estancia*, breakfast included, other meals extra and available for non-residents, English and Dutch spoken, runs tours to petrified forests at good prices, will collect guests from Sarmiento (same price as taxi). **E** *Musters*, Ing Coronel 215, T493097. **Camping** *Club Deportivo Sarmiento*, 25 de Mayo y Ruta 20, T4893103. *La Isla*, 1.5 km from centre, T15 647975

Río Mayo (Phone code: 02903; fuel and hotels **D-E**) is reached by Ruta 22 (paved) which branches southwest 84 km west of Sarmiento. From Río Mayo, a road continues west 114 km to the Chilean border at Coyhaique Alto for Coyhaique in Chile. For Sarmiento and Coyhaique from bus office in the centre. Monday-Friday at 0300 *Giobbi* buses take Ruta 40 north from Río Mayo direct to Esquel. *LADE* flights to Comodoro Rivadavia once a week, T420060. **South of Río Mayo** Ruta 40 is unpaved as far as Perito Moreno (124 km). There is no public transport and very few other vehicles even in mid-summer. At Km 31 on this road a turning leads west to Lago Blanco, to Chile via Paso Huemules and Balmaceda.

Perito Moreno
Phone code 02963
Colour map 9, grid B2
Population: 1,700
Altitude: 400 m

Not to be confused with the famous glacier of the same name near El Calafate, nor with nearby Parque Nacional Perito Moreno, **Perito Moreno** is a spruce little town, 25 km west of Lago Buenos Aires, the second largest lake in South America, and 60 km from border town Los Antiguos. Southwest is Parque Laguna, with varied bird life and fishing. But you're most likely to stop off here to see the **Cueva de las Manos** (see below). **Tourist office** at San Martín 1222, open 0700-2300, can advise on tours. T432222/020. Visit the www.scruz.gov.ar Also has information on Patagonian *estancias*, in English. Two ATMs, but nowhere to change travellers cheques.

Sleeping and eating **C** *Austral*, San Martín 1327, T432042. With breakfast, has a decent restaurant. Slightly better than *Belgrano*, San Martín 1001, T432019, also a pleasant place. Good food at *Pipach*, next to *Austral*, *Parador Bajo Caracoles*, or pizzas at *Nono's*, 9 de Julio y Saavedra. **Camping** Two campsites: Municipal site 2 km at Laguna de los Cisnes, T432072.
Outside of Perito Moreno Two estancias on RN40: 28 km south: **A** *Telken*, sheep station of the Nauta family, T02963-432079, telkenpatagonia@argentina.com or jarinauta@yahoo.com.ar Comfortable accommodation Oct-Apr, camping US$5, all meals available, breakfast US$3-6, Lunch US$10, dinner US$15, tea US$5-7, English and Dutch spoken, horse treks and excursions (Cueva de las Manos US$80, and others). Highly recommended. 60 km south, *Estancia Las Toldos*, 7 km off the road to Bajo Caracoles, T02963 432108, (011)4901 0436. Has *albergue* and *cabañas*, and organizes trips to see the cave paintings.

Transport **Air**: Airport 7 km east of town; take a taxi. *LADE* (Av San Martín 1207, T432055) flies to **Perito Moreno** from **Río Gallegos, Río Grande, Ushuaia, Calafate** and **Gob Gregores**. **Bus**: terminal on edge of town next to EG3 station, T432072. If crossing from Chile at Los Antiguos, 2 buses daily in summer, 1hr, US$2, *La Unión* T432133. Two companies to **El Chaltén**, *Chaltén Travel* even days 1000, and *Itinerarios y Travesías* twice a week, US$30. It's an unforgettable 14-hr, 582-km journey over the emptiness of Patagonia. To **Comodoro Rivadavia**, with *La Unión*, 6 hrs, US$12.

Border with
Chile – Los
Antiguos

From Perito Moreno Route 43 (paved) runs south of Lago Buenos Aires to **Los Antiguos**, 60 km west, 2 km from the Chilean border (Phone code 02963). **Sleeping**: **B** *Antigua Patagonia*, on Ruta 43, T491038, www.antiguapatagonia.om. ar Luxurious rooms with beautiful views, excellent restaurant. Also arranges small tours to the Cueva de las Manos and nearby Monte Cevallos. **D** *Argentino*, Av 11 de

Julio, T491132, comfortable, restaurant. **F**pp *Albergue Padilla*, San Martín 44 (just off main street) T491140. Cheapest, comfortable shared rooms, *quincho* and garden. Also camping. Sells El Chaltén travel tickets and receives passengers off the bus from El Chaltén. Also an outstanding *Camping Municipal*, 2 km from centre, T491308. T15 6211855, with hot showers, US$1.25 pp. **Tourist office** at Avenida 11 de Julio 446, no phone, open 0800-2200 in summer, morning only other times. www.losantiguos-sc.com.ar At Km 29, **A** *Hostería La Serena* offers very comfortable accommodation, excellent home-grown food, organizes fishing and trips in Chilean and Argentine Lake Districts, open October-June; further details from Geraldine des Cressonières, T02963-432340

Transport Buses: To **Comodoro Rivadavia**, US$9, *Co-op Sportman*, from near *Hotel Argentino*, daily, 7½ hrs, via **Perito Moreno** and **Caleta Olivia**. *Chaltén Travel* on even days to **El Chaltén** via Perito Moreno, US$40; *Albergue Padilla* sells tickets; *Itinerarios y Travesías* twice a week on same route. To **Chile**, *La Unión* to **Chile Chico**, 8 km west, US$1, 45 mins (for routes from Chile Chico to Coyhaique, see Chile chapter).

It is nearly impossible to hitchhike between Perito Moreno and Calafate. Hardly any traffic and few services

Argentina

Ruta 40 is unpaved and rough south of Perito Moreno; 118 km south, a marked road goes directly to the famous **Cueva de las Manos** (46 km northeast). In a beautiful volcanic canyon is an intriguing series of galleries with 10,000-year-old paintings of human hands and animals in red, orange, black, white and green. Worth the trip for the setting, especially early morning or evening. ■ *US$1.50, under 12 free. A ranger at the site gives information.*

Sleeping B *Hostería Cueva de Las Manos*, 20 km from the cave, T02963-432856/839 (Buenos Aires 4901 0436, F4903 7161). Open 1 Nov-5 Apr, closed Christmas and New Year, runs tours to the caves, horse riding. *Estancia Turística Casa de Piedra*, 75 km south of Perito Moreno on Ruta 40. Camping **G**, also has rooms **E**, hot showers, homemade bread, use of kitchen, excursions to Cueva de las Manos and volcanoes by car or horse, in Perito Moreno ask for Sr Sabella, Av Perón 941, T432199.

Tours from Perito Moreno *Itinerarios y Travesías* buses in El Chaltén (see under *Albergue Patagonia*), stop at the caves for 2 hrs on their journey north. For tours contact *Transporte Terrestre Guanacóndor*: Juan José Nauto, T432079, and *Transporte Lago Posados*, T432431. All day tour with option of collecting from Bajo Caracoles or *Estancia Los Toldos*, US$30-40. Both these operators also do the spectacular **Circuito Grande Comarca Noroeste**, one of the highlights of Santa Cruz, taking in some of the province's most dramatic scenery. From Perito Moreno to Bajo Caracoles, Cueva de las Manos, Lago Posada, Paso Roballos, Monte Cevallos, Los Antiguos.

Tourist office can advise: T02963-432222

After hours of spectacular emptiness, even tiny **Bajo Caracoles** (*Population*: 100) is a relief: a few houses with an expensive grocery store and very expensive fuel. (**D** *Hotel Bajo Caracoles*, hospitable, meals.) From here Ruta 41 goes 99 km northwest to **Paso Roballos**, continuing to Cochrane in Chile.

South of Bajo Caracoles, 101 km, is a crossroads. Ruta 40 heads southeast while the turning northwest goes to remote Parque Nacional Perito Moreno, at the end of a 90-km *ripio* track. There is trekking and abundant wildlife among the large, interconnected system of lakes below glaciated peaks, though much of the park is dedicated to scientific study only. Lago Belgrano, the biggest lake, is a vivid turquoise, its surrounding mountains streaked with a mass of differing colours. Ammonite fossils can be found. ■*Entrance is free. Park ranger, 10 km beyond the park entrance, has maps and information on wildlife, none in English. Camping is free: no facilities, no fires. There is no public transport into the park but it may be possible to arrange a lift with estancia workers from Hotel Las Horquetas. www.parquesnacionales.com has information. Park office in Gobernador Gregores, Av San Martín 409, T02962-491477.*

Parque Nacional Perito Moreno
Accessible only by own transport, Nov-Mar

Nearest accommodation is **B** full board *Estancia La Oriental*, T02962-452196, elada@uvc.com.ar Open November-March, with horse riding, trekking. See www.cielospatagonicos for other *estancias* in Santa Cruz: *Menelik* near PN Perito Moreno, and *El Cóndor*, on the southern shore of Lago San Martín, 120 km from Tres Lagos.

From the Parque Moreno junction to Tres Lagos, Ruta 40 improves considerably. East of the junction (7 km) is *Hotel Las Horquetas* (closed) and 15 km beyond is Tamel Aike village (police station, water). After another 34 km Ruta 40 turns sharply southwest, but if you need fuel before Tres Lagos, you must make a 72 km detour to Gobernador Gregores (always carry spare).

At **Tres Lagos** (accommodation at *Restaurant Ahoniken*, Av San Martín, **E**; camping at *Estancia La Lucia*, US$2.50, water, barbecue, 'a little, green paradise'; supermarket, fuel) a road turns off northwest to Lago San Martín. From Tres Lagos Ruta 40 deteriorates again and remains very rugged until after the turnoff to the Fitz Roy sector of Parque Nacional Los Glaciares. 21 km beyond is the bridge over Río La Leona, with delightful *Hotel La Leona* whose café serves good cakes.

Comodoro Rivadavia to Río Gallegos

Caleta Olivia (*Population*: 13,000) lies on the Bahía San Jorge, 74 km south of Comodoro Rivadávia, with hotels and a municipal campsite near beach. Only worth staying overnight to see the new sound sculptures, Ciudad Sonora, at **Pico Truncado** (a few simple hotels, campsite, tourist information T499 2202), 58 km southwest, where the wind sings through marble and metal structures, www.ciudad sonora.com.ar Daily bus service. *Hotel Robert*, San Martín 2152, T485 1452. Buses to Río Gallegos, *Pingüino*, US$8 overnight. Many buses to Comodoro Rivadavia, 1 hour, US$1.70 (*La Unión*, at terminal, T0297-485 1234), and 3 daily to Puerto Deseado. To El Calafate, 5 hours; to Perito Moreno and Los Antiguos, 5 hours, two daily.

The Monumento Natural Bosques Petrificados, in a bizarre lunar landscape surrounding the Laguna Grande, has the largest examples of petrified trees, araucarias 140 million years old, and it's astounding to think that this desert was once forest. There is a museum and a 1-km nature walk. ■ *1000-1800 , no charge but donations accepted; please do not remove 'souvenirs'. Tours from Puerto Deseado with* Los Vikingos, *address below. Access by Ruta 49 which branches off 86 km south of Fitz Roy. No facilities, and nearest campsite at Estancia la Paloma, 25 km before the entrance.*

Puerto
Deseado
Phone code: 0297
Colour map 9, grid B3
Population: 4,100

Puerto Deseado is a pleasant fishing port on the estuary of the Río Deseado, which drains, strangely, into the Lago Buenos Aires in the west. It's a stunning stretch of coastline and the estuary is a wonderful nature reserve, with Magellanic penguins, cormorants, and breeding grounds of Commerson's dolphin – one of the most beautiful in the world. **Cabo Blanco**, 72 km north, is the site of the largest fur seal colony in Patagonia, breeding season December-January. The **tourist office** is in the *vagón histórico*, San Martín 1525, T487 0220, turismo@pdeseado.com.ar

Sleeping and eating L *Estancia La Madrugada*, T011-5371 5555, lwalker@caminosturis-mo.com.ar or ats@caminosturismo.com.ar Accommodation and meals, excursions to sea lion colony and cormorant nesting area, English spoken. Highly recommended (see also www.cielospatagonicos.org). **C** *Los Acantilados*, Pueyrredón y España, T4872167. Beautifully located, good breakfast. **B** *Isla Chaffer*, San Martín y Mariano Moreno, T4872246. Modern, central. *Albergue Municipal la Ría*, Colón y Belgrano, T4870260. Eating places include *El Viejo Marino*, Pueyrredón 224. Considered best by locals. *La Casa de Don Ernesto*, San Martín 1245. Seafood and *parrilla*. *El Pingüino*, Piedrabuena 958. *Parrilla*.

Tour operators *Darwin Expediciones*, España 2601, T156 247554, www.darwin expediciones.com *Los Vikingos*, Estrada 1275, T156 245141/487 0020, vikingo@puertodeseado.com.ar Both offer excursions by boat to Ría Deseado reserve and Reserva Provincial Isla Pingüino.

The quiet Puerto San Julián is the best place for breaking the 834 km run from Comodoro Rivadavia to Río Gallegos. It has a fascinating history, little of which is visible today. The first mass in Argentina was held here in 1520 after Magellan had executed a member of his mutinous crew. Francis Drake also put in here in 1578, to behead Thomas Doughty, after amiably dining with him. There is much wildlife in the area: red and grey foxes, guanacos, wildcats in the mountains, rheas and an impressive array of marine life in the coastal Reserva San Julián. Recommended zodiac boat trip run by *Excursiones Pinocho*, Almte Brown 739, T452856, nonois@sanjulian.com.ar to see Magellanic penguins (September-March), cormorants and Commerson's dolphins. Ceramics are made at the **Escuela de Cerámica**; good handicraft centre at Moreno y San Martín. There is a regional museum at the end of San Martín on the waterfront. The **tourist office** is at San Martín 1126, T454396, centur@uvc.com.ar

Puerto San Julián
Phone code: 02962
Colour map 9, grid B2
Population: 4,480

Sleeping and eating B *Bahía*, San Martín 1075, T454028. Modern, comfortable, good value. Recommended. **B** *Municipal*, 25 de Mayo 917, T452300. Very nice, well run, good value, no restaurant. **B** *Res Sada*, San Martín 1112, T452013. Fine, hot water, but on busy main road, poor breakfast. Good municipal campsite Magallanes 650 y M Moreno, T452806. US$2 per site plus US$1 pp, repeatedly recommended, all facilities. Restaurants include *Sportsman*, Mitre y 25 de Mayo. Excellent value. *Rural*, Ameghino y Vieytes. Good, but not before 2100. A number of others. Also bars and tearooms.

   Inland B *Estancia La María*, 150 km northwest, offers transport, accommodation and meals and visits to fascinating caves with paintings of human hands, guanacos etc 4,000-12,000 years old, less visited than the Cueva de las Manos. Contact Fernando Behm, Saavedra 1163, T452328.

Transport Air: *LADE* (Berutti 985, T452137) flies weekly to **Comodoro Rivadavia**, **Gobernador Gregores**, **Puerto Deseado** and **Río Gallegos**. **Buses**: To/from Río Gallegos, *Pingüino*, 6 hrs, US$8.

Piedrabuena (*Population*: 2,600) on Ruta 3 is 146 km south of San Julián on the Río Santa Cruz. On Isla Pavón, south of town on Ruta 3 at the bridge over Río Santa Cruz, is a tourist complex, with popular wooded campsite and wildlife park, T497498, liable to get crowded in good weather; the river is popular for water sports. *Hostería Municipal Isla Pavón*, T02966-156 38380, is a new 4 star catering for fishers of steelhead trout. National trout festival in March. 36 km further south, a dirt road branches 22 km to **Monte León**, a provincial nature reserve (likely soon to be a National Park, owned by Douglas Tompkins (see Parque Pumalin in Chaitén, Chile) which includes the Isla Monte León, an important breeding area for cormorants and terns, where there is also a penguin colony and sea lions. There are impressive rock formations and wide isolated beaches at low tide. Campsite with basic facilities.

Río Gallegos and around

The capital of Santa Cruz Province, on the estuary of the Río Gallegos, this pleasant open town was founded in 1885 as a centre for the trade in wool and sheepskins, and boasts a few smart shops and some excellent restaurants. The delightful Plaza San Martín, 2 blocks south of the main street, Avenida Roca, has an interesting collection of trees, many planted by the early pioneers, and a tiny corrugated iron cathedral, with a wood-panelled ceiling in the chancel and stained glass windows. The small **Museo de los Pioneros**, Elcano y Alberdi, is worth a visit. Interesting tour given by the English-speaking owner, a descendent of the Scottish pioneers; great photos of the first sheep-farming settlers. ■ *Open daily 1000-2000, free.* **Museo de Arte Eduardo Minichelli**, Maipú 13, has work by local artists. ■ *Mon-Fri 0800-1900, Sat-Sun and holidays 1500-1900 (closed Jan/Feb).* **Museo Regional Provincial Manuel José Molina** , in the Complejo Cultural Santa Cruz, Av San Martín y

Phone code: 02966
Colour map 9, grid C2
Population: 75,000
232 km S of Piedrabuena

Argentina

Argentina

Ramón y Cajal 51, has rather dull rocks and fossils and a couple of dusty dinosaur skeletons.■ *Mon-Fri 1000-1800 1100-1900.* More stimulating, **Museo Malvinas Argentinas**, Pasteur 74, aims to inform visitors, with historical and geographical reasons, why the Malvinas are Argentine. ■ *Open Mon and Thu 0800-1300, Tue, Wed, Fri 1300-1800, 3rd Sun on month 1530-1830.*

Cabo Vírgenes, 134 km south of Río Gallegos, is where a nature reserve protects the second largest colony of Magellanic penguins in Patagonia. There's an informative self-guided walk to see nests among the *calafate* and *mata verde* bushes. Good to visit from November, when chicks are born, with nests under every bush, to January. ■ *US$2.30.* Great views from the Cabo Vírgenes lighthouse. *Confitería* close by with snacks and souvenirs Access from *ripio* Ruta 1 for 3½ hrs. 13 km north of Cabo Vírgenes is *Estancia Monte Dinero*, T428922, www.montedinero.com.ar where the English-speaking Fenton family offers accommodation (**A**), food and excursions; excellent. Tours to both with tour operators listed below, US$30 including lunch at Estancia Monte Dinero.

Sleeping
● *on map*

C *Apart Hotel Austral*, Roca 1505, T/F434314, www.apartaustral.com.ar Modern, very good value, particularly the superior duplexes, basic kitchen facilities, breakfast US$1.50 extra. **C** *Comercio*, Roca 1302, T422458, hotelcomercio@informacionrgl.com.ar Good value, including breakfast, nice design, comfortable, cheap *confitería*. **C** *Croacia*, Urquiza 431, T421218. Comfortable, huge breakfasts, helpful owners, a good choice. Recommended. **C** *Santa Cruz*, Roca 701, T420601, www.advance.com.ar/usuarios/htlscruz Good value, spacious rooms with good beds, full buffet breakfast. Recommended. **C** *Sehuen*, Rawson 160, T425683. Good, cosy, helpful, with breakfast. **D** *Covadonga*, Roca 1244, T420190. Small rooms with TV, with breakfast. **D** *Nevada*, Zapiola 480, T435790. Good budget option, simple rooms. **D** *París*, Roca 1040, T420111. Simple rooms, good value, breakfast extra. **Camping** *Camping ATSA* Ruta 3, en route to bus terminal, T420301, US$2.50 pp plus US$0.50 for tent. *Club Pescazaike*, Paraje Guer Aike, Ruta 3, T427366, US$2 pp per day, also *quincho* and restaurant, and *Chacra Daniel*, Paraje Río Chico, 3.5 km from town, T423970, US$4 pp per day, *parrilla* and facilities.

Río Gallegos

Buena Vista, Sarmiento y Gob Lista, T444114, near the river, looking across Plaza de la República. Most chic, not expensive, imaginative menu. Opposite the tourist office: *Puesto Molino*, Roca 862, inspired by *estancia* life, excellent pizzas (US$5 for two) and *parrilla* (US$10 for two). Next door, *El Horreo*, Roca 863, serves delicious lamb dishes and good salads. *El Dragón*, 9 de Julio 29. Cheap, varied *tenedor libre*. *La Vieja Esquina*, Sarsfield 90. For pizzas and pastas. *Confitería Díaz,* Roca 1157.

Eating
● *on map*
Excellent seafood, and some smart new inexpensive restaurants

Souvenirs and crafts: *Artesanías Keóken*, San Martín 336. Good leather and weavings. *Prepap* , Ramón y Cajal 51, and *Curtumbre Monte Aymond*, Roca 870, also fine traditional leather goods. Supermarkets: *La Anónima*, Roca y España, larger branch on Lisandro de la Torre, near bus terminal. *Alas*, Zapiola y Estrada.

Shopping

Macatobiano, Roca 908, T/F422466, macatobiano@macatobiano.com Air tickets and tours to Pingüinero Cabo Vírgenes, all day trip US$15, also to the Laguna Azul in a volcanic crater, a half day trip, to Estancia Monte Leon, as well as tickets to El Calafate and Ushuaia. *Tur Aike*, Zapiola 63, T422436. *Transpatagonia Expedición*, at the airport, T422504, transpatagonia@infovia.com.ar

Tour operators

Local Car rental: *Localiza*, Sarmiento 237, T424417. *Cristina*, Libertad 123, T425709. Essential to book rental in advance in season. **Taxis**: Taxi ranks plentiful, rates controlled, *remise* slightly cheaper.

    Long distance Air: Airport 10 km from centre. Taxi (*remise*) to/from town US$2.50. Now that the airport has opened at El Calafate, most flights go directly there. There are still regular flights to/from **Buenos Aires**, **Ushuaia** and **Río Grande** direct, with *AR*. *LADE* flies to **El Calafate**, **Ushuaia**, **Comodoro Rivadavia**, **Gobernador Gregores** and many other Patagonian airports once or twice a week. Book as far in advance as possible.

    Buses Terminal at corner of Ruta 3 and Av Eva Perón, 3 km from centre (crowded, no left luggage, *confitería*, toilets, kiosks); taxi to centre US$1, bus Nos 1 and 12 from posted stops around town. To **El Calafate**, 4-5 hrs, US$11, *Taqsa* and *Interlagos*. To **Los Antiguos**, *Sportman* daily at 2100, US$20. To **Comodoro Rivadavia**, *Pingüino* (T442169), *Don Otto* and *TAC*, 10 hrs, US$13. For **Bariloche**, *Transportadora Patagónica*, daily at 2130. To **Buenos Aires**, 33 hrs, several daily *Pingüino, Don Otto, TAC*, US$35. To **Río Grande** and **Ushuaia** *Tecni Austral*, Tue, Thu, Sat, at 1000, US$18-23, 8-10 hrs. **To Chile Buses**: to **Puerto Natales**, *Pingüino*, Wed, Sun, 7 hrs, US$7. *Bus-Sur* Tue, Thu 1700. To **Punta Arenas**, *Pingüino* and others, US$11 daily. **By car**: make sure your car papers are in order (go first to Tourist Office for necessary documents, then to the customs office at the port, at the end of San Martín, very uncomplicated). For road details, see Tierra del Fuego sections in Argentina and Chile.

Transport

Terminal information T442159
For all long distance trips, turn up with ticket 30 mins before departure

Airline offices *Aerolineas Argentinas* , San Martín 545, T422020/0810-222-86527. *LADE*, Fagnano 53, T422326. **Banks** 24-hr ATMs for all major international credit and debit cards all over town. *Banco Tierra del Fuego*, Roca 831, changes TCs. *Cambio El Pingüino*, Zapiola 469, and *Thaler*, San Martín 484. Both will change Chilean pesos as well as US$. **Communications** Internet: *J@va cybercafe* (next to British Club on Roca); also various *locutorios* offer internet services, US$0.60 per hr. **Post Office**: Roca 893 y San Martin. **Telephone**: *Locutorios* all over town, **Consulates** Chile, Mariano Moreno 136, Mon-Fri, 0900-1300. **Tourist offices** Provincial office at Roca 863, T438725, www.scruz.gov.ar/turismo Helpful, English spoken, has list of *estancias*, and will phone round hotels for you. Mon-Fri 0900-2100, Sat 1000-2000, Sun 1000-1500, 1600-2000. Also at airport, limited opening hours. Small desk at bus terminal, T442159.

Directory
Change TCs here if going to El Calafate, where it is even more difficult

El Calafate and around

This new town sits on the south shore of **Lago Argentino** and exists almost entirely as a tourist centre for the **Parque Nacional los Glaciares**, 50 km away. An ever-growing number of hotels, hostels and *cabañas* can't quite accommodate the hordes at times in January and February, but the town is empty and quiet all winter. It's neither cheap nor attractive, but the Lago Argentino is beautiful, and the shallow part at Bahía Redonda is good for birdwatching in the evenings.

Phone code: 02902
Colour map 9, grid B1
Population: 8,000
312 km NW of Río Gallegos

Argentina

For the main excursions to the glaciers, see Parque Nacional below. At **Punta Gualicho** (or Walichu) on the shores of Lago Argentino 7 km east of town, there are cave paintings (badly deteriorated). A recommended 30-minute walk is from the Intendencia del Parque, following Calle Bustillo up the new road among cultivated fields and orchards to **Laguna Nímez**, a bird reserve (fenced in), with flamingos, ducks, and abundant birdlife. Cecilia Scarafoni, T493196, ecowalks@ cotecal.com.ar, leads birdwatching walks, 2 km from town, two hours, US$5. There are several *estancias* within reach, offering a day on a working farm, *asado al palo*, horse riding. *Estancia Alice 'El Galpón'*, 21 km west, has a bird sanctuary, horse riding, sheep shearing and *asado* , English spoken. T492509, Buenos Aires 011-4774 1069, elgalpon@estanciaalice.com.ar *Estancia Quien Sabe* at beautiful Lago Roca, interesting fruit production, bees, *asado* lunch, English spoken. T492316 leutzturismo@cotecal.com.ar See also *Helsingfors*, in Sleeping below.

Sleeping
■ *on map*
Calafate is very popular in Jan-Feb, so book all transport and accommodation in advance. Best months to visit are Oct, Nov and Mar. Many hotels open only from Oct to Apr/May

Prepare to pay far more for accommodation here than elsewhere in Argentina. **L** *Los Alamos*, Moyano y Bustillo, T491145, posadalosalamos@cotecal.com.ar Extremely comfortable, charming rooms, good service, lovely gardens and without doubt the best restaurant in town. Recommended. **L** *Kosten Aike*, Gob Moyano 1243, T492424, www.kostenaike.com.ar Relaxed yet stylish, elegant rooms, jacuzzi, gym, excellent restaurant (open to non residents, US$10 for three courses), cosy bar, garden, English spoken. Recommended. **AL** *El Quijote*, Gob Gregores 1181 , T491017, www.hieos.com.ar Spacious, well-designed with traditional touches, tasteful rooms with TV, restaurant, Italian and English spoken. **AL** *Hostería Kau-Yatún*, 25 de Mayo (10 blocks from centre), T491259, kauyatun@cotecal.com.ar Many facilities, old *estancia* house, comfortable, restaurant and

El Calafate

To Punta Gualicho & Laguna Nímez

0 metres 100
0 yards 100

asados, horse riding tours with guides. **AL** *Sierra Nevada*, Libertador 1888, T493129, www.plusnoticias.com/hotel/sierranevada/ Breakfast included, well-equipped, TV, lake views, `smart-rustic' style. **A** *Michelangelo*, Espora y Gob Moyano, T491045, michelangelohotel@cotecal.com.ar Lovely, quiet, welcoming, TV, breakfast included, superb restaurant, US$10 for 2 courses. Recommended. **B** *ACA Hostería El Calafate*, Av del Libertador 1353, T491004, F491027. Modern, good view, open all year. **B** *Vientos del Sur*, up the hill at C 54 2317, T493563. Very hospitable, calm, comfortable, TV, good views, kind family attention. **C** *Cerro Cristal*, Gob Gregores 979 , T491088. Basic, central, modernized bathrooms, no TV, breakfast included. **C** *del Norte*, Los Gauchos 813, T491117. Open all year, kitchen facilities, comfortable, owner organizes tours. **C** *Hospedaje Sir Thomas*, Cte Espora 257, T492220. Modern, comfortable wood-lined rooms, breakfast $5 extra. **C** *Hostería Ariel*, Casimiro Bigua 35, T493131. Modern, functional, well maintained, TV with breakfast. **C** *Los Lagos*, 25 de Mayo 220, T491170, loslagos@cotecal.com.ar Very comfortable, cheerful, breakfast included; good value. **D** *Cabañas Nevis*, Libertador 1696, T493180. Nice cabins for 5 and 8, some with lake view, great value. Recommended.

B-F pp *Youth Hostel Albergue del Glaciar*, Los Pioneros 255, T/F491243 (reservations in Bs As T/F03488-469416, off season only), www.glaciar.com Discount for ISIC or HI members, open mid Sep to end May. The original and best, with accommodation for all budgets: doubles with bath, **B**, doubles with shared bath, **C**, shared dorms **F** pp. Many languages spoken, helpful staff, lots of bathrooms, internet access, kitchen facilities. *Punto de Encuentro* restaurant with good value fixed menu and vegetarian options. See Tour operators, below, for Alternative Glaciar Tour, booking service for *Navimag* and hotels and transport throughout Patagonia, free shuttle from bus terminal. Highly recommended. Book in advance in summer. **D** *Universo*, Libertador 1108, T491009. Central, old fashioned, a bit overpriced, basic rooms, no TV, attentive. **E** *Albergue Buenos Aires*, Buenos Aires 296, 200 m from terminal, T491147, hospbuenosaires@cotecal.com.ar Comfortable rooms for 4 or more, kitchen facilities, helpful, good hot showers, luggage store. **E** *Hosp Alejandra*, Cte Espora 60, T491328. Good value, shared bath, no breakfast - you can make your own. Also **E***pp, one flat for 5 with TV. Recommended.* **E** pp *Calafate Hostel*, Gob Moyano 1226, 300 m from bus terminal, T492450, www.hostelspatagonia.com The other big hostel, a huge place, dorms for 4-6 with shared bath, **C** doubles with bath. Also has **G** pp *refugio* space (take sleeping bag), kitchen facilities, internet access, lively sitting area. Book a month ahead for Jan-Feb, helpful travel agency, *Chaltén Travel*. **E** pp *Hostal Lago Argentino*, Campaña del Desierto 1050-61, T491139, hostellagoargentino@cotecal.com.ar Shared dorm, **D** pp in double, also has flats, near bus terminal, helpful **E** *Hosp Los Dos Pinos*, 9 de Julio 358, T491271. Popular place ranging from dorms, rather cramped, to cheap *cabañas* for 7(**C**), tiny little studio flats for 2 (**B**) and a campsite (**F**), all sharing the friendly TV room where you can cook, owner arranges tours to glacier.

In the Parque Nacional los Glaciares 80 km west of Calafate on the road to the Moreno glacier: **L** *Los Notros*, T/F499510, www.lastland.com With breakfast and transfers to the glacier *passarelas*. Wonderful view of the glacier, spacious rooms, transport from airport and other meals extra. (in Bs As: T011-4814 3934). **L** *Estancia Helsingfors*, T/F02966-420719, www.helsingfors.com Or BsAs T/F011-4824 46623/3634. With breakfast, fabulous place in splendid position on Lago Viedma, stylish rooms, welcoming lounge, delicious food, and excursions directly to glaciers and to Laguna Azul, by horse or trekking, plus boat trips.

Camping Municipal campsite behind YPF service station, at José Pantin s/n, T492622, campingmunicipal@cotecal.com.ar US$2 pp, hot water, security, restaurant, open 1 Oct-30 Apr. 2 campsites in the Park en route to the glacier: *Bahía Escondida*, 7 km east of the glacier, is the only one with full facilities, fireplaces, hot showers and shop. Crowded in summer, US$ 3 pp. Unmarked site at *Correntoso*, 10 km east of the glacier, no facilities but great location, no fires, US$2 pp. *Río Mitre*, near the park entrance, is a picnic ground only, no camping, no fires. *Lago Roca*, 50km from El Calafate, T499500, beautifully situated, US$3 pp, bike hire, restaurant/confitería. (*Ferretería Chuar*, Libertador 1242, sells gas for camping.)

Pura Vida, Av Libertador 2000 block, near C 17. Comfortable sofas, homemade Argentine food, vegetarian options, lovely atmosphere, lake view. Recommended. El Hornito, Buenos Aires 155. Intimate, opposite bus terminal, excellent pizzas and pastas. *El Rancho*, 9 de Julio

Eating
● *on map*

Argentina

y Gob Moyano. Cosy, popular, big cheap pizzas. *Mi Viejo*, Av Libertador 1111. Popular *parrilla,* US$6 for *tenedor libre.* *La Cocina*, Av Libertador 1245. *Pizzería,* pancakes, pasta, salads, warm atmosphere. Two lively packed places with good atmosphere: *Rick's Café*, Av Libertador 1105. *Tenedor libre* US$5, and *Casablanca*, 25 de Mayo y Av Libertador, jolly place for omelettes, hamburgers, vegetarian, US$4 for steak and chips. *Heladería Aquarela*, Av Libertador 1177. The best ice cream – try the *calafate. Shackleton Lounge*, Av Libertador 3287, on outskirts of town (US$1 in taxi). Recommended for drinks, lovely view of lake, old photos of Shakleton, good music. *Tango Sur*, 9 de julio 265, T491550, live music and tango show! US$3.50, Tue and Sun at 2030, 2300, in charming surroundings.

Tour operators Most agencies charge the same rates for excursions: to the Perito Moreno Glacier US$20; Minitrekking (on the glacier, with crampons included, recommended) US$50; Upsala Explorer (a full day visiting Upsala glacier by boat, then in 4WD, and trekking, superb lunch at the remote *Estancia Cristina* and boat trip, unforgettable) US$99; to Lago Roca, a full day including lunch at *Estancia Anita*, US$30; horse riding to Gualichó caves, 2 hrs, US$20. *Chaltén Travel*, Liertador 1174, T492212. Most helpful, huge range of tours: glaciers, *estancias*, trekking, and to El Chaltén. Also sell tickets along the Ruta 40 to Los Antiguos, English spoken.*Albergue del Glaciar*, address above. Alternative Glacier tour, entertaining, informative, includes walking, US$20. Recommended constantly. Also Supertrekking en Chaltén, 2-day hiking trip, featuring the best treks in the Fitz Roy massif, including camping and ice trekking. Highly recommended. *Hielo y Aventura*, Av Libertador 935, T491053, hieloyaventura@cotecal.com.ar Minitrekking includes walk through forests and 2-hr trek on glacier with crampons, US$50. Recommended. *Leutz Turismo*, Libertador 1341, T492316, leutzturismo@cotecal.com.ar Daily excursion to Lago Roca 1000-1800, US$20 pp, plus US$11 for lunch at *Estancia Quien Sabe*, interesting tour. *Mil Outdoor Adventure*, Av Libertador 1029, T491437. Excursions in 4WD, 4-6 hrs, US$20-40. *Upsala Explorer*, 9 de Julio 69, T491133, www.upsalaexplorer.com.ar Spectacular (if pricey) experience, superb food (vegetarians catered for on request), transfers from El Calafate not included. *Mundo Austral*, Libertador 1114, T492365, F492116. For all bus travel and glaciers, helpful bilingual guides.

Transport **Local   Car Hire**: *Cristina*, Libertador 1711, T491674. *Localiza*, Libertador 687, T491398. **Mountain bikes** can be hired from *Bike Way*, Espora 20, T492180, US$7 per day.

Long distance Air: Lago Argentino airport, T491220, 22 km east of town, *Aerobus* runs service from town to meet flights, T492492, US$3. Taxi (T491655/492005), US$7 *AR* flies daily to/from Buenos Aires. Many more flights in summer. To **Puerto Natales** *Aerovías Dap* Mon-Fri, summer only (Oct – Mar).

Buses Terminal on Roca, 1 block up stairs from Libertador. *Taqsa* (T491843) and *Interlagos* (T492197), run daily services to Perito Moreno glacier, the cheapest way to get there. To **Ushuaia** take bus to Río Gallegos, with *Taqsa* or *Interlagos*, several daily, US$11. To **El Chaltén**, with *Cal-Tur* or *Chaltén Travel*, 3 daily, US$14 return. Taxi (*remise*) to **Río Gallegos**, 4 hrs, US$100 irrespective of number of passengers, up to 5 people. Along Ruta 40 to Perito Moreno and Los Antiguos for Chile. *Chaltén Travel* (at terminal and see above) T491833, from El Chaltén to **Perito Moreno** and **Los Antiguos**, sometimes with a stop at Cueva de las Manos (goes north on odd days, south on even days). US$40, book a week in advance. Safari Route 40 to Bariloche (see under Bariloche, Buses) can be booked at *Albergue del Glaciar*, T491243, info@glaciar.com

Take passport when booking bus tickets to Chile

Direct services to Chile: To **Puerto Natales**, daily with either **Cootra** (T491444) or *Bus Sur* (T491631), US$16 (advance booking recommended, tedious border crossing). *Bus Sur* (Tue, Sat 0800) and *Zaahj* (Wed, Fri, Sun 0800) also run to Puerto Natales via Cerro Castillo (where you can pick up a bus to Torres del Paine in summer). **NB** Argentine pesos cannot be exchanged in Torres del Paine.

Directory **Banks** Best to take cash as high commission is charged on exchange, but there are ATMs at *Banco de la Provincia de Santa Cruz*, Libertador 1285, and at *Banco de Tierra del Fuego*, 25 de Mayo 34. *Thaler*, Libertador 1311 changes money and TCs. **Communications** Post Office: Libertador 1133 **Telephone**: *Open Calafate*,Libertador 996, huge locutorio for phone and also 20 fast internet places,

US$2 per hr. Open 0800-2400. **Tourist offices** In the bus terminal, T491090, www.elcalafate.gov.ar Helpful staff speak several languages and have a good map with accommodation shown. Oct-Apr daily 0700-2200. At the airport, T491230. See also www.calafate.com For information on the Parque Nacional los Glaciares, park office (Intendencia) is at Libertador 1302, T491005. Mon-Fri 0800-1600. www.apnglaciares@cotecal.com.ar

Parque Nacional Los Glaciares

This park, the second-largest in Argentina, extends over 660,000 ha. 40% of it is covered by ice fields (*hielos continentales*) from which 13 glaciers descend into two great lakes, Lago Argentino and, further north, Lago Viedma, linked by the Río La Leona, flowing south from Lago Viedma. The only accessible areas of the park are the southern area around Lago Argentino, accessible from El Calafate, and the northern area around Cerro El Chaltén (Fitz Roy). Access to the central area is difficult and there are no tourist facilities. Access to the southern part of the park is from El Calafate, entry US$3.

Argentina

At the western end of Lago Argentino (80 km from El Calafate) the major attraction is the Ventisquero Perito Moreno, until recently one of the few glaciers in the world that was advancing. It descends to the surface of the water over a 5-km frontage and a height of about 60 m. It once advanced across the lake, cutting the Brazo Rico off from the Canal de los Témpanos; then the pressure of water in the Brazo Rico would break through the ice and reopen the channel. Since February 1988 this spectacular rupture has not occurred, possibly because of global warming and increased water consumption with the demands of local services. It can be seen close up from a series of wooden walkways descending from the car park, and guardeparques guide an hour-long walk along the lake shore at 1530 and 1730 daily for a different view of the glacier.

Ventisquero Moreno
The vivid blue hues of the ice floes, with the dull roar as pieces break off and float away as icebergs from the snout, are spectacular, especially at sunset

Transport From Calafate there are buses by *Taqsa* or *Interlagos*. Many agencies in Calafate also run minibus tours (park entry not included) leaving 0800 returning 1800, giving three hours at glacier, return ticket valid if you come back next day (student discount available). For *Albergue del Glaciar*'s alternative trips and *Minitrekking Hielo y Aventura*, see Tour operators, above. Taxis, US$45 for four passengers round trip. At the car park facing the glacier is a reasonable restaurant. Boat trips on the lake are organized by Fernández Campbell, Av Libertador 867, T491155, with large boats for up to 60 passengers: 'Safari Náutico', US$10 pp, 1 hr offering the best views of the glacier.

Out of season, trips to the glacier are difficult to arrange, but you can gather a party and hire a taxi (remise taxis T491655

At the northwest end of Lago Argentino, 60 km long and 4 km wide, Upsala Glacier is considered the largest in South America and is a stunning expanse of untouched beauty. It can be reached by motor-boat from Punta Bandera, 50 km west of El Calafate, on a trip that also goes to Lago Onelli and Spegazzini glaciers. Small Lago Onelli is quiet and very beautiful, beech trees on one side, and ice-covered mountains on the other. The lake is full of icebergs of every size and sculpted shape. Tour boats usually operate a daily trip to the glacier, Fernández Campbell. The price includes bus fares and park entry fees (take food). Bus departs 0730 from El Calafate for Punta Bandera, time allowed for lunch at the restaurant (not included) near the Lago Onelli track. Return bus to El Calafate at 1930; a long but memorable day. See Tour operators also for the Upsala Explorer. Book through many agencies.

The Upsala Glacier
Out of season it is extremely difficult to get to the glacier

This small tourist town lies 230 km northwest of El Calafate in the north of the park, at the foot of the jagged peaks of the spectacular Fitz Roy massif, which soars steeply from the Patagonian steppe, its sides too steep for snow to stick. Chaltén is the Tehuelche name meaning the 'smoking mountain', and occasionally at sunrise the mountains are briefly lit up bright red for a few seconds, a phenomenon known as the 'sunrise of fire', or '*amanecer de fuego*'. The town is windy, expensive and unattractive, but it's the base for some of the country's finest trekking. If you haven't got a tent, you can easily rent all

El Chaltén
Phone code 02962; Take cash: No banks or ATMs, credit cards are not accepted. There's no internet access.0

you'll need. The tourist office is at Güemes 21, T493011, www.elchalten.com Excellent site with accommodation listed, but no email for queries. ■ *Office open Mon-Fri 0900-2000, Sat-Sun 1300-2000.* National Park office across the bridge at the entrance to the town, T493004. Both hand out helpful trekking maps of the area, with paths and campsites marked, distances and walking times.

The **Lago del Desierto**, 37 km north of El Chaltén, is surrounded by forests, a stunning virgin landscape. A short walk to a mirador at the end of the road gives fine views. Excursions from El Chaltén by Chaltén Travel daily in summer, and daily boat trips to the end of the lake, which you can combine with trekking. Campsite. Also daily boat trips on Lago Viedma to pass Glaciar Viedma, with possible ice trekking. The *estancia Hostería El Pilar* (see Sleeping) is a base for trekking up Río Blanco or Río Eléctrico, or try the multi activity adventure circuit. Highly recommended.

Note in high season places are likely to be full: book ahead

Sleeping AL *Hostería El Puma*, Lionel Terray 212, T542962, www.elchalten.com/elpuma A little apart, splendid views, lounge with log fire, tasteful stylish furnishings, comfortable, transfers and big American breakfast included. Can also arrange tours through their excellent agency *Fitz Roy Expeditions*, see **Climbing**, below. Recommended. **AL** *Hostería Posada Lunajuim*, Trevisán s/n, T/F493047, www.elchalten.com/lunajuim Stylish yet relaxed, comfortable (duvets on the beds!), lounge with wood fire, with full American breakfast. Recommended. **A** *Fitz Roy Inn*, T493062, caltur@cotecal.com.ar Overpriced place with pleasant but small rooms, often filled with package tour clients, breakfast included. Also travel agency *Cal Tur*. **B** *El Pilar* (see above), T/F493002, www.hosteriaelpilar.com.ar Country house in a spectacular setting at the meeting of Ríos Blanco and de las Vueltas, with clear views of Fitz Roy. A chance to sample the simple life with access to less-visited northern part of the park. Simple comfortable rooms, great food, very special. Owner Miguel Pagani is an experienced mountain guide. **C** *Hospedaje La Base*, Lago de Desierto 97, T493031. Basic doubles with bath, rooms for 3 or 4 **E**, tiny kitchen, self service breakfast included, great video lounge. **C** *Northofagus*, Hensen s/n, T493087, www.elchalten.com/northofagus/ Cosy bed and breakfast, simple rooms with shared bath, good value.

Hostels E *Albergue Patagonia*, T/F493019, www.elchalten.com/alberguepatagonia HI-affiliated, small and cosy, kitchen, video room, bike hire, laundry, very welcoming. Helpful information on Chaltén, also run excursions to Lago del Desierto. Next door is their restaurant *Fuegia*, with Patagonian dishes, curries and vegetarian food. Also friendly is **E** *Cóndor de los Andes*, Av Río de las Vueltas y Halvorsen, T493101, www.condordelosandes.com Nice little rooms for 6 with bath, sheets included, breakfast US$2, laundry service, library, kitchen, quiet. **E** *Albergue Rancho Grande*, San Martín s/n, T493005, rancho@cotecal.com.ar HI-affiliated, in a great position at the end of town with good open views and attractive restaurant and lounge, accommodates huge numbers of trekkers in rooms for 4, with shared bath, breakfast and sheets extra. Also **C** doubles, breakfast extra. Helpful, English and French spoken. Recommended. Reservations in *Calafate Hostel/Chaltén Travel*, Calafate. **Camping** *Camping Madsen* several km north, east of Río de las Vueltas, and *El Refugio*, off San Martín just before Rancho Grande (US$3 pp plus US$2 for hot shower). Neither has services. A gas/alcohol stove is essential for camping as open fires are prohibited in campsites in of the National Park. Take plenty of warm clothes and a good sleeping bag. It is possible to rent equipment in El Chaltén, ask at park office or *Rancho Grande*. Campsites in National Park: Confluencia, Poincenot, Capri, Lago Toro. None has services, all river water is drinkable. Pack out all rubbish, do not wash or bury waste within 70 m of rivers. *Camping Piedra del Fraile* on Río Eléctrico is behind park boundary, privately owned, has facilities.

Eating There's nowhere cheap to eat, but *Las Lengas*, Viedma y Güemes, opposite tourist office, is a little cheaper than most. Plentiful meals, basic pastas and meat dishes. US$3 for 2 courses. *Ruca Mahuida*, Lionel Terray s/n, widely regarded as the best restaurant with imaginative and well prepared food. *Patagonicus*, Güemes y Madsen, lovely warm place with salads, *pastas caseras* and fabulous pizzas for 2, US$4-7, open midday to midnight. Recommended. *Pangea*, Lago del Desierto 273 y San Martín, open for lunch and dinner, drinks and coffee, calm, good music, varied menu, US$3-7. Recommended. *Zafarancho* (behind *Rancho Grande*), bar-restaurant, good range and reasonably priced, also rents tents, sleeping bags and everything else, can arrange mountain guides. Coordinates with *Chaltén Travel* to sell bus tickets, adventure tourism, etc, www.hostelspatagonia.com **Josh Aike**, excellent *confitería*, homemade food, beautiful building. Recommended. **Domo Blanca**, Costanera y D'Agostini, for delicious home made ice cream. **Cervecería Bodegón El Chaltén**, San Martín s/n. Brews its own excellent beer, also coffee and cakes.

Shopping *El Gringuito* , Av Antonio Rojo, has the best choice. Many others around. Fuel is available. Equipment hire, *Zaffarancho* restaurant, see above.

Transport **Bus**: daily buses to **El Calafate**, 4 hrs, US$7 one way, run by **Chaltén Travel** (T493005) and **Cal Tur** (T493062). To **Los Antiguos**, *Itinerarios y Travesías* (T493088), overnight, includes trip to **Cueva de las Manos**, Sun 1730, and Wed 2200. *Chaltén Travel* travels north odd days 0730, 14hrs, US$40 single, bike US$5, returning even days. **Overland Patagonia** does trips to **Bariloche** in 4 days, staying at *estancias* and visiting Cueva de las Manos, www.overlandpatagonia.com Book through *Alaska Youth Hostel*, or *Periko's* in Bariloche. In 2003 a route to Chile was opened involving a 35-km hike and a boat trip to Villa O'Higgins; only every 2 weeks in 2003, but more regular service expected for 2004.

In summer, buses fill quickly: book ahead. Fewer services off season.

Trekking: The two most popular walks are to **1) Laguna Torre** (3 hours each way). After 90 minutes you'll come to Mirador Laguna Torre with great view of Cerro Torre, and 30 minutes more along side of lake, to busy Camping De Agostini where you have fantastic views. **2) Laguna de Los Tres** (4 hours each way). Walk up to Camping Capri (2 hours), great views of Fitz Roy, then another hour to Poincenot (3 hours). Just beyond it is Camping Río Blanco (only for climbers, by arrangement). From Río Blanco you can walk another hour to Laguna de los Tres where you'll get a spectacular view (not a good walk if it's cloudy). You can connect the two views of the two cordons by climbing past Capri (a detour to the side) and taking the signed path to your left, passing Laguna Madre and then Laguna Hija to reach the path that leads to Laguna Torre. From El Chaltén to Laguna Torre along this route takes about 7 hours. **3) Loma del Pliegue Tumbado** (4 hours each way). To a viewpoint where you can see both cordons and Lago Viedma: marked path from Park Ranger's office, a good day walk, best in clear weather. **4) Laguna Toro** (6 hrs each way). For more experienced trekkers, to wild glacial lake. **5) Up Río Blanco to Piedra del Fraile** (7 hrs each way). A beautiful walk to campsite with facilities, and Refugio Los Troncos, neither is free. Recommended. The best day walks are Laguna Capri, Mirador Laguna Torre, both of which have great views after an hour or so. Most paths are very clear and well worn, but a map is essential, even on short walks: the park information centre gives a helpful photocopied maps of treks, but the best is one published by *Zagier and Urruty*, 1992, US$6 (Casilla 94, Sucursal 19, 1419 Buenos Aires, F011-4572 5766) and is available in shops in El Calafate and El Chaltén. For trekking on horseback with guides: *Rodolfo Guerra*, T493020; *El Relincho*, T493007.

Trekking & climbing

The weather changes hourly, so don't wait for a sunny day to go hiking. Just be prepared for sudden deterioration in the weather. Don't stray from the paths

Climbing: base camp for Fitz Roy (3,375 m) is Campamento Río Blanco (see above). Other peaks include Cerro Torre (3,102 m), Torre Egger (2,900 m), Cerro Solo (2,121 m), Poincenot (3,002 m), Guillaumet (2,579 m), Saint-Exupery (2,558 m), Aguja Bífida (2,394 m) and Cordón Adela (2,938 m): most of these are for very experienced climbers. The best time is mid February to end March; November-December is very windy; January is fair; winter is extremely cold. Permits for climbing are available at the national park information office. Guides are availabe in Chaltén: ask Sr Guerra about hiring animals to carry equipment. *Fitz Roy Expediciones*, Lionel Terray 212, T493017, www.elchalten.com/fitzroy Owned by experienced guide Alberto del Castillo, organizes trekking and adventure excursions including on the *Campo de Hielo Continental*, ice climbing schools, horse riding, and fabulous longer trips. Must be fit, but no technical experience required; all equipment provided. Email with lots of notice to reserve. Highly recommended, English and Italian spoken. *Mermoz*, San Martín 493, T493098, for trips across Laguna del Desierto, including bus transfer, helpful.

Argentina

El Calafate to Chile

Argentina

Between El Calafate to Punta Arenas it is possible to see guanacos and condors

If travelling from El Calafate to Torres del Paine by car or bike, you'll cross this bleak area of steppe. About 40 km before reaching the border there are small lagoons and salt flats with flamingoes. From Calafate you can take the almost completely paved combination of Ruta 11, RN 40 and RN 5 to La Esperanza (165 km), where there's fuel, a campsite and a large but expensive *confitería* (accommodation **D** with bath). From La Esperanza, ripio Ruta 7 heads west along the valley of the Río Coyle. A shorter route (closed in winter) missing Esperanza, goes via El Cerrito and joins Ruta 7 at *Estancia Tapi Aike*. Ruta 7 continues to the border crossing at Cancha Carrera (see below) and then meets the good *ripio* road between Torres del Paine and Puerto Natales (63 km). For bus services along this route see under El Calafate.

Río Turbio
Colour map 9, grid C2
Population: 8,000
257 km W of Río Gallegos
30 km from Puerto Natales (Chile) Phone code 02902

A charmless place you're most likely to visit en route to or from Torres del Paine in Chile. The site of Argentina's largest coalfield hasn't recovered from the depression hitting the industry. It has a cargo railway, connecting it with Punta Loyola, and visitors can see Mina 1, where the first mine was opened. There is a ski centre: **Valdelén** has 6 pistes and is ideal for beginners, also scope for cross-country skiing between early June and late September. Tourist information in the municipality on San Martín.

Sleeping Hotels almost always full: Most recommendable is *De La Frontera*, 4 km from Rio Turbio, Paraje Mina 1, T421979. **C** *Hostería Capipe*, Dufour (9 km from town, T482930, www.hosteriacapipe.com.ar). In town, *Nazó*, Gob Moyano 464, T421800. *Restaurant El Ringo*, near bus terminal, will shelter you from the wind.

Transport Buses: To **Puerto Natales**, 2 hrs, US$2, several daily with *Cootra* (Tte del Castillo 01, T421448, cootra@oyikil.com.ar), *Bus Sur, Lagoper* (Av de Los Mineros 262, T411831). To **El Calafate**, same companies, *Expreso Pingüino* and *Taqsa* daily. US$7, 4½ hrs. **Río Gallegos**, 4 hrs, US$8 (*Taqsa*).

Border with Chile
1) Paso Mina Uno/Dorotea is 5 km south of Río Turbio. Open all year, 24 hours 31 November – 31 March, daytime only rest of year. On the Chilean side this runs south to join the main Puerto Natales-Punta Arenas road. **2) Paso Casas Viejas** is 33 km south of Río Turbio via 28 de Noviembre. Open all year, daytime only. On the Chilean side this runs east to join the main Puerto Natales-Punta Arenas road. **3) Paso Cancha Carrera** is 55 km north of Río Turbio, this is the most convenient crossing for Parque Nacional Torres del Paine. Open November-April only. Argentine customs are fast and friendly. On the Chilean side the road continues 14 km to the Chilean border post at Cerro Castillo, where it joins the road from Puerto Natales to Torres del Paine. Chilean immigration open 0830-1200, 1400-2000, November-March or April only.

Tierra del Fuego

The island at the extreme south of South America is divided between Argentina (east) and Chile (west), with the tail end of the Andes cordillera providing dramatic mountain scenery along the southern fringe of both countries. There are lakes and forests, mostly still wild and undeveloped, offering good trekking in summer and downhill or cross country skiing in winter. Until a century ago, the island was inhabited by four ethnic groups, Tehuelches, Onas, Alcalufes and Yaganes. All now extinct. They were removed by settlers who occupied their land to introduce sheep and many died from disease. Many of the sheep farming estancias which replaced the indigenous people can be visited. Ushuaia, the island's main city, is an attractive base for exploring the southwest's small national park, and for boat trips along the Beagle channel to Harberton, a fascinating pioneer estancia. There's good trout and salmon fishing, and a tremendous variety of bird life in summer. Autumn colours are spectacular in March-April.

Getting there There are no road/ferry crossings between the Argentine mainland and Argentine Tierra del Fuego. You have to go through Chilean territory. From Río Gallegos, Ruta 3 reaches the Chilean border at Monte Aymond (about 55 km; open 24hrs summer, 0800-2200 April to November), passing Laguna Azul. For bus passengers the border crossing is easy; hire cars need a document for permission to cross. 41 km into Chile is **Punta Delgada**, with a dock 16 km beyond for the 15-minute ferry-crossing over the Primera Angostura (First Narrows) to **Punta Espora** (cosy tea room *Bahía Azul*). Boats run every 40 minutes, 0830-2300. Some 145 km south is Chilean San Sebastián, and then 14 km east, across the border (24 hrs), is Argentine San Sebastián, with a basic **D** ACA motel, T02964-425542; service station open 0700-2300. From here the road is paved to Río Grande (see below). The other ferry crossing is **Punta Arenas-Porvenir**. RN255 from Punta Delgada goes west 103 km to the intersection with the Punta Arenas-Puerto Natales road. 5 km east of Punta Arenas, at Tres Puentes, there is a daily ferry crossing to Porvenir, from where a 225 km road runs east to Río Grande (six hours) via San Sebastián. For details of transport and hotels on Chilean territory, see the Chile chapter.

The main road from San Sebastián (Argentina) to Ushuaia is paved, apart from the 65km from **Tolhuin** to Rancho Hambre. All other roads are *ripio* (unsurfaced).

Ins & outs
Colour map 9, grid C3
Accommodation is sparse and planes and buses fill up quickly from Nov to Feb. Essential to book ahead
Fruit and meat may not be taken onto the island, nor between Argentina and Chile

Río Grande

Río Grande is a sprawling modern town in windy, dust-laden sheep-grazing and oil-bearing plains. (The oil is refined at San Sebastián in the smallest and most southerly refinery in the world.) The *frigorífico* (frozen meat) plant and sheep-shearing shed are among the largest in South America. Government tax incentives to companies in the 1970s led to a rapid growth in population; the subsequent withdrawal of incentives has produced increasing unemployment and emigration. The city was founded by Fagnano's Salesian mission in 1893, and you can visit the original building **La Candelaria**, 11 km north, whose museum has displays of indigenous artefacts and natural history. ■ *Mon-Sat 1000-1230,1500-1900, Sun 1500-1900, US$1.50. Afternoon teas, US$3. Taxi US$6 with wait.* Río Grande's **Museo de la Ciudad** is also recommended for its history of the pioneers, missions and oil. ■ *Mon-Fri 1000-1700. Alberdi 555.* **Local festivals**: Sheep shearing in January. Rural exhibition and handicrafts 2nd week February. Shepherd's day, with impressive sheepdog display first week March. Winter solstice, the longest night with fireworks and ice skating contests 20-21 June.

Phone code: 02964
Colour map 9, grid C2
Population: 35,000

B *Posada de los Sauces*, Elcano 839, T432895, info@posadadelossauces.com.ar Best by far, with breakfast, beautifully decorated, comfortable, good restaurant, cosy bar. **C** *Atlántida*, Belgrano 582, T431915, atlantida@netcombbs.com.ar Modern, uninspiring but good value, with breakfast, cable TV. **D** *Isla del Mar*, Güemes 963, T422883, www.hotelguia.com/hotelisladelmar On sea shore, bleak and a bit run down, but breakfast included and staff are friendly. **F** pp *Argentina*, San Martín 64, T422546, hotelargentino@yahoo.com More than a backpackers' youth hostel, best cheap place to stay, beautifully renovated 1920's building close to the sea front, kitchen facilities, owned by Graciela. Highly recommended. Recommended **eating** places: *La Nueva Colonial*, Fagnano 669, half a block from the plaza next to Casino Club. Delicious pasta, warm family atmosphere. *La Rueda*, Islas Malvinas 954, p 1. Excellent *parrilla*. Cheap fixed menu at *Leymi*, 25 de Mayo 1335. *La Nueva Piamontesa*, 24-hr grocery store at Belgrano y Mackinlay, T423620 (at the back), delivers food. Also try *Pope Pizzas*, Belgrano 383. Trendy **bar** *Epa!* on Rosalas just off the plaza.

For an authentic experience of Tierra del Fuego, **L** *Estancia Viamonte*, some 40 km southeast on the coast, T430861, www.estanciaviamonte.com Built in 1902 by pioneer Lucas Bridges, writer of *Uttermost Part of the Earth,* to protect the indigenous Ona peoples, this working *estancia* has simple and beautifully furnished rooms or a spacious cottage to let. Please reserve a week ahead, riding and trekking also arranged. Delicious meals extra.

Sleeping & eating
Book ahead, as there are few decent choices

Car hire: *Hertz Annie Millet* , Libertad 714, T426534, hertzriogrande@netcombbs.com.ar *Al Rent a Car International*, Belgrano 423, T430757, ai.rentcar@carletti.com.ar Also have 4WDs and *camionetas*. **Air** Airport 4 km west of town, T420600. Taxi US$2. To **Buenos**

Transport
Take passport when buying ticket

Aires, *AR* daily, 3½ hrs direct. **Buses** Buses leave from terminal , Elcano y Güemes, T420997, or from Tecni Austral's office Moyano 516, T430610. To **Porvenir**, Chile, 5 hrs, US$12, *Gesell*, T425611, Wed, Sun, 0800, passport and luggage control at San Sebastián. To **Punta Arenas**, Chile, via Punta Delgada, 10 hrs, *Pacheco*, Tue, Thu, Sat 0730, *Ghisoni* on other days but no bus Sun, US$20. To **Río Gallegos**, 3 times a week, US$18. To **Ushuaia**, *Tecni Austral* and *Líder*, 3-4 hrs, 2 daily, US$8. Also *Tolkeyen*, US$10.

Directory **Airline offices** *Aerolíneas Argentinas* , San Martín 607,T424467. **Banks** ATMs: 4 banks on San Martín between 100 and 300. Exchange is difficult: if coming from Chile, buy Argentine pesos there. **Communications** Post Office:Rivadavia 968. **Supermarkets** *La Nueva Piedmontesa*, see Eating, above. *Norte*, San Martín y Piedrabuena, good selection; also *La Anónima* on San Martín. **Tourist office** In hut on the plaza, at Rosales 350, T431324, rg-turismo@netcombbs.com.ar Mon-Fri 0900-2100, Sat 1000-1700.

Ushuaia and around

Phone code: 02901
Colour map 9, grid C2
Population: 44,976
234 km SW of Río Grande on new road via Paso Garibaldi

The most southerly town in Argentina and growing fast, Ushuaia is beautifully situated on the northern shore of the Beagle Channel, which is named after the ship in which Darwin sailed here in 1832. Its streets climb steeply towards snow-covered Cerro Martial and there are fine views over the Beagle Channel to the jagged peaks of Isla Navarino (Chile). First settled by missionary Thomas Bridges, whose son Lucas became a great defender of the indigenous peoples here, Ushuaia's fascinating history is still visible in its old buildings and at **Estancia Harberton**, 85 km west (see below). A penal colony for many years, the old prison, **Presidio**, Yaganes y Gob Paz, at the back of the Naval Base, houses the **Museo Marítimo**, with models and artefacts from seafaring days, and, in the cells, the **Museo Penitenciario**, which details the history of the prison. ■ *Mon-Sun 0900-2000, US$4 for foreigners.* **Museo del Fin del Mundo**, Maipú y Rivadavia, in the 1902 bank building, has small displays on indigenous peoples, missionaries and first settlers, as well as nearly all the birds of Tierra del Fuego (stuffed). Recommended. ■ *Daily 1000-1300, 1500-1930,US$ 1.50, students US$1, T421863.* The building also contains an excellent library with helpful staff. **Museo Yámana**, Rivadavia 56, fascinating scale models showing scenes of everyday life of indigenous peoples, also recommended. ■ *Daily 1000-2000 high season, otherwise closed lunchtime, US$1.50, T422874, www.tierradelfuego.org.ar/mundoyamana*

Parque Nacional Tierra del Fuego, just outside Ushuaia, is easily accessible; full details below. **Tren del Fin del Mundo** is the world's southernmost steam train, running new locomotives and carriages on track first laid by prisoners to carry wood to Ushuaia. A totally touristy experience with relentless commentary in English and Spanish, 50-minute ride from the Fin del Mundo station, 8 km west of Ushuaia, into Tierra del Fuego National Park (one way of starting a hike). ■ *4 departures daily in summer, 1 in winter. US$20 tourist, US$24 1st class return, plus US$4 park entrance and US$2 for bus to the station. Tickets at station, or from* Tranex *kiosk in the port, T431600, www.trendelfindelmundo.com.ar Sit on left outbound for the best views.*

Cerro Martial, about 7 km behind the town, offers fine views down the Beagle Channel and to the north. Take a chairlift (*aerosilla*) to the top, daily 1000-1800, US$2.20. To reach the chairlift, follow Magallanes out of town, allow 1½ hours. *Lautaro* and *Kaupen* run minibus services from the corner of Maipú and Roca, several departures daily in summer, US$2-4 return. From the top you can walk 90 minutes to **Glaciar Martial**. Splendid tea shop, *refugio* and *cabañas* at the Cerro. Excursions can also be made to **Lagos Fagnano** and **Escondido**.

The **Estancia Harberton**, the oldest on the island and run by descendents of British missionary, Thomas Bridges, whose family protected the indigenous peoples here, is 85 km from Ushuaia on Ruta J. It's a beautiful place, offering guided walks (US$3) through protected forest and delicious teas or lunch (reserve ahead), in the *Manacatush casa de té* overlooking the bay(T422742). The impressive **Museo Akatushún** has skeletons of South American sea mammals, the result of 23 years' scientific investigation in Tierra del Fuego, with excellent tours in English. You can camp free, with permission from the owners, or stay in cottages (see below). ■ *Daily, except Christmas, 1 Jan and Easter. Museum entrance US$2, T422742,* estanciaharberton@tierradelfuego.org.ar Access is from a good unpaved road which branches off Ruta 3, 40 km east of Ushuaia and runs 25 km through forest before the open country around Harberton; marvellous views, about 2 hours (no petrol outside of Ushuaia and Tolhuin). Boat trips to Harberton, twice weekly in summer, allow 2 hours on the estancia. Regular daily minibus service with *Bella Vista* and *Lautaro*, from Maipú and Juana Fadul, US$14 return.

Sea trips from Ushuaia are highly recommended, though the Beagle Channel can be very rough. These can be booked through most agencies, and leave from the *Muelle Turístico*. Trip to the sea lion colony at Isla de los Lobos, Isla de los Pájaros and Les Eclaireurs lighthouse: 2½ hours on catamaran, US$22, 4½-5 hours on the *Patagonian Adventure*, US$23 including 1 hour trekking on Bridges island and hot drink. To Isla de los Lobos, Isla de los Pájaros, Les Eclaireurs lighthouse, and the Isla Martillo penguin colony: 4½ hours on charming old boat *Barracuda*, US$18. To Isla de los Lobos, Isla de los Pájaros, Isla Martillo penguin colony, Les Eclaireurs light-house and Estancia Harberton: 8 hours round trip on catamaran, US$40, includes packed lunch Tuesday, Thursday, Saturday.

LL *Las Hayas*, Camino Glaciar Martial, Km 3, T430710, www.lashayas.com.ar Ushuaia's only 5 star, spectacular setting high up on the mountain, breakfast included, pool, sauna, gym, sports, shuttle from town and transfer from airport. Recommended. **B** *Cabo San Diego*, 25 de Mayo 368, T435600, www.cabosandiego.com.ar Apart-hotel with spacious apartments, equipped for cooking, comfortable. **B** *Canal Beagle*, Maipú y 25 de Mayo, T421117, hotelcanalbo@uolsinectis.com.ar Good value ACA hotel (discounts for members), clear views over the channel, reasonably priced restaurant. **B** *Cap Polonio*, San Martín 748, T422140, www.hotel cappolonia.com.ar Smart, central, modern, comfortable, TV, internet, restaurant/café *Marcopolo*, expensive (tango show Fri 2200). **B** *César*, San Martín 753, T421460, F432721, www.hotelcesarhostal.com.ar Central, often booked by groups, reasonable value, simple rooms, breakfast included. **B** *Las Lengas*, Florencia 1722, T423366 , laslengas@tierradelfuego.org.ar Superb setting. **B** *Hostal Malvinas*, Gob Deloqui 615, T/F422626, hotel malvinas@arnet.com.ar Comfortable, includes small breakfast, free tea and coffee, owner is sailing expert. **C** *Hostería Posada Fin del Mundo*, Valdez 281, T437345, posadafindelmundo@infovia.com.ar Family atmosphere, good value. **D** *Albergue Kayen*, Gob Paz 1410, T431497, www.alberguekayen.com.ar Good value, fine views over channel, shared bath, self service breakfast. **D** *B&B Nahuel*, 25 de Mayo 440, T423068, byb_nahuel@ yahoo.com.ar Views over channel, comfortable, great value. Recommended. **D** pp *El Nido de Cóndores*, Gob.Campos 795, T437753, www.companiadeguias.com.ar Simple rooms with shared bath, breakfast, relaxing café below, owners are walking guides (see *Compañía de Guías de Patagonia* in Tour operators). **E** pp *Amanecer de la Bahía* , Magallanes 594, T424405, www.ushuaiahostel.com Light, spacious, shared rooms for 4 and 6, also double and triples, internet, kitchen facilities, breakfast, discounts for students and members of Argentina Hostel Club. **F** pp *Albergue Cruz del Sur*, Deloqui 636, T423110, www.xdel sur.com.ar Relaxed, small, quiet library, kitchen. **F** pp *Los Troncos*, Gob Paz 1344, T/F421895. Family home, shared bath, use of kitchen, cable TV, with breakfast. **F** pp *Albergue Refugio de Mochilero*, 25 de Mayo 241, T436129, www.refugiodelmochilero.netfirms.com Dormitories with shared bath, kitchen facilities.

Accommodation in private homes Best of all is **D** *Galeazzi-Basily*, Gdor Valdez 323, T423213, fbasily@quasarlab.com.ar Beautiful family home, incredible welcome, in pleasant area 5 blocks from centre, breakfast included. Also **F** 5-bed *cabaña* in garden. Recommended. **F** pp *Familia Velásquez*, Juana Fadul 361, T421719. Basic rooms in cosy house, very cheap.

At Lago Escondido A *Hostería Petrel*, RN 3, Km 3186, T02901-433569, hpetrel@infovia.com.ar Secluded position in forest on the fjord-like lake, 50 km from Ushuaia towards Río Grande. Decent rooms with bath, good restaurant overlooking the lake, and tiny basic *cabañas*. Idyllic but pricey. 18 km from Ushuaia is **F** pp *Refugio Solar del Bosque*, RN3, Km 3020, T421228, solarbosque@tierradelfuego.org.ar A basic hostel for walkers.

Sleeping
■ *on map*
The tourist office has a comprehensive list of all officially registered accommodation and will help with rooms in private homes, campsites etc

Many people offer rooms in private houses at the airport

Argentina

At Lago Fagnano D *Cabañas Khami*, T02964-156 11243, T/F422296, www.cabaniaskhami.com.ar Well-equipped, rustic cabins, good value with linen. **D** *Parador Kawi Shiken*, 4 km south of Tolhuin on RN3, Km 2940, T156 11505, www.hotelguia. com/ hoteles/kawi-shiken/ Rustic, 3 rooms, shared bath, *salón de té* and restaurant, horse riding.

At Harberton A pp *Estancia Harberton*, T422742, estanciaharberton@tierradel fuego.org.ar Two restored buildings on the lakeside, simple, wonderful views, heating.

Camping On eastern edge of town is: *Camping Río Pipo*, Ushuaia Rugby Club (Km 4) US$2.50 pp, friendly owners, all facilities. On Ruta 3 heading for Río Grande: *Camping del Solar del Bosque* (Km 18), T421228, US$2.50 pp, hot showers. *Camping Haruwen*, in the Haruwen Winter Sports complex (Km 33), T/F424058, US$2.50 per tent, electricity, shop, bar, restaurant. Inside the Parque Nacional Tierra del Fuego (entry fee US$4) is *Camping Lago Roca*, 21 km from Ushuaia, by forested shore of Lago Roca, a beautiful site with good facilities, reached by bus Jan-Feb, expensive small shop, cafetería. There are also various sites with no facilities, eg: *Bahia Ensenada Camping* 16 km from Ushuaia; *Camping Las Bandurrias* and *Camping Laguna Verde*, both 20 km from Ushuaia.

Eating
● *on map*
Lots of restaurants along San Martín and Maipú
Ask around for currently available seafood, especially centolla (king crab) and cholga (giant mussels)

Expensive: Best restaurant in town is *Kaupé*, Roca 470 y Magallanes. Dishes, eg king crab, meat. **Mid-range**: *Los Pioneros, Bodegón Fueguino*, San Martín 859. Unusual *cazuelas, picadas* and dips in a renovated 1896 house. *El Rancho*, San Martín y Rivadavia. *Parrilla* with live music, popular with tourists. *Tante Sara Pizzas and Pastas*, San Martín 165. Bright and functional, tasty filling food. *Tía Elvira*, Maipú 349. Excellent seafood. *Volver*, Maipú 37. Delicious seafood in atmospheric 1898 house, with ancient newspaper all over the walls. **Cheap**: *Bar Ideal*, San Martín 393. Popular travellers' haunt. *El Náutico*, Maipú y Belgrano. For good lunch, US$4 set menu, on the waterfront. Of the two good *tenedor libres, Parrilla La Rueda*, San Martín y Rivadavia, is the best, great range. *La Estancia*, San Martín in the next block, is also cheery and good value. Both are packed in high season. *Moustaccio*, San Martín y Gdor Godoy. Long established, good for cheap fish. Of the **cafés** on San Martín, *Café Tante Sarah*, Fadul y San Martin opposite the tourist office, is best. Smart, good coffee, tasty sandwiches. Best fresh takeaway sandwiches at *La Baguette*, Don Bosco y San Martín, also delicious *empanadas* and *facturas* (pastries). Good places for a late night drink: *Lennon Pub*, on Maipú, with live music, and *U! Bar*, San Martín, trendy orange plastic sub-aquatic feel.

Ushuaia

Sleeping
1 Albergue Cruz del Sur
2 Albergue Kayen
3 Albergue Refugio de Mochilero
4 Amanecer la Bahía
5 B&B Nahuel
6 Cabo San Diego
7 Canal Beagle
8 Cap Polonio & Marcopolo Restaurant
9 César
10 El Nido de Cóndores
11 Familia Velásquez
12 Galeazzi-Basily
13 Hostal Malvinas
14 Hostería Posada Fin del Mundo

0 metres 200
0 yards 200

Lots of souvenir shops on San Martín and several offering good quality leather and silver ware. *World's End* , San Martín y Fadul, selection of books on the area, as well as T shirts and key rings. *Vraie* sells all kinds of clothes, *Atlántico Sur* is the (not especially cheap) duty free shop. *Popper*, opposite, sells outdoor clothes, camping and fishing gear. **Supermarkets** The *Norte*, 12 de Octubre y Karukinka, is good for take-away freshly-made food, has a fast-food diner.

Shopping
Ushuaia's tax free status doesn't produce as many bargains as you might hope

Sports Centre on Malvinas Argentinas on west side of town (close to seafront). **Fishing**: trout. Season 1 Nov-31 Mar, licences US$10 per week, US$5 per day. Contact **Asociación de Caza y Pesca** at Maipú y 9 de Julio, which has a small museum. **Skiing**, **hiking**, **climbing**: contact **Club Andino**, Fadul 50. **Skiing**: Ushuaia is becoming popular as a winter resort with several centres for skiing, snowboarding and husky sledging. By far the best is *Cerro Castor* complex, 27 km from town, T156 05595 www.cerrocastor.com 22 km of pistes, a vertical drop of 760 m and powder snow. Attractive centre with complete equipment rental for snowboarding and snowshoeing. Ski pass US$23 per day. Excellent cross country skiing, with various new centres at 19-22 km east of Ushuaia, of which *Tierra Mayor*, 21km from town T2901-437454, is recommended. In a beautiful wide valley between steep-sided mountains, offering half and full day excursions on sledges with huskies for hire, as well as cross country skiing and snowshoeing. Equipment hire and restaurant.

Sport & activities

All agencies charge the same fees for excursions; ask tourist office for a complete list: Tierra del Fuego National Park, 4 hrs, US$12 (entry fee US$4 extra); Lagos Escondido and Fagnano, 8 hrs, US$22 with lunch. With 3 or 4 people it might be worth hiring a *remise* taxi. *All Patagonia*, Juana Fadul 26, T430725, F430707, allpat@satlink.com Trekking, ice climbing, and tours. *Canal Fun & Nature*, Rivadavia 82, T437610, www.canalfun.com Huge range of activities, riding, 4WD excursions. Recommended. *Compañía de Guías de Patagonia* at *El Nido de los Cóndores*, Gob Campos 783, T432642, www.companiadeguias.com.ar The best agency for walking guides, expeditions for all levels, ice climbing (training provided), US$140 pp per day, including all equipment, transport. Recommended. *Rumbo Sur*, San Martín 350, T421139, www.rumbosur.com.ar Flights, buses, conventional tours, plus Antarctic expeditions, mid-Nov to mid-Mar (last minute reductions only available from Argentina, around US$2500 pp), English spoken. *Tolkar*, Roca 157, T431412, www.tolkarturismo.com.ar Flights, bus tickets to

Tour operators
Lots of companies now offer imaginative adventure tourism expeditions

Argentina

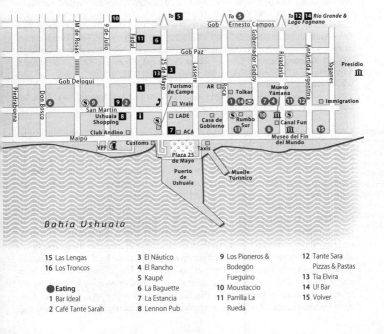

15 Las Lengas	3 El Náutico	9 Los Pioneros &	12 Tante Sara
16 Los Troncos	4 El Rancho	Bodegón	Pizzas & Pastas
	5 Kaupé	Fueguino	13 Tía Elvira
● **Eating**	6 La Baguette	10 Moustaccio	14 U! Bar
1 Bar Ideal	7 La Estancia	11 Parrilla La	15 Volver
2 Café Tante Sarah	8 Lennon Pub	Rueda	

Punta Arenas and Río Gallegos, conventional and adventure tourism, mountain biking to Lago Fagnano. *Travel Lab*, San Martín y 9 de Julio, T436555, travellabush@ speedy.com.ar Tren del Fin del Mundo, unconventional tours, mountain biking, trekking etc, English and French spoken, helpful. *Turismo de Campo*, 25 de Mayo 34, T/F437351, www.turismo decampo.com.ar Adventure tourism, English/French speaking guides, boat and trekking trips in the National Park, bird watching, horse riding, sailing.

Transport | **Car hire**: Most companies charge the same, around US$45 per day including insurance and 150 km per day.

Book ahead in summer; flights fill up fast. In winter flights often delayed.

Air Taxi to airport US$2.50 (no bus). Schedules tend to change from season to season. Airport tourist information T423970. To **Buenos Aires**, 4 hrs, **El Calafate**, 2 hrs, both with *AR* and *LADE*. Flights are usually available to **Río Gallegos**, 1 hr, and **Río Grande**, 1 hr, several a week, but check with agents. To **Punta Arenas**, 1 hr, *Aerovías DAP*.

Passport needed when booking international bus tickets

Buses To **Río Grande**, 3 hrs, *Tecni Austral*, book through *Tolkar* (address above), and *Líder* (Gob Paz 921, T436421), both US$8, 2 a day, and *Tolkeyen* (Maipú 237, T437073, tolkeyen@tierradelfuego.org.ar), US$10. To **Punta Arenas**, *Tecni Austral*, Mon, Wed, Fri 0600, and *Tolkeyen*, Tue, Thu, Sat, 0630, 12 hrs, US$30, via Punta Delgada ferry (15 mins' crossing). No through services to Río Gallegos. Go to Río Grande, then 8-10 hrs. Sometimes possible to book whole ticket in Ushuaia at *Tolkar*. **Taxi** *Tienda León*, San Martín 995, T422222, reliable.

Buses always booked up Dec-Mar; buy your ticket to leave as soon as you arrive

Boats To Puerto Williams (Chile) No regular sailings. Yachts might carry charter passengers in summer, returning the same day, fares US$25-35 one way. Enquire at *AIASN* agency for cruise through Beagle Channel. Spectacular luxury cruises around Cape Horn via Puerto Williams on the *Mare Australis* are operated by the Chilean company, *Cruceros Australis*, 7/8 days, US$1,260 (Carlos Pellegrini 989, p 6, Buenos Aires, T011-4325 4000, www.australis.com/flyer/). **To Antarctica**: Ushuaia is the starting point for a number of expeditions. Ask *Rumbo Sur, All Patagonia, Turismo de Campo* for itineraries and advice. Tickets are cheaper if bought here, than if booked in advance; weekly departures.

Directory | **Airline offices** *Aerolíneas Argentinas*, Roca 116, T421218. *Aerovías DAP*, 25 de Mayo 64, T431110. *LADE*, San Martín 542, shop 5, T/F421123. **Banks** Banks open 1000-1500 (in summer). ATMs are plentiful all along San Martín, using credit cards is easiest, changing TCs is difficult and expensive. *Banco de Tierra del Fuego*, San Martín 396, *Agencia de Cambio Thaler*, San Martín 877, also open weekends, 1000-1300, 1700-2030, and at *Oro Verde*, 25 de Mayo 50, also open Sat 1000-1300. **Communications Internet**: Many broadband cyber cafés and *locutorios* along San Martín. **Post Office**: San Martín y Godoy, Mon-Fri 0900-1300 and 1700-1900, Sat 0900-1300. **Telephone**: *Locutorios* all along San Martín. **Embassies and consulates** Chile, Malvinas Argentinas y Jainen, Casilla 21, T421279. Germany, Rosas 516. Italy, Yaganes 75. **Tourist offices** San Martín 674, esq Fadul, T/F432000., www.tierradelfuego.org.ar 'Best in Argentina', very helpful English speaking staff, who will find you accommodation in summer. Information available in English, French, German and Dutch. Mon-Fri 0800-2200, Sat, Sun and holidays 0900-2000. **Tierra del Fuego National Park Office**, San Martín 1395, T421315, has a small map but not much information.

Parque Nacional Tierra del Fuego

Even in the summer the climate can often be cold, damp and unpredictable, and remember that days are short in winter here

Covering 63,000 ha of mountains, lakes, rivers and deep valleys, this small but beautiful park stretches west to the Chilean border and north to Lago Fagnano, though large areas have been closed to tourists. Public access is allowed from the park entrance 12 km west of Ushuaia, where you'll be given a basic map with marked walks. 1) **Senda Costera**, 6.5 km, 3 hours each way. Along the shore from Ensenada (where boat trips start). From Lago Roca, continue along to Bahía Lapataia, crossing the broad green river. 2) **Sendo Hito XXIV**, along Lago Roca, 4 km, 90 minutes one way, lots of bird life. 3) **Cerro Guanaco**, 4 km, 4 hours one way. Challenging hike up through forest to splendid views. Campsite in a good spot at Lago Roca, with *confitería*, it's best to go early morning or afternoon to avoid the tour buses. You'll see geese, the torrent duck, Magellanic woodpeckers and austral parakeets. There are no legal crossing points to Chile. Helpful *guardeparque* (ranger) at Lago Roca. ■ *Entry US$4. In summer buses and minibuses, US$5 return to Lago Roca run by several companies, leaving from the tourist pier at Maipú y Roca. Tourist office has details and map of park, with walks. Topographical maps are sold at* Oficina Antárctica, *Maipú y Laserre. See above for Camping.*

Argentina (side margin)

Bolivia

Bolivia

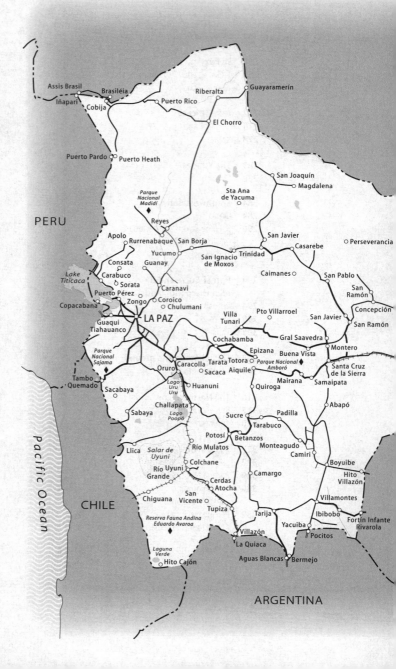

PERU

PACIFIC Ocean

CHILE

ARGENTINA

Assis Brasil
Iñapari
Brasiléia
Cobija
Puerto Rico
Riberalta
Guayaramerín
El Chorro
Puerto Pardo
Puerto Heath
San Joaquín
Magdalena
Parque Nacional Madidi
Sta Ana de Yacuma
Reyes
Apolo
Rurrenabaque
San Borja
San Javier
Casarebe
Perseverancia
Yucumo
Consata
Guanay
San Ignacio de Moxos
Trinidad
Caimanes
San Pablo
Lake Titicaca
Carabuco
Sorata
Caranavi
San Ramón
Puerto Pérez
Zongo
Coroico
Chulumani
Concepción
Copacabana
Guaqui
Tiahauanco
LA PAZ
Villa Tunari
Pto Villarroel
San Javier
San Ramón
Parque Nacional Sajama
Oruro
Caracolla
Tarata
Sacaca
Cochabamba
Epizana
Totora
Aiquile
Parque Nacional Amboró
Gral Saavedra
Buena Vista
Montero
Santa Cruz de la Sierra
Tambo Quemado
Sacabaya
Lago Uru Uru
Huanuni
Quiroga
Mairana
Samaipata
Challapata
Lago Poopó
Sucre
Padilla
Abapó
Sabaya
Potosí
Betanzos
Tarabuco
Llica
Salar de Uyuni
Río Mulatos
Monteagudo
Camiri
Colchane
Boyuibe
Río Uyuni Grande
Cerdas
Atocha
Camargo
Hito Villazón
Chiguana
San Vicente
Tupiza
Reserva Fauna Andina Eduardo Avaroa
Tarija
Villamontes
Ibibobo
Fortín Infante Rivarola
Yacuiba
Pocitos
Laguna Verde
Hito Cajón
Villazón
La Quiaca
Aguas Blancas
Bermejo

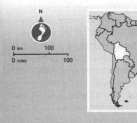

BRAZIL

Baia Grande

San Ignacio de Velasco

San Matías

Santa Ana

San Miguel

San Rafael

San José de Chiquitos

Quijarro/ Puerto Suárez Corumbá

Santiago

PARAGUAY

Bolivia

On Bolivia's Altiplano you are so far up it will make your head spin. Every day, the highest capital in the world transforms itself from a melée of Indian markets and modern business into a canyon of glittering stars as the lights come on at nightfall. On the largest salt flat on earth, a vast blinding-white expanse, you lose track of what is land and what is sky. In Bolivia, you learn to expect the unexpected. At La Diablada festival in Oruro dancers wear masks of the scariest monsters you could ever dream. To visit the mines at Potosí, once the silver lode for the Spanish Empire, you buy dynamite and coca leaves as presents for the labourers. Flamingoes feed from red and green lakes rimmed by volcanoes. Dalí-esque rock structures dot the Altiplano. Waterfalls crash down on vehicles on one of the most dangerous roads in the world. Turn the corner and you can swim with pink river dolphins in jungle waters, fish for piranhas in the pampas and fill your bags with everything from the beautiful autumnal colours of the textiles, to packs of dried llama foetuses, which protect homes from evil spirits.

Essentials

Planning your trip

Where to go **La Paz** is the best place to start, as many international flights land here and it is closest to the well-travelled overland routes from Peru and Chile. The capital is easy to explore, but you do need to adjust to the altitude, which will leave you temporarily breathless. La Paz is, after all, the highest capital city in the world. There are some good museums and churches, and an Indian market area. Daytrips include the pre-Inca city of **Tiahuanaco**, which is close to the beautiful **Lake Titicaca**. To appreciate the lake, a night or more on its shores is recommended. Northeast of La Paz, over the cordillera, are the **Yungas**, deep subtropical valleys, rich in vegetation, where a town like **Coroico** can provide welcome relief from the rigours of the Altiplano. Equally pleasant and lower than La Paz is **Sorata**, a good base for trekking and climbing.

South of La Paz is the mining city of **Oruro**, which hosts one of the most famous Latin American carnival celebrations, *La Diablada*, usually held in mid-to-late February. Southeast are the colonial cities of **Potosí**, where Spain garnered much of its imperial wealth from abundant silver deposits and present-day miners scour the mountain for more meagre pickings, and **Sucre**, Bolivia's official capital, with an array of fine buildings. **Uyuni**, further south again, is the jumping-off place for trips into stunning salt flats to see coloured lakes, flamingoes and horizons of volcanoes. **Tarija**, southeast of Potosí, is best known for its fruits and wine, dinosaur remains and Mediterranean climate (and thus its nickname, "the Andalucía of Bolivia"). Continuing beyond here you come to the Argentine border.

East of La Paz is **Cochabamba**, Bolivia's third largest city and centre of one of the country's main agricultural zones. The **Parque Nacional Toro Toro**, with its dinosaur tracks, rock paintings, canyons and waterfalls, is a tough but stunning excursion. Further east is **Santa Cruz**, now the country's most economically important (and largest) city, from where you can visit **Amboró**, **Noel Kempff Mercado** and other national parks, as well as follow in the footsteps of Che Guevara, take in **Samaipata**, the country's second most important archaeological site, see the beautiful **Jesuit missions** of the Chiquitanía, or take the aptly nicknamed "death train" to Corumbá in Brazil. Like its eastern neighbour, Bolivia has a **Pantanal** wetland, just now opening up to tourism, with opportunities to see a magnificent range of wildlife.

From La Paz you can fly into the Beni region, in the heart of the Bolivian Amazon. **Rurrenabaque** is the chief destination and starting point for the fantastic Chalalán Ecolodge in the **Parque Nacional Madidi**, which claims a greater bio-diversity than anywhere else on earth. Outside of Rurrenabaque, the further north you go the fewer tourists you will meet. April to October are the months to visit, although insects are year-round tenants.

When to go The most popular season for visitors is June-August, while some of the best festivals, e.g., Carnival and Holy Week, fall during the wet season, which is considered to be from December to March. The country has four climatic zones: (1) The Puna and Altiplano; average temperature, 10° C, but above 4,000 m may drop as low as -25° C at night in June-August. By day, the tropical sun raises temperatures to above 20° C. Rainfall on the northern Altiplano is 400 to 700 mm, much less further south. Little rain falls upon the western plateau between May and November, but the rest of the year can be wet. (2) The Yungas north of La Paz and Cochabamba, among the spurs of the Cordillera; altitude, 750-1,500 m; average temperature, 24° C. (3) The Valles, or high valleys and basins gouged out by the rivers of the Puna; average temperature, 19° C. Rainfall in the Yungas valleys is from 700 to 800 mm a year, with high humidity. (4) The tropical lowlands; altitude between 150 m and 750 m; rainfall is high but seasonal (heaviest November-March, but can fall at any season); large areas suffer from alternate flooding and drought. The climate is hot, ranging from 23° to 25° C in the south and to 30° C in the north. Occasional cold, dust-laden winds from the south, the *surazos*, lower the temperature considerably.

Finding out more

Tourism is under the control of the Dirección Nacional De Turismo, Edificio Ballivián, piso 18, Calle Mercado, La Paz, T236 7463/4, F237 4630. The Viceministerio de Turismo is at Avenida

Mcal Santa Cruz, Palacio de Comunicaciones, piso 16, La Paz, T236 7464, www.mcei.gov.bo/
web_mcei/Turismo/turismo.htm See under each city for addresses of tourist offices. For
national parks information: Sistema Nacional de Areas Protegidas, Edif El Cóndor, piso 13-
15, Batallón Coloradas 24, La Paz, T231 6077, F231 6230.

Tourism, culture and general information www.bolivia.com (in Spanish), for news, **Websites**
entertainment, tourism and information on regions.
www.boliviaweb.com (in English) has much general and travel-related information on
the entire country, with links to several related sites.
www.gorp.com/gorp/location/latamer/bolivia/basic_b.htm has an overview of the
country, with more detailed info on Amboró, Las Yungas, Choro Trail and jungle trips.
www.wtgonline.com/data/bol/bol.asp Information on travel, pre-Columbian cultures,
folk dances, festivals, traditional medicine and more.
www.boliviangeographic.com is an on-line magazine with good articles.
www.lanic.utexas.edu/la/sa/Bolivia/ is an excellent database on various topics
indigenous to Bolivia, maintained by the University of Texas, USA.
www.andes.org/ Quechua language lessons, music, songs, poems, stories and resources.
www.bolivianstudies.org Site of the *Bolivian Studies Association* with a journal, newsletter,
database and travellers' notes.
www.megalink.com For links to other Bolivian sites. www.boliviabiz.com on doing
business in Bolivia.

Sport and activities www.geocities.com/yosemite/gorge/1177/Information on
climbing, mountaineering and parapenting, from *Club de Montañismo Halcones* of Oruro.

Wildlife and nature www.megalink.com/fobomade/ Website of the *Foro Boliviano
sobre Medio Ambiente y Desarrollo*. For environmental issues, in Spanish.
www.bolivia-industry.com/sia/bolivia/datosgen/Areas.html,
www.eldiario.net/bolivia/medioamb and
www.ciedperu.org/agualtiplano/areas/apbolivia.htm are three sites with
information on a variety of national parks, in Spanish.

Lidema, Ecuador 2131, Sopocachi, La Paz, Casilla 11237, T241 9393, League for Environmental **Voluntary work**
Defence (Liga de Defensa del Medio Ambiente) is the umbrella organization for 27 NGOs
around the country, working in environmental areas, development, education, etc. Enquire
here for voluntary work opportunities. See also *Inti Wara Yassi* animal rescue centre, page 314.

Before you travel

A passport only is needed for citizens of almost all Western European countries, Israel, Japan, **Visas &**
North and South American countries (except Venezuela), South Africa, Australia and New **immigration**
Zealand. Irish citizens are advised to check with a Bolivian embassy before leaving home as, at
the time of writing, the Vice-Ministry of Tourism website said both that they did, and did not
require a visa. Many are granted 90 days on entry, others are entitled to only 30 (eg Australia,
Canada, the Czech Republic, Netherlands, Japan, New Zealand, South Africa). Extensions can
be easily arranged at immigration. Among those countries whose nationals require a visa and
must gain authorization from the Bolivian Ministry of Foreign Affairs (can take 3-5 weeks) are:
Bosnia, China, Croatia, India, Indonesia, Iran, Iraq, Laos, Lebanon, Libya, Malaysia, North Korea,
Palestine, Singapore, Slovenia, Syria, Taiwan, Thailand, Vietnam, Yemen and Yugoslavia, also
nationals of most African countries, the rest of Asia and former Soviet Union countries. Those
countries which require a visa but not authorisation include: Bangladesh, Cuba, Egypt, Haiti,
Hungary, Jordan, South Korea, Kuwait, Liechtenstein, Malta, Mexico, Oman, Pakistan, Panama,
Romania, Russia, Saudi Arabia, Tunisia and Venezuela. This takes 1-2 working days. The cost of
a visa varies from nationality to nationality. Visas (or permit to stay) can be renewed at any
migración office for up to 90 days at no cost. After this time renewal is at the discretion of the
immigration officer. If refused, leave the country and return. There should be a statutory 72

Bolivia

▶ *Bolivian embassies and consulates*

Belgium, *Avenue Louise N 176 Boite 6, 1050 Brussels, T2-647 2718*

Canada, *130 Albert Street, Suite 416, Ottowa, ON K1P 5G4, T613-236 5730, bolcan@iosphere.net*

France, *12 avenue Du President Kennedy, 75016 Paris 16, T01-4224 9344*

Germany, *Wichmannstrasse 6, 10787 Berlin, T263 9150, embolberlin@t-online.de/ or Konstantinstrasse 16, D5300, Bonn 2 – Germany T0228-362038*

Israel, *PO Box 2833, 90805 Mevasseret Zion, CPZ823, T2- 533 5195, F2-533 5196*

Italy, *Via Brenta 2/A, int18, 00198 Rome, T6-884 1001, embabolivia@cdc.it*

Japan, *No 38 Kowa Building, room 804, Nishi Azabu 4-12-24, Minato-Ku, Tokyo 106-0031, T3-3499 5441, emboltk@interlink.or.jp*

Netherlands, *Nassaulaan 5 2514 JS La Haya (The Hague), T70-361 6707*

Spain, *Velázquez 20, 7° piso, 28001 Madrid, T91-578 0835, EMBASSYboliviaespana@mad.servicom.es*

Sweden, *Södra Kungsvägen 60, 18132 Lidingö, Stockholm, T8-731 5830, em.bolivia@lidingo.mail.telia.com*

Switzerland, *7bis, rue du Valais, 1202 Geneva, T731 2725, mission.bolivia@itu.ch*

UK, *106 Eaton Square, London SW1 9AD, T0207-235 4248, F0207-235 1286, 100746.1347@compuserve.com*

USA, *3014 Massachusetts Avenue NW, Washington DC 20008, T202-483 4410, or 211 East 43 Road Street, Suite 702 New York, NY 10017, T212-499 7401, bolembus@erola.com*

hours period outside Bolivia before renewing a visa but 24 hours is usually acceptable. On arrival ensure that visas and passports are stamped with the same, correct date of entry or this can lead to 'fines' later. If you outstay your visa the current fine is US$1.50 per day. Business visitors (unless passing through as tourists) are required to obtain a visa from a Bolivian consulate. This costs £35 (or equivalent); applicants should check all requirements and regulations on length of stay and extensions in advance.

Duty-free 200 cigarettes, 50 cigars and 450 g tobacco. One bottle of unopened alcoholic drink.

Vaccinations Inoculate against typhoid. Visitors should have yellow fever vaccination when visiting Santa Cruz or the Oriente, although this is rarely asked for. A yellow fever vaccination certificate, at least 10 days old, is officially required for leaving and entering the country. Hepatitis and Chagas' Disease are widespread.

What to take **Clothing** Visitors to the Altiplano and the Puna should not underestimate the cold at night and take plenty of warm clothing. Tropical clothing will be needed for the Amazon and Eastern Lowlands. **NB** Contact lens solution is hard to find.

Money

Currency
Exchange rate in July 2003; US$1 = Bs 8.05

The unit of currency is the boliviano (Bs), divided into 100 centavos. There are notes for 200, 100, 50, 20, 10 and 5 bolivianos, and 5, 2 and 1 boliviano coins, as well as 50, 20 and 10 centavos. Bolivianos are often referred to as pesos; expensive items, including hotel rooms, are often quoted in dollars. When changing money, try to get notes in small denominations. Bs 100 notes are very difficult to change in La Paz and impossible elsewhere. Change is often given in forms other than money: eg, cigarettes, sweets, or razor blades. Watch out for forged currency, especially dollars (US$100 notes in particular) and Chilean pesos. It is difficult to buy dollars at points of exit when leaving or to change bolivianos in other countries. Establishments which change travellers' cheques are given in the text; outside major cities it can be impossible. Changing US$ cash presents no problems anywhere. It is not worth trying to change other currencies. All the larger *casas de cambio* will give US$ cash in exchange for travellers' cheques, usually with a commission. If arriving on Fri night, bring bolivianos or US dollars cash as it is difficult to change travellers' cheques at the weekend (in La Paz, try *El Lobo* restaurant, usually changes TCs at any time, good rates, or *Hotel Gloria*, good rates for most western currencies).

Credit/debit cards are commonly used in most cities to obtain cash. American Express is not as useful as Visa, or, to a lesser extent, MasterCard. In all cities and large towns there are plenty of 24-hour cash machines (ATMs). Those displaying the *Enlace* sign are the best, accepting both Visa, Visa Electron and MasterCard (and therefore pretty much every foreign card). You can draw US dollars or bolivianos. *Enlace* has a toll-free number for information about ATMs, 0800 3060. RedBank ATMs allow Visa holders to take out bolivianos or dollars, but MasterCard holders only bolivianos.

Credit/debit cards
For credit card purchases an extra charge, up to 10%, may be made

Bolivia is cheaper to visit than most neighbouring countries. Food, accommodation and transport are all cheap, though rents, appliances, some clothing, and especially toilet goods and medicines are relatively expensive. Budget travellers can get by on US$25-30 per person per day for two travelling together. A basic hotel costs as little as $5 per person, breakfast US$1-2, and a set lunch (*almuerzo*) costs around US$1.50-2.50.

Cost of travelling

Getting there

From Europe: fly to Lima, Rio de Janeiro, São Paulo or Buenos Aires for connections, or via Miami. **From North America**: *American Airlines* and *LAB* from Miami daily to La Paz with a continuing flight to Santa Cruz. Also *Varig*. From other North American cities, connect in Miami. **Within South America**: flights to Santa Cruz from all other South American capitals except those of Ecuador and Uruguay, as well as Rio de Janeiro and São Paulo in Brazil. There are also two Cusco-La Paz flights a week (*LAB*) and daily flights from Arica and Iquique, Chile, besides those from Santiago. Many international flights call at Cochabamba as well as Santa Cruz.

Air

From Peru: there are three overland routes from Puno (see page 277). **From Chile**: there are routes from Ollagüe to Uyuni (see page 290), from Arica to La Paz via Tambo Quemado or Visviri (see page 288). **From Argentina**: from Salta-Jujuy-La Quiaca to Potosí or Tarija, or from Salta via Bermejo or Yacuiba to Tarija or Santa Cruz, though these are dry weather only. **To Paraguay**: apart from the journey described on page 335 (also taken by Santa Cruz-Asunción buses), an alternative way of getting to Paraguay is to travel by bus to Salta or Orán (**Argentina**), then on to Asunción via Resistencia (**Argentina**). Travel to Paraguay at any time is problematic and roads are impassable during the rainy season.

Road

Touching down

A departure tax of US$25, payable in dollars or bolivianos, cash only, is levied on leaving by air. On internal flights an airport tax of US$2.25 must be paid. Tax on airline tickets 14.9%.

Airport taxes

Up to 10% in restaurants; in all other cases a tip is given in recognition of a service provided, eg, to a taxi driver who has been helpful (an extra Bs 0.50-1), to someone who has looked after a car or carried bags (usual tip Bs 0.50-1).

Tipping

Since 2001, civil disturbance in Bolivia has involved strikes and demonstrations in major cities, especially Cochabamba, and many road blocks throughout the country, some lasting a few hours, others weeks. Try to be flexible in your travel plans if you encounter such disruptions and make the most of the attractions where you are staying if overland transport is not running. The procedure for reporting a robbery is to go to the Departamento de Criminalística, or the office for stolen property, in the town where the theft took place. Purchase official paper from the police for them to write the report, then, with patience and politeness, you may get a report costing between US$1.30 and US$5.25. In the coca-growing territory around Villa Tunari (see page 314) the police advise not to stray from the main road. Violence between the *cocaleros* and military has increased since Sánchez de Lozada's re-election and although foreigners are not usually targeted, those from countries identified with anti-coca policies (eg USA) should be careful.

Safety
Also see warning under Rurrenabaque, page 318

Bolivia

Bolivia

▶ *Touching down*

Business hours *0900-1200 (sometimes 1230 in La Paz), and 1400-1800 (sometimes 1900 in La Paz). Saturday is a half day. Opening and closing in the afternoon are several hours later in the provinces.*
Banks *0900-1200, 1400-1630, 0900-1200, or 1300 on Saturday.*
Official time *Four hours behind GMT.*
IDD *591. Equal tones with long pauses*

means it is ringing. Equal tones with equal pauses indicate it is engaged.
Voltage *Varies considerably. Generally 110 volts, 50 cycles AC in La Paz, 220 volts 50 cycles AC elsewhere, but check before using any appliance. (You may even find 110 and 220 in the same room.) US-type plugs can be used in most hotels.*
Weights and measures *Metric.*

Where to stay

Hotels & hostels
See inside front cover of the book for hotel grade price guide. Prices listed include 20% tax and service charge

Hotels must display prices by law. The number of stars awarded each hotel is regulated by law as well and is a fairly accurate assessment of an establishment's relative status. Throughout Bolivia some hotels impose their own curfews. In La Paz it tends to be midnight (check) but it can be as early as 2130 in Copacabana. These locking-up times are strictly adhered to by hotel keepers. Ask for the hot water schedule; it changes with the season, water pressure, etc, although now even the cheapest hotels tend to have electric showers which offer hot/warm water all day. Clothes washing is generally not allowed in bathrooms but many of the cheaper hotels have a hand-washing area. Many mid-range hotels will keep money and valuables in the safe if there are no safety-deposit boxes. Cheaper hotels rarely have heating in the rooms. Youth hostels are not necessarily cheaper: many middle range *residenciales* are affiliated to the **HI**.

Camping
Camping is safe almost anywhere except near settlements (unless unavoidable). Warm sleeping gear essential, even in the lowlands in the winter. Sleeping bags are also useful for keeping warm on buses in the Andes. Camping gas-style and Epigas cannisters are available in La Paz and all large cities; white gas for Coleman stoves is difficult to find. Kerosene is much easier to find outside La Paz, even in small towns. *Alcohol potable* (meths) is widely available.

Getting around

Air
Internal air services are run by **Lloyd Aéreo Boliviano** (**LAB**), www.labairlines.com, **Aero Sur**, www.aerosur.com and – occasionally – the military air service, **TAM**. *LAB* and *Aero Sur* are generally reliable but *TAM* much less so (always reconfirm *TAM* flights); *TAM* is phasing out its civilian transport business. *LAB* offers a 30-day domestic airpass for US$296 for international travellers using *LAB* (or a foreign carrier with whom *LAB* may have a pooling arrangement) for a maximum of five flights between the main cities; note that many flights radiate from La Paz, Santa Cruz or Cochabamba. *LAB* have 5% discounts for family members if they travel together (take passport); *LAB* and *Aero Sur* also offer discounts of 5% to students under 26 and *Aero Sur* offer 20% discounts to passengers over 65. Note that a 'through' flight may require a change of plane, or be delayed waiting for a connecting flight coming from elsewhere. Only on international flights is overnight lodging provided during delays. Insure your bags heavily as they tend to get left around and *LAB* is reluctant to give compensation. If your internal flight is delayed keep your baggage with you and do not check it in until the flight is definitely announced. There are have been reports of theft.

Road
Only 5% of all Bolivian roads are paved and under 25% gravel-surfaced. In most instances the word road is a rather exaggerated description of what's on offer. Nearly all 'road' surfaces, even the paved sections, are bad, and after flooding or rough weather they are even worse. Even main roads may be closed in the rainy season. **NB** On election day no public transport runs whatsoever; only cars with a special permit may be on the road.

Bolivia

Bus

A small charge is made for use of major bus terminals; payment is before departure

Buses ply most of the roads (interurban buses are called *flotas*, urban ones *micros*, also minibuses and *trufis* (shared taxis). You should always try to reserve, and pay for, a seat as far as possible in advance and arrive in good time, but substantial savings can be made by buying tickets just before departure, as there is fierce competition to fill seats. In the wet season, bus travel is subject to long delays and detours, at extra cost, and cancellations are not uncommon. Obversely, in the dry season journeys can be very dusty. On all journeys, take food and toilet wipes. It is best to travel by day, not just so you can see the scenery and avoid arriving at your destination at night, but also because drivers work long hours and there is less chance of them falling asleep in daylight. Bus companies are responsible for any luggage packed on the roof.

Car

Road tolls vary from US$0.50 to US$2.50 for journeys up to 100 km

To bring a private vehicle into Bolivia temporary admission must be sought, but is not easily obtainable. A *carnet de passages* is recommended. You must also have an International Driving Permit. Car rental companies may only require your national licence but police controls may ask for an international licence. A hire company can arrange a 'blanket' driving permit for tourists which is valid for several days and destinations. Check with *Automóvil Club Boliviano*, corner of 6 Avenidos de Agosto and Arce, La Paz, T/F237 2139, for any special documents which may be required. Take great care when driving, especially at night. Too many truck drivers are drunk, almost never dip their headlights, and many private vehicles drive with faulty headlights. There are two grades of **petrol** (gasoline): 85 and 92 octane. 85 octane costs US$0.44, super US$0.56; diesel costs US$0.50 per litre. Costs are higher in the Amazon lowlands. **Trucks** congregate at all town markets, with destinations chalked on the sides. They can be cheaper than buses but this depends on the amount of competition. Think before hitching a ride as fatal accidents occur, especially in the Altiplano and Yungas regions, where mountainous terrain presents a hazard.

Train

Train tickets can be bought in advance

Empresa Nacional de Ferrocarriles (ENFE), was privatized in 1996 and La Paz railway station was closed in 1997. Trains to the Argentine border start at Oruro. The only other public railways of significance run from Santa Cruz to the Brazil border and southward. The new Santa Cruz terminal is amazingly efficient, and has connections with bus lines as well. For train information in La Paz T241 6545/6. Always check departure times in advance.

Maps

Instituto Geográfico Militar head office is at Estado Mayor General, Av Saavedra Final, Miraflores, La Paz, open Mon-Thu 0900-1100, 1500-1700, Fri 0900-1100, take passport to buy maps. Or go to Oficina 5, Juan XXIII 100 (mud track between Rodríguez y Linares), Mon-Thu 0800-1200 and 1430-1800, Fri 0800-1400. *IGM* map prices: 1:50,000 topographical sheet US$6.25 (photocopy US$4.70); 1:250,000 sheet US$7.00 (copy US$5.50); national communications map (roads and towns) US$7.80; 4-sheet Bolivia physical 1:1,000,000, US$14; 4 sheet political 1:1,500,000 US$14. *Liam P O'Brien* has a 1:135,000, full colour, shaded relief topographic map of the Cordillera Real, US$10 per copy, also a 1:2,200,000 full colour travel map of Bolivia highlighting the National Parks from map distributors (*Bradt, Stanfords*, etc). *Walter Guzmán Córdova* colour maps, 1:150,000, of Choro-Takesi-Yunga Cruz, Mururata-Illimani, Huayna Potosí Oruro-Potosi-Salar de Uyuni, Illampu-Ancohuma, Titicaca-Tiwanaku-Yungas, Nigruni-Condoriri, La Paz department, Santa Cruz department, Sajama and Mapa Físico- Político-Vial (1:2,250,000, road map), available from bookshops (US$6.70-7.50). The *German Alpine Club* (**Deutscher Alpenverein**) produces 2 maps of Sorata-Ancohuma-Illampu and Illimani, from *IGM* (US$6.50).

Keeping in touch

Internet Internet access is extensive and often easier than phoning. Every major town has an internet café. Outside La Paz connections can be slow, but persevere (see main text for details).

Post

Quipus, Casilla 1696, Calle Jáuregui 2248, T234 0062, is the Poste Restante for South American Explorers members

Post offices use the post box (*casilla*) system. Items sent by post should therefore bear, not the street address but the *casilla* number and town. Hours are Monday-Saturday 0800-2000, Sunday 0800-1200. For security, send mail 'certificado'. There is a national and international express post system; special counters and envelopes provided. Air-mail letters to and from Europe should take between five and 10 days. Letter/postcard up to 20 g to Europe US$0.90, to North America US$0.75, rest of the world US$1; letter over 30 g to Europe US$2.20, to North

Bolivia

America US$1.50, rest of the world US$2.30. Packages up to 2 kg can be posted from the ground floor of the main post office in La Paz between 1200-1430 when the main parcels department, downstairs, is taking lunch: to Europe a 2 kg parcel costs US$30, to North America US$20.30, to the rest of the world US$42. Surface mail parcels up to 2 kg cost US$16 to North America, US$19 to Europe and US$21 to the rest of the world. Parcels are checked by customs officers before being sealed. We have received reports of customs officers trying to charge for inspecting parcels: politely refuse to pay. After inspection and repacking parcels are wrapped in cloth and sewn up for security reasons; there is a small fee for this service.

Telephone

All phone numbers have seven digits. To dial long distance you must prefix each seven-digit number with a regional code: 02 in the departments of La Paz, Oruro and Potosí (the Occidente); 03 in Santa Cruz, Beni and Pando (the Oriente); 04 Cochabamba, Chuquisaca and Tarija (the Centro). Dialling from private phones requires an additional prefix, that of the telephone company you wish to use, between the zero and number of the regional code. The telephone company access numbers are: 10 for *Entel*, 11 for *AES*, 17 for *Telecel* and 13 for *Boliviatel*. Calling Bolivia from abroad conforms to systems elsewhere in the world. Dial the access code for Bolivia, 00-591 (011-591 from the US), then add the full long-distance 9-digit number minus its initial zero. All mobile numbers are now eight digits, starting with 7. If the person is local then dial their eight-digit number; if they are out of town you must dial a 0 first.

Direct calls are possible from major cities to Europe, USA, Australia and elsewhere, clear lines, delays minimal. Peak rate charges; US$2.10 per minute to Europe and Mexico, US$1.79 to USA and South America, US$2.25 to Australia. Fax to Europe costs US$5 per page, to the USA US$3.80, to Australia, New Zealand US$6. Phone calls within city limits are free for private calls from a private phone. For public phones, coins/*fichas* or phone cards are necessary. Many booths take cards only, as the coins and tokens are being phased out. Direct collect-call numbers: US AT&T 0800 1111, MCI 0800 2222, Sprint 0800 3333, IDB (TRT) 0800 4444; UK BT 0800 0044; Spain Telefónica 0800 0034; Brazil 0800 0055; Chile Entel 0800 0056; Canada Teleglobe 0800 0101; Japan KDD 0800 0081.

Media

In La Paz: morning papers – *Presencia*, daily, largely Catholic; *La Razón*, www.la-razon.com *El Diario* (sensationalist), www.eldiario.net *Ultima Hora*, and *Jornada* (evenings). In Cochabamba – *Los Tiempos*, www.lostiempos.com, and *Extra*. In Oruro – *La Patria*, mornings (except Monday). *El Día*, *La Estrella del Oriente*, *El Mundo* and *El Deber* are the Santa Cruz daily papers. *Deber* also appears in La Paz and Trinidad. In Sucre, *El Correo*. *Presencia*, *El Diario*, *El Mundo*, *La Razón* all have good foreign coverage. Weekly: *Nueva Economía*. La Paz papers are on sale in other cities. English language weekly *The Bolivian Times*, published Friday, US$1.50, available in big cities, local news reports (Jauregui 2248, Sopocachi, La Paz, Casilla 1696). International papers are available in La Paz. Also, there are about 85 radio stations, a government TV station and a university TV service.

Food and drink

Food
The normal international cuisine is found at most good hotels and restaurants

Bolivian highland cooking is usually very tasty and often *picante*. Local specialities which visitors should try include *empanadas* (cheese pasties) and *humitas* (maize pies); *pukacapas* are *picante* cheese pies. Recommended main dishes including *sajta de pollo*, hot spicy chicken with onion, fresh potatoes and *chuño* (dehydrated potatoes), *parrillada* (a Bolivian kind of mixed grill), *fricase* (juicy pork dish served with *chuño*), *silpancho* (fried breaded meat with eggs, rice and bananas), *saice*, a dish of minced meat with picante sauce, served with rice, potatoes, onions and tomatoes, *pique macho*, roast meat with chips, onion and pepper, and *ají de lengua*, ox-tongue with chilis, potatoes and *chuño* or *tunta* (another kind of dehydrated potato). The soups are also good, especially a *chairo* soup made of meat, vegetables, *chuño* and *ají* (hot pepper) to which the locals like to add *llajua* or *halpahuayca* (hot sauces always set on restaurant tables) to make it even more *picante*. *Salteñas* are meat or chicken pasties (originating from Salta, Argentina, but popular throughout the Andean countries), eaten regularly by Bolivians, mostly in the morning. Some are *muy picante* (very hot) with red chili peppers, but *medio picante* and *poco picante* ones can normally be obtained. *Marraqueta* is bread from La Paz, crusty, with a soft centre; *pan de Batallas* is a sandwich loaf.

Bolivia

Bolivia

In the lowland Oriente region, the food usually comes with cooked banana and yucca. The bread in this region is often sweet with cheese on top, and the rice bread is also unusual. In the north lowlands, many types of wild meat are served in tourist restaurants and on jungle tours. Bear in mind the turtles whose eggs are eaten are endangered and that other species not endangered soon will be if they stay on the tourist menu.

Eating out In the *pensiones* and cheaper restaurants a basic lunch (*almuerzo* – usually finished by 1300) and dinner (*cena*) are normally available. The *comida del día* is the best value in any class of restaurant. Good cheap and clean breakfasts are served in the markets in most towns (most restaurants do not open very early in the morning). Lunch can also be obtained in many of the modern market buildings in the main towns; eat only what is cooked in front of you. Dishes cooked in the street are not safe. Llama meat contains parasites similar to those in pork, so make sure it has been cooked for a long time and is hot when you eat it. Be very careful of salads, which may carry a multitude of amoebic life as well vile bacteria.

Drink The several makes of local, lager-type beer are recommendable; *Paceña* and *Ducal* are the best-selling brands. *El Inca* is a dark beer, sweet, like a stout, while *singani*, the national spirit, is distilled from grapes, and cheap and strong. *Chuflay* is *singani* and a fizzy mixer, usually 7 Up. Good wines are produced by La Concepción vineyard, near Tarija. *Chicha* is a fermented maize drink, popular around Cochabamba. It is not always alcoholic. In the countryside, look for the white flag outside the houses selling *chicha*. The hot maize drink, *api* (with cloves, cinnamon, lemon and sugar), is good on cold mornings. Bottled water, *Nataragua* and *Viscachani*, is easily available but make sure the seal is unbroken (rain water is sometimes offered as an alternative). There are also several brands of flavoured mineral water, *Cayacayani*, *La Cabaña*, *Mineragua*. The local tap water should not be drunk without first being sterilized. Local water purifier is 'Lugol Fuerte Solución', an iodine-based product, US$1.75 per small bottle; also *iodo* from *farmacias*, US$0.50. For milk, try sachets of *Leche Pil* (plain, chocolate or strawberry-flavoured), at US$0.25 each.

Shopping

Llama- and alpaca-wool knitted and woven items are at least as good as those from Peru and much cheaper. Ponchos, *mantas*, bags, *chullos* (bonnets), gold and silverware, musical instruments such as the *charango* (mandolin traditionally with armadillo-shell sound-box, now usually of wood) and the *quena* (Inca flute), and other wooden items, especially carvings (*tallados en madera*) made from the aromatic *guayacán* and *palo santo* woods.

Holidays and festivals

In Andean regions, *Carnaval Campesino* begins on **Ash Wednesday** and lasts for five days, ending with *Domingo de Tentación* in many small towns. Two weeks before Carnaval is *Jueves de Compadres* and one week before Jueves de Compadres, **Shrove Tuesday** is celebrated as *Martes de Challa*, when house owners make offerings to Pachamama and give drinks to passers-by. **2 February**: *Virgen de la Candelaria*, in rural communities, Copacabana, Santa Cruz. **Palm Sunday** (Domingo de Ramos) is the occasion for parades to the church throughout Bolivia; the devout carry woven palm fronds, then hang them outside their houses. *Corpus Christi* is also a colourful festival. **3 May**: *Fiesta de la Invención de la Santa Cruz*, various parts. **2 June**: *Santísima Trinidad* in Beni Department. **24 June**: *San Juan*, all Bolivia. **29 June**: *San Pedro y San Pablo*, at Tiquina and Tihuanaco. **28 July**: *Fiesta de Santiago* (St James), Altiplano and lake region; Achocalla a convenient place to go to. **16 August**: *San Roque*, patron saint of dogs; the animals are adorned with ribbons and other decorations. **1 and 2 November**: *All Saints and All Souls*, any local cemetery. **18 November**: *Beni's Departmental anniversary*, especially in Trinidad. For other festivals on the Altiplano enquire at hotels or tourist office in La Paz. Remember cities are very quiet on national holidays, but colourful celebrations will be going on in the villages. Beware of water-filled balloons thrown during carnival in even the coldest weather. Hotels are often full at the most popular places, for instance Copacabana on Good Friday; worth booking in advance.

1 January, New Year's Day; Carnival Week, Monday, Shrove Tuesday, Ash Wednesday; Holy Week: **Public holidays**
Thursday, Friday and Saturday; 1 May, Labour Day; Corpus Christi (movable); 16 July, La Paz
Municipal Holiday; 5-7 August, Independence; 2 November, Day of the Dead; Christmas Day.

Sport and activities

Climbing Bolivia has some of the best mountaineering in the world, but infrastructure is
not well-developed, so don't expect to be rescued if you get into trouble. With a dozen
peaks at or above 6,000 m and almost a thousand over 5,000 m, most levels of skill can find
something to tempt them. The season is May to September, with usually stable conditions
June to August. Proper technical equipment, experience and/or a competent guide are
essential to cross glaciers and climb snow and ice safely. The four ranges in which to climb
are: the **Cordillera Real**, which has 600 5,000 m plus mountains, including six at 6,000 m or
above: Illimani 6,439 m, Ancohuma 6,427 m, Illampu 6,368 m, Chearoco 6,104 m, Huayna
Potosí 6,088 m (the most popular) and Chachacomani 6,000 m. A week's acclimatization at
the height of La Paz or equivalent is necessary before attempting to climb above 5,000 m.
Access is easy from the flat Altiplano, but public transport is not always possible. **Quimza
Cruz**, southeast of La Paz, is hard to get to but offers some excellent possibilities. The
volcanic **Cordillera Occidental** contains Bolivia's highest peak, Sajama (6,542 m), plus
Parinacota and Pomerape, see under Sajama, page 288. The **Apolobamba** range,
northwest of La Paz, has many 5,000-m-plus peaks.

Mountain biking Bolivia is blessed with some of the most dramatic terrain in the world and
seven months of almost daily crystal clear skies and perfect weather for the sport. Nevertheless,
mountain biking is relatively new to Bolivia. Generally speaking, many areas have yet to be
explored properly and as of now there is no mountain biking guidebook. Hard-core,
experienced, fit and acclimatized riders can choose from a huge range of possibilities. Either
take a gamble and figure it out from a map, or find a guide and tackle the real adventure rides.
Some popular rides in the La Paz region, achievable by all levels of riders, are **La Cumbre to
Coroico**, down the so-called 'world's most dangerous road'; the **Zongo Valley** descent into the
Yungas; **Chacaltaya to La Paz**, down from the world's highest ski-slope; **Hasta Sorata**, to the
trekking paradise of Sorata. If you are planning on bringing your own mountain bike and doing
some hard riding, be prepared for incredibly abusive conditions (and that's in the dry season; in
the December-February wet season, the conditions are often so bad as to be unsafe). There is an
almost complete absence of spare parts and very few good bike mechanics. Alternatively, there
are now a number of operations offering guided mountain biking tours, but few agencies rent
good quality, safe machines. Furthermore, the wealth of good downhill rides has encouraged a
number of companies to opt for the 'quick buck' approach, using inappropriate and potentially
dangerous bicycles, inexperienced guides, insufficient guide-to-client ratios, and little or no
instruction during the ride. Choose a reputable company, guides who speak your language and
only opt for the best, US-made bikes.

Trekking There are many opportunities for trekking in Bolivia, from gentle one-day hikes in
foothills and valleys to challenging walks of several days from highlands to lowlands on Inca
or gold-diggers trails. The best known are: the **Choro**, **Takesi** and **Yunga Cruz** hikes, all of
whose starting points can be reached from La Paz; the **Mapiri Trail** and the **Illampu Circuit**,
both approached from Sorata; and the **Apolobamba** treks in the northwest. None of these
should be attempted without full planning and equipment. Various treks are outlined in the
text, especially near La Paz and from Sorata. Note that all these trails are remote in parts and
that robbery and violent attacks have been made on tourists and Bolivians alike. It is
advisable to hike these trails in large, organized groups. The local tourist office also produces
leaflets with sketch maps on walks in the vicinity of La Paz. There are also some excellent
guides available through local clubs. See also Books, in Background.

Nature tourism With more than 40 well-defined ecological regions and the transition
zones between them, there is ample scope for enjoying the wildlife of this remarkable

Bolivia

country. One of the most popular tours is the four-day trip to the **Salar de Uyuni** (salt flats), which includes the **Lagunas Colorada** and **Verde**. Not only will you see Andean bird life but also landscapes of unmatched, stark beauty and you will experience the bitter cold of the high altitudes. For seeing lowland birds and animals, the main options are **Rurrenabaque** in the lowlands of the river Beni, which is a centre for tours to the jungle (the **Parque Nacional Madidi**) and to the subtropical pampas, and the **Parque Nacional Amboró**, three hours west of Santa Cruz, containing ecosystems of the Amazon basin, Andean foothills and the savannahs of the Chaco plain. For table-top mountains, forests, *cerrado*, wetlands and a stunning array of wildlife, the remote **Parque Nacional Noel Kempff Mercado**, in northeast Santa Cruz, is worth making the effort to get to. Other opportunities include protected areas, wildlife refuges and rehabilitation centres, the sight of llamas and alpacas on any highland bus journey and even the tracks of dinosaurs.

Health

*See also
Essentials chapter
For vaccinations, see
page 242*

Whatever their age, travellers arriving in La Paz by air should rest for half a day, take very little food and alcoholic drink, drink plenty of clear, non-alcoholic fluids, and walk slowly when going uphill. Local remedies are *maté de coca*, *Sorojchi* and *Micoren* capsules (none is medically proven). Medical services are sketchy outside the towns and mining camps. Public hospitals charge Bs 5 for consultation, compared with up to and over US$100 in private hospitals. Epidemics are comparatively rare on the Altiplano, but cholera is a problem in times of drought. Malaria, cholera and yellow fever are still problems in the Oriente and Santa Cruz, and hepatitis and Chagas' disease are endemic in the warmer parts of the country. Take anti-malaria tablets if visiting the lowlands. A good remedy for stomach amoebas is *Tinidazol*.

La Paz

La Paz

*Phone code: 02
Colour map 6, grid A2
Population: 1.2 mn*

The minute you arrive in La Paz, the highest capital city in the world, you realise this is no ordinary place. La Paz's airport is at a staggering 4,000 m above sea level. The sight of the city, lying 500 m below, at the bottom of a steep canyon and ringed by snow-peaked mountains, takes your breath away – literally. For at this altitude breathing can be a problem.

The Spaniards chose this odd place for a city on 20 October 1548, to avoid the chill winds of the plateau, and because they had found gold in the Río Choqueyapu, which runs through the canyon. The centre of the city, Plaza Murillo, is at 3,636 m, about 400 m below the level of the Altiplano and the new city of El Alto, perched dramatically on the rim of the canyon.

Ins & outs
*For more detailed
information see
Transport, page 265*

Getting there La Paz has the highest commercial **airport** in the world, at El Alto, high above the city at 4,058 m; T281 0122/3. A taxi from the airport to the centre takes about 30 mins, US$7. There are 3 main **bus terminals**; the bus station at Plaza Antofagasta, the cemetery district for Sorata, Copacabana and Tiahuanaco, and Villa Fátima for Coroico and the Yungas.

Getting around There are 3 types of city bus: large Fiat buses run by the city corporation, on fairly limited routes; *micros* (dilapidated former US school buses), which charge US$0.18 in the centre, US$0.24 from outside centre; and the faster minibuses, US$0.20-0.34. *Trufis* are fixed route collective taxis which charge US$0.30-0.40 pp within city limits. Both taxis and *colectivos* are white, but recognize colectivos by red number plates.

Orientation The city's main street runs from Plaza San Francisco as Av Mcal Santa Cruz, then changes to Av 16 de Julio (more commonly known as the Prado) and ends at Plaza del Estudiante. The business quarter, government offices, central university (UMSA) and many of the main hotels and restaurants are situated in this area. The Prado is closed to vehicles every Sun from 0800 to 1700, when it is lined with handicraft sellers and bookstalls. From the Plaza del Estudiante, Av Villazón splits into Av Arce, which runs southeast towards the wealthier residential districts of Zona Sur and Av 6 de Agosto which runs through Sopocachi, an area full of restaurants, bars and clubs. Situated in the valley, 15 minutes south of the centre, is Zona Sur, home to the resident foreign community. It has international shopping centres, supermarkets with imported items and some of the best restaurants and bars in La Paz (see page 262). Zona Sur begins after the bridge at La Florida beside the attractive Plaza Humboldt. The main road, Av Ballivián, begins at C 8 and continues up the hill to San Miguel on C 21 (about a 20 min walk). Sprawled around the rim of the canyon is El Alto, now a city in its own right and reputedly the fastest growing in South America. Its popualtion is mostly indigenous immigrants from the countryside. El Alto is connected to La Paz by motorway (toll US$0.50, cycles free). Buses from Plaza Eguino and Pérez Velasco leave regularly for Plaza 16 de Julio, El Alto.

Tourist offices Information office at the bottom end of Av 16 de Julio (Prado) on Plaza del Estudiante on corner with C México. Helpful, English and French spoken, free leaflets, map of La Paz US$2.25. Open Mon-Fri 0830-1200, 1430-1900, Sat 0900-1200. There are smaller offices at Linares 932, which has a good selection of guide books for reference, purchase or exchange, and outside the main bus terminal.

Sights

There are few colonial buildings left in La Paz; probably the best examples are in **Calle Jaén** (see below). Late 19th/early 20th century architecture, often displayingEuropean influence, can be found in the streets around Plaza Murillo, but much of La Paz is modern. **The Plaza del Estudiante** (Plaza Franz Tamayo), or a bit above it, marks a contrast between old and new styles, between the commercial and the more elegant. The **Prado** itself is lined with high-rise blocks dating from the 1960s and 1970s.

Plaza Murillo, three blocks north of the Prado, is the traditional centre. Facing its formal gardens are the huge, graceful **Cathedral**, the **Palacio Presidencial** in Italian renaissance style, usually known as the **Palacio Quemado** (burnt palace) twice gutted by fire in its stormy 130-year history, and, on the east side, the **Congreso Nacional**. In front of the Palacio Quemado is a statue of former President Gualberto Villarroel who was dragged into the plaza by an angry mob and hanged in 1946. Across from the Cathedral on Calle Socabaya is the **Palacio de los Condes de Arana** (built 1775), with beautiful exterior and patio. It houses the **Museo Nacional de Arte**, which has a fine collection of colonial paintings including many works by Melchor Pérez Holguín, considered one of the masters of Andean colonial art, and which also exhibits the works of contemporary local artists. ■ *Tue-Fri 0900-1230, 1500-1900, Sat 1000-1230, 1500-1900, Sun 1000-1300, US$1, students US$0.25, T237 1177.* Calle Comercio, running east-west across the Plaza, has most of the stores and shops. West of Plaza Murillo is the **Museo Nacional de Etnografía y Folklore**, in the palace of the Marqueses de Villaverde, with exhibits on the Chipaya, Tarabuceño and Ayoreo Indians, quite good library adjoining. ■ *Tue-Fri 0900-1230, 1500-1900, Sat-Sun 0900-1300, Ingavi 916, T235 8559.*

Northwest of Plaza Murillo is **Calle Jaén**, a picturesque colonial street with many craft shops and home to four museums housed in colonial buildings. **Museo Costumbrista**, on Plaza Riosinio, at the top of Jaén, has miniature displays depicting incidents in the history of La Paz and well-known Paceños, as well as miniature replicas of reed rafts used by the Norwegian Thor Heyerdahl, and the Spaniard Kitin Muñoz, to prove their theories of ancient migrations. **Museo del Litoral Boliviano**, has artefacts of the War of the Pacific, and interesting selection of old maps. **Museo de Metales Preciosos** is well set out with Inca gold artefacts in basement vaults, also ceramics and archaeological exhibits, and **Museo Casa Murillo**, the erstwhile home of Pedro Domingo Murillo, one of the martyrs of the La Paz independence movement of 16 July 1809, has a good collection of paintings, furniture and national costumes. ■ *All four museums included on a single ticket from Museo Costumbrista; US$0.60, students US$0.15, free on Sat with children. All*

Around Plaza Murillo

Bolivia

museums Tue-Fri 0930-1230, 1500-1900, Sat and Sun 1000-1230. South of Jaén, near Plaza Mendoza, is the recommended **Museo Tambo Quirquincho**, in a restored colonial building with modern painting and sculpture, carnival masks, silver, early 20th century photography and city plans. Recommended. ■ *Tue-Fri, 0930-1230, 1500-1900, Sat-Sun, 1000-1230, US$0.15 (Sat and Sun students free), C Evaristo Valle.*

Plaza San Francisco up to the cemetery district

At the upper end of Avenida Mcal Santa Cruz is the **Plaza San Francisco** with the church and monastery of San Francisco, dating from 1549. This is one of the finest examples of colonial religious architecture in South America and well worth seeing. ■ *Opens at 1530. Local weddings can be seen on Sat 1000-1200 otherwise the church opens for Mass at 0700, 0900, 1100 and 1900, Mon-Sat and also at 0800, 1000 and 1200 on Sun.* Behind the San Francisco church a network of narrow cobbled streets rise steeply up the canyon walls. Much of this area is a permanent street market. Handicraft shops line the lower part of **Calle Sagárnaga**. The amazing **Mercado de**

Bolivia

La Paz

Detail map
A La Paz centre,
page 254

N

0 metres   100
0 yards   100

■ Sleeping	8 Galería	15 Italia *B2*
1 Andes *B1*	9 Hospedaje Milenio *A3*	16 La Joya *C1*
2 Continental *B2*	10 Hostal Claudia *D5*	17 La Paz City *D4*
3 Copacabana *D5*	11 Hostal	18 Libertador *B4*
4 El Dorado *D5*	Copacabana *C2*	19 Milton *C3*
5 España *D5*	12 Hostal La Estancia *C4*	20 Plaza *C5*
6 Estrella Andina *C2*	13 Hostal República *B4*	21 Posada El
7 Europa *C5*	14 Ingavi *A3*	Carretero *A3*

Hechicería, 'witchcraft market', on Calles Melchor Jiménez and Linares, which cross Santa Cruz above San Francisco, sells fascinating charms, herbs and more gruesome items like llama foetuses. At Linares 906, the excellent **Museo de la Coca** is devoted to the coca plant, its history, cultural significance, medical values, political implications, texts in Spanish and English. ■ *Daily1000-1900, US$1.05, shop with interesting items for sale.* Further up, from Illampu to Rodríguez and in neighbouring streets, is the produce-based **Rodríguez market**. ■*Daily, but best on Sun morning.* Turning right on Max Paredes, heading north, is **Avenida Buenos Aires**, one of the liveliest streets in the Indian quarter, where small workshops turn out the costumes and masks for the Gran Poder festival, and with great views of Illimani, especially at sunset. Continuing west along Max Paredes towards the **cemetery district**, the streets are crammed with stalls selling every imaginable item. Transport converges on the cemetery district (for more information see page 265).

Bolivia

22 Radisson Plaza *D6*	3 Casa de Chang *C4*	10 Jalapeños *D6*	17 Reineke Fuchs *D6*
23 Residencial Sucre *D4*	4 Club de la Prensa *C4*	11 La Bohème *D6*	18 Unicornio *C4*
24 Rosario *B2*	5 El Arriero *D6*	12 La Casa de	19 Vienna *C5*
25 Tambo de Oro *A2*	6 El Gaucho *D6*	los Paceños *A3*	20 Wagamama *D6*
	7 Eli's *C4*	13 La Quebecoise *D6*	
● Eating	8 Gringo	14 La Terraza *D6*	● Bars & clubs
1 Acuario *C3*	Limón *D6*	15 Mongo's *D6*	21 Pig & Whistle *D5*
2 Andrómeda *D6*	9 India *D6*	16 Pronto *D6*	

The Prado, Sopocachi, Miraflores & Zona Sur

On the Prado is the excellent **Museo de Arte Contemporáneo Plaza**, in a 19th-century house which has been declared a national monument. There is a good selection of contemporary art from national and international artists. Rotating exhibits, some work for sale. ■ *Daily 0900-2100, US$1.50, Av 16 de Julio 1698, T233 5905, www.museoplaza.com* Just off the Prado (go down the flight of stairs by the Hotel Plaza) is **Museo Tiahuanaco** (Tiwanaku), which contains good collections of the arts and crafts of ancient Tiwanaku and items from the eastern jungles. It also has a two room exhibition of gold statuettes and objects found in Lake Titicaca. ■ *Tue-Fri 0900-1230, 1500-1900, Sat 1000-1200, 1500-1830, US$0.75, students US$0.10.* In Sopocachi district, above Avenida 6 de Agosto, is **Casa Museo Marina Núñez del Prado**, with an excellent collection of her sculptures housed in the family mansion. ■ *Tue-Fri 0930-1300, 1500-1900, Sat-Mon 0930-1300, US$0.75, students US$0.30, T/F232 4906, Ecuador 2034.* On Avenida Libertador Simón Bolívar, from where there are great views of Mt Illimani, is the indigenous produce **Central Market** (called **Mercado Camacho**). Further east is the residential district of Miraflores where you'll find **Museo de Textiles Andinos Bolivianos** with good displays of textiles from around the country, detailed explanations and a knowledgeable owner. ■ *Mon-Sat 0800-1200, 1400-1830, Sun 1000-1300, T224 3601, Plaza Benito Juárez 488, Miraflores.* Outside the Hernan Siles national football stadium is the **Museo Semisubterráneo**, a sunken garden full of restored statues and other artefacts from Tiahuanaco, some of them badly eroded from traffic pollution. On Avenida del Ejército is the **Kusillo Cultural Complex** which features intereactive exhibits on Bolivian culture, shops selling native crafts, a Museum of Science and Play and a funicular railway. ■ *T222 6371, www.kusillo.com*

La Paz centre

0 metres 100
0 yards 100

Sleeping
1 Arcabucero
2 Austria
3 El Alem
4 El Lobo
5 Gloria
6 Gran Hotel París
7 Hospedaje Cactus & El Caminito
8 Hostal Happy Days
9 Hostal Naira & Banais Café
10 Hostería Blanquita
11 Julia Rojo Briseño
12 Majestic
13 Presidente
14 Residencial Plaza
15 Sagárnaga
16 Señorial
17 Torino

Eating
1 100% Natural
2 Alexander Coffee Shop
3 Angelo Colonial
4 Café Confitería de la Paz
5 Casa del Corregidor
6 Dos Laureles
7 El Calicanto
8 El Vegetariano
9 Jackie Chan
10 La Diligencia Churrascaría
11 Laksmi
12 Le Pot-Pourri des Gourmets
13 Los Escudos
14 Pizzería Romana
15 Sol y Luna
16 Wall St Bistro-Café
17 Yussef

Bolivia

Bolivia

▶ **Tiny treats**

One of the most intriguing items for sale in Andean markets is Ekeko, the god of good fortune and plenty and one of the most endearing of the Aymara folk legends. He is a cheery, avuncular little chap, with a happy face, a pot belly and short legs. His image, usually in plaster of Paris, is laden with various household items, as well as sweets, confetti and streamers, food, and with a cigarette dangling cheekily from his lower lip. Believers say that these statues only bring luck if they are received as gifts. The Ekeko occupies a central role in the festival of Alacitas, the Feast of Plenty, which takes place in La Paz at the end of January. Everything under the sun can be bought in miniature: houses, trucks, buses, suitcases, university diplomas; you name it, you'll find it here. The idea is to have your mini-purchase blessed by a Yatiri, an Aymara priest, and the real thing will be yours within the year.

Valle de la Luna
The climate in this valley is always much warmer than in the city

A worthwhile nearby excursion is to **Río Abajo**. Through the suburbs of Calacoto and La Florida follow the river road past picnic spots and through some weird rock formations, known as the Valle de la Luna, or 'Moon Valley'. About 3 km from the bridge at Calacoto the road forks. Get out of the minibus (see below) at the turning and walk a few minutes east to the Valle entrance, or get out at the football field which is by the entrance. Take good shoes and water. Just past the Valle de la Luna is **Mallasa** where there are several small roadside restaurants and cafés and the *Hotel Oberland* (see page 256). **The zoo** is on the road to Río Abajo, entrance just past Mallasa after Valle de la Luna, in beautiful, wide open park-like setting. Conditions for the animals and birds are relatively good, but the public is allowed to feed the animals. Quad biking is available behind the zoo. ■ *Zoo: daily 0900-1700, US$0.50 adults, US$0.25 children. Getting there: Minibus A can be caught on the Prado. If you do not want to walk in the valley, stay on the bus to the end of the line and take a return bus, 2 hrs in all. Alternatively take Micro 11 ('Aranjuez' large, not small bus) from C Sagárnaga, near Plaza San Francisco, US$0.65, and ask driver where to get off. Most of the local travel agents organize tours to the Valle de la Luna. These are very brief, 5 mins stop for photos in a US$15 tour of La Paz and surroundings; taxis cost US$6.*

Essentials

Sleeping
■ on map
Try to arrive early in the day as hotels, especially cheaper ones, can be hard to find

LL *Europa*, Tiahuanacu 64, T231 5656, PO Box 1800, behind *Plaza*, unico@hotel-europa-bolivia.com Difficult access but excellent facilities (*Summit Group*). Recommended. **LL** *Presidente*, Potosí y Sanjines 920, T240 6666, F240 7240. Includes breakfast, 'the highest 5-star in the world', pool, gym and sauna all open to non-residents, bar, disco, excellent service, comfortable, good food. **LL** *Radisson Plaza*, Av Arce 2177, T244 1111, radissonbolivia@usa.net 5-star hotel with all facilities, excellent buffet in restaurant (see Eating below). **L** *Plaza*, Av 16 de Julio 1789, T237 8311, plazabolivia@usa.net Good value restaurant (see below), peña show on Fri. **AL** *El Rey Palace*, Av 20 de Octubre 1947, T239 3016, hotelrey@caoba.intelnet.bo Includes breakfast, large suites, excellent restaurant, stylish, modern. **AL** *Gran Hotel París*, Plaza Murillo esq Bolívar, T220 3030, hparis@caoba.intelnet.bo Includes breakfast, elegant restaurant, English spoken. **A** *Gloria*, Potosí 909, T240 7070, www.hotelgloriabolivia.com 2 restaurants, 1 on top floor with good view, 1 vegetarian, excellent food and service (see below). Recommended. **A** *Libertador*, Obispo Cárdenas 1421, T231 3434, libertad@ceibo.entelnet.bo Good cheap restaurant, helpful, baggage stored. Highly recommended.

B *El Dorado*, Av Villazón, T236 3403, F239 1438. With breakfast, digital phones, safe luggage deposit, secure parking nearby. **B** *Galería*, C Santa Cruz 583, T246 1015, F246 1253. **C** without bath, lots of daylight, includes breakfast, quiet, good value. **B** *Hostal Naira*, Sagárnaga 161, T235 5645, F231 1214. Hot water, comfortable, cafeteria for breakfast, above *Peña Naira*. **B** *Oberland*, in Mallasa (see above), 12 km from centre, T274 5040, www.h-oberland.com, a Swiss-owned, chalet-style restaurant (excellent, not cheap) and hotel resort, gardens, cabañas, sauna, pool (open to public (US$2)), beach volley, tennis,

Bolivia

permits camping with vehicle. **B** *Rosario*, Illampu 704, Casilla 442, T245 1658, www.hotelrosario.com *Turisbus* travel agency downstairs (see Tour operators, page 265), 3-star, includes excellent buffet breakfast, very popular with foreigners, cable TV, modem connection, sauna, laundry, internet café *Jiwhaki* (free for guests, great view), good restaurant, stores luggage, very helpful staff. Highly recommended. Next door is **C** *Estrella Andina*, Illampu 716 esq Aroma, T456421, F451401. With breakfast, cheaper without bath, family run, tidy, helpful, internet access. **C** *Copacabana*, Av 16 de Julio 1802, T235 2244, F232 7390. Restaurant and grill room (lunch only at latter), good service, safe deposit, rooms a bit small. Recommended. **C** *Hostería Blanquita*, Santa Cruz 242, T/F245 7495. Includes breakfast, hot showers, comfortable. **C** *Sagárnaga*, Sagárnaga 326, T235 0252, F236 0831. **D** without bath, including basic restaurant, laundry, English spoken, lift, *peña*, ATM. **C-D** *Hostal República*, Comercio 1455, T220 2742, F220 2782. **D** without bath, old house of former president, hot water, inadequate shared bathrooms, luggage stored, helpful, laundry service, café, very popular with cyclists, usually full; separate house also available, **AL** sleeps 6, all facilities. **C-D** *La Joya*, Max Paredes 541, T245 3841, www.hotelajoya.com Phone, **E** without bath or TV, **E-F** pp in low season, modern and comfy, lift, laundry, includes breakfast, popular area with free pickup from town centre, close to bus and train station.

D *Arcabucero*, C Viluyo 307, Linares (close to Museo de Coca), T/F 231 3473. Pleasant new rooms in converted colonial house, excellent value, breakfast extra. **D** *Condeza*, Diagonal Juan XXII 190, entre Illampu y Linares, T231 1317. Hot water, TV, good.

D *Continental*, Illampu 626, T/F245 1176. **E** without bath, nice rooms, stores luggage. **D** *Hostal Copacabana*, Illampu 734, T245 1626, combicop@ceibo.intelnet.bo Hot water, **E** without bath, includes breakfast, changes TCs. **D** *El Alem*, Sagárnaga 334, T236 7400. Hot water, **E** pp without bath, secure, laundry service, includes breakfast, has travel agency. **D** *El Valle*, Evaristo Valle 153, T245 6085. **E** with shared bath, central, large rooms, quiet. . **D** *España*,

Bolivia

Av 6 de Agosto 2074, T244 2643, F244 1329. Hot water, cheaper without bath, very nice, quiet, restaurant. D*Hostal Claudia*, Av Villazón 1965, T237 2917. **E** without bath, secure. Recommended. **D** *Hostal La Estancia*, México 1559, T231 0336, F236 9242. With breakfast, TV, helpful, good restaurant. **D** *Latino*, Junín near Sucre, T228 2828, F228 0340. Hot water, TV, luggage stored, helpful. **D** *Majestic*, Santa Cruz 359 esq Ilampu T245 1628. Comfortable, laundry, safe. Recommended.**D** *Milton*, Illampu y Calderón No 1124, T236 8003, F236 5849, PO Box 5118. Hot water, includes breakfast, expensive laundry, safe parking around corner, popular, will store luggage, excellent views from roof. **D** *Res Sucre*, Colombia 340, on Plaza Sucre, T249 2038, F248 6723. Cheaper without bath, quiet area, hot water, big rooms, luggage stored, helpful. **D** *Señorial*, Yanacocha 540, Casilla 5081, T240 6042. Rooms with or without bath (also TV), hot water, kitchen, laundry, café, helpful, pleasant, good. **D** *Tambo de Oro*, Armentia 367, T228 1565, F228 2181. Near bus station, hot showers, TV, good value, safe for luggage.

E *Hostal Happy Days*, Sagárnaga 229, T231 4759, happydays@zuper.net Hot water, TV, popular, internet café next door. **E** *Ingavi*, Ingavi 727, T232 3645. Nice rooms with hot water, good value. **E** *Julia Rojo Briseño*, Murillo 1060, p 10, press 1001 on bellpush outside, T231 0236, juliarojo@hotmail.com Family house, 1 block from central post office, use of phone, fax and washing machine, includes breakfast (US$60 for a week for 2). **E** *Torino*, Socabaya 457, T240 6003. Ask for better rooms in new section, **F** without bath, run-down rooms in old section, free book exchange, good service, internet café and breakfast spot next door, 0100 curfew. **E-F** *El Lobo*, Santa Cruz 441 – see Eating. **F** *Alojamiento Illimani*, Av Illimani 1817. Hot water, quiet and safe, uncomfortable beds, laundry facilities, often full. **F** *Andes*, Av Manco Kapac 364, T245 5327. Cheaper without bath, hot water, includes breakfast, stores luggage, good restaurant. Recommended. **F** *Austria*, Yanacocha 531, T240 8540. Without bath, **G** pp in shared room, hot water but long queues for showers, safe deposit, laundry, TV, mainly dingy rooms (and no 18 is smelly from kitchen), book in advance, overpriced. **F** *Hospedaje Cactus*, Jiménez 818 y Santa Cruz, T245 1421. Shared showers (electric), helpful, kitchen facilities, luggage store, basic. **F** *Italia*, Av Manco Kapac 303, T245 6710. Hot water, luggage store, off-street motorcycle parking. Recommended, but noisy disco Fri and Sat night. **F** *La Paz City*, Acosta 487, T249 4565. Quiet, stores luggage, secure, basic, shared hot showers. **F** *Posada El Carretero*, Catacora 1056, entre Junín y Yanacocha, T228 5271. Double, single and dormitory rooms, safe deposit, laundry service, kitchen, reports book, information, backpackers' place, Spanish lessons with William Ortiz, internet. **F** *Res Plaza*, Plaza Pérez Velasco 785, T240 6099. Hot water, cheaper without bath, laundry and luggage storage facilities. **F** *El Solario*, Murillo 776, T236 7963, elsolariohotel@yahoo.com Central, good bathrooms, luggage store, use of kitchen, internet, international phone calls, laundry and medical services, taxi service, travel agency, good value. **G** *Res Imperial*, Pando 130, T245 7055. Hot water 24 hrs, stores luggage, cheap laundry. Recommended. **G** *Hospedaje Milenio*, Yanacocha 860, T228 1263. Without bath, family house, homely, helpful owner, quiet, kitchen, limited hot showers.

Youth Hostel *Asociación Boliviana de Albergues Juveniles*, ABAJ, has hostels around the country, which are given in the text. To use hostels you must have a Bolivian YHA card, US$2, 2 photos needed, available from ABAJ, which also sells international cards, US$20.

Camping No organized site, but Mallasa, at Valencia and Palca below the suburb of La Florida, has been recommended (Municipal Park, unmarked, turn left at Aldeas Infantiles SOS). For camping equipment and camping gas: *Andean Summits*, Comercio Doryan, Sagárnaga y Murillo, T/F242 2106, www.andeansummits.com, sells white gas, *bencina blanca*. *Caza y Pesca*, Edif Handal Center, no 9, Av Mcal Santa Cruz y Socabaya, T240 9209. Kerosene for pressure stoves is available from a pump in Plaza Alexander, Pando e Inca.

Eating
● *on map,*
Service charges
included on bill but
it's customary to leave
tip of 10%. Street
numbers in brackets

Av 16 de Julio *Alexander Coffee Shop*, Av 16 de Julio 1832, also Potosí 1091 and Av Mcal de Montenegro, Calacoto. Excellent coffee, muffins, cakes and good, cheap salads and sandwiches, open Mon-Fri 0800-2230, Sat and Sun 0900-2230. Recommended. *Eli's Pizza Express* 1400 block. English spoken, open daily including holidays (also at Comercio 914), very popular but not the best pizza in La Paz. Opposite Eli's is *Unicornio*. Great ice cream, lunch buffet upstairs. *Jackie Chan* , Cochabamba 100 (just south of Av Mcal Santa Cruz). Good value

Chinese, popular with locals. *Los Escudos* (1223, Edif Club de La Paz, T232 2028). Munich-type bierkeller with fixed 4-course lunch, good peña on Fri and Sat nights (2100-0100), US$5 cover charge. *La Fiesta* (1066). Good lunches. *Restaurant Verona*, esq Colón. Economical plato del día, popular in the evenings. *Utama*, in Plaza hotel (1789)Av Mcal Santa Cruz. Excellent salad bar, great value lunch, excellent view. Recommended.

South of the Prado *Angelo Colonial*, Linares 922. Excellent food and ambience, candle-light, antiques, internet access too, open early for breakfast, can get very busy. Also has a hostal on the Prado. *Banais*, Sagárnaga 161, same entrance as *Hostal Naira*. Coffee, sandwiches and juices. *Casa del Corregidor*, Murillo 1040, T236 3633. Centrally heated, Spanish colonial restaurant with Bolivian and European dishes, excellent food, bar. *Dos Laureles*, Evaristo Valle 120. Good cheap 4-course lunch. Recommended. *El Caminito*, Melchor Jiménez 812, entre Santa Cruz y Linares, Bolivian meat dishes, also vegetarian options, *almuerzo* US$2, all excellent. *El Lobo*, Santa Cruz 441. Huge portions, Israeli dishes, mid-price range, good meeting place, noticeboard, very popular (rooms to rent next door, E, F without bath). *Pizzería Romana*, Santa Cruz 260. Good pizzas and pastas, good value. *Le Pot-Pourri des Gourmets*, Linares 906, close to Sagárnaga. Bolivian and a variety of main courses including vegetarian, *almuerzo* US$2, pastries, snacks, hot and cold drinks, quiet, homely, music. *Sol y Luna*, Murillo 999 y Cochabamba. La Paz branch of a Copacabana café, good breakfasts. Recommended. *Tambo Colonial*, in Res Rosario (see above). Excellent local and international cuisine, good salad bar, huge buffet breakfast, peña at weekend. Recommended. *Yussef*, Sagárnaga 380, p 1 (poorly signed). Lebanese, great meze, good for vegetarians, good value.

North of the Prado *Café París*, restaurant in *Gran Hotel París*, Plaza Murillo esq Bolívar. Good food. *Club de la Prensa*, C Campero. In a pleasant garden, limited menu is typical Bolivian – meat only, in copious quantities – lively company. *Café Confitería de la Paz*, Camacho 1202, on the corner where Ayacucho joins Av Mcal Santa Cruz. Good tea room, traditional, meeting place for businessmen and politicians, great coffee and cakes. *Tranquera*, Potosí 1008, Centro Comercial Cristal, planta 3. Good set lunches US$3. *La Kantuta*, in *Hotel Presidente*, Potosí 920. Excellent food, good service. *Wall Street Bistro-Café*, Camacho 1363 entre Loayza y Colón. Good, not cheap (discount for ISIC card holders), owner speaks English and French (opens 0900 on Sun). *Casa de Chang*, Juan de la Riva 1522. Good, set Chinese meals. *El Calicanto*, Sanjines 467. Good food including regional specialities, renovated colonial house, live music at weekends, US$5. *La Casa de los Paceños*, Sucre 856. Excellent Bolivian food, but not cheap. There are many other eating places on C Comercio: for example *La Diligencia Churrascaría*, No 803, good grill and set meals, open 1200-2400 daily. Recommended.

Near Plaza del Estudiante *Luigi's Pizzería*, Villazón 2048. Good. *Andrómeda*, Av Arce 2116, T354723. European-style including a few vegetarian dishes, excellent US$3 lunch. *Jalapeños*, Arce 2549. Excellent Mexican dishes for US$5-6.50. Just behind it, Pasaje Pinilla 2557, is *Wagamama* (Tue-Sat 1200-1430, 1900-2000, Sun 1200-1500, closed Mon) which serves huge plates of sushi for under US$10. *Radisson Plaza Hotel*, Av Arce 2177, T244 1111, radissonbolivia@ usa.net Excellent buffet in 5-star setting, Mon and Wed, 2000-2300, US$5.50, delicious, friendly to backpackers. *Mongo's*, Hnos

VIENNA

RESTAURANT BAR

European style restaurant offering traditional cuisine and dining amid antiques, old prints and wood.

English and German spoken.

Our kitchen is open
Monday-Friday
12:00-14:00 18:30-22:00
Sundays
12:00-14:30

Federico Zuazo 1905 Casilla 56
Tel: 244 1660·Fax: 244 1572
La Paz - Bolivia

www.restaurantvienna.com
info@restaurantvienna.com

Bolivia

Manchego 2444, near Plaza Isabela la Católica. Open Mon-Thu 1000-0130, Fri-Sun 1800-0300, set lunch US$3-4, burgers and great fish and chips, 3 large fires, very Western, popular. *Chifa Emy*, Capitán Ravelo 2351, esq Belizario Salinas. Daily 1200-1500, 1800-2200 (Thu-Sat until 0200), best Chinese in town. *Vienna*, Federico Zuazo 1905, T244 1660, www.restaurantvienna.com German, Austrian and local food, excellent food and service, popular with Bolivians and foreigners, open Mon-Fri 1200-1400, 1830-2200, Sun 1200-1430.

In Sopocachi *Kuchen Stube*, Rosendo Gutiérrez 461. Excellent cakes, coffee and German specialities, Mon 1200-1900, Tue-Fri 0900-2000, Sat-Sun 1000-1230, 1430-1900. *La Terraza*, Av 6 de Agosto 2296, Av 16 de Julio and on Gutiérrez in Zona Sur. Excellent sandwiches and coffee. *Pronto*, Jáuregui 2248, T244 1369, in basement, Mon-Sat 1830-2230. Up-market Italian cuisine, beautiful decor, around US$10 pp, popular, good service. Opposite is *Reineke Fuchs*, Jáuregui 2241. Mon-Sat 1800-0100, many European beers and food. *La Bohème*, Guachalla 448, and adjacent *Confitería Creperie*, both French, good. *Restaurant Indio*, in front of Mercado Sopacachi, near the corner of Sánchez Lima. For curry, owners Bob and Sonya also have gourmet coffees and imported Earl Grey tea. *El Arriero*, Av 6 de Agosto 2535 (Casa Argentina). Best barbecue with large portions, US$11.50 pp. *El Gaucho*, Av 20 de Octubre 2041. Good steakhouse. *Gringo Limón*, 20 de Octubre esq Salazar. Food by weight, also take-away. *La Quebecoise*, 20 de Octubre 2355. French Canadian, good value, pleasant atmosphere.

Zona Sur *Puerto del Sol*, Av Ballivián, on the left, esq C 11, good Chinese. Opposite is an excellent arts and handicrafts shop, weavings, ceramics, silver etc. On Muñoz Reyes are *Chalet la Suisse*, No 1710, excellent fondue, steaks, expensive; and *El Nuevo Galeon*, No 1210, for excellent seafood. *Cevichería El Pulpo* at Galería Los Cántaros, Av Montenegro 1337, local 3, next to *Automanía*.

Vegetarian restaurants *Hotel Gloria*, Potosí 909. Very popular for *almuerzo*, US$3, be there by 1200 for a table, also buffet breakfast and dinner after 1900 for US$2.20, Sun 0700-1000 only. *Laksmi*, Sagárnaga 213, p 2. Vegetarian and vegan menu, set lunch US$1, closed Sun. Recommended. *100% Natural*, Sagárnaga 345. Full range of healthy, tasty fast foods, good breakfasts, closed Sun. *El Vegetariano*, Loayza 400 block, next to *Hotel Viena*. Good, breakfast, lunch (*almuerzo* US$1.25) and dinner.

For strictly limited budgets and strong stomachs is **Comedor Popular**, often referred to as *Comedor Familiar*, cheap but filling local meals around US$0.80-1.50, available at San Francisco, Camacho, Rodríguez and Lanza markets. Stalls in the markets sell cheap burgers but avoid *ají*, mayo or mustard and watch it being cooked. Bread from street vendors and Cochabamba wholemeal bread (*pan integral*), sold at the main markets, is recommended.

Entertainment
For up-to-the-minute information, check Quéhacer, free magazine with Saturday's La Razón, or visit www.la-razon.com

Peñas Best entertainment for visitors are the folk shows (*peñas*), which present the wide variety of local musical instruments. Enquire at the *Rumillajta* shop (in the *galería* close to San Francisco church) about future performances by the famous folk group of that name. Good *peña* at *Casa del Corregidor*, see under Eating above, dinner show Mon-Thu, no cover charge, Fri and Sat *peña* US$4, both 2100, colonial atmosphere, traditional music and dance. See under Eating for *Los Escudos* and *El Calicanto*. *Marko Tambo*, Jaén 710. US$7 all inclusive, repeatedly recommended (also sells woven goods). *El Parnaso*, Sagárnaga 189, T231 6827. Purely for tourists but a good way to see local costumes and dancing. *Bocaisapo*, Indaburo 654 y Jaén. Live music and no cover charge.

Bars and clubs *Equinoccio*, Sánchez Lima 2191. Top venue for live music and bar. *Café Montmartre*, Fernando Guachalla 399 y 20 de Octubre, next to *Alliance Française*, T244 2801. Fashionable bar with live music some weekends, good French menu, set lunch US$3.50, open 1200-1500, 1700-0200, closed Sun. *Pig and Whistle*, Goitia 155, T239 0429. Serves a selection of beers and whiskies. *Deadstroke*, Av 6 de Agosto 2460. US-style pub, café and billiards bar, food, drinks (good value for beer), billiards, pool and other games, opens 1700. *La Luna*, Oruro 197 esq Murillo. OK when quiet, opens 2200, good cocktails, can be very crowded, bring your own CDs. *Theolonius Jazz Bar*, 20 de Octubre 2172, T233 7806. Tue-Sat from 1700. *Café en Azul*, 20 de Octubre 2371. Oh, so boho atmosphere, cocktails. *Forum Disco*, Sanjinez 2908, a few blocks beyond Plaza España. Very popular, good variety of music, US$5 cover charge including couple of drinks. *La Salsa del Loro*, Rosendo Gutiérrez y Av 6 de Agosto. Open Thu, Fri and Sat evening. Good for salsa. *Underground*, Pasaje Medinacelli 2234, Sopocachi. Very popular nightclub with *paceños* and foreigners on Thu and Fri night. In Calacoto, on Av Ballivián on the left side between C 9 y 10 is *Rumors*, American/Mexican bar, restaurant, excellent music, popular late night place. Between C 15 y 16 on the left is *The Britannia*, open daily from 1700, closed Sun, cosy, popular, bar snacks. Next door No 969 is *Abracadabra*, open 7 days for lunch and dinner, great ribs and best hamburgers and pizza in town, American owner.

Cinemas Films mainly in English with Spanish subtitles. Best are *16 de Julio* (T244 1099) and *Monje Campero* (T233 0192; both on Av 16 de Julio) and *6 de Agosto* (Av 6 de Agosto, T244 2629). Expect to pay around US$2.50. The *Cinemateca Boliviana*, Capitán Ravelo y Rosendo Gutiérrez, 2 blocks from Puente de las Américas is La Paz's art film centre with festivals, courses, etc, US$1.20, students US$0.60.

Theatre *Teatro Municipal Alberto Saavedra Pérez* has a regular schedule of plays, opera, ballet and classical concerts, at Sanjines y Indaburo. The National Symphony Orchestra is very good and gives inexpensive concerts. Next door is the *Teatro Municipal de Cámara*, a small studio-theatre which shows dance, drama, music and poetry. *Casa Municipal de la Cultura 'Franz Tamayo'*, almost opposite Plaza San Francisco, hosts a variety of exhibitions, paintings, sculpture, photography, videos, etc, most of which are free. It publishes a monthly guide to cultural events, free from the information desk at the entrance. The *Palacio Chico*, Ayacucho y Potosí, in old Correo, operated by the *Secretaría Nacional de Cultura*, also has exhibitions (good for modern art), concerts and ballet, Mon-Fri 0900-1230, 1500-1900, closed at weekends, free. It is also in charge of many regional museums. Listings available in Palacio Chico.

Jan/Feb: the *Alacitas Fair*, from 24 Jan to first week of Feb, in Parque Central up from Av del Ejército, also in Plaza Sucre/San Pedro (see box). **End May/early Jun** *Festividad del Señor de Gran Poder*, the most important festival of the year, with a huge procession of costumed and masked dancers on the third Sat after Trinity. **Jul** *Fiestas de Julio*, a month of concerts and performances at the Teatro Municipal, offers a wide variety of music, including the University Folkloric Festival. **8 Dec**, festival around Plaza España, not very large, but colourful and noisy. On **New Year's Eve** fireworks are let off and make a spectacular sight; view from higher up. See also page 249 for national holidays and festivals outside La Paz.

Festivals

Up Sagárnaga, by the side of San Francisco church (behind which are many handicraft stalls in the Mercado Artesanal), are booths and small stores with interesting local items of all sorts, best value on Sun morning when prices are reduced. The lower end of Sagárnaga is best for antiques. At Sagárnaga 177 is an entire gallery of handicraft shops. *Millma*, Sagárnaga 225, and in *Hotel Plaza* for alpaca sweaters (made in their own factory) and antique and rare textiles. *Toshy* on Sagárnaga for top quality knitwear (closed Sat afternoon). *Mother Earth*, Linares 870; high-quality alpaca sweaters with natural dyes. Good quality alpaca goods also at *LAM* shops on Sagárnaga. *Artesanía Sorata*, Linares 862, and Sagárnaga 311. Mon-Sat 0930-1900 (and Sun 1000-1800 high season), specializes in dolls, sweaters and weavings. On Linares, between Sagárnaga and Santa Cruz, high quality alpaca goods priced in US$, also in *Comercio Doryan*, Sagárnaga y Murillo, eg *Wari*, unit 12, Comercio Doryan, always closes Sat afternoon. Will make to measure very quickly, English spoken, prices reasonable. *Comart Tukuypai*, Linares 958, T/F231 2686, www.terranova.nu/ comart high-quality textiles from an artisan community association. At *Kunturi*, Nicolás Acosta 783, T249 4350, you will find wonderful handicrafts produced by the Institute for the Handicapped, including embroidered cards. There are good jewellery stores throughout the city: for example *Joyería Cosmos*, Handal Center, Loc 13, Socabaya y Av Mcal Santa Cruz. Inca and Bolivian designs in gold and silver, colonial objects.

Shopping
Look around and bargain first.
In the low season many shops close Sat afternoon and Sun

Bookshops *Los Amigos del Libro*, Mercado 1315, T220 4321, also Av Montenegro y C 18 (San Miguel) and El Alto airport. They sell a few tourist maps of the region from Puno to the Yungas, and walking-tour guides, and will also ship books. *Gisbert*, Comercio 1270, libgis@ceibo.entelnet.bo Books, maps, stationery, will ship overseas. *Multi-Libro*, Loayza 233, T239 1996. Small, good for maps, politics, religion, psychology etc. *Librería Plural*, Pedro Salazar 489, Plaza Abaroa. Recommended. *Yachaywasi*, just below Plaza del Estudiante, opposite *Hotel Eldorado*. Large selection, popular with students. Historian Antonio Paredes-Candia has a bookstand selling rare historical works on a walkway below street level on Colón near Ayacucho (also on the Prado on Sun).

Bolivia

Markets In addition to those mentioned in the Sights section (page 253), the *Mercado Sopocachi* is a well-stocked covered market selling foodstuffs, kitchen supplies, etc. The 5-km square *El Alto* market is on Thu and Sun (the latter is bigger). Take a Ceja bus from along the Prado to Desvío. At the toll plaza on the autopista, change buses for one marked 16 de Julio; most other passengers will be doing the same, follow them. Arrive around 1000 and stay to 1600. Goods are cheap. Don't take anything of value, just a bin liner to carry your purchases.

Musical instruments *Rumillajta*, 1 of the Galería shops adjacent to the San Francisco church entrance. Many shops on Sagárnaga/Linares, for example *El Guitarrón*, Sagárnaga 303 esq Linares, *Marka 'Wi*, No 851.

Shopping malls *Shopping Norte*, Potosí y Socabaya, modern mall with restaurants and expensive merchandise. *Supermercado Ketal*, Ballivián esq C 15, Calacoto, is huge, also on C 21, San Miguel, and Av Arce, opposite *Jalapeños*. *Hipermaxi* in Miraflores, Cuba y Brazil, much cheaper and good for trekking food.

Sport & activities

Football: is popular and played on Wed and Sun at the *Siles Stadium* in Miraflores (Micro A) and at *Cañada Strongest*. There are reserved seats. **Golf**: *Mallasilla*, the world's highest course, 3,318 m. Non-members can play at Mallasilla on weekdays, when the course is empty, no need to book. Club hire, green fee, balls and a caddy (compulsory) also costs US$37. The course is in good condition and beautiful (take water). **Snooker/pool**: *San Luis*, Edif México, 2do Sótano, C México 1411. *Picco's*, Edif 16 de Julio, Av 16 de Julio 1566. Both have good tables and friendly atmosphere. *YMCA* sportsground and gymnasium: opposite the University of San Andrés, Av Villazón, and clubhouse open to the public, Av 20 de Octubre 1839 (table tennis, billiards, etc).

Tour operators

Those listed are all recommended. Flight tickets are the same price at airlines and agencies. Many agencies arrange excursions or travel to Peru (Puno, Cusco, Arequipa) as well as local tours

Akhamani Trek, Illampu 707, T237 5680, tourtrek@ceibo.entelnet.bo Trekking in Sorata and Coroico, also day trips, English spoken, safe, good porters, well-organized. *América Tours*, Av 16 de Julio 1490, Edificio Avenida PB, T237 4204, F231 0023, www.america-ecotours.com and *Gravity Assisted Mountain Biking*, www.gravitybolivia.com Cultural and ecotourism trips to many parts of the country (including the renowned Chalalan Lodge near Rurrenabaque, the Che Guevara Trail and Parque Nacional Noel Kempf Mercado), trekking, horse riding and mountain biking (including to Coroico, US$49), English spoken. Both companies are highly professional. *Bolivian Journeys*, Sagárnaga 363, p 1, T/F235 7848, , camping, mountain bike tours, equipment rental (with large shoe sizes), maps, English and French spoken, very helpful. *Camel Travel*, Murillo 904, T231 0070, www.boliviatrek.com Gravity assisted mountain biking, climbing, trekking, English and German spoken. *Carmoar Tours*, C Bueno 159, headed by Günther Ruttger T231 7202, carmoar@zuper.net Has information and maps for the Inca Trail to Coroico, rents trekking gear. *Crillon Tours*, Av Camacho 1223, T233 7533, www.titi caca.com With 24-hr ATM for cash on credit cards. In USA, 1450 South Bayshore Dr, suite 815, Miami, FL 33131, T305-358 5353, F305-372 0054, darius@titicaca.com Joint scheduled tours with Lima arranged. Full details of their Lake Titicaca services will be found on page 273. *Detour*, Av Mariscal Santa Cruz, Edif Camara

Bolivia

Nacional de Comercio, T236 1626. Good for flight tickets. *Diana Tours*, Sagárnaga 326, T235 1158, F236 0831. Some English spoken, tours to Coroico and Tiwanaku, bus to Puno US$12. *Explore Bolivia*, Sagárnaga 339, Galería Sagárnaga of 1, T/F239 1810, explobol@ ceiboentelnet.bo Adventure sports, good bikes (Trek). *Exprinter*, Av 6 de Agosto 2455 Edif Hilda p1, T244 2442, explpb@caoba.entlenet.bo Exchange facilities (helpful), trips to Cusco via Desaguadero with a stop in Puno. *Fremen*, C Pedro Salazar 537, Plaza Avaroa, T241 6336, F241 7327, Casilla 9682, www.amazoncharters.com (3530 Piedmont Rd, Suite 5-B, Atlanta GA 3035, USA T404-266 2180). Own *Flotel* in Trinidad for jungle cruises in the Beni and *Hotel El Puente* in the Chapare, run tours throughout country, English and French spoken.

Magri Turismo, Capitán Ravelo 2101, PO Box 4469, T244 2727, www.bolivianet.com/ magri/ Amex representative, gives TCs against American Express card but doesn't change TCs, offers Amex emergency services and clients' mail. Recommended for tours in Bolivia, travel services. *Nuevo Continente*, at *Hotel Alem*. Recommended for trip to Zongo, Clemente is a good driver, cheap service to airport, very helpful. *Pachamama Tours*, Sagárnaga 189 y Murillo Shopping Doryan p2, of35, T/F231 9740, www.megalink.com/ pachamama Cheap air fares within South America, very knowledgeable and professional, English spoken, also arranges cultural tours to indigenous groups. *Paititi*,Av 6 de Agosto, Edificio Santa Teresa, Casilla 106, T244 0586, www.paititravel.com Adventure travel, helpful, several languages spoken. *Sky Bolivia*, Sagárnaga 368, T/F231 0272, skyinter@kolla.net Mountain biking, trekking and jungle tours, owner Alejandro speaks good English. *Tauro Tours*, Mercado 1362, Galería Paladium Mezz, local 'M', T220 1846, F220 1881. Top end adventure tours, jeep trips everywhere, run by the highly experienced and trained Carlos Aguilar. *Tawa Tours*, Sagárnaga 161, T233 4290, vernay@ceibo.entelnet.bo French-run, run jungle tours to their own camp as well as the Salar de Uyuni, good guides. *Toñito Tours*, Sagárnaga 189, Comercio Doryan, T233 6250, www.bolivianexpeditions.com Tours of the **Salar**, also book bus and train tickets. *Transturin*, C Alfredo Ascarrunz 2518, Sopocachi, PO Box 5311, T242 2222, F241 1922, www.travelbolivia.com Full travel services, with tours ranging from La Paz to the whole country. Details of their Lake Titicaca services will be found on page 273. *Turisbus*, Illampu 704, Casilla 442, T245 1341, www.travelperubolivia.com Helpful, trekking equipment rented, agent for PeruRail, tickets to Puno and Cusco, also local and Bolivian tours. Recommended. *Turismo Balsa*, Capitán Ravelo 2104, T244 0817, turismo_balsa@megalink.com and Av 16 de Julio 1650, T235 4049, F237 1898. City and local tours (recommended), see also under Puerto Pérez, page 272.

Local Car hire: cars may be hired direct from *Imbex*, Av Montes 522, T245 5432, 706-47553 (mob), info@imbex.com Well-maintained Suzuki jeeps from US$60 per day, including 200 km free for 4-person 4WD. Highly recommended. *Kolla Motors*, Av Sánchez Lima 2321, T241 9141. Well-maintained 6-seater 4WD Toyota jeeps, insurance and gasoline extra. *Petita Rent-a-car*, Valentín Abecia 2031, Sopocachi Alto, T242 0329, T772 26481 (mob), www.rentacarpetita.com Swiss owners Ernesto Hug and Aldo Rezzonico. Recommended for well-maintained 4WD jeeps, etc, also offer adventure tours, German, French, English spoken. Recommended. Also arranges fishing trips. Ernesto also has garage for VW and other makes, Av Jaimes Freyre 2326, T241 5264. Highly recommended. Car Park on corner of Ingavi and Sanjines, US$1.35 for 24 hrs, safe and central.

Transport

For local buses, see page 250. See page 52 in Essentials for multinational car hire websites

Taxi: standard taxis charge US$0.75 pp for short trips within city limits. A *trufi* to Zona Sur will cost US$0.40 pp. Taxi drivers are not tipped. Don't let the driver turn the lights out at night. *Radio taxis* (e.g. *Alfa* T232 2427, *La Rápida* 239 2323) charge US$1.45 in centre and US$2.80 to suburbs. Also good value for tours for 3 people, negotiate price. *Eduardo Figueroa*, T278 6281, taxi driver and travel agent. Recommended. *Adolfo Monje Palacios*, in front of *Hotel El Dorado* or T235 4384. Highly recommended for short or long trips. *Oscar Vera*, Simón Aguirre 2158, Villa Copacabana, La Paz, T223 0453, specializes in trips to the Salar de Uyuni and the Western Cordillera, speaks English. Recommended.

Long distance Air: *Cotranstur* minibuses, white with 'Cotranstur' and 'Aeropuerto' written on the side and back, go from Plaza Isabel La Católica, anywhere on the Prado and Av Mcal Santa Cruz to the airport between 0800-0830 to 1900-2000, US$0.55 (allow about 1 hr), best to have little luggage, departures from the airport every 5 mins or so. Colectivos from

Bolivia

Plaza Isabel La Católica charge US$3.45 pp, carrying 4 passengers. Taxi is US$7 to airport. There is an *Enlace* ATM for Cirrus, Plus, Visa and MasterCard credit/debit cards in the international departures hall for taking out local cash and a bank which changes cash, OK rates. To change money when bank is closed, ask at the departure tax window near information. The international departures hall is the main concourse, with all check-in desks, and is the hall for all domestic arrivals and departures. Small tourist office at the Airport, some maps available, English spoken, helpful (when staffed). Bar/restaurant and café (cheaper) upstairs. For details of services, see under destinations. Note that *TAM* uses the nearby military airport.

Bus: For information, T228 0551. Buses to: **Oruro**, **Potosí**, **Sucre**, **Cochabamba**, **Santa Cruz**, **Tarija** and **Villazón**, leave from the main terminal at Plaza Antofagasta (micros 2, M, CH or 130), see under each destination for details. Taxi to central hotels, US$0.90. The terminal (open 0700-2300) has a tourist booth outside, internet, a post office, *Entel*, restaurant, luggage store (0530-2200) and agencies, such as *Turisbus*, *Diana*, *Vicuña* (cheaper than their offices in town). Touts find passengers the most convenient bus and are paid commission by the bus company. Buses to **Chokilla** and **Yanachi** leave from a street just off Plaza 24 de Septiembre at 0800 and 1500, 3-4 hrs, US$2.75.

Buses to **Sorata**, **Copacabana** and **Tiahuanaco** leave only from the Cemetery district. Companies include *Flota Copacabana*, *Manco Kapac*, *2 de Febrero*, *Ingavi*, *Trans Perla Andina*. To get to the Cemetery district, take any bus or minibus marked 'Cementerio' going up C Santa Cruz (US$0.17); the route is Santa Cruz, Max Paredes, Garita de Lima, Mariano Bautista, Plaza Félix Reyes Ortiz/Tomás Katari (look out for the cemetery arch on your left). On Plaza Reyes Ortiz are *Manco Kapac*, recommended (T235 0033) and *2 de Febrero* (T237 7181) for **Copacabana** and **Tiquina**. From the Plaza go up Av Kollasuyo and at the 2nd street on the right (Manuel Bustillos) is the terminal for minibuses to **Achacachi**, **Huatajata** and **Huarina**, and buses for **Sorata** (*Trans Unificada*, T301693). Several micros (20, J, 10) and min-ibuses (223, 252, 270, 7) go up Kollasuyo; look for 'Kollasuyo' on the windscreen in most, but not all cases. Buses to **Coroico and the Yungas** leave from Villa Fátima (25 mins by micros B,V,X,K, 131, 135, or 136, or *trufis* 2 or 9, which pass Pérez Velasco coming down from Plaza Mendoza, and get off at the service station, C Yanacachi 1434).

International buses from Plaza Antofagasta terminal: to **Buenos Aires**, US$110,daily at 1630, *San Roque*, T228 1959, via Yacuiba, or 1700, **San Lorenzo**, T228 2292, both take 2½ days. *Expresso Sur* (T228 1921) leaves at 1630 and charges U$10 more. Alternatively, go to Villazón and change buses in Argentina. To **Santiago**, *ChileBus* (T228 2168) leaves daily at 0630, arriving at Arica (1400) and Santiago 1700 1½ days later, US$43. To **Arica** via the frontier at Tambo Quemado and Chungará at 1300 Mon-Thu, with *Litoral*, T228 1920, 9 hrs on paved road, US$12. Also with *ChileBus* daily 0630, US$12 (good service), *Trans Salvador* daily, and *Transportes Cali*, 3 a week. To **Iquique**, take *Litoral's* Arica service, arriving 2200-2230, and continue to Iquique arriving 0400, US$15 including breakfast and lunch. To **Cusco**, *Litoral*, Wed, Fri, Sun, 0800, US$17, 12 hrs. Colectivos and agencies to **Puno** daily with different companies, most easily booked through travel agencies, US$12, 10 hrs. NB Of the various La Paz-Puno services, only *Transturin* does not make you change to a Peruvian bus once over the border. *Exprinter/Cruz del Sur*, T236 2708, go via Desaguadero Tue, Thu, Sat 0800, US$7.20. For luxury and other services to Peru see under Lake Titicaca below.

Directory **Airline offices** *Aerolíneas Argentinas*, Edif Gundlach, of 201, Reyes Ortiz 73, esq Federico Suárez, T235 1711, F239 1059. *Aero Sur*, Av 16 de Julio 616, T243 0430, F231 3957. *American Airlines*, Av 16 de Julio 1440, Edif Herman, T235 1316, www.aa.com *British Airways* and *Iberia*, Ayacucho 378, Edif Credinform p 5, T220 3885, F220 3950. *LanChile*, Av 16 de Julio 1566, p 1, T235 8377, www.lanchile.com *Lloyd Aéreo Boliviano (LAB)*, Camacho 1460, T0800-3001. *KLM* and *TAM*, Plaza del Estudiante 1931, T244 1595, F244 3487. *Lufthansa*, Av 6 de Agosto 2512 y P Salazar, T243 1717, F243 1267. *Swissair*, Edif Gundlach Torre Oeste, of 502, Reyes Ortiz 73, esq Federico Suárez, T235 0730, F239 1740. *Transportes Aéreo Militar (TAM)*, Av Montes 738 esq Serrano, T237 9286, Mon-Fri 0830-1200 and 1430-1830. *Varig*, Av Mcal Santa Cruz 1392, Edif Cámara de Comercio, T231 4040, F239 1131.

Banks *Citibank*, Av 16 de Julio 1434, T279 1414. Open Mon-Fri 0900-1600, cashes its own TCs, no commission, but will not advance cash against Citibank MasterCard. *Bisa*, Av Gral Camacho 1333, open 0830-1200, 1430-1800, Sat 1000-1300, good service, changes cash and Amex TCs. Cash advance (in bolivianos) on Visa at *Banco Santa Cruz* , also known as *BSCH* (branch in Shopping Norte is open Sat afternoon), *Banco Mercantil*, Mercado 1190 (good, quick service), *Banco Popular, Banco Nacional* and *Banco Boliviano Americano*, Camacho (good, quick service). *Visa*, Av Camacho 1448, p 11 y 12, T231 8585 (24 hrs), F281 6525, for cancelling lost or stolen credit cards. *Enlace* ATMs at many sites in the city. *Amex*, see *Magri Turismo* under Tour operators. **Exchange houses:** *Sudamer*, Colón 256 y Camacho, good rates also for currencies other than US$, 3% commission on TCs into dollars, no commission into bolivianos, frequently recommended. Very few deal in Argentine and Chilean pesos. Street changers on corners around Plaza del Estudiante, Camacho, Colón and Prado, OK rates. Sending money to Bolivia is easiest through *Giro Express*, Capitán Ravelo 2101. *Western Union*, Av Nicolás Acosta 547, Zona San Pedro, T248 9249, open 0830-1900, Sat 0900-1700, also useful, but more expensive. *Western Union*, however, has branches throughout city and country.

Communications Internet: There are many internet cafés in the centre of La Paz, opening and shutting all the time. Cost US$0.75-1 per hr. Internet connections are normally faster in the mornings and at weekends. Most open at 0900 and close anytime between 2100 and 2300; few open on Sun. Post Office: Correo Central, Av Mcal Santa Cruz y Oruro, Mon-Fri 0800-2000, Sat 0830-1800, Sun 0900-1200. Another on Linares next to Museo de Coca, 0830-2000. Stamps are sold only at the post offices. Good philately section/museum on 1st floor of Correo Central. There are a number of shops selling good postcards, etc, and one selling Walter Guzmán Córdova maps. *Poste Restante* keeps letters for 2 months, no charge. Check the letters filed under all parts of your name. For the procedure for sending parcels and for mailing prices, see page 246. Don't forget moth balls (difficult to buy – try C Sagárnaga) for textile items. To collect parcels costs US$0.15. Express postal service (top floor) is expensive. All firms pick up packets. *DHL*, Av Mcal Santa Cruz 1297, T0800-4020. *FedEx*, Rosendo Gutiérrez 113 esq Capitán Ravelo, T244 3537. *UPS*, Av 16 de Julio 1479, p 10. **Telephone:** *Entel* (T236 7474) office for telephone calls and fax is at Ayacucho 267, 0730-2300 (the only one open on Sun), and in Edif Libertad, C Potosí. Long wait for incoming calls. Many small *Entel* offices throughout the city, with quicker service. For international and national calls, rather than wait for a booth, buy a phonecard (Bs 5, 10, 20 or 100) and use it in the phones to the left in the main *Entel* office, also throughout the city. For local calls buy a *ficha* (US$0.10) from the person sitting next to red *Entel* phone booths; or use a phone in any shop or stall with 'teléfono' sign (US$0.20).

Cultural centres *Alliance Française*, Guachalla 399 esq Av 20 de Octubre T244 2075, F239 1950, French-Spanish library, videos, newspapers, and cultural gatherings information. Call for opening hours. *British Council*, Av Arce 2730, T243 1240, F243 1377, bcouncil@ceibo.entelnet.bo Café serves English breakfasts, open 0645-2100, 1600-2030, Mon-Fri, library with British newspapers and magazines, films every Wed 2000, also English classes. *Centro Boliviano Americano (CBA)*, Parque Zenón Iturralde 121, T235 1627/234 2582 (10 mins walk from Plaza Estudiante down Av Arce). Has public library and recent US papers (Mon-Wed 0900-1230, 1500-1930, till 2000 Thu and Fri). *Goethe-Institut*, Av 6 de Agosto 2118, T244 2453, www.goethe.de Library open Mon, Tue, Thu 1600-2000, Wed, Fri 1000-1300, 1600-2000; institute open Mon-Thu 0900-1300, 1500-1900, Fri 0900-1300. Excellent library, recent papers in German, CDs, cassettes and videos free on loan, German books for sale.

Cycle spares See *Gravity Assisted Mountain Biking* under *América Tours* in Tour operators, above, very knowledgeable, www.gravitybolivia.com In Calacoto: *Bicicar* (Trek Bikes), Av Montenegro y C 18, local 2. *Nosiglia Sport* (Cannondale), Av Costanera 28, T274 9904, nossport@ceibo.entelnet.bo *Massa* (Raleigh and Nishiki), C 21 No 8341, T/F279 7820.

Embassies and consulates Argentine Consulate, Sánchez Lima 497, T241 7737, 24 hrs for visa, 0900-1330. **Austrian Consulate**, Edif Petrolero, p 1, of 11, Av 16 de Julio 1616, T231 3953, 1430-1600. **Belgium**, Calle 9, No 6, Achumani, T277 0081, 0830-1700. **Brazil**, Av Arce, Edif Multicentro, T244 0202, 0900-1300, Mon-Fri (visas take 2 days). **Britain**, Av Arce 2732, T243 3424, F243 1073, Casilla 694, Mon-Fri 0900-1200, Mon, Tue, Thu also 1330-1630, visa section open 0900-1200 has a list of travel hints for Bolivia, doctors, etc. **Canadian Consulate**, Edif Barcelona p 2, Victor Sanjinez 2678, Plaza España, T241 4453, 0900-1200. **Chilean Consulate**, H Siles 5873, esq C 13, Obrajes district, T278 5275, open Mon-Fri 0900-1200, 1500-1700, visa same day if requested in the morning (take microbus N, A or L from Av 16 de Julio). **Danish Consulate**, Av Arce 2799 and Cordero, Edif Fortaleza, p 9, T243 2070, Mon-Fri, 0800-1600. **Finnish Consulate**, Av Sánchez Lima 2656, c/ John Deere office, T243 0170, Mon-Fri 0830-1200, 1400-1830. Only provides help if your passport is stolen; no free use of phone, fax or email (nearest embassy is in Peru). **French Consulate**, Av Hernando Siles 5390, esq C 08 Obrajes, T278 6189 (take microbus N, A or L down Av 16 de Julio), Mon-Fri 0830-1230, 1400-1600. **German**, Av Arce 2395, T244 0606, F244 1441, Mon-Fri 0900-1200. **Irish Honorary Consul**, Peter O'Toole, Av Sánchez Lima 2326,

Bolivia

T/F242 1408, Amtrac@ceibo.entelnet.bo **Israel**, Av Mcal Santa Cruz, Edif Esperanza, p 10, T237 4239, Casilla 1309/1320, Mon-Fri 0900-1600. *El Lobo* restaurant deals with mail for Israeli travellers. **Italy**, Av 6 de Agosto 2575, PO Box 626, T243 4955, F243 4975, Mon-Fri 1030-1230. **Japan**, Rosendo Gutiérrez 497, esq Sánchez Lima, PO Box 2725, T237 3151, Mon-Fri 0830-1145. **Netherlands Consulate**, Av 6 de Agosto 2455, Edif Hilda, p 7, T244 4040, F244 3804, Casilla 10509, nlgovlap@unete.com 0830-1700. **Norwegian Consulate**, C René Moreno 1096 in San Miguel, T/F277 0009, Mon-Fri 0900-1230, 1430-1700. **Paraguayan Consulate**, Edif Illimani, p 1, Av 6 de Agosto y P Salazar, good visa service, T243 2201, F243 3176, Mon-Fri 0800-1600. **Peru**, Edif Alianza office 110, Av 6 de Agosto 2190 y C F Guachalla, T244 0631, F244 4199, Mon-Fri 0900-1300, 1500-1700, visa US$10 in US$, issued same day if you go early. **Spanish Consulate**, Av 6 de Agosto 2827 and Cordero, T243 0118, Mon-Fri 0900-1330. **Swedish Consulate**, Av 14 de Septiembre 5080 y C5 Obrajes, T/F278 7903, Casilla 852, open 0900-1200. **Switzerland**, Edif Petrolero p 6, Av 16 de Julio 1616, T231 5617, F239 1462, Casilla 9356, Mon-Fri 0900-1200. **USA**, Av Arce 2780 y Cordero, T243 3520, F243 3854, Casilla 425, Mon-Fri 0800-1700.

Language schools *Alliance Française* (see also above). *Casa de Lenguas*, T/F+34-91 591 2393, www.casadelenguas.com (Also see Sucre, page 304). *Centro Boliviano Americano* (address under Cultural centres above), US$140 for 2 months, 1½ hrs tuition each afternoon. *Instituto de La Lengua Española*, María TeresaTejada, C Aviador esq final 14, No 180, Achumani, T279 6074, T715-56735 (mob), sicbol@caoba.entelnet.bo 1-to-1 lessons US$7 per hr. Recommended. *Speak Easy Institute*, Av Arce 2047, between Goitia and Montevideo, just down from Plaza del Estudiante, T/F244 1779, speakeasyinstitute@yahoo.com US$5 for private lessons, cheaper for groups and couples, Spanish and English taught. *The Spanish Language Learning Process*, C Murillo 1046 (p 3), T/F231 1471, T706-28016 (mob), www.spanishcourses.biz/index.html **Private Spanish lessons** from: *Cecilia Corrales*, José María Camacho 1664, San Pedro, T248 7458, besteaching75@hotmail.com *Isabel Daza Vivado*, Murillo 1046, p 3, T231 1471, T706-28016 (mob), maria_daza@hotmail.com US$3 per hr. *William Ortiz (ABC)*, Pisagua 634, T228 1175, T712-62657 (mob), williamor@hotmail.com US$5.50 per hr. *Enrique Eduardo Patzy*, Mendez Arcos 1060, Sopocachi, T241 5501 or 776-22210, epatzy@ hotmail.com US$6 an hr one-to-one tuition, speaks English and Japanese. Recommended.

For hospitals, doctors and dentists, contact your consulate or the tourist office for recommendations

Medical services Ambulance service: T222 4452. **Health and hygiene:** *Unidad Sanitaria La Paz*, on Ravelo behind *Hotel Radisson Plaza*, yellow fever shot and certificate for US$12. *Ministerio de Desarrollo Humano, Secretaría Nacional de Salud*, Av Arce, near *Radisson Plaza*, yellow fever shot and certificate, rabies and cholera shots, malaria pills, bring own syringe (US$0.20 from any pharmacy). *Centro Piloto de Salva*, Av Montes y Basces, T236 9141, 10 mins walk from Plaza San Francisco, for malaria pills, helpful. *Laboratorios Illanani*, Edif Alborada p 3, of 304, Loayza y Juan de la Riva, T231 7290, open 0900-1230, 1430-1700, fast, efficient, hygienic, blood test US$4.75, stool test US$9.50. Tampons may be bought at most *farmacias* and supermarkets. The daily paper, *Presencia*, lists chemists/pharmacies on duty (*de turno*). For contact lenses, *Optaluis*, Comercio 1089, well-stocked.

Useful addresses Immigration: to renew a visa go to **Migración Bolivia**, Av Camacho 1480, T0800-3007 (toll free). Mon-Fri 0830-1600, go early. Drop passport and tourist card at the booth on the right as you walk into the office in the morning and collect stamped passport in the afternoon. **Tourist Police:** Plaza del Estadio, Miraflores, next to *Love City* disco, T222 5016. Open 24 hrs, for insurance claims after theft, English spoken, helpful.

Trekking and climbing near La Paz

Start at **Ventilla** (see Transport, page 270), walk up the valley for about three hours **Takesi Trail** passing the village of Choquekhota until the track crosses the river and to the right of the road, there is a falling-down brick wall with a map painted on it. The Takesi and Alto Takesi trails start here, following the path to the right of the wall. The road continues to Mina San Francisco. In the first hour's climb from the wall is excellent stone paving which is Inca or pre-Inca, depending on who you believe, either side of the pass at 4,630 m. There are camping possibilities at *Estancia Takesi* and in the village of Kakapi you can sleep at the **G** *Kakapi Tourist Lodge*, 10 beds with good mattresses, solar shower and toilet. It is run by the local community and sponsored by Fundación Pueblo. It is also possible to camp. You also have to pass the unpleasant mining settlement of Chojlla, between which and Yanakachi is a gate where it is necessary to register and often pay a small 'fee'. Yanakachi has a number of good places to stay, several good hikes and an orphanage you can help at. The Fundación Pueblo office on the plaza has information. Buy a minibus ticket on arrival in Yanakachi or walk 45 minutes down to the La Paz-Chulumani road for transport. The trek can be done in one long day, especially if you organize a jeep to the start of the trail, but is more relaxing in two or three if you take it slowly though you'll have to carry camping kit. Hire mules in Choquekhota for US$8 per day plus up to US$8 for the muleteer. A 2-3 day alternative is from Mina San Francisco to El Castillo and the village of Chaco on the La Paz-Chulumani road. This trek is called La Reconquistada and has the distinction of including a 200 m disused mining tunnel.

Immediately before the road drops down from La Cumbre to start the descent to Las **Choro Trail (La** Yungas, there is a collapsing plastered brick wall on the left which marks the start of the **Cumbre to** trail. However, there is nothing to help you get across the featureless moonscape to the **Coroico)** *apacheta* where the trail starts properly. Cloud and bad weather are normal at La Cumbre (4,700 m): follow the left hand of the statue of Christ, take a map and compass or guide to get you to the start of the trail which is then well signposted. The trail passes Chucura, Challapampa (camping possible, US$0.40, wood and beer for sale), the Choro bridge and the Río Jacun-Manini (fill up with water at both river crossings). At Sandillani it is possible to camp in the carefully-tended garden of a Japanese man who keeps a book with the names of every passing traveller. He likes to see postcards and pictures from other countries. There is good paving down to Villa Esmeralda, after which is Chairo, then to Yolosa. It takes three days to trek from La Cumbre to Chairo and a further long day on foot to Coroico, unless you take a truck from Chairo to Yolosa (allegedly at 0600, or hire one if enough people: US$2.25 each). From Yolosa it is 8 km uphill to Coroico with regular transport for US$1 per person.

From Chuñavi follow path left (east) and contour gently up. Camping possible after **Yunga Cruz** two hours. Continue along the path staying on left hand side of the ridge to reach **(Lambate or** Cerro Khala Ciudad (literally, Stone City Mountain, you'll see why). Good paving **Chuñavi to** brings you round the hill to join the path from Lambate (this heads uphill for two days **Chulumani)** through Quircoma and then to Cerro Khala Ciudad after which you descend to join *Best but hardest* the path from Chuñavi). Head north to Cerro Cuchillatuca and then Cerro Yunga *of the 4 'Inca' trails* Cruz, where there is water and camping is possible. After this point water and camping *and therefore less* are difficult and normally impossible until you get down to Chulumani. The last water *popular, so less* and camping possibilities are all within the next hour, take advantage of them. Each *litter and begging* person should have at least two litres of water in bottles. For water purification, only use iodine-based preparations (iodine tincture, *iodo* in *farmacias* costs US$0.50: use 5 drops per litre.) There are some clearances on the way down but no water. Starting in Chuñavi saves two days' walking and makes the trek possible in three days but misses the best bits. Starting in Lambate the trek normally takes five days.

Transport **Takesi Trail** Take a Palca/Ventilla bus from outside *comedor popular* in C Max Paredes above junction with C Rodríguez, daily at 0530, US$1; or take any bus going to Bolsa Negra, Tres Ríos or Pariguaya (see Yunga Cruz below). Alternatively, take any micro or minibus to Chasquipampa or Ovejuyo and try hitching a lift with anything heading out of La Paz. If there isn't any transport, haggle with drivers of empty minibuses in Ovejuyo; you should be able to get one to go to Ventilla for about US$8. To Mina San Francisco: hire a jeep from La Paz; US$70, takes about 2 hrs. *Veloz del Norte* (T02-221 8279) leaves from Ocabaya and Av Las Américas in Villa Fátima, 0900 and 1400; 3½ hrs, continuing to Chojlla. Buses to La Paz (US$1.65) leave from Yanakachi at 0545 and 1245-1300 or 1400 daily.

Choro Trail To La Cumbre: take a bus or camión from Villa Fátima (US$1, about 1 hr); make sure the driver knows you want to get off at La Cumbre. Alternatively, get a radio taxi from central La Paz for about US$12, or hire a jeep for US$40.

Yunga Cruz Trail Take the bus to Pariguaya at 0900 Mon-Sat, from C Gral Luis Lara esq Venacio Burgoa near Plaza Líbano, San Pedro, US$2, 6 hrs to Chuñavi, US$2.25; 6½ hrs to Lambate (3 km further on). Buses to Tres Ríos and Bolsa Negra depart at same time but stop well before Chuñavi or Lambate. It's not possible to buy tickets in advance, be there between 0700 and 0800 on the day to ensure ticket.

Guides **Guides** must be hired through a tour company. *Club Andino Boliviano*, C México 1638,
& maps T232 4682, Casilla 5879 (closed Sat) can provide a list of guides and now works with the Bolivian association of mountain guides. Also recommended: *Ricardo Albert* at *Inca Travel*, Av Arce 2116, Edif Santa Teresa. *Dr Juan Pablo Ando*, Casillo 6210, T278 3495, trained in Chamonix, for mountaineering, rock climbing, trekking and ecological tours. *Iván Blanco Alba*, *Asociación de Guías de Montaña y Trekking*, C Chaco 1063, Casilla 1579, T235 0334. Trek Bolivia, C Sagárnaga 392, T/F231 7106. *Azimut Explorer*, Sagárnaga 173, Galery Gala Centro of 1, T/F329464/366155, PO Box 14907, azimexbo@wara.bolnet.bo Guide Juan Villarroel is one of the best. The *Club de Excursionismo, Andinismo y Camping*, helps people find the cheapest way to go climbing, trekking, etc; foreigners may join local groups, T278 3795, Casilla 8365, La Paz, or ask at the University. Each week there is a meeting and slide show.

Maps All treks in the Cordillera Real are covered by the map of the Cordillera Real, 1:135,000, Liam O'Brien. Takesi, La Reconquistada, Choro and Yunga Cruz are covered by the Walter Guzmán Córdova 1:150,000 map; see Maps in Essentials. There are also the *IGM* 1:50,000 sheets: for Takesi: Chojlla 6044 IV; for Choro: Milluni 5945 II, Unduavi 6045 III and Coroico; for Yunga Cruz: Lambate 6044 II and 6044. For guidebooks on trekking and climbing, see page 1479.

Huayna Potosí Huayna Potosí is normally climbed in two days, with one night camped on a glacier at
See Climbing in 5,600 m. There is a refugio *Huayna Potosí*, which costs US$10 per night, plus food,
Essentials, page 58, US$160 for three-day tour. Contact through office at *Hotel Continental*, Illampu 626,
and above for Casilla 731, T/F02-245 6717, bolclimb@mail.megalink.com or La Paz agencies for
details of guides further information. The starting point for the normal route is at Zongo, whose valley used to have a famous ice cave (now destroyed by global warming). ■ *It can be reached by transport arranged through tourist agencies (US$70) or the refugio. Camión from Plaza Ballivián in El Alto early morning or midday Mon, Wed, Fri (return next day), taxi (US$30), or minibus in the high season. If camping in the Zongo Pass area, stay at the site maintained by Miguel and family near the white house above the cross.*

Chacaltaya Chacaltaya was the highest ski run in the world. In 1999 skiing was discontinued as
90 mins by car there was not enough snow, but it's now becoming popular for downhill mountain
from La Paz (40 km) biking. Check at the Club Andino Boliviano (address above) if they still run excur-
Altitude: 5,345 m sions to their refuge on the mountain. You can walk to the summit of Chacaltaya for views of Titicaca on one side, La Paz on the other, and Huayna Potosí. Tiring, because of the altitude, but you have most of the day to do the climb and other peaks. Laguna Milluni, near Chacaltaya, is a beautiful lake to visit, but do not drink its heavily contaminated water. Take plenty of mineral water and protection against sun and ultra-violet light. For the really hardy, accommodation at the Chacaltaya ski station is free, but take very warm clothes, sleeping bag and bed roll, food and water,

as there is no heating or bedding. Meals are available at the hut at weekends. ■ *Taxi or minibus US$30 (whole car) for a ½-day trip, or similar to the top by rented car costs about US$70, and really only at weekends. However, the trip can be hair-raising, buses carry no chains. Often the buses and tours only go half way. Many agencies do day trips, US$12.50, often combined with Valle de la Luna.*

Tiahuanaco

This remarkable archaeological site, 72 km west of La Paz, near the southern end of Lake Titicaca, takes its name from one of the most important pre-Columbian civilizations in South America. It is now the most popular excursion fom La Paz. Many archaeologists believe that Tiahuanaco existed as early as 1600 BC, while the complex visible today probably dates from the eight to the 10th centuries AD. The site may have been a ceremonial complex at the centre of an empire which covered almost half Bolivia, south Peru, north Chile and northwest Argentina. It was also a hub of trans-Andean trade. The demise of the Tiahuanaco civilization, according to studies by Alan Kolata of the University of Illinois, could have been precipitated by the flooding of the area's extensive system of raised fields (*Sukakollu*), which were capable of sustaining a population of 20,000. The Pumapunka section, 1 km south of the main complex may have been a port, as the waters of the lake used to be much higher than they are today. The raised field system is being reutilized in the Titicaca area.

There is a small museum at the ticket office, the **Museo Regional Arqueológico de Tiahuanaco**, containing a well-illustrated explanation of the raised field system of agriculture. One of the main structures is the Kalasasaya, meaning 'standing stones', referring to the statues found in that part: two of them, the Ponce monolith (centre of inner patio) and the Fraile monolith (southwest corner), have been re-erected. In the northwest corner is the Puerta del Sol, originally at Pumapunku. Its carvings, interrupted by being out of context, are thought to be either a depiction of the creator God, or a calendar. The motifs are exactly the same as those around the Ponce monolith. The Templo Semisubterráneo is a sunken temple whose walls are lined with faces, all different, according to some theories depicting states of health, the temple being a house of healing; another theory is that the faces display all the ethnicities of the world. The Akapana, originally a pyramid, still has some ruins on it, but it has not been fully excavated. At Pumapunku, some of whose blocks weigh up to 132 tonnes, a natural disaster may have put a sudden end to the construction before it was finished. Most of the best statues are in the *Museo Tiahuanaco* or the *Museo Semisubterráneo* in La Paz (see page 254).

For the best light for photos, go before midday Taking a guide or a book on the area is recommended to make the most of the site

The nearby village of Tiahuanaco still has remnants from the time of independence and the 16th century church used pre-Columbian masonry. In fact, Tiahuanaco for a long while was the 'quarry' for the altiplano. For the festival on 21 June, before sunrise, there are colourful dances and llama sacrifices. On the 8th day of carnival (Sunday), there is a colourful carnival. Souvenirs for sale, bargain hard, do not take photographs. Market day in Tiahuanaco is Sunday; do not take photos then either.

■ *The site opens at 0900, US$2 for foreigners, including entry to museum. Allow 4 hrs to see the ruins and village. Guidebooks in English:* Tiwanaku, *by Mariano Baptista, Plata Publishing Ltd, Chur, Switzerland, or* Discovering Tiwanaku *by Hugo Boero Rojo. Guía Especial de Arqueología Tiwanaku, by Edgar Hernández Leonardini, a guide on the site, recommended. Written guide material is difficult to come by; hiring a good guide costs US$10. Map of site with historical explanation in English (published by Quipus) for sale at ticket office, US$2.50. Locals sell copies of Tiahuanaco figures; cheaper here than La Paz.*

Sleeping and eating There are a few places to sleep and eat, including **E** *Tiahuanco* and restaurant *Kala-Huahua* (on the southeast corner of the plaza). Next to the site museum is *La Cabaña del Puma* restaurant where lunch costs US$1.80.

Transport Take any Micro marked 'Cementerio', get out at Plaza Félix Reyes Ortiz, on Mariano Bautista (north side of cemetery), go north up Aliaga, 1 block east of Azin to find Tiahuanaco micros, US$1, 1½ hrs, every 30 mins, 0600 to 1700. Tickets can be bought in advance. Taxi for 2 costs about US$20-25 (can be shared), return, with unlimited time at site (US$30-40 including El Valle de la Luna). Some buses go on from Tiahuanaco to Desaguadero; virtually all Desaguadero buses stop at Tiahuanaco, US$0.65. Return buses (last back 1730-1800) leave from south side of the Plaza in village. Most tours from La Paz cost US$60 stopping at Laja and the highest point on the road before Tiahuanaco. Some tours include El Valle de la Luna.

La Paz

Bolivia

Lake Titicaca

See page 328 for recommended reading on the region. A paved road runs from La Paz to the Straits of Tiquina (114 km El Alto–San Pablo)

Lake Titicaca is two lakes joined by the Straits of Tiquina: the larger, northern lake (Lago Mayor, or Chucuito) contains the Islas del Sol and de la Luna at its southern end; the smaller lake (Lago Menor, or Huiñamarca) has several small islands. The waters are a beautiful blue, reflecting the hills and the distant cordillera in the shallows of Huiñamarca, mirroring the sky in the rarified air and changing colour when it is cloudy or raining. A trip on the lake is a must if you're in the area; boat services are given below.

La Paz to Copacabana

Puerto Pérez
72 km from La Paz

The closest point to the capital on Lake Titicaca, Puerto Pérez was the original harbour for La Paz. It was founded in the 19th century by British navigators as a harbour for the first steam boat on the lake (the vessel was assembled piece by piece in Puno). Colourful fiestas are held on New Year's Day, Carnival, 3 May and 16 July (days may change each year). There are superb views of the lake and mountains.

Sleeping and eating L *Hotel Las Balsas*, owned and operated by *Turismo Balsa* (see La Paz Tour Operators, page 264, or T/F02-2813226). In a beautiful lakeside setting, with views of the cordillera, all rooms have balcony over the lake, willing to negotiate out of season, fitness facilities including pool, jacuzzi, sauna. Excellent restaurant with fixed price lunch or dinner good value at US$12. Nearby on the Plaza is **C** *Hostería Las Islas*, same owners, shared bath, hot water, heated rooms, comfortable but can get crowded, *Blue Note* jazz bar next door.

Transport Regular minibus service from La Paz Cementerio district: across from the cemetery, above the flower market, ask for buses to Batallas, price US$0.75.

Huatajata

Further north along the east shore of the lake is Huatajata, with *Yacht Club Boliviano* (restaurant open to non-members, open Saturday, Sunday lunch only, sailing for members only) and *Crillon Tours International Hydroharbour* and *Inca Utama Hotel* (see below). Next to *Inca Utama*, is *Restaurant Huatajata Utama*, highly recommended. Then *Inti Raymi*, with fresh fish and boat trips (US$22 per boat); and others. The restaurants are of varying standard, most lively at weekends and in the high season. Máximo Catari's *Inti Karka* restaurant is on the road (full menu, open daily, average prices, good fish), also a hotel (**F**) on the waterfront, T0811 5058. Between Huatajata and Huarina (at Km 80 from La Paz) is the **B** *Hotel Titicaca*, T02-237 4877, F239 1225. Beautiful views, sauna, pool, good restaurant, very quiet

66 99 *The South American Handbook 1924*

On Lake Titicaca *It is curious after travelling for several days on the Southern Railway in the high altitudes of the Andes, to alight on the shores of Lake Titicaca and see at the pier a vessel which has the appearance and almost the size of an ocean liner.*

during the week (address in La Paz, Potosí y Ayacucho 1220, p 2). ■ Bus: La Paz-Huatajata/Tiquina, US$0.85, Transportes Titikaka, *Av Kollasuyo 16, daily from 0400, returning between 0700 and 1800.*

Beyond here is Chúa, where there is fishing, sailing and Transturin's catamaran dock (see below). The public telephone office, *Cotel*, is on the plaza just off the main road. About 2 km before Chúa is a turning to the right to *La Posada del Inca*. Open Saturday, Sunday and holidays for lunch only, in a beautiful colonial *hacienda*, good trout, average prices.

Crillon Tours (address under La Paz, Tour operators, page xxx) run a hydrofoil service on Lake Titicaca with excellent bilingual guides. Tours stop at their Andean Roots cultural complex at *Inca Utama*: the Bolivian History Museum includes a recorded commentary; a 15-min video precedes the evening visit to the Kallawaya (Native Medicine) museum. The **Inca Utama Hotel (AL)** has a health spa based on natural remedies; the rooms are comfortable, with heating, electric blankets, good service, bar, good food in restaurant, reservations through *Crillon Tours* in La Paz. *Crillon* is Bolivia's oldest travel agency and is consistently highly recommended). Also at *Inca Utama* is an observatory (*Alajpacha*) with two telescopes and retractable thatched roof for viewing the night sky, a floating restaurant and bar on the lake (*La Choza Náutica*), a 252-sq m floating island, a new colonial-style tower with 15 deluxe suites, panoramic elevator and 2 conference rooms. Health, astronomical, mystic and ecological programmes are offered. The hydrofoil trips include visits to Andean Roots complex, Copacabana, Islas del Sol and de la Luna, Straits of Tiquina and past reed fishing boats. See Isla del Sol below for *La Posada del Inca*. Trips can be arranged to/from Puno (bus and hydrofoil excursion to Isla del Sol) and from Copacabana via Isla del Sol to Cusco and Machu Picchu. Other combinations of hydrofoil and land-based excursions can be arranged (also jungle and adventure tours). Cost is US$173 from La Paz to Puno, US$145 for day excursion from La Paz; fascinating, not least for the magnificent views of the Cordillera on a clear day. All facilities and modes of transport connected by radio. In Puno, *Crillon*'s office is at *Arcobaleno Tours*, Lambayeque 175, T/F351052, arcobaleno@titicacalake.com where all documentation for crossing the border can be done.

Transturin (see also La Paz, Tour operators, page 264) run catamarans on Lake Titicaca, either for sightseeing or on the La Paz-Puno route. The catamarans are more leisurely than the hydrofoils of *Crillon* so there is more room and time for on-board entertainment, with bar, video and sun deck. From their dock at Chúa, catamarans run day and day/night cruises starting either in La Paz or Copacabana. Puno may also be the starting point for trips. Overnight cruises involve staying in a cabin on the catamaran, moored at the Isla del Sol, with lots of activities. On the island, *Transturin* has the *Inti Wata* cultural complex which has restored Inca terraces, an Aymara house and the underground *Ekako* museum. There is also a 50-passenger totora reed boat for trips to the Polkokaina Inca palace. Prices range from US$108-213; all island-based activities are for catamaran clients only. *Transturin* runs through services to Puno without a change of bus, and without many of the formalities at the border. **Transturin** has an office in Puno, Jr Libertad 176, T352771, F351316, www.travelbolivia.com and offers last

Lake Titicaca tours

Bolivia

minute, half-price deals for drop-in travellers (24-48 hrs in advance, take passport): sold in Copacabana only, half-day tour on the lake, continuing to Puno by bus, or La Paz; overnight Copacabana-Isla del Sol-Copacabana with possible extension to La Paz. Sold in La Paz only: La Paz-Isla del Sol-La Paz, or with overnight stay (extension to Puno possible on request).

Turisbus (see La Paz, Tour operators and *Hoteles Rosario*, La Paz, and *Rosario del Lago*, Copacabana) offer guided tours in the fast launches *Titicaca Explorer I* (28 passengers) and *II* (8 passengers) to the Isla del Sol, returning to Copacabana via the Bahía de Sicuani for trips on traditional reed boats (half-day US$29). Also La Paz-Puno, with boat excursion to Isla del Sol, boxed lunch and road transport (one day US$49), or with additional overnight at *Hotel Rosario del Lago* (US$79.50).

Islands of Lake Huiñamarca On **Suriqui** (1½ hours from Huatajata) in Lake Huiñamarca, a southeasterly extension of Lake Titicaca, you can visit the museum/craft shops of the Limachi brothers (now living at the *Inca Utama* cultural complex). The late Thor Heyerdahl's *Ra II*, which sailed from Morocco to Barbados in 1970, his *Tigris* reed boat, and the balloon gondola for the Nasca (Peru) flight experiment (see page 1149), were also constructed by the craftsmen of Suriqui. Reed boats are still made on Suriqui, probably the last place where the art survives. On **Kalahuta** there are *chullpas* (burial towers), old buildings and the uninhabited town of Kewaya. On **Pariti** there is Inca terracing and very good examples of weaving. Máximo Catari (see above) arranges boats to the islands in Lago Huiñamarca, Pariti, Kalahuta and Suriqui: prices from US$25-US$40, one hour boat trip US$7.50, sailing boat for three US$16-20 for a day (boat trips recommended). Boats can also be hired in Tiquina for trips to Suriqui, US$3 per person in a group.

From Chúa the main road reaches the east side of the Straits at **San Pablo** (clean restaurant in blue building, with good toilets). On the west side is San Pedro, the main Bolivian naval base, from where a paved road goes to Copacabana. Vehicles are transported across on barges, US$4. Passengers cross separately, US$0.35 (not included in bus fares) and passports are checked. Expect delays during rough weather, when it can get very cold.

Copacabana

Phone code: 02
Colour map 6, grid A2
158 km from La Paz
by paved road.
Beware of sunburn
especially on the
lake, even when it
does not feel hot.
You should never
walk alone in
the surrounding
countryside

An attractive little town on Lake Titicaca, Copacabana has a heavily restored, Moorish-style cathedral containing a famous 16th century miracle-working Dark Virgin of the Lake, also known as the Virgin of Candelaria, one of the patron saints of Bolivia. If going during Carnival or on a religious holiday, arrive early and be prepared to hold onto your place, as things tend to get very crowded. The cathedral itself is notable for its spacious atrium with four small chapels; the main chapel has one of the finest gilt altars in Bolivia. The basilica is clean, white, with coloured tiles decorating the exterior arches, cupolas and chapels. Vehicles are blessed in front of the church daily, especially on Sunday. There are 17th and 18th century paintings and statues in the sanctuary. Entrance at side of Basilica opposite *Entel*. ■ *Mon-Fri 1100-1200, 1400-1800, Sat-Sun, 0800-1200, 1400-1800, only groups of 8 or more, US$0.60.* On the headland which overlooks the town and port, Cerro Calvario, are the Stations of the Cross (a steep climb – leave plenty of time if going to see the sunset). On the hill behind the town (Cerro Sancollani) overlooking the lake, roughly southeast of the Basilica, is the **Horca del Inca**, two pillars of rock with another laid across them (probably a sun clock, now covered in graffiti), US$3. There is a path marked by arrows. Boys will offer to guide you: fix price in advance if you want their help. There's a lovely walk along the lakeside north to Yampupata, 15 km (allow 3½ hours), through unspoilt countryside. At the village, or at Sicuani ask for a rowing boat to Isla del Sol, or trip on the lake (US$3.50). José Quispe Mamani is helpful and provides a motor launch, plus meals and accommodation.

B *Gloria*, 16 de Julio, T/F862 2094, www.hotelgloriabolivia.com Same group as *Gloria* in La **Sleeping**
Paz, hot water, bar, café and restaurant with international and vegetarian food, gardens, ■ *on map*
money exchange. **B** *Rosario del Lago*, Rigoberto Paredes y Av Costanera, T862 2141,
reservaslago@hotelrosario.com Same ownership as *Rosario*, La Paz, includes breakfast, hot
water, *Turisbus* office (see above), small rooms with lake view, colonial style, beautifully furnished, internet café, handicrafts display, restaurant. Recommended. **B-C** *Chasqui de Oro*, Av
Costanera 55, T862 2343. Includes breakfast, lakeside hotel, café/breakfast room has great
views, trips organized, video room. **C-D** *La Cúpula*, C Michel Pérez 1-3, T862 2029,
www.hotelcupula.com 5 mins' walk from centre, price depends on room (most expensive
have kitchen and bath), sitting room with TV and video, fully-equipped kitchen, library, hot
water, book exchange, vegetarian restaurant (plus trout and some meat dishes, pricier than
others in town), great breakfast, offer local tours, run by Amanda and Martin Strätker whose
Centro Cultural Arco y Hamaca offers painting and sculpting classes and courses in Spanish,
English and German. Very warmly recommended. **D** *Utama*, Michel Pérez, T862 2013. With
breakfast, hot water, good showers, comfortable. **E** *Boston*, Conde de Lemos, near Basilica,
T862 2231. **F** without bath, good, quiet. **E** *Colonial del Lago*, Av 6 de Agosto y Av 16 de Julio,
T862 2270, titicacabolivia@yahoo.com Bright rooms, some with lake view, **F** without bath,
breakfast included, garden, restaurant and *peña*. **E** *Playa Azul*, 6 de Agosto, T862 2228, F862
2227. Rooms OK, but chilly, includes breakfast, tepid electric showers, water supply and toilets
poor, good food. **E** *Res Sucre*, Murillo 228, T862 2080. Hot water, parking, quiet, good cheap
breakfast, laundry US$1.20, offers tours of lake. **E-F** *Ambassador*, Bolívar y Jáuregui, T/F862
2216. Balcony, comfortable, heater US$2 per day, hot water, rooftop restaurant, reduction for
more than 1 night or with IH card, 10% with student card, luggage store, parking. Recommended. **G** *Res Pacha Aransaya*, Av 6 de Agosto 121, T862 2229. Being refurbished, basic, hot
shower but water problems, good trout in restaurant. **G** *Alojamiento Oasis*, Pando 222. With
bath, safe, good views. **G** *Emperador*, C Murillo 235, behind the Cathedral, T862 2083. Breakfast served in room for US$2, popular, laundry service and facilities, shared hot showers, helpful
for trips to Isla del Sol. Repeatedly recommended. **G** *Kota Kahuaña*, Av Busch 15. Shared hot
showers, quiet, kitchen facilities, some rooms with lake view, very hospitable. Recommended.
G *Hostal La Luna*, José P Mejía 260, T862 2051. Warm showers, laundry, breakfast in room on
request (US$1), can arrange discounts on trips to Isla del Sol. **G** *Res Porteñita*, by market on
Jáuregui. Safe. Recommended. Many other *residenciales* in **G** range.

Bolivia

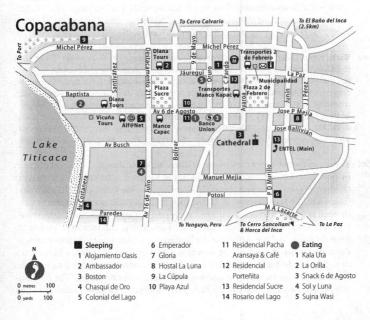

Copacabana

To Cerro Calvario
To El Baño del Inca (2.5km)

Michel Pérez
Diana Tours
Michel Pérez
Transportes 2 de Febrero
9 de Mayo
Jáuregui
Oruro
La Paz
C Pando
Plaza Sucre
Transportes Manco Kapac
Plaza 2 de Febrero
Municipalidad
Ayacucho
José P Mejía
Junín
J Pérez
Av 6 de Agosto
Manco Capac
Banco Union
Jose Ballivián
Cathedral
ENTEL (Main)
Av Busch
Bolívar
Lake Titicaca
Av Costanera
Av 16 de Julio
Manuel Mejía
Potosí
P D Murillo
M A Lazarte
Paredes
To Yunguyo, Peru
To Cerro Sancollani & Horca del Inca
To La Paz
To Port
Santiváñez
Destacamento 211
Baptista
Vicuña Tours
Alf@Net

N
0 metres 100
0 yards 100

Sleeping	6 Emperador	11 Residencial Pacha	● **Eating**
1 Alojamiento Oasis	7 Gloria	Aransaya & Café	1 Kala Uta
2 Ambassador	8 Hostal La Luna	12 Residencial	2 La Orilla
3 Boston	9 La Cúpula	Porteñita	3 Snack 6 de Agosto
4 Chasqui de Oro	10 Playa Azul	13 Residencial Sucre	4 Sol y Luna
5 Colonial del Lago		14 Rosario del Lago	5 Sujna Wasi

Eating

● *on map*
Very few places
open before 0800
and very few
vegetarian options

On Plaza 2 de Febrero *Napolés.* Reasonable prices, does vegetarian tortilla, changes money. **On 6 de Agosto** *Colonial*, corner of 16 de Julio. Decent lunch, good trout. *Snack* 6 de Agosto, 2 branches, good trout, big portions, some vegetarian dishes, serves breakfast. Also has good rooms for rent, **D** with bath, **E** without, breakfast extra, laundry facilities. *Kala Uta*, nice atmosphere, good vegetarian food. *Mankha Uta*, at lake end of avenue, warm, good service, cheap but uninspiring set meals, movies (poor picture quality on some), Play Station. *Nimbo*, No 684, near lake. Typical, international and vegetarian dishes, relaxing, warm, good music, good wine list and good value. *La Orilla*, tasty Mexican food, also stir fries and vegetarian options, cosy atmosphere, usually open 0700-2200. Recommended. *Pacha Café*, No 121, good. *El Trébol*, vegetarian, nice owner, generally well-regarded. *Sol y Luna*, Av 16 de Julio, in *Hotel Gloria*. Well-decorated bar with good music, internet, book exchange, guide books and CD library. *Sujna Wasi*, Jáuregui 127, open 0730-2300, excellent, good breakfasts and other meals, especially fish, in the market on C Abaroa.

Festivals

At these times hotel
prices quadruple

1-3 Feb *Virgen de la Candelaria*, massive procession, dancing, fireworks, bullfights. **Easter**, with candlelight procession on Good Friday. 23 Jun, **San Juan, also on Isla del Sol.** 4-6 Aug, *La Virgen de Copacabana*.

Transport

Road By car from **La Paz to Copacabana** (direct), 4 hrs, take exit to 'Río Seco' in El Alto. Agency buses: several agencies go from **La Paz to Puno**, stopping at Copacabana for lunch, or with an open ticket for continuing to Puno later. They charge US$12-15 and depart La Paz 0800; La Paz-Copacabana takes 4 hrs. Companies include: *Diana Tours*, Hotel Ambassador, Plaza Sucre. *Vicuña Tours*, 6 de Agosto, T862 2155. *Turisbus*, Rigoberto Paredes in *Hotel Rosario del Lago*. They continue to Peruvian border at Yunguyo and on to Puno, stopping for immigration formalities and changing money. 3½ hrs to Puno, US$3.30-4.25 depending on season, depart Copacabana around 1200-1400. It's also possible to catch a tour bus to **Cusco**, usually depart around 1400, tickets US$17-20, change bus in Puno, tour company arranges connection. **Public transport** to/from La Paz, US$2.05 plus US$0.35 for Tiquina crossing (also need to show passport), several departures daily between 0700-1800 with *Manco Capac*, T862 2234, or 245 3035, La Paz or *2 de Febrero*, T862 2233, or 237 7181, La Paz. Both have offices on Copacabana's main plaza and in La Paz at Plaza Reyes Ortiz, opposite entrance to cemetery. Buses also from main terminal, US$3. Buy bus tickets as soon as possible as all buses are usually full by day of travel, especially Sun. 1-day trips from La Paz are not recommended as they allow only 1½-2 hrs in Copacabana. (See also Frontier via Copacabana page 277.) Bus to Huatajata, US$2.10 and to Huarina, US$2.50.

Directory

Banks *Banco Unión*, 6 de Agosto opposite Oruro, reasonable rates of exchange, TCs at US$5 commission, cash advance on Visa and MasterCard 3% commission. Several *artesanías* on Av 6 de Agosto buy and sell US$ and Peruvian soles. **Communications** Internet: *Alcadi*, next to post office, opposite cathedral, US$2.40 per hr. *Alf@Net*, Av 6 de Agosto, next to *Hostal Colonial*, 0830-2200, US$2.95, very fast connection. In *Municipal building*, Plaza 2 de Febrero, US$2.95 per hr. *Ifa-Internet*, Av 16 de Julio y Jáuregui, Plaza Sucre. US$3.50 per hr. **Post Office:** Plaza 2 de Febrero, open (in theory) Tue-Sat 0900-1200, 1300-1800, Sun 0900-1500, *poste restante*. **Telephone:** *Entel*, open 0800-1230, 1330-2000, international phone and fax, accept US$. **Tourist office** Kiosk on Plaza 2 de Febrero, helpful when open.

Isla del Sol

It is not possible to
see all the sites on the
Isla del Sol and return
to Copacabana in 1
day; it's 3 hrs on foot
from one end of the
island to the other

The site of the main Inca creation myth (there are other versions) is a short distance by boat from Copacabana. Legend has it that Viracocha, the creator god, had his children, Manco Kapac and Mama Ocllo, spring from the waters of the lake to found Cusco and the Inca dynasty. A sacred rock at the island's northwest end is worshipped as their birthplace. On the east shore near the jetty for *Crillon Tours*' hydrofoils and other craft is the Fuente del Inca, a pure spring, and Inca steps leading up from the water. A 2 km walk from the landing stage takes one to the main ruins of Pilcocaina, a two storey building with false domes and superb views, US$1. Southeast of the Isla del Sol is the Isla de la Luna (or Coati), which also may be visited – the best ruins are an Inca temple and nunnery, both sadly neglected. The community-run Museo Comunitario de Etnografía celebrates costumes used in sacred dances. Director Esteban Quelima, an anthropolgist (museo_templodelsol@ latinmail.com), hopes in the future to expand the museum to include natural history. He also hopes to provide accommodation in local homes. ■ *Daily 0900-1200, 1300-1800, entry by voluntary contribution.*

Sleeping and eating   Most of the dozen *posadas* on the island are at Yumani, on the south side near the Inca steps. **D** *Casa de Don Ricardo*, with bath, heating and breakfast, good beds, nice atmosphere, small, Argentine-owned. At the peak of the hill above the village is **D** (**G** without bath) Puerta del Sol, very popular. Nearby is the owner's father's hostel, **G** *Templo del Sol*, with clean rooms, electric showers and a restaurant. **F** *El Imperio del Sol*, peach-coloured house, comfortable, no running water. Recommended. There are several others, all **G**, basic but clean, few have hot water (although the island now has electricity), meals provided US$1.50-2. *El Inti* restaurant, up the hill above the school, serves good food, including vegetarian. Next to Pilcocaina ruins is **G** *Albergue Inca Sama*, sleep on mattresses on floor, good food, also camping in typical tents (contact via *Hotel Playa Azul*, Copacabana, or La Paz T235 6566), Sr Pusari, offers boat service from Copacabana and trips to the north of island. Accommodation also at Challa, on the northeast coast, **G** *Posada del Inca*, right on the beach. 8 double rooms, very basic outside toilets, no showers, contact Juan Mamani Ramos through *Entel* office (T013-5006), food is provided and beer or *refrescos* are for sale. Several places to stay around the Plaza in Challapampa, at the north end of the island. Ask for Lucio Arias or his father, Francisco, who have opened 2 basic hostels (price depends on whether you have a shower or a bucket). Lucio can also arrange boat tickets. **G** *Posada Manco Kapac* has rooms for 35 people and a garden for camping, hot showers and views of Illampu. The second hostel has the same name but is further up the beach. *La Posada del Inca* is a restored colonial hacienda, owned by *Crillon Tours* and only available as part of a tour with *Crillon. Magri Turismo* also owns a hotel on the island. See La Paz, Tour operators on page 264. Rooms are offered by many families on the island. See also *Transturin's* overnight options on page 273.

It is worthwhile staying overnight for the many beautiful walks through villages and Inca terraces, some still in use

Transport   *Inca Tours* and *Titicaca Tours* run motor boats to the island; both have offices on Av 6 de Agosto in Copacabana, as do other companies. Boats leave Copacabana at 0815, arrive at the north end at 1000. They leave the south end of the island at 1600, arriving back at 1730-1800. This gives you enough time to walk the length of the island (take food and water). With the same ticket you can stay on the island and return another day. Other options are: half-day tours and tours which include north and south of Isla del Sol and Isla de La Luna in one day (not recommended, too short). Full-day tour US$3 pp (US$4.50 if you stay overnight). Other boats to the jetty by the Fuente del Inca leave at 0830 and 1330, returning punctually at 1600. Boats also depart to Isla del Sol from Yampupata (see page 274).

Border with Peru

The road goes from La Paz 91 km west to Guaqui, formerly the port for the Titicaca passenger boats. The road crosses the border at Desaguadero 22 km further west and runs along the shore of the lake to Puno. Bolivian immigration is just before the bridge and is open 0830-1230 and 1400-2030. Get exit stamp, walk a few hundred metres across the bridge then get entrance stamp on the other side. Get Peruvian visas in La Paz. There are a few basic hotels on both sides of the bridge, as well as restaurants. Money changers just over the bridge on Peruvian side give reasonable rates.

The west side of Lake Titicaca
There are three La Paz-Puno routes (see also page 1165)

Transport   Road paved all the way to Peru. Buses from La Paz to **Guaqui** and **Desaguadero** depart from same location as micros for Tiahuanaco (see above) every 30 mins, US$1.55, 1½-2 hrs. From Desaguadero to **La Paz** last bus departs 1700, buses may leave later if enough passengers, but charge a lot more.

From Copacabana a new, paved 'panoramic' highway leads south to the Bolivian frontier at Kasani, then to Yunguyo. Do not photograph the border area. For La Paz tourist agency services on this route see under International Buses (page 266)

Via Copacabana

Bolivia

and under Lake Titicaca above. The border is open 0830-1930 (Bolivian time). Buses/colectivos here and at the Peruvian side; or you can walk, 500 m, between the 2 posts. If crossing into Bolivia with a motorcycle, do not be fooled into paying any unnecessary charges to police or immigration.Going to Peru, money can be changed in Yunguyo at better rates than at the border. Coming into Bolivia, the best rates are at the border, on the Bolivian side. Soles can be changed in Copacabana (see above).

Transport In Peru, this starts at **Yunguyo**. Colectivo Copacabana-Kasani US$0.50 pp, Kasani-Yunguyo US$0.60 pp. Make sure, if arranging a through ticket La Paz-Puno, that you get all the necessary stamps en route, and find out if your journey involves a change of bus. Note the common complaint that through services La Paz-Puno (or vice versa) deteriorate once the border has been crossed, eg smaller buses are used, extra passengers taken on, passengers left stranded if the onward bus is already full, drivers won't drop you where the company says they will.

The east side of Lake Titicaca From Huarina, a road heads northwest to Achacachi (market Sunday; fiesta 14 September). Here, one road goes north across a tremendous marsh to Warisata, then crosses the altiplano to Sorata.

Sorata

Phone code: 02
Colour map 6, grid A2
Altitude: 2,578 m
163 km from La Paz

Sorata, a beautiful place set in a valley at the foot of Illampu, has lovely views and is ideal country for hiking and climbing. There is a delightful plaza, with views of the snow-capped summit of Illampu on a clear day. The market area is near the plaza, half block down Muñecas on the right. Market day is Sunday; fiesta 14 September. There are lots of walking possibilities, including day hikes. The most popular is to San Pedro cave, beyond the village of San Pedro. The cave is lit, but not up to much though you can swim in the underground 'lake'. ■ *0800-1700, US$1. Toilets at entrance; best not to go alone. It is reached either by road, a 12 km walk (2½ hrs) each way, or by a path along the Río San Cristóbal (about 3½ hrs one way). Get clear directions before setting out. Take water, at least 1 litre pp, or else take sterilizing tablets and fill up at the tap in San Pedro. There are also drinks for sale.*

Sleeping

D-E *Landhaus Copacabana*, 20 mins downhill from the centre (look for the signs), T/F813 5042, www.khainata.com/sorata **F** pp with shared bathroom, breakfast included, good restaurant, nice views, internet access US$3.60 per hr. Recommended. **E** *Res Sorata*, just off plaza, T/F813 5218, resorata@ceibo.entelnet.bo Cheaper with shared bath at the back, rambling old place (rather neglected) with original fittings, huge rooms, some with private bath, saggy beds, grubby mattresses in dormitories, bathrooms not always clean, also has modern section, restaurant with good lunch/dinner US$2.75, breakfast US$2, lovely big garden, washing machine US$1.80, owner Louis Demers from Quebec, internet access US$3.60 per hr, slow, not as well-regarded as it used to be. **F** *Gran Hotel Sorata* (Ex-*Prefectural*), on the outskirts immediately above the police checkpoint, T2817378, call from Plaza for free pick-up. Spacious although bathrooms (electric showers) a bit tired, free filtered water, large garden with great views, swimming pool (open to non-residents for US$0.50), games room, good restaurant, internet café, accepts credit cards. **F** pp *Paraíso*, Villavicencio 117, T813 5043. Pleasant, American breakfast US$1.80, hot water, restaurant. **G** *Alojamiento Chura*, Ingavi, 2 doors up from *Altai* restaurant, 1st and 2nd floors (no sign). Bright, hot showers (US$0.45). **G** pp *Hostal Mirador*, on Muñecas, same road and under same ownership as *Restaurant Terraza*, T813 5052. Good rooms, comfortable, clean showers and toilets, sun terrace. **G** *Hostal Panchita*, on plaza, T813 5038. Shared bath, large rooms, hot water, basic, good restaurant. At the road junction below *Café Illampu*, María Angela Sangines, T813 5055, mas1@ceibo.entelnet.bo has 3 self-catering bungalows (US$15 per night) for 4, minimum 1 week's stay, also has a deli with wines and cheeses from around the world.

Eating There are several small restaurants around the plaza, including *Pizzería Napolés*, Italian, and *Jalisco*, Mexican and Italian, good value. *Pete's Place*, Ingavi y Muñecas, mainly vegetarian, gringo-run, very good, set meal US$2, closed Mon. Same owners have *Oasis* restaurant, with camping and self-catering cabins 30 min walk from town by river, open 0830-2200. *Café Illampu*, on the way to San Pedro cave. Swiss-run, excellent sandwiches, bread and cakes, camping US$1 (an extra US$0.50 to hire tent), bikes for hire, closed Tue and Feb-Mar. *El Nuevo Ceibo*, on Muñecas. Good for fish and set meals. *La Terraza*, just below market. Cheap, good breakfast and lunch, some vegetarian dishes. *The Spider Bar*, 250 m west of plaza, near *Hostal Mirador*, www.geocities.com/ r_h_bryant The most popular drinking den, with snacks, English owner, book exchange, musical instruments.

Shopping For handicrafts, *Artesanía Sorata* on plaza, open Mon-Sat 0900-2000, Sun 0900-1600, also cashes TCs and accepts them as payment.

Transport **Bus** From La Paz with *Trans Unificada* (from C Manuel Bustillos, esq Av Kollasuyo, 2 blocks up from Cementerio in La Paz), 0430-1500, 4½ hrs, US$1.65; from Sorata every hour daily 0400-1400 (till 1700 Fri and Sun). To, or from **Peru**, change buses at Huarina for Copacabana.

Directory **Banks** Bank on the plaza changes US$ cash only, no ATM. Try *Artesanía Sorata, Res Sorata* or *Hotel Landhaus Copacabana*. **Communications** Internet: Various hotels as above. *María Angela Sangines*, road junction nr *Café Illampu*, US$3 per hr. **Post Office:** on north side of plaza, 0830-1230, 1500-1800. *Cotel*, next door, same hours, for local calls only. **Telephone:** *Entel*, on plaza at entrance to *Hostal Panchita*, for national and international calls, open daily 0700-2130. **Medical services** Hospital: Villamil de Rada e Illampu. Has oxygen and X-ray.

To Peru At Achacachi, another road runs roughly parallel to the shore of Lake Titicaca, through Ancoraimes (Sunday market), Carabuco (with colonial church), Escoma, which has an Aymara market every Sunday morning, to Kasiri Puerto Acosta on the Peruvian border. The area around Puerto Acosta is good walking country and the locals are friendly. From La Paz to Puerto Acosta the road is paved as far as Escoma, then good thereafter (best in the dry season, approximately May to October). North of Puerto Acosta towards Peru the road deteriorates and should not be attempted except in the dry season. There is an immigration office in Puerto Acosta, but it is advisable to get an exit stamp in La Paz first. There is one hotel (G) but no restaurants. There is a Peruvian immigration office 30 minutes' walk from the border, before Tilali.

Transport **Buses**: La Paz (Cementerio district)-Puerto Acosta, 5 hrs, US$3.25, Fri 1130, Sat/Sun 0630. Many trucks travel La Paz-Puerto Acosta on Tue and Fri afternoons. The only transport beyond Acosta is early on Wed and Sat morning when a couple of trucks go to the markets, some 25 km from Puerto Acosta on the border.

Trekking and climbing from Sorata

Armed robbery has been reported on the Illampu Circuit. It is much cheaper to go to Sorata and ask about trekking there than to book up a trek with an agency in La Paz. See warning in Hiking, page 240

Sorata is the starting point for climbing Illampu and Ancohuma but all routes out of the town are difficult, owing to the number of paths in the area and the very steep ascent. Experience and full equipment necessary and it's best to hire mule (see below). A highly recommended hike is to **Laguna Chillata** and **Inca Marka**, a strenuous full-day walk, climbing from Sorata to 4,207 m (either take plenty of water, or a water filter). Go with a guide because this is a sensitive area and the path is very hard to find; the lake is sacred and Inca Marka is a burial place, dating back to the pre-Columbian Mollu culture. Camping is forbidden; do not touch anything, not even bits of paper, bottles, etc, which may be offerings. This can be extended to a 3-day trek up to a glacier. The **Circuito Illampu**, a 4-7 day high-altitude trek (five passes over 4,500 m) around Illampu, is excellent. It can get very cold and it is a hard walk, though very beautiful with nice campsites on the way. Some food can be bought in Cocoyo on the third day. You must be acclimatized before setting out.

Sorata is the setting-off point for the very tough **Mapiri Trail**, a 7-8 day trek into the Yungas. It starts at Ingenio, four hours from Sorata by pick-up, US$6, and ending at Mapiri, an ugly mining town on the river of the same name. From Mapiri, you can continue to Guanay another mining town with several cheap hotels and places to eat (eg *Der Auslander Club*). Boats can be hired to go to Rurrenabaque, US$300 for up to 25 passengers. Alternatively, you can make an adventurous journey by road back to Sorata. The journey by *camioneta* from Sorata to Guanay via Consata and Mapiri is a three-day adventure in itself.

Guides Louis at *Residencial Sorata* can arrange guides and mules. *Club Sorata* (at *Hotel Landhaus Copacabana*) rents equipment and can arrange long and short treks, guides and mules, US$20 per person per day all inclusive, also quad bikes. *Sorata Guides Association*, President Eduardo Chura, office opposite side entrance of *Res Sorata* (T813 5044, F813 5218, guiasorata@ hotmail.com), for trekking guides only (very good, but not experienced for glacier climbing), porters, mules and equipment hire. Daily prices: guide US$15, porters and mules extra, remember you have to feed your guide/porter. When trekking avoid sedimented glacier melt water for drinking and treat with iodine all other water. For more information on trekking and walking in this area, see Books, page 328.

The Area Protegida Apolobamba forms part of the Cordillera Apolobamba, the north extension of the Cordillera Real. The range itself has many 5,000 m-plus peaks, while the conservation area of 483,744 ha protects herds of vicuña, huge flocks of flamingoes and many condors. The Area adjoins the Parque Nacional Madidi (see page 335). This is great trekking country and the five-day **Charazani to Pelechuco** trek is one of the best mountain treks in the country (see the *Bolivia Handbook* for details). It passes traditional villages and the peaks of the southern Cordillera Apolobamba. Charazani, the main starting point, is the biggest village in the region (3,200 m). Its three-day fiesta is around 16 July. There are some **G** *alojamientos*, restaurants and shops. Bus from Calle Reyes Cardona, Cemetery district, La Paz, Friday-Monday at 0600, 10 hours, US$4.40, returning Friday, Sunday, Monday, Wednesday at 0400, also 1900 on Monday. Pelechuco (3,600 m) is a basic village, also with **G** *alojamientos*, cafés and shops. Buses from La Paz (same street as for Charazani) leave on Wednesday, 1100, US$6, 18-24 hours, returning Friday 2000 and Saturday 1600. Jeeps charge US$250 to Charazani and US$300 to Pelechuco. The road to Pelechuco goes through the Area Protegida, passing La Cabaña, 5 km outside of which are the reserve's headquarters. Visitors are welcome to see the vicuñas and there is accommodation and food.

Cordillera Apolobamba

The Yungas

La Paz

Only a few hours from La Paz are the subtropical valleys known as The Yungas. These steep, forested slopes, squeezed in between the Cordillera and the Amazon Lowlands, provide a welcome escape from the chill of the capital. The warm climate of The Yungas is also ideal for growing citrus fruit, bananas, coffee and coca leaves for the capital.

The most commonly-used route to the Yungas is via **La Cumbre**, northeast of La Paz. The road out of La Paz circles cloudwards over La Cumbre pass at 4,725 m; the highest point is reached in an hour; all around are towering snowcapped peaks. Soon after Unduavi the paving ends, the road becomes 'all-weather' and drops over 3,400 m to the green subtropical forest in 80 km. The roads to Chulumani and Coroico divide just after Unduavi, where there is a *garita* (check point), the only petrol station, and lots of roadside stalls. From Unduavi leading to Yolosa, the junction 8 km from Coroico, is steep, twisting, clinging to the side of sheer cliffs, and it is slippery in the wet. It is a breathtaking descent (best not to look over the edge if you don't like heights) and its

La Paz to the Yungas

reputation for danger is more than matched by the beauty of the scenery. A new road from La Paz, including a 2½-km tunnel, is being built to Coroico via Chuspipata and Yolosa. It is creating a lot of damage and is unlikely to be completed until 2004. For the La Cumbre-Coroico hike (Choro), see page 269. *Gravity Assisted Mountain Biking* (address under La Paz, Tour operators, *América Tours*) run La Cumbre-Coroico with top quality bikes, guide, helmet, gloves and minibus to La Cumbre, US$49; four hours La Cumbre-Yolosa, then transport to Coroico. Recommended. Other companies do this trip, too, and taking a reputable organized tour is a sensible option. Cheap rented bikes may have inadequate (or no) brakes.

Coroico

Phone code: 02
Colour map 6, grid A3
There have been several incidents of young women being raped or attacked on the trails around Coroico; on no account hike alone in this area

The little town of Coroico is perched on a hill at 1,760 m amid beautiful scenery. The hillside is covered with orange and banana groves; coffee is also grown and condors circle overhead. It is a first-class place to relax with several good walks. There is horse riding with *El Relincho* (Reynaldo, T719-23814 mob) 100 m past *Hotel Esmeralda* (see below for location). A colourful 4-day festival is held on 19-22 October. On 2 November, All Souls' Day, the local cemetery is festooned with black ribbons. A good walk is up to the waterfalls, starting from El Calvario. Follow the stations of the cross by the cemetery, off Calle Julio Zuazo Cuenca, which leads steeply uphill from the plaza. Facing the chapel at El Calvario, with your back to the town, look for the path on your left. This leads to the falls which are the town's water supply (Toma de Agua) and, beyond, to two more falls. **Cerro Uchumachi**, the mountain behind El Calvario, can be climbed following the same stations of the cross, but then look for the faded red and white antenna behind the chapel. From there it's about 1½ hours' steep walk to the top (take water). A third walk goes to the pools in the Río Vagante, 7 km away off the road to Coripata; it takes about three hours to get there. The *Cámara Hotelera* on the plaza also functions as a tourist information centre.

Sleeping
Hotel rooms can be difficult to find at holiday weekends and prices are higher

B *El Viejo Molino*, T/F213 6004, valmar@waranet.com 2 km on road to Caranavi, 5-star, pool, jacuzzi, games room etc. **C** *Gloria*, C Kennedy 1, T/F213 6020, www.hotelgloria bolivia.com Spacious, large pool, breakfast extra, restaurant, internet, free transport from plaza (under renovation in 2003). **C** *Esmeralda*, T213 6017, www.hotelesmeralda.com 10 mins uphill from plaza (Casilla 9225, La Paz), cheaper without private bathroom and view, free pick-up service (ring from *Totai Tours*), German owned, English spoken, hikes arranged, Visa, Mastercard accepted (no commission), credit card phones, great views, fantastic hot showers, videos, breakfast US$2, restaurant and pizza oven, Finnish sauna, garden, pool, laundry service, free internet access, 2 hrs a night, some rooms noisy, best to book ahead. **D** *Bella Vista*, C Héroes del Chaco (2 blocks from main plaza), T715-69237 (mob). Beautiful rooms, beautiful views, **E** without bath but much smaller, 2 racquetball courts, terrace, bikes for rent, restaurant, covered pool. Recommended. **D** *Don Quijote*, 500 m out of town, on road to Coripata, T213

Bolivia

6007, quijote@mpoint.com.bo With bath, pool, quiet, English spoken. **D** *Hostal Kory*, at top of steps leading down from the plaza. Pool, terrace, **E** without bath, hot showers, kitchen, restaurant, good snacks, laundry. Recommended. **D** *Moderno*, C Guachalla (1 block from main plaza), T240 7864 (La Paz) for reservations. Large rooms, good views, pool. **E** *Cevra Verde*, Ayacucho 5037. With bath, pool, pick-up service. **E-F** pp *Sol y Luna*, 15-20 mins beyond *Hotel Esmeralda*, T715-61626 (mob), www.solyluna -bolivia.com 5 *cabañas* with bath and kitchen, splendid views, 5 rooms with shared bath for 1-4 people **G** pp, meals available, vegetarian specialities and Indonesian banquet, camping US$2 pp (not suitable for cars), lovely garden, pool, laundry service, massages, meditation, ceramics classes, TCs accepted, good value, Sigrid, the owner, speaks English, French, German and Spanish. Reserve through *Chuquiago Turismo*, Planta Baja, Edif La Primera, Av Santa Cruz 1364, Casilla 4443, La Paz, T236 2099. **F** *El Cafetal*, beside hospital, T719-33979 (mob). French-run, very nice, restaurant with excellent French/Indian/ vegetarian cuisine, good value. Highly recommended. **F** pp *La Casa Colonial*, on Pando. Shared bath, comfortable, good value. **F** *Las Hamacas*, Andrés Muñoz, esq P Salazar (1 block from main plaza), T241 7818. Basic, without bath, music and films at night, restaurant downstairs for pasta and vegetarian. **F** *Lluvia de Oro*, F Reyes Ortiz, T213 6005, 1 block from church. Good value, good food, pool. **G** *La Residencial Coroico*, F Reyes Ortiz. Without bath, basic, hot shower extra. Campsite by the small chapel on the hill overlooking the town.

La Casa, downhill from *Kory*, T213 6024. German-run, good food and setting, also hotel (**E**), vegetarian dishes, fondue and raclette for dinner (reserve in advance), wonderful views, pool, internet connection (US$3.50). Recommended. The convent opposite sells biscuits, peanut butter, wine and coffee liqueurs. *Deutsche Backstube*, opposite *Hostal Kory*. German pastries, set lunch (including vegetarian), breakfast, expensive (has house for rent for 1 month or more, T719 35594 mob), closed Tue and Wed. *La Taberna*, north side of plaza. Juices, American breakfast and banana pancakes recommended, shows videos.

Eating

From La Paz all companies are on C Yanacachi, beside YPFB station in Villa Fátima: *Turbus Totai* (T221 8385), US$2.25, 3 hrs, several daily from 0730-1630 each way, as does *Flota Yungueña* (T221 3275); worth booking in advance. Best views on left hand side on the descent to Yungas. Extra services run on Sun. It can be difficult to book journeys to La Paz on holidays and on Sun evenings/Mon mornings (though these are good times for hitching). Trucks and pick-ups from La Paz may drop you at Yolosa, 7 km from Coroico; there is usually transport Yolosa-Coroico, US$1, or you can walk, uphill all the way, 2 hrs. In Coroico trucks leave from the market. Buses, trucks and pick-ups run from Yolosa to **Rurrenabaque** via Caranavi, daily at 1500 with *Yungueña*, except Sun at 1730, with *Turbus Totai*, US$8.75, 13-15 hrs, the company will take you down to Yolosa to catch the bus from La Paz. *13 de Mayo* (on Virgen del Carmen, Villa Fátima) runs 4-6 day jeep tours of the Yungas.

Transport

Banks *Banco Mercantil*, on Central Plaza. Mon-Fri 0830-1230, 1430-1830, Sat 0900-1230, cash advances (no commission) on MasterCard and Visa. **Communications** Internet: Carlos, who lives on C Caja de Agua, T/F213 6041, has an internet café, will exchange Spanish for English lessons. **Post Office** on plaza. **Telephone:** *Entel*, on Sagárnaga next to *Flota Yungueña*, for international and local calls. Cotel, next to church, phones, public TV. **Language classes** *Siria León*, close to *Hotel Esmeralda*, planned lessons, speaks excellent English. **Medical services** Hospital: T213 6002, the best in the Yungas, good malaria advice. A **tourist office** called *Vagantes* provides information, guides and taxis to surrounding places of interest. A website is www.coroico-info.net On the main plaza are the **tour operators** *Eco Adventuras* and *Inca Land Tours*. **Police** East side of main plaza.

Directory

Chulumani

The capital of Sud Yungas is an attractive, relaxed little town with beautiful views and many hikes. Fiesta **24 August** (lasts ten days). The road from Unduavi goes through Puente Villa (**C** *Hotel Tamapaya*, T02-270 6099, just outside town, beautiful setting, with shower, good rooms, poo), where a road branches north to Coroico through Coripata. **Apa Apa Ecological Park**, 8 km away, is the last area of original Yungas forest

Phone code: 02
Colour map 6, grid A3
Altitude: 1,640 m
124 km from La Paz.

Lively market Sat/Sun

Bolivia

with lots of interesting wildlife. US$25 for up to five people park fee including transport and hiking guide (no reduction for fewer people); accommodation and campsite with bathrooms (US$5 per tent). The road to Irupana, a colonial village 1½ hours from Chulumani, passes the turn-off to the park; ask to get off and walk 15 minutes up to the *hacienda* of Ramiro Portugal and his wife, Tildi (both speak English); you can use their pool after trek. Or T 213 6106 to arrange transport from town; or T 279 0381 (La Paz) , or write to Casilla 10109, Miraflores, La Paz.

Sleeping & eating **B** pp *San Antonio*, 3 km out of town on La Paz road, T234 1809, F237 7896. Pleasant cabins and pool. **B-C** *San Bartolomé Plaza Resort*, 2 km from *tránsito* down Irupana road, arrange hotel transport beforehand if arriving by bus, no taxis, www.sanbartolome@usa.net Superb setting, swimming pool, can be booked through the *Hotel Plaza*, La Paz, T237 8311, ext 1221. **D** *Huayrani*, just off Junín, T213 6351. Lovely views, garden, more expensive in winter season. **E** *Country House*, 400 m out of town. Bed and breakfast, pool, good value, restaurant with home cooking, owner Xavier Sarabia has information on hikes. **E** *Hostal Familiar Dion*, Alianza, just off the plaza, T213 6070. Modern, roof terrace, includes breakfast, laundry facilities and use of kitchen, **F** without bathroom and breakfast, very good. **E** *Panorama*, at top of hill on Murillo, T213 6109. Some rooms with view, basic, garden, breakfast, pool. **G** *El Mirador*, on Plaza Libertad, T213 6117. Cheaper without bath, good beds, restaurant, noisy at weekends from disco. **G** *Alojamiento Danielito*, Bolívar. Hot water extra, laundry facilities, good view. *El Mesón*, on Plaza. Open 1200-1330 only, good cheap lunches. Also on Plaza, *Chulumani*, pleasant, good *almuerzo*. *La Hostería* on Junín close to the *tranca*, pizzas and hamburgers.

Transport **Buses from La Paz**: *Trans San Bartolomé*, Virgen del Carmen 1750, Villa Fátima, T221 1674, daily at 0800-1600 or when full, 4 hrs, US$2.50. *Trans Arenas*, daily at 0730-1800, US$2.25. *Trans 24 de Agosto micros*, 15 de Abril 408 y San Borja, T221 0607, 0600-1600, when full. Buses return to La Paz from the plaza, micros from the *tranca*.

Directory **Banks** On Plaza Libertad, *Banco Unión*, changes US$100 or more only in cash and TCs (5% commission), Mon-Fri 0830-1200, 1430-1800. *Cooperativa San Bartolomé*, changes cash Mon-Fri 0800-1200, 1400-1700, Sat-Sun 0700-1200. **Communications** Internet: in tourist office, US$1.05 per hr. The tourist office is in the centre of the main plaza, sells locally grown coffee, teas, jams and honey, allegedly open Mon-Fri 0900-1330, 1500-2200, Sat, Sun 0700-2200.

La Paz

Southwest Bolivia

The mining town of Oruro with its famous carnival of the devil, vast salt-flats, multi-coloured lakes, flamingoes and volcanoes are all found in this remote, starkly beautiful corner of Bolivia which borders Chile and Argentina.

Oruro

Phone code: 02
Colour map 6, grid A2
Population: 183,422
Altitude: 3,706 m

Phone companies Coteor and Entel operate in Oruro; Coteor uses prefix 52, Entel 51 before final 5 digits
30 km SE of La Paz

Although Oruro became famous as a mining town, there are no longer any working mines of importance. It is, however, a major railway junction and the commercial centre for the mining communities of the altiplano, as well as hosting the country's best-known carnival (see page 286). Several fine buildings in the centre hint at the city's former importance, notably the baroque concert hall (now a cinema) on Plaza 10 de Febrero and the **Casa de la Cultura**, built as a mansion by the tin baron Simón Patiño. It is now run by the Universidad Técnica de Oruro, and contains European furniture and a carriage imported from France, also houses temporary exhibitions. ■ *Mon-Fri 0900-1200, 1400-1830, US$0.30, Soria Galvarro 5755*. There is a good view from the Cerro Corazón de Jesús, near the church of the Virgen del Socavón, five blocks west of Plaza 10 de Febrero at the end of Calle Mier.

The **Museo Etnográfico Minero**, inside the Church of the Virgen del Socavón, contains mining equipment and other artefacts from the beginning of the century as well as a representation of *El Tío* (the devil.) ■ *Entry via the church 0900-1200, 1500-1800, US$0.50*. **Museo Antropológico**, south of centre on Av España (take *micro* A heading south or any *trufi* going south) has a unique collection of stone llama heads as well as impressive carnival masks. ■ *Mon-Fri 0900-1200, 1400-1800, Sat-Sun 1000-2000, 1500-1800, US$0.50, good guides. Recommended*. Museo Mineralógico, part of the University (take *micro* A south to the Ciudad Universitaria), with over 5,500 mineral specimens. ■ *Mon-Fri 0800-1200, 1430-1700, US$0.60*.

About 65 km south is the **Santuario de Aves Lago Poopó**, an excellent bird reserve on the lake of the same name. The lake dries up completely in winter. It can be visited from Challapata, 120 km south of Oruro on a paved road; buses from Oruro 0800 and 1430, 2½ hours, US$1. In Challapata is a gas station, basic lodging at main crossing opposite *Hotel Potosí* (**F**, good beds, basic restaurant); *fiesta* 15-17 July.

Bolivia

Oruro

Sleeping	
1 Alojamiento 15 de Octubre *B3*	2 Alojamiento San Gerardo *D3*
	3 América *D3*
	4 Bernal *A3*
	5 Gloria *C2*
	6 Gran Sucre *D2*
	7 Gutiérrez *A3*
	8 International Park *A3*
	9 Lipton *A3*
	10 Repostero *D3*
	11 Residencial San Miguel *D3*
	12 Residencial San Salvador *D3*

Eating
1 Café Sur *D3*
2 Caramello *C2*
3 Chifa Rosa *C2*
4 Club Social Arabe *C2*
5 El Nochero *C2*
6 Govinda *D2*
7 La Cabaña *C2*
8 La Casona *C2*
9 Libertador & El Huerto *D2*
10 Mateos *D2*
11 Nayjama *D3*
12 SUM Confitería *D2*

Bolivia

▶ *La Diablada festival*

On the Saturday before Ash Wednesday, Oruro Carnival stages the Diablada ceremony in homage to the miraculous Virgen del Socavón, patroness of miners, and in gratitude to Pachamama, the Earth Mother. The entire procession starts its 5 km route through the town at 0700, reaching the Sanctuary of the Virgen del Socavón at 0400 on Sunday. There the dancers invoke her blessing and ask for pardon. The company then proceeds to the Av Cívica amphitheatre, where the dancers perform two masques. Afterwards, the dancers all enter the sanctuary, chant a hymn in Quechua and pray for pardon. The Diablada was traditionally performed by Indian miners, but several other guilds have taken up the custom. The Carnival is especially notable for its fantastically imaginative costumes. The working-class Oruro district known as La Ranchería is particularly famous for the excellence of its costumes.

The Gran Corso del Carnaval takes place on the Sunday, a very spectacular display. Monday is El Día del Diablo y del Moreno in which the Diablos and Morenos, with their bands, compete against each other on Av Cívica in demonstrations of dancing. Every group seems to join in, in 'total marvellous chaos'. The action usually parades out of the amphitheatre, ending up at the Plaza de Armas. At dusk dancers and musicians go their separate ways, serenading until the early hours. By Tuesday the main touristic events have ended. Carnaval del Sur takes place, with ch'alla rituals to invoke ancestors, unite with Pachamama and bless personal possessions.

This is also the día del agua on which everyone throws water and sprays foam at everyone else (though this goes on throughout carnival; plastic tunics are sold for US$0.20 by street vendors).

The Friday before carnival, traditional miners' ceremonies are held at mines, including the sacrifice of a llama. Visitors may only attend with a guide and permission from Comibol, via the tourist office. The Sunday before carnival the groups practise and make their final pledges. In honour of its syncretism of Andean, precolumbian tradition and Catholic faith, La Diablada has been included on UNESCO's Heritage of Humanity list.

Seating Around the Plaza de Armas, along Avenida 6 de Agosto and on Avenida Cívica, seats cost US$5-10 a day, bought from the Alcaldía in the plaza, or whichever business has erected stands outside its building. Seats on Avenida Bolívar, etc, cost US$5 a day from the shops which built stands. You can wander freely among the dancers and take photographs.

Sleeping For the hotel of your choice it's best to book in advance for carnival; prices range from US$10 per person without bath, to US$20 per person with, to US$100 per person per day in the better places. The tourist office has list of all householders willing to let rooms; host and guest arrange the price, at least US$10 per person. Most hotels sell only three-night packages.

Transport Prices from La Paz triple. Organized day trips from La Paz cost US$30-45, including transport departing 0430, food and a seat in the main plaza, returning at 1600-1700 (missing the last 8-9 hours).

Sleeping
■ *on map*

In the centre B *Gran Sucre*, Sucre 510 esq 6 de Octubre, T527 6800, F525 4110. **D-E** without bath, includes breakfast, heaters on request. Recommended. **D** *Repostero*, Sucre 370 y Pagador, T525 8001. **E** without bath, hot water, includes breakfast, ageing but clean, parking. **E** *América*, Bolívar 347, T527 4707. Ring bell, cheaper without bath, TV, restaurant. **E** *Gloria*, Potosí 6059, T527 6250. 19th century building, basic but OK, hot water, open 24 hrs. **F** *Res San Miguel*, Sucre 331. Nice rooms, some with bath, restaurant. Recommended. **G** *Alojamiento 15 de Octubre*, 6 de Agosto 890, T527 6012. Without bath, hot showers, safe, good value. **Near the bus terminal B** *International Park*, above bus terminal, T527 6227, F525 3187. Best in town, includes breakfast, with bath, parking. **E** *Bernal*, Brasil 701, opposite terminal, T527 9468. Modern, good value, excellent hot showers, heaters on request, restaurant, tours arranged. **E** *Gutiérrez*, Bakovic 580, T525 6675, F527 6515. Open 24 hrs, cable TV, heaters on request, internet access US$0.90 per hr, good restaurant. E Lipton, Av 6 de Agosto 225, T527 6538. **G** pp without bath, secure, parking extra, open 24 hrs, good value.

Near the railway station F *Res San Salvador*, V Galvarro 6325, T527 6771. Hot water, best in this area. **G** *Alojamiento San Gerardo*, V Galvarro 1886, T525 6064. Cheapest and largest on this street, shared bath, renovations and internet café under way.

Mid-range: *La Cabaña*, Junín 609. Comfortable, smart, good international food, bar, Sun and Mon 1200-1530 only. *Nayjama*, Aldana esq Pagador. Best in town, huge portions. **Cheap**: *Club Social Arabe*, Junín 729 y Pres Montes. Good value lunches. *Govinda*, 6 de Octubre 6071. Excellent vegetarian, Mon-Sat 0900-2130. *El Huerto*, Bolívar 359. Good, vegetarian options, open Sun. A good *pizzería* is *La Casona*, Pres Montes 5970, opposite Post Office. *Libertador*, Bolívar 347. Excellent set lunch. *Chifa Rosa*, A Mier, north side of main plaza. Good value Chinese with large portions.

Eating
● *on map*

    Cafés and bars: *Caramello*, Junín y 6 de Octubre. Café-bar, good *almuerzos*, open till early hours for snacks, live music every 3 weeks, good atmosphere. Recommended. *El Nochero*, Av 6 de Octubre 1454, open 1700-2400, good coffee. *SUM Confitería*, Bolívar esq S Galvarro. Good coffee and cakes, popular at lunch, 0800-2300, Sun till 1600. *Café Sur*, Arce 163, near train station. Live entertainment, seminars, films, Tue-Sat, good place to meet local students.

Mercado Campero, V Galvarro esq Bolívar. Sells everything, cheap food in *comedor popular*, also *brujería* section for magical concoctions. *Mercado Fermín López*, C Ayacucho y Montes. Food and hardware, big *comedor popular*. C Bolívar is the main shopping street. *Micro Market Delicia*, A Meier y Soria Galvarro (off Plaza 10 de Febrero). Small supermarket well-stocked with good quality produce. On Av La Paz the 4 blocks between León and Belzu, 48-51, are largely given over to workshops producing masks and costumes for Carnival.

Shopping

Viajeros del Tiempo, Soria Galvarro 1220, T5271166, www.contactoenoruro.com They offer trips to the nearby mines, hot pools and other attractions, open Mon-Fri 0900-1230, 1500-1930, Sat 0900-1200.

Tour operators

Bus Bus terminal 10 blocks north of centre at Bakovic and Aroma, T525 3535, US$0.20 terminal tax to get on bus. Micro No 2 to centre, or any saying 'Plaza 10 de Febrero'. Daily services to: **La Paz** at least every hour 0400-2200, US$2, 3 hrs;. **Cochabamba** 0430-2230, US$2.25, 4½ hrs. **Potosí** 0800-1900, US$4.50, 8 hrs. **Sucre** 0845 and 2100, US$6, 12 hrs. **Uyuni** 2000, US$ 3, 9 hrs (longer in rainy season), several companies. **Santa Cruz** 0600-1530, US$10.45, 12 hrs. **Pisiga** (Chilean border) 1200, US$4.50, 5 hrs. **International buses** (US$2 to cross border): to Iquique via Pisiga, *Trans Salvador, T527 0280*, *semi-cama*, US$12, 14 hrs, Sun-Fri 1230, Wed also 2330. *Trans Paraíso, T527 0765*, *bus cama*, toilet, video, US$12.75, 10hrs, Mon-Sun 1230 and 2230. Arica via Tambo Quemado, *Trans Paraíso*, US$12.75, 14 hrs, Mon-Sun 1330.

Transport

    Train Two companies run services from Oruro to **Uyuni** and on to **Villazón** via Tupiza: *Nuevo Expreso del Sur*, Mon and Fri at 1530, arriving in Uyuni at 2156 (*Premier* US$7.75, *Salón* US$5.40); *Wara Wara del Sur* Sun and Wed at 1900, arriving in Uyuni at 0200 (*Salón* US$4.20). For details of trains from Uyuni to Villazón and for trains from Uyuni to Oruro, see Uyuni. For return times from Villazón, see page 294. Passengers with tickets Villazón-La Paz are transferred to a bus at Oruro. To check train times, call T5274605.

Banks *Enlace* ATM opposite *Banco Nacional de Bolivia*, La Plata 6153. TCs can be changed at *Banco Boliviano Americano*, 5% commission, or *Banco de Santa Cruz*, Bolívar 470 (also at *Pagador y Caro*, Sat 0900-1200). It is quite easy to change dollars (cash) on the street, or at shops in centre and around Mercado Campero displaying '*compro dolares*' signs. **Communications** Internet: *ICP*, Bolívar 469. *Ultranet*, 6 de Octubre 5864. **Post Office:** Presidente Montes 1456, half block from plaza. **Telephone:** *Entel*, Bolívar, esq S Galvarro. **Tourist office** Montes 6072, Plaza 10 de Febrero, T/F525 0144. Very helpful and informative. Mon-Fri 0800-1200 and 1400-1800. Another kiosk is outside *Entel* on C Bolívar (same hours). Colour map and guide (Spanish only), US$1. **Useful addresses** Immigration, Ayacucho 322, p2.

Directory
Exchange rates are the worst in Bolivia; up to 5% below the official rate

Bolivia

Parque Nacional Sajama

A one-day drive to the west of Oruro is the Parque Nacional Sajama, established in 1942 and covering 81,000 ha. The park contains the world's highest forest, consisting mainly of the rare Kenua tree (Polylepis Tarapana) which grows up to an altitude of 5,200 m. The scenery is wonderful and includes views of three volcanoes (Sajama – Bolivia's highest peak at 6,542 m – Parinacota and Pomerape). The road is paved and leads across the border into the Parque Nacional Lauca in Chile. You can trek in the park, with or without porters and mules, but once you move away from the Río Sajama or its major tributaries, lack of water is a problem. ■ *Park entry fee US$2.*

Sajama village
Population: 500
Altitude: 4,200 m

In Sajama village, Telmo Nina has a book with descriptions of the various routes to the summit. Basic accommodation is available with families and there are four *comedores* (no fresh food, so take plenty). It can be very windy and cold at night; a good sleeping bag, gloves and hat are essential. Crampons, ice axe and rope are needed for climbing the volcanoes and can be hired in the village. Horses can be hired, US$8 per day including guide. Good bathing in hot springs 7 km northwest of village; jeeps can be rented to visit, US$5-6. The Sajama area is a major centre of alpaca wool production and Telmo Nina works on a natural dye project (outlet in La Paz at Sagárnaga 177, local 4, founders Peter and Juana Brunhart).

Transport Take a La Paz-Oruro bus and change at Patacamayo, in front of *Restaurant Capitol*, for Lagunas on the road to Tambo Quemado, buses leave when full between 1000-1600, US$2.25. From Lagunas it's 12 km to Sajama, *Sajama Express* bus runs daily, or you can hire transport for US$5. Or take a La Paz-Arica bus, ask for Sajama, try to pay half the fare, but you may be charged full fare. Either way you have to walk 10 km from the road to Sajama village unless enough passengers on the Patacamayo-Tambo Quemado bus want to go into the village, US$0.75 extra. Walking not recommended: hot in day, extremely cold at night, and poor lighting. Flag a camion if possible.

By road to Chile

There are two routes from La Paz to Chile: the shortest and most widely used is the road to Arica via the border at Tambo Quemado (Bolivia) and Chungará (Chile). From La Paz take the highway south towards Oruro. Immediately before Patacamaya, turn right at green road sign to Puerto Japonés on the Río Desaguadero, then on to Tambo Quemado. Take extra petrol (none available after Chilean border until Arica), food and water. The journey is worthwhile for the breathtaking views.

Bolivian customs is at Lagunas, 12 km on from Sajama, a popular 'truck-stop'. Petrol available. Restaurant/bar *Lagunas* offers cheap set menu, helpful, friendly. Owner can usually find accommodation somewhere in the village, US$1, take your own sleeping bag, extra blankets, warm clothing. Facilities are at best very basic; you may well be sleeping on a straw mattress on a dirt floor. No water or electricity, gas lamps or candles are usual. It may be possible for men to sleep at the Puesto Militar, beside the new road, 100 m from village. Nights can be bitterly cold and very windy. In the daytime there are spectacular views of nearby snowcapped Mt Sajama. The Bolivian border control is at Tambo Quemado, 10 km on from Lagunas. Best to change a small amount of currency into Chilean pesos in La Paz. From Tambo Quemado there is a stretch of about 7 km of 'no-man's land' before you reach the Chilean frontier at Chungará. Here the border crossing, which is set against the most spectacular scenic backdrop of Lago Chungará and Volcán Parinacota, is strictly controlled; open 0800-2100. Expect a long wait behind lines of lorries. Avoid Sunday; best to travel midweek. Drivers must fill in 'Relaciones de Pasajeros', US$0.25 from kiosk at border, giving details of driver, vehicle and passengers. Do not take any livestock, plants, fruit, vegetables, or dairy products into Chile. Pets must have signed papers attesting to their health *before* crossing. Papers available in La Paz only.

An alternative route, on which there are no trucks, is to go by good road from La Paz via Viacha to Santiago de Machaco (130 km, petrol); then 120 km to the border at Charaña (F *Alojamiento Aranda*; immigration behind railway station), very bad road. In Visviri (Chile) there is no fuel, accommodation, electricity, ask for restaurant and bargain price. From Visviri a regular road runs to Putre, see Chile chapter.

Uyuni

Uyuni lies near the eastern edge of the Salar de Uyuni and is the jumping-off point for trips to the salt flats, volcanoes and multi-coloured lakes of southwest Bolivia. Still a commercial and communication centre, Uyuni was, for much of this century, important as a major railway junction. A statue of an armed railway worker, erected after the 1952 Revolution, dominates Av Ferroviaria. Most services are near the station. Market on Av Potosí between the clock and Avaroa sells everything almost every day. Fiesta 11 July. Train buffs should visit the Railway Cemetery: engines from 1907-1950s.

Phone code: 02
Colour map 6, grid B3
Population: 11,320
Altitude: 3,665 m

C *Kory Wasy*, Av Potosí, entre Arce y Sucre. **D** low season, rather basic for the price but good fun, sunny lobby, restaurant planned, tour agency. **C** *Toñito*, Av Ferroviaria 48, T693 2094, www.bolivianexpeditions.com Spacious rooms with good beds, **F** pp in rooms with shared bath, very helpful, "an oasis". **D** *Mágia de Uyuni*, Av Colón entre Sucre y Camacho, T693 2541 F693 2121, magia_uyuni@latinmail.com Includes breakfast. Recommended. **D** *Kutimuy*, Avaroa esq Av Potosí, near market, T693 2391. Includes continental breakfast, fair, electric showers, **F** without bath. **D** *Hostal Marith*, Av Potosí 61, T693 2174. **F** without bath, good budget option, hot showers, sunny patio with laundry sinks. Recommended. **E** *Avenida*, Av Ferroviaria 11, opposite the train station, T693 2078. Cheaper with shared bath, popular, good hot showers, laundry facilities, parking. **G** *Hospedaje El Salvador*, Av Arce 346. Family run, breakfast served, helpful, laundry, good. **G** pp *Hostal Europa*, Ferroviaria opposite train station. Good gas-powered showers, good beds, noisy in the early hours from people arriving off the train, basic kitchen facilities, storage, secure, English spoken. **G** *Residencial Sucre*, Sucre 132, T693 2047. Very welcoming and warm though the 3 stars on the sign is optimistic! **G** *Residencial Urkupiña*, Plaza Arce. Small, basic, quite clean, hot shower US$0.50.

Sleeping
Water is frequently cut off and may only be available between 0600 and 1200

On Plaza Arce: *Arco Iris*, good Italian food and atmosphere, occasional live music. *16 de Julio*, opens 0700, mid price, good food, meeting place. *Kactus*, good pancakes, omelettes, plus Bolivian dishes, heating, popular. *Urkupiña*, Plaza Arce, open for breakfast, good standard stuff. *Minuteman*, new pizza restaurant attached to *Toñito Hotel* (see above), good.

Eating
Avoid eating in market.This is not a good place to get ill

A road and railway line run south from Oruro, through Río Mulato, the junction for trains to Potosí, to Uyuni (323 km). The road is sandy and, after rain, very bad, especially south of Río Mulato. The train journey is quicker and more scenic. **Bus** Offices are on Av Arce, in the same block as the post office. To **La Paz**, change in Oruro, 2000 (also 1930 every day with *Belgrano* except 2100 on Thu), US$7.45, 11-13 hrs. *Panasur* direct Wed and Sun 1800, US$9, 13 hrs (*Panasur* from La Paz bus terminal daily 1730 via Oruro, direct Tue and Fri). Same schedule to **Oruro**, US$3, 8 hrs (bitterly cold trip; take blanket or sleeping bag). To **Potosí** 1000, 1900, US$4.50, 5-7 hrs, spectacular scenery. To **Sucre** 1000, 1900, US$5.20, 9½ hrs. To **Tupiza** Wed and Sun 0900, US$5.25, 10 hrs. To **Camargo** 1000, US$6.70, 11-12 hrs, via Potosí. Likewise to **Tarija** 1000, US$9, 14 hrs. No direct buses to the Argentine border.

Train Check services on arrival, as schedules are notoriously unreliable, T693 2153. *Nuevo Expreso del Sur* leaves for **Oruro** on Tue and Sat at 2352, arriving 0625 (*Premier* US$7.75; *Salón* US$5.40). *Wara Wara del Sur* service leaves on Mon and Thu at 0122, arriving 0825 (*Salón* US$4.20). To **Atocha, Tupiza** and **Villazón** *Expreso del Sur* leaves Uyuni on Mon and Fri at 2216, arriving, respectively, at 0015, 0315 and 0620 (*Premier* US$4.95, US$9.70, US$14.65; *Salón* US$1.95, US$4.17, US$6.40). *Wara Wara* leaves on Sun and Wed at 0235, arriving 0430, 0800 and 1135 (*Salón* US$1.65, US$3,45, US$5.10). The ticket office opens at 0830 and 1430 each day and one hour before the trains leave. It closes once tickets are sold – get there early or buy through a tour agent.

Transport
Bus tickets include a small 'bus station construction' charge Travel by day from La Paz to Uyuni if possible; accidents reported on night buses

Bolivia

Chile is 1 hr ahead of Bolivia from mid-Oct to Mar. Do not attempt to take coca leaves across the border; it is an arrestable offence.

Also Chile does not allow dairy produce, teabags (of any description), fruit or vegetables to be brought in

Travelling to Chile: the easiest way is to go via San Pedro de Atacama as part of your jeep trip to the Salar and *lagunas* (see below). Otherwise, there is a train service to **Calama** leaving between 0500 and 0800 Thu, US$13.45. It takes 1 hr to change trains at Avaroa, then it's 40 mins to Ollagüe, where Chilean customs take 2-4 hrs. All passports are collected and stamped in the rear carriage and should be ready for collection after 1-2 hrs; queue for your passport, no names are called out. After that it is an uncomfortable 6 hrs to Calama. On Mon an 0800 service runs only as far as Avaroa and you must organize your own change of trains; there is a service from there to Calama. *Predilecto* and *Trans 11 de Julio* each has a bus to Calama which leaves from its office Mon and Thu 0400, US$10.50, 15 hrs (depending on border crossing). *Colque Tours*, Av Potosí 54, T/F639 2199, www.colquetours.terra.cl, as well as running Salar and Lagunas tours that take you to **San Pedro de Atacama**, has a direct jeep leaving their office every day at 1900, US$25 pp, 16 hours. Whichever route you take, no exit stamp is needed in advance; the Bolivian border post charges US$2.50 on exit.

From Colchani it is about 60 km across to the west shore of the **Salar**. There are 2 or 3 parallel tracks about 100 m apart and every few kilometres stones mark the way; the salt is soft and wet for about 2 km around the edges. There is no real danger of getting lost, especially in the high season, but it is a hard trip and the road is impassable after rain. Nonetheless, keep to the road at all times, and never venture from the shoulder at night. There are still a few unmarked sections along the border that are mined, although both sides downplay this unfortunate situation. There is no gasoline between Uyuni and Calama (Chile). It is 20 km from the west shore to 'Colcha K', the military checkpoint. From there, a poor gravel road leads 28 km to San Juan, where tour groups spend the night (very cold, no heating), then the road enters the Salar de Chiguana, a mix of salt and mud which is often wet and soft with deep tracks which are easy to follow. 35 km away is Chiguana, another military post, then 45 km to the end of the Salar, a few kilometres before border at Ollagüe. This latter part is the most dangerous; very slippery with little traffic. Alternatively, *Toñito Tours* of Uyuni will let you follow one of their groups and even promise help in the event of a break-down.

Directory **Banks** *Banco de Crédito*, Av Potosí, entre Bolívar y Arce, does not change money. Instead, go to the exchange shop to its left, which changes dollars, Chilean pesos and TCs, as does a *cambio* almost opposite *M@c Internet Café* on Av Potosí. *Hotel Avenida* changes dollars cash. *Colque Tours*, Av Potosí 54, changes TCs. Tour agencies and some shops accept payment in TCs. **Communications** Internet: *M@cNet*, Av Potosí near Arce, open daily 0900-2300 or later if you ask, fast satellite connection. *Servinet*, Potosí y Bolívar, 0800-1300, 1400-2200 daily. Both US$1.50 per hr. **Post office:** Av Arce esq C Cabrera. **Telephone:** *Entel*, Av Arce above Av Potosí, 0830-2200. **Tourist office** In the public clocktower on Av Potosí with Plaza Arce, Mon-Fri 0900-1230, 1500-1930. The head office (go here if you want to complain about a tour) is nearby, at Av Potosí 13, Mon-Fri 0830-1200, 1400-1830, Sat-Sun 0830-1200. T693 2060 and ask for the tourist information office. **Useful addresses** Immigration: Av Sucre 94, corner of Av Potosí, open daily 0800-2000 for visa extensions.

Salar de Uyuni and Lagunas Colorada and Verde

The best map of the area is by Walter Guzmán Córdova (see page 246)

Crossing the Salar de Uyuni, the largest and highest salt lake in the world, is one of the great Bolivian trips. Driving across it is a fantastic experience, especially during June and July when the bright blue skies contrast with the blinding white salt crust. Farther south, and included on tours of the Salar, are the towering volcanoes and multi-coloured lakes (Colorada and Verde) that make up some of weirdest landscapes in South America. On the west side of the Salar, five hours from Uyuni, is the tiny village of Llica, not included on the tours. There are good llama wool handicrafts, but no shops or electricity and only a basic hotel (meals in private houses). Bus from Uyuni 1200 daily, truck 1100.

Some 346 km southwest of Uyuni, 10 hours straight driving over unmarked, rugged truck tracks, is **Laguna Colorada**, one of Bolivia's most spectacular and most isolated marvels. The shores and shallows are crusted with gypsum and salt, an arctic white counterpoint to the flaming red, algae-coloured waters (from midday) in which the rare James flamingoes, along with the more common Chilean and Andean flamingoes, breed and live. The 714,000-ha **Reserva Eduardo Avaroa** (REA) includes Laguna Colorada and the sparkling jade Laguna Verde near the Chilean border. It has an office at Potosí 23 in Uyuni, excellent map for sale, US$5 entry (not included in tour price; pay in bolivianos, write your name on the back of the ticket and do not surrender it on departure).

The standard tour (see below for operators) lasts four days. **Day 1**: Uyuni to Colchani, from there to the Salar, including a salt-mine visit, lunch on the cactus-studded Isla Pescado, and overnight at a village, eg San Juan, south of the Salar (simple lodging, eg **G** *Alojamiento Licancábur*, Teófilo Yucra, hot showers extra, helpful, electricity 1900-2100, running water). **Day 2**: to Laguna Colorada, passing active Volcán Ollagüe and a chain of small, flamingo-specked lagoons. Overnight at Laguna Colorada; demand to stay at *Reserva Eduardo Avaroa* headquarters US$4.50 per person, clean, comfortable, modern, quite warm – it's far better than Eustaquio Berna's hut which is also US$3 per person and favoured by the Uyuni agencies. There are two other places to stay, one good, one bad. Camping is not permitted here. **Day 3**: drive past belching geysers at Sol de Mañana (take care not to fall through the crust) and through the barren, surreal landscape of the Pampa de Chalviri at 4,800 m, via a pass at 5,000 m, to the wind-lashed jade waters of the Laguna Verde (4,400 m) at the foot of Volcán Licancábur (for best views arrive before 1100), and back to Laguna Colorada or further. At Aguas Termales Chalviri, between the two lakes, hot springs feed the salty water at about 30° C (hottest early morning). *Refugio* at Laguna Verde, US$2 per person, small, mattresses, running water, view of lake. **Day 4**: Return to Uyuni. A three day version eliminates the Salar de Uyuni or Laguna Verde, while an extension will permit ascent of Licancábur (not a difficult climb, guide compulsory, US$30).

Tours
Take a good sleeping bag, sunglasses, sun hat, sun protection, lots of warm clothing (record low measured in 1996 at Laguna Colorada: -30°C), water bottle, water purification tablets/iodine tincture, lots of film

Bolivia

Ask for a written contract which states a full day-by-day itinerary, a full meal-by-meal menu (vegetarians should be prepared for an egg-based diet), what is included in the price and what is not (accommodation is normally not included – add US$3-4.50 pp per night). If the tour doesn't match the contract, or when things go badly wrong, go back to the operator and demand a refund (unless you have been able to persuade them not to take the full price at the beginning). This seldom yields positive results, in which case complain to the tourism office in Uyuni (see above) and then to the *Director Regional de Turismo*, La Prefectura del Departamento de Potosí, C La Paz, Potosí (T02-622 7477). Trip prices are based on a 6-person group – it is easy to find other people in Uyuni, especially in high season, Apr-Sep. If there are fewer than 6 you each pay more. The standard 4-day trip (Salar de Uyuni, Lagunas Colorada and Verde) costs US$75-220 pp depending on agency, departure point and season. There is no refund for leaving for Chile after Laguna Verde. Shorter (including one day to the Salar) and longer trips are possible but 4 days in a jeep is enough for most people. Tours can also be arranged from Tupiza (see next page). Agencies in Potosí and La Paz also organize tours, but in some cases this may involve

Tour operators
Organization of tours from Uyuni is adequate at best and even good companies, their guides or vehicles have their off days, but the staggering scenery makes up for any discomfort

putting you on a bus to Uyuni where you meet up with one of the Uyuni agencies and get the same quality tour for a higher price. For the latest recommendations, speak to travellers who have just returned from a tour and try the following: *Colque Tours*, Av Potosí 54, T/F693 2199, Well-known but not always recommended, has its own hostal on the edge of the Salar. *Esmeralda*, Av Ferroviaria esq Arce, T693 2130. Good tours at the cheaper end of the market. *Kantuta*, Av Arce, T693 3084/3047. Run by 3 eager brothers, also run volcano-climbing tours. *Pamela*, Av Arce y Ferroviaria. Good tours. *Toñito Tours*, Av Ferroviaria 152, T693 2819, F693 2094, www.bolivianexpeditions.com Offers a variety of tours (also in La Paz, see page 265). *Tunupa/Discovery Bolivia*, Plaza Arce 15, T693 2099, T693 2823. *Uyuni Andes Travel Office*, Ayacucho 222, T693 2227. Good reports, run by Belgian Isabelle and Iver. *Wilson Tours*, Av Potosí 305, T693 2217. English-speaking guides, helpful, enthusiastic.

Crossing into Chile From Laguna Verde it is 7 km to Hito Cajón, the border post with Chile and all agencies now offer the option of crossing here . There is a Bolivian immigration post which will charge you US$2.65 for an exit stamp. Agencies will organize a bus (US$10 – your jeep driver should ensure you are safely on before leaving) both to the immigration post and on to San Pedro de Atacama in Chile, where the bus will wait for your lengthy immigration formalities to be completed. As with the train crossing, do not take any fresh fruit or coca leaves. Buy Chilean pesos in Uyuni, but don't change all your money as you'll need bolivianos for national park entry and the exit tax. A further 8 km is La Cruz, the junction with the east-west road between the borax and sulphur mines and San Pedro de Atacama (Chile). The meteorological station at Laguna Verde will radio for a pick-up from San Pedro. This service costs US$10 per person Hito Cajón-San Pedro. Transport Laguna Verde to Chile via Hito Cajón is becoming more plentiful and the crossing is getting much easier and popular. Do not underestimate the dangers of getting stuck without transport or lodging at this altitude. Do not travel alone.

Tupiza

Phone code: 02
Colour map 6, grid B3
Population: 20,000
Altitude: 2,990 m
200 km S of Uyuni

Set in a landscape of colourful, eroded mountains and stands of huge cacti, Tupiza is best known as the place from which to take Butch Cassidy and the Sundance Kid tours, but it's also the starting point for bike rides, horse and jeep tours in the surroundings, eg the Quebrada Palala with the nearby 'Stone Forest', the Valle de los Machos and the Quebrada Seca, and trips to the Uyuni salt flats (tour operators have details). The statue in the main plaza is to Avelino Aramayo (1802-82), of the Aramayo mining dynasty, pre-eminent in the late 19th, early 20th centuries. Chajra Huasi, a palazzo-style, abandoned home of the Aramayo family across the Río Tupiza, may be visited. Beautiful sunsets over the fertile Tupiza valley can be seen from the foot of a statue of Christ on a hill behind the plaza. Market days are Monday, Thursday and Saturday, with local produce sold in the northern part of town; there is also a daily market at the north end of Av Chichas. *IGM* office, for maps, is in the Municipal building to the right of the church, second floor.

For ecological reasons don't buy handicrafts made of cactus wood

Sleeping & eating

Tupiza is famous for its tamales, a delicious scrap of spicy dried llama meat encased in a ball of corn mash and cooked in the leaves of the plant

E *Mitru*, Av Chichas 187, T/F694 3001, with shared bath, **B** in suite with bath, breakfast, living room in new wing, in other rooms breakfast is extra. Best in town, hot water, pool, cable TV, parking, use of kitchen, luggage store, safes, takes credit cards, book exchange, has the only laundry in town (discount for hotel guests). Under same ownership, **E** *Mitru Anexo*, Abaroa next to station, T694 3002. Same services and prices, but no suites, parking or pool. **E** *Roca Colorada*, Av Chichas 220, T694 2633. **F** with shared bath, pleasant, good rooms, cable TV, electric showers. **E** *Hostal Valle Hermoso*, Av Pedro Arraya 478, T694 2592, hostalvh@hotmail.com Good hot showers, pleasant TV/breakfast room, book exchange, tourist advice, *Butch Cassidy* video, firm beds, cheaper with shared bath, motorbikes can be parked in restaurant, accepts credit cards and TCs (5% extra). **F** *Res Centro*, Av Santa Cruz 287, 2 blocks from station, T694 2705. Warm water, nice patio, motorbike and car parking. **F** *El Rancho*, Av Pedro Araya 86, T694 3116. **G** without bath, spacious, hot water, laundry facilities.

Los Helechos, next door to *Mitru Anexo* on Abaroa. Burgers and main courses, vegetarian options, good salad bar, closed alternate Suns. *Il Bambino*, Florida y Santa Cruz. Closed Sat and Sun evenings. *La Casa de Irma*, in supermarket *Frial Castro*, Florida. Lasagnes, chicken, meat and vegetarian dishes with an hour's notice, for US$2.25. *El Atajo*, Florida 157. Sandwiches and, at night, *chicharrón de pollo*, open Mon-Sat 0800-1200, 1500- 2200, internet US$2.10 per hr. Breakfasts in the market; dishes sold on the streets near market.

Local operators offer jeep tours to local sights for US$13 pp, horse riding, US$2.60 per hr, US$17 per day, and 2-days trips to San Vicente following Butch and Sundance's movements in 1908, US$35 pp. They also offer Salar de Uyuni tours but, as elsewhere, problems occur: vehicles may carry too many passengers (insist on 6) and Tupiza operators subcontract to Uyuni operators who may not have the same standards or competence. *Tupiza Tours*, in *Hotel Mitru* (address above), are the most experienced, also has additional tours: `triathlon' of riding, biking and jeep in the surroundings, US$19 pp, and extensions to the Uyuni tour, US$110-130). Also try *Valle Hermoso Tours*, opposite *Hostal Valle Hermoso*, T/F694 2592. **Tour operators**

Bus To **Villazón** 2 hrs, US$1.50, several daily. To **Potosí**, US$4.50, 8 hrs, daily 1000, 1030, 2030. Same schedule to **Oruro** and **Sucre**, both US$7.45. To **Uyuni**, Mon, Thu 1100, US$5.25, 10 hrs, poor road. *Expreso Tupiza* has a direct bus to **La Paz** at 1000, otherwise via Potosí, 14-17 hrs, US$8.95. A 2-way dirt road goes from Uyuni to **Atocha**. Road from Potosí which goes on south to Villazón is 2-way, dirt, with a bridge over the Río Suipacha. **Train** To **Villazón**: *Nuevo Expreso del Sur* Mon and Fri 0325, arriving 0620; *Wara Wara* Sun and Wed at 0835, arriving 1135. To **Atocha**, **Uyuni** and **Oruro**, *Expresso del Sur* Tue and Sat at 1800; *Wara Wara* Mon and Thu at 1900. The ticket office is open on Mon from 0730 for that afternoon's train; Mon from 1800 for train leaving on Tue; Wed 0800 for the Thu service; Fri 1500 for the Sat train. **Transport** *Train station in the centre. Bus station 5 blocks further south Book transport in advance.*

Banks Neither *Banco Mercantil*, south side of the plaza, nor *Banco Crédito*, opposite side, will change money. Many shops will change dollars and Argentine pesos at similar rates to Villazón. TCs can be changed on Av Abaroa, look for "Cambio TCs" sign. *Tupiza Tours* gives cash against Visa, Mastercard (no ATM) and TCs. **Communications Internet:** Many internet places, US$0.70 per hr. **Post office**: on Abaroa, northwest of plaza, Mon-Fri 0830-1800, Sat 0900-1700, Sun 0900-1200. **Telephone**: *Entel*, is at end of same street, Mon-Sat 0800-2300, Sun 0800-1300, 1500-2200. **Directory**

Tupiza is the centre of Butch Cassidy and the Sundance Kid country and there are tours following their last few days. On 4 November 1908, they held up an Aramayo company payroll north of Salo. (Aramayo *hacienda* in Salo, one hour north of Tupiza, still stands. Roadside kiosks serve roast goat, *choclo*, *papas*, soup.) Two days later they were killed by a four-man military police patrol in San Vicente. Shoot out site off main street – ask locals. Butch and Sundance are buried in the cemetery, but the grave has yet to be identified. An investigation of the supposed grave by the Nova project in 1991 proved negative, but see *Digging Up Butch and Sundance*, by Anne Meadows (Bison Books, 1996). Basic *alojamiento* on main street marked 'Hotel'. Restaurant *El Rancho* next door sells basic foodstuffs. Trucks from Avenida Chichas, Tupiza on Monday, Thursday and Saturday (market day) leave for the antimony mine at Chilcobija (60 km from San Vicente) and will go to San Vicente if there are enough people. **San Vicente** *Population: 400 Altitude: 4,500 m 103 km NW of Tupiza (4-6 hrs on good dirt road)*

South to Argentina

The Argentine border is here. There is not much to see (two cinemas and good indoor market). The border area must not be photographed. *Banco de Crédito*, Oruro 111, changes cash only; try the *casas de cambio* on Avenida República de Argentina, near border. Travellers' cheques can be exchanged at *Restaurante Repostero*, 20 de Mayo 190, 5% commission. Several internet cafés charge US$1.50 per hour. Post office and *Entel* are on Avenida Independencia, opposite side to bus station. The tourist office on the plaza is not very useful. *Diamante Tours*, Edificio de Turismo, Plaza 6 de Agosto, T/F596 2315, are helpful (also in Potosí and Uyuni.) **Villazón** *Phone code: 02; Cotevi phone company prefix 596, Entel 597 Population: 13,000 Altitude: 3,443 m 81 km S of Tupiza*

Sleeping & eating **D-E** *Res El Cortijo*, 20 de Mayo 338, behind post office, T596 2093. Breakfast included, some rooms with bath, intermittent hot water, restaurant. **E** *Grand Palace*, 25 de Mayo 52, 1 block southwest of bus terminal, T596 4693. Safe, **F** without bath. Recommended. **E** *Hostal Plaza*, Plaza 6 de Agosto 138, T596 3535. Modern, **F** without bath, TV, comfortable, good restaurant. **F** *Hostal Buena Vista*, Av Antofagasta 508, T596 3055. Good rooms, shared bath, hot showers US$1.05, close to the train and bus stations, above reasonable restaurant. **G** *Res Martínez*, 25 de Mayo 13, T596 3353, 1 block southwest of bus station. Well signed, shared bath, hot water. **G** *Res Panamericano*, C 20 de Mayo 384, T596 2612. Shared bath, risky electric showers, sagging beds, laundry facilities, parking. *Charke Kan*, J M Deheza, restaurant is good. Beside it is *Snack Pizzería Don Vicco*. *Chifa Jardín*, on the Plaza. Expensive but huge helpings. *El Repostero*, opposite market, serves good breakfasts and lunches. *Snack El Turista*, Edificio de Turismo, is open at 0900 for breakfast. Better to cross the border to La Quiaca to eat.

Transport
An unpaved road goes to Tarija, improved for the last 16 km. The road linking Potosí with Villazón via Camargo is in poor condition and about 100 km longer than the better road via Tupiza

Bus Bus terminal is near plaza, 5 blocks from the border. Taxi to border, US$0.35 or hire porter, US$1, and walk across. From **La Paz**, several companies, 25 hrs, US$7.50 (even though buses are called 'direct', you may have to change in Potosí, perhaps to another company), depart La Paz 1800, 1900, depart **Villazón** 0800, 0830. To **Potosí** several between 0800-0830 and 1800-1900, 10 hrs by day, 12 hrs at night, US$3-4.50 (terrible in the wet, can take 24 hrs; freezing at night). To **Tupiza**, several daily, US$1.50. To **Tarija**, beautiful journey but most buses overnight only, daily at 2000-2030, US$4.50, 6 hrs, very cold on arrival but passengers can sleep on bus until daybreak. **Train** Station about 1 km north of border on main road, taxi US$2.35. To **Tupiza**, **Atocha**, **Uyuni** and **Oruro**: *Nuevo Expreso del Sur* Tue, Sat, 1530, *Wara Wara del Sur* Mon, Thu 1530. Ticket office opens 0800, long queues.

Border with Argentina
Bolivian time is 1 hr behind Argentina

Bolivian immigration office is on Avenida República de Argentina just before bridge; open daily 0600-2000. They will issue an exit stamp. Officials are efficient, but be on your guard at all times. For Argentine immigration see page 152. Change all your bolivianos into dollars or pesos, because it is impossible to change them in Argentina. The Argentine consulate is at Avenida Saavedra 311; open Monday-Thursday 1000-1300.

Potosí, Sucre and the Southern Highlands

This is a region which boasts the World Cultural Heritage sites of Potosí, with its mining past and current mining misery, and Sucre, the white city. In the south, Tarija is known for its fruit and wines and its traditions which set it apart from the rest of the country.

Potosí

Phone code: 02
Colour map 6, grid B3
Population: 112,000
Altitude: 4,070 m

Potosí is the highest city of its size in the world. It was founded by the Spaniards on 10 April 1545, after they had discovered Indian mine workings at Cerro Rico, which dominates the city. Immense amounts of silver were once extracted. In Spain 'es un Potosí' (it's a Potosí) is still used for anything superlatively rich. By the early 17th century Potosí was the largest city in the Americas, but over the next two centuries, as its lodes began to deteriorate and silver was found elsewhere, Potosí became little more than a ghost town. It was the demand for tin – a metal the Spaniards ignored – that saved the city from absolute poverty in the early 20th century, until the price slumped because of over-supply. Mining continues in Cerro Rico – mainly tin, zinc, lead, antimony and wolfram.

Large parts of Potosí are colonial, with twisting streets and an occasional great mansion with its coat of arms over the doorway. UNESCO has declared the city to be 'Patrimonio de la Humanidad'. Some of the best buildings are grouped round the Plaza 10 de Noviembre. The old Cabildo and the Royal Treasury – Las Cajas Reales – are both here, converted to other uses. The **Cathedral** faces Plaza 10 de Noviembre. ■ *Mon-Fri 0930-1000, 1500-1730, Sat 0930-1000. Guided tour only, US$1.*

The **Casa Nacional de Moneda**, or Mint, is nearby, on Calle Ayacucho. Founded in 1572, rebuilt 1759-73, it is one of the chief monuments of civil building in Hispanic America. Thirty of its 160 rooms are a museum with sections on mineralogy, and an art gallery in a splendid salon on the first floor. One section is dedicated to the works of the acclaimed 17th-18th century religious painter Melchor Pérez de Holguín. Elsewhere are coin dies and huge wooden presses which made the silver strips from which coins were cut. The smelting houses have carved altar pieces from Potosí's ruined churches. You cannot fail to notice the huge, grinning mask of

Sights

Bolivia

Potosí

Sleeping	4 Claudia *A1*	13 Posada San Lorenzo *B2*
1 Alojamiento La Paz *B1*	5 El Turista *D2*	14 Residencial
2 Carlos V *C3*	6 Gran *A1*	Copacabana *A2*
3 Casa de María	7 Hostal Cerro Rico *D3*	15 Residencial Felcar *A2*
Victoria *D2*	8 Hostal Colonial *C3*	16 San Andrés *C1*
	9 Hostal Felimar *B2*	17 San Antonio *B1*
	10 Hostal Libertador *D3*	
	11 Hostal Santa María *A1*	**Eating**
	12 Jerusalem *B1*	1 Chaplin *C2*

2 Confitería Cherry's *C3*
3 El Fogón *C2*
4 Kaypichu *C3*
5 La Casona Pub *C2*
6 La Manzana
Mágica *B2*
7 Potocchi *C3*
8 Sumac Orcko *C2*
9 Sky Room *B2*

0 metres 100
0 yards 100

Bacchus over an archway between two principal courtyards. Erected in 1865, its smile is said to be ironic and aimed at the departing Spanish. Wear warm clothes, as it is cold inside. ■ *Tue-Fri 0900-1200, 1400-1830, Sat-Sun 0900-1300, US$3, US$3 to take photos, US$3 for video. Entry by regular, 2-hr guided tour only (in English at 0900, usually for 10 or more people), T622 2777.*

The **Convento y Museo de Santa Teresa** at Chicas y Ayacucho, T622 3847, has an interesting collection of colonial and religious art, obligatory guide.■ *0900--1100, 1500-1700, only by guided tour in Spanish or English, US$3.15, US$1.50 to take photos, US$25(!) for video.* Among Potosí's baroque churches, typical of 18th-century Andean or 'mestizo' architecture, are the Jesuit **Compañía** church, on Ayacucho, with an impressive bell-gable. ■ *0800-1200, 1400-1800.* **San Francisco** (Tarija y Nogales, T622 2539) with a fine organ, worthwhile for the views from the tower and roof, museum of ecclesiastical art, underground tunnel system. ■ *Mon-Fri 0900-1200, 1430-1700, Sat 0900-1200, US$1.50, US$1.50 to take photos, US$3 for video.* Also **San Lorenzo** (1728-44) with a rich portal, on Héroes del Chaco, fine views from the tower. **San Martín** on Hoyos, with an uninviting exterior, is beautiful inside, but is normally closed for fear of theft. Ask the German Redemptorist Fathers to show you around; their office is just to the left of their church. Other churches to visit include **Jerusalén**, Plaza del Estudiante, with **Museo Sacro** displaying gold work and painting. ■ *Mon-Sat 1430-1830, US$0.75.* On the opposite side of Plaza del Estudiante is **San Bernardo**, which houses the Escuela Taller Potosí where you can see a display of restoration work. ■ *Mon-Fri 0800-1200, 1400-1800.* **San Agustín** on Bolívar y Quijarro, with crypts and catacombs (the whole city was interconnected by tunnels in colonial times). ■ *Only by prior arrangement with tourist office. Tour starts at 1700, US$0.10.*

Teatro Omiste (1753) on Plaza 6 de Agosto has a fine façade. The **Museo Universitario**, Calle Bolívar 698, displays archaeology and some good modern Bolivian painting. ■ *Mon-Fri, 0800-1200, 1400-1800, US$0.75.* **Museo del Ingenio de San Marcos**, Betanzos y La Paz, is a well-preserved example of the city's industrial past, with machinery used in grinding down the silver ore. It also has a good restaurant, cultural activities and an exhibition of Calcha textiles. ■ *1000-2300; restaurant open 1200-2300, information office 1130-1230, 1430-1530, exhibition Mon-Sat 1300-2000, T622 2781.* **Museo Etno-indumentario** (also known as **Fletes**), Avenida Serrudo 152, and has a thorough display of the different dress and customs and their histories of Potosí department's 16 provinces. ■ *Mon-Fri 0900-1200, 1400-1800, Sat 0900-1200, US$1.10, includes tour in Spanish and basic German, very interesting, T622 3258.*

In Potosí, 2,000 colonial buildings have been catalogued. At Quijarro and Omiste is the Esquina de las Cuatro Portadas (two houses with double doors), or Balcón de Llamacancha. Off Junín, see the Pasaje de Siete Vueltas (the passage of the seven turns). There is a fine stone doorway (house of the Marqués de Otavi, now a bank) in Junín between Matos and Bolívar. At Lanza 8 was the house of José de Quiroz and of Antonio López de Quiroga (now a school). Turn up Chuquisaca from Lanza and after three blocks right into Millares; here on the left is a sculpted stone doorway and on the right a doorway with two rampant lions in low relief on the lintel. Turning left up Nogales you come to an old mansion in a little plaza. Turn left along La Paz and one block along there is another stone doorway with suns in relief. At La Paz y Bolívar is the Casa del Balcón de la Horca. Turn left for the Casa de las Tres Portadas.

Sleeping

■ *on map*
Unless otherwise stated hotels have no heating in rooms.
See also
Koala Tours

B *Claudia*, Av Maestro 322, out of centre, T622 2242, F622 5677. Helpful, modern. Recommended. **B** *Hostal Colonial*, Hoyos 8, T622 4265, F622 7146. A pretty colonial house near the main plaza, with heating, has names and telephone numbers of guides, very helpful, even if you're not staying there, very expensive for long-distance phone calls, best hotel in centre. Book in advance. **B** *Hostal Libertador*, Millares 58, T622 7877, hostalib@cedro.pts.entelnet.bo Central heating, quiet, helpful, comfortable, parking. Recommended. **C** *Hostal Cerro Rico*, Ramos 123 entre La Paz y Millares, T/F622 3539, www.hostalcerrorico.8k.com Very good rooms upstairs, heating, hot water, **D** without bath, cable TV, internet, helpful, parking. **C** *Jerusalem*, Oruro 143, T/F622 2600, hoteljer@ cedro.pts.entelnet.bo Pleasant, with breakfast, **F** without bath, helpful, *comedor*, parking, laundry, good value. **D** *Hostal Compañía de Jesús*, Chuquisaca 445, T622 3173. Central, attractive, good value, includes breakfast. **D** *Hostal Felimar*, Junín 14, T622 4357. Hot water, includes breakfast, 2 roof-top suites, basement rooms have no exterior windows but warm, quiet. **D** *Hostal Santa María*, Av Serrudo 244, T622 3255. Hot water, cold rooms, good cafeteria, popular. **E** *Gran*, Av Universitario 1002, T624 3483, opposite bus terminal. With bath, hot water, breakfast, TV, helpful. Recommended for early departures. **E** *El Turista*, Lanza 19, T622 2492, F622 2517. Also *LAB* office, helpful, hot showers, breakfast (US$1), great view from top rooms, good value. Recommended but poor beds. **E** *San Antonio*, Oruro 136, T622 3566. **G** without bath, 10% discount with valid IYHA card if sharing room, noisy. **F** *Res Felcar*, Serrudo 345 y Bustillos, T622 4966. Shared bath, hot water 0800-1600, popular, nice patio garden. **F** *Carlos V*, Linares 42 on Plaza 6 de Agosto, T622 5121. With breakfast, **F** without bath, occasional hot water 0700-1200, luggage store, 2400 curfew. **F** *Casa de María Victoria*, Chuquisaca 148, T22132. All rooms open onto colonial courtyard, **G** without bath, lukewarm water, stores luggage, popular with budget choice, arranges mine tours, owner speaks English, good breakfast, leave nothing unattended, poor beds. **F** *San Andrés*, Camacho 283, T622 9025. Helpful, shared bath, good. **G** *Res Copacabana*, Av Serrudo 319, T622 2712. Single or shared rooms, restaurant, separate hot showers, will change $ cash, safe car park (owner's son, Dr Hugo Linares Fuentes will give medical assistance). **G** *Alojamiento La Paz*, Oruro 262, T622 2632. Central, basic, 1 shower for the whole hotel, lukewarm water. **G** *Posada San Lorenzo*, C Bustillos 967, opposite market. Colonial building, nice courtyard, no showers.

Eating

La Casona Pub, Frías 34. Good food (meat fondue and trout recommended) and beer, open Mon-Sat 1000-1230, 1800-2400 (also owns *Café Plata* on C Hoyos, which is good for coffee and cakes). *Chaplin*, Quijarro y Matos 10. Pleasant, good breakfasts, best *tucumanos* before 1200, closed Sun. *Confitería Cherry's*, Padilla 8. Good cakes, very popular, good breakfast, cheap, open 0800. *Da Tong*, Oruro 526. Authentic Chinese, large portions, inexpensive. *El Fogón*, Oruro y Frías. Upmarket pub-restaurant, good food and atmosphere, open 1200-1500, 1800-2400. *Potocchi*, Millares 24, T22467. Great traditional food, opens 0800, *peña* most nights. Recommended. *The Sky Room*, Bolívar 701. Good views of the town and the Cerro, OK, slow service, opens 0800-2230 (1700 Sun). *Sumac* Orcko, Quijarro 46. Large portions, cheap set lunch, reasonably priced, very popular with travellers, heating. Vegetarian: *Kaypichu*, Millares 24. Stylish, open 0700-1300 and 1600-2100, closed Mon. *La Manzana Mágica*, Oruro 239. Good food and value, open 0700-2200, lunch US$2.

● on map
Good value food in Mercado Central, between Oruro, Bustillos, Héroes del Chaco and Bolívar, breakfast from 0700, fresh bread from 0600

Festivals

8-10 Mar is *San Juan de Dios*, with music, dancing, parades etc. In **May** there is a market on C Gumiel every Sun, with lotteries and lots of fun things for sale. *Fiesta de Manquiri*: on **3 consecutive Sat at the end of May/beginning of Jun** llama sacrifices are made at the cooperative mines in honour of *Pachamama*; the same occurs on **1 Aug**, the *Ritual del Espíritu*. *Carnaval Minero*, 2 weeks before carnival in Oruro, includes Tata Ckascho, when miners dance down Cerro Rico and El Tío (the *Dios Minero*) is paraded. *San Bartolomé*, or the Fiesta de Chutillos, is held from the middle of **Aug**, with the main event being processions of dancers on the weekend closest to the **24th-26th**; Sat features Potosino, and Sun national, groups. Costumes can be hired in *artesanía* market on C Sucre. Hotel and transport prices go up by 30% for the whole of that weekend. In **Oct**, *Festival Internacional de la Cultura*, in Potosí and Sucre. **10 Nov**, *Fiesta Aniversiario de Potosí*. Potosí is sometimes called the 'Ciudad de las Costumbres', especially at Corpus Cristi, Todos Santos and Carnaval, when special cakes are baked, families go visiting friends, etc.

Shopping

Mercado Central (see address above), sells mainly food and produce but silver is sold near the C Oruro entrance. *Mercado Artesanal*, at Sucre y Omiste, sells handwoven cloth and regional handicrafts. Some Fri the merchants organize music, food and drink (*ponche*), not to be missed. Tailor *Germán Laime*, Sucre 38, will make items (jackets, bags, etc) to customers' wishes.

Bolivia

Tour operators

Trips to the Salar de Uyuni, Laguna Colorada and Laguna Verde are expensive here. See page 290 for practical advice on booking a trip

The following have been recommended: *Amauta Expediciones*, Ayacucho 17, T622 5515. For trips to Uyuni, the lagoons and the mines. Gerónimo Fuentes has been recommended and speaks English. 15% of income goes to the miners. *Andes Salt Expediciones*, Plaza Alonso de Ibáñez 3. Recommended guides. Run by Raul Braulio who speaks English and who can also be contacted at Millares 96, T/F622 5175, turismo_potosi@hotmail.com *Carola Tours*, Quintanilla s/n, T622 8212. Guide Santos Mamani recommended. *Cerro Rico Travel*, Bolívar 853, T622 7044, T718-35083 (mob), jacky_gc@yahoo.com Jaqueline knows the mines well and speaks good English. Also English and French guides for trips to village *artesanía* markets north of the city and to colonial *haciendas*, horse and mountain bike hire, treks, trips to Toro Toro including cave visits. *Hidalgo Tours*, Junín y Bolívar 19, T622 5186, www.salaruyuni.com Upmarket and specialized services within the city and to Salar de Uyuni. Efraín Huanca has been recommended for mine tours. *Koala Tours*, Ayacucho 5, T/F622 2092. Run by Eduardo Garnica Fajardo who speaks English and French. Excellent mine tours by former miners, Juan Mamani Choque and Pedro Montes Caria have been recommended. Th company donates 15% of their fee to support on-site health-care facilities. Frequently recommended. They also have a hostal, *The Koala Den*, Junín 56, T622 6467, with heated dormitory and private rooms, shared showers and use of kitchen. And they have an internet café which serves meals. *Silver Tours*, Quijarro 12, Edif Minero, T622 3600, www.silvertours.8m.com One of the cheaper firms, guide Fredi recommended.

Transport

New road to La Paz under construction will reduce journey time to 6 hrs

Beware theft in the terminal area

A taxi in town costs US$1.

Air: The airport is 5 km out of town on the Sucre road. *Aero Sur* (C Hoyos 10, T622 2088), to **La Paz** 0800 Mon-Sat; *TAM* to/from La Paz, Mon. Flights frequently cancelled. **Bus**: The bus terminal is 20 mins downhill walk or a short taxi or micro ride from the centre of town on Av Universitaria below rail station, T624 3361, *Entel*, post office, police, US$0.10 terminal tax. When you buy your ticket you check your luggage into the operator's office and it is then loaded directly onto your bus. Daily services: to **La Paz** 1830-1930, US$4.50, 11 hrs, *buscama* with *Flota Copacabana* US$7.50. To travel by day, go to **Oruro**, 5 a day from 0700, US$4.50, 7 hrs. To **Cochabamba** 1830 and 1900, US$4.50, 12 hrs. To **Sucre** 4 daily 0700-1800, US$3, 3 hrs. Cars run to Sucre, taking 4 passengers, 2 hrs, US$4.25 pp, drop-off at your hotel. To **Santa Cruz** 1900 (change in Sucre or Cochabamba), US$12, 18 hrs. To **Villazón** 0800, 1900, US$3-4.50, 11 hrs. To **Tarija** 1800, US$6.70-7.45, 12 hrs. Buses to **Uyuni** leave from either side of the railway line (uphill the road is called Av Antofagasta or 9 de Abril, downhill it is Av Universitaria), daily 1100, 1830, US$4.50, 6 hrs, superb scenery; book in advance.

Directory

Banks There are ATMs around the centre. *Banco Nacional*, Junín 4-6. Exchange for US$ TCs and cash. *Banco Mercantil*, Sucre y Ayacucho. 1% commision on US$ TCs, no commission on Visa cash withdrawals. Almost opposite is *Casa Fernández* for cash exchange. *Banco de Crédito*, Bolívar y Sucre. Cash withdrawals on Visa. Many shops on Plaza Alonso de Ibáñez and on Bolívar, Sucre and Padilla display 'compro dólares' signs. **Communications Internet:** All US$0.75 per hr. *Café Candelaria*, Ayacucho 5, T622 8050, also crafts, postcards, book exchange. *Tuko's Café*, Junín 9, p 3, T622 5489/7, tuco25@hotmail.com Open 0800-2300, information, English spoken, popular music, videos, good food. Another opposite bus terminal. **Post Office:** Lanza 3, Mon-Fri 0800-2000, Sat till 1930, Sun 0900-1200. **Telephone:** *Entel*, on Plaza Arce at end of Av Camacho, T43496 (use of internet US$2.75 per hour). Also at Av Universitaria near bus terminal, and on Padilla, opposite *Confitería Cherys*. **Cultural centres** *Alianza Francesa*, Junín e Ingavi, French and Spanish lessons, *Le Boulevard* restaurant, Bolívar 853, with good set lunches (arrive early), 'impressive' toilets. **Tourist office** On Plaza 6 de Agosto, T622 7405, gobmupoi@cedro.pts.entelnet.bo Town maps US$0.40 (English, French, German and Spanish), better than glossy US$0.60 map (Spanish only), helpful. Open Mon-Fri 0800-1200, 1400-1800 (allegedly). **Useful addresses** *Migración*: Linares esq Padilla, T622 5989. Mon-Fri 0830-1630, closed lunchtime, beware unnecessary charges for extensions. **Police station:** on Plaza 10 de Noviembre.

Mine tours

By law all guides have to work with a travel agency and carry an ID card issued by the Prefectura

For many, the main reason for being in Potosí is to visit the mines of Cerro Rico. The state mines were closed in the 1980s and are now worked as cooperatives by small groups of miners. A 4½-hour morning tour to the mines and ore-processing plant involves meeting miners and seeing them at work in medieval conditions. It is a shocking but fascinating experience but you need to be fit and acclimatized and the tours are not recommended for claustrophobics or asthmatics. The guided tours run by Potosí agencies are conducted by former miners and they provide essential equipment – helmet, lamp and usually protective clothing (check when booking and ask about the level of difficulty of the tour). Wear old clothes and take torch and a handkerchief to filter the dusty air. The size of tour groups varies – some are as large as 20 people, which is excessive. The smaller the group the better. The price of tours is US$10 per person and includes transport. A contribution to the miners' cooperative is appreciated, as are medicines for the new health centre (*Posta Sanitaria*) on Cerro Rico. It is also a good idea to take presents for the miners – dynamite, coca leaves, cigarettes, Coca-cola, or water. Saturday and Sunday are the quietest days (Sunday is the miners' day off).

A good place to freshen up after visiting the mines (or to spend a day relaxing) is Tarapaya, where there are thermal baths, Tarapaya itself (in poor condition) and Miraflores (public, US$0.30, private, US$0.60). On the other side of the river from Tarapaya is a 50 m diameter crater lake, whose temperature is 30° C; take sun protection. Below the crater lake are boiling ponds but on no account swim in the lake. Several people have drowned in the boiling waters and agencies do not warn of the dangers. ■ *Buses, micros and colectivos from the bus terminal, outside Chuquimia market on Av Universitaria, every 30 minutes, 0700-1700, US$0.55. Taxi US$7.50 for a group. Last colectivo back to Potosí at 1800. Camping by the lake is possible and there is accommodation at Balneario Tarapaya.*

Tarapaya

Bolivia

Sucre

Charming Sucre, Bolivia's official capital, has grown rapidly since the mid-1980s following severe drought which drove campesinos from the countryside and the collapse of tin mining in 1985. Founded in 1538 as La Plata, it became capital of the audiencia of Charcas in 1559. Its name was later changed to Chuquisaca before the present name was adopted in 1825 in honour of the first president of the new republic. Sucre is sometimes referred to as La Ciudad Blanca, owing to the tradition that all buildings in the centre are painted in their original colonial white. This works to beautiful effect and in 1992 UNESCO declared the city a 'Patrimonio Histórico y Cultural de la Humanidad'. There are two universities, the older dating from 1624.

Phone code: 04
Colour map 6, grid B3
Population: 131,769
Altitude: 2,790 m

Juana Azurduy de Padilla **airport** is 5 km northwest of town (T645 4445). **Bus terminal** is on north outskirts of town, 2 km from centre on Ostria Gutiérrez, T645 2029; taxi US$0.75; Micro A or *trufi* No 8. Taxis cost US$0.45 pp within city limits. **Tourist office** At the bus station, allegedly open Mon-Fri 0800-1600, Sat 0800-1200; at the airport, to coincide with incoming flights; in town, at the municipal tourist booth, *Argentina y Olañeta*, Mon-Fri 0800-1200, 1400-1600, free pocket guide. More detailed information, at the *Casa de la Cultura*, Argentina 65, T642 7102 (same hours). Another office on Plaza 25 de Mayo 22, Mon-Fri 0830-1230, 1430-1830. For country maps try *Instituto Geográfico Militar*, Arce 172, 1st floor, T645 5514. Open Mon-Fri 0830-1200, 1430-1800.

Ins & outs
For more detailed information see Transport, page 304

Plaza 25 de Mayo is large, spacious, full of trees and surrounded by elegant buildings. Among these are the **Casa de la Libertad**, formerly the Assembly Hall of the Jesuit University, where the country's Declaration of Independence was signed. It contains a famous portrait of Simón Bolívar by the Peruvian artist Gil de Castro, admired for its likeness. ■ *Mon-Fri 0900-1115, 1430-1745, Sat 0930-1115, US$1.50 with guided tour; US$1.50 to take photographs, US$3 to use video, T645 4200.* Also on the Plaza is the beautiful 17th century **Cathedral**, entrance through the museum in Calle Ortiz. Worth seeing are the famous jewel-encrusted Virgin of Guadalupe, 1601, and works by Viti, the first great painter of the New World, who studied under Raphael. ■ *Mon-Fri 1000-1200, 1500-1700, Sat 1000-1200, US$1. If door is locked wait for the guide.*

Sights in the centre

Church opening times seem to change frequently, or are simply not observed

The neoclassical **San Felipe Neri church**, at Azurduy y Ortiz, is closed but ask the guide nicely to gain access. The roof (note the penitents' benches), which offers fine views over the city, is only open for an hour between 1630 and 1800 (times change). The monastery is used as a school. ■ *US$1 (extra charge for photos) with a free guide from Universidad de Turismo office on Plaza 25 de Mayo, T645 4333.* Diagonally opposite is the church of **La Merced**, which is notable for its gilded central and side altars. **San Miguel**, completed in 1628, has been restored and is very beautiful with Moorish-style carved and painted ceilings, *alfarjes* (early 17th century), pure-white walls and gold and silver altar. In the Sacristy some early sculpture can be seen. It was from San Miguel that Jesuit missionaries went south to convert Argentina, Uruguay and Paraguay. ■ *1130-1200. No shorts, short skirts or short sleeves.* **Santa Mónica** (Arenales y Junín) is perhaps one of the finest gems of Spanish architecture in the Americas, but has been converted into a *salón multiuso* (multipurpose space). **San**

Bolivia

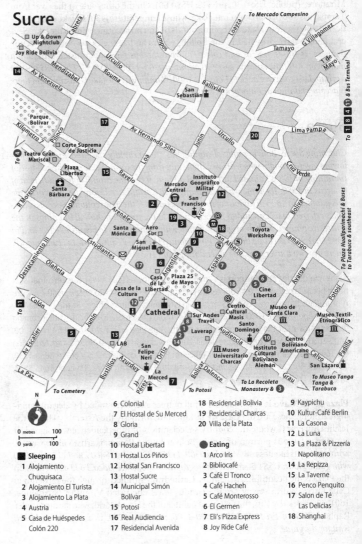

Sucre

N
0 metres 100
0 yards 100

■ Sleeping
1 Alojamiento Chuquisaca
2 Alojamiento El Turista
3 Alojamiento La Plata
4 Austria
5 Casa de Huéspedes Colón 220
6 Colonial
7 El Hostal de Su Merced
8 Gloria
9 Grand
10 Hostal Libertad
11 Hostal Los Piños
12 Hostal San Francisco
13 Hostal Sucre
14 Municipal Simón Bolívar
15 Potosí
16 Real Audiencia
17 Residencial Avenida
18 Residencial Bolivia
19 Residencial Charcas
20 Villa de la Plata

● Eating
1 Arco Iris
2 Bibliocafé
3 Café El Tronco
4 Café Hacheh
5 Café Monterosso
6 El Germen
7 Eli's Pizza Express
8 Joy Ride Café
9 Kaypichu
10 Kultur-Café Berlin
11 La Casona
12 La Luna
13 La Plaza & Pizzería Napolitano
14 La Repizza
15 La Taverne
16 Penco Penquito
17 Salon de Té Las Delicias
18 Shanghai

Francisco (1581) in Calle Ravelo has altars coated in gold leaf and 17th century ceilings; the bell is the one that summoned the people of Sucre to struggle for independence. ■ *0700-1200, 1500-1900*. **San Lázaro**, Calvo y Padilla (1538), is regarded as the first cathedral of La Plata (Sucre). On the nave walls are six paintings attributed to Zurbarán; it has fine silverwork and alabaster in the Baptistery. ■ *Daily for mass 0630-0730, 1830-1930.*

Between San Lázaro and Plaza 25 de Mayo is the excellent **Museo Textil-Etnográfico**, run by *Antropológicas del Surandino (ASUR)*, with displays of regional textiles and traditional techniques, craft shop sells local textiles. ■ *Mon-Fri 0830-1200, 1430-1800, Sat 0930-1200 (and Sat afternoon Jul/Aug/Sep), US$2, English, German and French-speaking guide; San Alberto 413 (Caserón de la Capellanía), T645 3841, www.bolivianet.com/asur* At Calvo 212 the **Museo de Santa Clara** displays paintings, books, vestments, some silver and musical instruments (including a 1664 organ); there is a window to view the church; small items made by the nuns on sale. ■ *Mon-Fri 0900-1200, 1500-1800, Sat 0900-1200, US$0.75.* A few blocks away, at Bolívar 698, the **Museo Universitario Charcas** has anthropological, archaeological and folkloric exhibits, and colonial collections and presidential and modern-art galleries. ■ *Mon-Fri 0800-2000, Sat 0900-1200, 1500-1800, Sun 0900-1200, US$1.50, photos US$1.50.*

Four blocks northwest of Plaza 25 de Mayo is the **Corte Suprema de Justicia**, the seat of Bolivia's national judiciary, and rationale behind the city's official status as being one of Bolivia's two capitals. ■ *Free but must be smartly dressed, leave passport with guard, guide can be found in library.* The nearby **Parque Bolívar** contains a monument and a miniature of the Eiffel tower in honour of one of Bolivia's richest 20th century tin barons, Francisco Argandoña, who created much of Sucre's latter-day splendour. The **obelisk** opposite the Teatro Gran Mariscal, in Plaza Libertad, was erected with money raised by fining bakers who cheated on the size and weight of their bread. Also on this plaza is the Hospital Santa Bárbara (1574).

Southeast of the city, at the top of Dalence, lies the Franciscan monastery of **La Recoleta** with good views over the city and the **Museo de la Recoleta**. It is notable for the beauty of its cloisters and gardens; the carved wooden choirstalls above the nave of the church are especially fine (see the martyrs transfixed by lances). In the grounds is the Cedro Milenario, a 1,400-year-old cedar. ■ *Mon-Fri 0900-1130, 1430-1630, US$1.20 for entrance to all collections, guided tours only, C Pedro de Anzúrez.* **Tanga Tanga** is an interactive children's museum with art, music, theatre, dance and books. It also has the excellent *Café Mirador* in the garden. ■ *Tue-Sun 1000-1800, Iturricha 297, La Recoleta, T644 0299.* Behind Recoleta monastery a road flanked by Stations of the Cross ascends an attractive hill, **Cerro Churuquella**, with large eucalyptus trees on its flank, to a statue of Christ at the top. In the cemetery are mausoleums of presidents and other famous people, boys give guided tours; take Calle Junín south to its end, 7 to 8 blocks from main plaza.

About 5 km south on the Potosí road is the **Castillo de la Glorieta**, the former mansion of the Argandoña family, built in a mixture of contrasting European styles with painted ceilings. Ask to see the paintings of the visit of the pope, in a locked room. ■ *Daily 0830-1200, 1400-1800. US$1. It is in the military compound. Take any bus marked 'Liceo Militar' from the Plaza, or bus or trufi 4 or E.* Some 7 km north of Sucre is **Cal Orcko**, an extensive area of dinosaur footprints found in the Fancesa cement works. Tracks from three types of dinosaur have been identified. ■ *Guided tours at 1000 and 1230. Tours in English are available for US$2. Recommended. Tour agencies charge US$10 pp as do taxi drivers who have trained as guides (untrained drivers charge US$7); ask tourist office for approved drivers. Dino Truck leaves daily 0930, 1200 from main plaza, US$4, minimum 5 people, good explanations in English, T645 1863.*

Sights outside the centre

A *Real Audiencia*, Potosí 142, T/F646 0823, realaudiencia2000@hotmail.com Modern, large rooms, excellent restaurant, heated pool. Recommended. **B** *El Hostal de Su Merced*,

Sleeping
■ *on map*

Bolivia

Azurday 16, T644 2706, sumerced@mara.scr.entelnet.bo Beautifully-restored colonial building, more character than any other hotel in the city, owner speaks fluent French and English, good breakfast buffet. Recommended. **B** *Paola Hostal*, C Colón 138, T645 4978, www.scr.cnb.net/~molincom Comfortable new hotel, with bath and jacuzzi, laundry, cafeteria for snacks, internet facilities, airport transfer. **B** *Refugio Andino Bramadero*, 30 km from the city, details from Raul y Mabel Cagigao, Avaroa 472, Casilla 387, T645 5592, bramader@yahoo.com Cabins or rooms, well-furnished, full board, drinks and transport included, excellent value, owner Raul is an astronomer and advises on hikes, book in advance. Recommended. **C** *Colonial*, Plaza 25 de Mayo 3, T645 4079, colonial@mara.scr.entelnet.bo Some rooms noisy, but generally recommended, good breakfast. **C** *Hostal Libertad*, Arce y San Alberto, p 1, T645 3101, F646 0128. Spacious comfortable rooms, hot water and heating, TV. Highly recommended. **C** *Hostal Sucre*, Bustillos 113, T645 1411, hosucre@mara.scr.entelnet.bo Rooms on patio noisy, breakfast for US$2.25. Recommended. **C** *Kantu Nucchu*, 21 km southwest of Sucre, details from Augusto Marion, San Alberto 237, T438 0312, tursucre@mara.scr.entelnet.bo With bath, kitchen, full board, **G** pp without meals, peaceful, colonial hacienda, hiking, swimming. Recommended. **C-D** *Municipal Simón Bolívar*, Av Venezuela 1052, T645 5508, F645 1216. Including breakfast in patio, helpful, restaurant. Recommended. **D** *Austria*, Av Ostria Gutiérrez 506, near bus station, T645 4202. Hot showers, redecorated, great beds and carpeted rooms, some with cable TV, cafeteria, parking, **F** rooms available and, next door, **G** in the *Alojamiento* (parking extra). **D** *Grand*, Arce 61, T645 2104, F645 2461, www.statusprd.com/grandhotel Comfortable (ask for room 18), hot showers, includes breakfast in room, good value lunch in *Arcos* restaurant, laundry, safe. Recommended. **D** *Hostal los Piños*, Colón 502, T645 4403, H-Pinos@mara.scr.entelnet.bo Comfortable, hot showers, nice garden, quiet, peaceful, includes breakfast, laundry, kitchen, parking.

E *Alojamiento Chuquisaca*, Av Ostria Gutiérrez 33, T645 4459. **G** shared bath, safe car parking (US$0.75 per day). **E** *Res Bolivia*, San Alberto 42, T645 4346, F645 3239. **F** without bath, spacious rooms, hot water, includes breakfast, clothes washing not allowed, safe and helpful. **E** *Casa de Huéspedes Colón 220*, Colón 220, T645 5823, colon220@bolivia.com Clean, laundry, helpful owner speaks English and German and has tourist information. **E** *Res Charcas*, Ravelo 62, T53972, F2496, hostalcharcas@latinmail.com **F** without bath, good value, breakfast, hot showers, runs bus to Tarabuco on Sun. **E** *Hostal San Francisco*, Av Arce 191 y Camargo, T645 2117, hostalsf@cotes.net.bo Meals available, includes breakfast, quiet, patio, laundry. **F** *Res Avenida*, Av H Siles 942, T645 2387. Hot showers, breakfast US$1, laundry, helpful, use of kitchen. **F** pp *Villa de la Plata*, Arce 369 (no sign). Rooms with shared kitchen, bath and living room, central, helpful, good value. **G** *Alojamiento El Turista*, Ravelo 118, T645 3172. Hot showers 0700-1200 only, basic, meeting place, cheap meals, use of kitchen, central rooms noisy, doors closed at 2300. **G** *Alojamiento La Plata*, Ravelo 32, T645 2102. Without bath, limited shower facilities, basic, noisy, good beds, popular with backpackers (lock rooms at all times). **G** *Gloria*, Av Ostria Gutiérrez 438, T645 2847, opposite bus station. Great value. **G** *Potosí*, Ravelo 262, T/F645 1975. Basic, popular, helpful, internet, good value.

Expensive **Arco Iris**, N Ortiz 42. Good service, good, *peña* on Sat, excellent *rösti*, live music some nights. **Mid-range** *El Asador*, Plaza Cumaná 485. Good steak and best fries. *El Chaqueño*, Av R Barrientos 749, Barrio Petrolero. Excellent steaks, best *charqui* (taxi US$1 each way). *El Huerto*, Ladislao Cabrera 86 (take a taxi at night). Good *almuerzo*. *Eli's Pizza Express*, España 130. Good. *La Casona*, Ostria Guitiérrez 401, near bus terminal. Stylish, *platos típicos*, good value. *La Plaza*, Plaza 25 de Mayo 33. Good food, live music on Fri nights, popular with locals, set lunch US$2.10, closed Mon. *La Repizza*, N Ortiz 78. Good value lunches, good pizzas in evening. *La Taverne* of the *Alliance Française*, Aniceto Arce 35, ½ block from plaza. Closed Sun evening, *peñas* Thu-Sat in Jul and Aug, good French food, also regular cultural events. *Pizzería Napolitano*, Plaza 25 de Mayo 30. Pizzas and pasta.

Cheap *Bibliocafé*, N Ortiz 50, near plaza. Good pasta and light meals, *almuerzo* US$3 1100-1600, closes 2000 (opens 1800 on Sun); music and drinks. *El Germen*, San Alberto 231. Vegetarian, set lunches (US1.80), excellent breakfast, US$1.05-2.10, open Mon-Sat 0800-2200, book exchange, German magazines. *Kaypichu*, San Alberto 168 y Bolívar. Good vegetarian, breakfast US$1.35-2.55, closed Mon and 1400-1700. Recommended. *Shanghai*, Calvo 70. Good, popular Chinese. **Cafés** *Amanecer*, Junín 855, German *pastelería*, run by social project supporting disabled children, opens 1530. *Café Al Tronco*, Topater 57, 100 m behind La Recoleta. Wide choice of meals and drinks, daily 1500-2400, tourist information. *Café Hacheh*, Pastor Sainz 233. Great coffee bar with art gallery, tasty lunch and fresh juices, open 1100-2400 (at 1700 on Sun). *Café Monterosso*, Bolívar 426. Open after 1900, delicious, cheap set dinner, good pasta, closed Sun. *Joy Ride Café*, N Ortiz 14, same Dutch owner as *Joy Ride Bolivia* (see Tour operators). Great food and drink, good salads, open 0800-0200. . *Kultur-Café Berlin*, Avaroa 326, open 0800-2400 (except Sun). Good breakfasts, German newspapers, *peña* every other Fri (in same building as *Instituto Cultural Boliviano Alemán – ICBA*), popular meeting place. *Penco Penquito*, Arenales 108. Excellent coffee and cakes. *Salon de Té Las Delicias*, Estudiantes 50. Great cakes and snacks, open 1600-1900. *Tertulias*, Plaza 25 de Mayo 59. Italian and other dishes, poor service. *La Vieja Bodega*, N Ortiz 38. Good value, cheapish wine.

Bars *Julyo's Chop*, Junín esq Colón. Popular bar, open late. *La Luna*, Argentina 65, back of Casa de la Cultura. Video pub with occasional live music, popular. **Clubs** *Mitsubanía*, Av del Maestro y Av Venzuela. Popular with local, younger, fashionable crowd, mixture of music with lots of *cumbia*, US$3 for men, women do not pay. **Folklore** Look out for the Ballet Folclórico of the Universidad San Francisco Xavier in the *Teatro Gran Mariscal*, Plaza Libertad.

24-26 May: *Independence* celebrations, most services, museums and restaurants closed on 25. **8 Sep:** *Virgen de Guadalupe*, 2-day fiesta. **Sep:** *Festival Internacional de la Cultura*, second week, shared with Potosí. **21 Sep:** *Día del Estudiante*, music around main plaza.

The central market is clean and colourful with many stalls selling *artesanía*, but beware theft. A bus from the central market will take you to the **Mercado Campesino** near football stadium. *Antropológicos del Surandino*, ASUR, San Alberto 413, T642 3841 (in the *Museo Textil-Etnográfico*). Weavings from around Tarabuco and from the Jalq'a. Weavings are more expensive, but of higher quality than elsewhere. *Artesanías Calcha*, Arce 103, opposite San Francisco church. Recommended, knowledgeable proprietor. *Fundación Aprecia*, Raul F de Córdova 49, just off Colón, T642 4718. A workshop for blind weavers making beautiful rugs (they can make to order with advance notice). Camping equipment can be bought at *Alfher*, San Alberto y Arce, and at *Sport Camping*, same entrance as *Hostal Libertad* (see above), but no gas.

Candelaria Tours, Audiencia No 1, C 322, T646 1661, F646 0289. Organizes excursions and also organizes Bolivian textile fashion shows, English spoken. *Joy Ride Bolivia*, Mendizábal 229, T642 5544, www.joyridebol.com Top quality quad and dirt bike trips, European standards of safety and bike-to-bike radio, insurance, take motorcycle licence for dirt bikes, car licence for quads. *Seatur*, Plaza 25 de Mayo 24, T/F646 2425, seatur@latinmail.com Local tours, English, German, French spoken. *Sur Andes* , NOrtiz 6, T645 3212, F644 2561. Organizes trekking from half a day to 5 days, eg to pre-Columbian sites such as **Pumamachay** and the **Camino Prehispánico** (take sleeping bag and good shoes, all else provided, but no porters).

Eating
● *on map*
Many fruit juice and snack stalls in the central market; clean stalls also sell cheap meals (US$0.75-1.40). The local sausages and chocolate are recommended

Bolivia

Bars & clubs

Festivals

Shopping
Famed local chocolate shops can be found on Arce and Arenales

Tour operators

Transport
164 km from Potosí (fully paved) 366 km to Cochabamba (for first hr from Sucre road is OK, terrible to Epizana, then paved)

Air: *Aero Sur* and *LAB* fly to **La Paz** and **Santa Cruz**, *LAB* also flies to **Cochabamba**. Few flights are daily. *Aero Sur*, Arenales 31, T646 2141 (Toll free 0800 3030). *LAB*, Bustillos 127, T645 4994 (Toll free 0800 3001). Airport minibus goes from entrance and will drop you off on Siles y Junín, and returns from here, 1½ hrs before flight (not always), US$0.70, 20-30 mins. Taxi US$4-5. *Trufis* No 1 and F go from entrance to H Siles y Loa, 1 block from main plaza, US$0.55, 25 mins. **Bus**: Daily to/from **La Paz** at 1430 (*10 de Noviembre*, 16 hrs via Potosí, US$6), 1730 (*Flota Copacabana*, *bus-cama*, 15hrs, US$7.50), 1730 (*Trans Copacabana*, *bus-cama*, 15hrs, US$10.45). To **Cochabamba**: several companies daily at 1830, arriving 0630, US$4.50-5.25 (*bus-cama*, US$8.90). To **Potosí**: 3 hrs on a paved road, frequent departures between 0630 and 1800, US$3. *Silito Lindo* taxis take 4 people to Potosí for US$4.25; T644 1014. To **Tarija**: several companies, 16hrs, US$5.25-6. To **Uyuni**: 0700 (*Emperador*), 0800 (*Trans Capital*), 10 hrs, US$5.20. Or catch a bus to Potosí and change; try to book the connecting bus in advance – see *Trans Real Audencia*. To **Oruro**: 1700 with *Emperador* via Potosí, arrives 0300, US$6 (*bus-cama*, US$8.95). To **Santa Cruz**: many companies go between 1600 and 1730, 15 hrs, US$6-7.50. To **Villazón**: at 1300 (*Transtin Dilrey*, direct) and 1400 (*Villa Imperial*, via Potosí) both 15 hrs, US$8.20. *Trans Real Audencia*, Arce 99 y San Alberto (same entrance as Hostal Libertad), T644 3119, for hassle-free bus tickets reservations to: **Potosí** (US$3), **Uyuni** (US$6.70), **Villazón** and **Tupiza** (US$7.45), **Tarabuco** (Sun 0700 from outside office, US$3 return).

Directory
For hospitals, doctors and dentists, contact your consulate or the tourist office for recommendations

Banks *Banco Nacional*, España esq San Alberto. Cash given on Visa and MasterCard US$3 commission, good rates for dollars, TCs changed, 5% commission. Diagonally opposite is *Banco Santa Cruz*. Good rates for cash, advances on Visa, MasterCard and Amex, US$10 fee. There are many *Enlace* 24hr ATMs around town. Travel agencies' rates are good and at *El Arca*, España 134, T646 0189, good rates for TCs, 3% commission into US $, free into bolivianos. *Casa de Cambio Ambar*, San Alberto 7, T645 1339. Good rates for TCs. Stalls at corner of Camargo and Arce buy and sell cash $ as well as Argentine, Chilean and Brazilian currency at good rates. Many shops and street changers on Hernando Siles/Camargo buy and sell $ cash. **Communications** Internet: Many around town, generally slow connections, average US$0.60 per hr. Also at *Alianza Francesa*, 0900-1200, 1500-1930, closed Sat pm and Sun. Post Office: Ayacucho 100 y Junín, open till 2000 (1600 Sat, 1200 Sun), good service. *Poste Restante* is organized separately for men and women. **Telephone:** *Entel*, España 252. Open 0730-2300. **Cultural centres** The *Instituto Cultural Boliviano-Alemán* (Goethe Institute), Avaroa 326, Casilla 304, T645 2091. Shows films, has German newspapers and books to lend (0930-1230 and 1500-2100), runs Spanish, German, Portuguese and Quechua courses and has the *Kulturcafé Berlín* (see above). Spanish lessons cost from US$6 for 45 mins for 1 person, with reductions the more students there are in the class. The *ICBA* also runs a folk music *peña* on Fri. *Centro Cultural Masis*, Bolívar 561, T645 3403, Casilla 463. Promotes the Yampara culture through textiles, ceramics, figurines and music. Instruction in Quechua, traditional Bolivian music (3 hrs a week for US$15 a month, recommended) and handicrafts; stages musical events and exhibitions; items for sale. Open Mon-Sat 1430-2000 (knock if door closed); contact the director, Roberto Sahonero Gutierres at the centre Mon, Wed and Fri. *Alianza Francesa*, Aniceto Arce 35, T645 3599. Offers Spanish classes. *Centro Boliviano Americano*, Calvo 301, T644 1608, cba@mara.scr.entelnet.bo Library open Mon-Fri 0900-1200, 1500-2000 (good for reference works). Recommended for language courses. The *Centro Cultural Hacheh* (see address for *Café Hacheh* above), run by Felix Arciénega, Bolivian artist who organizes folk and jazz concerts, conferences, exhibitions and discussions, and is the editor of an art and poetry journal 'Hacheh'. *Casa de la Cultura*, Argentina 65, presents art exhibitions, concerts, folk dancing etc, breakfast in café, open Mon-Fri 0830-1230, 1400-2200. **Embassies and consulates** France, Bustillos 206, T645 3018. Germany, Eva Kasewitz de Vilar, Rosendo Villa 54, T645 1369. Italy, Vice Consul, Dalence 19, T645 4280. Paraguay, Plaza 25 de Mayo 28, T645 2573. Perú, Avaroa 472, T642 0356. Spain, Pasaje Argandoña, T645 1435. **Language schools** *Academia Latinoamericana de Español*, Dalence 109, T646 0537, latino@cotes.net.bo Professional, good extracurricular activities, US$90 for 5 full days (US$120 for private teacher – higher prices if you book by phone or email). *Casa de Lenguas*, T/F5912393, www.casadelenguas.com (see also La Paz). *Margot Macias Machicado*, Olañeta 345, T642 3567, per hr. Recommended. *Sofia Sauma*, Loa 779, T645 1687, sadra@mara.scr.entelnet.bo US$5 per hr. **Useful addresses** Private teachers advertise in bars etc **Immigration:** Pastor Sáenz 117, T645 3647, Mon-Fri 0830-1630. **Police radio patrol:** T110 if in doubt about police or security matters.

Tarabuco
Colour map 6, grid B4 Altitude: 3,295 m

Tarabuco, 64 km southeast of Sucre, is best known for its colourful Indian market on Sunday, with local people in traditional dress. It starts around 0930-1000 and is very popular with tourists, but still an enjoyable experience. Those in search of a bargain should have an idea about the quality on offer. The *Phujllay* independence celebration in mid-March is very colourful and lively. No one sleeps during this fiesta. There is budget accommodation. Try the Plaza (*Snack Kuky*) or food stalls in market offering tasty local dishes. A good guide is *Alberto* from Sucre tourist office, US$45 for a full day in a car for four people. The market is not held at Carnival (when all Tarabuco is dancing in Sucre), Easter Sunday or on the holiday weekend in November.

Transport Buses (US$1.25) and trucks (very crowded) leave from 0630 or when full from Plaza Huallparimachi, Av Manco Capac, or across the railway (take micro B or C from opposite Mercado), 2½ hrs (or taxi, US$45). On Sunday only, at least one bus will wait on Ravelo by the market for travellers, charging US$3 return to Tarabuco. Shared trufi taxis can be arranged by hotels, with pick-up service, starting at 0700, US$3.25 return. First bus back 1300. *Andes Bus* run tourist services, departing 0800 (or when full), returning 1530, US$6, book at office, take food and drink. Transport more difficult on weekdays; take an early bus and return by truck.

A road runs southeast from Sucre, through Tarabuco, to **Monteagudo** where there are several hotels including **E** *Fortín*, Plaza 20 de Agosto 1-2, T647 2135, with bath, TV, includes breakfast, **F** *Alojamiento los Naranjos*, on road to bus terminal, hot showers, and a few restaurants. There are daily buses from Monteagudo to **Santa Cruz** (book early), US$8, 14 hours. The road then joins the road south from Santa Cruz to **Camiri** and **Boyuibe** (see page 335), from where a road heads east to the border with Paraguay at **Hito Villazón** (not to be confused with Villazón on the border with Argentina, see page 293). Most public transport goes south through Villamontes and a new road east to Paraguay, or continues south to **Yacuiba** on the border with Argentina (see page 336). The journey is beautiful through wild mountains. The easiest way to reach **Paraguay** from Sucre is to take a bus to Santa Cruz, then an international bus to **Asunción**. Alternatively, take the bus to Camiri (*Emperador* at 1730 or *Andes Bus*, 1800, on alternate days, 18 hrs, US$4.30). From Camiri take a colectivo to **Villamontes** (3 hrs, US$5), but stop in Boyuibe to get an exit stamp. In Villamontes, catch the Santa-Cruz-Asunción bus at about 0600. Bargain hard not to pay the full Santa Cruz-Asunción fare. (See also page 335.)

(margin) Sucre to Paraguay
Colour map 6, grid B4

Tarija

Tarija, a pleasant, small city, with a delightful climate and streets and plazas planted with flowering trees, is often called the ` Andalucía of Bolivia' for its resemblance to that region of Spain. The Indian strain is less evident here than elsewhere in Bolivia but Tarija has a strong cultural heritage. Founded 4 July 1574 in the rich valley of the Río Guadalquivir, the city declared itself independent of Spain in 1807, and for a short time existed as an independent republic before joining Bolivia. In Plaza Luis de Fuentes there is a statue to the city's founder, Capitán Luis de Fuentes Vargas.

(margin) Phone code: 04
Population: 109,000
Altitude: 1,840 m
Best time to visit: Jan onwards, when the fruit is in season

In the centre The oldest and most interesting church in the city is the **Basílica de San Francisco**, corner of La Madrid y Daniel Campos. It is beautifully painted inside, with praying angels depicted on the ceiling and the four evangelists at the four corners below the dome. The library is divided into old and new sections, the old containing some 15,000 volumes, the new a further 5,000. The oldest book is a 1501 *Iliad* incorporating other works. There are also old manuscripts and 19th century photograph albums. To see the library, go to the door at Ingavi 0137. ■ *0700-1000, 1800-2000, Sun 0630-1200, 1800-2000.* Tarija's **university museum**, Trigo y Lema, contains a palaeontological collection (dinosaur bones, fossils, remains of an Andean elephant), as well as smaller mineralogical, ethnographic and anthropological collections. ■ *Mon-Fri 0800-1200, 1500-1800 (Sat opens at 0900). Free, small donation appreciated.* The **Casa Dorada**, Trigo y Ingavi (entrance on Ingavi), or Maison d'Or, is now the Casa de Cultura, begun in 1886. It belonged to importer/exporter Moisés Narvajas and his wife Esperanza Morales and has been

(margin) Sights

(margin vertical) Bolivia

Bolivia

beautifully restored inside and out; the photography room contains pictures of Tarijan history and the restoration of the house. ■ *Mon-Fri 0900-1200, 1500-1800, Sat 0900-1200, guided tours only; voluntary donation (minimum US$0.30)* Near Parque Bolívar (shady, pleasant) is another of Narvajas' houses, the **Castillo de Beatriz**, Bolívar between Junín and O'Connor; much of house is off-limits, but ask the owner if it is possible to visit. If no answer, enquire at the museum.

Outside the centre The outskirts of the city can be a good place to look for **fossils**: take a micro or taxi in the direction of the airport. 5 km out of town, before the police control (*garita*), you see lovely structures of sand looking like a small canyon (*barrancos*). Here have been found bones, teeth, parts of saurian spines, etc; things come to the surface each year after the rains. You may have to go a long way from the city. About 15 km from the centre is the lovely village of **San Lorenzo**. Just off the plaza is the **Museo Méndez**, the house of the independence hero Eustaquio Méndez, `El Moto'. The small museum exhibits his weapons, his bed, his 'testimonio'. ■ *0900-1230, 1500-1830, minimum US$0.30 entry. At lunchtime on Sun, many court-yards serve cheap meals. Take a trufi from Barrio del Carmen, at the roundabout just north of San Juan Church. They return from San Lorenzo plaza; 45 mins, US$0.45.* The road to San Lorenzo passes **Tomatitas** (5 km) a popular picnic and river bathing area.

All bodegas are closed Sat afternoon and Sun There are also vineyard tours, see Tour operators

Bodegas *Aranjuez* bodega is a short walk across the river at Avenida Los Sauces 1976 (shop at 15 de Abril O-0241): ask Sr Milton Castellanos at the Agrochemical shop at Trigo 789 (Monday-Friday 1000-1200, 1500-1730, Saturday 0900-1200); he can also arrange visits to *Campos de Solana* (shop 15 de Abril E-0259). Farther afield is the *Rugero Singani* bodega at **El Valle de Concepción**, 36 km south of Tarija. An appointment must be made with Ing Sergio Prudencio Navarro, Bodegas y Viñedos de la Concepción at La Madrid y Suipacha s/n, T664 3763. Ing Prudencio will show visitors round the vineyards and the bodega. *Trufis* go from Parada del Chaco every 20-30 minutes, US$0.75, return from plaza.

Sleeping
Blocks west of C Colón have a small O before number (oeste), and all blocks east have an E (este); blocks are numbered from Colón outwards. All streets north of Av Las Américas are preceded by N

L *Los Parrales Resort*, Urb Carmen de Aranjuez Km 3.5, T664 8444 (ask for Lic Miguel Piaggio), only 5-star accommodation in southern Bolivia and worth it, European style amenities, can arrange city and vineyard tours and to Argentina, phone in advance for off-season discounts. **A** *Gran Hotel Tarija*, Sucre N-0770, T664 2684, F664 4777. Modernized, comfortable, parking, central. **A** *Los Ceibos*, Av Víctor Paz Estenssoro y La Madrid, T663 4430, F664 2461. Including excellent buffet breakfast, large rooms, mini-bar, good restaurant, pool and cocktail bar. **A** *Victoria Plaza*, on Plaza Luis de Fuentes, T664 2600, F664 2700. 4-star, includes buffet breakfast in Café-Bar La Bella Epoca, laundry service. **B** *Hostal Loma de San Juan*, Bolívar s/n (opposite Capela Loma de San Juan), T664 4522, F664 4206. Comfortable, pool, sumptuous buffet breakfast included. **C** *Gran Hostal Baldiviezo*, La Madrid O-0443, T/F663 7711. New, central. **D** *Hostal Carmen*, Ingavi O-0784 y R Rojas, T664 3372, vtb@olivo.tja.entelnet.bo Shower, good value, **E** without cable TV, some ground floor rooms without exterior windows, good breakfast, transfer stand at airport, tour agency, book in advance. **D** *Hostal Libertador*, Bolívar O-0649, T664 4231, F663 1016. Electric showers. **E** *Hostería España*, Alejandro Corrado O-0546, T664 1790. Hot showers, **F** without bath, pleasant. **E** *Res Rosario* (changing its name to *Amancayas*), Ingavi O-0777, T42942, residen_rosario@latinmail.com **F** without bath, showers, cable TV, quiet, good value. Recommended but for the laundry. **E** *Zeballos*, Sucre 0966, T664 2068. Nice atmosphere, **F** without bath, with breakfast, cable TV, quiet, safe, laundry, 5 mins from plaza. **G** *Alojamiento Familiar*, Rana S 0231 y Navajas, T664 0832. Shared hot shower, no breakfast, modern, helpful, close to bus terminal, traffic noise.

Eating
Many restaurants (and much else in town) close between 1400 and 1600

La Taberna Gattopardo, on main plaza. Pizza, *parrillada* with Argentine beef, local wines, snacks, excellent salads, good value, opens 0700-0200 daily. *Pizzería Europa*, main plaza west side. Internet (US$0.90 per hr), good *salteñas* in the morning. *Club Social Tarija*, east side of the plaza. Pleasant, old-fashioned, haunt of Tarija's business community, excellent *almuerzo* for US$1.80. Recommended. *Mateo's*, Trigo N-0610. Excellent *almuerzo* US$3 (includes salad bar), good value evening meals with a wide selection of local and international dishes, pasta a speciality, closed 1530-1900 and Sun. *Gringo Limón*, Trigo N-0345. Pay by weight, nothing special. *Chingo's*, on Plaza Sucre, is popular and serves cheap local food. Also on Plaza Sucre is *Bagdad Café* for live music at night. *Cabaña Don Pedro*, Padilla y Av Las Américas. Good typical, moderately-priced food. *Cabaña Don Pepe*, D Campos N-0138, near Av Las Américas. Excellent steaks at moderate prices, *peña* at weekends with local folk music. *Chifa Wang Fu*, D Campos N-0179, closed 1430-1800. Good Chinese. *Chifa New Hong Kong*, Sucre O-0235. Smart, good service, moderate prices. *El Solar,* Campero y V Lema. Vegetarian, set lunch, Mon-Sat 0800-1400 only. *La Fontana*, La Madrid y Campos, is good for ice cream, snacks and coffee. For a cheap breakfast try the market. Try the local wines, eg Aranjuez, La Concepción, Santa Ana de Casa Real or Kohlberg, the singani (a clear brandy, San Pedro de Oro and Rugero are recommended labels), also local beer, Astra.

Festivals Colourful processions take place on **15 Mar**, *Día de Tarija*. In **late Apr**, *Exposur* is held, approximately 20 km northwest of city; admission free; local and regional crafts, cuisine, and dances; much commercial activity as well. In the 3-day *San Roque* festival from the **first Sun in Sep** the richly-dressed saint's statue is paraded through the streets; wearing lively colours, cloth turbans and cloth veils, the people dance before it and women throw flowers from the balconies. Dogs are decorated with ribbons for the day. On **2nd Sun in Oct** the flower festival commemorates the *Virgen del Rosario* (celebrations in the surrounding towns are recommended, eg San Lorenzo and Padcaya). Another flower festival takes place in San Lorenzo in **Easter** week. Also in **Oct**, on 2 weekends mid-month, there is a *beer festival on Av de las Américas. La Virgen de Chaguaya, 15 Aug, people walk from Tarija to Santuario Chaguaya, south of El Valle, 60 km south of the city. For less devoted souls, Línea P* trufi from Plaza Sucre, Tarija, to Padcaya, US$1; bus to Chaguaya and Padcaya from terminal daily, 0700, returns 1700, US$1.35.

The city is famous for its colourful niño (child) processions

Tour operators *Internacional Tarija*, Sucre 721, T664 4446, F664 5017. Flights and tours, helpful. *Mara Tours*, Gral Trigo N-739, T664 3490, marvin@olivo.tja.entelnet.bo Helpful. *Viva Tours*, Sucre 0615, T663 8325, vivatour@cosett.com.bo Vineyard tours US$30 with lunch. *VTB*, at *Hostal Carmen* (see Sleeping above). All tours include a free city tour; 4-6 hr trips including singani bodegas, US$19 pp; comprehensive 10 hr "Tarija and surroundings in 1 Day", US$27; can also try your hand at an excavation with their palaeontology specialist!

Transport **Air** *LAB* flies to **Santa Cruz** and **Cochabamba**; *Aero Sur* flies to **La Paz** and **Santa Cruz**. Schedules change frequently; also flights are frequently cancelled and/or delayed. *LAB* office: Trigo N-0327, T644 2195. *TAM* office: La Madrid O-0470, T664 5899. *Aero Sur* office: Ingavi entre Sucre y Daniel Campos, T663 0894. Taxi to airport, US$3.75, or *micro* A from Mercado Central which drops you 1 block away. Some hotels have free transport to town, you may have to call them. On arrival at Tarija, reconfirm you return flight immediately. Airport information T664 3135. **Bus** The bus station is in the outskirts on Av de Las Américas (30 min walk from centre, 7-8 mins from airport), T663 6508. Daily on the 935 km route **Potosí-Oruro-La Paz**, depart 0700 and 1700 (24 hrs, US$15; check which company operates the best buses, eg *San Lorenzo* has heating). To **Potosí** (386 km), daily at 1630, 12 hrs, US$6.70-7.45 with *AndesBus*, *San Lorenzo*, *San Jorge* and *Emperador*. To **Sucre**, direct with *Andesbus* (recommended), *Emperador* and *Villa Imperial*, depart 1600-1630, 17-18 hrs, US$5.25-6, check if you have to change buses in Potosí. To **Villazón**, several companies daily, depart morning and afternoon, 7 hrs, US$4.50, unpaved road. To **Santa Cruz**, several companies, US$10.45-12, 24 hrs over rough roads, last 140 km from Abapó is paved; via Entre Ríos, Villamontes, Boyuibe and Camiri, between Entre Ríos and Villamontes is spectacular. Trucks to all destinations depart from Barrio La Loma, 10 blocks west of market.

Directory **Banks** *Banco Mercantil*, Sucre y 15 de Abril. Exchanges cash and gives cash against Visa and MasterCard (US$5 authorization charge). *Banco de Crédito*, Trigo N-0784, *Banco Nacional*, Av Trigo, all change TCs. Many ATMs accept foreign cards. Dollars and Argentine pesos can be changed at a number of casas de cambio on Bolívar between Campos and Sucre. **Communications** Internet: *Café Internet Tarija On-Line*, Campos N-0488, US$0.75 per hr. *Pizzería Europa* (see above), US$0.90 per hr. 2 on Plaza Sucre. **Post Office:** V Lema y Sucre. Also at bus terminal. **Telephone:** *Entel*, on main plaza, at V Lema y D Campos and at terminal. **Embassies and consulates** Argentina, Ballivián N-0699 y Bolívar, T664 4273, Mon-Fri, 0830-1230. **Germany**, Sucre N-0665, T664 2062, helpful. **Language classes** *Julia Gutiérrez Márquez*, T663 2857, gringo108@hotmail.com Recommended for language classes and information. **Tourist offices** On the main plaza in the Prefectura. Mon-Fri 0800-1200, 1430-1830, helpful, city map and guide for US$0.20 each, T663 1000. Also at Sucre y Bolívar.

To Argentina
Bolivia is 1 hr behind Argentina Crossing to Argentina, expect up to four hours to pass through customs and immigration. Electronic goods must be entered in your passport for later checks

The road to Villazón, 189 km, is the shortest route to Argentina, but a tiring six hours in all (only the first 15 km is paved). The alternative route via Bermejo is the most easily reached from Tarija, 210 km, the views are spectacular (sit on right); not recommended in the rainy season or a month or so after. The first 50 km out of Tarija, and the last 20 km to Bermejo are paved. Many buses daily, usually at night, some early morning, 4-5 hours, US$7.75, truck US$4.50. At **Bermejo** (*Population*: 13,000. *Altitude*: 415 m) there a few hotels and two *casas de cambio* on main street. Note there are thorough customs searches here and it's very hot. Cross river by ferry to Aguas Blancas, in Argentina. From Tarija to Yacuiba/Pocitos border is 290 km (see page 152). Daily buses to Yacuiba 0700-1800, 12 hours, US$5-8, mostly old buses, *Expresos Tarija* and *Narváez* are best.

Cochabamba and around

With its wonderful climate Cochabamba is an ideal half-way house between the cold of the altiplano and the tropical heat of the lowlands. It is 394 km from La Paz to Cochabamba by road, now completely paved. The fertile foothills surrounding the city provide much of the country's grain, fruit and coca and colonial villages and pre-Columbian sites are also within reach.

Cochabamba

Phone code: 04
Colour map 6, grid A3
Population: 594,790
Altitude: 2,570 m

Cochabamba deserves its unofficial title of 'City of Eternal Spring'. Set in a bowl of rolling hills at a comfortable altitude, its inhabitants enjoy a wonderfully warm, dry and sunny climate. Its parks and plazas are a riot of colour, from the striking purple of the bougainvillaea to the subtler tones of jasmin, magnolia and jacaranda. Bolivia's fourth largest city was founded in 1571. Today it is an important commercial and communications centre with many modern features, but it retains a small-town, rural feel.

Ins & outs
For more detailed information see Transport, page 312

Neither airport, nor bus station are far from the centre. Buses and taxis serve both. The central tourist office booth is at General Achá, next to *Entel*, helpful, photocopied city map and free guide; Mon-Fri 0830-1230, 1430-1815, Sat 0830-1230. Administration offices are at Colombia E-0340, between 25 de Mayo y España, T422 1793, Mon-Fri 0830-1630. The tourist police are here for complaints, also at Jorge Wilstermann airport. **Street numbering**: the city is divided into 4 quadrants based on the intersection of Av Las Heroínas running west to east, and Av Ayacucho running north to south. In all longitudinal streets north of Heroínas the letter N precedes the 4 numbers. South of Heroínas the numbers are preceded by S. In all transversal streets west of Ayacucho the letter O (Oeste) precedes the numbers and all streets running east are preceded by E (Este). The first 2 numbers refer to the block, 01 being closest to Ayacucho or Heroínas; the last 2 refer to the building's number. **NB** Recently there have been sporadic demonstrations and minor civil unrest in Cochabamba, largely as a result of the ongoing issues surrounding coca production in the neighbouring Chaparé region and the difficulty of obtaining a reliable source of potable water for the city. Also, you need to guard against theft around the markets and Plaza San Antonio.

At the heart of the old city is the arcaded **Plaza 14 de Septiembre** with the **Cathedral** **Sights**
dating from 1571, but much added to. Nearby are several colonial churches: **Santo**
Domingo (Santiváñez y Ayacucho) begun in 1778 and still unfinished; **San Francisco**
(25 de Mayo y Bolívar) 1581, but heavily modernized in 1926; the **Convent of Santa**
Teresa (Baptista y Ecuador) original construction 1760-90; and **La Compañía**
(Baptista y Achá), whose whitewashed interior is completely devoid of the usual riot of
late Baroque decoration.

    Museo Arqueológico, Jordán between Aguirre and Ayacucho, part of the
Universidad de San Simón, small but interesting display of artefacts including amerin-
dian hieroglyphic scripts and pre-Inca textiles, good 1½ hours tour. ■ *Tue-Sun*
0900-1800, US$2.25, free student guide (Spanish, French or English). **Casa de la**
Cultura, 25 de Mayo y Av Las Heroínas, has a library and first editions of newspapers.
Its museum with exhibitions of paintings colonial and modern, is now at Casona
Santiváñez, Santiváñez O-0156. ■ *Mon-Fri 0800-1200, 1430-1830, free, T425 9788*.

    From Plaza Colón, at the north end of the old town, the wide **Avenida Ballivián**
(known as **El Prado**) runs northwest to the wealthy modern residential areas. To the
north of Plaza Colón at Avenida Potosí 1450 (T243137) lies **Palacio de Portales**, the
Patiño mansion, now the *Centro Cultural Pedagócico Simón J Patiño*, reached by
micro G from Av San Martín. Built in French renaissance style, furnished from
Europe and set in 10 ha of gardens inspired by Versailles, the house was finished in
1927 but never occupied. ■ *Guided tours Mon-Fri 1700, 1730, 1800, Sat at 1100 in*
Spanish and English, US$1.50, don't be late, T424 3137, useful library. There is an
excellent art gallery in the basement. The gallery and gardens are open Mon-Fri
1700-1800, Sat-Sun 1000-1200.

    To the south of the old town lie the bus and train stations and some of the best
markets in Bolivia. These are very good for tourist items and souvenirs, but beware
pickpockets. The huge **La Cancha market** (San Martín, Punata, República y
Pulacayo) is packed on Wednesday and Saturday with campesinos and well worth a
visit. Woollen items are expensive but high quality (US$35-50 for an alpaca
sweater). The nearby **Incallacta market** is for fruit and vegetables but also sells tourist souvenirs. There is also a Saturday market at Avenida América y Libertador, best
before 0900. Overlooking the bus station is the **San Sebastián hill**, offering grand
views of the city. From here you can walk to the adjoining **La Coronilla hill**, topped
by an imposing monument commemorating the defence of Cochabamba by its
womenfolk against Spanish troops in 1812 (beware of robbery). At the east end of
Avenida Heroínas is another hill, the **Cerro de San Pedro**, with a statue to Cristo de
la Concordia. ■ *Sun 0800-2000, closed Mon, cable car 1000-1830, US$0.45; US$0.15*
to climb inside the statue for viewpoint.

Essentials

L-AL *Portales*, Av Pando 1271, T428 5444, F424 2071. 5-star, swimming pool open to non-resi- **Sleeping**
dents (US$4 a day, US$8 on Sun with buffet), a long way from centre. **AL** *Aranjuez*, Av Buenos ■ *on map*
Aires E-0563, T428 0076, F424 0158, Casilla 3056. 4-star, 2 blocks from Los Portales, small, colo- *There are many cheap*
nial style, good restaurant, jazz in the bar Fri and Sat night, small pool open to public (US$1). *and basic places to*
Recommended. **A** *Ambassador*, España N-0349, T425 9001, ambass@ *stay near the bus*
station, most are
comteco.entelnet.bo Modern, central and reasonable, includes breakfast, good restaurant. *short-stay and the*
A *Gran Hotel Cochabamba*, Plaza Ubaldo Anze, T428 2551, F428 2558. Beautifully set in the *area is unsafe*
north part of the city (2 blocks from Los Portales at La Recoleta), with garden, swimming pool
(US$3 for non-guests) and tennis courts, popular with tour groups. Recommended.
B *Americana*, Esteban Arce S-788, T425 0554, americana@ mail.infornetcbba.com.bo Fan,
helpful, lift, laundry, parking, *Rodizio* grill next door, good service. **C** *Boston*, C 25 de Mayo 0167,
T422 8530. Restaurant, luggage deposit, quiet rooms at back, safe parking. Recommended.
C *Ideal*, España N-0329, T425 9430, F425 7930. Includes breakfast, restaurant, comfortable,
good value. **C** *Regina*, Reza 0359, T425 7382, F411 7231. Spacious, efficient, breakfast extra,
restaurant. **C-D** *City*, Jordán E-0341, T422 2993. Central, includes breakfast, cheaper rooms on

upper floors, noisy but modern. **E** *Res Buenos Aires*, 25 de Mayo N-0329, T425 3911. **F** without bath, pleasant, clean communal baths, breakfast US$1.35. **E** *Hostal Elisa*, Agustín López S-0834, T423 5102. **F** without bath, good showers, hot water, good breakfast US$2.25, modern, garden, 2 blocks from bus station, laundry service, very popular with travellers. Recommended. **E** *Hostal Florida*, 25 de Mayo S-0583, T425 7911, floridah@elsito.com **F** without bath or cable TV, hot water, noisy, popular, laundry service, safe deposit box, internet, breakfast. **E** *Hostería Jardín*, Hamiraya N-0248, T424 7844. **F** without bath, garden, safe car-park, breakfast included, basic but good. **E** *Res Jordán*, C Antesana S-0671, T422 9294. Youth hostel, *ABAJ* affiliate, modern, basic, with cable TV and small pool. Annex (**D**) at 25 de Mayo S-0651, T422 5010. **F** *Colonial*, Junín N-0134, T422 1791. Garden and terrace, rooms with big balcony but run down, peaceful, secure, laundry service, breakfast served on terrace. **F** *Res Familiar*, Sucre E-0554, T422 7988, T422 7986. Pleasant, secure, good showers. Its annex at 25 de Mayo N-0234 (entre Colombia y Ecuador), is also pleasant, with a big courtyard, shared bath, hot water, comfortable. **F** *Maracaibo*, Agustín López S-0925, T422 7110. Close to bus terminal, popular, safe. **F** *Hostal Ossil*, Agustín López S-0915, close to bus terminal, T425 4476. New, good rooms, cooking facilities, helpful, good value. **G** *Res Agustín López*, Agustín López S-0859, T425 6926. Basic, hot water. **G** *Alojamiento Escobar*, Aguirre S-0749, T422 5812. Shared bath, good value (not to be confused with *Residencial* at Uruguay E-0213). **G** *Virgen de Copacabana*, Av Arce S-0875 y Brasil, T422 7929, near bus station. Hot showers, shared bath, good breakfast US$0.75, motorcycle parking, stores luggage. Recommended.

Eating

● *on map*
The bars and restaurants centre around España, Ecuador and Colombia Plaza Colón and Av Ballivián and north of Río Rocha near Av Santa Cruz. A few km north of the city, in the village of Tiquipaya, are many comida criolla restaurants, eg El Diente, recommended

Expensive *La Cantonata*, España N-0409. Italian. Highly recommended. *Suiza*, Av Ballivián 820. Popular, recommended for international cuisine, good value. **Mid-range** *BJ*, Av Libertador Bolívar 1580. International cuisine. Recommended. *Bufalo*, Torres Sofer, p 2, Av Oquendo N-0654. Brazilian *rodizio* grill, all-you-can-eat buffet for US$7.50, great service. Highly recommended. *Lai-Lai*, Recoleta E-0729. Chinese, also takeaway service. *Habana Café*, M Rocha E-0348. Genuine Cuban food and drinks, can get lively at night, open 1200-last person leaves. *Jacaranda*, Arce S-0628. Excellent food. *Marco's*, Av Oquenda entre Cabrera y Uruguay. Good Peruvian ceviche, Sat-Sun 1200-1500. *Metrópolis*, España N-0299. Good pasta dishes, huge portions, good vegetarian options, noisy. *Metrópolis Pizza* next door is good value. *Picasso*, España 327, entre Ecuador y Mayor Rocha. Good value Italian and Mexican. **Cheap** *Eli's Pizza Express,* 25 de Mayo N-0254. Son of the famous La Paz branch, great pizzas and serves Mexican fast food. *Incallacta market (see page 309) has excellent food for under US$1.* **Vegetarian** *Bohemia*, España casi Mayor Rocha. Lots of choice, set lunch US$2, excellent desserts, left luggage service, book exchange. *Comida Vegetariana*, M Rocha entre España y 25 de Mayo. Vegetarian food using soya milk, all-you-can-eat buffet for US$1.30. *Gopal*, C España 250, Galería Olimpia. Hare-krishna, vegetarian lunch 1200-1500, US$1.50, vegetarian in evening, English spoken, closed Sat and Sun night. *Snack Uno*, Av Heroínas E-0562. Good lunches and dinners including vegetarian. *Tulasi*, Av Heroínas E-0262. Open 0800-2200, till 1500 weekends, buffet lunch, US$1.50.

Cafés *Bambi*, 25 de Colombia y Colombia. Tea, cakes and ice cream. *Brazilian Coffee Bar*, Av Ballivián just off Plaza Colón. Upmarket, tables on pavement. *Café Express Bolívar*, Bolívar ente San Martín y 25 de Mayo. Great coffee. *Café Otoño*, 25 de Mayo y Mayor Rocha, T452 3903. Nicely decorated, simple but tasty dishes, good service. *Fragmento's Café*, Ecuador E-0325. Good coffee, snacks, nice atmosphere, popular with students, artists, occasional live music, cultural information. *Les Temps Modernes*, España N-0140. Fine coffee, French-style snacks, patisserie, Mon-Sat 1500-late. Recommended. *Dumbo*, Av Heroínas 0440. Good ice-cream parlour, popular eating and meeting spot, also does cheap meals. *Cristal*, 3 doors away, similar but smaller and quieter. Recommended. *Unicornio*, Heroínas y Baptista. Large, attractive, popular gringo hangout, pricey.

Bars & clubs *Chilimania*, M Rocha E-0333. Good for drinking and dancing. *Lujos*, Beni E-0330. Nice atmosphere; and *D'Mons*, Tarija y América. Mix of Latin, contemporary and classic American music, both open 2300, US$4 including first drink. *Panchos*, M Rocha E-0311, just off España. A lively dancing and drinking place. *Wunderbar*, Venezuela E-0635. Cable TV sports on Mon, music, darts upstairs, ribs, wings, subs, opens 1930.

Cochabamba

Bolivia

Entertainment **Peñas** *Totos*, M Rocha y Ayacucho, T452 2460. Fri night only, 2000-0300; may open on Sat. Free entry. **Theatre** Concerts and plays at the *Teatro Achá*, España y Las Heroínas, T422 1166. Popular productions (comedy, music, dance) at *Tra La La*, Plazuela 4 de Noviembre, T428 5030.

Festivals *Carnival* is celebrated 15 days before **Lent**. Rival groups (*comparsas*) compete in music, dancing, and fancy dress, culminating in El Corso on the last Sat of the Carnival. *Mascaritas* balls also take place in the carnival season, when the young women wear long hooded satin masks. **14 Sep:** *Day of Cochabamba*.

Shopping *Fotrama*, factory at Av Circunvalación 0413, T422 5468, outlet at Bolívar 0439. Cooperative for
Lots of antique shops alpaca sweaters, stoles, rugs, alpaca wool, etc (expensive). *Arizona*, Juan Capriles E-0133. A
on C España, near good bookshop is *Los Amigos del Libro*, Ayacucho S-0156, T450 4150, in *Hotel Portales* and
Plaza 14 de Septiembre *Gran Hotel Cochabamba*, in the Torres Sofer shopping centre and at Jorge Wilsterman airport. Stocks US and English magazines as well as *South American Handbook*. City map and guide in colour for US$2.50. *Ans Em Ex*, Heroínas O-0225, T422 9711. Camping equipment.

Tour *Turismo Balsa*, Av Heroínas O-0184, T422 7610, F422 5795. Daily city tours, excursions to
operators Quillacollo, Inca-Rakay, Samaipata, Totoro, etc, airline reservations (see also under La Paz Tour Operators). *Carve*, Ayacucho E-0637, T425 8627, and *Caxia Tours*, Arce 0563, T422 6148, caxiasrl@supernet.com.bo Both recommended. *Fremen*, Tumusla N-0245, T425 9392, F411 7790. City and local tours, specializes in travel in **Bolivian Amazonia**, using the *Reina de Enin* floating hotel out of Puerto Varador near Trinidad, also run *Hotel El Puente* in Villa Tunari (see below). *Vicuñita Tours*, Av Ayacucho 350, T452 0194, , specializing in local and regional travel, also overseas reservations (T03-334 0591 for Santa Cruz office).

Transport **Local** *Micros* and *colectivos*, US$0.20; *trufis*, US$0.30. Anything marked 'San Antonio' goes to the market. *Trufis* C and 10 go from bus terminal to the city centre. **Taxi**: about US$0.50 from anywhere to the Plaza, more expensive to cross the river; double after dark.

  Long distance Air: Jorge Wilstermann airport, T459 1820. Airport bus is Micro B from Plaza 14 de Septiembre, US$0.40; taxis from airport to centre US$3.60. Reconfirm all flights (and obtain reconfirmation number), and arrive early for international flights. Several flights daily to/from **La Paz** (30 mins) and **Santa Cruz** (45 mins) with *LAB* and *Aero Sur* (book early for morning flights). *LAB* also to **Guayaramerín, Sucre, Trinidad** and **Tarija**. International flights to **Asunción** and **Buenos Aires**. *LAB*, Heroínas, entre Sánchez y Baptista, open 0800, T0800-30011. *Aero Sur*, Av Villarroel 105, esq Av Oblitos (Pando), T440 0909/459 0077 (airport). **Bus**: the main bus terminal is on Av Ayacucho on opposite side from Montes and Punata (T155). To **Santa Cruz**, 10 hrs, from 0530-2200, US$3-4.50 (*buscama* US$7.50); only minibuses take the old mountain road via Epizana, from Av 9 de Abril y Av Oquendo, all day. See page 315, below. To/from **La Paz** many companies, shop around for best times, services and prices (about US$2.25-3.75, *buscama* US$4.50-6), by night or day, 7 hrs on paved road. Bus to **Oruro**, US$2.25-3, 4½ hrs, buses hourly. To **Potosí**, US$4.50-5.25 via Oruro, several companies 1830-2000. Daily to **Sucre**, US$4.50-5.25, 10 hrs, several companies between 1930 and 2030 (*Flota Copacabana* and *Trans Copacabana* recommended; latter *buscama* US$8.90). To **Sucre** by day; take a bus to Aiquile (see below), then a bus at midnight-0100 passing en route to Sucre (if you want to take a truck in daylight, wait till next day). Local buses leave from Av Barrientos y Av 6 de Agosto, near La Coronilla for **Tarata, Punata** and **Cliza**. Av República y Av 6 de Agosto to **Epizana** and **Totora**. Av Oquendo y 9 de Abril (be careful around this area), to **Villa Tunari**, US$2.70, 4-5 hrs, several daily; **Chimoré**, US$5.75; **Eterazama**, US$5.75; **Puerto Villarroel**, US$4, 6-8 hrs (from 0800 when full, daily); **Puerto San Francisco**, US$6.50.

Directory **Banks** Cash on Visa or MasterCard from many banks; no commission on bolivianos. Visa and MasterCard
For hospitals, doctors at *Enlace* cash dispensers all over the town (especially on Av Ballivián) and next to the bus terminal.
and dentists, contact *Exprint-Bol*, Plaza 14 de Septiembre S-0252, will change TCs into dollars at 2% commission. Money
your consulate or the changers congregate at most major intersections, especially outside *Entel*, and on Plaza Colón, .
tourist office for **Communications** Internet: Many cybercafés all over town, charging US$0.60 per hr. **Post Office:** Av
recommendations Heroínas y Ayacucho, next to *LAB* office (main entrance on Ayacucho), Mon-Fri 0800-2000, Sat

0800-1800, Sun 0800-1200. **Telephone:** *Entel*, Gral Achá y Ayacucho, international phone, fax (not possible to make AT&T credit card calls), open till 2300. **Cultural centres** Centro Boliviano **Americano**, 25 de Mayo N-0365, T422 1288. Library of English-language books, open 0900-1200 and 1430-1900; also offers language classes. **Alianza Francesa**, Santiváñez O-0187. **Instituto Cultural Boliviano-Alemán**, Sucre 693, Casilla 1700, T422 8431, F422 8890. Spanish classes offered. **Embassies and consulates** Argentina, F Blanco E-0929, T425 5859. Visa applications 0830-1300. **Brazil**, Edif Los Tiempos Dos, Av Oquendo, p 9, T425 5860. Open 0830-1130, 1430-1730. **Germany**, Edif La Promotora, p 6, of 602, T425 4024, F425 4023. **Italy**, Ayacucho, Gal Cochabamba p 1, T423 8650. 1800-1930 Mon-Fri. **Netherlands**, Av Oquendo 654, Torres Sofer p 7, T425 7362. 0830-1200, 1400-1630 Mon-Fri. **Paraguay**, Edif El Solar, 16 de Julio 211, T425 0183. 0830-1230, 1430-1830 Mon-Fri. **Peru**, Av Pando 1325, T424 0296. 0800-1200,1400-1800 Mon-Fri. **Spain**, Los Molles y Paraíso, Urb Irlandés, T425 5733. 1100-1200 Mon-Fri. **Sweden**, Barquisimeto, Villa La Glorieta, T/F424 5358. 0900-1200 Mon-Fri. **USA**, Av Oquendo, Torres Sofer p 6, T425 6714. 0900-1200 (will also attend to Britons and Canadians). **Language classes** *Sra Blanca de La Rosa Villareal*, Av Libertador Simón Bolívar 1108, esq Oblitas, Casilla 2707 (T424 4298). US$5 per hr. *Runawasi*, J Hinojosa, Barrio Juan XXIII s/n, Casilla 4034, T/F424 8923, www.runawasi.org Spanish and Quechua, also arranges accommodation. *Sra Alicia Ferrufino*, JQ Mendoza N-0349, T428 1006. US$10 per hour, *Elizabeth Siles Salas*, Casilla 4659, T423 2278, silessalas@latinmail.com *Reginaldo Rojo*, T424 2322, frojo@supernet.com.bo US$5 per hr. *María Pardo*, Pasaje El Rosal 20, Zona Queru Queru behind Burger King on Av América, T428 4615. US$5 per hr, also teaches Quechua. *Carmen Galinda Benavides*, Parque Lincoln N-0272, Casilla 222, T424 7072. *Maricruz Almanzal*, Av San Martín 456, T422 7923, maricruz_almanza@hotmail.com US$5 for 50 mins, special offers for extended tuition. See also Cultural centres, above. **Useful addresses Immigration Office:** Jordán y Arce, p 2, T422 5553, Mon-Fri 0830-1630.

Around Cochabamba

Quillacollo, 13 km west of the city, has a good Sunday market but no tourist items; the *campesinos* do not like being photographed. A few km beyond Quillacollo is a turn-off to the beautiful **Pairumani** *hacienda*, centre of the Patiño agricultural foundation, 8 km from Quillacollo. Known also as **Villa Albina**, it was built in 1925-32, furnished from Europe and inhabited by Patiño's wife, Albina. ■ *Mon-Fri 1500-1600, Sat 0900-1130. T426 0083 to check if it is open. Take bus 7 or 38, or trufi 211 from Cochabamba.* Some 27 km west of Cochabamba, near Sipe-Sipe, are **Inka-Rakay** ruins. The main attraction is the view from the site of the Cochabamba valley and the mountains around the ruins. **Tarata**, 33 km southeast of Cochambamba, is a colonial town with a traditional arcaded plaza on which stand the church, containing an 18th-century organ and other colonial artefacts (open 0800-1300 daily), the Casa Consistorial, and the Municipalidad. Inside the **Franciscan Convent** overlooking the town are the remains of the martyr, San Severino, patron saint of the town, more commonly known as the 'Saint of Rain'; festival, on the last Sunday of November, attracts thousands of people. Large procession on 3 May, day of La Santa Cruz, with fireworks and brass band. Market day Thursday (bus US$0.65, one hour, last return 1800). **Punata**, 48 km to the east, has a very lively and colourful market on Tuesday. It is famous for its Señor de los Milagros festival on 24 September. Behind the main church, which has many baroque/mestizo works of art, new vehicles are lined up to be blessed by the priest. The local speciality is *garapiña*, a mixture of *chicha* and ice-cream. Beyond Punata, at Villa Rivera, woven wall hangings are produced.

In the province of Potosí, but best reached from Cochabamba (135 km), is Torotoro, a small village, set amid beautiful rocky landscape (*Tinku* festival 25 June; *Santiago* 24-27 July). The village is in the centre of the Parque Nacional Torotoro. Attractions include caves, a canyon, waterfalls, pictographs, ruins, fossilized dinosaur tracks and rock paintings, some of which can be seen by the Río Toro Toro just outside the village (ask directions, or take a young guide). ■ *Entry to the park is US$3; local guide US$5 per day, plus his food for trips of over a day. Despite the difficulties of getting there, this trip is highly recommended. You should be able to speak Spanish and not be in a hurry. Tourist information is available at the national park office in Torotoro (open daily, ask here*

Parque Nacional Torotoro
Torotoro covers an area of 16,570 ha and was declared a National Park in 1989

▶ *Fiesta de la Virgen de Urkupiña, Quillacollo*

The festival lasts four days with much dancing and religious ceremony; its date varies each year between June and August. Plenty of transport from Cochabamba, hotels all full. Be there before 0900 to be sure of a seat, as you are not allowed to stand in the street. The first day is the most colourful with all the groups in costumes and masks, parading and dancing in the streets till late at night. Many groups have left by the second day and dancing stops earlier. The third day is dedicated to the pilgrimage. (Many buses, micros and trufis from Heroínas y Ayacucho, 20 minutes, US$0.30.)

about all tours, guides, etc). **Umajalanta cave**, which has many stalagtites and a lake with blind fish, is about 1½ hrs' walk northwest of Torotoro, with an hour's caving; a guide is necessary from the park office, US$5 per person in a group of 2-5 (take a head torch if possible). **El Vergel** waterfall can be reached without a guide, but you need good directions. The falls are fantastic, and the walk along the river bed is great fun if you like rock-hopping and skipping over pools. Fossils can be seen at Siete Vueltas, an afternoon's walk, but you need a guide. Mario Jaldín (Spanish speaking only) is knowledgeable. He lives two doors to the right of *Alojamiento Charcas*. He also leads a four-day trek to see canyons, condors, orchids, many birds and, if lucky, the Andean Bear and pumas; $80-100 per person, depending on the size of the group, includes camping gear and food, bring your own sleeping bag.

Sleeping and eating G *Alojamiento Charcas*, near bus terminal, with very good restaurant serving hot, filling meals, US$1 pp (order dinner in the morning). G *De Los Hermanos*, very basic rooms, supposedly running water, delightful owner with friendly pets. Lydia García's *Salón de Té* provides good meals with prior notice, good breakfasts, bakes bread and cakes, welcoming. There are 3 *tiendas* in the village.

Transport Travel to Torotoro is impossible overland in the wet season (end Nov-Mar), as flooded rivers wash out roads, but it is possible to fly quite cheaply as a group. Swiss pilot *Eugenio Arbinsona* charges US$120 for up to 5 passengers in his Cessna. It takes only 25 mins, but he may be persuaded to lengthen the journey by flying you through a canyon or two on the way. T424 6289 or T0717-23779 (mob). Check bus schedules at all times of year with Gonzalo Milán, *Comercial El Dorado*, Honduras 646, Cochabamba, T422 0207, also very helpful on accommodation and activities. Transport to **Torotoro** goes in convoy from Av República y 6 de Agosto at 0600 Sun and Thu, be there at 0530, US$4 in a bus or the cab of a truck, US$3 in the back, 10 uncomfortable hrs with stops at Cliza market and for lunch. Transport returns to Cochabamba every Mon and Fri, 0600. Groups can arrange with Gonzalo Milán to be picked up at a hotel. Alternatively, pay in advance and arrange to be picked up in Cliza where buses and trucks stop at 0800.

Cochabamba to Santa Cruz

Via Chapare
On this descent to the lowlands, the birdwatching is superb. The roads are manned by army and police and foreigners are subject to scrutiny. Always ask beforehand if the road is open throughout, as sections are frequently closed

The lowland road from Cochabamba to Santa Cruz runs through Villa Tunari, Sinahota and Chimoré (a centre for DEA operations; three hotels). The road is paved Villa Tunari-Santa Cruz. **Villa Tunari** is a relaxing place and holds an annual Fish Fair 5 and 6 August, music and dancing, delicious meals. **Parque Ecoturístico Machía** is just outside town and offers good trails through semi-tropical forest. ■ *Free, but donations welcome.* Beside the park is the animal refuge **Inti Wara Yassi**, where rescued animals are nursed back to health. Travellers can stay in G accommodation as volunteers (must be self-supporting), or just visit for the day. Highly recommended, especially for a 14-day working holiday. ■ *Daily 0900-1700, free, but donations welcome. There is a charge to take photos, US$2.25 and videos US$3.75. Contact Nena Beltazar in Villa Tunari, T04-413 4621, www.intiwarayassi.org* In 2003 the animal refuge is due to move to a new site, about 6 hours from Santa Cruz, 5

Bolivia

hours from Trinidad, near the village of Santa María, 30 minutes from Ascención de Guarayos. Its new name will be *Comunidad Ichepe Inti Warawara Yassi* (CIIWY). For transport from Cochabamba see page 312.

Sleeping and eating in Villa Tunari   A *Country Club Los Tucanes*, opposite turn-off for *El Puente*, T413 4108. Includes breakfast, a/c, 2 swimming pools. **B** *El Puente*, Av de la Integración, 3 km from town, T425 0302 (Cochabamba). With breakfast and bath, cabins from 2 people to family-size (book in advance at *Fremen* Travel Agency in Cochabamba or La Paz), pool, tours to Carrasco national park, the hotel has a stream and natural pools. **B** *Los Araras*, across bridge on main road to Santa Cruz. **C** midweek, large rooms, nice gardens, good breakfast. **C** *Las Palmas*, T413 4103, 1 km out of town. With breakfast, pool and good restaurant, changes US$ cash. Recommended. **F** *Las Palmas 2*, corner of plaza. With bath, breakfast, fan, swimming pool (not very clean). **G** *La Querencia*, pleasant terrace on river front, avoid noisy rooms at front, good cheap food, clothes-washing facilities. Several other hotels; also two internet cafés, *Entel* office and post office. Best restaurants are *El Bosque*, German, run by botanists, with orchid garden, west end of town, 1 km past toll booth, and *Cuqui*, 1 km west of town, fish specialities, also has tents for camping.

Before the Siberia pass, 5 km beyond Montepunco (Km 119), the 23 km road to Pocona and Inkallajta turns off. The Inca ruins of **Inkallajta** (1463-72, rebuilt 1525), on a flat spur of land at the mouth of a steep valley, are extensive and the main building of the fortress is said to have been the largest roofed Inca building. There are several good camping sites. The Cochabamba Archaeological Museum has some huts where visitors can stay, free, but take sleeping bag and food. Water available at nearby waterfall. **Totora**, on the Sucre road, is a beautiful, unspoiled colonial village. There is **G** *Residencial Colonial*, behind the church. Hot water in mornings, restaurant also. **Aiquile**, south of Totora and 217 km from Cochabamba, is famous for its wooden *charangos* and there's a festival in late October/early November, ask tourist office. Sunday market, for which the town fills up on Saturday. The town was devastated by an earthquake in 1998, so much of it remains in a partially re-built state. **F** *Hostal San Pablo*, one block from plaza, no sign but new, clean, family run and comfortable.

The mountain road
The 500 km road via the mountains and Epizana to Santa Cruz is not paved and the new lowland route is preferred by most transport

Transport: to Inkallajta   Best to go Thu or Sat when micros leave when full from 0700 from 6 de Agosto y República, Cochabamba, passing the sign to the ruins, from where it's a 12 km walk. Otherwise take a micro to the checkpoint 10 km from Cochabamba, then a truck to Km 119 sign, walk towards Pocona or take a truck for 15 km, to where a large yellow sign indicates the trail. After approximately 10 km the trail divides, take the downhill path and the ruins are a further 2 km. **To Totora**   Daily buses from Cochabamba, 6 de Agosto y República at 1600, also at 1430 on Saturday; return 0500 Monday-Saturday, 1100 Sunday. **To Aiquile**   Daily buses except Sun from Cochabamba with *Flotas Aiquile* (Av Barrientos S-2365) and *Trans Campero* (Av Barrientos S-2291, 100 m past Av 6 de Agosto junction , *trufis* 1, 10, 14, 16, 20 pass in front), 5 hrs; 1300, return at 1700. All nightly buses from Sucre to Cochabamba and Santa Cruz pass Aiquile between 2300 and 0130 (buses from Santa Cruz to Sucre pass 0400-0500); few sell tickets only to Aiquile. *Unificado* has an office on the main road in Aiquile beneath the shabby Aloj Turista with buses leaving every day for **Sucre** (0100), **Cochabamba** (1100) and **Santa Cruz** (2130). Daily bus from Totora at 1600.

Bolivia

La Paz

The Northern Lowlands

Bolivia's Northern lowlands account for about 70% of national territory. From scrubby east lowlands to dense tropical jungle in the north, this is pioneer country; home to missionaries, rubber tappers and cocaine refiners. Improved roads to Rurrenabaque and Trinidad are opening up the area and wildlife expeditions are becoming increasingly popular. Beni department has 53% of the country's birds and 50% of its mammals, but destruction of forest and habitat is proceeding at an alarming rate.

Caranavi to San Borja
From Caranavi, a road runs north to Sapecho. Beyond Sapecho, the road passes through Palos Blancos 7 km from the bridge (Saturday market day, several cheap lodgings). The road between Sapecho and Yucumo is now a very good all-weather gravel surface, three hours from Sapecho *tránsito*. There are *hospedajes* (F) and restaurants in **Yucumo** where a road branches northwest, fording rivers 13 times on its way to Rurrenabaque. From Yucumo it is 50 km (1-2 hours, truck at 0730) to **San Borja**, a small, wealthy-looking cattle-raising centre with hotels (D-F) and restaurants clustered near the plaza. From San Borja the road goes east to Trinidad via **San Ignacio de Moxos**. There are 5-6 river crossings and, in the wetlands, flamingoes, blue heron and waterfowl. The road passes through part of the Pilón Lajas Reserve (see below).

Transport *Flota Yungueña* daily except Thu at 1300 from Caranavi to La Paz (19 hrs); also to **Rurrenabaque** (*Buses 1 de Mayo*, T03-895 3467, US$4.40), **Santa Rosa**, **Riberalta**, **Guayaramerín** Thu, Sat, Sun. **Yucumo** is on the La Paz-Caranavi-Rurrenabaque and San Borja bus routes. Rurrenabaque-La Paz bus passes through about 1800. If travelling to Rurrenabaque by bus or truck take extra food in case there is a delay for river levels to fall. The road surface Caranavi-San Borja is good; San Borja-San Ignacio poor, long stretches are rutted and pot-holed; San Ignacio-Trinidad is good. Minibuses and *camionetas* run daily between San Borja and **Trinidad** throughout the year, US$15, about 7 hrs including 20 mins crossing of Río Mamoré on ferry barge (up to 14 hrs in wet season); *1 de Mayo* to **San Ignacio** (US$8), **Trinidad and Santa Cruz**. Gasoline available at Yolosa, Caranavi, Yucumo, San Borja and San Ignacio.

Parque Nacional Madidi
On tours, insect repellent and sun protection are essential. Visit www.ecobolivia.org/ for information on Madidi

Parque Nacional Madidi is quite possibly the most bio-diverse of all protected areas on the planet. It is the variety of habitats, from the freezing Andean peaks of the Cordillera Apolobamba in the southwest (reaching nearly 6,000 m), through cloud, elfin and dry forest to steaming tropical jungle and pampas (neo-tropical savannah) in the north and east, that account for the array of flora and fauna within the park's boundaries. In an area roughly the size of Wales or El Salvador are an estimated 1,000 bird species, 10 species of primates, five species of cat (with healthy populations of jaguar and puma), giant anteaters and many reptiles. Madidi is at the centre of a bi-national system of parks. The Heath river on the park's north-western border forms the Bolivia/Peru frontier and links with the Tambopata National Reserve in Peru. To the southwest the Area Protegida Apolobamba protects extensive mountain ecosystems.

Tours At San José de Uchupiamonas, in Madidi, 5 hrs up-river from Rurrenabaque, is Bolivia's top ecotourism project, *Chalalán Ecolodge*. It was founded by the local community, Conservation International and the Interamerican Development Bank. Accommodation is in thatched cabins, and activities include fantastic wildlife-spotting and birdwatching, guided and self-guided trails, river and lake activities, and relaxing in pristine jungle surroundings. A 5-day trip includes travel time from La Paz, but not air fares, US$260 in low season, US$350 in high season. Addresses: C Comercio, Rurrenabaque, T892 2519, chalalan@cibol.rds.org.bo In La Paz, T/F02-243 4058, or contact Jazmín Caballero (fluent English) at *América Tours* (address under La Paz Tour operators, page 264). See also *Conservation International*'s website: www.ecotour.org/destinations/chalalan.htm

Bolivia

Beyond the Beni River in the southeast runs the Pilón Lajas Biosphere Reserve and Indigenous Territory, home to several native groups. Together with Madidi, it constitutes approximately 60,000 sq km, one of the largest systems of protected land in the neotropics. Unfortunately, much of this land is under pressure from logging interests, and the government has allocated precious little resources to combat encroachment. The Pilón Lajas Biosphere Reserve and Indigenous Territory in the Beni, under the auspices of UNESCO, has been set up. The reserve has one of the continent's most intact Amazonian rainforest ecosystems, as well as an incredible array of tropical forest animal life. NGOs have been working with the people of La Unión, Playa Ancha, Nuevos Horizontes and El Cebó to develop sustainable forestry, fish farming, beekeeping, cattle ranching, *artesanía* and even fruit wines; tours are run by *Donato Tours* (see Tour operators, below), US$22 including lunch and transport. **B** pp *Mapajo*, a community-run eco-lodge 2 hours by boat from Rurrenebaque has 4 *cabañas* without electricity (take a torch and batteries), cold showers and a dining room serving traditional meals. You can visit the local community, walk in the forest, go birdwatching, etc. Take insect repellent, wear long trousers and strong footwear. Entry is about US$5 pp. For information contact *Vétérinaires sans Frontières* (VSF), T02-222 6640, or the *Mapajo-Asociación Indígena* (MAI) in Rurrenabaque, T/F8322 2524. Either may give permits for camping.

Pilón Lajas Biosphere Reserve & Indigenous Territory

Bolivia

Rurrenabaque

The charming, picturesque jungle town of Rurre, on the Río Beni, is the main jumping off point for tours in the Bolivian Amazon.

Phone code: 03
Population: 10,000

C-E *Beni*, by river, T892 2408, F892 2273. Best rooms have a/c and TV, hot showers extra, cheaper without bath or a/c (but with fan). Spacious, pleasant, good service. **C** *Hotel Safari*, on the outskirts by the river (a hot walk), T892 2410. Beautiful garden, pool, terrace. Recommended. **C** *Taquara*, on plaza. Generally better than others, pool, accepts credit cards. **D** *Asaí*, C Vaca Díez, T892 2439. Electric showers, laundry area, courtyard and hammocks, luggage store. **E** *El Porteño*, C Vaca Díez. Cheaper without bath, quite good. **E** *Oriental*, on plaza. Cheaper without bath, breakfast available, quiet. Recommended. **F** *Rurrenabaque*, 1 block east of plaza. Safe, cooking and laundry facilities, good. **F** *Santa Ana*, 1 block north of plaza on Avaroa, T892 2399. Cheaper without bath in hammock area, basic, hot showers extra, laundry, luggage store, pretty courtyard, car park. Recommended. **F** *Tuichi*, C Avaroa y Santa Cruz. **G** without bath, cold showers, luggage storage, laundry facilities, fan, good value, accepts TCs. **G** *Hostal Eden*, southern end of C Bolívar, T892 2452. With or without bath, hot water, breakfast available, has hammocks and kitchen, family run, good value. **G** pp *Jislene*, C Comercio, T892 2526. Erlan Caldera and family very hospitable, hot water, fan, basic, good breakfast if booked in advance, information, helpful.

Sleeping
Most hotels are noisy owing to all-night discos

Club Social Rurrenabaque, on Comercio 1 block north of Santa Cruz. Vegetarian dishes on request, good juices, fishburgers. *Café Motacu*, Av Santa Cruz beside *TAM*. Excellent meals, book exchange, closed Tue and Sun and 1200-1830. *Camila's*, Santa Cruz. Good Mexican and Italian food, fast food. *Bambi*, opposite *Flota Yungueña* office. Good meeting place; *heladería* which also does meals. *El Tacuara*, opposite *Camila's*. Good, also for breakfast. Just downriver from *El Porteño* is *Moskkito Bar*, good for ½-price cocktails 1900-2100; next door is an Italian restaurant, tasty food.

Eating
Good almuerzos and fruit juices in the market.

Jungle tours normally last 4 days and 3 nights (US$25 per day). The jungle is very hot and humid in the rainy season with many more biting insects and far fewer animals to be seen. You see a lot of wildlife on a 3-day Pampas tour (US$30 per day), which involves a 3½-hr jeep ride to the Río Yacuma, then a series of boat trips. You see howler, squirrel and capuchin monkeys, caiman, capybara, pink dolphins, possibly anacondas and a huge variety of birds. The weather and general conditions are more pleasant than in the jungle; season Jul to Oct. For pampas and jungle tours, 1-day trips are reportedly a waste of time as it takes 3 hrs to reach the jungle. Some

Tour operators
Mosquito nets can be bought here much more cheaply than in La Paz. It is cheaper to book tours in Rurrenabaque than La Paz

agencies offer ecologically unsound practices such as fishing, feeding monkeys, catching caiman; before signing up for a tour ask if the operator respects the environment. Pampas tours may involve wading through knee-deep water; wear appropriate shoes.

Warning We continue to receive reports of drugging and rape of foreign women by one guide in particular and though he has been convicted of rape he has so far eluded long-term imprisonment. Make enquiries about services and personnel, use only established tour operators and always go in company.

Agencia Fluvial, at *Hotel Tuichi*, T892 2372, runs jungle tours on the Río Tuichi, normally 4 days, but shorter by arrangement, US$25 pp per day (payable in dollars) including food, transport and mosquito nets (write to Tico Tudela, *Agencia Fluvial*, Rurrenabaque). Take swimming costume and insect repellent. Also 3-day 'Pampas Tours' on a boat to Río Yacuma, US$30 pp per day. Tico Tudela has opened *Hotel de la Pampa* near Lago Bravo, 2½ hrs from Rurrenabaque, as a base for visiting Lago Rogagua (birds) and Río Yacuma. Fully inclusive tours (including meals and accommodation) US$40 pp per day. *Aguila Tours*, Av Avaroa, T892 2478 (associated with *Flecha Tours*, Avaroa y Santa Cruz), jungle and pampas tours (can be booked through *Eco Jungle Tours*, C Sagárnaga, La Paz). *Bala Tours*, C Comercio, T892 2527. Arranges 'Pampas' and 'Jungle' tours, good base camp. Recommended. *Donato Tours*, C A Arce, T7179 5722/7779 5722 (mob). For regular tours and A Day for the Community.

Transport Air *TAM* (C Santa Cruz, T892 2398), 4 a week, US$65 one way from **La Paz** (also has charter for 8 people). Book all flights as early as possible and buy return to La Paz on arrival. Check flight times in advance; they change frequently. Expect delays and cancellations in wet season. Airport tax US$2. Motorcycle taxi from town, US$1. **Road** To/from **La Paz** via Caranavi daily at 1100 with *Flota Yungueña* and *Totai*; 18-20 hrs, US$8.20. Returns at 1100. *Flota Unificada* leaves La Paz (also from Villa Fátima) on Tue, Thu, Fri, Sat at 1030, same price. Continues to **Riberalta** and **Guayaramerín**; return departure time depends on road conditions. *Flota Yungueña* also has a 1030 bus which leaves Villa Fátima and continues to Riberalta and Guayaramerín. **Rurrenebaque-Riberalta** should take 12-18 hrs, but can take 6 days or more in the wet. Take lots of food, torch and be prepared to work. To **Trinidad**, Tue, Thu, Sat, Sun at 2230 with *Trans Guaya* via **Yucumo** and **San Borja**, US$18. **River** Boats to **Guanay**, US$16 pp; ask at any tour agency; take your own food.

Directory Banks No banks or *casas de cambio*. *Bala Tours* will give cash advance against credit cards at 7.5% commission. Try hotels or agencies for small amounts. TCs can be changed at *Micro Mercado* Masary, opposite *Flecha Tours*. Agencies will accept them as payment for tours, *TAM* also accepts them, or try *Agencia Fluvial*, 4% commission. **Communications Internet:** 2 next door to each other on C Santa Cruz, next to *Camila's*, US$3 per hr. Another on the same road, near the ferry. **Post office:** on C Bolívar. Both open Sat. **Telephone:** *Entel*, on C Comercio, 2 blocks north of plaza; also at Santa Cruz y Bolívar.

Riberalta
Phone code: 03
Colour map 3, grid B6
Population: 60,000
Altitude: 175 m

This town, at the confluence of the Madre de Dios and Beni rivers, is off the beaten track and a centre for brazil nut production. Change cash in shops and on street. Recent reports indicate an increase in theft and rape, worth knowing when the bus drops you in the middle of the night and everything is closed. Some 25 km away is Tumi-Chucua situated on a lovely lake. Nearby are the Nature Gardens. Here you can fish in the lake, good for birdwatching. They also have lots of information on the rainforest, the rubber boom and brazil nut production. Contact *Dr Willy Noack*, T/F352 2497 for further information.

Sleeping and eating Ask for a fan and check the water supply. **D** *Comercial Lazo*, NG Salvatierra, T852 8326. **F** without a/c, comfortable, laundry facilities, good value. **E** *Colonial*, Plácido Méndez 1. Charming colonial casona, large, well-furnished rooms, nice gardens and courtyard, comfortable, good beds, helpful owners. Recommended. **F** *Res Los Reyes*, near airport, T852 8018. With fan, safe, pleasant but noisy disco nearby on Sat and Sun. **G** *Res El Pauro*, Salvatierra 157. Basic, shared baths, good café. For eating, try, *Club Social Progreso*, on plaza. Good value *almuerzo*, excellent fish. *Club Social Riberalta*, on Maldonado. Good *almuerzo* US$3.50, smart dress only. *Quatro Ases*, Arce. Good. Tucunare, M Chávez/Martínez. Recommended. Good lunch at *comedor popular* in market, US$1.50.

Transport Air Expect delays in the wet season. *LAB* fly to **Santa Cruz**, **Guayaramerín**, **Trinidad** and **Cobija**; office at M Chávez 77, T852 2239 (0800-3001). *TAM* flies to **Cochabamba**, **Santa Cruz** and **La Paz**, Fri (US$100 to La Paz); office Av Suárez/Chuquisaca, T852 3924. Check all flight details in advance. **Road** Several companies (including *Yungueña*) to **La Paz**, via **Rurrenabaque** and **Caranavi** Tue-Sat at 1100, also Tue, Thu, Sat at 1000; US$22.40 (same price to Rurrenebaque, 18 hrs). To **Trinidad** with *8 de Diciembre* Mon, Wed, Thu, Sat, Sun at 0830, also *Trans Guaya* daily at 0930, via Rurrenabaque; to **Guayaramerín** daily, US$3, 3 hrs. To **Cobija** on Wed, Fri, Sat at 0900 with *8 de Diciembre*, Mon, Thu at 1000 with *Trans Amazonas*. Buses stop in Santa Rosa for meals. **River** Cargo boats carry passengers along the **Río Madre de Dios**, but they are infrequent. There are not many boats to Rurrenabaque.

Guayaramerín is a cheerful, prosperous little town on the bank of the Río Mamoré, opposite the Brazilian town of Guajará-Mirim. It has an important *Zona Libre*. Passage between the two towns is unrestricted; boat trip US$1.65 (more at night).

Guayaramerín
Phone code: 03
Colour map 4, grid C1

Bolivia

Sleeping and eating B *Esperanza* out of town in nearby Cachuela Esperanza, Casilla 171, reserve through *American Tours* in La Paz, T02-237 4204, F02-231 0023, www.america-ecoturs.com Eco-friendly. **C** *San Carlos*, 6 de Agosto, 4 blocks from port, T855 2152/3. With a/c (**D** without), hot showers, changes dollars cash, TCs and reais, swimming pool, reasonable restaurant. There are also **F-G** places, eg *Santa Ana*, close to the airport. The following eating places are all on the plaza: *Made in Brazil*, good coffee. *Gipsy*, good *almuerzo*. *Los Bibosis*, popular with visiting Brazilians. *Only*, 25 de Mayo/Beni, good *almuerzo* for US$2.50, plus Chinese. On road to airport *Heladería Tutti-Frutti*, excellent.

Transport Air *LAB* flies to **Trinidad**, **Riberalta**, **Santa Cruz**,and **Cobija**; office at 25 de Mayo 652, T855 3540 (0800-3001). *TAM* flies to **Cochabamba, Santa Cruz** and **La Paz**; office at 16 de Julio (road to airport). **Bus** To/from **La Paz**, *Flota Yungueña*, daily 0830 (1030 from La Paz), 36 hrs, US$22.40. Also *Flota Unificada*, leaving La Paz Tue, Thu, Fri, Sat 1030, US$26.90.To **Riberalta** 3 hrs, US$3, daily 0700-1730. To **Trinidad** Fri, 30 hrs, US$23. To **Rurrenabaque**, US$16. To **Cobija** 4 a week. To **Santa Cruz** via Trinidad, 1-2 a week, 2½ days. Buses depart from Gral Federico Román. Roads are very difficult in wet season. **River** Check the notice of boats leaving port on the Port Captain's board, prominently displayed near the immigration post on the riverbank. Boats up the Mamoré to **Trinidad** are fairly frequent – a 3-day wait at the most.

Bolivian immigration is on Avenida Costanera near port; open 0800-1100, 1400-1800. Passports must be stamped here when leaving, or entering Bolivia. On entering Bolivia, passports must be stamped at the Bolivian consulate in Guajará-Mirim. For Brazilian immigration, see page 553. The Brazilian consulate is on 24 de Septiembre, Guayaramerín, open 1100-1300; visas for entering Brazil are given here. Exchange money here (but not travellers' cheques) as this is very difficult in the State of Rondônia in Brazil.

Border with Brazil

The capital of the lowland Department of Pando lies on the Río Acre which forms the frontier with Brazil. As a duty-free zone, shops in centre have a huge selection of imported consumer goods at bargain prices. Brazilians and Peruvians flock here to stock up. As this is a this border area, watch out for scams and cons.

Cobija
Phone code: 03
Colour map 3, grid B5
Population: 15,000

Sleeping and eating E *Prefectural Pando*, Av 9 de Febrero, T842 2230. Includes breakfast, *comedor* does good lunch, manager Sr Angel Gil, helpful. **F** *Res Crocodilo*, Av Molina, T842 2215. Comfortable, good atmosphere, rooms with fan. **G** *Res Frontera*, 9 de Febrero, T842 2740. Good location, basic but clean, fan. *La Esquina de la Abuela*, opposite *Res Crocodilo*, good food, not cheap. Good cheap meals in *comedor popular* in central market.

Transport Local Taxis are very expensive, charging according to time and distance, eg US$10 to the outskirts, US$12 over the international bridge to Brasiléia. Besides taxis there are motorbike taxis (much cheaper). **Brasiléia** can also be reached by **canoe**, US$0.35. The bridge can be crossed on foot as well, although one should be dressed neatly in any case when approaching Brazilian customs. Entry/exit stamps (free) are necessary and yellow fever vaccination certificate also (in theory), when crossing into Brazil.

Long distance Air: *Aero Sur*, Av Fernández Molina, T842 3132, flies 3 days a week to **La Paz. *LAB*,** R Barrientos 343, T842 2170, twice a week to **Riberalta, Guayaramerín** and **Trinidad**. *TAM* office on 2 de Febrero, T842 2267 (check schedule). **Bus**: *Flota Yungueña* to **La Paz** via Riberalta and Rurrenabaque Sat at 0700 (check times first, T842 2318). To **Riberalta** with several bus companies and trucks, depart from 2 de Febrero, most on Wed, Fri, Sun at 0600; good all-weather surface; 5 river crossings on pontoon rafts, takes 10-11 hrs.

Directory Banks Lots of money changers along Av 2 de Febrero. Most shops will accept dollars or reais, or exchange money. **Communications** Internet: Internet place near the university, 100 m from the plaza. **Post Office**: on plaza. **Telephone**: *Entel*, on C Sucre, for telephone calls internal and abroad and fax, much cheaper than from Brazil.

Villa Tunari to the Lowlands Another route into Beni Department is via the lowland road between Cochabamba and Santa Cruz. At Ivirgazama, east of Villa Tunari, the road passes the turn-off to Puerto Villarroel, 27 km further north, from where cargo boats ply irregularly to Trinidad in about four to 10 days. You can get information from the Capitanía del Puerto notice board, or ask at docks. **E-G** *Amazonas Eco-hotel* with restaurant, T/F04-423 5105, boat trips arranged. There are very few stores in Villarroel. Sr Arturo Linares at the Cede office organizes boat trips to the jungle – not cheap.

Transport *Camionetas* go from the junction on the main road to **Puerto Villarroel** a few times a day, 1 hr, US$1.20. From Cochabamba you can get a bus to Puerto Villarroel (see Cochabamba Transport, Bus), **Puerto San Francisco**, or **Todos Santos** on the Río Chapare.

Trinidad

Phone code: 03
Colour map 6, grid A3
Population: 86,000
Altitude: 237 m

The hot and humid capital of the lowland Beni Department, founded 1686, is a dusty city in the dry season, with many streets unpaved. There are two ports, Almacén and Varador, check which one your boat is docking at. Puerto Varador is 13 km from town on the Río Mamoré on the road between Trinidad and San Borja; cross the river by the main bridge by the market, walk down to the service station by the police checkpoint and take a truck, US$1.70. Almacén is 8 km from the city. The main mode of transport in Trinidad (even for taxis, US$0.40 in city) is the motorbike; rental on plaza from US$2 per hour, US$8 per half day.

Hire a motorbike or jeep to go to the river; good swimming on the opposite bank; boat hire US$5. 8 km from town is the Laguna Suárez, with plenty of wildlife; the water is very warm, the bathing safe where the locals swim, near the café with the jetty (elsewhere there are stingrays and alligators). See under Eating, below. Motorbike taxi from Trinidad US$1.30.

About 17 km north is **Chuchini** with the Madriguera del Tigre, an ecological and archaeological centre, accessible by road in dry season and by canoe in wet season. Contact Efrem Hinojoso at Av 18 de Noviembre 543, T462 1811. Three days and two nights US$210 per person, including accommodation and meals; also including Museo Arqueológico del Beni, containing human remains, ceramics and stone objects from pre-Columbian Beni culture, said to be over 5,000 years old.

Sleeping **A** *Gran Moxos*, Av 6 de Agosto y Santa Cruz, T462 2240, F462 0002. Includes breakfast, a/c, fridge bar, cable TV, phone, good restaurant, accepts Visa and MasterCard. **C-D** *Hostal Aguahi*, Bolívar y Santa Cruz, opposite *TAM*, T462 5569. A/c, fridge, comfortable, swimming pool in pleasant garden. **C-D** *Monte Verde*, 6 de Agosto 76, T462 2738. With or without a/c, fridge bar, includes breakfast, owner speaks English. Recommended. **D** *Copacabana*, Tomás Villavicencio 627, 3 blocks from plaza, T462 2811. Good value, **F** pp without bath. **D-E** *Res Castedo*, Céspedes 42, T462 0937, 200 m from bus terminal. A/c or fan, cheaper without bath, breakfast. **D-E** Hostal Jarajorechi, Av 6 de Agosto y 27 de Mayo, Casilla 299, T462 1716. With bath and breakfast, comfortable, ecotourism centre offering jungle expeditions, equipment and transport hire. **F** *Paulista*, Av 6 de Agosto 36, T462 0018. Cheaper without bath, comfortable, good restaurant. **F** *Res Oriental*, 18 de Noviembre near Vaca Díez, T462 2534. Good value, shared bath, helpful, good food, but not very clean. **G** *Res 18 de Noviembre*, Av 6 de Agosto 135, T462 1272. Laundry facilities, OK but noisy.

Carlitos, on Plaza Ballivián. Recommended. *La Casona*, Plaza Ballivián. For good pizzas and set lunch, closed Tue. *Club Social 18 de Noviembre*, N Suárez y Vaca Díez on plaza. Good lunch for US$1.35. *La Estancia*, Barrio Pompeya, on Ibare entre Muibe y Velarde. Excellent steaks. *Pescadería El Moro*, Bolívar 707 y Natusch. Excellent fish. Also several good fish restaurants in Barrio Pompeya, south of plaza across the river. Burgers, ice cream and snacks at *Kivón* cafeteria on main plaza. Also on plaza, *Heladería Oriental*, good coffee, ice-cream, cakes, popular with locals. *Balneario Topacare* is a restaurant and bathing resort with swimming pool 10 mins out of town on Laguna Suárez, delicious local specialities, lunch or dinner, beautiful location, excellent bird watching, favourite spot for locals at weekends.

Eating
Cheap meals, includes breakfast, served at the fruit and vegetable market. Try delicious sugar cane juice with lemon

Fremen, Cipriano Berace 332, T462 1834. Run speed boat trips along the **Mamoré** and **Iboré rivers** and to **Parque Nacional Isiboro**, US$80 per day; their *Flotel Reina de Enin* offers tours of more than 1 day, US$80 pp per day, good food. Others on 6 de Agosto: *Tarope Tours*, No 57, T/F462 1468. For flights. *Moxos*, No 114, T462 1141. Recommended. *Paraíso Travel*, No 138, T/F462 0692, paraiso@sauce.ben.entelnet.bo Does 'Conozca Trinidad' packages. *Amazonia Holiday*, No 680, T462 5732, F462 2806. Good service. Most agents offer excursions to local *estancias* and jungle tours down river to *Amazonia*. Most *estancias* can also be reached independently in 1 hr by hiring a motorbike.

Tour operators

Air *AeroSur*, Nicolas Suárez, T462 0765, to **La Paz, Cochabamba, Santa Cruz, Riberalta** and **Guayaramerín**. *LAB*, Santa Cruz 234, T462 0595; to **La Paz, Cochabamba, Cobija, Guayaramerín, Santa Cruz** and **Riberalta**. *TAM*, Bolívar s/n entre 18 de Noviembre y Santa Cruz, T462 2363, at airport, T462 0355, to **Baures, Bella Vista, Magdalena** and **Huacaraje, Riberalta, Guayaramerín, Santa Cruz** and **La Paz** (do not leave any valuables in baggage that you check in). Airport, T462 0678. Taxi to airport US$1.20.

Transport

   Bus Bus station is on Rómulo Mendoza, between Beni and Pinto, 9 blocks east of main plaza. Motorbike taxis will take people with backpacks from bus station to centre for US$0.45. Several *flotas* daily to/from **La Paz** via San Borja and Caranavi, 20-21 hrs, depart 1730, US$17.50 (see also under San Borja, Transport). To **Santa Cruz** (12 hrs in dry season, US$5.80) and **Cochabamba** (US$11.60), with **Copacabana, Mopar** and **Bolívar** at 1700, 1730 and 1800; irregular morning service (generally 0900). Trinidad to Casarabe is paved and Santa Cruz to El Puente; otherwise gravel surface on all sections of unpaved road. To **Rurrenabaque** (US$18), **Riberalta** (US$21.15) and **Guayaramerín** (US$23), connecting with bus to **Cobija**; *Guaya Tours* Sun, Mon, Thu, Fri at 1030; road often impassable in wet season, at least 24 hrs to Rurrenabaque.

   River Cargo boats down the Río Mamoré to **Guayaramerín** take passengers, 3-4 days, assuming no breakdowns, best organized from Puerto Varador (speak to the Port Captain). *Argos* is recommended as friendly, US$22 pp, take water, fresh fruit and toilet paper. Ear-plugs are also recommended as hammocks are strung over the engine on small boats; only for the hardy traveller.

Banks *Banco Mercantil*, J de Sierra, near plaza. Changes cash and TCs, cash on Visa. *Banco Ganadero*, Plaza Ballivián. Visa agent. Street changers on 6 de Agosto (US dollars only). **Communications** Post and **telephone** (open daily till 1930) in same building at Av Barace, just off plaza. **Tourist office** In the Prefectural building at Joaquín de Sierra y La Paz, ground floor, T462 1305, ext 116, very helpful, sells guide and city map, US$2. Transport can be arranged from the airport.

Directory

Bolivia

**San Ignacio
de Moxos**
*90 km W of Trinidad
Electricity is supplied in
town from 1200- 2400*

This is known as the folklore capital of the Beni Department. The traditions of the Jesuit missions are still maintained with big *fiestas*, especially during Holy Week; 31 July is the town's patron saint's day, one of the country's most famous celebrations. *Macheteros*, who speak their own language, comprise 60% of the population. There are a few cheapish *residencias* (**E-F**) on the main plaza, several other basic *alojamientos* on and around plaza. Restaurants do not stay open late. *Isireri*, on plaza, good and cheap set lunches and delicious fruit juices. *Casa Suiza*, good European food. *Donchanta*, recommended for meat dishes. The Trinidad to San Borja bus stops at the *Donchanta* restaurant for lunch, otherwise difficult to find transport to San Borja. Minibus to Trinidad daily at 0730 from plaza, also *camionetas*, check times before.

**Magdalena &
Bella Vista**

This town northeast of Trinidad stands on the banks of the Río Itonama. There is an abundance of wildlife and birds in the surrounding area. The city's main festival, Santa María Magdalena, is on 22 July attracting many visitors from all over. There are some restaurants and basic hotels. Also **B** *Internacional*, T03-886 2210, info@hwz-inc.com with breakfast, pools, beautiful setting. Drinking water is available and electricity runs from 1800-2400. There is a bank (changes travellers' cheques), an *Entel* office and Post Office on the plaza. *LAB* flies from Trinidad (T886 3020). An unpaved road goes to Trinidad via San Ramón (pick-up US$10.50), passable only in the dry season. San Ramón to Magdalena takes six hours on motorbike taxi, US$16.

East of Magdalena, **Bella Vista** on the Río Blanco is considered by many to be one of the prettiest spots in northeast Bolivia. Lovely white sandbanks line the Río San Martín, 10 minutes' paddling by canoe from the boat moorings below town (boatmen will take you, returning later by arrangement; also accessible by motorcycle). Check that the sand is not covered by water after heavy rain. Other activities are swimming in the Río San Martín, canoeing, hunting, good country for cycling. **F** *Hotel Pescador*, owner Guillermo Esero Gómez very helpful and knowledgeable about the area, shared bath, provides meals for guests, offers excursions. Three well-stocked shops on plaza, but none sells mosquito repellent or spray/coils (bring your own, especially at the beginning of the wet season). No banks. There are *TAM* flights; ask at the office on the road nearest the river, 2-3 blocks east of plaza.

La Paz

Eastern Bolivia

The vast and rapidly-developing plains to the west of the Eastern Cordillera are Bolivia's richest area in natural resources. For the visitor, the pre-Inca ruins of Samaipata, the nearby Parque Nacional Amboró and the beautiful churches of former Jesuit missions east of Santa Cruz are worth a visit.

Santa Cruz de la Sierra

*Phone code: 03
Colour map 6, grid A4
Population: 1,160,000
Altitude: 437 m
851 km from La Paz*

As little as 50 years ago, Bolivia's second city was a remote backwater, but rail and road links ended its isolation and the exploitation of oil and gas in the Department of Santa Cruz has helped fuel the city's rapid development. Santa Cruz is far removed from most travellers' perceptions of Bolivia. Its sprawling suburbs full of new 4WD vehicles and expensive shops and restaurants seem out of place in South America's poorest country. The city centre, however, has retained much of its colonial air and during the lunchtime hiatus when the locals (who like to call themselves cambas) take refuge from the overwhelming heat, it can almost seem like its former self. Here, too, you can witness the incongruous sight of immigrant Mennonite farmers and their families, who fled persecution in the USA and Canada, going about their business in the presence of Bolivia's most open and laid-back population.

Bolivia

The Plaza 24 de Septiembre is the city's main square with the huge **Cathedral**, the Casa de Cultura and the Palacio Prefectural set around it. ■ *The Cathedral museum is open Tue, Thu 1000-1200, 1600-1800, Sun 1000-1200, 1800-2000, US$0.75.* **Casa de la Cultura** has occasional exhibitions, a museum, giftshop and also an archaeological display; also plays, recitals, concerts and folk dancing. The heart of the city, with its arcaded streets and buildings with low, red-tiled roofs and overhanging eaves, retains a colonial feel, despite the profusion of modern, air-conditioned shops and restaurants. Five blocks north of the Plaza is **Parque El Arenal** in which is a mural by the celebrated painter, Lorgio Vaca, depicting the city's history. Nearby is the **Museo Etno-Folklórico**, Beni y Caballero, which houses a collection of artefacts from lowland cultures. ■ *Mon-Fri 0830-1200, 1430-1830, US$0.75, T335 2078.* The **Museo de Historia Natural, Noel Kempff Mercado**, Av Irala s/n entre Velasco e Independencia, has a video library. Contact them for trips and information to Parque Nacional Noel Kempff Mercado (see page 332). ■ *Mon-Fri 0800-1200, also Mon-Tue 1500-1830. US$0.15, T/F336 6574.* Some 5 km out of town on the road to Cotoca are the **Botanical Gardens** (micro or colectivo from C Suárez Arana, 15 minutes).

Sights

The city has four ring roads, Anillos 1, 2, 3 and 4. Equipetrol suburb, where many hotels and bars are situated, is NW of the heart of the city between Anillos 2 and 3

Bolivia

L *House Inn*, Colón 643, T336 2323, Casilla 387, www.houseinn.com.bo 5-star suites with computer in each room, unlimited internet use, price includes taxes and breakfast, 2 pools, sauna, restaurant, a/c, parking, modern. **L** *Las Buganvillas*, Av Roca y Coronado 901, T355 1212, buganvillas@unete.com 5-star in all respects, all amenities, located between the Río Piraí and Feria Exposición complex. **L** *Los Tajibos*, Av San Martín 455 in Barrio Equipetrol out of town, 5-star, T342 1000, lostajib@ bibosi.scz. entelnet.bo A/c, *El Papagayo* restaurant good (*ceviche* is recommended), business centre, *Viva Club Spa* has sauna etc, swimming pool for residents only. **A** *Las Américas*, 21 de Mayo esq Seoane, T336 8778, americas@mail.zuper.net A/c, discount for longer stay, parking, arranges tours and car rental, restaurant, bar, 5-star service. **B** *Colonial*, Buenos Aires 57, T333 3156, F333 9223. A/c, breakfast, restaurant, comfortable. **B** *Viru-Viru* Junín 338, T333 5298, F336 7500. Includes breakfast, a/c, cheaper with fan.

C *Bibosi*, Junín 218, T334 8548, F334 8887. **D** with shared bath, breakfast included, internet. Recommended. **C** *Copacabana*, Junín 217, T332 1843, F333 0757. **B** with a/c, **E** without bath, cheap laundry service, includes breakfast, restaurant. **C** *Excelsior*, René Moreno 70, T332 5924, excelsior@cotas.net Includes breakfast, good rooms, good lunches.

E *Res 26 de Enero*, Camiri 32, T332 1818, F333 7518. **F** without bath, very clean. **E** *Res Sands*, Arenales 749, 7 blocks east of the main plaza, T337 7776. Unbelievable value, better than many in much higher price brackets, cable TV, fan, very comfortable beds, pool. **E** *Res Bolívar*, Sucre 131, T334 2500. Hot showers, some rooms with bath, lovely courtyard with hammocks, alcohol prohibited, excellent breakfast US$1.10. Recommended. **E** pp *Williams y Patricia Ribera*, Los Melones 622, T347 0909. Safe, convenient, good value, very helpful.

F *Res Ballivián*, Ballivián 71, T332 1960. Basic, shared hot showers (staff like to watch women guests going to and from the shower – harmless but off-putting), nice patio. Recommended. **F-G** *Res Cañada*, Cañada 145, near local bus terminal, T334 5541. Cheaper without bath. Recommended. **G** *Alojamiento Santa Bárbara*, Santa Bárbara 151, T332 1817. Hot showers, shared bath, helpful, will store luggage, good value. Recommended. **G** *Posada El Turista*, Junín 455, T336 2870. Small basic rooms, central, quiet.

Sleeping

■ *on map*
Accommodation is relatively expensive. It's hard to find good value mid and lower-range hotels

Expensive: *El Boliche*, Arenales 135. Open 1930 onwards, serves good crêpes. *Capri*, Irala 634, "The best pizzas in town". *Il Gatto*, 24 de Septiembre 285. Bright and clean, good pizzas, US$2.25 buffet 1200-1500. *Leonardo*, Warnes 366. Italian, also recommended. Mon-Sat 1900-2330. *Michelangelo*, Chuquisaca 502. Excellent Italian. Mon-Fri 1200-1400, 1900-2330, Sat evenings only. **Mid-range**: *La Buena Mesa*, Av Cristóbal de Mendoza 538, and *Churrasquería El Palenque*, Av El Trompillo y Santos Dumont,1200-1400,1830-2330, closed Tue, are both excellent for barbecued steak. There are many other barbecue restaurants around the Segundo Anillo, including *La Casa del Camba*, Cristóbal de Mendoza 539, "a must for the total camba experience." *El Fogón*, Av Viedma 434. Tue-Sun 1200-1400, 1900-2330, Mon only evening. *Café Irlandés*, Plaza 24 de Septiembre, Edificio Shopping Bolívar No 157 overlooking main plaza, T333 8118. Irish-themed restaurant,

Eating

● *on map*
Barrio Equipetrol is the area for the poshest restaurants and nightlife. Most restaurants close Mon. The bakeries on Junín, Los Manzanos and España sell the local specialities

Bolivia

English-speaking owner. Recommended. For truly superb filet mignon, go to *Pizzería Marguerita*, northwest corner of the plaza. A/c, good service, coffee, bar, also recommended, Mon-Fri 0900-2400, Sat-Sun 1600-2400. Finnish owner, speaks English, German. *Escuela Gastronómica Tatapy*, Av Santa Cruz 832, 2nd anillo. Gastronomy school restaurant with quality food at reasonable prices, tourist information. Two excellent Chinese restaurants are *Shanghai*, Av 26 de Febrero 27, and *Mandarin* 2, Av Potosí 793. One of the city's best restaurants is the *Yorimichi*, Av Busch 548, T334 7717. Japanese, could easily put some Tokyo restaurants to shame, call first, as hours are irregular. **Cheap**: Brazilian-style *por kilo* places are popular: eg *Rincón Brasil*, Libertad 358, every day 1130-1500, also (à la carte only) Tue-Sat from 1800, or *Sabor Brasil*, off Buenos Aires, entre Santa Bárbara y España, No 20. For fish, *La Esquina del Pescado*, Sara y Florida. US$1.60 a plate. *La Le Li Lo Lu*, Independencia 120, Mon-Sun 0800-2200. *La Palmera, Ayacucho y Callali*. Typical camba food, large portions. *El Patito Pekín*, 24 de Septiembre 307. Basic Chinese food, Mon-Sun 1100-1400, 1800-2000. *Tía Lía*, Murillo 40. US$1.50 (US$2.25 weekends) for all the beef, chorizos, pork

Santa Cruz

To Viru-Viru Airport & the North

2 Bibosi *B1*	11 Residencial Sands *B3*	5 Il Gatto *B2*
3 Colonial *B2*	12 Residencial 26	6 La Esquina
4 Copacabana *B1*	de Enero *C1*	del Pescado *B1*
5 Excelsior *B2*	13 Viru-Viru *B1*	7 La Palmera *B1*
6 House Inn *D1*		8 Leonardo *C3*
7 Las Américas *B2*	● **Eating**	9 Michelangelo *D2*
8 Posada El Turista *B1*	1 Capri *D1*	10 Pizzería Marguerita *B2*
9 Residencial	2 El Boliche *B2*	11 Sabor Brasil *B1*
Ballivián *B2*	3 El Patito Pekín *B2*	12 Tía Lía *B2*
10 Residencial Bolívar *B2*	4 Hawaii *B2*	13 Vegetariano *B1*

N

0 metres 200
0 yards 200

■ **Sleeping**
1 Alojamiento Santa Bárbara *B1*

and chicken you want from a *parrillada*, huge selection of salads, pasta and bean dishes, Mon-Fri 1100-1500, Sat-Sun 1100-1600. *Los Pozos market*, taking up the whole block between 6 de Agosto, Suárez Arana, Quijarro and Campero, is open daily, clean, good for midday meals, food aisles serve local and Chinese food.

Vegetarian: *Su Salud*, Quijarro 115. Tasty, filling lunches, huge portions. Recommended. *Vegetariano*, Ayacucho 444. Breakfast, lunch and dinner, good. *Vegetariano Cuerpomente*, Pari 228. Wide choice, good. Organic food sold at *La Alternativa* shop, Cuéllar 171. Helpful staff.

Bars and cafés: There are lots of very pleasant a/c cafés and ice cream parlours, where you can get coffee, ice cream, drinks, snacks and reasonably-priced meals. Among the best are: *Dumbo*, Ayacucho 247; *Hawaii*, Sucre 100 y Beni, open at 0730-2400 every day; *Heladería Pastelería Manolo*, 24 de Septiembre 170; and *Kivón*, Ayacucho 267. Highly recommended for ice cream; also at Quijarro 409 in Mercado Los Pozos. *Heladería Alpina,* Junín 229. For good coffee, go to *Alexander Coffee* at Av Monseñor Rivero 400 in Zona El Cristo. *Bar Irlandés Irish Pub*, 3o Anillo Interno 1216 (between Av Cristo Redentor and Zoológico), T343 0671. Irish-themed pub, food available, English-speaking owner (see also *Café Irlandes* on page 323), live music Wed and Sat evening.

Festivals
Cruceños are famous as fun-lovers and their music, the carnavalitos, can be heard all over South America

Of the various festivals, the brightest is *Carnival*, renowned for riotous behaviour, celebrated for the **15 days before Lent**: music in the streets, dancing, fancy dress and the coronation of a queen. Beware the following day when youths run wild with buckets and balloons filled with water – no one is exempt. The *mascaritas* balls also take place during the pre-Lent season at Caballo Blanco when girls have the right to demand that men dance with them, and wear satin masks covering their heads completely, thus ensuring anonymity. **24 Sep** is a holiday. *Misiones de Chiquitos* is an international music festival held every even year, concerts in Santa Cruz, San Javier, Concepción, among other places, including Renaissance and Baroque recitals. *International film festival* held every odd year in same locales. Contact *APAC* for info: T333 2287;

Shopping
Artesanía shops on Libertad and on Plaza 24 de Septiembre y Bolívar

Artecampo, Salvatierra 407 esq Vallegrande, T334 1843. Run by a local NGO, sells handicrafts made in rural communities in the department, high quality, excellent value. However, best local crafts are found at the *Museo de Historia* in the *Casa de Cultura*. Hours are sporadic, call ahead, T355 0611. All proceeds go to *La Mancomunidad*, a local outfit that supports indigenous craftsmen and their families. *Vicuñita Handicrafts*, Ingavi y Independencia, T333 7680. By far the best and biggest selection from altiplano and lowlands. Very honest, will ship. Gembol, in Casco Viejo, of 132 (esq 21 de Mayo y Junín), T336 8665. Outstanding selection of local and Brazilian stones. Honest, very reasonable prices, English spoken. Repeatedly recommended. *RC Joyas*, Bolívar 262, T333 2725. Jewellery and Bolivian gems, the manager also produces and sells good maps of Santa Cruz City and department. *Los Pozos market* (see under Eating) has plenty of smuggled Brazilian goods on sale, exchanged for Bolivian coca (beware of bag-snatching). *Bazar Siete Calles*, mainly for clothing, but food and fruit is sold outside, main entrance is in 100 block of Isabel La Católica, also on Camiri and Vallegrande, past Ingavi. There is a fruit and vegetable market at Sucre y Cochabamba, and a large Indian market on Sun near the bus terminal. *Los Amigos del Libro*, Igavi 14, T332 7937, sells foreign language books and magazines. *El Ateno*, Cañoto y 21 de Mayo, T333 3338. Books in English, access to internet. International magazines and newspapers often on sale in kiosks on main Plaza, eg *Miami Herald*, after arrival of daily Miami flight (0900).

Tour operators
Taking a taxi can work out much cheaper than using a tour and some taxi drivers speak English

Cambutur, René Moreno 8, T334 9999 (from airport 385 2042/2400), Best in city by far for local, regional, international. Ask for Cynthia Otalora; speaks English, French and Portuguese. She is a member of the *Asociación Cruceña – Guías de Turismo* and can arrange private city tours, T345 1741 or 773 44471 (mob). Exprinter, 21 de Mayo 327, T333 5133, xprintur@bibosi.scz.entelnet.bo *Magri Turismo*, Warnes esq Potosí, T334 5663, magri-srz@cotas.com.bo American Express agent. Recommended. *Fremen*, Beni 79, T333 8535, F336 0265. Local tours, also jungle river cruises. *Mario Berndt*, Casilla 3132, T342 0340, tauk@em.daitec-bo.com Does large-scale tailored tours off the beaten track, mostly to the

Bolivia

Altiplano, requires approx 3 months notice, speaks English, German and Spanish and is very knowledgeable about the area. *Jean Paul Ayala*, jpdakidd@roble.scz.entelnet.bo Recommended for birwatching trips, speaks English.

Transport **Local** Taxi: about US$1 inside first Anillo, US$1.20 inside 3rd Anillo, fix fare in advance. **Car hire:** *Aby's*, 3rd Anillo, esq Pasaje Muralto 1038 (opposite zoo), T345 1560, www.abys@khainata.com *Across*, 4th Anillo, esq Radial 27 (400 m from Av Banzer Oeste), T344 1617. US$70 per day for basic Suzuki 4x4 (200 km per day) with insurance. *Barron's*, Av Alemana 50 y Tajibos, T342 0160, www.rentacarbolivia.com

Long distance **Air**: The international airport is at **Viru-Viru**, about 16 km north of the city. Information T181; has Emigration/Immigration office, *Entel* office, luggage lockers, duty free shop, restaurant (expensive), bank open 0830-1830, changes cash and travellers' cheques, withdrawal on Visa and MasterCard (when closed try AASANA desk, where you pay airport tax). Airport bus every 20 mins from the bus terminal, 25 mins (US$0.70), also *colectivos*. Taxi, US$7.50. From airport take bus to bus terminal then taxi to centre. *LAB* flies at least twice daily to **La Paz** and **Cochabamba**, and to **Sucre**, **Tarija** and **Trinidad**. *Aero Sur* flies to **La Paz** (several daily), **Cochabamba, Sucre, Yacuiba** and **Puerto Suárez**. International destinations include most South American capitals, as well as **Salta** and **Córdoba, Rio de Janeiro, São Paulo** and **Manaus, Havana, Panama City, Cancún, Mexico City** and **Miami**. From **Trompillo airport** in the south part of the city, flights in small planes to local destinations. Service is scheduled to end in 2004.

Bus: Long distance buses leave from the new combined bus/train terminal, Terminal Bimodal, on the southeastern edge of the city between Av Brasil and Tres Pasos, between the second and third *anillos*. No 12 bus to/from the centre, taxi US$1.50. T336 0320. Local buses for the time being leave from terminal at Av Cañoto y Av Irala, T333 8391. Daily buses to **Cochabamba** (from US$3-4.50, 10 hrs), many *flotas* leave between 0600-0900 and 1630-2100. Direct to **Sucre** daily between 1700 and 1800, 14 hrs, US$6-7.50. **Oruro** and **La Paz** 16 hrs, US$10.45, between 1700-1930 (some are *buscama*). To **San Ignacio**, see page 331). To **Yacuiba** and **Tarija**, daily, several companies; 26-32 hrs to Tarija. To **Camiri, Cotoca, Montero**, many colectivos and micros from outside *Hotel España* (US$3.75 to Camiri). To **Trinidad**, several daily, 12 hrs, US$4.50, all depart 1700 or 1900. Many companies have offices in streets around terminal; eg *Expreso del Sur, San Lorenzo* and *Expresos Tarija*, but most of these are moving to the new terminal. **International**: *Empresa Yacyretá*, daily **Santa Cruz-Asunción**, US$65, 38 hrs in the dry, no upper limit in the wet. For information T334 9315. Also *Trans Suárez*, T333 7532, for **Asunción, Buenos Aires, Montevideo, Iguazú** and **São Paulo**. *Bolpar* 4 a week to **Asunción** at 1900 with connection to Buenos Aires, Av Monsignor Salvatierra 559, T/F336 6800, but poor service.

Train: Ferroviaria Oriental, T346 3900 ext 307/303. To **Quijarro** (for Brazil) and **Yacuiba** (for Argentina), see below.

Directory **Airline offices** *Aerolíneas Argentinas*, Edif Banco de la Nación Argentina, on main Plaza, T333 9776.

For hospitals, doctors and dentists, contact your consulate or the tourist office for recommendations

Aero Sur, Irala 616, T336 7400. *American Airlines*, Beni 167, T334 1314. *LAB*, Warnes y Chuquisaca, T334 4159. TAM, 21 de Mayo, T337 1999. **Banks** *Banco Mercantil*, René Moreno y Suárez de Figueroa. Cash advance on Visa, changes cash and TCs. *Banco de Santa Cruz*, Junín 154. TCs, bolivianos on Visa and MasterCard, no commission. *Banco Boliviano-Americano*, René Moreno 366 and Colón y Camiri (Siete Calles). *Enlace* cash dispenser for Visa and MasterCard. *Medicambio* on Plaza 24 de Septiembre will change TCs into dollars at 3% commission, excellent reputation. Also on main plaza, *Alemán* (changes TCs at 2% commission for $ or bolivianos). *Menno Credit Union*, 10 de Agosto 15, T332 8800, small office in Mennonite area of town, open 0900-1600, changes TCs, 1% commission, English, German and Dutch spoken. Street money changers on Plaza 24 de Septiembre and around bus terminal. ATMs in airport departure lounge and throughout downtown; also in Equipetrol. **Communications** Internet: cybercafés everywhere, US$0.40-0.80 per hr. **Post Office**: C Junín 146. **Telephone**: *Entel*, Warnes 36 (entre Moreno y Chuquisaca), T332 5526, local and international calls and fax, open Mon-Fri 0730-2330, Sat, Sun and holidays 0730-2200. Also small *Entel* office at Quijarro 267. **Cultural centres** Centro Boliviano Americano, Cochabamba 66, T334 2299. Library with US papers and magazines, English classes, some cultural events. **Instituto Cultural Boliviano Alemán** and **Alianza**

Francesa, 24 de Septiembre 266 (Boliviano Alemán T/F332 9906; Alianza Francesa T333 3392, afscz@roble.scz.entelnet.bo) Joint cultural institute with language courses, cultural events, library (internet access), both open Mon-Fri 0900-1200, 1530 (1600 Alemán)-2000, Francesa Sat 0900-1200. **Centro Iberoamericano de Formación**, Arenales 583, Casilla 875, T335 1322, F332 2217 (concerts, films, art exhibitions, lectures, etc), very good. **Embassies and consulates Argentina**, in Edif Banco de la Nación Argentina, Plaza 24 de Septiembre, Junín 22, T334 7133, Mon-Fri 0800-1300. **Belgium**, Av Cristo Redentor, T342 0662. **Brazil**, Av Busch 330, near Plaza Estudiantes, T333 44400, Mon-Fri 0900-1500. It takes 24 hrs to process visa applications, reported as unhelpful. **Canada**, contact Centro Menno, C Puerto Suárez 28, T334 3773. **Denmark**, Landívar 401, T352 5200, Mon-Fri, 0830-1230, 1430-1830. **France**, Alemania y Mutualista, off the 3rd ring, T343 3434, Mon-Fri 1630-1800. **Germany**, C Ñuflo de Chávez 241, T333 2485, Mon-Fri 0830-1200. **Israel**, Bailón Mercado 171, T342 4777, Mon-Fri 1000-1200, 1600-1830. **Italy**, Av El Trompillo 476, Edif Honnen p 1, T353 1796, Mon-Fri 0830-1200. **Netherlands**, Av Roque Aguilera 300, 3rd ring, between Grigotá and Paraí, Casilla 139, T358 1805, F358 1293, Mon-Fri 0900-1230. **Paraguay**, Manuel Ignacio Salvatierra 99, Edif Victoria, of 1A T336 6113. Colour photo required for visa, Mon-Fri 0730-1400. **Spain**, Monseñor Santiesteban 237, T332 8921, Mon-Fri 0900-1200. **Switzerland**, Cristo Redentador 470, T342 4000, Mon-Fri 0830-1200, 1430-1900. **UK**, Parapetí 28, 2nd floor, T334 5682. **USA**, Güemes Este 6, Equipetrol, T333 3072, Mon-Fri 0900-1130. **Tourist office** In *Prefectura del Departamento* (Direcciones), on the north side of the main plaza, T333 2770 ext 14. New and very impressive; videos; guided tours. *Guía Turística de Santa Cruz*, published by Editora Exclusiva (T336 8655), is available in bookshops. It gives all details on the city. **Useful addresses Immigration**: 3er Anillo Interno esq Av Cronenbold, opposite the zoo, T333 6442/2136, Mon-Fri 0830-1200, 1430-1800.

From Santa Cruz the spectacular old mountain road to Cochabamba runs along the Piray gorge and up into the highlands. Some 120 km from Santa Cruz is Samaipata, a great place to relax mid-week, with good lodging, restaurants, hikes and riding, and a helpful ex-pat community. Local *artesanías* include ceramics. At weekends the town bursts into life as crowds of Cruceños come to escape the city heat and to party.

Samaipata
Phone code: 03
Colour map M6,
grid A4
Altitude: 1,650 m

The **Centro de Investigaciones Arqueológicas y Antropológicas Samaipata** has a collection of pots and vases with anthropomorphic designs, dating from 200 BC to 200 AD and, most importantly, provides information on the nearby pre-Inca ceremonial site commonly called **El Fuerte**. ■ *Centro open daily 0930-1230, 1430-1830; El Fuerte 0900-1700, US$3 including El Fuerte, US$0.75 for Centro de Investigaciones only*. This sacred structure (1,970 m) consists of a complex system of channels, basins, high-relief sculptures, etc, carved out of one vast slab of rock. Latest research on dates is conflicting. Some suggests that Amazonian people created it around 1500 BC, but it could be later. There is evidence of subsequent occupations and that it was the eastern outpost of the Incas' Kollasuyo (their Bolivian Empire). It is no longer permitted to walk on the rock, so visit the museum first to see the excellent model. El Fuerte is 9 km from the town; 3 km along the highway, then 6 km up a rough, signposted road (taxi US$1.20); two hours' walk one way, or drive to the entrance. Pleasant bathing is possible in a river on the way to El Fuerte.

Sleeping and eating C *La Víspera*, 1.2 km south of town, T944 6082, vispera@entelnet.bo Dutch-owned organic farm with accommodation in 4 cosy cabins, camping US$3 (US$4 to hire tent), delicious local produce for breakfast, US$3 pp. Very peaceful; Margarita and Pieter know pretty much everything about the local area and can arrange all excursions through *Bolviajes*. Highly recommended. Across the road is **C** *Cabañas de Traudi*, T944 6094, traudiar@cotas.com.bo Cabins for 2-8, also **E** lovely rooms (**F** with shared bathroom), heated pool US$1.50 for non residents, sitting area with open fire, TV and music system, ceramics shop, great place. **C** *Campeche*, T944 6046, for 2-6 people, all self-catering, **D** midweek, **E** without kitchen. Most central of all the *cabañas* is **C** *Landhaus*, T944 6033. Beautiful place with a small pool, sun loungers, garden, hammocks, parking, internet and sauna (US$20 for up to 8 people), also rooms only with shared bathroom **F**; excellent restaurant and café. Several other *cabañas* west of town, but all very expensive. Hotels in town include **E** *Hostería Mi Casa*, Bolívar, T944 6292. Pretty flower patio, snack bar, **F** with shared bath, 1 *cabaña* (**D**). **F** *Don Jorge*, Bolívar, T944 6086. Cheaper with shared bath, hot showers, good beds, large shaded patio, good set

Rooms may be hard to find at weekends in high season. Most cabins listed have kitchen, bathroom, barbecue and hammocks

lunch. **F** *Aranjuez*, on the main road at the entrance to town, T944 6223. Upstairs terrace, clothes washing area, food available, includes breakfast, good value. **F** *Residencial Kim*, near the plaza, T944 6161. Use of kitchen, **G** with shared bath, good value. **G** *Alojamiento Vargas*, around corner from museum. Clothes-washing facilities, use of kitchen, includes breakfast, owner Teresa is helpful. Recommended. **G** *Paola*, western corner of plaza. Family-run, breakfast extra, good beds, warm showers, use of kitchen, good restaurant, can arrange guides to Amboró and El Fuerte and book microbus to Santa Cruz.

Café Hamburg, Bolívar. Laid back, bar, food (including vegetarian), well stocked book exchange, internet US$2.25 per hr (only after 1900), see *Roadrunners* tour agency below. *El Descanso en Los Alturas*. Wide choice including excellent steaks and pizzas. There are several restaurants on and around the plaza, most of which are cheap. Good *almuerzo* (US$1.05) at Media Vuelta. Dutch-owned *Chakana* bar/restaurant/café open every day 0900-late, relaxing, *almuerzos* for US$2.25, good snacks and salads, seats outside, a book exchange, cakes and ice cream. *Café Baden*, 1 km towards Santa Cruz, good for ice cream and tortes as well as steak and *schweizer würstsalat*. For superb biscuits, bread, home-made pastas, herbs, cheese, yoghurts and cold meats, try Swiss-run *Panadería Gerlinde*, open daily 0700-2200, which also has a weekend stall in the market.

All those in this list are recommended and offer trips to similar destinations. Expect to pay US$15-20 pp in a group of 4

Tour operators *Gilberto Aguilera*, T944 6050, considered the most knowledgeable local guide, good value tours. *Amboró Tours*, T/F944 6293, erickamboro@cotas.com.bo Run by Erick Prado who speaks only Spanish. *Michael Blendinger*, T944 6186, mblendinger@cotas.com.bo German guide who speaks English and Spanish, runs fully-equipped 4WD tours, short and long treks, horse rides, specialist in nature and archaeology. Accommodation in cabins available, also inclusive packages. *Roadrunners*, Olaf and Frank, T944 6193, speak English, enthusiastic, lots of information and advice, recommended tour of El Fuerte. See *La Vispera*, above, Margarita and Pieter, *Bolviajes*. All lead trips to Amboró and other interesting places.

Transport **Buses** leave Santa Cruz from the new bus station Mon-Sat 1600. *Colectivo* taxis run from Tundi 70 near the old terminal, 2 hrs, US$15 per taxi for 4 people. Departures are more frequent early in the day. *Colectivos* in Samaipata will pick you up from your hotel, or else take you from the petrol station. Buses and *micros* leaving Santa Cruz for **Sucre** pass through **Samaipata** between 1800 and 2000; tickets can be booked with 2 days' notice through *Roadrunners*. There's also a bus to Santa Cruz at 0430, 0445 and 0545 Mon-Sat from the plaza outside *El Tambo* store, US$2.25 (ask at *Roadrunners*), and sometimes an afternoon bus. Sun is much easier: buses leave 1100-1530. You can get to **Samaipata** by bus from Sucre; these leave at night and arrive soon after dawn, stopping in Mairana or Mataral for breakfast, about ½ hr before Samaipata.

La Higuera   Some 115 km south of the Santa Cruz-Cochabamba road is La Higuera, where Che Guevara was killed. On 8 October each year, people gather there to celebrate his memory. At *Hospital Nuestro Señor de Malta* you can see the old laundry building where Che's body was shown to the international press on 9 Ocotober 1967. Near the air strip you can see the results of excavations carried out in 1997 which finally unearthed his physical remains (now in Cuba)– ask an airport attendant to see the site. Pedro Calzadillo, headmaster of the school at La Higuera, will guide visitors to the ravine of El Churo, where Che was captured on 8 October 1967. ■ *No fee, but voluntary contribution to the health station, built on the site of the school where Che was held captive till his execution. Sr Calzadillo only speaks Spanish.*

Tours and transport *Flota Bolívar* has 4 daily buses from Santa Cruz to **Vallegrande** via **Samaipata**, 5 hrs, return most days at 0730 and/or 1300. Several pleasant, basic places to stay, all **F-G**, on or around the plaza. Good restaurant on corner of plaza, also several cheap places to eat near market. From Vallegrande market, a daily bus departs 0800 to **Pucara** (45 km), from where there is transport (12 km) to **La Higuera**. Taxi Vallegrande-La Higuera US$20-30. There are now several 'Che' tours of varying quality, including the 3-6-day 'Che

Guevara Trail', which follows the last movements of Che's band of guerrillas through the sub-tropical area bordering Santa Cruz and Chuquisaca departments. The full circuit is 815 km. If considering a tour, book locally, not from La Paz.

Parque Nacional Amboró

This vast (442,500 ha) protected area lies only three hours west of Santa Cruz. Amboró encompasses three distinct major ecosystems and 11 life zones and is home to thousands of animal, plant and insect species (it is reputed to contain more butterflies than anywhere else on earth). The park is home to 712 species of birds, including the blue-horned currasow, the very rare quetzal and cock-of-the-rock, red and chestnut-fronted macaws, hoatzin and cuvier toucans, and most mammals native to Amazonia, such as capybaras, peccaries, tapirs, several species of monkey, and jungle cats like the jaguar, ocelot and margay, and the increasingly rare spectacled bear. There are also numerous waterfalls and cool, green swimming pools, moss-ridden caves and large tracts of virgin rainforest. There are two places to base yourself for a trip into the park: Samaipata (see also page 327) and Buena Vista. Most entrances to the park involve crossing the Río Surutú, which is usually in flood in the wet season.

Much wading is required to get around the park, and there are many biting insects

Northwest of Santa Cruz by paved road is the sleepy town of Buena Vista. The most popular entrance to the park is Las Cruces, 35 km away, reached by a daily morning bus whose route runs alongside the Río Surutú for several km. From Las Cruces, the trail leads directly to the settlement of Villa Amboró, in the park's buffer zone. Also in the buffer zone is Macañucu which has the best services in the park, with horse riding, hiking trails, guides, camping, kitchen area and showers (US$20 per person per day), radio contact with the park office. There is a national park office just over a block from the plaza in Buena Vista, T932 2032 (permit free). Office is closed Sunday and siesta time. They can help with guides and suggestions.

Access from Buena Vista

Sleeping in Buena Vista L *Flora y Fauna*, known as '*Doble F*', T7194-3706 (mob), Casilla 2097, Santa Cruz. Hilltop cabins, viewing platforms for birdwatchers, specialist guiding (Robin Clark has written the definitive guide book to birds in Amboró). **B** *Pozoazul*, on the bypass, T03-932 2091. A/c, kitchen, pool, good restaurant, helpful, also camping US$14 including showers and pool. **D** *Sumuqué*, Av 6 de Agosto 250, T932 2080. Cabins in pleasant gardens, marked trails. **F** *Nadia*, T03-932 2049. Central, small, family run. There are other hotels, cabins and restaurants. In the park: *CARE* has funded cabins on the far bank of the Río Surutú just past Villa Aguiles on the road from Buena Vista to the river. Well-located in the multiple-use area with lots of flora and fauna; good trails.

Tour operators in Buena Vista *Amboró Tours*, near the park office, T03-932 2093, 716 33990 (mob), rodosoto@hotmail.com and *Amboró Adventures*, on the plaza, T03-932 2090, run excursions, US$27-33 pp per day for guide and transportation, not including food. For getting there, see Transport, below.

Transport Regular buses leave from beside Santa Cruz terminal hourly from 0500-1500 (also minibuses from Montero, US$1, and buses from Villa Tunari, US$5) to **Buena Vista**.

The park can be approached from the old Santa Cruz-Cochabamba road. If going on your own from Samaipata, first contact the *Fundación Amigos de la Naturaleza* (*FAN*), Sucre y Murillo, T03-944 6017, www.fan-bo.org, who can offer up-to-date information and will allow trekkers to use their radio telephone to contact the few park rangers in the area. Guides from the community of **La Yunga** charge US$15 per day to explore the park. There is also a *FAN* office in La Yunga near the plaza. Taxi Samaipata-La Yunga, 30 km, US$12 one way, or take a minibus to Mairana, 17 km from Samaipata, and a taxi from there. The village of **Quirusillas** is 1½-2 hours by minibus from Mairana over a bad, but beautiful road. As the area is close to the

Access from Samaipata

mountains, there is more rain than further east, with plenty of greenery and cloud forest. Quirusillas has two basic places to stay and a cemetery set on a hill overlooking a small valley. Lago Quirusillas is about 6 km away via a steep dirt road.

The Chiquitano Jesuit Missions

Six Jesuit churches survive east of Santa Cruz: San Javier, Concepción, Santa Ana, San Rafael, San Miguel and San José de Chiquitos. All are UNESCO World Heritage Sites. The first four were built by the Swiss Jesuit, Padre Martin Schmidt, the other two (plus the one at San Ignacio de Velasco, demolished in 1948, see below) were built by other priests. Besides organizing *reducciones* and constructing churches, for each of which he built an organ, Padre Schmidt wrote music (some is still played today on traditional instruments) and he published a Spanish-Idioma Chiquitano dictionary based on his knowledge of all the dialects of the region. He worked in this part of the then-Viceroyalty of Peru until the expulsion of the Jesuits in 1767 by order of Charles III of Spain.

Access to the mission area is by bus or train from **Santa Cruz**: a paved highway runs north to San Ramón (139 km) and on north, to San Javier (45 km), turning east here to Concepción (68 km) and San Ignacio (unpaved). One road continues east to San Matías and the Brazilian border; others head south either through San Miguel, or Santa Ana to meet at San Rafael for the continuation south to San José de Chiquitos. By rail, leave the Santa Cruz-Quijarro train at San José and from there travel north. The most comfortable way to visit is by jeep, in four days. The route is straightforward and fuel is available. For jeep hire, see page 326.

San Javier   The first Jesuit mission in Chiquitos (1691), its church completed by Padre Schmidt in 1750. The original wooden structure has survived more or less intact and restoration was undertaken between 1987 and 1993 by the Swiss Hans Roth. Subtle designs and floral patterns cover the ceiling, walls and carved columns. One of the bas-relief paintings on the high altar depicts Martin Schmidt playing the piano for his Indian choir. The modern town prospers from extensive cattle ranching. Many fine walks in the surrounding countryside; also good for cycling with an all-terrain bike. Local *fiesta*, 3 December.

Sleeping and eating C *Gran Hotel El Reposo del Guerrero*, T03-963 5022. More expensive Sat-Sun, cheaper with shared bath, includes breakfast, comfortable, restaurant, bar. **E-F** *Alojamiento Ame-Tauna*, on plaza opposite church. Cheaper with shared bath, hot showers, clean. Several hotels in **F-G** range in town and a few kilometres out of town is *Hotel Cabañas Totaitú*, T337 0880, totaitu@em.daitec-bo.com With pool, hot springs, tennis court etc, all included packages, more expensive that most, but has best amenities. Best restaurant is *Ganadero*, in Asociación de Ganaderos on plaza. Excellent steaks. Others on plaza.

Transport *Línea 31 del Este* micros from Santa Cruz, 4 hrs, US$3.50, several between 0800 and 1730; a few buses from the Terminal Bimodal, or from S Arana y Barron. To **Concepción** at 1130, 1830, 1½ hrs, US$1.40.

Concepción   The village is dominated by its magnificent cathedral, completed by Padre Schmidt in 1756 and totally restored by the late Hans Roth between 1975-82. The interior of this beautiful church has an altar of laminated silver. In front of the church is a bell-cum-clock tower housing the original bells and behind it are well-restored cloisters. On the corner of the beautiful plaza is an *Entel* office; also on the plaza is the Communications Centre, with public phones, fax and internet service. There is a tourist office, which can arrange trips to nearby ranches and communities.

Sleeping B *Gran Hotel Concepción*, on plaza, T964 3031, very comfortable, excellent service, including buffet breakfast, pool, bar. Highly recommended. **B** pp *Estancia La Pailita*, 7 km north of Concepción (15 mins by taxi), karin_meyer1960@yahoo.de Full board, Swiss-owned, German, French and English spoken, 2 guest rooms with solar power, Swiss, local and vegetarian food, activities include riding, swimming, nature treks, working on the farm. 1 block from the church is **D** *Apart Hotel Los Misiones*, T964 3021, pleasant rooms around a courtyard, good value. **D-F** *Colonial*, ½ block from plaza, T964 3050, also good value, with hot shower, garden, hammocks on veranda, breakfast extra. **F** *Residencial Westfalia*, 2 blocks from plaza, T9643040, cheaper without bath, German-owned, nice patio. Various restaurants.

Transport Many buses between Santa Cruz and San Ignacio pass through about midnight, but drop you at the gas station on the main road, several blocks from plaza; ask around for transport to centre. *Misiones del Oriente*, on the plaza to Santa Cruz and San Ignacio, *31 del Este micros*, 1 block from plaza, to **Santa Cruz** (US$4.50), and *Flota Jenecheru*, 2 blocks from plaza, buses to **Santa Cruz** and **San Ignacio** (3½ hrs, US$2.80).

A lack of funds for restoration led to the demolition of San Ignacio's Jesuit church in 1948. A modern replacement contains the elaborate high altar, pulpit and paintings and statues of saints. A museum in the Casa de la Cultura on the plaza has a few musical instruments from the old church. Laguna Guapomó on the outskirts of town is good for swimming, boating and fishing. *Entel* two blocks from plaza.

San Ignacio de Velasco

Sleeping and eating A-AL *La Misión*, Plaza 31 de Julio, T962 2333, hotel-lamision @unete.com Luxurious, colonial style with a/c, cable TV and pool, rooms of various standards and prices, includes buffet breakfast, tours arranged. **E** *Casa Suiza*, at the end of C Sucre, 5 blocks west of plaza (taxi US$0.75). Small guesthouse run by Horst and Cristina, German and French spoken, full board, excellent food, very comfortable, family atmosphere, hires horses. Highly recommended. **E** *Palace*, on the plaza. With hot shower, includes breakfast, comfortable, good value. Other hotels (**C-F**) and places to eat near plaza.

Transport Bus: from **Santa Cruz**, *Flota Chiquitana*, from new terminal 1900 daily, 10 hrs, US$6.70; also *Expreso Misiones del Oriente* daily at 1930, T337 8782. From **San Ignacio**: *Flota Chiquitano* and *Trans Velasco* at 1900; *Trans Joá* at 2030 (office on plaza). These companies and several others go to **San Matías** for Brazil (see below), 9 hrs, US$7.50; the final 92 km of road is poor. Some continue to **Cáceres**, 20½ hrs, US$28. To **San José de Chiquitos**, *Transical B*, Mon, Wed, Fri, Sat 1430, *Trans Bolivia*, Tue, Thu, Sun at 0700, US$4.25, 4½ hrs. Micros to **Santa Ana**, **San Rafael** and **San Miguel** from market area; also *Transical B* bus, 5 a day to **San Miguel**, 1 hr, US$1.40, and *Trans Bolivia* to **San Rafael** 0700, 1430, 1½-2 hrs, US$1.40.

Bus companies are based around the market

The church in **Santa Ana** (founded 1755, constructed after the expulsion of the Jesuits), is a lovely wooden building, currently being restored. Sr Luis Rocha will show you inside; ask for his house at the shop on the plaza where the bus stops. Two *alojamientos* in town and meals at Sra Silva's *Pensión El Tacú*, next to church. **San Rafael's** church was completed by Padre Schmidt in 1748. It is the most authentic (still retaining its original thatched roof), perhaps the best, and one of the most beautifully restored (Concepción's also vying for this title), with frescoes in beige paint over the exterior (*Hotel Paradita*, **F**, and two restaurants on plaza). The frescoes on the façade of the church (1766) at **San Miguel** depict St Peter and St Paul; designs in brown and yellow cover all the interior and the exterior side walls. The mission runs three schools and workshop; the sisters are very welcoming and will gladly show tourists around. Some 4 km away is the **Santuario de Cotoca**, beside a lake where you can swim; ask at *La Pascana* for transport. (*Alojamiento y Restaurant La Pascana*, on plaza, basic, cheap meals; just up the hill are two other *alojamientos* and *Entel*.) Most traffic from San Ignacio goes via San Miguel, not Santa Ana, to San Rafael. If visiting these places from San Ignacio, it's probably better to go to San Rafael first, then go back via San Miguel.

Santa Ana, San Rafael & San Miguel
A day trip by taxi from San Ignacio to these villages costs US$35-40 (negotiate)

Bolivia

San José de Chiquitos

Electricity is cut from 0200-0600; the town is lit when trains arrive

The whole of one side of the plaza of this dusty little town is occupied by the superb frontage of the Jesuit mission, begun in the mid-1740s. The stone buildings, in Baroque style, are connected by a wall. They are the restored chapel (1750); the church, unfinished at the expulsion of the Jesuits, with a triangular façade and side walls standing (restoration work in progress); the four-storey bell-tower (1748); the mortuary (*la bóveda* – 1754), with one central window but no entrance in its severe frontage. Behind is a long colonnaded hall. There is an *Entel* office and a hospital. On Monday, Mennonites bring their produce to sell to shops and to buy provisions. The colonies are 50 km west and the Mennonites, who speak English, German, plattdeutsch and Spanish, are happy to talk about their way of life.

About 2 km south from San José is the **Parque Nacional Histórico Santa Cruz la Vieja**, which includes the ruins of the original site of Santa Cruz (about 1540), a *mirador* giving views over the jungle and, 5 km into the park, a sanctuary. The park's heavily-forested hills contain much animal and bird life; various trails; guides available from the small village in the park (take insect repellent). About 1 km past the entrance, at the end of the road at the foot of high hills, is a large swimming pool fed by a mountain stream (open daily, free, no facilities other than changing rooms; take refreshments). The park and pool are best visited by car or taxi because it is a very hot, dusty walk there (allow over one hour on foot). ■ *Entry to park US$2, to pool US$0.40.*

Sleeping and eating C *Hotel Denisse*, 4 blocks east of plaza. Breakfast included, fan. D *Alojamiento San Miguel*, Velasco entre Gericke y 25 de Mayo. Good value, with fan. Recommended. **E-F** *Raquelita*, on the plaza, T972 2037. Good. *El Raffa* (formerly Casa e Paila), between *la tranca* and petrol station on outskirts of town is highly recommended for churrasco típico, inexpensive. Caseta de las Vivanderas, just outside train station. Open 2100-2400 (after train arrives), serves all typical favourites, inexpensive and recommended. *El Solar*, on plaza. Hamburgers, milanesa, salchipapa, cheap. *Romanazzi Pizzería*, Gericke. Run by elderly Italian-Bolivian who makes her own pizzas entirely from scratch. Visit at least 2 hrs before wishing to dine and describe what you'd like, very much worth the wait.

Transport **Train**: schedule from **Santa Cruz** as for Quijarro (see page 335), 8 hrs to San José, standard: Pullman US$6, 1st class US$3.15, 2nd class US$2.30; luxury: *cama* US$24.80, *semi-cama* US$20. To **Quijarro** daily except Sun at 2130; Pullman US$13.15, 1st class US$4.20, 2nd class US$3.30. Ferrobus Sun, Tue, Thu at 2340; *cama* US$21.35, *semi-cama* US$18.20. It is possible to reserve seats on either service at the train station up to a week in advance. Trains to San José are invariably delayed, often by upwards of 6 to 8 hrs and timetables are meaningless. Always reconfirm. **Bus**: to **San Ignacio**, *Transical B* and *Trans Bolivia*, 4½ hrs, US$4.25, each goes every day. Both go via **San Rafael** and **San Miguel**. Leave at 0700 and 1200; $3. Overnight bus to **Santa Cruz** during dry season only (May–Oct), $6 one way.

Parque Nacional Noel Kempff Mercado

In the far northeast corner of Santa Cruz Department, Parque Nacional Noel Kempff Mercado (named after a pioneer of conservation in Bolivia) is one of the world's most diverse natural habitats. It covers 1,583,809 ha (roughly the same size as Massachusetts) and encompasses seven ecosystems, within which are at least 130 species of mammals (including black jaguars), 620 species of birds (including nine types of macaw), 70 species of reptiles and 110 species of orchid. Highlights include the **Huanchaca** or **Caparú Plateau**, which with its 200-500 m sheer cliffs and tumbling waterfalls is another candidate for Sir Arthur Conan Doyle's Lost World (Colonel Percy Fawcett, who discovered the plateau in 1910, was a friend of the writer). The three best-known waterfalls are Arco Iris, Federico Ahlfeld on the Río Paucerna and the 150-m high Catarata del Encanto. The **Reserva Biológica Laguna Bahía**, in the southwest quadrant, has some tremendous hiking across the high plateau, through breathtaking scenery.

Getting there Until a paved road is completed from San Ignacio de Velasco to La Florida on **Ins & outs** the park's southwest edge, access is by plane from Santa Cruz to **Flor de Oro**, in the north/central sector, or to **Los Fierros**, the park's official headquarters, in the south. Flights also go to smaller places, but are irregular. All flights should be arranged through *FAN*. The road journey is long and arduous, eg 13-18 hrs by 4WD to Los Fierros from Santa Cruz, via Concepción and La Florida (40 km west of Los Fierros). Two weekly buses run from San Ignacio de Velasco to **Piso Firme** on the park's western edge (24 hrs, US$9), from where boats can be chartered to Flor de Oro, 5-9 hrs, US$250. Journey times depend on the season, state of the roads and river conditions. Tours can be arranged with operators in La Paz, Santa Cruz and, when the new road is finished, San Ignacio de Velasco. Prices for a 7-day/6-night tour range from US$915-1170, not including flights (*América Tours*, La Paz). Shorter tours are available.

Information Entry to park costs US$8. The *Fundación de Amigos de la Naturaleza* (*FAN*), C Agreda 1100 esq Burqueque, Casilla 2241, Santa Cruz, T03-332 9717, F332 9692, rvaca@ fan-bo.org, manages the park. Contact Richard Vaca, websites are www.noel kempff.com and www.mcei.gov.bo/web_mcei/turismo/destinos/ noelkemp.htm (in Spanish).

There are 2 lodges in the park: 15 beds at a renovated ranch at **Flor de Oro**, which gives **Sleeping** access to hiking in the pampas and forests, and river excursions to the Arco Iris and Federico Ahlfeld falls and to bays. At **Los Fierros** there are 30 beds at a more rustic facility, **B** pp including 3 meals. From here you can visit many different habitats and El Encanto falls. There are other lodging possibilities in small towns bordering the park and some camping is available. In all cases, contact *FAN*.

Travel to Brazil

There are three routes from Santa Cruz: by air to **Puerto Suárez**, by rail to **Quijarro**, or by road via **San Matías**. Puerto Suárez is near Quijarro and these two routes lead to Corumbá on the Brazilian side, from where there is access to the **southern Pantanal**. The San Matías road links to **Cáceres**, **Cuiabá** and the **northern Pantanal** in Brazil.

On the shore of Laguna Cáceres, this is a friendly, quiet, small town, with a shady **Puerto Suárez** main plaza. There is a nice view of the lake from the park at the north end of Avenida *Phone code: 03* Bolívar. The area around the train station is known as *Paradero*. Do not venture into *Colour map 6, grid B6* the market area unless you are looking to contract any one of innumerable intestinal *Population: 21,000* illnesses, and/or have your pockets picked. Fishing and photo tours to the ecologically-astonishing Pantanal can be arranged more cheaply than on the Brazilian side. You can also arrange river tours and day trips to Brazil; these are generally most easily done through a hotel, although they will add a 10-15% service charge (see below).

Sleeping and eating AL pp *Centro Ecológico El Tumbador*, T03-762 8699, T7106 7712 (mob), eltumbador@ yahoo.com A non-profit-making organization working for sustainable development in the Bolivian Lowlands runs ½-day to 4-day river, trekking and 4WD tours from its research station and lodge on the lake; prices from US$82 per person all-inclusive. **C** *Bamby*, Santa Cruz 31 y 6 de Agosto, T976 2015. A/c, **D** with fan, cheaper with shared bath, comfortable. **C** *Frontera Verde*, Vanguardia 24 y Simón Bolívar, T976 2468, F62470. Best in town, a/c, **D** with fan, breakfast included, parking, English spoken. **C-D** *Sucre*, Bolívar 63 on main plaza, T976 2069. A/c, with bath, pleasant, good restaurant. **D** *Beby*, Av Bolívar 111, T976 2270. A/c, **E** with shared bath and fan. **D** *Ejecutivo*, at south end of Bolívar, T976 2267. A/c, parking, cheaper with fan. **D** *Roboré*, 6 de Agosto 78, T976 2170. Fan, **E** with shared bath, basic, restaurant next door. **E** *Progreso*, Bolívar 21. Shared bath, basic. **E** *Res Puerto Suárez*, Bolívar 105. Shared bath, showers, basic. Beware the water, it is straight from the river. *Parillada Jenecherú*, Bolívar near plaza. Opposite is *Al Paso*, Bolívar 43. Very good value set meals and à la carte, popular. *El Taxista*, Bolívar 100 block. Several other small inexpensive restaurants nearby.

Tour operators *R B Travel*, Bolívar 65 by Plaza, T976 2014, for airline tickets, helpful.

Bolivia

Bolivia

Immigration office at airport issues Bolivian exit/entry stamps

Transport **Taxi**: to Paradero US$1.65; to airport US$2; to Quijarro or the border, US$5 (day), US$6 (night) or US$0.80 pp in a colectivo. **Air**: airport is 6 km north of town, T976 2347; airport tax US$2. Flights on Mon and Fri to/from Santa Cruz with *Aero Sur*. *TAM* to Santa Cruz, continues to Trinidad and La Paz. Do not buy tickets for flights originating in Puerto Suárez in Corumbá, you will have to pay more. **Train**: the station for Puerto Suárez is about 3 km from town. It is the first station west of Quijarro.

Directory Airline offices: *LAB*, La Paz 33, T976 2241. *Aero Sur*, Bolívar near plaza, T976 2581. *TAM*, C del Chaco s/n, T976 2205. **Banks**: *Supermercado Tocale* changes Bolivianos, reais and US$, cash only. **Embassies and consulates**: Brazilian Consulate, Santa Cruz entre Bolívar y 6 de Agosto.

Quijarro

Colour map 6, grid B6
Population: 15,000

The eastern terminus of the Bolivian railway, and the gateway to Brazil, is Quijarro, an unappealing town created around the railway station. There have been reports of drug trafficking and related problems in this border area and caution is recommended.

Water supply is often unreliable, try tap before checking in. Most people prefer to go on to Corumbá where hotels are better. The food stalls by the station and market are best avoided

Sleeping and eating **C** *Santa Cruz*, Av Brazil 2 blocks east of station, T978 2113, F978 2044. A/c, cheaper with fan, **D** with shared bath, good rooms, nice courtyard, good restaurant, parking. Highly recommended. **D** *Gran Hotel Colonial*, Av Brazil y Panamá, T/F978 2037. A/c, cheaper with fan, **E** with shared bath, good restaurant. **D** *Oasis*, Av Argentina 20, T978 2159. A/c, fridge, cheaper with shared bath and a/c, **E** with fan, OK. **D** *Yoni*, Av Brazil opposite the station, T978 2109. A/c, fridge, **E** with shared bath and fan, comfortable, mosquito netting on windows. **F** *Res Paratí*, Guatemala s/n. Shared bath, fan, laundry facilities. In Arroyo Concepción (see below) is **L** El Pantanal Resort, T978 2020 (ask for Keila Vieria), with all mod cons (poor internet connection), gateway to the Pantanal. They arrange cruises, tours and transport, expensive but worth it, discounts in dry season (very busy in Jan-Feb).

Tour operators *Santa Cruz*, in hotel of same name, sells airline tickets.

Transport **Taxi** to the border (Arroyo Concepción) US$0.40 pp; to Puerto Suárez US$0.80 pp, more at night. See Border with Brazil, below, for train details.

Directory **Banks**: Bolivianos, reais and US$ cash traded along Av Brazil opposite the station by changers with large purses sitting in lawn chairs; good rates, but beware of tricks. **Communications**: Telephone: *Entel*, at the south end of Av Naval, national and international calls, Mon-Sat 0700-2300, Sun 0700-2000. Also small office at Guatemala y Brazil near the station.

Border with Brazil

You can leave Bolivia at Quijarro when the border post is closed, but you have to return from Brazil for a Bolivian exit stamp within 8 days

The municipality by the border is known as Arroyo Concepción. You need not have your passport stamped if you visit Corumbá for the day. Otherwise get your exit stamp at Bolivian immigration (see below), formalities are straightforward. There are no formalities on the Brazilian side, you must get your entry stamp in Corumbá (see page 568); there is also an office at the bus station which is usually closed. Yellow Fever vaccination is compulsory to enter Bolivia and Brazil, have your certificate in hand when you go for your entry stamp, otherwise you may be sent to get revaccinated. Bolivian immigration is at the border at Arroyo Concepción, blue building on right just before bridge (opens 0700, closed for lunch 1130-1400) also at Puerto Suárez airport and in San Matías. Passports may be stamped at Santa Cruz station if leaving by train, which may avoid spurious exit charges at Quijarro. Money can be exchanged at the Quijarro border. You will probably only be able to sell bolivianos in Bolivia. The Brazilian consulate is in Santa Cruz, or in Puerto Suárez.

Transport **Air** The simplest way to Brazil is to fly to **Puerto Suárez** then share a taxi to the border, US$6 per car. See Puerto Suárez Transport above. *Servicio Aéreo Pantanal* flies daily from Santa Cruz to **San Matías** (office at El Trompillo airport, T03-353 1066).

Road The road route from Santa Cruz is via San Ignacio de Velasco to San Matías, a busy little town with hotels and restaurants then on to Cáceres and Cuiabá. From Santa Cruz it is a

3-day trip, roads permitting. See under San Ignacio, page 331, for bus information. Get your passport stamped in San Ignacio as there is no passport control in San Matías, but plenty of military checks en route. Once in Brazil go to immigration in Cáceres or, on Sun, to Polícia Federal in Cuiabá.

Train There is no direct service between Santa Cruz and Brazil. All trains from Santa Cruz go via San José de Chiquitos to Quijarro, from where travellers must go by *colectivo* to the border post (beware overcharging, fare should be US$0.40 pp), then by bus to Corumbá. Standard service, 20 hrs, leaves daily except Sun at 1530; Pullman US$16.25, 1st class US$7.20, 2nd class US$6; returns at 1500 Mon-Sat. A *ferrobus* runs Tue, Thu, Sun at 1900, returning Mon, Wed, Fri 1900, 13 hrs, US$31.55 *semi-cama*, 36.55 *cama* (not as luxurious as it claims). Take food, drinking water, insect repellent and a torch, whichever class you are travelling. From Mar-Aug take a sleeping bag for the cold; be prepared for delays. Tickets may be purchased the day prior to travel, counter opens at 0800, go early because queues form hours before and tickets sell fast. Take passport. At Quijarro station, Willy Solís Cruz, T978 2204, runs a left-luggage room, speaks English, very helpful, assists with ticket purchases for US$3 (has been known to let people sleep in the luggage room). The Quijarro ticket office sells tickets only on day of departure, open 0700-1600, queuing starts much earlier, it gets crowded, much pushing and shoving, touts resell tickets at hugely inflated prices. For a couple of dollars more you can buy tickets at agencies near the border without the queues. To buy tickets you must take your passport showing all relevant entry and exit stamps. Note that times of departure from Quijarro are approximate as they depend on when trains arrive. 500 m from station is a modern, duty-free a/c shopping complex with banks, restaurants and pool.

Travel to Paraguay

South of Santa Cruz the road passes through Abapó and Camiri. A paved road heads south from Camiri, through Boyuibe, Villamontes and Yacuiba to Argentina (see below). At Boyuibe another road heads east to Paraguay, used less now than a new road from Villamontes (see below) to Mariscal Estigarribia in the Paraguayan Chaco. It is possible, albeit foolish, to drive from Boyuibe into Paraguay direct on the old road in a truck or four-wheel drive, high clearance vehicle, carry insect repellent, food and water for a week. No help can be relied on in case of a breakdown; a winch is advisable, especially after rain. There are some rivers to ford and although they are dry in the dry season they can be impassable if there is rain in the area. The new route, once you leave the paved road at Villamontes, should be treated with the same respect. Boyuibe is the last town in Bolivia where exit stamps can be obtained if going to Paraguay (*Alojamiento Boyuibe*, has hot showers, restaurant, and two others, all **G**). All buses stop at *Parador-Restaurante Yacyretá*, on main road, owners are helpful, sell bus tickets to Asunción and have rooms to rent; change cash here (poor rates) or at immigration. Fuel and water are available. Passports are stamped at military checkpoint. If travelling by bus, passports are collected by driver and returned on arrival at Mcal Estigarribia, Paraguay, with Bolivian exit stamp. Paraguayan entry stamps are given in Pozo Colorado. As entry stamps are not given at Mcal Estigarribia, to visit the Chaco legally you must stay on the bus to Pozo Colorado, then return to the Chaco. Enquire locally for alternatives. See under Santa Cruz, page 326, for international bus services.

South of Boyuibe is Villamontes, renowned for fishing and infamous for its heat (second only to Villazón). It holds a Fiesta del Pescado in August. It is a friendly town on the edge of the Gran Chaco and is on the road and rail route from Santa Cruz to the Argentine border at Yacuiba. You can change buses here to/from Paraguay on the Santa Cruz-Yacuiba bus route, or to/from Tarija (Monday and Thursday), or if coming from Sucre. There are two banks (no ATM, exchange limited), *TAM* office (T672 2135) and internet café (next to *El Arriero* restaurant) on Plaza 15 de Abril. *Entel* is one block northeast of this plaza.

Villamontes
Phone code: 04
Colour map 6, grid B4
280 km E of Tarija

Bolivia

Sleeping and eating C pp *El Rancho*, 3 km from centre opposite station (taxi US$0.45) T672 2059, F672 2985. Lovely rooms, a/c, TV, excellent restaurant, also annexe **F** pp. Recommended. **C** *Gran Hotel Avenida*, 3 blocks east of Plaza 15 de Abril, T672 2297, F672 2412. A/c, includes breakfast, helpful owner, parking. **F** *Res Raldes*, 1 block from Plaza 15 de Abril, T672 2088. **G** pp without bath, neat rooms, poor showers. **E** *Res Miraflores*, 500 block of main Av. **F** without bath, basic, not very clean, owner Rolando Rueda arranges fishing trips. Good, cheap meals at *Parillada El Arriero*, Plaza 15 de Abril. For pizzas and grilled meat, *Churrasquería Argentina*, ½ block from same plaza. Locals favour *Bar Cherenta*, Plaza 15 de Abril, and for ice cream *Heladería Noelia*, halfway from the plaza to bus station.

Transport Air: *TAM* flies to **La Paz**, Sucre and Tarija on Sun and Santa Cruz on Sat. **Bus**: to **Tarija** via Entre Ríos (unpaved road, 10 hrs) Thu 0500 and 0600, Sun 0600, US$7.50; via Yacuiba 3 daily, 10 hrs. To **Santa Cruz** at 1030, 12 hrs, US$4.50, **Sucre** at 1930, US$7.50, and **La Paz** at 2000, US$9. Also to **Camiri**, **Tupiza**, **Villazón**. **Train**: for **Yacuiba** on Mon, Wed and Fri at 0400, US$1.20 and for **Santa Cruz** on Tue, Thu and Sat at 1930, US$11.35 (Pullman), US$5.25 (1st class), US$4.20 (2nd class). **Car**: the road to **Paraguay** runs east to Ibibobo. The first 80 km is an all-weather gravel surface. From Ibibobo to the frontier at Picada Sucre is 75 km, then it's 15 km to the border and another 8 km to the Paraguayan frontier post at Fortín Infante Rivarola. There are no police or immigration officials at the border.

Travel to Argentina

Yacuiba
Colour map 6, grid B4
Population: 11,000

From Santa Cruz the route goes Boyuibe, Villamontes and Yacuiba, a prosperous city at the crossing to Pocitos in Argentina. From Villamontes to Yacuiba road is paved, but no bridges; river crossings tricky in wet season. In Yacuiba, there is **C** *Hotel París*, Comercio y Campero, T682 2182, the best. **C** *Monumental*, Comercio 1270, T682 2088, includes breakfast. **D** *Valentín*, Avenida San Martín 1462, opposite rail station, T682 2645, F682 2317, **E** without bath, excellent value. Also *Entel* and post Correos. Argentine consul at Comercio y Sucre. The border crossing is straightforward. Passengers leaving Bolivia must disembark at Yacuiba, take a taxi to Pocitos on the border (US$0.40, beware unscrupulous drivers) and walk across to Argentina.

Transport   **Train** Santa Cruz-Yacuiba trains on Mon, Wed, Fri 1700, arrive 0600-0700, Pullman US$14, 1st class US$6.70, 2nd class US$5.40; return to Santa Cruz Tue, Thu, Sat 1700. **Bus** Good connections in all directions. To **Santa Cruz**, about 20 companies run daily services, mostly at night, 14 hrs, US$13. To **Tarija**, daily morning and evening. To **Potosí-Oruro-La Paz**, with *Trans Yacuiba* and *Expreso Tarija*. Daily to **Sucre** with *Flota Copacabana*.

Brazil

Brazil

Described as the sexiest nation on earth, Brazilians know how to flirt, flaunt and have fun. The Rio Carnival, with its intoxicating atmosphere and costumes to die for, is the most exuberant of a whole calendar of festivals. In this, the world's fifth largest country, football, looking good and dancing are the national passions. Everyone seems to be seduced by the sounds of samba...and by the beach.

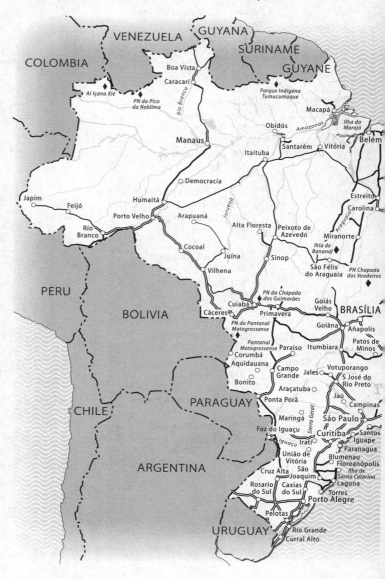

The coast of Brazil, all 7,408 km of it, has provided a suitable stretch of sand for every volley-ball champion, surfer, dune-buggy driver and party animal. Just off shore there are many islands to sail to, from the huge Marajó with its water buffalo, to highly developed Santa Catarina, to the marine paradise of Abrolhos National Park. Brazilians have a spiritual side to match their hedonistic streak. Many religions flourish, most obviously the African-based candomblé, which lives happily alongside Catholicism. In the 16th-18th centuries, when Brazil was rich in gold and diamonds, the Portuguese colonists expressed their faith in some of the most beautiful baroque buildings created anywhere at that time. For a change from cosmopolitan life, trek through the hills of the Chapada Diamantina, take the long road into the Pantanal wetlands and watch for hyacinth macaws and capybara, sling a hammock on a river boat up the mighty Amazon, or take a walk with the wildlife in the rainforest.

Essentials

Planning your trip

Where to go Rio de Janeiro was for a long time THE image of Brazil, with its beautiful setting – the Sugar Loaf and Corcovado overlooking the bay and beaches, its world renowned carnival, the nightlife and its *favelas* (slums – which are now being incorporated into tourism). It is still a must on many itineraries, but Rio de Janeiro state has plenty of other beaches, national parks and colonial towns (especially **Paraty**) and the imperial city of **Petrópolis**. **São Paulo** is the country's industrial and financial powerhouse; with some fine museums and its cultural life and restaurants are very good. All the São Paulo coast is worth visiting and inland there are hill resorts and colonial towns. The **state of Minas Gerais** contains some of the best colonial architecture in South America in cities such as Ouro Preto, Mariana, São João del Rei and Diamantina. All are within easy reach of the state capital, Belo Horizonte. Other options in Minas include national parks with good hill scenery and bird-watching and hydrothermal resorts.

The atmosphere of the **South** is dominated by its German and Italian immigrants. The three states, Paraná, Santa Catarina and Rio Grande do Sul have their coastal resorts, especially near Florianópolis, capital of Santa Catarina. **Rio Grande do Sul** is the land of Brazil's *gaúchos* (cowboys) and of its vineyards, but the main focus of the region is the magnificent **Iguaçu Falls** in the far west of Paraná, on the borders of Argentina and Paraguay.

The **Northeast** is famous for beaches and colonial history. Combining both these elements, with the addition of Brazil's liveliest African culture, is **Salvador de Bahia**, one of the country's most famous cities and a premier tourist destination. Huge sums of money have been lavished on the restoration of its colonial centre and its carnival is something special. Inland, Bahia is mostly arid *sertão*, in which a popular town is **Lençóis**, a historical monument with a nearby national park. The highlight of the southern coast of Bahia is the beach and party zone around **Porto Seguro**, while in the north the beaches stretch up to the states of Sergipe and Alagoas and on into Pernambuco. **Recife**, capital of Pernambuco, and its neighbour, the colonial capital **Olinda**; also mix the sea, history and culture, while inland is the major handicraft centre of Caruaru. Travelling around to the north-facing coast, there are hundreds of beaches to choose from, some highly developed, others less so. You can swim, surf or ride the dunes in buggies. Last stop before the mouth of the Amazon is **São Luís**, in whose centre most of the old houses are covered in colonial tiles.

Through the **North** flows the **Amazon**, along which river boats ply between the cities of Belém, Santarém and Manaus. From **Manaus** particularly there are opportunities for exploring the jungle on adventurous expeditions or staying in lodges. North of Manaus is the overland route through Boa Vista to Venezuela. The forest stretches south to the central tableland which falls to the **Pantanal** in the far west. This seasonal wetland, the highlight of the **Centre West**, is one of the prime areas for seeing bird and animal life in the continent. At the eastern end of the Centre West is **Brasília**, built in the 1960s and now a World Heritage Site in recognition of its superb examples of modern architecture. Also in this region is one of the largest river islands in the world (Bananal – a mecca for fishing) and the delightful hill and river landscapes of **Bonito** in Mato Grosso do Sul.

When to go Brazil is a tropical country, but the further south you go the more temperate the winters become and there are places in the coastal mountains which have gained a reputation for their cool climate and low humidity. The heaviest rains fall at different times in the different regions: November to March in the southeast, December to March in the centre west and April to August on the northeast coast around Pernambuco (irregular rainfall causes severe draughts). The rainy season in the north and Amazônia can begin in December and is heaviest March-May, but it is getting steadily shorter, possibly as a result of deforestation. It is only in rare cases that the rainfall can be described as either excessive or deficient: few places get more than 2,000 mm – the coast north of Belém, some of the Amazon Basin, and a small area of the Serra do Mar between Santos and São Paulo, where the downpour has been harnessed to generate electricity.

May to September is usually referred to as winter, but this is not to suggest that this is a bad time to visit. On the contrary, April to June and August to October are recommended times to go to most parts of the country. One major consideration is that carnival falls within the hottest, wettest time of year (in February), so if you are incorporating carnival into a longer holiday, it may be wet wherever you go. Also bear in mind that mid-December to February is the national holiday season, which means that hotels, planes and buses may be full and many establishments away from the holiday areas may be shut.

The average annual temperature increases steadily from south to north, but even on the Equator, in the Amazon Basin, the average temperature is not more than 27°C. The highest recorded was 42°C, in the dry northeastern states. From the latitude of Recife south to Rio, the mean temperature is from 23° to 27°C along the coast, and from 18° to 21°C in the Highlands. From a few degrees south of Rio to the boundary with Uruguay the mean temperature is from 17° to 19°C. Humidity is relatively high in Brazil, particularly along the coast.

Finding out more
Phone codes explained in Keeping in touch

The national **tourist board** is Embratur. Its head office is at Setor Comercial Norte, Quadra 02, Bloco G, 70712-907, Brasília, BF, Brazil; T0xx61-429 7777, F0xx61-429 7910, www.embratur.gov.br For information abroad, contact Brazil's representation overseas, see box on page 344. Tourist information bureaux are not usually helpful with information on cheap hotels and it is difficult to get information on neighbouring states. The expensive hotels provide tourist information magazines for their guests. Telephone directories (not Rio) contain good street maps.

National parks are run by Ibama, the Instituto Brasileiro do Meio Ambiente e dos Recursos Naturais Renováveis (Brazilian Institute of Environmental Protection): SCEN, Avenida L-4 Norte, Edifiço Sede de Ibama, CEP 70819-900, Brasília, DF, T0xx61-226 8221/9014, F0xx61-322 1058, www.ibama.gov.br The Institute is underfunded, understaffed and visitors may find it difficult to get information. National parks are open to visitors, usually with a permit from Ibama. See also the Ministério do Meio Ambiente website, www.mma.gov.br For further details, see individual parks.

Brazil

Useful websites www.ipanema.com Insider's guide to Rio in English. www.copacabana.com On Copacabana in Portuguese. Two websites for the English-speaking community in Rio: www.umbrellaonline.com.br More on lifestyle than the news-based www.expats. com.br www.maria-brazil.org is a fun site with info, tips, recommendations, mostly about Rio, but other regions, too. São Paulo: www.cityofsaopaulo.com Bahia: www.bahia tursa.ba.gov.br/ and www.uol.com.br/ agendasalvador Paraná: www.pr.gov.br/ turismo The following embassy sites have lots of information: www.brazil.org.au in Australia. www.brasilemb.org in Washington, DC. www.brazil.org.uk in London. www.at brazil.com is mostly a guide to hotels and resorts, but it has a currency converter and general info. www.brazilianmusic.com with introductions to musical styles and musicians, with more besides. www.brazilinfo.net is a portal in English. www.brazil-brasil.com is a wide-ranging site with news articles, chat room, culture and entertainment. www.vivabrazil.com a 'virtual trip', with news, history, chat. See www.terra.com.br/turismo/ for tourist information in Portuguese. www.wwf.org.br The World Wide Fund for Nature in Brazil.

Language
For the low-budget traveller, Portuguese is essential

The language is Portuguese. Efforts to speak it are greatly appreciated. If you cannot speak Portuguese, apologize and try Spanish, but note that the differences in the spoken languages are very much greater than appears likely from the printed page and you may well not be understood: you will certainly have difficulty in understanding the answers. One important point of spelling is that words ending in 'i' and 'u' are accented on the last syllable, though (unlike Spanish) no accent is used there. This is especially important in place names: Parati, Iguaçu. Note also that 'meia' (half) is frequently used for number six (ie half-dozen). There are Brazilian tutors in most cities (in London, see *Time Out* and *Leros*, the Brazilian magazine, for advertisements).

Volunteering In addition to suggestions in Essentials at the front of the Handbook, contact **RioVoluntário**, which supports 450 voluntary organizations, from environmental to healthcare. T +55-21-2262 1110, ask for Isadora or Fábio, www.riovoluntario.org.br in Portuguese and English.

Before you travel

Visas & immigration

Nationalities which do not need a visa Consular visas are not required for stays of up to 90 days by tourists from Andorra, Argentina, Aruba, Austria, Bahamas, Barbados, Belgium, Bermuda, Bolivia, Chile, Colombia, Costa Rica, Denmark, Ecuador, Finland, France, Germany, Greece, Iceland, Ireland, Israel, Italy, Liechtenstein, Luxembourg, Malaysia, Monaco, Morocco, Namibia, Netherlands, Norway, Paraguay, Peru, Philippines, Portugal, San Marino, South Africa, Spain, Suriname, Sweden, Switzerland, Thailand, Trinidad and Tobago, United Kingdom, Uruguay, the Vatican and Venezuela. For them, only the following documents are required at the port of disembarkation: a passport valid for at least six months (or *cédula de identidad* for nationals of Argentina, Chile, Paraguay and Uruguay); and a return or onward ticket, or adequate proof that you can purchase your return fare, subject to no remuneration being received in Brazil and no legally binding or contractual documents being signed. Venezuelan passport holders can stay in Brazil for 60 days on filling in a form at the border.

Visas US and Canadian citizens, Australians and New Zealanders and people of other nationalities, and those who cannot meet the requirements above, *must* get a visa before arrival, which may, if you ask, be granted for multiple entry. Visas are valid form date of issue. Visa fees vary from country to country, so apply to the Brazilian consulate, in the country of residence of the applicant. The consular fee in the USA is US$100. Do not lose the emigration permit they give you when you enter Brazil. Leaving the country without it, you may have to pay a fine.

Renewals Foreign tourists may stay a maximum of 180 days in any one year. 90-day renewals are easily obtainable, but only at least 15 days before the expiry of your 90-day permit, from the Polícia Federal. The procedure varies, but generally you have to fill out three copies of the tax form at the Polícia Federal, take them to a branch of Banco do Brasil, pay US$15 and bring two copies back. You will then be given the extension form to fill in and be asked for your passport to stamp in the extension. According to regulations (which should be on display) you should be able to show a return ticket, cash, cheques or a credit card, a personal reference and proof of an address of a person living in the same city as the office (in practice you simply write this in the space on the form). Some offices will only give you an extension within 10 days of the expiry of your permit. Some points of entry, such as the Colombian border refuse entry for longer than 30 days, renewals are then for the same period, insist if you want 90 days. For longer stays you must leave the country and return (not the same day) to get a new 90-day permit. If your visa has expired, getting a new visa can be costly (US$35 for a consultation, US$30 for the visa itself) and may take anything up to 45 days, depending on where you apply. If you overstay your visa, or extension, you will be fined US$7 per day, with no upper limit. After paying the fine to Polícia Federal, you will be issued with an exit visa and must leave within eight days. If you cannot pay the fine you must pay when you next return to Brazil. **NB** Officially, if you leave Brazil within the 90-day permission to stay and then re-enter the country, you should only be allowed to stay until the 90-day permit expires. If, however, you are given another 90-day permit, this may lead to charges of overstaying if you apply for an extension. For UK citizens a joint agreement allows visits for business or tourism of up to six months a year from the date of first entry.

Identification You must always carry identification when in Brazil; it is a good idea to take a photocopy of the personal details in your passport, plus that with your Brazilian immigration stamp, and leave your passport in the hotel safe deposit. Always keep an independent record of your passport details. It is a good idea to register with your consulate to expedite document replacement if yours gets lost or stolen.

Customs

Duty free allowance Clothing and personal articles are free of import duty. Cameras, movie cameras, portable radios, tape-recorders, typewriters and binoculars are also admitted free if there is not more than one of each. Tourists may also bring in, duty-free, 24 alcoholic drinks (no more than 12 of any one type), 400 cigarettes, 25 cigars, 280 g of perfume, up to 10 units of cosmetics, up to three each of any electronic item or watch, up to a total value of US$500 monthly. There is a limit of US$150 at land borders and a written declaration must be made to this effect. Duty free goods may only be purchased in foreign currency.

Vaccinations

Proof of vaccination against yellow fever is necessary if you are visiting Amazônia and the Centre-West, or are coming from countries with Amazonian territories, such as Bolivia, Colombia, Ecuador and Peru. It is strongly recommended to have an inoculation before visiting northern Brazil since those without a certificate will be inoculated on entering any of the northern and centre-western states. Although the vaccination is free it might be administered in unsanitary conditions. Yellow fever (see page 61) and some other vaccinations can be obtained from the Ministério da Saúde, R Cais de Pharoux, Rio de Janeiro. Less common ones can be obtained at Saúde de Portos, Praça 15 de Novembro, Rio de Janeiro. If visiting the Amazon basin, get vaccinations against hepatitis and typhoid. Poliomyelitis vaccination is required for children from three months to six years.

Money

Currency The unit of currency is the *real*, R$ (plural *reais*). It floats freely against the dollar. Any amount of foreign currency and 'a reasonable sum' in *reais* can be taken in; residents may only take out the equivalent of US$4,000. Notes in circulation are: 100, 50, 10, 5 and 1 *real*; coins 1 *real*, 50, 25, 10 and 5 centavos.

*real exchange rate with US$: 2.94, Jun 2003
Banks open 1000-1600 (1630 Mon-Fri)*

Banks In major cities banks will change cash and travellers' cheques. If you keep the exchange slips, you may convert back into foreign currency up to 50% of the amount you exchanged. This applies to the official markets only; there is no right of reconversion unless you have an official exchange slip. The black market, found in travel agencies, exchange houses and among hotel staff, was of marginal benefit compared with bank rates in 2001. Travellers' cheques are usually lower than for cash and they are less easy to change; commission may be charged. Many banks may only change US$300 minimum in cash, US$500 in travellers' cheques. Dollars cash are becoming more frequently used for tourist transactions and are also useful for those places where travellers' cheques cannot be

MONEY

▶ Brazilian embassies and consulates

Australia, *19 Forster Crescent, Yarralumla,
Canberra ACT 2600, T00612-6273 2372,
brazil@connect.net.au* **Consulate**, *St
Martins Tower L 17, 31 Market Street, Sydney
NSW 2000, T00612-9267 4414, F9267 4419,
consulado@brazilsydney.org*
Austria, *Am Lugeck 1/5/15, A-1010 Wien,
T00431-512 0631, F513 8374,
ausbrem@utanet.at*
Belgium, *350 Avenue Louise, 6eme Étage,
Boite 5-1050 Bruxelles, T00322-640 2015/
640 2111, F640 8134, brasbruxelas@beon.be*
Canada, *450 Wilbrod Street, Sandyhill,
Ottawa, ON K1N 6M8, T001613-237 1090,
F237 6144, mailbox@brasembottawa.org*
Denmark, *Ryvangs Alle, 24-2100 Kobenhavn,
T00453-920 6478, F927 3607,
embaixada@brazil.dk*
France, *34 Cours Albert I, 75008 Paris,
T00331-4561 6300, F4289 0345,
www.bresil.org*
Germany, *Kennedyallee 74, 53175 Bonn,
T0049228-959230, F373696,
brasil@brasemberlim.de*
Ireland, *Harcourt Centre, Europa House,
5th Floor, 41-54 Harcourt Street, Dublin 2,
T003531-475 6000/475 1338, F475 1341,
irlbra@iol.ie*
Israel, *Beit Yachin, 2 Kaplan Street, 8th Floor,
Tel Aviv, T009723-696 3934, F691 6060,
embrisra@netvision.net.il*
Italy, *14 Piazza Navona, 00186 Roma,
T003906-683981, F686 7858, brasital@tin.it*
Japan, *11-12 Kita-Aoyama 2-Chome,
Minato-Ku, Tokyo 107, T00813-3404 5211,
www.brasemb.or.jp*

Netherlands, *Mauritskade 19-2514 HD,
The Hague, T003170-302 3959,
F302 3950, brasemb@dataweb.nl*
New Zealand, *10 Brandon St,
Wellington 1, T00644-473 3516,
F473 3517, brasemb@ihug.co.nz*
Norway, *Sigurd Syrs Gate 4, 1st floor,
0244 Oslo, T0047-2254 0741,
F2254 0730, noruega@online.no*
Portugal, *Estrada das Laranjeiras,
144-1600 Lisboa, T003511-726 7777,
F726 7623, embrasilport@mail.telepac.pt*
Spain, *Calle Fernando El Santo,
6 DP 28010 Madrid, T00341-700 4650,
F700 4660, chanceleria@
embajadadebrasil.es*
Consulate*Carrer Consell de Cent, 357/
1a Ed Brasilia, 08007 Barcelona,
T0034-934-882288, F934-872645.*
Sweden, *Sturgegatan 11, 2 Tr, S114 36
Stockholm, T00468-234010, F234018,
stockholm@brasemb.se*
Switzerland, *Monbijouster 68-3007
Berne, T004131-371 8515,
F371 0525, brasbern@iprolink.ch*
UK, *32 Green Street, London WIY 4AT,
T004420-7399 9000, F7399 9100,
info@brazil.org.uk*
Consulate, *6 St Albans Street,
London SW1Y 4SQ, T004420-7930 9055,
F7839 8958.*
USA, *3006 Massachusetts Avenue
NW, Washington DC 20008-3699,
T001202-238 2700/2805,
F238 2827, webmaster@brasilemb.org
and consular@brasilemb.org*

changed and for when the banks go on strike: damaged dollars may be rejected. Parallel market and official rates are quoted in the papers and on TV news programmes. Tourists cannot change US$ travellers' cheques into US$ notes, but US$ travellers' cheques can be obtained on an American Express card (against official policy).

*MasterCard emergency
phone number
0800-891 3294
Visa emergency
number
000811-933 5589***Credit cards** Credit cards are widely used; Diners Club, MasterCard, Visa and American Express are useful. Banco Bradesco, subtitled Dia e Noite and Banco do Brasil handle the international Visa cash machine (ATM) network, Visa cash advances also at Banco do Brasil. HSBC handles international MasterCard cash machine network. Both Visa and MasterCard say that Banco 24 Horas machines will accept international credit cards. These kiosks advertise that they take a long list of credit cards in their ATMs, but they do not always accept international credit cards. Credit card transactions are charged at the tourist official rate. Cash advances on credit cards will only be paid in *reais* at the tourist rate, incurring a 1½% commission. ATMs are common in Brazil: it's worth remembering your PIN number since queues can be extremely long. Note however, that you may have to try many machines before being able to use your card.

Touching down

Business hours 0900-1800 Monday to Friday for most businesses, which close for lunch some time between 1130 and 1400. **Shops** open on Saturday till 1230 or 1300. **Government offices** 1100-1800 Monday to Friday. **Banks** 1000-1600, but closed on Saturday.

IDD: 55 Equal tones with long pauses means it is ringing; equal tones with equal pauses indicates engaged.

Official time Brazilian standard time is three hrs behind GMT; of the major cities, only the Amazon time zone, Manaus, Cuiabá, Campo Grande and Corumbá are different, with time five hrs behind GMT. The State of Acre is four hrs behind GMT. Clocks move forward one hr in summer for approximately five months (usually between October and February or March) but times of change vary. This does not apply to Acre.

Voltage This varies, see directory under individual towns.

Weights and measures The metric system is used by all.

Accommodation in every price range is good value. It should be easy finding a room costing US$10 pp, or less outside the cities and holiday centres. Eating is cheap and *comida a kilo* (pay by weight) restaurants are good value. Bus prices are reasonable, but because of long distances, costs can mount up. With lower internal air prices, some routes are cheaper than taking a bus. Prices are higher in Amazônia than elsewhere. **Cost of travelling**

Getting there

From Europe Rio de Janeiro and São Paulo are connected with the capitals of Europe by many major airlines, including *Varig*. *TAP* flies from Lisbon to Salvador, Recife and Fortaleza. **Air** *Regulations state that you cannot buy an air ticket in Brazil for use abroad unless you first have a ticket out of Brazil*

From USA Rio de Janeiro and São Paulo are connected to the USA direct by *Varig, TAM, Japan Airlines, American Airlines, Continental, Delta* and *United Airlines* from a number of US gateways. *Varig* flies Miami-Manaus twice a week. *Air Canada* flies Toronto-São Paulo.

From Latin America Most capitals are connected to São Paulo and Rio. If buying a ticket to another country but with a stopover in Brazil, check if two tickets are cheaper than one.

From elsewhere *South African Airways/Varig* fly between São Paulo and Johannesburg three times a week. There are regular flights between Tokyo and São Paulo (*Varig/All Nippon* and *Japan Airlines*). A consortium of Latin American airlines including *Varig* and *Aerolíneas Argentinas* operate the **Mercosur Airpass**, see page 43.

To drive in Brazil you need an international licence. A national driving licence is acceptable as long as your home country is a signatory to the Vienna and Geneva conventions. (See Motoring, Essentials.) There are agreements between Brazil and all South American countries (but check in the case of Bolivia) whereby a car can be taken into Brazil (or a Brazilian car out of Brazil) for a period of 90 days without any special documents; an extension of up to 90 days is granted by the customs authorities on presentation of the paper received at the border, this must be retained. This may be done at most customs posts and at the **Serviço de Controle Aduaneiro**, Ministério da Fazenda, Av Pres A Carlos, Sala 1129, Rio de Janeiro.# **Road**

For cars registered in other countries, the requirements are proof of ownership and/or registration in the home country and valid driving licence (as above). A 90-day permit is given by customs and procedure is very straightforward. Nevertheless, it is better to cross the border into Brazil when it is officially open because an official who knows all about the entry of cars is then present. You must specify which border station you intend to leave by, but application can be made to the Customs to change this.

Touching down

The amount of tax depends on the class of airport. All airports charge US$36 for international departure tax. First class airports charge R$9.50 domestic tax; second class airports R$7; domestic rates are lower still in third and fourth class airports. Tax must be paid on checking in, in *reais* or US dollars. Tax is waived if you stay in Brazil less than 24 hours. **Airport tax**

Brazil

Rules, customs & etiquette

Clothing It is normal to stare and comment on women's appearance, and if you happen to look different or to be travelling alone, you will attract attention. Single women are very unlikely to be groped or otherwise molested, but nevertheless Brazilian men can be extraordinarily persistent, and very easily encouraged. In general, clothing requirements in Brazil are less formal than in the Hispanic countries. It is, however, advisable for men visiting upmarket restaurants to wear long trousers (women in shorts may also be refused entry). As a general rule, it is better not to wear shorts in official buildings, cinemas, inter-state buses and on flights.

Conduct Men should avoid arguments or insults (care is needed even when overtaking on the road); pride may be defended with a gun. Gay men, while still enjoying greater freedom than in many countries, should exercise reasonable discretion.

Colour The people of Brazil represent a unique racial mix: it is not uncommon for the children of one family to be of several different colours. However, visitors of Afro-Caribibbean origin may encounter racial prejudice, or at least become the focus of some curiosity.

Tipping Tipping is usual, but less costly than in most other countries, except for porters. Restaurants, 10% of bill if no service charge but small tip if there is; taxi drivers, none; cloakroom attendants, small tip; cinema usherettes, none; hairdressers, 10-15%; porters, fixed charges but tips as well; airport porters, about US$0.50 per item.

Safety

Personal safety in Brazil has deteriorated in recent years, largely because of economic recession, and there are high rates of violent crime in large cities. Worst affected are *favelas* (slums), which should be avoided unless accompanied by a tour leader, or NGO. The situation is much more secure in smaller towns and in the country. Also steer well clear of areas of drug cultivation and red light districts. In the latter drinks are often spiked with a drug called `Goodnight Cinderella'. See the Safety section in Essentials at the beginning of the book for general advice.

Police There are three types of police: **Polícia Federal**, civilian dressed, who handle all federal law duties, including immigration. A subdivision is the **Polícia Federal Rodoviária**, uniformed, who are the traffic police. **Polícia Militar** is the uniformed, street police force, under the control of the state governor, handling all state laws. They are not the same as the Armed Forces' internal police. **Polícia Civil**, also state-controlled, handle local laws; usually in civilian dress, unless in the traffic division.

Where to stay

Hotels

See inside front cover for our hotel grade price guide.

NB Taxi drivers will try to take you to expensive hotels, who pay them commission for bringing in custom. Beware! Leave rooms in good time so frigobar bills can be checked; we have received reports of overcharging in otherwise good hotels

Usually hotel prices include breakfast; there is no reduction if you don't eat it. In the better hotels (category **B** and upwards) the breakfast is well worth eating: rolls, ham, eggs, cheese, cakes, fruit. Normally the *apartamento* is a room with bath; a *quarto* is a room without bath. *Pousadas* are the equivalent of bed-and-breakfast, often small and family run, although some are very sophisticated and correspondingly priced. The type known as *hotel familia*, to be found in the interior – large meals, communal washing, hammocks for children – is much cheaper, but only for the enterprising. The service stations (*postos*) and hostels (*dormitórios*) along the main roads provide excellent value in room and food, akin to truck-driver type accommodation in Europe, for those on a tight budget. The star rating system for hotels (five-star hotels are not price-controlled) is not the standard used in North America or Europe. Business visitors are strongly recommended to book in advance, and this can be easily done for Rio or São Paulo hotels with representation abroad. If staying more than three nights in a place in low season, ask for a discount. Motels are specifically intended for very short-stay couples: there is no stigma attached and they usually offer good value (the rate for a full night is called the *pernoite*), though the decor can be a little unsettling.

Roteiros de Charme In 31 locations in the Southeast and Northeast, this is a private association of hotels and *pousadas* which aims to give a high standard of accommodation in establishments which represent the town they are in. If you are travelling in the appropriate budget range (our **A** price range upwards), you can plan an itinerary which takes in these hotels, with a reputation for comfort and good food. Roteiros de Charme hotels are listed in the text and any one of them can provide information on the group. Alternatively, contact office in *Caesar Park Hotel* in Rio de Janeiro Av Vieira Souto 460, Ipanema, T0xx21-2525 2525 ext 501, 0800-251592, www.roteirosdecharme.com.br

For information about youth hostels contact **Federação Brasileira de Albergues da** **Youth hostels** **Juventude**, R dos Andrades 1137, conj 214, Porto Alegre, Rio Grande do Sul, CEP 90020-007, T0xx51-3228 3802/3226 5380, www.albergues.com.br Its annual book and website provide a full list of good value accommodation. Also see the **Internet Guide to Hostelling** which has list of Brazilian youth hostels: www.hostels.com/br.html Low-budget travellers with student cards (photograph needed) can use the Casa dos Estudantes network.

Members of the *Camping Clube do Brasil* or those with an international campers' card pay only **Camping** half the rate of a non-member, which is US$10-15 pp. The Club has 43 sites in 13 states and 80,000 members, www.campingclube.com.br For enquiries, **Camping Clube do Brasil**, R Senador Dantas 75, 29 andar, 20037-900 - Centro, Rio de Janeiro, T021-2210 3171, F2262 3143, ccb@campingclube.com.br In São Paulo, R Minerva 156, 05007-030 - Perdizes, T011-3864 7133, F3871 9749. In Curitiba, Al Dr Muricy 650, conj 161, CEP 80020-902, T/F041-224 7869. In Belo Horizonte, Av Amazonas 115, sala 1301, CEP 30180-000, T/F031-3201-6989. In Salvador, R Portugal 3, grupo 404/410, CEP 40015-000, T071-242 0482, F242 1954. It may be difficult to get into some Clube campsites during the high season (Jan-Feb). Private campsites charge about US$8 pp. For those on a very low budget and in isolated areas where there is no camp site, service stations can be used as camping sites (Shell stations recommended); they have shower facilities, watchmen and food; some have dormitories; truck drivers are a mine of information. There are also various municipal sites; both types are mentioned in the text. Campsites often tend to be some distance from public transport routes and are better suited to those with their own transport. Never camp at the side of a road; wild camping is generally not possible. Good camping equipment may be purchased in Brazil and there are several rental companies. Camping gas cartridges are easy to buy in sizeable towns in the south, eg in HM shops. Quatro Rodas' *Guia Brasil* lists main campsites, see page 341. Most sizeable towns have laundromats with self service. *Lavanderias* do the washing for you but are expensive.

Getting around

Because of the great distances, flying is often the most practical option. Internal air services are **Air** highly developed and the larger cities are linked several times a day. All national airlines offer *External tickets must* excellent service on their internal flights. The largest airlines are *TAM* (www.tam.com.br), *Varig* *be paid for in dollars* (www.varig.com.br), and *Vasp* (www.vasp.com.br). *Rio-Sul* and *Nordeste* (both allied to *Varig*) and *Transportes Aéreos Regionais* have extensive networks. In 2003 *TAM* and *Varig* began a flight-share programme to save costs.

Deregulation has reduced prices by about a third, so flying is fairly affordable. In addition, the no-frills, ticketless airline, *Gol* (T0300-789 2121, with English-speaking operators, or www.voegol.com.br, but website is in Portuguese), prvides a good service. Book *Gol* flights at a travel agent and pay by credit card. Double check all bookings (reconfirm frequently) and information given by ground staff. Economic cutbacks have led to pressure on ground service, including baggage handling (but not to flight service).

Internal flights often have many stops and are therefore quite slow. Most airports have left-luggage lockers (US$2 for 24 hrs). Seats are often unallocated on internal flights: board in good time. Available in all airports is the Protecto-Bag, US$8, a plastic wrapping which helps prevent opportunistic thieving.

Varig, *TAM* and *Vasp* offer 21-day air passes, but since deregulation these are not as good value as they used to be. The **Varig** and **TAM** airpasses cover all Brazil and each costs US$411 for four coupons. Additional coupons, up to a maximum of nine, cost US$100 each. All sectors must be booked before the start of the journey. Two flights forming one connection count as one coupon. The same sector may not be flown more than once in the same direction. Date or route changes are charged at US$30. There is no child discount, but infants pay 10%. For the *TAM* airpass, passengers may arrive in Brazil on any carrier. *Varig* passengers must arrive on a *Star Alliance* carrier. Routes must be specified before arrival. The **Vasp** air pass costs US$452 for five coupons. Extra coupons cost US$100 each, up to a maximum of nine. Date changes are free, route chages cost US$50. Two flights forming one connection count as one coupon. There is no child discount, but infants pay 10%. Passengers amy arrive in Brazil on any airline.

Brazil

All airpasses must be purchased outside Brazil, no journey may be repeated and none may be used on the Rio-São Paulo shuttle. Remember domestic airport tax has to be paid at each departure. Hotels in the *Tropical* and *Othon* chains, and others, offer discounts of 10% to Varig airpass travellers. Promotions on certain destinations offer a free flight, hotel room, etc; enquire when buying the airpass. Converting the voucher can take some hours, do not plan an onward flight immediately, check at terminals that the airpass is still registered, faulty cancellations have been reported. Cost and restrictions on the airpass are subject to change.

Small scheduled domestic airlines operate Brazilian-built *Bandeirante* 16-seater prop-jets into virtually every city and town with any semblance of an airstrip.

Road

Though the best paved highways are heavily concentrated in the southeast, those serving the interior are being improved to all-weather status and many are paved. Brazil has over 1.65 million km of highways, of which 150,000 km are paved, and several thousand more all-weather. Most main roads between principal cities are paved. Some are narrow and therefore dangerous. Many are in poor condition.

Bus

Many town buses have turnstiles which can be inconvenient if you are carrying a large pack. Urban buses normally serve local airports

There are three standards of bus: *comum* (conventional), which are quite slow, not very comfortable and fill up quickly; *executivo* (executive), which are a few reais more expensive, comfortable (many have reclining seats), but don't stop to pick up passengers en route and are therefore safer; and *leito* (literally, bed), which run at night between the main centres, offering reclining seats with foot and leg rests, toilets, and sometimes refreshments, at double the normal fare. For journeys over 100 km, most buses have chemical toilets. A/c can make *leito* buses cold at night, so take a blanket or sweater (and plenty of toilet paper); on some services blankets are supplied. Some companies have hostess service. Ask for window seats (*janela*), or odd numbers if you want the view.

Brazilian buses stop frequently (every 2-4 hrs) for snacks. The cleanliness of these *postos* is generally good, though less so in the poorer regions. Standards of comfort on buses and in *postos* vary, which can be important on long journeys. Take a drink on buses in the north.

Bus stations for interstate services and other long-distance routes are usually called *rodoviárias*. They are normally outside the city centres and offer snack bars, lavatories, left-luggage stores ('guarda volume'), local bus services and information centres. Buy bus tickets at rodoviárias (most now take credit cards), not from travel agents who add on surcharges. Reliable bus information is hard to come by, other than from companies themselves. Buses usually arrive and depart in very good time.

Car & car hire

Driving laws impose severe fines for many infringements of traffic regulations. Driving licences will be endorsed with points for infringements; 20 points = loss of licence

Fuel prices vary from week to week and region to region *gasolina comun* costs about US$1 per litre with *gasolina maxi* and *maxigold* a little more. *Alcool comun; alcool maxi* and diesel cost a little less. There is no unleaded fuel. **NB** It is virtually impossible to buy premium grades of petrol/gasoline anywhere. With alcohol fuel you need about 50% more alcohol than regular gasoline. Larger cars have a small extra tank for 'gasolina' to get the engine started; remember to keep this topped up. Fuel is only 85 octane, so be prepared for bad consumption and poor performance and starting difficulties in non-Brazilian cars in winter. Diesel fuel is cheap and a diesel engine may provide fewer maintenance problems. Service stations are free to open when they like. Very few open during Carnival week.

Car hire Renting a car in Brazil is expensive: the cheapest rate for unlimited mileage for a small car is about US$50 per day. Minimum age for renting a car is 21 and it is essential to have a credit card. Companies operate under the terms *aluguel de automóveis* or *autolocadores*. Compare prices of renting from abroad and in Brazil. Companies with nationwide coverage are **Avis** and **Localiza**, www.localiza.com.br

Taxi

Be wary of Moto Taxis. Many are unlicensed and a number of robberies have been reported

Taxi meters measure distance/cost in *reais*. At the outset, make sure the meter is cleared and shows tariff '1', except 2300-0600, Sun, and in Dec when '2' is permitted. Check the meter works, if not, fix price in advance. Radio taxi service costs about 50% more but cheating is less likely. Taxi services offered by smartly-dressed individuals outside larger hotels usually cost twice as much as ordinary taxis. If you are seriously cheated, note the taxi number and insist on a signed bill, threatening to go to the police; it can work.

Hitchhiking (*carona* in Portuguese) is difficult everywhere; drivers are reluctant to give lifts because passengers are their responsibility. Try at the highway-police check points on the main roads (but make sure your documents are in order) or at the service stations (*postos*).

Hitchhiking

The main areas where boat travel is practical (and often necessary) are the Amazon region, along the São Francisco River and along the Atlantic coast. There are also some limited transport services through the Pantanal.

Boat

There are 30,379 km of railways which are not combined into a unified system. Brazil has two gauges and there is little transfer between them. Two more gauges exist for the isolated Amapá Railway and the tourist-only São João del Rei line. There are passenger services in the state of São Paulo.

Train
Most passenger services have been withdrawn

Quatro Rodas, a motoring magazine, publishes an excellent series of maps and guides in Portuguese and English from about US$10. Its *Guia Brasil* is a type of Michelin Guide to hotels, restaurants (not the cheapest), sights, facilities and general information on hundreds of cities and towns in the country, including good street maps (we acknowledge here our debt to this publication). It also publishes a *Guia das Praias*, with descriptions of all Brazil's beaches. For information about the Quatro Rodas Guides and all their sister publications, www.abril.com.br

Maps & guides

Keeping in touch

Email is very common and public access to the internet is available in all towns and cities. The average hourly charge is US$3, but there are reduced rates for part of an hour. Many hotels offer internet service for their guests.

Internet

To send a standard letter or postcard to the USA costs US$0.75, to Europe US$0.85, to Australia or South Africa US$1. Air mail takes four to seven days to or from Britain or the US; surface mail takes four weeks. 'Caixa Postal' addresses should be used when possible. All places in Brazil have a post code, *CEP*; these are given in the text. Postes restantes usually only hold letters for 30 days. Franked and registered (insured) letters are normally secure, but check the amount franked is what you have paid, or the item will not arrive. Aerogrammes are most reliable. It may be easier to avoid queues and obtain higher denomination stamps by buying at the philatelic desk at the main post office. The Post office sells cardboard boxes for sending packages internally and abroad (they must be submitted open); pay by the kg; you must fill in a list of contents; string, official sellotape is provided. Courier services such as *DHL*, *Federal Express* and *UPS* (recommended) are useful, but note that they may not necessarily operate under those names.

Post

Important changes: All ordinary phone numbers in Brazil are changing from seven to eight figure numbers. The process will last until 2005. Enquire locally for the new numbers as in many cases whole numbers will change while others will simply add an extra digit. Where confirmed, 8-digit numbers have been included in the text. Where numbers have changed an electronic message should redirect callers. In addition, privatization of the phone system has led to increased competition. The consumer must now choose a phone company for long distance and international calls by inserting a two-digit code between the zero and the area code. **Phone numbers are now as follows: 0xx21 2540 5212.** 0 for a national call, followed by xx for the company code chosen, eg 21 for *Embratel*, followed by the two digit area code, eg 21 for Rio, followed by the seven, or eight digits of the number you are dialling. Thus the number for the Marina Palace Hotel in Rio would be: 021 21 2294 1644. For international calls: 00, 21 (*Embratel*), 44 (eg UK), then the city code and number.

Telephone

 Embratel (21) has national and international coverage. You can also choose a local operator for long distance calls but only if the call is made to a phone code within their area. For calls made within and between Rio de Janeiro, most of Minas Gerais, Espírito Santo, Bahia, Sergipe, Alagoas, Pernambuco, Paraíba, Rio Grande do Norte, Ceará, Piauí, Maranhão, Pará, Amapá, Amazonas and Roraima you can choose *Telemar* (31). *Intelig* for national and international calls (23). For calls made within and between Rio Grande do Sul, Santa Catarina, Paraná, Distrito

Brazil

Federal, Goiás, Tocantins, Mato Grosso do Sul, Mato Grosso, Rondônia and Acre use *Tele Centro-Sul* (14). For calls made within São Paulo you can choose *Telefônica* (15). *Embratel*: www.embratel.com.br *Telemar*: T0800 568888, or www.telemar.com.br *Telefônica*: www.telefonica.net.br *Intelig*: www.intellig.com

There are telephone boxes at airports, post offices, railway stations, hotels, most bars, restaurants and cafés, and in the main cities there are telephone kiosks *for local calls only* in the shape of large orange shells, for which *fichas* can be bought from bars, cafés and newsvendors; in Rio they are known as *orelhões* (big ears).

If you need to find a telephone number, you can dial 102 in any city (*auxílio à lista*) and the operator will connect you to a pre-recorded voice which will give the number. To find the number in a different city, dial the DDD code, followed by 121 (so, if you are in Salvador and want to know a Rio number, dial 0xx21 121). If your Portuguese is not up to deciphering spoken numbers, ask a hotel receptionist, for example, to assist you.

Phone cards are available from telephone offices, newstands, post offices and some chemists. Public boxes for intercity calls are blue; there are boxes within main telephone offices for international calls, make sure you buy a card worth at least 100 international units. To use the telephone office, tell the operator which city or country you wish to call, go to the booth whose number you are given; make your call and you will be billed on exit. Not all offices accept credit cards. Collect calls within Brazil can be made from any telephone – dial 9, followed by the number, and announce your name and city. Local calls from a private phone are normally free.

For international calls, make sure you buy at least one 90-unit card or pay at the desk after making your call from a booth. Calls are priced on normal and cheaper rates, depending on time of day. Check with local phone company. The rate to Europe is US$1-2 per min, to USA US$1. Phone companies have reduced rates usually between 2000 and 0600 and on Sunday.

Brazil is linked to North America, Japan and most of Europe by direct dialling. Codes are listed in the telephone directories. *Embratel* operates Home Country Direct, available from hotels, private phones or blue public phones to the following countries (prefix all numbers with 00080); Argentina 54, Australia 61, Belgium 03211, Bolivia 13, Canada 14, Chile 56 (*Entel*), 36 (*Chile Saturday*), 37 (*CTC Mundo*), Colombia 57, Costa Rica 50, Denmark 45, France 33, Germany 49, Holland 31, Hong Kong 85212, Israel 97, Italy 39, Japan 81 (*KDD*), 83 (*ITJ*), 89 (*Super Japan*), Norway 47, Paraguay 18, Peru 51, Portugal 35, Singapore 65, Spain 34, Sweden 46, Switzerland 04112, UK 44 (*BT Direct*), USA 10 (*AT&T*), 12 (*MCI*), 16 (*Sprint*), 11 (*Worldcom*), Uruguay 59, Venezuela 58. For collect calls from phone boxes (in Portuguese: 'a cobrar'), dial 107 and ask for the *telefonista internacional*. No collect calls are available to New Zealand.

Fax services operate in main post offices in major cities, at telephone offices, or from private lines. The international fax rates are as for phone calls; from the post office the rates are US$1.50 per page within Brazil, US$5 to Europe and the USA. To receive a fax costs US$1.40.

Mobile phones can be rented in Rio de Janeiro and São Paulo and pay-as-you-go phones are available. The systems in Brazil are mainly AMPS analog and TDMA digital.

Media **Newspapers** The main **Rio** papers are *Jornal do Brasil*, http://jbonline.terra.com.br *O Globo*, http://oglobo.globo.com *O Dia*, http://odia.ig.com.br and *Jornal do Commércio*, www.jornal docommercio.com.br **São Paulo** Morning: *O Estado de São Paulo*, www.estado.com.br *Folha de São Paulo*, www1.folha.uol.com.br/fsp/ *Gazeta Mercantil*, www.gazeta.com.br and *Diário de São Paulo*. Evening: *Jornal da Tarde, A Gazeta, Diário da Noite, Ultima Hora*. Around the country, the major cities have their own local press: *Diário de Pernambuco* in Recife, www.dpnet.com.br and the *Estado de Minas* in Belo Horizonte, www.em.com.br Foreign language papers include *The Brazilian Post* and *Sunday News* in English, and *Deutsche Zeitung* in German. In **Europe**, the *Euro-Brasil Press* is available in most capitals; it prints Brazilian and some news in Portuguese. London office 23 Kings Exchange, Tileyard Rd, London N7 9AH, T020-7700 4033, F7700 3540, eurobrasilpress@compuserve.com **Magazines** There are a number of good weekly news magazines: *Veja*: www.veja.abril.uol.com.br *Istoé*: www.terra. com.br/istoeonline/ *Exame*: http://portalexame.abril.com.br **Radio** English-language radio broadcasts daily at 15290 kHz, 19 m Short Wave (Rádio Bras, Caixa Postal 04/0340, DF-70 323 Brasília).

Food and drink

The most common dish is *bife (ou frango) com arroz e feijão*, steak (or chicken) with rice and the excellent Brazilian black beans. The most famous dish with beans is the *feijoada completa*: several meat ingredients (jerked beef, smoked sausage, smoked tongue, salt pork, along with spices, herbs and vegetables) are cooked with the beans. Manioc flour is sprinkled over it, and it is eaten with kale (*couve*) and slices of orange, and accompanied by glasses of *aguardente* (unmatured rum), usually known as *cachaça* (booze), though *pinga* (drop) is a politer term. Almost all restaurants serve the *feijoada completa* for Saturday lunch (that means up to about 1630).

Food
The main meal is usually taken in the middle of the day; cheap restaurants tend not to be open in the evening

Throughout Brazil, a mixed grill, including excellent steak, served with roasted manioc flour (*farofa*; raw manioc flour is known as *farinha* goes under the name of *churrasco* (it came originally from the cattlemen of Rio Grande do Sul), normally served in specialized restaurants known as *churrascarias* or *rodízios*; good places for large appetites

Bahia has some excellent fish dishes (see note on page 469); some restaurants in most of the big cities specialize in them. *Vatapá* is a good dish in the north; it contains shrimp or fish sauced with palm oil, or coconut milk. *Empadinhas de camarão* are worth trying; they are shrimp patties, with olives and heart of palm.

Minas Gerais has two splendid special dishes involving pork, black beans, *farofa* and kale; they are *tutu á mineira* and *feijão tropeiro*. A white hard cheese (*queijo prata*) or a slightly softer one (*queijo Minas*) is often served for dessert with bananas, or guava or quince paste. *Comida mineira* is quite distinctive and very wholesome and you can often find restaurants serving this type of food in other parts of Brazil.

Meals are extremely large by European standards; portions are usually for two and come with two plates. Likewise beer is brought with two glasses. If you are on your own and in a position to do so tactfully, you may choose to offer what you can't eat to a person with no food (observe the correct etiquette). Alternatively you could ask for an *embalagem* (doggy bag) or get a take away called a *marmita* or *quentinha*, most restaurants have this service but it is not always on the menu. Many restaurants now serve *comida por kilo* where you serve yourself and pay for the weight of food on your plate. Unless you specify to the contrary many restaurants will lay a *coberto opcional*, olives, carrots, etc, costing US$0.50-0.75. **Warning** Avoid mussels, marsh crabs and other shellfish caught near large cities: they are likely to have lived in a highly polluted environment. In a restaurant, always ask the price of a dish before ordering.

For vegetarians, there is a growing network of restaurants in the main cities. In smaller places where food may be monotonous try vegetarian for greater variety. Most also serve fish. Alternatives in smaller towns are the Arab and Chinese restaurants.

If travelling on a tight budget, remember to ask in restaurants for the *prato feito* or *sortido*, a money-saving, excellent value *table-d'hôte* meal. The *prato comercial* is similar but rather better and a bit more expensive. *Lanchonetes* are cheap eating places where you generally pay before eating. *Salgados* (savoury pastries), *coxinha* (a pyramid of manioc filled with meat or fish and deep fried), *esfiha* (spicey hamburger inside an onion-bread envelope), *empadão* (a filling – eg chicken – in sauce in a pastry case), *empadas* and *empadinhas* (smaller fritters of the same type), are the usual fare. In Minas Gerais, *pão de queijo* is a hot roll made with cheese. A *bauru* is a toasted sandwich which, in Porto Alegre, is filled with steak, while further north it has tomato, ham and cheese filling. *Cocada* is a coconut and sugar biscuit.

Imported drinks are expensive, but there are some fair local wines. Chilean and Portuguese wines are sometimes available at little more than the cost of local wines. The Brahma, Cerpa and Antárctica beers are really excellent, of the lager type, and are cheaper by the bottle than on draught. Buying bottled drinks in supermarkets, you may be asked for empties in return. The local firewater, *aguardente* (known as *cachaça* or *pinga*), made from sugar-cane, is cheap and wholesome, but visitors should seek local advice on the best brands; São Francisco, Praianinha, Maria Fulô, '51' and Pitu are recommended makes. Mixed with fruit juices of various sorts, sugar and crushed ice, *cachaça* becomes the principal element in a *batida*, a delicious and powerful drink; the commonest is a lime batida or *batida de limão*; a variant of

Drink

Brazil

this is the *caipirinha*, a *cachaça* with several slices of lime in it, a *caipiroska* is made with vodka. *Cachaça* with Coca-Cola is a *cuba*, while rum with Coca-Cola is a *cuba libre*. Some genuine Scotch whisky brands are bottled in Brazil; they are very popular because of the high price of Scotch imported in bottle; Teacher's is the most highly regarded brand. Locally made gin, vermouth and campari are very good.

There are plenty of local soft drinks. *Guaraná* is a very popular carbonated fruit drink. There is an excellent range of non-alcoholic fruit juices, known as *sucos: caju* (cashew), *pitanga*, *goiaba* (guava), *genipapo*, *graviola* (= *chirimoya*), *maracujá* (passion-fruit), *sapoti* and *tamarindo* are recommended. *Vitaminas* are thick fruit or vegetable drinks with milk. *Caldo de cana* is sugar-cane juice, sometimes mixed with ice. Remember that *água mineral*, available in many varieties at bars and restaurants, is a cheap, safe thirst-quencher (cheaper still in supermarkets). Apart from the ubiquitous coffee, good tea is grown and sold. **NB** If you don't want sugar in your coffee or *suco*, you must ask when you order it. *Água de côco* or *côco verde* (coconut water from fresh green coconut) cannot be missed in the Northeast.

Shopping

As a rule, shopping is easier, quality more reliable and prices higher in the shopping centres (mostly excellent) and in the wealthier suburbs. Better prices at the small shops and street traders; most entertaining at markets and on the beach. Bargaining (with good humour) is expected in the latter

Gold, diamonds and gemstones throughout Brazil. Innovative designs in jewellery: buy 'real' at reputable dealers (best value in Minas Gerais); cheap, fun pieces from street traders. Interesting furnishings made with gemstones, marble; clay figurines from the northeast; lace from Ceará; leatherwork; strange pottery from Amazônia; carvings in soapstone and in bone; tiles and other ceramic work, African-type pottery and basketwork from Bahia. Many large hotel gift shops stock a good selection of handicrafts at reasonable prices. Brazilian cigars are excellent for those who like the mild flavours popular in Germany, the Netherlands and Switzerland. Recommended purchases are musical instruments, eg guitars, other stringed, and percussion instruments. Excellent textiles: good hammocks from the northeast; other fabrics; design in clothing is impressive, though not equalled by manufacturing quality. Buy your beachwear in Brazil: it is matchless. For those who know how to use them, medicinal herbs, barks and spices from street markets; coconut oil and local skin and haircare products (fantastic conditioners) are better and cheaper than in Europe, but known brands of toiletries are exorbitant. Other bad buys are film (including processing), cameras and electrical goods (including batteries). Sunscreen, sold in department stores and large supermarkets, is expensive.

Holidays and festivals

For carnival freephone T0800-701 1250 (24 hrs, English, Spanish, Portuguese)

National holidays are 1 January (New Year); three days up to and including Ash Wednesday (Carnival); 21 April (Tiradentes); 1 May (Labour Day); Corpus Christi (June); 7 September (Independence Day); 12 October, Nossa Senhora Aparecida; 2 November (All Souls' Day); 15 November (Day of the Republic); and 25 December (Christmas). The local holidays in the main cities are given in the text. Four religious or traditional holidays (Good Friday must be one; other usual days: 1 November, All Saints Day; 24 December, Christmas Eve) must be fixed by the municipalities. Other holidays are usually celebrated on the Monday prior to the date.

Sport and activities

Birdwatching and nature tourism Birdwatching can be very rewarding and the possibilities are too numerous to cover in this brief introduction. Habitats include Amazonian rainforest, the Pantanal wetlands, the subtropical forest at Iguaçu, the *cerrado* of the central plateau, the arid northeast, the Lagoa dos Patos of Rio Grande do Sul and the few remaining pockets of *Mata Atlântica* of the east coast. None is difficult to get to, but it would be impossible to visit every type of environment in one trip to the country. A variety of birds can be seen, including many endemics. The system of national parks and protected areas, including those offshore (Abrolhos, Fernando de Noronha), is designed to allow access to Brazil's areas of outstanding beauty for education and recreation as well as scientific research. **Ibama**, address on page 341, can provide information. A tour operator specializing in bird-watching and environmentally responsible travel is ***Focus Tours***, 103 Moya Rd, Santa Fe, MN 87508, T505-466

4688, F505-466 4689, www.focustours.com The Focus Conservation Fund is a private, non-profit organization concerned with projects in the Pantanal (the Jaguar Ecological Reserve), the Amazon and the Caratinga region in Minas Gerais, www.focusconservation.org

Canoeing: This is supervised by the **Confederação Brasileira de Canoagem** (CBCa). It covers all aspects of the sport, speed racing, slalom, downriver, surfing and ocean kayaking. For downriver canoeing, go to **Visconde de Mauá** (Rio de Janeiro state) where the Rio Preto is famous for the sport; also the Rio Formoso at **Bonito** (Mato Grosso do Sul). A recommended river for slalom is the Pranhana, **Três Coroas**, Rio Grande do Sul. For kayak surfing the best places are Rio, the Ilha de Santa Catarina and Ubatuba, while ocean kayaking is popular in Rio, Búzios and Santos (São Paulo).

Caving There are some wonderful cave systems in Brazil and Ibama, the National Parks institute, has a programme for the protection of the national speleological heritage. National parks such as Ubajara (Ceará) and Chapada Diamantina (Bahia) and the state park of PETAR (São Paulo) have easy access for the casual visitor, but there are also many options for the keen potholer in the states of São Paulo, Paraná, Minas Gerais and the Federal District.

Climbing As Brazil has no mountain ranges of Andean proportions, the most popular form of climbing (*escalada*) is rock-face climbing. In the heart of Rio, you can see, or join, climbers scaling the rocks at the base of Pão de Açúcar and on the Sugar Loaf itself. Not too far away, the Serra dos Órgãos provides plenty of challenges, not least the Dedo de Deus (God's Finger). Rio de Janeiro is the state where the sport is most fully developed, but not far behind are Paraná, Minas Gerais, São Paulo and Rio Grande do Sul.

Cycling Brazil is well-suited to cycling. On main roads it is important to be on the look out for motor vehicles as cyclists are very much second-class citizens. Also note that when cycling on the coast you may encounter strong winds which will hamper your progress. There are endless roads and tracks suitable for **mountain biking**, and there are many clubs in major cities which organize group rides, activities and competitions.

Diving: The Atlantic coast offers many possibilities for scuba diving (*mergulho* in Portuguese). Offshore, the marine park of Abrolhos (Bahia) is a good site, but the prize above all others is **Fernando de Noronha** (Pernambuco) in the open Atlantic. The underwater landscape is volcanic, with cliffs, caverns and some corals, but the marine life that shelters here is magnificent. There are sharks, a protected breeding ground of hawksbill and green turtles and, the greatest draw for divers, a bay which is the home for a pod of several hundred spinner dolphin. In the archipelago there are a number of dive sites. Also in Pernambuco, **Recife** (where planes for Fernando de Noronha leave) is a diving centre, particularly for wrecks. The reef that protects the shore up to Recife provides sheltered swimming, natural pools and many rewarding diving spots. Full of marine life, this warm, clear, greenish-blue sea attracts global visitors as well as holidaymaking Brazilians, but, fortunately, is extensive enough to accommodate everyone without becoming overcrowded. Local fishermen still use hand-trawled nets and *jangadas* (sail-powered rafts which skim just below the water's surface). Visiting sea anglers are urged to respect local traditions: many species are in danger of extinction, as is the coral which is threatened by any disturbance and all forms of pollution. Moving south, Bahia's most popular dive sites are **Abrolhos** (already mentioned) and **Porto Seguro**. In the Southeast, **Búzios, Arraial do Cabo, Cabo Frio** to the north of Rio, and, south of the state capital, the island-filled bay of **Angra dos Reis**, together with **Ilha Grande**, and **Paraty** are all recommended. **Ilhabela/São Sebastião** in São Paulo state offers good opportunities for wreck diving and other places in the state include **Ubatuba, Laje de Santos** and **Ilha de Alcatrazes**. At Fernando de Noronha and Recife you can dive all year, although Recife (like anywhere on the coast) may be subject to strong currents. The further south you go, the lower the water temperatures become in winter (15-20°C). Currents and weather can affect visibility. In some areas in Brazil, diving includes underwater sport fishing; if you like this sort of thing, contact a company which specializes in fishing.

Ecotourism To some extent there is a mingling of ecotourism and adventure tourism in Brazil. This is partly because the adventurous activities nearly always take place in unspoilt parts of the country, but also because the term 'ecotourism' is applied to almost any outdoor activity. In Minas Gerais, **Amo-Te**, the Associação Mineira dos Organizadores do Turismo Ecológico, R Prof Morais 624, Apto 302, Savassi, Belo Horizonte, T0xx31-3281 5094, is helpful.

Fishing: Brazil has enormous potential for angling given the number and variety of its rivers, lakes and reservoirs. Add to this the scope for sea-angling along the Atlantic coast and it is not difficult to see why the sport is gaining in popularity. Officially, the country's fish stocks are under the control of Ibama (see above) and a licence is required for fishing in any waters. The states of Mato Grosso and Mato Grosso do Sul require people fishing in their rivers to get the states' own fishing permit, which is not the same as an Ibama licence. All details on prices, duration and regulations concerning catches can be obtained from Ibama; the paperwork can be found at Ibama offices, some branches of the Banco do Brasil and some agencies which specialize in fishing. In Mato Grosso and Mato Grosso do Sul information is provided by *Sema*, the Special Environment Secretariat, and documents may be obtained at fishing agencies or HSBC in Mato Grosso do Sul. Freshwater fishing can be practised in so many places that the best bet is to make local enquiries on arrival. You can then find out about the rivers, lakes and reservoirs, which fish you are likely to find and what types of angling are most suited to the conditions. Favoured rivers include tributaries of the Amazon, those in the Pantanal and the Rio Araguaia, but there are many others. Agencies can arrange fishing trips and there are local magazines on the subject.

Hang gliding and paragliding Hang gliding and paragliding are both covered by the **Associação Brasileira de Vôo Livre** (ABVL – Brazilian Hangliding Association, R Prefeito Mendes de Moraes s/n, São Conrado, Rio de Janeiro, T0xx21-3322 0266, www.abvl.com.br). There are state associations affiliated with ABVL and there are a number of operators who offer tandem flights for those without experience. Launch sites (called *rampas*) are growing in number. Among the best-known is Pedra Bonita at Gávea in Rio de Janeiro, but there are others in the state. Popular *rampas* can also be found in São Paulo, Espírito Santo, Minas Gerais, Paraná, Santa Catarina, Rio Grande do Sul, Ceará, Mato Grosso do Sul and Brasília.

Trekking This is very popular, especially in Rio de Janeiro, São Paulo, Minas Gerais, Paraná and Rio Grande do Sul. There are plenty of hiking agencies which handle hiking tours. Trails are frequently graded according to difficulty; this is noticeably so in areas where *trilhas ecológicas* have been laid out in forests or other sites close to busy tourist areas. Many national parks and protected areas provide good opportunities for trekking (eg the Chapada Diamantina in Bahia) and local information can easily be found to get you on the right track. Some of the best trails for **horse riding** are the routes that used to be taken by the mule trains that transported goods between the coast and the interior. A company like *Tropa Serrana* in Belo Horizonte (T0xx31-3344 8986/9983 2356, tropaserrana@hotmail.com) is an excellent place to start because their tours, including overnight horse treks, explore many aspects of the Minas Gerais countryside that visitors do not normally see.

Water sports Surfing: This can be enjoyed in just about every coastal state. It does not require permits; all you need is a board and the right type of wave. Brazilians took up surfing in the 1930s and have been practising ever since: in this beach-obsessed country, with 8,000 km of coastline, all shore and water sports are taken seriously. A favourite locale is **Fernando de Noronha**, the archipelago, 345 km out in the Atlantic, but the best waves are found in the south, where long stretches of the Atlantic, often facing the swell head-on, give some excellent and varied breaks. Many Brazilian surf spots are firmly on the international championship circuit: best known is **Saquarema**, in Rio de Janeiro state.

White water rafting: This started in Brazil in 1992. Companies offer trips in São Paulo state (eg on the Rios Juquiá, Jaguarí, do Peixe, Paraibuna), in Rio de Janeiro (also on the Paraibuna, at Três Rios in the Serra dos Órgãos), Paraná (Rio Ribeira), Santa Catarina (Rio Itajaí) and Rio Grande do Sul (Três Coroas).

Health

See also the Health section, Essentials at the beginning of the book, page 60 For information on vaccinations, see pages 56 and 334

If you are going to Amazônia, or to other low-lying forested areas, malaria prophylaxis is necessary (this can be difficult to obtain in some areas – the local name for *Paludrine* is *Doroprim*) and water purification tablets are essential. Dengue fever is now endemic in Brazil, and Rio de Janeiro is one of the worst places. Sporadic outbreaks of cholera have occurred in the Amazon region and on the northeast coast (eg Recife), but numbers have been in the tens, rather than the hundreds. Also, in the Amazon basin, sandflies abound. Be very careful about bathing in lakes or slow rivers anywhere in Brazil: harmful parasites abound (including the snails that carry schistosomiasis – this disease is rampant in Minas Gerais and most of central Brazil). South of the Amazon beware of *borrachudos*, small flies with a sharp bite that attack ankles and calves; coconut oil deters them.

Water should not be drunk from taps unless there is a porcelain filter attached or unless you have water sterilizing tablets (*Hydrosteril* is a popular local brand); there is mineral water in plenty and excellent light beer, known as 'chopp' (pronounced 'shoppi'), and soft drinks. For those who have been in Brazil for a while, *água gelada* (chilled water) is usually safe to drink, being filtered water kept in a refrigerator in most hotels, restaurants and stores. Avoid ice in cheap hotels and restaurants; it is likely to be made from unfiltered water. *Colestase* is the recommended local treatment for upset stomachs.

Brazilians are famous for their open sexuality: appearances can be deceptive, however, and attitudes vary widely. To generalize, the coastal cities are very easy-going, while in smaller towns and the interior, traditional morals are strictly enforced. HIV is widespread, primarily transmitted by heterosexual sex, and tolerance of male homosexuality is diminishing. You should take reliable condoms with you, even if you are sure you won't be needing them. Local condoms are reported not to be reliable..

Tampons are available, as are *Hydrocare* contact lens products (expensive). If staying in Brazil for any length of time, it is recommended to take out Brazilian health insurance; *Banco Económico* and *Citibank* are reported to provide good advice.

Rio de Janeiro

Brazilians say: God made the world in six days; the seventh he devoted to Rio. (Pronounced Heeoo by locals). Rio has a glorious theatrical backdrop of tumbling wooded mountains, stark expanses of bare rock and a deep blue sea studded with rocky islands. From the statue of Christ on the hunchbacked peak of Corcovado, or from the conical Pão de Açúcar (Sugar Loaf), you can experience the beauty of a bird's-eye view over the city which sweeps 220 km along a narrow alluvial strip on the southwestern shore of the Baía de Guanabara. Although best known for the curving Copacabana beach, for Ipanema – home to the Girl and beautiful sunsets, and for its swirling, reverberating, joyous Carnival, Rio also has a fine artistic, architectural and cultural heritage from its time as capital of both imperial and republican Brazil. But this is first and foremost a city dedicated to leisure: sport and music rule and a day spent hang-gliding or surfing is easily followed by an evening of jazz or samba.

Phone code: 0xx21
Colour map 4, grid C3
Population: 8 million

Getting there Most international flights stop at the **Aeroporto Internacional** Antônio Carlos Jobim (Galeão) on the Ilha do Governador. Left luggage only in Terminal 1. The air bridge from São Paulo ends at Santos Dumont airport in the town centre. Taxis from here are much cheaper than from the international airport. There are also frequent buses.

Ins & outs
See also Transport, page 382

International and buses from other parts of Brazil arrive at the **Rodoviária Novo Rio** (main bus station) near the docks.

Getting around Because the city is a series of separate districts connected by urban highways and tunnels, you will need to take public transport. Walking is only an option once you are in the district you want to explore. An underground railway, the **Metrô**, runs under some of the centre and the south and is being extended. Buses run to all parts, but should be treated with caution at night when taxis are a better bet.

Climate Rio has one of the healthiest climates in the tropics. Trade winds cool the air. Jun, Jul and Aug are the coolest months with temperatures ranging from 22°C (18° in a cold spell) to 32°C on a sunny day at noon. Dec to Mar is hotter, from 32°C to 42°C. Humidity is high. It is important, especially for children, to guard against dehydration in summer by drinking as much liquid as possible. Oct to Mar is the rainy season. Annual rainfall is about 1,120 mm.

Brazil

Tourist offices Riotur, R da Assembléia 10, 9th floor, T2217 7575, F2531 1872, www.rio.rj.gov.br/riotur Main information office: Av Princesa Isabel 183, Copacabana, T2541 7522, Mon-Fri 0900-1800, helpful with English and German spoken by some staff, has good city maps and a very useful free brochure *RIO*, in Portuguese and English. More information stands can be found at the international airport (0600-2400) and at Rodoviária Novo Rio (0800-2000), both very friendly and helpful in finding accommodation. *Alô Rio* is an information service in English and Portuguese, T2542 8080/0800-707 1808, daily from 0900-1800. **TurisRio**, R da Ajuda 5, 12th floor, T2215 0011, www.turisrio.rj.gov.br Information on the state of Rio de Janeiro, Mon-Fri 0900-1700, with stands at the bus station and Jobim airport. **Embratur**, R Uruguaiana 174, 8th floor, Centro, T2509 6017, www.embratur.gov.br Information on the whole of Brazil. The best guide to Rio, with excellent maps, is *Guia Quatro Rodas do Rio* in Portuguese and English (the *Guia Quatro Rodas do Brasil*, published annually in Nov, also has a good Rio section). *Trilhas do Rio*, by Pedro da Cunha e Meneses (Editora Salamandra, 2nd edition), US$22.50, describes walking trips around Rio. The guide *Restaurantes do Rio*, by Danusia Bárbara, published annually by Senac at around US$10.00 (in Portuguese only), is worth looking at for the latest ideas on where to eat in both the city and state of Rio. *Rio Botequim*, an annual guide to the best, most traditional bars and bistros, is published by the Prefeitura, US$12. Many hotels provide guests with the weekly *Rio This Month*. There is an online Favela news agency with news, comment and links, aimed at helping people understand better this aspect of the city: www.anf.org.br See also Tour operators.

Safety The majority of visitors enjoy Rio's glamour and the rich variety of experience it has to offer without any problems. It is worth remembering that, despite its beach culture, carefree atmosphere and friendly people, Rio is one of the world's most densely populated cities. If you live in London, Paris, New York or Los Angeles and behave with the same caution in Rio that you do at home, you will be unlucky to encounter any crime. The **Tourist Police**,

Rio de Janeiro

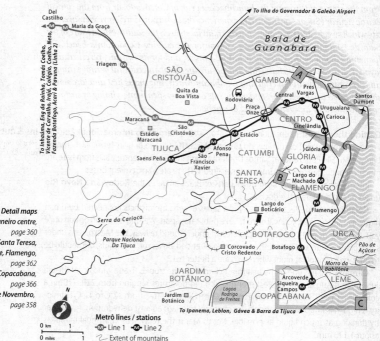

Detail maps
A Rio de Janeiro centre,
page 360
B Glória, Santa Teresa,
Catete, Flamengo,
page 362
C Copacabana,
page 366
Praça 15 de Novembro,
page 358

Metrô lines / stations
Ⓜ Line 1 Ⓜ Line 2
Extent of mountains

0 km   1
0 miles   1

Av Afrânio de Melo Franco 159, Leblon (in front of the Casa Grande theatre), T3399 7170 (24 hrs), publish a sensible advice leaflet (available from hotels and consulates: consulates also issue safety guidelines). Tourist police officers are helpful, efficient and multilingual. All the main tourist areas are patrolled. If you have any problems, contact the tourist police first.

History

The Portuguese navigator, Gonçalo Coelho, arrived at what is now Rio de Janeiro on 1 January 1502. Thinking that the Baía de Guanabara (the name the local Indians used) was the mouth of a great river, they called the place the January River. Although the bay was almost as large and as safe a harbour as the Baía de Todos Os Santos to the north, the Portuguese did not take of advantage of it. In fact, it was first settled by the French, who, under the Huguenot Admiral Nicholas Durand de Villegagnon, occupied Lage Island on 10 November 1555, but later transferred to Seregipe Island (now Villegagnon), where they built the fort of Coligny.

In early 1559-60, Mem de Sá, third governor of Brazil, mounted an expedition from Salvador to attack the French. The Portuguese finally took control in 1567. Though constantly attacked by Indians, the new city grew rapidly and when King Sebastião divided Brazil into two provinces, Rio was chosen capital of the southern captaincies. Salvador became sole capital again in 1576, but Rio again became the southern capital in 1608 and the seat of a bishopric.

Rio de Janeiro was by the 18th century becoming the leading city in Brazil. Not only was it the port out of which gold was shipped, but it was also the focus of the export/import trade of the surrounding agricultural lands. On 27 January 1763, it became the seat of the Viceroy. After independence, in 1834, it was declared capital of the Empire and remained the capital for 125 years.

Sights

The city is usually divided into north and south zones, Zona Norte and Zona Sul, with the historical and business centre, O Centro, in between. The parts that most interest visitors are the centre itself and the Zona Sul, which has the famous districts of Flamengo, Botafogo, Urca, Copacabana, Ipanema, Leblon and then out to the newer suburb of Barra de Tijuca.

The city's main artery is the Avenida Presidente Vargas, 4½ km long and over 90 m wide. It starts at the waterfront, divides to embrace the famous Candelária church, then crosses the Avenida Rio Branco in a magnificent straight stretch past the Central do Brasil railway station, with its imposing clock tower, until finally it incorporates a palm-lined, canal-divided avenue. The second principal street in the centre is the Avenida Rio Branco, nearly 2 km long, on which only a few ornate buildings remain, by Cinelândia and the Biblioteca Nacional. Some of the finest modern architecture is to be found along the Avenida República do Chile, such as the Petrobrás, the Banco Nacional de Desenvolvimento Econômico and the former Banco Nacional de Habitação buildings and the new Cathedral.

Around Praça 15 de Novembro
At weekends an antiques, crafts, stamp and coin fair is held from 0900-1900

Praça 15 de Novembro (often called Praça XV) has always been one of the focal points in Rio. Today it has one of the greatest concentrations of historic buildings in the city. The last vestiges of the original harbour, at the seaward end of the Praça, have been restored. The steps no longer lead to the water, but a new open space leads from the Praça to the seafront, beneath the Av Pres Kubitschek flyover. This space now gives easy access to the ferry dock for Niterói.

On Rua 1 de Março, across from Praça 15 de Novembro, there are three buildings related to the Carmelite order. The convent of the **Ordem Terceira do Monte do Carmo**, started in 1611, is now used as the Faculdade Cândido Mendes. The order's present church, the **Igreja da Ordem Terceira do Carmo**, also in R Primeiro de Março, the other side of the old cathedral (see below) from the convent, was built in 1754, consecrated in 1770 and rebuilt between 1797 and 1826. It has strikingly beautiful portals by Mestre Valentim, the son of a Portuguese nobleman and a slave girl.

Brazil

He also created the main altar of fine moulded silver, the throne and its chair and much else. ■ *Mon-Fri 0800-1400, Sat 0800-1200.*

Between the former convent and the Igreja da Ordem Terceira do Carmo is the old cathedral, the **Igreja de Nossa Senhora do Carmo da Antiga Sé**, separated from the Carmo Church by a passageway. It was the chapel of the Convento do Carmo from 1590 until 1754. A new church was built in 1761, which became the city's cathedral. In the crypt are the alleged remains of Pedro Alvares Cabral, the Portuguese explorer (though Santarém, Portugal, also claims to be his last resting place).

The **Paço Imperial** (former Royal Palace) is on the southeast corner of the Praça 15 de Novembro. This beautiful colonial building was built in 1743 as the residence of the governor of the Capitania. It later became the Paço Real when the Portuguese court moved to Brazil. After Independence it became the Imperial Palace. It has the *Bistro* and *Atrium* restaurants. Recommended. ■ *Tue-Sun 1100-1830, T2232 8333*

Igreja de São José (R São José e Av Pres Antônio Carlos), is considerably altered since its 17th century construction.The current building dates from 1824. ■ *Mon-Fri 0900-1200, 1400-1700, Sun 0900-1100.*

On the northwest side of Praça 15 de Novembro, you go through the Arco do Teles and the Travessa do Comércio to Rua do Ouvidor. The **Igreja Nossa Senhora da Lapa dos Mercadores** (R do Ouvidor 35) was consecrated in 1750, remodelled 1869-72 and has been fully restored. ■ *Mon-Fri 0800-1400.* Across the street, with its entrance at R 1 de Março 36, is the church of **Santa Cruz dos Militares**, built 1780-1811. It is large, stately and beautiful and has been well renovated in a 'light' baroque style.

The Church of **Nossa Senhora da Candelária** (1775-1810), on Praça Pio X (Dez), at the city end of Av Pres Vargas where it meets R 1 de Março, has beautiful ceiling decorations and romantic paintings. ■ *Mon-Fri 0730-1200, 1300-1630, Sat 0800-1200, Sun 0900-1300.*

With entrances on Av Pres Vargas and R 1 de Março 66, the **Centro Cultural Banco do Brasil (CCBB)** is highly recommended for good exhibitions. It has a library, multimedia facilities, a cinema, concerts (US$6 at lunchtime) and a restaurant ■ *Tue-Sun 1230-1900, T3808 2000.* Opposite is the **Espaço Cultural dos Correios**, R Visconde de Itaboraí 20, which holds temporary exhibitions and a

Praça 15 de Novembro

| 0 metres | 100 | ● Eating | 2 Confeitaria Colombo |
| 0 yards | 100 | 1 Bistro do Paço | 3 Rio Minho |

postage stamp fair on Saturdays. ■ *Tue-Sun 1300-1900, T2503 8770.* **Casa França-Brasil**, R Viscone de Itaboraí 253 and Av Pres Vargas, dates from the first French Artistic Mission to Brazil and it was the first neoclassical building in Rio. ■ *Tue-Sun 1200-2000, T2253 5366.* **Espaço Cultural da Marinha**, on Av Alfredo Agache at Av Pres Kubitschek. This former naval establishment now contains museums of underwater archaeology and navigation and the *Galeota*, the boat used by the Portuguese royal family for sailing around the Baía de Guanabara. Moored outside is the warship, *Bauru* and boats give access to the beautiful **Ilha Fiscal**. ■ *Tue-Sun 1200-1700. Boats to Ilha Fiscal, Fri, Sat, Sun, 1300, 1430, 1600, T3870 6879.*

Just north of Candelária, on a promontory overlooking the bay, is the **Mosteiro** (monastery) **de São Bento**, containing much of what is best in the 17th and 18th century art of Brazil. São Bento is reached either by a narrow road from R Dom Gerardo 68, or by a lift whose entrance is at R Dom Gerardo 40 (taxi to the monastery from centre US$5). The main body of the church is adorned in gold and red. The carving and gilding is remarkable, much of it by Frei Domingos da Conceição. The paintings, too, should be seen. The Chapels of the Immaculate Conception (Nossa Senhora da Conceição) and of the Most Holy Sacrament (Santíssimo Sacramento) are masterpieces of colonial art. The organ, dating from the end of the 18th century, is very interesting. ■ *Daily 0800-1230, 1400-1730, shorts not allowed. Every Sun at 1000, mass is sung with Gregorian chant and music, which is free, but you should arrive an hour early to get a seat. On other days, mass is at 0715.*

Around Largo da Carioca

The second oldest convent in the city is the **Convento de Santo Antônio**, on a hill off the Largo da Carioca, built between 1608 and 1615. Santo Antônio is a particular object of devotion for women looking for a husband and you will see them in the precincts. The church has a marvellous sacristy adorned with blue tiles and paintings illustrating the life of St Anthony. In the church itself, the baroque decoration is concentrated in the chancel, the main altar and the two lateral altars.

Separated from this church only by some iron railings is the charming church of the Ordem Terceira de **São Francisco da Penitência**, built in 1773. Its Baroque carving and gilding of walls and altar, much more than in its neighbour, is considered among the finest in Rio. There is also a Museu de Arte Sacra. Strongly recommended. ■ *Wed-Fri 1000-1600.*

Across Ruas da Carioca and 7 de Setembro is the Church of **São Francisco de Paula**, at the upper end of the R do Ouvidor. It contains some of Mestre Valentim's work. ■ *Mon-Fri 0900-1300.* One long block behind the Largo da Carioca and São Francisco de Paula is the **Praça Tiradentes**, old and shady, with a statue to Dom Pedro I. At the northeast corner of the praça is the **Teatro João Caetano** (T2221 0305). Shops nearby specialize in selling goods for *umbanda*, the Afro-Brazilian religion. South of the Largo da Carioca are the modern buildings on Avenida República do Chile including the new Cathedral, the **Catedral Metropolitana**, dedicated in November 1976. It is a cone-shaped building with capacity of 5,000 seated, 20,000 standing. The most striking feature is four enormous 60 m-high stained-glass windows. It is still incomplete. ■ *0800-1800.* Crossing Av República do Paraguai from the cathedral, is the Petrobrás building and the station, with museum, for the tram to Santa Teresa (entrance on R Senador Dantas – see below).

Avenida Rio Branco

Facing Praça Marechal Floriano is the **Teatro Municipal**, one of the most magnificent buildings in Brazil in the eclectic style. It was built in 1905-09, in imitation of the Opéra in Paris. The decorative features inside and out represent many styles, all lavishly executed. Opera and orchestral performances are given here (T2544 2900). To book a tour of the theatre, ask for extension – *ramal* – 935 in advance. ■ *Mon-Fri 0900-1700, US$2. The box office is at the right hand side of the building; ticket prices start at about US$15.* The **Biblioteca Nacional**, at Av Rio Branco 219 also dates from the first decade of the 20th century. The monumental staircase leads to a hall, off which lead the fine internal staircases of Carrara marble. It houses over nine

Brazil

million volumes and documents. ■ *Mon-Fri 0900, US$1, T2262 8255*. The **Museu Nacional de Belas Artes**, Av Rio Branco 199, was built between 1906 and 1908, in eclectic style. It has about 800 original paintings and sculptures and some thousand direct reproductions. One gallery, dedicated to works by Brazilian artists from the 17th century onwards, includes paintings by Frans Janszoon Post (Dutch 1612-80), who painted Brazilian landscapes in classical Dutch style, and the Frenchmen Debret and Taunay. Another gallery charts the development of Brazilian art in 20th century. ■ *Tue-Fri 1000-1800, Sat, Sun and holidays 1400-1800, US$1, T2240 0068*.

Praça Mahatma Gandhi, at the end of Av Rio Branco, is flanked on one side by the old cinema and amusement centre of the city, known as Cinelândia. Next to the praça is the **Passeio Público**, a garden planted in 1779-83 by the artist Mestre Valentim, whose bust is near the old former gateway. ■ *Daily 0900-1700*.

Museu do Instituto Histórico e Geográfico, Av Augusto Severo 8 (10th floor), just off Av Beira Mar, is across the street from the Passeio Público. It has an interesting collection of historical objects, Brazilian products and the artefacts of its peoples. ■ *Mon-Fri 1200-1700*.

Praça Marechal Âncora/Praça Rui Barbosa The **Museu Histórico Nacional**, which contains a collection of historical treasures, colonial sculpture and furniture, maps, paintings, arms and armour, silver and porcelain. ■ *Tue-Fri 1000-1730, Sat, Sun and holidays 1400-1800, US$1, T2550 9224,*

Rio de Janeiro centre

Detail map
A Praça 15 de
Novembro,
page 358

0 metres 200
0 yards 200

■ **Sleeping**
1 Itajubá

● **Eating**
1 Adega Flor de Coimbra

2 Al-kuwait
3 Café do Teatro

www.visualnet.com.br/mhr **Museu da Imagem e do Som**, also on Praça Rui Barbosa, has many photographs of Brazil and modern Brazilian paintings; also collections and recordings of Brazilian classical and popular music and a non-commercial cinema Friday-Sunday. ■ *Mon-Fri 1300-1800.*

Palácio do Itamaraty (Museu Histórico e Diplomático), Av Marechal Floriano 196, became the president's residence between 1889 and 1897 and then the Ministry of Foreign Affairs until the opening of Brasília. ■ *Guided tours Mon, Wed, Fri hourly between 1315 and 1615. Recommended.*

West of the centre

About 3 km west of the public gardens of the Praça da República (beyond the Sambódromo – see box, Carnival, page 376) is the **Quinta da Boa Vista**, formerly the Emperor's private park, from 1809 to 1889. If you are comfortable in crowds, perhaps the best time to visit is Saturday or Sunday afternoon. It is full of locals looking for fun and relaxation and therefore more police are on hand. ■ *Daily 0700-1800.*

Quinta da Boa Vista has had the problem of thieves operating by the park entrance and in the park itself

In the entrance hall of the **Museu Nacional** in the Quinta da Boa Vista is the famous Bendegó meteorite, found in the State of Bahia in 1888; its original weight, before some of it was chipped, was 5,360 kg. The museum also has important collections which are poorly displayed. The building was the principal palace of the Emperors of Brazil, but only the unfurnished Throne Room and ambassadorial reception room on the second

Brazil

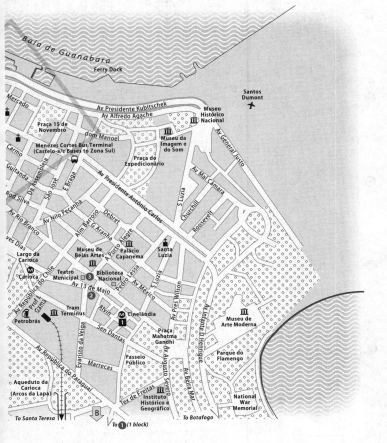

floor reflect past glories. The Museum contains collections of Brazilian Indian weapons, dresses, utensils etc, of minerals and of historical documents. There are also collections of birds, beasts, fishes and butterflies. Despite the need for conservation work, the museum is still worth visiting. ■ *1000-1600, closed Mon, US$2. The safest way to reach the museum is by taking a taxi to the main door. Having said that, it can be reached by Metrô to São Cristóvão, then cross the railway line and walk a few metres to the park. This is safer than taking a bus.* **Museu de Fauna**, also in the Quinta da Boa Vista, contains a most interesting collection of Brazilian fauna. ■ *Tue-Sun 1200-1700.*

Maracanã Stadium is one of the largest sports centres in the world, with a capacity of 200,000. Matches are worth going to if only for the spectators' samba bands. There are three types of ticket, but prices vary according to the game (expect to pay

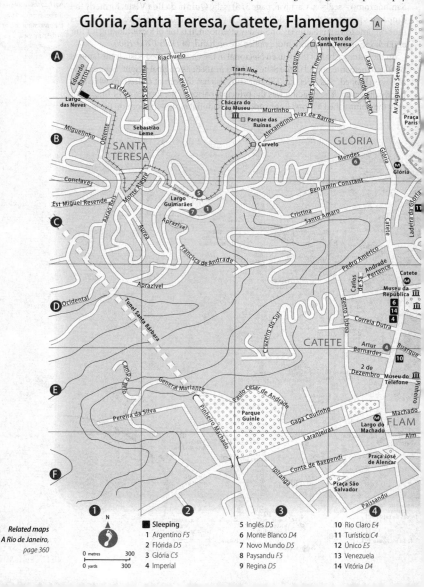

Glória, Santa Teresa, Catete, Flamengo

Related maps
A Rio de Janeiro,
page 360

0 metres 300
0 yards 300

■ **Sleeping**
1 Argentino *F5*
2 Flórida *D5*
3 Glória *C5*
4 Imperial

5 Inglês *D5*
6 Monte Blanco *D4*
7 Novo Mundo *D5*
8 Paysandu *F5*
9 Regina *D5*

10 Rio Claro *E4*
11 Turístico *C4*
12 Único *E5*
13 Venezuela
14 Vitória *D4*

US$7.50-10). Agencies charge much more for tickets than at the gate. It is cheaper to buy tickets from club sites on the day before the match. Seats in the white section have good views. Maracanã is now used only for major games; Rio teams play most matches at their home grounds (still a memorable experience, about US$2 per ticket). Hotels can arrange visits to football matches: a good idea on Sunday when the metrô is closed and buses are very full. ■ *0900-1700 (0800-1100 on match days). A guided tour of the stadium (in Portuguese) from Gate 16 costs US$2 and of the museum, US$0.50, T2568 9962. Highly recommended for football fans.*

The commercial district ends where the Av Rio Branco meets the Av Beira Mar. This avenue, with its royal palms, bougainvilleas and handsome buildings, coasting the Botafogo and Flamengo beaches, makes a splendid drive; its scenery is shared by the motorway, Av Infante Dom Henrique, along the beach over re-claimed land (the *Aterro*), leading to Botafogo and through two tunnels to Copacabana.

South of the centre

On the Glória and Flamengo waterfront, with a view of the Pão de Açúcar and Corcovado, is the **Parque do Flamengo**, designed by Burle Marx, opened in 1965 during the 400th anniversary of the city's founding and landscaped on 100 ha reclaimed from the bay. Security in the park is in the hands of vigilante policemen and it is a popular recreation area. At the city end of Parque Flamengo is the **Museu de Arte Moderna**, a spectacular building at Av Infante Dom Henrique 85, near the National War Memorial. It suffered a disastrous fire in 1978; the collection is now being rebuilt and several countries have donated works of art. ■ *Tue-Sun 1200-1700 (last entry 1630), US$2, T2240 4944, www.mamrio.com.br*

Beware armed robbery in Parque do Flamengo

The Monumento aos Mortos da Segunda Guerra Mundial/National War Memorial to Brazil's dead in the Second World War is at Av Infante Dom Henrique 75, opposite Praça Paris. The Memorial takes the form of two slender columns supporting a slightly curved slab, representing two palms uplifted to heaven. In the crypt are the remains of Brazilian soldiers killed in Italy in 1944-45. ■ *Crypt and museum open Tue-Sun 1000-1700, but beach clothes and rubber-thonged sandals are not permitted.* The beautiful little church on the Glória Hill, overlooking the Parque do Flamengo, is **Nossa Senhora da Glória do Outeiro**. It was the favourite church of the imperial family; Dom Pedro II was baptized here. The building is polygonal, with a single tower. It contains some excellent

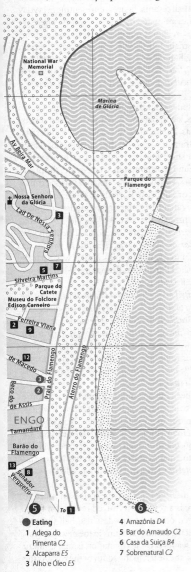

National War Memorial

Marina de Glória

Parque do Flamengo

Nossa Senhora da Glória

Av Beira Mar

Lad De Nossa Senhora

Silveira Martins

Parque do Catete

Museu do Folclore Edison Carneiro

Ferreira Viana

de Macedo

Beco de Assis

Praia do Flamengo

Aterro do Flamengo

ENGO

Tamandaré

Barão do Flamengo

Senador Vergueiro

To ●1

● **Eating**
1 Adega do Pimenta *C2*
2 Alcaparra *E5*
3 Alho e Óleo *E5*
4 Amazônia *D4*
5 Bar do Arnaudo *C2*
6 Casa da Suíça *B4*
7 Sobrenatural *C2*

Brazil

examples of blue-faced Brazilian tiling. Its main altar, of wood, was carved by Mestre Valentim. ■ *The church, 0800-1200 (only Sat-Sun) and 1300-1700 weekdays, is reached by bus 119 from the centre and 571 from Copacabana. The adjacent museum of religious art keeps the same hours, but is closed Mon, T2557 4600.*

Catete and north to the centre – Laranjeiras, Cosme Velho and Lapa – are being renovated 2001

Parque do Catete is a charming small park with birds and monkeys between Praia do Flamengo and the Palácio do Catete, which contains the **Museu da República**, R do Catete 153. The palace was built in 1858-66. In 1887 it was converted into the presidential seat, until the move to Brasília. The first floor is devoted to the history of the Brazilian republic. The museum is highly recommended. ■ *Tue-Sun 1200-1700, US$2.50, T2556 6434. Take bus 571 from Copacabana, or the Metrô to Catete station.*

Museu do Folclore Edison Carneiro, on R do Catete 181, houses a collection not to be missed. There is a collection of small ceramic figures representing everyday life in Brazil, some very funny, some scenes animated by electric motors. There are fine Candomblé and Umbanda costumes, religious objects, ex-votos and sections on many of Brazil's festivals. It has a small, but excellent library, with helpful, friendly staff for finding books on Brazilian culture, history and anthropology. ■ *Tue-Fri 1100-1800, Sat-Sun 1500-1800, free, T2285 0441. Photography is allowed, but without flash. Take bus 571 from Copacabana, or the Metrô to Catete station.*

Santa Teresa
A haven for artists and intellectuals

Known as the coolest part of Rio, this hilly inner suburb southwest of the centre, boasts many colonial and 19th century buildings, set in narrow, curving, tree-lined streets. Today the old houses are lived in by artists, intellectuals and makers of handicrafts. Most visitors in the daytime will arrive by tram. If you stay to the end of the line, Largo das Neves, you will be able to appreciate the small-town feel of the place. There are several bars here, including *Goiabeira*, simple and charming with a nice view of the praça. The essential stop is the Largo do Guimarães, which has some not to be missed eating places (see Eating.) The **Chácara do Céu**, or Fundação Raymundo Ottoni de Castro Maia, Rua Murtinho Nobre 93, has a wide range of art objects and modern painters, including Brazilian; exhibitions change through the year. ■ *Tue-Sun 1200-1700, US$1, T2285 0891, www.visualnet.com.br/cmaya   Take the Santa Teresa tram to Curvelo station, walk along Rua Dias de Barros, following the signposts to Parque das Ruínas.* The **Chalé Murtinho,** Rua Murtinho 41, was in ruins until it was partially restored and turned into a cultural centre called **Parque das Ruínas** in 1998. There are exhibitions, a snack bar and superb views. ■ *Daily 1000-1700.*

■ *Getting there: Santa Teresa is best visited on the traditional open-sided **tram**, the bondinho: take the Metrô to Cinelândia, go to R Senador Dantas then walk along to R Profesor Lélio Gama (look for Banco do Brasil on the corner). The station is up this street. Take the Paula Mattos line (a second line is Dois Irmãos) and enjoy the trip as it passes over the **Arcos da Lapa** aqueduct, winding its way up to the district's historic streets. At Largo das Neves, the tram turns round for the journey back to R Prof L Gama. Fare US$0.40 one way. **Bus**: Nos 206 and 214 run from Av Rio Branco in the centre to Santa Teresa. At night, only take a **taxi**.*

Security In recent years, visitors have been put off going to Santa Teresa because of a reputation for crime which has spilled over from neighbouring *favelas*. It would, however, be a great shame to miss this unique town-within-a-city. The crime rate has been reduced and normally a policeman rides each *bondinho*, but you are advised not to take valuables. A T-shirt, shorts and enough money for a meal should be sufficient. Avoid long walks far from the main centres of Largo das Neves and Largo do Guimarães. The area around *Hotel das Paineiras* is well-patrolled.

Pão de Açúcar (Sugar Loaf mountain)
The bird's eye view of the city and beaches is very beautiful

The Pão de Açúcar, or Sugar Loaf, is a massive granite cone at the entrance to Guanabara Bay that soars to 396 m. There is a restaurant (mixed reports on food, closes 1900) and a playground for children on the Morro da Urca, half way up, where there are also shows at night (consult the cultural sections in the newspapers). You can get refreshments at the top. The sea level cable car station is in a military area, so it is safe to visit. At Praia Vermelha, the beach to the south of the rock, is the

Círculo Militar da Praia Vermelha restaurant, which is open to the public (no sign). It has wonderful views, but is not so good for food or service; stop there for a drink anyway. From Praia Vermelha, the Pista Cláudio Coutinho runs around the foot of the rock. It is a paved path for walking, jogging and access to various climbing places. It is open until 1800, but you can stay on the path after that. Here you have mountain, forest and sea side-by-side, right in the heart of the city. You can also use the Pista Coutinho as a way of getting up the Pão de Açúcar more cheaply than the US$12.50 cable-car ride. About 350 m from the path entrance is a track to the left which leads though the forest to Morro de Urca, from where the cable car can be taken for US$10 (you can come down this way, too, but if you take the cable car from sea level you must pay full fare). You can save even more money, but use more energy, by climbing the Caminho da Costa, a path to the summit of the Pão de Açúcar. Only one stretch, of 10 m, requires climbing gear (even then, some say it is not necessary), but if you wait at the bottom of the path for a group going up, they will let you tag along. This way you can descend to Morro de Urca by cable car for free and walk down from there. There are 35 rock routes up the mountain, with various degrees of difficulty. The best months for climbing are April to August. See Sport, page 380, for climbing clubs; there is also a book on climbing routes.

■ *Getting there: Bus: Bus 107 (from the centre, Catete or Flamengo) and 511 from Copacabana (512 to return) take you to the cable-car station, Avenida Pasteur 520, at the foot.* **Cable car**: *Praia Vermelha to Morro de Urca: first car goes up at 0800, then every 30 mins (or when full), until the last comes down at 2200 (quietest before 1000). From Urca to Sugar Loaf, the first connecting cable car goes up at 0815 then every 30 mins (or when full), until the last leaves the summit at 2200; the return trip costs US$8 (US$6 to Morro da Urca, half-way up). The old cableway has been completely rebuilt. Termini are ample and efficient and the present Italian cable cars carry 75 passengers. Even on the most crowded days there is little queuing.*

Botafogo

The **Museu do Índio**, R das Palmeiras 55, houses 12,000 objects from many Brazilian Indian groups. There is also a small, well-displayed handicraft shop (shop closes for lunch 1200-1400). ■ *Tue-Fri 1000-1730, Sat-Sun 1300-1700, US$1.75, T2286 8899, www.museudoindio.org.br From Botafogo Metrô it's a 10-min walk; from Catete, bus 571 (Glória-Leblon) passes Ruas Bento Lisboa and São Clemente.*

Corcovado

Corcovado is a hunch-backed peak, 710 m high, surmounted by a 38 m high statue of Christ the Redeemer, O Cristo Redentor, which was completed on 12 October 1931. There is a superb view from the top (sometimes obscured by mist), to which there are a cog railway and road; taxis, cooperative minivans and train put down their passengers behind the statue. Private cars are only allowed as far as Paineiras, from where you can catch train or cabs. The 3.8 km railway itself offers fine views. Average speed is 15 kph on the way up and 12 kph on the way down. There is a new exhibition of the history of the railway. From the upper terminus there is a system of escalators, one with a panoramic view, to the top, near which there is a café (alternatively you can climb 220 steps up). To see the city by day and night ascend at 1500 or 1600 and descend on the last train, approximately 1815. Mass is held on Sunday in a small chapel in the statue pedestal. ■ *To reach the vast statue of Cristo Redentor at the summit of Corcovado, you have to go through Laranjeiras and Cosme Velho. The road through these districts heads west out of Catete.*

The **Museu Internacional de Arte Naïf do Brasil** (MIAN), R Cosme Velho 561, T205 8612, F205 8884, is one of the most comprehensive museums of Naïve and folk paintings in the world. It is only 30 m uphill, on the same street as the station for Corcovado. There is a permanent collection of some 8,000 works by Naïve artists from about 130 countries. ■ *Tue-Fri 1000-1800, Sat, Sun and holidays 1200-1800; closed Mon, T2205 8612. US$2.50; discounts for groups, students and senior citizens. Has a good shop at Av Atlântica 1998.*

Brazil

Those who want to see what Rio was like early in the 19th century should go to the **Largo do Boticário**, R Cosme Velho 822, a charming small square in neo-colonial style. Much of the material used in creating the effect of the square came from old buildings demolished in the city centre. The square is close to the terminus for the Corcovado cog railway.

Transport Take a Cosme Velho bus to the cog railway station at Rua Cosme Velho 513: from the centre or Glória/Flamengo No 180; from Copacabana take No 583, from Botafogo or Ipanema/Leblon No 583 or 584; from Santa Teresa Microônibus Santa Teresa. The train runs every 20-30 mins between 0800 and 1830, journey time 10 mins (cost: US$9 return; single tickets available). Taxis and minivans from Paineiras charge US$5 pp. Also, a 206 bus does the very attractive run from Praça Tiradentes (or a 407 from Largo do Machado) to Silvestre (the railway has no stop here now). An active walk of 9 km will take you to the top. For safety reasons go in company, or at weekends when more people are about. If going by car to Corcovado, the entrance fee is US$4 for the vehicle, plus US$4 pp. Coach trips tend to be rather brief and taxis, which wait in front of the station, offer tours of Corcovado and Mirante Dona Marta.

Copacabana

This celebrated curved beach is a must for visitors. Tourist police patrol Copacabana beach until 1700

Built on a narrow strip of land (only a little over four sq km) between mountain and sea, Copacabana has one of the highest population densities in the world: 62,000 per sq km, or 250,000 in all. Copacabana began to develop when the Túnel Velho (Old Tunnel) was built in 1891 and an electric tram service reached it. Weekend villas and bungalows sprang up; all have now gone. In the 1930s the Copacabana Palace Hotel was the only tall building; it is now one of the lowest on the beach. The opening of the

Copacabana

Sleeping
1 Atlantis
2 Benidorm Palace
3 Biarritz
4 Califórnia Othon
5 Castro Alves Othon
6 Copacabana Palace
7 Copacabana Rio
8 Debret
9 Lancaster Othon
10 Le Méridien
11 Rio Atlântica
12 Rio Copa
13 Rio Roiss
14 Sol
15 South American Copacabana
16 Toledo

Túnel Novo (New Tunnel) in the 1940s led to an explosion of population which shows no sign of having spent its force. Unspoilt Art Deco blocks towards the Leme (city) end of Copacabana are now under preservation order.

There is almost everything in this 'city within a city'. The shops, mostly in Avenida Nossa Senhora de Copacabana and the Rua Barata Ribeiro, are excellent. Even more stylish shops are to be found in Ipanema, Leblon and in the various large shopping centres in the city. The city's glamorous nightlife is beginning to move elsewhere and, after dark, Copacabana, has lost some of its former allure. A fort at the far end of the beach, Forte de Copacabana, was an important part of Rio's defences and prevents a seashore connection with the Ipanema and Leblon beaches. Parts of the military area are now being handed over to civilian use, the first being the Parque Garota de Ipanema at Arpoador, the fashionable Copacabana end of the Ipanema beach.

The world-famous beach is divided into numbered *postos*, where the lifeguards are based. Different sections attract different types of people, for example young people, artists and gays. The safest places are in front of the major hotels which have their own security, for instance the *Meridien* on Copacabana beach or the *Caesar Park* on Ipanema. The *Caesar Park* also has 24-hr video surveillance during the summer season, which makes it probably the safest patch of sand in Rio.

Transport Buses to and from the city centre are plentiful and cost US$0.40. The buses to take are Nos 119, 154, 413, 415, 455, 474 from Av Nossa Senhora de Copacabana. If you are going to the centre from Copacabana, look for 'Castelo', 'Praça 15', 'E Ferro' or 'Praça Mauá' on the sign by the front door. 'Aterro' means the expressway between Botafogo and downtown Rio (not open on Sun). From the centre to Copacabana is easier as all buses in that direction are marked. The 'Aterro' bus does the journey in 15 mins.

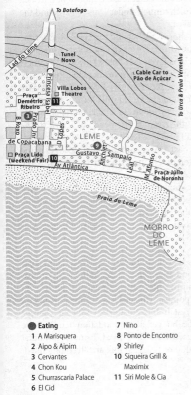

Ipanema & Leblon

Beyond Copacabana are the seaside suburbs of Ipanema and Leblon. The two districts are divided by a canal from the Lagoa Rodrigo de Freitas to the sea, beside which is the Jardim de Alá. Ipanema and Leblon are a little less built-up than Copacabana and their beaches tend to be cleaner. Praia de Arpoadar at the Copacabana end of Ipanema is a peaceful spot to watch surfers, with the beautiful backdrop of Morro Dois Irmãos; excellent for photography, walk on the rocks. There is now night-time illumination on these beaches. The seaward lane of the road running beside the beach is closed to traffic until 1800 on Sundays and holidays; this makes it popular for rollerskating and cycling (bicycles can be hired).

Backing Ipanema and Leblon is the middle-class residential area of **Lagoa Rodrigo de Freitas**, by a saltwater lagoon on which Rio's rowing and small-boat sailing clubs are active. The lake is too polluted for bathing, but the road which runs around its shores has pleasant views. The avenue on the eastern shore, Avenida Epitácio Pessoa, leads to the Túnel Rebouças which runs beneath Corcovado and Cosme Velho.

● **Eating**
1 A Marisquera
2 Aipo & Aipim
3 Cervantes
4 Chon Kou
5 Churrascaria Palace
6 El Cid
7 Nino
8 Ponto de Encontro
9 Shirley
10 Siqueira Grill & Maximix
11 Siri Mole & Cia

Well worth a visit are the **Jardim Botânico** (Botanical Gardens). These were founded in 1808. The most striking features are the transverse avenues of 30 m high royal palms. Among the more than 7,000 varieties of plants from around the world are examples of the *pau-brasil* tree, now endangered, and many other threatened species. There is a herbarium, an aquarium and a library (some labels are unclear). A new pavilion contains sculptures by Mestre Valentim transferred from the centre. Many improvements were carried out before the 1992 Earth Summit, including a new Orquidário and an enlarged bookshop. ■ *The gardens are open 0800-1700, US$2. They are 8 km from the centre; take bus No 170 from the centre, or any bus to Leblon, Gávea or São Conrado marked 'via Jóquei'; from Glória, Flamengo or Botafogo take No 571, or 172 from Flamengo; from Copacabana, Ipanema or Leblon take No 572 (584 back to Copacabana).*

The **Planetário** (Planetarium), on Padre Leonel Franco 240, Gávea, was inaugurated in 1979, with a sculpture of the Earth and Moon by Mario Agostinelli. ■ *Tours are given at 1400 and observations on Fri at 2000, Sat and Sun at 1630, 1800 and 1930. There are occasional chorinho concerts on Thu or Fri; check the press for details. T2274 0096, www.rio.rj.gov.br/planetario Getting there: Buses 176 and 178 from the centre and Flamengo; 591 and 592 from Copacabana.*

Transport Buses run from Botafogo Metrô terminal to Ipanema: some take integrated Metrô-Bus tickets; look for the blue signs on the windscreen. Many buses from Copacabana run to Ipanema and Leblon.

Leblon to Barra da Tijuca The Pedra Dois Irmãos overlooks Leblon. On the slopes is Vidigal *favela*. From Leblon, two inland roads take traffic west to the outer seaside suburb of Barra da Tijuca: the Auto Estrada Lagoa-Barra, which tunnels under Dois Irmãos, and the Estrada da Gávea, which goes through Gávea.

Parque da Cidade, a pleasant park a short walk beyond the Gávea bus terminus, has a great many trees and lawns, the *Museu Histórico da Cidade*, with views over the ocean. The proximity of the Rocinha favela (see below) means the park is not very safe. It is advisable to carry a copy of your passport here because of frequent police checks. ■ *Daily 0700-1700, free. Buses, Nos 593, 592, 174, 170, 546, leave you just short of the entrance, but it should be OK to walk the last part if in a group. Similarly, do not walk the trails in the park alone.* Beyond Leblon the coast is rocky. A third route to Barra da Tijuca is the Avenida Niemeyer, which skirts the cliffs on the journey past Vidigal, a small beach where the *Sheraton* is situated. Avenida Niemeyer carries on round the coast to São Conrado. On the slopes of the Pedra da Gávea, through which the Avenida Niemeyer has two tunnels, is the Rocinha favela.

The flat-topped **Pedra da Gávea** can be climbed or scrambled up for magnificent views, but beware of snakes. Behind the Pedra da Gávea is the Pedra Bonita. A road, the Estrada das Canoas, climbs up past these two rocks on its way to the Parque Nacional Tijuca. There is a spot on this road which is one of the chief hang-glider launch sites in the area (see Sport, page 380).

Barra da Tijuca
Although buses do run as far as Barra, getting to and around here is best by car. A cycle way links Barra da Tijuca with the centre of the city

This rapidly developing residential area is also one of the principal recreation areas of Rio, with its 20-km sandy beach and good waves for surfing. At the westernmost end is the small beach of Recreio dos Bandeirantes, where the ocean can be very rough. The channels behind the Barra are popular with jetskiers. It gets very busy on Sundays. There are innumerable bars and restaurants, clustered at both ends, campsites (see page 373), motels and hotels: budget accommodation tends to be self-catering. A bit further out is the **Museu Casa do Pontal**, Estrada do Pontal 3295, Recreio dos Bandeirantes, a collection of Brazilian folk art. Recommended. ■ *Sat and Sun only, 1400-1800.*

Transport Buses from the city centre to Barra, 1 hr, are Nos 175, 176; from Botafogo, Glória or Flamengo take No 179; Nos 591 or 592 from Leme; and from Copacabana via Leblon No 523 (45 mins-1 hr). A taxi to Zona Sul costs US$15 (US$22.50 after 2400). A comfortable bus, Pegasus, goes along the coast from the Castelo bus terminal to Barra da Tijuca and continues to Campo Grande or Santa Cruz, or take the free 'Barra Shopping' bus. Bus 700 from Praça São Conrado (terminal of bus 553 from Copacabana) goes the full length of the beach to Recreio dos Bandeirantes.

The Pico da Tijuca (1,022 m) gives a good idea of the tropical vegetation of the interior and a fine view of the bay and its shipping. A two to three hr walk leads to the summit: on entering the park at Alto da Boa Vista (0600-2100), follow the signposts (maps are displayed) to Bom Retiro, a good picnic place (1½ hours' walk). At Bom Retiro the road ends and there is another hour's walk up a fair footpath to the summit (take the path from the right of the Bom Retiro drinking fountain; not the more obvious steps from the left). The last part consists of steps carved out of the solid rock; look after children at the summit as there are several sheer drops, invisible because of bushes. The route is shady for almost its entire length. The main path to Bom Retiro passes the Cascatinha Taunay (a 30 m waterfall) and the Mayrink Chapel (built 1860). Beyond the Chapel is the restaurant *A Floresta*. Other places of interest not passed on the walk to the peak are the Paulo e Virginia Grotto, the Vista do Almirante and the Mesa do Imperador (viewpoints). Allow at least five to six hours for the excursion. Maps of the park are available. If hiking in the national park other than on the main paths, a guide may be useful if you do not want to get lost: *Sindicato de Guías*, T2267 4582.

Parque Nacional Tijuca
National park information, T208 4194

Transport Take bus No 221 from Praça 15 de Novembro, No 233 (which continues to Barra da Tijuca) or 234 from the rodoviária or from Praça Sáens Pena, Tijuca (the city suburb, not Barra – reached by Metrô), for the park entrance. Jeep tours are run by Atlantic Forest Jeep Tour, daily; T2495 9827, T9974 0218 (mob), or contact through travel agencies.

The island, the second largest in Guanabara Bay, is noted for its gigantic pebble shaped rocks, butterflies and orchids. At the southwest tip is the interesting Parque Darke de Mattos, with beautiful trees, lots of birds and a lookout on the Morro da Cruz. The island has several beaches, but ask about the state of the water before bathing. The only means of transport are bicycles and horse-drawn carriages (US$15 per hr, many have harnesses which cut into the horse's flesh). Neither is allowed into the Parque Darke de Mattos. A tour by *trenzinho*, a tractor pulling trailers, costs US$1.25, or just wander around on foot, quieter and free. Bicycles can be hired. The island is very crowded at weekends and on public holidays, but is usually quiet during the week. The prices of food and drink are reasonable.

Ilha de Paquetá
A paradise of giant pebbles, and home to butterflies and flowers

Transport Ferry services that leave more or less every two hrs from Praça 15 de Novembro, where there is a general boat terminal; there are boats from 0515 (0710 on Sun and holidays) to 2300, T2533 7524, or hydrofoils between 1000 and 1600, Sat and Sun 0800-1630 hourly, T2533 4343 or Paquetá 3397 0656 (fare US$0.85 by boat, 1 hr, US$2.50 by hydrofoil, 20 mins' journey, which more than doubles its price Sat, Sun and holidays). Buses to Praça 15 de Novembro: No 119 from Glória, Flamengo or Botafogo; Nos 154, 413, 455, 474 from Copacabana, or No 415 passing from Leblon via Ipanema. Other boat trips: Several agencies offer trips to Paquetá. Some also offer a day cruise, including lunch, to Jaguanum Island (see under Itacuruçá) and a sundown cruise around Guanabara Bay. Saveiros Tour, *Rua Conde de Lages 44, Glória, T2224 6990, www.saveiros.com.br, offers tours in sailing schooners around the bay and down the coast, also 'Baía da Guanabara Histórica' historical tours.*

Brazil

Essentials

Sleeping
See Telephone, page 349 for important phone changes
Price codes: see inside front cover

All hotels A-B and above in the following list are a/c. A 10% service charge is usually added to the bill and tax of 5% or 10% may be added (if not already included). Note that not all higher-class hotels include breakfast in their room rates. Economy hotels are found mainly in the 3 districts of Rio: Flamengo/Botafogo (best), Lapa/Fátima and Saúde/Maúa. The city is noisy. An inside room is cheaper and much quieter. Always ask for the actual room price: it usually differs from that quoted, frequently much lower.

■ *on map, page 366*
See Essentials for new telephone number changes

Copacabana LL to **L**: *Copacabana Palace*, Av Atlântica 1702, T2548 7070, www.copacabana palace.orient-express.com World famous hotel with distinguished guest list, tennis courts, popular pool. *Le Méridien*, Av Atlântica 1020, T3873 8888, sales@meridien.com.br World-renowned hotel chain but rooms quite small and better on upper floors, pool, huge breakfast. *Rio Atlântica*, Av Atlântica 2964, T2548 6332, rioatlan@netgate.com.br Excellent suites hotel, pool, 2 restaurants and other facilities. Recommended. *Rio Othon Palace*, Av Atlantica 3264, T2525 2500, F2525 1500, www.hoteis-othon.com.br

L-A: *Califórnia Othon*, Av Atlântica 2616, T/F2257 1900, gevenrio@othon.com.br good. *Copacabana Rio*, Av NS de Copacabana 1256, T2267 9900, www.copacabana riohotel.com.br Very convenient for Copacabana and Ipanema, roof-top pool, plenty of services and eating places nearby, superb breakfast, noisy a/c. *Lancaster Othon*, Av Atlântica 1470, T/F2543 8300, lancaster@othon.com.br Easy to change travellers' cheques, non-smoking rooms, balconies overlook the beach, helpful management, airline discount can cut price. Recommended. *Benidorm Palace*, R Barata Ribeiro 547, T2548 8880, hotelbenidorm@zipmail.com.br Suites and double rooms, sauna. Recommended. *Rio Roiss*, R Aires Saldanha 48, T2522 1142, rioroiss@tropicalbr.com.br Very good, restaurant. *South American Copacabana*, R Francisco de Sá 90, T2522 0040, southamerican@uol.com.br Good location 2 blocks from the beach, safe area, front rooms noisy, helpful front desk staff, highly rated.

A: *Castro Alves Othon*, Av Nossa Senhora de Copacabana 552, T/F2548 8815, srorio@othon.com.br Central, very comfortable and elegant. Recommended. *Debret*, Av Atlântica 3564, T2522 0132, sales@debret.com Good, helpful staff, some inner rooms dark. *Rio Copa*, Av Princesa Isabel 370, T2275 6644, riocopa@mtec.com.br Good value, English spoken. Recommended.

A-B: *Atlantis*, Av Bulhões de Carvalho 61, T2521 1142, atlantishotel@uol.com.br Very good, swimming pool, turkish bath, good breakfast, close to Ipanema and Copacabana beaches. *Biarritz*, R Ayres Saldanha 54, T2522 1087, biarritz@hoteisgandara.com.br Very reasonable considering good position close to beach. *Sol*, R Santa Clara 141, T2257 1840, www.copacabanasolhotel.com.br A/c, modern, safe, quiet, good breakfast, helpful. *Toledo*, R Domingos Ferreira 71, 1 block from beach, T2257 1995, F2257 1931. Good breakfast, single rooms are gloomy, but excellent value.

E pp *Novo Copa Chalet*, Rua Henrique Oswald, T2236-0047, www.copachalet.com.br Good location, breakfast included, English, French, German and Italian spoken.

Brazil

Ipanema and Leblon LL *Caesar Park*, Av Vieira Souto 460, T2525 2525, hotel@caesarpark-rio.com One of Rio's finest hotels, excellent service, beach patrol. **L** *Mar Ipanema*, R Visconde de Pirajá 539, Ipanema, 1 block from the beach, T2512 9898, maripa@domain.com.br Helpful, breakfast. **L** *Marina Palace*, Av Delfim Moreira 630, T22941794, F22941644, hotelmarina@callnet.com.br All rooms have sea view. Sauna, massage, pool. **L** *Sol Ipanema*, Av Vieira Souto 320, T2625 2020, www.solipanema.com.br Best Western. . **A** *Arpoador Inn*, Francisco Otaviano 177, T2523 0060, arpoador@ unisys.com.br. **A** *Ipanema Inn*, Maria Quitéria 27, behind *Caesar Park*, T2523 3092, F2511 5094. Good value and location. **B** *San Marco*, R Visconde de Pirajá 524, T/F2540 5032. 2-star, simple breakfast. **B** *Vermont*, R Visconde de Pirajá 254, T2522 0057, hoteisvermont@uol.com.br A/c, fancy, good value. At R Barão da Torre 175, 3 blocks from beach, are 3 guesthouses: **D** *Casa6ipanema*, casa 6, T2247 1384, www.casa6 ipanema.com 2 dormitories, one double (**B**), safe, quiet, English spoken, discount for long stay. **D** *Harmonia*, casa 18, T2523 4905, T9817 1331 (mob), hostelharmonia@hotmail.com doubles or dormitories, kitchen facilities, English, Spanish, German and Swedish spoken, good internet. And at casa 14, *Hostel Ipanema*, new in 2003.

São Conrado LL *Sheraton*, Av Niemeyer 121 (Vidigal), T2274 1122, res255sheratonsheraton.com Several restaurants located directly on beach front, 3 pools and full sports facilities, Gray Line travel agency and other services associated with 5-star hotel. Near the *Sheraton* is **D** *The White House*, Estrada de Vidigal 605, T2249 4421. Clean hostel accommodation.

Spectacular settings, but isolated and far from centre

Flamengo and Catete L *Glória*, R do Russel 632, T2555 7272, www.hotelgloriario.com.br Stylish and elegant old building, 2 swimming pools. **L** *Novo Mundo*, Praia Flamengo 20, T2557 6226, www.hotelnovomundo-rio.com.br Well recommended but noisy. **AL** *Flórida*, Ferriera Viana 71/81, T2556 5242, eventos.excelsior@windsor hoteis.com.br Sauna, pool, safe, quiet, good views, great breakfast. Recommended. **A** *Regina*, Ferreira Viana 29, T2556 1647,

■ *on map, page 362 Residential area between centre and Copacabana, with good bus and Metrô connections*

hotelregina@hotelregina.com.br Very safe, good breakfast. **B** *Argentina*, Cruz Lima 30, T2558 7233. Best rooms on 5th floor, cheapest on 1st, safe, English spoken, good breakfast. Recommended except for the tours. **B** *Paysandu*, Paissandu 23, T/F2558 7270. Comfortable and good value, helpful staff, good location, organized tours available. **D** *Turístico*, Ladeira da Glória 30, T2557 7698, F2558 9388. With breakfast, a/c, spacious, tourist information provided, helpful, favourable reports, ask about long-stay discounts. **C** *Inglês*, Silveira Martins 20, T2558 3052, F2558 3447. A/c, TV, breakfast. **C** *Único*, Buarque de Macedo 54, T/F2205 9932. TV, a/c, fridge. Recommended. On R do Catete: **D** *Monte Blanco*, No 160, T2225 0121, F2558 5042. Breakfast, a/c, helpful. **D** *Rio Claro*, No 233, T2558 5180. Small rooms, poor breakfast, a/c, safe. **D** *Vitória*, No 172, T2205 5397, F2557 0159. With breakfast, hot water, a/c, mixed reports.

In the **Botafogo** area is **AL-A** *O Veleiro*, T3473 3022, PO Box 62602, Praia de Botafogo, RJ 22252-970, www.oveleiro.com or www.brazilbedandbreakfast.com Address given only with reservation. An "oasis" of bed-and-breakfast accommodation, Canadian/Argentine/Carioca owned, pick-up and drop-off from airport, bus station, tours, guiding, very helpful. Recommended. **C** *El Misti Hostel*, Praia de Botafogo, 462, Casa 9, T2226-0991, www.elmistihostel.com Good location, friendly, helpful.

In **Santa Teresa**, an organization called Cama e Café has 11 bed-and-breakfast places, all in private homes (including the house Ronnie Biggs, the Great Train Robber, used to live in). Prices from **A-D**. All information and reservations through www.camaecafe.com

Between Lapa and Praça Tiradentes is an inner residential area, less desirable than Flamengo. Parts of this area are deserted from 2200 onwards

Lapa and Fátima Near Cinelândia Metrô station are a lot of cheap hotels, but many are hourly rentals. This area is not really recommended as it is not very safe and the nearby sites of interest should only be visited in daylight. In Cinelândia is **B** *Itajubá*, R Álvaro Alvim 23, T2210 3163, itahotel@Openlink.com.br Helpful staff, a little shabby, convenient for the centre. **D** *Marialva*, Gomes Freire 430, near New Cathedral, convenient for Av Rio Branco, buses etc, T2509 3187, F2509 4953. 2-star, a/c, breakfast in room. Recommended. **E** *Love's House*, Joaquim Silva, 87, T2509 5655. Ask for room with window, safe, respectable, good value.

If intending to stay between Christmas and Carnival, reserve youth hostels well in advance

Youth hostels **D** *Chave do Rio de Janeiro*, R Gen Dionísio 63, Botafogo, T2286 0303, www.riohostel.com.br HI, cheaper for members, clean showers, hot water, laundry and cooking facilities, but insufficient toilets. Superb breakfast. Noisy but frequently recommended. **D** pp *Che Lagarto*, www.chelagarto.com Has 2 hostels at: Barão de Jaguaripe St 208, Ipanema, T2247 4582; and Anita Garibaldi St 87, Copacabana, T2256 2778. Both with breakfast included, internet access, wheelchair friendly. **E** pp *Copacabana Praia*, R Tte Marones de Gusmão 85, Bairro Peixoto, T2353817, www.wcenter.com.br/cop_apraia Dormitory, apartments also available. Associations: **ALBERJ** (for Rio), R da Assembléia 10, l 61, T2531 2234, F2531 1943. **Federação Brasileira** (Brazil), at *Chave do Rio de Janeiro* hostel.

Self-catering apartments A popular form of accommodation in Rio, available at all price levels: eg furnished apartments for short-term let, accommodating up to 6, cost US$300 per month in Maracanã, about US$400 in Saúde, Cinelândia, Flamengo. Copacabana, Ipanema and Leblon prices range from about US$25 a day for a simple studio, starting at US$500-600 a

Brazil

month up to US$2,000 a month for a luxurious residence sleeping 4-6. Heading south past Barra da Tijuca, virtually all the accommodation available is self-catering. Renting a small flat, or sharing a larger one, can be much better value than a hotel room. Blocks consisting entirely of short-let apartments can attract thieves, so check the (usually excellent) security arrangements; residential buildings are called *prédio familial*. Higher floors (*alto andar*) are considered quieter.

Apart-Hotels are listed in the *Guia 4 Rodas* and *Riotur*'s booklet. Agents and private owners advertise in *Balcão* (like the UK's *Exchange and Mart*), twice weekly, *O Globo* or *Jornal do Brasil* (daily); under 'Apartamentos – Temporada'; advertisements are classified by district and size of apartment: 'vagas e quartos' means shared accommodation; 'conjugado' (or 'conj') is a studio with limited cooking facilities; '3 Quartos' is a 3-bedroom flat. There should always be a written agreement when renting.

The following rent apartments in residential blocks: **Copacabana Holiday**, R Barata Ribeiro 90A, Copacabana, T2542 1525, www.copacabanaholiday.com.br Recommended, well-equipped small apartments from US$500 per month, minumum 30 days let. **Fantastic Rio**, Av Atlântica 974, Suite 501, Copacabana, BR-22020-000, T/F2543 2667, hpcorr@hotmail.com All types of furnished accommodation from US$20 per day, owned by Peter Corr. **Fernando**, R Catete 214, casa 31/201, T9818 0396 (mob). Apartments in Flamengo and Catete, any length of stay, good value, Fernando speaks English and acts as a guide. **Paulo de Tarso**, Av Princesa Isabel, 236, Apto 102, T2542 5635, pauldetarso@ig.com.br Apartments near Copacabana beach from US$25 pp. **Yvonne Reimann**, Av Atlântica 4066, Apto 605, T2227 0281. Rents apartments, all with phone, near beach, a/c, maid service, English, French, German spoken, all apartments owned by agency, from US$50 per flat. **Rio Residences**, Av Prado Júnior 44, apto 508, T2541 4568, F2541 6462. Swiss run, includes airport transfer. Also *RIOFLATRENTAL*, Av Fleming 212, Barra da Tijuca, CEP 226110040, T2226 0991, www.rioflatrental.com

Camping Clube do Brasil, Av Sen Dantas 75, 29th floor, Centro, CEP 20037-900, T2210 3171, has 2 beach sites at Barra da Tijuca: Av Sernambetiba 3200, T2493 0628 (bus 233 from centre, 702 or 703 from the airport via Zona Sul, US$5 – a long way from the centre), sauna, pool, bar, café, US$12 (half price for members), during Jan and Feb this site is often full and sometimes restricted to members of the *Camping Clube do Brasil*; a simpler site at Estrada do Pontal 5900, T2437 8400, lighting, café, good surfing, US$6. Both have trailer plots. *Ostal*, Av Sernambetiba 18790, T2437 8350; and *Novo Rio*, at Km 17 on the Rio-Santos road, T2437 6518. If travelling by trailer, you can park at the Marina Glória car park, where there are showers and toilets, a small shop and snack bar. Pay the guards to look after your vehicle.

Camping

You can eat well for an average US$10-20 pp, less if you choose the *prato feito* at lunchtime (US$1.50-6), or eat in a place that serves food by weight (starting at about US$0.65 per gm). You can expect to pay US$20-40 pp in first-class places, more in the very best restaurants. While many of Rio's quality hotels offer world-class food and service, they may lack atmosphere and close at midnight. There are much livelier and cheaper places to eat if going out for an evening meal. Grill or barbecue houses (*churrascarias*) are relatively cheap, especially

Eating
● *Cariocas usually have dinner at 1900 or 2000, occasionally later at weekends after going out for the evening*

by European standards. There are many at São Conrado and Joá, on the road out to Barra da Tijuca (see page 368). *Galetos* are lunch counters specializing in chicken and grilled meat, very reasonable. Most less-expensive restaurants in Rio have basically the same type of food (based on steak, fried potatoes and rice) and serve large portions. *La Mole*, at 11 locations, serves good, cheap Italian food, very popular.

Many restaurants in this business district are open only for weekday lunch

Centre Expensive: *Republique*, Praça da República 63 (2nd floor). Chic, designed by the architect Chicô Gouveia, good food. **Mid-range**: *Art Station Grill*, Av Rio Branco 156 (downstairs in Shopping Avenida Central), www.artstation.com.br Carioca food, very good buffet lunch with wide variety of meat, fish and vegetables. *Café do Teatro*, Rio Branco, Teatro Municipal. Traditional cuisine served in the grand manner, no shorts or scruffy clothes allowed, weekday lunch only. **Cheap**: *Albamar*, Praça Marechal Âncora 184-6. Good, reasonably priced fish and seafood, with lovely views of the bay, 1130-1600 Mon, 1130-2200 Tue-Sat. *Al-kuwait*, Av Treze de Maio, T2240 1114. Charming Middle Eastern restaurant in unprepossessing alley off Treze de Maio, no English menu but helpful staff, closed Sat and Sun. *Bistro do Paço*, Praça 15 de Novembro 48 (Paço Imperial), T2262 3613. Good value food in attractive surroundings, Swiss-run. *Fiorino*, Av Heitor Beltrão 126, Tijuca, T25674476. Delicious, home-cooked Italian food with indulgent deserts. Recommended. *Mala e Cuia*, R Candelária 92. For *comida mineira*. Recommended. *Rio Minho*, R do Ouvidor 10, T2509 2338. For excellent seafood in historic building. **Seriously cheap**: Many *lanchonetes* offer good meals in the business sector. R Miguel Couto (opposite Santa Rita church) is called the *Beco das Sardinhas* because on Wed and Fri in particular it's full of people eating sardines and drinking beer. There are several Arab restaurants on Av Senhor dos Passos, which are also open Sat and Sun. *Luciano*, R das Marrecas 44. This functional all-you-can-eat buffet is one of several on this street.

Santa Teresa Mid-range: One of the best restaurants in Rio is the *Bar do Arnaudo*, in the Largo do Guimarães, R Almte Alexandrino 316, T2252 7246. Tue-Sat 1200-2200, Sun 1200-1600, it is decorated with handicrafts; the cuisine is northeastern, prices are reasonable and portions huge; try the *caipirinhas*, the *carne do sol* (sun-dried beef, or jerky) with *feijão de corda* (brown beans and herbs), or the *queijo coalho* (a country cheese, grilled). Also in the Largo do Guimarães is *Adega do Pimenta*, R Almte Alexandrino 296. Mon, Wed-Fri 1130-2200, Sun 1100-1800. A very small German restaurant with excellent sausages, sauerkraut and cold beer. On the same praça, *Sobrenatural*, R Almirante Alexandrino 432, T22241003. Daily 1200-2400, a charming rustic restaurant serving fish caught daily on the owner's boat, with a menu in English. For a light lunch, order a mix of excellent appetizers. Recommended.

Lapa and Glória Mid-range: *Adega Flor de Coimbra*, R Teotônio Regadas 34, Lapa. Founded 1938, serving Portuguese food and wines, speciality *bacalhau*. Very good. *Café Glória*, R do Russel 734, T2205 9647. Daily for lunch and dinner, beautiful Art Nouveau building, helpful staff, excellent food. *Casa da Suiça*, R Cândido Mendes 157, T2252 5182. Bar/restaurant, good atmosphere; several others on this street. **Flamengo and Catete Mid-range/cheap**: There are a lot of eating places on R do Catete: *Estação República*, No 104, good self-service. *Catelandia*, No 204, excellent and cheap, pay by weight. *Amazônia*, No 234B, downstairs, 1-price counter service, upstairs for good, reasonably priced evening meals. Recommended. *Catete Grill*, No 239, good. At Largo do Machado, *O Bom Galeto*, R do Catete 282, for chicken and meats. Next door is *Trattoria Gambino*, recommended for pasta, pleasant on summer evenings. *Adega Portugali*, Largo do Machado 30. Good food, red wine and *caipirinhas*. In the gallery at Largo de Machado 29 is *Rotisseria Sirio Libaneza*, ljs 32 e 33, very good value Arabic food. *Alcaparra*, Praia do Flamengo 144, elegant traditional Italian, reasonable. *Alho E Óleo*, R Buarque de Macedo 13. Fashionable, pleasant. Recommended. *Lamas*, Marquês de Abrantes 18A. Excellent value, good food, great atmosphere, opens late, popular with Brazilian arts/media people. Recommended.

Botafogo Mid-range: *Raajmahal*, R Gen Polidoro 29. Authentic Indian food. In Baixo Botafogo R Visconde de Caravelas has several interesting bars and restaurants, eg *Aurora*, corner of R Capitão Salomão 43 (cheap), and *Botequim*, No 184, varied menu, good food and value. Also here is *Cobal Humaitá*, a fruit market with many popular restaurants (Mexican *tacos*, pizzería, etc). Rio Sul Shopping has a lot of choice for food, including *Chez Michou*, crêpes and chopp, 4th floor, *Habib's*, Arabic fast-food, 2 branches of *Kotobuki* sushi bar (another branch on the road to Praia Vermelha, recommended) and *Chaika* for milkshakes, ice creams and sandwiches (4th floor, original branch on Praça Nossa Senhora da Paz, Ipanema).

Copacabana and Leme **Expensive**: *Shirley*, R Gustavo Sampaio 610, T2275 1398. Spanish, small, seafood, book in advance. *Churrascaria Marius*, Av Atlântica 290, also at R F Otaviano 96, Ipanema. Recommended. **Mid-range:**Chon Kou*, Av Atlântica 3880, T2287 3956. Traditional Chinese restaurant also offering an extensive sushi menu, a/c, sit upstairs for good views over Copacabana beach. *El Cid*, Min Viveiros de Castro 15B. Well-established for excellent steaks. *Churrascaria Palace*, R Rodolfo Dantas 16B, Long-established, 20 different kinds of meat, good food and value. *Nino*, Domingos Ferreira 242. Italian cuisine, Argentine beef, excellent. *Siqueira Grill*, R Siqueira Campos 16B. Pay-by-weight, wide selection, excellent value. **Cheap**: *Aipo & Aipim*, Av NS de Copacabana 391. Excellent food by weight at this popular chain with other branches on this road. *Al Capo*, Av NS de Copacabana e J Nabuco. Excellent fresh pasta. *Cervantes*, Barata Ribeiro 07-B e Prado Júnior 335B. Stand-up bar or sit-down, a/c restaurant, open all night, queues after 2200, said to serve the best sandwiches in town, a local institution. *A Marisquera*, Barata Ribeiro 232. Good seafood. *Maximix*, R Siqueira Campos 12, loja A. Buffet by weight, opens late, very popular. Recommended. *Ponto de Encontro*, Barata Ribeiro 750. Portuguese, try baked *bacalhau*. *Siri Mole & Cia*, R Francisco Otaviano 90. Brazilian cuisine, don't miss coffee after the meal from an old-fashioned coffee machine. *Taberna do Leme* , Princesa Isabel e Av NS Copacabana. Bar/restaurant with helpful waiters, comprehensive menu in English includes delicious crab pancakes. Warmly recommended for eating as well as drinking. **Seriously cheap**: There are stand-up bars selling snacks all around this area. *Marakesh*, Av NS de Copacabana 599. Good quality and value, pay by weight.

Ipanema **Expensive**: *Amarcord*, R Maria Quitéria 136. Recommended. *Pax Delícia*, Praça NS da Paz. Excellent light foods and salads, vegetarian options, lively crowd. Mon from 2000 and Tue-Sun from 1200. Recommended. **Mid-range**: *Grottamare*, R Gomes Carneiro 132. Good seafood. *Mostarda*, Av Epitácio Pessoa 980. Excellent food (often seasoned with mustard sauce), nightclub upstairs, entry fee can be avoided if you eat in the 1st floor restaurant before 2200-2300. Recommended. *Porcão*, Barão de Torre 218, a very good *churrascaria*, US$25 pp (another branch at Av NS de Copacabana 1144). *Satyricon*, R Barão da Torre 192, T2521 0627. Upmarket establishment specialising in Mediterranean cuisine.*Yemenjá*, R Visconde de Pirajá 128. Brazilian food from the Bahia region. *Casa da Feijoada*, Prudente de Morais 10. Serves an excellent *feijoada* all week. *La Frasca*, R Garcia d'Ávila 129. Good Italian, pleasant atmosphere. **Seriously cheap**: *Amarelinho*, R Farme de Amoedo 62. Great corner lanchonete with tables outside, fresh food, good value, friendly, open until 0300. Recommended.*Delicats*, Av Henrique Dumont 68. Good Jewish deli.

Ipanema is quieter than Copacabana, many nice places round Praça Gen Osório

Leblon **Mid-range**: *Ettore*, Av Ataulfo de Paiva 1321, loja A. Excellent Italian. *Mediterráneo*, R Prudente de Morais 1810. Excellent fish. *Un, Deux, Trois*, R Bartolomeu Mitre 123. Very fashionable, restaurant, nightclub. **Cheap**: *Celeiro*, R Dias Ferreira 199. Some of the best salads in the city, and light food, pay by weight.

Jardim Botânico and Lagoa **Expensive**: *Claude Troisgros*, R Custódio Serrão 62. Elegant French restaurant. Recommended. *Enotria*, R Frei Leandro 20. Excellent Italian food, service, atmosphere and prices. Recommended. **Mid-range**: *Mistura Fina*, Av Borges de Medeiros 3207, T2537 2844. Classy, popular, friendly nightclub upstairs.

Cafés For those who like their teas served English style, the sedate *Confeitaria Colombo*, R Gonçalves Dias 32, near Carioca Metrô station, is highly recommended for atmosphere, being the only one of its kind in Rio. Over 100 years old, it has the original Belle Epoque décor, 0900-1800, lunch available, no service charge so tip the excellent waiters. More

Brazil

▶ *Carnival*

Carnival in Rio is spectacular. On the Friday before Shrove Tuesday, the mayor of Rio hands the keys of the city to Rei Momo, the Lord of Misrule, signifying the start of a five-day party. Imagination runs riot, social barriers are broken and the main avenues, full of people and children wearing fancy dress, are colourfully lit. Areas throughout the city such as the Terreirão de Samba in Praça Onze are used for shows, music and dancing. Bandas and blocos (organized carnival groups) seem to be everywhere, dancing, drumming and singing.

There are numerous samba schools in Rio divided into two leagues, both of which parade in the Sambódromo. The 14 schools of the Grupo Especial parade on Sunday and Monday whilst the Grupos de Acesso A and B parade on Saturday and Friday respectively. There is also a mirins parade (younger members of the established schools) on Tuesday. The judging takes place on Wednesday afternoon and the winners of the various groups parade again on the following Saturday.

The Carnival parades are the culmination of months of intense activity by community groups, mostly in the city's poorest districts. Every school presents 2,500-6,000 participants divided into alas (wings) each with a different costume and 5-9 carros alegóricos, beautifully designed floats. Each school chooses an enredo (theme) and composes a samba (song) that is a poetic, rhythmic and catchy expression of the theme. The enredo is further developed through the design of the floats and costumes. A bateria (percussion wing) maintains a reverberating beat that must keep the entire school, and the audience, dancing throughout the parade. Each procession follows a set order with the first to appear being the comissão de frente, a choreographed group that presents the school and the theme to the public. Next comes the abre alas, a magnificent float usually bearing the name or symbol of the school. The alas and other floats follow as well as porta bandeiras and mestre salas, couples dressed in 18th century costumes bearing the school's flag, and passistas, groups traditionally of mulata dancers. An ala de bahianas, elderly women

with circular skirts that swirl as they dance is always included as is the velha guarda, distinguished members of the school who close the parade. Schools are given between 65 and 80 minutes and lose points for failing to keep within this time. Judges award points to each school for components of their procession, such as costume, music and design, and make deductions for lack of energy, enthusiasm or discipline. The winners of the Grupos de Acesso are promoted to the next higher group while the losers, including those of the Grupo Especial, are relegated to the next lowest group. Competition is intense and the winners gain a monetary prize funded by the entrance fees.

*The **Sambódromo**, a permanent site at R Marquês de Sapucai, Cidade Nova, is 600 m long with seating for 43,000 people. Designed by Oscar Niemeyer and built in 1983-84, it handles sporting events, conferences and concerts during the rest of the year.*

Rio's bailes (fancy-dress balls) range from the sophisticated to the wild. The majority of clubs and hotels host at least one. The Copacabana Palace hotel's is elegant and expensive whilst the Scala club has licentious parties. It is not necessary to wear fancy dress; just join in, although you will feel more comfortable if you wear a minimum of clothing to the clubs (crowded, hot and rowdy). The most famous are the Red & Black Ball (Friday) and the Gay Ball (Tuesday) which are both televised.

Bandas and blocos can be found in all neighbourhoods and some of the most popular and entertaining are Cordão do Bola Preta (meets at 0900 on Saturday in Rua 13 de Maio 13, Centro), Simpatia é Quase Amor (meets at 1600 Sunday in Praça General Osório, Ipanema) and the transvestite Banda da Ipanema (meets at 1600 on Saturday and Tuesday in Praça General Osorio, Ipanema). It is necessary to join a bloco in advance to receive their distinctive T-shirts, but anyone can join in with the bandas.

The expensive hotels offer special Carnival breakfasts from 0530. Caesar Park is highly recommended for a wonderful meal and a top-floor view of the sunrise over the beach.

Tickets The Sambódromo parades start at 1900 and last about 12 hrs. Gates (which are not clearly marked) open at 1800. There are cadeiras (seats) at ground level, arquibancadas (terraces) and camarotes (boxes). The best boxes are reserved for tourists and VIPs and are very expensive or by invitation only. Seats are closest to the parade, but you may have to fight your way to the front. Seats and boxes reserved for tourists have the best view, sectors 3, 5, 7, 9 and 11 all have good views (4, 7 and 11 house the judging points). 6 and 13 are at the end when dancers might be tired, but have more space. The terraces, while uncomfortable, house the most fervent fans, tightly packed; this is where to soak up the atmosphere but not take pictures (too crowded). Ticket prices for 2004 were not available at the time of going to press, but the arquibancadas are cheaper than the cadeiras. They are sold at banks and travel agencies as well as the Maracanã Stadium box office; expect to pay in the hundreds of dollars. Tickets are usually sold out before Carnaval weekend but touts outside can generally sell you tickets at inflated prices. Samba schools have an allocation of tickets which members sometimes sell, if you are offered one of these check its date. Tickets for the champions' parade on the Saturday following Carnival are much cheaper. Taxis to the Sambódromo are negotiable and will find your gate, the nearest metrô is Praça Onze and this can be an enjoyable ride in the company of costumed samba school members. You can follow the participants to the concentração, the assembly and formation on Avenida Presidente Vargas, and mingle with them while the queue to enter the Sambódromo. Ask if you can take photos.

Sleeping and security Visitors wishing to attend the Carnival are advised to reserve accommodation well in advance. Virtually all hotels raise their prices during Carnival, although it is usually possible to find a room. Your property should be safe inside the Sambódromo, but the crowds outside can attract pickpockets; as ever, don't brandish your camera, and only take the money you need for fares and food which is sold in the Sambódromo.) It gets hot so wear little.

Taking part Most samba schools will accept a number of foreigners and you will be charged upwards of US$200 (+ tax) for your costume as your money helps to fund poorer members of the school. You should be in Rio for at least two weeks before carnival. It is essential to attend fittings and rehearsals on time, to show respect for your section leaders and to enter into the competitive spirit of the event. For those with the energy and the dedication, it will be an unforgettable experience.

Rehearsals Ensaios are held at the schools' quadras from Oct onwards and are well worth seeing. It is wise to go by taxi, as most schools are based in poorer districts. Tour agents sell tickets for glitzy samba shows, which are nothing like the real thing. When buying a Carnival video, make sure the format is compatible (Brazilian format matches the USA; VHS PAL for most of Europe).

Samba Schools Acadêmicos de Salgueiro, R Silva Teles 104, Andaraí, T238 5564, www.salgueiro.com.br Beija Flor de Nilópolis, Pracinha Wallace Paes Leme 1025, Nilópolis, T791 2866, www.grupointernet.com.br/beija-flor/ Imperatriz Leopoldinense, R Prof. Lacê 235, Ramos, T270 8037. Mocidade Independente de Padre Miguel, R Coronel Tamarindo 38, Padre Miguel, T3332 5823. Portela, R Clara Nunes 81, Madureira, T3390 0471. Primeira Estação de Mangueira, R Visconde de Niterói 1072, Mangueira, T567 4637, www.mangueira.com.br Unidos da Viradouro, Av do Contorno 16, Niterói, T717 7540, www.viradouro.com

Useful information Riotur's guide booklet gives concise information on official and unofficial events in English. www.ipanema.com has a thorough explanation of how it all works. The entertainment sections of newspapers and magazines such as O Globo, Jornal do Brasil, Manchete and Veja Rio are worth checking. Liga Independente das Escolas de Samba do Rio de Janeiro, http://liesa.globo.com The book, Rio Carnival Guide, by Felipe Ferreira, has good explanations of the competition, rules, the schools, a map and other practical details. 21-24 Feb 2004, 5-8 Feb 2005, 26 Feb-1 Mar 2006 are the big parade days.

Brazil

modern but similar establishments in some of the main hotels, eg *Pergula*, *Copacabana Palace Hotel*, Av Atlântica 1702, Mon-Fri 1400-1700. Recommended. Also *Casarão*, Souza Lima 37A, Copacabana. *Traiteurs de France*, Av NS de Copacabana 386. Delicious tarts and pastries, not expensive.

Bars & clubs
A beer costs around US$1.50, but up to US$5 in expensive hotel bars. A cover charge of US$3-7 may be made for live music, or there might be a minimum consumption charge of around US$3; sometimes both. Snack food is always available

Copacabana, Ipanema and Leblon have many beach *barracas*, several open all night. The seafront bars on Av Atlântica are great for people-watching. The big hotels have good cocktail bars (*Copacabana Palace*, poolside, recommended). Seafront restaurant/bars in Ipanema: *Barril 1800*, Av Vieira Souto 110, T2523 0085. Good Brazilian menu, fish and meat, nice place to watch the sunset. *A Garota de Ipanema*, R Vinícius de Morais 49, is where the song 'Girl from Ipanema' was written, very lively. On the same street, No 39, 2nd floor, is *Vinícius*, live music and international cuisine from 1900. In Leblon is the *Academia da Cachaça*, R Conde de Bernadotte 26-G, with another branch at Av Armando Lombardi 800, Barra da Tijuca. Lots more bars are opening in districts to the south. *Bar Lagoa*, Av Epitácio Pessoa 1674, Lagoa. Recommended ('arty crowd', evenings only). On weekday evenings, Cariocas congregate at the bars around Praça Santos Dumont, Gávea. British ex-pats meet at *Porão*, under the Anglican church hall, R Real Grandeza 99, Botafogo, Fri only.

Lapa, once run-down and to be avoided at night, is now one of the trendiest districts to go for drinking and music: *Carioca da Gema*, Av Mem de Sá 79, Centro, T2221 0043. 1800 Mon-Fri and 2100 Sat, a 'musical café' with a varied programme, cover charge US$3.20 and minimum consumption US$3.20. Next door at No 81 is *Sacrilégio*, a 'cultural café' open from 1900 every night for cutting-edge theatre and other events, T2507 3898 for more information. *Semente*, R Joaquim Silva 138, T2242 5165. Popular for samba, choro and salsa from 2200 Mon-Sat, US$2.50 cover, minimum consumption US$2, book at weekends, great atmosphere inside and in the street outside. Recommended.

Rio nightlife is rich and infinitely varied, one of the main attractions for most visitors. If you are not in Rio for Carnival, it's worth seeing a samba show; entry is cheaper if you pay at the door

The usual system in **nightclubs** is to pay an entrance fee (about US$10) and then you are given a card onto which your drinks are entered. There is often a minimum consumption of US$10-15 on top of the entry charge. Do not lose your card or they may charge you more than you could possibly drink. Most places will serve reasonable snack food. Trendiest clubs playing contemporary dance music are *El Turf* (aka *Jockey Club*) , opposite the Jardim Botânico, Praça Santos Dumont 31. Opens 2100, gets going at 2300, you may have to wait to get in at the weekend if you arrive after midnight, no T-shirts allowed, very much a singles and birthday party place; another branch in Rio Sul Shopping Centre. *Fun Club*, also in Shopping Centre Rio Sul, 4th floor. *Le Boy*, Raul Pompéia 94, Copacabana, gay. *Papillon Club*, Inter Continental Hotel, Av Prefeito Mendes de Moraes 222, São Conrado, T3322 2200. *The Basement*, Av Nossa Senhora de Copacabana 1241, alternative. *W*, Visconde de Piraja, Ipanema, fashionable, good crowd. In Barra da Tijuca, *Rock 'n' Rio Café*, Barra Shopping. Good food, young crowd, a long way from the centre (taxis hard to find in the early morning). *Greenwich Village*, at Posto 6 on the beach front. Good reputation. There are dozens of other good clubs, most open Wed-Sun, action starts around midnight, lone women and male-only groups may have trouble getting in.

Gafieiras, for Samba dancing, including *Elite Club*, R Frei Caneca 4, 1st floor, Centro, also reggae. *Estudantina*, Praça Tiradentes 79, Thu-Sat. There are many cheaper *gafieiras*. All types of music and entertainment are represented: *Copa Show*, Av Nossa Senhora de Copacabana 435, has been recommended for forró and disco music (safe). *Reggae Rock Cafe*, Largo de São Conrado 20, T3322 4197. *Raizes*, Av Sernambetiba 1120, T3389 6240, for Afro-Brazilian beats. For samba, choro, forró, *Severyna*, R Ipiranga 54, Laranjeiras (also serves northeastern food), cover US$3. *Discoteca Fundição do Progresso*, downtown, near Lapa/Centro. Very trendy disco. Copacabana is full of discos where the girls are prostitutes. Sleazier shows are concentrated around Leme, as are gay clubs; many gay clubs also around Lapa (Cinelândia), but good ones exist all over the city.

Entertainment **Cinemas** New American releases (with original soundtrack), plus Brazilian and worldwide films and classics are all shown. See the local press. The normal seat price is US$4, discounts on Wed and Thu (students pay half price any day of the week).

Music Free concerts throughout the summer on Copacabana and Ipanema beaches, in Botafogo and at the parks: mostly samba, reggae, rock and MPB (Brazilian pop): no advance schedule, check the local press (see below). *Canecão* is a big, inexpensive venue for live concerts, most nights, see press for listings: R Venceslau Brás 215, Botafogo, T2543 1241. Rio's famous jazz, in all its forms, is performed in lots of enjoyable venues, see the press, which also lists who is playing at *Teatro Rival*, R Alvaro Alvim 33, Cinelândia, T2532 4192. *Centro Cultural Carioca*, R do Teatro, 37, T2242 9642, www.centroculturalcarioca.com 1830-the early hours, an exciting new venue, combining music (mostly samba) and dance, restored old house attracting a lovely mix of people. Professional dancers perform with musicians; after a few tunes the audience joins in. Thu is impossibly crowded; Sat calmer, bar food available, US$3 cover. Highly recommended. For purely local entertainment on Mon night, *Praia do Vermelha* at Urca. Residents bring musical instruments and chairs onto the beach for an informal night of samba from around 2100-midnight. Free. Bus no 511 from Copacabana.

Festivals Less hectic than Carnival, but very atmospheric, is the festival of *Iemanjá* on the night of **31 Dec**, when devotees of the *orixá* of the sea dress in white and gather on Copacabana, Ipanema and Leblon beaches, singing and dancing around open fires and making offerings. The elected Queen of the Sea is rowed along the seashore. At midnight small boats are launched as offerings to Iemanjá. The religious event is dwarfed, however, by a massive New Year's Eve party, called *Reveillon* at Copacabana. The beach is packed as thousands of revellers enjoy free outdoor concerts by big-name pop stars, topped with a lavish midnight firework display. It is most crowded in front of *Copacabana Palace Hotel*. Another good place to see fireworks is in front of *Le Meridien*, famous for its fireworks waterfall at about 10 mins past midnight. **NB** Many followers of *Iemanjá* are now making their offerings on 29 or 30 Dec and at Barra da Tijuca or Recreio dos Bandeirantes to avoid the crowds and noise of Reveillon. The festival of *São Sebastião*, patron saint of Rio, is celebrated by an evening procession on **20 Jan**, leaving Capuchinhos Church, Tijuca, and arriving at the cathedral of São Sebastião. On the same evening, an *umbanda festival* is celebrated at the Caboclo Monument in Santa Teresa. **Festas Juninas**: *Santo Antônio* on **13 Jun**, whose main event is a mass, followed by celebrations at the Convento do Santo Antônio and the Largo da Carioca. Throughout the state of Rio, the festival of *São João* is a major event, marked by huge bonfires on the night of **23-24 Jun**. It is traditional to dance the *quadrilha* and drink *quentão*, cachaça and sugar, spiced with ginger and cinnamon, served hot. The *Festas Juninas* close with the festival of *São Pedro* on **29 Jun**. Being the patron saint of fishermen, his feast is normally accompanied by processions of boats. **Oct** is the month of the feast of *Nossa Senhora da Penha*.

Jewellery *H Stern*, R Visconde de Pirajá 490/R Garcia Dávila 113, Ipanema, have 10 outlets, plus branches in major hotels. Next door is *Amsterdam Sauer*, R Garcia D'Ávila 105, with10 shops in Rio and others throughout Brazil. They offer free taxi rides to their main shop. There are several good jewellery shops at the Leme end of Av NS de Copacabana. For mineral specimens as against cut stones, try *Mineraux*, Av NS de Copacabana 195, Belgian owner.

Shopping
Buy precious and semi-precious stones from reputable dealers

Bookshops *Argumento*, R Dias Ferreira 417, Leblon, sells imported English books. *Da Vinci*, Av Rio Branco 185 lojas 2, 3 and 9, all types of foreign books. *Dazibão*, Praça 15 de Novembro and in Botafogo, Ipanema and Catete, www.dazibao.com.br Art, culture and history of Brazil. *FNAC* has a megastore at Barra Shopping, with French, English and other imported titles, CDs, etc. *Kosmos*, R do Rosário 155, good shop (in the centre and Av Atlântica 1702, loja 5). *Letras e Expressões*, R Visconde de Pirajá 276, Ipanema and Av Ataulfo 1292, Leblon, www.letras.com Wide selection of books and magazines (Brazilian and foreign), CDs, café, internet access, 24 hrs. *Saraiva* has a megastore at R do Ouvidor 98, T507 9500, also with a music and video shop and a café; other branches in Shopping Iguatemi and Shopping Tijuca. *Siciliano*, Av Rio Branco 156, loja 26. European books, also at Nossa Senhora de Copacabana 830 and branches; French books at No 298. Branches of *Sodiler* at both airports and Barra Shopping, Rio Sul, other shopping centres and at R São José 35, loja V. *Livraria da Travessa*, Travessa do Ouvidor 11-A, superb new branch at Av Rio Branco 44 and R Visconde de Pirajá 572, Ipanema. Excellent.

Markets Northeastern market at Campo de São Cristóvão, with music and magic, on Sun 0800-2200 (bus 472 or 474 from Copacabana or centre). A recommended shop for northeastern handicrafts is *Pé de Boi*, R Ipiranga 55, Laranjeiras, www.pedeboi.com.br Sat antiques market on the waterfront near Praça 15 de Novembro, 1000-1700. Also in Praça 15 de Novembro is *Feirarte II*, Thu-Fri 0800-1800. *Feirarte I* is a Sun open-air handicrafts market (everyone calls it the *Feira Hippy*) at Praça Gen Osório, Ipanema, 0800-1800, items from all over Brazil. A stamp, coin and postcard market is held in the Passeio Público on Sun, 0800-1300. Markets on Wed 0700-1300 on R Domingos Ferreira and on Thu, same hrs, on Praça do Lido, both Copacabana (Praça do Lido also has a *Feirarte* on Sat-Sun 0800-1800). Sun market on R da Glória, colourful, cheap fruit, vegetables and flowers; early-morning food market, 0600-1100, R Min Viveiros de Castro, Ipanema. There is a cheap market for just about anything, especially electronic goods, outside Metro stop Uruguaiana. Excellent food and household-goods markets at various places in the city and suburbs (see newspapers for times and places).

Saara is a multitude of little shops along R Alfândega and R Senhor dos Passos (between city centre and Campo Santana), where clothes bargains can be found (especially jeans and bikinis); it is known popularly as 'Shopping a Céu Aberto'. Little shops on Aires Saldanha, Copacabana (1 block back from beach), are good for bikinis and cheaper than in shopping centres.

Music For a large selection of Brazilian Music, jazz and classical, *Modern Sound Música Equipamentos*, R Barata Ribeiro 502D, Copacabana. *Toca do Vinícius*, R Vinícius de Moraes 129C, Ipanema. Specializes in Bossa Nova books, CDs, doubles as a performance space.

Shopping Malls The *Rio Sul*, at the Botafogo end of Túnel Novo, has almost everything the visitor may need. Some of the services in Rio Sul are: *Telemar* (phone office) for international calls at A10-A, Mon-Sat 1000-2200; next door is *Belle Tours Câmbio*, A10. There is a post office at G2. A good branch of *Livraria Sodiler* is at A03. For Eating and Entertainment, see above; live music at the *Terraço*; the *Ibeas Top Club* gym; and a cinema. A US$5 bus service runs as far as the *Sheraton* passing the main hotels, every 2 hrs between 1000 and 1800, then 2130. Other shopping centres, which include a wide variety of services, include: *Cassino* (Copacabana), *Norte Shopping* (Todos os Santos), *Plaza Shopping* (Niterói), *Barra* in Barra da Tijuca (see page 368). At São Conrado, *The Fashion Mall* is smaller and more stylish.

Sport & activities There are hundreds of gyms and sports clubs; most will not grant temporary (less than 1 month) membership. Big hotels may allow use of their facilities for a small deposit. **Cycling** Tours (hire available) with *Rio Bikers*, R Domingos Ferreira 81, room 201, T2274 5872. Bike rental from *Stop Bike*, T2275 7345, Copacabana. **Diving** *Squalo*, Av Armando Lombardi 949-D, Barra de Tijuca, T/F2493 3022, squalo1@hotmail.com Offers courses at all levels, NAUI and PDIC training facilities, also snorkelling and equipment rental. **Football** See under Maracanã stadium, above. **Hang-gliding** *HiltonFlyRio Hang Gliding Center*, T2278 3779/9964 2607 (mob), www.hiltonflyrio.com DeHilton Carvalho is an ABVL certified instructor, very experienced. *Just Fly*, T/F2268 0565, T9985 7540 (mob), www.justfly.lookscool.com US$80 for tandem flights with Paulo Celani (licensed by Brazilian Hang Gliding Association), pick-up and drop-off at hotel included, in-flight pictures US$15 extra, flights all year, best time of day 1000-1500 (5% discount for *South American* and *Brazil Handbook* readers on presentation of book at time of reservation). *Ultra Força Ltda*, Av Sernambetiba 8100, Barra da Tijuca, T3399 3114; 15 mins. **Horse racing and riding** *Jockey Club Racecourse*, by Jardím Botânico and Gávea, meetings on Mon and Thu evenings and Sat and Sun 1400, entrance US$1-2, long trousers required. Take any bus marked 'via Jóquei'. *Sociedade Hípico Brasileiro*, Av Borges de Medeiros 2448, T527 8090, Jardim Botânico – riding. **Parapenting** Tandem jumping (*Vôo duplo*); *Barra Jumping*, Aeroporto de Jacarepaguá, Av Ayrton Senna 2541, T3325 2494/9988 1566. Several other people offer tandem jumping; check that they are accredited with the Associação Brasileira de Vôo Livre. Ask for the *Parapente Rio Clube* at São Conrado launch site, tandem flight US$80. **Rock climbing and hill walking** *ECA*, Av Erasmo Braga 217, room 305, T2242 6857/2571 0484, personal guide US$100 per day; *Clube Excursionista Carioca*, also recommended for enthusiasts, R Hilário Gouveia 71, room 206, T2255 1348, meets Wed and Fri. *Paulo Miranda*, R Campos Sales 64/801, RJ20270-210, T/F2264 4501.

Turismo Clássico, Av NS de Copacabana 1059/805, T2523 3390, classico@infolink.com.br   **Tour operators**
Warmly recommended. *Metropol Viagens e Turismo*, R São José 46, T2533 5010, F2533 7160,
metropol@metropolturismo.com.br Eco, adventure and culture tours to all parts of Brazil.
Marlin Tours, Av NS de Copacabana office 1204, T2548 4433, bbm.robin@
openlink.com.br Recommended for hotel, flights and tours, Robin and Audrey speak English.
Rio Hiking, T9874 3698, www.riohiking.com.br Hiking tours to the top of Rio's mountains.
Organized trips to Samba shows cost US$50 including dinner, good, but it's cheaper to go
independently. *Fenician Tours*, Av NS de Copacabana 335, T2235 3843, offers a cheaper tour
than some at US$30 including transport from/to hotel. *Atlantic Forest Jeep Tour*, T2495 9827,
T9974 0218 (mob). As well as running jeep tours to the Parque Nacional Tijuca (see above), run
trips to coffee *fazendas* in the Paraíba Valley, trips to Angra dos Reis and offshore islands and
the Serra dos Órgãos. *Dantur*, Largo do Machado 29 (Galeria Condor) loja 47, T2557 7144. Helena speaks English and is friendly and helpful. *South America Experience*, R Raimundo Correia
36, T2548 8813, www.southamericaexperience.com Hop-on, hop-off coach service with local
guides for off-the-beaten track exploring in Rio de Janeiro and Bahia (part of the Adventure
Travel Network), day trips and 4-6 day trips, helpful. Recommended.

Favela Tour, Estr das Canoas 722, Bl 2, apt 125, CEP 22610-210, T3322 2727, T9989 0074
(mob 9772 1133), www.favelatour.com.br Guided tours of Rio's favelas, safe, different and
interesting, US$20, 3 hrs. Also ask Marcelo Armstrong, the owner, about eco tours, river rafting
and other excursions. He speaks English, French, Spanish, Italian and can provide guides in German and Swedish. For the best attention and price call Marcelo direct rather than through a
hotel desk. *Jeep Tours* also offer favela tours, T3890 9336, T9977 9610 (mob), www.jeep
tour.com.br Another favela tour, focussing on a tourism workshop in Rocinha, is offered by
Exotic Tours (Rejane Reis), T2422 2031, www.exotictours.com.br They also offer hang gliding,
ultralights, paragliding, sailing, diving, voodoo, and daytime tours. *Cultural Rio*, tours escorted
personally by Professor Carlos Roquette, R Santa Clara 110/904, Copacabana, T3322 4872,

T9911 3829 (mob), www.culturalrio.com English and French spoken, almost 200 options available. *Fábio Sombra* offers private and tailor-made guided tours focusing on the cultural aspects of Rio and Brazil, T2295 9220, T9729 5455 (mob), fabiosombra@hotmail.com *Itapora Ecoturismo*, T2245 4080/9387 4501 (mob), www.itaporaecotur.com.br Run by Geiza Monteiro, small group or individual tours and wlaks around Rio. *Rio Life*, R Visc de Pirajá 550, office 215, Ipanema, T2259 5532, T9637 2522 (mob), www.travelrio.com Good company offering personalised tours run by Luiz Felipe Amaral who speaks good English.

Helicopter sightseeing tours: *Helisight*, R Visconde de Pirajá 580, loja 107, Térreo, Ipanema, T2511 2141, www.helisight.com.br Prices from US$43 pp for 6-7 mins from Morro de Urca over Sugar Loaf and Corcovado, to US$148 pp for 30 mins over the city.

Transport

There are good services, but buses are very crowded and not for the aged and infirm during rush hours; buses have turnstiles which are awkward if you are carrying luggage. Hang on tight, drivers live out Grand Prix fantasies

Bus At busy times allow about 45 mins to get from Copacabana to the centre by bus. The fare on standard buses is R$1.10 (US$0.45) and suburban bus fares are US$0.75. Bus stops are often not marked. The route is written on the side of the bus, which is hard to see until the bus has actually pulled up at the stop. Private companies operate air-conditioned *frescão* buses which can be flagged down practically anywhere: *Real, Pegaso, Anatur*. They run from all points in Rio Sul to the city centre, Rodoviária and the airports. Fares are US$1.50 (US$1.80 to the international airport). *City Rio* is an a/c tourist bus service with security guards which runs between all the major parts of the city. Good maps show what sites of interest are close to each bus stop, marked by grey poles and found where there are concentrations of hotels. T0800 258060. Distances in km to some major cities with approximate journey time in brackets: Juiz de Fora, 184 (2¾ hrs); Belo Horizonte, 434 (7 hrs); São Paulo, 429 (6 hrs); Vitória, 521 (8 hrs); Curitiba, 852 (12 hrs); Brasília, 1,148 (20 hrs); Florianópolis, 1,144 (20 hrs); Foz do Iguaçu, 1,500 (21 hrs); Porto Alegre, 1,553 (26 hrs); Salvador, 1,649 (28 hrs); Recife, 2,338 (38 hrs); Fortaleza, 2,805 (48 hrs); São Luís, 3,015 (50 hrs); Belém, 3,250 (52 hrs).

For international car rental websites, see Car hire, Essentials, page 52

Car hire *Golden Car*, R Ronald de Carvalho 154B, Copacabana, T2275 4748, goldencar@riomaster.com.br *Interlocadora*, international airport T3398 3181, domestic airport T2240 0754; *Telecar*, R Figueiredo Magalhães 701, Copacabana, T2235 6778. Many agencies on Av Princesa Isabel, Copacabana. A credit card is essential for hiring a car. Recent reports suggest it is cheaper to hire outside Brazil. You may also obtain fuller insurance this way.

Motoring Service stations are closed in many places Sat and Sun. Road signs are notoriously misleading in Rio and you can end up in a *favela*. Take care if driving along the Estr da Gávea to São Conrado as it is possible to enter unwittingly Rocinha, Rio's biggest slum.

Metro The Metrô provides good service, clean, air conditioned and fast. Line 1: between the inner suburb of Tijuca (station Saens Peña) and Siqueira Campos (Copacabana - being extended to Ipanema), via the railway station (Central), Glória and Botafogo. Line 2: from Pavuna, passing Engenho da Rainha and the Maracanã stadium, to Estácio. It operates 0600-2300 Mon-Sat, closed Sun and holidays (except on special occasions). The fare is R$1.30 (US$0.45) single; multi-tickets and integrated bus/Metrô tickets are available. Changes in bus operations are taking place because of the extended Metrô system; buses connecting with the Metrô have a blue-and-white symbol in the windscreen.

Taxi The fare between Copacabana and the centre is US$7. Between 2300 and 0600 and on Sun and holidays, 'tariff 2' is used. Taxis have red number plates with white digits (yellow for private cars, with black digits) and have meters. Smaller ones (mostly Volkswagen) are marked TAXI on the windscreen or roof. Make sure meters are cleared and on tariff 1, except at those times mentioned above. Only use taxis with an official identification sticker on the windscreen. Don't hesitate to argue if the route is too long or the fare too much. Radio Taxis are safer but more expensive, eg *Cootramo*, T2560 5442, *Coopertramo*, T2260 2022, *Centro de Táxi*, T2593 2598, *Transcoopass*, T2560 4888. Luxury cabs are allowed to charge higher rates. Inácio de Oliveira, T2225 4110, is a reliable taxi driver for excursions, he only speaks Portuguese. Recommended. *Grimalde*, T2267 9812, has been recommended for talkative daytime and evening tours, English and Italian spoken, negotiate a price. Also *Eduardo*, T3361 1315 or 9708 8542, a/c taxi.

Air Rio has 2 airports: **Antônio Carlos Jobim International Airport** (T3398 4106), previously called Galeão, and the **Santos Dumont** airport on Guanabara Bay (T2814 7070), for domestic flights. Jobim international airport is situated on Governador Island some 16 km from the centre of Rio. It is in 2 sections: international and domestic. There is a *Pousada Galeão* (**A**), comfortable, good value if you need an early start, follow signs in airport.

Long distance
See also Ins and outs, page 355

Brazil

There are a/c taxis; *Cootramo* and *Transcopass* have fixed rates (US$18.75 Copacabana). Buy a ticket at the counter near the arrivals gate before getting into the car. Fixed rate taxi fares from Terminal 2 are US$8.50 to Centro, US$10 to Copacabana/Ipanema, US$15.50 to Barra da Tijuca. Credit cards accepted by some companies. The hire is for the taxi, irrespective of the number of passengers. Make sure you keep the ticket, which carries the number to phone in case of difficulty. Ordinary taxis also operate with the normal meter reading (about US$12.50, but some may offer cheaper rates from Copacabana to the airport, US$7-8.50). Do not negotiate with a driver on arrival, unless you are a frequent visitor. Beware pirate taxis which are unlicensed. It is better to pay extra for an official vehicle than run the risk of robbery.

The a/c 'Real' bus runs frequently from the first floor of the airport to Recreio dos Bandeirantes via the municipal rodoviária and city centre, Santos Dumont Airport, Flamengo, Copacabana, Ipanema and Leblon. Fares are collected during the journey; to Zona Sul US$1.75, to Santos Dumont US$1.50. The driver will stop at requested points (the bus runs along the seafront from Leme to Leblon), so it's worth checking a map so that you can specify your required junction. The bus returns by the same route. Town buses M94 and M95, *Bancários/Castelo*, take a circular route passing through the centre and the interstate bus station. They leave from the 2nd floor of the airport.

There are *câmbios* in the airport departure hall. There is also a *câmbio* on the first floor of the international arrivals area, but it gives worse rates than the Banco do Brasil, 24-hr bank, third floor, which has Visa ATMs and will give cash advances against Visa. Duty-free shops are well-stocked, but not especially cheap. Duty free is open to arrivals as well as departures. Only US dollars or credit cards are accepted on the air-side of the departure lounge. There is a wider choice of restaurants outside passport control.

The **Santos Dumont airport** on Guanabara Bay, right in the city, is used for Rio-São Paulo shuttle flights (US$150 single, US$300 return), other domestic routes, air taxis and private planes. The shuttle services operate every 30 mins from 0630 to 2230. Sit on the right-hand side for views to São Paulo, the other side coming back, book in advance for particular flights. The main airport, on Governador Island, some 16 km from the centre of Rio, is in 2 sections, international and domestic (including Vasp's jet shuttle from Rio to São Paulo).

Bus Rodoviária Novo Rio, Av Rodrigues Alves, corner with Av Francisco Bicalho, just past the docks, T2291 5151. Some travel agents sell interstate tickets, or will direct you to a bus ticket office in the centre. Agencies include: *Dantur Passagens e Turismo*, Av Rio Branco 156, subsolo loja 134, T2262 3424/3624; *Itapemirim Turismo*, R Uruguaiana 10, loja 24, T2509 8543, both in the centre; *Guanatur*, R Dias da Rocha 16A, Copacabana, T2235 3275, F2235 3664; and an agency at R Visconde de Pirajá 303, loja 114, Ipanema. They charge about US$1 for bookings. Buses run from Rio to all parts of the country. It is advisable to book tickets in advance. The rodoviária has a *Riotur* information centre, which is very helpful, T2263 4857. Left luggage costs US$3. There are *câmbios* for cash only. The local bus terminal is just outside the

The rodoviária attracts thieves

rodoviária: turn right as you leave and run the gauntlet of taxi drivers – best ignored. The air conditioned *Real* bus (opposite the exit) goes along the beach to São Conrado and will secure luggage. If you need a taxi collect a ticket, which ensures against overcharging, from the office inside the entrance (to Flamengo US$7.50). On no account give the ticket to the taxi driver. The main bus station is reached by buses M94 and M95, Bancários/Castelo, from the centre and the airport; 136, 172, Rodoviária/Glória/Flamengo/Botafogo; 127, 128, 136, Rodoviária/Copacabana; 170, Rodoviária/Gávea/São Conrado; 128, 172, Rodoviária/ Ipanema/Leblon.

International bus Asunción, 1,511 km via Foz do Iguaçu, 30 hrs (*Pluma*), US$50; **Buenos Aires** (*Pluma*), via Porto Alegre and Santa Fe, 48 hrs, US$82 (book 2 days in advance); **Santiago de Chile**, with *Pluma* US$135, or *Gen Urquiza*, about 70 hrs.

Hitchhiking To hitch to **Belo Horizonte** or **Brasília**, take a C-3 bus from Av Pres Antônio Carlos to the railway station, cross through the station to a bus station and catch the Nova Iguaçu bus. Ask to be let off at the Belo Horizonte turn off. For the motorway entrance north and south, take bus 392 or 393 from Praça São Francisco.

Directory

Airline offices *Aerolíneas Argentinas*, R São José 70, 8th floor, Centro, T2292 4131, airport T3398 3520. *Air France*, Av Pres Antônio Carlos 58, 9th floor, T2532 3642, airport T3398 3488. *Alitalia*, Av Pres Wilson 231, 21st floor, T2292 4424, airport T3398 3143. *American*, Av Pres Wilson 165, 5th floor, T0800-216176, airport T3398 4053. *Avianca*, Av Pres Wilson 165, offices 801-03, T2240 4413, airport T3398 3145. *British Airways*, T0800 176144, airport T3398 3888. *Continental*, R da Assembleia 10, sala 3711, T2531 1142, airport T3398 4105. *Delta*, R do Ouvidor 161, 14th floor, T0800 221121, airport T3398 3492. *Iberia*, Av Pres Antônio Carlos 51, 8th and 9th floors, T2282 1336, airport T3398 3168. *Lan Chile*, R da Assambleia 92, office 1301, T2220 0299/0800-554 900, airport T3398 3797. *LAB*, Av Calógeras 30A, T2220 9548/0800 118111. *Lufthansa*, Av Rio Branco 156D, T3687 5000, airport T3398 5910. *RioSul/Nordeste*, Av Rio Branco 85, 11th floor, T2507 4488 (has an advance check-in desk in Rio Sul Shopping). *TAM*, Praça Floriana 19, 28th floor, T2524 1717, airport T3398 2133. *TAP*, Av Rio Branco 311-B, T2210 1287, airport, T3398 3455. *United*, Av Pres Antônio Carlos 51, 5th floor, T3804 1200, airport T3398 4050. *Varig*, Av Rio Branco 277G, T2220 3821, information, T0800 997000 bookings; airport T3398 3522. *Vasp*, R Santa Luzia 735, T0800-998277

*Credicard phone line for Visa and MasterCard international: T0800 784456
Diners Club 0800 784444*

Banks *Citibank*, R Assembléia 100, T2291 1232, changes large US$ TCs into smaller ones, no commission, advances cash on Eurocard/MasterCard. *Banco do Brasil*, there are only 2 branches in Rio which will change US$ TCs, Praia de Botafogo, 384A, 3rd floor (minimium US$200) and the central branch at R Sen Dantas 105, 4th floor (minimum US$500 – good rates). *Banco do Brasil* at the International Airport is open 0800-2200. The international airport is probably the only place to change TCs at weekends. Visa cash withdrawals at *Banco do Brasil* (many ATMs at the R Sen Dantas branch, no queues) and *Bradesco* (personal service or machines). MasterCard and Cirrus cash machines at most *HSBC* branches in Centro, Copacabana, Ipanema and other locations. Some *BBV* branches have Visa and MasterCard ATMs. Also at Santos Dumont airport. *Lloyds TSB Bank*, R da Alfândega 332, 7th floor.

Money changers: *American Express*, Av Atlântica 1702, loja 1, T2548 2148 Mon-Fri 0900-1730, Av Pres Wilson 231, 18th floor, Centro, and at Jobim/Galeão airport, T3398 4251 (VIP room 1st floor), good rates (daily 0630-2230); credit card line 0800 785050. Most large hotels and reputable travel agencies will change currency and TCs. Copacabana (where rates are generally worse than in the centre) abounds with *câmbios* and there are many also on Av Rio Branco. *Câmbio Belle Tours*, Rio Sul Shopping, ground floor, loja 101, parte A-10, Mon-Fri 1000-1800, Sat 1000-1700, changes cash. In the gallery at Largo do Machado 29 are *Câmbio Nick* at loja 22 and, next door but one, *Casa Franca*.

Communications Internet: *@point*, Barra Shopping, Av das Americas 4666, Barra da Tijuca. Several places in Rio Sul Shopping, Botafogo. Many on Av NS de Copacabana and others on R Visconde de Pirajá, Ipanema. *Locutório* at R Francisco Sá 26, T2522 6343. Internet, phone, fax, open 0800-2000 daily. *Phone Serv*, Av NS de Copacabana 454 loja B. Internet and phone. *Tudo é Fácil*, 3 branches in Copacabana: R Xavier da Silveira, 19; Av Prado Júnior 78 and R Barata Ribeiro 396. Well-organized, with identification cards so once registered you can bypass the front desk, telephone booths and scanners, US$2 per hr, discounts for extended use. **Post** : The central Post Office is on R 1 de Março 64, at the corner of R do Rosário. Av NS de Copacabana 540 and many other locations. All handle international post. There is a post office at Galeão airport. Poste Restante: Correios, Av NS de Copacabana 540 and all large post offices (letters held for a month, recommended, US$0.10 per letter). *Federal Express*, Av Calógeras 23 (near Santa Luzia church) T2262 8565, is reliable. **Telephone**: International calls can be made at *Telemar* offices: Av NS de Copacabana 540, 2nd floor; Jobim international airport (24 hrs);

Novo Rio rodoviária; R Dias da Cruz 192, Méier-4, 24 hrs, 7 days a week; Praça Tiradentes 41, a few mins' walk from Metrô Carioca; R Visconde de Pirajá 111, Ipanema; R do Ouvidor 60, Centro. International telephone booths are blue. Larger *Embratel* offices have fax, as do many larger Correios.

Cultural centres British Council, R Elmano Cardim 10, Urca, T2295 7782, F2541 3693. **Sociedade Brasileira de Cultura Inglesa**, Av Graça Aranha 327 and in Copacabana, T2267 4048 (central information). **German Cultur-Institut** (Goethe), R do Psseio 62, 2nd floor, T2533 4862/9379, www.goethe.de/br/rio Tue-Wed 1000-1200, Thu 1530-2000, Fri 1530-1800, Sat 0900-1300.

Embassies and consulates Argentina, Praia de Botafogo 228, T2553 1646. Very helpful over visas, 1130-1600. **Australia** , Av Presidente Wilson 231, no 23, T3824 4624. Mon-Fri 9000-1300, 1430-1800. **Austria**, Av Atlântica 3804, T2522 2286. **Canada**, R Lauro Müller 116, T2543 3004, rio@dfait-maecigc.ca **Denmark**, Praia do Flamengo 66, T2558 6050, danmark@trip.com.br **France**, Av Pres Antônio Carlos 58, T2210 1272. **Germany**, R Pres Carlos de Campos 417, T2553 6777. **Ireland**, R 24 de Maio 347, Riachuelo, T2501 8455, rioconsulate@ireland.com **Israel**, Av NS de Copacabana 680, T2548 5432. **Japan**, Praia do Flemngo 200, 10th floor, T2265 5252. **Netherlands**, Praia de Botafogo 242, 10th floor, T2552 9028. **Paraguay**, same address, 2nd floor, T2553 2294. **Sweden**, **Finland** and **Norway**, Praia do Flamengo 344, 9th floor, T2553 5505. **Switzerland**, R Cândido Mendes 157, 11th floor, T2221 1867. **UK**, Praia do Flamengo 284, 2nd floor. T2555 3223 (consular section direct line)/5976, F2553 6850, consular section is open Mon-Fri 0900-1230 (the consulate's hrs are 0830-1700), Metrô Flamengo, or bus 170, issues a useful 'Guidance for Tourists' pamphlet. **Uruguay**, Praia de Botafogo 242, 6th floor, T2553 6030. **USA**, Av Pres Wilson 147, T2292 7117. Mon-Fri 0800-1100.

Language courses *Instituto Brasil-Estados Unidos*, Av Copacabana 690, 5th floor, 8-week course, 3 classes a week, US$200, 5-week intensive course US$260. Good English library at same address. *IVM Português Prático*, R do Catete 310, sala 302, US$18 per hr for individual lessons, cheaper for groups. Helpful staff. Recommended. *Cursos da UNE* (União Nacional de Estudantes), R Catete 243, include cultural studies and Portuguese classes for foreigners. Private lessons with *Camila Queiraz*, T8828 3196/3339 3485, reasonable prices.

Medical services Vaccinations at **Saúde de Portos**, Praça Mcal Âncora, T2240 8628/8678, Mon-Fri 1000-1100, 1500-1800 (international vaccination book and ID required). *Policlínica*, Av Nilo Peçanha 38. Recommended for diagnosis and investigation. A good public hospital for minor injuries and ailments is **Hospital Municipal Rocha Maia**, R Gen Severiano 91, Botafogo, T2295 2295/2121, near Rio Sul Shopping Centre. Free, but there may be queues. **Hospital Miguel Couto**, Mário Ribeiro 117, Gávea, T274 6050. Has a free casualty ward. **Health:** Dentist: English-speaking, *Amílcar Werneck de Carvalho Vianna*, Av Pres Wilson 165, suite 811. *Dr Mauro Suartz*, R Visconde de Pirajá 414, room 509, T2287 6745. Speaks English and Hebrew, helpful.

Useful addresses Immigration: Federal Police, Praça Mauá (passport section), entrance at Av Venezuela 2, T2291 2142. To renew a 90-day visa, US$12.50. **Ibama**, Praça 15 de Novembro 42, 8th floor, T2506 1734, edson.azeredo@ibama.gov.br *Student Travel Bureau*, Av Nilo Peçanha 50, SL 2417, Centro, T/F2544 2627, and R Visconde de Pirajá 550, lj 201, Ipanema, T2512 8577, www.stb.com.br (with offices throughout the country) has details of travel, discounts and cultural exchanges for ISIC holders.

Take note of local advice on water pollution. Air pollution also occurs

www.addresses.com.b r/ is a comprehensive guide to addresses in the city

Brazil

Rio de Janeiro State: East and Inland from Rio

This city is reached across Guanabara Bay by ferries which carry some 200,000 commuters a day. Founded in 1573, Niterói has various churches and forts, plus buildings associated with the city's period as state capital (until 1960). Many of these are grouped around the Praça da República. The **Capela da Boa Viagem** (1663) stands on a fortified island, attached by a causeway to the mainland. The most important historical monument is the **Fortaleza Santa Cruz** (16th century, still a military establishment), on a promontory which commands a fine view of the entrance to the bay. It is about 13 km from the centre of Niterói, on the Estrada Gen Eurico Gaspar Dutra, by Adão e Eva beach. ■ *Daily 0900-1600, US$1.50. Go with guide. T2710 7840.*

The **Museu de Arqueologia de Itaipu** is in the ruins of the 18th century Santa Teresa Convent and also covers the archaeological site of Duna Grande on Itaipu beach. It is 20 km from the city. ■ *Wed-Sun 1300-1800, T2709 4079.* **Museu de Arte Contemporânea-Niterói**, Mirante da Praia da Boa Viagem, is an Oscar Niemeyer

Niterói
Phone code: 0xx21
Colour map 7, grid B5
Population: 459,451

project and worth visiting. It is best seen at night, especially when the pond beneath the spaceship design is full of water. ■ *Tue-Sun 1100-1900, US$1, Sat 1300-1900, free, T2620 2400, www.macnit.com.br* The **Tourist office** is *Neltur*, Estrada Leopoldo Fróes 773, T2710 2727, in the São Francisco district, 5 km from ferry dock.

Transport Crossing from Rio: Ferry: from the 'barcas' at Praça 15 de Novembro (ferry museum at the terminal), ferry boats and launches cross every 10 mins to Niterói (15-20 mins, US$0.50). There are also catamarans ('aerobarcas') every 10 mins (about 3 mins, US$2.45). Of the frequent ferry and catamaran services from Praça 15 de Novembro, Rio, the slow, cheaper ferry gives the best views. **Bus/car**: the toll on the the Rio-Niterói bridge for cars is US$0.65. Bus 996 Gávea-Jurujuba, 998 Galeão-Charitas, 740-D and 741 Copocabana-Charitas, 730-D Castelo Jurujba, US$0.60-0.75.

Local beaches Take bus no 33 from the boat dock, passing Icaraí and São Francisco, both with polluted water but good nightlife, to the fishing village of Jurujuba. About 2 km further along a narrow road are the attractive twin beaches of Adão and Eva beneath the Fortaleza da Santa Cruz (see above). To get to the ocean beaches, take a 38 or 52 bus from Praça Gen Gomes Carneiro to Piratininga, Camboinhas, Itaipu (see the archaeology museum, above) and Itacoatiara. These are fabulous stretches of sand and the best in the area, about 40 minutes' ride through picturesque countryside.

Lagos Fluminenses To the east of Niterói lie a series of salt-water lagoons, the Lagos Fluminenses. The first major lakes, Maricá and Saquarema are muddy, but the waters are relatively unpolluted and wildlife abounds in the surrounding scrub and bush. An unmade road goes along the coast between Itacoatiara and Cabo Frio, giving access to the many long, open beaches of Brazil's **Costa do Sol**.

In the holiday village of **Saquarema**, the little white church of Nossa Senhora de Nazaré (1675) is on a green promontory jutting into the ocean. Saquarema is a fishing town and the centre for surfing in Brazil. Beware of strong currents, though. ■ *Mil e Um (1001) bus Rio-Saquarema, every 2 hrs 0730-1800, 2 hrs, US$3.40.*

The almost constant breeze makes the lake perfect for windsurfing and sailing

The largest lake is **Araruama** (220 sq km), famous for its medicinal mud. The salinity is extremely high, the waters calm, and almost the entire lake is surrounded by sandy beaches, making it popular with families looking for safe, unpolluted bathing. All around are saltpans and the wind pumps used to carry water into the pans. At the eastern end of the lake is **São Pedro de Aldeia**, which, despite intensive development, still retains much of its colonial charm.

There are many hotels, youth hostels and campsites in the towns by the lakes and by the beaches.

Cabo Frio
Phone code: 0xx24
Colour map 7, grid B5
Population: 126,828
156 km from Rio

Cabo Frio is a popular holiday and weekend haunt of Cariocas because of its cool weather, white sand beaches and dunes, scenery, sailing and good under-water swimming. Forte São Mateus, 1616, is now a ruin at the mouth of the Canal de Itajuru, which connects the Lagoa Araruama and the ocean. A small headland at its mouth protects the nearest beach to the town, Praia do Forte, which stretches south for about 7½ km to Arraial do Cabo. Tourist information is in a large orange building, Av do Contorno 200, Praia do Forte, T2647 1689, www.cabofrio.tur.br ■ *A new airport has opened linking the area with Belo Horizonte, Brasília, Rio de Janeiro and São Paulo. The rodoviária is 2 km from the centre. Bus from Rio every 30 mins, 2½ hrs, US$8. To Búzios, from the local bus terminus in the town centre, every hr, US$1.*

Sleeping A wide selection of hotels including: **L** *La Plage*, R dos Badejos 40, Praia do Peró, T/F26435690. Close to the beach, with restaurant and pool. **B** *Pousada Suzy*, Av Júlia Kubitschek 48, T2643 1742. Conveniently located 100 m from the rodoviária. **D** *Praia das Palmeiras*, Praia das Palmeiras 1, T/F2643 2866. **E** pp *Remmar Residence*, Av Teixeiroa e Souza 1203 (main route into town), close to beach and bus station, T2643 2313, F2645 5976. Short stay apartments with kitchen, bath and laundry. **Youth hostels** *São Lucas*, R Goiás 266,

Jardim Excelsior, T2645 3037, 3 mins from the rodoviária; reservations are necessary in Dec-Feb. **Camping** Clube do Brasil site at Estrada dos Passageiros 700, 2 km from town, T2643 3124. On the same road, at No 370 is *Camping da Estação*, T2643 1786. **Eating Mid-range**: *Picolino*, R Mcal Floriano 319. Good, local seafood with some international dishes in a pleasant setting. **Cheap**: *Do Zé*, on the canal quayside. Brazilian food, reliable. **Very cheap**: Fast food outlets can be found along the seafront (Av do Contorno) at Praia do Forte.

Búzios

Known as a lost paradise in the tropics, this village found fame in the 1964 when Brigite Bardot was photographed sauntering barefoot along the beach. The world's press descended on the sophisticated, yet informal resort, following the publicity. Originally a small fishing community, founded in 1740, Búzios remained virtually unknown until the 1950s when its natural beauty started to attract the Brazilian jet-set who turned the village into a fashionable summer resort. The city gets crowded at all main holidays, the price of food, accommodation and other services rises substantially and the traffic jams are long and stressful.

Phone code: 0xx24
Colour map 7, grid B5
Population: 18,208
192 km to Rio
37 km to Arraial do Cabo
For information
www.buzios channel.com.br

During the daytime, the best option is to head for one of the 25 beaches. The most visited are Geribá (many bars and restaurants; popular with surfers), Ferradura (blue sea and calm waters), Ossos (the most famous and close to the centre), Tartaruga and João Fernandes. To help you to decide two to three hr schooner trips pass many of the beaches: US$10-15. *Escuna Buziana*, T2623 6760, or *Escuna Queen Lory*, T2623 1179.

AL *Colonna Park*, Praia de João Fernandes, T2623 2245, colonna@colonna.com.br Top quality, fantastic view of the sea. **AL** *La Mandrágora*, Av J B Ribeiro Dantas 1010, Portal da Ferradura, T2623 1348, mandragora@uol.com.br One of the most famous in Búzios. **A** *Pousada Hibiscus Beach*, R 1, No 22, Quadra C, Praia de João Fernandes, T2623 6221, www.hibiscusbeach.com.br Run by its British owners, garden, pool, light meals available, help with car/buggy rentals and local excursions. **A-B** *Saint Germain*, Altos do Humaitá 5, Praia da Armação, T2623 1044, www.buzioschannel.com.br/saintgermain Includes breakfast, fully-equipped, 150 m from beach, family run, English, Italian, Spanish and Scandinavian languages spoken, discount for Handbook owners. **B** *Pousada dos Tangarás*, R dos Namorados 6, lote 4, Geribá, T2623 1275, tangaras@mar.com.br Good. **B** *Pousada La Coloniale*, R das Pedras 52, T2623 1434, lacoloniale@uol.com.br Ideally located for nightlife, but noisy until the early hrs. **D** *Pousada Axé*, R do Sossego 200, T2623 2008. Includes breakfast, a/c, TV, fridge, helpful, good value, pool. **D** *Brigitta's Guest House*, Rua das Pedras 131, T/F2623 6157, brigittas@mar.com.br Beautifully decorated little *pousada* with a nice restaurant, bar and tea house. **D** *Casa da Ruth*, R dos Gravatás, Geribá, T2623 2242, www.buziosturismo.com **Youth hostel E** *Praia dos Amores*, Av José Bento Ribeiro Dantas 92, T2623 2422. IYHA, not far from the bus station. Recommended. Several private houses rent rooms, especially in summer and holidays. Look for the signs: 'Alugo Quartos'.

Sleeping
Even though there are more than 150 pousadas, prior reservations are needed in summer, at holidays such as Carnival and the New Year's Eve, and weekends. For cheaper options and better availability, try Cabo Frio

Brazil

Eating

Restaurants on R das Pedras tend to be expensive. Cheaper options can be found in the surrounding streets

Expensive: *Estância Don Juan*, R das Pedras, 178. Grill and restaurant. *Moqueca Capixaba*, R Manoel de Carvalho 116, Centro. Brazilian seafood. *Kassai*, R das Pedras 275. Japanese. **Cheap**: *Bob's*, in front of *Shopping One*, R das Pedras. Hamburgers and chips to take away. *Chez Michou*, R das Pedras 90. Open-air bar with videos and music, pancakes accompanied by ice cold beer. *Skipper*, Av J B Ribeiro Dantas 392, Praia do Canto. Pizza. **Cheap** A few places on Praça Santos Dumont off R das Pedras offer sandwiches and self-service food, including *La Prima* on Av Manuel Turibo de Farias which doubles as a bakery.

Bars & clubs

A must in Búzios. R das Pedras has the best choice of restaurants, cafés, art galleries and bars. Crowded at weekends and holidays, especially after 2300. Good options are: *Zapata Mexican Bar*, R das Pedras. A Mexican theme bar and restaurant that serves as the only disco in town. *Ta-ka-ta ka-ta*, R das Pedras 256. One of the craziest bars in Búzios: owned by a foreigner who speaks fluent Portuguese, Spanish, English, German, Dutch, worth a visit.

Transport By car via BR-106 takes about 2½ hrs from Rio. **Bus**: *Mil e Um* from Novo Rio, go to T0xx21-2516 1001,US$ 8, 2½ hrs (be at the bus terminal 20 mins before departure). Departures every 2 hrs from 0700 to 1900 daily. You can also take any bus to Cabo Frio (many more during the day), from where it's 30 mins to Búzios. Buy the ticket in advance on major holidays. Búzios' rodoviária is a few blocks' walk from the centre. Some pousadas are within 10 mins on foot, eg La Coloniale, Brigitta's, while others need a local bus (US$0.50) or taxi. Buses from Cabo Frio run the length of the peninsula and pass several pousadas.

Directory **Communications** Internet: *buzios@internet*, Av J B Ribeiro Dantas, 97, close to *Shopping One* US$1.20 for 30 mins.

Petrópolis

Phone code: 0xx24
Post code: 25600
Colour map 7, grid B5
Population: 286,537
Altitude: 809 m
68 km N of Rio

A steep scenic mountain road from Rio leads to this summer resort, known for its floral beauty and hill scenery, coupled with adventure sports. Until 1962 Petrópolis was the 'summer capital' of Brazil. Now it combines manufacturing industry (particularly textiles) and tourism. There are possibilities for whitewater rafting, hiking, climbing, riding and cycling in the vicinity. Petrópolis celebrates its foundation on 16 March. Patron saint's day, *São Pedro de Alcântara*, 29 June.

The **Museu Imperial** (Imperial Palace) is Brazil's most visited museum. It is an elegant building, neoclassical in style, fully furnished and equipped. It is so well-kept

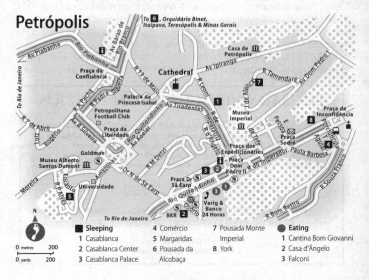

Petrópolis

To 6, *Orquidário Binot, Itaipava, Teresópolis & Minas Gerais*

	Sleeping		
1	Casablanca	4	Comércio
2	Casablanca Center	5	Margaridas
3	Casablanca Palace	6	Pousada da Alcobaça
		7	Pousada Monte Imperial
		8	York

	Eating	
1	Cantina Bom Giovanni
2	Casa d'Ángelo
3	Falconi

you might think the imperial family had left the day before, rather than in 1889. It's worth a visit just to see the Crown Jewels of both Pedro I and Pedro II. In the palace gardens is a pretty French-style tearoom, the *Petit Palais*. ■ *Tue-Sun 1100-1700, US$2, R da Imperatriz 220, T2237 8000*. The Gothic-style **Catedral de São Pedro de Alcântara**, completed in 1925, contains the tombs of the Emperor and Empress. The Imperial Chapel is to the right of the entrance; ■ *Tue-Sat 0800-1200, 1400-1800*. The summer home of air pioneer **Alberto Santos Dumont**, known as 'A Encantada', R do Encanto 22. ■ *Tue-Sun 0900-1700. US$1*. The interior of the **Casa de Petrópolis**, R Ipiranga 716, T2237 2133, is completely original and over-the-top, but has been lovingly restored. It holds art exhibitions and classical concerts. A charming restaurant in the old stables is worth a stop for coffee, if not for lunch. ■ *Tue-Sun 1100-1900, Sat 1100-1300, US$2*. **Orquidário Binot**, R Fernandes Vieira 390 (take bus to Vila Isabel), a huge collection of orchids from all over Brazil (plants may be purchased). ■ *Mon-Fri 0800-1100, 1315-1630, Sat 0700-1100*.

Sleeping
■ on map

L *Pousada da Alcobaça*, R Agostinho Goulão 298, Correas, T2221 1240, F222 3162. Delightful, family-run country house in flower-filled gardens, pool and sauna. Worth stopping by for tea on the terrace, or dinner at the restaurant. Recommended. **A** *Margaridas*, R Bispo Pereira Alves 235, T2242 4686, near Trono de Fátima. Chalet-style in lovely gardens with a swimming pool, charming proprietors. **A** *Casablanca*, R da Imperatriz 286, T2242 6662, F2242 5946. Most atmospheric of the 3 in this chain, cheaper rooms in modern extension, good restaurant, pool. **B** *Casablanca Center*, Gen Osório 28, T2242 2612, F2242 6298; and **B** *Casablanca Palace*, R 16 de Março 123, T2242 0162, F2242 5946. **A** *Pousada Monte Imperial*, R José de Alencar 27, T2237 1664, www.compuland.com.br/poumimpe Comfortable, TV, restaurant, bar, pool. **B** *York*, R do Imperador 78, T2243 2662, F2242 8220. A short walk from the Rodoviária, convenient, helpful, the fruit and milk at breakfast come from the owners' own farm. Recommended. **C** *Comércio*, R Dr Porciúncula 55, T2242 3500, opposite the Rodoviária. Shared bath, very basic.

Eating
● on map

Mid-range: *Falconi*, R do Imperador 757. Traditional Italian. Recommended. **Cheap**: *Cantina Bom Giovanni*, R do Imperador 729 upstairs. Popular, Italian, lunch and dinner. *Casa d'Ángelo*, R do Imperador 700, by Praça Dom Pedro II. Traditional tea house with self service food that doubles as a bar at night.

Transport

Bus From Rio every 15 mins throughout the day (US$3) with *Única Fácil*, Sun every hr, 1½ hrs, sit on the left hand side for best views. Return tickets are not available, so buy tickets for the return on arrival in Petrópolis. The ordinary buses leave from the rodoviária in Rio; a/c buses, hourly from 1100, from Av Nilo Peçanha, US$4. To **Teresópolis** for the Serra dos Órgãos, *Viação Teresópolis*, 8 a day, US$3. *Salutário* to **São Paulo**, daily at 2330.

Directory

Banks *Banco do Brasil*, R Paulo Barbosa 81. A Banco 24 Horas ATM is located by the *Varig* office at R Marechal Deodoro 98. Travel agencies with exchange: *BKR*, R Gen Osório 12, *Goldman*, R Barão de Amazonas 46, and *Vert Tur*, R 16 de Março 244, from 1000-1630. **Communications** Internet: *Compuland*, R do Imperador opposite Praça Dr Sá Earp. US$1.50 per hr. **Post Office**: R do Imperador 350. Telephone: *Telerj*, R Marechal Deodoro, just above Praça Dr Sá Earp. **Tourist offices**: Petrotur, in the Prefeitura de Petrópolis, at the rear of the Casa do Barão de Maúa, Praça da Confluência 03, T2243 3561/0800-241516, has a list of tourist sites and hotels and a good, free coloured map of the city. Mon-Fri 0900-1830, closed Sat and Sun. There is a tourist kiosk on Praça Dom Pedro II.

Serra dos Órgãos

The Serra dos Órgãos, so called because their strange shapes are said to recall organ-pipes, is an 11,000-ha national park (created in 1939, the second oldest in the country). The main attraction is the precipitous Dedo de Deus ('God's Finger') Peak (1,692 m). The highest point is the 2,263 m Pedra do Sino ('Bell Rock'), up which winds a 14-km path, a climb of three to four hours. The west face of this mountain is one of the hardest climbing pitches in Brazil. Another well-known peak is the Pedra do Açu (2,245 m) and many others have names evocative of their shape. Near the

Sub-Sede (see below) is the **Von Martius** natural history museum. ■ *0800-1700*. By the headquarters (Sede) entrance is the Mirante do Soberbo, with views to the Baía de Guanabara. To climb the Pedra do Sino, you must sign a register (under 18 must be accompanied by an adult and have authorization from the park authorities). ■ *Entrance US$1, with an extra charge for the path to the top. Open Tue-Sun 0800-1700. Best months for trekking Apr-Sep. For information from* Ibama, *T2642 1575*.

Sleeping *Ibama* has some hostels, US$5 full board, or US$3 first night, US$2 thereafter, a bit rough. There is also the *Refugio do Parque*, 2 km from park entrance of Teresópolis side, T9687 4539 (mob), refugiodoparque@bol.com.br Rooms with bath and dormitories with shower, breakfast and soup-and-bread supper included. **Camping** 2 sites in the Sub-Sede part, 1 close to the museum, the other not far from the natural swimming pool at Poço da Ponte Velha; 1 site in the Sede part.

Transport The park has 2 dependencies, both accessible from the BR-116: the Sede (headquarters, Av Rotariano, Alto Teresópolis, T/F2642 1575) is closer to Teresópolis, the highest city in the state of Rio de Janeiro, while the Sub-Sede is just outside the park proper, off the BR-116. **Rio-Teresópolis**: buses leave every 30 mins from the Novo Rio rodoviária. Book the return journey as soon as you arrive at Teresópolis; rodoviária at R 1 de Maio 100. Fare US$3.60. From Teresópolis to **Petrópolis**, 8 a day, US$3.

West from Rio

The Dutra Highway, BR-116, heads west from Rio towards the border with São Paulo. It passes the steel town of **Volta Redonda** and some 30 km further west, the town of **Resende**. In this region, 175 km from Rio, is **Penedo**, (five buses a day from Resende) which in the 1930s attracted Finnish settlers who brought the first saunas to Brazil. There is a Finnish museum, a cultural centre and Finnish dancing on Saturday. This popular weekend resort also provides horse riding, and swimming in the Portinho River. For tourist information, T0xx24-3352 1660, ext 305. (**B** *Bertell*, R Harry Bertell 47, T3351 1288, with meals. **B** *Pousada Penedo*, Av Finlândia, T3351 1309, safe, pool, recommended, and many others. There are two campsites.)

Parque Nacional Itatiaia
This is a good area for climbing, trekking and birdwatching

Founded 1937 on the Serra de Itatiaia in the Mantiqueira chain of mountains, the park was the first to be created in Brazil. Its entrance is a few km north of the Via Dutra (Rio-São Paulo highway). The town of Itatiaia is surrounded by picturesque mountain peaks and lovely waterfalls. Worth seeing are the curious rock formations of Pedra de Taruga and Pedra de Maçã, and the waterfalls Poranga and Véu de Noiva (many birds). There is a **Museu de História Natural**, ■ *1000-1600, closed Mon*, and a wildlife trail, **Três Picos**, which starts near the *Hotel Simon*.

For tourist information in the town of Itatiaia, T024-3352 1660

Ins and outs Information and maps can be obtained at the park office. The **Administração do Parque Nacional de Itatiaia** operates a refuge in the park which acts as a starting point for climbs and treks. Information from **Ibama**, T0xx24-2352 1461, F2352 1652, for the local headquarters. It is very difficult to visit the park without a car and some parts are only possible in a 4WD vehicle.

Sleeping Cabins and dorms available in the park; you will need to book in season by writing to **Administração do Parque Nacional de Itatiaia**, Caixa Postal 83657, Itatiaia 27580-970, RJ, telephone as above. **A** *Simon*, Km 13 on the road in the park, T3352 1122. With meals, lovely views, helpful with advice on getting around the park. Recommended. **A** *Hotel do Ypê*, on the road in the park, Km 14, T3352 1453, with meals. Recommended. **B** *Pousada do Elefante*, 15 mins walk back down hill from *Hotel Simon*. Good food, swimming pool, lovely views, may allow camping. Cheap lodging at R Maricá 255, T3352 1699, possibility of pitching a tent close to the national park. **D** *Hotel Alsene*, at 2,100 m, 2 km from the side entrance to the Park, take a bus to São Lourenço and Caxambu, get off at Registro, walk or hitchhike from there (12 km), very popular with climbing and trekking clubs, dormitory or camping, chalets available, hot showers, fireplace, evening meal after everyone returns, drinks but no snacks. **Camping** *Clube do Brasil* site is entered at Km 148 on the Via Dutra.

Transport Bus: a bus from Itatiaia, marked *Hotel Simon*, goes to the Park, 1200, returns 1700; coming from Resende this may be caught at the crossroads before Itatiaia. Through tickets to São Paulo are sold at a booth in the large bar in the middle of Itatiaia main street.

The Costa Verde or Emerald Coast

The Rio de Janeiro-Santos section of the BR101 is one of the world's most beautiful highways, hugging the forested and hilly Costa Verde southwest of Rio. It is complete through to Bertioga (see page 410), which has good links with Santos and São Paulo. Buses run from Rio to Angra dos Reis, Paraty, Ubatuba, Caraguatatuba, and São Sebastião, where it may be necessary to change for Santos or São Paulo. The coast is littered with islands, beaches, colonial settlements and mountain *fazendas*.

   Itacuruçá, 91 km from Rio, is a delightful place to visit. Separated from the town by a channel is the Ilha de Itacuruçá, the largest of a string of islands stretching into the bay. Further offshore is Ilha de Jaguanum, around which there are lovely walks. *Saveiros* (schooners) sail around the bay and to the islands from Itacuruça: *Passamar*, T9979 2420; *Rio Sightseeing*, T2680 7339. **C-D** *Resort Atlântico*, Praia do Axixá, T/F2680 7168, www.divingbrasil.com Dutch/Brazilian-owned pousada, helpful, good breakfast, English spoken, meals available, also offers diving courses (PADI). Ilha de Itacuruçá can also be reached from **Muriqui**, a popular beach resort 9 km from Itacuruçá. There are hotels on the island. **Mangaratiba**, 22 km down the coast, is half-way from Rio to Angra dos Reis. Its beaches are muddy, but the surroundings are pleasant and better beaches can be found outside town.

Transport Bus From Rio Rodoviária with *Costa Verde*, several daily, US$4.25. **Ferry** Daily boats to **Ilha Grande** (see below) at 0800, return 1730, US$30 return. This is a highly recommended trip. Check at the ferry station at Praça 15 de Novembro, Rio (see page 357).

Angra dos Reis

Said to have been founded on 6 January 1502 (O Dia dos Reis – The Day of Kings), this is a small port with an important fishing and shipbuilding industry. It has several small coves with good bathing within easy reach and is situated on an enormous bay full of islands. Of particular note are the church and convent of **Nossa Senhora do Carmo**, built in 1593 (Praça Gen Osório), the **Igreja Matriz de Nossa Senhora da Conceição** (1626) in the centre of town, and the church and convent of **São Bernardino de Sena** (1758-63) on the Morro do Santo Antônio. On the Largo da Lapa is the church of **Nossa Senhora da Lapa da Boa Morte** (1752), with a sacred art museum. Tourist information is opposite the bus station on the Largo da Lapa, very good, T3336 51175, ext 2186. On the Península de Angra, just west of the town, is the **Praia do Bonfim**, a popular beach, and a little way offshore the island of the same name, on which is the hermitage of Senhor do Bonfim (1780). **Boat trips** around the bay are available, some with a stop for lunch on the island of Gipóia (five hours). Several boats run tours from the Cais de Santa Luzia and there are agencies for *saveiros* in town, boats depart between 1030-1130 daily, U$10-12 (during January and February best to reserve in advance. T3365 1097). For **Diving**, *Aquamaster*, Praia da Enseada, T3365 2416, US$60 for two dives with drinks and food, take a 'Retiro' bus from the port in Angra.

Phone code: 0xx24
Post code: 23900
Colour map 7, grid B4
Population: 119,247
151 km SW of Rio

L *Frade*, on the road to Ubatuba (Km 123 on BR-101, 33 km from Angra), T3369 9500, F3369 2254. Luxury hotel on the Praia do Frade with restaurants, bar, sauna, sports facilities on land and sea. **A** *Pousada Marina Bracuhy*, at Km 115 on BR-101, 23 km from Angra, T3365 1485, F3363 1122. Lots of facilities for watersports, nightly shows and dancing during summer

Sleeping & eating

season or sailing events, restaurant. C *Pousada Tropicália*, R Silva Travassos 356, Frade, T3369 2424. With a/c, D without, F pp in dormitory, lovely building, helpful staff, also has restaurant/pizzeria, good. E pp *Rio Bracuí*, Estr Santa Rita 4, Bracuí, on the road to Santos at Km 115 (take bus to Paraty and ask driver to get off one stop after Marina Brachuy, just past the bridge), T3363 1234, ajriobracui@quick.com.br Youth hostel open all year. **In town** is: B *Caribe*, R de Conceição 255, T3365 0033, F3365 3450. Central. Recommended. C *Londres*, R Pompeia 75, T/F3365 0044. Comfortable, good breakfast and buffet lunch (US$2.50). *Bagdad Café*, R da Conceição 309. Good for lunch (US$3) with fish, meat or chicken options. *Taberna 33*, R Dr Moacir de Paula Lobo 25, Centro. Popular Italian restaurant with moderate prices.

Festivals In **Jan**: at New Year there is a *Festa do Mar*, with boat processions; on the 5th is the *Folia dos Reis*, the culmination of a religious festival that begins at **Christmas**; the 6th is the anniversary of the founding of the city. In **May** is the *Festa do Divino* and, on the second Sun, the *Senhor do Bonfim* maritime procession. As elsewhere in the state, the *Festas Juninas* are celebrated in **Jun**. **8 Dec**: the festival of *Nossa Senhora da Conceição*.

Transport **Bus** To **Angra** at least hourly from Rio's rodoviária with *Costa Verde*, several direct, T516 2437, accepts credit cards, comfortable buses take the 'via litoral', sit on the left, US$6, 2½ hrs. From Angra to **São Paulo**, 5 buses daily (3 on Sat), US$12. To **Paraty**, many buses leave from bus station or just flag the bus down at bus stops on the highway, US$3. To **Bracuí**, take Divisa Paraty, Frade and Residencial US$1, 35 minutes ride to the youth hostel. **Ferry** To Ilha Grande, 1½ hrs, daily at 1530, returns 1000, US$6.75. For day trips, go from Mangaratiba, see above. Fishing boats take passengers from Angra for about US$5. Also try the pier where the ferry leaves as there are often boats to Abraão carrying building material, US$3.

Ilha Grande
Phone code 0xx21
The island is covered
in Atlantic forest,
surrounded by
transparent green
waters

A two-hour ferry ride makes a most attractive trip through the bay to **Vila do Abraão**, the main village on Ilha Grande. There are about 100 beaches around the island, three dozen of which are regular tourist spots. The weather is best from March to June, it is best to avoid the peak summer months from December to February. There is a very helpful **tourist office** as you get off the boat, 0800-1100 and 1700-2100. It was once an infamous lair for European pirates, then a landing stage for slaves. In the 19th century, it was a leper colony and in the 20th century had one of Brazil's larger high security prisons (closed in 1994 and later destroyed). Most of it is now a state park, including the **Reserva Biológica da Praia do Sul**. Cars are not allowed on the island, so transport is either by boat, or on foot.

Sleeping and eating Many *pousadas* in **Abraão**: for example on R da Praia, none is large but all have a/c. A *Pousada do Canto*, 2 blocks from downtown, T3361 5115. Very good value, quiet location. Highly recommended. B *Tropicana*, R da Praia 28, T3361 5047, www.pousadatropicana.com A in high season, beachfront, French run, good open-air restaurant with great breakfast. B *Pousada Mata Nativa*, R das Flores 44, Abraão, T3361 5397, matanativa@ilhagrande.com Chalets and rooms, hot water, fridge, fan, TV, own generator, splendid breakfast. B *Solar da Praia*, R da Praia 32, T3361 5368. Raphael speaks English and will act as a trekking guide. Others in this range. C *Estalagem Costa Verde*, nice place in green surroundings, near beach, T0xx11-3104 7940 (São Paulo), speak to Marcia or Marly. C *Pousada Cachoeira*, at the end of the village, T3361 5083. Run by German-Brazilian couple, English spoken, bungalows in green surroundings, pleasant. C *Pousada Beija Flor*, R da Assambléia 70, Vila do Abraão, T9648 8177. Good breakfast, fridge, book exchange, laundry service. D *Pousada Over Nativa*, R Pres Vargas 517, T3361 5108, www.ilhagrande.com/br/pou_overnativa.html A/c rooms more expensive, fan, pretty, very welcoming. Rooms can be rented in Abraão. For eating, try *Casa da Sogra*, Travessa do Beto. Recommended. *Mar da Tranquilidade*, reasonably priced, vegetarian options. *Minha Deusa*, R Professor Alice Coury 7, next to church. Brazilian, excellent food, reasonable prices.

Transport **Ferry**: see above under Angra dos Reis and Mangaratiba. **Boat**: boat trips cost US$10 without food or drinks, but including fruit. Recommended boats are *Victória Régia* (owned by Carlos, contact at *Pousada Tropicana*), *Papyk* or *André Maru* (owned by André). There is some good scuba diving around the coast; instructor Alexandre at Bougainville shop No 5. **Bicycle**: can be hired and tours arranged; ask at *pousadas*.

Paraty

Paraty is a charming colonial town whose centre has been declared a national historic monument in its entirety. It was the chief port for the export of gold in the 17th century and a coffee-exporting port in the 19th century. It is reached by taking the road beyond Angra dos Reis, which continues 98 km along the coast past the nuclear-power plant at Itaorna. Much of the accommodation available is in colonial buildings, some sumptuously decorated, with flourishing gardens or courtyards.

Phone code: 0xx24
Post code: 23970
Colour map 7, grid B4
Population: 29,544

The town centre is out of bounds for motor vehicles; heavy chains are strung across the entrance to the streets. In spring the roads are flooded, while the houses are above the water level

There are four churches: **Santa Rita** (1722), built by the 'freed coloured men' in elegant Brazilian baroque, faces the bay and the port. It houses an interesting **Museum of Sacred Art**. ■ *Wed-Sun 0900-1200, 1300-1800, US$1.* **Nossa Senhora do Rosário e São Benedito** (1725, rebuilt 1757), R do Comércio, built by black slaves, is small and simple. ■ *Tue 0900-1200.* **Nossa Senhora dos Remédios** (1787-1873), is the town's parish church, the biggest in Paraty. ■ *Mon, Wed, Fri, Sat 0900-1200, Sun 0900-1500.* **Capela de Nossa Senhora das Dores** (1800) is a small chapel facing the sea that was used mainly by the wealthy whites in the 19th century (Ms Grassa will open it for visitors if requested in advance). There is a great deal of distinguished Portuguese colonial architecture in delightful settings. **R do Comércio** is the main street in the historical centre. The **Casa da Cadeia**, close to Santa Rita church, is the former jail and is being converted into a historical museum. On the northern headland is a small fort, **Forte do Defensor Perpétuo**, built in 1822. The town has plenty of souvenir and handicraft shops.

At **Fazenda Murycana**, an old sugar estate and 17th century *cachaça* distillery, you can taste and buy the different types of *cachaça*. It has an excellent restaurant. Mosquitoes can be a problem, take repellent and don't wear shorts. Take a Penha/Ponte Branca bus from the rodoviária, four a day; alight where it crosses a small white bridge and then walk 10 minutes along a signed, unpaved road. If short of time, the one *must* is to take a boat trip round the bay and to the stunning beaches at **Trindade** (30 km away). Other good beaches are **Paraty Mirim** (15 km south, frequent *Colitur* buses), **Prainha** (10 km towards Rio) and **Toca do Pastel** (11km). The **Gold Trail**, hiking on a road dating from the 1800s, can be done on foot or horseback. Many other adventure sports are available (see Tour operators).

AL *Pousada do Sandi*, Largo do Rosário 1, T3371 2100, F3371 1236. 18th century building, charming, spacious rooms. **A** *Morro do Forte*, R Orlando Carpinelli, T/F3371 1211. Lovely garden, good breakfast, pool, German owner Peter Kallert offers trips on his yacht. Recommended. **A** *Pousada Pardieiro*, R do Comércio 74, T3371 1370, F3371 1139. Attractive colonial building with lovely gardens, delightful rooms facing internal patios, extremely pleasant, swimming pool, calm, sophisticated atmosphere, but always full at weekends, does not take children under 15. **A** *Pousada Porto Imperial*, R do Comércio, T3371 1205, F3371 2111. Good value. Highly recommended. **B** *Pousada do Corsário*, Beco do Lapeiro 26, T3371 1866, F3371 1319. New building outside centre, tranquil, comfortable, pool. Recommended. to the the historical centre, pool, English and Japanese spoken. **B** *Pousada Mercado do Pouso*, Largo de Santa Rita 43, T/F3371 1114, close to the port and Santa Rita. Recommended. **B-C** *Pousada Missanga*, Praça João Miranda, 10 mins' walk from centre, T/F3371 1597. Small, colonial style, a/c or fan, pool, garden, good, English and German spoken. **C** *Pouso Familiar*, R José Vieira Ramos 262, T3371 1475. Run by Belgian (Joseph Yserbyt) and his Brazilian wife (Lucia), near bus station, laundry facilities, English, French, German and Flemish spoken. Recommended. **C** *Solar dos Gerânios*, Praça da Matriz, T/F3371 1550. Beautiful colonial building, good value, English spoken. Recommended. **C** *Varandas de Paraty*, R Mal Deodoro 50, T3371 1873. A/c, TV, pool, hammocks, very pleasant, with good breakfast.

Sleeping
Over 300 hotels and pousadas; in midweek look around and find a place that suits you best

D *Marendaz*, R Dr Derly Ellena 9, T3371 1369. With breakfast, family run, simple, charming, close to the historical centre. **D** *Pousada da Matriz*, R da Cadeia 334, close to corner with R do Comércio, in historic centre. Basic but clean rooms, with bath, without breakfast, friendly if a little noisy. **Youth hostel** at R Antonio Vidal 120, Chacara (walking distance from bus station), T3371 2223/9914 5506. **Camping** Two main campsites, one off Av Roberto Silveira and the other at Praia Jabaquara, T3371 2180.

Eating   **Expensive** *Do Hiltinho*, R Marechal Deodoro 233, T/F3371 1432, historical centre. Local dishes, excellent seafood, good service, expensive but worth it. **Mid-range** *Candeeiro*, R da Lapa 335. Good local food. *Chafariz*, Praça Chafariz. For Brazilian seafood, good value. *Corto Maltese*, R do Comércio 130. Italian, pasta. *Dona Ondina*, R do Comércio 2, by the river. Family restaurant, well-prepared simple food, good value (closed on Mon between Mar and Nov). *Punto Di Vino*, R Marechal Deodoro 129. Excellent Italian. *Thai Brasil*, R Dona Geralda 345. Excellent, delightful setting, English and German spoken. **Cheap** The less expensive restaurants, those offering *comida a quilo* (pay by weight) and the fast food outlets are outside the historical centre, mainly on Av Roberto Silveira. Eg *Sabor de Terra*, next to Banco do Brasil. Reliable, closes 2200.

Entertainment   *Bar Dinho*, Praça da Matriz at R da Matriz. Good bar, busy after midnight, live music Thu-Sat, mainly MPB. *Margarida*, Praça do Chafariz. Good food, best place for live music early in the week. *Paraty 33*, R da Lapa. Live music with bar and restaurant, popular but expensive. *Teatro Espaço, The Puppet Show*, R Dona Geralda 327, T3371 1575, ecparaty@ax.apc.org Wed, Sat 2100, US$8 (50% discount for students): this famous puppet show should not be missed.

Festivals   Feb/Mar: *Carnival*, excellent, plus, 2 Saturdays before Carnival, *Carnamar*, fancy dress, drinking and dancing on boats in the bay, and on the Sat before Carnival, *Bloco da Lama*, the mud procession from Praia Jabaquara to town; Mar/Apr: *Semana Santa*, with religious processions and folk songs. Jul: *Semana de Santa Rita*, traditional foods, shows, exhibitions and dances (different days each year). Aug: *Festival da Pinga*, the *cachaça* fair, plenty of opportunities to over-indulge. Sep (around the 8th): *Semana da Nossa Senhora dos Remédios*, processions and religious events. Sep/Oct: *Spring Festival of Music*. 31 Dec: *Reveillon*, a huge party with open-air concerts and fireworks (reserve accommodation in advance).

Tour operators   All can arrange schooner trips, bike hire, trekking in the rain forest and on the old gold trail, visits to Trindade beach and waterfalls, and transfers. They will also phone around for vacancies in hotels/pousadas. *Alcance*, Av Roberto Silveira 402, near bus station, T/F3371 6442, alcanceparaty@uol.com.br For flights and packages, also rafting, diving, hang gliding, kayaking (recommended), horse tgrekking, canyoning and abseiling. English spoken, very helpful. *Paraty Tours*, Av Roberto Silveira 11, T/F3371 1327. English and Spanish spoken.

Transport   **Bus** Rodoviária at the corner of R Jango Padua and R da Floresta. 9 buses a day go to **Rio** (241 km), 4½ hrs, US$10, *Costa Verde* – see under Angra dos Reis for details; to **Angra dos Reis** (98 km, 1½ hrs, every 1 hr 40 mins, US$4, also *Colitur*). 3 a day to **Ubatuba** (75 km, just over 1 hr, *Colitur*, US$4). To **São Paulo**, 4 a day (304 km via São José dos Campos, 5½ hrs, US$8.50, *Reunidas*, booked up quickly, very busy at weekends). To **São Sebastião**, 2 a day with*Normandy* (who also go to Rio twice a day). On holidays and in high season, the frequency of bus services usually increases.

Directory   **Banks** *Banco do Brasil*, Av Roberto Silveira, not too far from the bus station, exchange 1000-1500, long queues and commission. 2 ATMs in town for Visa and MasterCard, 0600-2200. Exchange also at *Atrium Turismo*, R da Lapa, 0900-1900 daily. **Communications** Internet: *Alcance Turismo* (see above); *Paraty Cyber Café*, Av R Silveira 17 (expensive but fast connection); *Paraty Web*, Shopping Colonial, next to bus station, T3371 2499 (fast broadband). **Post Office:** R Mcal Deodoro e Domingos Gonçalves de Abreu, 0800-1700, Sun 0800-1200. **Telephone:** *Telerj* for international calls, Praça Macedo Soares, opposite the tourist office. Local and long distance calls can be made from public phones. **Tourist office** Centro de Informações Turísticas, Av Roberto Silveira, near the entrance to the historical centre, T3371 2148.

São Paulo

Brasília

The overall aspect of the most populous city in South America is one of skyscrapers, long avenues, traffic and crowds. Most of its citizens are proud of São Paulo's high-rise architecture, of its well-lit streets and of the Metrô, but they also mourn the loss of innumerable historical buildings and green areas through short-sighted planning policies in the 1980s. The inhabitants of the city are called Paulistanos, to differentiate them from the inhabitants of the state, who are called Paulistas. The state of São Paulo is the industrial heart of Brazil. São Paulo city is the financial centre of Brazil and has much of cultural interest in the way of museums and the famous Butantã Snake Farm. On the coast there are fine beaches, although pollution is sometimes a problem. Inland there are hill resorts and an important area of caves.

Phone code: 0xx11
Colour map 7, grid B4
Population (city): 18 mn
Population (State): 37 mn

Until the 1870s São Paulo was a sleepy, shabby little town known as 'a cidade de barro' (the mud city), as most of its buildings were made of clay and packed mud. The city was transformed architecturally at the end of the 19th century when wealthy landowners and the merchants of Santos began to invest. Between 1885 and the end of the century the boom in coffee and the arrival of large numbers of Europeans transformed the state out of all recognition. By the end of the 1930s São Paulo state had one million Italians, 500,000 each of Portuguese and immigrants from the rest of Brazil, nearly 400,000 Spaniards and nearly 200,000 Japanese. It is the world's largest Japanese community outside Japan. In the early 20th century, numbers of Syrian-Lebanese came to São Paulo. Nowadays, it covers more than 1,500 sq km – three times the size of Paris.

History

Brazil

Ins and outs

There are air services from all parts of Brazil, Europe, North and South America to the international **airport** at Guarulhos, also known as Cumbica, Av Monteiro Lobato 1985, T6445 2945 (30 km from the city). *Varig* has its own, new terminal for international flights, adjoining the old terminal which all other airlines use. The local airport of Congonhas, 14 km from the city centre on Av Washington Luiz, is used for the Rio-São Paulo shuttle, some flights to Belo Horizonte and Vitória and private flights only, T5090 9195. The **main rodoviária** is Tietê (T235 0322 or 11-900 0096 toll free), which is very convenient and has its own Metrô station. There are three other bus stations for inter-state bus services.

Getting there
For more detailed information, see Transport, page 406

Much of the centre is pedestrianized, so there is no option other than to walk if you wish to explore it. All the rodoviárias (bus stations) are on the Metrô (underground railway), but if travelling with luggage, take a taxi. The shopping, hotel and restaurant centre embraces the districts of Av São Luis, the Praça da República, and R Barão de Itapetininga. The central commercial district, containing banks, offices and shops, is known as the Triângulo, bounded by R Direita, 15 (Quinze) de Novembro, São Bento and Praça Antônio Prado, but it is rapidly spreading towards the Praça da República. R Augusta begins close to Avenida São Luis, extends as far as **Av Paulista**, and continues beyond into one of the most affluent areas, Jardins. Both sides of R Augusta have a variety of shops, snackbars and restaurants, but the Jardins side contains the more exclusive boutiques and fashion houses, especially R Oscar Freire and R Haddock Lobo, while the part which leads to the centre is a rather curious but colourful mix of seedy bars, saunas and five-star hotels. Avenida Paulista is now Brazil's largest financial centre housing most banking head offices (most consulates as well), and the Museu de Arte de São Paulo (see below). It has become a new downtown area, more dynamic, but considerably less colourful than the old centre. Set to replace Avenida Paulista as the main centre is Avenida Faria Lima, at the southwest edge of Jardins 8 km from Praça da República. Newer still is the movement of offices to Avenida Luis Carlos Berrini, which is yet further southwest, parallel to the Avenida das Nações Unidas and the Rio Pinheiros. Other popular residential areas are Vila Madalena and Pinheiros, both west of the centre.

Getting around & orientation
Beware of assaults and pickpocketing in São Paulo. Thieves often use the mustard-on-the-back trick to distract your attention while someone else robs you. The areas around Luz station, Praça da República and Centro are not safe at night, and visitors should not enter favelas

Brazil

Tourist offices Information kiosks: **Praça da República**, very helpful, 0900-1800 daily. **Av Paulista** at Parque Trianon, 0900-1800 except Sat. **Av Brigadeiro Faria Lima** opposite the *Iguatemi Shopping Centre*, Mon-Fri 0900-1800. In *Ibirapuera park*, 0900-1800. At *Guarulhos* airport, 0600-2200, helpful. *Tietê* bus station, 0700-2000, also helpful, and *Lux* train station, 0900-1800. An excellent free map is given at all these offices. Head office: Av Olavo Fontoura 1209, Parque Anhembi, T6224 0400. **Tours of the city** three types of tour leave the kiosk on Praça da República each Sun, costing US$2: 3 to places of `green' interest, also historical and cultural, T6971 5000. Other tours leave R 15 de Novembro 347 Tue-Sun at 1000 and 1400, free. There are 2 different itineraries (2 hrs each). Tourist offices have free magazines in Portuguese and English: *Where* and *São Paulo This Month* (also available from most travel agencies and better hotels). Also recommended is Quatro Rodas' *Guia de São Paulo*. News stands sell a wide range of magazines and books which deal with tourism in the city and the state. Information on the web: www.cityofsaopaulo.com www.turismopaulista.sp.gov.br has links to all the municipalities in the state. **National parks**: Ibama, Alameda Tietê 637, Jardim Cerqueira César, T3066 2662, F3066 2675.

Climate There is ample rainfall; indeed, the highest rainfall in Brazil (3,810 mm) is over a small area between Santos and São Paulo; at São Paulo itself it is no more than 1,194 mm. Characteristic sharp changes of temperature cause people to catch cold often. In dry weather eyes and nose are continually troubled. The amount of air pollution can be exasperating and thermal inversions, in which a blanket of warm air prevents the dispersal of the industrial and automobile pollutants, are common.

Sights

An historic buildings walk is indicated on the city map

A focal point of the centre is the **Parque Anhangabaú**, an open space between the Triângulo and the streets which lead to Praça da República (Metrô Anhangabaú is at its southern end). Beneath Anhangabaú, north-south traffic is carried by a tunnel. Crossing it are two viaducts: **Viaduto do Chá**, which is open to traffic and links R Direita and R Barão de Itapetininga. Along its length sellers of potions, cures, fortunes and trinkets set up their booths. The **Viaduto Santa Ifigênia**, an iron bridge for pedestrians only, connects Largo de São Bento with Largo de Santa Ifigênia.

On **Largo de São Bento** is the **Igreja e Mosteiro de São Bento**, an early 20th century building (1910-22) on the site of a 1598 chapel. Due south of São Bento on R Líbero Badaró at Av São João is the **Martinelli building**, the city's first skyscraper. ■ *Mon-Sat 0900-1600, entry to 26th floor, free*. On Praça Antônio Prado stands the **Antigo Prédio do Banco do São Paulo**, the ground floor used for fairs and exhibitions. ■ *Mon-Fri 0900-1800*. The **Pátio do Colégio** is just east of Praça Padre Manuel da Nóbrega. This is the site of the founding of São Paulo and the present building is a reconstruction. It houses the **Capela de Anchieta** and the **Museu Casa de Anchieta**, which houses items from the Jesuit era, including paintings and relics. ■ *The chapel is open Mon-Fri 0730-1700; the museum Tue-Sun 1300-1630, US$1*.

A short distance southeast of the Pátio do Colégio is the **Solar da Marquesa de Santos**, an 18th-century residential building, which now contains the **Museu da Cidade**, R Roberto Simonsen 136. ■ *Tue-Sun, 0900-1700*. The **Praça da Sé** is a huge open area south of the Pátio do Colégio, dominated by the **Catedral Metropolitana**, a massive, peaceful space. The cathedral's foundations were laid over 40 years before its inauguration during the 1954 festivities commemorating the fourth centenary of the city. It was fully completed in 1970. This enormous building in neo-Gothic style has a capacity for 8,000 worshippers in its five naves. The interior is mostly unadorned, except for the two gilt mosaic pictures in the transepts: on the north side is the Virgin Mary and on the south Saint Paul.

West of the Praça da Sé, along R Benjamin Constant, is the Largo de São Francisco. Here is the **Igreja da Ordem Terceira de São Francisco**. The convent was inaugurated in 1647 and reformed in 1744. To the right is the Igreja das Chagas do Seráphico Pai São Francisco (1787), painted like its neighbour in blue and gold.

Across the Viaduto do Chá is the **Teatro Municipal**, one of the few distinguished early 20th-century survivors that São Paulo can boast (T223 3022). Viewing the interior may only be possible during a performance; as well as the full evening performances, look out for midday, string quartet and 'vesperais líricas' concerts.

It is easy to walk from Parque Anhangabaú to the Praça da República. Either go along Av São João (which is rather seedy in this part, with cinemas and sex shops) or, preferably, take the pedestrian streets from Viaduto do Chá. These streets tend to be crowded, but they have a wide variety of shops, places to eat and some hotels. In Praça da República the trees are tall and shady. There are also lots of police. Near the Praça is the city's tallest building, the **Edifício Itália** on the corner of Av Ipiranga and Av São Luís. There is a restaurant on top and a sightseeing balcony. Two blocks northwest of the Praça is the **Largo do Arouche**, by which is a large flower market. If you walk up Av São Luís, which has many airline offices and

Praça da República

Brazil

São Paulo

N

0 km   3
0 miles   3

○ **Open spaces**
1 Parque Ecológico do Tietê

2 Parque da Independência
3 Jardim Botânico
4 Jardim Zoológico & Simba Safári
5 Parque do Estado
6 Represa Billings
7 Autodromo de Interlagos
8 Represa de Guarapiranga

9 Parque do Ibirapuera
10 Jóquei Clube
11 Instituto Butantã
12 Ciudad Universitária
13 Campo de Marte
14 Parque Burle Marx

Ⓜ **Metro stations**
1 Tucuruvi
2 Tietê

3 Luz
4 Sé
5 Paraíso
6 Vila Mariana
7 Jabaquara
8 Barra Funda
9 Bresser
10 Itaquera
11 Clinicas
12 Vila Madalena

*Detail map
A Tietê to Liberdade,
page 401*

travel agencies (especially in the Galeria Metrópole), you come to Praça Dom José Gaspar, in which is the **Biblioteca Municipal Mário de Andrade**, surrounded by a pleasant shady garden.

North of the centre About 10 minutes' walk from the centre of the city is the old **Mercado Municipal** covering 27,000 sq m at R Cantareira 306. ■ *Mon-Sat 0400-1600.* **Parque da Luz** on Av Tiradentes (110,000 sq m) was formerly a botanical garden. It is next to the Luz railway station. There are two museums on Av Tiradentes, near the park: the **Museu de Arte Sacra** in the Convento da Luz, No 676, ■ *Tue-Sun 1300-1800, T3326 5393* and the **Pinacoteca do Estado** (State Art Collection) at No 141. ■ *Tue-Sun 1000-1800, free, T229 9844.* The **Igreja e Convento Nossa Senhora da Luz**, which houses the Sacred Art Museum, was built in 1774, one of the few colonial buildings left in São Paulo; the chapel dates from 1579.

Liberdade Directly south of the Praça da Sé, and only one stop on the Metrô, is Liberdade, the central Japanese district. The Metrô station is in Praça da Liberdade, in which there is an oriental market every Sunday (see Shopping). **Museu da Imigração Japonesa**, R São Joaquim 381, Liberdade (T3209 5465), is excellent, with a nice roof garden; ask at the desk for an English translation of the exhibits. ■ *Tue-Sun 1330-1730, free.*

São Paulo centre

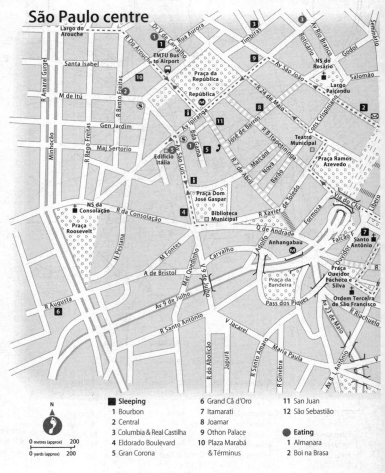

	Sleeping				
1	Bourbon	6	Grand Câ d'Oro	11	San Juan
2	Central	7	Itamarati	12	São Sebastião
3	Columbia & Real Castilha	8	Joamar		
4	Eldorado Boulevard	9	Othon Palace		Eating
5	Gran Corona	10	Plaza Marabá & Términus	1	Almanara
				2	Boi na Brasa

N

0 metres (approx)   200
0 yards (approx)   200

Either Metrô station Vergueiro or Paraíso is convenient for the southeastern end of Av Paulista, the highlight of which is **MASP**. This is the common name for The **Museu de Arte de São Paulo**, at Av Paulista 1578 (immediately above the 9 de Julho tunnel); the nearest Metrô is Trianon-MASP. The museum has major collections of European painters and sculptors, and some interesting work by Brazilian artists, including Portinari. Particularly interesting are the pictures of northeastern Brazil by Dutch artists during the Dutch occupation (1630-54): the exotic tropical land-scapes have been made to look incredibly temperate. Temporary exhibitions are also held and when a popular show is on, it can take up to an hour to get in. In this case, the later you go the better. ■ *Tue-Sun 1100-1800 (Thu 1100-2000, free), US$8; T251 5644. www.masp.art.br Bus 805A from Praça da República goes by MASP.*

Opposite MASP is **Parque Tenente Siqueira Campos**, which covers two blocks on either side of Alameda Santos; a bridge links the two parts of the park. ■ *Daily 0700-1830 and is a welcome green area in the busiest part of the city.* The **Museu da Imagem e do Som** (MIS) is at Av Europa 158. ■ *Tue-Fri 1400-1800.* It has photo-graphic exhibitions, archives of Brazilian cinema and music, and a nice café. Next to MIS is the **Museu Brasiliero da Escultura** (MuBE); free to temporary exhibitions and recitals in the afternoons. Av Europa continues to Av Brigadeiro Faria Lima, on which is the **Casa Brasileira**, Av Faria Lima 2705, T3032 2564, a museum of Brazilian furni-ture. ■ *Tue-Sun 1300-1800. It also holds temporary exhibitions.*

Avenida Paulista & the Jardins district

Brazil

The Parque do Ibirapuera, designed by Oscar Niemeyer and landscape art-ist Roberto Burle Marx for the city's fourth centenary in 1954, is open daily 0600-1730; entrance on Av Pedro Álvares Cabral. Within its 1.6 million sq m is the **Assembléia Legislativa** and a **planetarium** (shows at 1530 and 1730 at weekends and on holi-days, US$5, half price for those under 18, T273 5500, www.planetario. com.br). Also in the park is the **Museu de Arte Moderna** (MAM), with art exhibitions and sculpture garden (see Nuno Ramos' *Craca* – Barnacle). ■ *Tue, Wed, Fri 1200-1800, Thu 1200-2200, Sat-Sun 1000-1800, US$2, students half price, free all Tue and Fri after 1700, T5549 9688, www.mam. org.br* Bicycles can be hired from local character Maizena beside the city hall, *Prodam*, US$1.25 for a bike wthout gears, US$2 with gears, leave document as security. Buses to Ibirapuera, 574R from Paraíso Metrô station; 6364 from Praça da Bandeira. ; to Cidade Universitária 702U or 7181 from Praça da República. Every even-numbered year the **Bienal Internacional de São Paulo** (São Paulo Biennial) at Ibirapuera has the most important show of modern art in Latin America, usually in September (next in 2004).

Ibirapuera

3 Delícia Natural
  & Sabor Natural
4 Saúde Sabor
5 Terraço Itália

--►-- Historic buildings walk

Cidade Universitária & Morumbi The Cidade Universitária (university city) is on the west bank of the Rio Pinheiros, opposite the district of Pinheiros. The campus also contains the famous **Instituto Butantã** (Butantã Snake Farm and Museum), Av Dr Vital Brasil 1500, T3726 7222, www.butantan.gov.br The snakes are milked for their poison six times a day but you may not witness this. It also deals with spider and scorpion venom, has a small hospital and is a biomedical research institute. What visitors see is the museum of poisonous animals and public health, with explanations in Portuguese and English. ■ *Tue-Sun 0900-1700, US$1(children and students half price). From Praça da República take bus marked 'Butantã' or 'Cidade Universitária' (Nos 701U or 792U) along Av Paulista, and ask to be let out at Instituto Butantã.* The **Museu de Arte Contemporâneo** (MAC), with an important collection of Brazilian and European modern art, is in the Prédio Novo da Reitoria, T3818 3039, www.mac.usp.br ■ *Tue-Sat 1200-1800, Sun 1000-1800, free.* Also the **Museu de Arqueologia e Etnologia** (MAE), R Reitoria 1466, T3812 4001, with a collection of Amazonian and ancient Mediterranean material. Not far from the Butantã Institute, just inside Cidade Universitária, is the **Casa do Bandeirante** at Praça Monteiro Lobato, the reconstructed home of a pioneer of 400 years ago (T3031 0920).

On the west bank of the Rio Pinheiros, just southeast of the Cidade Universitária, is the palatial **Jóquei Clube/Jockey Club** racecourse in the Cidade Jardim area (Av Lineu de Paula Machado 1263, T3816 4011.) Take Butantã bus from República, among others). Race meetings are held on Monday and Thursday at 1930 and Saturday and Sunday at 1430. It has a **Museu do Turfe**. ■ *Tue-Sun, but closed Sat and Sun mornings.*

Morumbi is a smart residential district due south of the Cidade Universitária. In the area are the state government building, **Palácio dos Bandeirantes** (Av Morumbi 4500), the small, simple **Capela de Morumbi** (Av Morumbi 5387), and the Morumbi stadium of São Paulo Football Club, which holds 100,000 people. Motor racing fans might like to visit the Morumbi cemetery, last resting place of Ayrton Senna; take 6291 bus to R Profesor Benedito Montenegro.

Museu da Fundação Maria Luisa e Oscar Americano, Av Morumbi 3700, Morumbi, T842 0077, is a private collection of Brazilian and Portuguese art and furniture. The garden has fascinating paths, patios and native plants. ■ *Tue-Fri 1100-1830, Sat-Sun 1000-1830.* It is close to the Palácio dos Bandeirantes.

Burle Marx Park, Av Dona Helena Pereira de Moraes 200, Morumbi. Designed by famous landscape designer Burle Marx, it is the only place in the city where you can walk in trails in the Mata Atlântica (Atlantic Rain forest). ■ *Daily 0700-1900.*

Parque da Independência In the suburb of Ipiranga, 5½ km southeast of the city centre, the Parque da Independência contains the **Monumento à Independência**; beneath the monument is the Imperial Chapel, with the tomb of the first emperor, Dom Pedro I, and Empress Leopoldina ■ *Tue-Sun 1300-1700.* **Casa do Grito**, the little house in which Dom Pedro I spent the night before his famous cry of Ipiranga – 'Independence or Death' – is preserved in the park ■ *Tue-Sun 0930-1700.* The **Museu Paulista** contains old maps, traditional furniture, collections of old coins and of religious art and rare documents, and a department of Indian ethnology; ■ *Tue-Sun 0900-1645, US$1.* Behind the Museum is the **Horto Botânico/Ipiranga Botanical Garden** and the **Jardim Francês** ■ *Tue-Sun 0900-1700. Take bus 478-P (Ipiranga-Pompéia for return) from Ana Rosa, or take bus 4612 from Praça da República.*

Parque do Estado (Jardim Botânico) This large park, a long way south of the centre, at Água Funda (Av Miguel Estefano 3031-3687), contains the Jardim Botânico, with lakes and trees and places for picnics, and a very fine orchid farm worth seeing during November-December (orchid exhibitions in April and November). ■ *Wed-Sun 0900-1700, T5584 6300. Take Metrô to São Judas on the Jabaquara line, then take a bus.*

In Tremembé, a little beyond Cantareira, 30 minutes north of downtown, is the **Horto Florestal** (R do Horto 931, in Parque Estadual Alberto Löfgren, T952 8555), which contains examples of nearly every species of Brazilian woodland flora, 15 km of natural trails, a museum, a view of São Paulo from Pedra Grande on the right of the entrance to the park. ■ *Daily 0600-1800*. **Embu** (*M'Boy* – Big Snake), www.prefeituradeembu.com.br, 28 km from São Paulo, is a colonial town which has

Tietê to Liberdade

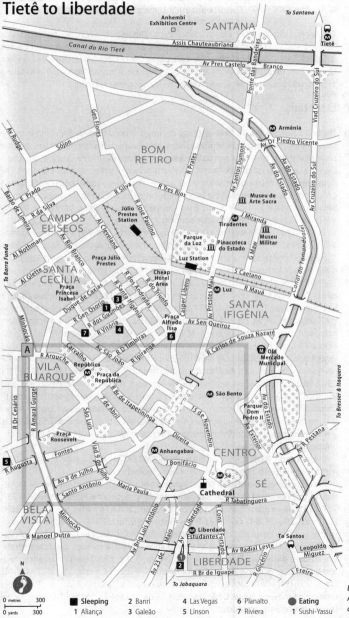

Brazil

*Detail map
A São Paulo centre
detail, page 398*

| 0 metres | 300 |
| 0 yards | 300 |

■ **Sleeping**   2 Banri   4 Las Vegas   6 Planalto   ● **Eating**
1 Aliança   3 Galeão   5 Linson   7 Riviera   1 Sushi-Yassu

become a centre for artists and craftsmen. The town itself, on a hill, is surrounded by industry and modern developments and the colonial centre is quite small. Many of the old houses are painted in bright colours and most contain arts, furniture, souvenir or antiques shops. There are many good restaurants (eg *Orixas* and *Garimpo* on R NS do Rosario). On Sunday afternoons there is a large and popular arts and crafts fair (0900-1800). On Monday almost everything is closed. In the Largo dos Jesuítas is the church of **Nossa Senhora do Rosário** (1690) and the **Museu de Arte Sacra** ■ *Sat-Sun 1200-1700*. Tourist office on R Capelinha, on the Largo 21 de Abril.

Transport From São Paulo, *Soamin* bus number 179 leaves from Av Cruzeiro do Sul between Tietê rodoviária and Metrô station (it is marked 'Embu-Engenho Velho'); departures between 0610 and 2310, US$2, 1 hr 45 mins. The route passes Clínicas Metrô, goes down Av Francisco Morato, then through Taboão da Serra: it is a long ride. A quicker alternative is to take a 'SP-Pinheiros' bus from Clínicas, which takes the main highway to Embu.

Essentials

Sleeping
See Essentials for new telephone number changes
■ *on maps, pages 401 & 398*
Price codes: see inside front cover

The best hotels are around Av Paulista and in Jardins. Around Praça da República there are some slightly cheaper, but still very good hotels and cheaper hotels can still be found on the pedestrian streets between Praça da República and Anhangabaú. In the daytime, this area is OK, but at night you should be careful. Ask your hotel which streets should be avoided. The Japanese district of Liberdade, south of Praça da Sé, has some pleasant hotels and is quite a good place to stay. Again, ask your hotel which directions are safest. The area between Av São João and Estação da Luz is where the cheapest hotels are. Some, but not all, are very seedy and the neighbourhood can be alarming at night.

Between Av Paulista and Praça Dom José Gaspar: The **LL** *Mofarrej Sheraton*, Al Santos 1437, T3253 5544, www.sheraton-sp.com On the south side of Av Paulista. Recommended. There are other international chain hotels. **L-A** *Grand Hotel Cà d'Oro*, R Augusta 129, T3236 4300, www.cadoro.com.br Extensive parking, good food and service, well decorated.

The following hotels are also good and are less expensive than the top flight establishments. They tend to be located closer to the downtown area. **LL** *Othon Palace São Paulo*, R Líbero Badaró 190, T3291 5000, F3107 7203, www.othon.com.br The only high-class hotel in the Triângulo, good. **AL** *Eldorado Boulevard*, Av São Luís 234, T3214 1833, www.hoteiseldorado.com.br/hbouleva.htm Excellent. **AL** *Bourbon*, Av Vieira de Carvalho 99, T3337 2000, hbnsao@uol.com.br Very smart, pleasant. **AL** *Linson* R Augusta 440, Consolação, T3256 6700, www.linson.com.br All apartments with double bed, kitchenette, sitting room, bath, TV, security system, restaurant, pool. **AL** *Planalto*, Cásper Líbero 117, Santa Ifigênia, T3311 7311, F3311 7916. Secure, helpful, good service, good dining room. **A** *Gran Corona*, Basílio da Gama 95/101, T3214 0043, in a small street just off Praça da República, www.grancorona.com.br Comfortable, good services, good restaurant. Warmly recommended. **A** *San Juan*, R Aurora 909, also near Praça da República, just behind Emtu airport bus terminal, T/F3225 9100, www.sanjuanhoteis.com.br Recommended. There are many other Aparthotels which are recommended for longer stays.

In **Liberdade**: **B** *Banri*, R Galvão Bueno 209, T3207 8877, www.banrohotel.com.br Near Metrô station Liberdade, good, Chinese owners. Recommended.

There are scores of hotels with prices below the luxury ranges, of which we include a selection. **In the vicinity of Praça da República** On Av Ipiranga are **B** *Plaza Marabá*, No 757, T3331 7811, www.plazamaraba.com.br recommended, and **B** *Términus*, No 741, T222 2226, F220 6162, also OK. **B-C**, *Columbia*, R dos Timbiras 492, T3331 3411, www.hotelcolumbia.com.br and *Real Castilha*, No 472, www.realcastilha.com.br A/c, minibar, internet connection, attention for businesswomen and handicapped guests, restaurant, bar, fitness centre. Under same ownership, **D** *Joamar*, R José de Barros 187, www.hoteljoamar.com.br Bed-and-breakfast, refurbished, TV, fan. **C-D** *Itamarati*, Av Vieira de Carvalho 150, T222 4133, 1½ blocks from Praça da República, www.hotelitamarati.com.br Good location, safe. Highly recommended and very popular. **C** *São Sebastião*, R 7 de Abril 364, T3255 1594. TV, fridge, phone, laundry service. Recommended.

Most of the cheaper hotels are in the area between Av São João and Estação Luz. The area can be approached either from Metrô República or Luz, but the red light district is in the blocks bounded by RR Santa Ifigênia, dos Andradas, dos Gusmões and Av Ipiranga, and is not recommended for women travelling alone. The area around Av Rio Branco is rather seedy and not entirely safe late at night. **C** *Riviera*, Av Barão de Limeira 117, T221 8077. Excellent value. Highly recommended. **D** *Central*, Av São João 288, T3335 6400, www.hotelcentral.com.br Cheaper without shower or TV, good, helpful, central. **D** *Center Plaza*, R Maestro Cardim 418, Bela Vista, near São Joaquim metro station, T/F289 3633, centerplaza@uol.com.br TV, fan, phone, accepts credit cards. **D** *Galeão*, R dos Gusmões 394, T3331 8211, www.hotelgaleao.sp.com.br Safe, helpful, hot showers. **D** *Las Vegas*, R Vitória 390 (corner Av Rio Branco), T221 8144. Also recommended. **E** *Aliança*, R Gen Osório 235, corner of Santa Ifigênia, T2204244. Nice, with breakfast, good value.

Apartment hotels can provide very good value. **B** *Paulistania Flat-Set*, Al Casa Branca 343, Jardim Paulista, T3148 2008, www.paulistaniaflat.com.br Modern, kitchenette, phone, cable TV, restaurant, pool, fitness centre, room service. **B** *Travel Inn Park Avenue*, Al Jaú 358, T3284 8622. **C** at weekends, similar to *Paulistania*, with gym, very nice. The *Parthenon* chain has modern apart-hotels in São Paulo and across Brazil, www.accorbrasil.com.br

Youth hostels Associação Paulista de Albergues da Juventude, R 7 de Abril 386, 2nd floor, Centro, T3258 0388, www.alberguesp.com.br Membership is US$15 per year. Hostel at *Magdalena Tagliaferro*, Estrada Turística do Jaguará 651, Km 18, via Anhangüera, 05161-000 São Paulo, T3258 0388. Open all year, reservations necessary, HI affiliated, take a Jaguará 8696 bus from Anhangabaú Metrô station to the Parque Estadual Jaguará, the hostel is 100 m from the entrance. **E** *Praça da Árvore*, Pageú 266, T/F5071 5148, www.spalbergue.com.br Member of Hostelling Internacional, kitchen, laundry, includes breakfast but not sheets, towels or luggage store, internet service (US$4.15), overpriced. An unaffiliated hostel is *Primavera* at R Mariz e Barros 350, Vila Santa Eulália, T215 3144 (bus 4491 from Parque Dom Pedro in the centre). US$10-15, cooking and washing facilities.

Camping A list of sites can be obtained from **Camping Clube do Brasil**, R Minerva 156, Perdizes, T3861 7133.

Apart from the international cuisine in the first-class hotels, here are a few recommendations out of many. The average price of a meal in 2002 was US$10-15 in trattorias, US$25-30 in first class places, but more in the very best restaurants; remember that costs can be cut by sharing the large portions served.

Brazilian *Bassi*, R 13 de Maio 666, T3104 2375, Bela Vista, for meat, US$25 pp midweek. *Paulista Grill*, R João Moura 257, Pinheiros, T853 5426. Top quality meat, excellent value, popular. *Vento Haragano*, Av Rebouças 1001, Jardim Paulista, T3085 6039. *Churrascaria rodizio*, very good, US$17 pp. *Moraes*, Al Santos 1105, Cerqueira César, T289 3347, and Praça Júlio de Mesquita 175, Vila Buarque (Centro), T221 8066. Traditional meat dishes. *Novilha de Prata*, Av 23 de Maio, corner Pedro Ivo 63, Paraíso (behind Shopping Paulista). Mid-range *rodizio*, good service, excellent meat, 5 other branches. *Sujinho*, R da Consolação 2068, T3259 1447. Very popular *churrascaria*, with another branch at No 2063. *Boi na Brasa*, R Bento Freitas by Praça da República. Very good, reasonable prices. *Dinho's Place*, Al Santos 45, Paraíso, T3284 5333. Fri seafood buffet, also meat, has daily bargains, also Av Morumbi 7976, T536 4299. *Dom Place*, Largo do Arouche 246. Good food and very good value (US$7 plus drinks). *Bolinha*, Av Cidade Jardim 53, Jardim Paulistano, T3061 2010. For *feijoadas* daily, and other dishes. *Oxalá*, Tr Maria Antônia 72, just off Consolação. Bahian specialities at modest prices.

French *Marcel*, R da Consolação 3555, T3064 3089. Sensational soufflés.

German *Arnold's Naschbar*, R Pereira Leite 98, Sumarezinho, T3672 5648. *Eisbein peruruca*. Recommended. *Bismarck*, Av Ibirapuera 3178, Moema, T5044 0313. Good food and excellent draught beer.

Italian *Il Sogno di Anarello*, R Il Sogno di Anarello 58, Vila Mariana, T5575 4266. Mon-Fri 1900-0100 only, excellent, typical *cantina paulistana*. *Lellis*, R Bela Cintra 1849, T3083 3588. Very good but pricey, *salada Lellis* is a must, and fresh squid in batter. *Massimo*, Al Santos 1826, Cerqueira César, T3284 0311, Italian and international cuisine. *L'Osteria do Piero*, Al Franca 1509, Cerqueira César, T3085 1082. Excellent. *Famiglia Mancini*, R Avanhandava 81, Bela Vista,

Eating
● *on maps 398 & 401*

Many restaurants now serve food by weight, even some of the better class places (but these are naturally more expensive per kg). You should compare prices carefully because an expensive per kg restaurant can work out more expensive than a normal one

Brazil

T3256 4320. Excellent, salads and cold dishes, always queues between 2000-2400. Its new branch, **Walter Mancini**, opposite, is more luxurious, also packed on Sun. **Gigetto**, Avanhandava 63, T256 9804. For pasta, reasonable prices. **La Trattoria**, R Antônio Bicudo 50, Pinheiros, T3088 3572. Closed Mon, midweek until 1900, Fri, Sat till 0100, reasonably priced food, strozzapreti a must. There are many Italian restaurants in the Bela Vista/Bixiga area, especially on R 13 de Maio; Among the best is Speranza, R 13 de Maio 1004, T3288 8502. Frequent award winner, pizza marguerita and antipasto tortano are supperb. Recommended pizzerias are **Capuano**, R Conselheiro Carrão 416, T288 1460, **Margherita**, Al Tietê 255, T3086 2556.

Portuguese Antiquarius, Al Lorena 1884, Cerqueira César, T3082 3015. Excellent.

Swiss **Chamonix**, R Pamplona 1446, Jardins, T3884 3025, and **Le Jardin Suisse**, Al Franca 1467, T5505 3110, both in Jardim Paulista. Expensive, very good.

Arabic **Almanara**, a chain of reasonably priced restaurants serving Middle Eastern/Lebanese food, Oscar Freire 523 (Cerqueiro César), R Basilio da Gama 70 and Av Vieira de Carvalho 109/123 (either side of Praça da República) and in Shoppings Iguatemi, Morumbi amd Paulista. **Bambi**, Al Santos 59, Paraíso, T284 4944. Mostly Arabic food. **Rubayat**, Al Santos 86, T289 6366. Excellent meat, fixed price meals.

Oriental (Japanese tends to be expensive) **Komazushi**, R São Carlos do Pinhal 241, loja 5, Cerqueiro César, T287 1820. Renowned for its sushi, closed weekends. **Kar Wua** Chinese restaurant, at R Mourato Coelho 44, Pinheiros, T3081 1581. Highly praised. **Suntory**, Al Campinas 600, Jardins, T283 2455. Japanese with separate salons for sushi and teppanyaki, piano bar, garden. **Sushi-Yassu**, R Tomaz Gonzaga 98, Liberdade, T3209 6622. Different styles, traditional, good reputation. Many other Chinese and Japanese restaurants in Liberdade, especially on R Tomaz Gonzaga, where there is a Japanese food market in the square by the Metrô station.

General **Terraço Itália**, on top of Edifício Itália (Ipiranga 344 e São Luis), 41 floors up, 1130-0100, fixed price lunch and other meals, dancing with excellent band and superb view (minimum consumption charge of US$10 to be allowed to see the view), US$85 pp including wine in dancing part, US$65-70 otherwise, dress smartly. **Mexilhão**, R 13 de Maio 626/8, Bela Vista, T3263 6135, seafood. **Charlô**, R Barã de Capanema 440, Jardim Paulista, mostly French but also Brazilian. **Restaurante do MASP**, Av Paulista 1578, in the basement of the museum, reasonably priced, often has live music. **Fran's Café**, 24 hrs, Av Paulista 358; R Heitor Penteado 1326 (Sumaré); R Haddock Lobo 586; Alameda Lorena 1271 (Jardim Paulista); R Tamandaré 744 (Liberdade), and others. A recommended chain for a meal, day or night.

Vegetarian Almost always the cheapest option in São Paulo. **O Arroz de Ouro**, Largo do Arouche 88. Shop as well, central. **Cheiro Verde**, Peixoto Gomilde 1413, Cerqueira César. More expensive than most. **Intergrão**, R Joaquim Antunes 377, Jardins. Macrobiotic. **Delícia Natural**, Av Rio Branco 211 (4th floor), corner of Av Ipiranga. Lunch only. **Sabor Natural**, same building, 1st floor, lunch only. **Folhas e Raizes**, Líbero Bádaro 370, Centro. Good value buffet lunch. **Saúde Sabor**, São Bento 500, Centro. Lunch only. 'Vida Integral' monthly newspaper gives details of some health food restaurants and stores in São Paulo.

Comida por kilo restaurants can be found all over the city; there are many on R Augusta: popular at lunchtime. One recommended local chain is **Viena**. In most shopping centres there is a Praça da Alimentação, where food counters are gathered together. **Frevinho Lanches**, R Augusta 1563, famous for its beirute (speciality of São Paulo), as well as many other toasted sandwiches. **Baguette**, Consolação 2418, near Av Paulista, opposite Belas Artes cinema. For sandwiches, especially lively around midnight, also at R 13 de Maio 68. **Absolute**, Al Santos 843. Among the best hamburgers in town. **Rock Dreams**, Av Brigadeiro Faria Lima 743. For hamburgers and sandwiches. **Casa da Fogazza**, R Xavier de Toledo 328 and R 7 de Abril 60 (both close to Praça da República). Calzone, with different fillings, juices. Recommended.

Bars & clubs São Paulo bars and clubs cater for all Bixiga is known as the 'Bohemian' area and is usually cheaper than Jardins and Pinheiros areas   **Balafon**, R Sergipe 160. Wed-Sun, small, Afro-Brazilian. **Banana-Banana Café**, Av 9 de Júlio 5872 (Jardim Paulista). Closed Mon. **B.A.S.E**, Av Brig Luís Antônio 1137, Bela Vista. Techno and dance music. **Blen-Blen**, R Cardeal Arcoverde 2958 (Pinheiros). Live Latin bands at weekends. **Café do Bexiga**, 13 de Maio 76 and lots of others in Bixiga/Bela Vista area with live music, eg **Café Piu Piu** (closed Mon) and **Café Pedaço**, at 13 de Maio 134 and 140. **Cervejaria Continental**, R dos Pinheiros 1275 and R Haddock Lobo 1573. Packed, mixed music. **Cha-Cha-Cha**, R Tabapuã 1236. Closed Mon, no Brazilian music, art on walls, candles, gay and straight.

Columbia upstairs, R Estados Unidos 1570. Lively. *DaDo Bier*, Av Juscelino Kubitschek 1203, Itaim. Beer made on the premises, live music or disco. *Finnegan's Pub*, R Cristiano Viana 358, Pinheiros, on an Irish theme, specializes in hamburgers and whiskey (not necessarily together). *Hell's Club* downstairs, opens 0400. Techno, wild. *Limelight Industry*, R Franz Schubert 93. Pop hits, Japanese restaurant upstairs. 5 other nightclubs on this street. *Love Club & Lounge*, R Pequetita 189, Vila Olímpa. Trance, house, drum 'n' bass. *Pé pra Fora*, Av Pompéia 2517, Sumarezinho, closed Sun, open-air. Recommended. *Reggae Night*, Av Robert Kennedy 3880, Interlagos. Thu-Sun, outdoors on lakeside. *Plataforma 1*, Av Paulista 424. Dinner and folkloric show, very touristy but extremely popular.

Cinema In cinemas entrance is usually half price on Wed; normal seat price is US$5 in the centre, US$7-8 in R Augusta, Av Paulista and Jardins. Cine clubs: *Cine SESC*, R Augusta 2075, and cinemas at the Museu da Imagem e do Som, Centro Cultural Itaú and Centro Cultural São Paulo. **Theatre** The *Teatro Municipal* (see Sights) is used by visiting theatrical and operatic groups, as well as the City Ballet Company and the Municipal Symphony Orchestra who give regular performances. There are several first-class theatres: *Aliança Francesa*, R Gen Jardim 182, Vila Buarque, T3259 8211; *Paiol*, R Amaral Gurgel 164, Vila Buarque, T221 2462; among others. Free concerts at *Teatro Popular do Sesi*, Av Paulista 1313, T3284 9787, at midday, under MASP (Mon-Sat); see also Museums.

Entertainment
See the Guia da Folha section of Folha de São Paulo and Veja São Paulo of the weekly news magazine Veja for listings

Foundation of the City 25 Jan. *Carnival* in Feb (most attractions are closed).This includes the parades of the escolas de samba in the Anhembi sambódromo – the São Paulo special group parades on the Fri and Sat and the Rio group on the Sun and Mon to maximise TV coverage. In Jun there are the *Festas Juninas* and the *Festa de São Vito*, the patron saint of the Italian immigrants. *Festa da Primavera* in Sep. In Dec there are various Christmas and New Year festivities. Throughout the year, there are countless anniversaries, religious feasts, international fairs and exhibitions, look in the press or the monthly tourist magazines to see what is on while you are in town. See Sights for the São Paulo Biennial.

Festivals

Handicrafts Souvenirs from *Casa dos Amazonas*, Al Jurupis 460. *Galeria Arte Brasileira*, Al Lorena 2163, galeria@dialdata.com.br Good value. *Ceará Meu Amor*, R Pamplona 1551, loja 7. Good quality lace from the northeast. There is a *Sutaco* handicrafts shop at República Metrô station; this promotes items from the State of São Paulo, Tue-Fri 1000-1900, Sat 1000-1500; there is a showroom at R Augusta 435, 6th floor.

   Jewellery There are many other shops selling Brazilian stones, including branches of *H Stern* and *Amsterdam Sauer*.

   Typical of modern development are the huge Iguatemi, Ibirapuera and Morumbi **shopping centres**. They include luxurious cinemas, snack bars and most of the best shops in São Paulo. Other malls include Paulista and Butantã. On a humbler level are the big supermarkets of *El Dorado* (Av Pamplona 1704) and *Pão de Açúcar* (Praça Roosevelt, near the *Hilton*); the latter is open 24 hrs a day (except Sun).

   Open-air markets 'Oriental' fair, Praça de Liberdade Sun 1000-1900, good for Japanese snacks, plants and some handicrafts, very picturesque, with remedies on sale, tightrope walking, gypsy fortune tellers, etc. The Sun `**hippy' market** on Praça da República has reopened but with stricter licensing than in the old days. Below the Museu de Arte de São Paulo, an **antiques market** takes place on Sun, 1000-1700. **Arts and handicrafts** are also sold in Parque Tenente Siqueira Campos/Trianon on Sun from 0900-1700. There are **flea markets** on Sun in the main square of the Bixiga district (Praça Don Orione) and in Praça Benedito Calixto in Pinheiros. The **Ceasa flower market** should not be missed, Av Doutor Gastão Vidigal 1946, Jaguaré, Tue and Fri 0700-1200.

   Bookshops *FNAC*, Av Pedroso de Morais 858, Pinheiros. Excellent range of foreign books. *Livraria Cultura*, Av Paulista 2073, loja 153, also at Shopping Villa-Lobos, Avdas Nacões Unidas 4777, Jardim Universale. New books in English, including guidebooks. *Livraria Freebook*, R da Consolação 1924, ring bell for entry, wide collection of art books and imported books in English. *Livraria Triângulo*, R Barão de Itapetininga 255, loja 23, Centro, sells books in English. *Livraria Kosmos*, Av São Luís 258, loja 6, international stock. In various

Shopping

São Paulo is relatively cheap for film and clothes (especially shoes)

Brazil

shopping malls *Livrarias Saraiva*, and *Laselva* (also at airports) sell books in English; *Siciliano*, at Shoppings Eldorado and Iguatemi. *Sodiler*, Shopping Market Place, Av Nações Unidas 13947, Brooklin, loja 121A, floor T. *Librairie Française*, R Barão de Itapetininga 275, ground floor, wide selection, also at R Professor Atilio Innocenti 920, Jardins. *Letraviva*, Av Rebouças 1986, Mon-Fri 0900-1830, Sat 0900-1400, specializes in books and music in Spanish. *Duas Cidades*, R Bento Freitas 158, near República, good selection of Brazilian and Spanish American literature.

Maps *Quatro Rodas*, *Mapograf*, *Cartoplam*, and the map given out by the tourist kiosks; *RGN Public Ltda* produces a map which is given out free in various places and which is adapted to show its sponsors' locations. A variety of maps and timetables are sold in news stands. Map shops: *Mapolândia*, 7 de Abril 125, 1st floor. There are 2 private map publishers: *Geo Mapas*, R Gen Jardim 645, 3rd floor, Consolação (40% discount for volume purchases, excellent 1988 1:5,000,000 map of Brazil, town maps), and *Editorial Abril*, R do Cartume 585, Bl C, 3rd floor, Lapa, CEP 05065-001.

Sport & activities The most popular sport, for spectators and for players, is association **football**. The most important matches are played at Morumbi and Pacaembu stadia. **Horse racing** (Jockey Club) is mentioned above. For **hiking excursions**, etc, *Free Way*, R Leôncio de Carvalho 267, Paraíso.

Transport **Local Bus**: these are normally crowded and rather slow, but clean. Maps of the bus and metro system are available at depots, for example Anhangabaú. Some city bus routes are run by trolley buses.

Car hire: See Car hire, Essentials for international car rental agencies, page 52. *Interlocadora*, several branches, São Luís T255 5604, Guarulhos T6445 3838, Congonhas T240 9287. **Driving**: the *rodízio*, which curbs traffic pollution by restricting car use according to number plate, may be extended beyond the winter months. Check.

Metrô: 2 main lines intersecting at Praça de Sé: north-south from Tucuruvi to Jabaquara; east-west from Corinthians Itaquera to Barra Funda (the interchange with *Fepasa* and *RFFSA* railways and site of the São Paulo and Paraná rodoviária); an extension east to Guaianases is under construction. A 3rd line runs from Vila Madalena in the west, along Av Paulista, to Ana Rosa in the south, joining the Jabaquara line at Paraíso and Ana Rosa. A 4th line is being built from Vila Sônia to Luz. The system is clean, safe, cheap and efficient; the 2 main lines operate from 0500-2400, Ana Madalena to Ana Rosa 0600-2030. Fare US$0.75, US$6 for a book of 10 tickets; backpacks are allowed. Combined bus and Metrô ticket are available, US$1, for example to Congonhas airport. Information T286 0111.

Taxi: display cards of actual tariffs in the window (starting price US$3). There are ordinary taxis, which are hailed on the street, or at taxi stations such as Praça da República, radio taxis and deluxe taxis. For **Radio Taxis**, which are more expensive but involve fewer hassles, *Central Rádio Táxi Comum*, T5063 0404; *São Paulo Rádio Táxi*, T5583 2000; *Fácil*, T6258 5947; *Aero Táxi*, T6461 4090; or look in the phone book; calls are not accepted from public phones.

Guarulhos International Airport,T6445 2945. Congonhas local airport, T5090 9000 **Long distance Air**: from the international airport Guarulhos (also known as Cumbica) there are airport **taxis** which charge US$35-40 on a ticket system (the taxi offices are outside Customs, 300 m down on the left; go to get your ticket then take your bags right back to the end of the taxi queue). Fares from the city to the airport are US$35-40 and vary from cab to cab. *Emtu* bus service (T6445 2505/0800-190088) every 30 mins from Guarulhos to Praça da República 343 (northwest side, corner of R Arouche), US$6.50, 30-45 mins, very comfortable (in the airport buy ticket at the booth in Domestic Arrivals); the same company runs services from Guarulhos to the main bus terminal, Tietê (hourly), US$6. Buses run to Bresser bus station from Guarulhos and there are other buses to Jabaquara bus terminal, without luggage space, usually crowded. Also *Airport Bus Service*, T0800-999701, www.airportbusservice.com.br US$6 to centre. Inter-airport bus US$12. From Congonhas airport, there are about 400 flights a week to Rio (US$100 one way). **Airport information** Money exchanges, in the arrivals hall, Guarulhos, 0800-2200 daily. Post office on the 3rd floor of *Asa A*. The *Infraero Sala VIP* has been recommended for coffee, cable TV for US$5. Mon-Fri 0800 to 1800. See Ins and outs above for the tourist office.

Trains: São Paulo has 4 stations: 1) **Estação da Luz** for commuter trains between the northwest and southeast of São Paulo state. There is also a Metrô stop here. A train runs from Luz 8 times a day to connect with the **tourist train** from Paranapiaçaba to Rio Grande da Serra, US$0.50. 2) **Barra Funda**, services go to São José do Rio Preto (overnight), Barretos, Londrina, Maringá, Sorocaba and Ponta Grossa. There is a Metrô station and a rodoviária at Barra Funda; 3) **Júlio Prestes** station, for commuter services to the west; T0800 550121 for these three. 4) **Roosevelt**, T6942 1199, for commuter trains to the east.

Bus: the main rodoviária is **Tietê**, which handles buses to the interior of São Paulo state, all state capitals (but see also under Barra Funda and Bresser below) and international buses. The **left luggage** charges US$0.80 per day per item. You can sleep in the bus station after 2200 when the guards have gone; tepid showers cost US$2.

Buses from Tietê: To **Rio**, 6 hrs, every 30 mins, US$12.50 (*leito*, 25), special section for this route in the rodoviária, request the coastal route via Santos ('via litoral') unless you wish to go the direct route. To **Florianópolis**, 11 hrs (US$23.75, *leito* 36.75). To **Porto Alegre**, 18 hrs, US$30 (*leito*, 51). **Curitiba**, 6 hrs, US$10.25-12.50. **Salvador**, 30 hrs, US$51 (executive, 64). **Recife**, 40 hrs, US$60-70. **Cuiabá**, 24 hrs, US$42. **Porto Velho**, 60 hrs (or more), US$75. **Brasília**, 16 hrs, US$30 (*leito*, 60). **Foz do Iguaçu**, 16 hrs, US$22. **São Sebastião**, 4 hrs US$8.85 (say 'via Bertioga' if you want to go by the coast road, beautiful journey but few buses take this route).

International buses from Tietê: to **Montevideo**, via Porto Alegre, with *TTL*, departs Mon, Thu, Sat 2200, 31 hrs, US$96, cold a/c at night, plenty of meal stops, bus stops for border formalities, passengers disembark only to collect passport and tourist card on the Uruguayan side (also *EGA*, same price, US$67 to **Chuy**, Tue, Fri, Sun). To **Buenos Aires**, *Pluma*, 36 hrs, US$74. To **Santiago**, *Pluma* or *Chilebus*, 56 hrs, US$130, *Chilebus*, poor meals, but otherwise good, beware overbooking. To **Asunción** (1,044 km), 18 hrs with *Pluma* (US$27-29, *leito* 61), *Brújula* or *RYSA* , all stop at Ciudad del Este. *Cometa del Amambay* runs to **Pedro Juan Caballero** and **Concepción**.

There are 3 other bus stations: **Barra Funda**, T3666 4682, with Metrô station, for buses from cities in southern São Paulo state, **Campo Grande**, 14 hrs, US$33, and many places in Paraná. **Bresser**, T6692 5191, on the Metrô, is for destinations in Minas Gerais. Buses from Santos arrive at **Jabaquara**, T5012 2256, at the southern end of the Metrô. To **Santos**, US$3.50, and destinations on the southern coast of São Paulo state, use Jabaquara station. Buses from here for Santos leave every 15 mins, taking about 50 mins, last bus at 0100, US$3.60. Buses at Bresser, *Cometa* (6967 7255) or *Transul* (T6693 8061) go to Minas Gerais: **Belo Horizonte**, 10 hrs, US$15.60, 11 a day (*leito* 31.20); 9 a day with *Gontijo*. *Translavras* and *Útil* also operate out of this station. Prices are given under destinations.

Airline offices *Aerolíneas Argentinas*, Araújo 216, 6th floor, T214 6022 (Guarulhos airport 6445 308). *Alitalia*, Av São Luís 50, cj 291, T3257 1922 (6445 3724). *American Airlines*, Araújo 216, 9th floor, T0800 703 4000 or 3214 4000 (6445 3808). *British Airways*, Av São Luís 50, 32nd floor, T3145 9700 (6445 2021). *Iberia*, Araújo 216, 3rd floor, T258 5333 (6445 2060). *JAL*, Av Paulista 542, 2nd floor, T251 5222 (6445 2040). *Lufthansa*, R Gomes de Carvalho 1356, 2nd floor, T3048 5800 (6445 2499). *Rio-Sul*, R Bráulio Gomes 151, T5561 2161. *TAM*, R da Consolação 247, 3rd floor, T0800 123100 (24 hrs), or 3155 6700 (6445 3474). *TAP*, Av São Luís 187, T255 5366 (6445 2150). *United*, Av Paulista 777, 9-10th floor, T3145 4200/0800-162323 (6445 3283). *Varig*, R da Consolação 362/372, Av Paulista 1765, T3231 9400 (Guarulhos 6445 3117, Congonhas 535 0216). *Vasp*, Praça L Gomes/Aurora 974, Av São Luís 72, T0800-998277.

Directory

Banks There are many national and international banks; most can be found either in the Triângulo, downtown, or on Av Paulista, or Av Brigadeiro Faria Lima. *Banco do Brasil* will change cash and TCs and will advance cash against Visa. All transactions are done in the foreign exchange department of any main branch (eg Av São João 32, Centro), but queues are long. *Citibank*, Av Ipiranga 855, or Av Paulista 1111 (1100-1500), cash on MasterCard. *Banespa*, for example at R Duque de Caxias 200, Centro, or Praça da República 295, accepts Visa, TCs and cash. *MasterCard*, cash against card, R Campo Verde 61, 4th floor, Jardim Paulistano. *MasterCard* ATMs at branches of *HSBC Bank*. *American Express*, Al Santos 1437 (*Hotel Mofarrej Sheraton*) T251 3383, Av Maria Coelho Aguiar 215, Bloco F, 8th floor, T3741 8478 and Guarulhos international airport, terminal 1, 1st floor of Asa A, T6412 3515. *Western Union* at Banco Itamarati, T0800-119837. **Money changers:** there are many *câmbios* on or

1000-1600; but some vary. All have different times for foreign exchange transactions (check at individual branches)

near Praça da República. There are none near the rodoviária or Tietê hotels. *Interpax*, Praça da República 177, loja 13, changes cash (many currencies) and TCs, 0930-1800, Sat 0930-1300. *Amoretur*, Praça da República 203, will change TCs. *Coraltur*, Praça da República 95. Most travel agents on Av São Luís change TCs and cash at good rates, but very few are open on Sat. *Avencatur*, Av Nações Unidas 1394, Morumbi, changes TCs, Deutschmarks, good rates.

Communications Internet: at Av Paulista 1499, conj 1001 (Mêtro Trianon), 1100-2200, English spoken, secondhand books; *Saraiva Megastore*, Shopping El Dorado, US$3; *Kiosknet*, Shopping Light, 4th floor, R Cel Xavier de Toledo 23, opposite Teatro Municipal, T3151 3645, US$2.50 per hr; *Monkey Paulista*, Al Santos 1217 (Jardins, off Av Paulista behind Citibank). Superfast connection, US$0.70-1.15 per hr, more expensive at weekends. *O Porão*, R Tamandaré 1066, near Vergueiro metro station. **Post Office:** Correio Central, Praça do Correio, corner Av São João and Prestes Máia. Booth adjoining tourist office on Praça da República, weekdays only 1000-1200, 1300-1600, for letters and small packages only. *UPS*, Brasinco, Alameda Jaú 1, 1725, 01420 São Paulo. *Federal Express*, Av São Luís 187, Galeria Metropole, loja 45, is reliable, also at Av das Nações Unidas 17891; *DHL*, Av Vereador José Diniz 2421. **Telephone:** *Telefônica*, R 7 de Abril 295, near Praça da República; many other offices. *Embratel*, Av São Luís 50, and Av Ipiranga 344. For the international operator dial 000111; for international collect calls dial 000107. Red phone boxes are for national calls, blue ones for international phone calls.

Cultural centres Centro Brasileiro Britânico, R Ferriera de Araújo 741, Pinheiros, T3039 0567. **American Library**, União Cultural Brasil-Estados Unidos, R Col Oscar Porto 208. **Goethe-Instituto**, R Lisboa 974 (Mon-Thu 1400-2030). **Centro Cultural Fiesp**, Av Paulista 1313, 0900-1900 Tue-Sun, has foreign newspapers and magazines. See under Entertainment for Alliance Française Theatre.

Consulates Argentina, Av Paulista 1106, T284 1355 (0900-1300, very easy to get a visa here). **Australia**, R Tenente Negrão 140, T3849 6281. **Bolivia**, R Oscar Freire 379, T3081 1618, www.embolivia.cjb.net 0900-1700. **Canada**, Av Nações Unidas 12901, T5509 4343, spalo-immigration@dfait-maeci.gc.ca 0800-1100, 1500-1600, Fri 0800-0930, 1200-1300. **Denmark**, R Oscar Freire 379, T3061 3625, 0900-1700, Fri until 1400 only. **France**, Av Paulista 1842, 14th floor, T287 9522, www.ambafrance.org.br 0830-1200. **Germany**, Av Brigadeiro Faria Lima 2092, T3814 6644, info@consuladoalemao-sp.com.br 0800-1130. **Italy**, Av Higienópolis 436, T3826 9022, notarile@italconsul.org.br **Israel**, Av Brig Faria Lima 1713, T3815 7788. **Japan**, Av Paulista 854, T287 0100, cgjsp@nethall.com.br **Netherlands**, Av Brigadeiro Faria Lima 1779, T3813 0522, 0900-1200. **New Zealand**, Av Campinas 579, T3148 0613, www.tradenz.govt.nz **Norway and Sweden**, R Oscar Freire 379, 3rd floor, T883 3322 (Norway), 3061 1700 (Sweden) (Caixa Postal 51626), 0900-1300. **Paraguay**, R Bandeira Paulista 600, 15th floor, T3849 0455, 0830-1600. **Peru**, R Votuverava 350, T3819 1793, viceconsulperu@originet.com.br 0900-1300. **UK**, R Ferreira Araújo 741, 2nd floor, Pinheiros, T3094 2700, correio@gra-bretanha.org.br **US**, R Padre João Manuel 933, Cerqueira César, T3081 6511, www.embaixada-americana.org.br 0800-1700.

Language courses *Universidade de São Paulo (USP)* in the Cidade Universitária has courses available to foreigners, including a popular Portuguese course, registry is through the **Comissão de Cooperação Internacional**, R do Anfiteatro 181, Bloco das Colméias 05508, Cidade Universitária.

Medical services Hospital Samaritano, R Conselheiro Brotero 1486, Higienópolis, T824 0022. Recommended. **Emergency and ambulance** T192, no charge. **Fire:** T193.

Useful addresses Police: Deatur, special tourist police, Av São Luís 91, T214 0209, R 15 de Novembro 347, T3107 8332. **Cepol**, civil police, T147. **Radio Patrol**, T190. **Federal Police**, Av Prestes Máia 700, 1000-1600 for visa extensions.

Santos

Phone code: 0xx13
Post code: 11000
Colour map 7, grid C4
Population: 417,983
72 km SE of São Paulo

Santos is a holiday resort with magnificent beaches and views. It is about 5 km from the open sea and the most important Brazilian port, best known for its commerce. Over 40% by value of all Brazilian imports and about half the total exports pass through it. The scenery on the routes crossing the Serra do Mar is superb. The roadway includes many bridges and tunnels. From Rio the direct highway, the Linha Verde (see pages 391 and 410) is also wonderful for scenery. The port is approached by the winding Santos Channel; at its mouth is an old fort (1709). The island upon which the city stands can be circumnavigated by small boats. The centre of the city is on the north side of the island. Due south, on the Baía de Santos, is **Gonzaga**, where hotels and bars line the beachfront. Between these two areas, the eastern end of the island curves round within the Santos Channel. At the eastern tip, a ferry crosses the estuary to give access to the beaches of the sophisticated resort of Guarujá.

The streets around **Praça Mauá** are very busy in the daytime, with plenty of cheap shops. In the centre is the **Bolsa Oficial de Café**, the coffee exchange, at R 15 de Novembro 95. Two churches in the centre are **Santo Antônio do Valongo** (17th century, but restored), which is by the railway station on Largo Monte Alegre, and the **Capela da Ordem Terceira de Nossa Senhora do Carmo** (1760, also later restored), Praça Barão do Rio Branco. **Monte Serrat**, just south of the city centre, has at its summit a semaphore station and look-out post which reports the arrival of all ships in Santos harbour. There is also a church, dedicated to Nossa Senhora da Monte Serrat. ■ *The top can be reached on foot or by funicular, which leaves every 30 mins, US$6.* **Museu do Mar**, R República do Equador 81, is in the eastern part of the city; with a collection that includes several thousand shells. In the western district of José Menino is the **Orquidário Municipal**, municipal orchid gardens, in the **Praça Washington** (flowering October-February, orchid show in November). ■ *Daily 0800-1745, the bird enclosure 0800-1100, 1400-1700, US$1 (children and senior citizens, free).*

The **Ilha Porchat**, a small island reached by a bridge at the far end of Santos/São Vicente bay, has beautiful views over rocky precipices, of the high seas on one side and of the city and bay on the other. At the summit is *Terraço Chopp*, a restaurant which has live music most evenings. On summer evenings the queues to get in can last up to 4 hours, but in winter, even if it may be a little chilly at night, the queues are non-existent (Al Ary Barroso 274, Ilha Porchat, São Vicente).

Itatinga, 30 km from Santos in the Serra do Mar, has remnants of Atlantic forest, mangrove and sandbanks. The area is full of wildlife. There are trails graded according to difficulty. ■ *Access is with one of the travel agencies officially permitted to lead groups: contact* Sictur *(the tourism department – see below). Access is either via the village of Itatinga by boat, 3 hours, then by street car. Or take the BR-101 (Santos-Rio) road, a 3-min crossing by boat and then 7.5 km by street car.*

Many beach front hotels on Av Pres Wilson, eg: **B** *Atlântico*, No 1, T3289 4500, www.atlantico-hotel.com.br Good, a/c, sauna, restaurant, bar. **C-D** *Hotel Natal*, Av Marechal Floriano Peixoto 104, T3284 2732, www.hotelnatal.com.br Comfortable, safe. with cable TV, fridge, full breakfast. There are many cheap hotels near the Orquidário Municipal (Praça Washington), 1-2 blocks from the beach. Restaurants (**cheap**: *Dona Mineira*, R Djalma Dutra 1, Gonzaga. Self service, excellent food, pleasant. *Point 44*, R Jorge Tibiriçá 44. Large, popular self-service. *Praia Gonzaga*, Av Mal F Peixoto 104a, Gonzaga. Self-service with *churrasco*, lunch only.

26 Jan, *Foundation of Santos; Good Friday; Corpus Christi; Festejos Juninos*. Throughout the summer there are many cultural, educational and sporting events. **8 Sep**, *Nossa Senhora de Monte Serrat*.

Local Bus: in Santos US$0.60; to São Vicente, US$0.90. **Taxi**: all taxis have meters. The fare from Gonzaga to the bus station is about US$5.

Long distance Bus: to São Paulo (50 mins, US$3.50) every 15 mins, from the rodoviária near the city centre, José Menino or Ponta da Praia (opposite the ferry to Guarujá). (The 2 highways between São Paulo and Santos are sometimes seriously crowded, especially at rush hours and weekends.) To Guarulhos/Cumbica airport, *Expresso* Brasileiro 3-4 daily, US$5, allow plenty of time as the bus goes through Guarulhos, 3 hrs. *TransLitoral* from Santos to Congonhas airport then to Guarulhos/Cumbica, 4 daily, US$7.25, 2 hrs. To **Rio** (*Normandy* company), several daily, 7½ hrs, US$22.50; to Rio along the coast road is via São Sebastião (US$7, change buses if necessary), Caraguatatuba and Ubatuba.

Banks *Banco do Brasil*, R 15 de Novembro 195, Centro, and Av Ana Costa, Gonzaga, Visa ATM. Generally ATMs are unreliable. Many **Money changers**. **Communications** Internet: *Viva Shop*, in Shopping Parque Balneario, Av Ana Costa, US$3 per hr. Main **post office** at R Cidale de Toledo 41, Centro, also at R Tolentino Filgueiras 70, Gonzaga. **Telephone: International calls:** can be made at R Galeão Carvalho 45, Gonzaga. **Embassies and consulates** Britain, R Tuiuti 58, 2nd floor, Caixa Postal 204, T3219 6622, daw@wilson.com.br Denmark, R Frei Gaspar 22, 10th floor, 106, CP 726, T3219 6455,

1000-1100, 1500-1700. **Tourist office** at the rodoviária, Praia do Gonzaga on the seafront (in a disused tram, very helpful) and Orquidário Municipal (limited opening). **Voltage** 220 AC, 60 cycles.

Beaches east of Santos

Population: 226,500

A vehicle ferry (free for pedestrians) crosses from Ponta da Praia to **Guarujá**, which becomes very crowded in summer. There are good seafood restaurants on the road (SP-061) between Guarujá and **Bertioga**, the next major beach centre up the coast (1 hr by bus). It, too, can be overcrowded in summer. A ferry crosses the mouth of the Canal de Bertioga. The town is on the north bank of the canal and beyond is a long sweeping bay with seven beaches divided by a promontory, the Ponta da Selada. The hills behind Bertioga are covered in forest which is now being used for walking in the Mata Atlântica by local agencies. **Sleeping** A *Marazul*, Av Tomé de Souza 825, Enseada, T3317 1109, good seafood restaurant; many others. **Tourist office**: *Diretoria de Turismo*, R Luiz Pereira de Campos s/n, T257 1157.

The coastal road beyond Bertioga is paved, and the Rio-Santos highway, 1 or 2 km inland, provides a good link to São Sebastião. Beyond Praia Boracéia are a number of beaches, including **Camburi**, surrounded by the Mata Atlântica, into which you can walk on the Estrada do Piavu (bathing in the streams is permitted, but use of shampoo is forbidden). There are a number of good hotels and restaurants in Camburi and at Praia de Boracéia, **B-C** *Chalés do Brasa*, Rua E No 99, T4330 3149/9331 4702, family chalets, garden setting, close to beach. ■ *Daily buses from São Paulo to Camburi, 160 km, en route to São Sebastiâo/Ilhabela, US$3.60.* The road carries on from Camburi, past clean beach **Maresias**, a fashionable place for surfers.

São Sebastião

Phone code: 0xx12
Post code: 11600
Colour map 7, grid B4
Population: 58,038

From Maresias it is 21 km to São Sebastião. In all there are 21 good beaches and an adequate, but not overdeveloped tourist infrastructure. The natural attractions of the area include many small islands offshore and a large portion of the **Parque Estadual da Serra do Mar** on the mainland, with other areas under protection for their different ecosystems. Trails can be walked through the forests. There are also old sugar plantations. In the colonial centre is a **Museu de Arte Sacra**, in the 17th century chapel of São Gonçalo (R Sebastião Neves 90). The town's parish church on Praça Major João Fernandes was built in the early 17th century and rebuilt in 1819. There is a **Museu do Naufrágio** near the church (entrance free) exhibiting shipwrecks and natural history of the local area. **Tourist office**: Av Dr Altino Arantes 174, T452 1808.

The beaches within 2-3 km of São Sebastião harbour are polluted; others to the south and north are clean and inviting. Ilhabela tends to be expensive in season, when it is cheaper to stay in São Sebastião.

Sleeping B *Hotel Roma*, on the main Praça, T452 1016. Excellent. Warmly recommended. C *Bariloche*, R Três Bandeirantes 133. Basic but clean. 6 km south of São Sebastião is *Camping do Barraqueçaba Bar de Mar de Lucas*, hot showers, English spoken, cabins available. .

Transport Bus: 2 buses a day from **Rio** with *Normandy*, 0830 and 2300 (plus 1630 on Fri and Sun), to Rio 0600 and 2330, heavily booked in advance, US$12.60 (US$5 from Paraty); 4 a day from **Santos**, 4 hrs, US$7; 4 *Litorânea* buses a day also from **São Paulo**, US$8.85, which run inland via São José dos Campos, unless you ask for the service via Bertioga, only 2 a day (bus to Bertioga US$3.50). Free **ferry** across the narrow strait to Ilhabela for foot passengers, see below.

Ilha de São Sebastião

The island abounds in tropical plants and flowers, and many fruits grow wild, whose juice mixed with cachaça (firewater) and sugar makes as delicious a cocktail

The island of São Sebastião, known popularly as Ilhabela, is of volcanic origin, roughly 390 sq km in area. The four highest peaks are Morro de São Sebastião, 1,379 m, Morro do Papagaio, 1,309 m, Ramalho, 1,28 m, and Pico Baepi, 1,025 m. All are often obscured by mist. Rainfall on the island is heavy, about 3,000 mm a year. The slopes are densely wooded and 80% of the forest is protected by the Parque Estadual de Ilhabela. The only settled district lies on the coastal strip facing the mainland, the Atlantic side being practically uninhabited except by a few fisherfolk. The terraced **Cachoeira da Toca** waterfalls amid dense jungle close to the foot of the Baepi peak give cool freshwater bathing; lots of butterflies (US$4, includes insect repellent).

Brazil

You can walk on a signed path, or go by car; it's a few kilometres from the ferry dock. The locals claim there are over 300 waterfalls on the island, but only a few of them can be reached on foot. In all shady places, especially away from the sea, there thrives a species of midge known locally as *borrachudo*. A locally sold repellent (*Autan*) keeps them off for some time, but those allergic to insect bites should remain on the inhabited coastal strip. There is a small hospital (helpful) by the church in town.

No alterations are allowed to the frontage of the main township, **Ilhabela.** It is very popular during summer weekends, when it is difficult to find space for a car on the ferry. It is, however, a nice place to relax on the beach, with good food and some good value accommodation. The **tourist office** *Secretaria Municipal de Turismo* is at R Bartolomeu de Gusmão 140, Pequeá, T472 7102/8523.

Phone code: 0xx12 Population: 20,836; the island's population rises to 100,000 in high season

Visit the old **Feiticeira** plantation, with underground dungeons. The road is along the coast, sometimes high above the sea, towards the south of the island (11 km from the town). You can go by bus, taxi, or horse and buggy. A trail leads down from the *fazenda* to the beautiful beach of the same name. Another old *fazenda* is **Engenho d'Água**, which is nearer to the town, which gives its name to one of the busiest beaches (the *fazenda* is not open to the public).

Beaches and watersports On the mainland side the beaches 3-4 km either side of the town are polluted: look out for oil, sandflies and jellyfish on the sand and in the water. There are some three dozen beaches around Ilhabela, only about 12 of them away from the coast facing the mainland. **Praia dos Castelhanos**, reached by the rough road over the island to the Atlantic side (no buses), is recommended. Several of the ocean beaches can only be reached by boat. The island is considered the **Capital da Vela** (of sailing) because its 150 km of coastline offers all types of conditions. There is also plenty of adventure for divers.

Sleeping and eating A *Ilhabela*, Av Pedro Paulo de Morais 151, T/F472 1083, hoibela@mandic.com.br Good breakfast. Recommended. Next door is **AL** *Itapemar*, No 341, T472 1329, F472 2409. Windsurfing equipment rented. **B** *Pousada dos Hibiscos*, same avenue No 714, T472 1375. Good atmosphere, swimming pool. Recommended. Others in this price range and some other less expensive hotels in the **A-B** range, mostly on the road to the left of the ferry. **D** *Estância das Bromélias Pousada*, Av Col José Vicente Faria Lima 1243, Perequê, T3896 3353, www.estanciadasbromelias.com.br Welcoming, chalets for 5, great breakfast, garden, pool, horse riding and jeep excursions, very good. **Camping** in addition to Pedras do Sino, there are campsites at Perequê, near the ferry dock, and at Praia Grande, a further 11 km south. A reasonable eating place is *Perequê*, Av Princesa Isabel 337. *Farol*, Av Princesa Isabel 1634, Perequê. Good, especially seafood. Recommended.

Transport Bus A bus runs along the coast facing the mainland. *Litorânea* from São Paulo connects with a service right through to Ilhabela; office in Ilhabela at R Dr Carvalho 136. **Ferry** At weekends and holidays the 15-20 min ferry between São Sebastião and Perequê runs non-stop day and night. During the week it does not sail between 0130 and 0430 in the morning. Passengers pay nothing; the fare for cars is US$7 weekdays, US$10 at weekends.

On the Santos-Rio road is São Francisco da Praia, opposite the northern end of Ilhabela, beyond which begin the beaches of **Caraguatatuba** (*Phone code*: 0xx12). In all there are 17 good beaches to the northeast and southwest, most divided between two sweeping bays. As well as watersports, Caraguatatuba is known for hang-gliding. It is a popular place at weekends and in the summer, with good hotels, restaurants, bars and campsites. For tourist information visit *Setur*, Praça Diógenes Ribeiro de Lima 140, T420 8142. There are several youth hostels: *Recanto das Andorinhas*, R Engenheiro João Fonseca 112, Centro, 11660-000, T422 6181, one street from the central bus terminal, 50 m from the beach. ■ *Direct buses to Caraguatatuba from Rio (US$12, same schedule as for São Sebastião), São Paulo and Santos; direct buses from São Paulo go via São José dos Campos.*

North of São Sebastião

Brazil

Ubatuba

Phone code: 0xx12
Post code: 11680
Colour map 7, grid B4
Population: 66,861

This is one of the most beautiful stretches of the São Paulo coast with a whole range of watersports on offer. In all, there are 72 beaches, some large, some small, some in coves, some on islands. They are spread out over a wide area, so if you are staying in Ubatuba town, you need to use the buses which go to most of them. The commercial centre of Ubatuba is at the northern end of the bay. Here are shops, banks, services, lots of restaurants (most serving pizza and fish), but few hotels. These are on the beaches north and south and can be reached from the Costamar bus terminal.

Saco da Ribeira, 13 km south, is a natural harbour which has been made into a yacht marina. Schooners leave from here for excursions to **Ilha Anchieta** (or dos Porcos), a popular 4-hr trip. On the island are beaches, trails and a prison, which was in commission from 1908-52. Agencies run schooner trips to Ilha Anchieta and elsewhere. Trips leave Saco da Ribeira at 1000, returning 1500, 4-hr journey, US$20 per person. A 6-hr trip can be made from Praia Itaguá, but in winter there is a cold wind off the sea in the afternoon, same price. The *Costamar* bus from Ubatuba to Saco da Ribeira (every 20 mins, 30 mins, US$0.85) drops you at the turn-off by the *Restaurante Pizzaria Malibu*.

Sleeping

At all holiday times it is expensive, with no hotel less than US$30

Beach hotels On many of the beaches there are hotels and *pousadas*, ranging from luxury resorts to more humble establishments. **AL** *Saveiros*, R Laranjeira 227, Praia do Lázaro, 14 km from town, T442 0172, F442 1327. Pool, restaurant, English spoken.

In town The main hotels in the centre are **A** *São Charbel*, Praça Nóbrega 280, T432 1090, F432 1080. Very helpful and comfortable, a/c, TV, restaurant, bar, swimming pool, etc. **A** *São Nicolau*, R Conceição 213, T432 5007, F432 3310. Good, TV, fridge, good breakfast. **A** *Xaréu*, R Jordão Homem da Costa 413, T/F432 3060. Pleasant, quiet. Recommended. These three are all convenient for the town beach, restaurants and services, and their prices fall to **B** in the low season. **D** *Pousada Taiwan*, R Felix Guisard Filho 60, T432 6448. Fan or a/c, with breakfast, TV, refrigerator.

Youth hostels *Cora Coralina*, Rodovia Oswaldo Cruz, Km 89, CEP 11680-000, T011-258 0388. 0800-2300, near the Horto Florestal. *J S Brandão*, R Nestor Fonseca 173, Jardim Sumaré, CEP 11880-000, T432 2337. 0700-2300, near the Tropic of Capricorn sign south of town. **Camping** 2 *Camping Clube do Brasil* sites at Lagoinha (25 km from town), T443 1536, and Praia Perequê-Açu, 2 km north, T432 1682. There are about 8 other sites in the vicinity.

Tour operators

Companies offer trekking tours graded according to difficulty lasting from 2 hrs to 2 days. More details from the guide association, T9141 3692, www.ubatuba.com.br/ecoturismo

Transport

Bus There are 3 bus terminals: 1) Rodoviária Costamar, at R Hans Staden e R Conceição, which serves all local destinations; 2) Rodoviária at R Profesor Thomaz Galhardo 513 for São José buses to Paraty, US$2.25, some *Normandy* services (to Rio, US$9) and some *Itapemirim* buses; 3) Rodoviária Litorânea, the main bus station: go up Conceição for 8 blocks from Praça 13 de Maio, turn right on R Rio Grande do Sul, then left into R Dra Maria V Jean. Buses from here go to **São Paulo**, 3½ hrs, frequent, US$8, **Caraguatatuba**, US$2.

Taxis in town are a rip-off, for example US$6 from the centre to the main bus terminal.

Directory

Communications Internet: *Chat and Bar*, upper floor of *Ubatuba Shopping*, US$3 per hr. **Post Office**: is on R Dona Maria Alves between Hans Staden and R Col Dominicano. **Telephone**: *Telesp*, is on Galhardo, close to *Sérgio* restaurant. **Tourist office** Comtur, on Av Iperoig opposite R Profesor Thomaz Galhardo, T432 4255, very helpful.

Straddling the border of São Paulo and Rio de Janeiro states is the **Parque Nacional Serra da Bocaina**, which rises from the coast to its highest point at Pico do Tira (or Chapéu) at 2,200 m, encompassing three strata of vegetation. ■ *Permission to visit must be obtained in advance from Ibama, T0xx12-3117 2183/88 in São José do Barreiro, the nearest town.*

It is 8 km from São Vicente to **Praia Grande**, the beach most used by Paulistanos. Next comes Mongaguá then, 61 km from Santos, **Itanhaém** (*Phone code*: 0xx13), with its pretty colonial church of Sant'Ana (1761), Praça Narciso de Andrade, and the Convento da Nossa Senhora da Conceição (1699-1713, originally founded 1554), on a small hill. There are several good seafood restaurants along the beach, hotels and camping. There are more beaches 31 km south of Itanhaém at **Peruíbe**, where the climate is said to be unusually healthy owing to a high concentration of ozone in the air. Local rivers have water and black mud which has been proven to contain medicinal properties. There are plenty of places to stay in Peruíbe (none close to the bus station), including **C** Vila Real, Av Anchieta 6625, T458 2797 breakfast, shower. Also, there are places to eat. Peruíbe marks the northernmost point of the **Estação Ecológico Juréia-Itatins**, 820 sq km of protected Mata Atlântica, "as it was when the Portuguese arrived in Brazil". The station was founded in 1986. The four main ecosystems are *restinga*, mangrove, Mata Atlântica and the vegetation at 900 m on the Juréia mountain range. ■ *Contact the Instituto Florestal, R do Horto 931, CEP 02377-000, São Paulo, T0xx11-6997 5000, for permission to visit the ecological station.*

At the southern end of Juréia-Itatins is the town of Iguape founded in 1538. Typical of Portuguese architecture, the small **Museu Histórico e Arqueológico** is housed in the 17th-century Casa da Oficina Real de Fundição, R das Neves 45. ■ *Tue-Sun 0900-1730.* There is also a **Museu de Arte Sacra** in the former Igreja do Rosário, Praça Rotary. ■ *Sat-Sun 0900-1200, 1330-1700.* The **tourist office** is at 9 de Julho 63, T6841 3358.

Opposite Iguape is the northern end of the **Ilha Comprida** with 86 km of beaches (some dirty and disappointing). This Área de Proteção Ambiental is not much higher than sea level and is divided from the mainland by the Canal do Mar Pequeno. The northern end is the busiest and on the island there are good restaurants, hotels, supermarkets – fresh fish is excellent. There is also accommodation. The Ibama office of the *Area de Proteção Ambiental Cananéia-Iguape-Peruíbe* is at R da Saúde s/n, Canto do Morro, Iguape, T6841 2692/2388.

Sleeping B-C *Silvi*, R Ana Cândida Sandoval Trigo 515, T6841 1421, silvihotel@virtualway.com.br With bath and breakfast, good. There is a **campsite** at Praia da Barra da Ribeira, 20 km north, and wild camping is possible at Praia de Juréia, the gateway to the ecological station.

Transport Bus To **Iguape**: from São Paulo, Santos, or Curitiba, changing at Registro. **Sea** A continuous ferry service runs from Iguape to Ilha Comprida (free but small charge for cars); buses run until 1900 from the ferry stop to the beaches. From Iguape it is possible to take a boat trip down the coast to Cananéia and Ariri (see below). Tickets and information from **Dpto Hidroviário do Estado**, R Major Moutinho 198, Iguape, T841 1122. It is a beautiful trip, passing between the island and the mainland.

At the southern end of Ilha Comprida, across the channel, is Cananéia. The colonial centre, around Praça Martim Afonso de Souza and neighbouring streets, contains the 17th-century church of **São João Batista** and the **Museu Municipal**. To the south are a number of good beaches and the waterways are popular with fisherfolk. For guides, contact *Manoel Barroso*, Avenue Independencia 65, T013-851 1273, Portuguese only. Recommended. Cananéia has several hotels, starting in price range **B**.

To reach the densely wooded Ilha do Cardoso, which is a Reserva Florestal e Biológica, take a ferry from the dock at Cananéia, 4 hours, three services daily (*R Princesa Isabel*, T841 1122). Alternatively, drive 70 km along an unpaved road, impassable when wet, to **Ariri**, from where the island is 10 mins by boat. The tiny village of Marujá, which has no electricity, has some very rustic *pousadas* and restaurants. Camping is allowed at designated places.

Southwest from Santos

Iguape
Phone code: 0xx13
Colour map 7, grid C3
Population: 27,427

Brazil

Cananéia & Ilha do Cardoso
Colour map 7, grid C3
Population: 12,298
270 km from São Paulo

There are lots of idyllic beaches; best for surfing is Moretinho

Campinas

Phone code: 0xx19
Post code: 13000
Colour map 7, grid B3
Population: 969,396
88 km from São Paulo

Bus to São Paulo, US$3

An industrial centre linked with São Paulo by the fine Via Anhangüera highway, Campinas is important as a clearing point for coffee. Visits can be made to the **Instituto Agronômico** to see all the aspects of coffee; Av Barão de Itapura 1481, Guanabara. ■ *Mon-Fri 0800-1100, 1300-1700, T3231 5330.* The Viracopos international airport is 11 km from Campinas, which also has its own airport. See the fine **Catedral Metropolitana Nossa Senhora da Conceição**, built in 1883 in neoclassical style with baroque elements (Praça José Bonifácio), and the **Mercado Municipal** (old market, 1908) on Av Benjamin Constant. There are several museums: **Carlos Gomes**, R Bernardino de Campos 989, T3231 2567, of arts and sciences. In the Bosque de Jequitibás are the **Museus de História Naturaldo e Folclore**. The arts centre in the **Centro de Convivência Cultural**, Praça Tom Jobim, T3252 5857, has a noted symphony orchestra. **Tourist information**, T3256 0399, Monday-Friday 0800-1800.

Tourist trains 25 km from Campinas, at **Jaguariúna**, is a railway preservation group with steam engines and wagons. ■ *Every weekend and public holiday two trains (three on Sun) run between Jaguariúna and Campinas on a 2-hr trip. You can either take an hourly bus from Campinas to Jaguariúna, or take the steam train itself from Campinas (station behind Carrefour, Anhumas, reached by town bus). For schedules and information, T3253 6067.*

The Via Anhangüera continues northwest from Campinas to **Ribeirão Preto**, 319 km from São Paulo (4-5 hours by bus, US$20). The **Museu do Café**, in the former Fazenda Monte Alegre on the campus of the Universidade de São Paulo, tells the history of coffee in the area. ■ *On the road to Sertãozinho, T633 1986.* Some 115 km northwest of Ribeirão Preto, **Barretos** is where, in the third week in August, the **Festa do Peão Boiadeiro** is held. This is the biggest annual rodeo in the world. The town is taken over as up to a million fans come to watch the horsemanship, enjoy the concerts, eat, drink and shop in what has become the epitome of Brazilian cowboy culture. Tours from the UK are run by *Last Frontiers*, see page 44.

Minas Gerais

Minas Gerais was once described as having a heart of gold and a breast of iron. Half the mineral production of Brazil comes from the state, including most of the iron ore. Diamonds and gold are still found. Minas Gerais also produces 95% of all Brazil's gemstones. All this mineral wealth has left the state a legacy of sumptuous colonial cities built on gold and diamond mining, but there are other attractions: rugged national parks, which are great for trekking, lots of festivals and a famous cuisine, the comida mineira. The State of Minas Gerais is somewhat larger than France, is mountainous in the south, rising to the 2,787 m peak of Agulhas Negras in the Mantiqueira range, and in the east, where there is the Parque Nacional ParCaparaó containing the Pico da Bandeira (2,890 m). The capital, Belo Horizonte is culturally very active. From Belo Horizonte north are undulating grazing lands, the richest of which are in the extreme west: a broad wedge of country between Goiás in the north and São Paulo in the south, known as the Triângulo Mineiro.

Belo Horizonte

Phone code: 0xx31
Post code: 30000
Colour map 7, grid B5
Population: 4.8 million
Altitude: 800 m

Belo Horzonte is surrounded by mountains and enjoys an excellent climate (16°-30°C) except for the rainy season (December-March). It was founded on 12 December 1897 and is one of Brazil's fastest growing cities, now suffering from atmospheric pollution. The city celebrates *Maundy Thursday*; *Corpus Christi*; 15 August, *Assunção* (Assumption); 8 December, *Conceição* (Immaculate Conception). The third largest city in Brazil is a hilly city with streets that rise and fall and trees lining many of the central avenues. The large **Parque Municipal** is an oasis of green in the heart of downtown; closed at night and on Monday, except for a small section in the southwest corner. The main commercial district is around Av Afonso Pena; at night the *movimento* shifts to Savassi, southwest of the centre, where all the good eating places are.

The principal building in the Parque Municipal is the **Palácio das Artes**, Afonso Pena 1537, T3237 7234, which contains the **Centro de Artesanato Mineiro** (with craft shop), an exhibition of painting in Minas Gerais, a cinema, three theatres and temporary exhibitions. ■ *Mon 1300-1800, Tue-Fri 0900-2100, Sat 0900-1300, Sun 1000-1400*. On the stretch of Av Afonso Pena outside the Parque Municipal an open-air market operates each Sunday morning (0800-1400). The avenue is transformed by thousands of coloured awnings covering stalls selling every conceivable type of local handicraft. Six blocks up Av João Pinheiro from Av Afonso Pena is the **Praça da Liberdade**, which is surrounded by fine public buildings, some in eclectic, *fin-de-siècle*-style, others more recent. At the end of the Praça is the **Palácio da Liberdade**. ■ *Sun 0900-1800 only*. The Praça itself is very attractive, with trees, flowers, fountains which are lit at night and joggers and walkers making the most of the paths. The **railway station**, with a museum on the 2nd floor showing a model railway, is part of a complex which includes a number of buildings dating from the 1920s around the **Praça da Estação** (also called Praça Rui Barbosa).

Museu Mineiro, Av João Pinheiro 342, houses religious and other art. ■ *Tue-Fri 1230-1830, Sat-Sun 1000-1600, T3269 1168*. **Museu Histórico Abílio Barreto**, R Bernardo Mascarenhas, Cidade Jardim, T3296 3896, in an old *fazenda* which is the last reminder of Belo Horizonte's predecessor, the village of **Arraial do Curral d'el Rey**, houses historical exhibits (take bus 2902 from Av Afonso Pena).**Museu de História Natural**, Instituto Agronómico, R Gustavo da Silveira 1035, Santa Inês, has geological, palaeontological and archaeological displays (take bus 8001). ■ *Mon-Thu 0800-1130, 1300-1630, Sat-Sun 0900-1600*. Also here is the **Jardim Botânico**.

About 8 km northwest from the centre is the picturesque suburb of **Pampulha**, famous for its modern buildings and the artificial lake, created in the 1930s by Brasilia architect Oscar Niemeyer and landscaped by Roberto Burle Marx. The **Igreja São Francisco de Assis**, Av Otacílio Negrão de Lima Km 12, T3491 2319, was inaugurated in 1943. The painter Cândido Portinari installed beautiful blue and white tiles depicting Saint Francis' life on the exterior. On the wall behind the altar is a powerful composition also by Portinari. On the opposite shore is the glass and marble **Museu de Arte de Pampulha** (MAP), at Av Octacílio Negrão de Lima 16585 ■ *Tue-Sun 0800-1800, free, T3277 7946*. It has a fine collection of modern art from Minas Gerais. The **Casa do Baile** is a perfect example of Niemeyer's fascination with the curved line. Just south of the lake is the **Mineirão** stadium, about 750 m away. This is the second largest stadium in Brazil after the Maracanã stadium in Rio. Seats cost between US$5 and US$10. Nearby is the 25,000-seater Mineirinho stadium and multi-sport facility.

In the southern zone of the city, just 3 km from the central area, the **Parque de Mangabeiras** is on the Serra do Curral at between 1,000 m and 1,400 m above sea level. There are good views of the city, especially from the Mirante da Mata. Three forest trails have been laid out. ■ *Thu-Sun 0800-1800*. The natural amphitheatre, Praça do Papa, where the Pope spoke in 1980, is on the way up to Parque Mangabeiras; there is an iron monument marking the occasion.

LL *Othon Palace*, Av Afonso Pena 1050, T3247 0000, F3247 0001, www.hoteis-othon.com.br Deluxe, modern, glass-fronted, excellent, safe deposit boxes, good restaurant, pool on roof, helpful staff, rooms on lower floors can be noisy. **L** *Grandville*, R Espírito Santo 901, T0800-311188, F3248 1100. Convenient for city centre. **L-AL** *Normandy*, R dos Tamóios 212, T3201 6166, normandyhotel@ig.com.br Excellent grill. **AL** *Sol Meliá*, R da Bahia 1040, T/F3274 1344, www.solmeliabh.com.br Comfortable, all facilities, pool and sauna. **AL** *Boulevard Plaza*, Av Getúlio Vargas 1640, Savassi district (chic shopping area), T3269 7000, www.boulevardhoteis.com.br Very nice. **A** *Wembley Palace*, R Espírito Santo 201, T3273 6866, www.hotelwembley.co.br Central. **B** *Ambassy*, R dos Caetés 633, near Rodoviária, T3279

Sights

As in any large city watch out for sneak thieves in the centre and at the bus station. Take taxis.
The Parque Municipal is not too safe, so it is best not to go alone

Sleeping

■ *on map*
You may spend the night in the rodoviária only if you have an onward ticket (police check at midnight)

See Essentials for new telephone number changes

Brazil

Brazil

5000. Helpful, good value, safe, English spoken. **B** *Esplanada*, Av Santos Dumont 304, T3273 5311, F3222 7725 **D** without bath, restaurant, garage, good value. **C** *Continental*, Av Paraná 241, T3201 7944, F3201 7336. Central, quieter interior rooms recommended. **C** *Financial*, Av Afonso Pena 571, Centro, T3270 4000, hotel@hotelfinancial. com.br Large, dated, but good value. **C** *Magnata*, R Guarani 124, T3201 5368. With breakfast, near rodoviária, hot shower, safe deposit. **D** *São Cristovão*, Av Oiapoque 284, T3201 4860. Quiet, breakfast. **D** *Madrid*, R Guarani 12, T3201 1088/6330. Recommended, but in a noisy location. Near the rodoviária and in R Curitiba many hotels are for very-short-stay couples. **E** *São Salvador*, R Espírito Santo 227, T3222 7731. **E** *Gontijo*, R dos Tupinambás 731, T3272 1177. With bath and breakfast, TV, safe.

Youth hostels *Pousadinha Mineira*, R Araxá 514, Floresta, T3423 4105, ajpousadinhamineira@backpacker.com.br or vieira77@hotmail.com 15 mins from the rodoviária, very helpful, popular with Brazilians, HI, bedding and towels can be hired, breakfast extra on request. Recommended. *Chalé Mineiro*, R Santa Luzia 288, Santa Efigênia, T3467 1576. Attractive, splash pool, recommended. **Federação Brasileira de Albergues Juveniles**, R Sergipe 1449, Savassi, T3284 9958.

Eating
● *on maps*
Comida mineira is the local speciality

Chico Mineiro, R Alagoas 626, corner of Av Brasil, T3261 3237. Local chicken specialities, good, closed Sun. *Dona Lucinha*, R Sergipe 811, T3261 5930. Recommended, also at R Padre Odorico 38, Savassi, T3227 0562. *Farroupilha Grill*, Av Afonso Pena, Mangabeiras, T3225 5050. Excellent *rodízio* with good meat at good value (mid-range), 2 other branches. *Interior*

Belo Horizonte & Pampulha

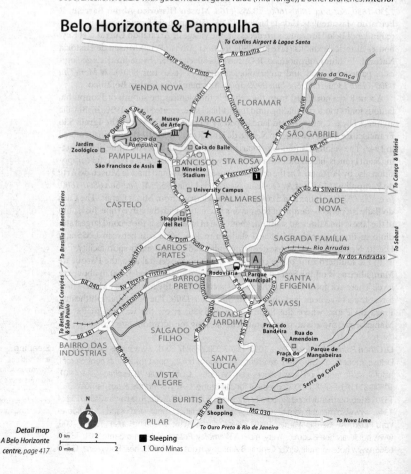

Detail map
A Belo Horizonte
centre, page 417

0 km   2
0 miles   2

■ **Sleeping**
1 Ouro Minas

de Minas, R Rio de Janeiro 1191. Central, good for lunch, good value, also at Av Olegário Maciel 1781, Lourdes. *Mala e Cuia*, a chain of restaurants serving good *comida mineira*, for example at R Gonçalves Dias 874, Savassi, Av Antônio Carlos 8305, Pampulha, Av Raja Gabaglia 1617, São Bento. **Other Brazilian** *La Greppia*, R da Bahia 1204 (Centro). Lunch only, good. *Flor de Líbano*, R Espírito Santo 234. Cheap and good. *Tampa*, R Tupis between Av Curitiba and R São Paulo. Cheap, pizza, dish of the day, open evenings. *Aquarius*, Av Curitiba between R dos Carijós and R dos Tamoios. Cheap, simple food, open Sun evenings. The Cidade Shopping mall on R Rio de Janeiro has 2 good food courts.

International *Santa Felicidade*, R Profesor Morais 659 (Savassi). Pastas, fish, grill, buffet, open for lunch and in the evening. **Italian** *Buona Távola*, R Santa Rita Durão 309 (Savassi), T3227 6155. Excellent. *Dona Derna*, R Tomé de Souza 1380 (Savassi), T3223 6954. Highly recommended. *Pizzarela*, Av Olegário Maciel 2280, Lourdes, T3222 3000. Good for pizzas. *Vecchio Sogno*, R Martim de Carvalho 75/R Dias Adorno, Santo Agostinho, T3292 5251, under the Assembléia Legislativo. Good food, top wine list, closed Sun. **French** *Taste Vin*, R Curitiba 2105, Lourdes. Recommended. **German** *Alpino*, Av Contorno 5761 (Savassi). Good value and popular. **Oriental** *Yun Ton*, Chinese, R Santa Catarina 946, T3337 2171. Recommended. *Kyoto*, Japanese, R Montes Claros 323, Anchieta. Recommended. **Vegetarian** *Mandala*, R Cláudio Manoel 875, Savassi, T3261 7056.

Cafés *Café Belas Artes*, R Gonçalves Dias 1581, Lourdes, in the foyer at Unibanco Belas Artes Liberdade. Popular. *Café Belas Artes Nazaré*, R Guajaras 37, near Av Afonso Pena, in the Unibanco Nazaré Liberdade cinema. *Café Três Corações*, Praça Diego de Vasconcelos, Savassi. Coffees and snacks. *Koyote Street Bar*, R Tomé de Souza 912. Street café.

Belo Horizonte centre

	Sleeping				
1 Ambassy	3 Esplanada	5 Madrid	7 Normandy	9 Sol Meliá
2 Continental	4 Grandville	6 Magnata	8 Othon Palace	10 Wembley Palace

Bars Recommended bars are *Alambique*, Av Raja Gabaglia 3200, Chalé 1D, Estoril, T3296 7188. Specializes in *cachaça*, with *mineira* appetizers, designed like a country house. *Amoricana*, R Pernambuco 1025. *Entre Folhas*, R Floralia 40. Outdoor café bar with live music, US$1.50, open until midnight Tue-Sun. Recommended. *Bar Nacional*, Av Contorno 1076, Barro Preto. Good value. *Heaven*, Av Getúlio Vargas 809.

Entertainment **Theatres** The city prides itself on its theatre and dance companies (look out for the *Grupo Galpão*) and has at least a dozen theatres. The local press and tourist literature give details of shows and events.

Shopping *Mercado Central*, Av Augusto de Lima 744, is large and clean, open every day. See above for the Sun *handicraft fair* on Av Afonso Pena. A **flower market** is held at Av Bernardo Monteiro, near Av Brasil, every Fri from 1200 to 2000. For **gemstones**, try *Manoel Bernardes*, Av Contorno 5417, Savassi, very reasonable. For **music**, *Cogumelo*, Av Augusto de Lima 399. **Bookshops** *Daniel Vaitsman*, R Espírito Santo 466, 17th floor, for English language books. Foreign language books at *Livraria Van Damme*, R das Guajajaras 505, also good local and Portuguese selection. Used foreign-language books at *Livraria Alfarrábio*, R Tamóios 320.

Tour operators *Master Turismo* (Amex representative), R da Bahia 2140, T3330 3655, www.masterturismo.com.br At Sala VIP, Aeroporto de Confins, and Av Afonso Pena 1967, T3330 3603 (very helpful). Oasis Turismo, A de Lima 479/815, Centro, T3274 6422. Very helpful, manager Jacqueline. *Ouro Preto Turismo*, Av Afonso Pena 4133, T3287 0505, F3287 0103, www.ouropretotour.com and *Revetur*, R Espírito Santo 1892, 1st floor, Lourdes, T3337 2500, www.revetour.com.br Both have been recommended. *Ametur*, R Alvarengo Peixoto 295, loja 102, Lourdes, T/F3275 2139, 0900-1200, 1400-1900, has information on *fazendas* which welcome visitors and overnight guests. **Ecotourism and adventure sports:** *Amo-Te*, *Associação Mineira dos Organizadores do Turismo Ecológico*, R Prof Morais 624, Apto 302, Savassi, T3281 5094, oversees ecotourism in Minas Gerais. For companies which arrange trekking, riding, cycling, rafting, jeep tours, canyoning, visiting national parks, or *fazendas*, speak to *Amo-Te* in the first instance. For recommended **horse riding** tours, contact *Tropa Serrana*, Tullio Marques Lopes Filho, T3344 8986, T9983 2356 (mob).

Transport **Local** **Bus**: the city has a good public transport system: red buses run on express routes and charge US$0.75; yellow buses have circular routes around the Contorno, US$0.50; blue buses run on diagonal routes charging US$0.65. There are also buses which integrate with the regional, overground Metrô. A new system is being introduced, in which all routes will feed into an *estação*, or route station; passengers will purchase tickets before boarding the bus.

Taxi: are plentiful, although hard to find at peak hrs.

Long distance **Air**: the international airport is near Lagoa Santa, at Confins, 39 km from Belo Horizonte, T3689 2700. Taxi to centre, US$50, cooperative taxis have fixed rates to different parts of the city. Airport bus, either *executivo* from the exit, US$11, or comfortable normal bus (*Unir*) from the far end of the car park hourly, US$2.20, both go to/from the rodoviária.

Closer to the city is the national airport at Pampulha, which has shuttle services from several cities, including Rio and São Paulo, T3490 2001. Urban transportation to/from this airport is cheaper than from Confins. From Pampulha airport to town, take blue bus 1202, 25 mins, US$0.65, passing the rodoviária and the cheaper hotel district.

Train: to **Vitória**, daily 0700, tickets sold at 0530, US$17.50 *executivo*, US$11.50 1st class, US$7.80 2nd, 12 hrs.

Bus: the rodoviária is by Praça Rio Branco at the northwest end of Av Afonso Pena, T3271 3000/8933. The bus station has toilets, post office, phones, left-luggage lockers (attended service 0700-2200), shops and is clean and well-organized. Buses leave from the rather gloomy platforms beneath the ticket hall. Do not leave belongings unattended.

To **Rio** with *Cometa* (T3201 5611) and *Útil* (T3201 7744), 6½ hrs, US$12.75 (ordinary), *leito*, US$25.50. To **Vitória** with *São Geraldo* (T3271 1911), US$14.50 and *leito* US$29. To

Brasília with *Itapemirim* (T3291 9991) and *Penha* (T3271 1027), 10 hrs, 6 a day including 2 *leitos*, only one leaves in daylight (0800), US$19.25, *leito* US$38.50. To **São Paulo** with *Cometa* and *Gontijo* (T3201 6130), 10 hrs, US$15.60. To **Foz do Iguaçu**, US$42, 22 hrs. To **Salvador** with *Gontijo*, US$40, 24 hrs, at 1900 daily, and *São Geraldo* at 1800. *São Geraldo* also goes to **Porto Seguro**, 17 hrs, direct, via Nanuque and Eunápolis, US$33. To **Recife** with *Gontijo*, 2000, US$41. To **Fortaleza**, US$63. To **Natal**, US$66. To **Belém** with *Itapemirim* at 2030, US$72. To **Campo Grande** with *Gontijo* (at 1930) and *Motta* (3 a day), US$31-36, a good route to Bolivia, avoiding São Paulo. All major destinations served. For buses within Minas Gerais, see under each destination.

Airline offices *American*, Av Bernardo Monteiro 1539, Funcionários, T3274 3166.*TAM*, Av Cristóvão **Directory** Colombo 485, 7th floor, T3228 5500, Pampulha T3441 8100. *United*, Av Getúlio Vargas 840, T3339 6060, Confins T3689 2736. *Varig/Rio Sul/Nordeste*, Av Getúlio Vargas 840, T3339 6000/0800-997000, Confins airport T3689 2350. *Vasp*, Av Getúlio Vargas 1492, T0800-998277, Confins T3689 2394. **Banks** *Banco do Brasil*, R Rio de Janeiro 750, Av Amazonas 303; cash is given against credit cards at *Banco Itaú*, Av João Pinheiro 195. *Citibank*, R Espírito Santo 871. Visa ATM at *Bradesco*, R da Bahia 947. *Master Turismo*, see Tour operators, above. American Express representative. Changing TCs is difficult, but hotels will change them for guests at a poor rate. **Communications** Internet: *Internet Café Club*; R Fernandes Tourinho 385, Plaza Savassi, US$5 per hr. Post Office: Av Afonso Pena 1270, with fax, philatelic department and small museum, service is slow (unless the quick counter is open), closes 1800; poste restante is behind the main office at R de Goiás 77 (unhelpful). The branch office on R da Bahia is less busy. **Telephone:** *Telemig*, Av Afonso Pena 1180, by the Correios, daily 0700-2200; also at the rodoviária, Confins airport, R Caetés 487 and R Tamóios 311 in the centre; R Paraíba 1441, Savassi. **Embassies and consulates** Austria, R José Américo Cançado Bahia 199, T3333 5363, F3333 1046. **Denmark**, R Paraíba 1122, 5th floor, T3286 8626, F3269 8785. **Finland**, Av Contorno 6283, salas 602/4, T3281 1052, F3281 9514. **France**, R Bernardo Guimarães 1020, lj 3, Funcionários, T3261 7805, F3261 7806. **Germany**, R Timbiras 1200, 5th floor, T3213 1568. Italy, Av Afonso Pena 3130, 12th floor, T3281 4211. **Netherlands**, R Sergipe 1167, loja 5, T3227 5275. **Spain**, R Curitiba 778, sl 701, T/F3212 3759. **UK**, R dos Inconfidentes 1075, sala 1302, Savassi, T3261 2072, F3261 0226, britcon.bhe@terra.com.br **Language classes** *Carlos Robles*, T3281 1274, gatirobles@vol.com.br Has a network of schools in Brazil, speaks good English. **Medical services** *Mater Dei*, R Gonçalves Dias 2700, T3339 9000. Recommended. **Tourist offices** Belotur, the municipal information office, is at R Pernambuco 284, Funciários, T3277 9797, F3277 9730, www.pbh.gov.br/belotur/index.htm Very helpful, with lots of useful information and maps. The monthly *Guia Turístico* for events, opening times etc, is freely available. Belotur has offices also at the southwest corner of Parque Municipal, at Confins and Pampulha airports, and at the rodoviária (particularly polyglot). **Turminas**, Praça Rio Branco 56, T3272 8573, F3272 5605, www.turminas.mg.gov.br The tourism authority for the state of Minas Gerais is very helpful. **Ibama**, Av do Contorno 8121, Cidade Jardim, CEP 30110-120, Belo Horizonte, T3337 2624, F3335 9955. **Voltage** 120-220 AC, 60 cycles.

Around Belo Horizonte

The **Parque Natural de Caraça** is a remarkable reserve about 120 km east of Belo **Nature** Horizonte. It has been preserved so well because the land belongs to a seminary, part **reserves** of which has been converted into a hotel. The rarest mammal in the park is the maned wolf; the monks feed them on the seminary steps in the evening. Also endangered is the southern masked titi monkey. Other primates include the common marmoset and the brown capuchin monkey. Some of the bird species at Caraça are endemic, others rare and endangered. The trails for viewing the different landscapes and the wildlife are marked at their beginning and are quite easy to follow. ■ *0700-2100; if staying overnight you cannot leave after 2100. US$5 per vehicle.*

Sleeping and eating The seminary hotel, *Hospedaria do Caraça*, has pleasant rooms; room rates vary, **AL-B**, full board. For reservations write to Santuário do Caraça, Caixa Postal 12, 35960-000 – Santa Bárbara, MG, T0xx31-837 2698, or phone 101 and ask the operator to connect you to PS1 do Caraça. There is a restaurant serving good food which comes from farms within the seminary's lands. Lunch is served 1200-1330.

Transport Turn off the BR-262 (towards Vitória) at Km 73 and go via Barão de Cocais to Caraça (120 km). There is no public transport to the seminary. Buses go as far as Barão de Cocais, from where you have to take a taxi, US$12 one way. You must book the taxi to return for you, or else hitch (which may not be easy). The park entrance is 10 km before the seminary. The alternatives are either to hire a car, or take a guide from Belo Horizonte, which will cost about US$75 (including guiding, transport and meals). It is possible to stay in **Santa Bárbara** (D *Hotel Karaibe*. D *Santa Inés*), 25 km away on the road to Mariana and hitchhike to Caraça. 11 buses a day from Belo Horizonte – Santa Bárbara (fewer on Sat and Sun).

About 105 km northeast of Belo Horizonte, **Parque Nacional da Serra do Cipó**, 33,400 sq km of the Serra do Espinhaço, has scenic beauty and several endemic plants, insects and birds. In the last category, the Cipó Canestero is only found in one small area in the south of the park. The predominant habitat is high mountain grassland, with rocky outcroppings. Full details from *Ibama*, T0xx31 3718 7228. ■ *The park can be reached via road MG-010. This road continues unpaved to Serro (see page 429); buses run on this route. Agencies offer excursions from the city to the park. It is recommended to take a guide because the trails are unmarked; ask locally.*

Sabará
Colour map 7, grid B5
Population: 115,352

East of the state capital by 23 km is the colonial gold-mining (and steel-making) town of Sabará, strung along the narrow steep valleys of the Rio das Velhas and Rio Sabará. For tourist information, visit the *Secretaria de Turismo*, R Pedro II 200, T671 1522. www.sabara.mg.gov.br ■ *Viação Cisne bus No 1059 from R Catete, Belo Horizonte, US$0.75, 30 mins, circular route.*

Worth seeing is R Dom Pedro II, which is lined with beautiful 18th-century buildings. Among them is the **Solar do Padre Correa** (1773) at No 200, now the **Prefeitura**; the **Casa Azul** (also 1773), No 215; and the **Teatro Municipal**, former Opera House (1770 – the second oldest in Brazil). At the top of R Dom Pedro II is the Praça Melo Viana, in the middle of which is **Nossa Senhora do Rosário dos Pretos** (left unfinished at the time of the slaves' emancipation). There is a museum of religious art in the church. ■ *Church and museum: Tue-Sun 0800-1100, 1300-1700.* To the right of the church as you face it is the **Chafariz do Rosário** (the Rosário fountain). In R da Intendência is the museum of 18th century gold mining in the **Museu do Ouro**. It contains exhibits on gold extraction, plus religious items and colonial furniture. ■ *Tue-Sun 1200-1730, US$1.* Another fine example is the **Casa Borba Gato**, R Borba Gato 71; the building currently belongs to the Museu do Ouro.

The church of **Nossa Senhora do Carmo** (1763-74), with doorway, pulpits and choirloft by Aleijadinho (see below) and paintings by Athayde, is on R do Carmo ■ *US$1; includes a leaflet about the town.* **Nossa Senhora da Conceição** (begun 1701, construction lasting until 1720), on Praça Getúlio Vargas, has much visible woodwork and a beautiful floor. The carvings have much gilding, there are painted panels and paintings by 23 Chinese artists brought from Macau. The clearest Chinese work is on the two red doors to the right and left of the chancel. ■ *Free.* **Nossa Senhora do Ó**, built in 1717 and showing Chinese influence, is 2 km from the centre of the town at the Largo Nossa Senhora do Ó (take local bus marked 'Esplanada' or 'Boca Grande').

If you walk up the Morra da Cruz hill from the *Hotel do Ouro* to a small chapel, the Capela da Cruz or Senhor Bom Jesus, you can get a wonderful view of the whole area.

Sleeping B *Pousada Solar das Sepúlvedas*, R da Intendência 371, behind the Museu do Ouro, T671 2708. Grand, rooms with TV, pool. D *Hotel do Ouro*, R Santa Cruz 237, Morro da Cruz, T671 5622. With bath, hot water, with breakfast, marvellous view, best value.

Caeté
Colour map 7, grid B5
Population: 36,299
60 km from
Belo Horizonte

A further 25 km is Caeté, which has several historical buildings and churches. On the Praça João Pinheiro are the **Prefeitura** and **Pelourinho** (both 1722), the **Igreja Matriz Nossa Senhora do Bom Sucesso** (1756 rebuilt 1790) ■ *Daily 1300-1800*, and the **Chafariz da Matriz**. Also on the Praça is the tourist information office in the Casa da Cultura (T6511855). Other churches are **Nossa Senhora do Rosário**

(1750-68), with a ceiling attributed to Mestre Athayde, and **São Francisco de Assis**. The **Museu Regional**, in the house of the Barão de Catas Altas, or Casa Setecentista, R Israel Pinheiro 176, contains 18th and 19th century religious art and furniture. ■ *Tue-Sun 1200-1700*.

Ouro Preto

Founded in 1711, this famous former capital of the state has cobbled streets that wind up and down steep hills which are crowned with 13 churches. Mansions, fountains, churches, vistas of terraced gardens, ruins, towers shining with coloured tiles, all blend together to maintain a delightful 18th century atmosphere. From October-February the climate is wet, but the warmest month of the year is February (30°C on average). The coldest months are June, July and August, with lowest temperatures being in July (10°C).

Phone code: 0xx31
Post code: 35400
Colour map 7, grid B5
Population: 66,277
Altitude: 1,000 m

In the central **Praça Tiradentes** is a statue of the leader of the **Inconfidentes**, Joaquim José da Silva Xavier. Another Inconfidente, the poet Tomás Antônio Gonzaga lived at R Cláudio Manoel 61, close to São Francisco de Assis church. On the north side of the praça (at No 20) is a famous **Escola de Minas** (School of Mining), founded in 1876, in the fortress-like **Palácio dos Governadores** (1741-48); it has the interesting **Museu de Mineralogia e das Pedras**, with 23,000 stones from around the world. ■ *Tue-Sun 1200-1700*. On the south side of the Praça, No 139, is the **Museu da Inconfidência**, a fine historical and art museum in the former **Casa de Câmara e Cadeia**, which has some drawings by Aleijadinho and the Sala Manoel da Costa Athayde, in an annex. ■ *Mon-Fri 0800-1800, US$1.50*. **Casa das Contas**, R São José 12, built between 1782-87, is the Centro de Estudos do Ciclo de Ouro (Centre for Gold Cycle Studies) and a museum of money and finance. ■ *Tue-Sat 1230-1730, Sun and holidays 0830-1330, US$0.50*. The **Casa Guignard**, R Conde de Bobadela 110, displays the paintings of Alberto da Veiga Guignard. ■ *Tue-Sat 1230-1730, Sun 0830-1330, free*. The **Teatro Municipal** in R Brigadeiro Musqueiro, is the oldest functioning theatre in Latin America. It was built in 1769. ■ *Daily 1230-1800*.

Sights
Photography is prohibited in all the churches and museums
Churches are all closed Mon

São Francisco de Assis (1766-96), Largo de Coimbra, is considered to be one of the masterpieces of Brazilian baroque. Aleijadinho worked on the general design and the sculpture of the façade, the pulpits and many other features. Mestre Athayde (1732-1827) was responsible for the painted ceiling. ■ *0830-1145, 1330-1640, US$1; the ticket also permits entry to NS da Conceição (keep your ticket for admission to the museum)*. **Nossa Senhora da Conceição** (1722) is heavily gilded and contains Aleijadinho's tomb. It has a museum devoted to him. ■ *0830-1130, 1330-1645, Sun 1200-1645*. **Nossa Senhora das Mercês e Perdões** (1740-72), R das Mercês, was rebuilt in the 19th century. Some sculpture by Aleijadinho can be seen in the main chapel. ■ *1000-1400*. **Santa Efigênia** (1720-85), Ladeira Santa Efigênia e Padre Faria; Manuel Francisco Lisboa (Aleijadinho's father) oversaw the construction and much of the carving is by Francisco Xavier de Brito (Aleijadinho's mentor). ■ *0800-1200; has wonderful panoramic views of the city*. **Nossa Senhora do Carmo**, R Brigadeiro Mosqueira (1766-72); museum of sacred art with Aleijadinho sculptures. ■ *1330-1700*. **Nossa Senhora do Pilar** (1733), Praça Mons Castilho Barbosa, which also contains a religious art museum. ■ *1200-1700, entry is shared with São Francisco de Paula, Ladeira de São José (1804)*. **Nossa Senhora do Rosário**, Largo do Rosário, dated from 1785, has a curved façade. The interior is much simpler than the exterior, but there are interesting side altars.

The **Mina do Chico Rei**, R Dom Silvério is not as impressive as some other mines in the area, but is fun to crawl about in; restaurant attached. ■ *0800-1700, US$1.50*. Near the Padre Faria Church (NS do Rosário dos Brancos) is another small mine, **Mina Bem Querer**, with a swimming pool with crystal clear water that runs through the mine. ■ *US$1*. (Between Ouro Preto and Mariana is the **Minas de Passagem**

▶ *O Aleijadinho*

Antônio Francisco Lisboa (1738-1814), the son of a Portuguese architect and a black slave woman, was known as O Aleijadinho (the little cripple) because in later life he developed a maiming disease (possibly leprosy) which compelled him to work in a kneeling (and ultimately a recumbent) position with his hammer and chisel strapped

to his wrists. His finest work, which shows a strength not usually associated with the plastic arts in the 18th century, is probably the set of statues in the gardens and sanctuary of the great Bom Jesus church in Congonhas do Campo, but the main body of his work is in Ouro Preto, with some important pieces in Sabará, São João del Rei and Mariana.

gold mine, dating from 1719. ■ *A guided tour visits the old mine workings and underground lake (take bathing suit), entrance US$7.50, visiting hours 0900-1730, last admissions at 1645.)*

Sleeping

Prices indicated here are for high season; many hotels offer, or will negotiate lower prices outside holiday times or when things are quiet

Ask at the tourist office for accommodation in *casas de família*, reasonably priced. Avoid touts who greet you off buses and charge higher prices than those advertised in hotels; it is difficult to get hotel rooms at weekends and holiday periods.

AL *Pousada Solar de NS do Rosário*, Av Getúlio Vargas 270, T3551 5200, rosario@bis.com.br Fully restored historic building with a highly recommended restaurant, bar, sauna, all facilities in rooms. **AL-A** *Pousada do Mondego*, Largo de Coimbra 38, T3551 2040, F3551 3094. Beautifully kept colonial house in a fine location by São Francisco church, room rates vary according to view, small restaurant, Scotch bar, popular with groups (a Roteiro de Charme hotel), the hotel runs a *jardineira* bus tour of the city, 2 hrs, minimum 10 passengers, US$10 for non-guests. Recommended. **B** *Pousada Casa Grande*, R Conselheiro Quintiliano, 96, T/F3551 4314. TV, fridge, including breakfast, safe, good views. **B** *Grande*, R Senador Rocha Lagoa 164, T/F3551 1488, www.hotelouropreto.com.br Largest hotel in town and the only modern structure, designed by Oscar Niemeyer, the feel of the place is somehow more dated than the colonial buildings that surround it, but that is no reflection on the service. **C** *Pouso Chico Rei*, R Brigadeiro Musqueira 90, T3551 1274. A fascinating old house with Portuguese colonial furnishings, very small and utterly delightful, book in advance (room No 6 has been described as a 'dream'). **C** *Solar das Lajes*, R Conselheiro Quintiliano 604, T/F3551 3388, www.solardaslajes.com.br A little way from centre, excellent view, swimming pool, well run. **C** *Colonial*, Travessa Cônego Camilo Veloso 26, T3551 3133, colonial@ ouropreto.feop.com.br Close to Praça Tiradentes, with new rooms and older rooms refurbished, pleasant. **C** *Pousada Itacolomi*, R Antônio Pereira 43, T3551 2891. Small, TV in rooms. Recommended. **C** *Pousada Nello Nuno*, R Camilo de Brito 59, T3551 3375. Cheaper without bath, charming owner Annamélia speaks some French. Highly recommended. **C** *Hospedária de Ouro Preto*, R Xavier da Veiga 1, T3551 2203. A restored colonial house. Recommended. **C** *Pousada Ouro Preto*, Largo Musicista José dos Anjos Costa 72, T3551 3081, www.asminasgerais.com.br Small, laundry facilities, English spoken by owner, Gérson Luís Cotta (most helpful), good views. Recommended. **C** *Pousada Tiradentes*, Praça Tiradentes 70, T3551 2619. Comfortable, TV, fridge, rooms a bit spartan and small, very convenient. **D** *Pousada dos Bandeirantes*, R das Mercês 167, T551 1996, F551 1962, behind São Francisco de Assis. Beautiful views, TV, fridge, very pleasant. **D** *Pousada dos Inconfidentes*, Praça Tiradentes 134, T3551 5276. Comfortable, quiet, good breakfast, very nice. **D** *Pousada São Francisco de Paula*, Padre JM Pena 202 (next to the São Francisco de Paula church), T3551 3456, pousadas@hotmail.com In a garden, panoramic view, veranda with hammock, multilingual staff, trips organized to nearby villages, mountains, mines, waterfalls, 8 rooms including a dormitory, with or without a simple breakfast, private or communal bathroom, full breakfast and snacks available. **Youth hostel**: R Costa Sena 30-A, Largo de Coimbra, T/F3551 6705, www.users.task.com.br/albergue **F** pp *Brumas*, Ladeira São Francisco de Paula 68, 150 m downhill from rodoviária, just below São Francisco de Paula church, T3551 2944, brumasonline@hotmail.com Dormitory, kitchen, superb views. Don't walk down from bus station after dark.

Students can stay, during holidays and weekends, at the self-governing student hostels, known as *repúblicas*. The Prefeitura has a list of over 50 *repúblicas* with phone numbers, available at the *Secretaria de Turismo*. Many are closed between Christmas and Carnival.

Camping Camping Clube do Brasil, 2 km north of the city at Rodovia dos Inconfidentes Km 91, T551 1799, is quite expensive but very nice.

Casa Grande and *Forno de Barro*, both on Praça Tiradentes (Nos 84 and 54 respectively). **Eating** Good local dishes. *Pasteleria Lampião*, Praça Tiradentes. Good views at the back (better at lunchtime than in the evening). *Tacho de Ouro*, Conde de Bobadela 76. Good lunch buffet, popular. *Casa do Ouvidor*, Conde de Bobadela 42, above Manoel Bernardis jewellery shop. Good. *Satélite*, R Conde de Bobadela 97. Restaurant and pizzeria, bar next door, good value. *Pizzaria Zebão*, R Paraná 43. *Ouro Grill*, R Senador Rocha Lagoa 61. Self-service at lunchtime, US$5, good value, restaurant after 1600. *Vide Gula*, R Senador Rocha Lagoa 79A. Food by weight, good, friendly atmosphere. Recommended. *Taverna do Chafariz*, R São José 167. Good local food. *Café & Cia*, R São José 187. Closes 2300, very popular, *comida por kilo* at lunchtime, good salads, juices. Recommended. *Chale dos Caldos*, R Pandia Calogera between *Pousada Circolo de Ouro* and *Pousada Ouro Preto*. Good soups, pleasant setting. *Arqueiro Bar*, R Direita. Bar and, through the small hallway to the backyard, great pizzas. *Adega*, R Teixeira Amaral 24. 1130-1530, vegetarian smorgasbord, US$5, all you can eat. Highly recommended. *Beijinho*, Direita 134A. Recommended for pastries and cakes. Try the local *licor de jaboticaba*.

Ouro Preto is famous for its **Holy Week** processions, which in fact begin on the Thu before **Festivals** Palm Sunday and continue (but not every day) until Easter Sunday. The most famous is that commemorating Christ's removal from the Cross, late on Good Friday. Many shops close during this holiday, and on winter weekends. Attracting many Brazilians, *Carnival* here is also memorable. In Jun, *Corpus Christi* and the *Festas Juninas* are celebrated. Every **Jul** the city holds the *Festival do Inverno da Universidade Federal de Minas Gerais (UFMG)*, the Winter Festival, about 3 weeks of arts, courses, shows, concerts and exhibitions. Also in **Jul**, on the 8th, is the *anniversary of the city*. 15 Aug: *Nossa Senhora do Pilar*, patron saint of Ouro Preto. 12-18 Nov: *Semana de Aleijadinho*, a week-long arts festival.

Gems are not much cheaper from freelance sellers in Praça Tiradentes than from the shops, **Shopping** and in the shops, the same quality of stone is offered at the same price – *Gemas de Minas* and *Manoel Bernardis*, Conde de Bobadela 63 and 48 respectively, are recommended. If buying on the street, ask for the seller's credentials. Buy soapstone carvings at roadside stalls and bus stops rather than in cities; they are much cheaper. Many artisans sell carvings, jewellery and semi-precious stones in Largo de Coimbra in front of São Francisco de Assis church.

Bus The rodoviária is at R Padre Rolim 661, near São Francisco de Paula chruch, T3551 1081. A **Transport** 'Circular' bus runs from the rodoviária to Praça Tiradentes, US$0.40. Taxi US$2.30. 11 buses a *Don't walk from* day from Belo Horizonte (2 hrs, *Pássaro Verde*), US$3.50, taxi US$30. Day trips are run. Book *the rodoviária to* your return journey to **Belo Horizonte** early if returning in the evening; buses get crowded. *town at night;* Bus from **Rio**, *Útil* at 0830 or 2330 (US$15, 7.5 hrs), return bus to Rio at 2330 (book in advance). *robberies have* There are also *Útil* buses to **Conselheiro Lafaiete**, 3-4 a day via Itabirito and Ouro Branco (see *occurred* below), US$3.75, 2¾ hrs, for connections to **Congonhas do Campo**. Other *Útil* services to Rio, Barbacena, Conselheiro Lafaiete and Congonhas go via Belo Horizonte. Direct buses to **São Paulo**, 3 a day with *Cristo Rei*, 11 hrs, US$19.25. *Gontijo* go to Salvador via Belo Horizonte.

Banks *Banco do Brasil*, R São José 189, high commission, changes TCs. *Bradesco*, corner of Senador **Directory** Rocha Lagoa and Padre Rolim, opposite the Escola de Minas. *Banco 24 Horas*, Praça Alves de Brito, next to Correios. **Communications** Internet: *Point* Language School, Xavier da Veiga 501. **Post Office:** Praça Alves de Brito. **Tourist offices** Praça Tiradentes 41 (opens 0800, Portuguese only spoken), very helpful, T3551 2655. The *Secretaria de Turismo* is in the Casa de Gonzaga, R Cláudio Manoel 61, T3559 3282, F3559 3251. It has lists of hotels, restaurants and local sites and a map. **Guidebooks**: Bandeira's *Guia de Ouro Preto* in Portuguese and English, normally available at tourist office. Also available is Lucia Machado de Almeida's *Passeio a Ouro Preto*, US$6 (in Portuguese, English and French). The tourist office sells a guide with maps to Ouro Preto and Mariana, *Guia Prático*, for US$5. A local guide for a day, **Associação de Guias de Turismo** (*AGTOP*), can be obtained through the tourist office (a recommended guide is *Cássio Antunes*), T3551 2655 at the tourist office, or T3551 1544 ext 269. The **Guiding Association** (T3551 2504, or T3551 1544 ext 205) offers group tours of US$30 for 1 to 10 people, US$45 for more than 10. If taking a guide, check their accreditation. **Voltage** 110 volts AC.

Mariana

Streets are lined with beautiful, two-storey 18th century houses in this old mining city, which is much less hilly than Ouro Preto. Twelve kilometres east of Ouro Preto, on a road which goes on to join the Rio-Salvador highway, Mariana's historical centre slopes gently uphill from the river and the Praça Tancredo Neves, where buses from Ouro Preto stop. The first street parallel with the Praça Tancredo Neves is R Direita, and is home to the 300-year-old houses. At No 54 is the **Casa do Barão de Pontal**, whose balconies are carved from soapstone, unique in Minas Gerais. The ground floor of the building is a museum of furniture. ■ *Tue 1400-1700*. At No 35 is the **Museu-Casa Afonso Guimarães** (or Alphonsus de Guimaraens), the former home of a symbolist poet: photographs and letters. ■ *Free.* No 7 is the **Casa Setecentista**, which now belongs to the Patrimônio Histórico e Artístico Nacional.

R Direita leads to the Praça da Sé, on which stands the **Cathedral**, Basílica de Nossa Senhora da Assunção. The portal and the lavabo in the sacristy are by Aleijadinho. The painting in the beautiful interior and side altars is by Manoel Rabello de Sousa. Also in the cathedral is a wooden German organ (1701), a gift to the first diocese of the Capitania de Minas do Ouro in 1747. ■ *Organ concerts are given on Fri at 1100 and Suns at 1200, US$7.50.* On R Frei Durão is the **Museu Arquidiocesano**, which has fine church furniture, a gold and silver collection, Aleijadinho statues and an ivory cross ■ *0900-1200, 1300-1700, closed Mon, US$1.50. Opposite is the* **Casa da Intendência/Casa de Cultura**, No 84, which holds exhibitions and has a museum of music. ■ *0800-1130, 1330-1700.* On the south side of Praça Gomes Freire is the **Palácio Arquiepiscopal**, while on the north side is the **Casa do Conde de Assumar**, who was governor of the Capitania from 1717 to 1720.

From Praça Gomes Freire, Travessa São Francisco leads to Praça Minas Gerais and one of the finest groups of colonial buildings in Brazil. In the middle of the Praça is the **Pelourinho**, the stone monument to Justice, at which slaves used to be beaten. On one side of the square is the fine **São Francisco** church (1762-94), with pulpits designed by Aleijadinho, paintings by Mestre Athayde, who is buried in tomb No 94, a fine sacristy and one side-altar by Aleijadinho. ■ *Daily 0800-1700.* At right angles to São Francisco is **Nossa Senhora do Carmo** (1784), with steatite carvings, Athayde paintings, and chinoiserie panelling. ■ *Daily 1400-1700.* Across R Dom Silvério is the **Casa da Cámara e Cadéia** (1768), at one time the Prefeitura Municipal. On Largo de São Pedro is **São Pedro dos Clérigos** (begun in 1753), one of the few elliptical churches in Minas Gerais. Restoration is under way.

Capela de Santo Antônio, wonderfully simple and the oldest in town, is on R Rosário Velho. It is some distance from the centre. Overlooking the city from the north, with a good viewpoint, is the church of **Nossa Senhora do Rosário**, R do Rosário (1752), with work by Athayde and showing Moorish influence.

Sleeping & eating **B** *Pousada Solar dos Corrêa*, R Josefá Macedo 70 and R Direita, T/F3557 2080. Central, with breakfast, TV, fridge in room, parking. **C** *Pousada do Chafariz*, R Cônego Rego 149, T3557 1492. TV, fridge, parking, breakfast included, family atmosphere. Recommended. **C** *Providência*, R Dom Silvério 233, T3557 1444. Run by nuns, small rooms, pool, quiet. **C** *Central*, R Frei Durão 8, T/F3557 1630. **C** without bath, on the attractive Praça Gomes Freire, pleasant, quiet. Recommended but avoid downstairs rooms. The modern service station (*Posto Mariana*) on the highway above the town offers good clean rooms (**D**) with hot showers. **D** pp *Müller*, Av Getúlio Vargas 34, T3557 1188. Across the river from the Terminal Turístico. Recommended. Restaurants: *Mangiare della Mamma*, D Viçoso 27, Italian.

Recommended. *Tambaú*, R João Pinheiro 26. typical meals. *Engenho Nôvo*, Praça da Sé 26. Bar at night, English spoken by the owners and clients. Recommended by English travellers. *Panela de Pedra* in the Terminal Turístico serves food by weight at lunchtime.

Bus From Escola de Minas, Ouro Preto, for Mariana, every 30 mins, US$0.60, all passing Minas de Passagem. Buses stop at the new rodoviária, out of town on the main road, then at the Posto Mariana, before heading back to centre of Mariana at Praça Tancredo Neves. Buses from Mariana to Ouro Preto can be caught by the bridge at the end of R do Catete. **Transport**

Tourist offices In the *Terminal Turístico Manoel Costa Athayde*, Praça Tancredo Neves, is the local guides' association (**AGTURB**, T3557 1158), who run tours for US$40. There is also a small tourist office; map US$1.50. A free monthly booklet, *Mariana Agenda Cultural*, has details of the historical sites, accommodation, restaurants, shopping, transport etc, plus articles, poems and a calendar of events. **Directory**

This hill town is connected by a paved 3½ km road with the Rio-Belo Horizonte highway. Most visitors spend little time in the town, but go straight to **O Santuário de Bom Jesus de Matosinhos**, which dominates Congonhas. The great pilgrimage church was finished in 1771; below it are six linked chapels, or *pasos* (1802-18), showing scenes with life-size Passion figures carved by Aleijadinho and his pupils in cedar wood. These lead up to a terrace and courtyard. On this terrace (designed in 1777) stand 12 prophets, sculpted by Aleijadinho between 1800 and 1805. Carved in soapstone with dramatic sense of movement, they constitute one of the finest works of art of their period in the world. Inside the church, there are paintings by Athayde and the heads of four sainted popes (Gregory, Jerome, Ambrose and Augustine) sculpted by Aleijadinho for the reliquaries on the high altar. To the left of the church, as you face it, the third door in the building alongside the church is the Room of Miracles, which contains photographs and thanks for miracles performed. ■ *Tue-Sun 0700-1900. There are public toilets on the Alameda das Palmeiras. The information desk at the bus station will guard luggage.*

Congonhas do Campo
Phone code: 0xx31
Post code: 36404
Colour map 7, grid B5
Population: 41,256
Altitude: 866 m

Brazil

On the hill are a tourist kiosk, souvenir shops, the *Colonial Hotel* and *Cova do Daniel* restaurant. From the hotel the Alameda das Palmeiras sweeps round to the **Romarias**, which contains the Espaço Cultural, the headquarters of the local tourist office (*Fumcult*, T3731 1300 ext 114 or 3731 3133), workshops, the museums of mineralogy and religious art and the Memória da Cidade. To get there take bus marked 'Basílica' which runs every 30 minutes from the centre of the rodoviária to Bom Jesus, 5 km, US$0.45. A taxi from the rodoviária costs US$5, US$10 return including the wait while you visit the sanctuary. In town, the bus stops in Praça JK. You can walk up from Praça JK via Praça Dr Mário Rodrigues Pereira, cross the little bridge, then go up Ruas Bom Jesus and Aleijadinho to the Praça da Basílica.

Sleeping and eating D *Colonial*, Praça da Basílica 76, opposite Bom Jesus, T3731 1834. Comfortable but noisy, breakfast extra, cheaper without bath, fascinating restaurant (*Cova do Daniel*) downstairs is full of colonial handicrafts and local food. E *Freitas*, R Marechal Floriano 69, T3731 1543. Basic, with breakfast, cheaper without bath. *Estalagem Romaria*, 2 mins from *Hotel Colonial* in the Romarias, good restaurant and pizzeria, reasonable prices.

Festivals Congonhas is famous for its **Holy Week** processions, which have as their focus the Bom Jesus church. The most celebrated ceremonies are the meeting of Christ and the Virgin Mary on the Tue, and the dramatized Deposition from the Cross late on Good Friday. The pilgrimage season, first half of **Sep**, draws thousands. **8 Dec**, *Nossa Senhora da Conceição*.

Transport Bus The Rodoviária is 1½ km outside town; bus to town centre US$0.40; for 'Basílica', see above. To/from **Belo Horizonte**, 1½ hrs, US$3, 8 times a day. To **São João del Rei**, 2 hrs, US$3.60, tickets are not sold until the bus comes in. Bus to **Ouro Preto**: go via Belo Horizonte or Conselheiro Lafaiete. Whether going from Ouro Preto or Rio to Congonhas do Campo, there is no direct bus; you have to change at **Conselheiro Lafaiete**. Frequent service Conselheiro Lafaiete-Congonhas do Campo, US$1.

São João del Rei

Phone code: 0xx32
Post code: 36300
Colour map 7, grid B5
Population: 78,616

This colonial city is at the foot of the Serra do Lenheiro. A good view of the town and surroundings is from Alto da Boa Vista, where there is a Statue of Christ (Senhor dos Montes). São João del Rei is very lively at weekends. Through the centre of town runs the Corrego do Lenheiro; across it are two fine stone bridges, A Ponte da Cadeia (1798) and A Ponte do Rosário (1800).

There are five 18th century churches in the town, three of which are splendid examples of Brazilian colonial building. **São Francisco de Assis** (1774), Praça Frei Orlando: the façade, with circular towers, the doorway intricately carved and the greenish stone framing the white paint to beautiful effect was designed by Aleijadinho. Inside are two sculptures by Aleijadinho, and others of his school. The six side altars are in wood; restoration has removed the plaster from the altars, revealing fine carving in sucupira wood. ■ *0830-1200 and some afternoons, US$1.*

Basílica de Nossa Senhora do Pilar (the Cathedral, R Getúlio Vargas – formerly R Direita), built 1721, has a 19th century façade which replaced the 18th century original. It has rich altars and a brightly painted ceiling. In the sacristy are portraits of the Evangelists. ■ *Open afternoons.* **Nossa Senhora do Carmo**, Praça Dr Augusto Viegas (Largo do Carmo), very well restored, is all in white and gold. Construction commenced in 1733. ■ *Open afternoons.* Almost opposite São Francisco is the house of **Bárbara Heliodora** which contains the **Museu Municipal Tomé Portes del Rei**, with historical objects and curios, and, downstairs, the tourist office: *Secretaria de Turismo*, T3371 7833, 0900-1700, free map. The **Museu Ferroviário** (railway museum), Av Hermílio Alves 366, T371 8004, (see below for the train to Tiradentes) is well worth exploring. The museum traces the history of railways in general and in Brazil in brief. You can walk along the tracks to the round house, in which are several working engines in superb condition, an engine shed and a steam-operated machine shop, still working. It is here that the engines get up steam before going to couple with the coaches for the run to Tiradentes. On days when the trains are running, you can get a good, close-up view of operations even if not taking the trip; highly recommended. ■ *Tue-Sun 0900-1130, 1300-1700, US$0.50.*

Sleeping & eating

A *Lenheiros Palace*, Av Pres Tancredo Neves 257, T/F3371 8155, www.mgconecta.com.br/lenheiros/index.html A modern hotel with good facilities, parking, *Lenheiros Casa de Chá* tea house, breakfast, no restaurant. **B** *Ponte Real*, Av Eduardo Magalhães 254, T/F3371 7000. Also modern, comfortable, sizeable rooms, good restaurant. **C** *Pousada Casarão*, opposite São Francisco church, in a converted mansion, Ribeiro Bastos 94, T3371 7447, F3371 2866. Firm beds, TV, fridge, swimming pool, games room, delightful. **C** *Aparecida*, Praça Dr Antônio Viegas 13, T3371 2540. Central, by the bus and taxi stop, has a restaurant and *lanchonete*. **D** *do Hespanhol*, R Mcal Deodoro 131, T3371 4677. Also central, price varies according to room. **E** *Brasil*, Av Presidente Tancredo Neves 395, T3371 2804. In an old house full of character and staircases, on the opposite side of the river from the railway station, cheap. Recommended but basic, no breakfast. **E** *Pousada São Benedito*, R Marechal Deodoro 254, T371 7381. Shared rooms only, shared bath. *Quinto do Ouro*, address as *pousada* above, good regional food, reasonable prices; also on Praça Severiano de Resende is *Churrascaria Ramón*, No 52, good. Several restaurants and bars on Av Tancredo Neves.

Festivals

Apr, *Semana Santa*; 15-21 Apr, *Semana da Inconfidência*. May or Jun, *Corpus Christi*. First 2 weeks of Aug, *Nossa Senhora da Boa Morte*, with baroque music (novena barroca). Similarly, 12 Oct, *Nossa Senhora do Pilar*, patron saint of the city. 8 Dec, *founding of the city*. FUNREI, the university (R Padre José Maria Xavier), holds *Inverno Cultural* in Jul.

Transport

Rodoviária is 2 km west of centre of São João

Bus Buses to **Rio**, 5 daily with *Paraibuna* (3 on Sat and Sun), 5 hrs, US$10-12. *Cristo Rei* to **São Paulo**, 8 hrs, 5 a day (also to Santos), and *Translavras*, 4 a day (also to Campinas), US$12.50. **Belo Horizonte**, 3½ hrs, US$6.60. To **Tiradentes** with *Meier*, 8 a day, 7 on Sat, Sun and holidays, US$0.65.

Banks *Bemge*, Av Pres Tancredo Neves 213, has exchange, 1100-1600. **Directory**
Communications Telephone: *Telemig* at Av Pres Tancredo Neves 119, 0700-2200.

Tiradentes

This charming little town, 15 km from São João, with its nine streets and eight | Phone code: 0xx32
churches, is at the foot of the green Serra São José. It is very busy during Holy Week, | Post code: 36325
when there are numerous religious processions. It was founded as São José del Rei | Population: 5,759
on 14 January 1718. After the ousting of the emperor in 1889 the town was renamed
in honour of the martyr of the Inconfidência.

The **Igreja Matriz de Santo Antônio** (1710-36) contains some of the finest gilded | **Sights**
wood carvings in the country. The church has a small but fine organ brought from | *The tourist office is*
Porto in the 1790s. The upper part of the reconstructed façade is said to follow a | *in the Prefeitura,*
design by Aleijadinho. In front of the church are also a cross and a sundial by him. | *R Resende Costa 71*
■ *Daily 0900-1700.* **Santuário da Santíssima Trindade**, on the road which leads
up behind the Igreja Matriz de Santo Antônio, is 18th century, while the room of
miracles associated with the annual Trinity Sunday pilgrimage is modern.

The charming **Nossa Senhora do Rosário** church (1727), on a small square on R
Direita, has fine statuary and ornate gilded altars. ■ *Thu-Mon 1200-1600, US$0.50.*
São João Evangelista is on the Largo do Sol, a lovely open space. It is a simple
church, built by the Irmandade dos Homens Pardos (mulattos). ■ *Thu-Mon
0900-1700.* Beside Igreja São João Evangelista is the **Museu Padre Toledo**, the
house of one of the leaders of the Inconfidência Mineira. It exhibits some good
pieces of furniture. At the junction of R da Câmara and R Direita is the **Sobrado
Ramalho**, said to be the oldest building in Tiradentes. It has been beautifully
restored as a cultural centre. **Nossa Senhora das Mercês** (18th century), Largo das
Mercês, has an interesting painted ceiling and a notable statue of the Virgin (Sunday
0900-1700). The magnificent **Chafariz de São José** (the public fountain, 1749) is
still used for drinking, clothes washing and watering animals. You can follow the
watercourse into the forest of the Serra de São José (monkeys and birds can be seen).

The **train** on the line between São João del Rei and Tiradentes (13 km) has been in
continuous operation since 1881, using the same locomotives and rolling stock,
running on 76 cm gauge track, all lovingly cared for. The maximum speed is 20 km
per hr. ■ *Tickets cost US$13 return interior, US$6.50 return meia. The train runs on
Fri, Sat, Sun and holidays, 1000 and 1415 from São João del Rei, returning from
Tiradentes at 1300 and 1700.*

AL-A *Solar da Ponte*, Praça das Mercês (proprietors John and Anna Maria Parsons), T3355 | **Sleeping**
1255, www.roteirosdecharme/sol.htm Has the atmosphere of a country house, the price
includes breakfast and afternoon tea, only 12 rooms, fresh flowers in rooms, bar, sauna,
lovely gardens, swimming pool, light meals for residents only, for larger meals, the hotel rec-
ommends 5 local restaurants (it is in the Roteiros de Charme group). Recommended.
A *Pousada Três Portas*, R Direita 280A, T3355 1444, F3355 1184. There are more expensive
suites, has sauna, thermal pool, hydromassage, heating. **A** *Pousada Mãe D'Água*, Largo das
Forras 50, T3355 1206, F3355 1221. Including breakfast but not tax, very nice.
B *Pousada Maria Barbosa*, R Antônio Teixeira Carvalho 144, T/F3355 1227,
www.idasbrasil.com.br Near bridge that leads out of town, pool, very pleasant, price
includes breakfast, lunch and evening snack, during the week it is **C** (breakfast only). **B** *Hotel
Ponto do Morro*, Largo das Forras 88, T3355 1342, F3355 1141. With pool, sauna, fridge, TV,
phone, also has 2 chalets, the hotel has a nice entry. There are lots of other *pousadas*.

Quartier Latin, R São Francisco de Paula 46, Praça da Rodoviária. French, cordon bleu chef, | **Eating**
excellent but expensive. *Quinto de Ouro*, R Direita 159. Recommended. *Virados do Largo*,
Largo do Ó. Good food and service. *Estalagem*, R Ministro G Passos 280. *Padre Toledo*, R
Direita 202. *Pasta & Cia*, R Frederico Ozanan 327. Beautiful restaurant with excellent freshly

cooked meals served in glazed tile earthenware. Recommended. *Aluarte*, Largo do Ó 1, is a bar with live music in the evening, nice atmosphere, US$4 cover charge, garden, sells handicrafts. Recommended. There are other restaurants, snack bars and *lanchonetes* in town.

Transport **Bus** Last bus back to São João del Rei is 1815, 2230 on Sun; fares are given above. **Taxi** To São João del Rei costs US$10. Around town there are pony-drawn taxis; ponies can be hired for US$5. For horse-riding treks, contact John Parsons at the *Solar da Ponte*.

The most remote of the colonial cities to the north of the State capital is reached from Belo Horizonte by taking the paved road to Brasília (BR-040). Turn northeast to **Curvelo**, beyond which the road passes through the impressive rocky country of the Serra do Espinhaço.

Diamantina

Phone code: 0xx38
Post code: 39100
Colour map 7, grid A5
Population: 44,259
Altitude: 1,120 m

This centre of a once active diamond industry Diamantina has excellent colonial buildings. Its churches (difficult to get into, except for the modern Cathedral) are not as grand as those of Ouro Preto, but it is possibly the least spoiled of all the colonial mining cities, with carved overhanging roofs and brackets. This very friendly, beautiful town is in the deep interior, amid barren mountains. It is lively at weekends. President Juscelino Kubitschek, the founder of Brasília, was born here. His house, R São Francisco 241, has been converted into a museum. ■ *Tue-Thu 0900-1700, Fri-Sat 0900-1800, Sun 0900-1400*. Local festivals are *Carnival*. 12 September is *O Dia das Serestas*, the Day of the Serenades, for which the town is famous; this is also the anniversary of Kubitschek's birth.

Sights
The office will arrange a free tour of churches with guide who has keys (tip guide)

The oldest church in Diamantina is **Nossa Senhora do Rosário**, Largo Dom Joaquim, built by slaves in 1728. **Nossa Senhora do Carmo**, R do Carmo, dates from 1760-65 and was built for the Carmelite Third Order. It is the richest church in the town, with fine decorations and paintings and a pipe organ, covered in gold leaf, made locally.

São Francisco de Assis, R São Francisco, just off Praça JK, was built between 1766 and the turn of the 19th century. It is notable for its paintings. Other colonial churches are the **Capela Imperial do Amparo** (1758-76), **Nossa Senhora das Mercês** (1778-84) and **Nossa Senhora da Luz** (early 19th century). The **Catedral Metropolitana de Santo Antônio**, on Praça Correia Rabelo, was built in the 1930s in neo-colonial style to replace the original cathedral.

After repeated thefts, the diamonds of the **Museu do Diamante** (Diamond Museum), R Direita 14 (US$1), have been removed to the Banco do Brasil. The museum does house an important collection of the materials used in the diamond industry, plus other items from the 18th and 19th centuries. The **Casa de Chica da Silva** is at Praça Lobo Mesquita 266, ■ *Free*. Chica da Silva was a slave in the house of the father of Padre Rolim (one of the Inconfidentes). She became the mistress of João Fernandes de Oliveira, a diamond contractor. Chica, who died on 15 February 1796, has become a folk-heroine among Brazilian blacks.

Behind the 18th century building which now houses the **Prefeitura Municipal** (originally the diamonds administration building, Praça Conselheiro Matta 11) is the **Mercado Municipal** or **dos Tropeiros** (muleteers), Praça Barão de Guaicuí. The **Casa da Glória**, R da Glória 297, is two houses on either side of the street connected by an enclosed bridge. It contains the Instituto Eschwege de Geologia.

Walk along the **Caminho dos Escravos**, the old paved road built by slaves between the mining area on Rio Jequitinhonha and Diamantina. A guide is essential (ask at the Casa de Cultura – cheap), and beware of snakes and thunderstorms. Along the river bank it is 12 km on a dirt road to **Biribiri**, a pretty village with a well-preserved church and an abandoned textile factory. It also has a few bars and at weekends it is a popular, noisy place. About half-way, there are swimming pools in the river; opposite them, on a cliff face, are animal paintings in red. The age and origin are unknown. The plant life along the river is interesting and there are beautiful mountain views.

Sleeping & eating

C *Dália*, Praça JK (Jota-Ka) 25, T3531 1477. Fairly good. C *Tijuco*, Macau do Melo 211, T/F3531 1022. The best, with good food. **E** pp *JK*, opposite the rodoviária, with limited breakfast, hot showers, simple but spotless. **E** *Pensão Comercial*, Praça M Neves 30. Basic. Wild camping is possible near the waterfall just outside town. A recommended eating place is *Capistrana*, R Campos Carvalho 36, near Cathedral square. *Santo Antônio* in the centre has a good self-service *churrasco* and salad for US$3 during the week.

Entertainment

Serestas (serenades) are sung on Fri and Sat nights. Many young people hang out in the bars in Beco da Mota. *Taverna de Gilmar* is recommended for a good mix of music, although it gets packed quickly. *Cavernas Bar*, Av Sílvio Felício dos Santos, is good for *pagode* on Sat and Sun from late afternoon.

Transport

6 buses a day to **Belo Horizonte**, via Curvelo, with *Pássaro Verde*: 2½ hrs to **Curvelo**, US$3, to **Belo Horizonte**, US$10, 5½ hrs. To Bahia, take the *Gontijo* Belo Horizonte-Salvador bus to **Araçuaí** (**D** *Pousada Tropical*, opposite rodoviária behind the policlínica, T3731 1765, with bath, good) and change there, US$11.50 but you have to check an hr or so beforehand to see if there is space in the bus. The bus passes Diamantina at about 1330-1400, or 0200. It's a very bumpy ride through Couto de Magalhães de Minas and Virgem da Lapa. From Araçuaí take a bus to Itaobim (US$2.65, 2 hrs) then connect to Vitória da Conquista (US$5.50, 4 hrs).

Directory

Useful information Tourist office Departamento de Turismo, is in the Casa de Cultura, Praça Antônio Eulálio 53, 3rd floor, T3531 1636, F3531 1857; pamphlets and a reliable map are available, information about churches, opening times, friendly and helpful. **Voltage** 110 AC.

Serro

Phone code: 0xx38
Post code: 39150
Colour map 7, grid B5
Population: 21,012

From Diamantina, 92 km by paved road and reached by bus from there or from Belo Horizonte, is this unspoiled colonial town on the Rio Jequitinhonha. It has six fine baroque churches, a museum and many beautiful squares. It makes *queijo serrano*, one of Brazil's best cheeses, being in the centre of a prosperous cattle region. The most conspicuous church is **Santa Rita** on a hill in the centre of town, reached by a long line of steps. On the main Praça João Pinheiro, by the bottom of the steps, is **Nossa Senhora do Carmo**, arcaded, with original paintings on the ceiling and in the choir. The town has two large mansions: those of the **Barão de Diamantina**, Praça Presidente Vargas, now in ruins, and of the **Barão do Serro** across the river on R da Fundição, beautifully restored and used as the town hall and Casa de Cultura. ■ *Tue-Sat 1200-1700, Sun 0900-1200.* The **Museu Regional Casa dos Ottoni**, Praça Cristiano Ottoni 72, is an 18th century house now containing furniture and everyday objects from the region.

Southern and eastern Minas

São Tomé das Letras

Phone code: 0xx35
Colour map 7, grid B4
Population: 6,204
The average maximum temperature is 26°C, the minimum is 14°C.
Rainy season: Oct-Mar

A beautiful hilltop town in **southern Minas**, one of the five highest places in Brazil, São Tomé has attracted many new age visitors and its hotels are graded in UFOs instead of stars. It is said to be a good vantage point for seeing UFOs, which draw crowds at weekends. Nearby are caves with inscriptions, which some say are extraterrestrial in orgin. It is believed that there are many places with special energies. Behind the town are rocky outcrops on which are the Pyramid House, the Cruzeiro (Cross, 1,430 m, with good 360° views), the Pedra da Bruxa and paths for walking or, in some parts, scrambling. A quarry town since the beginning of the 20th century, there is evidence of the industry everywhere you look.

The bus stops at the main Praça, on which is the frescoed 18th-century **Igreja Matriz** beside the fenced cave in which are the faded red rock paintings ('letras') of the town's name. A second church, the **Igreja das Pedras** (Nossa Senhora do Rosário – 18th century) is on a Praça to the left as you enter town (R Ernestina Maria

Brazil

de Jesus Peixoto). It is constructed in the same style as many of the charming old-style buildings, with slabs of the local stone laid on top of each other without mortar. The post office and *Bemge Bank* are in the group of buildings at the top right of the Praça, facing the Gruta São Tomé. Tourist office R José Cristiano Alves 4.

Tours In the surrounding hills are many caves, waterfalls and rapids. Some of these places make a good hike from the town, but you can also visit several in a day on an organized tour. T3237 1283 or enquire at *Néctar* shop on R José Cristiano Alves. Tours run on weekends and holidays from the Praça at 1000 and 1400 to waterfalls, caves, etc, T3237 1353 and ask for Jaime or Iraci. The Carimbado cave is especially rich in myths and legends. Shangri-lá, which is a beautiful spot, is also called the Vale do Maytréia. There are three daily buses (two on Sunday) to São Tomé from Tres Corações, the birthplace of Pelé, the legendary football star (to whom there is a statue in Praça Col José Martins), US$1.65, 1½ hours. The first 30 mins is on a paved road. Tres Corações has hotels and regular buses to Belo Horizonte, US$10, 5½ hrs, and São Paulo, US$8.

Note that streets are hard to follow because their names seem to change almost from one block to the next; numbering is also chaotic

Sleeping There are lots of *pousadas* and rooms to let all over town: **C** *Pousada Arco-Iris*, R João Batista Neves 19, T/F3237 1212. Rooms and chalets, sauna, swimming pool. **D** *dos Sonhos II* (do Gê), Trav Nhá Chica 8, T3237 1235. Very nice, restaurant, swimming pool, sauna. Recommended. **E** *Hospedaria dos Sonhos I*, R Gabriel Luiz Alves. With bath, restaurant, shop, groups accommodated. On the main Praça is the shop of the *Fundação Harmonia*, whose headquarters are downhill, on the road to Sobradinho (4 km). The community emphasizes several disciplines for a healthy lifestyle, for mind and body, 'new age', workshops, massage, excursions, vegetarian food, clean accommodation (**D** pp). Address Estrada para Sobradinho s/n, Bairro do Canta Galo, São Tomé das Letras, CEP 37418-000, T3237 1280. There are many restaurants and bars.

Parque Nacional Caparaó

The park, surrounded by coffee farms, features rare Atlantic rainforest in its lower altitudes and Brazilian alpine on top

In this park in **eastern Minas** are the Pico da Bandeira (2,890 m), Pico do Cruzeiro (2,861 m) and the Pico do Cristal (2,798 m). From the park entrance (where a small fee has to be paid) it is 6 km on a good unpaved road to the car park at the base of the waterfall. From the hotel (see below) jeeps (US$20 per jeep) run to the car park at 1,970 m (2½ hours' walk), then it's a three to four hour walk to the summit of the Pico da Bandeira, marked by yellow arrows; plenty of camping possibilities, the highest being at Terreirão (2,370 m). This is good walking country. It is best to visit during the dry season (April-October). It can be quite crowded in July and during Carnival. ■ *Contact R Vale Verde s/n, Alto do Caparaó, CEO 36836-000, T0xx32-3747 2555.*

Sleeping **B** *Caparaó Parque*, T(PS-101)741 2559, 2 km from the park entrance, 15 mins' walk from the town of Alto Caparaó, nice. Ask where **camping** is permitte. In **Manhumirim** **D** *São Luiz*, good value, but *Cids Bar*, next door, Travessa 16 do Março, has better food.

Transport Parque Nacional Caparaó is 49 km by paved road from Manhuaçu (about 190 km south of Governador Valadares) on the Belo Horizonte-Vitória road (BR-262). There are buses from Belo Horizonte (twice daily with *Pássaro Verde*), Ouro Preto or Vitória to **Manhumirim** (*Population*: 20,025), 15 km south of Manhuaçu. From Manhumirim, take a bus direct to Alto Caparaó, 8 a day, US$1. By car from the BR-262, go through Manhumirim, Alto Jaqutibá and Alto Caparaó village, then 1 km further to the *Hotel Caparaó Parque*.

Governor Valadares

Phone code: 0xx33
Post code: 35100
Colour map 7, grid B5
Population: 247,131
Altitude: 170 m
324 km from Belo Horizonte

A modern planned city, Governador Valadares is a good place to break the Belo Horizonte-Salvador journey. It is a centre of gemstone mines and lapidation, as well as for the cut-crystal animals one finds in tourist shops all around Brazil. It is also one of the world's top cross-country paragliding/hang-gliding sites; hitch a ride up to the launch site at 1000, but take a blue Rio Doce bus from the road near the landing site back to town. Several **A-B** hotels and many cheap hotels near the bus station. *JB* restaurant, R Israel Pinheiro 1970. Recommended. On same street, *Dom de Minas*, No 2309, *churrascaria*, pay by weight. ■ *The airport is on the BR-381, 6 km* *from the city centre with flights to Belo Horizonte and Ipatinga. Bus: 5½ hrs from Belo Horizonte with* Gontijo, *US$11.50, US$21 leito.*

Teófilo Otoni, 138 km from Governador Valadares, is a popular buying spot for dealers of crystals and gemstones, with the best prices in the state. **C** *Pousada Tio Miro*, R Dr Manoel Esteves 389, T3521 4343, relaxed atmosphere. Recommended. ■ *Buses from Belo Horizonte with* Gontijo, *US$15.50, leito US$29; to Porto Seguro via Nanuque (can break Belo Horizonte-Salvador journey here.* **D** Hotel Minas, *at the rodoviária, adequate, and others nearby).*

Phone code: 0xx33
Post code: 39800
Colour map 7, grid A6
Population: 129,424
Altitude: 335 m

Espírito Santo

The coastal state of Espírito Santo is where mineiros head to for their seaside holidays. Five bridges connect the island on which Vitória stands with the mainland. The state capital is beautifully set, its entrance second only to Rio's, its beaches quite as attractive, but smaller, and the climate is less humid. Port installations at Vitória and nearby Ponta do Tubarão have led to some beach and air pollution at places nearby. It is largely a modern city: The upper, older part of town, reached by steep streets and steps, is much less hectic than the lower harbour area which suffers dreadful traffic problems.

Vitória &
around
Phone code: 0xx27
Post code: 29000
Colour map 7, grid B6
Population: 292,304

On Av República is the huge **Parque Moscoso**, an oasis of quiet, with a lake and playground. Colonial buildings still to be seen in the upper city are the **Capela de Santa Luzia**, R José Marcelino (1551), now an art gallery; the church of **São Gonçalo**, R Francisco Araújo (1766) and the ruins of the **Convento São Francisco** (1591). In the **Palácio do Governo**, or **Anchieta**, Praça João Climaco (upper city) is the tomb of Padre Anchieta, one of the founders of São Paulo. The **Teatro Carlos Gomes**, on Praça Costa Pereira, often presents plays, also jazz and folk festivals. **Vila Velha**, reached by a bridge across the bay, has an excellent beach. Although built up and noisy at times, it is safer than Vitória: take a bus from Vitória marked Vilha Velha. See the mostly ruined, fortified monastery of **Nossa Senhora da Penha** (1558), on a high hill above Vila Velha; the views are superb. There is also a pleasant ferry service to Vila Velha. Urban beaches such as **Camburi** can be affected by pollution, but it is quite pleasant, with a fair surf. 10 km south of Vila Velha is **Barra do Jucu**, which has bigger waves and the **Reserva de Jacarenema**, which preserves coastal ecosystems.

Santa Leopoldina or **Domingos Martins**, both around 45 km from Vitória, are less than an hour by bus (two companies run to the former, approximately every three hours). Both villages preserve the architecture and customs of the first German and Swiss settlers who arrived in the 1840s. Domingos Martins (also known as Campinho) has a Casa de Cultura with some items of German settlement. Santa Leopoldina has an interesting museum covering the settlers' first years in the area. ■ *Tue-Sun 0900-1100, 1300-1800.* **Santa Teresa** is a charming hill town 2½ hours, 90 km by bus from Vitória (US$6 a beautiful journey). There is a hummingbird sanctuary at the **Museu Mello Leitâo**, Av José Ruschi 4, which is a library including the works of the hummingbird and orchid scientist, Augusto Ruschi. Hummingbird feeders are hung outside the library. ■ *0800-1200, 1300-1700, T259 1182.*

Sleeping C *Avenida*, Av Florentino Avidos 350, T3223 4317. With breakfast. Recommended. **D** *Europa*, 7 de Setembro, corner Praça Costa Pereira. Noisy but cheap, good value restaurant (nearby is a good value vegetarian restaurant and a money changer, ask at hotel). Adequate hotels can be found opposite the rodoviária. Other hotels are located in beach areas, Camburi to the north, Vila Velha to the south, both 15 mins from city centre. **D** *Itaparica Praia*, R Itapemirim 30, Coqueiral de Itaparica, Vila Velha, T3329 7385. Quiet, safe and good. **Youth hostel** *Jardim da Penha*, R Hugo Viola 135, T3324 0738, F3325 6010, take 'Universitário' bus, get off at first University stop. In Vila Velha, *Forte Príncipe* , R Aracruz 169, Coqueiral de Itaparica, 8 km from Vitória, T3339 1605, www.forteprincipe.com.br Convenient for services, beach and buses.

Brazil

Eurico Salles airport at Goiaberas, 11 km from city. The rodoviária is a 15-min walk west of the centre

Transport Trains Daily passenger service to **Belo Horizonte**, 14 hrs, US$17.50 *executivo* (very comfortable), US$11.50 1st class, US$7.80 2nd. **Bus** Rio, 8 hrs, US$15 (*leito* 25). **Belo Horizonte**, US$14.50 (*leito* 29). São Paulo, US$20, 16 hrs. **Salvador**, 18 hrs, US$27; **Porto Seguro** direct 11 hrs with lots of stops, US$18 (also *leito* service); alternatively, take a bus to Eunápolis, then change to buses which run every hr.

Directory Tourist offices Setur, Av Desembargador Santos Neves 1267, Prara do Canto, T3382 6900, myrian@setur.es.gov.br In Vila Velha, T3289 0202.

Guarapari
Colour map 7, grid B6
Population: 88,400

South of Vitória (54 km) is Guarapari, whose beaches are the closest to Minas Gerais, so they get very crowded at holiday times. The beaches also attract many people seeking cures for rheumatism, neuritis and other complaints, from the radioactive monazitic sands. Information about the sands can be found at *Setuc*, in the Casa de Cultura, Praça Jerônimo Monteiro, T3261 3058, and at the Antiga Matriz church on the hill in the town centre, built in 1585.

A little further south (20 km) is the fishing village of **Ubu**, then, 8 km down the coast, **Anchieta**. Near here are Praia de Castelhanos (5 km east, on a peninsula) and **Iriri**, a small village with two beaches, Santa Helena and Inhaúma. There is accommodation in these places. The next spot down the coast, 5 km, is **Piúma**, a calm, little-visited place, renowned for its craftwork in shells. About 3 km north of the village is Pau Grande beach, where you can surf. The resort town of **Marataízes**, with good beaches, hotels and camping, is 30 km south of Piúma. It is just north of the Rio state border.

Turtle beaches

The **Reserva Biológica Comboios**, 104 km north of Vitória via Santa Cruz, is designed to protect the marine turtles which frequent this coast (for information, contact *Ibama* in Vitória, Av Marechal Mascarenhas 2487, CP 762, CEP 29000, T3324 1811, or T0xx27-984 3788, camboios@tamar.org.br). **Regência**, at the mouth of the Rio Doce, 65 km north of Santa Cruz, is part of the reserve and has a regional base for *Tamar*, the national marine turtle protection project.

Linhares, 143 km north of Vitória on the Rio Doce, has good hotels (**E** *Modenezi*, opposite bus terminal, with bath) and restaurants. It is a convenient starting place for the turtle beaches. Besides those at the mouth of the Rio Doce, there is another *Tamar* site at **Ipiranga**, 40 km east of Linhares by an unmade road.■ *For information, also contact* Tamar *at Caixa Postal 105, CEP 29900-970, Linhares, ES.*

Conceição da Barra
Colour map 7, grid B6
Population: 26,494
261 km N of Vitória

The most attractive beaches in the state are around this town. Corpus Christi (early June) is celebrated with an evening procession for which the road is decorated with coloured wood chips. Viewed from its small port, the sunsets are always spectacular. Conceição da Barra has pleasant beach hotels, also **D** *Caravelas*, Avenue Dr Mário Vello Silvares 83, T762 1188, one block from the beach, basic, shared bathroom, light breakfast. Recommended. **E** *Pousada Pirámide*, next to rodoviária, T762 1970, good value, 100 m from beach. *Camping Clube do Brasil* site with full facilities, Rodovia Adolfo Serra, Km 16, T762 1346.

Itaúnas, 27 km north by road, or 14 km up the coast, has been swamped by sand dunes, 30 m high. From time to time, winds shift the sand dunes enough to reveal the buried church tower. Itaúnas has been moved to the opposite river bank. The coast here, too, is a protected turtle breeding ground (*Tamar*, Caixa Postal 53, Conceição da Barra, T0xx27-762 1124). There are a few *pousadas* and a small campsite at Itaúnas. At Guaxindiba, 3 km north, is **A** *Praia da Barra*, Av Atlântica 350, T0xx27-762 1100; and others. ■ *Bus from the bakery in Conceição da Barra at 0700, returns 1700.*

Southern Brazil: Paraná

Brasília

Paraná has one of the premier tourist sites in South America, the Iguaçu Falls. The state has a short coastline and its main port, Paranaguá, is connected with the capital, Curitiba, by one of the best railways in South America. The culture of Paraná has been heavily influenced by its large immigrant communities including Japan, Poland, Italy, Syria and the Ukraine.

Population: 9.5 million

Curitiba

One of the three cleanest cities in Latin America, the capital of Paraná state has extensive open spaces and some exceptionally attractive modern architecture. The commercial centre is the busy R 15 de Novembro, part of which is a pedestrian area called **Rua das Flores**. The **Boca Maldita** is a particularly lively part where local artists exhibit. On Praça Tiradentes is the **Cathedral**, R Barão do Serro Azul 31, T222 1131, built in neo-gothic style and inaugurated in 1893 (restored in 1993). Behind the cathedral, near Largo da Ordem, is a pedestrian area with a flower clock and old buildings, very beautiful in the evening when the old lamps are lit – nightlife is concentrated here. The oldest church in Curitiba is the **Igreja de Ordem Terceira da São Francisco das Chagas**, built in 1737 in Largo da Ordem. Its most recent renovation was in 1978-80. In its annex is the **Museu de Arte Sacra** (T223 7545). The **Igreja de Nossa Senhora do Rosário de São Benedito** was built in the Praça Garibáldi in 1737 by slaves and was the Igreja dos Pretos de São Benedito. It was demolished in 1931 and a new church was inaugurated in 1946. A mass for tourists, Missa do Turista, is held on Sunday at 0800.

Phone code: 0xx41
Post code: 80000
Colour map 7, grid C2
Population: 1,587,315
Altitude: 908 m

Museu Paranaense, Praça Generoso Marques, includes documents, manuscripts, ethnological and historical material, stamps, works of art, photographs and archaeological pieces. ■ *Tue-Fri 1000-1800, other days 1300-1800, closed first Mon of each month, T323 1411*. **Museu de Arte Contemporânea**, R Desembargador Westphalen 16, Praça Zacarias, displays Brazilian contemporary art in its many forms, with an emphasis on artists from Paraná. ■ *Tue-Fri 0900-1900, Sat-Sun 1400-1900, T222 5172*. **Museu de Arte do Paraná**, in the Palácio São Francisco, exhibits the work of many of Paraná's artists. ■ *T2343172*. **Museu de História Natural**, R Benedito Conceição 407, natural history with lots of zoology and scientific collections, also details on endangered species in the State. ■ *T366 3133*.

There is a small fish fair on Saturday mornings at **Praça Generosa Marques**, and an art market in **Praça Garibáldi** on Sunday mornings. The **Centro Cívico** is at the end of Av Dr Cândido de Abreu, 2 km from the centre: a monumental group of buildings dominated by the **Palácio Iguaçu**, headquarters of the state and municipal governments. In a patio behind it is a relief map to scale of Paraná. The **Bosque de João Paulo II** behind the Civic Centre on R Mateus Leme, was created in December 1980 after the Pope's visit to Curitiba. It also contains the **Memorial da Imigração Polonesa no Paraná** (Polish immigrants memorial). All that remains of the old **Palácio Avenida**, Travessa Oliveira Belo 11, is the façade, which was retained during remodelling works in 1991. Nowadays it has offices, an auditorium for 250 people and cultural activities. The **Solar do Barão**, built in 1880-83, is used for concerts in the auditorium and exhibitions, R Presidente Carlos Cavalcanti 53. ☆ *T322 1525*.

A fine example of the use of steel and glass is **Rua 24 Horas**, where the whole street is protected by an arched roof. The street's shops, bars and restaurants never close. The **Passeio Público**, in the heart of the city (closed Monday), inaugurated in 1886. It has three lakes, each with an island, and playground. About 4 km east of the rodoferroviário, the **Jardim Botânico Fanchette Rischbieter** has a fine glass house, inspired by Crystal Palace in London. The gardens are in the French style and there is also a **Museu Botánico**, R Ostoja Roguski (Primeira Perimetral dos Bairros), T321 8646, 362 1800 (museum). Take the orange Expreso buses from Praça Rui Barbosa.

Brazil

Sleeping

■ on map
There are some
incredibly good value
hotels in the city in the
C and B categories

L *Bourbon & Tower*, Cândido Lopes 102, T322 4001, www.bourbon.com.br Most luxurious in centre. **A** *Lancaster*, R Voluntários da Pátria 91, T/F322 8953. Wood-panelled, very comfortable, caters to business clients as well as tourists. **B** *Costa Brava Palace*, R Francisco Torres 386, T262 7172. Good restaurant. Recommended. **B** *Curitiba Palace*, R Ermelino de Leão 45, T322 8081, curitibapalace@cwb.palm.com.br Central, polished and cosy with vast rooms, 24-hr restaurant, pool, good value. **B** *Del Rey*, R Ermelino de Leão 18, T/F322 3242. On Rua das Flores, upmarket yet relaxed, large rooms, good restaurant, fantastic value. Recommended. **C** *King's*, Av Silva Jardim 264, T322 8444. Good apartment hotel, secure. Highly recommended. **C** *O'Hara*, R 15 de Novembro 770, T232 6044. Good location, fan, excellent breakfast, parking. **C** *Tourist Universo*, Praça Gen Osório 63, T322 0099, F223 5420. On one of the city's most attractive squares, very smart for price, with sauna and pool, intimate and excellent value. Recommended. **D** *Cervantes*, R Alfredo Bufrem 66, T222 9593. Central, small, but cosy. **D** *Estação Palace*, R Des Westphalen 126, T322 9840, F324 5307. Excellent for price, 24-hr room service and internet. Recommended. **E** pp *Inca*, R João Negrão 370, T223 8563. Breakfast OK, safe, good. **E** pp *Nova Lisboa*, Av 7 de Setembro 1948, T264 1944. With breakfast, cheaper without breakfast. Recommended. **F** pp *Maia*, Av Presidente Afonso Camargo 360 block, opposite Rodoferroviária, T264 1684. Quiet, with breakfast, cheapest. **F** *Pensão PP*, Rua Gen Carneiro 657, T263 1169. Basic, no breakfast. Recommended. **F** Pousada Flor do Campo, R Amintas de Barros 483/503, T262 6725. Shared bath, TV, comfortable, breakfast.

Youth hostels **E** pp *AJ de Curitiba*, Av Padre Agostinho 645, Mercês, Curitiba PR, T233 2746, ajcwb@uol.com.br IYHA. **F** *Casa do Estudante Luterano Universitario*, R Pr Carlos Cavalcanti 239, T324 3313. Good. This hostel is fully booked Jan and the week before Christmas. **Associação Paranaense de Albergues de Juventude**, Av Padre Agostinho 645, Curitiba PR, CEP 80.410, T233 2746. **Camping** Camping Clube do Brasil, 16 km, BR-116, Km 84.5, direction São Paulo, T358 6634.

Curitiba

■ Sleeping	4 Curitiba Palace	8 King's	12 O'Hara	● Eating
1 Bourbon & Tower	5 Del Rey	9 Lancaster	13 Pousada Flor	1 Badida
2 Cervantes	6 Estação Palace	10 Maia	do Campo	2 Churrascão
3 Costa Brava Palace	7 Inca	11 Nova Lisboa	14 Tourist Universo	Colónial

Brazil

Mid-range *Baviera*, Alameda Augusto Stellfield, corner with Al Dr Murici. Intimate and atmospheric in style of beer cellar, cantina, pizzeria and delivery service established over 30 years, open 1800-2300. *Jangil*, Praça Osório 45, upper floor. Quirky place at top of stairwell, with balcony overlooking lovely main praça. Go for a drink, tapas or dinner (pizza, pasta, fish and churasco) served by fatherly figures in white dinner jackets. *Saccy*, R São Franscisco 350, corner with Mateus Leme 12. Pizza, tapas and lively bar with live music. *Salmão* , R Emiliano Perneta 924. In historic house, delicious fish and pizza, often special promotions, live music every night, open till 0100. Short taxi ride from centre. **Churrascarias** all recommended: *Badida*, Av Batel 1486, Batel, T243 0473. *Churrascão Colônia*, Av Manoel Ribas 3250, Vista Alegre, T335 8686. *Devon's* , R Lysimaco Ferreira da Costa 436, Centro Cívico, T254 7073. *Scavollo*, R Emiliano Perneta 924, Batel, T225 2244. Recommended for pizza. Local and Italian food and local red wine in nearby Santa Felicidade northeast of the centre, for example *Madalosso*, Av Manoel Ribas 5875, T372 2121. Enormous Italian *rodizio*, allegedly the 2nd largest in the world, cheap. Recommended. *Dom Antônio*, same street No 6121, T273 3131. Excellent; and others. *Cantina do Eisbein*, Av dos Estados 863, Água Verde. Owner Egon is friendly, duck specialities highly recommended. Closed Mon. *Oriente Arabe*, R Ebano Pereira 26 (1st floor), T223 2708. Excellent, huge Arab lunch. **Cheap** *Kisco*, 7 de Setembro near Tibagi. Good, huge *prato do dia*, friendly. Cheap food also near the old railway station and good meals in the bus station. Close to the Rodoferroviária is the market, where there are a couple of *lanchonetes*. Hot sweet wine sold on the streets in winter keeps out the cold. For addicts, there are *McDonald's*, and takeaway Chinese and pizzas. *Happy Rango*, Av Visconde de Nacar 1350, near R 24 horas. Brightly lit, basic corner joint selling fast food and pizzas, open 24 hrs. *Mister Sheik*, Av Vicente Machado 534. Arabic fast food in pitta with salad, popular for deliveries. Recommended. Cheap food near old railway station and a good meal in the bus station. Close to the Rodoferroviária is the market, where there are a couple of *lanchonetes*. Hot sweet wine sold on the streets in winter helps keep out the cold. Restaurants offering buffets are usually good value at around US$12.

Eating
● *on map*

Vegetarian Most closed at night. *Vherde Jante*, R Pres Faria 481, Centro, T225 1627. Very good (open in evening). *Super Vegetariano*, R Presidente Faria 121, T223 6277, Cruz Machado 217, R Dr Murici 315, lunch and dinner Mon-Fri, very good and cheap buffet. *Greenland*, R 15 de Novembro 540, T232 3813. Recommended. *Panini*, R da Glória 307. Recommended for buffet lunches (US$4 with meat; US$2.50 vegetarian) in a charming house.

A cluster of bars at the Largo da Ordem have tables and chairs on the pavement, music, and bar food: *Fire Fox*, Av Jaime Reis 46, flanked by *Tuba's* and *The Farm*.

Bars

There are several modern **theatres**: the *Teatro Guaíra*, R 15 de Novembro, T322 2628, for plays and revues (also has free events – get tickets early in the day), the *Teatro Paiol* in the old arsenal, R Col Zacarias, T322 1525, the *Ópera de Arame* opera house on R João Gava, T252 9637, and others. A theatre festival takes place in Mar. There are **cinemas** in several shopping centres, and other places showing international films. Tickets are usually US$4-5 Mon-Thu,

Entertainment

Brazil

3 Devon's
4 Dom Antônio
5 Happy Rango
6 Jangil
7 Madalosso
8 Mister Sheik
9 Orient Arabe
10 Saccy
11 Scavollo
● Bars & clubs
12 Fire Fox

and US$6-8 at weekends. Best to look in the newspaper for music and what's on in the bars, clubs and theatres; *Gazeta do Povo* has a what's on section called *Caderno G*.

Shopping For souvenirs and handicrafts, try *Lojas Leve Curitiba*, at several locations, R 24 Horas, Afonso Pena airport, Ópera de Arame, Jardim Botánico, Memorial de Curitiba. *Lojas de Artesanato*, Casa de Artesanato Centro, R Mateus Leme 22, T352 4021. *Lojas de Artesanato 'Feito Aquí'*, Dr Muricy 950, International Airport and Shopping Mueller. *Feira de Arte e Artesanato*, Praça Garibáldi, Sun 0900-1400. Curitiba is a good place to buy clothes and shoes. *H Stern* jewellers at Mueller Shopping Centre. **Bookshops** *Livraria Saraiva*, in Shopping Crystal, has a large selection of books and music as well as a cyber café. Also *Ginghone* and *Curitiba* on Rua 15 and at Shoppings Curitiba and Crystal. *Figaro*, R Lamenha Lins 62, buys and sells second hand paperbacks in English and German. *Trovutare*, R de São Francisco 48. Good choice of books in English, Dutch, Spanish and French.

Tour operators *BMP Turismo*, R Brigadeiro Franco, 1845, T322 8566, American Express representative, emergency cash available with Amex. *Rostel*, R 13 de Maio 894, Alto São Francisco, T322 2610, www.rostelturismo.com.br Very helpful. In same building is *Scubasul*, T232 0198, www.scubasul.com.br Advice on diving, courses arranged, reasonable prices.

Transport **Local** There are several route types on the integrated transport system and you are advised to pick up a map with details. **Express** are red and connect the transfer terminals to the city centre, pre-paid access, they use the silver 'tubo' bus stops; **Feeder** orange conventional buses connect the terminals to the surrounding neighbourhoods; **Interdistrict** green buses run on circular routes connecting transfer terminals and city districts without passing through the centre; **Direct or speedy** silver grey buses use the 'tubo' stations to link the main districts and connect the surrounding municipalities with Curitiba; **Conventional** yellow buses operate on the normal road network between the surrounding municipalities, the Integration Terminals and the city centre; **City circular** white mini buses, *Linha Turismo,* circle the major transport terminals and points of interest in the traditional city centre area. US$3.50 (multi-ticket booklets available), every 30 mins from 0900-1700, except on Mon. First leaves from R das Flores, narrow street in front of McDonalds. Three stops allowed.

Long distance **Air**: Afonso Pena (21 km away) for international and national flights, T381 1515. Silver Ligeirinho bus 'Aeroporto' leaves from 'tubo' stop near Circulo Militar to airport, stopping at rodoferroviária every 30 mins, US$0.60, 50 mins.
Bus: Short-distance bus services within the metropolitan region (up to 40 km) begin at Terminal Guadalupe at R João Negrão s/n, T321 8611. The Terminal Rodoviário/Estação Rodoferroviária is on Av Afonso Camargo s/n, T320 3000, for other cities in Paraná and other states. Restaurants, banks, bookshops, shops, phones, post office, pharmacy, tourist agency, tourist office and public services are all here. Frequent buses to **São Paulo** (6 hrs, US$10-12.50) and **Rio** (12 hrs, US$25, *leito* US$42). To **Foz do Iguaçu**, 10 a day, 10 hrs, US$15. **Porto Alegre**, 10 hrs, US$17.50. **Florianópolis**, US$12, 4½ hrs; **Blumenau** 4 hrs, US$6.50, 3 daily with *Penha/Catarinense*. Good service to most destinations in Brazil. *Pluma* bus to **Buenos Aires** (change buses at Foz de Iguaçu) and to **Asunción**. *TTL* runs to **Montevideo**, 26 hrs, 0340 departure (*semi-cama*).
Train: Rodoferroviária, Av Afonso Camargo s/n, T323 4007 (Serra Verde Express). Passenger trains to Paranaguá, see below.

Directory **Airline offices** *Lufthansa*, Barão do Cerro Azul 325, T322 8227. *TAM*, Ermelino de Leão 75, 1st floor,
Visa extensions: T234 1234/323 5201. *Varig*, T0800-997000. *Vasp*, R 15 de Novembro 537, T221 7422/0800-998227.
Federal police, **Banks** *Bradesco*, R 15 de Novembro 155, Visa ATM. Plus or Cirrus associated credit cards can cash
Dr Muricy 814, money at *Citibank*, R Marechal Deodoro 711 or at Buenos Aires 305 near Shopping Curitiba. *Sigla*
1000-1600 *Turismo*, R Marechal Deodoro 427, Centro, popular for exchange. *Diplomata*, R Presidente Faria 145 in the arcade. *Câmbio*, 15 de Novembro 467, Edif Carvalho Lorreiro. **Communications Internet**: at *Livraria Saraiva* in Shopping Crystal, *Livraria Curitiba*, R das Flores (US$2 per hr), and Estação Plaza Shopping (four blocks from Rodoferroviária) after 1100. Also in R 24 Horas at *Digitando o Futuro*, free

access but you need to book in advance T350 6366, and *Internet 24 Horas*, in the bookshop, open 24 hrs, US$3 per hr. *Monkey*, Av Vicente Machado 534, corner with R Brigadeiro. Cool, modern with lots of computers and internet games, open daily till 2400. **Post Office:** main post office is at Mal Deodoro 298; post offices also at R 15 de Novembro and R Pres Faria. *UPS*, T2626180. **Telephone:** *Tele Centro-Sul* information, T102. *Embratel*, Galeria Minerva, R 15 de Novembro. **Cultural centres** Sociedade **Brasileira de Cultura Inglesa** (British Council), R Gen Carneiro 679 (Caixa Postal 505). **Instituto Goethe**, R Schaffenberg, near Military Museum, Mon-Thu 1500-1900, Library, Mon-Tue till 2130. **Embassies and consulates** Austria, R Cândido Hartmann 570, Ed Champagnat, 28th floor, T336 1166, Mon-Fri 1000-1300. **Britain**, R Pres Faria 51, 2nd floor, T322 1202, F322 3537, consulado.britanico@mais.sul.con.br Mon-Fri 0830-1200, 1400-1730. **Denmark**, R Prof Francisco Ribeiro 683, Caixa Postal 321, T843 2211, F843 1443. **Germany**, R Emiliano Perneta 297, 2nd floor, T222 6920, Mon-Fri 0800-1200. **Netherlands**, Av Candido de Abreu 469, conj 1606, T254 7846, consul Tony Bruinjé, open 1400-1700, except emergencies. **Uruguay**, R Voluntários da Pátria 475, 18th floor. **Medical services** Emergency: T190 for Police and T193 for ambulance or fire. The *Cajuru Hospital* is at Av São José 300, T362 1100, and the *Evangélico* is at Al Augusto Stellfeld 1908, T322 4141, both of which deal with emergencies. **Tourist offices**: Secretaria de Turismo, R da Glória 362, 3rd floor, T352 8000 (free map, good information, English spoken). Kiosk in R 24 Horas (0800-2400, 2200 at weekends). **Paranatur**, R Deputado Mário de Barros 1290, 3rd floor, Centro Cívico, Edif Caetano Munhoz da Rocha, T254 7273/6933, F254 6109; www.pr.gov.br/turismo **Disque Turismo** T1516 (for the state), T352 8000 (for the city); there are also booths at the airport (T381 1153) and Rodoferroviária (0700-1300). *Guía Turística de Curitiba e Paraná*, annual, US$4, on sale at all kiosks; free weekly leaflet, *Bom Programa*, available in shops, cinemas, paper stands. **Voltage** 110 V, 60 cycles.

Brazil

This route can be done by paved road or rail to Paranaguá. The railway journey is the most spectacular in Brazil. There are numerous tunnels with sudden views of deep gorges and high peaks and waterfalls as the train rumbles over dizzy bridges and viaducts. Near Banhado station (Km 66) is the waterfall of Véu da Noiva; from the station at Km 59, the mountain range of **Marumbi** can be reached, see below.

Curitiba to Paranaguá

There are 2 trains running on the line from Curitiba to Paranaguá: the **Litorina**, a modern a/c railcar with on-board service with bilingual staff, which stops at the viewpoint at the Santuário da Nossa Senhora do Cadeado and Morretes; hand luggage only; tickets can be bought 2 days in advance; departs Sat-Sun and holidays 0900, returns 1430, US$25 one way tourist class, 3½ hours (advanced booking is very bureaucratic, allow 2 hours). Also the **Trem Classe Convencional**, which stops at Marumbi and Morretes, buy tickets 2 days in advance, departs Tue-Sun 0800, returns 1500, *turístico*, US$12, 4 hours. The train also leaves on Mon from Jan until Carnival. Schedules change frequently; check times in advance. For information and reservations, *Serra Verde Express*, T323 4007, tickets sold at the Rodoferroviária, Portão 8, Curitiba, open Mon-Sat 0800-1800, Sun 0700-1000. Sit on the left-hand side on journey from Curitiba. On cloudy days there's little to see on the higher parts. The train is usually crowded on Sat and Sun. *Serra Verde Express* also gives information about trips by car on the Estrada de Graciosa.

Return by bus (see below), if you do not want to stay 4½ hrs in Paranaguá

Marumbi Park is one of the largest remaining preserved Atlantic rainforests in Brazil and is a UNESCO World Heritage site and Biosphere Reserve. The forest in the 2,343 ha park is covered in banana trees, palmito and orchids. There are rivers and waterfalls and among the fauna are monkeys, snakes and toucans. A climbing trail reaches 625 m to Rochedinho (2 hours). Hands need to be free to grasp trees, especially during the rainy season (December-March), when trails are muddy. The last 5 minutes of the trail is a dangerous walk along a narrow rock trail. ■ *At the park entrance, notify administration of your arrival and departure. There is a small museum, video, left luggage and the base for a search and rescue unit at weekends. Volunteer guides are available at weekends. Call Marumbi T432 2072. In Curitiba ask for Harvey T262 6488. Wooden houses can be rented for US$55 a night. Arrange with Harvey; take torch. Camping is free. To get there take the Paranaguá train from Curitiba at 0800, arriving Marumbi at 1000. Return at 1800 to Curitiba. If continuing*

Parque Nacional Marumbi

*the next day to Paranaguá your Curitiba-Marumbi ticket is valid for the onward jour-
ney. NB Inform conductor you want to stop at Marumbi and notify him of your return
time as the train does not stop unless there are passengers.*

You can also visit **Antonina** (a port, not on the main route) and **Morretes** (on the
main route), two sleepy colonial towns which can be reached by bus on the old
Graciosa road, which is almost as scenic as the railway. In Morretes, try *barreado*, beef
cooked for 24 hours, especially good in the two restaurants on the river bank, highly
recommended. ■ *Buses from Paranaguá to Antonina stop en route at Morretes, 6 a day
(US$1.50). 12 buses daily Morretes-Curitiba US$2; 11 buses a day Curitiba-Antonina.
No exchange faciilties at all in Morretes.*

About 14 km north of Morretes is the beautiful village of **São João de Graciosa**, 2
km beyond which is a flower reserve. The Graciosa road traverses the **Marumbi**
range for 12 km, with six rest stops with fire grills, shelters and camping. You can
also hike the original trail which follows the road and passes the rest-stops. Take
food, water and plenty of insect repellent. (See above.)

Paranaguá

Phone code: 0xx41
Post code: 83200
Colour map 7, grid B3
Population: 127,339
268 km S of Santos

Chief port of the state of Paraná and one of the main coffee-exporting ports,
Paranaguá was founded in 1585. It is on a lagoon 29 km from the open sea and is
approached via the Baia de Paranaguá, dotted with picturesque islands. Paranaguá
is a free port for Paraguay. *Banco do Brasil* is at Largo C Alcindino 27. *Câmbio*, R
Faria Sobrinho, for cash. Tourist offices are outside the railway station (1100-1700,
free maps), also at the docks in front of the pier where boats to IIha do Mel leave,
T422 6882, 0800-1900: boat schedules, toilet, and left luggage.

The **fort of Nossa Senhora dos Prazeres** was built in 1767 on a nearby island;
one hr's boat trip. The former Colêgio dos Jesuitas, a fine baroque building, has been
converted into a **Museu de Arqueologia e Artes Populares**. ■ *Tue-Sun
1200-1700, US$1*. Other attractions are a 17th century fountain, the church of **São
Benedito**, and the shrine of **Nossa Senhora do Rocio**, 2 km from town. There are
cruises on Paranaguá Bay by launch, daily between 0900-1300, minimum 15 people,
US$5 from Cais do Mercado.

Matinhos, 40 km south, is invaded by surfers in October for the Paraná surf competition; several hotels, including **B** *Praia e Sol*, R União 35, T452 1922, recommended. There are four camp sites in the vicinity. ■ *8 buses a day from Paranaguá.*

*There are cheap
restaurants in the old
market building,
and plenty of cheap
ones near the markets
on the waterfront*

Sleeping and eating **AL** *Hotel Camboa*, R Jõao Estevao, T423 2121. Large colonial building,
near bus station. **A** *Portofino*, Av Atlântica s/n, T/F458 1488, Balneário Portofino, 35 km from
Paranagu. Very nice. **D** *Palacio*, R Correia de Freitas 66, T422 5655, F423 2518. Good value.
Recommended. **D** *Karibe*, F Simas 86, T422 1177. Good value. **E** *Litoral*, R Correia de Freitas
68. Without breakfast, comfortable. **Camping** *Arco Iris* at Praia de Leste, on the beach, 29 km
south of Paranaguá, 30 mins. T458 2001. For eating, try *Bobby's*, Faria Sobrinho 750.
Danúbio Azul, 15 de Novembro 91, good, open 24 hrs, view of river, *prato do mar* US$8.50
for 1 person, US$12 for 2. *Dirienzo Cucina*, Praça Leoncio Corrreia 16, good *comida por kilo*,
nice setting at harbour, Italian owner with Beverly Hills background. *Tres Irmãos*, Av Gabriel
de Lara 40, good but not cheap seafood, rodizio style.

Transport Bus All buses operated by *Graciosa*. To **Curitiba**, US$4.15, many, 1½ hrs (only
the 1500 to Curitiba takes the old Graciosa road). Also direct buses to **Rio** and **Joinville**.

Ilha do Mel

Ilha do Mel is at the mouth of the Baía de Paranaguá and was of strategic use in the
18th century. The Fortaleza da Barra was built in 1767 on the orders of King José I of
Portugal, to defend what was one of the principal ports in the country. The island is
now an ecological reserve (no cars permitted and visitors limited to 5,000 per day),
but is well-developed for tourism. Its four villages, **Nova Brasília**, **Praia das
Encantadas**, **Praia da Fortaleza** and **Farol** are linked by pathways. The beaches,
caves, bays and hill walks are beautiful. The hike to the fort is very rewarding.
December-March are very rainy months here and there are very persistent *mutucas*

(biting insects) in November, so April-October is the best time to visit. There is electricity on the island 1000-0200. In summer and at holiday times the island is very crowded with an active nightlife and *Forró* dancing; at other times it is very quiet.

Sleeping and eating There are 18 *pousadas* at Praia do Farol, 12 at Praia das Encantadas and a few others at Nova Brasília, and Praia da Fortaleza. There are mini **campsites** with facilities at Encantadas, Farol and Brasília. Camping is possible on the more deserted beaches. At Praia das Encantadas, you can rent a fisherman's house – ask for *Valentim's Bar*, or for Luchiano. Also **E** *Coração da Ilha*, Praia das Encantadas, T457 9601. With good breakfast. At Praia do Farol, **B** *Pousadinha*, on the road to Praia do Farol, T978 3366, excellent breakfast, delightful rooms, good beds, fan, bath, mosquito nets, owner Marcos speaks English. **B** *Pousada Praia do Farol*, T978 3433, or **C** *Estalagem Ancoradouro*, T978 3333, both with breakfast. If camping, watch out for the tide, watch possessions and beware of the *bicho de pé* which burrows into feet (put foot in hot water to soften skin, remove with a needle and alcohol) and of the *borrachudos* (discourage with *Autan* repellent). *Lanchonete Paraíso*, nice meeting place, good food and music; more expensive restaurant next door to *Forró Zorro*, Praia das Encantadas. Restaurant *Toca do Abutre*, 1 km from Nova Brasília, Praia do Farol das Conhas, and bar *Barranco*.

Transport By ferry from Paranaguá, Sat at 1000, Mon and Fri at 1500, Sat and Sun at 0900 from Dec until Carnival, US$3,1 hr 40 mins, boats leave from R Gen Carneiro (R da Praia) in front of the Tourist Information kiosk; by ferry from Pontal do Paraná (Pontal do Sul), daily from 0800 to 1800, every 40 mins, 30 mins. From Paranaguá, take the bus to Pontal do Sul (many daily, 1½ hrs, US$0.60), then wait for the ferry, US$3.25. The last bus back to Paranaguá leaves at 2200. Alternatively, go the small harbour in Paranaguá and ask for a boat to Ilha do Mel, US$5 one way (no shade). Make sure the ferry goes to your chosen destination (Nova Brasília or Encantadas are the most developed areas).

The island of Superagui is a national park and a UNESCO World Heritage Site. With its neighbour Peças it is one of the principal research stations investigating Atlantic forest. Wildlife includes the rare yellow-fronted alligator and the black-faced monkey, and many species of threatened and migratory birds.

Parque Nacional Superagui

There is also an Indian village at the top of the island's hill; other inhabitants are mostly of European descent, living off fishing. There is a certain amount of resentment that the wildlife receives more help than the community (*Population*: 1,200). There are some 10 *pousadas* on Superagui: most popular with foreigners is **E** pp *Carioca*, T9978 4213, cheaper without bath, breakfast, lots of information. Booking necessary at holiday times, January-February; can arrange rooms elsewhere if full. **E** pp *Bella Ilha*, T9998 2953, with breakfast. **F** pp *Golfinhos*, T9959 8852, with breakfast. Camping US$1.50. Take torch and mosquito repellent. The *Restaurante dos Golfinhos* (blue, on beach) can arrange boat trips for the Indian village, ask for Lurdinho or Nagibe, US$12 slow boat, US$15 motor boat, arrange pick-up time. Another restaurant is *Crepúsculo*. In both cases book lunch or dinner in advance. No dollars or credit cards accepted on the island. ■ *Getting there: Boat from Paranaguá on Sat 1000 arriving 1400, return Sun 1530 (2 stops en route), US$6 one way. Private boats from Ilha do Mel run if the weather is good.*

West of Curitiba on the road to Ponta Grossa is the **Museu Histórico do Mate**, an old water-driven mill where mate was prepared. ■ *Free, 20 km, at Km 119.* On the same road is Vila Velha, 91 km from Curitiba: the sandstone rocks have been weathered into most fantastic shapes. 4 km away are the Furnas, three water holes, the deepest of which has a lift (US$1 – not always working) which descends almost to water level. ■ *US$0.20.* Also in the park is the Lagoa Dourada (surrounded by forest) whose water level is the same as that in the Furnas. ■ *The park office (phone, toilets, lanchonete, tourist information) is 300 m from the highway and the park a further 1½ km (entrance – also to Furnas, keep the ticket – US$2 – opens 0800).*

Parque Nacional Vila Velha
Colour map 7, grid C2
Allow all day if visiting all 3 sites (unless you hitch, or can time the buses well, it's a lot of walking)

Brazil

Transport Take a bus from Curitiba to the park, not to the town of Ponta Grossa 26 km away. *Princesa dos Campos* bus from Curitiba 0730 and 1400, 1½ hrs, US$5.65 (the last bus leaves the park at 1600). One bus from Vila Velha between 1530-1600, US$0.65, 4½ km to turn-off to Furnas (another 15 mins' walk) and Lagoa Dourada. Bus Mon-Sat 1330 to Furnas – Ponta Grossa that passes the car park at the top of the park. On Sun, 1200,1620,1800. It may be advisable to go to Ponta Grossa and return to Curitiba from there (114 km, 6 buses a day, US$4.25, *Princesa dos Campos*, also with buses to Foz do Iguaçu, 9 hrs).

Iguaçu Falls

The Iguaçu Falls are the most stunning waterfalls in South America. Their magnitude, and the volume of water that thunders over the edge, is incredible. They are 32 km from the city of Foz do Iguaçu. For a description of the falls, maps and an account of road links between Argentina, Brazil and Paraguay, see the Argentina chapter, page184.

Parque Nacional Foz do Iguaçu
Colour map 7, grid C1

The Brazilian national park was founded in 1939 and the area was designated a World Heritage Site by UNESCO in 1986. Fauna most frequently encountered are little and red brocket deer, South American coati, white-eared opossum, and a sub-species of the brown capuchin monkey. The endangered tegu lizard is common. Over 100 species of butterflies have been identified, among them the electric blue Morpho, the poisonous red and black heliconius and species of Papilionidae and Pieridae. The bird life is especially rewarding for birdwatchers. Five members of the toucan family can be seen.

Take a bus or taxi to the park's entrance, 17 km from Foz. There's a smart modern **visitors centre** here, with toilets, ATM, a small café and a large souvenir shop, but little information on the park or wildlife. Also a *Banco do Brasil câmbio* (0800-1900). Entry is US$6.30, payable in pesos, reais, dollars or euros, and the park is open daily, apart from Monday 0800-1700 in winter, and to 1800 in summer. If possible, visit on a weekday when the walks are less crowded. From the entrance, shuttle buses leave every 10-15 minutes for the 8-km journey to the falls, stopping first at the start of the **Macuco Safari** (see below). From there it's another 10 minutes' drive to the *Hotel Tropical das Cataratas* and the start of a 1.2 km paved walk to the falls. This is an easy walk, taking you high above the Rio Iguaçu, giving splendid views of all the falls on the Argentine side from a series of galleries. At the end of the path, you can walk down to a viewing point right almost under the powerful Floriano Falls, a dramatic view, since you're in the middle of the river, though you will get completely soaked. A catwalk at the foot of the Floriano Falls goes almost to the middle of the river to give a good view of the Garganta del Diablo. From here, there are 150 steps up to the **Porto Canoas** complex (lift under renovation mid-2003), but for those who find stairs difficult, you can return the way you came, and walk a little further along the road. The Porto Canoas complex consists of a big souvenir shop, toilets, a café, a fast food place (mixed reports) and smart restaurant (3-course lunch US$7.30, open 1130-1600 Tuesday-Sunday, good value), all with good view of the river above the falls. Return to the visitor centre and entrance either by the free shuttle bus, by walking back along the forest path as far as *Hotel das Cataratas* (good lunch with a view of the falls for US$13) and take the bus from there. The whole visit will take around 2 hrs, plus time for lunch.

Tours The **Macuco Safari Tour**, 1 hr 40 mins, US$33, involves a ride down a 3-km path through the forest in open electric jeeps. Then a fast motor boat whisks you close to the falls themselves (similar to *Jungle Explorer* on the Argentine side, but more expensive and the guides aren't as good). Portuguese, English and Spanish spoken, take insect repellent. Helicopter tours over the falls leave from near the entrance, US$20 pp, 8 mins. Apart from disturbing visitors, they disturb bird life and so the altitude has been increased, making the flight less attractive. Lots of companies on both sides organize conventional tours to the falls, useful more for convenience rather than information, since they collect you from your hotel. Half day, US$10, plus park entrance price.

Transport Buses leave from the Terminal Urbana in Foz, Av Juscelino Kubitschek and República Argentina, every 40 mins from 0730-1800, and are clearly marked `400, Parque Nacional'. You can get on or off at any point on the route past the airport and *Hotel das Cataratas*, 40 mins, US$0.80 one way, payable in reais only (the driver waits at the Park entrance while passengers purchase entry tickets, which are checked by a park guard on the bus). Taxi US$4, plus US$5.50 per hr for waiting.

Foz do Iguaçu and around

A small, modern city, 28 km from the falls, with a wide range of accommodation and good communications by air and road with the main cities of southern Brazil and Asunción in Paraguay. The **Parque das Aves** bird zoo, at Rodovia das Cataratas Km 16, 100 m before the entrance to the park, has received frequent good reports. It contains Brazilian and foreign birds, many species of parrot and beautiful toucans, in huge aviaries through which you can walk, with the birds flying and hopping around you. There are other birds in cages and a butterfly and hummingbird house. ■ *0830-1700, US$8, T/F529 8282, www.parquedosaves.com.br*

Phone code 0xx45
Population 258,543
For tourist information, see Directory

The **Itaipu dam**, on the Río Paraná 12 km north, is the site of the largest single power station in the world built jointly by Brazil and Paraguay. Construction of this massive scheme began in 1975 and it became operational in 1984. The main dam is 8 km long, creating a lake which covers 1,400 sq km. The 18 turbines have an installed capacity of 12,600,000 Kw and produce about 75 bn Kwh a year, providing 80% of Paraguay's electricity and 25% of Brazil's. The Paraguayan side may be visited from

Brazil

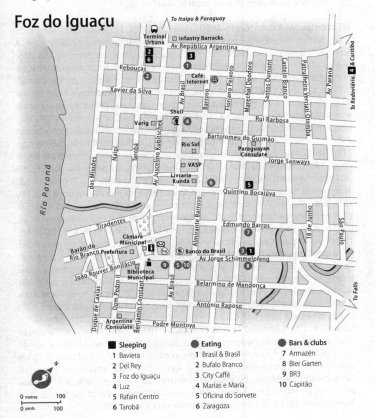

Foz do Iguaçu

To Itaipu & Paraguay

Terminal Urbana
Infantry Barracks
Av República Argentina
Rebouças
Café Internet
Xavier da Silva
Av Brasil
Barros
Floriano Peixoto
Marechal Deodoro
Castelo Branco
Santos Dumont
Patulheiro Veriliati Otemba
Av Paraná
To Rodoviária, 4 & Curitiba
Shell
Varig
Av Juscelino Kubitschek
Tarobá
das Missões
Napi
Rio Sul
VASP
Livraria Kunda
Rui Barbosa
Bartolomeu do Gusmão
Paraguayan Consulate
Jorge Sanways
Quintino Bocaiúva
Rio Paraná
Tiradentes
Almirante Barroso
Edmundo Barros
18 de Junho
São Paulo
Câmara Municipal
Barão do Rio Branco
Prefeitura
Banco do Brasil
Av Jorge Schimmelpfeng
João Rouver Bonifácio
Biblioteca Municipal
Av Brasil
Belarmino de Mendonça
Duque de Caxias
Dom Pedro II
Benjamin Constant
Antônio Raposo
Argentine Consulate
Padre Montoya
To Falls

0 metres 100
0 yards 100

■ Sleeping	● Eating	● Bars & clubs
1 Baviera	1 Brasil & Brasil	7 Armazén
2 Del Rey	2 Bufalo Branco	8 Bier Garten
3 Foz do Iguaçu	3 City Caffé	9 BR3
4 Luz	4 Marias e Maria	10 Capitão
5 Rafain Centro	5 Oficina do Sorvete	
6 Tarobá	6 Zaragoza	

Ciudad del Este. ■ *Buses run from outside the Terminal Urbano to a village 200 m away from the visitor centre, US$0.50. A short film is shown at the visitor centre 10 mins before each guided visit, all free, at 0800, 0900, 1000, 1400, 1500, 1600, Mon-Sat. Check times with tourist office, and take passport. Night visits are also arranged on Fri and Sat. The Noelia company in Puerto Iguazú includes Itaipu in its tours of the Brazilian side of the falls, US$11, T422722.* There is also the **Ecomuseu de Itaipu**, Avenida Tancredo Neves, Km 11, ■ *Mon 1400-1700, Tue-Sat 0900-1100, 1400-1700* and Iguaçu Environmental Education Centre are geared to educate about the preservation of the local culture and environment, or that part which isn't underwater. ■ *Free with guide, recommended.*

Sleeping

■ *on map*
Av Juscelino Kubitschek and the streets south of it, towards the river are unsafe at night. Many prostitutes around R Rebouças and Almirante Barroso. Taxis are only good value for short distances when you are carrying all your luggage

Outside Foz do Iguaçu: **L-AL** *Hotel das Cataratas (Tropical)*, directly overlooking the Falls, 28 km from Foz, T521 7000, www.tropicalhotel.com.br Some discount may be offered in slack periods for holders of the Brazil Air Pass. Generally recommended but caters for lots of groups, attractive colonial-style building with pleasant gardens (where a lot of wildlife can be seen at night and early morning) and pool. Non-residents can eat here, midday and evening buffets; also à-la-carte dishes and dinner with show. On the road to the Falls (Rodovia das Cataratas) are **AL** *San Martin*, Km 17, T529 8088, www.hotelsanmartin.com.br Attractive 4-star, a/c, TV, pool, sports, nightclub, several eating options, luxury, comfortable. Recommended. A *Carimã*, Km 10, T521 3000, www.carima.com.br 4-star, popular with groups, well laid out, lots of facilites, good restaurant, pool, bars, good value. Recommended. A *Colonial*, Km 16, T529 7711, www.colonialhotel.com.br 1 km from the airport, spacious, fine location, price includes breakfast and mediocre dinner, no English. **C** *Panorama*, Km 12, T529 8200, www.hotelpanoramaresort.com.br Good value, pool.

In Foz do Iguaçu: A *Rafain Centro*, Mal Deodoro 984, T/F523 1213, www.rafaincentro.com.br Smart, comfortable, attractive pool area, good restaurant, although rooms rather worn. **A** *Suíça*, Av Felipe Wandscheer 3580, T525 3232, www.hotelsuica.com.br Some way out of the city, but charming, comfortable, Swiss manager, helpful with tourist information, attractive pool. **B** *Foz do Iguaçu*, Av Brasil 97, T523 4455, www.hotelfozdoiguazu.com.br Smart, attractive pool and terrace, well-designed rooms, good value. **B** *Foz Presidente*, R Xavier da Silva 1000, T/F572-4450, www.fozpresidentehoteis.com.br Good value, decent rooms, restaurant, pool, with breakfast, convenient for buses. **C** *Baviera*, Av Jorge Schimmelpfeng 697, T523 5995, hotelbavieraiguassu@foznet.com.br Chalet-style exterior, on main road, central for bars and restaurants, comfortable, if rather gloomy rooms. **C** *Foz Plaza Hotel*, R Marechal Deodoro 1819, T/F523 1448, fozplaza@challengerhoteis.com.br Serene and very nice. **D** *Del Rey*, R Tarobá 1020 e República Argentina, T523 2027. Nothing fancy, but perennially popular, little pool, great breakfasts. Recommended. **D** *Luz*, Av Costa e Silva Km 5, near Rodoviária, T522 3535, www.luzhotel.com.br Recommended. **D** *San Remo*, Kubitschek e Xavier da Silva 563, T523 1619, F523-5120. A/c, good breakfast. **D** *Tarobá*, R Tarobá 1048, T523 9722, www.hoteltaroba.com.br Bright and welcoming, small pool, nice rooms, helpful, a/c, good breakfast. Recommended. **E** *15 de Julho*, Almte Barroso 1794, T574 2664, F574 2237. A/c, TV, hot water, pool, German and some English spoken, excellent value. Recommended. **F** *Pousada Evelina Navarrete*, R Irlan Kalichewski 171, Vila Yolanda, T/F574 3817. Lots of tourist information, English, French, Italian, Polish and Spanish spoken, lots of information, good breakfast and location, near Chemin Supermarket, near Av Cataratas on the way to the falls. Warmly recommended. **F** pp *Pousada Vitória*, R Nereu Ramos 285, Parque Presidente, near bus station, T573 4664/9967 6183 (mob). Hot shower, helpful, Spanish and English spoken.

Youth hostel E pp (in high season IYHA members only): *Paudimar Campestre*, Av das Cataratas Km 12.5, Remanso Grande, near airport, T/F529 6061, www.paudimar.com.br From airport or town take Parque Nacional bus (0525-0040)and get out at Remanso Grande bus stop, by *Hotel San Juan*, then take the free shuttle (0700-1900) to the hostel, or 1.2 km walk from main road. Camping as well, pool, soccer pitch, quiet, kitchen and communal meals, breakfast. Highly recommended. For assistance, ask for owner, Gladis. The hostel has telephone, fax and internet for guests' use. Tours run to either side of the falls, US$8 to Argentine side 0830-1700 (good value). *Paudimar* desk at rodoviária.

Camping E Pousada Internacional, R Manêncio Martins, 600 m from turnoff, T523 8183, www.campinginternacional.com.br For vehicles and tents, helpful staff, English, German and Spanish spoken, pool, restaurant. Recommended. *Camping Clube do Brasil*, by the national park entrance 17 km from Foz, T529 9206, US$10 pp (half with International Camping Card), pool, clean. Park vehicle or put tent away from trees in winter in case of heavy rain storms, no restaurants, food there is not very good, closes at 2300.

Camping
Camping is not permitted by the Hotel das Cataratas and falls

Expensive *Cabeça de Boi*, Av Brasil 1325. Live music, buffet, churrasco, but coffee and pastries also. *Rafain*, Av das Cataratas, Km 6.5, T523 1177, closed Sun. Out of town, take a taxi or arrange with travel agency. Set price for excellent buffet with folkloric music and dancing (2100-2300) from throughout South America, touristy but very entertaining. Recommended. *Zaragoza*, R Quintino Bocaiúva 882. Large and upmarket, for Spanish dishes and seafood. Recommended. **Mid-range** *Bier Garten*, Av Jorge Schimmelpfeng 550. Pizzeria and *choparia*, beer garden in name only but some trees. *Boulevard*, Av das Cataratas 1118. Food court open daily from 1700, and all day Sun. *Brasil & Brazil*, Brasil 157. A handful of food stalls, with live music and dancing 2000 to 0200, bingo. *Búfalo Branco*, R Rebouças 530. Superb all you can eat churrasco, includes filet mignon, bull's testicles, salad bar and desert. Sophisticated surroundings and attentive service. Highly recommended.*Tropicana*, Av Juscelino Kubitschek 228. All-you-can-eat pizza or *churrascaria* with salad bar, good value. **Cheap** *City Caffé*, Av Jorge Schimmelpfeng 898. Stylish café open daily 0800-2330 for sandwiches, Arabic snacks and pastries. *Marias e Maria*, Av Brasil 50. Good *confeitaria*. *Oficina do Sorvete*, Av Jorge Schimmelpfeng 244, open daily 1100-0100. Excellent ice-creams, a popular local hang-out.

Eating
● on map

Bars, all doubling as restaurants, concentrated on Av Jorge Schimmelpfeng for two blocks from Av Brasil to R Mal Floriano Peixoto. Wed to Sun are best nights; crowd tends to be young. *Alquimia*, No 334, T5723154. Popular, nightclub, *Dancing*, attached, open 2400-0500, US$3. *BR3*, corner with Av Brasil. Modern, open till 2400. *Capitão Bar*, No 288 and Almte Barroso, large, loud and popular, nightclub attached. *Armazém*, R Edmundo de Barros 446. Intimate and sophisticated, attracts discerning locals, good atmosphere, mellow live music, US$1 cover. Recommended.*Oba! Oba!*, Av das Cataratas 3700, T529 6596 (Antigo Castelinho). Live samba show Mon-Sat 2315-0015, very popular, US$9 for show and 1 drink.

Bars & clubs

Kunda Livraria Universitária, R Almte Barroso 1473, T523 4606. Guides and maps of the area, books on the local wildlife, novels etc in several languages.

Shopping

There are many travel agents on Av Brasil. *Caribe Tur* at the airport and *Hotel das Cataratas*, T523 1612, runs tours from the airport to the Argentine side and *Hotel das Cataratas* (book hotel direct, not at the airport desk). *Jaha Iguassu Explorer*, T523 1484, T9106 6985 (mob), 24 hrs, chilelindo7@hotmail.com Provides bus information for all sights, visits to Paraguay (full day, US$25), Argentinian falls (in mini-van, US$10, includes lunch but not guide or entrance fee), bike tours to Argentina, horse riding and overnight stays in national park. Ruth Campo Silva, *STTC Turismo*, Hotel Bourbon, Rodovia das Cataratas, T/F529 8580 American Express).

Tour operators
Beware of overcharging for tours by touts at the bus terminal

Air Iguaçu international airport, 18 km south of town near the falls, T521 4200. In Arrivals is *Banco do Brasil* and *Caribe Tours e Câmbio*, car rental offices, tourist office and an official taxi stand, US$10 to town centre (US$11 from town to airport). All buses marked Parque Nacional pass the airport in each direction, US$0.50, 0525-0040, does not permit large amounts of luggage but backpacks OK. Many hotels run minibus services for a small charge. Daily flights to **Rio**, **São Paulo**, **Curitiba** and other Brazilian cities.

Transport

Bus For transport to the falls see above under Parque Nacional Foz do Iguaçu. Long distance terminal (Rodoviária), Av Costa e Silva, 4 km from centre on road to Curitiba, T522 2590; bus to centre, any bus that says 'Rodoviária', US$0.65. Taxi US$4. Book departures as soon as possible. As well as the tourist office (see below), there is a *Cetreme* desk for tourists who have lost their documents, Guarda Municipal (police) and luggage store. To **Curitiba**, *Pluma*,

Brazil

Sulamericana, 9-10 hrs, paved road, US$15. To **Guaíra** via Cascavel only, 5 hrs, US$10. To **Florianópolis**, *Catarinense* and **Reunidas**, US$28, 14 hrs. *Reunidas* to **Porto Alegre**, US$26-30. To **São Paulo**, 16 hrs, *Pluma* US$30, executivo 6 a day, plus one *leito*. To **Rio** 22 hrs, several daily, US$38. *Cambio Corimeira*, Almte Barroso 2037, T523 3550, sells national bus tickets in the centre.

Directory   **Airline offices** *Rio Sul*, J Sanways 779, T574 6080. *TAM*, R Rio Branco 640, T523 8500 (offers free transport to Ciudad del Este for its flights, all cross-border documentation dealt with). *Varig*, Av Juscelino Kubitschek 463, T523 2111. *Vasp*, Av Brasil 845, T523 2212 (airport 529 7161). **Banks** It is difficult to exchange on Sun but quite possible in Paraguay where US dollars can be obtained on credit cards. There are plenty of banks and travel agents on Av Brasil. *Banco do Brasil*, Av Brasil 1377. Has ATM, high commission for TCs. *Bradesco*, Av Brasil 1202. Cash advance on Visa. *HSBC*, Av Brasil 1151, for MasterCard ATM. *Banco 24 Horas* at Oklahoma petrol station. *Itaú*, Av Kubitschek e Bocaiúva. Câmbio at *Vento Sul*, Av Brasil 1162, no TCs, good rates for cash. Also *Corimeira*, see Bus, above. **Communications** Internet: *Boulevard* cinema complex, Av das Cataratas 1118, T5234245. Open from 1700 and all day Sun. *Cafe Internet*, R Rebouças 950, T/F523 2122, 0900-2300, US$1.50 per hr, open 0900-2300 and Sun pm. *Café Pizzanet*, R Rio Branco 412, corner with Av Juscelino Kubitschek, US$2 per hr. Pizzaria too. *Zipfoz.com*, R Barão do Rio Branco 412, corner with Av Juscelino Kubitschek. Smart, a/c, US$1.50 per hr. Post Office: Praça Getúlio Vargas 72. **Telephone:** *Tele Centro Sul* on Edmundo de Barros. **Embassies and consulates** Argentina, Travessa Eduardo Bianchi 26, T574 2969. Open Mon-Fri 1000-1430. **France**, R Federico Engels 48, Villa Yolanda, T574 3693, 0900-1200, 1400-1700. **Paraguay**, Bartolomeu de Gusmão 738, T523 2898. **Medical services** Free 24-hr clinic, Av Paraná 1525, opposite Lions Club, T573 1134. Few buses: take taxi or walk (about 25 mins). **Tourist offices** Secretaria Municipal de Turismo, new location (Jun 2003) on Av Jorge Schimmelpfeng, T521 1455, 0700-2300, very helpful, English spoken. There is a 24-hr tourist help line number, T0800-451516. Very helpful. Airport tourist information is also good, open for all arriving flights, gives map and bus information, English spoken. Helpful office, free map, at the rodoviária, English spoken. **Delegacia do Turista e da Mulher** (police station for tourists and women), Av Brasil 1374, opposite Banco do Brasil, T523 3036. A newspaper, *Triplice Fronteira*, carries street plans and other tourist information. **Voltage** 110 volts a/c.

Border with This crossing via the Puente Tancredo Neves is straightforward. Even if crossing on
Argentina a day visit, you must have your passport stamped. If you need a visa to enter Brazil, you will not be allowed into the country without it, even for a day visit. Between October-February Brazil is 1 hr ahead of Argentina. It takes about 2 hours to get from Foz to the Argentine falls, very tiring when the weather is hot.

Transport Buses marked 'Puerto Iguazú' run every 20 mins from the Terminal Urbana, crossing the border bridge; 30 mins' journey, 3 companies, including *Pluma* and *Três Fronteiras*, US$1. When you get out of the bus to get your passport stamped at immigration, the bus waits. **NB** Be sure you know when the last bus departs from Puerto Iguazú for Foz (usually 1900). Combined tickets to Puerto Iguazú and the falls cost more than paying separately. For buses to **Buenos Aires**, see Puerto Iguazú, Transport for the options. There is a *Pluma* bus direct from Foz and you can also go to **Posadas** via Paraguay.

Border with The *Ponte de Amizade/Puente de Amistad* (Friendship Bridge) over the Río Paraná,
Paraguay 6 km north of Foz, leads straight into the heart of Ciudad del Este. Paraguayan and
Brazil is 1 hr ahead Brazilian immigration formalities are dealt with at opposite ends of the bridge. Ask
of Paraguay for relevant stamps if you need them.

Transport Bus: (marked Cidade-Ponte) leave from the Terminal Urbana, Av Juscelino Kubitschek, for the Ponte de Amizade (Friendship Bridge), US$0.40. To **Asunción**, *Pluma* (0700), *RYSA* (direct at 1430, 1830), from Rodoviária, US$11 (cheaper if bought in Ciudad del Este). **Motoring**: If crossing by private vehicle and only intending to visit the national parks, this presents no problems. Another crossing to Paraguay is at **Guaíra**, at the northern end of the Itaipu lake. It is 5 hrs north of Iguaçu by road and can be reached by bus from Campo Grande and São Paulo. Ferries cross to Saltos del Guaira on the Paraguayan side (see page 1023).

Santa Catarina

Brasília

Famous for its beaches and popular with Argentine and Paraguayan holidaymakers in high summer, this is one of the best stretches of Brazilian coast for surfing, attracting 1½ million visitors to the 170 beaches just in the summer months of January and February. For the rest of the year they are pleasant and uncrowded. Immigrant communities, such as the German, give a unique personality to many towns and districts with the familiar European pattern of mixed farming. Rural tourism is important and the highlands, 100 km from the coast, are among the coldest in Brazil, giving winter landscapes reminiscent of Europe, or Brazil's southern neighbours

Florianópolis

Half way along the coast of Santa Catarina is the state capital and port of Florianópolis, founded in 1726 on the Ilha de Santa Catarina. The island is joined to the mainland by two bridges, one of which is Ponte Hercílio Luz, the longest steel suspension bridge in Brazil (closed for repairs). The newer Colombo Machado Salles bridge has a pedestrian and cycle way beneath the roadway. The natural beauty of the island, beaches and bays make Florianópolis a magnet for holidaymakers in summer. The southern beaches are usually good for swimming, the east for surfing, but be careful of the undertow.

Phone code: 0xx48
Colour map 5,
grid B5
Population: 342,315

In the 1960s Florianópolis port was closed and the aspect of the city's southern shoreline was fundamentally changed, with land reclaimed from the bay. The two main remnants of the old port area are the late 19th-century **Alfândega** and **Mercado Público**, both on Rua Conselheiro Mafra, fully restored and painted ochre. In the Alfândega is a handicraft market. ■ *Mon-Fri 0900-1900, Sat 0900-1200, T224 6082.* The market is divided into *boxes*, some are bars and restaurants, others shops. ■ *Mon-Fri 0600-1830, Sat 0600-1300, a few fish stalls open on Sun, T225 3200.* The **Cathedral** on Praça 15 de Novembro was completed in 1773. **Forte Santana** (1763), beneath the Ponte Hercílio Luz, houses a **Museu de Armas Major Lara Ribas**, with a collection of guns and other items, mostly post Second World War. ■ *Tue-Sun 0830-1200, 1400-1800 (Mon 1400-1800), free, T229 6263.* **Museu Histórico**, in the 18th-century Palácio Cruz e Souza, on Praça 15 de Novembre, contains furniture, documents and objects belonging to governors of the state. ■ *Tue-Fri 0800-1900, Sat 1300-1900, Sun 1530-1900, T221 3504.* **Museu de Antropologia**, at the Trindade University Campus, has a collection of stone and other archaeological remains from the cultures of the coastal Indians. ■ *Mon-Fri 0900-1200, 1300-1700, T331 8821.* **Museu do Homem Sambaqui**, at the Colégio Catarinense, R Esteves Júnior 711, exhibits pieces from the *sambaqui* culture and fossils. ■ *Mon-Fri 1330-1630, T224 9190.* There is a look-out point at **Morro da Cruz** (take *Empresa Trindadense* bus, US$0.60, waits 15 mins, or walk).

Boat trips can be made in the bay with Scuna Sul, T225 1806, www.scunasul.com.br From US$7.50

A *Castelmar*, R Felipe Schmidt 1260, T225 3228, F225 3126 www.iaccess.com.br/castelmar Pool, a/c, TV, laundry, restaurant. **A** *Faial*, R Felipe Schmidt 603, T225 2766, F225 0435, faial@interspace.com.br Good restaurant. **A** *Florianópolis Palace*, R Artista Bittencourt 14, T224 9633, F223 0300. Recommended. **A** *Mercure Diplomata*, Av Paulo Fontes 1210, T225 4455, F225 5082. Very good views, 4-star hotel but prices sometimes negotiable. **A-B** *Valerim Plaza*, R Felipe Schmidt 705, T/F225 3388, valerim@iaccess.com.br Three-star, more modern than *Valerim Center*, buffet restaurant open till 2300. **B** *Oscar*, Av Hercílio Luz 760, T222 0099, F222 0978, oscarhotel@oscarhotel.com.br A/c, TV, safe, central. **B** *Porto da Ilha*, R Dom Jaime Câmara 43, T322 0007, hotel@portodailha.com.br Central, comfortable. Recommended. **B** *Valerim Center*, R Felipe Schmidt 554, T225 1100. Large rooms, hot water, hard beds. **C** *Pousada Recanto da Costa*, R 13 de Maio 41. With breakfast, hot water, laundry facilities, parking, 15 mins' walk from centre. **D** *Central Sumaré*, R Felipe Schmidt 423, T222

Sleeping
■ *on map*

5359. Breakfast, good value, rooms vary from **C** with bath, to **F. D-E** *Felippe*, R João Pinto 132, 1 block from 15 de Novembro, by Terminal Urbano, T222 4122. Small rooms, some with no windows, breakfast is just a cup of coffee, dirty bathrooms.

Youth hostels E pp *Ilha de Santa Catarina*, R Duarte Schutel 227, T222 3781, F225 1692, alberguesfloripa@uol.com.br HI. Recommended, breakfast included, cooking facilities, clean, some traffic noise, very friendly, will store luggage. Prices rise in Dec-Feb; more expensive for non-members.

Camping *Camping Clube do Brasil*, São João do Rio Vermelho, north of Lagoa da Conceição, 21 km out of town; also at Lagoa da Conceição, Praia da Armação, Praia dos Ingleses, Praia Canasvieiras. 'Wild' camping allowed at Ponta de Sambaqui and Praias Brava,

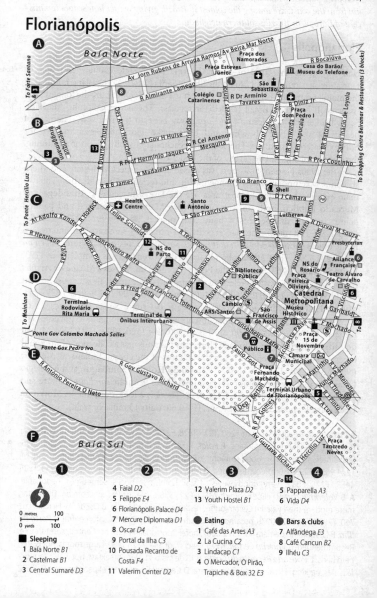

Florianópolis

Sleeping
1 Baía Norte *B1*
2 Castelmar *B1*
3 Central Sumaré *D3*
4 Faial *D2*
5 Felippe *E4*
6 Florianópolis Palace *D4*
7 Mercure Diplomata *D1*
8 Oscar *D4*
9 Portal da Ilha *C3*
10 Pousada Recanto de Costa *F4*
11 Valerim Center *D2*
12 Valerim Plaza *D2*
13 Youth Hostel *B1*

Eating
1 Café das Artes *A3*
2 La Cucina *C2*
3 Lindacap *C1*
4 O Mercador, O Pirão, Trapiche & Box 32 *E3*
5 Papparella *A3*
6 Vida *D4*

Bars & clubs
7 Alfândega *E3*
8 Café Cancun *B2*
9 Ilhéu *C3*

Aranhas, Galheta, Mole, Campeche, Campanhas and Naufragados; 4 km south of Florianópolis, camping site with bar at Praia do Sonho on the mainland, beautiful, deserted beach with an island fort nearby. 'Camping Gaz' cartridges from *Riachuelo Supermercado*, on R Alvim and R São Jorge.

Take a walk along Rua Bocaiúva, east of R Almte Lamego, to find the whole street filled with Italian restaurants, barbecue places and an exclusive fish restaurant, *Toca da Garoupa* (turn on to R Alves de Brito 178). *Don Pepé Forno a Lenha* is a great place to go for a quiet romantic meal with a *serenador* (cover charge added to bill for singer). Shrimp dishes are good everywhere. A popular place to start a night out (after 2100) is the *Nouvelle Vague*, more commonly known as *A Creperia*, buzzing every weekend, wide selection of sweet and savoury pancakes. **Mid-range** *Lindacap*, R Felipe Schmidt 1132 (closed Mon). Recommended, good views. *Macarronada Italiana*, Av Beira Mar Norte 2458. Good. Next door is *Pizza da Piedra*. *Papparella*, Almte Lamego 1416. Excellent giant pizzas. In the Mercado Público: *O Mercador*, Box 33/4. Self-service specializing in fish and seafood. *O Pirão* overlooks the market square. Elegant, self-service, open 1100-1430. *Trapiche*, Box 31. Also self-service fish and seafood (see also Bars, below). **Cheap** *Café das Artes*, nice café at north end of R Esteves Junior, No 734. With excellent cakes. *Kayskidum*, Av Beira Mar Norte 2566. Lanchonete and crêperie, very popular. *Mirantes*, R Alvaro de Carvalho 246, Centro. Self-service buffet, good value. For a wide selection of juices and snacks: *Cía Lanches*, Ten Silveira e R Trajano, downstairs, and, in Edif Dias Velho al R Felipe Schmidt 303, *Laranja Madura*, *Sabor e Sucos* and *Lanchonete Dias Velho*.

Vegetarian *La Cucina*, R Padre Roma 291. Buffet lunch, Mon-Sat, pay by weight, good, vegetarian choices. Recommended. *Vida*, R Visc de Ouro Preto 298, next to Alliance Française. Good.

Eating
● *on map*

Brazil

The Mercado Público in the centre, which is alive with fish sellers and stalls during the day, has a different atmosphere at night; the stall, *Box 32*, is good for seafood and becomes a bar specializing in *cachaça* for hard working locals to unwind. *Empórium*, Bocaiúva 79, is a shop by day and popular bar at night. To find out about events and theme nights check the Beiramar centre for notices in shop windows, ask in surf shops or take a trip to the University of Santa Catarina in Trindade and check out the noticeboards. The news-paper *Diário Catarinense* gives details of bigger events, eg Oktoberfest. *Ilhéu*, Av Prof Gama d'Eça e R Jaime Câmara. Bar and club open until early hrs, tables spill outside, very popular with locals, fills up quickly, music a mixture of 1980s and 1990s hits but dance floor shamefully small. *Café Cancun*, Av Beira Mar Norte, T225 1029. Wed-Sat from 2000, bars, restaurant, dancing, sophisticated.

Bars & clubs
Free open air concert every Sat morning at the market place near the bus terminal

In **Dec** and **Jan** the whole island dances to the sound of the *Boi-de-Mamão*, a dance which incorporates the puppets of Bernunça, Maricota (the Goddess of Love, a puppet with long arms to embrace everyone) and Tião, the monkey. The Portuguese brought the tradition of the bull, which has great significance in Brazilian celebrations. Around **Easter** is the Festival of the Bull, *Farra de Boi*. It is only in the south that, controversially nowadays, the bull is killed on Easter Sunday. The festival arouses fierce local pride and there is much celebration.

Festivals

Local Bus: there are 3 bus stations for routes on the island, or close by on the mainland: Terminal de Ônibus Interurbano between Av Paulo Fontes and R Francisco Tolentino, west of the Mercado Público; Terminal Urbano between Av Paulo Fontes and R Antônio Luz, east of Praça Fernando Machado; a terminal at R Silva Jardim and R José da Costa. Yellow micro buses (*Transporte Ejecutivo*), starting from the south end of Praça 15 de Novembro and other stops, charge US$0.75-US$1.45 depending on destination. Similarly, normal bus fares vary according to destination, from US$0.65.

Car hire: *Auto Locadora Veleiros*, R Silva Jardim 1050, T225 8207, veleiros@brasilnet.net *Interlocadora*, T236 1595 at the airport, rates from US$40 a day before supplements.

Transport

Long distance Air: international and domestic flights arrive at Hercílio Luz airport, Av Deomício Freitas, 12 km from town, T331 4000. Take *Ribeiroense* bus 'Corredor Sudoeste' from Terminal Urbano.

Bus: international and buses from other Brazilian cities arrive at the rodoviária Rita Maia on the island, at the east (island) end of the Ponte Colombo Machado Salles, T224 2777.

Daily buses to **Porto Alegre** (US$16, 7 hrs), **São Paulo**, 9 hrs (US$23.75, *leito* US$36.25), **Rio**, 20 hrs (US$31 *convencional*, US$42 *executive*, US$55 *leito*); to **Foz de Iguaçu** (US$28, continuing to **Asunción** US$30), to **Curitiba** US$12. To **Blumenau** US$7, 3 hrs. To **São Joaquim** at 1145, 1945 with *Reunidos*, 1815 with *Nevatur*, 5-6 hrs, US$9.30; to **Laguna** US$5.25.

International buses: Montevideo, US$52, daily, by *TTL*. **Buenos Aires**, US$55, *Pluma*, buses very full in summer, book 1 week in advance.

Directory   **Airline offices** *Aerolíneas Argentinas*, R Tte Silveira 200, 8th floor, T224 7835. *Nordeste/Rio Sul*, Av Rio Branco 883, T0800-492004. *TAM*, at airport, T236 0003. *Varig*, Av Rio Branco 796, T224 7266/0800-997000. *Vasp*, Av Osmar Cunha 105, T224 7824/0800-998277. **Banks** *Banco do Brasil*, Praça 15 de Novembro, exchange upstairs, 1000-1500, huge commission on cash or TCs. ATMs downstairs, some say Visa/Plus. *Banco Estado de Santa Catarina*, (BESC) câmbio, R Felipe Schmidt e Jerônimo Coelho, 1000-1600, no commission on TCs. *Lovetur*, Av Osmar Cunha 15, Ed Ceisa and *Centauro Turismo* at same address. *Açoriano Turismo*, Jaime Câmara 106, T2243939, takes Amex. Money changers on R Felipe Schmidt outside BESC. ATM for MasterCard/Cirrus at *Banco Itaú*, Shopping Centre Beiramar (not in the centre, bus Expresso). **Communications** Internet:*Moncho*, Tiradentes 181. Internet café on R Felipe Schmidt 700 block, opposite *Lav Lev* laundry, US$1.55 per hr. Post Office: Praça 15 de Novembro 5. Telephone: Praça Pereira Oliveira 20. **Tourist offices** Setur, head office at Portal Turístico de Florianópolis, mainland end of the bridge, Av Eng Max de Souza 236, Coqueiros, T244 5822 or 224 1516 information line, open 0800-2000 (Sat/Sun 1800). Office in the Mercado Público, T244 5822, Mon-Fri 0800-1200, 1330-1800, Sat-Sun 0800-1200. At Rodoviária, Av Paulo Fontes, T223 2777, and airport, maps available, free, 0700-1800 (0800 Sat/Sun). www.guiafloripa.com.br *Santur*, Edif ARS, R Felipe Schmidt 249, 9th floor, T212 6300, F222 1145, helpful, www.sc.gov.br/santacatarina/turismo/contrastes/index.html **Voltage** 220 volts AC.

Ilha de Santa Catarina

Colour map 7, grid C3   There are 42 beaches around the island. The most popular are the surfers' beaches such as Praia Moçambique; for peace and quiet try Campeche or the southern beaches; for sport, the Lagoa de Conceição has jet skis and windsurfing. You can walk in the forest reserves, hang glide or paraglide from the Morro da Lagoa, sandboard in the dunes of Joaquina. Surfing is prohibited 30 April-30 July because of the migration of the island's largest fish, the *tainha*.

Lagoa da Conceição has beaches, sand dunes, fishing, church of NS da Conceição (1730), market every Wednesday and Saturday, post office. Tandem hang gliding, *Lift Sul Vôo Livre*, T232 0543. From the Centro da Lagoa on the bridge there are daily boat trips to Costa da Lagoa which run until about 1830, check when you buy your ticket, US$4 return, the service is used mostly by the local people who live around the lake and have no other form of public transport.

Across the island at **Barra da Lagoa** is a pleasant fishing village and beach, surfing, lively in the summer season, with plenty of good restaurants, which can be reached by 'Barra da Lagoa' bus (Transol No 403, every 15 mins from Terminal Urbano, 55 mins, US$0.75). The same bus goes to beaches at **Mole** (good for walking, soft sand beach, surfing) and at **Joaquina** (surfing championships in January).

There is a pleasant fishing village at **Ponta das Canas**, walk 1 km to Praia Brava for good surfing, and the beach at **Canasvieiras** is good. Also in the north of the island, is **Praia dos Ingleses** (bus 602). **Forte São José da Ponta Grossa** is beautifully restored with a small museum. ■ *US$1.50. Buses to Jureré and Daniela beaches go there, 1 hr.*

In the south of the island are **Praia do Campeche**, 30 mins by bus (Pantano do Sul or Costa de Dentro) from Florianópolis, **Praia da Armação** with, just inland, **Lagoa do Peri** (a protected area). Further south is **Pântano do Sul**, an unspoilt fishing village with a long, curved beach, lovely views, several *pousadas*, bars and restaurants, though not much nightlife. From here it's a good 4-km walk over rocks and a headland to beautiful **Lagoinha do Leste**. **Praia dos Naufragados**: take bus to Caieira da Barra do Sul and then a one hr walk through fine forests. **Forte Nossa Senhora da Conceição** is on a small island just offshore. It can be seen from the lighthouse near Praia dos Naufragados or take a boat trip with Scuna Sul from Florianópolis.

Lagoa da Conceição D *Pousada Zilma*, R Geral da Praia da Joaquina 279, T232 0161. Quiet, safe. Recommended. *Ricardo*, R Manoel S de Oliveira 8, CEP 88062, T232 0107, rents self-contained apartments, can arrange houses also. Recommended. Restaurants: *Bodeguita*, Av das Rendeiras 1878, very good value and atmosphere. *Oliveira*, R Henrique Veras, excellent seafood dishes.

Barra da Lagoa C *Pousada Floripaz*, Estrada Geral (across hanging bridge at bus station, take bus 403 from terminal municipal), T232 3193. Book in advance, safe, family run, helpful owners, will organize tours by boat and car on island. Highly recommended. **D** *Pousada-Lanchonete Sem Nome*, Praia do Moçambique. In 4-bunk rooms, bathrooms separate, kitchen, laundry. Recommended. **D** *Albergue do Mar*. Basic, good for lone travellers. *Camping da Barra*, T232 3199. Beautiful clean site, helpful owner. Restaurant: *Meu Cantinha*, R Orlando Shaplin 89, excellent seafood.

Joaquina A *Joaquina Beach*, R A Garibaldi Santiago, T232 5059. Pleasant. **Ponta das Canas A** *Hotel Moçambique*, T/F266 1172. In centre of village, noisy at weekends. Houses to let from Frederico Barthe, T266 0897. **Canasvieiras Praia dos Ingleses A** *Sol e Mar*, T262 1271. Excellent. Recommended. **Praia de Campeche AL** *Hotel São Sebastião da Praia*, Av Campeche 1373, T/F237 4066, hotel@hotelsaosebastiao.com.br Resort hotel on splendid beach, offers special monthly rate Apr to Oct, excellent value. **Near Pântano do Sul B** *Pousada dos Tucanos*, Estrada Geral da Costa de Dentro 2776, T237 5084, Caixa Postal 5016. English, French, Spanish spoken, spacious bungalows in garden setting, excellent organic food. Very highly recommended. Take bus to Pântano do Sul, walk 6 km or telephone and arrange to be picked up by German owner. Hostelling International **F** *Albergue do Pirata*, R Rosalia P Ferreira 4973, Pântano do Sul, T389 2727, www.megasites.com.br/pirata With breakfast, natural surroundings, lots of trails.

Sleeping & eating

Throughout the summer the beaches open their bars day and night. The beach huts of Praia Mole invite people to party all night (bring a blanket). Any bars are worth visiting in the Lagoa area (around the Boulevard and Barra da Lagoa).

Bars & clubs

On the coast north of Florianópolis there are many resorts. They include Porto Belo, a fishing village on the north side of a peninsula settled in 1750 by Azores islanders, with a calm beach and a number of hotels and restaurants. Around the peninsula are wilder beaches reached by rough roads: Bombas, Bombinhas, Quatro Ilhas (quieter, 15 mins' walk from Bombinhas), Mariscal, and, on the southern side, Zimbros (or Cantinho). Many of the stunning beaches around **Bombinhas** are untouched, accessible only on foot or by boat. Its clear waters are marvellous for diving.

Porto Belo Beaches
Phone code: 0xx47
Population: 10,704

Sleeping Porto Belo: **D** *Pousada Trapiche*, no breakfast. Lots of apartments, mostly sleep 4-6, in **B** range, good value for a group. **Zimbros**: **B** *Pousada Zimbros*, R da Praia 527, T369 3225/1225. Cheaper off season, on beach, sumptuous breakfast, restaurant, spear fishing guide. Highly recommended. **Camping**: There are lots of camp sites around the peninsula.

Transport Bus Florianópolis to Porto Belo, several daily with *Rainha*, fewer at weekends, more frequent buses to Tijuca, Itapema and Itajaí, all on the BR-101 with connections. Buses from Porto Belo to the beaches on the peninsula.

This is now the most concentrated development on Brazil's southern coast. From 15 December to end-February it is very crowded and expensive; the rest of the year it is easy to rent furnished apartments by the day or week. A few kilometres south, at Lojas Apple, there is Parque Cyro Gevaerd, a museum (archaeology, oceanography, fishing, arts and crafts) and aquarium; and Meia Praia, which is quieter and cleaner than Camboriú. A *teleférico* has been built to Praia Laranjeiras, previously deserted; US$5 return from Barra Sul shopping centre to Laranjeiras via Mata Atlântica

Camboriú
Phone code: 0xx47
Colour map 7, grid C3
Population: 41,445
80 km N of Florianópolis

Brazil

Brazil

station. Between Camboriú and Itajaí is the beautiful, deserted (and rough) beach of Praia Brava. ■ *Buses from Florianópolis, Joinville and Blumenau. TTL buses Montevideo-São Paulo stop here at about 1800, a good place to break the journey.*

Blumenau

Phone code: 0xx47
Post code: 89100
Colour map 7, grid C3
Population: 261,808
61 km by paved
road from Itajaí
Voltage: 220 AC

Some 47 km up the Rio Itajaí-Açu is this prosperous city, where hightech and electronics industries are replacing textiles as the economic mainstay. The surrounding district was settled mostly by Germans. It is clean and orderly with almost caricatured Germanic architecture. See the **Museu da Família Colonial**, German immigrant museum, Av Duque de Caxias 78. ■ *Mon-Fri 0800-1130, 1330-1730, Sat morning only, US$0.15.* Also worth a visit is the **German Evangelical Church**, and the houses, now **museums** (open 0800-1800), of **Dr Bruno Otto Blumenau** and of **Fritz Müller** (a collaborator of Darwin), who bought the Blumenau estate in 1897 and founded the town.

Oktoberfest, the second largest street party in Brazil, after Carnival is usually held in the first half of October. During the day the narrow streets are packed around the Molemann Centre, which contains a mixture of bars, live music and of course, Chopp beer. At 1900 the doors of the Oktoberfest pavilion open for different events, including drinking competitions, the 'sausage Olympics', traditional dress and cake making competitions. There is also a fun fair and folk dancing shows. Visitors report it is worth attending on weekday evenings but weekends are too crowded. It is repeated, but called a 'summer festival', in the three weeks preceding Carnival.

At **Pomerode**, 33 km west of Blumenau, the north German dialect of Plattdeutsch is still spoken and there are several folkloric groups keeping alive the music and dance of their ancestors. The Museu Pomerano, Rodovia SC 418, Km 3, T387 0477, tells the story of the colonial family. Museu Ervin Kurt Theichmann, R 15 de Novembro 791, T387 0282, has sculptures. The *Confeitaria Torten Paradies*, R 15 de Novembro 211, serves excellent German cakes. *Festa do Pomerania* in January. ■ *Coletivos Volkmann (T387 1321) Blumenau-Pomerode daily US$0.75, 1 hr; check schedule at tourist offices.*

Sleeping
Reservations are essential during Oktoberfest

C *Blumenau Turist Hotel*, R Francisco Margarida 67, T323 3554, 200 m from bus station. Helpful. **C** *Glória*, R 7 de Setembro 954, T326 1988, F326 5370. German-run, excellent coffee shop, best deal is 'meal of soups', US$2.30 for salad bar, 4 soups, dessert and wine. **D** *Herrmann*, Floriano Peixoto 213, T322 4370, F326 0670. One of the oldest houses in Blumenau, rooms with or without bath, excellent big breakfast, German spoken. Many cheap hotels do not include breakfast. Youth hostel *Grün Garten Pousada*, R São Paulo 2457, T323 4332, 15 mins' walk from rodoviária. **Camping** Municipal campsite, 3 km out on R Pastor Osvaldo Hesse; Paraíso dos Poneis, 9 km out on the Itajaí road, also Motel; Refúgio Gaspar Alto, 12 km out on R da Glória.

Eating

Good German food at *Frohsinn*, Morro Aipim (panoramic view) and *Cavalinho Branco*, Av Rio Branco 165, huge meals. International eating at *Moinho do Vale*, Paraguai 66. *Amigo*, Peixoto 213, huge cheap meals. *Deutsches Eck*, R 7 de Septembro 432. Recommended, especially carne pizzaiola. *Gruta Azul*, Rodolfo Freygang 8. Good, popular, not cheap. *Internacional*, Nereu Ramos 61. Chinese, very good, moderate prices. *Chinês*, R 15 de Novembro 346, near Tourist office. Good. *Tunga*, R 15 de Novembro. Patio, live music. *Patisseria Bavaria*, Av 7 Septembro y Zimmerman. Very good cakes and fruit juices, friendly and caring staff.

Transport

Bus Rodoviária is 7 km from town (get off at the bridge over the river and walk 1 km to centre). Bus to the rodoviária from Av Presidente Castelo-Branco (Beira Rio). There are connections in all directions from Blumenau. To **Curitiba**, US$6.50, 4 hrs, 3 daily (*Penha* and *Catarinense*).

Directory

Banks *Câmbios*/travel agencies: *Vale do Itajaí Turismo e Cambio*, Av Beira Rio 167, very helpful, German spoken. **Tourist office** T387 2627. *Tilotur Turismo*, Alameda Rio Branco e 15 de Novembro, 2nd floor, T326 7999.

80 km up the coast at the mouth of the Baia de Babitonga, São Francisco do Sul is the port for the town of Joinville, 45 km inland at the head of the Rio Cachoeira. There is an interesting **Museu Nacional do Mar** reflecting Brazil's seafaring history. The centre has over 150 historical sites and has been protected since 1987. The **cathedral** was built between 1699 and 1719 and still has its original walls made with sand, shells and whale oil. There are some excellent **beaches** nearby. **AL-A** Zibamba, R Fernandes Dias 27, T/F444 2020, central, good restaurant. ■ *Bus terminal is 1½ km from centre. Direct bus* (Penha) *daily to Curitiba at 0730, US$6, 3½ hrs.*

São Francisco do Sul
Phone code: 0xx47
Colour map 7, grid C3
Population: 32300

Joinville itself (*Phone code*: 0xx47) is the state's largest city. It lies 2 km from the main coastal highway, BR-101, by which Curitiba and Florianópolis are less than two hours away. The industry does not spoil the considerable charm of the city. The **Alameda Brustlein**, better known as the **R das Palmeiras**, is an impressive avenue of palm trees leading to the **Palácio dos Príncipes**. The trees have been protected since 1982. The **Cathedral** on Av Juscelino Kubitscheck with R do Príncipe (T433 3459), is futuristic with spectacular windows recounting the story of man. The **Casa da Cultura** (Galeria Municipal de Artes 'Victor Kursansew'), R Dona Fransisca 800, also contains the School of Art 'Fritz Alt', the School of Music 'Vila Lobos' and the School of Ballet. ■ *Mon-Fri 0900-1800, Sat 0900-1300.* A number of museums and exhibition centres reflect the history of, and immigration to the area and the city's artistic achievements. In July, Joinville hosts the largest dance festival in the world, which attracts around 4,000 dancers who stay for 12 days and put on shows and displays ranging from jazz, folklore, classical ballet and other styles.There is also an annual beer festival, *Fenachopp*, in October. There are many good restaurants and good air and road links to other parts of Brazil. **Tourist offices** Corner Praça Nereu Ramos with R do Príncipe, T433 1511/1437, F433 1491. *Promotur*, in Centreventos Cau Hansen, A José Vieira 315, sala 20, T423 2633, www.promotur.com.br Also www.joinville.sc.gov.br

Brazil

A *Tannenhof*, Visconde de Taunay 340, T/F433 8011, www.tannenhof.com.br 4-star, pool, gym, traffic noise, excellent breakfast, restaurant. **A** *Anthurium Parque*, São José 226, T/F433 6299, www.anthurium.com.br Colonial building, once home to a bishop, good value, English spoken, pool, sauna. **D** *Mattes*, 15 de Novembro 801, T422 3582, www.hotelmattes.com.br Good facilities, big breakfast. **E** *Novo Horizonte*, at bus station, basic, clean.

Sleeping

Southern Santa Catarina

At **Praia do Rosa**, 101 km south of Florianópolis, is the headquarters of the Right Whale Project (*Projeto Baleia-franca*) and one of Brazil's prime **whale-watching** sites. The right whales come to the bay to calve from May to November and trips can be arranged to see them. The project's base is the *Pousada Vida, Sol e Mar*, T354 0041/355 6111, which has cabins, pool, restaurant and surf school. For packages contact *Rentamar Turismo*, 338 Milton Rd, Cambridge, CB4 1LW, UK, T/F+44-1223 424244, Glauce.UK@tesco.net There are other lodgings at Praia do Rosa and other fine beaches in the area. The nearest major town is Imbituba. Ibama: *Area de Proteção Ambiental da Baleia Franca*, Av Mauro Ramos 1113, CCP660, 88020-301 Florianópolis, T212 3300, F224 9549.

Some 15 km from Tubarão is the small fishing port of **Laguna**. The town, founded in 1676, was the capital of the Juliana Republic in 1839, a short-lived separatist movement led by Italian idealist Guiseppe Garibáldi. At Laguna is the **Anita Garibáldi Museum**, containing documents, furniture, and personal effects of Garibáldi's devoted lover. ■ *Buses to/from Porto Alegre, 5½ hrs, with Santo Anjo Da Guarda; same company goes to Florianópolis, 2 hrs, US$5.25, 6 daily.*

Laguna
Phone code: 0xx48
Colour map 7, grid C3
Population: 47,568
124 km S of Florianópolis

About 16 km away (by ferry and road) are beaches and dunes at **Cavo de Santa Marta**. Also from Laguna, take a *Lagunautor* or *Auto Viação São José* bus to **Farol** (four buses a day Monday-Friday, one on Saturday, US$1.50, beautiful ride). You

Brazil

have to cross the mouth of the Lagoa Santo Antônio by ferry (10 mins) to get to Farol; look out for fishermen aided by dolphins (*botos*). Here is a fishing village with a lighthouse (Farol de Santa Marta), built by the French in 1890 of stone, sand and whale oil. It is the largest lighthouse in South America and has the third largest view in the world. ■ *Guided tours available (taxi, US$10, not including ferry toll). It may be possible to bargain with fishermen for a bed, or there are campsites at Santa Marta Pequena by the lighthouse, popular with surfers.*

Sleeping C *Turismar*, Av Beira Mar 207, T647 0024, F647 0279. 2-star, view over Mar Grosso beach, TV. **D** *Recanto*, Av Colombo 17, close to bus terminal. With breakfast, modern but basic. **D** *Beiramar*, T644 0260, 100 m from *Recanto*, opposite Angeloni Supermarket. No breakfast, TV, rooms with view over lagoon.

São Joaquim
Colour map 7, grid C2
Population: 22,836
Altitude: 1,360 m

Buses from the coalfield town of Tubarão (27 km from Laguna) go inland to Lauro Müller, then over the Serra do Rio do Rastro (beautiful views of the coast in clear weather) to **Bom Jardim da Serra** which has an apple festival every April. The road continues to **São Joaquim**. The highest town in southern Brazil, it regularly has snowfalls in winter; a very pleasant town with an excellent climate. 11 km outside the town on the way to Bom Jardim da Serra is the **Parque Ecológico Vale da Neve** (Snow Valley). It is an easy hike and very beautiful, the entrance is on the main road, US$3, and there is a restaurant. The owner is American and an English speaking guide will take you for a 1½ hr walk through the forest. The **Parque Nacional de São Joaquim** in the Serra Geral (33,500 ha, on paper only, much of the land is still private) has canyons containing sub-tropical vegetation, and araucaria forest at higher levels. There is no bus (local *Ibama* office, T048-278 4002, *Secretaria de Turismo de São Joaquim*, T049-233 0258).

Sleeping In São Joaquim: D *Nevada*, T/F233 0259. Expensive meals. **D** *Maristela*, T233 007, French spoken, no heating so can be cold, helpful, good breakfast; both on R Manoel Joaquim Pinto, 190 and 220 respectively (5 mins' walk from rodoviária). In **Bom Jardim da Serra**, **E** *Moretti*, family atmosphere, owner very helpful. **Camping** *Clube do Brasil* site.

Transport Bus to **Florianópolis** 0700 and 1700 via Bom Retiro (*Reunidos*) and 0800 via Tubarão (*Nevatur*), 5½ hrs, US$9. Florianópolis-Bom Jardim da Serra, US$10.

Rio Grande do Sul

Population: 10.2 million

Rio Grande do Sul is gaúcho country; it is also Brazil's chief wine producer. The capital, Porto Alegre, is the most industrialized city in the south, but in the surroundings are good beaches, interesting coastal national parks and the fine scenery of the Serra Gaúcha. On the border with Santa Catarina is the remarkable Aparados da Serra National Park. In the far west are the remains of Jesuit missions. Look out for local specialities such as comida campeira, te colonial and quentão. In southern Rio Grande do Sul there are great grasslands stretching as far as Uruguay to the south and Argentina to the west. In this distinctive land of the gaúcho, or cowboy (pronounced ga-oo-shoo in Brazil), people feel closer to Uruguay and Argentina than Brazil (except where football is concerned). The gaúcho culture has developed a sense of distance from the African-influenced society of further north. This separationist strain was most marked in the 1820s and 1830s when the Farroupilha movement, led by Bento Gonçalves, proclaimed the República Riograndense in 1835.

Porto Alegre

The capital of Rio Grande do Sul is where cowboy culture meets the bright lights. It lies at the confluence of five rivers (called Rio Guaíba, although it is not a river in its own right) and thence into the great freshwater lagoon, the Lagoa dos Patos, which runs into the sea. The freshwater port is one of the most up-to-date in the country and Porto Alegre is the biggest commercial centre south of São Paulo. It is also one of the richest and best educated parts of Brazil and held the first three World Social Forums (2001-2003), putting the city in a global spotlight. Standing on a series of hills and valleys on the banks of the Guaíba, it has a temperate climate through most of the year, though the temperature at the height of summer can often exceed 40°C and drop below 10°C in winter.

Phone code: 0xx51
Colour map 7, inset
Population: 1,360,590
The market area in
Praça 15 de Novembro
and the bus terminal
are dangerous at
night. Thefts have
been reported in
Voluntários da Pátria
and Praça Parcão

The older residential part of the town is on a promontory, dominated previously by the **Palácio Piratini** (Governor's Palace) and the imposing 1920s **cathedral** on the Praça Marechal Deodoro (or da Matriz). Also on, or near this square, are the neo-classical **Theatro São Pedro** (1858), the **Solar dos Câmara** (1818, now a historical and cultural centre), the **Biblioteca Pública** – all dwarfed by the skyscraper of the **Assembléia Legislativa** – and the **Museu Júlio de Castilhos**, Duque de Caxias 1231, which has an interesting historical collection about the state of Rio Grande do Sul. ■ *Tue-Sun 0900-1700.* Down Rua General Câmara from Praça Marechal Deodoro is the **Praça da Alfândega**, with the old customs house and the Museu de Arte de Rio Grande do Sul (see below). A short walk east of this group, up Rua 7 de Setembro, is Praça 15 de Novembro, on which is the neoclassical **Mercado Público**, selling everything from religious artefacts to spice and meat. For art from the state, visit the **Museu de Arte do Rio Grande do Sul**, Praça Senador Florêncio (Praça da Alfândega). ■ *Tue 1000-2100, Wed-Sun 1000-1700, free.* **Museu de Comunicação Social**, Rua dos Andradas 959, in the former *A Federação* newspaper building, deals with the development of the press in Brazil since the 1920s. ■ *Mon-Fri 1200-1900, T3224 4252.*

Sights
On Sun there are guided
walks from Praça da
Alfândega and on Sat
from Praça da Matriz,
1500 or 1600, free,
contact Central de
Informações Turísticas,
R Vasco da Gama 153,
Bom Fim,
T0800-517686, or in the
Mercado Público.

A large part of **Rua dos Andradas** (Rua da Praia) is permanently closed to traffic and by around 1600 it is jammed full of people. Going west along Rua dos Andradas, you pass the wide stairway that leads up to the two high white towers of the church of **Nossa Senhora das Dores**. At the end of the promontory, the **Usina do Gasômetro** has been converted from a thermoelectric station into a cultural centre. Its enormous chimney has become a symbol for the city. There is a café in the bottom of it. The sunset from the centre's balcony is stunning. In the **Cidade Baixa** quarter are the colonial **Travessa dos Venezianos** (between Ruas Lopo Gonçalves and Joaquim Nabuco) and the **house of Lopo Gonçalves**, Rua João Alfredo 582, which houses the **Museu de Porto Alegre Joaquim José Felizardo**, a collection on the history of the city. ■ *Tue-Sun 0900-1700, free.*

The central **Parque Farroupilha** (called Parque Redenção) which has many attractions and on Sundays there is a *feira* of antiques, handicrafts and all sorts at the José Bonifácio end. The **Jardim Botânico** (Bairro Jardim Botânico, bus 40 from Praça 15 de Novembro), is on Rua Salvador França 1427, *zona leste.*

The 5-km wide **Rio Guaíba** lends itself to every form of boating and there are several sailing clubs. Two boats run trips around the islands in the estuary: *Cisne Branco*, from Cais do Porto, near Museu de Arte de Rio Grande do Sul, T3224 2802, several sailings on Sunday, fewer mid-week, one hr, US$5; and *Noiva do Caí*, from the Usina do Gasômetro, T3211 7662, several on Sunday, fewer mid-week, one hr, US$2 (check winter schedules). You can see a good view of the city, with glorious sunsets, from the **Morro de Santa Teresa** (take bus 95 from the top end of Rua Salgado Filho, marked 'Morro de Santa Teresa TV' or just 'TV'). Another good sunset-viewing spot is the Usina do Gasômetro.

Brazil

Sleeping

AL *Continental*, Lg Vespasiano Júlio Veppo 77, T3211 2344, www.hoteiscontinental.com.br High standards, pool, gym. Recommended. **B** *Açores*, R dos Andradas 885, T3221 7588, F3225 1007. Central, cramped but friendly. **B** *Lancaster*, Trav Acelino de Carvalho 67, T3224 4737, F3224 4630. Central, quiet, a/c, restaurant. **B** *Ritter*, Lg Vespasiano Júlio Veppo 55, opposite rodoviária, T3228 4044, F3228 1610. Four-star and 3-star wings, English, French, German spoken, bar, small pool, sauna. Fine restaurant, good service. Recommended. **C** *Savoy*, Av Borges Medeiros 688, T3224 0843, hotelsavoy@terra.com.br Good value, garage. **D** *Elevado*, Av Farrapos 65, T/F3224 5250, www.hotelelevado.cjb.net Youth hostel association member, big rooms, microwave and coffee, good value. **D** *Palácio*, Av Vigário José Inácio 644, T3225 3467. Central, hot water, safe. **E** *América*, Av Farrapos 119, T/F3226 0062, www.hotelamerica.com.br Bright, large rooms with sofas, garage. Recommended. **E** *Erechim*, Av Júlio de Castilhos 341, near Rodoviária, T3228 7044, www.hotelerechim.com.br Youth hostel member, with or without bath, good value. **Camping** Praia do Guarujá, 16 km out on Av Guaíba.

Eating

Churrasco *Moinhos de Vento*, R Dona Laura 424, T3331 1847. Closed Sun afternoon. *Coqueiros*, R João Alfredo 208, T3227 1833. 1130-1430, 1930-2400, closed Sun and Mon evening. Cheap and cheerful. **General** *Le Bon Gourmet*, Av Alberto Bins 514 (in *Plaza São Rafael Hotel*), 1900-2300, closed Sun. Steaks, pasta and fine fish, mid-range. 24-hour *514 Bar* is at back of hotel lobby. *Chalé da Praça 15*, Praça 15 de Novembro. Average gaúcho food but recommended for early evening drinks and snacks. *Komka*, Av Bahia 1275, San Geraldo, T3222 1881. 1130-1430, 1900-2300, closed Sun, also do churrasco. Recommended. The Central Market along the Praça is lined with *lancherias*.**German** *Chopp Stübel*, R Quintino Bocaiúva 940, Moinhos de Vento, T3332 8895. Open 1800-0030, closed Sun, Recommended. *Wunderbar*, R Marquês do Herval 5981, Moinhos de Vento, T3222 4967. Very busy 1830 till last diner leaves.

Porto Alegre

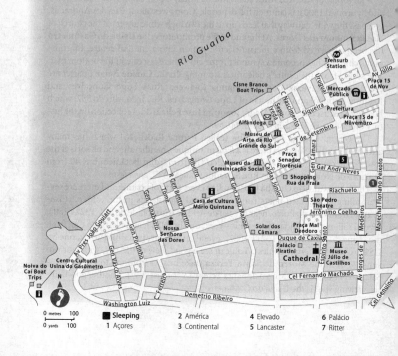

■ **Sleeping**	2 América	4 Elevado	6 Palácio
1 Açores	3 Continental	5 Lancaster	7 Ritter

Recommended, welcoming, mid-range. **Italian** *Al Dente*, R Mata Bacelar 210, Auxiliadora, T3343 1841. Expensive northern Italian cuisine. *Atelier de Massas*, R Riachuelo 1482. Lunch and dinner, closed Sun, fantastic pastas and steaks, excellent value. *Spaguetti Express*, Centro Comercial Nova Olária, Lima e Silva 776. Good. **Regional** *Gambrinus*, Central Market ground level, Praça 15 de Novembro. T32266914. Lunch and dinner, closed Sun. Cheap. In Casa de Cultura Mário Quintana, R dos Andrades 736, *Café Dos Cataventos* in courtyard and *Restaurant Majestic* on roof. Both serve good drinks, snacks and meals. Fantastic rooftop sunsets. 1200-2300.The café in Usina do Gasômetro is also very good for sandwiches and speciality coffee. Cheap. *Lancheria Primavera*, Av Farrapos 187. Good breakfasts (toasties and juice) if staying nearby. 0630-1930 closed Sun. Cheap. Staff also run red metal shack round corner on R Dr Barros Cassal serving tasty German hotdogs and burgers. **Vegetarian** *Ilha Natural*, R Gen Câmara 60, T3224 4738. Self-service, cheap, lunch only Mon-Fri. *Nova Vida Restaurant Alternativo*, Av Borges de Medeiros 1010.1100-1500, closed Sun, good lasagne. Also at Demetrio Ribeiro 1182. Cheap.

Bars & clubs

Bar do Goethe, R 24 de Outubro 112, Moinhos de Vento, T3222 2043, www.compuserve.com.br/bardogoethe/ Reunion each Tue, 2030, for foreign language speakers. *Bar do Nito*, Av Cel Lucas de Oliveira 105, Moinhos de Vento. T3333 4600. Popular music bar. *Cía Sandwiches*, Getúlio Vargas 1430, T3233 7414. 1800-0200, beer, sandwiches and music. *João de Barro*, R da República 546, Cidade Baixa. Good jazz. *Sargeant Peppers*, Dona Laura 329, T3331 3258. Live music Thu-Sat, closed Mon. On weekend nights, thousands spill out of the huge beer bars and clubs along Av Goethe between R Vasco de Gama and R Dona Laura in Rio Branco (a US$2 taxi ride from the centre). **Nightclubs**: *Dr Jekyll*, Travessa do Carmo 76, Cidade Baixa. T32269404. Open from 2200. Closed Sunday. Nearby is *Ossip*, Av República 677 e João Afredo. Pleasant wine bar. Gay bars and clubs include *Doce Vício*, R Vieira de Castro 32. Three floors with games room, bar, restaurant, 1830-0230, closed Mon. *Fly*, R Gonçalvo de Carvalho 189. Predominantly male, attractive bar with art exhibition, sophisticated, open 2100-0200, closed Tue. *Wanda Bar*, R Comendador Coruja 169, Floresta. T3224 4755. Open from 2030.

Entertainment

Art galleries *Casa de Cultura Mário Quintana*, R dos Andrades 736, T3221 7147. A lively centre for the arts, with exhibitions, theatre, pleasant bar etc, open 0900-2100, 1200-2100 Sat-Sun. **Theatre** *São Pedro*, Praça Mal Deodoro, T3227 5100. Free noon and late afternoon concerts Sat, Sun, art gallery, café.

Festivals

The main event is on **2 Feb** (a local holiday), with the festival of *Nossa Senhora dos Navegantes* (Iemanjá), whose image is taken by boat from the central quay in the port to the industrial district of Navegantes. *Semana Farroupilha* celebrates *gaúcho* traditions with parades in traditional style, its main day being on **20 Sep**. The Carnival parade takes place in Av A do Carvalho, renamed Av Carlos Alberto Barcelos (or Roxo) for these 3 days only, after a famous carnival designer.

Brazil

To Guaíba Bridge

To Museu de Porto Alegre Joaquim José Felizardo

● **Eating**
1 Atelier de Massas   2 Le Bon Gourmet

Shopping The Praia de Belas shopping centre, among the largest in Latin America, is a US$1.50 taxi ride from town. There is a street market (leather goods, basketware etc) in the streets around the central Post Office. Good leather goods are sold on the streets. Sun morning handicraft and bric-a-brac market (plus sideshows) Av José Bonifácio (next to Parque Farroupilha). There is a very good food market. **Bookshops** *Livraria Londres*, Av Osvaldo Aranha 1182. Used books in English, French and Spanish and old *Life* magazines. *Saraiva Megastore*, in Shopping Praia de Belas. *Siciliano*, R dos Andradas 1273 and other branches. Each year a *Feira do Livro* is held in Praça da Alfândega, Oct-Nov.

Transport **Local Bus** 1st-class minibuses (*Lotação*), painted in a distinctive orange, blue and white pattern, stop on request, fares about US$0.60. Safer and more pleasant than normal buses (US$0.35). **Air** The international airport is on Av dos Estados, 8 km from the city, T3342 1082. There are regular buses to the rodoviária and a metrô service, *Trensurb*, to the Mercado Público, via the rodoviária, US$0.40.

Long Distance Bus International and interstate buses arrive at the rodoviária at Largo Vespasiano Júlio Veppo, on Av Mauá with Garibáldi, T145, www.rodoviaria-poa.com.br Facilities include a post office and long-distance telephone service until 2100. There are 2 sections to the terminal; the ticket offices for interstate and international destinations are together in 1 block, beside the municipal tourist office (very helpful). The intermunicipal (state) ticket offices are in another block; for travel information within the state, ask at the very helpful booth on the station concourse.

To **Rio**, US$60, 24 hrs with Itapemirim; **São Paulo**, US$30 (*leito* US$51), 18 hrs; **Florianópolis**, US$16, 7 hrs with *Santo Anjo* (take an *executivo* rather than a *convencional*, which is a much slower service); **Curitiba**, from US$17.50 *convencional* to US$30 *leito*, coastal and *serra* routes, 11 hrs; **Rio Grande**, US$10, every 2 hrs from 0600, 4 hrs. **Foz do Iguaçu**, US$26-30, 13 hrs. To **Jaguarão** on Uruguayan border at 2400, 6 hrs, US$10. **Uruguaiana**, US$17.50, 8 hrs. Many other destinations.

Take your passport and tourist card when purchasing international bus tickets

International buses To **Montevideo**, with *TTL executivo* daily 2030 US$44 (*leito* Fri only at 2100), alternatively take an ordinary bus to border town of Chuí at 1200 or 2330 daily, 7 hrs, US$13, then bus to Montevideo (US$8). To **Asunción** with *Unesul* at 1900, Tue, Fri, 18 hrs via **Foz do Iguaçu**, US$24. There are bus services to **Buenos Aires**, US$50-70, 19 hrs (depending on border) with *Pluma*, 1805 daily, route is Uruguaiana, Paso de los Libres, Entre Ríos and Zárate. For **Misiones** (Argentina), take 2100 bus (not Sat) to Porto Xavier on the Río Uruguay, 11 hrs, US$15, get exit stamp at police station, take a boat to San Javier, US$2, go to Argentine immigration at the port, then take a bus to Posadas (may have to change in Leandro N Além).

Road Good roads radiate from Porto Alegre, and Highway BR-116 is paved to Curitiba (746 km). To the south it is paved (mostly in good condition), to Chuí on the Uruguayan border, 512 km. In summer visibility can be very poor at night owing to mist, unfenced cows are a further hazard. The paved coastal road to Curitiba via Itajaí (BR-101), of which the first 100 km is the 4-lane Estrada General Osório highway, is much better than the BR-116 via Caxias and Lajes. The road to Uruguaiana is entirely paved but bumpy.

Directory **Banks** *Banco do Brasil*, Av dos Estados 1515, T371 1955 (also has Visa/Plus ATM), and Av Assis Brasil 2487, T341 2466. 1000-1500, good rates for TCs. Branch at Uruguai 185 has Visa/Plus ATM. Many branches of *Bradesco* have Visa ATMs; also branches of *Banco Bilbao Vizcaya Argentaria Brasil*. *Citibank*, R7 de Setembro 722, T3220 8619. *MasterCard* ATMs at any *HSBC* branch or *Banco 24 Horas*. *MasterCard*, cash against card, R 7 de Setembro 722, 8th floor, Centro. *Exprinter*, R Hilário Ribeiro 292 (best for cash). For other addresses consult tourist bureau brochure. **Communications** Internet: *Com Cyber Café*, R da Praia Shopping, S17, Rua dos Andradas 1001, T3286 4244, www.com-cybercafe.co.br US$3 per hr. *Ciber Café*, Câncio Gomes e C Colombo 778, T3346 3098, 0900-2300. *Livraria Saraiva Megastore*, Shopping Praia de Belas, Mon-Sat 1000-2200. *PC2*, Duque de Caxias 1464, T3227 6853, US$2 per hr. *Portonet*, R Mal Floriano 185, T3227 4696, 0900-2100. US$2.50 per hr. **Post office**: R Siqueira Campos 1100, Centro, Mon-Fri 0900-1800, Sat 0900-1230. **UPS**, T434 972 (Alvaro). **Telephone**: R Borges de Medeiros 475, and upstairs at rodoviária. **Cultural centres** Sociedade Brasileira da Cultura Inglesa, Praça Mauricio Cardoso 49, Moinhos de Vento. Instituto Goethe, 24 de

Outubro 122. Mon-Fri, 0930-1230, 1430-2100, occasional concerts, bar recommended for German *Apfelkuchen*. **Embassies and consulates** Argentina, R Coronel Bordini 1033, Moinhos de Vento, T/F3321 1360. 0900-1600. **Germany**, R Prof Annes Dias 112, 11th floor, T3224 9255, F3226 4909. 0830-1130. **Italy**, Praça Marechal Deodoro 134, T3228 2055. 0900-1200. **Japan**, Av João Obino 467, Alto Petrópolis, T3334 1299, F3334 1742. 0900-1230, 1500-1700. **Portugal**, R Prof Annes Dias 112, 10th floor, T/F3224 5767. 0900-1500. **Spain**, R Ildefonso Simões Lopes 85, Três Figueiras, T3338 1300, F3338 1444. 0830-1330. **Sweden**, Av Viena 279, São Geraldo, T3222 2322, F3222 2463, 1400-1745. **UK**, R Itapeva 110, Sala 505, Edif Montreal, Bairro Passo D'Areia, T/F3341 0720, 0900-1200, 1430-1800. **Uruguay**, Av Cristóvão Colombo 2999, Higienópolis, T 3325 6200, F3325 6200, 0900-1500. **USA**, R Riachuelo 1257, 2nd Floor, T3226 3344, 1400-1700. **Language courses** Portuguese and Spanish, *Matilde Dias*, R Pedro Chaves Barcelos 37, Apdo 104, T3331 8235, malilde@estadao.com.br US$9 per hr. **Tourist offices** Tourist information T0800-517686, www.portoalegre.rs.gov.br/turismo *Central de Informações Turísticas*, R Vasco da Gama 153, Bom Fim, open daily 0900-2100. *Setur*, Borges de Medeiros 1501, 10th floor, T3228 5400; also at airport; rodoviária, very helpful (free city maps); Casa de Cultura Mário Quintana, open Tue-Fri 0900-2100, Sat-Sun 1200-2100; Usina do Gasômetro, open daily 1000-1800; Mercado Público, Mon-Sat 0900-1600.

Porto Alegre beach resorts

The main beach resorts of the area are to the east and north of the city. Heading east along the BR-290, 112 km from Porto Alegre is **Osório**, a pleasant lakeside town with a few hotels. From here it is 18 km southeast to the rather polluted and crowded beach resort of **Tramandaí** (5 buses daily from Porto Alegre, US$3.50). The beaches here are very popular, with lots of hotels, bars, restaurants, and other standard seaside amenities. Extensive dunes and lakes in the region provide an interesting variety of wildlife and sporting opportunities. The beach resorts become less polluted the further north you travel, and the water is clean by the time you reach Torres (see below). Among the resorts between the two towns is **Capão da Canoa**, with surfing at Atlântida beach. The Lagoa dos Quadros, inland, is used for windsurfing, sailing, water-skiing and jet-skiing.

Torres

Phone code: 0xx51
Colour map 7, inset
Population: 30,880

Torres is a well developed resort, with a number of beaches, several high class, expensive hotels, a wide range of restaurants, professional surfing competitions and entertainment. Torres holds a ballooning festival in April. There is an annual independence day celebration, when a cavalcade of horses arrives in town on 16 September from Uruguay. Torres gets its name from the three huge rocks, or towers, on the town beach, Praia Grande. Fishing boats can be hired for a trip to **Ilha dos Lobos**, a rocky island 2 km out to sea, where sea lions spend the winter months. Dolphins visit Praia dos Molhes, north of the town, the year round and whales can occasionally be seen in July. The tourist office is at R Rio Branco 315, T664 1219/626 1937. ■ *Bus Porto Alegre-Torres, 9 a day, US$6.*

There is a paved road running south from Tramandaí along the coast to Quintão, giving access to many beaches. Of note is **Cidreira**, with *Hotel Farol* on the main street (**D** with bath). Bus from Porto Alegre US$3.40.

Serra Gaúcha

Population: Canela, 33,625; Gramado, 29,593

The Serra Gaúcha boasts stunningly beautiful scenery, some of the best being around the towns of **Canela** and **Gramado**, about 130 km north of Porto Alegre. There is a distinctly Swiss/Bavarian flavour to many of the buildings in both towns. It is difficult to get rooms in the summer/Christmas. In spring and summer the flowers are a delight, and in winter there are frequently snow showers. This is excellent walking and climbing country among hills, woods, lakes and waterfalls. For canoeists, the Rio Paranhana at Três Coroas is renowned, especially for slalom. Local crafts include knitted woollens, leather, wickerwork, and chocolate.

Gramado, at 850 m on the edge of a plateau with views, provides a summer escape from the 40° C heat of the plains. It lives almost entirely by tourism and the main street, Av Borges de Medeiros, is full of kitsch artisan shops and fashion boutiques. In the summer, thousands of hydrangeas (*hortênsias*) bloom. About 1.5 km along Av das

Hortênsias towards Canela is the **Prawer Chocolate Factory**, Av das Hortênsias 4100. ■ *Free tours of the truffle-making process and free tasting. T2861580, www.prawer.com.br 0830-1130, 1330-1700, closed weekends.* Opposite is the incongruous but good **Hollywood Dream Car Automobile Museum** (No 4151, T2864-515, 0900-1900 US$2.10) with a collection of dating back to a 1929 Ford Model A and Harley Davidson motorbikes from 1926. For a good walk/bike ride into the valley, take the dirt road Turismo Rural 28, *Um Mergulho no Vale* (A Dive into the Valley), which starts at Av das Hortênsias immediately before Prawer. Each August, Gramado holds a festival of Latin American cinema. Internet at *Cyber*, Av Borges de Medeiros 2016, T286 9559, 1300-2300, US$2.80 per hour. Tourist offices at Av das Hortênsias (Pórtico), T286 1418 and Praça Maj Nicoletti/Av Borges de Medeiros 1674, T286 1475. www.gramadosite.com.br ■ *Frequent bus service to Canela, 10 mins.*

A few kilometres along the plateau rim, **Canela** has been spared the plastic make-over of its neighbour. Seven km away is the **Parque Estadual do Caracol**, (T278 3035, 0830-1800, US$1.75) with a spectacular 130-m high waterfall where the Rio Caracol tumbles out of thick forest. A 927-step metal staircase ("equivalent to a 45-storey building") leads to the plunge pool. There is an 18-km circular bike route continuing on to **Parque Ferradura**, where there is a good view into the canyon of the Rio Cai. From the Ferradura junction, take the right to continue to the Floresta Nacional run by Ibama, T282 2608, 0800-1700, free. From here, the dirt road continues round to Canela. Another good hike or bike option is the 4-km track southeast of Canela past Parque das Sequóias to Morro Pelado. At over 600 m, there are spectacular views from the rim edge.■ *Tourist office, Laga da Fama 227, T282 2200, www.canela.com.br Voltage is 220 V AC.*

All those listed are recommended **Sleeping Gramado**: Plenty of hotels and places to eat (mostly expensive). **B** *Chalets do Vale*, R Arthur Reinheimer 161 (off Av das Hortênsias at about 4700), T 286 4151, chaletsdovale@via-rs.net 3 homely chalets in lovely setting, kitchen, TV, good deal for groups of 4/ families. **C Pousada Pertuti**, Av Borges de Medeiros 3571, T286 2513. Good breakfast, use of kitchen. **E** *Albergue Internacional de Gramado,* Av das Hortênsias 3880, T295 1020. Cosy and new. **Canela**: On R Oswaldo Aranha: **B** *Bela Vista*, No 160, T/F282 1327, near rodoviária. Good breakfasts. **D** *Turis Café*, No 223, T282 2774. Breakfast, English speaking staff. **D** *Pousada Schermer*, Travessa Romeu 30, T282 1746. Very good indeed. **D** pp*Pousada do Viajante*, R Ernesto Urbani 132, T2822017. Kitchen facilities. **Camping** *Camping Clube do Brasil*, 1 km from waterfall in Parque do Caracol, 1 km off main road, signposted (8 km from Canela), T282 4321; excellent honey and chocolate for sale here. *Sesi*, camping or cabins, R Francisco Bertolucci 504, 2½ km outside Canela, T/F282 1311. Clean, restaurant.

Parque Nacional de Aparados da Serra *Colour map 7, inset* The major attraction at the Parque Nacional de Aparados da Serra is a canyon, 7.8 km long and 720 m deep, known locally as the Itaimbezinho. Here, two waterfalls cascade 350 m into a stone circle at the bottom. For experienced hikers (and with a guide) there is a difficult path to the bottom of Itaimbezinho. One can then hike 20 km to Praia Grande in Santa Catarina state. As well as the canyon, the park, its neighbour, the **Parque Nacional da Serra Geral**, and the surrounding region have several bird specialities. The park is 80 km from São Francisco de Paula (18 km east of Canela, 117 km north of Porto Alegre). ■ *Wed-Sat 0900-1700, US$2.10 plus US$1.75 for car, T251 1262. Further information from Porto Alegre tourist office or Ibama, R Miguel Teixeira 126, Cidade Baixa, Caixa Postal 280, Porto Alegre, CEP 90050-250, T3225 2144.*

Tourist excursions, mostly at weekends, from **São Francisco de Paula** (hotel: **A** *Veraneio Hampal*, RS-235 road to Canela, Km 1, T244 1363; **E** *Hotel e Churrascarria Mirão*, B Constant 492, T244 1273, basic; tourist information at southern entrance to town). At other times, take a bus to Cambará do Sul (0945, 1700, 1¼ hrs, US$2) : several *pousadas* and **D** *Pousada dos Pinheiros*, Estrada Morro Agudo, T9967 2567, 12 km from Cambará, off road to Aparados da Serra and Praia Grande turn right (signposted) for 2 km, rustic cabins, breakfast and dinner at isolated farm amid stunning scenery. Recommended.

Caxias do Sul and around

This city's population is principally of Italian descent and it is an expanding and modern city, the centre of the Brazilian wine industry. Vines were first brought to the region in 1840 but not until the end of the century and Italian immigration did the industry develop. The church of **São Pelegrino** has paintings by Aldo Locatelli and 5 m-high bronze doors sculptured by Augusto Murer. There is a good **Museu Municipal** at R Visconde de Pelotas 586, with displays of artefacts of the Italian immigration. ■ *Tue-Sat 0830-1130, 1330-1700, Sun 1400-1700, T221 2423.* Italian roots are again on display in the **Parque de Exposições Centenário**, 5 km out on R Ludovico Cavinato. January-February is the best time to visit. There is a tourist information kiosk in Praça Rui Barbosa. ■ *Rodoviária, R Ernesto Alves 1341, T228 3000, is a 15-min walk from the main praça, but many buses pass through the centre.*

Caxias do Sul's festival of grapes is held in February-March. Many *adegas* accept visitors (but do not always give free tasting). Good tour and tasting (six wines) at *Adega Granja União*, R Os 18 de Forte 2346. Visit also the neighbouring towns and sample their wines: **Farroupilha** 20 km from Caxias do Sul. **Nova Milano**, 6 km away (bus to Farroupilha, then change – day trip). **Bento Gonçalves**, 40 km from Caxias do Sul. **Garibáldi**, which has a dry ski slope and toboggan slope – equipment hire, US$5 per hr. A restored steam train leaves Bento Gonçalves Tuesday, Wednesday and Saturday at 1400 and 1500 for **Carlos Barbosa**; called *'a rota do vinho'* (the wine run), it goes through vineyards in the hills. US$25 round trip, including wines, with live band; reserve in advance through *Giordani Turismo*, R 13 de Maio 581, T455 2788. Another worthwhile trip is to **Antônio Prado**, 1½ hours by *Caxiense Bus*. The town is now a World Heritage Site because of the large number of original buildings built by immigrants in the Italian style.

Phone code: 0xx54
Post code: 95000
Colour map 7, inset
Population: 360,419
122 km from
Porto Alegre

Sleeping **Caxias do Sul** **D** *Peccini*, R Pinheiro Machado 1939. Shared bath, good breakfast. **D** *Pérola*, Marquês de Herval 237, T223 6080. Good value. Hotels fill up early in the afternoon. **Farroupilha** **D** *Grande*, R Independência 1064, T/F261 1025, 2 blocks from the church where the buses from Caxias do Sul stop, no breakfast, clean. And others. **Bento Gonçalves** **D** *Somensi*, R Siba Paes 367, T453 1254, near the Pipa Pórtico and Cristo Rei church in the upper town. Youth hostel **E** *Pousada Casa Mia*, Trav Niterói 71, T451 1215. HI. **Camping** *Palermo*, 5 km out on BR-116 at Km 118, T222 7255. *Recanto dos Pinhais*, on BR-453 towards Lajeado Grande at Km 23. At Garibáldi, Camping Clube do Brasil, estrada Gen Buarque de Macedo 4 km.

Western Rio Grande do Sul

West of **Passo Fundo**, 'the most *gaúcho* city in Rio Grande do Sul', are the **Sete Povos das Missões Orientais**. The only considerable Jesuit remains in Brazilian territory (very dramatic) are at **São Miguel das Missões**, some 50 km from **Santo Ângelo**. At São Miguel, now a World Heritage Site, there is a church, 1735-45, and small museum. ■ *0900-1800.* A *son et lumière* show in Portuguese is held daily, in winter at 2000, and later in summer, although all times rather depend on how many people there are. The show ends too late to return to Santo Ângelo. *Gaúcho* festivals are held on some Sunday afternoons, in a field near the Mission.

Jesuit Missions
Colour map 7, grid C1
Colour map 8, grid A6

Sleeping Santo Ângelo: **A** *Maerkli*, Av Brasil 1000, T/F312 2127. Recommended. **D-E** *Hotel Nova Esperança*, Trav Centenário 463, T3312 1173, behind bus station, without breakfast. **D** *Brasil*, R Mal F Peixoto 1400, T3312 1299, and **E** *Comércio*, Av Brasil 1178, T3312 2542, good for the price, a bit run down. **São Miguel:** **C** *Hotel Barichello*, Av Borges do Canto 1567, T3381 1272. Nice and quiet, restaurant with *churrasco* for lunch. Youth hostel, **E**, next to the ruins, *Pousada das Missões*, T3381 1030, pousada.missoes@terra.com.br Very good. In the evening it is difficult to find a good place to eat, try one of the 2 snack bars for hamburgers.

Brazil

Border with Argentina
Colour map 8, grid A6

Exchange rates are better in the town than at the border

In the extreme west are **Uruguaiana**, a cattle centre 772 km from Porto Alegre, and its twin Argentine town of Paso de los Libres, also with a casino. A 1,400 m bridge over the Rio Uruguai links the cities. Brazilian immigration and customs are at the end of the bridge, five blocks from the main praça; exchange and information in the same building. In 2003 this border crossing was not recommended as Paso de los Libres was not safe. Should you cross here, there are hotels in each town.

Transport Taxi or bus across the bridge about US$3.50. Buses connect the bus stations and centres of each city every 30 mins; if you have to disembark for visa formalities, a following bus will pick you up without extra charge. There are buses to Porto Alegre. *Planalto* buses run from Uruguaiana via Barra do Quaraí/Bella Unión to Salto and Paysandú in Uruguay.

South of Porto Alegre

Colour map 7, inset

South of Quintão (see above), a track runs to the charming town of **Mostardas** (**E** *Hotel Mostardense*, R Bento Conçalves 200, T673 1368, good), thence along the peninsula on the seaward side of the Lagoa dos Patos to São José do Norte, opposite Rio Grande (see below). Mostardas is a good base for visiting the national park **Lagoa do Peixe**, one of South America's top spots for migrating birds. Flamingos and albatross are among the visitors. The main lake (which has highest bird concentration) is about 20 km from Mostardas and the town of **Tavares**. ■ *Free, park has no infrastructure Park info from Praça Luís Martins 30, Mostardas, T673 1464. For local transport José Carlos Martins Cassola T673 1186, Itamar Velho Sessin T673 1431. From Mostardas you can hop off the 1045 bus which passes through the northern end of the park on its way to the beach (basic hotels and restaurants). Three buses a week between Mostardas/Tavares and São José do Norte (130 km), via Bojuru.*

São Lourenço do Sul
Phone code: 0xx53
Population: 43,691

40 km to the south (towards Rio Grande) begins the Costa Doce of the Lagoa dos Patos. São Lourenço is a good place to enjoy the lake, the beaches, fish restaurants and watersports. The town hosts a popular four-day festival in March. **C** *Vilela*, R Almte Abreu 428, T251 3335, family hotel. ■ *Bus from Porto Alegre US$6.50, six a day.* On the BR-116, **Pelotas** is the second largest city in the State of Rio Grande do Sul, 271 km S of Porto Alegre, on the Rio São Gonçalo which connects the shallow Lagoa dos Patos with the Lagoa Mirim. There are many good hotels and transport links to all of the state and the Uruguay border at Chuí.

South of Pelotas on the BR-471, is the **Taim** water reserve on the Lagoa Mirim. Many protected species, including black swans and the *quero-quero* (the Brazilian lapwing). Information from Ibama in Porto Alegre.

Rio Grande
Phone code: 0xx53
Colour map 7, inset
Population: 186,544
274 km S of Porto Alegre

Some 59 km south of Pelotas, at the entrance to the Lagoa dos Patos, is this city. It is the distribution centre for the southern part of Rio Grande do Sul, with significant cattle and meat industries. During the latter half of the 19th century Rio Grande was an important centre, but today it is a rather poor town, notable for the charm of its old buildings. The **Catedral de São Pedro** dates from 1755-75. **Museu Oceanográfico**, has an interesting collection of 125,000 molluscs, 2 km from centre on Av Perimetral, bus 59 or walk along waterfront. ■ *Daily 0900-1100, 1400-1700, T231 3496.* The tourist kiosk is at junction of R Duque de Caxias and R Gen Becaleron.

Excursions To **Cassino**, a popular seaside town on the ocean, 24 km, over a good road. Travelling south, beaches are Querência (5 km), Stela Maris (9 km), Netuno (10 km), all with surf. The breakwater (the Barra), 5 km south of Cassino, no bus connection, through which all vessels entering and leaving Rio Grande must pass, is a tourist attraction. Barra-Rio Grande buses, from the east side of Praça Ferreira pass the Superporto. Across the inlet from Rio Grande is the little-visited settlement of **São José do Norte**, founded in 1725. ■ *There are ferries every half hour, 30 mins, São José to Rio Grande; there are also 3 car ferries daily, T232 1500. Tourist information from R Gen Osório 127. Buses run north to Tavares and Mostardas.*

Brazil

Sleeping and eating Rio Grande A *Atlântico Rio Grande*, R Duque de Caxias 55, T231 3833. Recommended, good value. **D** *Paris*, R Mal F Peixoto 112,. Old, charming and recommended. For eating, try *Rio's*, R Val Porto 393. Vast but good *churrascaria*. *Barrillada Don Lauro*, R Luís Loréa 369. Uruguayan steak in nice restaurant, fairly cheap. *China Brasil*, R Luís Loréa 389. Good Chinese. *Blue Café*, R Luis Loréa 314. Expresso machine and good cake. 0830-1930 (2300 Fri when jazz/blues music). Mid-range. *Tia Laura*, 29 km from town on BR-392 north to Pelotas. Excellent, specializes in home cooking and *café colonial*.

Transport Bus: Frequent daily buses to and from **Pelotas** (56 km), 1 hr, US$1.75 , **Bagé** (280 km), **Santa Vitória** (220 km), and **Porto Alegre** (5 a day, US$10, 4 hrs). All buses to these destinations go through Pelotas. Road to Uruguayan border at **Chuí** is paved, but the surface is poor (5 hrs by bus, at 0700 and 1430). Bus tickets to Punta del Este or Montevideo at 2330 from rodoviária or *Benfica Turismo*, Av Silva Paes 373, T232 1807.

The Brazilian border town is **Chuí**. The BR-471 from Porto Alegre and Pelotas skirts the town and carries straight through to Uruguay, where it becomes Ruta 9. The main street crossing west to east, Av Internacional (Av Uruguaí on the Brazilian side, Av Brasil in Uruguay) is lined with clothes and household shops in Brazil, duty free shops and a casino in Uruguay. São Miguel fort, built by the Portuguese in 1737, now reconstructed with period artefacts, is worth a visit. A lighthouse 10 km west marks the Barro do Chuí inlet, which has uncrowded beaches and is visited by sea lions. Brazilian immigration is about 2½ km from the border, on BR-471, road to Pelotas. Buses stop at customs on both sides of the border, except those from Pelotas, on which you must ask the bus to stop for exit formalities. International buses make the crossing straightforward: the company holds passports; hand over your visitor's card on leaving Brazil and get a Uruguayan one on entry. Have luggage available for inspection. Make sure you get your stamp, or you will have trouble leaving Brazil.

> **Border with Uruguay: coastal route**
> *Colour map 7, inset*
> *Population: 5,167*

Entering Brazil From Uruguay, on the Uruguayan side, the bus will stop if asked, and wait while you get your exit stamp (with bus conductor's help); on the Brazilian side, the appropriate form is completed by the rodoviária staff when you purchase your ticket into Brazil. The bus stops at Polícia Federal (BR-471) and the conductor completes formalities while you sit on the bus.

Sleeping C *Bertelli Chuí*, BR-471, Km 648, 2 km from town, T053-265 1266, F265 1207. Comfortable, with pool. **E** *Rivero*, Colômbia 163-A, T265 1271. With bath, without breakfast. **E** *San Francisco*, Av Colombia e R Chile. Shower, restaurant. *Spetu's Churrascaria*, Panamá 193, 2 blocks off main street, for meat.

Transport Bus: Rodoviária on R Venezuela. Buses run from Chuí to **Pelotas** (6-7 daily, US$6, 4 hrs), **Rio Grande** (0700, 1400, 5 hrs, US$6) and **Porto Alegre** (1200, 2400, 7¾ hrs, US$13).

At **Aceguá**, 60 km south of Bagé, there is a crossing to the Uruguayan town of Melo, and further east, **Jaguarão** with the Uruguayan town of **Rio Branco**, linked by the 1½ km long Mauá bridge across the Rio Jaguarão.

> **Border with Uruguay: inland routes**
> *Colour map 8, grid A6*

Entering Uruguay Before crossing into Uruguay, you must visit Brazilian *Polícia Federal* to get an exit stamp; if not, the Uruguayan authorities will send you back. The crossing furthest west is **Barra do Quaraí** to Bella Unión, via the Barra del Cuaraim bridge. This is near the confluence of the Rios Uruguai and Quaraí. Thirty kilometres east is another crossing from **Quaraí** to **Artigas** in a cattle raising and agricultural area.
The southern interior of the state is the region of the real *gaúcho*. Principal towns of this area include **Santana do Livramento**. Its twin Uruguayan city is Rivera. All one need do is cross the main street to Rivera, but by public transport this is not a straightforward border. ■ *The town has hotels and a youth hostel. Bus to Porto Alegre, 2 daily, 7 hrs, US$20; 3 daily to Uruguaiana (4 hrs, US$10), services also to São Paulo and other destinations. Rodoviária is at Gen Salgado Filho e Gen Vasco Alves.*

Brasília

Salvador de Bahia

Phone code: 0xx71
Post code: 40000
Colour map 5, grid C5
Population:
3.02 million

Salvador, the third largest city in Brazil, is capital of the state of Bahia, dubbed 'Africa in exile' for its mixture of African and European which finds its most powerful expression in Carnival. Often referred to as Bahia, rather than Salvador, the city is home to a heady mix of colonial buildings, beautiful beaches, African culture and pulsating musical rhythms. It stands on the magnificent Bahia de Todos os Santos, a sparkling bay dotted with 38 islands. The bay is the largest on the Brazilian coast covering an area of 1,100 sq km. Rising above the bay on its eastern side is a cliff which dominates the landscape and, perched on top, 71 m above sea level, are the older districts with buildings dating back to the 17th and 18th centuries. Beyond the state capital are many fine beaches, particularly in the south around Porto Seguro, while inland is the harsh sertão, traversed by the Rio São Francisco.

Ins & outs
For more detailed information, see Transport, page 476

Getting there Luis Eduardo Magalhães **Airport** is 32 km from city centre. The **Rodoviária** is 5 km from the city with regular bus services to the centre and Campo Grande; the journey can take up to 1 hr especially at peak periods.

Getting around The broad peninsula on which the city of Salvador is built is at the mouth of the Bahia de Todos Os Santos. On the opposite side of the bay's entrance is the Ilha de Itaparica. The commercial district of the city and its port are on the sheltered, western side of the peninsula; residential districts and beaches are on the open Atlantic side. The point of the peninsula is called Barra, which is itself an important area. The centre of the city is divided into 2 levels, the Upper City (or Cidade Alta) where the Historical Centre lies, and the Lower City (Cidade Baixa) which is the commercial and docks district. The 2 levels are connected by a series of steep hills called *ladeiras*. The easiest way to go from one level to the other is by the 74-m high **Lacerda** lift which connects Praça Cairu in the lower city with Praça Municipal in the upper (renovated 2003). There is also the Plano Inclinado Gonçalves, a funicular railway which leaves from behind the Cathedral going down to Comércio, the commercial district (closes 1300 on Saturday and all Sunday). Most visitors limit themselves to the Pelourinho and historical centre, Barra, the Atlantic suburbs and the Itapagipe peninsula, which is north of the centre. The roads and avenues between these areas are straightforward to follow and are well-served by public transport. Other parts of the city are not as easy to get around, but have less of a tourist interest. If going to these areas a taxi may be advisable until you know your way around.

Climate Temperatures range from 25°C to 32°C, never falling below 19°C in winter. Humidity can be high, which may make the heat oppressive. It rains somewhat all the year but the main rainy season is between May and Sep. Nevertheless, the sun is never far away.

Tourist offices Bahiatursa, R das Laranjeiras 12, Historical Centre, T321 2133, open daily 0830-2200, English and German spoken. Rodoviária, T450 3871, good, English spoken; airport, T204 1244, open daily 0800-2245, friendly; in the Mercado Modelo, T241 0242, Mon-Sat 0900-1800; Sac Shopping Centre, Av Centenario 2992, T264 4566. Useful information (often only available in Portuguese) includes *BahiaCultural*, the month's programme of events with maps of themed points of interest. *Bahiatursa* has lists of hotels and accommodation in private homes. Map, US$1.20, not all streets marked; also a free map, clear map of the historic centre. Offices have noticeboards for messages. The offices also have details of travel throughout the State of Bahia. T131, *Disque Turista* for tourist information in English or Portuguese. **Maps:** from **Departamento de Geografia e Estadística**, Av Estados Unidos (opposite Banco do Brasil, Lower City): also from news stands including the airport bookshop, US$1.50. See also www.uol.com.br/agendasalvador, for what's on.

Security Be very careful of your money and valuables at all times and in all districts. There have been reports of armed muggings on the sand dunes surrounding Lagoa do Abaeté. Do not visit them alone. At night, the areas around and in the lifts and buses are unsafe. Leave valuables securely in your hotel, particularly at night (including wristwatch and cameras if possible: disposable cameras are widely available). Carry a small amount of money that you can hand over if you are threatened. Do not walk down any of the links between the old and new city, especially the Ladeira de Misericôrdia, which links the Belvedere, near the Lacerda Lifts, with the lower city. Should a local join you at your table for a chat, leave at once if drugs are mentioned. The civil police are reported to be very sympathetic and helpful and more resources have been put into policing the old part of the city and Barra, which are now well-lit at night. Police are little in evidence after 2300, however.

Background

On 1 November 1501, All Saints' Day, the navigator Amérigo Vespucci sailed into the bay. As the first European to see it, he named it after the day of his arrival. The first Governor General, Tomé de Sousa, arrived on 23 March 1549 to build a fortified city to protect Portugal's interest from constant threats of Dutch and French invasion. Salvador was formally founded on 1 November 1549 and remained the capital of Brazil until 1763. By the 18th century, it was the most important city in the Portuguese Empire after Lisbon, ideally situated in a safe, sheltered harbour along the trade routes of the 'New World'.

The city's first wealth came from the cultivation of sugar cane and tobacco, the plantations' workforce coming from the West coast of Africa. For three centuries Salvador was the site of a thriving slave trade. Even today, Salvador is described as the most African city in the Western Hemisphere and the University of Bahia boasts the only chair in the Yoruba language in the Americas. The influence permeates the city: food sold on the street is the same as in Senegal and Nigeria, Bahian music is fused with pulsating African polyrhythms, men and women nonchalantly carry enormous loads on their heads, fishermen paddle dug-out canoes in the bay, the pace of life is a little slower than elsewhere. The pulse of the city is *candomblé*, an Afro-Brazilian religion in which the African deities of Nature, the Goddess of the sea and the God of creation are worshipped. These deities (or *orixás*) are worshipped in temples (*terreiros*) which can be elaborate, decorated halls, or simply someone's front room with tiny altars to the *orixá*. *Candomblé* ceremonies may be seen by tourists – but not photographed – on Sunday and religious holidays. Contact the tourist office, *Bahiatursa*, or see their twice monthly calendar of events. Salvador today is a city of 15 forts, 166 Catholic churches, 1,000 *candomblé* temples and a fascinating mixture of old and modern, rich and poor, African and European, religious and profane. It is still a major port exporting tropical fruit, cocoa, sisal, soya beans and petrochemical products. Its most important industry, though, is tourism. Local government has done much to improve the fortunes of this once rundown, poor and dirty city and most visitors feel that the richness of its culture is compensation enough for any problems they may encounter. The Bahianas – black women who dress in traditional 18th century costumes – are street vendors who sit behind their trays of delicacies, savoury and seasoned, made from the great variety of local fish, vegetables and fruits. Their street food is one of the musts for visitors.

Sights

There is much more of interest in the Upper than in the Lower City. From Praça Municipal to the Carmo area 2 km north along the cliff is the Centro Histórico (Historical Centre), now a national monument and also protected by UNESCO. It was in this area that the Portuguese built their fortified city and where today stand some of the most important examples of colonial architecture in the Americas. This area is undergoing a massive restoration programme funded by the Bahian state government and UNESCO. Colonial houses have been painted in pastel colours. Many of the bars have live music which spills out onto the street on every corner. Patios have been created in the open areas behind the houses with open air cafés and bars. Artist ateliers, antique and handicraft stores have brought new artistic blood to what was once the bohemian part of the city. Many popular traditional restaurants and bars from other parts of Salvador have opened new branches here. Its transformation has also attracted many tourist shops and the area can get crowded.

Centro Histórico

**Praça
Municipal,
Praça de Sé
& Terreiro
de Jesus**

Dominating the Praça Municipal is the old Casa de Câmara e Cadeia or **Paço Municipal** (Council Chamber – 1660), while alongside is the **Palácio Rio Branco** (1918), once the Governor's Palace now the headquarters of Bahiatursa, the state tourist board (no office open to the public). Leaving it with its panoramic view of the bay, R Misericôrdia goes north passing the **Santa Casa Misericôrdia** (1695 – see the high altar and painted tiles, open by arrangement 0800-1700, T322 7666) to Praça da Sé. This praça with its mimosa and flamboyant trees leads into Terreiro de Jesus, a picturesque praça named after the church which dominates it. Built in 1692, the **church of the Jesuits** became the property of the Holy See in 1759 when the Jesuits were expelled from all Portuguese territories. The façade is one of the earliest examples of baroque in Brazil, an architectural style which was to dominate the churches built in the 17th and 18th centuries. Inside, the vast vaulted ceiling and 12 side altars in baroque and rococo frame the main altar completely leafed in gold. The tiles in blue, white and yellow in a tapestry pattern are also from Portugal. It houses the tomb of Mem de Sá. The church is now the city Cathedral (**Catedral Basílica**); parts are currently being renovated. ■ *0900-1100, 1400-1700.* On the eastern side of the square is the church of **São Pedro dos Clérigos** which is beautifully renovated, while close by, on the south-side, is the church of the **Ordem Terceira de São Domingos** (Dominican Third Order), which has a beautiful painted wooden ceiling and fine tiles. ■ *Mon-Fri 0800-1200, 1400-1700, US$0.25.* Nearby is **Museu Afro-Brasileiro**, in the former Faculty of Medicine building, Terreiro de Jesus, compares African and Bahian Orixás (deities) celebrations, beautiful murals and carvings, all in Portuguese. ■ *Mon-Fri 0900-1700, US$1, students US$0.50.*

Facing Terreiro de Jesus is Praça Anchieta and the church of **São Francisco**. Its simple façade belies the treasure inside. The entrance leads to a sanctuary with a

Brazil

Salvador

*Related map
A Centro
Histórico,
page 467*

spectacular painting on the wooden ceiling, by local artist José Joaquim da Rocha (1777). The main body of the church is the most exuberant example of baroque in the country. The cedar wood carving and later gold leaf was completed after 28 years in 1748. The cloisters of the monastery are surrounded by a series of blue and white tiles from Portugal. ■ *0830-1700, entry to cloisters US$1, students US$0.50, church free.* Next door is the church of the **Ordem Terceira de São Francisco** (Franciscan Third Order – 1703) with its façade intricately carved in sandstone. Inside is a quite remarkable Chapter House with striking images of the Order's most celebrated saints. ■ *0800-1200, 1300-1700, US$1, students US$0.50.*

Leading off the Terreiro de Jesus is R Alfredo Brito, a charming, narrow cobbled street lined with fine colonial houses painted in different pastel shades. This street leads into the Largo do Pelourinho (Praça José Alencar), which was completely renovated in 1993. Considered the finest complex of colonial architecture in Latin America, it was once the site of a pillory where unscrupulous tradesmen were publicly punished and ridiculed. After the cleaning of the area, new galleries, boutiques and restaurants are opening, and at night the Largo is lively, especially on Tuesday (see Nightlife below). **Nosso Senhor Do Rosário Dos Pretos** church, the so-called Slave Church, dominates the square. It was built by former slaves over a period of 100 years. The side altars honour black saints. The painted ceiling is very impressive, the overall effect being one of tranquillity in contrast to the complexity of the Cathedral and São Francisco. ■ *Small entry fee.*

Largo do Pelourinho

At the corner of Alfredo Brito and Largo do Pelourinho is a small museum to the work of Jorge Amado, who died in 2002, **Casa da Cultura Jorge Amado**. Information is in Portuguese only, but the café walls are covered with colourful copies of his book jackets. ■ *Mon-Sat 0900-1900, free.* The Carmo Hill is at the top of the street leading out of Largo do Pelourinho. **Museu Abelardo Rodrigues**, Solar Ferrão, Pelourinho (R Gregório de Mattos 45), is a religious art museum, with objects from the 17th, 18th and 19th centuries, mainly from Bahia, Pernambuco and Maranhão. ■ *1300- 1900 except Mon, US$0.40.* **Museu da Cidade**, Largo do Pelourinho, has exhibitions of arts and crafts and old photographs. From the higher floors of the museum you can get a good view of the Pelourinho. ■ *Weekdays except Tue 0930-1800, Sat 1300-1700, Sun 0930-1300, free.* **Casa do Benin**, below NS do Rosario dos Pretos, shows African crafts, photos, a video show on Benin and Angola. ■ *Mon-Fri 1000-1800.*

The **Carmo** (Carmelite Third Order) church (1709) houses one of the sacred art treasures of the city, a sculpture of Christ made in 1730 by a slave who had no formal training, Francisco Xavier das Chagas, known as O Cabra. One of the features of the piece is the blood made from whale oil, ox blood, banana resin and 2,000 rubies to represent the drops of blood. ■ *Mon-Sat 0800-1130 and 1400-1730, Sun 1000-1200, US$0.30.* **Museu do Carmo,**

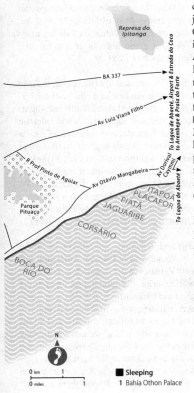

Represa do Ipitanga

BA 337 ··· To Lagoa de Abaeté, Airport & Praia do Forte
Estrada do Coco
Airport & Estrada do Coco

Av Luiz Viana Filho

Av Dorival Caymmi To Arembepe & Praia do Forte

R Prof Pinto de Aguiar

Av Otávio Mangabeira

Parque Pituaçu

ITAPOÃ
PLACAFOR
PIATÃ
JAGUARIBE

To Lagoa de Abaeté

CORSÁRIO

BOCA DO RIO

N

0 km 1
0 miles 1

■ **Sleeping**
1 Bahia Othon Palace

Brazil

in the Convento do Carmo, has a collection of icons and colonial furniture. ■ *Mon-Sat 0800-1200, 1400-1800, Sun 0800-1200, US$0.10.*

South of the Praça Municipal
Rua Chile leads to **Praça Castro Alves**, with its monument to Castro Alves, who started the campaign which finally led to the Abolition of Slavery in 1888. Two streets lead out of this square, Av 7 de Setembro, busy with shops and street vendors selling everything imaginable, and, parallel to it, R Carlos Gomes. **Museu de Arte Sacra** is in the 17th century convent and church of Santa Teresa, at the bottom of the steep Ladeira de Santa Teresa, at R do Sodré 276 (off R Carlos Gomes). Many of the 400 carvings are from Europe, but some are local. Among the reliquaries of silver and gold is one of gilded wood by Aleijadinho (see page 422). ■ *Mon-Fri 1130-1730, US$1.50.* **Museu Arqueológico e Etnográfico**, in the basement of the same building, houses archaeological discoveries from Bahia (stone tools, clay urns etc), an exhibition on Indians from the Alto Rio Xingu area (artefacts, tools, photos), recommended. There is a museum of medicine in the same complex. ■ *Mon-Fri 0900-1700, US$0.40.*

São Bento church (rebuilt after 1624, but with fine 17th century furniture) is on Av 7 de Setembro. Both eventually come to **Campo Grande** (also known as Praça Dois de Julho). In the centre of the praça is the monument to Bahian Independence, 2 July 1823. Av 7 de Setembro continues out of the square towards the Vitória area. There are some fine 19th century homes along this stretch, known as Corredor da Vitória. The **Museu de Arte Moderna**, converted from an old sugar estate house and outbuildings off Av Contorno, is only open for special exhibitions. The restaurant (*Solar do Unhão*) is still there and the buildings are worth seeing for themselves (take a taxi there as access is dangerous). ■ *Tue-Fri 1300-2100, Sat 1500-2100 and Sun 1400-1900, T329 0660.* **Museu Costa Pinto**, Av 7 de Setembro 2490, is a modern house with collections of crystal, porcelain, silver, furniture etc. It also has the only collection of *balangandãs* (slave charms and jewellery), highly recommended. ■ *Weekdays 1430-1900, but closed Tue, Sat-Sun 1500-1800, US$2.* **Museu de Arte da Bahia**, Av 7 de Setembro 2340, Vitória, has interesting paintings of Brazilian artists from the 18th to the early 20th century. ■ *Tue-Fri 1400-1900, Sat-Sun 1430-1900, US$1.20.*

Barra
From Praça Vitória, the avenue continues down Ladeira da Barra (Barra Hill) to Porto da Barra. The best city beaches are in this area. Also in this district are the best bars, restaurants and nightlife. The Barra section of town has received a facelift with a new lighting system. The pavements fill with people day and night and many sidewalk restaurants and bars are open along the strip from Porto da Barra as far as the Cristo at the end of the Farol da Barra beach. Great attention to security is given. A little further along is the **Forte de Santo Antônio da Barra** and **lighthouse**, 1580, built on the spot where Amérigo Vespucci landed in 1501. It is right at the mouth of the bay where Bahia de Todos Os Santos and the South Atlantic Ocean meet and is the site of the first lighthouse built in the Americas. The interesting **Museu Hidrográfico** is housed in the upper section of the Forte de Santo Antônio, fine views of the bay and coast, recommended. ■ *Tue-Sat 1300-1800, US$1. It has a good café for watching the sunset.*

Atlantic beach suburbs
The promenade leading away from the fort and its famous lighthouse is called Av Oceânica, which follows the coast to the beach suburbs of Ondina, Amaralina and Pituba. The road is also called Av Presidente Vargas, but the numbering is different. Beyond Pituba are the **best ocean beaches** at Jaguaripe, Piatã and Itapoã. En route the bus passes small fishing colonies at Amaralina and Pituba where *jangadas* can be seen. A *jangada* is a small raft peculiar to the northeastern region of Brazil used extensively as well as dug-out canoes. Near Itapoã is the **Lagoa do Abaeté**, surrounded by brilliant, white sands. This is a deep, freshwater lake where local women traditionally come to wash their clothes and then lay them out to dry in the sun. The road leading up from the lake offers a panoramic view of the city in the distance, the coast, and the contrast of the white sands and fresh water less than 1 km from the sea and its golden beaches. **NB** See Security, above. Near the lighthouse at   **Itapoã** there are two

campsites on the beach. A little beyond the campsites are the magnificent ocean beaches of Stella Maris and Flamengo, both quiet during the week but very busy at the weekends. Beware of strong undertow at these beaches. Apart from Porto da Barra, all the beaches before Itapoã are polluted with sewage (a new system is under construction). The Sunday paper, *A Tarde*, publishes the condition of the beaches.

See also the famous church of **Nosso Senhor do Bonfim** on the Itapagipe peninsula in the suburbs north of the centre, whose construction began in 1745. It draws endless supplicants (particularly on Friday and Sunday) offering favours to the image of the Crucified Lord set over the high altar; the number and variety of ex-voto offerings is extraordinary. The processions over the water to the church on the third Sunday in January are particularly interesting. Also on the Itapagipe peninsula is a colonial fort on **Monte Serrat** point, and at Ribeira the church of **Nossa Senhora da Penha** (1743). The beach here has many restaurants, but the sea is polluted (bus from Praça da Sé or Av França).

Bonfim & Itapagipe

Brazil

Salvador Centro Histórico

N
Not to scale

■ **Sleeping**
1 Albergue das Laranjeiras
2 Paris
3 Pousada da Praça
4 Solara

● **Eating**
1 Coffee Shop

2 Gramado
3 Jardim das Delícias

✝ **Churches**
1 Conceição de Praia
2 Igreja do Desterro
3 Nossa Senhora da Ajuda
4 Nossa Senhora do Rosário dos Pretos
5 Ordem Terceira de São Domingos
6 Ordem Terceira de São Francisco

7 Palma
8 Santa Casa Misericórdia
9 Sant'Ana
10 São Francisco
11 São Pedro dos Clérigos

🏛 **Museums**
1 Abelardo Rodrigues
2 Afro-Brasileiro
3 Arqueológico e Etnográfico, Arte de Bahia, Arte

Moderna, Arte Sacra, Casa do Benin, Convento do Carmo, Costa Pinto, Hidrográfico, Medicine
4 Casa da Cultura Jorge Amado
5 Casa do Benin
6 Cidade
7 Convento do Carmo
8 Museu de Arte Sacra

╫╫╫ Funicular Railway

To Convent of Santa Teresa, 🏛 8, *Church of São Bento & Campo Grande*

Essentials

Sleeping

■ *on map*
This includes the old city of Pelhourino and the main shopping area

A 10% service charge is often added to the bill. Check which credit cards are accepted. All luxury hotels have swimming pools

City centre B *Palace*, R Chile 20, T322 1155, palace@e-net.com.br Traditional, a little past its best, good breakfast. **C** *Imperial*, Av 7 de Setembro 751, Rosário, T/F329 3127. A/c, helpful, breakfast. Recommended. **C** *Pousada da Praça*, Rui Barbosa, 5, T321 0642, gifc@zaz.com.br Simple, pretty old colonial house, quiet, secure, big breakfast , rooms with and without bath. Recommended. **D** *Arthemis*, Praça da Sé 398, Edif Themis, 7th floor, T322 0724, arthemis@arthemis.com.br Fan, wonderful views over bay and old city. Recommended restaurant with French chef. **D** *Internacional*, R Sen Costa Pinto 88, T321 3514. Convenient, good value. **D** *Paris*, R Rui Barbosa 13, T321 3922. A/c rooms more expensive, shared showers, breakfast, restaurant in same building. Recommended. **D** *São Bento*, Largo de São Bento 3, T243 7511. Good cheap restaurant. Cheaper hotels on Av 7 de Setembro: **D** *São José*, No 847. Safe. Recommended. **F** pp *Pousada*, No 2349. Warmly recommended. Near the Praça da Sé the following have been recommended: **C** *Pelourinho*, R Alfredo Brito 20, T243 2324. Run down but charismatic. **D** *Solara*, R José Alencar 25, Largo do Pelourinho, T326 4583. With shower, breakfast, laundry facilities. **E** *Ilhéus*, Ladeira da Praça 4, 1st floor, T322 7240. Breakfast.

This quiet district just 5 mins walk NE of Pelourinho has attracted Europeans who have set up pousadas in beautifully restored buildings. Without exception, they are imaginatively designed and full of character; all are recommended. This is now undoubtedly the ideal, if not the cheapest, area to stay

Santo Antônio A *Pousada Redfish*, R Direita do Santo Antônio, T/F243 8473, www.hotelredfish.com Incredibly stylish, modern design. English-owned, some rooms with terraces and open-air showers. **B** *Pousada das Flores*, R Direita de Santo Antônio 442, near Santo Antônio fort, T/F243 1836. Brazilian/French owners, excellent breakfast, beautiful old house. **B** *Pousada do Boqueirão*, R Direita do Santo Antônio 48, T241 2262, www.pousadaboqueirao.com.br Family-run, beautiful house overlooking the bay, remodelled, relaxed atmosphere, most European languages spoken, great food, first class in all respects. **B** *Pousada Villa Carmo*, R do Carmo 58, T/F241 3924. Italian/Brazilian owned, many European languages spoken, very comfortable, rooms with fan or a/c. **B-C** *Pousada Baluarte*, R Baluarte, 13, T327 0367. Bohemian household, lovely owners, 5 rooms, cheaper without bath, the home made breakfasts are excellent. **D** *Pensão Von Sandt Platz*, R Direita de Santo Antônio 351, T/F316 6551, manaschu@cpunet.com.br Relaxing family house of Nazaré Schubeler, sumptuous breakfasts, legendary caipirinhas, free email facilities, laundry, "prepare to be mothered", being extended in 2003. **F** pp *Nalvas*, R Direita de Santo Antônio 22. 4-bed rooms, fan, no towel, use of kitchen, related travel agency at No 22, good value.

Upmarket residential area, between Barra and city centre, convenient for museums

Campo Grande/Vitória L *Tropical Hotel da Bahia*, Av 7 de Setembro 1537, Campo Grande, T255 2031, www.tropicalhotel.com.br Well-run, convenient for city centre, very much a business hotel. **A** *Bahia do Sol*, Av 7 de Setembro 2009, T338 8800, F336 7776. Comfortable, safe and frigobar in room, family run, good breakfast and restaurant, bureau de change. Highly recommended (no pool). **D** *Caramuru*, Av 7 de Setembro 2125, Vitória, T336 9951. Cosy, with lounge and terrace, safe parking. Recommended.

Barra has fallen a little from favour in recent years, so unless you are desperate to be by the beach, stay in Pelhourino to enjoy its unique nightlife and travel here by bus during the day. Taxis are recommended after dark. Care should be taken on Sun when the beaches are busy

Barra All recommended: **A-C** *Mansion Villa Verde*, R da Palmeira 190, T264 3597, www.pousadavillaverde.com **C-D** in low season, reduced rates for longer stay, a/c studios with kitchen and double room with fan, garden, terrace, hammocks, safe, very good. On Av 7 de Setembro: **B** *Barra Turismo*, No 3691, Porto da Barra, T245 7433. Breakfast, a/c, fridge, on beach. **C-E** *Pousada Santa Maria*, No 3835, T264 4076, pousadasmaria@hotmail.com Excellent breakfast, English and German spoken, TV, laundry service, internet, restaurant/bar, exchange, car rental. **C** *Pousada Malu*, No 3801, T264 4461. Small and homely, with breakfast, cooking facilities and laundry service. **C** *Pousada Ambar*, R Afonso Celso 485, T264 6956, www.ambarpousada.com.br Good service, breakfast, convenient, run by Paulo and Christine (French, also speaks English). **C** *Villa Romana*, R Lemos Brito 14, T336 6522, F247 6748. Good location, pool, a/c. **C** *Enseada Praia da Barra*, R Barão de Itapoã 60, Porto da Barra, T235 9213. Breakfast, safe, money exchanged, accepts credit cards, laundry bills high, otherwise good value, near beach. **E** Rooms to let in private apartments: *Carmen Simões*, R 8 de Dezembro 326. Safe, helpful. *Gorete*, R 8 de Dezembro 522, Apt 002, Edif Ricardo das Neves, Graça, T264 3584/3016, gorete@cpunet.com.br Convenient, use of kitchen, patio, internet, safe.

Atlantic Suburbs LL *Bahia Othon Palace*, Av Presidente Vargas, 2456, Ondina, T203 2000, T0800 7010098, F2454877, www.hoteis-othon.com.br **LL-A** *Pestana Bahia*, R Fonte de Boi 216, Rio Vermelho, T/F453 8000, www.pestanahotels.com.br One of the best in Salvador, all comfort and facilties including for the disabled. **A** *Catharina Paraguaçu*, R João Gomes 128, Rio Vermelho, T247 1488. Charming, small, colonial-style, tastefully decorated. **A** *Ondina Plaza*, Av Pres Vargas 3033, Ondina, T245 8158, F247 7266. A/c, pool, good value, on beach. **C** *Mar*, R da Paciência 106, Rio Vermelho, T331 2044, F245 4440. Good nightlife in the area.

This modern suburban area runs along the coast from Ondina to Itapoã for 20 km towards the airport. The best beaches are after Pituba. All hotels recommended

In **Itapoã**: **LL-A** *Sofitel*, R Passargada s/n, T374 8500, www.sofitel.com Another superb hotel, in a park with 9-hole golf course, 5 mins from airport, shuttle bus to centre, all facilities. **A** *Villa do Farol*, Praia do Pedra do Sol, T374 2618, F374 0006. Small Swiss-run *pousada*, pool, homely, great restaurant, 1 block from beach. First class. **B** *Grão de Areia*, R Arnaldo Santana 7, Piatã, T375 4818. A/c, pool, near good beach. **D** *Pousada Glória*, R do Retiro 46, T/F375 1503. No breakfast, near beach.

Youth hostels Albergues de Juventude, **D-F** pp including breakfast, but sometimes cheaper if you have a HIHA membership card. Prices are higher and hostels very full at carnival. **Pelourinho**: *Albergue das Laranjeiras*, R Inácio Acciolli 13, T/F321 1366, www.alaranj.com.br In a beautiful colonial building in the heart of the historical district, can be noisy, café downstairs, English spoken. Good for meeting other travellers. Warmly recommended. *Vagaus*, R Alfredo Brito 25, Pelourinho, T321 6398, vagaus@elitenet.com.br Independent youth hostel, all rooms collective with breakfast, internet access available. Recommended. *Barra*, R Dr Arturo Neiva 4, T245 2600, www.alberguebarravento.com.br HI, 30 m from beach, cheaper for memebers and in low season, suites and dorms, breakfast US$1, cyber café, kitchen and laundry. The following can be booked through www.hostels.com/en/br.sa.html *Albergue Bahia*, R Alfredo Brito 41, Pelourinho, internet, laundry; *Nega Maluca*, R dos Marchantes 15, Santo Antônio, with breakfast, internet, laundry, kitchen, bar, safe, tourist information; *Casa da Barra*, R Afonso Celso 447, Barra, laundry, internet, takes credit cards.

On the beaches: *Albergue do Porto*, R Barão de Sergy 197, T264 6600, www.alberguedoporto.com.br One block from beach, short bus ride or 20 minutes on foot from historical centre. IYHA hostel in beautiful turn-of-the-century house, breakfast, convenient, English spoken, double room with a/c and bath available, kitchen, laundry facilities, safe, TV lounge, games room, internet, courtyard. Highly recommended. *Casa Grande*, R Minas Gerais 122, Pituba, T248 0527, F240 0074. Laundry and cooking facilities. *Pousada Marcos*, Av Oceânica 281, T235 5117. Youth hostel-style, great location near the lighthouse, very busy, notices in Hebrew for potential travelling companions, efficient.

Pensionatos are places to stay in shared rooms (up to 4 per room); part or full board available. Houses or rooms can be rented for US$5-35 a day from *Pierre Marbacher*, R Carlos Coqueijo 68A, Itapoã, T249 5754 (Caixa Postal 7458, 41600 Salvador), he is Swiss, owns a beach bar at Rua K and speaks English. At Carnival it's a good idea to rent a flat; the tourist office has a list of estate agents. They can also arrange rooms in private houses; however, caution is advised as not all householders are honest.

Camping *Camping Clube do Brasil*, R Visconde do Rosário 409, Rosário, T242 0482. *Ecológica*, R Alameida da Praia, near the lighthouse at Itapoã, take bus from Praça da Sé direct to Itapoã, or to Campo Grande or Barra, change there for Itapoã, about 1 hr, then 30 mins walk, T3743506. Bar, restaurant, hot showers. Highly recommended.

Sea bathing is dangerous off shore near the campsites

Local specialities The main dish is *moqueca*, seafood cooked in a sauce made from coconut milk, tomatoes, red and green peppers, fresh coriander and *dendê* (palm oil!). It is traditionally cooked in a wok-like earthenware dish and served piping hot at the table. Served with *moqueca* is *farofa* (manioc flour) and a hot pepper sauce which you add at your discretion, it's usually extremely hot so try a few drops before venturing further. The *dendê* is somewhat heavy and those with delicate stomachs are advised to try the *ensopado*, a sauce with the same ingredients as the *moqueca*, but without the palm oil.

Eating
● *on map*

Brazil

Brazil

Nearly every street corner has a Bahiana selling a wide variety of local snacks, the most famous of which is the *acarajé*, a kidney bean dumpling fried in palm oil which has its origins in West Africa. To this the Bahiana adds *vatapá*, a dried shrimp and coconut milk paté (also delicious on its own), fresh salad and hot sauce (*pimenta*). For those who prefer not to eat the palm oil, the *abará* is a good substitute. *Abará* is steamed, wrapped in banana leaves. Seek local advice on which are most hygienic stalls to eat from. Two good Bahianas are *Chica*, at Ondina beach (on the street at the left side of *Mar A Vista Hotel*) and *Dinha* at Largo da Santana (very lively in the late afternoon), who serves *acarajé* until midnight, extremely popular. Bahians usually eat *acarajé* or *abará* with a chilled beer on the way home from work or on the beach at sunset. Another popular dish with African origins is *Xin-Xin de Galinha*, chicken on the bone cooked in *dendê*, with dried shrimp, garlic and squash.

Recommended places to eat

Pelourinho (Historical Centre) Expensive: *Bargaço*, R das Laranjeiras 26, T242 6546. Traditional seafood restaurant, Bahian cuisine, open daily except Tue. *Casa do Benin*, Praça José Alencar 29. Afro-Bahian, great surroundings, try the shrimp in the cashew nut sauce, closed Mon and 1600-1900. *Maria Mata Mouro*, R Inácio Accioly 8, T321 3929. International menu, excellent service, relaxing atmosphere, closed Sun night. *Pizzeria Micheluccio*, R Alfredo Brito 31, T323 0078. Best pizzas in Pelourinho, open daily 1200 till late. *Uauá*, R Gregório de Matos 36, T321 3089. Elegant, colonial restaurant and bar, typical Bahian cuisine. **Mid-range**: *Jardim das Delícias*, R João de Deus, 12, T321 1449. Elegant restaurant and antiques shop with tropical garden, very reasonable for its setting, classical or live music. *Senac*, Praça José Alencar 8, Largo do Pelourinho. State-run catering school, a selection of 40 local dishes, buffet, lunch 1130-1530, dinner 1830-2130, all you can eat for US$16, inconsistent quality but very popular, folkloric show Thu-Sat 2030, US$5. *Quilombo do Pelô*, R Alfredo Brito 13, T322 4371. Rustic Jamaican restaurant, open daily from 1100, good food with relaxed, if erratic service, vegetarian options. *Mamabahia*, R Alfredo Brito 21. Good open-air steak house. Near the Carmo church: *Casa da Roça*, R Luis Viana 27. Pizzas, caipirinhas and live music at weekend. **Cheap**: *Bahiacafe.com*, Praça da Sé 20. Funky, Belgian-run internet café, good breakfasts, excellent food, English spoken. *Coffee Shop* , Praça da Sé. Cuban-style café serving sandwiches; main attraction is excellent coffee, and tea served in china cups, doubles as cigar shop. *Gramado*, Praça da Sé. One of few food-by-weight restaurants in area, basic, lunch only. *Atelier Maria Adair*, R J Castro Rabelo 2. Specializing in coffees and cocktails, owner Maria is a well known artist whose highly original work is on display. Good wholemeal snacks and juices at *Bar da Tereza*, No 16, open daily 0900-2330. *Dona Chika-Ka*, No 10, 1100-1500 and 1900-0200. Good local dishes. Open gates beside *Dona Chika-Ka* lead to an open square, Largo de Quincas Berro d'Água (known locally as Quadra 2M) with many bars and restaurants. On the next block down is *Tempero da Dadá*, R Frei Vicente 5. Open daily 1130 till late, closed Tue, Bahian cuisine, owners Dadá and Paulo are genial hosts, extremely popular. Across the street is *Quereres*, a restaurant and bar with good live music. *Kilinho*, Ribeiro dos Santos 1. Fresh salads, popular with locals. *Restaurante e lanchonete Xango*, Praça Cruzeiro de São Francisco. Good for fruit juices. *Carvalho*, R Conselheiro Cunha Lopez 33, Centro. *Comida a kilo*, tasty, excellent fish, clean, cheap. *Casa da Gamboa*, R João de Deus 32, 1st floor. 1200-1500 and 1900-2400, closed Mon. Also at R Newton Prado 51 (Gamboa de Cima), beautifully located in old colonial house overlooking the bay, good reputation, open Mon- Sat 1200-1500, 1900-2300, not cheap. Good *feijoada* at *Alaide do Feijão*, R Fransisco Muniz Barreto 26, daily 1100-2400. Also at *da Dinha* on Praça José Alencar 5, Mon-Sat 0800-2000. *Encontro dos Artistas*, R das Laranjeiras 15, T321 1721, Ribeiro dos Santos 10, Passo – Pelourinho, cheap. *Galeria Villa Manhattan e Bistro*, Rua das Laranjeiras 52. Good pasta.

Between the Historical Centre and Barra Expensive: *Chez Bernard*, R Gamboa de Cima, 11. French cuisine, open daily except Sun. **Mid-Range** Among the best *churrascarias* in Salvador is *Baby Beef*, Av AC Magalhães, Iguatemi. Top class restaurant, excellent service, extremely popular, open daily 1200-1500 and 1900-2300. An excellent Japanese restaurant is *Beni-Gan*, Praça A Fernandes 29, Garcia, intimate atmosphere, Tue-Sun 1900 till midnight. *Casa D'Italia*, corner of Av 7 and Visconde de São Lourenço. Reasonable prices, good service. *Recanto das Coroas*, underneath the *Hotel Arthemis* (see above), looks uninviting but the food is excellent. *Ristorante d'Italia*, Av 7 de Setembro, 1238, Campo Grande has won awards. Very reasonable, with large portions, closed Sun night, music some evenings. **Cheap**: There are some good snack bars on Av 7 de Setembro: *Kentefrio*, No 379, the best, clean, counter service only, closed Sun.

At the bottom of the Lacerda Lift is Praça Cairu and the famous *Mercado Modelo*: on the upper floor of the market are 2 very good restaurants, *Camafeu De Oxossi* and *Maria De São Pedro*, both specializing in Bahian dishes, great atmosphere, good view of the port, daily 1130 till 2000, Sat lunchtime is particularly busy. Opposite the Mercado Modelo, the Paes Mendonça supermarket self-service counter is good value, 1100-1500, 1st floor. *Divino Gula*, Av Francia 414, 400 m from the *Mercado Modelo* is good and frequented by locals. On Av Contorno, *Solar Do Unhão*, in a beautiful 18th century sugar estate on the edge of the bay, lunch and dinner (fair Bahian cuisine) with the best folklore show in town, expensive; also good for sunset drinks.

Barra Expensive: *Caranguejo do Farol*, Av Oceânica 231, raised above the road. Specializing in crab, extremely busy. A little further along is *Restaurante do Sergipe*, also very busy. **Mid-range**: *Ban Zai*, Av 7 de Setembro 3244, Ladeira da Barra, T336 4338, by the yacht club. Sushi bar, always busy, open daily except Mon. *Oceânia*, Av Oceânica. Street café, noisy, good people watching, open every day until late. Almost next door is *Don Vitalone Pizzaria*, No 115, excellent pizzas. *Don Vitalone Trattoria*, T235 7274, is a block away, part of the same chain. Great Italian food, open daily for lunch and evening meal. *Pizzaria Il Forno*, R Marques de Leão 77 (parallel to the promenade), T247 7287. Italian food at a good price, good service, open daily for lunch and evening meal. *Yan Ping*, on R Airosa Galvão, T245 6393. Good Chinese, open daily 1100 until midnight, reasonably priced, generous portions. **Cheap**: *Mediterrânio*, R Marques de Leão 262. Pay by weight, open daily. *A Porteira*, R Afonso Celso 287, T235 5656. Open for lunch only, pay by weight northeastern Brazilian food. *Nan Hai*, Av 7 de Setembro 3671. Good Chinese, lunch and dinner (Porto da Barra). In Shopping Barra: *Califa's* , first floor, basic Arabian place. *Pizza e Cia*, ground floor, good selection of fresh salads, also good pizzas, good value. Opposite is *Perini*, great ice cream, chocolate, savouries and cakes. *Saúde Brasil*, top floor (L3), for very good wholefood snacks, cakes and a wide variety of juices. Near the lighthouse at the mouth of the bay (Farol Da Barra) there are a number of good fast food places: *Micheluccio*, Av Oceânica 10, good pizza, always busy. Next door is *Baitakão*, good hamburgers and sandwiches. *Mon Filet*, R Afonso Celso 152. Good steaks, pastas, open 1830-2400. On the same street, *Pastaxuta*, pizza, pasta, reasonable prices, and a number of other good cheap restaurants, for example *Maná*, opens 1100 till food runs out, different menu each day, closed Sun, popular, owner Frank speaks a little English. The best Bahian restaurant in the area is *Frutos Do Mar*, R Marquês de Leão 415. A very good vegetarian restaurant is *Rama*, R Lord Cochrane, great value.

In Ondina *Extudo*, Largo Mesquita 4, T237 4669. Good varied menu, lively bar at night, attracts interesting clientèle, open 1200-0200, closed Mon, not expensive. *Manjericão*, R Fonte do Boi (the street leading to *Pestana*). Excellent wholefood menu, Mon-Sat 1100-1600. *Margarida*, R Feira de Santana, Parque Cruz Aguiar. Open daily for lunch 1130-1500, original dishes, pasta, seafood, meat, imaginative salads, pay by weight, great desserts, very friendly owners, attracts interesting clientèle. *Postudo*, R João Gomes 87, T245 5030. Over a small shopping mall called *Free Shop*, open daily except Sun, reasonably priced good food in an interesting setting, always busy. Across the street at the base of the hill in Largo da Santana is *Santana Sushi Bar*, T237 5107. Open Tue-Sat, authentic. There is an interesting fish market at Largo da Mariquita with a number of stalls serving food from noon until the small hrs, clean, good atmosphere, popular with locals. *Cantina Famiglia-Salvatore*, Largo da Mariquita 45. Delicious, authentic Italian pasta, 2 other branches.

Further along Av Oceânica *Brisa*, R Sargento Astrolábio 150, Pituba. Mon-Sat, 1100-1500, excellent wholefood restaurant, small, simple, cheap, owner Nadia is very friendly, organizes a small organic market Thu 0700-1000. *Rodeio*, Jardim dos Namorados, Pituba, T240 1762. Always busy, good value 'all you can eat' *churrascaria*, open daily from 1130-midnight. At **Jardim Armação**:Boi Preto, Av Otávio Mangabeira e Av Yemenjá. Top quality *churrascaria*, open 1200-1600, 1830-0100. *Yemanjá*, Av Otávio Mangabeira 4655, T461 9010, a 20-minute taxi ride from the centre. Excellent Bahian

There are a number of restaurants specializing in crab, along the sea front promenade

Brazil

seafood, open daily from 1130 till late, very typical, always busy, reasonably priced, good atmosphere. *Deutsches Haus*, Av Otávio Mangabeira 1221. Good German cooking. *Rincão Gaúcho*, R Pedro Silva Ribeiro s/n, T231 3800. Excellent *churrascaria*, huge selection of salads, many different cuts of meat, very popular with locals.

A Porteira at Boca do Rio. Specializes in northeastern dishes, 1200-1600 and 1800-2300, seafood dishes also served. Nearby on the same street is *Bar Caribe* (more commonly known as *Pimentinha*). Zany décor, little comfort, hard to believe that it could be so busy, extremely busy on Mon (its best night), tables on the street, blessings given by the owner, a *pai de santo*, no other bar like this anywhere, food served, healthy portions, expect delays though. In Itapoã near the lighthouse, 2 good restaurants are *Mistura Fina*, R Professor Souza Brito 41, T249 2623, seafood, pasta dishes, open daily 1000-midnight and *O Lagostão*, R Agnaldo Cruz 12, T375 3646, Bahian cuisine, open daily 1100 till midnight. *Casquinha De Siri* at Piatã beach. Daily from 0900, live music every night, cover charge US$2, very popular. The beaches from Patamares to Itapoã are lined by *barracas*, thatched huts serving chilled drinks and freshly cooked seafood dishes, ideal for lunch and usually very cheap. Try *Ki-Muqueca*, Av Otávio Mangabeira 36 (Av Oceânica), for large helpings of excellent Bahian food in attractive surroundings. *Dadá*, on Patamares beach. New, opened by famous chef Dadá, excellent Bahian food, great setting. *La Marina*, Stella Maris (after Itapoã; take dirt road to beach opposite Stella Market mall). Basque owned, best paella, freshest fish.

Bars & clubs

Much of the nightlife is concentrated in the historical centre, especially the compact network of cobbled streets around R João de Deus

The best time to hear and see artists and groups is during carnival but they are also to be seen outside the carnival period. Busy nights in the Pelourinho are Tue, with live music 2000-2330 in the Largos Quincas Berro d'Água and Pedro Arcanjo, and weekends, plus every night throughout the summer in several places. Sat nights are very busy, the most popular band being the *Fred Dantas Orchestra*, which plays a fusion of big band music and Latin rhythms. Reggae hangs in the air of Pelourinho with many reggae bars such as *Bar do Reggae*, *Casa do Olodum* and *Bar do Olodum*, all within a short walk of each other. *Casa do Olodum*, R Gregório de Matos, is a bar and dance floor where the band *Olodum* performs on Tue to packed crowds (hang out on the pavement outside if you don't want to pay the entrance fee); the rest of the week it's open to all. Almost directly opposite at No 15 is: *NR*, a great after-hours bar with live music (which is not always so great). There's a US$0.50 charge if you sit down. A good jam session takes place every Sat night (Aug-Mar) in the grounds of the *Solar do Unhão*, Av Contorno. Guest musicians are welcome. It is best to go by taxi as bus connections are difficult.

Busy nights in the Pelourinho are Tue and weekends

Pelourinho *Cantina da Lua*, Terreiro de Jesus. Open daily, popular, good place to meet, flower boxes and more security ensure less hassle for open-air diners. Many bars on the Largo de Quincas Berro d'Água (see above). Good café and great chocolate at *Cailleur*, R Gregório de Matos 17, open daily 0930-2100, bar service continues till 0100. **Barra** *Mordomia Drinks*, Ladeira Da Barra. Enter through a narrow entrance to an open air bar with a spectacular view of the bay, very popular. Most Barra nightlife happens at the Farol da Barra (lighthouse). R Marquês de Leão is very busy, with lots of bars with tables on the pavement: *Habeas Copos*, R Marquês de Leão 172. Famous and traditional street side bar, very popular.. *Barra Vento 600* is a popular open air bar on the beachfront. Bar in the ICBA (Goethe Institute), has good light snacks, attracts a young bohemian clientèle, closes 2300, very pleasant courtyard setting. **Rio Vermelho** Once the bohemian section of town, where Jorge Amado lived and Caetano Veloso still has a house, the nightlife in this region rivals Pelourinho. Try *Porto Seguro* at *Salvador Praia Hotel*, T245 5033. *New Fred's*, Av Visconde de Itaboraí 125, T248 4399 (middle-aged market, singles bar).

Entertainment

Cinema The main shopping malls at Barra, Iguatemi, Itaigara and Brotas, and *Cineart* in Politeama (Centro), run more mainstream movies. The impressive Casa do Comércio building near Iguatemi houses the *Teatro do SESC* with a mixed programme of theatre, cinema and music Wed-Sun. The **Fundação Cultural do Estado da Bahia** edits *Bahia Cultural*, a monthly brochure listing the main cultural events for the month. These can be found in most hotels and Bahiatursa information centres. Local newspapers *A Tarde* and *Correio da Bahia* have good cultural sections listing all events in the city.

Brazil

Music Every Tue night *Banda Olodum*, a drumming troupe made famous by their innovative powerhouse percussion and involvement with Paul Simon, Michael Jackson and Branford Marsalis, rehearse in the Largo Teresa Batista in front of packed crowds. Starts 1930, US$14. They also rehearse free of charge in the Largo do Pelourinho on Sunday; T321 5010. Established in Liberdade, the largest suburb of the city, *Ilê Aiyê* is a thriving cultural group dedicated to preserving African traditions which under the guidance of its president Vovô is deeply committed to the fight against racism. Rehearsals take place mid week at Boca do Rio and on Saturday nights in front of their headquarters at Ladeira do Curuzu in Liberdade. *Araketu* hails from the sprawling Periperi suburb in the Lower City. Once a purely percussion band *Araketu* has travelled widely and borrowed on various musical forms (samba, candomblé, soukous etc) to become a major carnival attraction and one of the most successful bands in Bahia. Rehearsals take place on Wed nights on Av Contorno.As these get very full, buy tickets in advance from Av Oceânica 683, Barra Centro Comercial, Sal 06, T247 6784. Neguinho do Samba was the musical director of *Olodum* until he founded *Didá*, an all-woman drumming group based along similar lines to *Olodum*. They rehearse on Fri nights in the Praça Teresa Batista, Pelourinho. Starts 2000, US$10. *Filhos de Gandhi*, the original African drumming group and the largest, was formed by striking stevedores during the 1949 carnival. The hypnotic shuffling cadence of *Filhos de Gandhi*'s *afoxé* rhythm is one of the most emotive of Bahia's carnival. *Carlinhos Brown* is a local hero. He has become one of the most influential musical composers in Brazil today, mixing great lyrics, innovative rhythms and a powerful stage presence. He played percussion with many Bahian musicians, until he formed his own percussion group, *Timbalada*. He has invested heavily in his native Candeal neighbourhood: the Candy All Square, a centre for popular culture, is where the *Timbalada* rehearsals take place every Sun night. 1830, US$20 from Sep to Mar. Not to be missed. During the winter (July-September) ring the *blocos* to confirm that free rehearsals will take place.

Artists and bands using electronic instruments and who tend to play in the *trios eléctricos* draw heavily on the rich rhythms of the drumming groups creating a new musical genre known as *Axé*. The most popular of such acts is Daniela Mercury, following the steps to international stardom of Caetano Veloso, Maria Bethânia, João Gilberto, Gilberto Gil. Other newer, interesting acts are Margareth Menezes who has travelled extensively with David Byrne. Gerónimo was one of the first singer/songwriters to use the wealth of rhythms of the Candomblé in his music and his song 'E d'Oxum' is something of an anthem for the city. All the above have albums released and you can find their records easily in most record stores. See Shopping in the Pelourinho. Also try *Billbox* in Shopping Barra on the 3rd floor.

Theatre *Castro Alves*, at Campo Grande (Largo 2 de Julho), T339 8000, seats 1400 and is considered one of the best in Latin America. It also has its own repertory theatre, the *Sala de Coro*, for more experimental productions. The theatre's *Concha Acústica* is an open-air venue used frequently in the summer, attracting the big names in Brazilian music. *Teatro Vila Velha*, Passéio Público, T336 1384, Márcio Meirelles, the theatre's director works extensively with Grupo Teatro Olodum; although performed in Portuguese productions here are very visual and worth investigating. *Instituto Cultural Brasil-Alemanha* (ICBA) and the *Associação Cultural Brasil Estados Unidos* (ACBEU), both on Corredor de Vitória have a varied programme, the former with a cinema. In the Pelourinho is the *Teatro XVIII*, R Frei Vicente, T 332 0018, an experimental theatre. *Teatro Gregório de Matos* in Praça Castro Alves offers space to new productions and writers. *Balé Folclórico da Bahia*, R Inácio Acioly 11, T322 1962. Good selection of dances, 2000 daily, US$2.50.

Festivals 6 Jan (*Epiphany*); *Ash Wednesday* and *Maundy Thursday*, half-days; 2 Jul (*Independence of Bahia*); 30 Oct; *Christmas Eve*, half-day. An important local holiday is *Festa do Nosso Senhor do Bonfim*; it takes place on the second Sun after Epiphany, but the washing or *lavagem* of the Bonfim church, with its colourful parade, takes place on the preceding Thu (usually **mid-Jan**). The *Festa da Ribeira* is on the following Mon. Another colourful festival is that of the fishermen of Rio Vermelho on **2 Feb**; gifts for Yemanjá, Goddess of the Sea, are taken to sea in a procession of sailing boats to an accompaniment of *candomblé* instruments. The Holy Week processions among the old churches of the upper city are also interesting.

Brazil

Brazil

▶ *Carnival in Bahia*

Carnival officially starts on Thursday night at 2000 when the keys of the city are given to the Carnival King 'Rei Momo'. The unofficial opening though is on Wednesday with the Lavagem do Porto da Barra, when throngs of people dance on the beach. Later on in the evening is the Baile dos Atrizes, starting at around 2300 and going on until dawn, very bohemian, good fun. Check with Bahiatursa for details on venue, time etc (see under Rio for carnival dates).

Carnival in Bahia is the largest in the world and it encourages active participation. It is said that there are 1½ million people dancing on the streets at any one time.

There are two distinct musical formats. The **Afro Blocos** are large drum-based troupes (some with up to 200 drummers) who play on the streets accompanied by singers atop mobile sound trucks. The first of these groups was the Filhos de Gandhi (founded in 1949), whose participation is one of the highlights of Carnival. Their 6,000 members dance through the streets on the Sunday and Tuesday of Carnival dressed in their traditional costumes, a river of white and blue in an ocean of multicoloured carnival revellers. The best known of the recent **Afro Blocos** are Ilê Aiye, Olodum, Muzenza and Malê Debalê. They all operate throughout the year in cultural, social

and political areas. Not all of them are receptive to foreigners among their numbers for Carnival. The basis of the rhythm is the enormous surdo (deaf) drum with its bumbum bumbum bum anchorbeat, while the smaller repique, played with light twigs, provides a crack-like overlay. Ilê Aiye take to the streets around 2100 on Saturday night and their departure from their headquarters at Ladeira do Curuzu in the Liberdade district is not to be missed. The best way to get there is to take a taxi to Curuzu via Largo do Tanque thereby avoiding traffic jams. The ride is a little longer in distance but much quicker in time. A good landmark is the Paes Mendonça supermarket on the corner of the street from where the bloco leaves. From there it's a short walk to the departure point.

The enormous **trios eléctricos** 12 m sound trucks, with powerful sound systems that defy most decibel counters, are the second format. These trucks, each with its own band of up to 10 musicians, play songs influenced by the **afro blocos** and move at a snail's pace through the streets, drawing huge crowds. Each **Afro Bloco** and **bloco de trio** has its own costume and its own security personnel who cordon off the area around the sound truck. The **bloco** members can thus dance in comfort and safety.

Shopping **Shopping in Pelourinho** The major carnival *afro blocos* have boutiques selling T-shirts etc. *Boutique Olodum*, on Praça José Alencar, *Ilê Aiyê*, on R Francisco Muniz Barreto 16 and *Muzenza* next door. On the same street is *Modaxé*, a retail outlet for clothes manufactured by street children under the auspices of the Projeto Axé, expensive. Márcia Ganem, R das Laranjeiras 10. Original Bahian fashion designs, women's wear only, unusual combinations of materials. *Brazilian Sound*, R Francisco Muniz Barreto 18, for the latest in Brazilian and Bahia music, CDs mainly. Good music shops in nearby Praça da Sé are *Mini Som* and an unnamed shop between R da Misericórdia and R José Gonçalves, helpful, CDs only with discounts for multiple purchases. The record shop at the Rodoviária is also good for regional Bahian music.

Instituto Mauá, R Gregório de Matos 27. Open Tue-Sat 0900-1800, Sun 1000-1600, good quality Bahian handicrafts at fair prices, better value and better quality for traditional crafts than the Mercado Modelo. A similar store is *Loja de Artesanato do SESC*, Largo Pelourinho (T321 5502). Mon-Fri 0900-1800 (closed for lunch), Sat 0900-1300. *Rosa do Prado* , R Inacio Aciolly, 5. Cigar shop packed with every kind of Brazilian 'charuto' imaginable. *Scala* , Praça da Sé, T/F321 8891. Handmade jewellery using locally mined gems (eg. acquamarine, amythyst and emerald), workshop at back. Other jewellery stores are *Lasbonfim* (T242 9854) and *Simon* (T242 5218), both in the Terreiro de Jesus. They both have branches in the nearby Carmo district. *Casa Moreira* , Ladeira da Praça, just south of Praça da Sé. Exquisite jewellery and antiques, most very expensive, but some affordable charms. Also for antiques and modern jewellery, *Oxum Casa de Arte*, R Gregório de Matos. Excellent hand-made lace products at *Artesanato Santa Bárbara*, R Alfredo Brito 7. For local art the best stores are *Atelier Portal*

The traditional Carnival route is from Campo Grande (by the Tropical Hotel da Bahia) to Praça Castro Alves near the old town. The **blocos** go along Avenue 7 de Setembro and return to Campo Grande via the parallel R Carlos Gomes. Many of the trios no longer go through the Praça Castro Alves. The best night at Praça Castro Alves is Tuesday (the last night of Carnival) when the famous 'Encontro dos trios' (Meeting of the Trios) takes place. Trios jostle for position in the square and play in rotation until dawn (or later!) on Ash Wednesday. It is not uncommon for major stars from the Bahian (and Brazilian) music world to make surprise appearances.

There are grandstand seats at Campo Grande throughout the event. Day tickets for these are available the week leading up to Carnival. Check with Bahiatursa for information on where the tickets are sold. **Tickets** are US$10 (or up to US$30 on the black market on the day). The blocos are judged as they pass the grandstand. There is little or no shade from the sun so bring a hat and lots of water. Best days are Sunday to Tuesday. For those wishing to go it alone, just find a barraca in the shade and watch the blocos go by. Avoid the Largo da Piedade and Relogio de São Pedro on Avenue 7 de Setembro: the street narrows here, creating human traffic jams.

The other major centre for Carnival is Barra to Ondina. The **blocos alternativos** ply this route. These are always **trios eléctricos** connected with the more traditional blocos who have expanded to this now popular district. Not to be missed here is Timbalada (see **Music** in Bahia).

Recommended Blocos Traditional Route (Campo Grande): Mel, T245 4333, Sunday, Monday, Tuesday; Cameleão, T336 6100 (www.cameleao.com.br), Sunday, Monday, Tuesday; Pinel, T336 0489, Sunday, Monday, Tuesday; Internacionais, T245 0800, Sunday, Monday, Tuesday; Cheiro de Amor, T336 6060, Sunday, Monday, Tuesday. **Afro Blocos** Araketu: T237 0151, Sunday, Monday, Tuesday; Ilê Aiye, T388 4969, Saturday, Monday; Olodum, T321 5010, Friday, Sunday. **Blocos Alternativos** Timbalada, T245 6999, Thursday, Friday, Saturday; Nana Banana, T245 1000, Friday, Saturday; Melomania, T245 4570, Friday, Saturday.

Prices range from US$180 to US$450 (including costume). The quality of the **bloco** depends who plays on the **trio**. A related website is www.meucarnaval.com.br

da Cor, Ladeira do Carmo 31 (T242 9466), run by a co-operative of local artists, Totonho, Calixto, Raimundo Santos, Jô, good prices. Recommended. Also across the street at **Casa do Índio**, Indian artefacts and art, restaurant and bar open here till late, good surroundings. Good wood carvings on R Alfredo Brito, next to Koisa Nossa (No 45), by a co-operative of sculptors, Palito and Negão Barão being the most famous. Hand-made traditional percussion instruments (and percussion lessons) at **Oficina de Investigação Musical**, Alfredo Brito 24 (T322 2386), Mon-Fri 0800-1200 and 1300-1600, US$15 per hr.

Bookshops Livraria Brandão, R Ruy Barbosa 104, Centre, T243 5383. Secondhand English, French, Spanish and German books. **Livraria Civilização Brasileira**, Av 7 de Setembro 912, Mercês, and in the Barra, Iguatemi and Ondina Apart Hotel shopping centres have some English books. Also **Graúna**, Av 7 de Setembro 1448, and R Barão de Itapoã 175, Porto da Barra, many English titles. **Livraria Planeta**, Carlos Gomes 42, loja 1, sells used English books. The bookshop at the airport has English books and magazines. **Sabor dos Saberes**, R das Laranjeiras 5, Pelourinho. Very good selection of cultural titles, knowledgeable owner, Olympio, nice coffee shop upstairs.

Markets The **Mercado Modelo**, at Praça Cairu, lower city, offers many tourist items such as wood carvings, silver-plated fruit, leather goods, local musical instruments. Lace items for sale are often not handmade (despite labels), are heavily marked up, and are much better bought at their place of origin (for example Ilha de Maré, Pontal da Barra and Marechal Deodoro). Cosme e Damião, musical instrument sellers on 1st floor, has been recommended, especially if you want to play the instruments. Bands and dancing, especially Sat (but very much for money from tourists taking photographs), closed at 1200 Sun. There is a photograph exhibition of the

Brazil

old market in the basement. (Many items are often cheaper on the Praça da Sé.) The largest and most authentic market is the *Feira de São Joaquim*, 5 km from Mercado Modelo along the sea front: barkers, trucks, *burros*, horses, boats, people, mud, all very smelly, every day (Sun till 1200 only), busiest on Sat morning; interesting African-style pottery and basketwork; very cheap. (The car ferry terminal for Itaparica is nearby.) *Iguatemi Shopping Centre* sells good handicraft items, it is run by the government so prices are fixed and reasonable. Similarly at *Instituto Mauá*, Porto da Barra. Every Wed from 1700-2100 there is a **handicrafts fair** in the 17th century fort of Santa Maria at the opposite end of Porto da Barra beach. On Fri from 1700-2100, there is an open air market of handicrafts and Bahian food in **Porto da Barra**, a popular event among the local young people. Mosquito nets from *Casa dos Mosquiteros*, R Pedro Sá 6F, Calçada, T226 0715.

Sport & activities **Capoeira**, a sport developed from the traditional foot-fighting technique introduced from Angola by African slaves. The music is by drum, tambourine and *berimbau*; there are several different kinds of the sport. If you want to attempt Capoeira, the best school is *Mestre Bimba*, R das Laranjeiras, T322 0639, open 0900-1200, 1500-2100, basic course in *Capoeira regional*, US$25 for 20 hours. Another *Capoeira regional* school is *Filhos de Bimba*, R Durval Fraga, 6, Nordeste, T345 7329. There are schools in Forte de Santo Antônio behind Pelourinho which teach *Capoeira Angola*, but check addresses at the tourist office. Exhibitions take place in the Largo do Pelourinho every Friday evening around 2000, very authentic, in the upper city. You can also see *capoeiristas* in public spaces like the Pelourinho, outside the Mercado Modelo and at Campo Grande. They may be picturesque but are not always genuine experts; they often expect a contribution, too, but real Capoeira should be free. Negotiate a price before taking pictures. At the Casa da Cultura at Forte de Santo Antônio there is also free live music on Saturday night.

Tour operators Bus tours are available from several companies: *LR Turismo*, T264 0999, also offers boat trips, *Itaparica Turismo*, T2483433, *Tours Bahia*, Praça Jose Anchieta 4, T322 3676 (Austrian guide Victor Runa has been recommended), and *Alameda Turismo*, T248 2977, city tour US$15 pp. *Bahiatours'* Bahia by Night including transport to the *Senac* restaurant, a show, dinner and a night-time walk around Pelourinho (US$15 pp). All-day boat trip on Bahia de Todos Os Santos last from 0800-1700 including a visit to Ilha dos Frades, lunch on Itaparica (US$10 extra), US$15 pp. *Tatur Turismo*, Av Tancredo Neves 274, Centro Empresarial Iguatemi, Sala 228, Bloco B, Salvador 41820-020, Bahia Brasil. T450 7216, F450 7215, tatur@svn.com.br Run by Irishman, Conor O'Sullivan. English spoken. Specializes in Bahia, arranges private guided tours and can make any necessary travel, hotel and accommodation arrangements. Highly recommended. *Kontik*, Av Tancredo Neves 969, sala 1004, T341 2121, F341 2071. A recommended guide who speaks German, English and Portuguese is *Dieter Herzberg*, T334 1200.

Transport **Local Bus**: local buses US$0.70, *executivos*, a/c, US$1.40, US$1.50 or US$3 depending on the route. On buses and at the ticket-sellers' booths, watch your change and beware pickpockets (one scam used by thieves is to descend from the bus while you are climbing aboard). To get from the old city to the ocean beaches, take a 'Barra' bus from Praça da Sé to the Barra point and walk to the nearer ones; the Aeroporto *executivo* leaves Praça da Sé, passing Barra, Ondina, Rio Vermelho, Amaralina, Pituba, Costa Azul, Armação, Boca do Rio, Jaguaripe, Patamares, Piatã and Itapoã, before turning inland to the airport. The glass-sided Jardineira bus goes to Flamengo beach (30 km from the city) following the coastal route; it passes all the best beaches; sit on the right hand side for best views. It leaves from the Praça da Sé daily 0730-1930, every 40 mins, US$1.50. For beaches beyond Itapoã, take the *executivo* to Stella Maris and Flamengo beaches. These follow the same route as the Jardineira. During Carnival, when most streets are closed, buses leave from Vale do Canela (O Vale), near Campo Grande.

If renting a car check whether credit card or cash is cheapest. See page 52, for multinational car rental agencies

Car hire: *Interlocadora*, at airport, T377 2550/204 1019, in the centre T377 4144. *Unidas*, Av Oceânica 2456, Ondina, T336 0717.

Taxi: taxi meters start at US$0.50 for the 'flagdown' and US$0.10 per 100 m. They charge US$15 per hr within city limits, and 'agreed' rates outside. Taxi Barra-Centro US$3 daytime; US$4 at night. Watch the meter, especially at night; the night-time charge should be 30 higher than daytime charges. *Chame Táxi* (24-hr service), 241 2266, and many others.

Long distance Air: an a/c bus service every 30-40 mins between the new Luis Eduardo Magalhães Airport (T 204 1244) and the centre, a distance of 32 km, costs US$1.20. It takes the coast road to the city, stopping at hotels en route. Service starts from the airport at 0500 (last bus 2200, 0600-2200 at weekends) and from Praça da Sé at 0630 (last bus 2100). Also ordinary buses, US$0.50. 'Special' taxis to both Barra and centre (buy ticket at the airport desk next to tourist information booth), US$50; normal taxis (from outside airport), US$20, bus-taxi service, US$10. Allow plenty of time for travel to the airport and for check-in. ATMs are in a special area to the extreme right as you arrive, a good place to get money. *Banco do Brasil* is to the extreme left, open Mon-Fri 0900-1500. *Jacarandá* exchange house is in front of international arrivals, open 24 hrs a day, but poor rates and only good for changing a small amount (count your money carefully). Tourist information booth open 24 hrs, English spoken, has list of hotels and useful map.

Daily flights to all the main cities. *Nordeste* have daily flights to Porto Seguro and several flights a week to destinations in the interior of Bahia. *Tam* and *VASP* also fly to Porto Seguro.

Bus: bus from the Rodoviária (T450 4500); bus RI or RII, 'Centro-Rodoviária-Circular'; in the centre, get on in the Lower City at the foot of the Lacerda lift; buses also go to Campo Grande (US$0.70). A quicker executive bus from Praça da Sé or Praça da Inglaterra (in front of McDonalds), Comércio, run to Iguatemi Shopping Centre, US$1.50, weekdays only, from where there is a walkway to the rodoviária (take care in the dark, or a taxi, US$10). To **Belém** US$48 *comercial* with *Itapemirim*. To **Recife**, US$18-25, 13 hrs, 2 a day and 1 *leito*, *Itapemirim*, T358 0037. To **Rio** (28 hrs, US$45.50, *leito* US$91, *Itapemirim*, good stops, clean toilets, recommended). **São Paulo** (30 hrs), US$51, *leito* US$64 (0815 with *Viação Nacional*, 2 in afternoon with São Geraldo, T358 0188). To **Fortaleza**, 19 hrs, US$33 at 0900 with *Itapemirim*. **Ilhéus**, 7 hrs, *Aguia Branca*, T358 7044, *comercial* US$14.50, *leito* US$29, several. To **Lençóis** 0700, 1200, 2330, 8 hrs, US$12 with *Real Expresso*, T358 1591. **Belo Horizonte**, *Gontijo*, T358 7448, at 1700, US$40 *comercial*, US$50 *executivo*, São Geraldo at 1800. There are daily bus services to **Brasília** along the fully paved BR-242, via Barreiras, 3 daily, 23 hrs, *Paraíso*, T358 1591, US$40. Frequent services to the majority of destinations; a large panel in the main hall lists destinations and the relevant ticket office.

Airline offices *Nordeste/Rio Sul*, R Almte das Espadtodias 100, Camino das Arvores, T0800-992004. *TAM*, Praça Gago Coutinho, T0800-123100. *TAP*, Edif Ilheus, sala 401, Av Estados Unidos 137, T243 6122. *Varig* have a handy booth in Shopping Barra, 1st floor. T0800-997000. *Vasp*, R Chile 27, T0800-998277.

Directory

Banks Don't change money on the street especially in the Upper City where higher rates are usually offered. Changing at banks can be bureaucratic and time-consuming. *Citibank*, R Miguel Calmon 555, Comércio, centre, changes TCs. Branch at R Almte Marquês de Leão 71, Barra, has ATM. Visa ATMs at branches of *Bradesco* and *Banco do Brasil*, whose *câmbios* are in Pelourinho, Iguatemi Shopping (opposite Rodoviária) and Pituba (high commission on TCs). MasterCard at *Credicard*, 1st floor, Citibank building, R Miguel Calmon 555, Comércio. MasterCard ATMs at branches of *HSBC*, eg Av 7 de Setembro

Banks are open 1000-1600 Between 2100-0700 ATMs give maximum R$150/US$50

Brazil

136, and any *Banco 24 Horas*. ATMs for all major cards in the Rodoviária. *Iguatemi Cambio e Turismo*, Shopping Iguatemi, 2nd floor. Changes all brands of TCs at good rates. *Figueiredo*, opposite *Grande Hotel da Barra* on Ladeira da Barra will exchange cash at good rates. *Shopping Tour* in Barra Shopping centre changes dollars, as will other tour agencies. If stuck, all the big hotels will exchange, but at poor rates.

Communications Internet: *Bahiacafe.com*, Praça da Sé (see Eating, above). US$1.20 for 30 mins. *Internetcafe.com*, Av 7 de Setembro 3713, Porto da Barra and R João de Deus 2, historical centre. US$2 per hr, closed Sun. *Internet Access* , R Alfonso Celso 447, Barra. US$1.20 per hr. *Novo Tempo*, Ladeira do Carmo 16, Centro Histórico. **Post Office:** main post office and poste restante is in Praça Inglaterra, in the Lower City, open Mon-Fri 0800-1700, Sat 0800-1200, F243 9383 (US$1 to receive fax). Several other offices, including R Alfredo Brito 43, Mon-Sat 0800-1700, Sun 0800-1200, has a philatelic section; rodoviária; airport; Barra and Iguatemi Shopping Malls. **Telephone:** *Embratel*, R do Carro 120. *Telemar* has branches at Campo da Pôlvora, Trav Joaquim Maurício 81, open 0630-2400, on R Hugo Baltazar Silva (open 0700-2200 daily), airport (daily 0700-2200) and rodoviária (Mon-Sat 24 hrs and Sun 0700-2200).

Cultural centres Cultura Inglesa, R Plínio Moscoso 357, Jardim Apipema. **Associação Cultural Brasil-Estados Unidos**, Av 7 de Setembro 1883, has a library and reading room with recent US magazines, open to all, free use of internet for 30 mins, and at No 1809 on the same avenue is the German **Goethe Institut**, also with a library and reading room; both have cafés. **Alliance Française**, Ladeira da Barra, top end. Exhibition centre, theatre, classes, open-ari café, beautiful view.

Embassies and consulates Austria, R Jardim Armacao, T371 4611. **Belgium**, Av Trancredo Neves 274A, sala 301, Iguatemi, T623 2454. **Denmark**, Av 7 de Setembro 3959, Barra, T336 9861. Mon-Fri 0900-1200, 1400-1700. **Finland**, Jardim Ipiranga 19, T247 3312, Mon-Fri 0800-1000 and after 1900. **France**, R Francisco Gonçalves 1, sala 805, Comércio, T241 0168, Mon, Tue, Thu morning only. **Germany**, R Lucaia 281, 2nd floor, Rio Vermelho, T334 7106, Mon-Fri 0900-1200. **Holland**, Av Santa Luzia, 1136 Ed Porto Empresarial, Sala 302, T341 0410, Mon-Fri 0800-1200. **Italy**, Av 7 de Setembro 1238, Centro, T329 5338, Mon, Wed, Fri 1500-1800. **Norway**, Av Estados Unidos, 14, 8th floor, T326 8500 , Mon-Fri 0900-1200, 1400-1600. **Portugal**, Largo Carmo 4, Sto Antônio, T241 1633. **Spain**, R Mal Floriano 21, Canela, T336 1937, Mon-Fri 0900-1400. **Sweden**, Av Estados Unidos 357, Ed Joaquim Barreto, sala 501, Comércio, T242 4833. **Switzerland**, Av Tancredo Neves 3343, 5th floor, sala 506b, T341 5827. **UK**, Av Estados Unidos 4, 18B, Comércio, T243 7399, Mon-Thu, 0900-1100, 1400-1600, Fri 0900-1100. **USA**, R Pernambuco 51, Pituba, T345 1545, Mon-Fri, 0900-1130, 1430-1630.

Language classes *Casa do Brasil*, R Milton de Oliveira 231, Barra, T264 5866, www.casa-do-brasil.net *Superlearning Idiomas*, Av Sete de Setembro 3402, Ladeira da Barra, T337 2824, www.allways.com.br/spl Uses music and relaxation as learning techniques.

Medical services Clinic: Barão de Loreto 21, Graça. *Dr Argemiro Júnior* speaks English and Spanish. First consultation US$40, 2nd free. **Medical:** yellow fever vaccinations free at **Delegação Federal de Saúde**, R Padre Feijó, Canela. Israeli travellers needing medical (or other) advice should contact *Sr Marcus* (T247 5769), who speaks Hebrew.

Useful addresses Immigration: (for extensions of entry permits), Policia Federal, Av O Pontes 339, Aterro de Água de Meninos, Lower City, T319 6082, open 1000-1600. Show an outward ticket or sufficient funds for your stay, visa extension US$17.50. **Tourist Police:** R Gregório de Matos 16, T320 4103. **Delegacia de Proteção ao Turista**, R Gregório de Matos 1, T242 3504.

Itaparica

Phone code: 071
Colour map 5, grid C5

Across the bay from Salvador lies the island of Itaparica, 29 km long and 12 km wide. The town of Itaparica is very picturesque, with a fair beach in the town, and well worth a visit. Take a bus or kombi by the coast road (Beira Mar) which passes through the villages of Manguinhos, Amoureiras and Ponta de Areia. The beach at Ponta de Areia is one of the best on the island and is very popular. There are many *barracas* on the beach, the best and busiest is *Barraca Pai Xango*, always very lively.

In Itaparica there are many fine residential buildings from the 19th century, plus the church of **São Lourenço**, one of the oldest in Brazil, and there are delightful walks through the old town. During the summer months the streets are ablaze with the blossoms of the beautiful flamboyant trees. The beaches at Mar Grande are fair but can be dirty at times. There are many *pousadas* in Mar Grande and at the nearby beaches of Ilhota and Gamboa (both to the left as you disembark from the ferry).

From Bom Despacho there are many buses, kombis and taxis to all parts of the island, inlcuding beaches at Ponta de Areia, Mar Grande, Berlinque, Aratuba and Cacha Pregos. Kombi and taxis can be rented for trips but be prepared to bargain. There are also buses to other towns such as Nazaré das Farinhas, Valença (see below) and also **Jaguaribe**, a small, picturesque colonial port. Both of these towns are on the mainland connected by a bridge on the southwest side of the island, turn off between Mar Grande and Cacha Pregos (bus company, *Viazul*). There are good beaches across the bay on the mainland, but a boat is needed to reach these (US$12).

A good simple *pousada* at Amoureiras is **C** *Pousada Pé na Praia*, T831 1389. Good breakfast, good sized rooms, English and French spoken. There are few *pousadas* in the town. The best is **A** *Quinta Pitanga*, T831 1554. Beautifully decorated by the owner Jim Valkus, 3 suites and 2 singles, beachfront property, a retreat, excellent restaurant. Expensive but highly recommended, accepts day visitors. **D** *Pousada Icaraí*, Praça da Piedade, T831 3119. Charming, good location. **Mar Grande** The following are all recommended: **A** *Pousada Arco Íris*, Estrada da Gamboa 102, T833 1130. Magnificent building and setting in mango orchard, expensive, good if slow restaurant, *Manga Rosa*. They have camping facilities next door, shady, not always clean. **C** *Pousada Estrela do Mar*, Av NS das Candeias 170, T833 1108. Good rooms, fan or a/c. **D** *Pousada Sonho do Verão*, R São Bento 2, opposite *Pousada Arco Íris*, T833 1616. Chalets and apartments, cooking facilities, French and English spoken. Like other *pousadas* they rent bicycles (US$3 per hr); they also rent horses (US$5 per hr). Near the church in the main praça is the **D** *Pousada Casarão da Ilha*, T833 1106. Spacious rooms with a great view of Salvador across the bay, swimming pool, a/c. **E** *Pousada Samambaia*, AV NS das Candeias 61. Good breakfast, French spoken.

   Aratuba D *Pousada Zimbo Tropical*, Estrada de Cacha Pregos, Km 3, Rua Yemanjá, T/F8381148. French/Brazilian-run, good breakfast, evening meals available. Recommended.

   Cacha Pregos *Club Sonho Nosso*, T837 1040 or T226 1933. Very clean huts on clean beach, good service, collect you from anywhere on the island – also Bom Despacho. Kombis stop in front of entrance, a 5-min walk. Recommended. **C** *Pousada Babalú*, T837 1193. Spacious bungalows, frigobar, fan, good breakfast. Recommended. **D** *Pousada Cacha Pregos*, next to the supermarket, T837 1013. With fan, bath, no breakfast, good.

Sleeping

Good restaurants in Mar Grande are *Philippe's Bar and Restaurant*, Largo de São Bento, French and local cuisine, information in English and French. *O Pacífico* is peaceful. *Restaurant Rafael* in the main praça for pizzas and snacks. Also pizzas at *Bem Me Quer*, opposite *Pousada Samambaia*, down an alley. There are many Bahianas selling acarajé in the late afternoon and early evening in the main praça by the pier.

Eating

Ferry The main passenger ferry leaves for Bom Despacho from São Joaquim (buses for Calçada, Ribeira stop across the road from the ferry terminal; the 'Sabino Silva – Ribeira' bus passes in front of the Shopping Barra). First ferry from Salvador at 0540 and, depending on demand, at intervals of 45 mins thereafter; last ferry from Salvador at 2230. Returning to Salvador the 1st ferry is at 0515 and the last at 2300. In summer ferries are much more frequent. Enquiries at the **Companhia de Navegação Bahiana** (CNB), T321 7100 from 0800 to 1700. A one way ticket for foot passengers Mon-Fri is US$1, Sat-Sun US$1.20. Catamarans depart for Bom Despacho twice daily, US$3. **Mar Grande** can be reached by a smaller ferry (*Lancha*) from the Terminal Marítimo in front of the Mercado Modelo in Salvador. The ferries leave every 45 mins and the crossing takes 50 mins, US$1.80 return.

Transport

The area around Salvador, known as the Recôncavo Baiano, was one of the chief centres of sugar and tobacco cultivation in the 16th century. Some 73 km from Salvador is **Santo Amaro da Purificação**, an old sugar centre sadly decaying, noted for its churches (often closed because of robberies), municipal palace (1769), fine main

The Recôncavo

Brazil

praça, birthplace of the singers Caetano Veloso and his sister Maria Bethania and ruined mansions including Araújo Pinto, former residence of the Barão de Cotegipe. Other attractions include the splendid beaches of the bay, the falls of Vitória and the grotto of Bom Jesus dos Pobres. The festivals of **Santo Amaro**, 24 January-2 February, and **Nossa Senhora da Purificação** on 2 February itself are interesting. There is also the **Bembé do Mercado** festival on 13 May. Craftwork is sold on the town's main bridge. There are no good hotels or restaurants.

Cachoeira & São Félix

At 116 km from Salvador and only 4 km from the BR-101 coastal road are the towns of Cachoeira (Bahia's 'Ouro Preto', *Population*: 30,416) and São Félix (*Population*: 13,699), on either side of the Rio Paraguaçu below the Cachoeira dam. Cachoeira was twice capital of Bahia: once in 1624-25 during the Dutch invasion, and once in 1822-23 while Salvador was still held by the Portuguese. There are beautiful views from above São Félix.

Cachoeira's main buildings are the **Casa da Câmara e Cadeia** (1698-1712), the **Santa Casa de Misericórdia** (1734 – the hospital, someone may let you see the church), the 16th-century **Ajuda** chapel (now containing a fine collection of vestments), and the Convent of the **Ordem Terceira do Carmo**, whose church has a heavily gilded interior. Other churches are the **Matriz** with 5 m-high *azulejos*, and **Nossa Senhora da Conceição do Monte**. There are beautiful lace cloths on the church altars. All churches are either restored or in the process of restoration. The **Museu Hansen Bahia,** R Ana Néri, houses fine engravings by the German artist who made the Recôncavo his home in the 1950s. There is a great wood-carving tradition in Cachoeira. The artists can be seen at work in their studios. Best are Louco Filho, Fory, both in R Ana Néri, Doidão, in front of the Igreja Matriz and J Gonçalves on the main praça. A 300 m railway bridge built by the British in the 19th century spans the Rio Paraguaçu to São Felix where the Danneman cigar factory can be visited to see hand-rolling. Tourist office: Casa de Ana Néri, Cachoeira. ■ *Buses from Salvador (Camurjipe) every hr or so from 0530; Feira Santana, 2 hrs, US$3.*

Sleeping and eating Cachoeira **A** *Pousada do Convento de Cachoeira*, T725 1716. In a restored 16th-century convent, good restaurant. **D** *Santo Antônio*, near the rodoviária. Basic, safe, laundry facilities. Recommended. **E** *Pousada Tia Rosa*, near Casa Ana Neri, T725 1692. With breakfast, very basic. *Cabana do Pai Thomaz*, 25 de Junho 12, excellent Bahian food, good value, also an hotel, **C** with private bath and breakfast. *Gruta Azul*, Praça Manoel Vitorino. Lunch only. *Do Nair*, R 13 de Maio. Delicious food and sometimes Seresta music. *Casa do Licor*, R 13 Maio 25. Interesting bar, try the banana-flavoured spirit. **São Félix** *Xang-hai*, good, cheap food. Warmly recommended. Try the local dish, *maniçoba* (meat, manioc and peppers).

Festivals *São João* (**24 Jun**), 'Carnival of the Interior' celebrations include dangerous games with fireworks. *Nossa Sehora da Boa Morte* (**early Aug**) is also a major festival. A famous *candomblé* ceremony at the Fonte de Santa Bárbara is held on **4 Dec**.

Lençóis

Phone code: 0xx75
Colour map 5, grid C4
Population: 8,910
400 km W of
Salvador on BR-242

This historical monument and colonial gem was founded in 1844 to exploit the diamonds in the region. While there are still some *garimpeiros* (gold prospectors), it is not precious metals that draw most visitors, but the climate, which is cooler than the coast, the relaxed atmosphere and the wonderful trekking and horseriding in the hills of the Chapada Diamantina. A few of the options are given below under Excursions, and *pousadas* and tour operators offer guiding services to point you in the right direction. This is also a good place for buying handicrafts.

Sleeping **A** *Recanto das Águas*, Av Senhor dos Passos s/n, T/F334 1154. Comfortable, good location, swimming pool, a/c or fan. Recommended. **A** *Hotel de Lençóis*, R Altinha Alves 747, T/F334 1102. With breakfast, swimming pool. Recommended. **C** *Pousalegre*, R Boa Vista 95, T334

1124/1245. With good regional breakfast, dormitories only, safe, hot showers, good vegetarian restaurant. **C** *Estalagem de Alcino*, R Gen Vieira de Morais 139, T334 1171. **D** pp shared bath, beautiful, restored 19th-century house, superb breakfast. Highly recommended. **D** *Pousada Casa da Geleia*, R Gen Viveiros 187, T334 1151. 2 excellent chalets set in a huge garden at the entrance to the town, and 4 very nice rooms, English spoken, good breakfast (Ze Carlos is a keen birdwatcher and an authority on the region, Lia makes excellent jams). **D** *Casa de Hélia*, R das Muritiba 102, T334 1143. Attractive and homely, English and some Hebrew spoken, good facilities, renowned breakfast. Recommended. **D** *Tradição*, R José Florêncio, T334 1137. Breakfast, fridge, mosquito net, pleasant. **D** *Pousada Violeiro*, R Prof Assis 70, T334 1259. Nice rooms with fan, some with bath, good view and breakfast. **E** *Pousada dos Duendes*, R do Pires s/n, T/F334 1229, oliviadosduendes@zaz.com.br Welcoming, very comfortable, run by the ever helpful Olivia Taylor who will sort out all trekking and walking activities for visitors, rooms with bath, fan, some with veranda, hot showers, small campsite, excellent food, vegetarian and vegan options, basically a home from home for all road-weary travellers. Olivia's travel agency, *H2O*, organizes day trips, hikes and kayaking. Highly recommended. **E** *Pousada Diangela*, R dos Mineiros 60, T334 1192. With good breakfast and vegetarian dinner. Juanita on R do Rosário rents rooms with access to washing and cooking facilities, US$3.50 pp. Cláudia and Isabel, R da Baderna 95, T334 1229, rent a house on the main praça in front of the Correios, US$4 pp without breakfast; they also have an agency with sort and long-term rents. **Camping**: *Alquimia*, 2 km before Lençóis, T334 1241, and *Camping Lumiar*, near Rosário church in centre, friendly. Recommended.

Picanha na Praça, opposite the bandstand on the square above the main praça. *Artistas da* **Eating**
Massa, R Miguel Calmon. Italian. *O Xente Minina*, 100 m past the *Recanto das Águas* on the road out of town. Excellent pizzas and ambience. *Goody*, R da Rodoviária s/n. Good simple cooking. *Grisante*, on main praça. Good local food. The best night spots are *Veneno Café Bar*, on main praça. For drinks and sandwiches, plays good music. At weekends there is a local nightclub called *Inferninho* on R das Pedras. Not up to much but can be amusing, R$1 for men, free for girls. *Dom Oba*, at the top of town. Bar with good music and *churrasco*.

Artesanato Areias Coloridas, R das Pedras, owned by Taurino, is the best place for local sand **Shopping**
paintings made in bottles. These are inexpensive. They will make one as you wait. For ceramic *The Mon morning*
work, the most original is *Jota*, who has a workshop which can be visited. Take the steps to the *market is*
left of the school near the *Pousada Lençóis*. There is a local craft market just off the main praça *recommended*
every night. *O Tempo*, R São Benedito 123. Works by local artists, closed Mon.

H2O, see Sleeping. *Lentur*, Av 7 de Setembro 10, T/F334 1271. Organizes day trips to nearby **Tour operators**
caves and to see the sunset at Morro do Pai Inácio. Recommended. *Pé de Trilha Turismo Aventura*, Praça dos Nagos opposite the market building, T334 1124. Guiding, trekking, rents camping equipment, etc, can make reservations for most of the *pousadas* in the Chapada Diamantina (see below), represented in Salvador by *Tatur Turismo* (see above). Guides: *Edmilson* (known locally as Mil), R Domingos B Souza 70, T334 1319; he knows the region extremely well and is very knowledgeable. *Roy Funch*, T334 1305, royfunch@gd.com.br, the ex-director of the Parque Nacional Chapada Diamantina, is an excellent guide and can be found at his craft shop, *Funkart*, in the main praça (he and his wife also offer quiet and comfortable accommodation with a good breakfast at their home at Rua Pé da Ladeira 212). Likewise *Gyl*, who has a workshop and guesthouse, *Ateliê Casa Fénix* at R Prof Assis 40, close to bus station, T334 1070, ateliecasafenix@ligbr.com.br Gyl guides regular and unusual trips. Recommended. *Índio*, recommended, T334 1348, or ask around. Each *pousada* generally has a guide attached to it to take residents on tours, about US$20-30.

Real Expresso bus from Salvador; buses also from Recife, Ibotirama, Barreiras or Brasília, 16 hrs, US$33. **Transport**

Banks *Banco do Brasil*, 0900-1300 Mon-Fri, Visa ATM and changes TCs and US$ cash. No MasterCard. **Directory**
Communications Post Office: main square, 0900-1700, Mon-Fri. **Tourist office Sectur**, is on Praça Oscar Maciel, next to the church across the river from town, T334 1327.

Brazil

Parque Nacional da Chapada Diamantina
Colour map 5, grid C4

Palmeiras, 50 km from Lençóis, is the headquarters of the Parque Nacional da Chapada Diamantina (founded 1985), which contains 1,500 sq km of mountainous country. There is an abundance of endemic plants, waterfalls, large caves (take care, and a strong torch, there are no signs and caves can be difficult to find without a guide), rivers with natural swimming pools and good walking tours. ■ *Information,* Ibama, *R Ruy Barbosa 5, Palmeiras, T0xx75-332 2229, F332 2187.*

Excursions near Lençóis and in the Chapada Diamantina Near the town, visit the **Serrano** with its wonderful natural pools in the river bed, which give a great hydro massage. A little further away is the **Salão de Areia**, where the coloured sands for the bottle paintings come from. **Ribeirão do Meio** is a 45-min walk from town; here locals slide down a long natural water chute into a big pool (it is best to be shown the way it is done and to take something to slide in). **Gruta do Lapão**, 3 hours from Lençóis, guide essential, is in quartz rock and therefore has no stalagmites. Some light rock climbing is required. **Cachoeira da Primavera**, two very pretty waterfalls close to town, recommended. **Cachoeira Sossego**, 45 mins from town, a 'picture postcard' waterfall, swimming pool, recommended. **Morro de Pai Inácio**, 30 km from Lençóis, has the best view of the Chapada, recommended at sunset (bus from Lençois at 0815, 30 mins, US$1). In the park is the **Cachoeira da Fumaça** (Smoke Waterfall, also called **Glass**), 384 m, the second highest in Brazil. To see it, go by car to the village of **Capão** and walk 2½ hours. The view is astonishing; the updraft of the air currents often makes the water flow back up creating the 'smoke' effect. Olivia Taylor at the *Pousada dos Duendes* offers a three-day trek, the village of Capão and Capivara and Palmital falls from US$45. ■ *Local guides can often arrange transport to the more remote excursions, certainly this is possible when groups are involved.*

Sleeping Capão: C *Candombá*, F0xx75-332 2176, or through *Tatur Turismo* in Salvador. Good breakfast, excellent food, home-grown vegetables, run by Claude and Suzana (Claude speaks French and English and guides in the region). **D** *Pousada Verde*, at entrance to town. Very good breakfast. Recommended. **E** *Pouso Riacho do Ouro*. Recommended. **E** *Tatu Feliz*. No breakfast. **Mucugê: A** *Alpina Resort*, on a hill above the town, T0xx75-338 2150, www.alpinamucuge.com.br Panoramic views, log fires, helpful staff. Recommended.

South of Salvador

Valença
Phone code: 0xx71
Colour map 7, grid A6
Population: 77,509
271 km from Salvador via paved road

This small, attractive town stands at the mouth of the Rio Una. Two old churches stand on rising ground; the views from Nossa Senhora do Amparo are recommended. The town is in the middle of an area producing black pepper, cloves and piaçava (used in making brushes and mats). Other industries include the building and repair of fishing boats (*saveiros*). The Rio Una enters an enormous region of mangrove swamps. The main attraction of Valença are the beaches on the mainland (Guabim, 14 km north) and on the island of Tinharé. Avoid touts at the rodoviária. Better to visit the friendly tourist office opposite (T741 3311).

Sleeping B *do Porto*, Av Maçônica 50, T741 3066. Helpful, safe, good breakfast, good restaurant. **C** *Rafa*, Praça da Independência, T741 1816. Large rooms. Recommended. Next door is **D** *Guabim*, Praça da Independência, T741 3804. Modest with bath and buffet breakfast. good *Akuarius* restaurant. **D** *Valença*, R Dr H Guedes Melo 15, T741 1807. Comfortable, good breakfast. Recommended.

Long-distance buses from new rodoviária, Av Maçônica, T741 1280. Local buses from the old rodoviaria

Transport Many buses a day to/from **Salvador**, 5 hrs, US$6, several companies including *Aguia Branca* (T450 4400). For the shortest route to Valença, take the ferry from São Joaquim to Bom Despacho on Itaparica island, from where it is 130 km to Valença via Nazaré das Farinhas. To/from Bom Despacho on Itaparica, *Camarujipe* and *Águia Branca*, 16 a day, 1 hr 45 mins, US$3.60.

Brazil

Tinharé and Morro de São Paulo

Tinharé is a large island separated from the mainland by the estuary of the Rio Una and mangrove swamps, so that it is hard to tell which is land and which is water. The most popular beaches and *pousadas* are at Morro de São Paulo. Immediately south is the island of **Boipeba**, separated from Tinharé by the Rio do Inferno. On this island, too, there are lovely beaches and a small fishing village, also called Boipeba.

1½ hrs south of Valença by boat

Morro de São Paulo is situated on the headland at the northernmost tip of Tinharé, lush with ferns, palms and birds of paradise. The village is dominated by the lighthouse and the ruins of a colonial fort (1630), built as a defence against European raiders. It has a landing place on the sheltered landward side, dominated by the old gateway of the fortress. From the lighthouse a path leads to a ruined look out with cannon, which has panoramic views. The fort is a good point to watch the sunset from. Dolphins can be seen in August. Fonte de Ceu waterfall is reached by walking along the beach to **Gamboa** then inland. Watch the tide; it's best to take a guide, or take a boat back to Morro (US$0.50-1). No motor vehicles are allowed on the island. On 7 September there's a big festival with live music on the beach.

There is a port tax of US$1 payable at the prefeitura on leaving the island; this is resented by many

Sleeping

Expensive Dec-Mar, cheaper and more tranquil during the rest of the year. Very crowded during public holidays

Morro de São Paulo There are many cheap *pousadas* and rooms to rent near the fountain (Fonte Grande) but this part of town is very hot at night. **C** *Pousada Gaúcho*. Huge breakfast, shared bath. A little further along and up some steep steps to the left is **B** *Pousada Colibri*. Cool, always a breeze blowing, excellent views, only 6 apartments, Helmut, the owner, speaks English and German.

Beach hotels The beaches on Morro de São Paulo are at the bottom of the main street where one turns right on to the first beach (Primeira Praia). **A** *Pousada Vistabella*, T0xx73-783 1001. Owner Petruska is extremely welcoming, good rooms, those to the front have good views and are cooler, all have fans, hammocks. **B** *Pousada Farol do Morro*, T483 1036, F243 4207. All rooms with sea view, cool. **C** *Pousada Ilha da Saudade*. Good breakfast, simple. **C** *Pousada Ilha do Sol*. Good views. On third beach (Terceira Praia) is **A** *Pousada Fazenda Caeira*, T0xx75-4411272. Large grounds, private, well stocked library with snooker and other games. **D** *Pousada Aradhia*. Balconies with ocean view. **E** *Pousada Govinda*. Simple, good breakfast, other meals available, English and Spanish spoken.

In **Boipeba A** *Pousada Tassimirim*, T9981 2378 (R Com Madureira 40, 45400-000 Valença), www.ilhaboipeba.org.br Bungalows, bar, restaurant, including breakfast and dinner, secluded. **D** *Pousada Luar das Águas* (T9981 1012). Simple, good.

Eating

Mid-range *Bahiana*, on the main square, good food. *Belladonna* on the main street is a very good Italian restaurant with great music, a good meeting point, owner Guido speaks Italian, English and French, and is a willing source of information on the Morro, open daily from 1800 till the small hours. *Morena Bela*, good for *moqueca*. *Restaurant Gaúcho* for good, reasonably priced, typical regional cooking. **Cheap** *Casablanca* is a good simple restaurant, open daily till late, good breakfasts at *Comida Natural*, on the main street, *comida a kilo*, good juices. Good pasta dishes at *Club do Balango* on the second beach, where many beach huts offer cool drinks and meals. *Barraca Caita* opens till late with good music at weekends. They have snorkelling equipment for hire, popular meeting point, potent cocktail parties every night! Another *barraca* is *Ponto da Ilha* alongside. There are many other *barracas* on the third beach.

Transport

Part of the trip is on the open sea, which can be rough

Air taxi from Salvador airport US$40 1-way, 20 mins, Adey T377 2451, Aero Star 377 4406.

From Salvador, several companies operate a ferry (1 hr 30 mins) and catamaran (30 mins) service from the Terminal Marítimo in front of the Mercado Modelo to Morro de São Paulo. Times vary according to the weather and season. Lancha Farol do Morro, T241 7858 and *Catamara Gamboa do Morro*, T9975 6395. **Boats** leave every day from Valença for Gamboa (1½ hrs) and Morro de São Paulo (1½ hrs) from the main bridge in Valença 5 times a day (signalled by a loud whistle). The fare is US$2.50. A *lancha rápida* taking 25 mins travels the route between Valença and Morro, US$8. Only buses between 0530-1100 from Salvador to Valença connect with ferries. If not stopping in Valença, get out of the bus by the main bridge in town, don't wait till you get to the rodoviária, which is a long way from the ferry. Private boat hire can be arranged if you miss the ferry schedule. A responsible local boatman is *Jario*,

T0xx75-741 1681. He also offers excursions to other islands, especially Boipeba. There is a regular boat from Valença to Boipeba on weekdays 1000-1230 depending on tide, return 1500-1700, 3-4 hrs.

Ilhéus

Phone code: 0xx73
Post code: 45650
Colour map 7, grid A6
Population: 222,127
462 km S of Salvador

At the mouth of the Rio Cachoeira, the port serves a district which produces 65% of all Brazilian cocoa. Shipping lines call regularly. A bridge links the north bank of the river with Pontal, where the airport is located. The local beaches are splendid, but the central beach is polluted. It is the birthplace of Jorge Amado (1912-2002) and the setting of one of his most famous novels, *Gabriela, cravo e canela* (*Gabriela, Clove and Cinnamon*). There is a tourist office on the beach opposite Praça Castro Alves (a few minutes from the cathedral), T634 3510, friendly, maps US$2, recommended. *Festa de São Sebastião* (17-20 January), *Carnival, Festa de São Jorge* (23 April), *Foundation day,* 28 June, and *Festa do Cacau* throughout October. The church of **São Jorge** (1556), the city's oldest, is on the Praça Rui Barbosa; it has a small museum. The cathedral of **São Sebastião**, on the Praça Dom Eduardo, near the seashore, is a huge, early 20th-century building. In Alto da Vitória is the 17th century **Nossa Senhora da Vitória**, built to celebrate a victory over the Dutch. Ask in travel agencies for trips to Rio de Engenho to visit **Santana** church (1537).

North of Ilhéus, two good beaches are Marciano, with reefs offshore and good surfing, and Barra, 1 km further north at the mouth of the Rio Almada. South of the river, Pontal beaches can be reached by 'Barreira' bus; alight just after *Hotel Jardim Atlântico* (**AL**). Between Ilhéus and **Olivença** are fine beaches, such as Cururupe, Batuba (good surfing) and Cai n'Água in Olivença itself (also good surfing).

Try the local drink, coquinho, coconut filled with cachaça. Also try suco de cacau at juice stands

Sleeping and eating A *Hotel Barravento* on Malhado beach, R NS das Graças 276, T/F634 3223. Ask for the penthouse – usually no extra charge, including breakfast and refrigerator. **A** *Ilhéus Praia*, Praça Dom Eduardo (on beach), T634 2533. Pool, helpful. Recommended. **B** *Pousada Sol Atlântico*, Av Lomanto Júnior 1450, Pontal T231 8059. Good view over bay, fan, TV, balcony. Plenty of cheap hotels near the municipal rodoviária in centre, also **D** *Hotel Atlântico Sul*, R Bento Berilo 224, Centro, T231 4668. Good bar/restaurant. Recommended. **D** *Cacau D'Ouro*, R Vieiro 33, T231 3713. With bath and breakfast, restaurant with good views of the town. **Campsite** *Estância das Fontes*, 19 km on road south to Olivença, T212 2505. Cheap, shady. A recommended eating place is *Os Velhos Marinheiros*, Av 2 de Julho, on the waterfront. *Vesúvio*, Praça Dom Eduardo, next to the cathedral, made famous by Amado's novel (see above). Good but pricey. *Nogar*, Av Bahia 377, near sea. Pizzas and pasta.

Transport Bus: Rodoviária is 4 km from the centre on Itabuna road. Several daily to **Salvador**, 7 hrs, US$14.40 (*leito* US$29, *Expresso São Jorge*); 0620 bus goes via Itaparica, leaving passengers at Bom Despacho ferry station on the island – thence 50-mins ferry to Salvador. To **Eunápolis**, 5 hrs, US$5.40, this bus also leaves from the central bus terminal. Other destinations served; local buses leave from Praça Cairu. Insist that taxi drivers have meters and price charts.

Porto Seguro

Phone code: 0xx73
Post code: 45810
Colour map 7, grid A6
Population: 95,721

About 400 km south of Ilhéus on the coast is the old town of Porto Seguro. Building is subject to controls on height and materials, in keeping with traditional Bahian styles (colonial or Indian). In the area are remains of original Atlantic coastal forest, with parrots, monkeys, marmosets and snakes.

Town beaches are not recommended. The best beaches are north of town along the Santa Cruz de Cabrália road (known as Av Beira Mar – BR-367)

Pedro Álvares Cabral sighted land at Monte Pascoal south of Porto Seguro. As the sea here was too open, he sailed north in search of a secure protected harbour, entering the mouth of the Rio Burnahém to find the harbour he later called Porto Seguro (safe port). Where the first mass was celebrated, a cross marks the spot on the road between Porto Seguro and Santa Cruz Cabrália. A tourist village, Coroa Vermelha, has sprouted at the site of Cabral's first landfall, 20 mins by bus to the north of Porto Seguro. It has souvenir shops selling Pataxó-Tupi Indian items, beach bars, hotels and rental houses, all rather uncoordinated.

Brazil

From the roundabout at the entrance to Porto Seguro take a wide, steep, unmarked path uphill to the historical city, **Cidade Histórica**, three churches (Nossa Senhora da Misericórdia-1530, Nossa Senhora do Rosário-1534, and Nossa Senhora da Pena-1718), the former jail and the monument marking the landfall of Gonçalo Coelho; a small, peaceful place with lovely gardens and panoramic views. There are *borrachudos*, little flies that bite feet and ankles in the heat of the day; coconut oil keeps them off; at night mosquitoes can be a problem (but there is no malaria, dengue or yellow fever).

Guided tours of the area can be arranged with *BPS*, at the Shopping Centre, T288 2373. *Companhia do Mar* (Praça dos Pataxós, T288 2981) does daily trips by schooner to coral reefs. The most popular is to Recife de Fora, with good snorkelling; it leaves daily at 1000, returns 1630, about US$10, US$2.50 extra for snorkelling gear.

The town is a popular holiday resort with many charter companies flying in directly from Rio and São Paulo. Room capacity of the local hotel industry is greater than that of Salvador.

A *Pousada Imperador*, Estrada do Aeroporto, T288 2759, F288 2900. 4-star, all facilities, interesting architecture, above the city, great views from pool deck. **A** *Estalagem Porto Seguro*, R Marechal Deodoro 66, T288 2095, F288 3692. In an old colonial house, relaxing atmosphere, a/c, TV, pool, good breakfast. Highly recommended. **A** *Pousada Casa Azul*, 15 de Novembro 11, T/F288 2180. TV, a/c, good pool and garden, quiet part of town. **A** *Pousada Alegrete*, Av dos Navegantes 567, T/F288 1738. All facilities. Recommended. **B** *Pousada Las Palmas*, Praça Antônio Carlos Magalhães 102, T/F288 2643. A/c, TV, no pool. Highly recommended. **B** *Pousada Jandaias*, R das Jandaias 112, T288 2611, F288 2738. Fan, great breakfast, tranquil. **B** *Pousada dos Raizes* (**C** without breakfast), Praça dos Pataxós 196, T/F288 4717. **C** *Pousada Coral*, R Assis Chateaubriand 74, T/F288 2630. A/c, TV, good location. **C** *Pousada Da Orla*, Av Portugal 404, T/F288 1131. Fan, good breakfast, great location. Highly recommended. **C** *Pousada do Francês*, Av 22 de Abril 180, T/F288 2469. A/c, TV, breakfast. Recommended. **C** *Pousada Mar e Sol*, Av Getúlio Vargas 223, T/F288 2137. Fan in most apartments, a/c in a few. **C** *Pousada dos Navegantes*, Av 22 de Abril 212, T288 2390, F288 2486, www.portonet.com.br/navegantes, a/c, TV, pool, conveniently located. Recommended. **D** *Pousada da Praia*, Av Getúlio Vargas 153, T/F288 2908. A/c, TV, pool, breakfast, comfortable. **D** *Pousada Aquárius*, R Pedro Álvares Cabral 174, T/F288 2738. No breakfast, family run, central. **D** *Estalagem da Yvonne*, R Marechal Deodoro 298, T/F288 1515. Some rooms with a/c. **E** *Porto Brasília*, Praça Antônio Carlos Magalhães 234. Fans, mosquito nets, with breakfast, **E** without. **F** *Pousada Alto Mar*, R Bela Vista, behind the cathedral. Cheaper without breakfast, hot water, safe, good views of the port. **F** *Pousada Casa Grande*, Av dos Navegantes 107, Centro, T288 2003. Comfortable, multilingual, breakfast. **Youth hostels** *Porto Seguro*, R Cova da Moça 720, T/F288 1742, and *Maracaia*, Coroa Vermelha on road to Santa Cruz Cabrália, T672 1155. Both aj.maracaia@uol.com.br and both HI. **Camping** *Camping dos Marajas*, Av Getúlio Vargas, central. *Camping Mundaí Praia*, US$8 per night, T879 2287. *Tabapiri Country*, BR-367, Km 61.5, next to the rodoviária on the road leading to the *Cidade Histórica*, T288 2269.

Sleeping
Prices rise steeply Dec-Feb and Jul. Off-season rates can drop by 50%, for stays of more than 3 nights: negotiate. Outside Dec-Feb rooms with bath and hot water can be rented for US$150 per month

Expensive *Cruz de Malta*, R Getúlio Vargas 358. Good seafood. **Mid-range** *Anti-Caro*, R Assis Chateaubriand 26. Good. Recommended. Also antique shop, good atmosphere. *Les Agapornis*, Av dos Navegantes 180. Wide selection of crêpes and pizzas. *Prima Dona*, No 247. Italian, good. *Tres Vintens*, Av Portugal 246. Good imaginative seafood dishes. Recommended. *Vida Verde*, R Dois de Julho 92, T2882766. Vegetarian food, open 1100-2100 except Sunday. **Cheap** Good breakfast at *Pau Brasil*, Praça dos Pataxós. *Preto Velho*, on Praça da Bandeira. Good value à la carte or self-service. On Praça Pataxós: *da Japonêsa*, No 38. Excellent value with varied menu, open 0800-2300. Recommended. *Ponto do Encontro*, No 106. Good simple food, owners rent rooms, open 0800-2400.

Eating

Porto Seguro is famous for the *lambada*. A good bar for live music is *Porto Prego* on R Pedro Álvares Cabral, small cover charge. *Sotton Bar*, Praça de Bandeira, is lively as are *Pronto Socorro do Choppe*, *Doce Letal 50* and *Studio Video Bar*. There are lots of bars and street cafés on Av Portugal.

Entertainment

Brazil

Tour operators *Brazil travel*, Av 22 de Abril 200, T/F288 1824/679 1276 braziltravel@braziltravel.tur.br Dutch-run travel agency, all types of trips organized, English, German, Dutch, French and Spanish spoken. Several agencies at the airport. **Diving**: *Portomar Ltda*, R Dois de Julho 178. Arranges diving and snorkelling trips to the coral reefs offshore, professional instructors, equipment hire.

Transport **Rentals** **Car hire:** Several companies at the airport. **Bicycles**, *Oficina de Bicicleta*, Av Getúlio Vargas e R São Pedro, about US$10 for 24 hrs. Also at Praça de Bandeira and at 2 de Julho 242.

Airport T288
1877/2010
    Air Daily except Sat from Rio, with *Gol*, via Belo Horizonte; *Gol* Sat and Sun from São Paulo; *Nordeste* and *TAM* daily from Salvador and São Paulo; *Vasp* three a week to Salvador and São Paulo. Taxi airport-Porto Seguro, US$7. Also buses.

At Brazilian holiday
times, all transport
north or south
should be booked
well in advance
    Bus From Porto Seguro: **Salvador** (*Águia Branca*), daily, 12 hrs, US$22.25. **Vitória**, daily, 11 hrs, US$18. **Ilhéus**, daily 0730, 5½ hrs, US$11. **Eunápolis**, 1 hr, US$2. For **Rio** direct buses (*São Geraldo*), leaving at 1745, US$35 (*leito* 70), 18 hrs, from Rio direct at 1600 (very cold a/c, take warm clothes), or take 1800 for Ilhéus and change at Eunápolis. To **Belo Horizonte** daily, direct, US$33 (*São Geraldo*). Other services via Eunápolis (those going north avoid Salvador) or Itabuna (5 hrs, US$9).

    The rodoviária has reliable luggage store and lounge on the 3rd floor, on the road to Eunápolis, 2 km from the centre, regular bus service (30 mins) through the city to the old rodoviária near the port. Local buses US$0.30. Taxis charge US$5 from the rodoviária to the town or ferry (negotiate at quiet times). For local trips a taxi is an economic proposition for 2 or more passengers wishing to visit various places in 1 day.

Directory **Banks** *Banco do Brasil*, Av Beira Mar, open 1000-1500, changes TCs and US$ cash, also Visa ATM. Also at airport. *Bradesco*, Av Getúlio Vargas, Visa ATM. **Communications** Internet: *Ellisnet*. **Post Office:** In the mini-shopping centre on the corner of R das Jandaias and Av dos Navegantes **Telephone:** *Telemar* service, post, Praça dos Pataxós beside ferry terminal, open daily 0700-2200, cheap rates after 2000, receives and holds faxes, 288 3915. **Tourist office** Secretaria de Turismo de Porto Seguro, T288 4124, turismo@portonet.com.br A website for the entire coast is www.portonet.com.br

Only 10 mins north of Coroa Vermelha, **Santa Cruz Cabrália** is a delightful small town at the mouth of the Rio João de Tiba, with a splendid beach, river port, and a 450-year-old church with a fine view. A good trip from here is to Coroa Alta, a reef 50 minutes away by boat, passing along the tranquil river to the reef and its crystal waters and good snorkelling. Daily departure at 1000. A recommended boatman is Zezé (T/F282 1152) on the square by the river's edge, helpful, knowledgeable. The trip costs around US$15 without lunch. *Secretaria de Turismo*, T282 1122. A 15-minute river crossing by ferry to a new road on the opposite bank gives easy access to the deserted beaches of **Santo André** and **Santo Antônio**. There are two *pousadas*: *Victor Hugo*, T9985 5292 (mob) and *Tribo da Praia*, T282 1002, helpful American owner. Hourly buses from Santa Cruz to Porto Seguro (23 km).

Sleeping C *Pousada do Mineiro*, T282 1042. A/c, pool, sauna, good *churrascaria*. Recommended. On the hill overlooking the town: **C** *Pousada Atobá*, T/F282 1131. A/c, pool, sauna.

Arraial da Ajuda

Colour map 7, grid A6
Each Aug there is
a pilgrimage to the
shrine of Nossa
Senhora da Ajuda
Across the Rio Buranhém south from Porto Seguro is the village of Arraial da Ajuda, the gateway to the idyllic beaches of the south coast. Set high on a cliff, there are great views of the coastline from behind the church of Nossa Senhora da Ajuda in the main praça. Ajuda has become very popular with younger tourists (especially Israelis; many restaurant menus in Hebrew) and there are many *pousadas*, from the very simple to the very sophisticated, restaurants, bars and small shops. Parties are held almost every night, on the beach or in the main street, called the *Broadway*. Drugs are said to be widely available, but easily avoided. At Brazilian holiday times (especially New Year and Carnival) it is very crowded.

The beaches, several protected by a coral reef, are splendid. The nearest is 15 mins' walk away. During daylight hours those closest to town (take 'R da Praia' out of town to the south) are extremely busy; excellent *barracas* sell good seafood, drinks, and play music. The best beaches are Mucugê, Pitinga ('*bronzeamento irrestrito*' or nude sunbathing!), Lagoa Azul (with medicinal white mud) and Taipé.

A *Pousada Pitinga*, Praia Pitinga, T575 1067, F575 1035. Bold architecture amid Atlantic forest, a hideaway, great food and pool, a Roteiros de Charme hotel. **A** *Pousada Canto d'Alvorada*, on road to Ajuda, T575 1218. **C** out of season, Swiss run, 7 cabins, restaurant, laundry facilities. **B** *Pousada Caminho do Mar*, Estrada do Mucugê 246, T/F575 1099. Owners helpful. **B** *Pousada do Robalo*, T575 1053, F575 1078. Good grounds, welcoming, good pool. **B** *Pousada Arquipélago*, T/F575 1123. Reading library, relaxed atmosphere. **B** *Ivy Marey*, near centre on road to beach, T575 1106. 4 rooms and 2 bungalows, showers, nice décor, good bar, French/Brazilian owned. Nearby is **B** *Le Grand Bleu*, T575 7272. Same owner, good *pizzaria*. **B** *Sole Mio*, T575 1115, just off the beach road leading from the ferry to Arraial. French owners, English spoken, laid back, 4 chalets, excellent *pizzaria*.

C *Pousada Erva Doce*, Estrada do Mucugê 200, T575 1113. Good restaurant, well appointed chalets. **C** *Pousada Natur*, T288 2738. Run by a German environmentalist, English spoken. **C** *Pousada Tubarão*, R Bela Vista, beyond the church on the right, T575 1086. Good view of the coastline, cool, good restaurant. **C** *Pousada Mar Aberto*, Estrada do Mucugê 554, T/F575 1153, very near Mucugê beach, 400 m from centre of village. Set in lush gardens.

D *Pousada Flamboyant*, Estrada do Mucugê 89, T575 1025. Pleasant, good breakfast. **D** *Pousada Flor*, on praça, T575 1143. Owner Florisbela Valiense takes good care of female guests. **D** *Pousada Gabriela*, Travessa dos Pescadores, T575 1237. With breakfast. **D** *Pousada do Mel*, Praça São Bras, T575 1309. Simple, good breakfast. **D** *Pousada Porto do Meio*, on the road between the ferry and the village, T/F575 1017, portodomeio@ uol.com.br Close to beach, a/c, good breakfast, small pool, laundry facilities, Swiss run, English, French, German and Spanish spoken. **D** *Pousada Corujão*, on the way to the beach, T/F575 1508. Bungalows, cooking facilities, laundry, restaurant and book exchange.

Camping *Praia*, on Mucugê Beach, good position and facilities. *Chão do Arraial*, 5 mins from Mucugê beach, shady, good snack bar, also hire tents. Recommended. Also *Camping do Gordo*, on the left shortly after leaving the ferry, on a beach which is not as good as Mucugê. Generally, Arraial da Ajuda is better for camping than Porto Seguro.

Sleeping

At busy times, don't expect to find anything under US$15 pp in a shared room for a minimum stay of 5-7 days. Camping is best at these times. All hotels in the list are recommended

Mid-range: *São João*, near the church, is the best typical restaurant. *Mão na Massa*, Italian restaurant, behind the church. Recommended. *Fatta em Casa*, 5 mins by taxi or 15-min walk from centre. Delicious homemade pastas, sauces and desserts, good atmosphere and value. *Los Corales*, Travessa dos Pescadores 167, Spanish, *paella* a speciality. **Cheap**: *Paulinho Pescador*, open 1200-2200, seafood, also chicken and meat, US$5, English spoken, good service, very popular. *Café das Cores*, on way to the beach, good cakes and snacks, expresso coffee. *Manda Brasa*, on Broadway, good snack bar. Recommended *barracas* are *Tem Q Dá* and *Agito* on Mucugê beach and *Barraca de Pitinga* and *Barraca do Genésio* on Pitinga.

Eating

At the *Jatobar* bar the *lambada* is danced, on the main praça, by the church (opens 2300 – *pensão* at the back is cheap, clean and friendly). There is also a *capoeira* institute; ask for directions. *Gringo Louco* is a good bar as is *Duere*, great dance bar. Many top Brazilian bands play at the beach clubs at Praia do Parracho during the summer.

Entertainment

Ferries across the Rio Buranhém from Porto Seguro take 15 mins to the south bank, US$0.60 for foot passengers, US$3.60 for cars, every 30 mins day and night. It is then a further 5 km to Arraial da Ajuda, US$0.50 by bus; kombis charge US$0.75 pp; taxis US$5.

Transport

Banks Mobile *Banco do Brazil* in the main square during high season. **Communications** Internet: *Ellisnet*, Shopping Ajuda, Caminho da Praia. Also long distance calls. **Telephone**: *Telemar* on main praça, 0800-2200; faxes number is 575 1309, US$1.50 to receive.

Directory

Brazil

Trancoso
*25 km S of
Porto Seguro
Phone code 0xx73*

Some 15 km from Ajuda is Trancoso. It is a 3-hr walk along the beach, but watch out for the tides. This pretty, peaceful village, with its beautiful beaches (Praia dos Nativos is recommended, Pedra Grande is nudist), is popular with Brazilian tourists and many Europeans have built or bought houses there. There are good restaurants around the main praça. From the end of Praça São João there is a fine coastal panorama. Trancoso has an historic church, São João Batista (1656). Between Ajuda and Trancoso is the village of Rio da Barra. ■ *Trancoso can be reached by bus (1 every hr, from 0800, last returns 1800, US$1.25, 1 hr, more buses and colectivos in summer), colectivo, or by hitchhiking. Colectivos run hourly from Trancoso to Ajuda, US$1.15. Arriving from the south, change buses at Eunápolis from where the newly paved Linha Verde road runs.*

Sleeping A *Caipim Santo*, T668 1122, to the left of the main praça. With breakfast, the best restaurant in Trancoso. Recommended. **B** *Pousada Calypso*, Parque Municipal, T668 1113. Good apartments, comfortable, rooms at lower price also available, good library, German and English spoken. Recommended. **B** *Pousada Terra do Sol*, main praça, T668 1036. Without breakfast, good. Recommended. **C** *Pousada Canto Verde*, T0xx24-243 7823. With breakfast, restaurant only in high season. Recommended. Also on the main praça, **C** *Gulab Mahal*, oriental style, lovely garden, vast breakfast, good restaurant. Recommended. **D-E** *Pousada do Bosque*, on the way to the beach. English, German and Spanish spoken, cabins with hammocks and showers, hot water, with breakfast, camping facilities also available, good value. **E** *Pousada Beira Mar*. With bath, restaurant serving *prato feito*.

About 500 m inland away from main praça (known as the 'quadrado') lies the newer part of Trancoso (known as the 'invasão') with 2 good value *pousadas*: **D** *Pousada Quarto Crescente*, about 25 mins from beach. English, German, Dutch and Spanish spoken, cooking facilities, laundry, helpful owners, library. **D** *Luna Pousa*, further along on the left. With breakfast, well ventilated, only 4 rooms. There are many houses to rent, very good ones are rented by Clea who can be contacted at *Restaurant Abacaxi*.

*Apart from restaurants
which serve breakfast
most open at 1500
until 2200 or so*

Eating *Urano*, just before the main praça. Good portions. *Rama* has also been recommended, also *Silvana e Cia* in the historical centre. *Abacaxi* on the main praça does breakfasts, snacks and crêpes. Good breakfast at *Pé das Frutas*, *Maré Cheia* next door for simple dishes, great *moqueca*. *Pacha* on the seafront does a *prato feito*. Ice cream at *Tão Vez*.

Caraíva
*65 km S of
Porto Seguro*

This atmospheric, peaceful fishing village on the banks of the Rio Caraíva and near the Pataxó Indian Reserve has no wheeled vehicles, no electricity nor hot water, but has marvellous beaches and is a real escape from the more developed Trancoso and Porto Seguro. Despite the difficulty of getting there, it is becoming increasingly popular. Good walks are north to Praia do Satu (Sr Satu provides an endless supply of coconut milk), or 6 km south to a rather sad Pataxó Indian village (watch the tides). Horses can be hired from *Pousada Lagoa* or *Pizzaria Barra Velha*. Boats can be hired for US$40 per day from Zé Pará to Caruípe beach, snorkelling at Pedra de Tatuaçu reef and Corombau (take your own mask and fins) or for diving (best December to February). Prainha river beach, about 30 minutes away, and mangrove swamps can also be visited by canoe or launch. The high season is December-February and July; the wettest months are April-June and November. Use flip-flops for walking the sand streets and take a torch. There are no medical facilities and only rudimentary policing.

Low season prices

Sleeping and eating D *Pousada Lagoa*, T/F0xx73-9965 6662. Chalets and bungalows under cashew trees, good restaurant, popular bar, own generator. The owner, Hermínia, speaks English and is very helpful and can arrange local trips and excursions. **D** *Pousada da Terra*, far end of village near Indian reserve. With breakfast. Recommended. Similar is *Pousada da Barra*. Simpler lodging: *Pousada da Canoa*, attached to *Bar do Pará*, by the river, which serves the best fish in the village, US$7-8 (try *sashimi* or *moqueca*). *Santuzzi*, 100 m from *Canaá* grocery store. *Oasis*, run by taxi driver Batista. Other good restaurants are *Natal* by *Bar do Pará*, and *Pizzaria Barra Velha*, by the canoe crossing. There is forró dancing 0100-0600 at *Pelé* and *Ouriços* on alternate nights in season.

Brazil

Transport Caraíva can only be reached by canoe across the river. Access roads are poor and almost impossible after heavy rain. From Porto Seguro either go to Arraial da Ajuda and take the Rio Buranhém ferry crossing, or take the detour to the Eunápolis road then on to Trancoso, after which the road is bad, especially after the turn-off to Oteiro das Brisas, 13 km before Caraíva. *Aguia Azul* bus company takes this route from Porto Seguro at 1500. Taxis are unwilling to go from Porto Seguro or Arraial, so call Batista in Caraíva, who charges US$60. If arriving by bus from the south, change to *Aguia Azul* bus in Itabela, departs at 1500, or take a taxi, about 50 km. Drivers should leave the BR-101 at Monte Pascoal (Km 769, 800 m past the Texaco station) and drive 41 km to Caraíva.

South of Porto Seguro, reached by a 14 km paved access road at Km 796 of the BR-101, the Parque Nacional de Monte Pascoal set up in 1961 to preserve the flora, fauna and birdlife of the coastal area in which Europeans made landfall in Brazil (Caixa Postal 24, CEP 45836-000 Itamaraju, T0xx73-294 1110). The Pataxó Indian reservation is located at Corombau village, on the ocean shore of the park. Corombau can be reached by schooner from Porto Seguro. A small luxury resort has been built at Corombau. ■ *From Caraíva there is a river crossing by boats which are always on hand. Buses run from Itamaraju 16 km to the south, at 0600 on Fri-Mon.*

Parque Nacional de Monte Pascoal
Colour map 7, grid A6

Further south still, 107 km from Itamaruju (93 km south of Eunápolis), is this charming little town, rapidly developing for tourism, but a major trading town in 17th and 18th centuries. Caravelas is in the mangroves; the beaches are about 10 km away at Barra de Caravelas (hourly buses), a fishing village. Teresa and Ernesto (from Austria) organize boat trips (US$40 per day), jeep and horse hire (turn left between the bridge and the small supermarket). 'Alternative' beach holidays (organic vegetarian food, yoga, meditation, other activities) with Beky and Eno on the unspoilt island of Coçumba. Recommended. Contact *Abrolhos Turismo*, Praça Dr Imbassahi 8, T297 1149, rents diving gear and arranges boat trips. Helpful tourist information at *Ibama Centro de Visitantes*, Barão do Rio Branco 281. ■ *Buses to Texeira de Freitas (4 a day), Salvador, Nanuque and Prado. Flights from Belo Horizonte, São Paulo and Salvador to Caravelas; otherwise fly to Porto Seguro.*

Caravelas
Colour map 7, grid A6
Population: 20,103

Sleeping C *Pousada Caravelense*, 50 m from the rodoviária, T297 1182. TV, fridge, good breakfast, excellent restaurant. Recommended. **D** *Shangri-la*, Barão do Rio Branco 216. Bath, breakfast. **Barra de Caravelas C** *Pousada das Sereias*. French-owned. **E** *Pousada Jaquita*. Use of kitchen, big breakfast, bath, airy rooms, the owner is Secka who speaks English. There are some food shops, restaurants and bars.

The **Parque Nacional Marinho dos Abrolhos** is 70 km east of Caravelas. Abrolhos is an abbreviation of Abre os olhos: 'Open your eyes' from Amérigo Vespucci's exclamation when he first sighted the reef in 1503. Established in 1983, the park consists of five small islands (Redonda, Siriba, Guarita, Sueste, Santa Bárbara), which are volcanic in origin, and several coral reefs. The park is best visited in October-March. Humpback whales breed and give birth from July to December. Diving is best December-February. The archipelago is administered by *Ibama* and a navy detachment mans a lighthouse on Santa Bárbara, which is the only island that may be visited. Permission from *Parque Nacional Marinho dos Abrolhos*, Praia do Kitombo s/n, Caravelas, Bahia 45900, T0xx73-297 1111, or Ibama, Av Juracy Magalhães Junior 608, CEP 41940-060, Salvador, T/F0xx71-240 7913. Visitors are not allowed to spend the night on the islands, but may stay overnight on schooners.

The warm current and shallow waters (8-15 m deep) make a rich undersea life (about 160 species of fish) and good snorkelling

Transport The journey to the islands takes between 1 and 6 hrs depending on the boat. Mestre Onofrio Frio in Alcobaça, Bahia, T0xx73-293 2195 is authorized by the Navy to take tourists. Tours also available from *Abrolhos Turismo*, see above, Caravelas (about US$170 for a slow 2½ day tour by *saveiro*). 1-day tours can be made in a faster boat (US$100) from Abrolhos or the Marina Porto Abrolhos.

Brazil

Brazil

North from Salvador

The paved BA-099 coast road from near Salvador airport is known as the Estrada do Coco (Coconut Highway, because of the many plantations) and for 50 km passes some beautiful beaches. The best known from south to north are Ipitanga (with its reefs), Buraquinho, Jauá (with reefs, surfing, pools at low tide, clean water; **D** *Lagoa e Mar*, Praia de Jauá, T/F672 1573, www.hotellagoaemar.com.br Very good breakfast, spacious bungalows, swimming pool, 350 m to beach, restaurant, helpful, transport to airport, 10% discount to Footprint owners), Arembepe (with a Tamar turtle protection project, famous hippy village in 1960s), Guarajuba, Itacimirim, Castelo Garcia D'Ávila (with its 16th century fort) and Forte. Regular buses serve most of these destinations.

Praia do Forte The fishing village, 80 km north of Salvador, takes its name from the castle built by a Portuguese settler, Garcia D'Ávila, in 1556 to warn the city to the south of enemy invasion. Praia do Forte is now a charming, tranquil fishing village with sand streets and lovely beaches. There is a strong emphasis on preservation of the local flora and fauna. Inland from the coast is a *restinga* forest, which grows on sandy soil with a very delicate ecosystem. Near the village is a small *pantanal* (marshy area), which is host to a large number of birds, caymans and other animals. Birdwatching trips on the *pantanal* are rewarding. The Tamar Project preserves the sea turtles which lay their eggs in the area. Praia do Forte is now the headquarters of the national turtle preservation programme and is funded by the Worldwide Fund for Nature. There is a visitors' centre at the project; its address is Caixa Postal 2219, Rio Vermelho, CEP 40210-990, Rio Vermelho, Salvador, Bahia, T0xx71-876 1045, F876 1067. ■ *Buses to Praia do Forte from Salvador (US$2): Santa Maria/Catuense leave 5 times daily from rodoviária, 1½ hrs.*

Prices rise steeply in the summer season. Most hotels are in the AL price range. It may prove difficult to find cheaper accommodation

Sleeping and eating **LL** *Praia do Forte EcoResort*, Av do Farol, T676 4000, reservas@ pfr.com.br Polynesian-inspired and deserving of its name, spacious, beautiful beachfront grounds and full programme of activities (including humpback whale and turtle watching), 5 pools. Recommended. **A** *Pousada Praia do Forte*, Al do Sol, T676 1116, F876 1033. Chalets in peaceful setting, on beach. Recommended. **A** *Pousada Solar da Lagoa*, R do Forte, T676 1029. Good location, spacious rooms. **A** *Pousada Sobrado da Vila*, Al do Sol, T/F676 1152. Pleasant, good value restaurant. **B** *Pousada Tatuapara*, Praça dos Artistas, T676 1015. Friendly. **B** *Pousada João Sol*, R da Corvina, T676 1054. Owner speaks English, Spanish and German, good, only 6 apartments, great breakfast. Recommended. **B** *Pousada da Sereia*, R da Corvina, T676 1032. With fan, good breakfast. **B** *Pousada Sol Nascente*, on the street parallel to the main street. Good, bath, frigobar, fan, breakfast. **C** *Tia Helena*, Helena being the motherly proprietor who provides an excellent meal and enormous breakfast, nice rooms. Highly recommended. 2-bedroom apartments at *Solar dos Arcos* on the beach, US$90, with pool, gardens, lawns. Warmly recommended. **Youth Hostel D** *Albergue da Juventude Praia do Forte*, R da Aurora 3, T676 1094, praiadoforte@ albergue.com.br With bathroom, fan, breakfast, kitchen and shop, more expensive for non-HI members. *Bar Da Souza*, on the right as you enter the village. Best seafood in town, open daily, live music at weekends, reasonably priced. Recommended. *Brasa Na Praia*. Specializes in grilled seafood and meat, open daily, peaceful setting. Recommended. *La Crêperie*. Excellent crêpes, Tue to Sun, good music, popular, owner Klever very friendly. *Pizzaria Le Gaston*. Good pizza and pasta, also good home-made ice-creams, open daily.

Tour operators *Odara Turismo*, in the *EcoResort Hotel*, T676 1080, F676 1018. Imaginative tours to surrounding areas and outlying villages and beaches using 4WD vehicles. They are very friendly and informative. Recommended. The owners, Norbert and Papy, speak English and German. *Bahia Adventure*, T676 1262, baadventure@svn.com.br Ecotourism, abseiling and Land Rover trips. Praia do Forte is ideal for windsurfing and sailing owing to constant fresh Atlantic breezes.

The Linha Verde (the extension of the Estrada do Coco) runs for 142 km to the **The coast** bordern of Sergipe, the next state north; the road is more scenic than the BR-101, **road north** especially near Conde. There are very few hotels or *pousadas* in the more remote villages. The most picturesque are **Imbassaí**, **Subaúma**, **Baixio** (very beautiful, where the Rio Inhambupe meets the sea) and **Conde**. Sítio do Conde on the coast, 6 km from Conde, has many *pousadas*, but the beaches are not very good. Sítio do Conde is an ideal base to explore other beaches at Barra do Itariri, 12 km south, at the mouth of a river (fine sunsets). The last stop on the Linha Verde is **Mangue Seco**. Access from Sergipe is by boat or canoe on the Rio Real from Pontal (10 min crossing).

The Northeast

The eight states north of Bahia are historically and culturally rich, but generally poor economically. Steeped in history are, for instance, Recife, Olinda, or São Luís and cultural heritage abounds (eg 'Forró' and other musical styles, many good museums, lacework, ceramics). There is a multitude of beaches: those in established resorts tend to be polluted, but you don't have to travel far for good ones, while off the beaten track are some which have hardly been discovered.

Sergipe and Alagoas

On the BR-101, 247 km north of Salvador and almost midway between the Sergipe-Bahia border and Aracaju, is **Estância**, one of the oldest towns in Brazil. Its colonial buildings are decorated with Portuguese tiles. The month-long festival of **São João** in June is a major event. There are pleasant hotels, but most buses stop at the Rodoviária, which is on the main road (four hours from Salvador).

Capital of Sergipe founded 1855, it stands on the south bank of the Rio Sergipe, **Aracaju** about 10 km from its mouth. In the centre is a group of linked, beautiful parks: **Praça** *Phone code: 0xx79* **Olímpio Campos**, in which stands the cathedral, **Praça Almirante Barroso**, with *Post code: 49000* the Palácio do Governo, and **Praças Fausto Cardoso** and **Camerino**. Across Av Rio *Colour map 5, grid C5* Branco from these two is the river. There is a handicraft centre, the **Centro do** *Population: 461,534* **Turismo** in the restored Escola Normal, on Praça Olímpio Campos, Rua 24 Horas; *327 km N of Salvador* the stalls are arranged by type (wood, leather, etc). ■ *0900-1300, 1400-1900*. The city's beaches are at **Atalaia**, 16-km by road, and the 30-km long **Nova Atalaia**, on Ilha de Santa Luzia across the river. It is easily reached by boat from the Hidroviária (ferry station), which is across Av Rio Branco from Praça Gen Valadão.

São Cristóvão is the old state capital, 17 km southwest of Aracaju on the road to Salvador. It was founded in 1590 by Cristóvão de Barros. It is the fourth oldest town in Brazil. Built on top of a hill, its colonial centre is unspoiled: the **Museu de Arte Sacra e Histórico de Sergipe** contains religious and other objects from the 17th to the 19th centuries; it is in the **Convento de São Francisco**. ■ *Tue-Fri 1000-1700, Sat-Sun 1300-1700*. Also worth visiting (and keeping the same hours) is the **Museu de Sergipe** in the former **Palácio do Governo**; both are on Praça de São Francisco. Also on this square are the churches of **Misericórdia** (1627) and the **Orfanato Imaculada Conceição** (1646, permission to visit required from the Sisters), and the **Convento de São Francisco**. On Praça Senhor dos Passos are the churches **Senhor dos Passos** and **Terceira Ordem do Carmo** (both 1739), while on the Praça Getúlio Vargas (formerly Praça Matriz) is the 17th century **Igreja Matriz Nossa Senhora da Vitória**. ■ *Tue-Fri 1000-1700, Sat-Sun 1500-1700*.

Sleeping and eating There is a range of hotels in the centre, including **A** *Grande*, R Itabaianinha 371, T/F211 1383. A/c, TV, fridge, central, *Quartier Latin* restaurant. **B** *Brasília*,

Brazil

R Laranjeiras 580, T224 8022. Good value, good breakfasts. Recommended. *Gonzaga*, Rua Santo Amaro 181, T224 7278. Lunch only, good value, popular, excellent traditional dishes.

Transport Interstate rodoviária is 4 km from centre, linked by local buses from adjacent terminal (buy a ticket before going on the platform). To **Salvador**, 6-7 hrs, 11 a day with *Bonfim*, US$11-14. To **Maceió**, US$9 with *Bonfim*.

Directory Tourist offices: *Emsetur*, Travessa Baltazar Góes 86, 11th floor, T214 4039, emsetur@emsetur.com.br For **tourist information** in Portugese, check the state's portal, www.se.gov.br

Penedo

Phone code: 0xx82
Post code: 57200
Colour map 5, grid C6
Population: 56,993

A more interesting crossing into Alagoas can be made by frequent ferry (car and foot passengers) from **Neópolis** in Sergipe, to Penedo some 35 km from the mouth of the Rio São Francisco. This charming town, with a nice waterfront park, Praça 12 de Abril, was originally the site of the Dutch Fort Maurits (built 1637, razed to the ground by the Portuguese). The colonial town stands on a promontory above the river. Among the colonial architecture, modern buildings on Av Floriano Peixoto do not sit easily. On the Praça Barão de Penedo is the neoclassical **Igreja Matriz** (closed to visitors) and the 18th century **Casa da Aposentadoria** (1782 – the tourist office is here, T551 2827, ext 23). East and a little below this square is the Praça Rui Barbosa, on which are the **Convento de São Francisco** (1783 and later) and the church of **Santa Maria dos Anjos** (1660). As you enter, the altar on the right depicts God's eyes on the world, surrounded by the three races, one Indian, two negroes and the whites at the bottom. The church has fine *trompe-l'oeil* ceilings (1784). The convent is still in use. Guided tours are free. The church of **Rosário dos Pretos** (1775-1816), on Praça Marechal Deodoro, is open to visitors. **Nossa Senhora da Corrente** (1764), on Praça 12 de Abril, and **São Gonçalo Garcia** (1758-70) are on Av Floriano Peixoto. n *Mon-Fri 0800-1200, 1400-1700*. Also on Av Floriano Peixoto is the pink **Teatro 7 de Setembro** (No 81) of 1884. The **Casa de Penedo**, at R João Pessoa 126 (signs point the way up the hill from F Peixoto), displays photographs and books on, or by, local figures. ■ *Tue-Sun 0800-1800, T551 2516.*

Sleeping A *São Francisco*, Av Floriano Peixoto, T551 2273, F551 2274. Standard rooms have no a/c, TV, fridge. Recommended except for poor restaurant. **B** *Pousada Colonial*, Praça 12 de Abril 21, T551 2355, F551 3099. *Luxo* and suite have phone, TV and fridge, suites have a/c, spacious, good cheap restaurant, front rooms with view of Rio São Francisco. **D** *Turista*, R Siqueira Campos 143, T551 2237. With bath, fan, hot water. Recommended.

Transport Bus: 451 km from **Salvador** (US$12-14, 6 hrs, daily bus 0600, book in advance), at same time for **Aracaju** (US$6). Buses south are more frequent from Neópolis, 6 a day (0630-1800) to Aracaju, 2 hrs, US$3.60. 115 km from **Maceió**, 5 buses a day in either direction, US$5.40-6.60, 3-4 hrs. Rodoviária: Av Duque de Caxias, behind Bompreço supermarket.

Maceió and around

Phone code: 0xx82
Post code: 57000
Colour map 5, grid C6
Population: 797,759
294 km NE of Aracaju
285 km S of Recife
Voltage: 220 volts AC,
60 cycles

The capital of Alagoas state is mainly a sugar port. Two of its old buildings, the **Palácio do Governo**, which also houses the **Fundação Pierre Chalita** (Alagoan painting and religious art) and the church of **Bom Jesus dos Mártires** (1870 – covered in tiles), are particularly interesting. Both are on the Praça dos Martírios (or Floriano Peixoto). The **cathedral**, Nossa Senhora dos Prazeres (1840), is on Praça Dom Pedro II.

Lagoa do Mundaú, a lagoon whose entrance is 2 km south at **Pontal da Barra**, limits the city to the south and west: excellent shrimp and fish are sold at its small restaurants and handicraft stalls; a nice place for a drink at sundown. Boats make excursions in the lagoon's channels.

Beyond the city's main dock the beachfront districts begin; within the city, the beaches are smarter the further from the centre you go. The first, going north, is **Pajuçara** where there is a nightly craft market. At weekends there are wandering musicians and entertainers. Further out, **Jatiúca**, **Cruz das Almas** and **Jacarecica** (9 km from centre) are all good for surfing. The beaches, some of the finest and most popular in Brazil, have a protecting coral reef a kilometre or so out. Bathing is much better three days before and after full or new moon, because tides are higher and the water is more spectacular. *Jangadas* take passengers to a natural swimming pool 2 km off Pajuçara beach (**Piscina Natural de Pajuçara**), at low tide you can stand on the sand and rock reef (beware of sunburn). You must check the tides, there is no point going at high tide. *Jangadas* cost US$5 per person per day (or about US$20 to have a *jangada* to yourself). On Sunday or local holidays in the high season it is over-crowded (at weekends lots of *jangadas* anchor at the reef selling food and drink).

By bus (22 km south) past Praia do Francês to the attractive colonial town and former capital of Alagoas, **Marechal Deodoro**, which overlooks the Lagoa Manguaba. The 17th century **Convento de São Francisco**, Praça João XXIII, has a fine church (Santa Maria Magdalena) with a superb baroque wooden altarpiece, badly damaged by termites. You can climb the church's tower for views. Adjoining it is the **Museu de Arte Sacra**. ■ *Mon-Fri 0900-1300, US$0.30, guided tours available, payment at your discretion.* Also open to visitors is the **Igreja Matriz de Nossa Senhora da Conceição** (1783). The town is the birthplace of Marechal Deodoro da Fonseca, founder of the Republic; the modest house where he was born is on the R Marechal Deodoro, close to the waterfront. ■ *Mon-Sat 0800-1700, Sun 0800-1200, free.* On a day's excursion, it is easy to visit the town, then spend some time at beautiful **Praia do Francês**. The northern half of the beach is protected by a reef, the southern half is open to the surf. Along the beach there are many *barracas* and bars selling drinks and seafood; also several *pousadas*.

AL *Sete Coqueiros*, Av A Gouveia 1335, T231 8583, F231 7467. 3-star, a/c, TV, phone, popular restaurant, pool. **AL** *Enseada*, Av A Gouveia 171, T231 4726, enseada@ vircom.com.br Recommended. **A** *Velamar*, Av A Gouveia 1359, T327 5488, velamar@threenet.com.br A/c, TV, fridge, safes in rooms. **A** *Laguna Praia*, R Jangadeiros Alagoanos 1231, T231 6180. Highly recommended. **B** *Buongiorno*, R Jangadeiros Alagoanos 1437, T231 7577, F231 7577. A/c, fridge, English-speaking owner, helpful. **C** *Casa Grande da Praia*, R Jangadeiros Alagoanos 1528, T231 3332. A/c and TV, cheaper without. Recommended. **C** *Costa Verde*, R Jangadeiros Alagoanos 429, T231 4745. Bath, fan, good family atmosphere, English, German spoken. Further from the centre, **C** *Pousada Cavalo Marinho*, R da Praia 55, Riacho Doce (15 km from the centre), facing the sea, T/F355 1247, pcavalomarinho@uol.com.br Use of bicycle, canoes and body boards including, hot showers, German and English spoken, tropical breakfasts, Swiss owner. Very highly recommended (nearby is *Lua Cheia*, good food and live music at night). There are many hotels on Praia Pajuçara, mostly along Av Dr Antônio Gouveia and R Jangadeiros Alagoanos.

Youth hostels *Nossa Casa*, R Prefeito Abdon Arroxelas 327, T231 2246. *Pajuçara*, R Quintino Bocaiúva 63, Pajuçara, T231 0631. *Stella Maris*, Av Desembargador Valente de Lima 209, Mangabeiras, T325 2217. All IH affiliated, all require reservations Dec-Feb, Jul and Aug. **Camping** There is a *Camping Clube do Brasil* site on Jacarecica beach, T235 3600, a 15-min taxi drive from the town centre. *Camping Pajuçara* at Largo da Vitória 211, T231 7561, clean, safe, food for sale, recommended.

Sleeping
It can be hard to find a room during the Dec-Mar holiday season, when prices go up

Ao Lagostão, Av Duque de Caxias 1348. Seafood, fixed price (expensive) menu. *Pizzeria Sorrisa*, Praça Visconde Sinimbu 207. Very cheap, good food, popular with Brazilians. **Vegetarian** *O Natural*, R Libertadora Alagoana (R da Praia) 112. *Nativa*, Osvaldo Sarmento 56, good views. Many good bars and restaurants in Pajuçara, eg on Av Antônio Gouveia. The beaches for 5 km from the beginning of Pajuçara to Cruz das Almas in the north are lined with *barracas* (thatched bars), providing music, snacks and meals until midnight (later at weekends). Vendors on the beach sell beer and food during the day: clean and safe. There are many other bars and *barracas* at Ponto da Barra, on the lagoon side of the city.

Eating
Local specialities include oysters, pitu, a crayfish (now becoming scarce), and sururu, a kind of cockle. Local ice cream, Shups, recommended

Brazil

Festivals 27 Aug: *Nossa Senhora dos Prazeres*; 16 Sep: *Freedom of Alagoas*; 8 Dec: *Nossa Senhora da Conceição*; 15 Dec: *Maceiofest*, 'a great street party with *trios eléctricos*'; *Christmas Eve*; *New Year's Eve*, half-day.

Transport **Local Bus**: Frequent buses, confusingly marked, serve all parts of the city. Bus stops are not marked: it is best to ask where people look as if they are waiting. The 'Ponte Verde/Jacintinho' bus runs via Pajuçara from the centre to the rodoviária, also take 'Circular' bus (25 mins Pajuçara to rodoviária); Taxis from town go to all the northern beaches, but buses run as far as Ipioca (23 km). The Jangadeiras bus marked 'Jacarecica-Center, via Praias' runs past all the beaches as far as Jacarecica. From there you can change to 'Riacho Doce-Trapiche', 'Ipioca' or 'Mirante' buses for Riacho Doce and Ipioca. To return take any of these options, or take a bus marked 'Shopping Center' and change there for 'Jardim Vaticana' bus, which goes through Pajuçara. Buses and kombis to Marechal Deodoro, Praia do Francês and Barra de São Miguel leave from R Zacarias Azevedo, near the ferroviária: bus US$0.75, kombi US$1 to Marechal Deodoro, 30 mins, calling at Praia do Francês in each direction. Last bus back from Praia do Francês to Maceió at 1800.

Long distance **Air**: 20 km from centre, taxi about US$25. Buses to airport from near *Hotel Beiriz*, R João Pessoa 290 or in front of the Ferroviária, signed 'Rio Largo'; alight at Tabuleiro dos Martins, then 7-8 mins walk to the airport, bus fare US$0.75.

Buses: The rodoviária is 5 km from centre, on a hill with good views and cool breezes. Taxi, US$7 to Pajuçara. Bus to **Recife**, 10 a day, 3½ hrs express (more scenic coastal route, 5 hrs) US$9. To **Aracaju**, US$9, 5 hrs (potholed road). To **Salvador**, 10 hrs, 4 a day, US$20 (*rápido* costs more).

Directory **Tourist offices** Ematur (Empresa Alagoana de Turismo), Av Dr A Gouveia 1143, Pajuçara, T216 1501, turismo@ematur.al.gov.br Also at the airport and rodoviária . Helpful. The municipal tourist authority is **Emturma**, R Saldanha da Gama 71, Farol, T223 4016; information post on Pajuçara beach, opposite *Hotel Solara*, www.maceio.com.br

North to Pernambuco There are many interesting stopping points along the coast between Maceió and Recife. **Barra de Santo Antônio**, 45 km north, is a busy fishing village, with a palm fringed beach on a narrow peninsula, a canoe-ride away. The beaches nearby are beautiful: to the south, near the village of Santa Luzia, are Tabuba and Sonho Verde. To the north is Carro Quebrado, from which you can take a buggy to Pedra do Cebola, or further to Praia do Morro, just before the mouth of the Rio Camaragibe.

Beyond Barra do Camaragibe, a coastal road, unpaved in parts, runs to the Pernambuco border and São José da Coroa Grande. The main highway, BR-101, heads a little inland from Maceió before crossing the state border to Palmares.

Recife

Phone code: 0xx81
Post code: 50000
Colour map 5, grid B6
Population:
1.42 million
285 km N of Maceió
839 km N of Salvador

The capital of Pernambuco State was founded on reclaimed land by the Dutch prince Maurice of Nassau in 1637 after his troops had burnt Olinda, the original capital. The city centre consists of three portions, Recife proper, Santo Antônio and São José, and Boa Vista and Santo Amaro. The first two are on islands formed by the rivers Capibaribe, Beberibe and Pina, while the third is made into an island by the Canal Tacaruna, which separates it from the mainland. The centre is always very busy by day; the crowds and the narrow streets, especially in the Santo Antônio district, can make it a confusing city to walk around. Recife has the main dock area, with commercial buildings associated with it. South of the centre is the residential and beach district of Boa Viagem, reached by bridge across the Bacia do Pina. Olinda, the old capital, is only 7 km to the north (see page 503).

Recife orientation

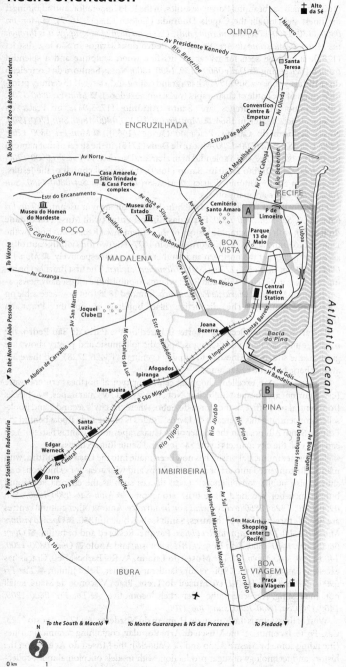

To Northern Beaches

✝ Alto
da Sé

OLINDA

J Nabuco

Av Presidente Kennedy

Rio Beberibe

☐ Santa
Teresa

Av Olinda

ENCRUZILHADA

Convention
Centre &
Empetur

Estrada de Belém

Gov A Magalhães

Av Cruz Cabugá

Rio Beberibe

RECIFE

To Dois Irmãos Zoo & Botanical Gardens

Av Norte

Estrada Arraial

Casa Amarela,
Sítio Trindade
& Casa Forte
complex

Av Rosa e Silva

Estr do Encanamento

Museu do
Estado 🏛

Cemitério
Santo Amaro

A

P de
Limoeiro

A Lisboa

Museu do Homen
do Nordeste 🏛

Bonifácio

Av Rui Barbosa

BOA
VISTA

Parque
13 de
Maio

POÇO

Rio Capibaribe

To Várzea

MADALENA

Gov A Magalhães

Av João de Barros

Av Caxanga

Dom Bosco

Central
Metrô
Station

Joquei
Clube ☐

Av San Martim

Estr dos Remédios

Joana
Bezerra

Dantas Barreto

Bacia
do Pina

To the North & João Pessoa

M Gonçalves da Luz

R Imperial

A de Góis

H Bandeira

Av Abdias de Carvalho

Afogados
Ipiranga

B

Mangueira

R São Miguel

PINA

Atlantic Ocean

Santa
Luzia

Rio Tijipió

Rio Jordão

Rio Pina

Av Boa Viagem

Five Stations to Rodoviária

Edgar
Werneck

Av Central

Barro

Dr J Rufino

Av Recife

IMBIRIBEIRA

Av Marechal Mascarenhas Morais

Av Sul

Av Domingos Ferreira

BR 101

Gen MacArthur

Shopping
Center
Recife ☐

IBURA

Canal Jordão

BOA
VIAGEM

Praça
Boa Viagem ■ ✝

N

To the South & Maceió

To Monte Guararapes & NS das Prazeres

To Piedade

0 km   1
0 miles   1

Brazil

Detail maps ☐
A *Recife,* page 497
B *Boa Viagem,*
page 499

Sights

Many churches close to visitors on Sun because of services. Many are in need of repair

The best sights are the churches of **Santo Antônio do Convento de São Francisco** (1606), which has beautiful Portuguese tiles, in the R do Imperador, and adjoining it the finest sight of all, the **Capela Dourada** (Golden Chapel, 1697). ■ *Mon-Fri 0800-1130, 1400-1700, Sat morning only, US$1, no flash photography; it is through the Museu Franciscano de Arte Sacra.* **São Pedro dos Clérigos** in São José district (1782), should be seen for its façade, its fine wood sculpture and a splendid *trompe-l'oeil* ceiling. ■ *Daily 0800-1130, 1400-1600.* **Nossa Senhora da Conceição dos Militares**, R Nova 309 (1771), has a grand ceiling and a large 18th century primitive mural of the battle of Guararapes (museum next door). ■ *Mon-Fri 0800-1700.* Other important churches are **Santo Antônio** (1753-91), in Praça da Independência, rebuilt in 1864. ■ *Mon-Fri 0800-1200, 1400-1800, Sun 1700-1900.* **Nossa Senhora do Carmo**, Praça do Carmo (1663). ■ *Mon-Fri 0800-1200, 1400-1900, Sat-Sun 0700-1200.* **Madre de Deus** (1715), in the street of that name in the district of Recife, with a splendid high altar, and sacristy. ■ *Tue-Fri 0800-1200, 1400-1600.* The **Divino Espírito Santo** (1689), the original church of the Jesuits, Praça 17 in Santo Antônio district. ■ *Mon-Fri 0800-1630, Sat 0800-1400, Sun 1000-1200.* There are many others.

Forte do Brum (built by the Dutch in 1629) is an army museum. ■ *Tue-Fri 0900-1600, Sat-Sun 1400-1600.* **Forte das Cinco Pontas** (with **Museu da Cidade do Recife**), with a cartographic history of the settlement of Recife, was built by the Dutch in 1630 and altered by the Portuguese in 1677. The two forts jointly controlled access to the port at the northern and southern entrances respectively. ■ *Mon-Fri 0900-1800, Sat-Sun 1300-1700, US$0.50 donation advised.* The first Brazilian printing press was installed in 1706 and Recife claims to publish the oldest daily newspaper in South America, *Diário de Pernambuco*, founded 1825 (but now accessible on www.dpnet.com.br/). The distinctive lilac building is on the Praça da Independência.

The artists' and intellectuals' quarter is based on the **Pátio de São Pedro**, the square round São Pedro dos Clérigos. Sporadic folk music and poetry shows are given in the square Wednesday to Sunday evenings (T3426 2728) and there are atmospheric bars and restaurants.

The square is an excellent shopping centre for typical northeastern craftware (clay figurines are cheapest in Recife). Not far away, off Av Guararapes, two blocks from central post office, is the **Praça do Sebo**, where the city's second-hand booksellers concentrate; this Mercado de Livros Usados is off the R da Roda, behind the Edifício Santo Albino, near the corner of Av Guararapes and R Dantas Barreto. You can also visit the city markets in the São José and Santa Rita sections.

The former municipal prison has now been made into the **Casa da Cultura**, with many cells converted into art or souvenir shops and with areas for exhibitions and shows (also public conveniences). Local dances such as the ciranda, forró and bumba-meu-boi are held as tourist attractions. ■ *Mon-Sat 0900-1900, Sun 0900-1400. T3284 2850 to check what's on in advance.* Among other cultural centres are Recife's three traditional **theatres**, **Santa Isabel**, built in 1850. ■ *Open to visitors Mon-Fri 1300-1700, Praça da República.* **Parque.** Restored and beautiful. ■ *Open 0800-1200, 1400-1800, R do Hospício 81, Boa Vista;* and **Apolo** ■ *Open 0800-1200, 1400-1700, R do Apolo 121.* The **Museu do Estado**, Av Rui Barbosa 960, Graças has excellent paintings by the 19th-century landscape painter, Teles Júnior. ■ *Tue-Fri 0900-1700, Sat-Sun 1400-1700.* **Museu do Trem**, Praça Visconde de Mauá, small but interesting, especially the Henschel locomotive. ■ *Tue-Fri 0800-1200, 1400-1700, Sat 0900-1200, Sun 1400-1700.*

West of the centre is the **Museu do Homem do Nordeste**, Av 17 de Agosto 2223, Casa Forte. It comprises the **Museu de Arte Popular**, containing ceramic figurines (including some by Mestre Alino and Zé Caboclo); the **Museu do Açúcar**, on the history and technology of sugar production, with models of colonial mills, collections of antique sugar bowls and much else; the **Museu de Antropologia**, the **Nabuco Museum** (at No 1865) and the modern museum of popular remedies,

Farmacopéia Popular. ■ *Tue-Fri 1100-1700, Sat-Sun 1300-1700, US$1*. Either take the 'Dois Irmãos' bus (check that it's the correct one, with 'Rui Barbosa' posted in window, as there are two) from in front of the Banorte building near the post office on Guararapes, or, more easily, go by taxi.

Boa Viagem, the main residential and hotel quarter, is currently being developed at its northern end. The 8-km promenade commands a striking view of the Atlantic, but the beach is backed by a busy road, is crowded at weekends and not very clean.

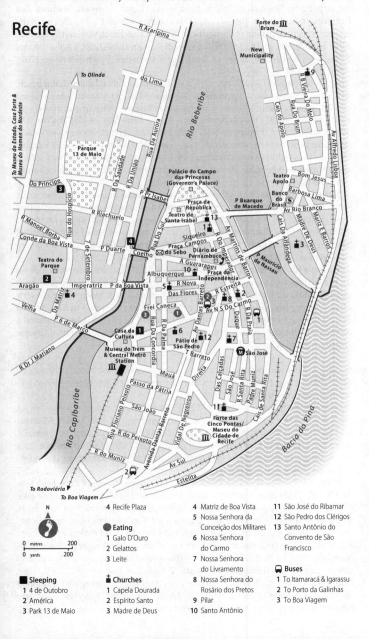

Recife

Brazil

During the January breeding season, sharks come close to the shore. You can go fishing on *jangadas* at Boa Viagem with a fisherman at low tide. The main praça has a good market at weekends. Take any bus marked 'Boa Viagem'; from Nossa Senhora do Carmo, take buses marked 'Piedade', 'Candeias' or 'Aeroporto' – they go on Av Domingos Ferreira, two blocks parallel to the beach, all the way to Praça Boa Viagem (at Av Boa Viagem 500). Back to the centre take buses marked 'CDU' or 'Setubal' from Av Domingos Ferreira. 14 km south of the city, a little beyond Boa Viagem and the airport, on Guararapes hill, is the historic church of **Nossa Senhora dos Prazeres**. It was here, in 1648-49, that two Brazilian victories led to the end of the 30-year Dutch occupation of the northeast in 1654. The church was built by the Brazilian commander in 1656 to fulfil a vow. ■ *Tue-Fri 0800-1200, 1400-1700, Sat 0800-1200, closed to tourists on Sun.* Boa Viagem's own fine church dates from 1707.

Beaches south of Recife About 30 km south of Recife, beyond Cabo, is the beautiful and quiet **Gaibu** beach, with scenic Cabo de Santo Agostinho on the point 5 km east of town. It has a ruined fort. To get there, take bus 'Centro do Cabo' from the airport, then frequent buses – 20 mins – from Cabo. **C** *Pousada Aguas Marinhas*, Av Beira Mar 56, T3522 6346. A/c, comfortable, fridge, **E** without bath, with breakfast, French spoken, very nice. **Itapuama** beach is even more empty, both reached by bus from **Cabo** (*Population:* 140,765), Pernambuco's main industrial city, which has interesting churches and forts and a **Museu da Abolição.** At nearby **Suape** are many 17th-century buildings and a biological reserve.

Porto de Galinhas, further south still, is a beautiful beach. It has cool, clean water, and waves. Because of a reef close to the shore, swimming is only possible at high tide (take heed of local warnings) and a rash of recently built upmarket resorts is changing its rustic atmosphere. Humberto Cavalcanti, T3426 7471/9944 0196, has two small houses for rent. ■ *Porto de Galinhas is reached by bus from the southern end of Av Dantas Barreto, 8 a day, 7 on Sun, 0700-1700, US$1.25.*

Igarassu (Colour map 5, grid B6; Population: 82,277), 39 km north of Recife on the road to João Pessoa, has the first church built in Brazil (SS Cosme e Damião, built in 1535), the Livramento church nearby, and the convent of Santo Antônio with a small museum next door. The church of Sagrado Coração is said to have housed Brazil's first orphanage. Much of the town (founded in 1535) has been declared a National Monument. ■*Buses leave from Av Martins de Barros, in front of Grande Hotel, Recife, 45 mins, US$1.*

Sleeping Boa Viagem is the main tourist district and the best area to stay. All hotels listed in this area are
■ *on maps* within a block or two of the beach. There is not much reason to be in the city centre and accom-
Opportunistic theft modation here is of a pretty low standard.
is unfortunately
common in the streets   **Centre A** *Recife Plaza*, R da Aurora 225, T3231 1200, Boa Vista. Overlooking the Rio
of Recife and Olinda Capibaribe, every comfort, fine restaurant (popular at lunchtime). **B** *4 de Outubro*, R Floriano
(especially on the Peixoto 141, Santo Antônio, T3224 4900, F3424 2598. 4 standards of room, hot water, TV,
streets up to phone, a/c. **C** *Hotel Park 13 de Mayo*, Rua do Hospício, T3231 7627. Safe, OK. **D** *América*, Praça
Alto da Sé). Maciel Pinheiro 48, Boa Vista, T221 1300. Cheaper without a/c, front rooms pleasanter, quiet.
Keep hold of bags
and cameras, and do   **Boa Viagem A** *Recife Monte*, R Petrolina e R dos Navegantes 363, T3465 7422, F3465
not wear a watch. 8406. Very smart and good value for category, caters to business travellers. **B** *Aconchego*, Félix
Prostitution is de Brito 382, T3326 2989, aconchego@novaera.com.br Motel style rooms around pleasant
reportedly common in pool area, a/c, sitting home, English-speaking owner, will collect you from the airport.
Boa Viagem, so choose **C** *Coqueiral*, R Petrolina, 43, T3326 5881. Dutch-owned (Dutch, English, French spoken), a/c,
nightclubs with care small and homely with pretty breakfast room. Recommended. **C** *Uzi Praia*, Av Conselheiro
Aguiar 942, T/F3466 9662. A/c, cosy, sister hotel across the road. **D** *Navegantes Praia* , R dos
Navegantes 1997, T3326 9609, F3326 2710. One block from beach, basic but a/c, TV and room
service. Good value **D** *Pousada da Julieta*, R Prof Jose Brandão 135, T3326 7860,
hjulieta@elogica.com.br One block from beach, very good value. Recommended. **D** *Pousada
da Praia*, Alcides Carneiro Leal 66, T3326 7085. A/c, TV, safe, a/c, rooms vary (some tiny), very
helpful, popular with Israelis. Roof-top breakfast room.

Boa Viagem

To Recife Centre

Boa Viagem detail

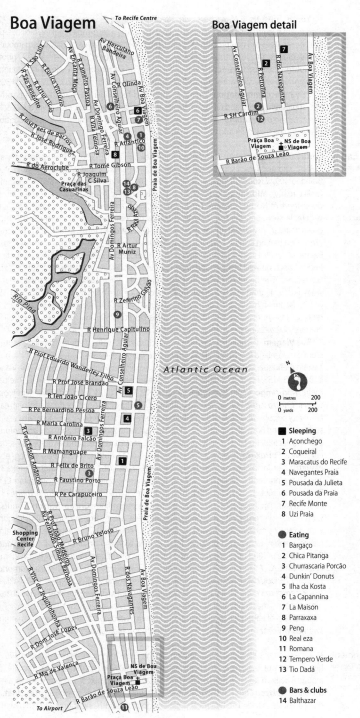

Atlantic Ocean

N

0 metres 200
0 yards 200

■ **Sleeping**
1 Aconchego
2 Coqueiral
3 Maracatus do Recife
4 Navegantes Praia
5 Pousada da Julieta
6 Pousada da Praia
7 Recife Monte
8 Uzi Praia

● **Eating**
1 Bargaço
2 Chica Pitanga
3 Churrascaria Porcão
4 Dunkin' Donuts
5 Ilha da Kosta
6 La Capannina
7 La Maison
8 Parraxaxa
9 Peng
10 Real eza
11 Romana
12 Tempero Verde
13 Tio Dadá

● **Bars & clubs**
14 Balthazar

Brazil

Brazil

Youth hostels E *Maracatus do Recife*, R Maria Carolina 185, T3326 1221, alberguemaracatus@yahoo.com Good breakfast, no hot water, simple, cooking facilities, pool, safe, mosquitoes can be a problem. Membership information from Associação Pernambucano de Albergues da Juventude (APEAJ), from Empetur (see below – take 2 photos). **Camping** There is no camping within the city. For information on camping throughout Pernambuco state, call **Paraíso Camping Clube**, Av Dantas Barreto 512, loja 503, T3224 3094.

Private accommodation During Carnival and for longer stays at other times, private individuals rent rooms and houses in Recife and Olinda; listings can be found in the classified ads in *Diário de Pernambuco*, or ask around the streets of Olinda. This accommodation is generally cheaper, safer and quieter than hotels.

Eating
● *on maps*
There are many good restaurants, at all prices, in the city, and along beach at Boa Viagem

Centre Expensive: *Leite* (lunches only), Praça Joaquim Nabuco 147/53 near Casa de Cultura. Old and famous, good service, smart (another branch in Boa Viagem, at Prof José Brandão 409). *Lisboa á Noite*, R Geraldo Pires 503. Good, reasonable, open Sun evenings (unlike many). **Mid-range**: *Galo D'Ouro*, Gamboa do Carmo 83. Well-established, international food. At No 136, *Casa de Tia*, lunch only, must arrive by 1215, try *cosido*, a meat and vegetable stew, enough for 2. *Tivoli*, R Matias de Albuquerque, Santo Antônio. Lunches downstairs, a/c restaurant upstairs, good value. *O Vegetal*, R Cleto Campelo e Av Guararapes (2nd floor) behind Central Post Office, lunch only, closed Sat-Sun. **Cheap**: *Casa dos Frios*, da Palma 57, loja 5. Delicatessen/sandwich bar, salads, pastries etc. *Buraquinho*, Pátio de Sao Pedro. Lunch only, all dishes good, generous servings of *caipirinha*, friendly. *Savoy Bar*, Av Guararapes. The haunt of Pernambucan intellectuals since 1944, with poetry all over the walls and the legend that Sartre and De Beauvoir once ate there, buffet Mon-Sat 1100-1500, US$2, also lunch by weight. *Lanchonetes* abound in the city, catering to office workers, but tend to close in evening. *Gelattos*, Av Dantas Barreto, 230. Great *sucos* (try the delicious *guarana do amazonas* with nuts), hamburgers and sandwiches.

Boa Viagem Restaurants on the main beach road of Av Boa Viagem are pricey; venture a block or two inland for cheaper deals. **Expensive**: *Bargaço*, Av Boa Viagem 670. Typical northeastern menu specialising in seafood, sophisticated with small bar. *La Maison*, Av Boa Viagem, 618, T3325 1158. Fondue restaurant in low-lit basement, with rosé wine and peach melba on menu. **Mid-range**: *Chica Pitanga*, R Petrolina, 19, T3465 2224. Upmarket, excellent food by weight. *Churrascaria Porcão*, Av Eng Domingos Ferreira 4215. Good for meat and salad eaters alike, very popular. *Ilha da Kosta*, R Pe Bernardino Pessoa, 50, T3466 2222. Self-service seafood, sushi, pizza and Brazilian cuisine, open 1100 to last client and all afternoon. *La Capannina*, Av Cons Aguiar 538, T3465 9420. Italian, pizzas, salad, pasta and sweet and savoury crêpes, delivery service. *Parraxaxa*, R Baltazar Pereira, 32, T9108 0242. Rustic-style, award-winning, northeastern buffet, including breakfast. Recommended. *Pizza Hut*, Av Eng. Domingos Ferreira 3742 and Shopping Centre Recife, T3267 1515 for deliveries, open 1200-2400. Shopping Center Recife (open 1000-2200, T3464 6000) in Boa Viagem has a range of options, eg. *Sushimi*, T3463 6500. Classic, Japanese fast-food in suitably sterile surroundings. **Cheap**: *Dunkin' Donuts*, Av Cons Aguiar, on corner with R Atlântico. Good coffee, a/c, try Brazilian-style mini doughnuts with goiaba or canela filling. *Peng* , Av Domingos Ferreira, 1957. Self-service, some Chinese dishes, bargain, rather than gourmet food, in area with few other restaurants. *TioDadá*, R Baltazar Pereira 100. Loud, TV screens, good value portions of beef. *Realeza*, Av Boa Viagem, on corner with Av Atlântico. Beachfront location, hamburgers, snacks and pizza. *Romana*, R Setubal 225. Deli/bakery with a few tables and chairs, pastries, coffee, yoghurt for breakfast or snack. *Tempero Verde*, R S H Cardim, opposite *Chica Pitanga*. Where the locals go for a bargain meal of beans, meat and salad, US$1.50, simple, self-service, pavement tables.

Be careful of eating the local small crabs, known as *guaiamum*; they live in the mangrove swamps which take the drainage from Recife's *mocambos* (shanty towns).

Entertainment
Agenda Cultural details the cultural events for the month, free booklet from tourist offices

Most bars (often called 'pubs', but nothing like the English version) stay open until dawn. The historic centre of *Recife Antigo* has been restored and is now an excellent spot for nightlife,. Bars around R do Bom Jesus such as *London Pub*, No 207, are the result of a scheme to renovate the dock area. *Calypso Club*, R do Bom Jesus, US$5, has live local bands playing anything from traditional music to rock. The two most popular nightclubs (both enormous, 2300 to dawn) are

Downtown Pub, R Vigário Tenório, disco, live music, US$5, and *Fashion Club*, Av Fernando Simões Barbosa 266, Boa Viagem in front of *Shopping Centre Recife*, T3327 4040, US$8. Techno and rock bands. The Graças district, west of Boa Vista, on the Rio Capibaribe, is popular for bars and evening entertainment. Discos tend to be expensive and sophisticated. Best times are around 2400 on Fri or Sat, take a taxi. The Pina zone, north of the beginning of Boa Viagem, is one of the city's major hang-out areas with lively bars, music and dancing. In Boa Viagem, *Baltazar*, R Baltazar Pereira 130, T3327 0475. Live music nightly, bar snacks, large and popular. Open 1600 to early hours. Try to visit a northeastern *Forró* where couples dance to typical music, very lively especially Fri and Sat, several good ones at Candeias. *Papillon Bar*, Av Beira Mar 20, Piedade, T3341 7298. Forró Wed-Sat. **Theatre** Shows in the Recife/Olinda Convention Center, US$10, traditional dances in full costume.

1 Jan, *Universal Brotherhood*. 12-15 Mar, parades to mark the city's foundation. Mid-Apr,   **Festivals** *Pro-Rock Festival*, a week-long celebration of rock, hip-hop and manguebeat at Centro de Convenções, Complexo de Salgadinho and other venues. Check *Diário de Pernambuco* or *Jornal do Comércio* for details. Jun, *Festejos Juninos*. The days of Santo Antônio (13 Jun), São João (24 Jun), São Pedro and São Paulo (29 Jun), form the nuclei of a month-long celebration whose roots go back to the Portuguese colony. Intermingled with the Catholic tradition are Indian and African elements. The annual cycle begins in fact on São José's day, **19 Mar**, historically the first day of planting maize; the harvest in June then forms a central part of the festejos juninos. During the festivals the *forró* is danced. This dance, now popular throughout the Northeast, is believed to have originated when the British builders of the local railways held parties that were 'for all'. 11-16 Jul, *Nossa Senhora do Carmo*, patron saint of the city. Aug is the *Mes do Folclore*. Oct, *Recifolia*, a repetition of carnival over a whole weekend; dates differ each year. 1-8 Dec is the festival of *Iemanjá*, with typical foods and drinks, celebrations and offerings to the goddess; also 8 Dec, *Nossa Senhora da Conceição*.

Markets The permanent craft market is in the *Casa da Cultura*; prices for ceramic figurines   **Shopping** are lower than Caruaru. *Mercado São José* (1875) for local products and handicrafts. *Hippy fair* at Praça Boa Viagem, on the sea front, wooden statues of saints, weekends only. Sat craft fair at *Sítio Trindade*, Casa Amarela. On 23 Apr, here and in the Pátio de São Pedro, one can see the *xangô* dance. Herbal remedies and spices at Afogados market. *Cais de alfandega*, Recife Barrio, market of local work, 1st weekend of every month. *Domingo na Rua*, Sun market in Recife Barrio, with stalls of local artesanato and performances. **Bookshops** *Livraria Brandão*, R da Matriz 22 (used English books and some French and German), and bookstalls on the R do Infante Dom Henrique. *Livro 7*, R do Riachuelo 267. An emporium with an impressive stock. *Sodiler* at Guararapes airport has books in English, newspapers, magazines; also in the *Shopping Center Recife*. *Livraria Saraiva*, Rua 7 de Setembro 280. The best selection of Brazilian literature in the city. *Almanque Livros*, Largo do Varadouro 418, loja 58. Bohemian atmosphere, sells food and drink. A local character, *Melquísidec Pastor de Nascimento*, has a second-hand stall at Praça do Sebo. Shopping malls *Shopping Center Recife* between Boa Viagem and the airport. *Shopping Tacaruna*, in Santo Amaro, buses to/from Olinda pass it.

Diving Offshore are some 20 wrecks, including the remains of Portuguese galleons; the   **Sport &** fauna is very rich. *Mergulhe Coma*, T3552 2355, T9102 6809 (mob), atlanticdivingasr@   **activities** hotmail.com English speaking instructors for PADI courses. *Seagate*, T3426 1657/9972 9662, www.seagaterecife.com.br Daily departures and night dives.

Local Bus: city buses cost US$0.30-60; they are clearly marked and run frequently until about   **Transport** 2300 weekdays, 0100 weekends. Many central bus stops have boards showing routes. CID/SUB or SUB/CID signs on the front tell you whether buses are going to or from the suburbs from/to the city centre (cidade). On buses, especially at night, look out for landmarks as street names are written small and are hard to see. Integrated bus-**metrô** (see Train below) routes and tickets (US$1) are available. Urban transport information, T158. See below for buses to Olinda and other destinations outside the city. Taxis are plentiful; fares double on Sun, after 2100 and on holidays; number shown on meter is the fare; don't take the taxi if a driver tells you it is km.

Long distance Air: the principal international and national airlines fly to Guararapes airport, 12 km from the city in Boa Viagem. T3464 4188. Internal flights to all major cities. Bus to airport, No 52, US$0.40. Airport taxis cost US$5 to the seafront. There is a bank desk before customs which gives much the same rate for dollars as the moneychangers in the lobby.

Train: commuter services, known as the **Metrô** but not underground, leave from the central station; they serve the rodoviária (frequent trains, 0500-2300, US$0.40 single). To reach the airport, get off the Metrô at Central station (not Joana Bezerra, which is unsafe) and take a bus or taxi (US$8) to Boa Viagem.

Bus: the rodoviária, mainly for long-distance buses, is 12 km outside the city at São Lourenço da Mata (it is called Terminal Integrado dos Passageiros, or TIP, pronounced 'chippy'). T3452 1999. There is a 30-min metrô connection to the central railway station, entrance through Museu do Trem, opposite the Casa da Cultura, 2 lines leave the city, take train marked 'Rodoviária'. From Boa Viagem a taxi all the way costs US$20, or go to Central Metrô station and change there. Bus US$1, 1 hr, from the centre or from Boa Viagem. The train to the centre is much quicker than the bus. Bus tickets are sold at Cais de Santa Rita (opposite EMTU) and *Fruir Tur*, at Praça do Carmo, Olinda.

To **Salvador**, daily 1930, 12 hrs, US$18-25. To **Rio**, daily 2100, 44 hrs, US$58-65. To **São Paulo**, 1630 daily, 50 hrs, US$60-70. To **Santos**, daily 1430, 52 hrs, US$60. To **Foz do Iguaçu**, Fri and Sun 1030, 55 hrs, US$90. To **Curitiba**, Fri and Sun, 52 hrs, US$76. To **Brasília**, daily 2130, 39 hrs, US$49-60. To **Belo Horizonte**, daily 2115, 34 hrs, US$41. To **João Pessoa**, every 20-30 mins, 2 hrs, US$2.50. To **Carauru**, every hr, 3 hrs, US$3. Buses to Olinda, see below; those to the beaches beyond Olinda from Av Dantas behind the post office. To **Cabo** (every 20 mins) and beaches south of Recife from Cais de Santa Rita.

Directory Airline offices. *Gol*, T3464 4793. *RioSul/Nordeste*, Av Domingos Ferreira 801, loja 103-5, T(Nordeste) 3465 6799, T(Rio Sul) 3465 8535. *TAM*, airport T3462 6799/0800-123100. *TAP*, Praça Min Salgado Filho, Imbiribeira, T3465 0300. *Varig*, R Conselheiro Aguiar 456, T3464 4440. Vasp, Av Manoel Borba 488, Boca Viagem, T32126 2000.

Banks open 1000-1600, hours for exchange vary between 1000 and 1400, sometimes later

Banks **Banco do Brasil**, Shopping Centre Boa Viagem (Visa), helpful. *MasterCard*, cash against card, Av Conselheiro Aguiar 3924, Boa Viagem. *Citibank*, Av Marques de Olinda 126 and Av Cons Aguiar 2024, MasterCard with ATM. Also at branches of *HSBC*, eg Av Conde de Boa Vista 454 and Av Cons Aguiar 4452, Boa Viagem, and at *Banco 24 Horas*. **Lloyds TSB Bank**, Rua A.L. Monte 96/1002. *Bradesco*, at: Av Cons Aguiar 3236, Boa Viagem; Av Conde de Boa Vista; Rua da Concórdia 148; Getúlio Vargas 729; all have credit card facility, 24-hr ATMs but no exchange. **Exchange:** *Anacor*, Shopping Center Recife, loja 52, also at Shopping Tacaruna, loja 173. *Norte Câmbio Turismo*, Av Boa Viagem 5000, and at Shopping Guararapes, Av Barreto de Menezes.

Communications Internet: Internet access in bookshop (signposted) in Shopping Centre Recife in Boa Viagem. Also, *lidernet* , Shopping Boa Vista, city centre. *popul@r.net*, R Barão de Souza Leão, near junction with Av Boa Viagem. Open daily 0900-2100. **Post Office:** including poste restante, Central Correios, 50001, Av Guararapes 250. In Boa Viagem, Av Cons Aguiar e R Col Sérgio Cardim. **Telephone:** *Embratel*, Av Agamenon Magalhães, 1114, Parque Amorim district; also Praça da Independência. **International telephones:** *Telemar*, Av Conselheiro Aguiar, Av Herculano Bandeira 231, and Av Conde da Boa Vista, all open 0800-1800.

Cultural centres British Council, Domingos Ferreira 4150, Boa Viagem, T3465 7744, F3465 7271, www.britcoun.org/br 0800-1500, reading room with current English newspapers, very helpful. **Alliance Française**, R Amaro Bezerra 466, Derby, T/F3222 0918.

Embassies and consulates Denmark, Av M de Olinda 85, Ed Alberto Fonseca 2°, T3224 0311, F3224 0997. Open 0800-1200, 1400-1800. **Finland**, R Ernesto de Paula Santos 1327, T3465 2940, F3465 2859. **France**, Av Conselheiro Aguiar 2333, 6th floor, T3465 3290. **Japan**, R Padre Carapuceiro 733, 14th floor, Boa Viagem, T3327 7264. **Netherlands**, Av Conselheiro Aguiar 1313/3, Boa Viagem, T3465 6764. **Sweden**, R Ernesto de Paula Santos, Boa Viagem, T3465 2940. **Switzerland**, Av Conselheiro Aguiar 4880, loja 32, Boa Viagem, T3326 3144. **UK**, Av Cons Aguiar 2941, 3rd floor, Boa Viagem, T3465 0230, F3465 0247, recife@britishconsulate.org.br 0800-1130. **US**, Gonçalves Maia 163, Boa Vista, T3421 2441, F3231 1906.

Dengue fever has been resurgent in Recife

Medical services Unimed, Av Bernardo Vieira de Melo 1496, Guararapes, T3462 1955/3461 1530, general medical treatment. *Unicordis*, Av Conselheiro Aguiar 1980, Boa Viagem, T3326 5237, equipped for cardiac emergencies; also at Av Conselheiro Roas e Silva 258, Aflitos, T421 1000. **Tourist offices** **Empetur** (for the State of Pernambuco), main office, Complexo Viário Vice-Governador Barreto Guimarães s/n, Salgadinho, T3427 8000, between Recife and Olinda, www.empetur.gov.br Branches at airport – 24 hrs, T3224 2361 (helpful but few leaflets, English spoken), and Praça of Boa Viagem, T3463 3621 (English spoken, helpful). Maps are available, or can be bought at newspaper stands in city; also sketch maps in monthly guides *Itinerário Pernambuco* and *Guia do Turista*. For the **Secretaria de Turismo da Prefeitura do Recife**, T3425 8605/8070. **Secretaria de Indústria, Comércio e Turismo**, Av Rui Barbosa 458, Graças, T3231 4500, F3231 4537, www.pernambuco.gov.br Hours of opening of museums, art galleries, churches etc are published in the *Diário de Pernambuco* and *Jornal do Comércio*. The former's website has lots of tourist information, www.dpnet.com.br/turismo/ **Useful addresses Ibama**, Av 17 de Agosto 1057, Casa Forte, T3441 6338, F3441 5033. **Tourist Police**, T3326 9603/3464 4088. **Voltage** 220 volts AC, 60 cycles.

Olinda

The old capital of Brazil founded in 1537 and named a World Heritage Site by UNESCO in 1982 is about 7 km north of Recife. A programme of restoration, partly financed by the Netherlands government, was initiated in order to comply with the recently conferred title of National Monument, but many of the buildings are still in desperate need of repair. The compact network of cobbled streets is steeped in history and invites wandering. This is a charming spot to spend a few relaxing days and a much more appealing base than Recife.

Phone code: 0xx81
Post code: 53000
Colour map 5, grid B6
Population: 367,902

Brazil

The **Basílica e Mosterio de São Bento**, R São Bento, was founded 1582 by the Benedictine monks, burnt by the Dutch in 1631 and restored in 1761. This is the site of Brazil's first law school and the first abolition of slavery. The magnificent gold altar was on loan to New York's Guggenheim Museum at the time of writing. ■ *Mon-Fri 0830-1130, 1430-1700. Mass Sat 0630 and 1800; Sun 1000, with Gregorian chant. Monastery closed except with written permission.* Despite its weathered exterior, the **Convento de São Francisco** (1585), Ladeira de São Francisco, has splendid woodcarving and paintings, superb gilded stucco, and azulejos in the Capela de São Roque within the church of **Nossa Senhora das Neves** in the same building. ■ *Tue-Fri 0700-1130, 1400-1700, Sat 0700-1200, US$0.40. Mass Tue 1900, Sat 1700 and Sun 0800.* Make the short, but very steep, climb up to the **Alto da Sé** for memorable views of the city and the coastline stretching all the way to Recife. Here, the simple **Igreja da Sé** (1537), a cathedral since 1677, was the first church to be built in the city, ■ *Mon-Fri 0800-1200, 1400-1700.* Nearby, the **Igreja da Misericórdia**(1540), R Bispo Coutinho, has fine tiling and gold work. ■ *Daily 1145-1230, 1800-1830.* On a small hill overlooking Praça do Carmo, the **Igreja do Carmo** church (1581) has been closed for several years, with restoration planned.

There are some houses of the 17th century with latticed balconies, heavy doors and brightly-painted stucco walls, including a house in Moorish style at **Praça João Alfredo 7**, housing the *Mourisco* restaurant and a handicrafts shop, *Sobrado 7*. The local colony of artists means excellent examples of regional art, mainly woodcarving and terracotta figurines, may be bought in the Alto da Sé, or in the handicraft shops at the **Mercado da Ribeira**, R Bernardo Vieira de Melo (Vieira de Melo gave the first recorded call for independence from Portugal, in Olinda in 1710). Handicrafts are also sold at good prices in the Mercado Eufrásio Barbosa, by the junction of Av Segismundo Gonçalves and Santos Dumont, Varadouro. There is a **Museo de Arte Sacra** in the former Palacío Episcopal (1696), R Bispo Coutínho. ■ *Tue-Fri 0900-1300.* At R 13 de Maio 157, in the 18th century jail of the Inquisition, is the **Museu de Arte Contemporânea** (same hours as Museu Regional). The **Museu Regional**, R do Amparo 128, is excellent. ■ *Tue-Fri, 0900-1700, Sat and Sun 1400-1700.* **Museu do Mamulengo**, Amparo 59, has Pernambucan folk puppetry. ■ *0900-1800, Sat-Sun 1100-1800.*

The **beaches** close to Olinda are reported to be seriously polluted. Those further north from Olinda, beyond Casa Caiada, are beautiful, usually deserted, palm-fringed; at **Janga**, and **Pau Amarelo**, the latter can be dirty at low tide (take either a 'Janga' or 'Pau Amarela' bus, Varodouro bus to return). At many simple

Sights
Many of the historic buildings have irregular opening hours, but can be viewed from the outside.
The Tourist Office provides a complete list of all historic sites with a useful map, Sítio Histórico Guides with identification cards wait in Praça do Carmo. They are former street children and half the fee for a full tour of the city (about US$12) goes to a home for street children. If you take a guide you will be safe from mugging which, unfortunately, occurs

cafés you can eat *sururu* (clam stew in coconut sauce), *agulha frita* (fried needle-fish), *miúdo de galinha* (chicken giblets in gravy) and *casquinha de carangueijo* (seasoned crabmeat and *farinha de dendê* served in crabshells). Visit the Dutch fort on Pau Amarelo beach; small craft fair here on Saturday nights.

Sleeping

■ *on map*
Prices at least triple during Carnival when 5-night packages are sold. Rooms at regular prices can often be found in Boa Viagem during this time. All of the following, and even most of the cheaper hotels outside the old city, have a pool

Historic cientre Accommodation is mostly in converted mansions that are full of character. If you can afford it, staying in one of these *pousadas* is the ideal way to absorb Olinda's colonial charm. **AL** *Pousada do Amparo*, R do Amparo 199, T3439 1749, www.pousado amparo.com.br Olinda's best hotel, 18th century house full of atmosphere, distinctive rooms with a/c and fridge, some with jacuzzi, flower-filled garden, sauna, good view, very helpful, English spoken, romantic restaurant, in *Roteiros de Charme* group (see page 346). Highly recommended. **AL** *7 Colinas*, Ladeira de Sao Francisco 307, T/F3439 6055, 7colinas@hotel7 colinas.com.br Spacious, new hotel in beautiful grounds with large swimming pool, an oasis with full facilities. **B-C** *Pousada dos Quatro Cantos*, R Prudente de Morais 441, T3429 0220, www.pousada4cantos.com.br Converted mansion with original furniture; full of character, yet homely, garden, terraces and restaurant open till 2100. Highly recommended. **C** *Pousada d'Olinda*, P João Alfredo 178, T/F3494 2559. Nice pool area, sociable, 10% discount for *Footprint Handbooks* owners, 2 communal rooms with good view (**E**), restaurant, English, French, German and Spanish spoken. Recommended. **C-D** *Pousada Peter*, R do Amparo 215, T/F3439 2171, www.pousadapeter.com.br A/c, pool, German owner, family atmosphere, good value.

Outside the historic centre Hotels on R do Sol and in Bairro Novo are below the old city and on the roads heading north. **B** *Oh! Linda Pousada*, Av Ministro Marcos Freire 349, Bairro Novo, T3439 2116. Recommended. **C** *Cinco Sóis*, Av Ministro Marcos Freire 633, Bairro Novo, T/F3429 1347. A/c, fridge, hot shower, parking. **C** *Hospedaria do Turista*, Av Marcos Freire 989, T3429 1847. Excellent. **C** *Pousada São Francisco*, R do Sol 127, T3429 2109, F3429 4057. Comfortable, pool. Recommended, modest restaurant. **D** *São Pedro*, Praça Cons João Alfredo 168, T3429 2935. Cosy, helpful, laundry, Danish run, English spoken. Recommended. **D** *Pousada Alquimia*, R Prudente de Morais 292, T3429 1457. Simple, lovely house, good breakfast, caring owners whose son is a painter with a workshop at the front.

Brazil

Olinda

■ Sleeping		● Eating
1 7 Colinas	6 Pousada dos	1 Goya
2 Alberque de Olinda	Quatro Cantos	2 Maison do Bonfim
3 Pousada Alquimia	7 Pousada Peter	3 Marola
4 Pousada d'Olinda	8 Pousada São Francisco	4 Mourisco
5 Pousada do Amparo		5 Oficina do Sabor

Not to scale

Youth hostels **D** *Cheiro do Mar*, Av Ministro Marcos Freire 95, T3429 0101.Very good small hostel with some double rooms (room No 1 is noisy from the disco), cooking facilities, ask driver of 'Rio Doce/Piedade' or 'Bairra de Jangada/Casa Caiada' bus (see below) to drop you at Albergue de Juventude on the sea front. **E** *Albergue de Olinda*, R do Sol 233, T3429 1592, www.alberguedeolinda.com.br Popular, suites with bath (**C**) and communal bunk rooms, laundry facilities, discounts for HI members. Highly recommended.

Camping *Olinda Camping*, R Bom Sucesso 262, Amparo, T3429 1365. US$5 pp, space for 30 tents, 5 trailers, small huts for rent, quiet, well-shaded, on bus route, recommended.

Expensive *Oficina do Sabor*, R do Amparo, 355. Consistently wins awards, pleasant terrace overlooking city, food served in hollowed-out pumpkins and lots of vegetarian options. *Goya*, R do Amparo, 157. Regional food, particularly seafood, beautifully presented. **Mid-range** *Maison do Bomfim*, R do Bonfim, 115. Serene, fan-cooled, rustic-style restaurant, French cuisine, as well as Brazilian and Italian. *Samburá*, Av Min Marcos Freire 1551. With terrace, try *caldeirada* and *pitu* (crayfish), also lobster in coconut sauce or daily fish dishes, very good. **Cheap** *Mourisco*, Praça João Alfredo 7. Excellent, good value food by weight in lovely, part-covered, garden, delicious deserts. Warmly recommended. Several *lanchonetes* and fast-food options along the seafront. The traditional Olinda drinks, *Pau do Índio* (which contains 32 herbs) and *Retetel*, are both manufactured on the R do Amparo. Also try *tapioca*, a local dish made of manioc with coconut or cheese.

Eating
● *on map*

Cantinho da Sé, Ladeira da Sé 305. Lively, good view of Recife, food served. *Farandola*, R Dom Pedro Roeser 190, behind Carmo church. Mellow bar with festival theme and 'big-top' style roof. Warmly recommended. *Marola*, Trav. Dantas Barreto 66. Funky wooden *barraca* on rocky shoreline specializing in seafood, great *caiprifrutas* (frozen fruit drink with vodka – try the cashew), can get crowded. Recommended. *Pernambucanamente*, Av Min Marcos Freire 734, Bairro Novo. Live, local music every night. Beginning at dusk, but best after 2100, the Alto da Sé becomes the scene of a street fair, with arts, crafts, makeshift bars and barbecue stands, and impromptu traditional music; even more animated at Carnival.

Bars & clubs
Every Fri night bands of wandering musicians walk the streets serenading passers-by. Each Sun from 1 Jan to Carnival there is a mini Carnival in the streets

At Olinda's *carnival* thousands of people dance through the narrow streets of the old city to the sound of the *frevo*, the brash energetic music which normally accompanies a lively dance performed with umbrellas. The local people decorate them with streamers and straw dolls, and form themselves into costumed groups to parade down the R do Amparo; *Pitombeira* and *Elefantes* are the best known of these groups. *Foundation Day* is celebrated with 3 days of music and dancing, **12-15 Mar**, night time only.

Festivals

Viagens Sob O Sol, Prudente de Moraes 424, T3429 3303, transport offered to all parts, any type of trip arranged, also car hire. *Victor Turismo*, Av Santos Domont 20, Loja 06, T3494 1467. Day and night trips to Recife.

Tour operators

Bus **From Recife**: take any bus marked 'Rio Doce', No 981 which has a circular route around the city and beaches, or No 33 from Av Nossa Senhora do Carmo, US$0.60 or 'Jardim Atlântico' from the central post office at Siqueira Campos; from Boa Viagem, take bus marked 'Piedade/Rio Doce' or 'Bairra de Jangada/Casa Caiada' (US$0.60, 30 mins). Change to either of these buses from the airport to Olinda: take 'Aeroporto' bus to Av Domingos Ferreira, Boa Viagem, and ask to be let off; and from the Recife Rodoviária: take the metrô to Central station and then change. In all cases, alight in Praça do Carmo. Taxi drivers between Olinda and Recife try to put meters onto rate 2 at the Convention Centre (between the 2 cities), but should change it back to 1 when queried (taxi to Recife US$8, US$12 to Boa Viagem at night).

Transport

Banks *Banco do Brasil*, R Getúlio Vargas 1470. *Bradesco*, R Getúlio Vargas 729, Visa ATM. *Bandepe* on the same Av has MasterCard ATM. **Communications** Internet: *Study Web*, Praça do Carmo, US$1.20, 30 mins, a/c. *Olind@.com*, Av Beira Mar 15, US$1.50, 30 mins. Post Office: Praça do Carmo, open 0900-1700. Telephone: International calls can be made at *Telemar* office on Praça do Carmo, Mon-Sat 0900-1800. **Tourist offices** *Secretaria de Turismo*, Praça do Carmo, T3429 9279, open daily 0900-2100.

Directory
There are no facilities to change TCs, or ATMs in the old city

Brazil

West of Recife

Caruaru
Colour map 5, grid C6
Population: 253,634
Altitude: 554 m
134 km W of Recife

The paved road from Recife passes through rolling hills, with sugar cane and large cattle *fazendas*, before climbing an escarpment. As the road gets higher, the country-side becomes drier, browner and rockier. Caruaru is a busy, modern town, one of the most prosperous in the *agreste* in Pernambuco. It is also culturally very lively, with excellent local and theatre and folklore groups.

Caruaru is most famous for its markets. The *Feira da Sulanca* is basically a clothes market supplied mostly by local manufacture, but also on sale are jewellery, souve-nirs, food, flowers and anything else that can go for a good price. The most impor-tant day is Monday. There is also the *Feira Livre* or *do Troca-Troca* (free, or barter market). On the same site, Parque 18 de Maio, is the *Feira do Artesanato*, leather goods, ceramics, hammocks and basketware, all the popular crafts of the region. It is tourist-oriented but it is on a grand scale and is open daily 0800-1800.

The little clay figures (*figurinhas* or *bonecas de barro*) originated by Mestre Vitalino (1909-63), and very typical of the *Nordeste*, are the local speciality; most of the local potters live at Alto da Moura 6 km away, where a house once owned by Vitalino is open (the **Casa Museu Mestre Vitalino**), with personal objects and pho-tographs, but no examples of his work. ■ *Bus, 30 mins, bumpy, US$0.50.*

Sleeping and eating A *Grande Hotel São Vicente de Paulo*, Av Rio Branco 365, T3721 5011, F3721 5290. Good, central, a/c, laundry, garage, bar, restaurant, pool, TV. **C** *Central*, R Vigário Freire 71, T3721 5880. Suites or rooms, all with a/c, TV, good breakfast, in the centre. Recommended. **C** *Centenário*, 7 de Setembro 84, T3722 4011, F3721 1033. Also suites, good breakfast, pool, in the town centre so not very quiet, otherwise recommended. Cheap *hospedarias* are around the central Praça Getúlio Vargas. Lots of cheap lunch restaurants in the centre.

Festivals 17 Dec-2 Jan, *Festas Natalinas*; Semana Santa, Holy Week, with lots of folklore and handicraft events; 18-22 May, city's anniversary. 13 Jun *Santo Antônio* and 24 Jun *São João*, the latter a particularly huge forró festival, are part of Caruaru's Festas Juninas. Sep, *Micaru*, a street carnival; also in Sep, *Vaquejada* (a Brazilian cross between rodeo and bull fighting), biggest in the northeast.

Transport The rodoviária is 4 km from the town; buses from Recife stop in the centre. Bus from centre, at the same place as Recife bus stop, to rodoviária, US$0.40. Many buses from TIP in **Recife**, 2 hrs, US$3. Bus to **Fazenda Nova** 1030, 1 hr, US$2, returns for Caruaru 1330.

Directory Useful information The *Cultura Inglesa Caruaru*, Av Agamenon Magalhães 634, Maurício de Nassau, CEP 55000-000, T3721 4749 (cultura@netstage.co.br) will help any visitors with information.

Fernando de Noronha

Many unspoilt beaches and interesting wildlife. Excellent scuba-diving and snorkelling. The rains are from Feb-Jul; the island turns green and the sea water becomes lovely and clear. The dry season is Aug- Mar, but the sun shines all year round

This small archipelago 345 km off the northeast coast was declared a Marine National Park in 1988. Only one island is inhabited and is dominated by a 321 m peak. It is part of the state of Pernambuco administered from Recife. The islands were discovered in 1503 by Amérigo Vespucci and were for a time a pirate lair. In 1738 the Portuguese built the Forte dos Remédios (begun by the Dutch), later used as a prison in this century, and a church to strengthen their claim to the islands. Remains of the early fortifications still exist.

Vila dos Remédios, near the north coast, is where most people live and socialize. At Baía dos Golfinhos is a lookout point for watching the spinner dolphins in the bay. On the south side there are fewer beaches, higher cliffs and the whole coastline and offshore islands are part of the marine park.

■ *All development is rigorously controlled by* Ibama, *to prevent damage to the nature* *reserve. Many locals are dependent on tourism and most food is brought from the mainland; prices are about double. Entry to the island is limited to 100 tourists per day. A maximum of 420 tourists is allowed on the island at any one time. There is a daily tax of US$13 for the first week of your stay. In the second week the tax increases each day. Take sufficient reais as dollars are heavily discounted. For information, contact the park office, Al do Boldró s/n Fernando de Noronho, T0xx81-3619 1176, F3619 1210.*

One hr behind Brazilian Standard Time. No repellent available for the many mosquitoes

B *Estrela do Mar*, T3619 1366, with breakfast, excursions arranged. Also **Pousada Verde** *Riviere*, T3619 1312. Owner Sra Helena Maria, good food, especially fresh tuna. Independent travellers can go much cheaper as many local families rent out rooms with full board, from about US$50 pp per day. The home owners have an association, **Associação das Hospedarias Domiciliares de Fernando de Noronha**, T0xx81-3619 1142. There are 3 restaurants, *Anatalício*, *Ecológico* and *Miramar*. The speciality of the island is shark (*tubarão*), which is served in bars and at the port (Noronha Pesca Oceânica). There aren't many bars, but a good one is **Mirante Bar**, near the hotel, with a spectacular view over Boldró beach; it has loud music and at night is an open-air disco.

Sleeping & eating

Diving Diving is organized by *Atlantis Divers*, T0xx81-3619 1371, *Águas Claras*, T3619 1225, in the hotel grounds, and *Noronha Divers*, T3619 1112. Diving costs between US$50-75 and equipment rental from US$50. This is the diving mecca for Brazilian divers with a great variety of sites to explore and fish to see.

Sport & activities

Boat trips and jeep tours are available; it is also possible to hire a beach buggy (US$100 a day without a driver, US$30 with driver). Motorbikes can be rented for US$80 a day. You can hitch everywhere as everyone stops. There are good hiking, horse riding and mountain biking possibilities, but you must either go with a guide or ranger in many parts.

Tours

Air Daily flights from Recife with *Varig*, 2 hrs, US$400, and daily flights from Recife and Natal with *Transporte Regional do Interior Paulista*.

Transport

João Pessoa

It is a bus ride of two hours through sugar plantations over a good road from Recife (126 km) to João Pessoa, capital of the State of Paraíba on the Rio Paraíba. It is a capital that retains a small town atmosphere. In the **Centro Histórico** is the São Francisco Cultural Centre (Praça São Francisco 221), one of the most important baroque structures in Brazil, with the beautiful church of **São Francisco** which houses the Museu Sacro e de Arte Popular. ■ *Tue-Sat 0800-1100, Tue-Sun 1400-1700, T221 2840*. Other tourist points include the **Casa da Pólvora**, now the **Museu Fotográfico Walfredo Rodríguez** (Ladeira de São Francisco). ■ *Mon-Fri 0800-1200, 1330-1700*. Also the **Teatro Santa Roza** (1886), Praça Pedro Américo, Varadouro, T241 1230. ■ *Mon-Fri 1400-1800*. João Pessoa's parks include the 17-ha **Parque Arruda Câmara**, north of the centre, and **Parque Solon de Lucena** or **Lagoa**, a lake surrounded by impressive palms in the centre of town, the city's main avenues and bus lines go around it.

Phone code: 0xx83 Post code: 58000 Colour map 5, grid B6 Population: 597,934

The beachfront stretches for some 30 km from Ponta do Seixas (south) to the port of **Cabedelo** (north), on a peninsula between the Rio Paraíba and the Atlantic Ocean. This is Km 0 of the Transamazônica highway. The ocean is turquoise green and there is a backdrop of lush coastal vegetation. 7 km from the city centre, following Av Presidente Epitáceo Pessoa is the beach of **Tambaú**, which has many hotels and restaurants. ■ *Bus No 510 'Tambaú' from outside the rodoviária or the city centre, alight at* Hotel Tropical Tambaú. Regional crafts, including lace-work, embroidery and ceramics are available at *Mercado de Artesanato*, Centro de Turismo, Almte Tamandaré 100. About 14 km south of the centre is the Cabo Branco lighthouse at Ponta do Seixas, the most easterly point of continental Brazil and South America;

Brazil

there is a panoramic view from the cliff top. **Cabo Branco** is much better for swimming than **Tambaú**. Take bus 507 'Cabo Branco' from outside the rodoviária to the end of the line; hike up to the lighthouse.

Sleeping
■ *on map*
Hotels in the centre tend to cater to business clients

Centre C *Guarany*, R Almeida Barreto 181 and 13 de Maio, T/F241 5005, guarany@ bomguia.com.br Cheaper without a/c and TV, cheaper still in low season, pleasant, safe, extremely good value, own self service restaurant. Recommended. **D** *Aurora*, Praça João Pessoa 51, T241 3238. A/c, cheaper with fan, on attractive square, pleasant enough. **D** *Ouro Preto*, Idaleto 162, T221 5882, Varadouro near rodoviária. With bath, fan. Cheaper hotels can be found near the rodoviária. **G** *Pousada Fênix*, R 13 de Maio, 588, T222 1193. 'Love hotel', rents rooms by hr, but spotless and real bargain.

The town's main attractions are its beaches, where most tourists stay

Tambaú AL *Tropical Tambaú*, Av Alm Tamandaré 229, T2473660, F2471070, reservas.tambau@tropicalhotel.com.br Enormous round building, looks like a rocket launching station and a local landmark, comfortable, good service. Recommended. **A** *Sol-Mar*, Rui Carneiro 500, T226 1350, F226 3242. Pool, superb restaurant (**C** in low season). **B** *Tambia Praia*, R Carlos Alverga 36, T247 4101. Central, 1 block from beach, intimate, balconies with sea view. Recommended. **E** *Pousada Mar Azul*, Av João Maurício 315, T226 2660. Beachfront, with fan, large room, no breakfast but a bargain.

All are across from the beach, along Av Cabo Branco unless otherwise noted

Cabo Branco B *Pouso das Águas*, No 2348, T/F2265103. Homely atmosphere, landscaped areas, pool. **B** *Pousada Casa Rosada*, No 1710, T2472470. With fan, **C** with shared bath, family run. Accommodation can also be found in the outer beaches such as Camboinha and Seixas, and in Cabedelo.

Eating
■ *on map*

There are few options in the centre, other than the stalls in Parque Solon de Lucena next to the lake. **Tambaú Expensive**: *Adega do Alfredo*, Coração de Jesus. Excellent, popular, Portuguese. *Sagaranda*, Av Tamandaré near *Hotel Tambaú*. Very good *cozinha criativa* (similar to *nouvelle cuisine*). **Mid-range**: *Apetito Tratoria*, Osório Paes 35. Very good Italian, charming atmosphere. *Cheiro Verde*, R Carlos Alverga 43. Self-service, well-established, regional food. **Cheap**: Every evening on the beachfront, stalls are set up selling all kinds of snacks and barbecued meats.

Festivals
Pre-carnival celebrations are renowned: the bloco *Acorde Miramar* opens the celebrations the Tue before Carnival and on Wed, known as *Quarta Feira de Fogo*, thousands join the *Muriçocas de Miramar*. Celebrations for the patroness of the city, *Nossa Senhora das Neves*, take place for 10 days around **5 Aug**.

João Pessoa centre

N
Not to scale

■ Sleeping
1 Aurora 2 Guarany

Half-day city tours (US$6), day trips to Tambaba (US$8) and Recife/Olinda (US$12) organized **Tour operators**
by *Vida Mansa*, T226 1141. *Roger Turismo*, Av Tamandaré 229, T247 1856. A range of tours,
some English-speaking guides. *Preocupação Zero Turismo*, Av Cabo Branco 2566, T226
4859, F226 4599. Local and regional tours, floating bars. *Navegar*, Artur Monteiro de Paiva
97, Bessa, T/F246 2191. Buggy tours (US$25 to Jacumã).

Local Bus: Most city buses stop at the rodoviária and go by the Lagoa (Parque **Transport**
Solon de Lucena). Take No 510 for Tambaú, No 507 for Cabo Branco.

Long distance Air: Aeroporto Presidente Castro Pinto, Bayeux, 11 km from centre, T232
1200; national flights. Taxi to centre costs US$8, to Tambaú US$12.
    Bus: Rodoviária is at R Francisco Londres, Varadouro, 10 mins from the centre, T221 9611;
luggage store; PBTUR information booth is helpful. Taxi to the centre US$1.50, to Tambaú
US$5. To **Recife** with *Boa Vista* or *Bonfim*, every 30 mins, US$2.50, 2 hrs. To **Natal** with
Nordeste, every 2 hrs, US$6 *convencional*, US$7.50 *executivo*, 3 hrs. To **Fortaleza** with
Nordeste, 2 daily, 10 hrs, US$18. To **Juazeiro do Norte** with *Transparaíba*, 2 daily, US$14,
10 hrs. To **Salvador** with *Progresso*, 4 weekly, US$30, 14 hrs. To **Belém** with *Guanabara*,
daily at 1000, US$46, 36-39 hrs.

Airline Offices *TAM*, Av Senador Rui Carneiro 512, T247 2400 (airport T232 2747). *Varig*, Av Getúlio **Directory**
Vargas 183, Centro, T221 1140, 0800-997000. *Vasp*, Parque Solon de Lucena 530, Centro, T221 1140
(airport 247 2400). **Banks** *Banco do Brasil*, Praça 1817, 3rd floor, Centro, helpful, or Isidro Gomes 14,
Tambaú, behind Centro de Turismo, poor rates. MasterCard Cirrus and Amex cashpoints at *Banco 24
Horas* kiosk in front of Centro de Turismo, Tambaú, and *HSBC*, R Peregrino de Carvalho 162, Centro. *PB
Câmbio Turismo*, Visconde de Pelotas 54C, Centro, T241 4676, open Mon-Fri 1030-1630, cash and TCs.
Communications Internet: Many cybercafés in Tambaú: at telephone office in Centro de Turismo,
Almte Tamandaré 100. **Post Office**: main office is at Praça Pedro Américo, Varadouro; central office is at
Parque Solon de Lucena 375; also by the beach at Av Rui Carneiro, behind the Centro de Turismo.
Telephone: Calling stations at: Centro de Turismo, Tambaú; Av Epitácio Pessoa 1487, Bairro dos Estados;
rodoviária and airport. **Tourist offices** PBTUR, at the Centro de Turismo, Tambaú, T226 7078,
pbtur@pbtur.pb.gov.br Branches at rodoviária and airport, all open 0800-2000. Basic maps.

The best known beach of the state is **Tambaba**, the only official nudist beach of the
Northeast, 49 km south of João Pessoa in a lovely setting. Two coves make up this
famous beach: in the first bathing-suits are optional, while the second one is only for
nudists. Strict rules of conduct are enforced. Between Jacumã (many hotels, restaurants) and Tambaba are several nice beaches such as **Tabatinga** which has summer
homes on the cliffs and **Coqueirinho**, surrounded by coconut palms, good for bathing, surfing and exploring caves.

Natal

Natal sits on a peninsula between the Rio Potengi and the Atlantic Ocean, and is one *Phone code: 0xx84*
of the most attractive cities of Brazil's northeast coast. The oldest part of the city is *Post code: 59000*
the **Ribeira** along the riverfront where a process of renovation has been started. The *Colour map 5, grid B6*
Cidade Alta, or Centro, is the main commercial centre and Av Rio Branco its princi- *Population: 712,317*
pal artery. The main square is made up of **Praças João Maria**, **André de Albuquer-** *185 km N of*
que, **João Tibúrcio** and **7 de Setembro**. At Praça André de Albuquerque is the old *João Pessoa*
cathedral (inaugurated 1599, restored 1996). The modern cathedral is on Av
Deodoro s/n, Cidade Alta. The church of **Santo Antônio**, R Santo Antônio 683,
Cidade Alta, dates from 1766, and has a fine, carved wooden altar and a sacred art
museum. ■ *Tue-Fri 0800-1700, Sat 0800-1400*.
    The **Museu Câmara Cascudo**, Av Hermes de Fonseca 1440, Tirol (T212 2795),
has exhibits on archaeological digs, Umbanda rituals and the sugar, leather and
petroleum industries. ■ *Mon 1400-1700, Tue-Fri 0800-1100, 1400-1700, Sat
1000-1600, US$1.50*. The **Forte dos Reis Magos** (16th century) at Praia do Forte,
the tip of Natal's peninsula, is open daily 0800-1630; between it and the city is a

military installation. It is possible to walk along the beach to the fort, or to go in a tour, or by taxi; it is worth it for the views. ■ *US$1.50*. **Museu do Mar**, Av Dinarte Mariz (Via Costeira), Praia de Mãe Luiza, has aquariums with regional sea life and exhibits with preserved specimens. ■ *Mon-Fri 0800-1700, Sat 0800-1400, T215 4433*. At Mãe Luiza is a lighthouse with beautiful views of Natal and surrounding beaches (take a city bus marked Mãe Luiza; get the key from the house next door).

Natal has excellent beaches some of which are also the scene of the city's night life. The urban beaches of Praia do Meio, Praia dos Artistas and Praia de Areia Preta have recently been cleaned up and a beachside promenade built. The **Via Costeira** runs south along the ocean beneath the towering sand dunes of **Parque das Dunas** (access restricted to protect the 9 km of dunes), joining the city to **Ponta Negra**, 12 km from the centre, the most popular beach. It is 20 mins by bus from centre; pleasant and 'quaint' atmosphere; the northern end of the beach is good for surfing, while the southern end is calmer and good for bathing. At the south end of the beach is **Morro do Careca**, a 120 m high dune with a sand skiing slope surrounded by vegetation (crowded on weekends and holidays, but not safe to wander alone when deserted, as there are robberies).

Brazil

Sleeping

The Via Costeira is a strip of enormous, upmarket beachfront hotels, which are very isolated. Ponta Negra is the ideal place to stay, with its attractive beach and concentration of restaurants. Economical hotels are easier to find in the city proper but otherwise there is not much reason to stay here

Centre B *Casa Grande*, R Princesa Isabel 529, Centro, T211 0555. With a/c, cheaper without bath (also low season discounts), good breakfast, pleasant, excellent value. Recommended. **B** *Oassis Swiss*, R Joaquim Fabrício 291, Casa 08, Petrópolis, T/F202 2455. Swiss-owned, a/c, cheaper with fan (cheaper still in low season), pool, massive breakfasts, exceptional value. **D** *Fenícia*, Av Rio Branco 586, Centro, T211 4378. More expensive with a/c, with breakfast and shower, English spoken, low season discount. Several near **rodoviária**: **B** *Pousada Esperança*, Av Capt Mor Gouveia 418, T205 1955. Cheaper with fan and without bath. **D** *Cidade do Sol*, Piancó 31, T205 1893. Cheaper with fan. **E** *Pousada Beth Shalom*, R Patos 45, T205 1141. Fan. **Praia do Meio, Praia dos Artistas and Praia de Areia Preta** Unless stated hotels are on the beachfront Av Pres Café Filho (the numbering of which is illogical); all recommended: **A** *Praia do Sol*, No 750, Praia do Meio, T211 4562, F222 6571. Opposite beach, quiet, a/c, TV. **B** *Bruma*, No 1176, T/F211 4308, www.hotelbruma@zaz.com.br Slick, intimate, beachfront balconies, pool, terrace. **D** *Beira Mar*, Av Pres Café Filho, Praia do Meio, T202 1470. With breakfast, a/c, small pool, good value, popular. **F** *Pousada do Pax*á, No 11, T2022848, www.paxaturismo.hpg.com.br Beachfront, breakfast extra, real bargain. **D** *Parque das Dunas*, R João XXIII 601 (take Bus 40, alight at Farol, 40 mins from the centre), T202 1820. Excellent breakfast (good value dinner on request), safe, **E** in low season.

At Ponta Negra L *Manary Praia*, R Francisco Gurgel 9067, T/F219 2900, manary@digi.com.br Stylish, beachfront rooms and pool/terrace, a Roteiro de Charme hotel. **A** *Hotel e Pousada O Tempo e o Vento*, R Elias Barros 66, T/F219 2526. A/c (**B** in low season), fridge, cheaper with fan, pool, camping, US$5 pp. **B** *Pousada Castanheira*, R da Praia 221, T/F236 2918, www.pousadacastanheira.com.br Small, comfortable, safe, most hospitable, English owned, pool. Recommended. **B** *Ingá Praia*, Av Erivan França 17, T219 3436, www.ingapraiahotel.com.br Comfortable, cosy. Recommended. **B** *Miramar*, Av da Praia 3398, T2362079. Clean, English spoken. **C** *Pousada Porta do Sol*, R Francisco Gurgel 9057, T236 2555, F205 2208. Room with bar, TV, breakfast, pool, steps down onto beach, good value. Recommended. **D** *Pousada Maravista*, R da Praia, 223, T236 4677, marilymar@hotmail.com Good breakfast, English spoken, TV, fridge. **D** *Maria Bonita 2*, Estrela do Mar 2143, T236 2941, F219 2726. With a/c, **E** with fan. Recommended. **E** *Pousada Porto Seguro*, Av Pres Café Filho 1174, T9412 1039. Very sociable, beachfront terrace, good rooms and good value.

Youth hostels D pp: *Lua Cheia*, R Dr Manoel Augusto Bezerra de Araújo 500, Ponta Negra, T236 3696, www.luacheia.com.br Includes breakfast, HI. Outstanding. *Verdes Mares*, R das Algas 2166, Conj Algamar, Ponta Negra, T236 2872. HI, includes breakfast.

Eating

Centre and central beaches Expensive: *Raro Sabor*, R Seridó 722, Petrópolis. Exclusive bistro. *Chaplin*, Av Pres Café Filho 27, Praia dos Artistas. Traditional, seaviews, good seafood, part of leisure complex with bar, English pub and nightclub. *Estação Trem de Minas*, Av Pres Café Filho 197, Praia dos Artistas. Charming rustic style, 40 brands of cachaça, live music nightly, self-service lunch and dinner. **Mid-range** *Bella Napoli*, Av Hermes da Fonseca 960, Tirol. Good Italian food. *Camarões Express*, Av Sen Salgado Filho 2234, Natal Shopping. Literally, fast-food prawns in 15 styles. Open for lunch only at weekends. *Carne de Sol Benigna Lira*, R Dr José Augusto Bezerra de Medeiros 09, Praia do Meio. Traditional, regional cuisine. *Peixada da Comadre*, R Dr José Augusto Bezerra de Medeiros 4, Praia dos Artistas. Seafood, popular with visitors. **Cheap** *Bob's*, Av Sen Salgado Filho, 2234, Natal Shopping. Hamburger chain open daily 1000-2200. *A Macrobiótica*, Princesa Isabel 524, vegetarian, shop, lunch only. *Saint Antoine*, R Santo Antônio 651, Cidade Alta. Self-service by kg. For snacks, try the stalls along the beaches.

Ponta Negra Expensive: *Tereré*, Estr de Pirangi 2316. All-you-can-eat barbecue, including Argentine beef, ribs, as well as fish and salad. **Mid-range**: *Atlântico*, No 27. Relaxed, semi-open air, beachfront, Italian and Portugese dishes, fish and carne do sol. Recommended. *Barraca do Caranguejo*, No 1180. Live music nightly from 2100, 8 prawn dishes for US$8. *Camarões*, Av Eng Roberto Freire 2610, also at Natal Shopping Centre. Touristy, but very good seafood. *Cipó Brasil*, jungle theme, 4 levels, sand floors, lantern-lit, very atmospheric, average food (pizzas and crêpes), good for cocktails, live music nightly after 2100. *Ponta Negra Grill*, No 20. Large, several terraces, popular, lively, steaks, seafood and cocktails. **Cheap**: Beach *baracas* for snacks and fast food. *Ponta Negra Mall*, stalls sell sandwiches and snacks.

Street numbering is not logical, but all restaurants are on Av Erivan França, the short beach road

Brazil

Baraonda, Av Erivan França, 44, Ponta Negra, T9481 3748. Live music nightly (closed Tue), including swing and ambiente from 2300 to last customer. *Taverna Pub*, R Dr Maneol A B de Araújo 500, Ponta Negra, T236 3696. Medieval-style pub in youth hostel basement, eclectic (rock, Brazilian pop, Jazz, etc), live music Tue-Sun from 2200, best night Wed. The *Centro de Turismo* (see Shopping) has *Forró com Turista*, a chance for visitors to learn this fun dance, Thu 2200; many other enjoyable venues where visitors are encouraged to join in. In Ribeira, Centro, there are two popular bar/nightclubs in restored historic buildings on Rua Chile: *Blackout B52*, No 25, T221 1282, '40s theme, best night is 'Black Monday', and *Downtown Pub*, No 11, 4 bars, dancefloor, games area, cybercafé, live bands Thu-Sat. *Novakapital*, Av Pres Café Filho 872, Praia dos Artistas, T202 7111. *Forró*, live music, especially rock, foam parties, US$4, from 2400.

Bars & clubs
Ponta Negra beach is lively at night and the venue for a full-moon party, when there is live music all night

In **Jan** is the *Festa de Nossa Senhora dos Navegantes* when numerous vessels go to sea from Praia da Redinha, north of town. In **mid-Oct** there is a country show, *Festa do Boi*, bus marked Parnamirim to the exhibition centre, it gives a good insight into rural life. **Mid-Dec**: *Carnatal*, a lively 4-day music festival with dancing in the streets.

Festivals

Centro de Turismo, R Aderbal de Figueiredo s/n, off R Gen Cordeiro, Petrópolis, T211 6149; a converted prison with a wide variety of handicraft shops, art gallery, antique shop and tourist information booth; good views; open daily 0900-1900; bus No 46 from Ponta Negra or No 40 from rodoviária. *Centro Municipal de Artesanato*, Av Presidente Café Filho s/n, Praia dos Artistas, daily 1000-2200. *Natal Shopping*, Av Sen Salgado Filho 2234, between Ponta Negra and Via Costeira. Large mall with restaurants, ATMs, cinemas and 140 shops, free shuttle bus service to major hotels.

Shopping

Local Bus The old rodoviária on Av Junqueira Aires, by Praça Augusto Severo, Ribeira, is a central point where many bus lines converge. Buses to some of the beaches near Natal also leave from here.

Long distance Air: Aeroporto Augusto Severo, in Parnamirim, 15 km south from centre, T644 1000. "Parnamirim-A" minibus every 30 mins from the old rodoviária near the centre US$0.65, taxi US$25 to centre, US$20 to Ponta Negra.

Bus: Rodoviária, Av Capitão Mor Gouveia 1237, Cidade da Esperança, T205 4377, about 6 km southwest of the centre. Buses from the south pass Ponta Negra first, where you can ask to be let off. Luggage store. Regional tickets are sold on street level, interstate on the 2nd floor. City bus 'Cidade de Esperança Av 9', 'Areia Preta via Petrópolis' or 'Via Tirol' to centre. Taxi US$6 to centre, US$9 to Ponta Negra.

Transport
Unlike most Brazilian cities, in Natal you get on the bus in the front and get off at the back

To **Recife** with *Napoles*, 5 daily, US$6.60 *convencional*, US$9 *executivo*, 4 hrs. To **Fortaleza**, US$15 *convencional*, US$18 *executivo*, US$29 *leito*, 8 hrs. To **João Pessoa**, every 2 hrs, US$6 *convencional*, US$7.50 *executivo*, 3 hrs. To **Salvador**, US$32.50 *executivo*, 20 hrs. To **Belém**, US$45, 32 hrs.

Directory **Airline Offices** *Nordeste*, at airport, T272 6814. *TAM*, Av Campos Sales, 500, Tirol, T201 2020 (airport 643 1624) 0800-123100. *Varig*, R Mossoró 598, Centro, T201 9339 (airport 743 1100), 0800-997000. *Vasp*, R João Pessoa 220, Centro, T221 4453 (airport 643 1441). **Banks** *Banco do Brasil*, seafront ATM, Ponta Negra for Cirrus/MasterCard and Visa/Plus. Also Av Rio Branco 510, Cidade Alta, US$ cash and TCs at poor rates, cash advances against Visa, Mon-Fri 1000-1600. MasterCard ATM at *HSBC*, Av Deodoro 745, and *Banco 24 Horas* ATMs (eg *Natal Shopping*). *Sunset Câmbio*, Av Hermes da Fonseca 628, Tirol, T212 2552, cash and TCs, 0900-1700. *Dunas Câmbio*, Av Roberto Freire 1776, Loja B-11, Capim Macio (east of Parque das Dunas), T219 3840, cash and TCs, 0900-1700. **Communications** Internet: *Sobre Ondas*, Av Erivan França 14, Ponta Negra, 0900-2400, 10 centavos/1 min. Cybercafés in *Praia Shopping*, Av Eng Roberto Freire 8790, Ponta Negra and *Natal Shopping*, see above. **Post Office:** R Princesa Isabel 711, Centro; Av Rio Branco 538, Centro; Av Praia de Ponta Negra 8920, Ponta Negra. **Telephone:** international phone calls, *Telemar*, R Princesa Isabel 687 e R João Pessoa, Centro; Av Roberto Freire 3100, Ponta Negra, Shopping Cidade Jardim, Av Roberto Freire, Ponta Negra; and rodoviária. **Tourist office** Secretaria Estadual de Turismo (Setur/RN): main office, Av Afonso Pena 1155, Tirol, T232 2496, www.turismorn.com.br Information booths at Centro de Turismo, T211 6149 (see Shopping above), Av Presidente Café Filho s/n, Praia dos Artistas (0800-2100 daily), Cajueiro de Pirangi (see Rota do Sul below), rodoviária (T205 4377) and airport (T643 1811). For information dial 1516. *Setur* publishes a list of prices for tourist services such as tours, taxi fares, food and drinks. **Useful address** Tourist Police: Delegacia do Turista, T232 2851, 24 hrs. **Voltage** 220 volts AC, 60 cycles.

Rota do Sul The *Rota do Sol/Litoral Sul* (RN-063) follows the coastline south of Natal for some 55 km and is the access to beaches south of Ponta Negra: **Pirangi do Norte**, 28 km (30 mins from new rodoviária, US$0.60) is near the world's largest cashew nut tree (*cajueiro*); branches springing from a single trunk cover an area of some 7,300 sq m. The snack bar by the tree has schedules of buses back to Natal. There are calm waters and it is popular for water sports. Land or boat tours of the Litoral Sul usually include a stop at Pirangi.

Beyond **Barreta**, 55 km, is the long, pristine beach of **Malenbar** or **Guaraíra**, access walking or by 10-min boat ride across the Rio Tibau to the south end. One of the most visited areas of the southern coast, because of its great natural beauty, is that surrounding **Tibau do Sul** (*Population*: 7,749). Lovely beaches circled by high cliffs, lagoons, Atlantic forest and dolphins are among its attractions. Access is via the BR-101 south from Natal or north from João Pessoa, as far as **Goianinha**, then east 18 km to Tibau do Sul. **Praia da Pipa**, 3 km further south (85 km from Natal), is a popular resort with many *pousadas* and charming restaurants. Recommended as good value are: **D** *Pomar da Pipa*, R da Mata s/n, T246 2256, www.pomarda pipa.hpg.com.br Comfortable, fan, English and Spanish spoken. **D** *Vera My House*, T246 2295. Room or dormitory, use of kitchen, no breakfast, English spoken. **F** pp *Manolo*, T246 2328, manolopousada@uol.com.br Helpful, great breakfast. Just north of town, on a 70 m-high dune, is the **Santuário Ecológico de Pipa**, a 60 ha park conserving the *mata atlântica* forest; there are several trails and lookouts over the cliffs which afford an excellent view of the ocean and dolphins. ■ *0800-1600, US$3*.

The coast north of Natal is known for its many impressive, light-coloured sand dunes. A 25-min ferry crossing on the Rio Potengi or a 16 km drive along the *Rota do Sol/Litoral Norte* goes to **Redinha**, the nearest beach on the north coast. The best known beach in the state is **Genipabu**, 30 km north of the city; access from Redinha via RN-304. Its major attractions are very scenic dunes, the Lagoa de Genipabu (a lake surrounded by cashew trees and dunes) and many bars and restaurants on the sea shore. ■ *Buggy tours of the Litoral Norte cost US$100 per buggy split between four and are a good way to see many of the beaches and sights in one day. Buggy rental from* Associação dos Bugueiros, *T225 2077, US$25.*

Fortaleza

Fortaleza, the fifth largest city in Brazil, is a busy metropolis with many high-rise buildings. It has an important clothes manufacturing industry with many hotels and restaurants and a lively nightlife. Fishermen's *jangadas* still dot the turquoise ocean across from the beach and transatlantic cruise ships call in for refuelling. The mid-day sun is oppressive, tempered somewhat by a constant breeze; evening temperatures can be more pleasant, especially by the sea.

Phone code: 0xx85 (0xx88 outside metropolitan Fortaleza) Post code: 60000 Colour map 5, grid B5 Population: 2.1 million

Praça do Ferreira, from which pedestrian walkways radiate, is the heart of the commercial centre. The whole area is dotted with shady squares. **Fortaleza Nossa Senhora da Assunção**, Av Alberto Nepomuceno, originally built in 1649 by the Dutch, gave the city its name. ■ *Daily 0800-1100, 1400-1700, T251 1660*. Near the fort, on R Dr João Moreira, is the 19th century **Passeio Público** or Praça dos Mártires, a park with old trees and statues of Greek deities. West of here, a neoclassical former prison (1866) houses the **Centro de Turismo do Estado** (Emcetur), with museums, theatre and craft shops. ■ *Av Senador Pompeu 350, near the waterfront, T0800-991516, closed Sun*. It houses the **Museu de Arte e Cultura Populares** and the **Museu de Minerais**. ■ *Mon-Fri 0800-1700, Sat 0800-1400, US$0.50, T212 3566*. Further west along R Dr João Moreira, at **Praça Castro Carreira**, is the nicely refurbished train station **Estação João Felipe** (1880).

The **Teatro José de Alencar**, on the praça of the same name, was inaugurated in 1910; this magnificent iron structure was imported from Scotland and is decorated in neo-classical and art nouveau styles. It also houses a library and art gallery. ■ *Mon-Fri 0800-1700, hourly tours, some English speaking guides, US$1, Wed free, T2291989*. The new **cathedral**, completed in 1978, in gothic style but built in concrete, stands beside the new **Mercado Central** with beautiful stained glass windows (Praça da Sé, Av Alberto Nepomuceno).

The **Museu do Maracatu**, Rufino de Alencar 231, at Teatro São José, houses costumes of this ritual dance of African origin. The new and exciting **Centro Dragão do Mar de Arte e Cultura** at R Dragão do Mar 81, Praia de Iracema hosts music concerts, dance, and art and photography exhibitions. ■ *Tue-Thu 100-1730, Fri-Sun 1400-2130. T488 8600, dragao@dragaodomar.org.br Free on Sun.*. In the Palácio da Abolicão is the **mausoleum of President Castelo Branco** (1964-67), Av Barão de Studart 505. ■ *0800-1800 daily*.

Sights

Tourists should avoid the Serviluz favela between the old lighthouse (Av Vicente de Castro), the favela behind the railway station, the Passeio Público at night. Av Abolição at its eastern (Nossa Senhora da Saúde church) and western ends. Also be careful at Mucuripe and Praia do Futuro. Generally, though, the city is safe for visitors

Fortaleza has 25 km of beaches, many of which are the scene of the city's nightlife; those between Barra do Ceará (west) and Ponta do Mucuripe (east) are polluted. **Eastern beaches Praia de Iracema** is one of the older beach suburbs with some original turn-of-the-century houses. East of Iracema, the **Av Beira Mar** (Av Presidente Kennedy) connects Praia do Meireles with Volta da Jurema and **Praia do Mucuripe**, 5 km from the centre. Fortaleza's main fishing centre, *jangadas*, bring in the catch here. **Praia do Futuro**, 8 km southeast of the centre, is the most popular bathing beach, 8 km long, with strong waves, sand dunes and fresh-water showers, but no natural shade; there are many vendors and straw shacks serving local dishes. A *Jardineira* or city bus marked 'P Futuro' from Praça Castro Carreira, 'Praia Circular', does a circular route to Praia do Futuro; a bus marked 'Caça e Pesca' passes all southeast beaches on its route. About 29 km southeast of the centre is **Praia Porto das Dunas**, popular for watersports including surfing; the main attraction is **Beach Park**, a water park (admission US$20; *jardineira* bus from centre or Av Beira Mar).

Western beaches Northwest of the centre is **Praia Barra do Ceará**, 8 km, where the Rio Ceará flows into the sea. Here are the ruins of the 1603 Forte de Nossa Senhora dos Prazeres, the first Portuguese settlement in the area. The beaches west of the Rio Ceará are cleaner, lined with palms and have strong waves. A new bridge across this river gives better access to this area, for example, **Praia de Icaraí**, 22 km, and **Tabuba**, 5 km further north. Beyond Tabuba, 37 km from Fortaleza, is **Cumbuco**, a lively

Urban beaches

Various minibus day tours to beaches, $US4; they gather along seafront. Also agency CPVTUR, Av Mons Tabosa 1001

Brazil

beach, dirty in high season, bars, horse riding, dunes which you can sandboard down into a rainwater lake, palm trees. ■ Jardineira *minibus, US$1.15, leaves from beside the* Ideal Clube *at west corner of Av Rui Barbosa and Av Raimundo Girão.*

Sleeping
■ *on map*
Most hotels offer reduced prices in the low season

LL *Imperial Othon Palace*, Av Beira Mar 2500, Meireles, T242 9177, F242 7777, www.hoteis-othon.com.br, beach front location (recommended *feijoada* on Sat). **A** *Colonial Praia*, R Barão de Aracati 145, Iracema, T455 9600, F219 3501. 4-star, pleasant grounds and big pool, laundry service (10 mins walk from Av Beira Mar). **A** *Zen Praia*, Av Abolição 1894, Meireles, T244 3213, F261 2196. A/c, pool, restaurant. Recommended.

B *Chevalier*, Av Duque de Caxias 465, T231 4611. Fan, pleasant. **B** *Pousada Jardim*, Idelfonso Albano 950, Aldeota, T226 9711, www.hoteljardim.com.br No sign outside, by Iracema beach, nice garden, excursions arranged, many languages spoken. Warmly recommended, 20% discount for Handbook users. **B** *Nordeste Palace*, R Assunção 99 in centre, T/F221 1999. Large rooms, good value. **B** *Ondas Verdes*, Av Beira Mar 934, Iracema, T219 0871. Fan, TV. Recommended. **C** *Abrolhos Praia*, Av Abolição 2030, Meireles, T/F2481217, abrolhos@rotaceara.com.br Pleasant, one block from beach, internet access. **C** *Pousada Jambo*, R Antônia Augusto 141, T219 3873, T9929481 (mob). Very private, no sign, quiet street, variety of rooms, some with kitchens at no extra cost, small pool, a/c, cheaper with fan, Swiss run, changes cash and TCs. Warmly recommended. **C** *Pousada da Praia*, Av Monsenhor Tabosa 1315, Iracema, 2 blocks from beach, T248 5935, F261 1104. With a/c, fridge, OK. **C** *Villamaris*, Av Abolição 2026, Meireles, T248 3834, villamaris@fortalnet.com.br Cosy, security guard, TV, fridge, small rooftop pool, one block from beach. **D** Pousada Beleza Tropical, R Dom Joaquim 132, T219 0515, www.btropical.hpg.com.br A/c, hot water, TV, fridge, breakfast by the pool, good. **D** *Caxambu*, Gen Bezerril 22, T/F226 2301. A/c, with breakfast, central (opposite Cathedral), good value. **D** *Dom Luis*, R Ildefonso Albano 245, T/F219 1321. Quiet street, small terrace/garden and bar, TV, a/c, fridge, laundry, good value. Recommended. **D** *Passeio*, R Dr João

Fortaleza

■ **Sleeping**	3 Caxambu	7 Imperial Othon Palace
1 Abrolhos Praia	4 Chevalier	8 Nordeste Palace
& Villamaris	5 Colonial Praia	9 Ondas Verdes
2 Beleza Tropical	6 Dom Luis	10 Passeio

Moreira 221, Centro, T226 9640, F253 6165. Opposite lovely park and Centro Turismo, homely, rooms with high ceilings, a/c or fan, good value. Recommended.

Youth hostel D Pousada Atalaia, Av Beira Mar 814, Iracema, T/F219 0658, alberguedajuventude@task.com.br HI, **F** in dormitory, a/c, fan, TV, good breakfast, prices rise in high season. *Coqueiro Verde*, R Frei Monsueto 531, Meireles, T3081 1973. Dormitories, kitchen, laundry facilities, cheap but not very clean, poor breakfast.

Camping *Fortaleza Camping Club*, R Pedro Paulo Moreira 505, Parque Manibura, Água Fria, 12 km, T273 2544, many trees for shade, US$7 pp. *Barra Encantada*, Praia do Barro Preto, Iguape, 42 km southeast (reservations in Fortaleza, T370 1173), US$9 pp, Camping Club members US$4 pp, see East Coast below. *Fazenda Lagoa das Dunas*, Uruaú (115 km southeast), T244 2929, US$4 pp Camping Club members, US$9 pp others; also rents rooms. See Beberibe, East Coast below.

Expensive Several good fish restaurants at Praia de Mucuripe, where the boats come ashore between 1300 and 1500. Recommended on Av Beira Mar, Meireles are: *Alfredo*, No 4616, and, next door, No 4632, *Peixada do Meio*. *Francés-Italiano*, Av Des Moreira 155. Good lobster. **Mid-range** *Amici's*, R Dragão do Mar 80. Pasta, pizza and lively atmosphere in music-filled street, evenings only. *Carneiro de Ordones*, R Azevedo Bolão 571, Parquelândia, near North Shopping. Crowded with locals at weekends for every kind of lamb dish. **Cheap** *Churrascaria Picanha de Veras*, R Carlos Vasconcelos 660, Aldeota. Good for chicken. *Dom Pastel*, R Carlos Vasconcelos 996, Aldeota. Pay-by-weight. *R Julo Ibiapina*, this street in Meireles, one block behind beach, has pizzerias, fast food restaurants and sushi bars. *Casa Nossa*, Barão de Aracati, adjacent to *Holiday Inn*, self-service (lunch only), part-covered courtyard, where the locals eat, excellent value. Recommended. *Habib*, Antônio Justa Abolição, corner with Av Barão de Studart. Modern middle-eastern fast-food restaurant, excellent service, set menus are a bargain, good deserts. Highly recommended. **Centre Expensive** Emcetur restaurant, *Xadrez*, in

Eating
● *on map*
At Praia de Iracema, good outdoor nightlife and a collection of cafés on the beach serve good fast food and great coffee

Brazil

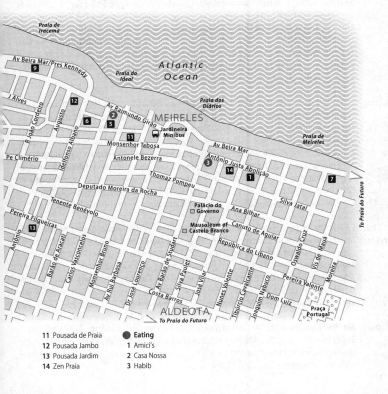

11 Pousada de Praia
12 Pousada Jambo
13 Pousada Jardim
14 Zen Praia

● **Eating**
1 Amici's
2 Casa Nossa
3 Habib

the old prison, good atmosphere, overpriced, open to 2400, reported safe to 2100. **Cheap** Several options around and in the railway station. *Alivita*, Barão do Rio Branco 1486. Good for fish and vegetarian, lunch only, Mon-Fri. *Fonte de Saúde*, R Pedro 339. Excellent vegetarian food, sold by weight, and a wide range of fruit juices.

Bars & clubs

Fortaleza is renowned for its night life and prides itself with having the liveliest Mon night in the country

Some of the best areas for entertainment, with many bars and restaurants are: the Av Beira Mar, Praia de Iracema, the hill above Praia de Mucuripe and Av Dom Luís. The streets around Centro Cultural Dragão do Mar on R Dragão do Mar are lively every night of the week. Brightly painted, historic buildings house restaurants where musicians play to customers and the pavements are dotted with cocktail carts. *Caros Amigos*, R Dragão do Mar, 22. Live music at 2030: Tue, Brazilian instrumental; Wed, jazz; Thu, samba; Sun, Beatles covers, $US1. *Chopp do Bixiga* , lively outdoor corner bar. Some recommended bars: *Espaço Cultural Diogo Fontenelle*, R Gustavo Sampaio 151, art gallery and bar with live music.

Festivals

6 Jan, *Epiphany*; *Ash Wednesday*. 19 Mar, *São José*; *Christmas Eve*; *New Year's Eve*, half-day. The *Festas Juninas* in Ceará are much livelier than carnival. A festival, the *Regata Dragão do Mar*, takes place at Praia de Mucuripe on the last Sun in Jul, during which the traditional *jangada* (raft) races take place. Also during the last week of Jul, the out-of-season Salvador-style carnival, *Fortal*, takes place along Avs Almte Barroso, Raimundo Giro and Beira Mar. On 15 Aug, the local Umbanda *terreiros* (churches) celebrate the *Festival of Iemanjá* on Praia do Futuro, taking over the entire beach from noon till dusk, when offerings are cast into the surf. Well worth attending (members of the public may 'pegar um passo' – enter into an inspired religious trance – at the hands of a *pai-de-santo*).

Sport & activities

Diving *ASPA (Atividades Subaquáticas e Pesquisas Ambientais)*, R Eduardo Garcia 23, s 13, Aldeota, T268 2966. Or *Projeto Netuno*, R do Mirante 165, Mucuripe, T/F263 3009. **Surfing** Surfing is popular on a number of Ceará beaches. *Projeto Salva Surf*, a surfers rescue service operated by the fire department, may be reached by dialing 193. **Trekking** The Fortaleza chapter of the *Trekking Club do Brasil* has walks once a month to different natural areas; visitors welcome, US$20 for transport and T-shirt, T212 2456. **Windsurfing** A number of Ceará beaches are excellent for windsurfing; equipment can be rented in some of the more popular beaches such as Porto das Dunas and in the city from *Windclub*, Av Beira Mar 2120, Praia dos Diários, T982 5449, lessons also available.

Shopping

Fortaleza has an excellent selection of locally manufactured textiles, which are among the cheapest in Brazil, and a wide selection of regional handicrafts. The local craft specialities are lace and embroidered textile goods; also hammocks (US$15 to over US$100), fine alto-relievo wood carvings of northeast scenes, basket ware, leatherwork and clay figures (*bonecas de barro*). Bargaining is OK at the *Mercado Central*, Av Alberto Nepomuceno (closed Sun), and the *Emcetur Centro de Turismo* in the old prison. Crafts also available in shops near the market. The *Sine* shop, at R Dr João Moreira 429, is part of a state government initiative to promote small independent producers. Every night (1800-2300) there are stalls along the beach at Praia Meireiles. Crafts also available in the commercial area along Av Monsenhor Tabosa.

Tour operators

City and beach tours: *Lavila*, Rui Barbosa 1055, T261 4777. Recommended. *Lafuente Turismo*, Av Senador Virgílio Távora 496, T242 1010. Boat tours: *Ceará Saveiro*, Av Beira Mar 4294, T263 1085. Sailboat and yacht trips, daily 1000-1200 and 1600-1800 from Praia de Mucuripe. *Martur*, Av Beira Mar 4260, T263 1203. Sailing boat and schooner trips, from Mucuripe, same schedule as above. Tours to the interior by rail and bus: *Turistar*, Praça Castro Carreira at the railway station, T212 3090/982 4675, F212 2456. Helpful with general information. *BIC*, R Sen Virgílio Távora 480, T242 4599. American Express representative.

Transport

Air Aeroporto Pinto Martins, Praça Eduardo Gomes, 6 km south of centre, T477 1200. Direct flights to major cities. Bus 404 from airport to Praça José de Alencar in the centre, US$0.65, also 066 Papicu to Parangaba and 027 Papicu to Siqueira, or luxury Guanabara service from Beira Mar via Iracema, a/c, US$0.75; taxis US$10.

Bus Rodoviária at Av Borges de Melo 1630, Fátima, 6 km south from centre, T186, ATM outisde left luggage. Many city buses (US$0.65) including 'Aguanambi' 1 or 2 which go from Av Gen Sampaio, 'Barra de Fátima-Rodoviária' from Praça Coração de Jesus, 'Circular' for Av Beira Mar and the beaches. Taxi to Praia de Iracema, US$5. No luggage store, only lockers.

Nordeste: To **Natal**, 7 daily, US$15 *convencional*, US$18 *executivo*, US$29 *leito*, 8 hrs. **João Pessoa**, 3 daily, US$18 *convencional*, 10 hrs. **Guanabara**, to **Recife**, 5 daily, US$27 convencional, US$33 executivo, US$40 *leito*, 12 hrs, book early for weekend travel. *Itapemirim* to **Salvador**, US$33, 21 hrs. *Timbira* and *Boa Esperança*: to **Teresina**, several daily, US$13.50, 10 hrs. To **Belém**, 2 daily, US$35 *convencional*, US$40.25 *executivo*, 23 hrs (Expresso Timbira also sells Belém-Manaus boat tickets). **Piripiri**, for Parque Nacional de Sete Cidades, US$11, 9 hrs, a good stop en route to Belém. *Guanabara* to **São Luís**, 3 daily, US$27, 18 hrs.

Car hire *HM*, R Vicente Leite 650, Aldeota, T261 7799, cars and buggies. *Loc Car*, Av Virgílio Távora 206, Aldeota, T224 8594, cars and buggies. *Loca Buggy*, Av Beira Mar 2500, Meireles, T/F242 6945.

Directory

Brazil

Airline offices On Av Santos Dumont, Aldeota are: *Varig*, No 2727, T266 8000. *Vasp*, No 3060, sala 803, T244 6222/0800-998277. *TAM*, Av Santos Dumont 2849, T261 0916. **Banks** *Banco do Nordeste*, R Major Facundo 372, a/c, helpful, open 0900-1630. Recommended. TCs exchanged and cash with Visa at *Banco do Brasil*, R Barão do Rio Branco 1500, also on Av Abolição. *Banco Mercantil do Brasil*, Rua Major Facundo 484, Centro, Praca do Ferreira: cash against MasterCard. Cirrus/MasterCard ATM at international airport; others at *HSBC* and *Banco 24 Horas* throughout the city. ATM for Cirrus/MasterCard and Visa outside cinema at Centro Cultural Dragão do Mar. Also at Av Antonio Sales and *Iguatemi Shopping*. Exchange at *Tropical Viagens*, R Barão do Rio Branco 1233, T221 3344, *Libratur*, Av Abolição 2794. Recommended. *ACCtur*, has exchange booths for dollars (cash and TCs) throughout the city, main office Av Dom Luís 176, Aldeota, T261 9955. **Communications** Internet: Cybercafés at Av Beira-Mar 2120, Aldeota, open 0800-2230, US$3.50 per hr, and outside Avenida Shopping, Av Dom Luís 300, US$2.50 per hr. *Abrolhos Praia*, Av Abolição 2030, Meireles, part of hotel of same name, US$2.50 per hr, open daily, closes 1400 Sun. **Post Office:** main branch at R Senador Alencar 38, Centro; Av Monsenhor Tabosa 1109, Iracema; at train station. Parcels must be taken to Receita Federal office at Barão de Aracati 909, Aldeota (take 'Dom Luiz' bus). **Telephone:** international calls from *Emcetur* hut on Iracema beach and from offices of *Telemar*; at rodoviária and airport. **Embassies and consulates** Belgium, R Eduardo Garcia 609, Aldeota, T264 1500. **Denmark**, R Inácio Capelo 50, Colônia, T228 5055, open 0800-1800. **France**, R Bóris 90, Centro, T254 2822. **Germany**, R Dr Lourenço 2244, Meireles, T246 2833. **Sweden** and **Norway**, R Leonardo Mota 501, Aldeota, T242 0888. **Switzerland**, R Dona Leopoldina 697, Centro, T226 9444. **UK**, c/o Grupo Edson Queiroz, Praça da Imprensa s/n, Aldeota, T466 8580, F261 8763, annette@edson queiroz.com.br **US**, Nogueira Acioli 891, Centro, T252 1539. **Medical services** Instituto Dr José Frota (IJF), R Barão do Rio Branco 1618, T255 5000. Recommended public hospital. **Tourist offices** Setur, state tourism agency; Centro Administrativo Virgílio Távora, Cambeba, T488 3900, www.setur.ce.gov.br Information booths at Centro de Turismo, T488 7411, has maps, information about beach tours (0700-1800, Sun 0700-1200); rodoviária, T256 4080 (0600-1800 daily), airport, T477 1667 (24 hrs) and Farol de Mucuripe, T263 1115 (0700-1730). Tourist police, R Silva Paulet 505, Aldeota, T261 3769/445 8112.

Aquiraz, 31 km east of Fortaleza, first capital of Ceará which conserves several colonial buildings and has a religious art museum, is the access point for the following beaches: **Prainha**, 6 km east, a fishing village and 10 km long beach with dunes, clean and largely empty. You can see *jangadas* coming in daily in the late afternoon. The village is known for its lacework: you can see the women using the *bilro* and *labirinto* techniques at the **Centro de Rendeiras**. 18 km southeast of Aquiraz is **Praia Iguape**, another fishing and lacework village, 3 km south of which is **Praia Barro Preto**, wide, tranquil, with sand dunes, palms and lagoons. All these beaches have accommodation. ■ *Daily bus service to all these beaches from Fortaleza rodoviária; Prainha, 11 daily, US$1; Iguape, hourly between 0600 and 1900, US$1.10.*

Eastern coast
For bus information in Fortaleza, T272 1999

Cascavel (Colour map 5, grid B5), 62 km southeast of Fortaleza (Saturday crafts fair), is the access point for the beaches of **Caponga and Águas Belas**, where traditional fishing villages coexist with fancy weekend homes and hotels. ■ *Direct bus from Fortaleza rodoviária (4 a day, US$1.30) or take a bus from Fortaleza to Cascavel (80 mins) then a bus from Cascavel (20 mins); bus information in Caponga T334 1485.*

Some 4 km from **Beberibe**, 78 km from Fortaleza, is **Morro Branco**, with a spectacular beach, coloured craggy cliffs and beautiful views. *Jangadas* leave the beach at 0500, returning at 1400-1500, lobster is the main catch in this area. The coloured sands of the dunes are bottled into beautiful designs and sold along with other crafts such as lacework, embroidery and straw goods. *Jangadas* may be hired for sailing (one hr for up to six people US$30). Beach buggies (full day US$100) and taxis are also for hire. The beach can get very crowded at holiday times. Recommended hotels: **B** *Recanto Praiano*, T224 7118, and **C** *Pousada Sereia*, T330 1144. You can rent fishermen's houses. Meals can also be arranged at beach-front bars. South of Morro Branco and 6 km from Beberibe is **Praia das Fontes**, which also has coloured cliffs with sweet-water springs; there is a fishing village and a lagoon. South of Praia das Fontes are several less developed beaches including **Praia Uruaú** or **Marambaia**. The beach is at the base of coloured dunes, there is a fishing village with some accommodation. Just inland is Lagoa do Uruaú, the largest in the state and a popular place for watersports. Buggy from Morro Branco US$45 for four.

Transport *São Benedito* bus from Fortaleza to Morro Branco, US$2.15; 2½ hrs, 5 a day. To Natal, take 0600 bus to Beberibe, then 0800 bus (only 1) to Aracati, US$0.60, then on to Natal.

Canoa Quebrada

Colour map 5, grid B5
The town's telephone numbers are 421 1401 and 421 1761, 3-digit numbers below are extension numbers

On the shores of the Rio Jaguaribe, **Aracati** is the access point to the southeast-ern-most beaches of Ceará; it is along the main BR-304. The city is best known for its Carnival and for its colonial architecture. **B** *Pousada Litorânea*, R Col Alexandrino 1251, T421 1001, a/c, **D** with fan, near rodoviária. ■ *Natal-Aracati bus via Mossoró, 6 hrs, US$7.50; from Mossoró (90 km) US$2.50, 2 hrs; Fortaleza-Aracati (142 km), São Benedito, Guanabara or Nordeste many daily, US$4, 2 hrs; Aracati-Canoa Quebrada from Gen Pompeu e João Paulo, US$0.60; taxi US$3.60.*

About 10 km from Aracati is Canoa Quebrada on a sand dune, famous for its *labirinto* lacework and coloured sand sculpture, for sand-skiing on the dunes, for the sunsets, and for the beaches. There are many bars, restaurants and *forró* establishments. To avoid biting insects (*bicho do pé*), wear shoes. There is nowhere to change money except *Banco do Brasil* in Aracati. In the second half of July the *Canoarte Festival* takes place, it includes a *jangada* regatta and music festival. ■ *Fortaleza-Canoa Quebrada, São Benedito, 3 daily, US$4.25. Fortaleza-Majorlândia, São Benedito, 4 daily, US$4.25.*

The town's telephone number is 421 1748, 3-digit numbers are extensions

South of Canoa Quebrada and 13 km from Aracati is **Majorlândia**, an attractive village, with many-coloured sand dunes and a wide beach with strong waves, good for surfing; the arrival of the fishing fleet in the evening is an important daily event; lobster is the main catch. It is a popular weekend destination with beach homes for rent and Carnaval here is lively. (**C** *Pousada Esquina das Flores*, T188. **D** *Pousada do Gaúcho*, R do Jangadeiro 323, T195, with restaurant. **D** *Pousada e Restaurante Requinte*, 100 m before beach on main road, airy rooms with or without bath, use of kitchen.)

Sleeping Canoa Quebrada: **B** *Pousada Latitude*, R Dragão do Mar, T323. A/c, fridge, cheaper with fan, restaurant. **C** *Pousada do Rei*, R Nascer do Sol 112, T316. Fan, fridge. Highly recommended. **C** *Pousada Maria Alice*, R Dragão do Mar, T421 1852. Fan, restaurant, safe. **C** *Pousada Alternativa*, R Francisco Caraço, T335. With or without bath, central. Recommended. **C** *Pousada Via Láctea*, off the main street (so quieter). Beautiful view of beach which is 50 m away, some rooms with hot shower, fridge, fan, good breakfast, safe parking, horse and buggy tours, English spoken. Highly recommended. **C** *Tenda do Cumbe*, at end of the road on cliff, T421 1761. Thatched huts, restaurant. Warmly recommended. **D** *Pousada do Holandês*, R Nascer do Sol. Rooms without bath (**E**), no breakfast, kitchen use. **E** *Pousada California*, R Nascer do Sol 136, T/F416 1039, california@secrel.com.br A/c, TV, pool, bar, jeep tours, horse riding available. **F** *Pousada Quebramar*, on the beach front, T416 1044. With breakfast, safe, hot water. Villagers will let you sling your hammock or put you up cheaply (Verónica is recommended, European books exchanged; Sr Miguel rents good clean houses for US$10 a day).

Paracuru, a fishing port which has the most important Carnaval on the northwest coast, is 2 hours by bus from Fortaleza and . West of Paracuru, about 120 km from Fortaleza and 12 km from the town of Paraipaba, is **Lagoinha**, a very scenic beach, with hills, dunes and palms by the shore; a fishing village is on one of the hills. ■ *Bus from Fortaleza, 3 daily, US$3.15, T272 4483*. Some 7 hours by bus and 230 km from Fortaleza is the sleepy fishing village of **Almofala**, home of the Tremembés Indians who live off the sea and some agriculture. There is electricity, but no hotels or restaurants, although locals rent hammock space and cook meals. Bathing is better elsewhere, but the area is surrounded by dunes and is excellent for hiking along the coast to explore beaches and lobster-fishing communities. In Almofala, the church with much of the town was covered by shifting sands and remained covered for 50 years, reappearing in the 1940s; it has since been restored. There is also a highly praised turtle project. ■ *From Fortaleza 0700 and 1530 daily, US$6, T272 2728.*

Jijoca de Jericoacoara (Gijoca) near the south shore of scenic Lagoa Paraíso (or Lagoa Jijoca) is the access point for **Jericoacoara**, or Jeri as the locals call it (Phone code: 0xx88). One of the most famous beaches of Ceará and all Brazil, it has towering sand dunes, deserted beaches with little shade, cactus-covered cliffs rising from the sea and interesting rock formations. Its atmosphere has made it popular with Brazilian and international travellers, with crowds at weekends mid-December to mid-February, in July and during Brazilian holidays. Electricity depends on generators until it is fully installed. Jericoacoara is part of an environmental protection area which includes a large coconut grove, lakes, dunes and hills covered in *caatinga* vegetation.

Watching the sunset from the top of the large dune just west of town, followed by a display of capoeira on the beach, has become a tradition among visitors

Western coast

Sleeping

A *Hippopotamus*, R do Forró, T268 2722. With pool, light, fan, restaurant, tours. **B** *Capitão Tomáz*, on east end of beach, T621 0538. Good. Recommended apart from breakfast. **C** *Casa Nostra*, R das Dunas, T961 5509. Nice rooms, good breakfast, can pay with US$ or German marks, money exchange, Italian spoken. Recommended. **C** *Casa do Turismo*, R das Dunas, T669 2000, www.jericoacoara.com Cabins, information, tours, horse rental, bus tickets, telephone calls, post office, exchange. **C** *Papagaio*, Beco do Forró, T/F268 2722 (Fortaleza). Recommended, runs tours. **C** *Pousada Renata*, T621 0554. Patio with hammocks, breakfast, English, Italian and German spoken. **D** *Calanda*, R das Dunas, T621 0544. With solar energy, Swiss run, good rooms, good breakfast, good views, helpful, German, English and Spanish spoken, full moon party every month. Warmly recommended. **D** *Isalana Praia*, R Principal, T669 2009, isalana@jericoacoara.tur.br A/c, minibar, TV, very helpful, ask for Will Louzada. **E** *Por do Sol*, Bairro Novo Jeri, 1 street west of R das Dunas, behind main dune. Basic, good value. **F** *Pousada Tirol*, R São Francisco 202, T669 2006, www.jericoacoara-tirol.com HI-affiliated, with breakfast, hot water, safe, helpful, great fun. Recommended.

Many establishments operate during high season, only about half close at other times when hotel prices go down some 30%. The town's calling centre telephone number is (0xx88) 621 0544; you can leave a message for most hotels through this number

Eating

There are several restaurants serving vegetarian and fish dishes: *Alexandre* (R Oceano Atlântico), *Isabel* (R do Forró), both on the beach, good seafood, pricey. *Acoara do Jerico*, R Principal by the beach, reasonable. Home cooking, all on R Principal: *Samambaia*, good value. *Catavento*, good. *Espaço Aberto*, delicious seafood, pleasant atmosphere. Recommended. *Naturalmente*, on the beach, nice atmosphere, wonderful crêpes. Recommended. *Sorrisa de Natureza* cheap, tasty food. Recommended. Italian food and pizza at: *Pizza Banana*, R Principal, good. *Senzala*, same street, nice, pleasant atmosphere (allows **camping** in its grounds). *Taverna*, opposite *Planeta Jeri*, lovely pasta and pizza. *Cantinho da Masa*, R do Forró, good. Several shops sell basic provisions, so camping is possible.

Bars & clubs

Forró nightly in high season at R do Forró, Wed and Sat in low season, 2200. Action moves to bars when *forró* has stopped about 0200. There are also frequent parties to which visitors are welcome. Once a week in high season there is a folk dance show which includes *capoeira*.

Transport

A *jardineira* (open-sided 4WD truck) meets *Redenção* bus from/to Fortaleza, at Jijoca: 1½ hrs, US$1.05, from Jijoca at 1400, 0200, from Jericoacoara at 0600, 2200, from R das Dunas by Casa do Turismo. At other times pick-ups can be hired in Jijoca, US$6 pp. For a direct connection take the *Redenção* bus leaving Fortaleza 0900 (arrive Jeri 1600) or 2100 (arrive Jeri 0330,

It is not possible to ride from Jijoca to Jericoacoara on a motorcycle

Brazil

Brazil

US$7.50); the 0600 bus from Jeri arrives in Fortaleza 1430, the 2200 bus arrives between 0430 and 0600, from the rodoviária it goes to Praia Iracema; night buses are direct, while daytime ones make many stops; Fortaleza-Jericoacoara US$8.50. 2 or 3-day tours from Fortaleza are available, book through travel agencies. If coming from Belém or other points north and west, go via Sobral (from Belém US$28.25, 20 hrs), where you change for Cruz, 40 km east of Jijoca, a small pleasant town with basic hotels (Sobral-Cruz: Mon-Sat at 1200; Cruz-Sobral: Mon/Wed/Fri at 0400, Tue/Thu/Sat at 0330; US$7.25; 3-4 hrs). Continue to Jijoca the next day (Cruz-Jijoca, daily about 1400, US$1.25, meets *jardineira* for Jeri, Cruz-Jericoacoara, US$2.20).

Western Ceará

At 348 km from Fortaleza is **Ubajara** with an interesting Sunday morning market selling produce of the *sertão*; and 3 km from town is **Parque Nacional Ubajara**, with 563 ha of native highland and *caatinga* brush. The park's main attraction is the Ubajara cave on the side of an escarpment. Fifteen chambers totalling 1,120 m have been mapped, of which 400 m are open to visitors. Access is along a footpath and steps (2-3 hours, take water) or with a cablecar which descends the cliff to the cave entrance. ■ *0830-1630, US$4*. Lighting has been installed in nine caverns of the complex, but a torch and spare batteries may be useful. An *Ibama* guide leads visitors in the cave; the *Ibama* office at the park entrance, 5 km from the caves, is not always helpful and not always open, T0xx85-634 1388. The views of the *sertão* from the upper cablecar platform are superb; beautiful walks among forest and waterfalls and old sugar-mills scattered around the plateau.

Camping is not allowed in the park

Sleeping and eating   Near the park B *Pousada da Neblina*, Estrada do Teleférico, 2 km from town, T/F634 1270. In beautiful cloud forest, swimming pool, with breakfast and private shower (**C** without breakfast) restaurant open 1100-2000. Meals recommended. Campground (US$15 per tent). Opposite is **C** *Pousada Gruta da Ubajara*, rustic, restaurant. Recommended. **D** *Sítio do Alemão*, take Estrada do Teleférico 2 km from town, after the Pousada da Neblina turn right, 1 km to Sítio Santana, in the coffee plantation of *Herbert Klein*, on which there are 3 small chalets, with full facilities, excursions, bicycle hire offered, if chalets are full the Kleins accommodate visitors at their house (Caixa Postal 33, Ubajara, CE, CEP 62350-000). Warmly recommended. **Ubajara** town   **C** *Le Village*, on Ibiapina road 4 km south from town, T634 1364. Restaurant, pool, sauna, good value. **D** *Pousada da Neuza*, R Juvêncio Luís Pereira 370, T634 1261. Small restaurant.

Parnaíba

Phone code: 0xx86
Post code: 64200
Colour map 5, grid A4
Population: 132,282

Parnaíba is a relaxed, friendly place, with a regular connection here to Tutóia, for boats across the Parnaíba delta (see page 521). A tour in the delta costs US$20 per person. There is a tourist office, *Peimtur* T321 1532, at Porto das Barcas, a pleasant shopping and entertainment complex with several good restaurants and a large open-air bar on the riverside. **L** *Cívico*, Av Gov Chagas Rodrigues, T322 2470, F322 2028. With a/c, good breakfast. Recommended. **A** *Pusada dos Ventos*, Av São Sebastião 2586, Universidade, T/F322 2177/4880. Pool. Recommended. **D** *Rodoviária*, and other basic hotels in the centre.

Teresina

Phone code: 0xx86
Post code: 64000
Colour map 5, grid B3
Population: 715,360

About 435 km up the Rio Parnaíba is the state capital. The city is reputed to be the hottest after Manaus (temperatures rise to 42°C). The **Palácio de Karnak** (the old governor's palace), just west of Praça Frei Serafim, contains lithographs of the Middle East in 1839 by David Roberts RA. ■ *Mon-Fri 1530-1730*. Also see the Museu do Piauí, Praça Marechal Deodoro. ■ *Tue-Fri 0800-1730, Sat-Sun 0800-1200, US$0.60*. There is an interesting **open market** by the Praça Marechal Deodoro and the river is picturesque, with washing laid out to dry along its banks. The market is a good place to buy hammocks, but bargain hard. Every morning along the river bank there is the **troca-troca** where people buy, sell and swap. An undercover complex (**Mercado Central do Artesanato**) has been built at R Paissandu 1276 (Praça Dom Pedro II). ■ *Mon-Fri 0800-2200*. Most of the year the river is low, leaving sandbanks known as *coroas* (crowns). There is a good, clean supermarket on Praça Marechal Deodoro 937 with fresh food. Local handicrafts include leather and clothes.

L *Rio Poty*, Av Marechal Castelo Branco 555, Ilhota, T223 1500, F222 6671, 5-star. Recommended. **B** *Sambaíba*, R Gabriel Ferreira 230-N, 2-star, T222 6711. Central, good. **D** *Fortaleza*, Felix Pacheco 1101, Praça Saraiva, T222 2984. Fan, basic. Recommended. **D** *Santa Terezinha*, Av Getúlio Vargas 2885, opposite rodoviária, T219 5918. With a/c, cheaper with fan. Many other cheap hotels and *dormitórios* around Praça Saraiva. **D** *Grande*, Firmino Pires 73, very friendly and clean. Many cheap ones in R São Pedro and in R Alvaro Mendes. For fish dishes, *Pesqueirinho*, R Domingos Jorge Velho 6889, in Poty Velho district. *Camarão do Elias*, Av Pedro Almeida 457, T232 5025. Good seafood. *Sabores Rotisserie*, R Simplício Mendes 78, Centro. By kg, good quality and variety. Many eating places for all pockets in Praça Dom Pedro II.

Sleeping & eating

Teresina is proud of its *Carnival*, which is then followed by *Micarina*, a local carnival in Mar. There is much music and dancing in Jul and Aug, when there is a *Bumba-meu-Boi*, the Teresina dance festival, *Festidanças*, and a convention of itinerant guitarists.

Festivals

Air Flights to Fortaleza, Brasília, Rio, São Paulo, São Luís, Belém, Manaus. Buses from outside the airport run straight into town and to the rodoviária. **Bus** The bus trip from **Fortaleza** is scenic and takes 9 hrs (US$13.50). There are direct buses to **Belém** (13 hrs, US$23.40), **Recife** (16 hrs, US$27) and to **São Luís** (7 hrs, US$12).

Transport

Banks There are ATMs for both Visa and MasterCard, eg *Banco 24 Horas – TecBan*, Av João XXIII 2220 **Tourist offices** Piemtur, R Acre s/n, Centro de Convenções, Cabral, T222 6202, piemtur@piemtur.pi.gov.br Information office at R Magalhães Filho s/n (next to 55 N, English spoken); kiosks at rodoviária and airport. **Singtur** (Sindicato dos Guías de Turismo de Piauí), R Paissandu 1276, T221 2175, has information booths at the Centro de Artesanato (helpful), the Encontro das Águas, Poty Velho and on the shores of the Rio Poty.

Directory

Unusual eroded rock formations decorated with mysterious inscriptions are to be found in the Parque Nacional de Sete Cidades, 12 km from Piracuruca. The rock structures are just off the Fortaleza-Teresina road. From the ground it looks like a medley of weird monuments. The inscriptions on some of the rocks have never been deciphered; one theory suggests links with the Phoenicians, and the Argentine Professor Jacques de Mahieu considers them to be Nordic runes left by the Vikings. There is plenty of birdlife, and iguanas, descending from their trees in the afternoon. For park information, contact Ibama, Rod Min Vicente Fialho, Piripiri, CEP 64260-000, T343 1342. Colourful brochures with good map, entrance US$1 plus US$3.30 for compulsory guide. Ibama hostel in the park, **E** pp, pleasant, good restaurant, natural pool nearby, camping (US$5). Local food is limited and monotonous: bring a few delicacies, and especially fruit. Free Ibama bus service leaves the Praça da Bandeira in Piripiri (26 km away), at 0700, passing Hotel Sete Cidades at 0800 (at Km 63 on BR-222, T0xx86-276 2222; also has a free pick-up to the park), reaching the park 10 minutes later. Return at 1630, or hitchhike (to walk takes all day, very hot, start early). Piripiri is a cheap place to break the Belém-Fortaleza journey; several good hotels.

Parque Nacional de Sete Cidades
Colour map 5, grid B4
190 km NE of Teresina

Transport Taxi from Piripiri, US$15, or from Piracuruca, US$21. Bus Teresina-Piripiri and return, throughout the day 2½ hrs, US$4. Bus São Luís-Piripiri, 3 a day, 10 hrs, US$15. Several daily buses Piripiri-Fortaleza, 9 hrs, US$11. Bus Piripiri-Ubajara (see above), marked 'São Benedito', or 'Crateús', 2½ hrs; US$4, first at 0700 (a beautiful trip).

Crossing the Parnaíba delta, which separates Piauí from Maranhão, is possible by boat arriving in Tutóia: an interesting trip through swamps sheltering many birds. This park has 155,000 ha of beaches, lakes and dunes, with very little vegetation and largely unstudied wildlife. It is a strange landscape of shifting white dunes, stretching about

Parque Nacional Lençóis Maranhenses
Colour map 5, grid A3

Brazil

140 km along the coast between **Tutóia** and Primeira Cruz, west of **Barreirinhas**. The best time to visit is during the rainy season (June-September), when the dune valleys fill with water. Reflections of the sky make the water appear vivid blue, a spectacular contrast against brilliant white sand. ■ *Ribamar at Ibama, Av Jaime Tavares 25, São Luís, T231 3010, is helpful on walks and horse rides; national park office: Av Joaquim Soeiro de Carvalho 746, CEP 65590-000, Barreirinhas, T0xx98-349 1155, F231 4332.*

Sleeping Tutóia: **D** *Pousada Em-Bar-Cação*, R Magalhães de Almeida 1064, T479 1219. On the beach, breakfast US$3. Recommended for good food and *tiquira*, a drink made of manioc. **Barreirinhas D** *Pousada Lins*, central praça, T0xx98-349 1203. Shared bath, good but shop around before taking their tours. **D** *Pousada do Baiano*, T0xx98-349 1130. *Pousadas* at Praia Cabure, 5 hrs by boat from Barreirinhas (or truck from Tutóia), friendly, fresh seafood daily.

Transport Parnaíba-Tutóia: bus, 4 hrs, US$6; river boat up the Parnaíba delta, 8 hrs, US$6. Recommended. Private boat hire is also possible. São Luis-Barreirinhas: bus, 4 hrs on a new road, US$12. Private tour buses, US$24, organized bus tours cost US$72.50. Plane (single propeller), 1 hr, US$75. Recommended. A fabulous experience giving panoramic views of the dunes, pilot **Amirton**, T225 2882. Agencies charge about US$200 for a tour with flight. **Boat** Excursions from/to Barreirinhas: regular boat service between Barreirinhas and Atins (7 hrs return, US$5): boat along Rio Preguiça, 4 hrs then 1 hr walk to the dunes, US$12. The only forms of transport that can get across the dunes right into the park are a **jeep** or a **horse**, both about US$15. It is a 2-3 hr walk from Barreirinhas to the park; you will need at least another 2 hrs in the dunes. At Mandacuru, a popular stop on tours of the area, the lighthouse gives a very impressive view.

São Luís

Phone code: 0xx98
Post code: 65000
Colour map 5, grid A3
Population: 870,028
1,070 km W
of Fortaleza
806 km SE of Belém

The capital of Maranhão state, founded in 1612 by the French and named after St Louis of France, is in a region of heavy tropical rains, but the surrounding deep forest has been cut down to be replaced by *babaçu* palms. It stands upon São Luís island between the bays of São Marcos and São José. The urban area extends to São Francisco island, connected with São Luís by three bridges. An old slaving port, the city has a large black population, and has retained much African culture.

Sights   The old part, on very hilly ground with many steep streets, is still almost pure colonial. The historical centre is being restored with UNESCO support and the splendid results (eg the part known as Reviver) rival the Pelourinho of Salvador. The damp climate stimulated the use of ceramic tiles for exterior walls, and São Luís shows a greater variety of such tiles than anywhere else in Brazil, in Portuguese, French and Dutch styles. The commercial quarter (R Portugal, also called R Trapiche) is still much as it was in the 17th century. The best shopping area is R de Santana near Praça João Lisboa. There is a *Funai* shop at R do Sol 371 and a *Centro do Artesanato* in the main street of the São Francisco suburb, over the bridge from the city.

The **Palácio dos Leões** (Governor's Palace), Av Dom Pedro II, has beautiful floors of dark wood (*jacarandá*) and light (*cerejeira*), great views from terrace. ■ *Mon, Wed and Fri 1500-1800.* The restored **Fortaleza de Santo Antônio**, built originally by the French in 1614, is on the bank of the Rio Anil at Ponta d'Areia. The **Fábrica Canhamo**, a restored factory, houses an arts and crafts centre, R São Pantaleão 1232, Madre de Deus, near Praia Grande. ■ *Mon-Fri 0900-1900, T232 2187.* The **Centro da Creatividade Odylo Costa Filho**, R da Alfândego 200, Praia Grande, is an arts centre with theatre, cinema, exhibitions, music, a bar and café; a good meeting place. ■ *Mon-Fri 0800-2200, T231 4058.*

The best colonial churches are the **Cathedral** (1629) on Praça Dom Pedro II, and the churches of **Carmo** (1627), Praça João Lisboa, **São João Batista** (1665), Largo São João, **Nossa Senhora do Rosário** (1717 on R do Egito), and the 18th century **Santana**, R de Santana. On Largo do Desterro is the church of **São José do Desterro**, finished in 1863, but with some much older parts.

The **Cafua das Mercês**, R Jacinto Maia 43, is a museum housed in the old slave market, worth the effort to find: a building opposite the Quartel Militar. ■ *Mon-Fri 1330-1700*. Also visit the Casa dos Negros, next door. **Museu de Artes Visuais**, Av Portugal 289, shows ceramics and post war art. ■ *Mon-Fri 0800-1300, 1600-1800*.

B *Pousada Colonial*, R Afonso Pena 112, T232 2834. In a beautiful restored, tiled house. Recommended. **B** *São Marcos*, Saúde 178, T232 3768. Restored colonial house, a/c, family-run. Recommended. **B** *Vila Rica*, Praça D Pedro II 299, T232 3535, F232 7245, www.hotelvilarica.com.br Central, many amenities. Recommended. **C** *Lord*, R Nazaré 258, T/F221 4655, facing Praça Benedito Leite. Comfortable, good breakfast. Recommended. **D** *Pousada Solar dos Nobres*, R 13 de Maio 82, Centro, T232 5705. Bright, welcoming, superb breakfast, very good. **E** *Hotel Casa Grande*, Rua Isaac Martins 94, Centro, T232 2432. Basic, single, double, triple rooms. Recommended. Many cheap hotels can be found in R da Palma, very central (eg **G** *Pousada Ilha Bela*, safe), and R Formosa. **Youth hostels E-F** *Solar das Pedras*, R da Palma 127, T/F232 6694, aj.solardaspedras.ma@bol.com.br

Sleeping
● *on map*

Base de Edilson, R Alencar Campos 31. Shrimp only, excellent. *Tia Maria*, Av Nina Rodrigues 1 (Ponta d'Areia). Seafood. Recommended. *Base da Lenoca*, R Don Pedro II 181. Good view, seafood, big portions. *La Bohème*, R Isaac Martins 48. Very good food, live music, expensive, popular. *Beiruth 2*, Av Castelo Branco 751-B, T227 8447. Recommended. *Naturalista Alimentos*, R do Sol 517. Very good, natural foods shop and restaurant, open till 1900. *Cia Paulista*, R Portugal e R da Estrela. Good, simple food, cheap. R da Estrela has many eating places with good food and outdoor terraces. There is further choice in the São Francisco district, just across bridge.

Eating
● *on map*

Brazil

São Luís historic centre

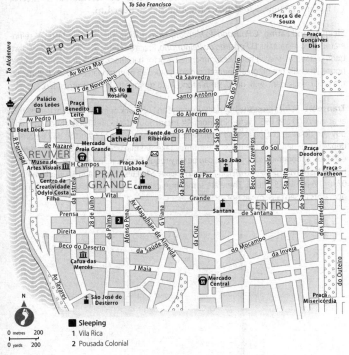

Sleeping
1 Vila Rica
2 Pousada Colonial

0 metres 200
0 yards 200

Festivals On **24 Jun** (São João) is the *Bumba-Meu-Boi*. For several days before the festival street bands parade, particularly in front of the São João and São Benedito churches. There are dances somewhere in the city almost every night in Jun. In **Aug**, *São Benedito*, at the Rosário church.

Transport **Air** Internal flights only, 15 km from centre; buses ('São Cristovão') to city until midnight, US$0.75. **Bus** Rodoviária is 12 km from the centre on the airport road, 'Rodoviária via Alemanha' bus to centre (Praça João Lisboa), US$0.50. Bus to **Fortaleza**, US$27, 4 a day, 18 hrs. To **Belém**, 13 hrs, US$20, *Transbrasiliana*. Also to **Recife**, US$45, 25 hrs, all other major cities and local towns.

Directory **Banks** TCs at *Banco do Brasil*, Praça Deodoro. *HSBC*, off Praça João Lisboa. Accepts MasterCard/Maestro. *Agetur*, R do Sol 33-A, T231 2377. **Communications** Telecommunications: Embratel, Av Dom Pedro II 190. **Language courses** Portuguese lessons: Sra Amin Castro, T227 1527. Recommended. **Medical services** Clínica São Marcelo, R do Passeio 546, English speaking doctor. **Tourist office**, Av Jerónimo de Albuquerque s/n, Ed Clodomir 5th floor, Calhau, T227 5564, planomaior@geplan.ma.gov.br

Alcântara
Colour map 5,
grid A3
Population: 21,291

Some 22 km away by boat is Alcântara the former state capital, on the mainland bay of São Marcos. Construction of the city began at the beginning of the 17th century and it is now a historical monument. There are many old churches, such as the ruined **Matriz de São Matias** – 1648, and colonial mansions (see the **Casa**, and **Segunda Casa, do Imperador,** also the old cotton barons' mansions with their blue, Portuguese tiled façades). In the Praça Gomes de Castro is the pillory, the **Pelourinho** (1648), also a small museum (0900-1300, US$0.20) and the **Forte de São Sebastião** (1663) now in ruins. See also the **Fonte de Mirititiua** (1747). Canoe trips go to **Ilha do Livramento**, good beaches, good walking around the coast (can be muddy after rain), mosquitoes after dark. A rocket-launching site has been built nearby. Principal festivals: **Festa do Divino**, at Pentecost (Whitsun); 29 June, **São Pedro**; early August, **São Benedito**.

Sleeping and eating C *Pousada do Mordomo Régio*, R Grande 134, T337 1197. TV, refrigerator, good restaurant. **D** *Pousada do Pelourinho*, Praça de Matriz 55, T337 1257. Breakfast, good restaurant, shared bath. Recommended. Ask for hammock space or rooms in private houses, friendly but no great comfort; provide your own mineral water. *Bar do Lobato*, on the praça, is pleasant, with good, simple food, fried shrimps highly recommended.

Transport Ferries cross the bay daily, leaving São Luís dock or from São Francisco district at about 0700 and 0930, returning from Alcântara about 0815 and 1600: check time and buy the ticket at the *hidroviária* (west end of R Portugal, T232 0692) the day before as departure depends on the tides. The journey takes 90 mins, return US$15, worth paying extra for 'panorámica' seat. The sea can be very rough between Sep and Dec. Old wooden boats the *Newton Bello* and *Mensageiro da Fé* leave São Luís at 0630 and 1600 returning at 0730 (1½ hrs, US$5 return). There are sometimes catamaran tours bookable through tour operators in São Luís, meals not included.

Northern Brazil

Brasília

The area is drained by the mighty Amazon, which in size, volume of water – 12 times that of the Mississippi – and number of tributaries has no equal in the world. At the base of the Andes, far to the west, the Amazonian plain is 1,300 km in width, but east of the confluences of the Madeira and Negro rivers with the Amazon, the highlands close in upon it until there is no more than 80 km of floodplain between them. Towards the river's mouth – about 320 km wide – the plain widens once more and extends along the coast southeastwards into the state of Maranhão and northwards into the Guianas.

Brazilian Amazônia, much of it still covered with tropical forest, is 56% of the national area. Its jungle is the world's largest and densest rain forest, with more diverse plants and animals than any other jungle in the world. It has only 8% of Brazil's population, and most of this is concentrated around Belém (in Pará), and in Manaus, 1,600 km up the river. The population is sparse because other areas are easier to develop.

Successive modern Brazilian governments have made strenuous efforts to develop Amazônia. Roads have been built parallel to the Amazon to the south (the Transamazônica), from Cuiabá (Mato Grosso) northwards to Santarém (Pará), and northeast from Porto Velho through Humaitá to the river bank opposite Manaus. Unsuccessful attempts were made to establish agricultural settlements along these roads; major energy and mining projects for bauxite and iron ore are bringing rapid change. More environmental damage has been caused to the region by gold prospectors (*garimpeiros*), especially by their indiscriminate use of mercury, than by organized mining carried out by large state and private companies using modern extraction methods. The most important cause of destruction, however, has been large scale deforestation to make way for cattle ranching, with logging for hardwoods for the Asian markets coming a close second.

There is a gradually growing awareness among many Brazilians that their northern hinterland is a unique treasure and requires some form of protection and recently some encouraging moves have been made. On the other hand, government is still intent upon some form of development in the region, as its seven-year Avança Brasil programme demonstrated. Scientists argued in 2001 that if the plan went ahead, its road improvement and other elements would lead to a loss of between 28% and 42% of Amazon rainforest by 2020, with only about 5% of the region untouched. This report led to a reassessment of the plan.

Background

Northern Brazil consists of the states of Pará, Amazonas, Amapá and Roraima. The states of Rondônia and Acre are dealt with under Southern Amazônia

Climate

The rainfall is heavy, but varies throughout the region; close to the Andes, up to 4,000 mm annually, under 2,000 at Manaus. Rains occur throughout the year but the wettest season is between Dec and May, the driest month is Oct. The humidity can be extremely high and the temperature averages 26°C. There can be cold snaps in Dec in the western reaches of the Amazon basin. The soil, as in all tropical forest, is poor.

Up the Amazon River

Rivers are the arteries of Amazônia for the transport of both passengers and merchandise. The two great ports of the region are Belém, at the mouth of the Amazon, and Manaus at the confluence of the Rio Negro and Rio Solimões. Manaus is the hub of river transport, with regular shipping services east to Santarém and Belém along the lower Amazon, south to Porto Velho along the Rio Madeira, west to Tabatinga (the border with Colombia and Peru) along the Rio Solimões and northwest to São Gabriel da Cachoeira along the Rio Negro. There is also a regular service connecting Belém and Macapá, on the northern shore of the Amazon Delta, and Santarém and Macapá. The size and quality of vessels varies greatly, with the largest and most comfortable ships generally operating on the Manaus-Belém route. Hygiene, food and service are reasonable on most vessels but **overcrowding** is a common problem.

The Amazon system is 6,577 km long, of which 3,165 km are in Brazilian territory. Ships of up to 4-5,000 tonnes regularly negotiate the Amazon for a distance of about 3,646 km up to Iquitos, Peru

Many of the larger ships offer air-conditioned berths with bunkbeds and, for a higher price, 'suites', with a private bathroom (in some cases, this may also mean a double bed instead of the standard bunkbed). The cheapest way to travel is 'hammock class'; on some routes first class (upper deck) and second class (lower deck) hammock space is available, but on many routes this distinction does not apply. Some new boats have air-conditioned hammock space. Although the idea of swinging in a hammock may sound romantic, the reality is you will probably be squeezed in with other passengers, possibly next to the toilets, and have difficulty sleeping because of **noise** and an aching back. Most boats have some sort of rooftop bar serving expensive drinks and snacks.

Riverboat travel is no substitute for visiting the jungle. Except for a few birds and the occasional dolphin, little wildlife is seen. However, it does offer an insight into the vastness of Amazônia and a chance to meet some of its people, making a very pleasant experience. Extensive local inquiry and some flexibility in one's schedule are indispensable for river travel. **Agencies** on shore can inform you of the arrival and departure dates for several different ships, as well as the official (highest) prices for each, and they are sometimes amenable to bargaining. Whenever possible, **see the vessel** yourself (it may mean a journey out of town) and have a chat with the captain or business manager to confirm departure time, length of voyage, ports of call, price, etc. Inspect cleanliness in the kitchen, toilets and showers. All boats are cleaned up when in port, but if a vessel is reasonably clean upon arrival then chances are that it has been kept that way throughout the voyage. You can generally arrange to sleep on board a day or two before departure and after arrival, but be sure to secure carefully your belongings when in port. If you take a berth, lock it and keep the key even if you will not be moving in right away. If you are travelling hammock class, board ship at least 6-8 hrs before sailing in order to secure a good spot (away from the toilets and the engine and check for leaks in the deck above you). Be firm but considerate of your neighbours as they will be your intimate companions for the duration of the voyage. Always keep your gear locked. Take some light warm clothing, it can get very chilly at night.

Compare fares for different ships and remember that prices may fluctuate with supply and demand. Most ships sail in the evening and the first night's supper is not provided. Empty cabins are sometimes offered to foreigners at reduced rates once boats have embarked. **Payment** is usually in advance. Insist on a signed ticket indicating date, vessel, class of passage, and berth number if applicable.

All ships carry cargo as well as passengers and the amount of cargo will affect the length of the voyage because of weight (especially when travelling upstream) and loading/unloading at intermediate ports. All but the smallest boats will transport vehicles, but these are often damaged by rough handling. Insist on the use of proper ramps and check for adequate clearance. Vehicles can also be transported aboard cargo barges. These are usually cheaper and passengers may be allowed to accompany their car, but check about food, sanitation, where you will sleep (usually in a hammock slung beneath a truck), and adequate shade.

Prices vary according to the vessel; generally it is not a good idea to go with the cheapest fare you are quoted

The following are the **major shipping routes** in Amazônia, indicating intermediate ports, average trip durations, and fares. Facilities in the main ports are described in the appropriate city sections below. Not all ships stop at all intermediate ports. There are many other routes and vessels providing extensive local service. All **fares shown are one-way only** and include all meals unless otherwise stated; berth and suite fares are for two people, hammocks per person. Information is generally identical for the respective return voyages (except Belém-Manaus, Manaus-Belém).

Boat services   **Belém-Manaus** via Breves, Almeirim, Prainha, Monte Alegre, Curua-Uná, Santarém, Alenquer, Óbidos, Juruti, and Parintins on the lower Amazon. 5-6 days upriver, 4 days downriver, including 18-hr stop in Santarém, suite US$315 upriver, 225 down, double berth US$165 upriver, 135 down, hammock space US$67 upriver, US$60 down. Vehicles: small car US$225, combi US$300 usually including driver, other passengers extra, 4WD US$415 with 2 passengers; motorcycle US$70. The Belém-Manaus route is very busy. Try to get a cabin.

Belém-Santarém, same intermediate stops as above. 2½ days upriver, 1½ days downriver, fares suite US$135, berth US$125, hammock US$40 up river, US$35 down. All vessels sailing Belém-Manaus will call in Santarém.

Santarém-Manaus, same intermediate stops as above. 2 days upriver, 1½ days downriver, fares berth US$77, hammock US$27. All vessels sailing Belém-Manaus will call in Santarém and there are others operating only the Santarém-Manaus. Speedboats (*lanchas*) are sometimes available on this route, 16 hrs sitting, no hammock space, US$30.

Belém-Macapá (Porto Santana) non-stop, 24 hrs on large ships, double berth US$100, hammock space US$27 pp, meals not included but can be purchased onboard (expensive), vehicle US$80, driver not included. Same voyage via Breves, 36 to 48 hrs on smaller riverboats, hammock space US$22.50 pp including meals. See page 531.

Macapá (Porto Santana)-Santarém via Vida Nova, Boca do Jari, Almeirim, Prainha, and Monte Alegre on the lower Amazon (does not call in Belém), 2 days upriver, 1½ days downriver, berth US$118, hammock US$36.

Manaus-Porto Velho via Borba, Manicoré, and Humaitá on the Rio Madeira. 4 days upriver, 3½ days downriver (up to 7 days when the river is low), double berth US$165, hammock space US$60 pp, vehicle US$200. Many passengers go only as far as Humaitá and take a bus from there to Porto Velho, much faster.

Manaus-Tefé via Codajás and Coari, 24 to 36 hrs, double berth US$63, hammock space US$18 pp. Boats every other day to Tabatinga (also Varig flights Manaus-Tefé-Tabatinga).

Manaus-Tabatinga via Fonte Boa (3 days), Foz do Jutaí, Tonantins (4 days), Santo Antônio do Içá, Amaturá, Monte Cristo, São Paulo de Olivença (5 days) and Benjamin Constant along the Rio Solimões. Up to 8 days upriver (depending on cargo), 3 days downriver, suite US$180, double cabin US$120, hammock space US$60 pp upriver, cheaper down (the *Voyager* fleet is recommended).

Manaus-São Gabriel da Cachoeira via Novo Airão, Moura, Carvoeiro, Barcelos, and Santa Isabel do Rio Negro along the Rio Negro. Berth US$162, hammock US$55, most locals prefer to travel by road.

What to take A hammock is essential on all but the most expensive boats; it is often too hot to lie down in a cabin during day. Light cotton hammocks seem to be the best solution. Buy a wide one on which you can lie diagonally; lying straight along it leaves you hump-backed. A climbing carabiner clip is useful for fastening hammocks to runner bars of boats. It is also useful for securing baggage, making it harder to steal.

Health
See also Health, Essentials, page 60

There is a danger of malaria in Amazônia. Mosquito nets are not required when in motion as boats travel away from the banks and too fast for mosquitoes to settle, though repellent is a boon for night stops. From Apr to Oct, when the river is high, the mosquitoes can be repelled by *Super Repelex* spray or *K13*. A yellow-fever inoculation is strongly advised; it is compulsory in some areas and may be administered on the spot with a pressurized needle gun. The larger ships must have an infirmary and carry a health officer. Drinking water is generally taken on in port (ie city tap water), but taking your own mineral water is a good idea.

Food Ample but monotonous, better food is sometimes available to cabin passengers. Meal times can be chaotic. Fresh fruit is a welcome addition; also take plain biscuits, tea bags, seasonings, sauces and jam. Fresh coffee is available; most boats have a bar of sorts. Plates and cutlery may not be provided. Bring your own plastic mug as drinks are served in plastic beakers which are jettisoned into the river. A strong fishing line and a variety of hooks can be an asset for supplementing one's diet; with some meat for bait, *piranhas* are the easiest fish to catch. Negotiate with the cook over cooking your fish. The sight of you fishing will bring a small crowd of new friends, assistants, and lots of advice – some of it useful.

66 99 *The South American Handbook 1924*

On travelling up the Amazon *Ocean liners of 7,000 tons regularly negotiate the Amazon for a distance of 1,000 miles up to Manáos, well in the heart of the continent. Travelling by Booth Lines steamer from Liverpool the passenger penetrates the Equatorial forests of Brazil without change of cabin.*

In Amazônia Inevitably fish dishes are very common, including many fish with Indian names, eg *pirarucu, tucunaré,* and *tambaqui,* which are worth trying. Also shrimp and crab dishes (more expensive). Specialities of Pará include duck, often served in a yellow soup made from the juice of the root of the manioc (*tucupi*) with a green vegetable (*jambu*); this dish is the famous *pato no tucupi,* highly recommended. Also *tacaca* (shrimps served in *tucupi*), *vatapá* (shrimps served in a thick sauce, highly filling, simpler than the variety found in Salvador), *maniçoba* (made with the poisonous leaves of the bitter cassava, simmered for 8 days to render it safe – tasty). *Caldeirada,* a fish and vegetable soup, served with *pirão* (manioc puree) is a speciality of Amazonas. There is also an enormous variety of tropical and jungle fruits, many unique to the region. Try them fresh, or in ice creams or juices. Avoid food from street vendors.

Belém

Phone code: 0xx91
Post code: 66000
Colour map 5,
grid A1
Population:
1.3 million

Belém (do Pará) is the great port of the Amazon. It is hot (mean temperature, 26°C), but frequent showers freshen the streets. There are some fine squares and restored historic buildings set along broad avenues. Belém used to be called the 'City of Mango Trees' and there are many such trees remaining. The largest square is the **Praça da República** where there are free afternoon concerts; the main business and shopping area is along the wide Av Presidente Vargas leading to the river and the narrow streets which parallel it. The neoclassical **Teatro da Paz** (1868-74) is one of the largest theatres in the country. It stages performances by national and international stars and also gives free concert and theatre shows; worth visiting, recently restored. ■ *Tue-Fri 0900-1800, tours US$1.50.* Visit the **Cathedral** (1748), another neoclassical building which contains several remarkable paintings. ■ *Mon 1500-1800, Tue-Fri 0800-1100, 1530-1800.* It stands on Praça Frei Caetano Brandão, opposite the 18th-century **Santo Aleixandre** church which is noted for its wood carving. The 17th-century **Mercês** church (1640), near the market, is the oldest church in Belém; it forms part of an architectural group known as the Mercedário, the rest of which was heavily damaged by fire in 1978 and is being restored.

Belém

■ **Sleeping**
1 Central
2 Hilton & Restaurante Açaí
3 Itaoca
4 Le Massilia
5 Novo Avenida
6 Palácio das Musas
7 Regente
8 Sete-Sete
9 Ver-o-Peso
10 Vitória Régia
11 Zoghbi Park

● **Eating**
1 Cantina Italiana
2 Casa Portuguesa
3 Churrascaria Rodeio
4 Churrascaria Tucuruvi
5 Círculo Militar
6 Lá em Casa
7 Miako

Brazil

The **Basílica of Nossa Senhora de Nazaré** (1909), built from rubber wealth in romanesque style, is an absolute must for its stained glass windows and beautiful marble. ■ *Mon-Sat 0500-1130, 1400-2000, Sun 0545-1130, 1430-2000*. It is on Praça Julho Chermont on Av Magalhães Barata. A museum at the basilica describes the Círio de Nazaré religious festival. The **Palácio Lauro Sodré** or **Museu do Estado do Pará**, on Praça Dom Pedro II, a gracious 18th-century Italianate building, contains Brazil's largest framed painting, 'The Conquest of Amazônia', by Domenico de Angelis. ■ *Mon-Fri 0900-1800, Sat-Sun 1900-1200, T225 3853*. The **Palácio Antônio Lemos**, **Museu da Cidade**, which houses the **Museu de Arte de Belém** and is now the **Prefeitura**, was originally built as the Palácio Municipal between 1868 and 1883. In the downstairs rooms there are old views of Belém; upstairs the historic rooms, beautifully renovated, contain furniture, paintings etc, all well explained. ■ *Palácio: Tue-Fri 0900-1200, 1400-1800, Sat-Sun 0900-1300*.

The Belém market, known as 'Ver-o-Peso' was the Portuguese Posto Fiscal, where goods were weighed to gauge taxes due (hence the name: 'see the weight'). It now has lots of gift shops selling charms for the local African-derived religion, *umbanda*; the medicinal herb and natural perfume stalls are also interesting. It is one of the most varied and colourful markets in South America; you can see giant river fish being unloaded around 0530, with frenzied wholesale buying for the next hour; a new dock for the fishing boats was built just upriver from the market in 1997. The area around the market swarms with people, including many armed thieves and pickpockets.

In the old town, too, is the **Forte do Castelo**, Praça Frei Caetano Brandão 117. ■ *Daily 0800-2300, T223 0041*. The fort overlooks the confluence of the Rio Guamá and the Baía do Guajara and was where the Portuguese first set up their defences. It was rebuilt in 1878. The site also contains the *Círculo Militar* restaurant (entry US$1; drinks and *salgadinhos* served on the ramparts from 1800 to watch the sunset; the restaurant serves Belém's best Brazilian food). At the square on the waterfront below the fort the *açaí* berries are landed nightly at 2300, after picking in the jungle (*açaí* berries ground up with sugar and mixed with manioc are a staple food in the region).

At the **Estação das Docas**, the abandoned warehouses of the port have been restored into a complex with an air-conditioned interior and restaurants outside. The Terminal Marítimo has an office of *Valverde Tours*, which offers sunset and nighttime boat trips. The Boulevard das Artes contains the *Cervejaria Amazon* brewery, with good beer and simple meals, an archaeological museum and arts and crafts shops. The Boulevard de Gastronomia has smart restaurants and the 5-star *Cairu* ice cream parlour (try *açaí* or the *Pavê de Capuaçu*). Also in the complex are ATMs, internet café, phones and good toilets.

The **Bosque Rodrigues Alves**, Av Almte Barroso 2305, is a 16-ha public garden (really a preserved area of original flora), with a small animal collection; yellow bus marked 'Souza' or 'Cidade Nova' – any number – 30 minutes from 'Ver-o-Peso' market, also bus from Cathedral. ■ *0900-1700, closed Mon, T226 2308*. The **Museu Emílio Goeldi**, Av Magalhães Barata 376, takes up a city block and consists of the museum proper (with a fine collection of Marajó Indian pottery, an excellent exhibition of Mebengokre Indian lifestyle) and botanical exhibits including Victoria Régia lilies. ■ *Tue-Thu 0900-1200, 1400-1700, Fri 0900-1200, Sat-Sun 0900-1700, US$1, additional charges for specialist areas. Take a bus from the Cathedral.*

A return trip on the ferry from Ver-o-Peso to **Icaoraci** provides a good view of the river. Several restaurants here serve excellent seafood; you can eat shrimp and drink coconut water and appreciate the breeze coming off the river. Icaoraci is 20 km east of the city and is well-known as a centre of ceramic production. The pottery is in Marajoara and Tapajonica style. Take the bus from Av Presidente Vargas to Icaoraci (one hr). Open all week but best on Tuesday-Friday. Artisans are friendly and helpful, will accept commissions and send purchases overseas.

The nearest beach is at **Outeiro** (35 km) on an island near Icaoraci, about an hour by bus and ferry (the bus may be caught near the Maloca, an Indian-style hut near the docks which serves as a nightclub). A bus from Icaoraci to Outeiro takes 30 mins.

Belém has its share of crime and is prone to gang violence. Take sensible precautions especially at night. Police for reporting crimes, R Santo Antônio e Trav Frei Gil de Vila Nova

Brazil

Further north is the island of **Mosqueiro** (86 km) accessible by an excellent highway, with many beautiful sandy beaches and jungle inland. It is popular at weekends when traffic can be heavy (also July) and the beaches can get crowded and polluted. ■ *Buses Belém-Mosqueiro every hr from rodoviária, US$1.45, 80 mins.* Many hotels and weekend villas are at the villages of Mosqueiro and Vila; recommended (may be full weekends and July). Camping is easy and there are plenty of good places to eat.

Sleeping
● *on map*
Many cheap hotels close to waterfront, none too safe. Several others near the rodoviária which are generally OK

A *Itaoca*, Av Pres Vargas 132, T241 3434, F241 0891. Charming, a/c, ask for a quiet room. **A** *Regente*, Av Governador José Malcher 485, T241 1222, F241 1333, hregente@zaz.com.br 3-star, modest, comfortable, good breakfast. **B** *Le Massilia*, R Henrique Gurjão 236, T224 7147. Also has French restaurant. **C** *Novo Avenida*, Av Pres Vargas 404,T/F223 8893, avenida@hotel novoavenida.com.br Central, on busy street, a/c, fridge, cheaper with fan, very well looked after. **C** *Zoghbi Park*, R Padre Prudêncio 220, T/F241 1800, zoghbi@zoghbi.com.br Smart if dated, spacious, good value, small pool, restaurant, caters to business clients. Recommended. **D** *Central*, Av Pres Vargas 290, T242 4800. With a/c (**E** without bath), on busy street, some rooms noisy, but comfortable, good meals, a must for art-deco fans. **D** *Sete-Sete*, Trav 1 de Março 673, T222 7730, F224 2346. Comfortable, safe (but the neighbourhood is not), with breakfast. Recommended. **D** *Ver-o-Peso*, Av Castilho França 308, T241 1022. Functional, rooftop restaurant, TV and fridge, not too clean, but good position near port and Ver-o-Peso market. **D** *Vitória Rêgia*, Trav Frutuoso Guimarães 260, T/F212 2077. With breakfast, more with a/c, fridge (**E** without), safe. **E** *Palácio das Musas*, Trav Frutuoso Guimarães 275, T212 8422. Big rooms, shared bath. **F** *Akemi*, Av Ceará, near rodoviária, T246 4211. With fan, OK.

Eating
● *on map*

Expensive: All the major hotels have upamrket restaurants; the *Açaí* at the *Hilton* is recommended for regional dishes and others, Sun brunch or daily lunch, dinner with live music. *Lá em Casa*, Av Governador José Malcher 247 (also in Estação das Docas). Try *menu paraense*, good cooking, fashionable. **Mid-range**: *Cantina Italiana*, Trav Benjamin Constant 1401. Very good Italian, also delivers. *Casa Portuguesa*, R Sen Manoel Barata 897. Good, Portuguese dishes. *Churrascaria Rodeio*, Trav Pres Eutíquio 1308 and Rodovia Augusto Montenegro Km 4. Excellent meat, salad bar. *Churrascaria Tucuruvi*, Trav Benjamin Constant 1843, Nazaré. Good value. *Miako*, Trav 1 de Março 766, behind Praça de República. Very good Japanese, oriental and international food. *Okada*, R Boaventura da Silva 1522, past R Alcindo Cacela. Japanese, excellent, try 'Steak House', various types of meat, rice and sauces, vegetables, all you can eat, also try *camarão à milanesa com salada*. *Pizzaria Napolitano*, Praça Justo Chermont 12. Pizzas and Italian dishes. **Cheap**: *Nectar*, Av Gentil Bittencourt, Travessa P Eutíquio 248, pedestrian zone. Good vegetarian, lunch only. *Tempero*, R Ò de Almeida, 348. Self-service, some Middle-Eastern dishes, real bargain. Warmly recommended. Specially recommended are some very good snack-bars, mostly outdoors, where you can buy anything up to a full meal, much cheaper than restaurants: *Charlotte*, Av Gentil Bittencourt 730, at Travessa Quintino Bocaiúva, for best *salgadinhos* in the city, also good desserts, very popular. Many buffet-style restaurants along R Santo Antônio pedestrian mall and elsewhere in the *Comércio* district including *Doce Vida Salgado*, 1 de Março 217, good food and prices; generally lunch only, good variety, pay by weight. *Sabor Paranse*, R 13 de Maio, 450. food by weight, lunch only.

Bars & clubs

Many venues around Av Doca de Souza Franco, often just called 'Doca', especially popular Thu. *African Bar*, Praça Waldemar Henrique 2. Rock or Samba, weekends only. *Baixo Reduto*, R Quintino Bocaiúva, Reduto. Blues on Wed; Brazilian pop, Thu; rock, Fri and jazz, Sa. The Reduto district has recently become the place to go at night. *Cachaçaria Água Doce*, R Diogo Móia 283 esq Wandenkolk. Specializes in fine cachaças, good appetizers, live music, informal atmosphere. *Bar Teatro Bora Bora*, R Bernal do Couto 38, restaurant, bar and nightclub. MPB and Pagode open from 2100 until late Thu-Sun. *Colarinho Branco Chopperia*, Av Visconde de Souza Franco 80, near the river. Open Tue-Sun 1800 to last customer, nightly perfomers of Brazilian popular music. *Escapóle*, Rodovia Augusto Montenegro 400. Huge dance hall with various types of music, live and recorded, frequented by all age groups, open Wed-Sat from 2200 (take a radio taxi for safety), no a/c, dress informally. *Olê Olá*, Av Tavares Bastos 1234. Disco, live music and dance floor. Thu-Sun, 2230 to last customer.

Brazil

Círio, the Festival of Candles in **Oct**, is based on the legend of the Nossa Senhora de Nazaré, whose image was found on the site of her Basílica around 1700. On the second Sun in Oct, a procession carries a copy of the Virgin's image from the Basílica to the cathedral. On the Mon, 2 weeks later, the image is returned to its usual place. There is a Círio museum in the crypt of the Basílica, enter at the right side of the church; free. (All hotels are fully booked during Círio.) **Festivals**

Parfumaria Orion, Trav Frutuoso Guimarães 268, has a variety of perfumes from Amazonian plants, much cheaper than tourist shops. The *Complexo São Brás* on Praça Lauro Sodré has a handicraft market and folkloric shows in a building dating from 1911. Belém is a good place to buy hammocks, look in the street parallel to the river, 1 block inland from Ver-o-Peso. Bookshop on Av Presidente Vargas with English titles in arcade next to *Excelsior Hotel*. **Shopping**

Amazon Star, R Henrique Gurjão 236, T/F212 6244, amazonstar@amazonstar.com.br City and river tours, Ilha de Marajó, very professional, good guides, jungle tours. Repeatedly recommended. *Amaz*ônia *Sport & Ação*, Av 25 de Setembro, 2345, T226 8442. Extreme sports, diving, rock-climbing. *Angel*, in *Hilton*, T224 2111, angel@datanetbbs.com.br Tours, events, issues ISIC and HI cards. **Tour operators**

Air Bus 'Perpétuo Socorro-Telégrafo' or 'Icoaraci', every 15 mins from the Prefeitura, Praça Felipe Patroni, to the airport, 40 mins, US$0.50. Taxi to airport, US$10 (ordinary taxis are cheaper than Co-op taxis, buy ticket in advance in Departures side of airport). ATMs for credit cards in the terminal. T257 0626. **Transport**

Daily flights south to **Brasília** and other Brazilian cities, and west to **Santarém** and **Manaus**. To **Paramaribo** and **Cayenne**, 3 a week with *Surinam Airways*. Travellers entering Brazil from Guyane may need a 60-day visa (takes 2 days) before airlines will confirm their tickets. Internal flights also offered by *Varig, Vasp, Nordeste*and *TAM*.

Bus The rodoviária is at the end of Av Governador José Malcher 5 km from the centre (T246 8178). Take Aeroclube, Cidade Novo, No 20 bus, or Arsenal or Canudos buses, US$0.50, or taxi, US$5 (day), US$7 (night) (at rodoviária you are given a ticket with the taxi's number on it, threaten to go to the authorities if the driver tries to overcharge). It has a good snack bar and showers (US$0.10) and 2 agencies with information and tickets for riverboats. Regular bus services to all major cities. To **Santarém**, via Marabá (on the Transamazônica) once a week (US$45, more expensive than by boat and can take longer, goes only in dry season). *Transbrasiliana* go direct to Marabá, 16 hrs, US$20. To **São Luís**, 2 a day, US$20, 13 hrs, interesting journey through marshlands. To **Fortaleza**, US$35-40 (24 hrs), several companies. To **Recife**, US$52, 34 hrs.

River services To **Santarém, Manaus**, and intermediate ports (see River Transport, Amazônia, page 526). All larger ships berth at Portobrás/Docas do Pará (the main commercial port) at Armazém (warehouse) No 10 (entrance on Av Marechal Hermes, corner of Av Visconde de Souza Franco). The guards will sometimes ask to see your ticket before letting you into the port area, but tell them you are going to speak with a ship's captain. Ignore the touts who approach you. *Macamazónia*, R Castilho Franca, sells tickets for most boats, open Sun. There are 2 desks selling tickets for private boats in the rodoviária; some hotels recommend agents for tickets. Purchase tickets from offices 2 days in advance. Smaller vessels (sometimes cheaper, usually not as clean, comfortable or safe) sail from small docks along Estrada Nova (not a safe part of town). Take a Cremação bus from Ver-o-Peso.

To **Macapá (Porto Santana)**, the quickest (12 hrs) are the catamaran *Atlântico I* or the launches *Lívia Marília* and *Atlântico II* (slightly slower), all US$27-40 and leaving at 0700 on alternate days. Other boats take 24 hrs: *Silja e Souza* (Wed) of Souzamar, Trav Dom Romualdo Seixas corner R Jerônimo Pimentel, T222 0719, and *Almirante Solon* (Sat) of Sanave (Serviço Amapaense de Navegação, Castilho Franca 234, opposite Ver-o-Peso, T222 7810), slightly cheaper, crowded, not as nice. Via Breves, ENAL, T224 5210 (see River Transport in Amazônia, page 526). Smaller boats to Macapá also sail from Estrada Nova.

Airline offices *Varig*, Av Pres Vargas 768, T224 3344, airport T257 0481. *Vasp*, T0800-998277, airport 257 0944. *Surinam Airways*, R Gaspar Viana 488, T212 7144, airport 211 6038, English spoken, helpful with information and documentation. **Banks** *Banco do Brasil*, Av Pres Vargas (near *Hotel Central*), good **Directory**

Brazil

rates, Visa ATMs, and other Brazilian banks (open 0900-1630, but foreign exchange only until 1300). *HSBC*, Av Pres Vargas near Praça da República has MasterCard Cirrus and Amex ATMs. *Banco de Amazônia* (Basa), on Pres Vargas, gives good rates for TCs (Amex or Citicorp only), but does not change cash. *Itaú*, R Boaventura 580, good TCs and cash rates. Since 2002 all *Casas de câmbio* have been closed, so money can only be changed at banks during the week. At weekends hotels will only exchange for their guests, while restaurants may change money, but at poor rates. Exchange rates are generally the best in the north of the country. **Communications** Internet: *Amazon*, 2nd floor of Estação das Docas. In *Shopping Iguatemi*, US$1.40 per hr. **Post Office:** Av Pres Vargas 498, but international parcels are only accepted at the Post Office on the praça at the corner of Trav Frutuoso Guimarães e R 15 de Novembro, next door to NS das Mercês (hard to find). **Telephone:** telegrams and fax at the Post Office, Av Pres Vargas. For phone calls: *Telemar*, Av Presidente Vargas. **Embassies and consulates** Denmark (Consul Arne Hvidbo), R Senador Barata 704, sala 1503, T241 1588 (PO Box 826). Finland, Av Sen Lemos 529, T222 0148. France, R Pres Pernambucio 269, T224 6818, also for Guyane. Germany, Campos Sales 63, sala 404, T222 5666. Netherlands, R José Marcelino de Oliveira 399, T255 0088. Suriname, R Gaspar Viana 490, T212 7144. Sweden, Av Sen Lemos 529, mailing address Caixa Postal 111, T241 1104, open 1600-1800. UK, Robin Burnett, Ed Palladium Centre, room 410/411, Av Governador José Malcher 815, T222 5074, F212 0274, open at 1130. USA, Av Osvaldo Cruz 156, T223 0800. Venezuela, opposite French Consulate, Av Pres Pernambuco 270, T222 6396 (Venezuelan visa for those entering overland takes 3 hrs, costs US$30 for most nationalities, but we are told that it is better to get a visa at Manaus, Boa Vista or before you leave home. **Medical services** Health: a yellow fever certificate or inoculation is mandatory. It is best to get a yellow fever vaccination at home (always have your certificate handy) and avoid the risk of recycled needles. Medications for malaria prophylaxis are not sold in Belém pharmacies. Bring an adequate supply from home. **Clínica de Medicina Preventativa**, Av Bras de Aguiar 410 (T222 1434), will give injections, English spoken, open 0730-1200, 1430-1900 (Sat 0800-1100). **Hospital Ordem Terceira**, Trav Frei Gil de Vila Nova 2, doctors speak some English, free consultation but it's a bit primitive. Surgery open Mon 1300-1900, Tue-Thu 0700-1100, 24 hrs for emergencies. The British consul has a list of English-speaking doctors. **Tourist offices** Belemtur, Av José Malcher 592, T242 0900, belemtur@cinbesa.com.br Also at airport, T211 6151. **Paratur**, Praça Maestro Waldemar Henrique s/n, T212 9135, www.paratur.pa.gov.br Helpful, many languages spoken; has a good map of Belém in many languages (but some references are incorrect). Town guidebook, US$2.75. **Ibama**, Av Conselheiro Furtado 1303, Batista Campos, CEP 66035-350, T241 2621, F223 1299. **Voltage** 110 AC, 60 cycles.

Ilha do Marajó

Colour map 5, grid A1   At almost 50,000 sq km, the world's largest island formed by fluvial processes is flooded in rainy December-June and provides a suitable habitat for water buffalo, introduced from India in the late 19th century. They are now farmed in large numbers (try the cheese and milk). It is also home to many birds, crocodiles and other wildlife, and has several good beaches. It is crowded at weekends and in the July holiday season. The island was the site of the pre-Columbian Marajoaras culture.

Ponta de Pedras   Boats leave Belém (near Porto do Sal, seat US$3.25, cabin US$35 for two, five hours) most days for Ponta de Pedras (D *Hotel Ponta de Pedras*, good meals, buses for Soure or Salvaterra meet the boat). Bicycles for hire (US$1 per hr) to explore beaches and the interior of the island. Fishing boats make the eight-hr trip to Cachoeira do Arari (one pousada, **D**) where there is a Marajó museum. A 10-hr boat trip from Ponta de Pedras goes to the Arari lake where there are two villages, Jenipapo built on stilts, forró dancing at weekends, and Santa Cruz which is less primitive, but less interesting (a hammock and a mosquito net are essential). There is a direct boat service to Belém twice a week.

Soure   The 'capital' of the island has fine beaches: Araruna (2 km – take supplies and supplement with coconuts and crabs, beautiful walks along the shore), do Pesqueiro (bus from Praça da Matriz, 1030, returns 1600, eat at *Maloca*, good, cheap, big, deserted beach, 13 km away) and Caju-Una (15 km). Small craft await passengers from the Enasa boats, for Salvaterra village (good beaches and bars: seafood), 10 minutes, or trips are bookable in Belém from *Mururé*, T241 0891. There are also 17th-century Jesuit ruins at Joanes as well as a virgin beach.

Colour map 5, grid A1
Population: 19,958

B *Ilha do Marajó*, 15 mins' walk from centre, T/F741 1315. A/c, bath, pool. **a Branca**, Rua 4, T741 1414. A/c, **E** with fan, breakfast, dirty, good food. **D** P̄o., .úfalo, Trav 17, T741 1113. A/c, cheaper with fan, breakfast, bar, restaurant. **F** *Casa Alemão*, ∂a Rua, T741 1234. German/Brazilian owned, hospitable, tourist information. *Canecão*, Praça da Matriz, sandwiches, meals. Recommended. **Salvaterra A** *Pousada das Guarãs*, Av Beira Mar, Salvaterra, T/F765 1133, www.pousadadosguaras.com.br Well-equipped, tour programme, on beach. **Joanes D** *Pousada Ventania do Rio-Mar*, take bus, US$1.20 from Foz do Cámara, T9992 5716, pousadas@hotmail.com Near the beach, with bath and breakfast, arranges tours on horseback or canoe, Belgian and Brazilian owners.

Transport Ferry: From Belém docks the Enasa ferry sails to Soure on Fri at 2000 (4 hrs, US$5). There are daily boats to Foz do Cámara at 0630, 0700 and 1300 (1½-3 hrs US$4). Then take a bus to Salvaterra and a ferry to Soure. Boats return from Foz do Cámara at 0800 and 1100. There is a 'taxi-plane' service to Soure leaving Belém at 0630 returning 1600, US$30.

Macapá

The capital of Amapá State is situated on the northern channel of the Amazon Delta and is linked to Belém by boat and daily flights. Along with Porto Santana it was declared a Zona Franca in 1993 and visitors flock to buy cheap imported electrical and other goods. Each brick of the **Fortaleza de São José do Macapá**, built between 1764 and 1782, was brought from Portugal as ballast; 50 iron cannons remain. Today it is used for concerts, exhibits, and colourful festivities on the anniversary of the city's founding, 4 February. In the handicraft complex (**Casa do Artesão**), Av Azárias Neto, craftsmen produce their wares onsite. A feature is pottery decorated with local manganese ore, also woodcarvings, leatherwork and Indian crafts. ■ *Mon-Sat 0800-1900*. **São José Cathedral**, inaugurated by the Jesuits in 1761, is the city's oldest landmark.

The riverfront is a very pleasant place for an evening stroll. The **Complexo Beira-Rio** has food and drink kiosks, and a nice lively atmosphere. The pier (*trapiche*) has been rebuilt and is a lovely spot for savouring the cool of the evening breeze, or watching sunrise over the Amazon. There is a monument to the equator, **Marco Zero** (take Fazendinha bus). The equator also divides the nearby enormous football stadium in half, aptly named O Zerão. South of here, at Km 12 on Rodovia Juscelinho Kubitschek, are the **botanical gardens**. **Fazendinha** (16 km from the centre) is a popular local beach, very busy on Sunday. **Curiarú**, 8 km from Macapá, was founded by escaped slaves, and is popular at weekends for dancing and swimming.

Sleeping & eating

L-AL *Centro Equatorial de Turismo Ambiental Amazônico (Ceta)*, R do Matodouro 640, Fazendinha, T227 3396, turismoambiental@zaz.com.br All furniture made on site, a/c, sports facilities, gardens with sloths and monkeys, ecological trails. Highly recommended. **A** *Ekinox*, R Jovino Dinoá 1693, T222 4378, j-f@uol.com.br Nice atmosphere, a/c, book and video library, excellent meals and service, riverboat tours available. Recommended. **B** *Mara*, R São José 2390, T222 0859. With bath, a/c, TV, fridge, good, breakfast. **C** *Glória*, Leopoldo Machado 2085, T222 0984. A/c, minibar, TV. **C** *Mercúrio*, R Cândido Mendes 1300, 2nd floor, T223 1699. With breakfast, cheaper without a/c. Recommended. **D** *Santo Antônio*, Av Coriolano Jucá 485, T222 0226, near main praça. Cheaper with fan, **E** with shared bath, good breakfast extra; **F** in dormitory. *Cantinho Bahiano*, Av Beira-Rio 1, Santa Inês. Good seafood. Many other good fish restaurants on the same road, eg *Martinho's Peixaria*, No 810. *Chalé*, Av Pres Vargas 499. Nice atmosphere. *Bom Paladar Kilo's*, Av Pres Vargas 456. Good pay-by-weight buffet. *Sorveteria Macapá*, R São José 1676, close to centre. Excellent ice cream made from local fruit. *Rithimus*, R Odilardo Silva e Av Pres Vargas. Thu night popular with local rhythm *Brega*.

Festivals

Marabaixo is the traditional music and dance of the state of Amapá; a festival held 40 days after Easter. The *sambódromo*, near Marco Zero, is used by Escolas de Samba during Carnaval and by Quadrilhas during the São João festivities.

Changing mone, is only possible a. very poor rates. Take plenty of insect repellent

Phone code: 0xx96
Post code: 68900
Colour map 2, grid C6
Population: 283,308

Brazil

Brazil

Tour operators *Awara*, Av Presidente Vargas 2396-B, T/F222 0970, www.awara.com.br Recommended .. city and river tours, English and French spoken. *Marco Zero*, R São José 2048, T223 1922, F222 3086. Recommended for flights.

Transport **Air** *Varig* (R Cândido Mendes 1039, T223 4612), *TAM* (T223 2688), and *Vasp* (R Independência 146, T224 1016), all fly to Belém and other Brazilian cities. *Gol* fly to Belém, Brasília and São Paulo.

Boat Ships dock at Porto Santana, 30 km from Macapá (frequent buses US$1.30, or share a taxi US$15). To **Belém**, *Silja e Souza* of Souzamar, Cláudio Lúcio Monteiro 1375, Santana T281 1946, and *Almirante Solon* of Sanave, Av Mendonça Furtado 1766, T223 0244. See under Belém, River Services, for other boats. Purchase tickets from offices 2 days in advance. Also smaller and cheaper boats. The faster (12 hr) catamaran *Atlântico I* or launches leave for Belém most days. *São Francisco de Paula I* sails to **Santarém** and **Manaus**, not going via Belém.

Bus New rodoviária on BR-156, north of Macapá. To **Amapá** (US$15) and **Calçoene** (US$20) daily at 1500. To **Oiapoque** (US$25) daily at 0630, another at 2000 except Sun. Oiapoque buses stop in Calçoene, but not Amapá.

Directory **Banks** *Banco do Brasil*, R Independência 250, cash, Visa, ATM and TCs. Visa ATM also at *Bradesco*, Cândido Mendes 1316. MasterCard and Amex ATM at *HSBC*, Av Pres Vargas. *Casa Francesa*, Independência 232, changes euros (euros can be bought in Macapá and Belém). **Communications** Post Office: Av Coriolano Jucá. International calls can be made at São José 2050, 0730-1000. **Embassies and consulates** For the French honorary consul, ask at *Pousada Ekinox*, visas for Guyane have to be obtained from Brasília which can take a while. **Tourist offices** CEIT/AP, R Cândido Mendes 1131, T212 5335, detur@prodep.org.br Offices at the airport and rodoviária. **Useful addresses** Ibama, R Hamilton Silva 1570, Santa Rita, CEP 68.906-440, Macapá, T/F214 1100.

Border with Guyane
Colour map 2, grid B6

The main road crosses the Rio Caciporé and continues to the border with Guyane at **Oiapoque**, on the river of the same name. It is 90 km inland from the Parque Nacional Cabo Orange, Brazil's northernmost point on the Atlantic coast. About 7 km to the west is Clevelândia do Norte, a military outpost and the end of the road in Brazil. Oiapoque is remote, with its share of contraband, illegal migration, and drug trafficking. It is also the gateway to gold fields in the interior of both Brazil and Guyane. As it is quite a rough place, the visitor should be cautious, especially late at night. Prices here are high, but lower than in neighbouring Guyane. The **Cachoeira Grande Roche** rapids can be visited, upstream along the Oiapoque River, where it is possible to swim, US$25 per motor boat. The road north to the Guyane border (BR-156) is unpaved from Tatarugalzinho and is difficult in parts, especially during the wet season (but open throughout the year). It is advisable to carry extra fuel, food and water from Macapá onwards.

Sleeping and eating **C** *Oiapoque*, on the waterfront opposite the petrol station. With breakfast, fridge, restaurant. **D** *Amapá*, R Lélio Silva 298, near the Praça (1 block from the bus stop), T521 1768. A/c, bath, no breakfast. Recommended. **D** *Pousada Central*, Av Coracy Nunes 209, one block from the river, T521 1466. A/c, bath, **F** with fan and shared bath. **E** *Mini Hotel*, Av Coaracy Nunes, near bus stop, T521 1241. Fan, bath. Other cheap hotels along the waterfront are mainly used by Brazilians waiting to cross to Guyane. *Pantanal Bar*, next to the monument at riverfront, has dancing at weekends.

Transport **Air**: Flights to Macapá Mon-Fri with *Penta*, office on the waterfront, T/F521 1117. While waiting for flights to Cayenne from St-Georges, it is much cheaper to stay on the Brazilian side. **Bus**: leave for Macapá at 1400 and 1800 Mon-Sat, 12 hrs (dry season), 14-24 hrs (wet season), US$25. You may be asked to show your Polícia Federal entry stamp and Yellow Fever vaccination certificate either when buying a ticket from the offices on the waterfront or at the bus station when boarding for Macapá. **Crossing to Guyane**: motorized canoes cross to St-Georges de L'Oyapock, 10 mins downstream, US$4 pp, bargain for return fare. A vehicle ferry will operate until a bridge is eventually built.

Directory Banks Exchange: It is possible to exchange US$ and reais to euros, but dollar rates are low and TCs are not accepted anywhere. *Banco do Brasil*, Av Barão do Rio Branco, open 1000-1500, and *Bradesco*, have Visa facilities to withdraw reais which can be changed into euros. *Casa Francesa*, on the riverfront, and one *câmbio* in the market sell reais for US$ or euros. Rates are worse in St-Georges. Best to buy euros in Belém, or abroad. **Communications Post Office:** Av Barão do Rio Branco, open 0900-1200, 1400-1700. **Useful addresses Immigration:** Polícia Federal, for Brazilian exit and entry stamps, is on the road behind the church about 500 m from the river.

A few hours up the broad river from Belém, the region of the thousand islands is entered. The passage through this maze of islets is known as 'The Narrows' and is perhaps the nicest part of the journey. The ship winds through 150 km of lanes of yellow flood with equatorial forest within 20 m or 30 m on both sides. On one of the curious flat-topped hills after the Narrows stands the little stucco town of **Monte Alegre**, an oasis in mid-forest (airport; some simple hotels, **E**). There are lagoon cruises to see lilies, birds, pink dolphins; also village visits (US$25-40 per day).

Belém to Manaus

Santarém

The third largest city on the Brazilian Amazon is small enough to walk around. It was founded in 1661 as the Jesuit mission of Tapajós; the name was changed to Santarém in 1758. There was once a fort here and attractive colonial squares overlooking the waterfront remain. Standing at the confluence of the Rio Tapajós with the Amazon, on the southern bank, Santarém is half-way (two or three days by boat) between Belém and Manaus. Most visitors breeze in and out on a stopover by boat or air.

Phone code: 0xx91
Post code: 68000
Colour map 4, grid A5
Population: 262,538

The yellow Amazon water swirls alongside the green-blue Tapajós; the **meeting of the waters**, in front of the market square, is nearly as impressive as that of the Negro and Solimões near Manaus. A small **Museu dos Tapajós** in the old city hall on the waterfront, now the **Centro Cultural João Fora**, downriver from where the boats dock, has a collection of ancient Tapajós ceramics, as well as various 19th century artefacts. The unloading of the fish catch between 0500 and 0700 on the waterfront is interesting. There are good beaches nearby on the Rio Tapajós.

A *Amazon Park I*, Av Mendonça Furtado 4120, T523 2800, amazon@stm.interconect.com.br Swimming pool, 4 km from centre, taxi US$4. **C** *Brasil Grande Hotel*, Trav 15 de Agosto 213, T522 5660. Family-run, with restaurant. **C** *New City*, Trav Francisco Correia 200, T523 3149. A/c, frigobar, good, will collect from airport. **C** *Santarém Palace*, Rui Barbosa 726, T523 2820. A/c, TV, fridge, comfortable. **D** *Mirante*, Trav Francisco Correa, 115, T523 3054/08007073054, www.mirantehotel.com Homely, a/c, fridge, TV, some rooms with balcony, individual safes, internet, good value. Recommended. **D** *Brasil*, Trav dos Mártires 30, T523 5177. Nice, family-run, includes breakfast, communal bath, good food, good service. **D** *Horizonte*, Trav Senador Lemos 737, T522 5437, horizontehotel@bol.com.br With a/c, **F** with fan, modern. **D** *Rios*, R Floriano Peixoto 720, T522 5701. Large rooms, comfortable, a/c, fridge and TV. Recommended. *Mascote*, Praça do Pescador 10. Open 1000-2330, restaurant, bar and ice cream parlour. *Santa Antonio*, Av Tapajós 2061. Churrasco and fish. *Mascotinho*, Praça Manoel de Jesus Moraes, on riverfront. Bar/pizzeria, popular, outside seating, good view. *Lucy*, Praça do Pescador. Good juices and pastries. Recommended.

Sleeping & eating

Santarém 29 Jun, *São Pedro*, with processions of boats on the river and boi-bumbá dance dramas. **Alter do Chão** 2nd week in Jul, *Festa do Sairé*, religious processions and folkloric events. .

Festivals

Amazon Tours, Trav Turiano Meira, 1084, T522 1928, amazontours@amazonriver.com The owner Steve Alexander is a very friendly, helpful man who can give you lots of hints on what to do. He also organizes excursions for groups to remote areas which are quite expensive. Recommended. *Coruá-Una Turismo*, R Dr Hugo Mendonça 600, T518 1014. Offers various tours, Pierre d'Arcy speaks French. Recommended. *Santarém Tur*, in *Amazon Park*, and at R Adriano Pimental 44, T522 4847, F522 3141. Owned by Perpétua and Jean-Pierre Schwarz

Tour operators

Brazil

(speaks French), friendly, helpful, also group tours (for a group of 5 US$50 per day pp). Recommended. *Gil Serique*, Praça do Pescador 131, T522 5174. English-speaking guide. Recommended. *Tapam Turismo*, Trav 15 de Agosto, 127 A, T523 2422. Recommended.

Transport **Air** 15 km from town, T523 1021. Internal flights only. Buses run to the centre or waterfront. From the centre the bus leaves in front of the cinema in Rui Barbosa every 80 mins from 0550 to 1910, or taxis (US$8 to waterfront). The hotels *Amazon Park* and *New City* have free buses for guests; you may be able to take these.

Bus Rodoviária is on the outskirts (T522 3392), take 'Rodagem' bus from the waterfront near the market, US$0.25. Santarém to **Marabá** on the Rio Tocantins with *Transbrasiliana*. From Marabá there are buses east and west on the Transamazônica. Enquire at the rodoviária for other destinations. Road travel during rainy season is always difficult, often impossible.

Shipping services To **Manaus**, **Belém**, **Macapá**, **Itaituba**, and intermediate ports (see River transport, page 526). Boats to Belém and Manaus dock at the Cais do Porto, 1 km west, take 'Floresta-Prainha', 'Circular' or 'Circular Externo' bus; taxi US$4. Boats to other destinations, including Macapá, dock by the waterfront by the centre of town. Local service to **Óbidos**, US$10, 4 hrs, Oriximiná US$12.50, Alenquer, and **Monte Alegre** (US$10, 5-8 hrs).

Directory **Airline offices** *Penta*, Trav 15 de Novembro 183, T523 2532. *Varig/Nordeste*, Av Rui Barbosa, 790, T523 2488. **Banks** Cash withdrawals on Visa at *Banco do Brasil*, Av Rui Barbosa 794. It is very difficult to change dollars (impossible to change TCs anywhere), try travel agencies. **Communications** Internet: *Tapajós On Line*, Mendonça Furtado 2454, US$3.50 per hr. **Post Office**: Praça da Bandeira 81. **Telephone**: *Posto Trin*, R Siquiera Campos 511. 0700-1900 Mon-Sat, 0700-2100 Sun. **Tourist office**: COMTUR, R Floriano Peixoto 343, T/F523 2434, good information available in English.

Alter do Chão Some 34 km west of Santarém is this friendly village on the Rio Tapajós, at the outlet of Lago Verde. Of particular interest is the **Centro do Preservação de Arte Indígena**, R Dom Macedo Costa, T527 1110, which has a substantial collection of artefacts from tribes of Amazônia and Mato Grosso. ■ *0800-1200, 1300-1700*. Good swimming in the Tapajós from the beautiful, clean beach. **B** *Pousada Tupaiulândia*, Pedro Teixeira 300, T0xx91-527 1157. A/c, unimpressive but OK, very helpful, good breakfast for US$5, next to telephone office opposite bus stop. **E** *Pousada Villa Praia*, first on the right as you enter the village. Large rooms, a/c, very helpful staff, good value. *Lago Verde*, Praça 7 de Setembro, good fresh fish, try *caldeirada de tucunaré*, huge portions.

Transport Bus tickets and information from the bus company kiosk opposite Pousada Tupaiulândia. From Santarém: bus stop on Av São Sebastião, in front of Colégio Santa Clara, US$1, about 1 hr.

Óbidos
Population: 46,490

At 110 km up-river from Santarém (5 hours by boat), Óbidos is located at the narrowest and deepest point on the river. It is a picturesque and clean city with many beautiful, tiled buildings and some nice parks. Worth seeing are the **Prefeitura Municipal** (T547 1194), the cuartel and the **Museu Integrado de Óbidus**, R Justo Chermont 607. ■ *Mon-Fri 0700-1100, 1330-1730*. There is also a **Museu Contextual**, a system of plaques with detailed explanations of historical buildings throughout town. The airport has flights to Manaus, Santarém and Parintins. **C** *Braz Bello*, R Corrêia Pinto, on top of the hill, shared bath, full board available. **C** *Pousada Brasil*, R Correia Pinto, basic with bath, cheaper without and others in same price range.

Just across the Pará-Amazonas border, between Santarém and Manaus, is **Parintins** (*Phone code: 0xx92. Post code: 69150-000*), 15 hours by boat upriver from Óbidos. Here, on the last three days of June each year, the **Festa do Boi** draws over 50,000 visitors. Since the town has only two small hotels, everyone sleeps in hammocks on the boats that bring them to the festival from Manaus and Santarém. The festival consists of lots of folkloric dancing, but its main element is the competition between two rival groups, the Caprichoso and the Garantido, in the *bumbódromo*, built in 1988 to hold 35,000 spectators. ■ *Apart from boats that call on the Belém-Manaus route, there are irregular sailings from Óbidos (ask at the port). Journey times are about 12-15 hrs from Manaus and 20 from Santarém. There is also a small airport with flights to Manaus, Óbidos and Santarém.*

Manaus

The next city upriver is Manaus, capital of Amazonas State – the largest in Brazil. Once an isolated urban island in the jungle, it now sprawls over a series of eroded and gently sloping hills divided by numerous creeks (igarapés). The city is growing fast and 20-storey modern buildings are rising above the traditional flat, red-tiled roofs, but an impressive initiative in 2001 saw the start of a significant restoration programme in which historic buildings have been given a new lease of life and theatres, cultural spaces and libraries created. Manaus is an excellent port of entry for visiting the Amazon. Less than a day away are river islands and tranquil waterways. The opportunities for canoeing, trekking in the forest and meeting local people should not be missed and, once you are out of reach of the urban influence, there are plenty of animals to see. There is superb swimming in the natural pools and under falls of clear water in the little streams which rush through the woods, but take locals' advice on swimming in the river (electric eels and various other kinds of unpleasant fish, apart from the notorious piranhas, abound and industrial pollution of the river is growing).

Phone code: 0xx92
Post code: 69000
Average temp: 27°C
Colour map 4, grid A3
Population: 1.4 million

Brazil

Getting there Boats sock at different locations depending on where they have come from. The **docks** are quite central. The **airport** is 18 km from the centre, the **bus terminal** 9 km. Both are served by local buses and taxis.

Ins & outs
See Transport, page 542 for further details
Manaus time is 1 hr behind Brazilian standard time (2 hours behind Oct-Feb, Brazil's summer time)

    Getting around All city bus routes start below the cathedral in front of the port entrance; just ask someone for the destination you want. The city centre is easily explored on foot.

    Tourist office Av Eduardo Ribeiro 666, near *Teatro Amazonas*, T231 1998. Open Mon-Fri 0800-1800, Sat 0800-1300. Limited English and information. **Secretaria de Estado da Cultura e Turismo**, Av 7 de Setembro 1546, Vila Ninita, behind *Centro Cultural Palácio Rio Negro*, T633 2850, sec@visitamazonas.com.br Open Mon-Fri 0730-1700. At the airport, open daily 0700-2300, T652 1120. Also in Amazonas Shopping Center and in a trailer opposite Palácio da Policia. Town map from *Amazon Explorers*, or news kiosks. Weekend editions of *A Crítica*, newspaper, list local entertainments and events.

    Security Manaus is a friendly, if busy city and a good deal safer than the big cities of southern Brazil. As in any city, the usual precautions against opportunist crime should be taken, especially when arriving at night (see River transport in Amazônia on staying on boats in port). Bars along R Joaquim Nabuco are reported particularly unsafe. This street, R dos Andrades, R 10 de Julho and the port area are not places to hang around after dark. A tourist police force, **Politur**, assists visitors. See below for advice on choosing a jungle tour.

Dominating the centre is a **Cathedral** built in simple Jesuit style on a hillock; very plain inside or out. Nearby is the main shopping and business area, the tree-lined Av Eduardo Ribeiro; crossing it is Av 7 de Setembro, bordered by ficus trees. The opulent **Teatro Amazonas**, on the Praça São Sebastião, was completed in 1896 during the great rubber boom following 15 years of construction. It has been restored four times and should not be missed. There are ballet, theatre and opera performances several times a week and free popular Brazilian music on Monday nights, June-December. ■ *Mon-Sat 0900-1600, 20-min tour US$7. Recommended. About same price for a concert, for information on programmes T622 2420.* **Igreja São Sebastião** on the same praça, has an unusual altar of two giant ivory hands holding a water lily of Brazil wood.

Sights

    On the waterfront, the **Mercado Adolfo Lisboa**, R dos Barés 46, was built in 1902 as a miniature copy of the now demolished Parisian Les Halles. The wrought ironwork which forms much of the structure was imported from Europe and is said to have been designed by Eiffel. The remarkable **harbour installations**, completed in

1902, were designed and built by a Scottish engineer to cope with the up to 14 m annual rise and fall of the Rio Negro. The large passenger ship floating dock is connected to street level by a 150 m-long floating ramp, at the end of which, on the harbour wall, can be seen the high water mark for each year since it was built. When the water is high, the roadway floats on a series of large iron tanks measuring 2½m in diameter. The large yellow **Alfândega** (Customs House) on R Marquês de Santa Cruz stands at the entrance to the city when arriving by boat. It was entirely prefabricated in England, and the tower once acted as lighthouse. ■ *Mon-Fri 0800-1300.*

The **Biblioteca Pública Estadual** (Public Library) at R Barroso 57, inaugurated in 1871, features an ornate European cast iron staircase. It is well stocked with 19th century newspapers, rare books and old photographs, and worth a visit. ■ *Mon-Fri 0730-1730, T234 0588.* The **Centro Cultural Pálacio Rio Negro**, Av 7 de Setembro was the residence of a German rubber merchant until 1917 and later the state government palace. It now holds various cultural events, including exhibitions, shows and films; there is also a café. ■ *Tue-Fri 1000-1700, Sat-Sun 1600-2100, T232 4450.*

There is a curious little church, **Igreja do Pobre Diabo**, at the corner of Avenidas Borba and Ipixuna in the suburb of Cachoeirinha; it is only 4 m wide by 5 m long, and was built by a tradesman, the 'poor devil' of the name. Take Circular 7 Cachoeirinha bus from the cathedral to Hospital Militar.

Manaus

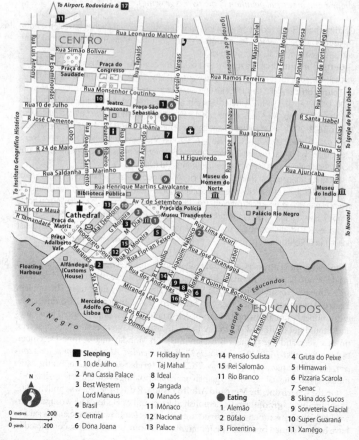

■ Sleeping	7 Holiday Inn	14 Pensão Sulista	4 Gruta do Peixe
1 10 de Julho	Taj Mahal	15 Rei Salomão	5 Himawari
2 Ana Cassia Palace	8 Ideal	11 Rio Branco	6 Pizzaria Scarola
3 Best Western	9 Jangada		7 Senac
Lord Manaus	10 Manaós	**● Eating**	8 Skina dos Sucos
4 Brasil	11 Mônaco	1 Alemão	9 Sorveteria Glacial
5 Central	12 Nacional	2 Búfalo	10 Super Guaraná
6 Dona Joana	13 Palace	3 Fiorentina	11 Xamêgo

On Praça da Polícia is the very small **Museu Tiradentes**, run by the military police and holds selected historical items and old photographs. ■ *Mon 1400-1800, Tue-Fri 0800-1200, 1400-1800, T234 7422.* A short distance away is **Museu do Homem do Norte**, Av 7 de Setembro 1385 (near Av J Nabuco), which reviews the way of life of the Amazonian population; social, cultural and economic aspects are displayed with photographs, models and other pieces. ■ *Mon-Thu 0900-1200, 1300-1700, Fri 1300-1700, T232 5373, US$1.* **Instituto Geográfico e Histórico do Amazonas**, located in a fascinating older district of central Manaus, houses a museum and library of over 10,000 books which thoroughly document Amazonian life through the ages, R Bernardo Ramos 117 (near Prefeitura). ■ *Mon-Fri 0800-1200, US$0.20, T232 7077.* **Museu do Índio**, kept by the Salesian missionaries: this interesting, if rather run down, museum's collection includes handicrafts, ceramics, clothing, utensils and ritual objects from the various Indian tribes of the upper Rio Negro, R Duque de Caxias (near Av 7 Setembro); excellent craft shop. ■ *Mon-Fri 0800-1200, 1400-1700, Sat 0830-1130, T234 1422, US$3.*

Botanic Gardens, Instituto Nacional de Pesquisas Amazonas (INPA), Estrada do Aleixo, at Km 3, not far from the Museu de Ciências Naturais da Amazônia, is the centre for scientific research in the Amazon; labs here (not open to the public) investigate farming, medicines and tropical diseases in the area. There is a small museum and restaurant, lots of birds, named trees and manatees (best seen Wednesday and Friday mornings when the water is changed), caimans and giant otters; worth a visit. ■ *Mon-Fri 0900-1100, 1400-1630, Sat-Sun 0900-1600, T643 3377/643 3192, US$2, take any bus to Aleixo.* The **Museu de Ciências Naturais da Amazônia** has a pavilion with insects and fish of the region and is located at Al Cosme Ferreira, Colonia Cachoeira Grande, 15 km from the city. ■ *Mon-Sat 0900-1700, US$4, T644 2799, difficult to get to, take 'São José-Acoariquarape/Tropolis' bus 519 to Conjunto Petro, then 2 km walk. Best to combine with a visit to INPA, and take a taxi from there.* **Jardim Botânico 'Chico Mendes'** (Horto Municipal). The botanical gardens contain a collection of plants from the Amazon region. Av André Araujo s/n. ■ *Daily 0800-1200, 1400-1700, buses 'Aleixo', 'Coroado'.* The **zoo**, Estrada Ponta Negra 750 (look for the life-size model jaguar), is run by CIGS, the army jungle-survival unit. It has been expanded and improved and has a 800-m trail which leads into the zoo itself. ■ *Tue-Sun 0900-1630, US$0.65, plus US$1 for trail. Take bus 120 or 207, 'Ponta Negra', from R Tamandaré, US$0.70.*

About 15 km from Manaus is the confluence of the yellow-brown Solimões (Amazon) and the blue-black Rio Negro, which is itself some 8 km wide. The two rivers run side by side for about 18 km (says one traveller) without their waters mingling. Tourist agencies run boat trips to this spot (US$60-160). The simplest route is to take a taxi or No 713 'Vila Buriti' bus to the Careiro ferry dock, and take the car ferry across. The ferry (very basic, with no shelter on deck and no cabins) goes at 0700 returning 1000, and 1500 returning 1800 (approximately). Small private launches cross, 40 mins journey, US$10-15 per seat, ask for the engine to be shut off at the confluence, you should see dolphins especially in the early morning. Alternatively, hire a motorized canoe from near the market (US$15 approximately; allow 3-4 hours to experience the meeting properly). A 2-km walk along the Porto Velho road from the Careiro ferry terminal will lead to a point from which Victoria Regia water lilies can be seen in April/May-September in ponds, some way from the road. Agencies can arrange tours.

Arquipélago de Anavilhanas, the largest archipelago in a river in the world, is in the Rio Negro, some 100 km upstream from Manaus, near the town of Novo Airão. There are hundreds of islands, covered in thick vegetation. When the river is low, white sand beaches are revealed, as well as the roots and trunks of the trees. Tour companies arrange visits to the archipelago (US$195-285, one day).

Essentials

Sleeping

L *Tropical*, Praia de Ponta Negra, T658 5000, F658 5026, ghathm@tropicalhotel.com.br A lavish, 5-star Varig hotel 20 km outside the city (taxi to centre, US$20). Wave pools, beach with new dock, departure point for river cruises, tennis courts, *churrascaria*, pool, 24-hr coffee shop, open to well-dressed non-residents. Take minibus from R José Paranaguá in front of Petrobras building at the corner of Dr Moreira, US$5 return, 0830, 0930, 1130 to hotel, 1200, 1400, 1500, 1800 to town, or take Ponta Negra bus, US$0.70, then walk. It is rarely full, except in Jan-Feb.

Central hotels L *Holiday Inn Taj Mahal*, Av Getúlio Vargas 741, T633 1010, tajmahal@internext.com.br Large, impressive, one of best hotels in city, popular, tour agency, revolving restaurant, massage and high level of service. Recommended. **A** *Ana Cassia Palace*, R dos Andradas 14, T622 3637, F234 4163. Gloriously faded, large rooms, some with great views of port, restaurant, pool. **A** *Best Western Lord Manaus*, R Marcílio Dias 217, T622 7700, bwmanaus@internext.com.br Conveniently located in heart of Zona Franca, comfortable, bar. **A** *Manaós*, Av Eduardo Ribeiro 881, T6335744, manaos@argo.com.br Good option near *Teatro Amazonas*. **A** *Mônaco*, R Silva Ramos 20, T622 3446, F622 3637. Rooms have good view, pleasant (some rooms noisy), rooftop restaurant/bar, delicious breakfast. **B** *Brasil*, Av Getúlio Vargas 657, T233 6575, hotel-brasil@internext.com.br Mid-market option close to centre. **B** *Central*, R Dr Moreira 202, T622 2600, hcentral@zaz.com.br Dated, high ceilings, quiet. **D** *Nacional*, R Dr Moreira 59, T232 9206. Fine for price. **D** *Palace*, Av 7 de Septembro 593, T622 4522, palace@argo.com.br Recently restored, simple, traditional rooms with high ceilings, some with wrought iron balconies, excellent location on praça overlooking cathedral. Highly recommended. **D** *Rei Salomão*, R Dr Moreira 119, T234 7374. In commercial centre, modern, quiet, a/c, restaurant, excellent value. Recommended. **E** *Dona Joana*, R dos Andradas 553, T233 7553, alberto.dionizio@interlins.com.br A/c, fridge, TV, newly decorated, homely and helpful, good value, the hotel is safe although the area is not. **E** *Ideal*, R dos Andradas 491, T/F233 9423. A/c, **F** with fan. **E** *Pensão Sulista*, Av Joaquim Nabuco 347, T234 5814. Run down, a/c, **F** with fan and shared bathroom. **E** *Rio Branco*, R dos Andradas 484, T/F233 4019. Basic, uncooperative, laundry facilities, a/c. **E** *10 de Julho*, R Dez de Julio 679, T232 6280, htdj@horizon.com.br Near opera house, a/c, new rooms in 2003, good value and breakfast, tours arranged (independent of all guides on the street). Recommended. **F** *Jangada*, R dos Andradas 473, T622 0264. Basic, a bargain, a/c and TV. Recommended.

Camping There are no campsites in or near Manaus; it is difficult to find a good, safe place to camp wild.

Eating

Expensive *La Barca*, R Recife 684. Wide variety of fish dishes, very swanky, popular, often has live music. *Himawari*, R 10 de Julho 618. Swish, sushi and Japanese food, attentive service, opposite *Teatro Amazonas*, open Sun night, when many restaurants close. Recommended. Japanese at *Miako*, R São Luís 230. *Restaurant Tarumã* in Tropical Hotel (see above). Dinner only. **Mid-range** *Búfalo*, *churrascaria*, Av Joaquim Nabuco 628. Best in town, US$7, all you can eat Brazilian barbecue. *Canto da Peixada*, R Emílio Moreira 1677 (Praça 14 de Janeiro). Superb fish dishes, lively atmosphere, unpretentious, close to centre, take a taxi. *Fiorentina*, R José Paranaguá 44, Praça da Polícia. Fan-cooled, traditional Italian, including vegetarian dishes, average food but one of best options in centre, watch out for the mugs of wine! Great *feijoada* on Sat, half-price on Sun. *Pizzaria Scarola*, R 10 de Julho, corner with Av Getúlio Vargas. Standard Brazilian menu, pizza delivery, popular. *São Francisco*, Blvd Rio Negro 195, 30 mins walk from centre (or bus 705), in Educandos suburb. Good fish, huge portions. *Suzuran*, R Teresina, 155, Adrianópolis, Japanese cuisine, closed Tue, take taxi. **Cheap** *Alemã*, R José Paranaguá, Praça da Policia. Food by weight, great pastries, hamburgers, juices, sandwiches. *Brasil*, next to hotel of same name, see above. Food by weight, juice and sandwich kiosk outside hotel. *Gruta do Peixe*, R Saldanha Marinho 609. Self-service and *pratos* in attractive basement, lunch only. Recommended. *Senac*, R Saldanha Marinho, 644. Cookery school, self-service, open daily, lunch only. Highly recommended. *Sorveteria Glacial*, Av Getúlio Vargas 161 and other locations. Recommended for ice cream. *Skina dos Sucos*, Eduardo Ribeiro e 24 de Maio. Juices and snacks. *Super Guaraná*, R Guilherme Moreira 395. Guaraná with juice, hamburgers, pies. *Xamêgo*, Av Getúlio Vargas, corner with R Dez de Julio. Basic self-service, popular with locals.

Entertainment

Boiart's, R José Clemente 500, next to *Teatro Amazonas*. Touristy, popular disco with jungle theme and shows. Cachoeirinha has a number of bars offering music and dancing, liveliest at weekends. *Tucano* nightclub in the *Tropical Hotel* attracts Manaus's wealthy citizens on Thu-Sat, as does its bingo club. Nearby Ponta Negra beach becomes extremely lively late on weekend nights and during holidays, with outdoor concerts and samba in the summer season. *Studio 5*, R Contorno, Distrito Industrial, T2378333, disco, part of leisure complex with several cinema screens. **Performing Arts** For *Teatro Amazonas* and *Centro Cultural Pálacio Rio Negro*, see above. *Teatro da Instalação*, R Frei José dos Inocentes, T/F2344096. Performance space in recently restored historic buildings with free music and dance (everything from ballet to jazz), Mon-Fri May-Dec at 1800. Charge for performances Sat and Sun. Recommended. In Praça da Saudade, R Ramos Ferreira, there is a Sunday **funfair** from 1700; try prawns and calaloo dipped in *tacaca* sauce.

Festivals

6 Jan: *Epiphany*; *Ash Wednesday*, half-day; *Maundy Thursday*; 24 Jun: *São João*; 14 Jul; 5 Sep; 30 Oct; 1 Nov, *All Saints Day*, half-day; *Christmas Eve*; *New Year's Eve*, half-day. Feb: *Carnival* dates vary – 5 days of Carnival, culminating in the parade of the Samba Schools. 3rd week in **Apr**: *Week of the Indians*, Indian handicraft. In **Jun**: *Festival do Amazonas*; a celebration of all the cultural aspects of Amazonas life, indigenous, Portuguese and from the northeast, especially dancing; 29 Jun: *São Pedro*, boat processions on the Rio Negro. In **Sep**: *Festival da Bondade*, last week, stalls from neighbouring states and countries offering food, handicrafts, music and dancing, SESI, Estrada do Aleixo Km 5. **Oct**: *Festival Universitário de Música – FUM*, the most traditional festival of music in Amazonas, organized by the university students, on the University Campus. **8 Dec**: *Processão de Nossa Senhora da Conceicão*, from the Igreja Matriz through the city centre and returning to Igreja Matriz for a solemn mass.

Shopping

Since Manaus is a free port, the whole area a few blocks off the river front is full of electronics shops. All shops close at 1400 on Sat and all day Sun

Bookshops *Livraria Nacional*, R 24 de Maio 415, stocks some French books. *Usados CDs e Livros*, Av Getúlio Vargas 766. Selection of used books, English, German, French and Spanish. *Valer*, R Ramos Ferreira 1195. A few English classics stocked, best bookshop in city. Maps from *Paper Comunicação*, Av J Nabuco 2074-2. **Markets and souvenirs** Go to the *Mercado Adolfo Lisboa* (see above) early in the morning when it is full of good quality regional produce, food and handicrafts, look out for *guaraná* powder or sticks, scales of *pirarucu* fish (used for manicure), and its tongue used for rasping *guaraná* (open Mon-Sat 0500-1800, Sun and holidays 0155-1200). In the Praça do Congresso, Av E Ribeiro, there is a very good Sun craftmarket. There is a good supermarket at the corner of Av Joaquin Nabuco and Av Sete de Setembro. *Shopping Amazonas*, outside the city, is a mall with cinema, supermarket, fast food. *Artesanato da Amazônia*, R José Clemente 500, loja A, opposite *Teatro Amazonas*. Good, reasonably priced, selection of regional products. The *Central Artesanato*, R Recife s/n, near Detran, has local craft work. The souvenir shop at the INPA has some interesting Amazonian products on sale. *Selva Amazônica*, Mercado Municipal, for wood carvings and bark fabric. For hammocks go to R dos Andradas, many shops.

Sport & activities

Swimming: for swimming, go to Ponta Negra beach by *Soltur* bus for US$0.70, though the beach virtually disappears beneath the water in Apr-Aug; popular by day and at night with outdoor concerts and samba in the summer season. Every Sun, boats leave from the port in front of the market to beaches along Rio Negro, US$2, leaving when full and returning at end of the day. This is a real locals' day out, with loud music and food stalls on the sand. Good swimming at waterfalls on the Rio Tarumã, where lunch is available, shade, crowded at weekends. Take Tarumã bus from R Tamandaré or R Frei J dos Inocentes, 30 mins, US$0.80 (very few on weekdays), getting off at the police checkpoint on the road to Itacoatiara.

Tour operators

Check agencies' licences from Embratur and ABAV If in the least doubt, use only a registered company

Amazon Clipper Cruises, R Sucupira 249, Conj Kissia, Planalto, T656 1246. Informed guides, well-planned activities, comfortable cabins and good food. *Amazon Explorers*, R Nhamundá 21, Praça NS Auxiliadora, T633 3319, www.amazonexplorers.com.br Day tour including 'meeting of the waters', Lago do Janauari, rubber collecting and lunch. *Espaço Verde Turismo*, R Costa Azevedo 240, T6334522, rogerio-evtur@internext.com.br Opposite *Teatro Amazonas*, river boat tours, one day US$30, including lunch; flights; trips to lodges, English spoken, helpful. *Heliconia*, R Col Salgado 63, Aparecida, T234 5915, alternatur@internext.com.br Run by French researcher Thérèse Aubreton. *Iguana*, R 10 de Julho 667, T633 6507, iguanatour@hotmail.com Short and long tours, plenty of activities, many languages spoken. *Jaguar Adventure Tours* R Marciano Armond, Vila Operária 23A, Cachoeirinha, www.objetivonet.com.br/jaguartours Carlos Jorge Damasceno, multilingual, deep jungle exploration with an ecological slant and visits to remote historical and Indian settlements. *Swallows and Amazons*, R Quintino Bocaiúva 189, Suite 13, T/F622 1246, www.swallowsandamazonstours.com Mark and Tania Aitchison offer a wide range of riverboat tours and accommodation (up to 15 days), prices start at US$65-120 per day; they have their own houseboat *Dona Tania*, covered motorized canoe and 8-room private jungle lodge, *The Over Look Lodge*, just before the Anavilhanas islands. Very comprehensive service, with full assistance for travellers (reservations, email, transfers, medical, etc), English, French and Spanish speaking guides. *The Global Heritage Expeditions*, R Floriano Peixoto 182, T233 3010, www.amazonpda.hpg.com.br Sandro Gama speaks English, small group tours in the Amazon basin. **Guides** are licensed to work only through tour agencies, so it is safest to book guides through approved agencies.

Transport

Local flights leave from airport terminal 2; make sure in advance of your terminal Airport T652 1120

Air International flights: *LAB* to Miami and Santa Cruz (Bolivia), twice a week. *Varig* flies four times a week to Caracas. To the Guyanas, *Meta* (no office in town) flies from the small Eduardinho airport (by main airport) twice a week to Georgetown (US$90) and Paramaribo (US$140), via Boa Vista. **Internal flights**: there are frequent internal flights with *Varig, Vasp, Penta, TAM* and *Tavaj*. Domestic airport tax US$7.

The taxi fare to or from the airport is US$7.50, fixed rate, buy ticket at airport and in most hotels; or take bus 306 marked `Aeroporto Internacional' from R Tamandaré near the cathedral, US$0.50, or 1107 from Ed Garagem on Av Getúlio Vargas every 30 mins. No buses 2300-0700. (Taxi drivers often tell arrivals that no bus to town is available, be warned!) It is

sometimes possible to use the more regular, faster service run by the *Tropical Hotel*; many tour agencies offer free transfers without obligation. Check all connections on arrival. **NB** Check in time is 2 hrs in advance. Allow plenty of time at Manaus airport, formalities are very slow especially if you have purchased duty-free goods. The restaurant serves good à la carte and buffet food through the day. Many flights depart in the middle of the night and while there are many snack bars there is nowhere to rest.

Bus Manaus rodoviária is 9 km out of town at the intersection of Av Constantino Nery and R Recife. Take a local bus from centre, US$0.50, marked 'Aeroporto Internacional' or 'Cidade Nova' (or taxi, US$5). Local buses to Praça 14 or the airport leave from Praça Adalberto Vale (take airport bus and alight just after Antárctica factory) or take local bus to Ajuricaba.

Road Hitchhiking with truckers is common, but not recommended for women travelling alone. To hitch, take a Tarumã bus to the customs building and hitch from there, or try at 'posta 5', 2 km beyond the rodoviária. The Catire Highway (BR 319) from Manaus to Porto Velho (868 km), has been officially closed since 1990. Enquire locally if the road is passable for light vehicles; some bridges are flimsy. The alternative for drivers is to ship a car down river on a barge, others have to travel by boat (see below).

Shipping To Santarém, Belém, Porto Velho, Tefé, Tabatinga (for Colombia and Peru), São Gabriel da Cachoeira, and intermediate ports (see River Transport, page 526). Almost all vessels now berth at the first (downstream) of the floating docks which is open to the public 24 hrs a day. A tourist office in a purpose-built shopping complex on the dockside will help travellers buy tickets (avoiding touts) and will translate for you as you look over the boats. Bookings can also be made up to 2 weeks in advance at the ticket sales area by the port's pedestrian entrance (bear left on entry). The names and itineraries of departing vessels are displayed here as well as on the docked boats themselves; travellers still recommend buying tickets from the captain on the boat itself. The port is relatively clean, well organized, and has a pleasant atmosphere.

ENASA (the state shipping company) sells tickets for private boats at its office in town (prices tend to be high here), T633 3280. Local boats and some cargo barges still berth by the concrete retaining wall between the market and Montecristi. Boats for São Gabriel da Cachoeira and Novo Airão go from São Raimundo, up river from the main port. Take bus 101 'São Raimundo', 112 'Santo Antônio' or 110, 40 mins; there are 2 docking areas separated by a hill, the São Raimundo *balsa*, where the ferry to Novo Airão, on the Rio Negro, leaves every afternoon (US$10); and the Porto Beira Mar de São Raimundo, where the São Gabriel da Cachoeira boats dock (most departures Fri). **NB** Departures to the less important destinations are not always known at the **Capitânia do Porto**, Av Santa Cruz 265, Manaus. Be careful of people who wander around boats after they've arrived at a port: they are almost certainly looking for something to steal.

Immigration For those arriving by boat who have not already had their passports stamped (eg from Leticia), the immigration office is on the first of the floating docks. Take the dock entrance opposite the cathedral, bear right, after 50 m left, pass through a warehouse to a group of buildings on a T section.

Directory

Airline offices *TAM*, Av Tarumã, 433, T233 1828. *Varig*, Marcílio Dias 284, T622 4500, English spoken, helpful. *Vasp*, Av 7 de Setembro 993, T622 3470/633 2213.

Banks *Banco do Brasil*, Guia Moreira, and airport changes US$ cash, 8% commission, both with ATMs for Visa/Plus, Cirrus/MasterCard. Most offices shut at 1500; foreign exchange operations 0900-1200 only, or even as early as 1100. *Bradesco*, Av 7 de Setembro 895/293, for Visa ATM. *HSBC*, R Dr Moreira,226. ATM for Visa, Cirrus, MasterCard and Plus. *Credicard*, Av Getúlio Vargas 222 for Diner's cash advances. Cash at main hotels; *Câmbio Cortez*, 7 de Setembro 1199, converts TCs into US$ cash, good rates, no commission. Do not change money on the streets.

Communications Internet: Free internet access available from all public libraries in city, eg *Biblioteca Arthur Reis*, Av 7 de Setembro 444, open 0800-1200, 1400-1700, with virtual Amazon library and English books. *Amazon Cyber Cafe*, Av Getúlio Vargas 626, corner with R 10 de Julho, US$1.50 per hr. Another at No 188, 0800-2300, US$2 per hr. *Discover Internet*, R Marcílio Dias 304, next to Praça da Polícia, cabins in back of shop with Internet phones and scanners, US$1.50 per hr. *Internext*, R 24 de Maio 220, US$3 per hr. Post Office: main office including poste restante on Marechal Deodoro. On the 1st floor is the philatelic counter where stamps are sold, avoiding the long queues downstairs. Staff

Brazil

don't speak English but are used to dealing with tourists. For airfreight and shipping, Alfândega, Av Marquês Santa Cruz (corner of Marechal Deodoro), Sala 106. For airfreight and seamail, Correio Internacional, R Monsenhor Coutinho e Av Eduardo Ribeiro (bring your own packaging). **UPS** office, T232 9849 (Custódio). **Telephone:** International calls can be made from local call boxes with an international card. Also *Telemar*, Av Getúlio Vargas 950 e R Leo Malcher.

Embassies and consulates Austria, Rua 5, 4 Qde Jardim Primavera T642 1939/236 6089. **Belgium,** 13 qd D conj Murici, T236 1452. **Colombia**, R 24 de Maio 220, Rio Negro Center, T234 6777, double check whether a Colombian tourist card can be obtained at the border. **Denmark**, R Miranda Leão 45, T622 1365, also handles **Norway**. **Finland**, R Marcílio Dias 131, T234 5084. **France**, R Joaquim Nabuco 1846, Bl A sala 2, T233 6583. **Germany**, Av 24 Maio 220, Ed Rio Negro Centre, sala 812, T234 9045, 1000-1200. **Italy**, R Belo Horizonte 240, T611 4877. **Japan**, R Fortaleza 460, T234 8825. **Netherlands**, R M Leão 41, T622 1366. **Peru**, R KL c/6, Morada do Sol, Aleixo, T642 1646. **Portugal**, R Terezina 193, T633 1577. **Spain**, R Mons Coutinho 941, T234 4144. **Sweden**, R M Leão 45, T633 1371. **UK**, Swedish Match de Amazônia, R Poraquê 240, Distrito Industrial, T237 7869/613 1819, F613 1420, vincent@internext.com.br **US**, R Recife 1010, T234 4546; will supply letters of introduction for US citizens. **Venezuela**, R Rio Jetau 868, T233 6004, F233 0481, 0800-1200. Everyone entering Venezuela overland needs a visa. The requirements are: 1 passport photo, an onward ticket and a yellow fever certificate, US$30 (check with a Venezuelan consulate in advance for changes to these regulations).

Medical services *Clínica São Lucas*, R Alexandre Amorin 470, T622 3678, reasonably priced, some English spoken, good service, take a taxi. *Hospital Tropical*, Av Pedro Teixeira (D Pedro I) 25, T656 1441. Centre for tropical medicine, not for general complaints, treatment free, some doctors speak a little English. Take buses 201 or 214 from Av Sete de Setembro in the city centre. *Pronto Soccoro 28 de Agosto*, R Recife, free for emergencies. **Useful addresses** Police: to extend or replace a Brazilian visa, take bus from Praça Adalberto Vale to Kissia Dom Pedro for Polícia Federal post, people in shorts not admitted. **Ibama:** R Ministro João Gonçalves de Souza s/n, BR-319, Km 01, Distrito Industrial, Caixa Postal 185, CEP 69900-000, T237 3718, F237 5177. **Voltage** 110 volts AC. Some hotels 220 volts AC, 60 cycles.

Tours from Manaus

There are **two types** of tours: those based at jungle lodges and river boat trips. Most tours, whether luxury or budget, combine river outings on motorised canoes with piranha fishing, caiman spotting, visiting local families and short treks in the jungle. Specialist tours include fishing trips and those aimed specifically at seeing how the people in the jungle, *caboclos*, live. Booking in advance on the internet is likely to secure you a good guide (who usually works for several companies and may get booked up). Be sure to ascertain in advance the exact itinerary of the tour, that the price includes everything (even drink and tips), that guides are knowledgeable and will accompany you themselves and that there will be no killing of anything rare. Ensure that others in your party share your expectations and are going for the same length of time. Choose a guide who speaks a language you can understand. A shorter tour may be better than a long, poor one. Packaged tours, booked overseas, are usually of the same price and quality as those negotiated locally.

NB There are many hustlers at the airport and on the street (particularly around the hotels and bars on Joaquim Nabuco and Miranda Leão), and even at the hotels. It is not wise to go on a tour with the first friendly face you meet; all go-betweens earn a commission so recommendations cannot be taken at face value. Employing freelance guides not attached to a company is potentially dangerous. Make enquiries and check for Embratur and ABAV (Brazilian Association of Travel Agents) credentials personally. *Secretaria de Estado da Cultura e Turismo* is not allowed by law to recommend guides, but can provide you with a list of legally registered companies. Unfortunately, disreputable operations are rarely dealt with in any satisfactory manner and most continue to operate. When you are satisfied that you have found a reputable company, book direct with the company itself and ask for a detailed, written contract if you have any doubts.

Flights over the jungle give a spectacular impression of the extent of the forest. Bill Potter, resident in Manaus, writes: "opposite Manaus, near the junction of the Rio Negro and the Rio Solimões, lies the **Lago de Janauri**, a small nature reserve. This is where all the day or half-day trippers are taken, usually combined with a visit to the 'meeting of the waters'. Although many people express disappointment with this area because so little is seen and/or there are so many 'tourist-trash' shops, for those with only a short time it is worth a visit. You will see some birds and with luck dolphins. In the shops and bars there are often captive parrots and snakes. The area is set up to receive large numbers of tourists, which ecologists agree relieves pressure on other parts of the river. Boats for day trippers leave the harbour constantly throughout the day, but are best booked at one of the larger operators. Remember that in the dry season, one-day tours may not offer much to see if the river is low."

Those with more time can take the longer cruises and will see various ecological environments. To see virgin rainforest, a five-day trip by boat is needed. Most tour operators operate on both the Rio Solimões and the Rio Negro. The Rio Negro is considered easier to navigate, more pristine, generally calmer and with fewer biting insects. This area has more visible upland rainforest and it is easier to see animals such as sloths because there are fewer people. The Solimões, which is flooded for six months of the year, has more birds, piranha and alligators, but you're likely to be constantly fighting the mosquitoes and sandflies. Another alternative is to go upriver to one of the jungle hotels. From the base, you can then take short trips into the forest or along the river channels.

Generally, between Apr and Sep excursions are only by boat; in the period Oct-Mar the Victoria Regia lilies virtually disappear. Fishing is best between Sep and Mar (no flooding). If using a camera, do remember to bring a fast film as light is dim.

Prices vary, but usually include lodging, guide, transport, meals and activities. The recommended companies charge within the following ranges (pp): one day, US$50-100; three days, eg to Anavilhanas Archipelago, US$195-285. Longer, specialized, or more luxurious excursions will cost significantly more. Most river trips incorporate the meeting of the waters on the first day, so there is no need to make a separate excursion.

What to take

Leave luggage with your tour operator or hotel in Manaus and only take what is necessary for your trip. Long sleeves, long trousers, shoes and insect repellent are advisable for treks where insects are voracious. A hat offers protection from the sun on boat trips. Bottled water and other drinks are expensive in the jungle, so you may want to take your own supplies.

Lodges

There are several lodges within a few hrs boat or car journey from Manaus. Most emphasize comfort (although electricity and hot water is limited) rather than a real jungle experience and you are more likely to enjoy a nice buffet in pleasant company than come face to face with rare fauna. Nevertheless, the lodges are good if your time is limited and you want to have a brief taste of the Amazon rainforest. Agencies for reservations are also listed.

L *Amazon Ecopark Lodge*, Igarapé do Tarumã, 20 km from Manaus, 15 mins by boat, jungle trails; 60 apartments with shower, bar, restaurant, T/F233 2559, www.amazon copark.com.br Nearby is the **Amazon Monkey Jungle**, an ecological park where many monkey species are treated and rehabilitated in natural surroundings. The Living Rainforest Foundation, which administers the *Ecopark*, also offers educational jungle trips and overnight camps (bring your own food). Entrance US$15. **L** *Acajatuba Jungle Lodge*, Lago Acajatuba 4 hrs up the Rio Negro from Manaus, 30 apartments with shower, bar, restaurant, contact T233 7642, www.acajatuba.com.br **L** *Amazon Village*, Lago de Puraquequara, 60 km, 2 hrs by boat from Manaus, a comfortable lodge on dry land, with nice cabins, 32 apartments with cold shower, restaurant. Recommended. Contact T633 1444. **A** *Amazon Lodge*, a floating lodge on Lago do Juma, 80 km from Manaus, 30 mins by Careiro ferry, then 1½ hrs by bus, then 2 hrs by boat, 12 basic apartments with cold shower, restaurant, good excursions. Highly recommended. Contact T656 3357. **L** *Ariaú Amazon Towers*, Rio Ariaú, 2 km from Archipélago de Anavilhanas, 60 km and 2 hrs by boat from Manaus on a side channel of the Rio Negro. Complex of towers connected by walkways, beach (Sep-Mar), trips to the Anavilhanas islands in groups of 10-20. Rates pp: US$280 for 2-days/1-night, US$400, 3 nights/4 days. Highly recommended. Manaus office at R Leonardo Malcher 699, Centro, T2121 5000/0800-925000, www.ariau.tur.br **A** *Boa Vida Jungle Resort*, 53 km from Manaus by route AM-10, direction Itacoatiara, 7 apartments and 6 chalets, shower, fridge, bar, restaurant, fishing, boating; contact T234 5722, F232 2482. *Pousada dos Guanavenas* on Ilha de Silves, 300 km from Manaus on the road to Itacoatiara then by boat along the Rio Urubu, views of Lago Canacari, 33 rooms, a/c, fridge, electric showers, T656 1500. **A** *Rainforest Lodge*, on the banks of Lago Januacá, 4 hrs from Manaus, 14 bungalows with fans, pool, restaurant, snack bar, contact

MS Empreendimentos, T233 9182, rflodge@n3.com.br **L** *Juna Lodge*, small lodge on the Riuo Juma, 2½ hrs south of Manaus by road and boat, all-inclusive packages, contact 0xx11-3088 1937, www.jumahotel.com.br **A** *Lago Salvador Lodge*, Lago Salvador, 30 km from Manaus, 40 mins by boat from the *Hotel Tropical*, 12 apartments, shower, bar, restaurant; T659 5119.

Amazon Youth Hostel, near the town of Maués, southeast of Manaus. US$75 per week in dormitory, US$150 per week in cabin, 5-day backpacking tours US$250, kitchen, lounge, hiking, canoeing. Contact Doña Nailê or Joe Maldonado, www.amazon-hostal.com *Rico Airlines*, T652 1553, fly Manaus-Maués US$75, 1 hr, or boat at 1600, arrive 1100 next day, US$25 (take own hammock) or US$65 in cabin. In Maués go to *Casa Quixada* store and take a water taxi to the hostel, US$30 per group.

Mamiraua sustainable development reserve, at the confluence of the Rios Solimões, Japurá and Auti-Paraná, is one of the best places to see the Amazon. It protects flooded forest (*várzea*) and is listed under the Ramsar Convention as an internationally important wetland. In the reserve *Uakari* is a floating lodge with 10 suites. Lots of mammals and birds to see, including cayman, dolphin and harpy eagles, also the endangered *piraracu* fish. Visitors are accompanied by guides the whole time. ■ *4-day, 3-night package US$360 all inclusive. Reservations through www.mamiraua.org.br All profits go to local projects and reseach. Daily flights Manaus-Tefé, then 1½ hrs by boat to lodge.*

Manaus to Colombia and Peru

Colour map 3, grid A5 **Benjamin Constant** is on the border with Peru, with Colombian territory on the opposite bank of the river. ■ *Boat services from Manaus, 7 days, or more; to Manaus, 4 days, or more.* **Sleeping** Recommended hotels: **B** *Benjamin Constant*, beside ferry. A/c, some rooms with hot water and TV, good restaurant, arranges tours, postal address Apto Aéreo 219, Leticia, Colombia. **D** *Márcia Maria*. With bath, a/c, fridge. **E** *Hotel São Jorge*. Meals available. **E** *Hotel Lanchonete Peruana*, good food. Eat at *Pensão Cecília*, or *Bar-21 de Abril*, cheaper.

Tabatinga is 4 km from Leticia (Colombia). The Port Captain in Tabatinga is reported as very helpful and speaks good English. **NB** The port area of Tabatinga is called Marco. A good hammock will cost US$15 in Tabatinga (try Esplanada Teocides) or Benjamin Constant. A mosquito net for a hammock is essential if sailing upstream from Tabatinga; much less so downstream. ■ *Airport to Tabatinga by minibus, US$1.* Varig *to Manaus 3 times a week. See also under Leticia (Colombia) page 851. Regular minibus to Leticia, US$0.60.*

Sleeping and eating **D** *Residencial Aluguel Pajé*. With bath, fan. **D** *Solimões*. Military-run, close to airport, with breakfast, other meals available if ordered in advance, excellent value. VW colectivo from barracks to centre, harbour and Leticia. **F** pp *Rio Mar*, at the dockside. Run by Sr Dixon, who speaks English, with bath and fan. There are decent places to stay near the boat companies for Peru. Excellent *Canto do Peixado*, on main street. Highly recommended. *Lanchonete e Sorveteria Mallet*, fresh juices, ice creams, burgers, popular.

Directory Banks: no exchange facilities at Tabatinga port. Best to change money in Leticia. Dollars are accepted everywhere; Colombian pesos are accepted in Tabatinga, Peruvian soles rarely accepted.

Border with Brazil, Colombia & Peru

In this area, carry your passport at all times

It is advisable to check all requirements and procedures before arriving at this multiple border. Travellers should enquire carefully about embarkation/disembarkation points and where to go through immigration formalities. If waiting for transport, Tabatinga has convenient hotels for early morning departures, but Leticia has the best money changing facilities and the only internet in the region (try the bookshop next to the church). **NB** When crossing these borders, check if there is a time difference (for example, Brazilian summer time, usually mid-October to mid-February). **Consulates** Brazilian, C 11, No 10-70, Leticia, T27531, 1000-1600,

Brazil

Monday-Friday, efficient, helpful; onward ticket and 2 black-and-white photos needed for visa (photographer nearby); allow 36 hours. Peruvian, Cra 11, No 6-80, Leticia, T27204, F27825, open 0830-1430; no entry or exit permits are given here.

Brazilian immigration Entry and exit stamps are given at the *Policía Federal*, 2 km from the Tabatinga docks, best to take a taxi, 24 hours. Proof of US$500 or an onward ticket may be asked for. There are no facilities in Benjamin Constant. One-week transit in Tabatinga is permitted. The Colombian consulate is near the border on the road from Tabatinga to Leticia, opposite *Restaurant El Canto de las Peixadas*. Open 0800-1400. Tourist cards are issued on presentation of 2 passport photos.

If coming from Peru, you must have a Peruvian exit stamp and a yellow fever certificate

Transport Travel between Tabatinga and Leticia is very informal; taxis between the two towns charge US$5 (more if you want to stop at immigration offices, exchange houses, etc; beware of taxi drivers who want to rush you expensively over the border before it 'closes'), or US$0.80 in a colectivo (more after 1800). **Boat** From Manaus to Benjamin Constant boats normally go on to Tabatinga, and start from there when going to Manaus. They usually wait 1-2 days in both Tabatinga and Benjamin Constant before returning to Manaus; you can stay on board. It's quicker to get off the river boat in Benjamin Constant and take a fast ferry, US$1.50, 2 hrs, to Tabatinga, than stay on the river boat for the crossing from Benjamin Constant. Boats arrive in Benjamin Constant at 0600, so you can take the 0700 ferry and have a enough time in Tabatinga to get exit stamps and book the launch to Iquitos for the next day. For information on boats to/from Manaus, see Manaus Shipping and River Transport in Amazônia.

Colombian immigration DAS, C 9, No 8-32, T27189, Leticia, and at the airport. Exit stamps to leave Colombia by air or overland are given by DAS no more than 1 day before you leave. If flying into Leticia prior to leaving for Brazil or Peru, get an exit stamp while at the airport. Check both offices for entry stamps before flying into Colombia. To enter Colombia you must have a tourist card to obtain an entry stamp, even if you are passing through Leticia en route between Brazil and Peru (the Colombian consul in Manaus may tell you otherwise; try to get a tourist card elsewhere). The Colombian Consular Office in Tabatinga issues tourist cards; 24-hr transit stamps can be obtained at the DAS office. If visiting Leticia without intending to go anywhere else in Colombia, you may be allowed to enter without immigration or customs formalities (but travellers' cheques cannot be changed without an entry stamp). ■ *Travel between Colombia and Brazil and Peru is given above and below respectively. Travel from/into Colombia is given under Leticia.*

There are no customs formalities for everyday travel between Leticia and Tabatinga

Peruvian immigration Entry/exit formalities take place at Santa Rosa. Every boat leaving and entering Peru stops here. There is also an immigration office in Iquitos (Mcal Cáceres 18th block, T235371), where procedures for leaving can be checked. There is no Brazilian consulate in Iquitos No exchange facilites in Santa Rosa; reais and dollars are accepted, but soles are not accepted in Leticia and only occasionally in Tabatinga.

Transport Boats Santa Rosa-Tabatinga or Leticia, US$1 (in reais, soles or pesos). Between Tabatinga and Iquitos in Peru there are 3 companies with 20-seater speedboats, US$50 one way, buy ticket 1 day in advance. They take 11-12 hrs. Departure from Tabatinga is 0530 (be there 0500). There are also cheaper, slower *lanchas*, which 2 days (US$15-17.50 hammock, US$25-30 cabin). Boat services are given under **Iquitos** in the Peru chapter. Passengers leaving and entering Peru must visit immigration at Santa Rosa when the boat stops there. For entry into Brazil, formalities are done in Tabatinga; for Colombia, in Leticia.

The road which connects Manaus and Boa Vista (BR-174 to Novo Paraíso, then the Perimetral, BR-210, rejoining the BR174 after crossing the Rio Branco at Caracaraí) can get badly potholed. There are service stations with toilets, camping, etc, every 150-180 km, but all petrol is low octane. Drivers should take a tow cable and spares, and bus passengers should prepare for delays in the rainy season. At Km 100 is

Manaus to Venezuela & Guyana

Presidente Figueiredo, with many waterfalls and a famous cave with bats, shops and a restaurant. About 100 km further on is a service station at the entrance to the **Uaimiri Atroari Indian Reserve**, which straddles the road for about 120 km. Private cars and trucks are not allowed to enter the Indian Reserve between sunset and sunrise, but buses are exempt from this regulation. Nobody is allowed to stop within the reserve at any time. At the northern entrance to the reserve there are toilets and a spot to hang your hammock (usually crowded with truckers overnight). At Km 327 is the village of Vila Colina with *Restaurante Paulista*, good food, clean, you can use the shower and hang your hammock. At Km 359 there is a monument to mark the equator. At Km 434 is the clean and pleasant *Restaurant Goaio*. Just south of Km 500 is *Bar Restaurante D'Jonas*, a clean, pleasant place to eat, you can also camp or sling a hammock. Beyond here, large tracts of forest have been destroyed for settlement, but already many homes have been abandoned.

At **Caracaraí**, a busy port with modern installations on the Rio Branco, a bridge crosses the river for traffic on the the the Manaus-Boa Vista road. It has hotels in our **D-E** range. ■ *Buses from Caracaraí to Boa Vista costs US$9, 3 hrs.* Boa Vista has road connections with the Venezuelan frontier at Santa Elena de Uairén (237 km, paved, the only gasoline 110 km south of Santa Elena) and Bonfim for the Guyanese border at Lethem. Both roads are open all year.

Boa Vista

Phone code: 0xx95
Post code: 69300
Colour map 2, grid B2
Population: 200,568
785 km N of Manaus

The capital of the extreme northern State of Roraima has a modern functional plan, which often necessitates long hot treks from one function to another. It has an interesting modern cathedral; also a museum of local Indian culture (poorly kept). There is swimming in the Rio Branco, 15 mins from the town centre (too polluted in Boa Vista), reachable by bus only when the river is low.

Sleeping
Accommodation is generally expensive. Economic hardship has caused an increase in crime, sometimes violent

B *Aipana Plaza*, Praça Centro Cívico 53, T224 4800, aipana@technet.com.br Modern, a/c, good service, best food in town, buffet US$7.20-8. **C** *Eusébio's*, R Cecília Brasil 1107, T224 0300, F623 8690 Run down in 2001, a/c, restaurant, swimming pool, free transport to rodoviária or airport. **C** *Itamaraty*, Av NS da Consolata 1957, T/F224 9757, itamaraty@ osite.com.br A/c, parking, good. **C** *Roraima*, Av Cecília Brasil e Benjamin Constant, T224 9843. Recommended. The restaurant opposite is also recommended. **C** *Uiramutam Palace*, Av Capt Ene Garcez 427, T/F224 9912. Good service, a/c, restaurant, pool. **D** *Três Nações*, Av Ville Roy 1885, T/F224 3439. Close to the rodoviária, some rooms a/c, refurbished, basic. Often recommended. **E** *Imperial*, Av Benjamin Constant 433, T224 5592. A/c, cheaper with fan, welcoming, safe motorcycle parking. **E** *Terraço*, Av Cecília Brasil 1141. Without bath, noisy, friendly. **Camping** Rio Caaumé, 3 km north of town (unofficial site, small bar, clean river, pleasant).

Eating
Most restaurants close at night, except for pizza, including delivery

Ver O Rio, R Floriano Peixoto 116. For best fish dishes. In same area are *Makuchic*, also for fish, and *Black and White*, fixed price lunch and more expensive by weight. *Café Pigalle*, R Cecília Brasil, just off central praça, next to *Eusébio's*. Good food, drinks and atmosphere, open till all hrs. *Churrascaria La Carreta*, R Pedro Rodrigues 185, 500 m from *Eusébio's*. Good, US$3 buffet, nice atmosphere. Recommended. *La Góndola*, Benjamin Constant e Av Amazonas. Good. *Vila Rica*, R Ville Roy, near the rodoviária. Good cheap lunch. *Catequeiro*, Araújo Filho e Benjamin Constant. Recommended *prato feito*. *Café com Leite Suíço*, at Santa Cecilia, 15 mins by car on road to Bom Fim. Open 0630-1300 for regional food, US$4, good.

Transport

Air *Varig* daily to and from São Paulo and Manaus. Confirm flights before reaching Boa Vista as they are fully booked. Aircraft maintenance, baggage checking and handling are unreliable. No left luggage, information or exchange facilities at the airport, which is 4 km from the centre. Bus 'Aeroporto' from the centre is US$0.40. Taxi to rodoviária, US$5, to centre US$7, 45 mins walk.

Bus (See also Border Crossings below.) Rodoviária is on the town outskirts, 3 km at the end of Av Ville Roy; taxi to centre, US$5, bus US$0.45, 10 mins (marked '13 de Setembro' or 'Joquey Clube' to centre). The local bus terminal is on Av Amazonas, by R Cecília Brasil, near the central

Brazil

praça. It is difficult to get a taxi or bus to the rodoviária in time for early morning departures; as it's a 25-min walk, book a taxi the previous evening. To **Manaus**, US$26-32.50, several companies including *Eucatur/União Cascavel* (T224 0505), 12 hrs, at least 6 daily, *executivo* service at 1800/1900 with meal stop. Advisable to book. **Boa Vista-Caracaraí** US$9, 3 hrs.

Hitchhiking To Santa Elena, Venezuela, is not easy; either wait at the bridge and police checkpoint on the road to the border, or try to find a Venezuelan driver on the praça. Hitching from Boa Vista to Manaus is fairly easy on the many trucks travelling south; try from the Trevo service station near the rodoviária. Truck drivers ask for approximately half the bus fare to take passengers in the cab (bargain), much cheaper or free in the back. The view from the truck is usually better than from the bus and you can see the virgin forest of the Indian Reserve in daylight. Take some food and water.

Airline offices *META*, Praça Santos Dumont 100, T224 7677. *Varig*, R Araújo Filho 91, T224 2269. **Banks** US$ and Guyanese notes can be changed in Boa Vista. TCs and cash in *Banco do Brasil*, Av Glaycon de Paiva 56, 1000-1300 (minimum US$200), has Visa/Plus ATM. There is no official exchange agency and the local rates for bolívares are low: the Banco do Brasil will not change bolívares. *HSBC*, Av Ville Roy 392, MasterCard ATM. *Bradesco*, Av Jaime Brasil 441, Visa ATM. Best rate for dollars, *Casa Pedro José*, R Araújo Filho 287, T224 9797, also changes TCs and bolívares; *Timbo's* (gold and jewellery shop), Av B Constant 170, T224 4077, will change money. **Embassies and consulates** Venezuela, Av Benjamin Constant 525E, T224 2182, Mon-Fri 0830-1300, but may close earlier. **Medical services** Yellow fever inoculations are free at a clinic near the hospital. **Tourist offices** Information is available at the rodoviária; also R Col Pinto 241, Centro, T623 1234, turismo@tecnet.com.br At the rodoviária, Leyla King at *Maikan Turismo* is very helpful; she speaks English and can arrange tours. Information and free hammock space from Klaus, T9963 7915/9111 3339/623 9960, or ask for Lula at *Guri Auto Elétrica*, R das Mil Flores 738, near rodoviária. **Tour Guide** boat trips on Rio Branco and surrounding waterways (jungle, beaches, Indian reservations), *Acqua*, R Floriano Peixoto 505, T224 6576. Guide Elieser Rufino is recommended.

Directory

Border with Venezuela

Border searches are thorough and frequent at this border crossing. If entering Brazil, ensure in advance that you have the right papers, including yellow fever certificate, before arriving at this border. Officials may give only two months' stay and car drivers may be asked to purchase an unnecessary permit. Ask to see the legal documentation. Everyone who crosses this border must have a visa for Venezuela. Check beforehand. Current procedure is to take filled out visa form, two photos and deposit slip from *Banco do Brasil* (US$75) to the Venezuelan consulate (address above), be prepared to wait an hour, but it may be possible to get a visa at the border; check requirements in advance. There is another Venezuelan consulate in Manaus which issues one-year, multiple entry visas.

On the Brazilian side there is a basic hotel, *Pacaraima Palace*, a guest house, camping and a bank. ■ *One bus a day goes from Boa Vista rodoviária to Santa Elena de Uairén, stopping at all checkpoints, US$15, 4 hrs, take water. It is possible to share a taxi. There are through buses to Ciudad Guayana, Ciudad Bolívar (eg* Caribe)*, US$33.*

Border with Guyana
Colour map 2, grid B3
Population: 9,326

The main border crossing between Brazil and Guyana is from **Bonfim**, 125 km (all paved) northeast of Boa Vista, to Lethem. The towns are separated by the Rio Tacutu, which is crossed by small boats for foot passengers; vehicles cross by ferry on demand, US$4 return. The river crossing is 2.5 km from Bonfim, 1.6 km north of Lethem. A bridge is under construction. Formalities are generally lax on both sides of the border, but it is important to observe them as people not having the correct papers may have problems further into either country.

Brazilian immigration is at Polícia Federal (closed for lunch): from the rodoviária in Bonfim take a taxi, obtain exit stamp, then walk to the river. Once across, do not go to the Guyanese police for immigration, but to the airport. Brazilian customs is at Ministério da Fazenda checkpoint, before entering Bonfim; jeeps from here charge US$1 to immigration. There is no Guyanese consul in Boa Vista, so if you need a visa for Guyana, you must get it in São Paulo or Brasília (see Guyana Documents in Essentials). *Reais* can be changed into Guyanese dollars in Boa Vista. There are no exchange facilities in Lethem, but *reais* are accepted in town.

Brazil

Sleeping and eating D *Bonfim*, owned by Mr Myers, who speaks English and is very helpful, fan, shower. *Domaia*. There is a café at the rodoviária, opposite the church, whose owner speaks English and gives information. *Restaurante Internacional*, opposite the rodoviária, on other side from church; another restaurant a bit further from the rodoviária serves good food. Local speciality, fried cashew nuts. English-speaking teacher, Tricia Watson, has been helpful to bewildered travellers.

Transport Bus: Boa Vista-Bonfim 6 a day US$6, 2½ hrs; colectivos charge US$18. **Ferry**: to cross the river, take a canoe (see above), US$0.25 (no boats at night).

Southern Amazônia

Rondônia and Acre, lands which mark not just the political boundaries between Brazil and Peru and Bolivia, but also developmental frontiers between the forest and colonization. Much of Rondônia has been deforested. Acre is still frontier country with great expanses of forest in danger of destruction.

Porto Velho

Phone code: 0xx69
Post code: 78900
Colour map 4, grid B1
Population: 334,661
Malaria is common; the drinking water is contaminated with mercury (from gold panning)

This city stands on a high bluff overlooking a curve of the Rio Madeira. It prospered during the local gold and timber rush but this has slowed. At the top of the hill, on Praça João Nicoletti, is the **Cathedral**, built in 1930, with beautiful stained glass windows; the **Prefeitura** is across the street. The principal commercial street is Av 7 de Setembro, which runs from the railway station and market hall to the upper level of the city, near the rodoviária. The centre is hot and noisy, but not without its charm, and the port and old railway installations are interesting. In the old railway yards known as Praça Madeira-Mamoré are the **Museus Ferroviário** and **Geológico** (both 0800-1800), the **Casa do Artesão** (see Shopping) and a promenade with bars by the river, a wonderful place to watch the sunset. A neoclassical **Casa do Governo** faces Praça Getúlio Vargas, while Praça Marechal Rondon is spacious and modern. There are several viewpoints overlooking the river and railway yards: **Mirante I** (with restaurant) is at the end of R Carlos Gomes; **Mirante II** (with a bar and ice cream parlour), at the end of R Dom Pedro II. There is a clean fruit and vegetable market at the corner of R Henrique Dias and Av Farquhar and a dry goods market three blocks to the south, near the port.

Five km northeast of the city is the **Parque Nacional Municipal**, a small collection of flora in a preserved area of jungle and one of very few parks in the city. The **Cachoeira de Santo Antônio**, rapids on the Rio Madeira, seven km upriver from Porto Velho, is a popular destination for a swim during the dry season; in the rainy season the rapids may be underwater and swimming is dangerous. ■ *Access is by boat, taking a tour from Porto Cai N'Água, one hr; or by city bus No 102, Triângulo, which runs every 50 mins from the city bus terminus or from the bus stop on R Rogério Weber, across from Praça Marechal Rondon.* Gold dredges may be seen working near Porto Velho, ask around.

Sleeping

The city is relatively safe for tourists, but take care in the evenings and even during the day near the railway station and port

A *Rondon Palace*, Av Gov Jorge Teixeira corner Jacy Paraná, away from the centre, T/F223 3420/3422. A/c, fridge, restaurant, pool, travel agency. **C** *Central*, Tenreiro Aranha 2472, T224 2066, F224 5114. A/c, TV, fridge, reliable. Recommended. **D** *Líder*, Av Carlos Gomes, near rodoviária. Honest, welcoming, reasonably clean, fan, coffee. Recommended. **E** *Tía Carmen*, Av Campos Sales 2995, T221 7910. Very good, honest, good cakes in *lanche* in front of hotel. Recommended. From the rodoviária, take bus No 301 'Presidente Roosevelt' (outside *Hotel Pontes*), which goes to railway station at riverside, then along Av 7 de Setembro as far as Av Marechal Deodoro, passing: **C** *Pousada da Sete*, No 894, T221 8344. A/c, cheaper with fan, **D** with shared bath. **D** *Guaporé Palace*, Av G Vargas 1553, T221 2495. A/c, restaurant. **D** *Missionero*, No 1180, T221 4080. Good, a/c, cheaper with fan, **E** with shared bath, fan. Recommended. **E** *Laira*, Joaquim Nabuco, just off 7 de Setembro. Good, cheap. **F** *Yara*, Av 7 do Septembre y R Gonçalves Dias. Shared room with breakfast, safe, helpful staff.

Almanara, R José de Alencar 2624. Good authentic Lebanese food, popular, not cheap. Recommended. *Chá*, Av Presidente Dutra 3024. By kilo buffet, pricey. *Churrascaria Natal*, Av Carlos Gomes 2783. Good meat and chicken. *Assados na Brasa*, Carlos Gomes 2208. Similar. *Emporium*, Av P Machado e Av Dutra. Mid-range, nice atmosphere, good meats and salads, expensive drinks, open 1800-2400. *Mister Pizza II*, Carlos Gomes e José de Alencar. Good. For cheap pizza, *Casa d'Italia*, Av P Machado 821, T224 4616. A number of good restaurants around the intersection of Dom Pedro II and Av Joaquim Nabuco: *Champagne*, recommended for pizzas, and a good Chinese, Joaquim Nabuco 2264. *Bella Italia*, Joaquim Nabuco 2205. Italian, pizza and *comida caseira*. Many *lanches* in town: recommended is *Petiskão*, Av 7 de Setembro e Joaquim Nabuco. Excellent juices. *Novaroma*, Av 7 de Setembro 1650. Good coffee and cakes. *Panificadora Popular*, Av Marechal Deodoro between 7 de Setembro e Dom Pedro II. Good juices and soups. *Xalezinho*, opposite, for an even bigger bowl of soup.

Eating

Avoid eating much fish because of mercury contamination

Indian handicrafts *Casa do Índio*, R Rui Barbosa 1407 and *Casa do Artesão*, Praça Madeira-Mamoré, behind the railway station, Thu-Sun 0800-1800. **Bookshop** *Livraria da Rose*, Av Rogério Weber 1967, opposite Praça Marechal Rondon, exchanges English paperbacks; Rose, the proprietor, speaks English, friendly. Other bookshops nearby. *Supermercado Maru*, 7 de Setembro e Joaquim Nabuco.

Shopping

Ecoporé, R Rafael Vaz e Silva 3335, Bairro Liberdade, T221 5021, carol@ronet.com.br For ecotourism projects in rubber tappers' communities on the Brazil/Bolivia border, US$50 pp per day, full details from Carol Doria, who speaks English.

Tour operators

Air Airport 8 km west of town, T225 1339. Take bus marked 'Aeroporto' (last one between 2400-0100). Daily flights to many Brazilian cities.
Bus Rodoviária is on Jorge Teixeira between Carlos Gomes and Dom Pedro II. From town take 'President Roosevelt' bus No 301 (if on Av 7 de Setembro, the bus turns at Av Marechal Deodoro); 'Aeroporto' and 'Hospital Base' (No 400) also go to rodoviária. Health and other controls at the Rondônia-Mato Grosso border are strict. To break up a long trip is much more expensive than doing it all in one stretch.

Bus to **Humaitá**, US$5, 3 hrs. To **São Paulo**, 60-plus hrs, US$75. To **Cuiabá**, 23 hrs, US$45, expensive food and drink is available en route. To **Guajará-Mirim**, see below. To **Rio Branco**, *Viação Rondônia*, 6 daily, 8 hrs, US$7. Daily bus with *Eucatur* from **Cascavel** (Paraná, connections for Foz do Iguaçu) via Maringá, Campo Grande and Cuiabá to Porto Velho (Porto Velho-Campo Grande 36 hrs, US$60). To **Cáceres** for the Pantanal, 18 hrs, US$30. Hitching is difficult, try the gasoline stations on the edge of town.

River services See River Transport, page 526. Passenger service from *Porto Cai N'Água* (which means 'fall in the water', watch out or you might!), for best prices buy directly at the boat, avoid touts on the shore. Boat tickets for Manaus are also sold in the rodoviária. The Rio Madeira is fairly narrow so the banks can be seen and there are several 'meetings of waters'. Shipping a car: São Matheus Ltda, Av Terminal dos Milagros 400, Balsa, takes vehicles on pontoons, meals, showers, toilets, cooking and sleeping in your car is permitted.

Car hire *Silva Car*, R Almte Barroso 1528, Porto Velho, T221 1423/6040, US$50 per day.

Transport

Road journeys are best done in the dry season, the 2nd half of the year

Airline offices *TAM*, RJ Castilho 530, T221 6666. *Varig*, Av Campos Sales 2666, T224 2262/225 1675, F224 2278, English spoken. *Vasp*, R Tenheiro Aranha 2326, T224 4566/225 3226. **Banks** Banks are open in the morning only; *Banco do Brasil*, Dom Pedro II 607 e Av José de Alencar, cash and TCs with 2% commission, minimum commission US$15, minimum amount exchanged US$200. *Marco Aurélio Câmbio*, R José de Alencar 3353, T221 4922, T984 0025 (mob), efficient, good rates, Mon-Fri 0900-1500. *Parmetal* (gold merchants), R Joaquim Nabuco 2265, T221 1566, cash only, good rates, open Mon-Fri 0730-1800, Sat 0730-1300. Exchange is difficult elsewhere in Rondônia. **Communications** Post Office:

Directory

Brazil

Av Presidente Dutra 2701, corner of Av 7 de Setembro. **Telephone:** *Tele Centro Sul*, Av Presidente Dutra 3023 e Dom Pedro II, 0600-2300 daily. **Medical services** Hospital Central, R Júlio de Castilho 149, T/F224 4389, 24 hr emergencies. **Dentist:** at Carlos Gomes 2577; 24-hr clinic opposite. **Tourist office** Setur/Ro, Av Pdte Dutra 3004, Caiari, CEP 78900-550, T223 3496, seturo@zipmail.com.br **Fundação Cultural do Estado de Rondônia** (*Funcer*) is at same address. Also www.terra.com.br/cidades/pvh/ **Voltage** 110 volts AC, Guajará-Mirim also, elsewhere in Rondônia 220 volts.

The BR-364

Colour map 4, grid C2
At the Mato Grosso
state border, proof
of yellow-fever
inoculation is required:
if no proof is presented,
a new shot is given

The Marechal Rondon Highway, BR-364, is fully paved to Cuiabá, 1,550 km. A result of the paving of BR-364 is the development of farms and towns along it; least population density is in the south between Pimenta Bueno and Vilhena. From Porto Velho south, the towns include **Ariquemes** (202 km from Porto Velho. (*Phone code* 0xx69. *Post code:* 78930; buses hourly from 0600, 3-4 hours, hotels, bank); **Ji Paraná** (376 km.*Post code:* 78960. *Phone code:* 0xx69; bus to Porto Velho, US$16.25, 16 hours; to Cuiabá, 15 hours, US$28), on the shores of the Rio Machado, a pleasant town with a small riverside promenade, which has several bars, lively at night; several hotels.

Parque
Nacional
Pacaás Novos
765,800 ha

The Parque Nacional Pacaás Novos, lies west of the BR-364; it is a transitional zone between open plain and Amazonian forest. The majority of its surface is covered with *cerrado* vegetation and the fauna includes jaguar, brocket deer, puma, tapir and peccary. The average annual temperature is 23°C, but this can fall as low as 5°C when the cold front known as the *friagem* blows up from the South Pole. Details from *Ibama*, Av Jorge Teixeira 3559, CEP 78.904-320, T0xx69-223 3597, Porto Velho, or Ibama head office, same avenue No 3477, T0xx69-223 3607, F229 6511.

The Madeira-
Mamoré
Railway

Porto Velho was the terminus of the Madeira-Mamoré railway. It was supposed to go as far as Riberalta, on the Rio Beni, above that river's rapids, but stopped short at Guajará Mirim. The BR-364 took over many of the railway bridges, leaving what remained of the track to enthusiasts to salvage what they could. The line no longer works, but the roundhouse, recently restored, has two antique locomotives on display. Mr Johnson at the station speaks English.

Guajará Mirim
Phone code: 0xx69
Colour map 4, grid B1
Population: 38,045

From Porto Velho, the paved BR-364 continues 220 km southwest to Abunã (hotels **E**), where the BR-425 branches south to Guajará Mirim. The BR-425 is a fair road, partly paved, which uses the former rail bridges (in poor condition). It is sometimes closed March-May. Across the Mamoré from Guajará Mirim is the Bolivian town of Guayaramerín, which is connected by road to Riberalta, from where there are air services to other Bolivian cities. Guajará Mirim is a charming town. The **Museu Municipal** is at the old Guajará Mirim railway station beside the ferry landing; interesting and diverse. Highly recommended. ■ *0500-1200, 1400-1800, T541 3362. Banco do Brasil* only changes money in the morning.

Sleeping and eating **C** *Jamaica*, Av Leopoldo de Matos 755, T/F541 3721. A/c, fridge, parking. **C** *Lima Palace*, Av 15 de Novembro 1613, T541 3421, F541 2122. A/c, fridge, parking. **C** *Mini-Estrela*, Av 15 de Novembro 460, T541 2399. A/c, parking. **D** *Chile*, Av Q Bocaiúva. Good value, includes breakfast. Recommended. **D** *Fénix Palace*, Av 15 de Novembro 459, T541 2326. Highly recommended. **D** *Mamoré*, R M Moraes, T541 3753. Clean, friendly. **Youth hostel** *Centro Deportivo Afonso Rodrigues*, Av 15 de Novembro, T541 3732. There is a basic dorm, **E**, opposite the rodoviária. Best to eat is *Oasis*, Av 15 de Novembro 460. Recommended (closed Mon). *Lanchonates*, self-service, good value. Recommended.

Transport **Bus** From Porto Velho to Guajará Mirim, 5½ hrs or more depending on season, 8 a day with *Viação Rondônia*, US$18. Taxi from Porto Velho rodoviária, US$25 pp for 4-5, 3 hrs, leaves when full.

Get Brazilian exit and entry stamps from Polícia Federal, Av Presidente Dutra 70, corner of Av Quintino Bocaiúva, T541 4021. The Bolivian consulate is at Av C Marquês 495, T541 2862, Guajará Mirim; visas are given here. ■ *Speedboat across the Rio Mamoré (border), US$1.65, 5-min crossing, operates all day, tickets at the waterside; ferry crossing for vehicles, T541 3811, Mon-Sat 0800-1200, Mon-Fri 1400-1600, 20-min crossing.*

Border with Bolivia

Rio Branco

The BR-364 runs west from Porto Velho to Abunã (239 km), then in excellent condition, 315 km to Rio Branco the capital of the State of Acre. This intriguing state, rich in natural beauty, history and the *seringueiro* culture, is still very much off the beaten track. During the rubber boom of the late 19th century, many *Nordestinos* migrated to the western frontier in search of fortune. As a result, the unpopulated Bolivian territory of Acre was gradually taken over by Brazil and formally annexed in the first decade of the 20th century. In compensation, Bolivia received the Madeira-Mamoré railroad, as described above. In 1913, Rio Branco became capital of the new Território Federal do Acre, which attained statehood in 1962. The chief industries remain rubber and *castanho-de-pará* (Brazil nut) extraction, but timber and ranching are becoming increasingly important and improved road access is putting the state's tropical forests at considerable risk. Despite improved air and road links, Rio Branco remains at the 'end of the line', a frontier outpost whose depressed economy, high unemployment and prevalent drug-running make the city unsafe at night.

Post code: 69900
Phone code: 0xx68
Colour map 3, grid B6
Population: 253,059

NB Rio Branco time is one hour behind Porto Velho and Manaus time; this means two hours behind Brazilian Standard Time

The Rio Acre is navigable upstream as far as the Peru and Bolivia borders. It divides the city into two districts called Primeiro (west) and Segundo (east), on either side of the river. In the central, Primeiro district are **Praça Plácido de Castro**, the shady main square; the **Cathedral**, Nossa Senhora de Nazaré, along Av Brasil; the neo-classical **Palácio Rio Branco** on R Benjamin Constant, across from Praça Eurico Gaspar Dutra. There is a market off R Epaminondas Jácome. Two bridges link the districts. In the Segundo district is the **Calçadão da Gameleira**, a pleasant promenade along the shore, with plaques and an old tree marking the location of the original settlement. There are several large parks in the city; the **Horto Forestal**, popular with joggers, in Vila Ivonete (1° distrito), 3 km north of the centre ('Conjunto Procon' or 'Vila Ivonete' city-buses), has native Amazonian trees, a small lake, paths and picnic areas.

Museu da Borracha (Rubber Museum), Av Ceará 1177, in a lovely old house with a tiled façade, has information about the rubber boom, archaeological artefacts, a section about Acreano Indians, documents and memorabilia from the annexation and a display about the Santo Daime doctrine (see excursions below). Recommended. ■ *Mon-Sat 0730-1900.* **Casa do Seringueiro**, Av Brasil 216, corner of Av Getúlio Vargas, has a good exhibit on rubber tappers and on **Chico Mendes** in particular; the Sala Hélio Melo has a display of Melo's paintings, mainly on the theme of the forest.

In 1° distrito (west bank) A *Pinheiro Palace*, Rui Barbosa 91, T224 7191, pinheiro@ mdnet.com.br A/c, pool. Recommended. B *Rio Branco*, R Rui Barbosa 193, T224 1785, F224 2681, by Praça Plácido de Castro. A/c, fridge, TV, nice but simple. C *Triângulo*, R Floriano Peixoto 727, T224 9265, F224 4117. A/c, TV, fridge, restaurant. C *Albemar*, R Franco Ribeiro 99, T224 1938. A/c, fridge, TV, good breakfast, good value. Recommended. D *Xapuri*, Nações Unidas 187, T225 7268. Shared bath, fan, basic, 15 mins' walk from the centre. In 2° distrito (east bank), in Cidade Nova by the rodoviária B *Rodoviária*, R Palmeiral 268, T224 4434. A/c, fridge TV, D with shared bath, fan, good value. C *Skina*, Uirapuru 533, T224 0087. A/c, fridge, TV, fan. D *Nacional*, R Palmeiral 496, T224 4822. Fan, both cheaper with shared bath.

Sleeping
Few economical hotels in the centre, but a reasonable selection of these by the rodoviária

Kaxinawa, Av Brasil at Praça Plácido de Castro. The best in town for Acreano regional food. *Pizzaria Tutti Frutti*, Av Ceará 1132, across from the Museu da Borracha. Pizzas, ice cream, not cheap. *Casarão*, Av Brasil 310, next to the telephone office. Good food and drink. *Churrascaria*

Eating

Brazil

Triângulo, R Floriano Peixoto 727. As much charcoal-grilled meat as you can eat. Recommended. *Remanso do Tucunaré*, R José de Melo 481, Bairro Bosque. Fish specialties. *Anexos*, R Franco Ribeiro 99, next to *Albemar Hotel*. Popular for meals and drinks. For ice cream *Sorveteria Arte Sabor*, Travessa Santa Inés 28, corner Aviarsio, 1° distrito, 15 mins' walk from the centre. Excellent home made ice cream, many jungle fruit flavours. Recommended. **Local specialities** *Tacacá*; a soup served piping hot in a gourd (*cuia*) combines manioc starch (*goma*), cooked *jambu* leaves which numb the mouth and tongue, shrimp, spices and hot pepper sauce; recommendation from Sra Diamor, Boulevar Augusto Monteiro 1046, Bairro 15 in the 2° distrito (bus Norte-Sul from the centre), other kiosks in town, ask around.

Transport

Prices for car rentals with the nationwide agencies are higher in Acre than in other states

Air The airport is on AC-40, Km 1.2, in the 2° distrito. Taxi from the airport to the centre US$20 flat rate, but going to the airport the meter is used, which usually comes to less. By bus, take 'Norte-Sul' or 'Vila Acre'. Flights with *Varig* and *Vasp* daily to **Porto Velho**, Manaus, Brasília and São Paulo. *Nordeste* daily to **Cruzeiro do Sul**.

Bus Rodoviária on Av Uirapuru, Cidade Nova, 2° distrito (east bank); city bus 'Norte-Sul' to the centre. To **Porto Velho**, *Viação Rondônia*, 6 daily, 8 hrs, US$7. To **Guajará Mirim**, daily with *Rondônia* at 1130 and 2200, 5-6 hrs, US$10; or take *Inácio's Tur* shopping trip, 3 per week. From Rio Branco the BR-364 continues west (in principle) to Cruzeiro do Sul and Japim, with a view to reaching the Peruvian frontier further west when completed.

Directory **Airline offices** *Varig*, T224 1182/0800-997000. **Communications** **Post Office:** on the corner of R Epaminondas Jácome and Av Getúlio Vargas. **Telephone:** on Av Brasil between Marechal Deodoro and Av Getúlio Vargas, long delays for international calls. **Tourist offices** **SEICT/AC**, R Mal Deodoro 219 4th floor, Centro, T223 1390, seict@ac.gov.br

Border with Bolivia & Peru

The BR-317 from Rio Branco heads south and later southwest, parallel to the Rio Acre; it is paved as far as **Xapuri** (the location of the Fundação Chico Mendes); one very basic lodging and two restaurants. The road continues to **Brasiléia** (four buses daily to/from Rio Branco, five hours in the wet, faster in the dry, US$5; three hotels, two basic lodgings, several restaurants – La Felicitá is good, Polícia Federal give entry/exit stamps), opposite the Bolivian town of Cobija on the Rio Acre. It is possible to stay in Epitaciolândia (**D** *Hotel Kanda*, 5 minutes' walk from the police post) and cross into Bolivia early in the morning.

The road ends at Assis Brasil where the Peruvian, Bolivian and Brazilian frontiers meet. Across the Rio Acre are Iñapari (Peru), border crossing difficult, even out of the wet season, and Bolpebra, Bolivia. A bus service operates only in the dry season beyond Brasiléia to Assis Brasil, access in the wet season is by river. In **Assis Brasil**, there are two hotels (one basic but clean, friendly, **E**), two restaurants, some shops, a bank which does not change US dollars (the hotel owner may be persuaded to oblige). You get between Iñapari and Assis Brasil by canoe, or by wading across the river. **NB** There is no Polícia Federal in the village, get entry/exit stamps in Brasília. Take small denomination dollar bills or Peruvian soles as there is nowhere to change money on the Peruvian side.

The Centre West

The Centre West is the frontier where the Amazon meets the central plateau. It is also Brazil's frontier with its Spanish American neighbours. Lastly, it contains the border between the expansion of agriculture and the untouched forests and savannahs. On this region's eastern edge is Brasília, the symbol of the nation's commitment to its empty centre.

Brasília

The purpose-built federal capital of Brazil succeeded Rio de Janeiro (as required by the Constitution) on 21 April 1960. The creation of an inland capital had been urged since the beginning of the 19th century, but it was finally brought into being after President Kubitschek came to power in 1956, when a competition for the best general plan was won by Professor Lúcio Costa, who laid out the city in the shape of a bent bow and arrow. (It is also described as a bird, or aeroplane in flight.) Only light industry is allowed in the city and its population was limited to 500,000; this has been exceeded and more people live in a number of shanty towns, with minimal services, located well away from the main city, which is now a UNESCO World Heritage Site. Brasília is on undulating ground in the unpopulated uplands of Goiás, in the heart of the undeveloped Sertão. The official name for central Brasília is the Plano Piloto.

Phone code: 0xx61
Post code: 7000
Colour map 7, grid A3
Population: 2.1 million (2000)
Altitude: 1,171 m
960 km from Rio

Orientation The Eixo Monumental divides the city into Asa Sul and Asa Norte (north and south wings) and the Eixo Rodoviário divides it east and west. Buildings are numbered according to their relation to them. For example, 116 Sul and 116 Norte are at the extreme opposite ends of the city. The 100s and 300s lie west of the Eixo and the 200s and 400s to the east; Quadras 302, 102, 202 and 402 are nearest the centre and 316, 116, 216 and 416 mark the end of the Plano Piloto. Residential areas made up of large six-storey apartment blocks, called the 'Super-Quadras'. All Quadras are separated by feeder roads, along which are the local shops. There are also a number of schools, parks and cinemas in the spaces between the Quadras (especially in Asa Sul), though not as systematically as was originally envisaged. The main shopping areas, with more cinemas, restaurants and so on, are situated on either side of the city bus station (rodoviária). There are now several green areas. The private residential areas are west of the Super-Quadras, and on the other side of the lake. At right angles to these residential areas is the 'arrow', the 8-km long, 250 m wide **Eixo Monumental**. The main north-south road (Eixo Rodoviário), in which fast-moving traffic is segregated, follows the curve of the bow; the radial road is along the line of the arrow – intersections are avoided by means of underpasses and cloverleaves. Motor and pedestrian traffic is segregated in residential areas.

Ins & outs

Climate The climate is mild and the humidity refreshingly low, but overpowering in dry weather. The noonday sun beats hard, but summer brings heavy rains and the air is usually cool by night.

At the tip of the arrow is the **Praça dos Três Poderes**, with the Congress buildings, the Palácio do Planalto (the President's office), the Palácio da Justiça and the Panteão Tancredo Neves. Nineteen tall Ministry buildings line the Esplanada dos Ministérios, west of the Praça, culminating in two towers linked by a walkway to form the letter H, representing Humanity. They are 28 storeys high: no taller buildings are allowed in Brasília. Where the bow and arrow intersect is the city bus terminal (rodoviária), with the cultural and recreational centres and commercial and financial areas on either side. There is a sequence of zones westward along the shaft of the arrow; a hotel centre, a radio city, an area for fairs and circuses, a centre for sports, the **Praça Municipal** (with the municipal offices in the Palácio do Buriti) and, lastly (where the nock of the arrow would be), the combined bus and railway station (rodoferroviária) with the industrial area nearby. The most impressive buildings are all by Oscar Niemeyer, Brazil's leading architect.

Sights

The **Palácio da Alvorada**, the President's official residence (not open to visitors), is on the lakeshore. The 80-km drive along the road round the lake to the dam is attractive. There are spectacular falls below the dam in the rainy season. Between the Praça dos Três Poderes and the lake are sites for various recreations, including golf, fishing and yacht clubs, and an acoustic shell for shows in the open air. The airport is at the eastern end of the lake. Some 395 ha between the lake and the northern residential area (Asa Norte) are reserved for the Universidade de Brasília, founded in 1961. South of the university area, the Av das Nações runs from the Palácio da

Brazil

Alvorada along the lake to join the road from the airport to the centre. Along it are found all the principal embassies. Also in this area is the attractive vice-presidential residence, the **Palácio do Jaburu** (not open to visitors). This area is very scenic.

It is worth telephoning addresses away from the centre to ask how to get there. An urban railway, Metrô, runs to the southwest suburbs

A fine initial view of the city may be had from the **television tower**, which has a free observation platform at 75 m up; also bar and souvenir shop. ■ *Mon 1400-2000, Tue-Sun 0800-2000, West Eixo Monumental.* If the TV tower is closed, the nearby *Alvorada* hotel has a panoramic terrace on the 12th floor (lift to 11th only): ask at reception. A good and cheap way of seeing Brasília is by taking bus rides from the municipal rodoviária at the centre: the destinations are clearly marked. The circular bus routes 106, 108 and 131 go round the city's perimeter. If you go around the lake by bus, you must change at the Paranoá dam; to or from Paranoá Norte take bus 101, 'Rodoviária', and to and from Sul, bus 100, bypassing the airport. Tours from 1300-1700, start from the downtown hotel area and municipal rodoviária (US$12-20). Many hotels arrange city tours (see also Tour operators). ■ *Some buildings are open 1000-1400 Sat-Sun with guided tours in English, well worth going.*

Town clothes (not shorts or minis) should be worn when visiting all these buildings

Praça dos Três Poderes: **Congress** is open to visitors, who may attend debates when Congress is in session (Friday morning). Excellent city views from the 10th floor in Annex 3. ■ *Mon-Fri 0930-1200, 1430-1630 (take your passport), guides free of charge (in English 1400-1700).* The **Palácio do Planalto** may also be visited. ■ *Sun 0930-1330, 30-min tours. The guard is changed ceremonially at the Palácio do Planalto on Friday at 1730.* The President attends if he is available. Opposite the Planalto is the Supreme Court building, **Supremo Tribunal Federal**. **Museu Histórico de Brasília** is really a hollow monument, with tablets, photos and videos telling the story of the city. ■ *Tue-Sun and holidays 0900-1800.* The sculpture 'Os Candangos' in front of the Planalto is a symbol of the city. By Bruno Giorgi, it pays homage to the *candangos*, or pioneer workers who built Brasília on empty ground. The marvellous building of the Ministry of Foreign Affairs, the **Itamarati**, has modern paintings and furniture and beautiful water gardens. ■ *Guided visits Mon, Wed, Fri 1500-1700, free.* Opposite the Itamarati is the **Palácio da Justiça**, with artificial cascades between its concrete columns. ■ *Mon-Fri, 0900-1200, 1500-1700.* The **Panteão Tancredo Neves** is a 'temple of freedom and democracy', built 1985-86 by Niemeyer. It includes an impressive

Brasília: Plano Piloto

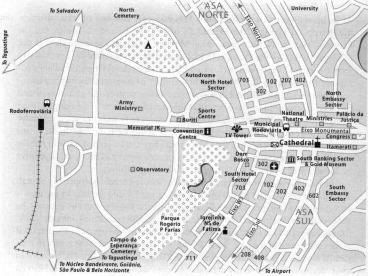

homage to Tiradentes, the precursor of Brazilian independence. **Espaço Lúcio Costa** contains a model of Plano Piloto, sketches and autographs of the designer's concepts and gives the ideological background to the planning of Brasília.

The **Catedral Metropolitana**, on the Esplanada dos Ministérios, is a spectacular circular building in the shape of the crown of thorns. Three aluminium angels, suspended from the airy, domed, stained-glass ceiling, are by the sculptor Alfredo Ceschiatti, who also made the five life-sized bronze apostles outside. The baptistery, a concrete representation of the Host beside the cathedral, is connected to the main building by a tunnel (open Sundays only). The outdoor carillon was a gift from the Spanish government: the bells are named after Columbus's ships. ■ *0800-1930, T224 4073.*

South of the TV tower on Av W3 Sul, at Quadra 702, is the Sanctuary of **Dom Bosco**, a gothic-style building with narrow windows filled with blue glass mosaics, purple at the four corners; the light inside is most beautiful. ■ *0800-1800, T223 6542.*

The **Templo da Boa Vontade**, Setor Garagem Sul 915, lotes 75/76, is a seven-faced pyramid topped by one of the world's largest crystals, a peaceful place dedicated to all philosophies and religions. ■ *T245 1070, open 24 hrs. Take bus 151 from outside the Centro do Convenções or on Eixo Sul to Centro Médico.*

A permanent memorial to Juscelino Kubitschek, the '**Memorial JK**', contains his tomb and his car, together with a lecture hall and exhibits. ■ *Daily 0900-1745, US$0.50, has toilets and* lanchonete. The **Monumental Parade Stand** has unique and mysterious acoustic characteristics (the complex is north of the Eixo Monumental, between the 'Memorial JK' and the rodoferroviária). There are remarkable stained glass panels, each representing a state of the Federation, on the ground floor of the Caixa Econômica Federal.

Some 15 km out along the Belo Horizonte road is the small wooden house, known as '**O Catetinho**', in which President Kubitschek stayed in the late 1950s during his visits to the city when it was under construction; it is open to visitors and most interesting. Northwest of Brasília, but only 15 minutes by car from the centre, is the **Parque Nacional de Brasília** (about 28,000 ha), founded in 1961 to conserve the flora and fauna of the Federal Capital. Only a portion of the park is open to the public without a permit. There is a swimming pool fed by clear river water, a snack bar and a series of trails through gallery forest (popular with joggers in the early morning and at weekends). The rest of the park is grassland, gallery forest and *cerrado* vegetation. Large mammals include tapir, maned wolf and pampas deer; birdwatching is good. ■ *Contact the park's Ibama office, BR 040 SMU, T465 2013.*

Lago Do Paranoá

Palácio da Alvorada
Palácio do Jaburu
Palácio do Planalto
Praça dos Três Poderes
Avenida das Nações

0 metres 200
0 yards 200

Sleeping

In the Southern Hotel Sector **L** *Nacional*, Quadra 1 bloco A, T321 7575, hotelnacional@ hotelnacional.com br Cavernous, old-fashioned and a city landmark with many tour agencies located outside. **A** *Alvorada*, Quadra 4 bloco A, T332 1122, alvoradahotel@ zaz.com.br Comfortable high rise with good view from roof terrace. **A** *Bristol*, Qd 4 bloco F, T321 6162, bristolh@tba.com.br Very traditional, piano bar, 24 hr room service. **D** *Pousada da Nilza*, W3 Sul, quadra 703, bloco A, casa 54, T226 5786, F225 5902. Family-run, range of rooms, functional, but one of few cheaper options in area.

Prices include breakfast, but 10% must be added. Weekend discounts of 30% are often available, but must be asked for. It is not advisable to walk around at night

See Essentials for new telephone number changes

Brazil

In the Northern Hotel Sector AL *Aracoara*, Qd 5 bloco C, T3289222, F3289067, www.aracoara.com.br Four-star, 24-hr room service and international restaurant. One road gives access to: **A** *Aristus*, Quadra 2 bloco O, T328 8675, F326 5415. Good, a/c, TV, phone, money exchange, small restaurant. **A** *Casablanca*, Qd 3 bloco A, T3288586, casablanca@brasilia.com.br More intimate than most of hotels in this area. **B** *El Pilar*, Quadra 3 bloco F, T328 5915, F328 9088. A/c or fan, TV. **C** *Mirage*, Quadra 2 lote N, T225 7150. Fan, good value. And others. Moderately-priced hotels can be found in the Northern Hotel Sector only. **D** *Cury's Solar*, HIGS 707, Bloco I, Casa 15, T11362 52/244 1899, www.conectanet.com.br/curyssolar Cramped but helpful, safe, around 30 mins from the centre (Eixo Monumental) along W3 Sul. Recommended. **D** *Pensão da Zenilda*, W3 Sul Quadra 704, Bloco Q, Casa 29, T224 7532. Safe.

Teresa Tasso, SQN312-'K'-505, T273 4844 or 272 4243, offers accommodation in an apartment in the Asa Sul at US$20 pp (sleeps 5, kitchen, bath, laundry facilities), excellent value, Teresa gives city tours for US$15-20 pp for 3-4 hrs, and will collect you at the airport if you phone in advance (bus to flat from centre, 5 mins). Rooms to let (**D-C**) from: *Getúlio Valente*, warmly recommended, Av W3 Sul, HIGS 703, Bl N casas 10, 34, near the TV tower, good, cheap meals available, Portuguese speakers T226 8507/225 5021 and Getúlio will pick you up; otherwise, turn right off Av W3 Sul between 703 and 702, then take first left (an unpaved driveway). The tourist office has a list of *pensões*.

Camping The city's main site is 2 km out of the centre, by the Centro Esportivo, near the motor-racing track, with room for 3,100 campers, mixed reports. Take bus 109 (infrequent) from municipal rodoviária. Água Mineral Parque, 6 km northwest of city, direct buses only at weekend, mineral pool, showers. **Associação Brasileira de Camping** (Edif Márcia, 12th floor, Setor Comercial Sul, T225 8768) has two sites: one at Km 19 on the Belo Horizonte road and one 25 km northeast of Brasília at Sobradinho. *Camping Clube do Brasil* has a site at Itiquira waterfall, 100 km northeast of the city, near Formosa; information from Edif Maristela, room 1214, Setor Comercial Sul, T223 6561.

Eating

Southern Hotel Sector tends to have more restaurants than the Northern. At weekends few restaurants in central Brasília open

Asa Norte Expensive: All the large hotels in this area have upmarket restaurants, most catering to business visitors. **Mid-range**: *Boa Saúde*, Av W3 Norte Quadra 702, Edif Brasília Rádio Center. Vegetarian open Sun-Fri 0800-2000. *Bom Demais*, Av W3 Norte, Qd 706. Comfortable, serving fish, beef and rice etc, live music at weekends (cover charge US$0.50). *Churrascaria do Lago*, SHTN, Conj 1-A, by Palácio da Alvorada, a number of Brazilian restaurants and some serving Amazonian food. *El Hadj*, in Hotel Torre Palace, Setor Hoteleiro Norte, Qd 4 bloco A. Very good Arabic food. **Cheap**: *Conjunto Nacional*, SDN, Cj A, enormous mall and food court with 50 restaurants. *Habib's*, SCN Quadra 4. Arabic food and pizzas at bargain prices at this upmarket chain restaurant. Recommended. The municipal rodoviária provides the best coffee and *pasteis* in town (bottom departure level).

Asa Sul Expensive: *Gaf*, Centro Gilberto Salomão, Lago Sul, excellent international food, especially meat dishes. *Le Français*, Av W3 Sul, Qd 404, bloco B. French food served in bistro atmosphere, classic and modern dishes. *La Chaumière*, Av W3 Sul, quadra 408, bloco A. Traditional French cuisine in suitable surroundings, established 1966, no smoking. *Porcão*, Sector de Clubes Sul, Trecho 2, cj 35, lt 2B. Upmarket chain restaurant specialising in *churrasco*, piano bar, large veranda. **Mid-range**: *China in Box*, Comércio local Sul 402, bloco C, loja 13. Reliable Chinese, delivery service. *Kazebre 13*, Av W3 Sul, Qd 504, loja 2. Traditional Italian. *O Espanhol*, Av W3 Sul, Qd 404, bloco C, loja 07. Spanish paella and seafood, open daily. *Roma*, Av W3 Sul, Qds 501 and 511. Good value Italian. **Cheap**: *Cedro do Líbano*, SCS, Qd 6, bloco A, loja 218. Self-service, some Arabic dishes, friendly, closes 2200. Recommended. *Centro Venâncio 2000* at the beginning of Av W3 Sul, has several budget options, including *Salada Mista*, lunch only. *Coisas da Terra*, SCS, Qd 5, bloco B, loja 41. Comfortable self-service, lunch only. Recommended. There are many cheap places on Avenida W3 Sul, eg at Blocos 502 and 506.

Snack bars: (ie those serving *prato feito* or *comercial*, cheap set meals) can be found all over the city, especially on Av W3 and in the Setor Comercial Sul. Other good bets are the Conjunto Nacional and the Conjunto Venâncio, 2 shopping/office complexes on either side of the municipal rodoviária. Tropical fruit flavour ice cream can be found in various parlours, eg Av W3 Norte 302. Freshly made fruit juices in all bars.

Gates Pub, Av W3 Sul 403, T2254576, with disco; and *London Tavern*, Av W3 Sul 409. The **Bars & clubs**
Grenada bar near the *Hotel Nacional* has good pavement atmosphere in early evening.
Nightclubs in Conjunto Venâncio, Centro Gilberto Salomão and in the main hotels. *Bier Fass*,
SHS Q 5, bloco E, loja 52/53, cavernous restaurant/bar with wine cellar, live music Tue-Sun,
open to 0200. *Dom Quichopp Choparia*, SLCS 110, bloco A, loja 17, open Tue-Sun
1630-0300, sports theme bar.

Information about entertainment etc is available in 2 daily papers, *Jornal de Brasília* and *Correio* **Entertainment**
Brasiliense. Any student card (provided it has a photograph) will get you into the cinema/thea-
tre/concert hall for half price. **Cinema** *Pier 21*, SCSS, Trecho 2, Cj 32/33, is an enormous complex with 13 cinema screens, nightclubs, restaurants, video bars and children's theme park.
Theatre There are 3 auditoria of the *Teatro Nacional*, Setor Cultural Norte, Via N 2, next to the
bus station, T325 6109, foyer open 0900-2000, box office open at 1400; the building is in the
shape of an Aztec pyramid. The Federal District authorities have 2 theatres, the *Galpão* and
Galpãozinho, between Quadra 308 Sul and Av W3 Sul. There are several other concert halls.

For handicrafts from all the Brazilian states try *Galeria dos Estados* (which runs underneath **Shopping**
the *eixo* from Setor Comercial Sul to Setor Bancário Sul, 10 mins' walk from municipal
rodoviária, south along Eixo Rodoviário Sul). For Amerindian handicrafts, *Artíndia*, SRTVS, Qd
702, also in the rodoviária and at the airport. There is a *feira hippy* at the base of the TV tower
Sat, Sun and holidays: leather goods, wood carvings, jewellery, bronzes. English books (good
selection) at *Livraria Sodiler* in Conjunto Nacional and at the airport.

Buriti Turismo, SCLS 402, bloco A, lojas 27/33, Asa Sul, T225 2686, American Express repre- **Tour operators**
sentative. *Presmic Turismo*, SHS Q 1 Bloco A, loja, 35, T225 5515. Full, half-day and *Many tour operators*
night-time city tours (0845, 1400 and 1930 respectively). *Toscana* SCLS 413, Bloco D, loja *have their offices in the*
22/24, T242 9233. Recommended as cheap and good. 3-4 hr city tours with English com- *shopping arcade of the*
mentary can also be booked at the airport by arriving air passengers – a convenient way of *Hotel Nacional*
getting to your hotel if you have heavy baggage. Some tours have been criticized as too
short, others that the guides speak poor English, and for night-time tours, the flood lighting
is inadequate on many buildings.

Air Airport, 12 km from centre, T354 9000. Frequent daily flights to **Rio** and **São Paulo** (1½ **Transport**
hrs in both cases) and to main cities. Bus 102 or 118 to airport, regular, US$0.65, 30 mins. Taxi
is US$10 (meter rate 2 used to airport), worth it. Left luggage facilities at airport (tokens for
lockers, US$0.50).
   Bus The bus terminal (rodoferroviária, T363 2281) beside the railway station, from which
long-distance buses leave, has post office (0800-1700, Sat 0800-1200) and telephone facilities.
Bus 131 between rodoviária, the municipal terminal, and rodoferroviária, US$1.25; taxi
rodoferroviária to Setor Hoteleiro Norte, US$9. There are showers (US$0.50). Both bus stations
have large luggage lockers. To **Rio**: 17 hrs, 6 *comuns* (US$32) and 3 *leitos* (about US$64) daily.
To **São Paulo**: 16 hrs, 7 *comuns* (about US$30) and 2 *leitos* (about US$60) daily (*Rápido Federal* recommended). To **Belo Horizonte**: 12 hrs, 9 *comuns* (US$20) and 2 *leitos* (US$40) daily.
To **Belém**: 36 hrs, 4 daily (US$55, *Trans Brasília* T233 7589). To **Salvador**: 24 hrs, 3 daily
(US$40). To **Cuiabá**: 17½ hrs (US$30) daily at 1200 with *São Luís*. For **Mato Grosso**: generally
Goiânia seems to be the better place for buses. **Barra do Garças**: 0830 and 2000, takes 9 hrs
with *Araguarina*, T233 7598, US$13.20 return. All major destinations served. Bus tickets for
major companies are sold at the city rodoviária.
   Car hire: all large companies are represented at the airport and the Car Rental Sector.
Multinational agencies and *Interlocadora*, airport, T365 2511.*Unidas*, T365 3343, and at airport, T365 1412.

Airline offices *GOL*, airport, T364 9370, premium rate number, T0300-7892121. *Rio-Sul/Nordeste*, **Directory**
SCLN 306, bloco B, loja 24, T242 2590; airport T365 9020. *TAM/Brasil Central*, SHN Hotel Nacional,
Gallery Store, 36/37, T325 1300; airport, T365 1000. *Varig*, SCN Qd 4, bloco B, T329 1240; airport, T364
9219. *Vasp*, SCLN 304, bloco E, lojas 80/100, T329 0404; airport, T365 3037.

Banks Foreign currency (but not always Amex cheques) can be exchanged at branches of: *Banco Regional de Brasília*, SBS Q 1, Bl E, T412 8282 and *Banco do Brasil*, Setor Bancário Sul, latter also at airport (ATM, bank open weekends and holidays), charges US$20 commission for TCs. *American Express*, SCS Q 6, Edif Federação do Comércio, 1st floor, T321 6570. *MasterCard* office, SCRN 502, Bl B, loja 31-32, T225 5550, for cash against card; ATMs at *Citibank*, SCS Quadra 06, bloco A, loja 186, T215 8000, *HSBC*, SCRS 502, bloco A, lojas 7/12, and *Banco 24 Horas* at airport, and all over the city, including the Rodoferroviária. Good exchange rates at *Hotel Nacional* and hotels with 'exchange-turismo' sign.

Communications Internet: *Café.Com.Tato*, CLS 505, bloco C, loja 17, Asa Sul, open daily. *Liverpool Coffee Shop*, CLS 108, R da Igreijinha. **Post Office**: Poste restante, Central Correio, 70001; SBN-Cj 03, BL-A, Ed Sede da ECT, the central office is in the Setor Hoteleiro Sul, between *Hotels Nacional* and *St Paul*. Another post office is in Ed Brasília Rádio, Av 3 Norte

Cultural centres British Council, Setor C Sul, quadra 01, Bloco H, 8th floor, Morro Vermelho Building, T323 6080. **Cultura Inglesa**, SEPS 709/908 Conj B, T243 3065. **American Library**, Casa Thomas Jefferson, Av W4 Sul, quadra 706, T243 6588. **Aliança Francesa**, Sul Entrequadra 707-907, Bloco A, T242 7500. **Instituto Cultural Goethe**, Edifício Dom Bosco, Setor Garagem Sul 902, Lote 73, Bloco C, T224 6773, Mon-Fri, 0800-1200, also 1600-2000, Mon, Wed, Thu.

Embassies and consulates **Australia**: Caixa Postal 11-1256, SHIS QI-09, Conj 16, Casa 1, T248 5569. **Austria**: SES, Av das Nações 40, T243 3111. **Canada**: SES, Av das Nações 16, T321 2171. **Denmark**: Av das Nações 26, T443 8188, 0900-1200, 1400-1700. **Finland**: SES, Av das Nações, lote 27, T443 7151. **Germany**: SES, Av das Nações 25, T443 7330. **Greece**: SES, Av das Nações, T443 6573. **Guyana**: SDS, Edifício Venâncio III, 4th floor, sala 410/404, T224 9229. **Netherlands**: SES, Av das Nações 5, T321 4769. **New Zealand**, SHIS Q1 09, conj 16, casa 01, Lgo Sul, T248 9900, F248 9916, zelandia@terra.com.br **South Africa**: SES, Av das Nações, lote 06, T312 9503. **Sweden**: Av das Nações 29, Caixa Postal 07-0419, T243 1444. **Switzerland**: SES, Av das Nações 41, T443 5500. **UK**: SES, Quadra 801, Conjunto K (with British Commonwealth Chamber of Commerce), Av das Nações, T225 2710, F225 1777, www.reinounido.org.br **US**: SES, Av das Nações 3, T321 7272. **Venezuela**: SES, Av das Nações 13, T223 9325.

Tourist offices At the Centro de Convenções, 3rd floor, **Adetur**, helpful, good map of Brasília, open to public 0800-1200, 1300-1800, some English spoken, T325 5700, F225 5706; small stand at rodoferroviária (open daily 0800-2000), friendly but not very knowledgeable. Airport tourist office, T325 5730, open daily 0800-2000, will book hotels, limited English and information, no maps of the city. **Embratur** head office, Setor Comercial Norte, Quadra 02, bloco G, CEP 70710-500, T224 9100, F323 8936, webmaster@embratur.gov.br The information office in the centre of Praça dos Tres Poderes has a colourful map and lots of useful text information. The staff are friendly and have interesting information about Brasília and other places in Goiás – only Portuguese spoken. **Maps** 'Comapa', Venâncio 200 business complex, 2nd floor, have expensive maps.

Leaving Brasília From Saída Sul (the southern end of the Eixo) the BR-040/050 goes to **Cristalina** where it divides; the BR-040 continues to Belo Horizonte and Rio, the BR-050 to Uberlândia and São Paulo (both paved). Also from Saída Sul, the BR-060 goes to **Anápolis**, Goiânia and Cuiabá. At 10 km outside Anápolis (Population: 265,000), on the Goiânia road, is the **Centro de Gemologia de Goiás**, Quadra 2, Módulo 13, Daia, with a fine collection of gemstones, sales and lapidary courses and how to tell real gems from fakes. ■ *Mon-Fri 0730-1130, 1330-1730*. From Anápolis the BR-153 (Belém-Brasília) heads north to Belém and from Goiânia the BR-153 goes south through the interior of the states of São Paulo and Paraná (also paved).

From Saída Norte (the northern end of the Eixo) the BR-020 goes northeast to **Formosa** (1½ hours by frequent buses from Brasília, cheap hotels and restaurants), Barreiras (*colour map 5, grid C2*), and after Barreiras on the BR-242 (all paved) to Salvador and Fortaleza. The BR-020 is in good condition for 120 km. At Alvorada do Norte (130 km) there are cheap but very basic hotels. **Posse** (295 km, *colour map 5, grid C2*) is picturesque (accommodation on Av Padre Trajeiro).

Parque Nacional Chapada dos Veadeiros & Emas In the elevated region 200 km north of Brasília is the popular **Chapada dos Veadeiros**. The main attractions are a number of high waterfalls complete with palm-shaded oases and natural swimming pools, and the varied wildlife: capybara, rhea, tapir, wolf, toucan, etc. ■ *US$0.50, Ibama, Rodovia GO 239, Km 33, Zona Rural, Alto Paraíso, T0xx62-459 3388*. There is a small hotel (**D**) by the rodoviária in Alto Paraíso and a very basic *dormitório* in São Jorge (take sleeping bag or hammock). The best season to visit is May-October. The park is reached by paved state highway 118 to Alto Paraíso de Goiás, then gravel road west towards Colinas for 30 km where a sign marks the turnoff (just before São Jorge village). Buses Brasília-Alto Paraíso 1000 and 2200, US$3.60; occasional local buses Alto Paraíso-São Jorge, includes 1600 departure, then 5-km walk to entrance.

In the far southwest of the state, covering the watershed of the Araguaia, Taquari and Formoso rivers, is the small **Parque Nacional Emas**, 98 km south of Mineiros just off the main BR-364 route between Brasília and Cuiabá (112 km beyond Jataí). Almost 132,868 ha of undulating grasslands and *cerrado* contain the **world's largest concentration of termite mounds**. Pampas deer, giant anteater, greater rhea, or 'ema' in Portuguese, and maned wolf are frequently seen roaming the grasses. The park holds the greatest concentration of blue-and-yellow macaws outside Amazônia, and blue-winged, red-shouldered and red-bellied macaws can also be seen. (There are many other animals and birds.) Along with the grasslands, the park supports a vast marsh on one side and rich gallery forests on the other. As many of the interesting mammals are nocturnal, a spotlight is a must. ■ *Permission to visit from Ibama R 229 No 95, Setor Universitário, 74605-090 Goiânia, T0xx64-634 1704. Day trips are not recommended, but 4-day, 3-night visits to the Park can be arranged through agencies (eg Focus Tours, see page 352).*

Sleeping Mineiros A *Pilões Palace*, Praça Alves de Assis, T661 1547. Restaurant, comfortable. **C** *Boi na Brasa*, R Onze 11, T661 1532. No a/c, good *churrasco* restaurant attached. Next door **D** *Mineiros Hotel*, with bath and huge breakfast, good lunch. Recommended. Dorm accommodation at the park headquarters; kitchen and cook available but bring own food.

Transport The park is 6 hrs by car from Campo Grande, about 20 hrs from Goiânia, paved road poor. The road to the park is paved; twice weekly bus from Mineiros.

The Rio Araguaia: north of Goiânia

Brazilians are firmly convinced that the 2,630-km-long Rio Araguaia is richer in fish than any other in the world. A visit to the 220-km stretch between **Aruanã** (a port 180 km northwest of Goiás Velho by paved road), and the Ilha do Bananal during the fishing season is quite an experience. As the receding waters in May reveal sparkling white beaches, thousands of Brazilian and international enthusiasts pour into the area. As many as 400 tent 'cities' spring up, and vast quantities of fish are hauled in before the phenomenon winds down in September, when the rivers begin to rise again and flood the surrounding plains.

Yellow-fever vaccination is recommended for the region. Borrachudas, tiny biting insects, are an unavoidable fact of life in Central Brazil in June and July; repellent helps a little

Bananal is the **world's largest river island**, located in the state of Tocantins. The island is formed by a division in the south of the Rio Araguaia and is approximately 320 km long. The entire island was originally a national park (**Parque Nacional Araguaia**), but it has been reduced from two million ha to its current size of 562,312 ha. The island, and especially the park, form one of the more spectacular wildlife areas on the continent, in many ways similar to the Pantanal. The vegetation is a transition zone between the *cerrado* (woody savanna) and Amazon forests, with gallery forests along the many waterways. There are several marshlands throughout the island. The fauna is also transitional. More than 300 bird species are found here, including the hoatzin, hyacinthine macaw, harpy eagle and black-fronted piping guan. The giant anteater, maned wolf, bush dog, giant otter, jaguar, puma, marsh deer, pampas deer, American tapir, yellow anaconda and South American river turtle also occur here. The island is flooded most of the year, with the prime visiting (dry) season being from June to early October, when the beaches are exposed. Unfortunately, the infrastructure for tourism aside from fishing expeditions is very limited. ■ *Permission to visit the park should be obtained in advance from Ibama, R 229, No 95, Setor Universitário, 74605-800 Goiânia, T0xx62-224 2488, F225 5035.*

Ilha do Bananal
Colour map 5, grid C1
Home to a variety of rare wildlife

Brazil

São Félix do Araguaia
Colour map 5, grid C1
Mosquito nets are highly recommended: high incidence of malaria

Bananal can be visited from São Félix do Araguaia . Many Carajás indians are found in town; a depot of their handicrafts is between the *Pizzaria* and *Mini Hotel* on Av Araguaia. With permission from Funai in the town, you cross the river to the Carajá village of **Santa Isabela de Morra** and ask to see the chief, who can tell you the history of the tribe. **Tours** Many river trips are available for fishing or to see wildlife. Another access to Bananal is through the small but pleasant town of **Santa Teresinha** which is north of São Felix. A charming hotel is the **A** *Bananal*, Praça Tarcila Braga 106, CEP 78395 (Mato Grosso), with full board.

Sleeping and eating Recommended is **C** *Xavante*, Av Severiano Neves 391, T522 1305. A/c, shower, frigobar, excellent breakfast, delicious *cajá* juice, Sr e Sra Carvalho very hospitable. A good restaurant is the *Pizzaria Cantinho da Peixada* on Av Araguaia, next to the Texaco station, overlooking the river: the owner, Klaus, rents rooms, **E**, better than hotels, T522 1320, he also arranges fishing trips. Recommended.

Transport Bus to São Félix from Barra do Garças, see above. Rodoviária is 3 km from the centre and waterfront, taxi US$5; buses to Barra do Garças at 0500, arrive 2300, or 1730, arrive 1100 next day.

The Brasília-Belém highway runs through the new state of Tocantins (277,322 sq km). **Palmas** is the state capital and the newest city in Brazil. It is not really on the tourist trail yet. There are hotels and restaurants and waterfalls in the surrounding mountains and beaches on the River Tocantins. For tourist information *Secretaria de Tursimo TO*, Av NS 2 Conj 4 lote, 1t floor, CEP 77100-050, Palmas, TO, T0xx63- 218 2310, seturto@terra.com.br At Fátima, on the BR-153, a paved road heads east 52 km to a new bridge over the Rio Tocantins to **Porto Nacional** (*Post code*: 77500-000. *Phone code*: 0xx63). From here a road runs north to Palmas, 55 km. Porto Nacional has hotels, restaurants and a regional airport.

Mato Grosso do Sul and Mato Grosso

To the west of Goiás are the states of Mato Grosso and Mato Grosso do Sul, with a combined area of 1,231,549 sq km (larger than Bolivia) and a population of only about 4.6 million, or about three people to the sq km. The two states are half covered with forest, with the large wetland area called the Pantanal (roughly west of a line between Campo Grande and Cuiabá), partly flooded in the rainy season (see page 570). The Pantanal, which covers a staggering 230,000 sq km (more than half the size of France), is a mecca for wildlife tourism or fishing. Whether land or river-based, seasonal variations make a great difference to the practicalities of getting there and what you will experience. A road runs across Mato Grosso do Sul via Campo Grande to Porto Esperança and Corumbá, both on the Rio Paraguai; much of the road is across the wetland, offering many sights of birds and other wildlife. Other worthwhile places to go are the ancient landscapes of the Chapada dos Guimarães and the lovely area around Bonito. Cattle ranching is very important, with over 21 million head of beef cattle on 16 million ha of free range pasture in Mato Grosso do Sul alone.

Campo Grande

Phone code: 0xx67
Post code: 79000
Colour map 7, grid B1
Population: 663,621

Capital of the State of Mato Grosso do Sul. It was founded in 1899. It is a pleasant, modern city. Because of the *terra roxa* (red earth), it is called the 'Cidade Morena'. In the centre is a shady park, the **Praça República**, commonly called the Praça do Rádio after the Rádio Clube on one of its corners. Three blocks west is **Praça Ari Coelho**. Linking the two squares, and running through the city east to west, is Av Afonso Pena; much of its central reservation is planted with yellow ypé trees. Their blossom covers the avenue, and much of the city besides, in spring.

Museu Dom Bosco (Indian Museum), R Barão do Rio Branco 1843, is superb. Its exhibits from the five Indian groups with which the Salesian missionaries have had contact in the 20th century all have explanatory texts. There are also collections of shells, stuffed birds, butterflies and mammals from the Pantanal, as well as a two-headed calf. Each collection is highly recommended. ■ *Mon-Sat 0800-1700, Sun 1200-1700, US$0.50, T383 3994*. **Museu do Arte Contemporâneo**, Marechal Rondón e Calógeras, has modern art from the region. ■ *Mon-Fri 1300-1800, free*.

A *Exceler Plaza*, Av Afonso Pena 444, T321 0102, F321 5666. Very comfortable, traditional hotel that caters to tourists and business visitors, small pool, tennis. **A** *Vale Verde*, Av Afonso Pena 106, T321 3355. Pleasant and well-maintained, small pool. Recommended. **B** *Advanced*, Av Calógeras 1909, T321 5000, F325 7744. A/c, small pool, **C** with fan, a bit faded. **C** *Concord*, Av Calógeras 1624, T384 3081, F382 4987. Very good, pool, mini bar. **E** *Americano*, R 14 de Julho 2311 and Mcal Rondón, T321 1454. A/c, fridge, cheaper with fan, a bit run down, in main shopping area. **E** *Pousada LM*, R 15 de Novembro 201, T321 5207, lmhotel@enersulnet.com.br Nice rooms motel-style around courtyard, TV, fridge, terrace, on busy road, **F** with fan, **G** single room, also rents by the month. Good value. Recommended.

Near the rodoviária There is a wide variety of hotels in the streets around the rodoviária so it is easy to leave bags in the *guarda volumes* and shop around. **A** *Internacional*, Allan Kardec 223, T384 4677, F321 2729, **B** with fan. Modern, comfortable, small pool. **B** *Saigali*, Barão do Rio Branco 356, T384 5775. A/c, mini bar, parking, cheaper with fan, comfortable. Recommended. **D** *Iguaçu*, R Dom Aquino 761, T384 4621, F321 3215. A/c, bar **E** with fan, modern, pleasant, internet for guests US$4 per hr. Recommended. **D** *Nacional*, R Dom Aquino, 610, T383 2461. A/c, **E** with fan, shared bath, or single, busy, includes breakfast, real bargain. **F** *Cosmos*, R Dom Aquino 771, T384 4270. Nice, quieter than others in area, good value. Recommended. **Youth hostel**: **E** Large block opposite rodoviária. Laundry, kitchen, reception open 24 hrs. Recommended.

Mid-range *Cantina Romana*, R da Paz 237. Established over 20 years, Italian and traditional cuisine, good atmosphere. *Casa Colonial*, Av Afonso Pena 3997, on corner with R Paraíba. Traditional, regional and Italian cuisine, with large dessert menu. *Dom Leon*, Av Afonso Pena 1907. Large *churrascaria*, pizzeria and restaurant, self-service lunch, live music evenings. *Largo de Ouro*, R 14 de Julho 1345. No-frills, large pizzeria and restaurant that does brisk trade. *Morada dos Bais*, Av Noroeste 5140, corner with Afonso Pena, behind

Sleeping
■ *on map*
Large, mid-range hotels, many with small pools and restaurants, and all very traditional, are found along Av Calógeras, away from the bus station and its budget options

This area is not safe at night

Brazil

Eating
● *on map*

Campo Grande

■ **Sleeping**	3 Concord	6 Iguaçu	9 Pousada LM	● **Eating**
1 Americano	4 Cosmos	7 Internacional	10 Vale Verde	1 Dom Leon
2 Advanced	5 Exceler Plaza	8 Nacional	11 Youth Hostel	

Not to scale

tourist office. Pretty courtyard, Brazilian and Italian dishes, US$2 lunch Tue-Sat. **Cheap** *Shopping Campo Grande*, Av Afonso Pena, has a wide selection of restaurants in this category, including *Pão de Queijo Express*. There are also lots of good, cheap options around the bus station and Praça Ari Coelho, and several self-service restaurants on R Cândido Mariano, Nos 1660 to 2512. **Local specialities** *Caldo de piranha* (soup), *chipa* (Paraguayan cheese bread), sold on streets, delicious when hot, and the local liqueur, *pequi com caju*, which contains *cachaça*.

Shopping
There is a market (Feira Livre) on Wed and Sat

Local native crafts, including ceramics, tapestry and jewellery, are good quality. A local speciality is Os Bugres da Conceição, squat wooden statues covered in moulded wax. Very good selections are found at *Casa do Artesão*, Av Calógeras 2050, on corner with Av Afonso Pena, housed in an historic building, Mon-Fri 0800-2000, Sat 0800-1200 (also has maps and information), and *Barroarte*, Av Afonso Pena 4329. Also *Arte do Pantanal*, Av Afonso Pena 1743.

Tour operators

Asteco Turismo, R 13 de Maio, 3192, T321 0077, www.ecotur-ms.com.br/com/as Two-day (1-night) trips from US$60-US$75, depending on activities and hotel. *Ecological Expeditions*, R Joaquim Nabuco 185, T321 0505, www.pantanaltrekking.com Attached to youth hostel at bus station, see above. Budget camping trips (sleeping bag needed) for 3/4/5 days ending in Corumbá. Recommended. *Impacto*, R Padre João Crippa 1065, sala 101, T325 1333. Helpful, Pantanal and Bonito tour operators, prices vary according to standard of accommodation; a wide range is offered. Two-day packages for 2 people from US$190-600. Transfers and insurance included. *Time Tour*, R Joaquim Murtinho 386, T312 2500, American Express representative.

Transport
Car hire agencies on Av Afonso Pena and at airport

Air Daily flights to most major cities. Airport T368 6000. City bus No 158, 'Popular' stops outside airport. Taxi to airport, US$6. *Banco do Brasil* at airport exchanges dollars. Post office, fax and phones in same office. It is safe to spend the night at the airport. *Varig*, R Barão do Rio Branco 1356, Centro, T0800-997000, airport 763 1213.

Bus Rodoviária is in the block bounded by Ruas Barão do Rio Branco, Vasconcelos Fernandes, Dom Aquino and Joaquim Nabuco, T383 1678, all offices on 2nd floor. At the V Fernandes end are town buses, at the J Nabuco end state and interstate buses. In between are shops and *lanchonetes*, 8 blocks' walk from Praça República. Cinema in rodoviária, US$1.20. (Taxi to rodoviária, US$3.60.)

Good connections throughout the country

São Paulo, US$33, 14 hrs, 4 buses daily, 1st at 1030, last at 2200, *leito* US$40. **Cuiabá**, US$21, 10 hrs, 12 buses daily, *leito* at 2100 and 2200 US$50. To **Brasília**, US$32, 23 hrs at 1000 and 2000. To **Goiânia**, *São Luís* 1100, 2000, 15 hrs on 1900 service, US$32, others 24 hrs, US$1 cheaper. **Corumbá**, with *Andorinha* (T782 3420), 8 daily from 0600, 6 hrs, US$14. Campo Grande-Corumbá buses connect with those from Rio and São Paulo, similarly those from Corumbá through to Rio and São Paulo. Twice daily direct service to **Foz do Iguaçu** (17 hrs) with *Integração*, US$27. To **Pedro Juan Caballero** (Paraguay), *del Amambay*, 0600, US$8.50. *Amambay* goes every Sun morning to **Asunción**.

Directory

Banks ATMs at *Banco do Brasil*, 13 de Maio e Av Afonso Pena, open 1000-1500, commission US$10 for cash, US$20 for TCs, regardless of amount exchanged. And *Bradesco*, 13 de Maio e Av Afonso Pena. *HSBC*, R 13 de Maio 2837, ATM. *Banco 24 horas*, R Maracaju, on corner with 13 de Junho. Also at R Dom Aquino e Joaquim Nabuco. *Overcash Câmbio*, R Rui Barbosa 2750, open Mon-Fri 1000-1600. **Communications** Internet: *Cyber Café Iris*, Av Alfonso Pena 1975. **Post Office**: on corner of R Dom Aquino e Calógeras 2309 and Barão do Rio Branco corner Ernesto Geisel, both locations offer fax service, US$2.10 per page within Brazil. **Telephone**: *Tele Centro Sul*, R Dom Aquino 1805, between P Celestino and Rui Barbosa, open 0600-2200. **Embassies and consulates** Bolivia, R João Pedro de Souza 798, T382 2190. **Paraguay**, R 26 Agosto 384, T324 4934. **Medical services** Yellow and Dengue fevers are both present in Mato Grosso do Sul. Get your immunizations at home. **Tourist offices** Maps and books for sale at the municipal **Centro de Informação Turística e Cultural**, Av Noroeste 5140 corner Afonso Pena, T/F324 5830, pensao@ms.sebrae.com.br Housed in Pensão Pimentel, a beautiful mansion built in 1913, also has a database about services in the city and cultural information. Open Tue-Sat 0800-1900, Sun 0900-1200. Kiosk at airport, open 24 hrs, T363 3116. State tourist office at R 14 de Julho 992, Vila Glória, T321 7504, embraturms@zipmail.com.br

Brazil

There is a paved road from Campo Grande to the Paraguayan border to Ponta Porã (*Post code*: 79900. *Phone code*: 0xx67), separated from Pedro Juan Caballero in Paraguay only by a broad avenue. With paved streets, good public transport and smart shops, Ponta Porã is more prosperous than its neighbour, although Brazilians cross the border to play the casino. *Banco do Brasil* changes travellers' cheques. Many banks in the centre of town (but on Sundays change money in hotels).

Ponta Porã
Voltage is 220 volts AC

Sleeping B *Porta do Sol Palace*, R Paraguai 2688, T431 3341, F431 1193. A/c, pool, very nice. B *Guarujá*, R Guia Lopes 63, T431 1619. Recommended. Opposite is C *Barcelona*, No 45, T/F431 3061. Maze-like building, a/c, restaurant, pool. C *Alvorada*, Av Brasil 2977, T431 5866. Good café, close to post office, good value but often full. C *Internacional*, R Internacional 1267, T431 1243. D without a/c, hot water, good breakfast. Recommended. Brazilian hotels include breakfast, Paraguayan ones do not.

Transport Bus: To **Campo Grande**, 9 a day from 0100-2130, 5 hrs, US$10; the rodoviária is 3 km out on the Dourados road ('São Domingos' bus, taxi US$3).

There are no border posts between the two towns and people pass freely for local visits. The Brazilian general police office for entry and exit visas is on the second floor of the white engineering supply company building at R Marechal Floriano 1483, T431 1428. ■ *Weekdays 0730-1130, 1400-1700.* The two nations' consulates face each other on R Internacional (border street), a block west of **Ponta Porã**'s local bus terminal; some nationalities require a visa from the Paraguayan consul (next to *Hotel Internacional*), open only 0800-1200 Monday-Friday. **Check requirements carefully**, and ensure your documents are in order: without the proper stamps you will inevitably be sent back somewhere later on in your travels. ■ *Taking a taxi between offices can speed things up if pressed for time; drivers know border crossing requirements; US$4.25.*

Border with Paraguay
Colour map 7, grid B2

Brazil

Bonito

The municipality of Bonito in the Serra do Bodoquena yields granite and marble and is clad in forest. The area's main attractions are in its rivers, waterfalls and caves. There are spectacular walks through mountains and forest, rafting and snorkelling in clear rivers and wildlife such as birds, rheas, monkeys, alligators and anaconda. Bonito has become very popular with Brazilian vacationers, especially during December-January, Carnival, Easter, and July (advance booking is essential). Prices are high. The wet season is January-February; December-February is hottest, July-August coolest.

Phone code: 0xx67
Post code: 79290
Colour map 6, grid B6
Population: 16,956
248 km from Campo Grande

Caves Lagoa Azul, 26 km from Bonito, has a lake 50 m long and 110 m wide, 75 m below ground level. The water, 20°C, is a jewel-like blue as light from the opening is refracted through limestone and magnesium. Prehistoric animal bones have been found in the lake. The light is at its best January-February, 0700-0900, but is fine at other times. A 25-ha park surrounds the cave. ■ *You must pay a municipal tax, US$5; if not using your own transport, a car for 4 costs US$20.* Also open is **Nossa Senhora Aparecida cave**, which has superb stalactites and stalagmites; no tourism infrastructure.

The **Balneário Municipal** on the Rio Formoso (7 km on road to Jardim), with changing rooms, toilets, camping, swimming in clear water, plenty of fish to see (strenuous efforts are made to keep the water and shore clean), US$5. **Hormínio** waterfalls, 13 km, eight falls on the Rio Formoso, suitable for swimming; bar and camping, entry US$0.15. **Rafting** on the Rio Formoso: 2½ hours, minimum four people, US$15 per person, a mixture of floating peacefully downriver, swimming and shooting four waterfalls, lifejackets available; arranged by many agencies. The **Aquário Natural** is one of the springs of the Rio Formoso; to visit you must have authorization from the owners; you can swim and snorkel with five types of fish (US$25). Do not swim with suntan oil on. Other tours are: from the **springs of the Rio Sucuri** to its meeting with the Formoso (permission required to visit), about 2 km of crystal-clear water, with

River excursions

Brazil

swimming or snorkelling, birdwatching, very peaceful; **Aquidaban**, a series of limestone/marble waterfalls in dense forest; **Rio da Prata** a spring with underground snorkelling for 2 km, stalactites, bats, very beautiful, also parrots and other animals can be seen on the trip, US$24. The **fishing** season is from 1 March-31 October. In late October, early November is the *piracema* (fish run), when the fish return to their spawning grounds. Hundreds can be seen jumping the falls. **NB** Bonito's attractions are nearly all on private land and must by visited with a guide. Owners also enforce limits on the number of daily visitors so, at busy times, pre-booking is essential.

Sleeping **A** *Canaã*, Pilad Rebuá 1293, T255 1255, F255 1282, hcanaa@ bonitonline.com.br Parking, TV, a/c, fridge, phone, restaurant and *churrascaria*. **A** *Tapera*, Estrada Ilha do Padre, Km 10, on hill above Shell station on road to Jardim, T255 1700, F255 1470, taperahotel@bonitonline.com.br Fine views, cool breezes, peaceful, a/c, very comfortable, own transport an advantage. **A-B** *Pousada Olho d'Água*, just outside Bonito, Km 1 on road to Três Morros, T255 1430, F255 1741, bonito@pousadaolhodagua.com.br 3 km from town, accommodation in cabins, including breakfast, fan, showers with solar-heated water, fruit trees, fresh vegetables, small lake, own water supply, horse riding, bicycles. Recommended. **B** *Bonanza*, R Col Pilad Rebuá (main street) 1876, T/F255 1162, hbonanza@bonitonline.com.br Suites and family rooms available, a/c. Frequently recommended. **D** pp *Pousada Muito Bonito*, Pilad Rebuá 1448, T/F255 1645, muitobonito@uol.com.br With bath, or rooms with bunkbeds, nice patio, excellent, helpful owners, including breakfast, also with tour company (Mario Doblack speaks English, French and Spanish). Warmly recommended. Also on Rebuá at 1800 is a hostal **E**, owned by the Paraíso tour agency, T255 1477, shared bath. Recommended. **E** *Pousada São Jorge*, Av Col Pilad Rebuá 1605, T255 1956, saojorge@ bonitonline.com.br Hot water, tropical breakfast, a/c, cheaper with fan, car parking, internet access, international telephone, laundry. Recommended. **F** pp *Pousada Rio do Peixe*, R 29 de Maio 820, T255 2212, www.pousada riodopeixe.hpg.com.br More expensive with TV, Italian-owned, very helpful, excellent breakfast, tours arranged. **Youth hostel** *Bonito Hostelling International*, R Lúcio Borralho 716, T/F255 1022, www.ajbonito.com.br Pool, kitchen and laundry facilities, English spoken.

Camping At *Ilha do Padre*, 12 km north of Bonito, T/F255 1430. Very pleasant, no regular transport. 4 rustic cabins with either 4 bunks, or 2 bunks and a double, US$10 pp, youth hostel with dorms, US$6 pp, same price for camping, toilets, showers, clothes' washing, meals available, bar, electricity, can swim anywhere, to enter the island for a day US$3. Camping also at *Poliana* on Rio Formosa, 100 m past Ilha do Padre, T255 1267. Very pleasant.

Eating *Tapera*, Pilad Rebuá 1961, T255 1110, good, home-grown vegetables, breakfast, lunch, pizzas, meat and fish dishes, opens 1900 for evening meal. *Comida Caseira*, Luís da Costa Leite e Santana do Paraíso, good local food, lunch and dinner, not open Sun afternoon. *Verdo-Frutos e Sucos Naturais*, Pilad Rebuá 1853, good juices and fruits.

Tour operators Sérgio Ferreira Gonzales, R Col Pilad Rebuá 628, T255 1315, is an authority on the caves. Recommended. *Hapakany Tour*, Pilad Rebuá 628, T/F255 1315. Jason and Murilo, for all local tours. Diving trips US$40 per day. *Sub Mundo*, R Pilad Rebuá 2148, T255 2040, www.submundodive.com.br Specializes in dives on Rio Formoso, lakes and in caves, very professional, good equipment, courses available. Recommended. *Tapera Tour*, R Col Pilad Rebuá 1961, T255 1757. Guides, information, tours, clothes shop. Recommended. For information in English and French, contact Henrique Ruas, T/F255 1430, see *Ilha do Padre* or *Pousada Olho d'Água* above.

The Associação dos Guias de Turismo can be reached on T255 1837

Transport **Bus** Rodoviária is on the edge of town, T255 1606. From **Campo Grande**, US$11, 5½-6 hrs, 1500, returns at 0530. Bus uses MS-345, with a stop at Autoposto Santa Cruz, Km 60, all types of fuel, food and drinks available. For Aquidauana, take Campo Grande bus. Bus Corumbá-Miranda-Bonito-Jardim-Ponta Porã, Mon-Sat, leaves either end at 0600, arriving Bonito 1230 for Ponta Porã, 1300 for Miranda; can change in Jardim (1400 for 1700 bus) or Miranda (better connections) for Campo Grande; fare **Corumbá**-Bonito US$12.50. Also connections on 1230 route in Bela Vista at 2000 for Asunción and Col Oviedo.

Banks *Banco do Brasil*, R Luiz da Costa Leite 2279, for Visa. Hoteliers and taxi drivers may change money. **Communications** Post Office: R Col Pilad Rebuá. **Telephone:** Santana do Paraíso. **Tourist office** Comtur, R Col Pilad Rebuá 1780, T255 1850. On the web see www.portalbonito.com.br **Directory**

Campo Grande to Corumbá and Bolivia

BR-262 is paved most of the way from Campo Grande to Corumbá and the Bolivian border. The scenery is marvellous.

There are several daily buses from Campo Grande. Turn south here to Jardim, with connections to Paraguay, and for one route to Bonito. Aquidauana is a gateway to the Pantanal. Excursions in fishing boats negotiable around US$50 per person a day, or via *Chalanatur*, T241 3396.

Aquidauana
Colour map 7, grid B1
Population: 43,440
131 km W of
Campo Grande

Sleeping and eating D *Fluminense*, R Teodoro Rondon 865, T241 2038. With fan and breakfast, a/c more expensive. D *Lord*, R Manoel Paes de Barros 739, T241 1857. Shared bathroom in single room, private bath in double room. Recommended. *O Casarão (grill)*, R Manoel Paes de Barros 533, T241 2219. Recommended.

Tour operators *Buriti Viagens e Turismo Ltda*, R Manoel Paes de Barros 720, T241 2718, F241 2719. *Lucarelli Turismo Ltda*, R Manoel Paes de Barros 552, T241 3410. *Cordon Turismo*, R Búzios, T384 1483. Organizes fishing trips into the Pantanal. *Panbratur*, R Estevão Alves Correa 586, T/F241 3494. Tour operator in southern Pantanal.

All recommended

Further west by 77 km is **Miranda** another entrance to the Pantanal. There is a *jacaré* farm, *Granja Caimã*, which is open to visitors. ■ US$1. A road heads south to Bodoquena and on to Bonito. ■ *Bus Campo Grande-Miranda, seven a day with Expresso Mato Grosso, US$5.10, and others*. The Campo Grande-Corumbá road crosses the Rio Miranda bridge (two service stations before it) then carries on, mostly paved to cross the Rio Paraguai.

Corumbá

Situated on the south bank by a broad bend in the Rio Paraguai, 15 minutes from the Bolivian border, the city offers beautiful views of the river, especially at sunset. It is hot and humid (70%); cooler in June-July, very hot from September to January. It has millions of mosquitoes in December-February.

Phone code: 0xx67
Post code: 79300
Colour map 6, grid B6
Population: 95,701

There is a spacious shady **Praça da Independência** and the port area is worth a visit. Av Gen Rondon between Frei Mariano and 7 de September has a pleasant palm lined promenade which comes to life in the evenings. The **Forte Junqueira**, the city's most historic building, which may be visited, was built in 1772. In the hills to the south is the world's greatest reserve of manganese, now being worked. Corumbá is the best starting point for the southern part of the Pantanal, with boat and jeep trips and access to the major hotel/farms.

B *Internacional Palace*, R Dom Aquino Correia 1457, T/F231 6247. A/c, fridge, pool, sauna, parking, cafe. **B** *Nacional Palace*, R América 936, T231 6868, F231 0202. A/c, fridge, good pool, parking. **B** *Carandá*, R Dom Aquino Corrêa 47, T/F231 2023. A/c, fridge, pool, good, helpful, restaurant. **B** *Laura Vicunha*, R Cuiabá 775, T231 5874, T231 2663. A/c, fridge, **C** for simpler room, parking, modern. Recommended. **D** *Beira Rio*, R Manoel Cavassa 109, T231 2554. A/c, cheaper with fan, by the port, popular with fishermen. **D** *Pensâo do Tato*, R 13 de Junho 720, T231 7727. A/c, cheaper with fan, small rooms. **D** *Timoneiro*, R Cabral 879, T231 5530, between rodoviária and centre. A/c, **E** with fan, cheaper with shared bath. **E** *Angola*, R Antônio Maria 124, T231 7233. A/c, **F** with fan, restaurant. **E-F** *City*, R Cabral 1031, T231 6373, between rodoviária and centre. A/c, **C** with fan, cheaper with shared bath, parking. **Near the rodoviária are D** *Internacional*, R Porto Carreiro 714, T231 4654. Shared bath, fan, basic, simple breakfast,

Sleeping
The city is unsafe late at night

Brazil

owner organizes fishing trips. **E** *Beatriz*, R Porto Carreiro 896, T231 7441. Fan, cheaper with shared bath, small rooms, simple. **E** *Irure*, R 13 de Junho 776. Small and clean.

Eating There are several good restaurants in R Frei Mariano. *Churrascaria do Gaúcho*, No 879. Good value. *Peixaria do Lulú*, R Dom Aquino Correia 700. Good fish. *Churrascaria Rodéio*, 13 de Junho 760. Very good, lunchtime buffet. Recommended. *Viva Bella*, R Arthur Mangabeira 1 (behind Clube Corumbaense 1 block from Gen Rondon). Fish, meat, pizza, home made pastas, drinks, magnificent views over the river especially at sunset, live music Wed-Sat, opens at 1700, good food and atmosphere. Recommended. *Almanara*, R America 964 next to *Hotel Nacional*. Good Arabic food. On the waterfront you can eat good fish at *Portal do Pantanal*. Lots of open-air bars on the river front. Many good ice cream parlours: *Cristal*, R 7 de Setembro e Delamaré. Recommended.

Local specialities These include *peixadas corumbaenses*, a variety of fish dishes prepared with the catch of the day; as well as ice cream, liquor and sweets made of *bocaiúva*, a small yellow palm fruit, in season Sep-Feb.

Festivals **2 Feb**, *Festa de Nossa Senhora da Candelária*, Corumbá's patron saint, all offices and shops are closed. **24 Jun**, *Festa do Arraial do Banho de São João*, fireworks, parades, traditional food stands, processions and the main event, the bathing of the image of the saint in the Rio Paraguai. **21 Sep**, Corumbá's anniversary, includes a Pantanal fishing festival held on the eve.

Shopping *Casa do Artesão*, R Dom Aquino Correia 405. Open Mon-Fri 0800-1200, 1400-1800, Sat
Shops tend to open 0800-1200, good selection of handicrafts, small bookshop, friendly staff but high prices.
early and close by 1700 *CorumbArte*, Av Gen Rondon 1011. For good silk-screen T-shirts with Pantanal motifs. *Livraria Corumbaense*, R Delamaré 1080. For state maps. **Supermarkets** *Ohara*, Dom Aquino 621. *Frutal*, R 13 de Junho 538, open 0800-2000.

Tour operators Corumbá has many travel agencies selling tours to the Pantanal. For more information see page 572: *Pantur*, R Frei Mariano 1013, T231 2000, F231 6006. Tours, agents for *Hotel Fazenda Xaraés* in Nhecolândia, sells train tickets to Santa Cruz. *Taimã*, R Antônio M Coelho 786, T/F231 2179. River trips, flights over Pantanal, airline tickets.

Transport **Air** Airport, R Santos Dumont, 3 km, T231 3322. Daily flights to Campo Grande, Londrina and São Paulo with TAM. No public transport from airport to town, you have to take a taxi.
Buses The rodoviária is on R Porto Carreiro at the south end of R Tiradentes, next to the railway station. City bus to rodoviária from Praça da República.
Car hire: *Unidas*, R Frei Mariano 633, T/F231 3124.
Taxi: are extortionate, but moto-taxis only charge US$0.65. *Andorinha* services to all points east. To **Campo Grande**, 7 hrs, US$14, 13 buses daily, between 0630 and midnight, interesting journey ('an excursion in itself') – take an early bus to see plentiful wildlife, connections from Campo Grande to all parts of Brazil. To **Ponta Porã**, 12 hrs, US$20, via Bonito (6 hrs, US$12.50) and Jardim (9 hrs, US$15), Mon-Sat at 0600; ticket office open 0500-0600 only, at other times call T231 2383.

Directory **Banks** *Banco do Brasil*, R 13 de Junho 914, ATM, 15% commission on exchange. *HSBC*, R Delamare 1068, ATM. **Communications** Internet: *Caffe.com*, R Frei Mariano 635, T231 7730. *PantanalNET*, Rua América 403,Centro, US$2.50 per hr. **Post Office:** main at R Delamaré 708 (has fax service); branch at R 15 de Novembro 229. **Telephone:** *Tele Centro Sul*, R Dom Aquino 951, near Praça da Independência, open 0700-2200 daily. To phone Quiarro/Puerto Suárez, Bolivia, it costs slightly more than a local call, dial 214 + the Bolivian number.

Border with Over the border from Corumbá are Arroyo Concepción, Puerto Quijarro and Puerto
Bolivia Suárez. From Puerto Quijaro a 650-km railway runs to Santa Cruz de la Sierra. There is
Go to R 7 de Setembro, a road of sorts. There are flights into Bolivia from Puerto Suárez.
Corumbá, for a yellow **Brazilian immigration** Formalities are constantly changing so check procedures
fever inoculation

in advance. You need not have your passport stamped to visit Quijarro or Puerto Suárez only for the day. Otherwise, get your passport stamped by Brazilian Polícia Federal at Praça da Republica 37, next to NS da Candelária, 0800-1130, 1400-1730. The visa must be obtained on the day of departure. If leaving Brazil merely to obtain a new visa, remember that exit and entry must not be on the same day. Money changers at the border and in Quijarro offer the same rates as in Corumbá. The Bolivian consulate is at R Antônio Maria Coelho 881, Corumbá, T231 5605. ■ *Mon-Fri, 0700-1100, 1500-1730, Sat and Sun closed.* A fee is charged to citizens of those countries which require a visa. A yellow fever vaccination certificate is required.

Transport Leaving Brazil, take Canarinho city bus marked Fronteira from the port end of R Antônio Maria Coelho to the Bolivian border (15 mins, US$0.45), walk over the bridge to Bolivian immigration (blue building), then take a colectivo to Quijarro or Puerto Suárez. When travelling from Quijarro, take a taxi or walk to the Bolivian border to go through formalities. Just past the bridge, on a small side street to the right, is the bus stop for Corumbá, take bus marked Fronteira or Tamengo to Praça da República, US$0.45, every 45 mins between 0630 and 1915, don't believe taxi drivers who say there is no bus. Taxi to centre US$6. Find a hotel then take care of Brazilian formalities at Polícia Federal, address above.

The schedules of **trains** from Puerto Quijarro to Santa Cruz are given on page 335. Timetables change frequently, so check on arrival in Corumbá. It may be best to stay in Quijarro to get a good place in the queue for tickets.

Pantanal

This vast wetland, measuring 230,000 sq km between Cuiabá, Campo Grande and the Bolivian frontier, is one of the **world's great wildlife preserves**. Parts spill over into neighbouring Bolivia and Paraguay, and the entire area has been opened up to tourism.

Similar in many ways to the Amazon basin, though because of the more veldt-like open land, the wildlife can be viewed more easily than in the dense jungle growth. Principal life seen in this area is about 650 species of birds, including the hyacinth macaw, jabiru stork (the *tuiuíu*, almost 1.2 m tall), plumbeous ibis, both blue-throated and red-throated piping guans, rhea, curasow and roseate spoonbill. Easy to see on the river-banks are the ubiquitous capybara, a kind of giant aquatic guinea-pig, and caiman (*jacaré*). You may also come across otters, anteaters, opossums, armadillos, bare-eared marmosets, black-and-gold howler monkeys and marsh deer. Harder to spot are maned wolf, South American coati, ocelot, margay, jaguarundi and even pumas, jaguars and yellow anacondas. There are some 230 varieties of fish, from the giant *pintado*, weighing up to 80 kg, to the tiny, voracious *piranha*. Fishing here is exceptionally good (best May-October). The extraordinary thing is that man and his domesticated cattle thrive together with the wildlife with seemingly little friction. Local farmers protect the area jealously.

Wildlife
For the Pantanal on the web see www.geocities.com/ RainForest/1820/ (Portuguese and English)

Only one area is officially a national park, the **Parque Nacional do Pantanal Matogrossense** in the municipality of Poconé, 135,000 ha of land and water, only accessible by air or river. Hunting in any form is strictly forbidden throughout the Pantanal and is punishable by four years imprisonment. Fishing is allowed with a licence (enquire at travel agents for latest details); it is not permitted in the spawning season or *piracema* (1 October to 1 February in Mato Grosso do Sul, 1 November to 1 March in Mato Grosso). Like other wilderness areas, the Pantanal faces important threats to its integrity. Agro-chemicals and *garimpo* mercury washed down from the neighbouring *planalto* are a hazard to wildlife. Visitors must share the responsibility of protecting the Pantanal and you can make an important contribution by acting responsibly and choosing your guides accordingly: take out your rubbish, don't fish out of season, don't let guides kill or disturb fauna, don't buy products made from endangered species and report any violation of these norms to the authorities.

Permission to visit the park needs to be obtained at Ibama, Av Principal do CPA, Cuiabá, CEP 78000-000, T648 9100, F644 2210

When to go   The Pantanal is good for seeing wildlife year-round. However, the dry season between Jul and Oct is the ideal time as animals and birds congregate at the few remaining areas of water. During these months you are very likely to see jaguars. This is the nesting and breeding season, when birds form vast nesting areas, with thousands crowding the trees, creating an almost insupportable cacophony of sounds. The white sand river beaches are exposed, caiman bask in the sun, and capybaras frolic amid the grass. Jul sees lots of Brazilian visitors who tend to be noisy, decreasing the chances of sightings. From the end of Nov to the end of Mar (wettest in Feb), most of the area, which is crossed by many rivers, floods. At this time mosquitoes abound and cattle crowd on to the few islands remaining above water. In the southern part, many wild animals leave the area, but in the north, which is slightly higher, the animals do not leave.

What to take   Most tours arrange for you to leave your baggage in town, so you need only bring what is necessary for the duration of the tour with you. In winter (Jun-Aug), temperatures fall to 10°, warm clothing and covers or sleeping bag are needed at night. It's very hot and humid during summer and a hat and sun protection is vital. Wear long sleeves and long trousers and spray clothes as well as skin with insect repellent. Insects are less of a problem Jul-Aug. Take insect repellent from home as mosquitoes, especially in the North Pantanal, are becoming immune to local brands. Drinks are not included in the price of packages and tend to be over-priced, so if you are on a tight budget bring your own. Mostly importantly, try to get hold of a pair of binoculars.

Getting there   The Pantanal is not easy or cheap to visit. The best starting points are Corumbá, Cuiabá, and to a lesser extent Campo Grande, from where one finds public transport all around the perimeter, but none at all within. Wild camping is possible if you have some experience and your own transport. Remember that the longer you stay and the further you go from the edges (where most of the hotels are located), the more likely you are to see rare wildlife.

From Corumbá there is access to the Pantanal by both road and river, offering a variety of day trips, luxury house boat excursions, and connections to many surrounding *fazendas*. Along the road from Corumbá to Campo Grande (BR-262) are Miranda and Aquidauana, both important gateways to various fishing and tourist lodges. The BR-163 which connects Campo Grande and Cuiabá skirts the east edge of the Pantanal. Coxim, 242 km north of Campo Grande, offers access via the Rio Taquari but few facilities. From Cuiabá there is year-round road access to Barão de Melgaço and Poconé, both of which can be starting points for excursions. The Transpantaneira Highway runs south from Poconé to Porto Jofre, through the heart of the Pantanal, providing access to many different lodges, but does not have any bus service. During the rainy season, access is restricted between Pixaim and Porto Jofre. Finally Cáceres, 215 km west of Cuiabá at the northwest corner of the Pantanal, offers access along the Rio Paraguai to one of the least developed parts of the region.

Types of tour
Whatever your budget, take binoculars   Tourist facilities in the Pantanal currently cater to four main categories of visitors. **Sport fishermen** usually stay at one of the numerous speciality lodges scattered throughout the region, which provide guides, boats, bait, ice and other related amenities. Bookings can be made locally or in any of Brazil's major cities. **All-inclusive tours** combining air and ground transportation, accommodation at the most elaborate *fazendas*, meals, guided river and land tours, can be arranged from abroad or through Brazilian travel agencies. This is the most expensive option. **Moderately priced tours** using private guides, camping or staying at more modest *fazendas* can be arranged locally in Cuiabá (where guides await arrivals at the airport) or through the more reputable agencies in Corumbá. **The lowest priced tours** are offered by independent guides in Corumbá, some of whom are unreliable and travellers have reported at times serious problems here (see below). For those with the minimum of funds, a glimpse of the Pantanal and its wildlife can be had on the bus ride from Campo Grande to Corumbá, by lodging or camping near the ferry crossing over the Rio Paraguai (Porto Esperança), and by staying in Poconé and day-walking or hitching south along the Transpantaneira.

Choosing a tour   Most tours combine 'safari' jeep trips, river-boat trips, piranha fishing and horse riding with accommodation in lodges. As sunset and sunrise are the best times for spotting bird and wildlife, excursions often take place at these times. A two-day trip, with a full day taken up with travel each way, allows you to experience most of what is on offer. Longer tours tend to have the same activities spread out over a longer period of time.

Many budget travellers en route to or from Bolivia make Corumbá their base for visiting the Pantanal. Such tourists are often approached, in the streets and at the cheaper hotels, by salesmen who speak foreign languages and promise complete tours for low prices. They then hand their clients over to agencies and/or guides, who often speak only Portuguese, and may deliver something quite different. Some travellers have reported very unpleasant experiences and it is important to select a guide with great care anywhere. By far the best way is to speak with other travellers who have just returned from a Pantanal tour. Most guides also have a book containing comments from their former clients. Do not rush to sign up when first approached, always compare several available alternatives. Discuss the planned itinerary carefully and try to get it in writing (although this is seldom possible – threaten to go to someone else if necessary). Try to deal directly with agencies or guides, not salesmen (it can be difficult to tell who is who). Always get an itemized receipt. Bear in mind that a well-organized three-day tour can be more rewarding than four days with an ill-prepared guide. There is fierce competition between guides who provide similar services, but with very different styles. Although we list a few of the most reputable guides below, there are other good ones and most economy travellers enjoy a pleasant if spartan experience. Remember that travellers must shoulder part of the responsibility for the current chaotic guiding situation in Corumbá. Act responsibly and don't expect to get something for nothing. (See also Corumbá guides section.)

It appears to be the case that once a guide is recommended by a guidebook, he ceases to guide and sets up his own business working in promoting and public relations, using other guides to work under his name. Guides at the airport give the impression that they will lead the tour, but they won't. Always ask who will lead the party and how big it will be. Less than four is not economic and he will make cuts in boats or guides.

From Campo Grande **LL** full board *Pousada São Francisco*, 135 km from Aquidauana in the Rio Negro area of Nhecolândia, T241 3494, accessible only by air during the wet, with bath, fan, screening, horse riding, price including transport, meals, tours, bookings through *Impacto Turismo*, Campo Grande, T/F0xx67-725 1333 (full address above). **LL** full board *Refúgio Ecológico Caiman*, 36 km from Miranda, 236 km from Campo Grande, first class, full board, excursions, T0xx67-687 2102, T/F687 2103, or São Paulo 3079 6622, F3079 6037, www.caiman.com.br A Roteiro de Charme hotel. **L** full board *Pousada Aguapé*, Fazenda São José, 59 km north of Aquidauana, 202 km from Campo Grande, T686 1036, farmhouse hotel, screened rooms, some with a/c, pool, horse riding, boat trips, trekking, meals and tours included, bookings through *Impacto Turismo*, as above, or T241 2889, F241 3494. **AL** *Fazenda Salobra*, T0xx67-242 1162, 6 km from Miranda, 209 km from Corumbá, 198 km from Campo Grande, is recommended, with bath, including all meals, tours, boat rentals and horses are extra; it is by the Rio Salobra (clear water) and Rio Miranda, with birds and animals easily seen. Take bus from Campo Grande to Miranda, and alight 50 m from the bridge over Rio Miranda, turn left for 1,200 m to the *Fazenda*. **B** *Fazenda Toca da Onça*, 10 km from Aquidauana on the shores of the Rio Aquidauana, cabins, a/c, restaurant, boats, bookings through *Panbratur*, Aquidauana, as above, or T986 0189. *Pousada Pequi*, 42 km from the BR 262, 1 km from the Rio Aquidauana, T686 1042, www.pantanalpequi.com.br A/c, restaurant, tours and excursions, on a farm. **B** *Pousada Águas do Pantanal*, Av Afonso Pena 367, Miranda, T/F0xx67-241 4241/1702, contact Fátima or Luis Cordelli. Very good, good food, restaurant serves *jacaré* legally. There is a good campsite 30 km past Miranda. There are also several camping possibilities along the shores of the Rio Aquidauana including *Camping Baía*, 50 km from Aquidauana, T241 3634, on a bay on the river, trees for shade, boats. *Camping Itajú*, 18 km from Aquidauana, sandy beach, cabins, lanchonete, shower, electricity, boat rental. **Camping allows you to see the wildlife at its greatest period of activity** – dawn and dusk, but protection against mosquitoes is essential. Care should also be taken to avoid dangerous animals: snakes (especially in the rainy season), piranhas (especially in the dry season), killer bees and the larger jacarés.

Sleeping

The inexperienced should not strike out on their own. Many lodges with fair to good accommodation, some only approachable by air or river; most are relatively expensive. One option is to hire a car and check for yourself: in Jun-Sep, especially Jul, book in advance. An ordinary vehicle should be able to manage the Transpantaneira out of Cuiabá throughout most of the year, but in the wet season you should be prepared to get stuck, and muddy, pushing your car from time to time

Trips from Corumbá Some of Corumbá's many agencies are listed on page 568. Tours out of Corumbá are of 3-4 days, costing up to US$100 (includes all food, accommodation and transport).1 day river trips are also available on river boats with a capacity of 80 passengers, US$25 half-day; US$50 full day, including transfers and hot fish meal. Smaller boats US$15 pp for 3 hrs. Tickets at travel agents and by port. Boats may be hired, with fishing tackle and guide, at the port (US$100 per day, up to 3 people, in season only). There are also hotels specializing in fishing, all reached from Corumbá by road.

Lodges **LL** full board *Pousada do Pantanal*, T0xx67-725 5267/231 5212, 125 km from Corumbá near the Campo Grande road at *Fazenda Santa Clara*. A working cattle ranch, very comfortable, easy access by bus, reservations from all agencies in Corumbá. **LL** full board *Hotel Fazenda Xaraés*, T0xx67-231 4094, Rio Abobral, 130 km from Corumbá, luxurious, a/c, pool, restaurant, horses, boats. **A** *Fazenda Santa Blanca*, on the Rio Paraguai, 15 mins by boat south of Porto Esperança (where the BR-262 crosses the Rio Paraguai), full board, good kayak excursions, horse riding, information from R 15 de Novembro 659, 79300 Corumbá, T231 1460.

Tour operators Travel is in the back of a pick-up (good for seeing animals), up to a maximum of 6. Accommodation is in a hammock under a palm thatch on a *fazenda*. Food can be good. If you want flushing toilets, showers or luxury cabins, approach an agency. Guides provide bottled mineral water (make sure enough is carried), but you must take a hat, sun screen and mosquito repellent. Some guides go to *fazendas* without permission, have unreliable vehicles, or are inadequately equipped, so try to check their credentials. Agencies sometimes subcontract to guides over whom they have no control. If you are asked to pay half the money directly to the guide check him out as if he were independent and ask to see his equipment. Guides will generally not make the trip with fewer than 5 people, so if you have not already formed a group, stay in touch with several guides. This is most important during Mar-Oct, when very few tourists are around and many agencies shut up shop for the low season. Decide on your priorities: try to ensure that your guide and other group members share your ideas. We list below those guides who have received positive reports from travellers: *Greentrack*, R Antônio João 216, T231 2258, greentk@terra.com.br Run by guide Katu, who is recommended, has a hostel, mixed reports for agency. *Saldanha Tour*, R Porto Carreiro 896B, T231 16891, saldanha_v@hotmail.com Owner Eliane is very helpful to travellers. *Carola Alice Reimann*, creimann@hotmail.com Speaks English, knowledgeable. There are many other guides not listed here; lots have received criticisms from travellers. There may be others on whom we have received no feedback.

Cuiabá to Pantanal

Colour map 6, grid A6 A paved road turns south off the main Cuiabá-Cáceres road to **Poconé** (102 km from Cuiabá, hotels, 24-hr gas station – closed Sunday). From here, the Transpantaneira runs 146 km south to Porto Jofre (just a gas station, gasoline and diesel, but no alcohol available). At the entrance to the Pantanal, there is a gate across the road where drivers are given a list of rules of conduct. The road is of earth, in poor condition, with ruts, holes and many bridges that need care in crossing. Easiest access is in the dry season (July-September), which is also the best time for seeing birds and, in September, the trees are in bloom. In the wet, especially January-February, there is no guarantee that the Transpantaneira will be passable. The wet season, however, is a good time to see many of the shyer animals because more fruit, new growth and other high calorie foods are available, and there are fewer people.

Campos de Jofre, about 20 km north of Porto Jofre, is said to be magnificent between August and October. In Poconé one can hitch to Porto Jofre, or hire a vehicle in Cuiabá. You will get more out of this part of the Pantanal by going with a guide; a lot can be seen from the Transpantaneira in a hired car, but guides can take you into *fazendas* some 7 km from the Transpantaneira and will point out wildlife. Recommended guides in Cuiabá are under Tour operators. Although there are gas stations in **Pixaim** (a bridge across the Rio Pixaim, two hotels and a tyre repair shop) and Porto Jofre, they are not always well stocked, best to carry extra fuel.

Brazil

In Pixaim and The Transpantaneira **L** *Pantanal Mato Grosso*, T/F0xx65-321 9445. Mod- **Sleeping**
ern cabins, 35 rooms for 3-6 people, with full board, fan, hot water (also family-size apartments
with a/c), pool, good home-grown food, in radio contact with office on R Barão de Melgaço in
Cuiabá, camping possible, boat rental with driver US$30 per hr. **AL** *Hotel-Fazenda Cabanas
do Pantanal*, 142 km from Cuiabá, 50 km from Poconé by the Rio Pixaim, on the northern edge
of the Pantanal. 10 chalet bedrooms with bath, restaurant, boat trips (few in dry season),
horse-riding, fishing, helpful proprietor and staff, everything except boat trips and bar drinks
included in price (booking: *Confiança*, Cuiabá). **A** *Araras EcoLodge*, Km 32 on Transpantaneira,
T682 2800, F682 1260, 14 rooms with bath, pool, good food, home-made *cachaça*, well-
informed guides, can book through *Expeditours* in Cuiabá. Recommended. **A** *Pousada
Pantaneira*, full board, 7 rooms with 2-3 bunk beds each, bath, simple, owned and operated
by *pantaneiros* (reservations through *Faunatur* in Cuiabá), about 45 km from Pixaim. Next to
Pousada Pantaneira is the private Jaguar Ecological Reserve, owned by *pantaneiros*, funded by
donation, an excellent place to see jaguars; all further details through *Focus Tours* (see page
352). **A** *Pousada Pixaim*, built on stilts, T721 1899. Full board (meals also available separately),
10 rooms with a/c or fan, mosquito-netted windows, hot water, electricity 24 hrs, pleasant setting, boat trips – US$30 per hr with driver, camping possible US$10 per tent or free if you eat in
the restaurant. **E** *Pousada Piuval*, at Fazenda Ipiranga, Matogrossense, Rod Transpantaneira
Km 10, T983 7425. A/c, with bath, **G** for camping with outside shower, horse riding, boat trips.

On Rio Cuiabá, 130 km from Cuiabá (*TUT* bus at 0730 and 1500, US$6.50), Barão de **Barão de**
Melgaço is reached by two roads: the shorter, via Santo Antônio de Leverger, unpaved **Melgaço**
from Santo Antônio to Barão (closed in the wet season), or via São Vicente, longer, but *Colour map 7, grid A1*
more pavement. The way to see the Pantanal from here is by boat down the Rio
Cuiabá. Boat hire, for example from *Restaurant Peixe Vivo* on waterfront, up to US$85
for a full day; or enquire with travel agencies in Cuiabá. The best time of day would be
sunset, but it would need some organizing to be in the best part at the best time, without too much boating in the dark. Protect against the sun when on the water. Initially
the river banks are farms and small habitations, but they become more forested, with
lovely combinations of flowering trees (best seen September-October). After a while, a
small river to the left leads to the Baia and Lakes Chacororé and Sia Mariana, which
join each other. Boats can continue beyond the lakes to the Rio Mutum, but a guide is
essential because there are many dead ends. The area is rich in birdlife and the
waterscapes are beautiful.

Sleeping **L** *Pousada Passárgada*, programmes from 3 days up, full board, boat, car and trekking expeditions, transport from Barão de Melgaço, owner speaks English, French and German,
food excellent, closed Dec to Feb; reservations T713 1128, in Barão de Melgaço on riverside, or
through *Nature Safaris*, Av Marechal Rondon, Barão de Melgaço. Much cheaper if booked direct
with the owner, Maré Sigaud, Mato Grosso, CEP 786807, *Pousada Passárgada*, Barão de
Melgaço. Highly recommended. **L** *Sapé Pantanal Lodge*, Caixa Postal 2241 – CEP 78020.970,
Cuiabá, T0xx65-391 1442, www.sapehotel.com.br Basic, self-contained accommodation,
meals buffet-style, sport fishing, wildlife observation and photography excursions. A complete
programme includes road transport from Cuiabá airport to Barão de Melgaço (wet season), or
Porto Cercado (dry season) with onward river transportation (about 1½ hrs); outboard powered boats with experienced guides at guests' disposal; optional trekking and horse riding in
dry season, paddling in wet; English, French, Spanish spoken. *Sapé*, which is recommended, is
closed 20 Dec-31 Jan. Reservations can be made through agencies at favourable rates.

Cuiabá

The capital of Mato Grosso state on the Rio Cuiabá, an upper tributary of the Rio *Phone code: 0xx65*
Paraguai, is in fact two cities: Cuiabá on the east bank of the river and Várzea *Post code: 78000*
Grande, where the airport is, on the west. It is very hot; coolest months for a visit are *Colour map 7, grid A1*
June, July and August, in the dry season. *Population: 483,346*
Altitude: 176 m

Cuiabá has an imposing government palace and other fine buildings round the green **Praça da República**. On the square is the **Cathedral**, with a plain, imposing exterior, two clock-towers and, inside, coloured-glass mosaic windows and doors. Behind the altar is a huge mosaic of Christ in majesty, with smaller mosaics in side chapels. Beside the Cathedral is the leafy **Praça Alencastro**. On **Praça Ipiranga**, at the junction of Avs Isaac Póvoas and Tenente Col Duarte, a few blocks west of the central squares, there are market stalls and an iron bandstand from Huddersfield, UK. On a hill beyond the praça is the church of **Bom Despacho**, built in the style of Notre Dame de Paris (in poor condition, closed to visitors). In front of the Assembléia Legislativa, Praça Moreira Cabral, is a point marking the **Geogedesic Centre of South America** (see also under Chapada dos Guimarães). **Museus de Antropologia, História Natural e Cultura Popular**, in the Fundação Cultural de Mato Grosso, Praça da República 151, has historical photos, a contemporary art gallery, stuffed Pantanal fauna, Indian, archaeological finds and pottery. ■ *Mon-Fri 0800-1730, US$0.50*. At the entrance to Universidade de Mato Grosso, 10 minutes by bus from the centre, is the small **Museu do Índio/Museu Rondon** (by swimming pool), with well-displayed exhibits.

Sleeping
■ *on map*
The port area is best avoided day and night

AL *Áurea Pálace*, Gen Mello 63, T623 1826, F623 7390, aureaph@zaz.com.br swimming pool, good. **AL** *Best Western Mato Grosso Pálace*, Joaquim Murtinho 170, T614 7000, F321 2386, pwmt@zaz.com.br A/c, fridge, central, restaurant. **B** *Jaguar Pálace*, Av Getúlio Vargas 600, T624 4404, jaguarph@zaz.com.br New extension with rooms around large pool, older rooms are large with sofas and old-fashioned (once used by prospectors who paid for their room in gold nuggets), comfortable and good value. **C** *Samara*, R Joaquim Murtinho 270, T322 6001. Central, with bath, hot shower, fan, basic but good, cheaper with shared bath. **C** *Mato Grosso*, R Comandante Costa 2522, T614 7777, bwmt@zaz.com.br Excellent value, with breakfast, a/c, **D** with fan, good restaurant, English spoken, luggage stored whilst guests tour Chapada or Pantanal. **E** *Pousada Ecoverde*, R Pedro Celestino 391, T624 1386, joelsouza@terra.com.br 5 rooms with shared bath around a courtyard in colonial family house, breakfast, kitchen, laundry and garden with hammocks. **E** *Presidente*, Barão de Melgaço e Av G Vargas, T624 1386. On a busy central corner, convenient but run down, a/c, **F** with fan, cheaper with shared bath. By the rodoviária, on Jules Rimet are: **A** *Skala Pálace*, at No 26, T322 4347. With a/c, fridge, restaurant, front rooms noisy. **B** *Brazil*, No 20, T621 2703. A/c, fridge, parking, **D** with fan, cheaper with shared bath, ground floor rooms best. **C** *Ipanema*, s/n, T621 3069. A/c, **D** with fan, cheaper with shared bath, good value, good breakfast. **D** *Grande*, No 30, T621 3852. A/c, **E** with fan, cheaper with shared bath, basic. Others in same area.

Cuiabá

Sleeping
1 Áurea Pálace
2 Best Western Mato Grosso Pálace
3 Brazil
4 Grande
5 Ipanema
6 Jaguar Pálace
7 Mato Grosso
8 Pousada Ecoverde
9 Presidente
10 Samara
11 Skala Pálace

Eating
1 Cedros
2 Choppão
3 Getúlio
4 Hong Kong

N

0 metres 100
0 yards 100

Youth hostel E *Portal do Pantanal*, Av Isaac Povoas 655, T/F624 8999, www.portaldopantanal.com.br IYHA, with breakfast, cheaper with fan, internet access US$2.50 per hr, laundry, kitchen.

Eating

● *on map*
City centre restaurants only open for lunch. On Av CPA are many good restaurants and small snack bars

Expensive *Getúlio*, Av Getúlio Vargas 1147. Somewhat pretentious a/c restaurant with pavement tables, dance floor and sushi bar, excellent food, with meat specialties and pizza. **Mid-range** *Cedros*, Praça 8 de Abril 750, Goiabeiras. Fan-cooled, popular place offering wide selection of Arabic food, including *tabule* salad and 'pizza' made with pitta bread. Delivery service, T624 9134. Recommended. *China in Box*, Av Lavapés,70, T623 8400. Chinese food with a Brazilian twist, also fish dishes and desserts. Open daily for lunch and dinner; delivery service. *Choppão*, Praça 8 de Abril. Go for the huge portions of food or just for thebeer. Recommended. *Lig-China*, R Presidente Marques 960. Sophisticated, a/c restaurant with standard Chinese and Japanese menu, open daily for lunch and dinner till 2400, also delivers. **Cheap** There are several restaurants and *lanchonetes* on R Jules Rimet across from the rodoviária. *Hong Kong*, Av G Vargas 647, opposite *Jaguar Hotel*. Self-service Chinese, good quality for price. *Lanchonete Presidente*, Hamburgers and sandwiches, next to hotel of same name, open late.

Bars & clubs

Cuiabá is quite lively at night, bars with live music and dance on Av CPA. *Bierhaus*, Isaac Póvoas 1200. Large, sophisticated, semi open-air bar/restaurant with music. *Tucano* bar/restaurant, Av CPA, beautiful view, specializes in pizza. Recommended. Av Mato Grosso also has many bars and restaurants. 4 cinemas in town.

Shopping

Handicrafts in wood, straw, netting, leather, skins, Pequi liquor, crystallized *caju* fruit, compressed *guaraná* fruit (for making the drink), Indian objects on sale at the airport, rodoviária, craft shops in centre, and daily market, Praça da República, interesting. The *Casa de Artesão*, Praça do Expedicionário 315, T321 0603, sells all types of local crafts in a restored building. Recommended. Fish and vegetable market, picturesque, at the riverside.

Tour operators

All these agencies arrange trips to the Pantanal; for longer or special programmes, book in advance

Anaconda, R Mal Deodoro 2142, T624 4142, anaconda@anacondapantanal.com.br Upmarket agency providing airport transfers, all meals and high standard of accommodation both in Cuiabá before departure and on trips (guide Fábio Mendes, multilingual, has been recommended).1-3 day tours to Pantanal, day tour to Chapada dos Guimarães or Águas Quentes, Amazon trips to Alta Floresta/Rio Cristalino region (price does not include airfare). Recommended. *Ametur*, R Joaquim Murtinho 242, T/F624 1000. Very helpful, good for air tickets. Adriana Coningham of *Ararauna Turismo Ecológica*, Av Lavapes 500, loja 07, T/F626 1067. Highly recommended. *Confiança*, R Cândido Mariano 434, T623 4141. Very helpful travel agency, tours to Pantanal US$75 per day. Also recommended. *Ecological Pantanal Tours*, R Itapuã Qd 15, Bl A3, Apto 202, Várzea Grande, ecotours@terra.com.br Owner Judy Sueni, who also guides, good tours, helpful. *Pantanal Explorers*, Av Governador Ponce de Arruda 670, T682 2800. Sightseeing, fishing trips for 4-5 days by boat.

Recommended guides (in alphabetical order): *Sérgio Alves*, F623 5258. Speaks English, birdwatching and other tours. *Paulo Boute*, R Getúlio Vargas 64, Várzea Grande, near airport, T686 2231. Speaks Portuguese, English, French, also sells Pantanal publications. *Marcus W Kramm*, R Franklin Cassiano da Silva 63, Cuiabá, T/F321 8982. Speaks Portuguese, English, German. *Djalma dos Santos Moraes*, R Arnaldo Addor 15, Coophamil, 78080 Cuiabá, T/F625 1457. US$100 pp per day. *Laércio Sá*, *Fauna Tour*, T682 0101, T9983 7475 (mob 24 hrs), faunatur@zaz.com.br Very well-informed, helpful and knowledgeable about environmental issues. Speaks English, Spanish and Italian, 2 and 3-day Pantanal tours (including transport, accommodation in farmhouses rather than hotels, meals, all activities). Has own car, can arrange longer tours and camping (Aug-Oct) on request, also excursions to Chapada dos Guimarães. *Gregório de Silva*, T9975 3347 (mob). 20 years experience of guiding in the Pantanal, multilingual. *Joel Souza*, owner of *Pousada Ecoverde*, see above. Can be contacted at Av Getúlio Vargas 155A, next to *Hotel Presidente*, T646 1852, T9956 7229 (mob), joelsouza@terra.com.br Speaks English, German and Italian, knowledgeable, checklists for flora and fauna provided, will arrange all transport, accommodation and activities, tends to employ guides rather than guiding himself.

All guides work freelance for other companies as well as employing other guides for trips when busy. Most guides await incoming flights at the airport; compare prices and services in town if you don't wish to commit yourself at the airport

Brazil

Transport **Local Bus**: many bus routes have stops in the vicinity of Praça Ipiranga. To/from airport, see below; bus 501 or 505 (Universidade) to University museums (ask for 'Teatro') from Av Tenente Col Duarte by Praça Bispo Dom José, a triangular park just east of Praça Ipiranga. To rodoviária, No 202 from R Joaquim Murtinho behind the cathedral, 20 mins.

Long distance Air Airport in Várzea Grande, T682 2213. By air to most major cities. ATMs outside include Banco do Brasil for Visa, MasterCard/Cirrus; there is a post office. Taxi to centre US$8, bus US$0.40 (take any white Tuiuiú bus, name written on the side, in front of the airport to Av Tenente Col Duarte; to return take 'Aeroporto' bus from Praça Ipiranga). *Varig*, R 15 de Novembro 230, Bairro Porto, T624 6498, airport T682 1140/3672.

    Bus: Rodoviária is on R Jules Rimet, Bairro Alvorada, north of the centre; town buses stop at the entrance. Comfortable buses (toilets) to **Campo Grande**, 10 hrs, US$20, 12 buses daily, *leito* at 2000 and 2100, US$50. **Goiânia**, 14 hrs, US$25; direct to **Brasília**, 24 hrs, US$30, *leito* US$60. To **Porto Velho**, 6 *União Cascavel* buses a day (T621 2551), US$45, 21 hrs. *Andorinha* (T621 3416) 1700 bus São Paulo-Cuiabá connects with Porto Velho service. Several to **São Paulo**, eg *Motta* (T621 1159), US$42. To **Barra do Garças**, *Xavante* (T621 2755) 0800, 1300 and 2030, US$15, also *Barattur*, T621 1300. Connections to all major cities.

Directory **Banks** *Banco do Brasil*, Av Getúlio Vargas e R Barão de Melgaço, commission US$10 for cash, US$20 per transaction for TCs, very slow for TCs, but best rates, also has ATM; *Incomep Câmbio*, R Gen Neves 155, good rates. It is difficult to get cash advances on credit cards especially MasterCard, for Visa try *Banco do Brasil*. **Communications** Internet: *Copy Grafic*, Praça Alencastro 32, fax and email, English spoken, friendly. *Netnave*, in Três Américas shopping centre, Av Brasília 200, 2nd floor. Not central but fast access, multimedia machines, US$2.50 per hr. Free short-term access at the tourist office. **Post Office:** main branch at Praça da República, fax service. **Telephone:** *Tele Centro Sul*, R Barão de Melgaço 3209, 0700-2200, also at rodoviária, 0600-2130, international service. **Embassies and consulates** Bolivia: Av Isaac Póvoas 117, T623 5094, open Mon-Fri.e **Tourist offices** Secretaria de Desenvolvimento do Turismo, *Sedtur*, Praça da República 131, next to the post office building, T/F624 9060, www.sedtur.mt.gov.br Mon-Fri, 0700-1800. Good maps, helpful, contact them if you have any problems with travel agencies; also book hotels and car hire, some English and Spanish spoken. Also at the airport, T682 2213, ext 2252. *Ramis Bucair*, R Pedro Celestino 280, is good for detailed maps of the region. **Voltage** 110 volts AC, 60 cycles.

Chapada dos Guimarães

Phone code: 065
Post code: 78195
Colour map 7, grid A1
Population: 15,755

Some 68 km northeast of Cuiabá lies one of the oldest plateaux on earth. It is one of the most scenic areas of Brazil and visitors describe it as a mystical, energising place. The pleasant town of Chapada dos Guimarães, the main population centre, is a base for many beautiful excursions in this area; it has the oldest church in the Mato Grosso, **Nossa Senhora de Santana** (1779), a bizarre blending of Portuguese and French baroque styles, and a huge spring-water public swimming pool (on R Dr Pem Gomes, behind the town). Formerly the centre of an important diamond prospecting region, today Chapada is a very popular destination for Cuiabanos to escape the heat of the city at weekends and on holidays. It is a full day excursion from Cuiabá through lovely scenery with many birds, butterflies and flora. There is a post office at R Fernando Corrêa 848. The *Festival de Inverno* is held in last week of July, and Carnival is very busy. Accommodation is scarce and expensive at these times.

    The Chapada is an immense geological formation rising to 700 m, with rich forests, curiously-eroded rocks and many lovely grottoes, peaks and waterfalls. A **national park** has been established in the area just west of the town, where the **Salgadeira** tourist centre offers bathing, camping and a restaurant close to the Salgadeira waterfall. The beautiful 85 m **Véu da Noiva** waterfall (Bridal Veil), 12 km before the town near Buriti (well-signposted, ask bus from Cuiabá to let you off), is reached by a short route, or a long route through forest. Other sights include the **Mutuca** beauty spot, **Rio Claro**, the viewpoint over the breathtaking 80 m-deep **Portão do Inferno** (Hell's Gate), and the falls of **Cachoeirinha** (small restaurant) and **Andorinhas**.

About 8 km east of town is the **Mirante do Ponto Geodésico**, a monument officially marking the Geodesic Centre of South America, which overlooks a great canyon with views of the surrounding plains, the Pantanal and Cuiabá's skyline on the horizon; to reach it take R Fernando Corrêa east, drive 8 km then turn right (there is no sign anymore). Continuing east, the road goes through agricultural land and later by interesting rock formations including a stone bridge and stone cross. 45 km from Chapada you reach the access for **Caverna do Francês** or Caverna Aroe Jari ('the dwelling of the souls' in the Bororo language), a sandstone cave over 1 km long, the second largest in Brazil; it is a 1-km walk to the cave, in it is Lagoa Azul, a lake with crystalline blue water. Take your own torch/flashlight (guides' lamps are sometimes weak). A guide is necessary to get through *fazenda* property to the cave, but not really needed thereafter.

Other excursions are to the **Cidade de Pedra** rock formations, 25 km from town along the road to the diamond prospecting town of Água Fria. Nearby is a 300 m wall formed by the Rio Claro and 60 km from town are the **Pingador** and **Bom Jardim** archaeological sites, caverns with petroglyphs dating back some 4,000 years.

Tours The **Secretaria de Turismo e Meio Ambiente** office, R Quinco Caldas 100, near the praça, provides a useful map of the region and organizes tours. José Paulino dos Santos is a guide working with this office (weekdays 0800-1100, 1300-1800, T791 1245). Recommended tours with Jorge Belfort Mattos from Ecoturismo Cultural, Praça Dom Wunibaldo 464, T/F301 1393; he speaks English and knows the area well (however not all of the other guides speak English); several 4-6 hr itineraries from US$20-50 pp (minimum 4 people or prices increase). Cássio Martins of *AC Tour*, R Tiradentes 28, T791 1122, often waits at the rodoviária. 4-hr tours are about US$20 pp, minimum 5 persons; 7- 8 hr tours, US$25 pp, minimum 5; horseback day tour, US$25 pp, minimum 2; an 8-10 km hike with a guide, US$20 pp, minimum 2; bicycle tour with guide, US$20 pp, minimum 2. Tours from Cuiabá cost US$35-40 pp, but a one-day tour is insufficient for a full appreciation of what the area has to offer.

Sleeping A *Pousada Pequizeiro*, 1 km from centre on unmarked road, T301 3333, www.terra.com.br/chapadadosguimaraes/pequizeiro A/c, fridge, TV, small pool, breakfast, new and good. B *Hotel da Chapada*, R Fernando Correia 1065, 2 km out on Cuiabá road (MT 251, Km 63), T791 1171, F791 1299. A/c, fridge, cheaper with fan, restaurant, bar, pool, sports facilities, parking. B *Estância San Francisco*, at the entrance to town from Cuiabá (MT 251, Km 62), T791 1102, F791 1537. On 42-ha farm with 2 lakes, a/c, fridge, breakfast fresh from the farm. B *Rio's Hotel*, R Tiradentes 333, T791 1126. A/c, fridge, C with fan, cheaper with shared bath, good breakfast. Recommended. B *Chapadense*, R Vereador José de Souza 535, T/F791 1410. A/c, fridge, C with fan, restaurant. C *Turismo*, R Fernando Corrêa 1065, a block from rodoviária, T791 1176, F791 1383, hotelturismo@ chapadadosguimaraes.com A/c, fridge, cheaper with fan, restaurant, breakfast and lunch excellent, very popular, German-run, Ralf Goebel, the owner, is helpful in arranging excursions. C *Pousada Bom Jardim*, Praça Bispo Dom Wunibaldo s/n, T791 1244. Fan, parking, good breakfast. Recommended. D *São José*, R Vereador José de Souza 50, T791 1152. Fan, cheaper with shared bath and no fan, hot showers, basic, good, owner Mário sometimes runs excursions. E *Dormitório*, R Tiradentes s/n. Basic, no fan, cheaper with shared bath. **Camping** E pp *Aldeia Velha*, in the Aldeia Velha neighbourhood at the entrance to town from Cuiabá, T322 7178 (Cuiabá). Fenced area with bath, hot shower, some shade, guard.

Eating *Nivios*, Praça Dom Wunibaldo 631. Good regional food, closed Mon. *Fogão da Roça*, Praça Dom Wunibaldo 488. *Comida mineira*, generous portions, good quality. Recommended. *O Mestrinho*, R Quinco Caldas 119. Meat, regional dishes, *rodízio* at weekends. *Choppada* (*O Chopp da Chapada*), R Cipriano Curvo s/n near praça. Drinks and meals, regional dishes, live music at weekends. *Trapiche*, R Cipriano Curvo 580. Pizza, drinks, regional dishes. *O Mestrinho*, *Peixaria Serrano*, R Dr Pem Gomes 505 (near pool). Fish specialities and *comida caseira*, cheaper than those near the praça. *Veu da Noiva*, R Dr Pem Gomes 524. Regional dishes, fish in season (*piracema* fishing ban 1 Oct-1 Mar). *Pequi* is a regional palm fruit used to season many foods; *arroz com pequi* is a rice and chicken dish.

Brazil

Shopping   Crafts, artefacts, sweets and honey from *Casa de Artes e Artesanato Mato Grossense* (Praça Dom Wunibaldo). Regional sweets from *Doceria Olho de Sogra*, Praça Dom Wunibaldo 21.

Transport   Seven bus departures daily to and from **Cuiabá** (*Rubi* 0700-1900, last back to Cuiabá 1800), 1½ hrs, US$2.75.Hiring a car in Cuiabá is the most convenient way to see many of the scattered attractions, although access to several of them is via rough dirt roads which may deteriorate in the rainy season; drive carefully as the area is prone to dense fog. Hitchhiking from Chapada town to the national park is feasible on weekends and holidays.

Cáceres

Phone code: 065
Post code: 78200
Colour map 6, grid A6
Population: 85,857
200 km W of Cuiabá

Situated on the banks of the Rio Paraguai, Cáceres is very hot but clean and hospitable. The city has many well mantained 19th century buildings, painted in pastel colours.

The **Museu Histórico de Cáceres** (R Antônio Maria by Praça Major João Carlos) is a small local history museum. The main square, Praça Barão de Rio Branco, has one of the original border markers from the Treaty of Tordesillas, which divided South America between Spain and Portugal; it is pleasant and shady during the day. In the evenings, between November and March, the trees are packed with thousands of chirping swallows (*andorinhas*). The praça is surrounded by bars, restaurants and ice cream parlours and comes to life at night. The city is known for its many bicycles as most people seem to get around on two wheels. Until 1960, Cáceres had regular boat traffic, today it is limited to a few tour boats and pleasure craft. The town is at the edge of the Pantanal. Vitória Regia lilies can be seen north of town, just across the bridge over the Rio Paraguai along the BR-174. Local festivals are *Piranha Festival*, mid-March; *International Fishing Festival* in mid-September; annual cattle fair.

Sleeping   **A** *Ipanema*, R Gen Osório 540, T223 1177, F223 1743. With a/c, fridge, garage, restaurant. **A** *Caiçaras*, R dos Operários 745, corner R Gen Osório, T223 3187, F223 2692. A/c, **B** without fridge and TV, parking. **B** *Fênix*, R dos Operários 600, T223 1027, F221 2243. Fridge, a/c. **B** *Rio*, Praça Major João Carlos 61, T223 3387, F223 3084. A/c, **C** without fridge, TV, **D** with shared bath, fan. **C** *Charm*, Col José Dulce 405, T/F223 4949. A/c, **D** with shared bath. Near the rodoviária: **C** *Capri*, R Getúlio Vargas 99, T223 1711. A/c, comfortable. **C** *Gasparin*, Av Sangradouro 162, T223 4579. A/c, fridge, cheaper with fan. **D** *União*, R 7 de Setembro 340. Fan, **E** with shared bath, basic. **D** *Rio Doce*, R 7 de Setembro. A/c, cheaper with shared bath, good value.

Eating   *Corimbá*, R 15 de Novembro s/n, on riverfront. Fish specialities, good, not cheap. *Kaskata*, floating restaurant at the end of R Col José Dulce, by the port. Fish and *jacaré* specialties, expensive. *Gulla's*, R Cel José Dulce 250. Buffet by kilo. Recommended. *Hispano*, Praça Barão de Rio Branco 64. Buffet by kilo. *Panela de Barro*, R Frei Ambrósio 34, near rodoviária. *Comida caseira*.

Transport   **Bus** Rodoviária, T224 1261. *Colibri/União Cascavel* buses Cuiabá-Cáceres, US$9, many daily between 0630-2400 (book in advance), 3½ hrs. Cáceres-Porto Velho, US$32. **River** For information on sailings, ask at the **Capitânia dos Portos**, on the corner of the main square at waterfront. At the waterfront you can hire a boat, US$5 per hr pp, minimum 3.

Directory   **Banks** *Banco do Brasil*, R Cel José Dulce 234. *HSBC*, R Cel José Dulce 145. *Casa de Câmbio Mattos*, Comandante Bauduino 180, next to main praça, changes cash and TCs at good rates. **Communications** **Telephone:** Praça Barão de Rio Branco s/n.

Border with **Bolivia**   An unpaved road runs from Cáceres to the Bolivian border at San Matías. Brazilian immigration is at R Col Farías, Cáceres, for exit and entry formalities; when closed, go to *Polícia Federal*, Av Rubens de Medarca 909. Leaving Bolivia, get your passport stamped at Bolivian immigration (1000-1200, 1500-1700), then get your passport stamped at Cáceres, nowhere in between, but there are luggage checks for drugs.

Transport Bus: the bus fare Cáceres-San Matías is US$9 with *Transical-Velásquez*, Mon-Sat at 0630 and 1500, Sun 1500 only (return at same times), 3 hrs.

Chile

Chile

Chile is a ribbon of land squashed between the Pacific and the Andes. Its landscape embraces glacial wilderness and moonscapes, lakes and volcanoes, beaches and salt flats. The north is characterised by the burnt colours of the driest desert in the world. Should rain fall in this barren land, flower seeds that have lain in wait seize the moment to bloom, bringing brilliant colours where no life seemed possible. Snow-capped volcanoes in the Lauca National Park seem close enough to touch in the rarefied air. In one day it is possible to scale a mountain with ice axe and crampons, soak off the exhaustion in a thermal bath and rest beneath the stars of the Southern Cross. Real stargazers will want to visit the astronomical observatories near La Serena, while lovers of mystery will head south for the folklore of Chiloé, Land of Seagulls - and rain. The Chilean Lake District is the homeland of the Mapuche, the people who resisted the Spaniards and who proudly maintain their culture and traditions. The lakes themselves are beautiful, set in farm land, overlooked by yet more snow-capped volcanoes. Before the road peters out, blocked by fjords and icefields, the Carretera Austral reveals ancient woodlands, hot springs beside the sea, mountains like castles and raging, emerald rivers - a paradise for fishing and cycling. To reach the ultimate goal of trekkers and birdwatchers, the fabulous granite towers and spires of the Torres del Paine National Park, you have to take a boat, or fly, or make the long haul through Argentina. There are seaports of every size, with their fishing boats, pelicans and sea lions. The most romantic is Valparaíso, described by one observer as 'a Venice waiting to be discovered', with its warren of streets and brightly painted houses, its singular lifts up to the clifftops and its old bars.

Like Chilean geography, Valparaíso is a contradiction in itself. It ranges from being ordered and well-to-do by the port, to chaotic and anarchic in the hills above. Perhaps inevitably, it was in this uniquely atmospheric city that the symbols of Chilean political extremes were both born and raised in the early years of the 20th century: Salvador Allende and Augusto Pinochet.

Chile is often written off as a European country disguised as a South American one. Its citizens even call themselves 'the English of South America'. But those who doubt its magical qualities need only take a short boat trip to the island of Chiloé. Here, the islanders have an entire mythology all of their own, including goblins, ghost ships, mermaids and witches, who fly to the graveyards at night and eat the bodies of the recently interred.

Chile

Essentials

Planning your trip

Where to go A great many of Chile's attractions are out of doors, in the national parks, adventure sports, etc, but the capital, **Santiago**, has a rich cultural life (museums, restaurants, handicrafts shopping) and is a good base for visiting nearby areas. These include the vineyards of the Maipo Valley, the Andean foothills in the Cajón del Maipo and the ski resorts. The port of Valparaíso and the beach resorts to north and south, principally Viña del Mar, are only a couple of hours away.

North of Santiago is La Serena, a popular seaside resort, from which can be reached the Elqui Valley, where Chilean *pisco* is made, and three major astronomical observatories. Heading north, the land becomes more barren, but after rain, usually September-October, the flowers that have lain dormant in the desert burst into bloom; if you are in the area, a sight not to be missed. Inland from Antofagasta, the next main city, a road goes to Calama, the huge copper mine at Chuquicamata and the isolated Andean town and popular tourist resort of San Pedro de Atacama. Its attractions are lunar landscapes, hot geysers, salt flats and the way of life at high altitude. Alternatively, from Antofagasta you can take the spectacular coast road to the **Far North** and the ports of Iquique, near which are several archaeological sites, thermal springs and abandoned nitrate mines, and Arica, the last main town before Peru. The road route into Bolivia from Arica passes through the magnificent Parque Nacional Lauca, with its wealth of Andean bird and animal life, high lakes and remote volcanoes.

South of Santiago, the longitudinal highway runs south through the Central Valley passing a number of cities, such as Rancagua, Talca, Chillán and Concepción (the country's second city). There are national parks which deserve a visit in both the Andean foothills and in the coastal range of mountains. You can visit vineyards, thermal springs, unspoilt beaches or simply enjoy real Chilean rural life.

The Lake District is home to the most popular lakes are Villarrica and Llanquihue, but there are many others with much less development. Protected areas of great beauty and first-class opportunities for adventure sports and fishing abound. Temuco, at the northern end of this region, is also the centre of the Mapuche culture, with a huge product market. Wooded Valdivia, near the coast, is worth a detour for the trip to the mouth of the river to see the ruined Spanish forts that protected this outpost of the empire. The southern gateway to the Lake District is Puerto Montt, also the starting point for the long haul south. The city's fishing harbour, Angelmó, with its market and food stalls, is not to be missed. From Puerto Montt you can cross to Argentina by road and ferries on Lago Todos los Santos and neighbouring Lagos Frías and Nahuel Huapi on the way to Bariloche.

The island of **Chiloé**, a short bus and ferry ride from Puerto Montt, has a distinctive culture and a green landscape which is the result of more than enough rain. On the mainland, running south from Puerto Montt, the Carretera Austral has opened up an area of forests, lakes and rivers, linking small communities of settlers. The biggest town is Coyhaique and there is a regular excursion by sea to the stunning glacier at the Laguna San Rafael. A four-day sea voyage from Puerto Montt takes you to Puerto Natales in **Chilean Patagonia**, near Chile's most dramatic national park, the **Torres del Paine**. Hiking around the vertical mountains with their forested slopes, past lakes and glaciers, in the presence of a multitude of southern Andean wildlife is an unforgettable experience (but do allow for the unpredictability of the weather). If you prefer not to venture this far south by ship, there are regular flights to the main city of Chilean Patagonia, Punta Arenas, and there is no problem crossing from Argentina by road or by ferry from **Tierra del Fuego**. The contrast between this southernmost part of the country with the dry, desert north could not be greater.

When to go The best times to visit vary according to geographical location. For the heartland, any time between October and April is good, but the most pleasant seasons are spring (September-November) and autumn (March-April). In Santiago itself, summers (December-February) are roasting hot and winters (June-August) polluted. The heat of the north is less intense from June to September. In the south December to March, summer, is the best time. In the far south this is the only realistic time to travel because at other times ferry schedules are restricted and in mid-winter many transport services do not run at all. Also bear in mind that January-February in the Lake District and further south are the busiest months, with raised prices, hotels and buses full, lots of backpackers on the road and advance booking often essential. In this holiday season business visitors may find making appointments difficult, but otherwise any time of year is good for working in Santiago.

Finding out more

The national secretariat of tourism, **Sernatur**, has offices throughout the country (addresses given in the text), www.sernatur.cl City offices provide town maps and other information. A recommended book is *Turistel*, published annually in four parts, *Norte, Centro, Sur* and a camping guide with road map, with information and a wealth of maps covering the whole country and neighbouring tourist centres in Argentina (eg Mendoza, San Martín de los Andes, Bariloche), in Spanish only. Each volume costs between US$11-15, depending where you buy it, but buying the whole set is better value; they can be found in bookshops and news stands in the centre of Santiago. See www.turistel.cl (in Spanish). *Matassi* maps (*JLM Mapas*), usually with a red cover, are good value but often contain errors, US$5.50-6.50, F02-236 4808, jmatassi@interactiva.cl **Conaf** (the Corporacíon Nacional Forestal), Presidente Bulnes 291, p 1, Santiago, T390 0126, www.conaf.cl publishes a number of leaflets and has documents and maps about the national park system. **CODEFF** (Comité Nacional Pro-Defensa de la Fauna y Flora), Bilbao 691, Providencia, T251 0262, can also provide information on environmental questions.

www.chile.cl (Spanish); www.gochile.cl (English and Spanish); www.prochile.cl **Websites** (Spanish); and www.chileinfo.com (English), www.visitchile.org (English, Spanish); www.chilelindo.com (Spanish)

The government's site is **www.gobiernodechile.cl** **www.tnet.cl** is Chilean version of Terra, which covers much of Latin America in Spanish. Its tourism page is **www.tnet.cl/turismo/**

www.hotelschile.com For hotel information, reservations, advice and tours.

See also **www.chip.cl**, the site of *Chile Information Project*, Av Santa María 227, of 12, Recoleta, Santiago, T777 5376, which gives access to *The Santiago Times* English-language daily, travel information, hotels, history, wine and LOM books. Gay travellers should visit **www.gaychile.com**

For information and loads of links in Patagonia, visit **www.chileaustral.com**

For Valparaíso, visit **www.valparaisochile.cl**

For the outdoors, **www.chile-outdoors.cl**

www.ancientforests.org *Ancient Forest International*, Box 1850, Redway, CA 95560, T/F707-923 4475, USA, can be contacted regarding Chilean forests. See also **www.greenpeace.cl** for environmental issues (in Spanish).

The local pronunciation of Spanish, very quick and lilting, with the 's' dropped and final **Language** syllables cut off, can present difficulties to the foreigner.

Before you travel

Passport (valid for at least six months) and tourist card only are required for entry by all **Visas &** foreigners except citizens of Guyana, Haiti, Dominica, Kuwait, Egypt, Saudi Arabia and United **immigration** Arab Emirates, most African countries, Cuba and some former Eastern bloc countries (excluding Croatia, the Czech Republic, Estonia, Hungary, Poland, Slovak Republic, Slovenia and Yugoslavia), who require visas. It is imperative to check tourist card and visa requirements before travel. National identity cards are sufficient for entry by citizens of Argentina, Brazil, Paraguay, and Uruguay. Tourist cards are valid for 90 days. For nationals of Greece, Indonesia and Peru validity is 60 days; Belize, Costa Rica, Malaysia and Singapore 30 days. Tourist cards can be obtained from immigration offices at major land borders and Chilean airports; you must surrender your tourist card on departure. If you wish to stay longer than 90 days (as a tourist), you must buy a 90-day extension from the Departamento de Extranjería (address under Santiago Useful addresses), or

Chile

any local *gobernación* office. It costs US$100. To avoid this, make a day-trip to Argentina, Bolivia or Peru and return with a new tourist card (the authorities don't like it if you do this more than 3-4 times). An onward ticket is required. Tourist card holders may change their status to enable them to stay on in employment if they have a contract; they need to contact the Extrangería in whichever province they will be working. On arrival you will be asked where you are staying in Chile. **NB** On arrival by air, US citizens will be charged an administration fee of US$100, Canadians US$55, Australians US$30 and Mexicans US$15 (this is a reciprocal tax payable because Chileans have to pay the equivalent amount when entering these countries). This tax is not charged at land borders. The permission is valid for multiple entry and for the life of the passport. The tax should be paid in cash, but cheques are accepted. For some nationalities a visa will be granted within 24 hours upon production of an onward ticket, for others (eg Guyana), authorization must be obtained from Chile. For other nationalities who need a visa, a charge is made. To travel overland to or from Tierra del Fuego a multiple entry visa is essential since the Argentine- Chilean border is crossed more than once (it is advisable to get a multiple entry visa before arriving, rather than trying to change a single entry visa once in Chile). A student card is useful for getting discounts on buses, etc. They can be obtained from Hernando de Aguirre 201, of 602, Providencia and cost US$8, photo and proof of status required; www.isic.cl

Customs **Duty free allowance** 500 cigarettes, 100 cigars, 500 gms of tobacco, three bottles of liquor, camera, and all articles of personal use. Unlike neighbouring countries, Chile's agricultural sector is free of many diseases, so fruit, vegetables, meat, flowers and milk products may not be imported. These will be confiscated at all land borders, where there are searches. This applies even to those who have had to travel through Argentina in the far south to get from one part of Chile to another. **NB** There are internal customs checks for all travellers going south from Region I in the far north. This is to inspect for duty-free goods from Iquique, but fruit, vegetables, meat, flowers and milk products will be confiscated.

Vaccinations Inoculation against hepatitis and typhoid is a wise precaution.

Chilean embassies and consulates

Australia, 10 Culgoa Circuit,
O'Malley 2606, ACT, PO Box 69,
Monaro Crescent, ACT2603,
T61-6-6286 2430, F6286 1289,
www.embachile-australia.com
Belgium, 40 rue Montoyer, 1000 Brussels,
T32-2-280 1620, F280 1481,
embachile.belgica@skynet.be
Canada, 50 O'Conner Street, suite 1413,
Ottawa, K1 P6L2, T1-613-235 4402,
F235 1176, www.chile.ca
Denmark, Kastelsvej 15, 3, 2100
Copenhagen, T45-3526 1535,
F3538 4201, www.chiledk.dk
France, 2 ave de la Motte Picquoet,
75007 Paris, T33-1-4418 5960, F4418 5961,
echile@amb-chili.fr
Germany, Lepziger Strasse 63, 10117 Berlin
Israel, Havkook N 7, Tel Aviv, T972-3-602
0131, F602 0133, www.embachile-israel.org.il
Japan, Nihon Seimei Akabanebashi Bldg,
8F 3-1-14 Shiba, Minato-Ku, Tokyo 105,
T81-3-3452 7561, F3452 4457,
embajada@chile.or.jp

Netherlands, Mauritskade 51, 2514 HG,
The Hague, T31-70-312 3640, F361 6227,
echilenl@euronet.nl
New Zealand, 1-3 Willeston Street,
Willis Coroon House 7th floor, PO Box 3861,
Wellington, T64-4-471 6270, F472 5324,
www.prochinz.co.nz
Norway, Meltzers Gate 5, 0257 Oslo,
T47-2244 8955, F2244 2421,
www.home.online.no/~embachile
Spain, Lagasca 88, p 6, Madrid 28001,
T34-1-431 9160, F455 4833, echilees@tsai.es
Sweden, Sturegatan 8, 3rd floor,
11435 Stockholm, T46-8-679 8280, F679 8540,
www.chileemb.se
Switzerland, Eigerplatz 5, 12th floor,
3007 Bern, T41-31-371 0745, F372 0025,
echilech@swissonline.ch
UK, 12 Devonshire Street, London, W1N 2DS,
T020-7580 6392, F020-7436 5204,
www.echileuk.demon.co.uk
USA, 1140 Connecticut Avenue NW,
Washington, suite 703, DC 20036, T1-202-785
1746, F1-202-887 5579, www.chile-usa.org

Chile

What to take

Warm days and cool nights are usual during most of the year, but the two main exceptions are at altitude in the far north, where nights can be bitterly cold, and in the far south where the climate is wet, windy and very changeable. Be prepared for cold and rain in this region. In the central area dress as you would for Spring in Continental Europe during the Chilean winter (June to mid-September). Light clothing is best for summer (December to March). Remember that temperatures are always more moderate on the coast than inland. If camping, trekking, cycling or skiing, consider taking all your own equipment because, although it may be available in Chile, it will be expensive. Also note that in the Lake District and Chiloé, between mid-December and mid-January, huge horseflies (*tavanos*) can be a real problem when camping, hiking and fishing: do not wear dark clothing. APS film is generally very hard to find.

Money

Currency

peso exchange rate with US$: 747.1 MasterCard emergency T1230-020-2012; Visa emergency T1230-020-2136; Amex emergency T02-695 2422

The unit is the peso, its sign is $. Notes are for 1,000, 5,000, 10,000 and 20,000 pesos and coins for 1, 5, 10, 50, 100 and 500 pesos. Small businesses and bus drivers do not look kindly upon being presented with high denomination notes, especially in the morning. **Banks**   The easiest way to obtain cash is by using ATMs which operate under the sign Redbanc (www.redbanc.cl for a full list); they take Cirrus (MasterCard) and Plus (Visa) and permit transactions up to US$400 per day. Instructions are available in English. Diners' Club, Visa and MasterCard are common in Chile (Bancard, the local card, is affiliated to the last two; *Banco del Estado* accepts Mastercard, with ATM, in most towns). American Express is less useful. Travellers' cheques are most easily exchanged in Santiago, but you get better value for cash dollars. Outside Santiago, use *casas de cambio* in main tourist centres to change TCs, not banks, which usually charge commission. Even slightly damaged US dollar notes may be rejected for exchange. Exchange shops (*casas de cambio*) are open longer hours and often give slightly better rates than banks. It is always worth shopping around. Rates get worse as you go north from Santiago. Official rates are quoted in *La Tercera*. Prices may be quoted in US dollars; check if something seems cheap. Remember that in some hotels foreigners who pay with US dollars cash or travellers' cheques are not liable for VAT.

▶ **Touching down**

Business hours Banks: 0900-1400, closed on Saturday. **Government offices:** 1000-1230 (the public is admitted for a few hours only). **Business hours:** 0830-1230, 1400-1800 (Monday to Friday). **Shops (Santiago):** 1030-1930, 0930-1330 Saturday. **IDD** 56. A double ring repeated regularly means it is ringing; equal tones with equal pauses means it is engaged.

Official time GMT minus four hours; minus three hours in summer. Clocks change from mid-September or October to early March.
VAT 18%
Voltage 220 volts AC, 50 cycles.
Weights and measures The **metric** system is obligatory but the quintal of 46 kg (101.4 lbs) is used.

Cost of travelling

Santiago tends to be more expensive for food and accommodation than other parts of Chile

The average cost for a traveller on an economical budget is about US$25 per day for food, accommodation and land transportation (more for flights, tours, car hire etc). Cheap accommodation costs US$6-12. Breakfast in hotels, if not included in the price, is about US$2 (instant coffee, roll with ham or cheese, and jam). *Alojamiento* in private houses and hostels (bed, breakfast and often use of kitchen) costs US$7-10 per person (bargaining may be possible). Southern Chile is much more expensive between 15 December and 15 March.

Getting there

Air **From Europe** There are regular flights to Santiago from Paris, Barcelona and Madrid, and Frankfurt with *LanChile* and/or European carriers. Connections from London and other European cities can be made in the above, USA, Bogotá, Brazil or Buenos Aires.

  From North America Several airlines have flights from Miami, New York, Atlanta, Dallas and Los Angeles to Santiago. From other US cities make connections in Miami, New York or Los Angeles. From Canada, make onward connections in New York, Miami or Los Angeles.

  Transpacific routes *LanChile* flies two to four times a week, depending on season, between Tahiti and Santiago; they stop over at Easter Island. For flights from Japan, make connections in the USA. *LanChile* and *Qantas* have a code-share from Sydney, Australia, to Santiago, via Auckland, New Zealand.

  Within Latin America All the South American capitals, plus Córdoba and Mendoza (Argentina), Guayaquil (Ecuador), Santa Cruz (Bolivia) and Rio de Janeiro and São Paulo (Brazil), have regular flights to Santiago. In addition, *LanChile* fly to Arica and Iquique from La Paz.

Road **Overland from neighbouring countries** : roads connect Santiago with Mendoza, Temuco with Zapala, Osorno and Puerto Montt with Bariloche, and Punta Arenas with Río Gallegos in Argentina. Less good road connections north and south of Santiago are described in the main text. The main route connecting northern Chile with Bolivia (Arica-La Paz) is paved. Similarly, the road route Arica-Tacna (Peru) is paved. Other routes are poor. Note that any of the passes across the Andes to Argentina can be blocked by snow from Apr onwards.

Train There are usually passenger services only on Calama-Uyuni (Bolivia) and Arica-Tacna (Peru).

Touching down

Airport tax Airport tax is US$26 for international flights; US$13 for domestic flights.

Tipping In restaurants, if service is not included in the bill, tip 10%; tip a few pesos in bars and soda fountains. Railway and airport porters: US$0.15 a piece of luggage, or US$1 for the service. Taxi-drivers are not tipped.

Safety Chile is generally one of the safest countries in South America for the visitor. **Law enforcement** officers are *Carabineros* (green military uniforms), who handle all tasks except immigration. Investigaciones, in civilian dress, are the detective police who deal with everything except traffic. **Policia Internacional**, a division of Investigaciones, handle immigration (head office Gral Borgoña 1052, Santiago, T737 2443/1292).

Where to stay

On hotel bills service charges are usually 10%, and IVA(VAT) on bills is 18%. Check on arrival whether hotel rates include VAT. When booking in make certain whether meals are included in the price or only breakfast or nothing at all, and don't rely on the posted sheet in the bedroom for any prices. It is often worth asking for a discount, especially out of season. Particularly in North and Central Chile breakfast is likely to be instant coffee and bread or toast. In popular tourist destinations, especially in the south in high season, large numbers of families offer accommodation: these are usually advertised by a sign in the window. People often meet buses to offer accommodation, which varies greatly in quality and cleanliness etc. Have a look before committing. See *Backpacker's Bed & Breakfast, Best of Chile*, www.back packersbest.cl in English, German and Spanish, for suggestions on good accommodation at reasonable prices throughout Chile (T09-441 5019); it also has information on homestays. In summer especially, single rooms can be hard to find. Most motels are short stay only.

Sleeping
In expensive hotels, if you pay in US$ cash or TCs, you may not have to pay IVA, but unless the establishment has an agreement with the government, hotels are not obliged to exclude IVA for dollar payments

Camping is easy but not always cheap at official sites. A common practice is to charge US$10 for up to 5 people, with no reductions for any less. 'Camping Gaz International' stoves are recommended, since replaceable cylinders are widely available in hardware shops; for good value try the *Sodimac* chain of DIY stores. *Copec* run a network of 33 'Rutacentros' along Ruta 5 which have showers, cafeterias and offer free camping. Free camping is also available at many filling stations.

Camping

There are youth hostels throughout Chile; average cost about US$5-10 pp. Although some hostels are open only from Jan to the end of Feb, many operate all year round. The IH card is usually readily accepted, but YHA affiliated hostels are not necessarily the best. In summer they are usually crowded and noisy, with only floor space available. Chilean YHA card costs US$5. A Hostelling International card costs US$15. These can be obtained from the ***Asociación Chilena de Albergues Turísticos Juveniles***, Hernando de Aguirre 201, of 602, Providencia, Santiago, T233 3220/234 3233, www.hostelling.cl, together with a useful guidebook of all Youth Hostels in Chile, *Guía Turística de los Albergues Juveniles*. In summer there are makeshift hostels in many Chilean towns, usually in the main schools; they charge US$3-4 pp.

Youth hostels

Getting around

Most flights of *LanChile* and its subsidiary, *Lan Express*, between Santiago and major towns and cities, are given in the text. The newest airline on the domestic market is *Sky*, whose network is not as extensive as *LanChile*. Try to sit on the left flying south, on the right flying north to get the best views of the Andes. *LanChile* offers a 30-day 'Visit Chile' ticket. It must be purchased abroad in conjunction with an international ticket and reservations made well ahead since many flights are fully booked in advance. If arriving in Chile on *LanChile* or *Iberia*, three coupons cost US$250, if on another carrier US$350. Extra coupons cost US$60, or US$80 respectively. The maximum number of coupons is six. Rerouting charge US$30. Travel must commence within 14 days of arriving in Chile. There is a special sector fare of US$525 if using *LanChile* translantic for Santiago-Easter Island-Santiago. **NB** Book well in advance (several months) for flights to Easter Island in Jan-Feb. If arriving in Chile on *LanChile*, ask about discounts on individual sector, domestic flights. Check with the airlines for matrimonial, student and other discounts.

Air
It is best to confirm domestic flights at least 24 hrs before departure

The road network is 79,293 km, much of it in good condition and many roads paved. The region round the capital and the Central Valley are the best served. The main road is the Panamericana (Ruta 5), which is now dual carriageway from La Serena to Puerto Montt. A paved coastal route running the length of Chile is also being constructed, which should be ready by 2007.

Road

Chile

Bus

Since there is lots of competition between bus companies, fares may be bargained lower, particularly just before departure

Buses are frequent and on the whole good. Apart from holiday times, there is little problem getting a seat on a long-distance bus. *Salón-cama* services run between main cities on overnight services; *TurBus* and *Pullman* have the most extensive networks. *Turbus* itineraries can be checked and tickets bought online at www.turbus.cl Generally avoid back seats near toilet due to smell and disruption of passing passengers. *Salón-cama* means 25 seats, *semi-cama* means 34 and *Salón-ejecutivo* means 44. Stops are infrequent. Prices are highest between Dec-Mar and fares from Santiago double during the Independence celebrations in Sep. Students may get discounts, amount varies, but not usually in high season. Most bus companies will carry bicycles, but may ask for payment (on *TurBus* payment is mandatory).

Car

Carabineros are strict about speed limits (100-120 kph on motorways): Turistel maps mark police posts, make sure you are not speeding when you pass them. Car drivers should have all their papers in order and to hand since there are frequent checks, but fewer in the south

For drivers of private vehicles entering Chile, customs will type out a *título de importación temporal de vehículos* (temporary admission), valid for three months, or in accordance with the length of stay granted by immigration. Your immigration entry/exit card is stamped 'entrada con vehículo' so you must leave the country with your vehicle (so you cannot make an excursion to Bariloche, for example, without your car). There are very strict controls for fresh fruit, vegetables, meat, fish, etc. Insurance is obligatory and can be bought at borders.

Fuel and spares Gasoline (sold in litres) costs the equivalent of US$0.55-0.70 a litre (depending on international oil prices); it becomes more expensive the further north and further south you go. Unleaded fuel, 93, 95 and 97 octane, is available in all main cities. Diesel fuel is widely available. Esso service stations usually accept credit cards. Other companies may not; always ask beforehand. When driving in the south (on the Carretera Austral particularly), and in the desert north, always top up your fuel tank and carry spare petrol/gasoline. Car hire companies may not have fuel cans. These are obtainable from some supermarkets but not from service stations. Tyres need to be hard-wearing (avoid steel belt); it is recommended to carry more than one spare and additional tubes. A *carnet de passages* is not officially required for foreign-owned **motorcycles**: a temporary import paper is given at the border.

Car hire

Many agencies, both local and international, operate in Chile. Vehicles may be rented by the day, the week or the month, with or without unlimited mileage. Rates quoted may not include insurance or 18% VAT. Make sure you know what the insurance covers, in particular third-party insurance. Often this is only likely to cover small bumps and scratches. Ask about extra cover for a further premium. If you are in a major accident and your insurance is inadequate, your stay in Chile may well be prolonged beyond its intended end. A small car, with unlimited mileage costs about US$300 a week in high season, a pick-up much more. In some areas rates are much lower off-season. (At peak holiday times, eg Independence celebrations, car hire is very difficult.) Shop around, there is much competition and reputable Chilean companies offer much better value than the well-known international ones. Note that the *Automóvil Club de Chile* has a car hire agency (with discounts for members or affiliates) and that the office may not be at the same place as the Club's regional delegation. On the motorways (eg the Panamericana), tolls are very expensive, often more than a bus ticket for one person (but the charge does include towing to the next city and free ambulance in case of accident). Also, the car hire companies charge way too much to pick up the car from a city other than the place of rental (can easily be US$200), so, even though car rental may be cheaper in Santiago, unless you intend to make a round trip, it makes economic sense to travel by public transport, then rent a car closer to your real destination. **NB** If intending to leave the country in a hired car, you must obtain authorization from the hire company, otherwise you will be turned back at the border. When leaving Chile this is exchanged for a quadruple form, one part of which is surrendered at each border control. (If you plan to leave more than once you will need to photocopy the authorization.)

Hitchhiking

Hitchhiking is generally easy and safe throughout Chile, although you may find that in some regions traffic is sparse, so you are less likely to catch a lift.

Taxis

Taxis have meters, but agree beforehand on fares for long journeys out of city centres or special excursions. In some places a surcharge is applied late at night. Taxi drivers may not know the location of any streets away from the centre. There is no need to tip unless some extra service, like the carrying of luggage, is given. Black colectivos (collective taxis) operate on fixed routes

Chile

identified by numbers and destinations. They have fixed charges, often little more expensive than buses, which increase at night and which are usually advertised in the front windscreen. They are flagged down on the street corner (in some cities such as Puerto Montt there are signs). It is best to take small change as the driver takes money and offers change while driving. Yellow colectivos also operate on some interurban routes, leaving from a set point when full.

There are 6,560 km of line, of which most are state owned. Passenger services in the south go **Train** from Santiago to Temuco. Passenger services north of the Valparaíso area have ceased, though there are regional train lines in the Valparaíso and Concepción areas. Trains in Chile are moderately priced, and not as slow as in other Andean countries. See Santiago, Transport, Long Distance, Trains for rail company offices.

The **Instituto Geográfico Militar**, Dieciocho 369, Santiago, T698 7278, has published a *Guía* **Maps** *Caminera*, with roads and city plans (available only at IGM offices, not 100% accurate). The *Turistel* Guides are very useful for roads and town plans, but note that not all distances are exact and that the description 'ripio' (gravel) usually requires high clearance; 'buen ripio' should be OK for ordinary cars. Good road maps are also published by Turbus and Copec.

Keeping in touch

Internet access is becoming widely available; in cyber cafés expect to pay US$0.80-2 per hour.   **Internet**

Airmail takes 3-4 days from Europe. Seamail takes 8-12 weeks. There is a daily airmail service **Post** to Europe with connections to the UK. Poste restante only holds mail for 30 days, then returns it to sender. *Lista de Correos* in Santiago, Central Post Office, is good and efficiently organized. Rates: letters to Europe/North America US$0.60, aerogrammes US$0.55. To register a letter, recommended, costs US$0.75.

There are eight main phone companies (*portadores*, carriers) offering competing rates **Telephone***Online* (widely advertised). Callers choose companies by dialling an access code before the city code. *telephone directory* Access codes: *Entel* 123; *CTC Mundo* 188, *CNT* (*Telefónica del Sur* – in Regions X and XI) 121; *www.blancas.cl* *VTR* 120; *Chilesat* 171; *Bell South Chile* 181; *Iusatel Chile* 155; *Transam Comunicaciones* 113. For international calls you dial the company code, then 0, then the country code. International calls are cheap. For visitors, long distance and international calls should be made from *centros de llamadas*, call centres (ubiquitous), or with special calling cards available from kiosks (carriers 113 and 155 are cheapest).
   Telephone boxes can be used to make local and long-distance calls, for making collect calls and receiving calls. To make a local call, simply dial the number you require and pay the rate charged , US$0.15 for 3 minutes. To call mobiles, use phone boxes, US$0.25-30 per minute. To make an inter-urban call, dial '0' plus the area code (DD) and the number.

Newspapers Santiago daily papers *El Mercurio* (centre-right) www.emol.com *La Nación* **Media** (liberal-left), *La Segunda*, *La Tercera* www.tercera.cl, and *La Quarta*. *Las Ultimas Noticias*. *La Hora*. Online is *El Mostrador*, www1.elmostrador.cl In English is *The News Review*, published weekly on Friday, sold at selected kiosks; Casilla 151/9, Santiago, T236 1423, F236 2293. There is a German-language magazine, *Cóndor*, www.condor.cl Weekly magazines; *Hoy*, *Qué Pasa*, *Ercilla*, www.ercilla.cl **Television** TV channels include UCTV (Universidad Católica) on Channel 13, the leading station; TVN (government operated) on Channel 7; on the web www.tvn.cl/24horas; Megavisión (private) on Channel 9 and La Red (private) on Channel 4.

Food and drink

A very typical Chilean dish is *cazuela de ave*, a nutritious stew containing large pieces of **Food** chicken, potatoes, rice, and maybe onions, and green peppers; best if served on the second day. *Valdiviano* is another stew, common in the south, consisting of beef, onion, sliced potatoes and eggs. Another popular Chilean dish is *empanadas de pino*, which are turnovers

Chile

filled with a mixture of raisins, olives, meat, onions and peppers chopped up together. *Pastel de choclo* is a casserole of meat and onions with olives, topped with a maize-meal mash, baked in an earthenware bowl. *Humitas* are mashed sweetcorn mixed with butter and spices and baked in sweetcorn leaves. *Prieta* is a blood sausage stuffed with cabbage leaves. A normal *parrillada* or *asado* is a giant mixed grill served from a charcoal brazier. *Bistek a lo pobre* (a poor man's steak) can be just the opposite: it is a steak topped by a fried egg, mashed potatoes, onions and salad. The Valparaíso speciality is the *chorillana*, chips topped with fried sliced steak, fried onions and scrambled eggs, while in Chiloé you can enjoy a *curanto*, a meat, shellfish and potato stew traditionally cooked in a hole in the ground.

What gives Chilean food its personality is the seafood. The delicious *congrio* fish is a national dish, and *caldillo de congrio* (a soup served with a massive piece of conger, onions and potato balls) is excellent. A *paila* can take many forms (the *paila* is simply a kind of dish), but the commonest are made of eggs or seafood. *Paila Chonchi* is a kind of bouillabaisse, but has more flavour, more body, more ingredients. *Parrillada de mariscos* is a dish of grilled mixed seafood, brought to the table piping hot on a charcoal brazier. Other excellent local fish are the *cojinoa*, the *albacora* (swordfish) and the *corvina* (bass). A range of mussels (*choritos/cholgas*) is available, as are abalone (*locos*), clams (*almejas*) and razor clams (*machas*). Some bivalve shellfish may be periodically banned because they carry the disease *marea roja* (which is fatal in humans). *Cochayuyo* is seaweed, bound into bundles, described as 'hard, leathery thongs'. The *erizo*, or sea-urchin, is also commonly eaten as are *picorocos* (sea barnacles) and the strong flavoured *piure*. *Luche* is dried seaweed, sold as a black cake, like 'flakey bread pudding' to be added to soups and stews.

Avocado pears, or *paltas*, are excellent, and play an important role in recipes. Make sure that vegetables are included in the price for the main dish; menus often don't make this clear. Always best, if being economical, to stick to fixed-price *table d'hôte* meals or try the local markets. Local fast food is excellent and many international players are struggling. *Completos* are hot dogs with a huge variety of fillings. A *barros jarpa* is a grilled cheese and ham sandwich and a *barras luco* is a grilled cheese and beef sandwich. *Sopaipillas* are cakes made of a mixture which includes pumpkin, served in syrup (traditionally made in wet weather). *Ice cream* is very good; *lúcuma* and *chirimoya* are highly recommended flavours.

Breakfast is poor: instant coffee or tea with bread and jam are common, although some hostels serve better fare. Lunch is about 1400 and dinner not before 2030. *Onces* (Elevenses) is tea taken at 1700, often accompanied by a snack. Good, cheap meals can be found in Casinos de Bomberos, or around the market. Most restaurants offer a cheaper set meal at lunchtime; it is called *colación* or *el menú* and may not be included on the menu (*la carta*).

Coffee is generally instant except in expresso bars including popular chains of cafés such as **Café Haiti, Café Brasil** and **Tío Pepe**, found in major cities. Elsewhere specify *café-café, expresso* or *cortado*. Tea is widely available. If you order '*café*', or *té, con leche*', it will come with all milk; to have just a little milk in either, you must specify that. After a meal, instead of coffee, try an *agüita* (infusion) – hot water in which herbs such as mint, or aromatics such as lemon peel, have been steeped. There is a wide variety, available in sachets, and they are very refreshing.

Drink

Tap water is safe to drink in main cities but bottled water is safer for the north

The local wines are very good; the best are from the central areas. The bottled wines cost from US$1.50 upwards. The *Guía de vinos de Chile*, published every year in January (English edition available) has ratings and tasting notes for all Chilean wines on the market. Beer is quite good and cheap (about US$0.80 for a litre bottle, plus US$0.30 deposit in shops). Draught lager is known as Schop. Chilean brewed beers include *Cristal* and *Royal Guard* (light), *Escudo* (Amber), *Austral* (good in the far south) and *Heineken*. In Valdivia, *Kunstmann* brews three types of beer, good. *Malta*, a brown ale, is recommended for those wanting a British-type beer.

Pisco, made from grapes, is the most famous spirit. It is best drunk as a 'Pisco Sour' with lime or lemon juice and sugar. *Manzanilla* is a local liqueur, made from *licor de oro* (like Galliano); *crema de cacao*, especially Mitjans, has been recommended. Two popular drinks are *vaina*, a mixture of brandy, egg and sugar and *cola de mono*, a mixture of *aguardiente*, coffee, milk and vanilla served very cold at Christmas. *Chicha* is any form of alcoholic drink made from fruit, usually grapes. Cider (*chicha de manzana*) is popular in the south. *Mote con huesillo*, made from wheat hominy and dried peaches, is refreshing in summer.

Holidays and festivals

1 January, New Year's Day; Holy Week (two days); 1 May, Labour Day; 21 May, Navy Day; 15 August, Assumption; 18, 19 September, Independence Days; 12 October, Columbus' arrival in America; 1 November, All Saints Day; 8 December, Immaculate Conception; 25 December.

Sport and activities

Climbing There are four different terrains: rock climbing; high mountains; ice climbing; and volcanoes. Some volcanoes and high mountains are difficult to get to and, being in border areas, need permission to climb. Other volcanoes, like Villarrica and Osorno are popular excursions, although access is controlled by *Conaf* (see Finding out more). The Federación de Andinismo de Chile and the Escuela Nacional de Montaña are both at Almirante Simpson 77A in Santiago.

Fishing The lakes and rivers of Araucanía, Los Lagos and Aisén offer great opportunities for trout and salmon fishing. The season runs from mid-Nov to the first Sun in May (or from mid-Sep on Lago Llanquihue). A permit must be obtained, usually from the local Municipalidad, police or angling associations. The price of a permit is about US$12 for foreigners and is valid for the whole country. Some of the world's best fishing is in the Lake District, but this is a very popular region. Better still, as they are less-heavily fished, are the lakes and rivers south of Puerto Montt. Some fish are catch and release only. Premiums might have to be paid to fish in private areas, or specially designated zones. Sea fishing is popular between Puerto Saavedra (Araucania) and Maullín (Los Lagos). The mountain resort of Río Blanco is where residents of Santiago and Valparaíso go to fish.

Horseriding Treks on horseback in the mountains can be organized in Santiago, but south of Concepción and north, the the the Elqui and Hurtado valleys, there are more opportunities and a number of companies organize riding holidays. A popular national pastime in the centre and south is rodeo and events are held throughout the summer in stadia known as *media lunas* (half moons), culminating in the national finals in Rancagua in March. There is also horse racing throughout the country.

Mountain biking This is a popular sport locally as there are lots of opportunities in the mountains and the Lake District. The Carretera Austral is also a great ride. Bikes are manufactured locally, but quality is variable.

Nature tourism Birdwatching can be extremely rewarding with opportunities which vary from the flamingoes and wildfowl of the altiplano, as found in the Parque Nacional Lauca in the far north, to the birds of the forests in the south, to the condors, geese and other species in the Torres del Paine. Mammals include those of the camel family, the llama, alpaca, vicuña and guanaco, and some rare deer, the miniature pudú and the huemul. The trees of Chile are another attraction: many deciduous varieties, the araucaria, or monkey-puzzle tree, and areas of very ancient forest, more and more of which are being protected. Also, as mentioned above, the flowering of the desert is a sight to look out for.

Rafting and kayaking Over 20 rivers between Santiago and Tierra del Fuego are excellent for white water rafting. Some run through spectacular mountain scenery, such as the Río Petrohué, which flows through temperate rainforest beneath the Osorno and Calbuco volcanoes. Rafting is generally well organized and equipment is usually of a high standard. Access to headwaters of most rivers is easy. For beginners, many agencies in Santiago, Puerto Varas and Pucón offer half-day trips on Grade 3 rivers. The best Grade 4 and 5 rafting is in Futaleufú, near Chaitén. Sea kayaking is best enjoyed in the waters between Chiloé and the mainland and in the sheltered fjords off the northernmost section of the Carretera Austral. Kayaking and other watersports such as windsurfing take place in many lakes in the Lake District, notably Lagos Villarrica and Llanquihue, which holds an annual kayaking regatta.

Sailing Apart from sailing on the lakes, ocean sailing is best, again, in the sheltered waters south of Puerto Montt. There is ample scope for yachting in the waters east of Chiloé. Things get more adventurous is you sail down the coast to Cape Horn and expertise is needed for such a trip. Most coastal towns on the entire Chilean coast have yacht clubs.

Chile

Addresses of ski federations, clubs and operators are given under Santiago, Sports, page 606

Skiing The season is from Jun to September/October, weather permitting. The major international ski resorts are in the Andes near Santiago, Farellones, El Colorado, La Parva, Valle Nevado, Portillo and Lagunillas. South of Santiago, skiing is mostly on the slopes of volcanoes. The larger resorts are Termas de Chillán, Villarrica/Pucón and Antillanca, but there are a great many smaller places with limited facilities which are worth the effort to get to for some adventurous fun. Details of the major resorts and some smaller ones are given in the text.

Trekking Trekking possibilities are endless, ranging from short, sign-posted trails in national parks to hikes of several days, such as the circuit of the Parque Nacional Torres del Paine. There is a project to build a trekking/mountain biking path running the whole length of Chile. Pilot sections have been completed in all 13 regions, and the path is complete in the metropolitan region. See www.senderodechile.cl for more information.

Santiago and around

Santiago, the political, economic and financial capital of Chile, is one of the most beautifully set of any South American city, standing in a wide plain with the magnificent chain of the Andes in full view for much of the year – rain and pollution permitting. Nearly 70% of Chileans live in and around Santiago, which is now the fifth largest city in South America. It's a modern industrial capital, full of skyscrapers, bustle, noise and traffic, and smog is a problem especially between April and September. Santiago bursts with possibilities, with its parks, museums, shops and hectic nightlife, and is also within easy reach of vineyards, beaches and Andean ski resorts.

Ins & outs

Phone code: 02
Colour map 8, grid B1
Population: over 5 million
Altitude: 600 m

See also Transport on page 627

Getting there US$2, and *Centropuerto*, US$1.50. There are also shuttle services to/from hotels and private addresses (US$5-7) and taxis (US$15-17).

The **railway station**, Estacíon Central, which only serves the south of the country, is on the Alameda, as are the 4 main **bus terminals**. All can be reached by buses, taxi or the Metro. The bus terminals are Alameda, for *Pullman-Bus* and *TurBus* services; next door is Terminal Santiago, for the whole country and some international destinations (metro Universidad de Santiago); San Borja, for northern and some national destinations (metro Estación Central); Los Héroes (nearest the centre, metro Los Héroes) for some southern, northern and international routes.

Getting around The **Metro** (underground railway) has 3 lines, Line 1 east-west, Lines 2 and 5 north-south. Fares range from US$0.40 to US$0.60 depending on time of day. The east-west line follows the main axis, linking the bus and train stations, the centre, Providencia and beyond. Metrobus services connect the subway with outlying districts. **City buses**: other than the blue metrobuses, yellow buses serve the whole city. Fares are US$0.50. **Taxis** are abundant and not expensive (minimum charge around US$0.60, plus US$0.12 per 200 m). **Colectivos** (collective taxis) run on fixed routes to the suburbs, US$0.75-1.50.

Tourist offices Servicio Nacional de Turismo (*Sernatur* – the national tourist board), Av Providencia 1550 (Casilla 14082), between metros Manuel Montt and Pedro de Valdivia, next to Providencia Municipal Library, T731 8300, F251 8469. English and German spoken and maps (road map US$1.50), brochures and posters are available. Good notice board. Mon-Fri 0845-1830, Sat 0900-1800. Kiosk on Ahumada near Agustinas (erratic opening times). Information office also at the airport, open 0900-2100 daily. **Municipal Tourist Board**, Casa Colorada, Merced 860, T336700/330723. Has a good free booklet, *Historical Heritage of Santiago: A Guide for Tourists* in English and Spanish, on historic buildings.

Orientation The centre of the old city lies between the Mapocho and the Avenida O'Higgins, which is usually known as the **Alameda**. From the **Plaza Baquedano** (usually called **Plaza Italia**), in the east of the city's central area, the Mapocho flows to the northwest and the Alameda runs to the southwest. From Plaza Italia the C Merced runs due west to the **Plaza de Armas**, the heart of the city, 5 blocks south of the Mapocho. The **airport** is 26 km northwest of the centre. Regular bus services run to the centre, Tur Bus,

Best time to visit There is rain during the winter, but the summers are dry. The rain increases to the south. On the coast at Viña del Mar it is 483 mm a year, but is less inland. Temperatures, on the other hand, are higher inland than on the coast. There is frost now and then, but very little snow falls. Temperatures can reach 33°C in January, but fall to 13°C (3°C at night) in July. Days are usually hot, the nights cool.

Security Like all large cities, Santiago has problems of theft. Pickpockets and bagsnatchers, who are often well-dressed, operate especially on the Metro and around the Plaza de Armas. Tourist offices in small, summer-only resorts outside Santiago are closed in winter, so stock up on information here.

Sights

On the eastern and southern sides of the Plaza de Armas there are arcades with shops; on the northern side is the Post Office and the Municipalidad; and on the western side the Cathedral and the archbishop's palace. The **Cathedral**, much rebuilt, contains a recumbent statue in wood of San Francisco Javier, and the chandelier which lit the first meetings of Congress after independence; it also houses an interesting museum of religious art and historical pieces (0930-1230, 1530-1830, free). In the **Palacio de la Real Audiencia** on the Plaza de Armas is the **Museo Histórico Nacional**, covering the period from the Conquest until 1925. ■ *Tue-Sat 1000-1745, Sun 1000-1600, US$1.70, No 951.*

Just west of the Plaza is the **Museo Chileno de Arte Precolombino**, Bandera 361, in the former Real Aduana: a representative exhibition of objects from the pre-Columbian cultures of Central America and the Andean region, highly recommended for the quality of the objects and their presentation. ■ *Tue-Sat 1000-1800, Sun and holidays 1000-1400, US$3, T688 7348. Displays in English.* The **former Congress** building, a block west of the Cathedral, is now occupied by the Ministry of Foreign Affairs (the new Congress building is in Valparaíso). At Calle Merced 864, close to the Plaza de Armas, is the **Casa Colorada**, built in 1769, the home of the Governor in colonial days and then of Mateo de Toro, first President of Chile. It is now the **Museo de Santiago** (history of Santiago from the Conquest to modern times), with excellent displays and models, guided tours. ■ *Tue-Sat 1000-1900, Sun and holidays, 1000-1400, US$1.* From the Plaza de Armas Paseo Ahumada, a pedestrianized street lined with cafés runs south to the Alameda four blocks away, crossing Huérfanos, which is also pedestrianized.

Four blocks north of the Plaza de Armas is the interesting **Mercado Central**, at 21 de Mayo y San Pablo. The building faces the Parque Venezuela, on which is the Cal y Canto metro station, the northern terminus of Line 2, and, at its western end, the former **Mapocho Railway Station**, now a cultural centre. If you head east from Mapocho station, along the river, you pass through the Parque Forestal (see below), before coming back to Plaza Italia.

The Alameda runs through the heart of the city for over 3 km. It is 100 m wide, and ornamented with gardens and statuary: the most notable are the equestrian statues of Generals O'Higgins and San Martín; the statue of the Chilean historian Benjamín Vicuña MacKenna who, as mayor of Santiago, beautified Cerro Santa Lucía (see below); and the great monument in honour of the battle of Concepción in 1879.

From the Plaza Italia, where there is a statue of Gen Baquedano and the Tomb of the Unknown Soldier, the Alameda skirts, on the right, Cerro Santa Lucía, and on the left, the Catholic University. Beyond the hill the Alameda goes past the neo-classical **Biblioteca Nacional** on the right, Moneda 650 (good concerts, temporary exhibitions). Beyond, on the left, between Calles San Francisco and Londres, is the oldest church in Santiago: the red-walled church and monastery of **San Francisco**. Inside is the small statue of the Virgin which Valdivia carried on his saddlebow when he rode from Peru to Chile. The **Museo Colonial San Francisco**, beside Iglesia San Francisco, houses religious art, including one room with 54 paintings of the life of St Francis; in

Around the Plaza de Armas
Almost all museums are closed on Mon and on 1 Nov

Chile

Along the Alameda

the cloisters is a room containing Gabriela Mistral's Nobel medal. ■ *Tue-Sat 1000-1330, Sun and holidays 1500-1800, US$1.50, T639 8737, Londres 4, some information in English.* South of San Francisco is the Barrio París-Londres, built in 1923-1929, now restored. Two blocks north of the Alameda on Calle Agustinas is the **Teatro Municipal**. ■ *Guided tours Tue 1300-1500, Sun 1100-1400, US$3.*

A little further west along the Alameda, is the **Universidad de Chile**; the **Club de la Unión** is almost opposite. Nearby, on Calle Nueva York is the **Bolsa de Comercio** ■ *Open to the public 1000 to 1200 weekdays.* One block further west is the Plaza de la Libertad. To the north of this Plaza, hemmed in by the skyscrapers of the Centro Cívico, is the **Palacio de la Moneda** (1805), the Presidential Palace containing historic relics, paintings and sculpture, and the elaborate 'Salón Rojo' used for official receptions. Although the Moneda was damaged by air attacks during the military coup of 11 September 1973 it has been fully restored. (Ceremonial changing of the guard every other day, 1000, never on Sunday; Sunday ceremony is performed Monday. The courtyards, with sculptures and carabineros in dress uniform, are open to all – entry from the north – guided tours available.)

West of the centre **Barrio Brasil**, with Plaza Brasil at its heart and the Basílica del Salvador two blocks from the plaza, is one of the earliest parts of the city. It has some fine old buildings, especially around C Concha y Toro, but also modern amenities with plenty of places to stay and eat (Metro República). Five blocks south of the Alameda at this point is the **Palacio Cousiño**, a large mansion in French rococo style with a superb Italian marble staircase and other opulent items. ■ *Tue-Fri 0930-1330, 1430-1700, Sat, Sun and holidays 0930-1330, US$2. C Dieciocho 438. Guided tours only, in Spanish, English and Portuguese, visitors have to wear cloth bootees to protect the floors. Recommended.*

Parque O'Higgins lies about 10 blocks south of Alameda. It has a small lake, playing fields, tennis courts, swimming pool (open from 5 December), an open-air stage, a club, the racecourse of the Club Hípico, an amusement park, *Fantasilandia* (admission US$7-9, unlimited rides, open at weekends until 2000 only in winter, and not when raining), kite-flying contests on Sunday, good 'typical' restaurants, craft shops, an aquarium, an insect, reptile and shellfish museum and the **Museo del Huaso**, a collection of criollo clothing and tools. On 19 September there is a huge military parade in the park. ■ *Museum: Tue-Fri 1000-1300, 1430-1715, Sat, Sun and holidays 1000-1800, free.To the park, take Metro Line 2 to Parque O'Higgins station. Bus from Parque Baquedano via Avs MacKenna and Matta.*

The Alameda continues westwards to the **Planetarium**. ■ *US$2.50, shows Tue-Sun 1800, 2000, Alameda 3349, T776 2624.* Opposite it on the southern side, the railway station (Estación Central or Alameda). On Avenida Matucana, running north from here, is the very popular **Parque Quinta Normal** (at Avenida D Portales). It was founded as a botanical garden in 1830. In or near the park is **Museo de la Solidaridad Salvador Allende**, Herrera 360, T681 7542, www.mssa.cl A well-presented collection of works donated to Chile by Latin American and European artists (including Matta, Miró and Saura) between 1970 and 1973 to demonstrate solidarity with Allende's government. Recommended. ■ *Tue-Sun 1000-1900, US$1, good café*

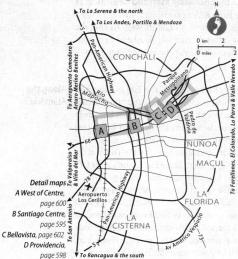

Santiago orientation

To La Serena & the north
To Los Andes, Portillo & Mendoza

0 km   2
0 miles   2

CONCHALI

Pan-American Highway
To Aeropuerto Comodoro Arturo Merino Benítez
Río Mapocho
Parque Metropolitano
Pedro de Valdivia
68
To Valparaíso & Viña del Mar
To Farellones, El Colorado, La Parva & Valle Nevado

A   B   C/D

NUÑOA
MACUL

Aeropuerto Los Cerrillos
78
To San Antonio
Pan-American Highway

LA FLORIDA

LA CISTERNA

5
To Rancagua & the south

Av Américo Vespucio
78

Detail maps
A West of Centre, page 600
B Santiago Centre, page 595
C Bellavista, page 602
D Providencia, page 598

Chile

with set lunch, US$3. Information sheet in English. Closed in summer. **Museo Artequín**, nearby at Avenida Portales 3530, in the Chilean pavilion built for the 1889 Paris International Exhibition, containing prints of famous paintings and activities and explanations of the techniques of the great masters, recommended. ■ *Tue-Fri 0900-1700, Sat, Sun and holidays 1100-1800, US$2.50.*

Cerro Santa Lucía, bounded by Calle Merced to the north, Alameda to the south, Calles Santa Lucía and Subercaseaux, is a cone of rock rising steeply to a height of 70 m. It can be climbed from the Caupolicán esplanade, on which, high on a rock, stands a statue of that Mapuche leader, but the ascent from the northern side of the hill, where there is an equestrian statue of Diego de Almagro, is easier. A plaque to Darwin, who climbed the hill, has a quotation giving his impressions. There are striking views of the city from the top (reached by a series of stairs), where there is a fortress, the Batería Hidalgo (closed to the public). ■ *The Cerro closes at 2100.* It is best to descend the eastern side, to see the small Plaza Pedro Valdivia with its waterfalls and statue of Valdivia.

East of the centre

Chile

Santiago centre

Detail maps
A Bellavista, page 602
B West of Centre,
page 600

	3 Galerías *D3*	11 Res Londres *D3*
	4 Indiana *A1*	12 Santa Lucía *C3*
	5 Libertador *D3*	
	6 Majestic *B1*	**● Eating**
	7 Nuevo Valparaíso *A2*	1 Acuario *D3*
	8 Olicar *A2*	2 Café Brasil *C2*
■ Sleeping	9 París *D3*	3 Café Caribe *C2*
1 Carrera *C1*	10 Plaza San	4 Café Santos *C2*
2 El Marqués	Francisco *D3*	5 Da Carla & San Marco *B3*
del Forestal *A3*		

6 El 27 de Nueva York *D2*
7 El Naturista *D3*
8 El Vegetariano *C3*
9 La Caleta de Done Beno *D2*
10 Las Tejas *D2*
11 Lung Fung *C3*
12 Masticón *D2*
13 Pastelería Colonial *C3*
14 Sena *D2*

Parque Forestal lies due north of Santa Lucía hill and immediately south of the Mapocho. **Museo Nacional de Bellas Artes**, in an extraordinary example of neo-classical architecture, has a large display of Chilean and foreign painting and sculpture; contemporary art exhibitions are held several times a year. ■ *Tue-Sat 1000-1800, Sun and holidays 1100-1800, US$0.80. Quiet café.* In the west wing of the building is the **Museo de Arte Contemporáneo**. **Parque Balmaceda** (Parque Gran Bretaña), east of Plaza Italia, is perhaps the most beautiful in Santiago (the Museo de los Tajamares, which holds monthly exhibitions, is here).

Between the Parque Forestal, Plaza Italia and the Alameda is the **Lastarria** neighbourhood (Universidad Católica Metro). For those interested in antique furniture, objets d'art and old books, the area is worth a visit, especially the **Plaza Mulato Gil de Castro** (Calle José V Lastarria 305). Occasional shows are put on in the square, which has a mural by Roberto Matta and a new visual arts museum. The **Museo Arqueológico de Santiago**, in Plaza Mulato Gil de Castro, exhibits Chilean archaeology, anthropology and pre-Columbian art. ■ *Mon-Fri 1000-1400, 1530-1830, Sat 1000-1400, US$1.50. Lastarria 307.* Nearby, on Lastarria, is the **Jardín Lastarria**, a cul-de-sac of craft and antique shops.

The **Bellavista** district, on the north bank of the Mapocho from Plaza Italia at the foot of Cerro San Cristóbal (see below), is the main focus of nightlife in the old city. Around Calle Pío Nono are restaurants and cafés, theatres, entertainments, art galleries and craft shops (especially those selling lapis lazuli). **La Chascona**, was the house of the poet Pablo Neruda and is now headquarters of the Fundación Pablo Neruda. ■ *Daily except Mon, 1000-1300, 1500-1800, US$3 guided visits only. T777 8741, F Márquez de la Plata 0192, Bellavista (see page 624).*

Providencia

East of Plaza Italia, the main east-west axis of the city becomes **Avenida Providencia** which heads out towards the residential areas, such as **Las Condes**, at the eastern and upper levels of the city. It passes through the neighbourhood of Providencia, a modern area of shops, offices, bars and restaurants around Pedro de Valdivia and Los Leones metro stations (particularly Calle Suecia), which also contains the offices of Sernatur, the national tourist board. At Metro Tobalaba it becomes Avenida Apoquindo. Here, in **El Bosque Norte**, there are lots more good, mid-range and expensive restaurants.

Museo Ralli, Sotomayor 4110, **Vitacura** (further east still), has an excellent collection of works by modern European and Latin American artists, including Dali, Chagall, Bacon and Miró. ■ *Tue-Sun 1030-1600, closed in summer, free.*

The sharp, conical hill of **San Cristóbal**, forming the **Parque Metropolitano**, to the northeast of the city, is the largest and most interesting of the city's parks. There are two entrances: from Pío Nono in Bellavista and further east from Pedro de Valdivia Norte. On the summit (300 m) stands a colossal statue of the Virgin, which is floodlit at night; beside it is the astronomical observatory of the Catholic

University which can be visited on application to the observatory's director. Further east in the Tupahue sector there are terraces, gardens, and paths; in one building there is a good, expensive restaurant (*Camino Real*, T232 1758) with a splendid view from the terrace, and an Enoteca (exhibition of Chilean wines: you can taste one of the three 'wines of the day', US$1.50 per glass, and buy if you like, though prices are higher than in shops). Nearby is the Casa de la Cultura which has art exhibitions and free concerts at midday on Sunday. There are two good swimming pools (see **Sports** below). East of Tupahue are the Botanical Gardens, with a collection of Chilean native plants, guided tours available. ■ *Getting there: by **funicular**: every few mins from Plaza Caupolicán at the northern end of C Pío Nono (it stops on its way at the Jardín Zoológico near the Bellavista entrance), US$2, 1000-1900 Mon-Fri, 1000-2000 Sat and Sun (closed for lunch 1330-1430). By **teleférico** from Estación Oasis, Av Pedro de Valdivia Norte via Tupahue to San Cristóbal, the funicular's upper station, 1030-1900 at weekends, 1500-1830 weekdays except Tue (in summer only), US$2. A combined funicular/teleférico ticket is US$4. An open bus operated by the teleférico company runs to San Cristóbal and Tupahue from the Bellavista entrance with the same schedule as the teleférico itself. To get to Tupahue at other times you must take the funicular or a taxi (or walk to/from Pedro de Valdivia Metro station, about 1 km). By taxi either from the Bellavista entrance (much cheaper from inside the park as taxis entering the park have to pay entrance fee), or from Metro Pedro de Valdivia.*

Situated in the barrio of Recoleta, just north of the city centre, this cemetery contains the mausoleums of most of the great figures in Chilean history and the arts, including Violeta Para, Víctor Jara and Salvador Allende. There is also an impressive monument to the victims, known as "desaparecidos" (disappeared) of the 1973-90 military government. ■ *Take any Recoleta bus from Calle Miraflores to get there.*

Cementerio General

Chile

Essentials

Santiago Centre LL *Carrera*, Teatinos 180, T698 2011, hotel.carrera@chilnet.cl Art-deco lobby, pool, rooftop restaurant (good buffet lunch), helpful staff and great atmosphere. **LL** *Galerías*, San Antonio 65, T638 4011, galerias@entelchile.net Excellent, welcoming. **LL** *Plaza San Francisco*, O'Higgins 816, T639 3832, F639 7826. Lufthansa-affiliated, excellent breakfast, good, LanChile office. **AL** *Conde Ansúrez*, Av República 25, T696 0807, F671 8376, Metro República. Convenient for central station and bus terminals, helpful, safe, luggage stored. **AL-A** *Majestic*, Santo Domingo 1526, T695 8366, hotelmajestic@entelchile.net With breakfast, good Indian restaurant open to non-residents, pool, English spoken. **A** *Monte Carlo*, Subercaseaux 209, T633 9905, info@hotelmontecarlo.cl At foot of Santa Lucía, modern, restaurant, with heating, stores luggage, good. **A-B** *Da Carlo*, Manuel Thompson 3940, 2 blocks from Universidad de Santiago Metro, T776 4523, F778 7329. Very good suites, tasteful, helpful.

Sleeping
■ *on maps*
Check if breakfast and 18% tax are included in the price quoted. . Cheap places do not charge the 18% tax

B *El Márques del Forestal*, Ismael Valdés Vergara 740, opposite Parque Forestal, T633 3462. Good value, several rooms with cooker and sink, all have TV, phone. **B** *Foresta*, Subercaseaux 353, T639 6261, F632 2996. Heating, laundry service, restaurant, bar. **B** *Hostal Río Amazonas*, Rosas 2234, T698 4092, www.hostalrioamazonas.cl Convenient, central, good, charming hosts, internet access. **B** *Hostal Vía Real*, Marín 066, T635 4676, F635 4678. Charming, small, TV, laundry. Recommended. **B** *Libertador*, O'Higgins 853, T639 4212, info@hotellibertador.cl Helpful, stores luggage, good restaurant. **B** *Santa Lucía*, San Antonio 327 y Huérfanos, p 4, T639 8201, santalucia@terra.cl Garage 2 blocks away, comfortable, small, quiet restaurant. **B** *Tokio*, Almte Barroso 160, T671 4516, F698 4500. Lovely garden, convenient location but overpriced, good breakfast, Japanese and English spoken, no credit cards. **C** *Hostal Americano*, Compañía 1906, T/F698 1025, hostal@ mi.terra.cl Breakfast extra, bath shared between 2 bedrooms, convenient. **C-D** *París*, París 813, T/F639 4037, www.hotelparis.cl Great location, good meeting place, luggage store. Recommended. **D** *Res Gloria*, Latorre 449 (no sign), T698 8315, Metro Toesca. Including breakfast. Recommended. **D** pp *Olicar*, San Pablo 1265, T698 3683. Laundry, kitchen, quiet, a bit run down, another branch at Teatinos 741, with kitchen.

E *Indiana*, Rosas 1339, T688 0008, hostal_indiana@ hotmail.com Kitchen facilities, popular, internet US$2-3 per hr, convenient but noisy, cold, basic, mixed reports. **E** pp *Res Londres*, Londres 54, T/F638 2215, unico54@ctcinternet.cl Old mansion with original features in lovely area, perfect location, without breakfast, cheaper without bath, pleasant common rooms, good, safe, laundry service, often full, often refuses to take advance bookings. Recommended.**F** pp *La Casa Roja*, Agustinas 2113, Barrio Brasil, T696 4241, info@lacasaroja.tie.cl In dormitory, **D** in double room, huge converted historic house, great location, kitchen facilities, meals extra, internet, convenient for metro and lots of amenities, fun, but not if you want a quiet time. **F** pp *Nuevo Valparaíso*, Morandé 791, T671 5698. Basic gringo meeting place, central, hot water, safe, poor beds, use of kitchen (no utensils), cable TV, popular. **F** pp *Res Alemana*, República 220 (no sign), T671 3668, residencial.alemana@usa.net Metro República,

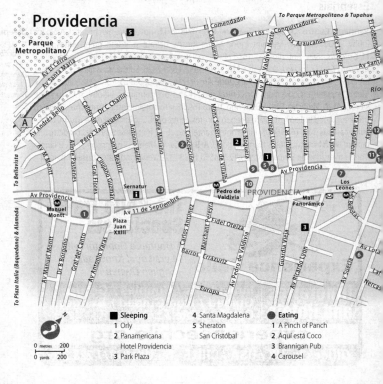

Sleeping
1 Orly
2 Panamericana
  Hotel Providencia
3 Park Plaza
4 Santa Magdalena
5 Sheraton
  San Cristóbal

Eating
1 A Pinch of Panch
2 Aquí está Coco
3 Brannigan Pub
4 Carousel

pleasant patio, heating on request, good cheap meals available. Recommended. **F** pp *San Patricio*, Catedral 2235, T695 4800.Cheaper without bath, hot shower, with breakfast, "rough and ready" but safe and quiet, good value, parking.

Providencia LL *Hyatt Regency Santiago*, Av Kennedy N 4601, T218 1234, info@hyatt.cl Superb, beautifully decorated, large outdoor pool, gym, Thai restaurant. **LL** *Sheraton San Cristóbal*, Santa María 1742, T233 5000, guest@stgusheraton.cl Best in town, good restaurant, good buffet lunch, and all facilities. **L** *Park Plaza*, Ricardo Lyon 207, T233 6363, bookings@ parkplaza.cl 5-star, good. **L** *Santa Magdalena Apart Hotel*, Helvecia 244, Las Condes, T374 6875, www.santamagdalena.cl **AL** *Panamericana Hotel Providencia*, Francisco Noguera 146, T233 2230/7, www.panamericanahoteles.cl Helpful, good restaurant. **AL-A** *Orly*, Pedro de Valdivia 027, Metro Pedro de Valdivia, T231 8947, www.orlyhotel.com Fully renovated, comfortable, *Cafetto* café attached with cheap food. **A** *Atton*, Alonso de Córdova 5199, T422 7979. Good, very helpful, full disabled access.

Near bus terminals and Estación Central D *Res Mery*, Pasaje República 36, off 0-100 block of República, T696 8883, m.mardones@entelchile.net Big green building down an alley, without bath, quiet. Recommended. **E** pp *Alojamiento Diario*, Salvador Sanfuentes 2258 (no sign), T699 2938. Safe, kitchen facilities. **E** pp *Hostal Internacional Letelier*, Cumming 77, 3 blocks from Alameda, T965 6861. Very helpful, no meals, internet, Spanish lessons arranged. **F** pp family *hostal* at Sazie 2048, casa 1, T695 3570, large rooms, big breakfast. **F** pp *Res Sur*, Ruiz Tagle 055, T776 5533. Pleasant, helpful, meals available.

On north side of Alameda opposite bus terminals **F** pp *Federico Scoto* 130, T779 9364. Use of phone and fax, good meals, cooking facilities, often full. Highly recommended. **F-G** pp *SCS Habitat, Scott's Place*, San Vicente 1798, T683 3732, scshabitat@yahoo.com Kitchen, laundry facilities, lots of interesting information, huge breakfast, popular, English spoken, maps and camping equipment sold/rented, cycles for hire, safe bike parking. To get there take taxi from bus station. **G** *Apabalza*, Federico Scoto 41, T764 7601. Very helpful, use of kitchen, hot water.

Near airport B pp *Hacienda del Sol y La Luna*, 4 Hijuela 9978, Pudahuel, T/F601 9254. English, German, French spoken..

Accommodation with families C pp *Antonio y Ana Saldivia*, Guillermo Tell 5809, La Reina, T226 6267. Breakfast, dinner extra, quiet, take bus 244 from Alameda. **C** pp *Marilu's Bed & Breakfast*, Rafael Cañas 246-c, Providencia T235 5302, tradesic@ intermedia.cl French and English spoken, good breakfast, comfortable. **C** pp *Urania's B&B*, Bocaccio 60, Las Condes, T537 1596, F201 2922, uraniae@hotmail.com Comfortable, good breakfast. **D** *Cecilia Parada*, Llico 968, T522 9947, F521 6328.1 block from Metro Departamental, washing machine, gardens, quiet. **D** pp *Rodrigo Sauvageot*, Gorbea 1992, dept 113, T672 2119. Includes breakfast, phone first. **D** *Sra Marta*, Amengual 035, Alameda Alt 4.400, T779 7592 (Metro Ecuador). Good, hospitable, kitchen facilities, motorcycle parking.**E** pp *Sra Fidela*, San Isidro 261, Apt H, T222 1246. Shared bathroom, breakfast. Recommended.

Recommended accommodation in comfortable family guest houses through Amigos de Todo el Mundo, Libertad 371 (Metro U Latinoamericana), Casilla 52861, Correo Central Sgto, T681 7638, F698 1474, Sr Arturo Navarrete

5 Cafetto	10 La Pizza Nostra
6 Centre Catalá	11 Louisiana River Pub
7 Coppelia	12 Mr Ed
8 El Huerto	13 Phone Box Pub
9 Gatsby	14 Red Pub

Chile

E pp *Sra Lucía*, Catedral 1029, p 10, dept 1001, T696 3832. Central, safe, cooking facilities, wonderful views. **E** pp *Sra Marta*, Catedral 1029, dept 401, T672 6090, half a block from main plaza. Basic, safe, good breakfast. Recommended.

Longer stay accommodation See the classified ads in *El Mercurio*; flats, homes and family *pensiones* are listed by district, or in *El Rastro* (weekly), or try the notice board at the tourist office. Estate agents handle apartments, but often charge ½ of the first month's rent as commission, while a month's rent in advance and 1 month's deposit are required. Recommended apartments are **Santa Magdalena**, see Sleeping, Las Condes. Also **Edificio San Rafael**, Miraflores 264, T633 0289, F222 5629. US$30 a day double, minimum 3 days, very central.

Youth hostels **E** pp *Hostelling Internacional Santiago*, Cienfuegos 151, T671 8532, F672 8880, histgoch@ entelchile.net (5 mins from Metro Los Héroes). Modern, satellite TV, no cooking facilities, sterile, cafeteria, parking. Information from Youth Hostel Association, Hernando de Aguirre 201, of 602, Providencia, T233 3220/234 3233, hostelling@hostelling.cl (worth getting a list of YH addresses around the country as these change). Supplies student cards (2 photos required and proof of student status, though tourist card accepted), US$16.

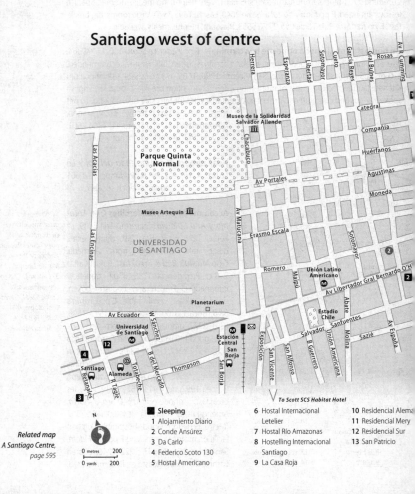

Santiago west of centre

Related map
A Santiago Centre,
page 595

0 metres 200
0 yards 200

■ Sleeping
1 Alojamiento Diario
2 Conde Ansúrez
3 Da Carlo
4 Federico Scoto 130
5 Hostal Americano

6 Hostal Internacional
  Letelier
7 Hostal Río Amazonas
8 Hostelling Internacional
  Santiago
9 La Casa Roja

10 Residencial Alema
11 Residencial Mery
12 Residencial Sur
13 San Patricio

Camping Excellent facilities about 70 km southwest from Santiago at Laguna de Aculeo, called *Club Camping Maki*: including electricity, cold water, swimming pool, boat mooring, restaurant, but only available to members of certain organizations. An alternative site is *El Castaño* camping (with casino), 1 km away, on edge of lake, very friendly, café sells fruit, eggs, milk, bread and kerosene, good fishing, no showers, water from handpump.

Santiago centre Mid-range *Acuario*, París 817. Excellent seafood, attentive service, good value set lunch. *Da Carla*, MacIver 577. Italian food, good; and *San Marco*, 2 doors away, better still. *El 27 de Nueva York*, Nueva York 27. Central, good, live music. *El Lagar de Don Quijote*, Morandé y Catedral. Bar, restaurant, *parrillada*, good, popular. *Faisán d'Or*, Plaza de Armas. Good *pastel de choclo*, pleasant place to have a drink and watch the world go by. *Fra Diavolo*, París 836. Lunches only, excellent food and service, popular. *Guimas*, Huérfanos y Teatinos. Good value *almuerzo*. *Las Vacas Gordas*, Cienfuegos 280, Barrio Brasil. Good value grilled steaks. *Les Assassins*, Merced 297. French, very good. Highly recommended. *Los Adobes de Argomedo*, Argomedo 411 y Lira, T222 2104 for reservations. Hacienda-style, good Chilean food and floor show including cueca dancing, salsa and folk, Mon-Sat, only place in winter which has this type of entertainment on a Mon. *Lung Fung*, Agustinas 715. Delicious oriental food, large cage in the centre with noisy parrots. *Ostras Azócar*, Gral Bulnes 37. Reasonable prices for oysters. For something different, take a tour with Elizabeth Caskey, *Tercer Chakra*, Lucrecia Valdés 359, loft 201, T681 1799, www.tercerchakra.com Off the beaten track cultural and culinary tours, including market and gourmet lunch.

Cheap *Bar Central*, San Pablo 1063. Cheap, typical food. Recommended. *Bar Nacional No 1*, Huérfanos 1151 and *Bar Nacional No 2*, Bandera 317. Popular, local specialities, good for quantity. *Círculo de Periodistas*, Amunátegui 31, p 2. Unwelcoming entrance, good value lunches. Recommended. *El Rápido*, next to *No 2*, specializes in *empanadas*, good food, good fun, "happening locals' joint". *Mermoz*, Huérfanos 1048. Good for lunches. *Nuria*, MacIver 208. Wide selection, large portions. *Torres*, Alameda 1570. Traditional bar/restaurant, good atmosphere, live music at weekends.

Seriously cheap On C San Diego, south of the Alameda: *La Caleta de Done Beno*, No 397, *parrilladas*, seafood, popular, a bit pricy. *Las Tejas*, No 234, for typical dishes and drinks, rowdy. *Masticón*, No 152, good service, excellent value. *Sena*, No 145, wide choice, good cocktails. *Tercera Compañía de Bomberos*, Vicuña Mackenna 097.

East of the centre Expensive López de Bello *El Otro Sitio*, No 53. Peruvian, excellent food, elegant. *La Divina Comida*, No 93. Italian with 3 rooms – Heaven, Hell and Purgatory, good seafood. *Le Coq au Vin*, No 0110. French, excellent, good value. Highly recommended. *R*, José V Lastarria 307. Fine food and service, cheaper fixed menu. *San*

Eating
● *on maps*
Some of the best seafood restaurants are to be found in the Mercado Central (by Cal y Canto Metro, lunches only), at the Vega Central market on the opposite bank of the Mapocho and on Av Cumming and C Reyes in Barrio Brasil

Chile

● **Eating**
1 Las Vacas Gordas
2 Ostras Azócar

Visit El Mercurio online, www.emol.com, and go to "tiempo libre", to search for types of restaurants and areas of the city

Fruttuoso, Mallinckrodt 180. Italian, recommended. **Mid-range** *Calamar*, Pío Nono 241. Recommended. *Como Agua para Chocolate*, Constitución 88. Good food and value. *El Rincón Español*, just off C Rosal. Spanish, good *paella*. Next door is *El Bar Escondido*, small and pleasant (closed Sun in summer). *Eladio*, Pío Nono 251. Good steaks, Argentine cuisine, excellent value. *Gatopardo*, Lastarria 192. Good value. Highly recommended. *La Pergola de la Plaza* in Plaza Mulato Gil de Castro. Cosy. *La Tasca Mediterránea*, Purísima 165. Good food. Recommended. Next door is *Libro Café Mediterráneo*, popular with students, lively, cheap. *Off the Wall*, López de Bello 155. Recommended for fish. *Tragaluz*, Constitución 124. Good Chilean food, not cheap. *Venezia*, Pío Nono, corner of López de Bello, huge servings, good value. **Cheap** *Café Universitario*, Alameda 395 y Subercaseaux (near Santa Lucía). Good *almuerzos*, lively at night, rock videos, very pleasant. *Fuente Alemana*, Av O'Higgins 58 (Metro Baquedano). Huge sandwiches, burgers, hotdogs, juices and beer, good value.

It is difficult to eat cheaply in the evening apart from fast food, so budget travellers should make the almuerzo their main meal

Providencia Expensive *Aquí está Coco*, La Concepción 236. Good seafood, reservation advised. *Au Bon Pain*, 11 de Septiembre 2263. "French bakery café", very good, has other branches. *Carousel*, Los Conquistadores 1972. French cuisine. Very good, nice garden. *Centre Catalá*, Av Suecia 428 near Lota. Good food and décor, reasonably-priced set lunch. *Cuerovaca*, El Mañío 1659. Fantastic tender steaks, Argentine and Chilean cuts, expensive. *da Renato*, Mardoqueo Fernández 138 (Metro Los Leones). Good. *El Giratorio*, 11 de

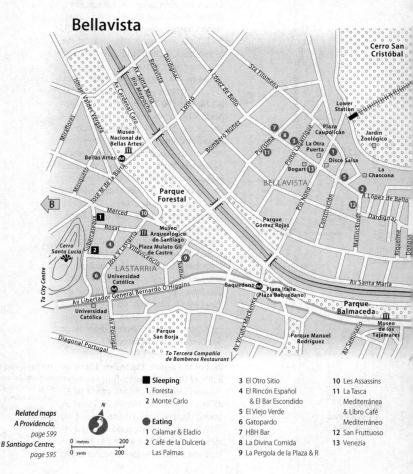

Bellavista

Related maps
A Providencia,
page 599
B Santiago Centre,
page 595

0 metres 200
0 yards 200

■ **Sleeping**
1 Foresta
2 Monte Carlo

● **Eating**
1 Calamar & Eladio
2 Café de la Dulcería
   Las Palmas

3 El Otro Sitio
4 El Rincón Español
   & El Bar Escondido
5 El Viejo Verde
6 Gatopardo
7 HBH Bar
8 La Divina Comida
9 La Pergola de la Plaza & R

10 Les Assassins
11 La Tasca
   Mediterránea
   & Libro Café
   Mediterráneo
12 San Fruttuoso
13 Venezia

Septiembre 2250, p16. French restaurant with good food. *El Madroñal*, Vitacura 2911, T233 6312. Spanish, excellent, booking essential. *El Mesón del Calvo*, corner with Roger de Flor, expensive seafood. *La Pez Era*, No 1421. Seafood, smart but not too expensive. *La Pizza Nostra*, Av Providencia 1975. Pizzas and good Italian food, real coffee, also at Av Las Condes 6757 and Luis Thayer Ojeda 019. *Lomit's*, Av Providencia 1980. Good food and service. *Oriental*, Manuel Montt 584. Excellent Chinese. Highly recommended. *Sakura*, Vitacura 4111. Japanese, sushi, very good. *Salvaje*, Av Providencia 1177. Good international menu, open-air seating, good value. Warmly recommended. **Mid-range** *A Pinch of Panch*, Gral del Canto 45. Very good seafood. *Delmónico*, Vitacura 3379. Excellent, reasonably priced. *Gatsby*, Av Providencia 1984. American food, as-much-as-you- can-eat buffet and lunch/dinner, snack bar open till 2400, tables outside in warm weather, good (also has a good branch at the airport). *Le Fournil*, Vitacura 3841. Excellent French bakery and restaurant, popular a lunchtime. *Mare Nostrum*, La Concepción 281. Good for seafood. *Praga*, Vitacura 3917. Czech. *The Wok House*, Vitacura 4355. Chinese, take-away available. **On Isadora Goyenechea**: *La Cascade*, No 2930. French, excellent. *Pinpilinpausha*, No 2900. Good. *Puerto Marisco*, No 2928. Seafood, good. *Taj Mahal*, No 3215 (Metro El Golf). Indian, expensive but excellent.

Vegetarian *El Huerto*, Orrego Luco 054, Providencia, T233 2690. Open daily, live music Fri and Sat evenings, varied menu, very good but not cheap, popular. Recommended. Its sister café, La Huerta, next door, is cheaper. *El Naturista*, Moneda 846. Excellent, closes 2100.

╫╫╫ Funicular railway

Santiago centre *Bombón Oriental*, Merced 345. Superb Turkish, specialities, coffee, Falafel and cakes. *Café Paula*, several branches, eg Estado at entrance to Galería España. Excellent coffee, cakes and ice cream, good breakfast. *Café Santos*, Huérfanos 830. Popular for 'onces' (afternoon tea), many branches. *New York*, Moneda y Tenderini. Good coffee, helpful. On San Antonio opposite the Teatro Municipal is *Pastelería Colonial*, MacIver 133. *Tip-Top Galetas*, recommended for biscuits, branches throughout the city, eg Merced 867. **East of the centre** *Café de la Dulcería Las Palmas*, López de Bello 190. Good pastries and lunches. *La Chimenea*, Pasaje Príncipe de Gales 90. Hidden away upstairs in a small street, meals during the day, lively. **Providencia** *Country Village*, Av Las Condes y Estoril. *Le Flaubert*, Orrego Luco 125. Good *salón de té* and restaurant. *Salón de Té Tavelli*, drugstore precinct, No 2124. **For snacks and ice cream** Several good places on Av Providencia including *Coppellia*, No 2211, *Bravissimo*, No 1406, and *El Toldo Azul*, No 1936.

Listings in weekend newspapers, particularly *El Mercurio* and *La Tercera*. Also *Santiago What's On*. Lively areas to head for are: Bellavista, good selection of varied restaurants, bars, clubs and salsotheques. Reasonable prices (Metro Baquedano). Avs Suecia and Gral Holley, much of it pedestrianized. Lots of bars and some restaurants, clubs and salsotheques (Metro Los Leones). El Bosque

Cafés & bars
For good coffee try Café Haití, Café Brasil and Café Caribe, all on Paseo Ahumada and elsewhere in centre and Providencia, mainly for men – look at the waitresses to see why – women advised to go escorted. Almost all hotel bars are closed on Sun

Bars & clubs
For all entertainments, nightclubs, cinemas, restaurants, concerts, El Mercurio Online website has all listings and a good search feature, www.emol.com

Chile

Norte, chic bars and expensive restaurants for the Chilean jetset (Metro Tobalaba). Barrio Brasil, a number of bars and restaurants dotted around the Plaza Brasil and on Avs Brasil and Cumming. Popular with Chilean students (Metro República). Plaza Ñuñoa. A number of good bars dotted around the Plaza in the middle-class suburb of Ñuñoa.

Bogart, Av López de Bello 34, disco-rock bar. *Caribbean*, Av López de Bello 40, reggae pub-club. *Club de Jazz de Santiago*, Av Pedro Alessandri 85, Ñuñoa, www.clubdejazz.cl Regular live jazz in candle-lit bar, pleasant. *Disco Salsa*, Pío Nono 223, salsa and classes. *Flannery's Irish Geo Pub*, Encomenderos 83. With beer and food, live music Wed and Fri, internet. *Golden Bell Inn*, Hernando Aguirre 27. Popular with expatriates. Bavarian-style beer brewed to traditional recipes in Temuco at *HBH Bars*, Pío Nono 129 and Purísima y López de Bello, also at Irarrázaval 3176, near Plaza Ñuñoa, and Gral Holley 124, Providencia. Many good bars on Av Suecia including *Brannigan Pub*, No 35, good beer, live jazz, *Louisiana River Pub*, Suecia y Gral Holly, live music, and *Mr Ed*, No 1552. *Heaven*, Recoleta 345. Expensive. *Ilé Habana*, Bucaré, just off Suecia. Bar with salsa, often live, and a good dance floor. *La Otra Puerta*, Pío Nono 348. Lively salsoteca. *Morena*, Av Suecia 0120. Good dance floor and sound system, techno, open till 0200, live music weekends. *Peña Nano Parra*, San Isidro 57. Good folk club, cheap. *Phone Box Pub*, Av Providencia 1652. Serves imported British beers, popular with locals and gringos. *Red Pub*, No 29. Further east on Av Las Condes at Paseo San Damián are several popular bar-restaurants including *T'quila* (annex of *Santa Fe*, No 10690, a colourful, popular Mexican restaurant). *Tu Tu Tango*, Pío Nono 127. Good value.

Entertainment

Good guide to daily cinema in the free newspapers, La Hora and tmg, given out at metro stations on weekday mornings

Cinemas 'Ciné Arte' (quality foreign films) is popular and 7 small cinemas specialize in this type of film: *AIEP*, Miguel Claro 177, T264 9698. *Casa de Extensión UC*, Alameda 390, T635 1994. *Espaciocal* and *Lo Castillo*, Candelaría Goyenechea 3820, T246 1562/244 5856. *El Biógrafo*, Lastarria 181, T633 4435. *Normandie*, Tarapacá 1181, T697 2979. *Tobalaba*, Av Providencia 2563, T231 6630. Try also Goethe-Institut (address below). Many multiplex cinemas across the city show mainstream releases, nearly always in the original English with subtitles. Seats cost US$4-6 with reductions on Wed (elsewhere in the country the day varies).

Free classical concerts are sometimes given in San Francisco church in summer. Arrive early for a seat. Theatres and events are listed in El Mercurio and La Tercera

Theatres *Teatro Municipal*, Agustinas y San Antonio. Stages international opera, concerts by the Orquesta Filarmónica de Santiago, and the Ballet de Santiago, throughout the year. On Tue at 2100 there are free operatic concerts in the Salón Claudio Arrau; tickets range from US$7 for a very large choral group with a symphony orchestra, and US$8 for the cheapest seats at the ballet, to US$70 for the most expensive opera seats. Some cheap seats are often sold on the day of concerts. *Teatro Universidad de Chile*, Plaza Italia, is the home of the Orquesta y Coro Sinfónica de Chile and the Ballet Nacional de Chile. There are a great number of theatres which stage plays in Spanish, either in the original language or translations. *Santiago Stage* is an English-speaking amateur drama group. Outdoor rock concerts are held at the *Estadio Nacional*, Av Grecia y Pedro de Valdivia, at the *Teatro Teletón*, Rosas 325 (excellent sound system), and elsewhere.

Festivals

During **Nov** there is a free art fair in the Parque Forestal on the banks of the Río Mapocho, lasting a fortnight. In **Oct** or **Nov** there are a sumptuous flower show and an annual agricultural and industrial show (known as Fisa) in Parque Cerrillos. Religious festivals and ceremonies continue throughout Holy Week, when a priest washes the feet of 12 men. The image of the *Virgen del Carmen* (patron of the Armed Forces) is carried through the streets by cadets on **16 Jul**.

Shopping

Book prices are high compared with neighbouring countries and Europe

Bookshops *Apostrophes*, Merced 324, T/F632 3569, apos@cybercenter.cl Specializes in French books, book exchange, internet service. Second-hand English books from *Books*, Av Providencia 1652, Metro Pedro de Valdivia, T235 1205, exchange for best deal (the artist's shop in same precinct sells attractive cards). Next to *Books* is *Chile Ilustrado*, No 1652, T235 8145, chileil@tnet.cl Specializes in books relating to Chile, flora, fauna, history and anthropology (mostly in Spanish). *Feria Chilena del Libro*, Huérfanos 623, T639 6758, and in Drugstore precinct, Providencia 2124. Good for travel books and some maps. *Librería Albers*, Vitacura 5648, Las Condes, T218 5371, F218 1458. Spanish, English and German, good selection, cheaper than most, helpful, stocks Footprint Handbooks, also German and Swiss newspapers. *Librairie*

Française, books and newspapers, Estado 337. For cheap English books, try the second-hand book kiosks on San Diego between Eleuterio Ramírez and Cóndor, 4 blocks south of Plaza Bulnes, or *Drago*, Rosas 3260, near Parque Quinta Normal. *Librería Inglesa*, Huérfanos 669, local 11, Pedro de Valdivia 47, Providencia 2653, Vitacura 5950, www.libreriainglesa.cl Good selection of English books. *Librería Universitaria*, Alameda 1050, T687 4216, in unmistakable yellow building next to Universidad de Chile metro. Good selection of books in Spanish. *LOM Ediciones*, Estación Mapocho. Very good, large stock from its own publishing house (literature, history, sociology, art, politics), also bar and reading room with recent Chilean papers and magazines, Mon-Fri 1000-2000, Sat 1000-1400. *South American Way*, Apoquindo 6856, Las Condes, T211 8078. Sells books in English.

Camping equipment Standard camping gas cartridges can be bought at *Fabri Gas*, Bandera y Santo Domingo. **Mountain Service**, Santa Magdalena 75, of 306, Providencia, T234 3439, F234 3438, www.mountainservice.cl Metro Los Leones. English spoken, tents, stoves, clothing, equipment rental, recommended.

Imported camping goods from *Club Andino* and *Federación de Andinismo* (see below): *Outdoors & Travel*, Encomenderos 206, Las Condes, T/F335 7104. German/Chilean owned, clothing, equipment, maps. *Industria Yarur*, Rosas 1289 y Teatinos, T672 3696 (metro Cal y Canto). Sells wide range of *Doite* products (Chilean, good value). *La Cumbre*, Apoquindo 5258, Las Condes, T678 4285/220 9907, la_cumbre@email.com Dutch-owned, very helpful. *Reinaldo Lippi*, Av Italia 1586, Ñuñoa, T344452. Makes tents, sleeping bags, packs, etc, sells secondhand kit, repairs, helpful. Repair of camping stoves at *Casa Italiana*, Tarapacá 1120. For second-hand equipment look for adverts in cheaper hotels or try Luz Emperatriz Sanhuela Quiroz, Portal Lyon, Loc 14, Providencia 2198 (Metro Los Leones), expensive for new equipment, as is *Patagonia Retail Store*, Helvecia 210 e Ebro, near Metro Tobalaba, T335 1716. Try also the arcades around the Central railway station.

Crafts *Cooperativa Almacén Campesino*, Purísima 303, Bellavista, T737 2127. A cooperative association in an attractive colonial building, selling handicrafts from all over Chile, including attractive Mapuche weavings, wood carvings, pottery and beautiful wrought copper and bronze. Highly recommended for variety, quality and value. Prices are similar to those in similar shops in Temuco. Ask about shipping. The gemstone lapis lazuli can be found in shops on C Bellavista between Pío Nono and Yáñez, but is cheaper in the arcades on south side of the Plaza de Armas and in the *Centro Artesanal Santa Lucía* (Santa Lucía Metro, south exit) which also has a wide variety of woollen goods, jewellery, some folk music and other miscellanea. *Amitié*, Ricardo León y Av Providencia (Metro Los Leones) and *Dauvin Artesanía Fina*, Providencia 2169, Local 69 (Metro Los Leones) have also been recommended. *Cema-Chile* (Centro de Madres), Portugal 351 and at Universidad de Chile Metro stop, *Manos Chilensis*, Portugal 373, *Artesanías de Chile*, Varas 475, *Artesanía Popular Chilena*, Av Providencia 2322 (near Metro Los Leones), and *Artesanía Chilena*, Estado 337, all have a good selection of handicrafts. *Chile Vivo*, Dardignac 15, Bellavista, T735 0227, chilevivo@latinmail.com Typical handicrafts, jewellery making, art gallery, internet café, owner Doris Berdichevsky is very helpful. *Prisma de los Andes*, Santo Domingo 1690 T673 0540, Metro Santa Ana. Textiles, crafts, tapestries, rucksacks, bags, kids clothes etc. Antique stores in Plaza Mulato Gil de Castro and elsewhere on Lastarria (Merced end).

Beside and behind the Iglesia de los Dominicos, on Av Apoquindo 9085, is *Los Graneros del Alba*, or *El Pueblo de Artesanos*. Open 1030-2100 in summer, 1000-1900 in winter. All types of ware on sale, classes given in some shops, interesting. To get there, take a No 326 or 327 bus from Av Providencia, marked 'Camino del Alba'; get out at the children's playground at the junction of Apoquindo y Camino del Alba, at the foot of the hill leading up to the church, and walk up. *Plaza Artesanos de Manquehue*, Av Manquehue Sur, block 300-600, just off Apoquindo. Good range of modern Chilean crafts from ceramics to textiles. Take any bus east from Providencia or Escuela Militar which goes via Apoquindo.

Maps *Automóvil Club de Chile*, Vitacura 8620. Route maps of Chile, 7 maps in total, US$6 each or US$3 each if affiliated to motor organization. *Instituto Geográfico Militar*, Dieciocho 369, T460 8222. Has detailed geophysical and topographical maps of the whole of Chile, very useful for climbing. Expensive (US$11 each), but the Biblioteca Nacional, Alameda 651 (T360 5200) has copies and will allow you to photocopy parts of each map. *Mapas*, Gral del Canto 105, of 1506, Providencia, T236 4808, jmattassi@interactiva.cl Sells good comprehensive maps available for the whole of Chile. Some specialize in marking trekking routes, especially in national parks where maps are produced in conjunction with *Conaf*. Maps are US$6 each. Purchase direct from small office on 15th floor of highrise just off Providencia. Mon-Fri 1000 –1330 and 1430-1700. Basic plans of central Santiago can be obtained free from tourist info centres in Vitacura, Paseo Ahumada and airport. More detailed and extensive ones can be bought at same places. *Atlas de Chile* street map, from bookshops and news stands, has been recommended, US$6.50. Telefónica Plano de Santiago in booklet format recommended, US$6. See also Finding out more in Essentials.

Markets For **food**: *Mercado Central*, between Puente y 21 de Mayo by the Río Mapocho (Cal y Canto Metro) is excellent but quite expensive. There is a cheaper market, the *Vega Central*, on the opposite bank of the river. There are **craft markets** in an alleyway, 1 block south of the Alameda between A Prat and San Diego, on the 600 to 800 blocks of Santo Domingo (including pieces from neighbouring countries) and at Pío Nono y Santa María, Bellavista. The shopping arcade at the Central Station is good value, likewise the street market outside. The *Bío Bío* flea market on C Bío Bío, Metro Franklin (follow the crowds) on Sat and Sun morning is huge; everything under the sun sold, lots of it having fallen off the back of a lorry! A good outside fruit market is at Puente 815, by *Frutería Martínez*.

Music *Feria de Disco*, Paseo Ahumada and in numerous malls. The biggest chain, often sell tickets for rock concerts. *Musimundo*, Huérfanos 930 (complete with listening stations) and Providencia 2266, megastores.

Shopping malls Numerous: most central is *Mall del Centro*, Rosas 900 block, just north of the Plaza de Armas. *Alto Las Condes*, Av Kennedy 9001; *Apumanque*, Manquehue y Apoquindo; *Parque Arauco*, Av Kennedy 5413, north of Metro Escuela Militar; *Plaza Vespucio* at terminus of Línea 5, Bellavista de La Florida. Generally open daily 1000-2100.

Wine *El Mundo del Vino*, Isidora Goyenechea 2931, T244 8888, for all types of Chilean wines, good selection across the price range. Similar at *Vinopolis*, El Bosque Norte 038 and Pedro de Valdivia 036. Mon-Fri 0900-2300, Sat 1000-2300, Sun 1000-2200. Also at airport. *The Wine House*, Vitacura 2904, Mall Parque Arauco, loc 333.

Sport & activities **Cycling**: for new models, parts and repairs at best prices go to San Diego, 800 and 900 blocks, south of the Alameda. **Cricket**: Sat in summer at *Club Príncipe de Gales*, Las Arañas 1901 (bus from Tobalaba Metro), US$5, membership not required. **Football**: main teams including Colo Colo who play at the Estadio Monumental, T688 3244 (reached by any bus to Puente Alto; tickets from Cienfuegos 41), Universidad de Chile, Campo de Deportes, Ñuñoa, T239 2793 (Estadio Nacional, Grecia 2001, T238 8102) and Universidad Católica who play at San Carlos de Apoquindo, reached by bus from Metro Escuela Militar, tickets from Andrés Bello 2782, Providencia, T231 2777. **Horse racing**: *Club Hípico*, Blanco Encalada 2540, highly recommended, entry to main stand US$6, every Sun and every other Wed; Hipódromo Chile every Sat. **Skiing and climbing**: *Club Alemán Andino*, El Arrayán 2735, T242 5453. Open Tue and Fri, 1800-2000, May-Jun. *ClubAndino de Chile,* Enrique Foster 29, ski club (open 1900-2100 on Mon and Fri). *Federación de Andinismo de Chile*, Almte Simpson 77A (T222 0888, F222 6285). Open daily (frequently closed Jan/Feb), has a small museum, library (weekdays except Wed 1930-2100), shop selling guides and equipment. *Escuela Nacional de Montaña* (ENAM), at same address, T222 0799, holds seminars and courses and has the addresses of all the mountaineering clubs in the country. It has a mountaineering school. Also try *Skitotal*, Apoquindo 4900, of 32,33,43, T246 0156, for 1-day excursions and good value ski hire. Equipment hire is much cheaper in Santiago than in ski resorts. Sunglasses are essential. For ski resorts in the Santiago area see below page 612. **Swimming**: *Tupahue* (large pool with cafés, entry US$10 but worth it) and *Antilen*, both on Cerro San Cristóbal. Open daily in summer except Mon 1000-1500 (check if they are open in winter, one usually is). In Parque O'Higgins, 1330-1830 summer only, US$3. Olympic pool in Parque Araucano (near Parque Arauco Shopping Centre, Metro Escuela Militar), open Nov-Mar Tue-Sat 0900-1900. **Tennis**: Municipal courts in Parque O'Higgins. Estadio Nacional, Av Grecia y Av Marathon, has a tennis club which offers classes.

A number of agencies offer day trips from Santiago. Typical excursions are to the Wine Valleys, **Tour**
Valparaíso and Viña del Mar, Isla Negra (Pablo Neruda's seaside villa), visits to nearby haciendas **operators**
and adventure tours such as whitewater rafting, rock climbing or trekking in the Cajón del
Maipo, southeast of the city. Many agencies advertise in the **Sernatur** tourist office (see above).

Asatej Student Flight Centre, H de Aguirre 201, Oficina 401, T335 0395, www.sertur.cl For
cheap flights and youth travel. Recommended. *Blanco Viajes*, Gral Holley 148, T636 9100,
blancoviajes@blancoviajes.cl American Express representative for TCs, funds transfer,client
mail. *Eurotur*, Huérfanos 1160, local 13, www.eurotur.com For cheap air tickets to Europe.
Ladatco, USA T800-327-6162, www.ladactco.com Runs South-American wide tours.
Passtours, Huérfanos 886, of 1110, T639 3232, F633 1498. Helpful. *Tajamar*, Orrego Luco 023,
Providencia, T336 8000. Good for flights. *Turismo Cocha*, El Bosque Norte 0430, PO Box
191035, Providencia, Metro Tobalaba, T464 1000, www.cocha.com *Turismo Joven*, 11 de
Septiembre 2305, local 11, Providencia, T232 3174, turjoven@mailnet.rdc.cl Youth travel ser-
vices for young people and students for travel, studies, leisure with links in Latin America and
worldwide. *Wagons-Lits* , Carmencita, Providencia, T233 0820. Recommended.
Hotelschile.com, and *experiencechile.org*, T313 3389, hotels and tours.

For adventure tours and trekking: *Altue Expediciones*, Encomenderos 83, p 2, Las
Condes (above *Geo Pub*), T232 1103, altue@entelchile.net For wilderness trips including tour
of Patagonia. Recommended. *Andina del Sud*, Bombero Ossa 1010, p 3, of 301, T697 1010,
F696 5121. For tours in the Lake District. *Antu Aventuras*, Casilla 24, Santiago, T271 2767.
Climbing and adventure tours in the Lake District and elsewhere. *Azimut 360*, General Salvo
159, Providencia, T236 3880/1612, emergency 235 3085, www.azimut.cl www.terraluna.cl
Adventure and ecotourism including mountaineering all over Chile, low prices. Highly recom-
mended. *Catamaranes del Sur*, Isidora Goyenechea 3250, of 802, Las Condes, T333 7127, F232
9736, offers tours of Chilean Patagonia. At Puerto Montt: Km 13, Chinquihue, T482308 and Av
Diego 510, T267533; at Chaitén: Av Padre Juan Todesco 180, T731199; at Puerto Chacabuco:
José Miguel Carrera 50, T351112, www.catamaranesdelsur.cl *Lime Light Tour*, Av 11 de
Septiembre 1945, of 1213, Providencia, T3811510, F3811509, www.limelighttour.cl, offers
tours of Chilean Patagonia. *Mountain Service* (see under skiing and climbing). *Nicole
Aventuras*, Nicole Schoenholzer, Mar del Plata 1957-42, Providencia, T/F225 6155, www.fis.
puc.cl/~gtarrach/avenic 1 and 3-day trips to national parks, trekking and adventure tours in
precordillera and coastal mountain range, English, French, German spoken. *Patagonia Connection SA*, Fidel Oteíza 1921, of 1006, Providencia (Metro Pedro de Valdivia), T225 6489,
www.patagoniaconnex.cl For excursion by boat Puerto Montt- Coyhaique/Puerto
Chacabuco-Laguna San Rafael. *Racies*, Plaza Corregidor Zañartu 761, T/F638 2904. Cultural
tours, including Robinson Crusoe Island and Antarctica. *Southern Cross Adventure*, J M de la
Barra 521, 4E, T/F639 6591, www.scadventure.com Climbing, riding, trekking, overland expeditions, fishing in Patagonia. *Sportstours*, Moneda 970, p 14, T549 5200, www.sportstour.cl German-run, 5-day trips to Antarctica (offices also at Hotels *Carrera*, and *San Cristóbal*), only for
tours organized from abroad. *Turismo Cabo de Hornos*, Av Vitacura 2898, Las Condes, T335
0550, hornos@chilesat.net For DAP flights and Tierra del Fuego/ Antarctica tours. *Valle
Nevado*, T206 0027, www.vallenevado.com Skiing, trekking and mountain biking.

Local Buses are called *micros*. Destinations are marked clearly on the front. In theory pas-   **Transport**
sengers put the exact change in a ticket machine to get a printed ticket. In practice this is only   *Hang on to your*
one of three options, the other two being that you give the money to the driver who will   *bus ticket, inspectors*
arrange a printed ticket, or the driver will give you an old-style paper ticket. There are also   *occasionally ask*
colectivos (collective taxis) on fixed routes to the suburbs, US$0.75-1.50. Routes are dis-   *for them*
played with route numbers. **Taxis** (black with yellow roofs) are abundant, and not expensive, with a minimum charge of US$0.60, plus US$0.12 per 200 m. For short trips within the
centre, it is convenient to go by taxi, especially if there are 2-4 of you. Note in the immediate
centre of the city, taxis are not allowed to pick up, only set down (the limits of this zone are
marked by white bollards). Taxi drivers are permitted to charge more at night, but in the daytime check that the meter is set to day rates. At bus terminals, drivers will charge more – best
to walk a block and flag down a cruising taxi. Avoid taxis with more than one person in them
especially at night. For journeys outside the city arrange the charge beforehand. The private

Chile

taxi service which operates from the bottom level of *Hotel Carrera* has been recommended (same rates as city taxis), as has **Radio Taxis** Andes Pacífico, T225 3064/2888; similarly *Rigoberto Contreras*, T638 1042, ext 4215, but rates above those of city taxis.

Tax of 18% is charged but usually not included in price quoted. If possible book a car in advance. Information boards full of flyers from companies at airport and tourist office

Car hire: prices vary a lot so shop around first. Main international agencies and others are available at the airport (see Essentials, page 52 for agency web addresses). *Just Rent a Car*, Helvecia 228, Las Condes, T232 0900. English and Portuguese spoken. *Costanera*, Av Andrés Bello 1255, T235 7835. **Automóvil Club de Chile** car rental from head office (see Maps), discount for members and members of associated motoring organizations. *Seelmann*, Las Encinas 3057, Ñuñoa, T09-331 0591. English and German spoken. A credit card is usually asked for when renting a vehicle. Remember that in the capital driving is restricted according to licence plate numbers; look for notices in the street and newspapers.

See next page for Metro map

Metro: (www.metro-chile.cl) There are 3 lines: Line 1 which runs west-east between San Pablo and Escuela Militar, under the Alameda; Line 2 which runs north-south from Cal y Canto to Callejón Ovalle; Line 5, from Santa Ana via Baquedano south to La Florida (an extension to Quinta Normal is due for completion by 2004). The trains are fast, quiet, and very full. The first train is at 0630 (Mon-Sat), 0800 (Sun and holidays), the last about 2230. Fares vary according to time of journey; there are 2 charging periods: high 0715-0900, 1800-1900, US$0.60; economic, at all other times, US$0.40. The simplest solution is to buy a *boleto valor/carnet*, US$4 for 10 journeys. Blue *metrobus* services connect with the metro at Lo Ovalle, Las Rejas, Pila de Ganso, Caly Canto, Salvador, Escuela Militar and La Florida for outlying districts, fare US$0.50.

Airport information T601 9709

Long distance Air: International and domestic flights leave from Arturo Merino Benítez Airport at Pudahuel, 26 km northwest of Santiago, off Ruta 68, the motorway to Viña del Mar and Valparaíso. The terminal has most facilities, including *Afex cambio* (poor rates, change only what you need), ATMs, *Sernatur* office which will book accommodation and a fast-food plaza. **Left luggage** US$2.50 per bag per day.

Airport taxi, about US$15-17 but bargain hard and agree fare beforehand: more expensive with meter. Taxi to airport is much cheaper, US$10-12, if flagged down in the street rather than booked by phone. Frequent bus services to/from city centre by 2 companies:*Tur Bus* (buses from Terminal Alameda) US$2, every 30 mins; and *Centropuerto* (T601 9883, from Metro Los Héroes), US$1.50, first from centre 0600, last from airport 2330, every 10 mins. Buses leave from outside airport terminal and, in Santiago, call at Plazoleta Los Héroes (near the yellow 'Línea 2' sign), Estación Central, the Terminal Santiago and most other regular bus stops. (Beware the bus marked *Aeropuerto* which stops 2 km short of the Airport). *Delfos* runs shuttle bus for larger groups and cars for 1 or 2 people, fare from centre US$13, book in advance, T601 1111. *Navett*, Av Ejército Libertador 21 (nearest Metro Los Héroes), T695 6868 has a round-the-clock service, US$7. For domestic flights from Santiago, see under destinations. *Transfer* runs minibuses from your house or hotel to airport (or vice-versa), any time day or night, US$6 to centre, US$7 Providencia, US$8 Las Condes, T777 7707 for reservation (cheaper than taxi). Recommended.

Check if student rates are available (even for non-students), or reductions for travelling same day as purchase of ticket; it is worth bargaining over prices, especially shortly before departure and out of summer season

Buses: There are frequent, and good, interurban buses to all parts of Chile. Take a look at the buses before buying the tickets (there are big differences in quality among bus companies); ask about the on-board services, many companies offer drinks for sale, or free, and luxury buses have meals and wine, videos, headphones. Reclining seats are standard and there are also *salón cama* sleeper buses. Fares from/to the capital are given in the text. On Fri evening, when night departures are getting ready to go, the terminals can be chaotic. There are 4 bus terminals: 1) **Terminal de Buses Alameda**, which has a modern extension called Mall Parque Estación, O'Higgins 3712, Metro Universidad de Santiago, T270 7150. All *Pullman-Bus* and *TurBus* services go from here, they serve almost every destination in Chile, good quality but prices a little higher than others. 2) **Terminal de Buses Santiago**, O'Higgins 3878, 1 block west of Terminal Alameda, T376 1755, Metro Universidad de Santiago. Services to Valparaíso, Viña del Mar and all parts of Chile, including Punta Arenas with *Turibus*. Also international departures. The best place to start shopping around for prices. 3) **Terminal San Borja**, O'Higgins y San Borja, 1 block west of Estación Central, 3 blocks east of Terminal Alameda, Metro Estación Central (entrance is, inconveniently, via a busy shopping centre), T776 0645. Some national departures and buses to outlying parts of Región Metropolitana and Region 5. Booking offices and departures organized according to destination. Left luggage US$1.50 per piece per day. 4) **Terminal Los Héroes** on Tucapel Jiménez, just north of the Alameda, Metro Los Héroes, T420 0099. Booking offices of 8 companies, to the north, the south and Lake District and some international services (Lima, Asunción, Montevideo, Buenos Aires, Bariloche, Mendoza). Some long-distance buses call at Las Torres de Tajamar, Providencia 1108, which is more convenient if you are planning to stay in Providencia. *Cruz del Sur*and *Pullman Express* have offices on Paseo Los Leones.

See the note under Taxis about not taking expensive taxis parked outside bus terminals, but note that official *Turbus* taxis are good and reliable.

International buses There are frequent services from Terminal Santiago through the Cristo Redentor tunnel to **Mendoza** in Argentina, 6-7 hrs, US$12, many companies, departures around 0800, 1200 and 1600, touts approach you in Terminal Santiago. There are also collective taxis from the Terminal Los Héroes and from the 800/900 blocks of Morandé (*Chi-Ar* taxi company, Terminal Santiago of 62, T776 0048, recommended; *Chilebus*, Morandé 838; *Cordillera Nevada*, Morandé 870, T698 4716), US$15, 5 hrs, shorter waiting time at customs. To **Buenos Aires**, US$40, 22 hrs (eg *Tas Choapa* and *Ahumada* from Los Héroes terminal); to **Montevideo**, involving a change in Mendoza, *El Rápido*, 27 hrs; to **Córdoba** direct, US$28, 18 hrs, several companies including *Tas Choapa* and *TAC* (El Rápido not recommended); to **San Juan**, *TAC*, *Tas Choapa*, US$20; To **Lima**, *Ormeño* (Terminal Santiago Sur of 83, T779 3443), 51 hrs, US$70, it is cheaper to take a bus to Arica, a colectivo to Tacna, then bus to Lima.

Most services leave from Terminal Santiago, though there are also departures from Terminal Los Héroes

Trains: All trains leave from Estación Central at O'Higgins 3170. The line runs south to Rancagua, San Fernando, Curicó, Talca, Linares, Parral, Chillán, Concepción and Temuco. Trains are still fairly cheap and generally very punctual, although 1st class is generally more expensive than bus; meals are good but not cheap. Trains can be cold and draughty in winter and spring. There are also frequent local *Metrotren* services to Rancagua. For reservations T376 8500, efereservas@entelchile.net, www.efe.cl Booking offices: for *State Railways*, at Universidad de Chile Metro station, local 10, T688 3284, Mon-Fri 0830-1900, Sat 0900-1300; Estación San Bernardo, Baquedano 590, T859 1977; or *Agencia Traveller Zone*, Paseo Las Palmas 2229, local 18, Providencia, T946 1835 *Dormitorio* carriages were built in Breslau (now Wroclaw, Poland) in 1929, with sleeping compartments (*departamento*), bunks (comfortable) lie parallel to rails, US-Pullman-style (washrooms at each end, one with shower-bath – for hot water give the steward 15 mins notice); an attendant for each car. Also a car-transporter service to Chillán and Temuco. **Left luggage** office at Estación Central.

Schedules change with the seasons, so check timetables in advance. Summer services are booked up a week in advance

Ferry companies: *Navimag*, Av El Bosque Norte 0440, p 11, Las Condes, T442 3120, F203 5025, www.navimag.com, for services from **Puerto Montt** to **Puerto Natales** and vice versa. *Transmarchilay*, Av Providencia 2653, loc 24, T600-600 8687/88, www.tmc.cl For services between **Chiloé** and the mainland and ferry routes on the Carretera Austral. M/n *Skorpios*: Augusto Leguía Norte 118, Las Condes, T231 1030, F232 2269, www.skorpios.cl For luxury cruise out of Puerto Montt to **Laguna San Rafael**. *Transmarchilay* also sail to the Laguna San Rafael in summer.

Check schedules with ferry companies lines rather than Sernatur

Directory

Airline offices *Aerolíneas Argentinas*, Moneda 756, T639 5001, www.aerolineas.com.ar *American Airlines*, Huérfanos 1199, and Bosque Norte 0107, T679 0000. *Avianca*, Santa Magdalena 116, Providencia, T270 6600. *British Airways*, Isidora Goyenechea 2934, Oficina 302, T330 8600, 232 9560 (for confirmation). *Continental*, Nueva Tajamar 481, T204 4000. *Delta*, Vitacura 2700 (Metro Tobalaba), T0800-532892. *Ecuatoriana*, T234 2350. *Iberia*, Bandera 206, p 8, T698 3950. *KLM*, San Sebastián 2839, of 202, T233 0011 (233 0991 reservations). *LAB*, Moneda 1170, T688 8680. *Lacsa*, Dr Barros Borgoño 105, T235 5500. *LanChile*, sales office: Huérfanos 926, T526 2000, Mon-Fri 0900-1900, Sat 0900-1230 (to avoid queues, buy tickets at the office in the airport). *Lufthansa*, Moneda 970, p 16, T630 1655. *United*, El Bosque 0177, T337 0000. *Varig*, El Bosque Norte 0177, T707 8000.

Banks For Cirrus/MasterCard, Visa ATMs go to any bank or *Copec* petrol station with Redbanc sign. Visa at *Corp Banca*, Huérfanos y Bandera, but beware hidden costs in 'conversion rate', and *Banco Santander*, Av Providencia y Pedro de Valdivia, no commission. For stolen or lost Visa cards go to *Transbank*, Huérfanos 770, p 10. *Banco de Chile*, Ahumada 251 and other branches, minimum of formalities. *Citibank*, Av Providencia 2653. *American Express*, see *Blanco Viajes*, above. *Casas de Cambio* (exchange houses) in the centre are mainly situated on Agustinas and Huérfanos. Use them, not banks, for changing TCs. *Exprinter*, Bombero Ossa 1053, good rates, low commission. *Transafex*, Moneda 1140, good rates for TCs. In Providencia several on Av Pedro de Valdivia Some *casas de cambio* in the centre open Sat morning (but check first). Dollars can only be bought for Chilean pesos in *casas de cambio*. Most *cambios* charge 3% commission to change US$ TCs into US$ cash; check beforehand. Only residents can buy dollars against credit cards. Always avoid street money changers (particularly common on Ahumada and Agustinas): they pull any number of tricks, or will usually ask you to accompany them to somewhere obscure. The passing of forged notes and muggings are reported.

Communications Internet: *463@café*, Av Brasil 463, 1000-2200 daily. *Banda Ancha*, República 16, also in Cienfuegos 161 next to Youth Hostel, Mon-Sat 0930-2300, Sun 1730-2300, and at Salvador Sanfuentes 2150, Mon-Sat 1000-2300, Sun 1730-2300. *Cafeaquí*, Providencia y E Yáñez, 0800-2000. Small access point in Bus Terminal Alameda in *CTC Telefónica* office, lower floor of attached shopping gallery. *Café Phonet*, Gral Holley 2312 and San Sebastián 2815, 0900-2300 daily. *Chileinternet*, López de Bello 45, T732 0699. Email, scanning service, chat lines, phones and café. *Connections*, López de Bello entre Pío Nono y Constitución. *Cyber Station*, Brasil 167, Mon-Fri 0900-2200, Sat-Sun 1000-2200. *Dazoca*, Monjitas 448, 1000-2400 daily, also *Dazoca* at Providencia 1370 y Almte Pastene, p 2, 1000-2400 daily. *ES Computación*, S Sanfuentes 2352, T688 7395, metro República, nine@ctc.internet.cl Helpful. *La Araña*, San Isidro 171, Casa 2, in Mall del Centro (Santo Domingo with Puente). Also at Ramón de Corvalán 119, just south of Alameda near Plaza Italia. Agustinas 869, p2. 60 flat-screen computers, US$1.50 per hr, open 0700-2300 daily, popular. *Sicosis*, José M de la Barra 544. *Sonnets*, Londres 43, of 11, T664 4725, www.2central.com 1000-2100 daily, helpful, many languages spoken, book exchange. Post Office: Plaza de Armas and Moneda between Morandé and Bandera. Also sub offices in Providencia at Av 11 de Septiembre 2092, Manuel Montt 1517, Pedro de Valdivia 1781, Providencia 1466, and in Estación Central shopping mall. These open Mon-Fri 0900-1800, Sat 0900-1230. Poste restante well organized (though only kept for 30 days), US$0.20, passport essential, list of letters and parcels received in the hall of central Post Office (one list for men, another for women, indicate Sr or Sra/Srta on envelope); Plaza de Armas office also has philatelic section, 0900-1630, and small stamp museum (ask to see it). If sending a parcel, the contents must first be checked at the Post Office. Paper, tape etc on sale. Telephone: *CTC*, Moneda 1151, closed Sun. International phone calls also from: *Entel*, Huérfanos 1133. Mon-Fri 0830-2200, Sat 0900-2030, Sun 0900-1400, calls cheaper 1400-2200. Fax upstairs, fax also available at *CTC* offices, eg Mall Panorámico, 11 de Septiembre, 3rd level (phone booths are on level 1). There are also *CTC* phone offices at some metro stations, La Moneda, Escuela Militar, Tobalaba, Universidad de Chile and Pedro de Valdivia for local, long-distance and international calls. There are also phone boxes in the street from which overseas calls can be made.

Cultural centres Instituto Chileno Británico de Cultura, Santa Lucía 124, T638 2156. 0930-1900, except 1330-1900 Mon, and 0930-1600 Fri, has British papers and library (also in Providencia, Darío Urzúa 1933, and Las Condes, Renato Sánchez 4369), runs language courses. British Council, Eliodoro Yáñez 832, near Providencia, T223 4622, www.britcoun.cl/index.htm Instituto Chileno Francés de Cultura, Merced 298, T639 8433. In a beautiful house. Instituto Chileno Alemán de Cultura, Goethe-Institut, Esmeralda 650, T638 3185. Instituto Chileno Norteamericano de Cultura, Moneda 1467, T696 3215. Good for US periodicals, cheap films on Fri. Also runs language courses and free Spanish/English language exchange hours (known as Happy Hours) which are a good way of meeting people. (Ask also about Mundo Club which organizes excursions and social events.)

Embassies and consulates Argentina, Miraflores 285, T633 1076. Consulate Vicuña MacKenna 41, T222 6853. Australians need letter from their embassy to get visa here, open 0900-1400 (visa US$25, free for US citizens), if you need a visa for Argentina, get it here or in the consulates in Concepción, Puerto Montt or Punta Arenas, there are no facilities at the borders. Australia, Gertrudis Echeñique 420, T228 5065, 0900-1200. Austria, Barros Errázuriz 1968, p 3, T223 4774. Belgium, Av Providencia 2653, depto 1104, T232 1071. Bolivia, Santa María 2796, T232 8180 (Metro Los Leones). 0930-1400. Canada, Nueva Tajamar 481, p 12, T362 9660, www.dfait-maeci.gc.ca/santiago (prints a good information book). Denmark, Jaques Cazotte 5531, T218 5949. France, Condell 65, T225 1030. Germany, Apoquindo 4445, of 302, T207 3585. Israel, San Sebastián 2812, T750 0500. Italy, Román Díaz 1270, T225 9439. Japan, Av Ricardo Lyon 520, T232 1807. Netherlands, C Las Violetas 2368, T223 6825. 0900-1200. New Zealand, Av El Golf 99, of 703, Las Condes, T290 9802, nzembassychile@adsl.tie.cl Norway, San Sebastián 2839, T234 2888. Peru, Andrés Bello 1751, T235

2356 (Metro Pedro de Valdivia). **South Africa**, Av 11 de Septiembre 2353, Edif San Román, p 16, T231 2862. **Spain**, Av Andrés Bello 1895, T235 2755. **Sweden**, 11 de Septiembre 2353, Torre San Ramón, p 4, Providencia, T231 2733, F232 4188. **Switzerland**, Av Americo Vespucio Sur 100, p 14, T263 4211, F263 4094, metro Escuela Militar. Open 1000-1200. **United Kingdom**, El Bosque Norte 0125 (Metro Tobalaba), Casilla 72-D, T231 3737/370 4100, F335 5988, www.britemb.cl Will hold letters, consular section (F370 4170) open 0930-1230. **United States**, Andrés Bello 2800, T232 2600, F330 3710. Consulate, T710133, Merced 230 (visa obtainable here).

Language schools *Centro de Idiomas Bellavista*, Crucero Exeter 0325, T737 5102, www.cib.in.cl Group and individual courses, accommodation with families, free activities. *Escuela de Idiomas Violeta Parra*, Ernesto Pinto Lagarrigue 362, Recoleta-Barrio Bellavista, T735 8240, www.tandemsantiago.cl Courses aimed at budget travellers, information programme on social issues, arranges accommodation and visits to local organizations and national parks. *Instituto Chileno-Suizo de Idiomas y Cultura*, José Victorino 93, p 2 (Metro Universidad Católica), T638 5414, www.chilenosuizo.cl Coordinates stays in Chile for foreign-language students, courses in several languages, *La Araña* cybercafé (see above), *La Cafetería* meeting place, *El Rincón del Libro* study area and art gallery. *Natalis English Centre*, Vicuña Mackenna 6, p 7, T222 8721, natalislang@hotmail.com Many **private teachers**, including *Lucía Araya Arévalo*, T749 0706 (home), 731 8325 (office), 09-480 3727 (Mob), lusara5@hotmail.com Speaks German and English. *Carolina Carvajal*, Av El Bosque Sur 151, dpto Q, Las Condes, T734 7646, ccarvajal@interactiva.cl Exchange library, internet access. Highly recommended. *Patricio Ríos*, Tobalaba 7505, La Reina, T226 6926. Speaks English. Recommended. *Patricia Vargas Vives*, JM Infante 100, of 308, T/F244 2283. Qualified and experienced (US$12.50 per hr).

Medical facilities **Hospitals** Emergency hospital at Marcoleta 377 costs US$60. For yellow fever vaccination and others (but not cholera). **Hospital San Salvador**, J M Infante 551, T225 6441, Mon-Thu 0800-1300, 1330-1645, Fri 0800-1300, 1330-1545. Also **Vaccinatoria Internacional**, Hospital Luis Calvo, MacKenna, Antonio Varas 360. **Clínica Central**, San Isidro 231, T222 1953, open 24 hrs.

If you need to get to a hospital, it is better to take a taxi than wait for an ambulance

Useful addresses **Immigration** For extension of tourist visa, or any enquiries regarding legal status, go to **Departamento de Extranjería**, Teatinos 950 (near Estación Mapocho), T674 4000. Mon-Fri 0900-1200. They will give you the information you need. Then, to get the paperwork done, you will have to go round the back of the building and queue. Office open 0900-1300. Make sure you are in the queue before 0800 and take a good book. **Policía Internacional**: For lost tourist cards, etc, Gral Borgoño 1052, T737 2443/1292.

Around Santiago

In this little town, pottery can be bought and the artists can be seen at work. The area is rich in clay and the town is famous for its cider in the apple season, for its *chicha de uva* and for its Chilean dishes, highly recommended. From Santiago take the *Melipilla* bus from outside the San Borja terminal, every few minutes, US$1 each way, Rutabus 78 goes on the motorway, 1 hr, other buses via Talagante take 1 hour 25 minutes (alight at side road to Pomaire, 2-3 km from town, colectivos every 10-15 minutes – these buses are easier to take than the infrequent, direct buses).

Pomaire
65 W of Santiago

Several vineyards in the Santiago area can be visited. *Cousiño-Macul*, Av Quilin 7100 on east outskirts of the city, offers tours Monday-Saturday at 1100, phone first T248 1011, vtaparticular@cousinomacul.cl Take bus 390 from Alameda, or 391 from Merced, both marked Peñalolén. *Concha y Toro* at Pirque, near Puente Alto, 40 km south of Santiago, T821 7069, rpublicas@conchaytoro.cl Short tour (2 a day in Spanish, 2 in English), Monday-Saturday. Entry US$4, includes free wine glass and 3 tastings; book 1 day in advance, 1 week for Saturday. Take Metro to Bellavista de La Florida (end of Línea 5), then blue Metrobus to Pirque. The *Undurraga* vineyard at Santa Ana, southwest of Santiago, T372 2811, sproduccion@undurraga.cl Six tours in English and Spanish daily (reserve 2 days in advance), 1000-1600 on weekdays (tours given by the owner-manager, Pedro Undurraga). Take a Melipilla bus (but not Rutabus 78) to the entrance. *Viña Santa Rita*, Padre Hurtado 0695, Alto Jahuel, Buín, 45 km south, T362 2520, rrivas@santarita.cl Good tour in English and Spanish, US$4 (free if you dine in the restaurant), reserve 2 days in advance, daily except Sunday at specific times. Take a bus from Terminal San Borja to Alto Jahuel.

Visits to vineyards
The Maipo Valley is considered by many experts to be the best wine producing area of Chile

Upper Maipo Valley

If visiting this area or continuing further up the mountain, be prepared for military checks

Southeast of Santiago is the rugged, green valley of the Cajón del Maipo. A road runs through the villages of San José de Maipo, Melocotón and San Alfonso, near which is the Cascada de Animas waterfall. At **El Volcán** (1,400 m), 21 km beyond San Alfonso, there are astounding views, but little else (the village was wiped away in a landslide). From El Volcán the road (very poor condition) runs east to the warm natural baths at **Baños Morales**. ■ *Open from Oct, entry to baths US$2.* 12 km further east up the mountain are **Baños Colina**, hot thermal springs. ■ *Horses for hire.* This area is popular at weekends and holiday times, but is otherwise deserted.

Sleeping and eating At **Baños Morales D** pp *Hostería Baños Morales*, full board, hot water. **D** pp *Res Los Chicos Malos*, T288 5380, comfortable, fresh bread, good meals; free campsite. **E** *Pensión Díaz*, T861 1496, basic, good food. Excellent café in the village, serving homemade jam, it closes at Easter for the winter. 14 km east of El Volcán, just after Baños Morales, **B** pp *Refugio Alemán Lo Valdés*, T220 7610, stone-built chalet accommodation, full board, own generator, good food, a good place to stay for mountain excursions, open all year. A splendid region which deserves the journey required to get there. At **Baños Colina**: **D** pp *Res El Tambo*, full board, restaurant, also camping. No shops so take food.

Transport Buses from Metro Parque O'Higgins to **El Volcán** daily at 1200 (US$2) and on to **Baños Morales**, US$4, 3 hrs, returns at 1745; buy return on arrival to ensure seat back.

Ski resorts

Manzur Expediciones, T777 4284, run buses to all ski resorts from metro Baquedano, Wed, Sat, Sun 0830

There are six main ski resorts near Santiago, four of them around the mountain village of Farellones. **Farellones**, situated on the slopes of Cerro Colorado at 2,470 m, only 32 km from the capital and reached by road in under 90 minutes, was the first ski resort built in Chile. Now it is more of a service centre for the three other resorts, but it provides accommodation, has a good beginners area with fairly basic equipment for hire and is connected by lift to El Colorado. Popular at weekends, it has several large restaurants. It offers beautiful views for 30 km across 10 Andean peaks and incredible sunsets. Daily ski-lift ticket, US$30; a combined ticket for all four resorts is also available, US$40-50 depending on season. Equipment can be rented for$US20 per day; 1-day return shuttles are available from Santiago, US$9; enquire Ski Club Chile, Goyenechea Candelaria 4750, Vitacura (north of Los Leones Golf Club), T211 7341.

El Colorado is 8 km further up Cerro Colorado and has a large ski lodge at the base, offering all facilities, and a restaurant higher up. There are nine lifts giving access to a large intermediate ski area with some steeper slopes. Lift ticket US$37. For information on the state of the pistes, T02-246 3344. **La Parva**, nearby at 2,816 m, is the upper class Santiago weekend resort with 13 lifts, 0900-1730. Accommodation is in a chalet village and there are some good bars in high season. Good intermediate to advanced skiing, not suitable for beginners. Lift ticket, US$40; equipment rental, US$15-25 depending on quality. For information on the state of the slopes, T02-220 9530.

In summer, this is a good walking area, but altitude sickness can be a problem

Valle Nevado is 16 km from Farellones and owned by Spie Batignolles of France. It offers the most modern ski facilities in Chile. There are 34 runs accessed by nine lifts. The runs are well prepared and are suitable for intermediate level and beginners. There is a ski school and heli skiing. Lift ticket US$30 weekdays, US$42 weekends.

Transport Buses from Santiago to Farellones, El Colorado, La Parva and Valle Nevado leave from in front of Omnium building, Av Apoquindo, 4 blocks from Escuela Militar Metro, daily at 0800-0830, essential to book in advance, Ski Total T246 6881, ot Buses Clarck T218 2946, US$9-11. It is easy to hitch from the junction of Av Las Condes/El Camino Farellones (petrol station in the middle), reached by a Barnechea bus.

Portillo, 2,855 m, is 145 km north of Santiago and 62 east of Los Andes near the customs post on the route to Argentina. One of Chile's best-known resorts, Portillo is on the Laguna del Inca, 5½ km long and 1½ km wide; this lake, at an altitude of 2,835 m, has no outlet, is frozen over in winter, and its depth is not known. It is surrounded on three sides by accessible mountain slopes. The runs are varied and well prepared, connected by 12 lifts, two of which open up the off-piste areas. This is an excellent family resort, with a highly regarded ski school. Cheap packages can be arranged at the beginning of and out of season. Lift ticket US$35, equipment hire US$30. There are boats for fishing in the lake (afternoon winds can make the homeward pull much longer than the outward pull). Out of season this is another good area for walking, but get detailed maps before setting out.

Lagunillas is 67 km southeast of Santiago in the Cajón del Maipo. Accommodation is in the lodges of the Club Andino de Chile (see **Skiing** above). Lift ticket US$25; long T-bar and poma lifts; easy field. Being lower than the other resorts, its season is shorter, but it is also cheaper.

Sleeping and eating Farellones B pp *Refugio Club Alemán Andino* (address under **Skiing and Climbing**, above), hospitable, good food. **AL** *Posada Farellones*, T Santiago 201 3704. And others. **El Colorado** **L** *Edificio Los Ciervos* and *Edificio Monteblanco*, in Santiago, San Antonio 486, of 151, T233 5501, F231 6965. **La Parva** **L** *Condominio Nueva Parva*, good hotel and restaurant, reservations in Santiago: Roger de Flor 2911, T212 1363, F220 8510. Three other restaurants. **Valle Nevado** Several hotels and restaurants. *Casa Valle Nevado*, Gertrudis Echeñique 441, T206 0027, F228 8888. **Portillo** **L-AL** *Hotel Portillo*, cinema, nightclub, swimming pool, sauna and medical service, on the shore of Laguna del Inca. Lakefront suites, family apartments and bunk rooms without or with bath (from **C** up), parking charges even if you go for a meal, jacket and tie obligatory in the dining room, self-service lunch, open all year. Reservations, Roger de Flor 2911, T231 3411/263 0606, F231 7164, Santiago. **AL** *Hostería Alborada*, includes all meals, tax and service. Reservations, Agencia Tour Avión, Agustinas 1062, Santiago, T726184, or C Navarro 264, San Felipe, T 101-R. Cheaper accommodation can be found in Los Andes but the road is liable to closure due to snow. **Eating at El Portillo** Cheaper than the hotels are *Restaurant La Posada* opposite *Hotel Portillo*, open evenings and weekends only. *Restaurant Los Libertadores* at the customs station 1 km away.

Chile

Chile

Transport To Portillo: Portillo is easily reached by taking any bus from Santiago or Los Andes to Mendoza; you may have to hitch back. Or try Portillo Travel, Málaga 115, of 510, T236 0806.For the resort, www.skiportillo.com **To Lagunillas**: public transport goes up to San José de Maipo, 17 km west of the resort. Bus from Metro Parque O' Higgins, Av Norte-Sur, or west side of Plaza Ercilla, every 15 mins, US$1, 2 hrs. www.skilagunillas.cl

Santiago to Argentina The route across the Andes via the Redentor tunnel is one of the major crossings to Argentina. Before travelling check on weather and road conditions beyond Los Andes. See under Santiago, International Buses. Some 77 km north of Santiago is the farming town of Los Andes. There is a monument to the Clark brothers, who built the Transandine Railway to Mendoza (now disused) and several workshops where hand-painted ceramics are made (the largest is *Cala*, Rancagua y Gen Freire). Tourist office is on the main plaza, opposite the post office. A *Baños El Corazón*, at San Esteban, 2 km north, T421371. With full board, use of swimming pool but thermal baths extra, take bus San Esteban/El Cariño (US$0.50). The bus terminal is 1 block from the plaza. To Santiago US$2.50, also to Mendoza (Argentina); any Mendoza bus will drop you off at Portillo ski resort, US$6. The road to Argentina follows the Aconcagua valley for 34 km until it reaches the village of **Río Blanco** (1,370 m). East of Río Blanco the road climbs until Juncal where it zig-zags steeply through a series of 29 hairpin bends at the top of which is Portillo. This can be reached by hourly buses to Saladillo.

Border with Argentina: Los Libertadores The old pass, with the statue of Christ the Redeemer (**Cristo Redentor**), is above the tunnel on the Argentine side. On the far side of the Andes the road descends 203 km to Mendoza. The 4 km long tunnel is open 24 hours September-May, 0700-2300 Chilean time June-August, toll US$3. The Chilean border post of Los Libertadores is at Portillo, 2 km from the tunnel. Bus and car passengers are dealt with separately. Bicycles must be taken through on a pick-up. There may be long delays during searches for ot be imported into Chile. For Argentine formalities, see page 160. A Casa de Cambio is in the customs building in Portillo.

Santiago

Valparaíso and around

Pacific beaches close to the capital include the international resort of Viña del Mar, Reñaca, Concón and several others. On the same stretch of coast are the ports of Valparaíso and San Antonio. This coastline enjoys a Mediterranean climate; the cold sea currents and coastal winds produce much more moderate temperatures than in Santiago and the central valley. Rainfall is moderate in winter and the summers are dry and sunny.

Valparaíso

Phone code: 032
Colour map 8, grid B1
Population: 290,000

Sprawling over a crescent of forty-two hills (*cerros*) that rear up from the sea, Valparaíso, the capital of V Región, is unlike any other Chilean city. The main residential areas obey little order in their layout and the *cerros* have a bohemian, slightly anarchic atmosphere. Here you will find mansions mingling with some of Chile's worst slums and many legends of ghosts and spirits. It is an important naval base and, with the new Congress building, it is also the seat of the Chilean parliament.

❝❞ *The South American Handbook 1924*

On Valparaiso ...there may continually be seen porters and carters in bare feet, the latter with spurs on the left foot; horsemen with broad-brimmed straw hats, ponchos, leather gaiters with silver fastenings, and lasso attached to the saddle; ladies in native black "mantos"; strings of carts with postilion-riders; trains of heavily-laden mules...

Inaugurated in 1542 (but not officially 'founded' until the end of the 20th century), Valparaíso became, in the colonial period, a small port used for trade with Peru. It was raided by pirates, including Sir Francis Drake, at least seven times in the colonial period. The city prospered from independence more than any other Chilean town. It was used in the 19th century by commercial agents from Europe and the United States as their trading base in the southern Pacific and became a major international banking centre as well as the key port for US shipping between the East Coast and California (especially during the gold rush) and European ships that had rounded Cape Horn. Its decline was the result of the development of steam ships which stopped instead at the coal mines around Concepción and the opening of the trans-continental railway in the United States and then the Panama Canal in 1914. It then declined further owing to the development of a container port in San Antonio, the shift of banks to Santiago and the move of the middle-classes to nearby Viña del Mar, but Valparaíso is now reviving. It is officially the Cultural Capital of Chile and much work is being done to renovate the historical centre and museums and to build new galleries. **History**

Little of the city's colonial past survived the pirates, tempests, fires and earthquakes of the period. Most of the principal buildings date from after the devastating earthquake of 1906 (further serious earthquakes occurred in July 1971 and in March 1985) though some impression of its 19th century glory can be gained from the banking area of the lower town which known as **El Plan**. This is the business centre, with once fine office buildings on narrow streets strung along the edge of the bay. Above, covering the hills ('cerros'), is a fantastic, multicoloured agglomeration of fine mansions, tattered houses and shacks, scrambled in oriental confusion along the narrow back streets. Superb views over the bay are offered from most of the 'cerros'. The lower and upper cities are connected by steep winding roads, flights of steps and 15 *ascensores* or funicular railways dating from the period 1883-1914. The most unusual of these is **Ascensor Polanco** (entrance from Calle Simpson, off Avenida Argentina, a few blocks from the bus station), which is in two parts, the first of which is a 160 m horizontal tunnel through the rock, the second a vertical lift to the summit on which there is a *mirador*. Bag-snatching is common in El Puerto and around the ascensores. One of the best ways to see the lower city is on the historic **trolley bus**, which takes a circular route from the Congress to the port (US$0.20). Some of the cars, imported from Switzerland and the US, date from the 1930s. Another good viewpoint is from top of Ascensor Barón, near the bus terminal. **Sights**

The old heart of the city is the **Plaza Sotomayor**, dominated by the former **Intendencia** (Government House), now used as the seat of the admiralty. Opposite is a fine monument to the 'Heroes of Iquique' (see page 645). Bronze plaques on the Plaza illustrate the movement of the shoreline over the centuries and an opening, protected by a glass panel, shows parts of the original quay, uncovered when a car park was being excavated. The modern passenger quay is one block away (with poor, expensive handicraft shops) and nearby is the railway station for trains to Viña del Mar and Limache – see the huge mural. The streets of El Puerto run on either side from Plaza Sotomayor. Serrano runs northwest for two blocks to the Plaza Echaurren, the oldest plaza in Valparaíso, once the height of elegance, today the home of sleeping drunks. Near it stands the low-built stucco church of **La Matriz**, built in 1842 on the site of the first church in the city. Remnants of the old colonial city can be found in the hollow known as El Puerto, grouped round La Matriz. **Museo del Mar Almirante Cochrane**, housing a collection of naval models built by local Naval Modelling Club, has good views over the port. ■ *Tue-Sun 1000-1800, free. Take Ascensor Cordillera from C Serrano, off Plaza Sotomayor, to Cerro Cordillera; at the top, Plazuela Eleuterio Ramírez, take C Merlet to the left, No 195.*

Between Plazas Echaurren and Aduana is the `barrio chino' or red light district pretty seedy at night

Further northwest, along Bustamante lies the Plaza Aduana from where Ascensor Artillería rises to the bold hill of **Cerro Artillería**, crowned by a park, the huge Naval Academy and the **Museo Naval** (naval history 1810-1880, exhibitions on Chile's two naval heroes, Lord Cochrane and Arturo Prat). ■ *Tue-Sun*

Chile

1000-1800, US$0.35. Avenida Altamirano runs along the coast at the foot of Cerro Playa Ancha to **Las Torpederas**, a popular, picturesque bathing beach. The **Faro de Punta Angeles**, on a promontory just beyond Las Torpederas, was the first lighthouse on the West Coast. ■ *Permit to go up from Edificio de la Armada on Plaza Sotomayor.*

UNESCO is considering declaring **Cerros Concepción** and **Alegre** (and the El Puerto-Matriz sector), World Heritage Sites. Both cerros have fine architecture and scenic beauty. Artists and students are being attracted to live there, lending them a slightly bohemian feel, and the cerros are becoming deservedly very popular with tourists. A signed, 2-km walk starts at the top of Ascensor Turri (Cerro Concepción), leading to Paseo Mirador Gervasoni and Calle Pupudo through a labyrinth of narrow streets and stairs (the municipal tourist office has a good map). Two museums on these hills are: **Museo Municipal de Bellas Artes**, with Chilean landscapes and seascapes and some modern paintings by Chilean and contemporary artists, housed in the impressive Palacio Baburizza, Paseo Yugoslavo, Cerro Alegre. ■ *To reopen after refurbishment end 2003. Take Ascensor El Peral from Plaza de la Justicia, off Plaza Sotomayor.* **Casa de Lukas**, Paseo Mirador Gervasoni 448, Cerro Concepción, is a beautiful villa dedicated to the work of Chile's most famous caricaturist and recommended. ■ *US$0.60. Tue-Sun, summer 1100-2200, winter 1030-1400, 1530-1830.*

Southeast of Plaza Sotomayor Calles Prat, Cochrane and Esmeralda run through the old banking and commercial centre to Plaza Aníbal Pinto, around which are several of the city's oldest bars. On Esmeralda, just past the Turri Clock Tower and Ascensor is the building of **El Mercurio de Valparaíso**, the world's

Chile

Valparaíso

Detail map
A El Puerto, Cerro Alegre & Concepción,
page 618

0 metres 200
0 yards 200

■ **Sleeping**
1 Hostal Kolping
2 Prat
3 Robinson Crusoe
4 Villa Kunterbunt

● **Eating**
1 Bambú
2 Bogarín
3 Coco Loco
4 Gioco
5 J Cruz

oldest Spanish-language newspaper still in publication, first published in 1827. Further east is the Plaza Victoria with the Cathedral. Near Plaza Victoria is the **Museo de Historia Natural** and **Galería Municipal de Arte**, both in 19th century Palacio Lyon, Condell 1546. ■ *Tue-Fri 1000-1300, 1400-1800, Sat 1000-1800, Sun 1000-1400.* Above Plaza Victoria on Cerro Bellavista is the **Museo al Cielo Abierto**, a collection of 20 street murals on the exteriors of buildings, designed by 17 of Chile's most distinguished contemporary artists. It is reached by the Ascensor Espíritu Santo at the end of Calle Huito, or by walking downhill from **Casa "La Sebastiana"**, former house of Pablo Neruda. This has interesting displays, guides in English, wonderful views and is worth a visit (see also his house at Isla Negra, below). It has an art gallery and a small café. ■ *Tue-Fri 1030-1410, 1530-1800. Sat, Sun, holidays, 1030-1800. In summer, Tue-Sun 1030-1850, US$2.50, Tue-Fri students half-price. Ferrari 692, Av Alemania, Altura 6900 on Cerro Florida, T256606. Bus O from Av Argentina, US$0.30, or colectivo from Plazuela Ecuador, US$0.60.* East of Plaza Victoria, reached by following Calle Pedro Montt is Plaza O'Higgins (antiques market on Sunday mornings – see **Shopping**), which is dominated by the huge square arch of the imposing new **Congreso Nacional**. Small boats make 30-minute tours of the harbour from near Plaza Sotomayor. ■ *US$1.50 pp, or US$15 to hire a whole boat, recommended.*

El Jardín Suizo or **Pümpin** is a botanical garden and nursery set in eight acres in the middle of Valparaíso. Beyond are hills that have been left almost entirely untouched, giving a glimpse of what Valparaíso must have looked like before the rise of the port. It's a good place for a picnic. ■ *Closed Sun and holidays. To get there, take green bus M going inland from Av Argentina.*

Chile

6 La Costeñita
7 La Otra Cocina
8 Los Porteños

9 Marco Polo
10 Pizzería Napoletana

╫╫╫╫╫╫ Funicular railways (Ascensores)

Sleeping

■ *on map*
The best option is to stay on one of the Cerros, eg Alegre or Concepción
The bus terminal area is quite rough and dirty
El Plan is noisy and not too safe at night
After dark C Chacabuco is frequented by rent boys and transvestites

Cerros Alegre and Concepción B *Brighton*, Paseo Atkinson 151, T223513, brighton-valpo@entelchile.net New building in traditional style, good views, small rooms, live tango and bolero music in the bar at weekends. **B/C** *Templeman Apartments*, Pierre Loti 65, T257067, chantalderementeria@hotmail.com Stylish self-contained apartments, peaceful. Recommended. **F** pp *Casa Aventura*, Pasaje Gálvez 11, off Calle Urriola, Cerro Concepción, T755963, casatur@ctcinternet.cl In restored traditional house, good breakfast, German and English spoken, Spanish classes offered, good value tours, informative, kitchen facilities. Highly recommended. **E** pp *Casa Latina*, Papudo 462. Bed and breakfast, comfortable. **F** pp *La Bicicleta*, Almte Montt 213. Basic, bright rooms, lovely patio, French run. **F** pp *Sr Juan Carrasco*, Abtao 668, T210737. Dingy but great views from terrace. **F** pp *Luna Sonrisa*, Templeman 833, Co Alegre, T734117, www.lunasonrisa.cl **C** with private bath, newly restored, bright, comfortable, large kitchen, patio, tours arranged, English, French spoken, good breakfast (fresh juice, wholemeal bread, real coffee etc), helpful and informative, already popular.

Other Cerros: **A** *Robinson Crusoe*, Héctor Calvo Jofre 389, Co Bellavista. T495499, robinsoncrusoeinn@hotmail.com Beautiful rooms and spectacular views, new 2002. **F** pp*Villa Kunterbunt*, Av Quebrada Verde 192, Co Playa Ancha,T288873. Lovely building, fine views from top floor, with breakfast, garden, English and German spoken. Highly recommended. Bus 1, 2, 5, 6, 17, 111, N, *colectivo* 150, 151, 3b all pass by.

El Plan A *Puerta de Alcalá*, Pirámide 524, T227478. Good standard of facilities, but restaurant has mixed reports. **C** *Prat*, Condell 1443, T253081, F213368. Comfortable, good restaurant with good value *almuerzo*. **C** *Condell*, Pasaje Pirámide, T253081. **C** *Hostal Kolping*, Valdés Vergara 622, T216306, kolpingvalparaiso@yahoo.es Without bath, pleasant, quiet, good

El Puerto, Cerros Alegre & Concepción

● Sleeping	● Eating	10 Playa
1 Brighton	1 Bar Inglés	11 Puerto Escondido
2 Casa Aventura	2 Bote Salvavidas	12 Turri
3 Juan Carrasco	3 Café Riquet	13 Valparaíso Mi Amor
4 Luna Sonrisa	4 Cinzano	
5 Puerta de Alcalá	5 Color Café	● Bars & clubs
6 Templeman	6 El Dominó	14 Axe Havana
Apartments	7 El Rincón Sueco	15 Café Vinilo
	8 La Colombina	16 Gremio
	9 Le Filou Montpelier	17 La Piedra Feliz

value. **Near the terminal E** pp *Res El Rincón Universal*, Argentina 825, T/F235184, www.elrinconuniversal.cl With breakfast, laundry, study, cable TV, internet, good, the area can be intimidating at night. **F** pp *Castillo family*,12 de Febrero 315, T220290, T09-6347239 (mob). Hot showers, good local knowledge. **F** pp *María Pizarro*, Chacabuco 2340, Casa No 2, T230791. Lovely rooms, central, quiet, kitchen. Frequently recommended. Also her neighbour, *Elena Escobar*, Chacabuco 2340, Casa No 7, T214193, same price. Recommended. **F** pp *Res Eliana*, Av Brasil 2164, T250954. Large old house, without breakfast. Recommended, slightly rough area. **F** pp *Sra Mónica Venegas*, Av Argentina 322, Casa B, T215673, 2 blocks from bus terminal. Often booked up. Recommended. **F** pp *Sra Silvia*, Pje La Quinta 70, Av Argentina, 3 blocks from Congress, T216592. Quiet, kitchen facilities. Not safest area at night.

Cerros Alegre and Concepción Expensive: *La Colombina*, Paseo Yugoeslavo 15, Cerro Alegre, T236254. Fish and seafood, good food and wines, fine views. *Turri*, Templeman 147, Cerro Concepción, T259198. Good food and service, wonderful views, lovely place. **Mid-range**: *El Rincón Sueco*, Lautaro Rosas y Templeman. Swedish, good. *Puerto Escondido*, Pasaje Gálvez. Pasta. **Cheap**: *Gloria Vuscovic*, Monte Alegre 280. Offers good set lunches in a delightful old house. *Le Filou Montpellier*, Almte Montt 382. French-run, Saturday menu deservedly popular. *Valparaíso Mi Amor*, C Papudo. Chilean.

Other Cerros Expensive: *Gato Tuerto*, in Fundación Valparaíso building, Calvo 205, Co Bellavista. Thai and oriental food. *Porto Fino*, Bellamar 301, Co Esperanza, T669939. Great views, best restaurant in Valparaíso.

El Plan Expensive: *Bote Salvavidas*, by Muelle Prat. Elegant fish restaurant. *Coco Loco*, Blanco 1781 pisos 21 y 22, T227614. Plush revolving restaurant 70 m above the bay. **Mid-range**: *Bar Inglés*, Cochrane 851 (entrance also on Blanco Encalada). Historic bar dating from the early 1900s, a chart shows the ships due in port. Good food and drink. Recommended. *Cinzano*, Plaza Aníbal Pinto 1182. The oldest bar in Valparaíso, also serving food. Flamboyant live music at weekends, noted for tango (no dancing by guests allowed). Service can be awful. *J Cruz*, Condell 1466. Valparaíso's most traditional restaurant/museum, famous for its *chorillana*, open all night, very popular. *La Costeñita*, Blanco 86. Good seafood, kitsch décor. *La Otra Cocina*, Yungay near Francia. Good seafood. *Los Porteños*, Valdivia 169 and Cochrane 102, perennial favourite for fish and shellfish, terse service but good food. *Pizzería Napoletana*, Pedro Montt 2935, in front of Congress. Good, try the vegetarian pizza. At Caleta Membrillo, 2 km northwest of Plaza Sotomayor (take any Playa Ancha bus), there are several good fish restaurants including *Club Social de Pescadores*, Altamirano 1480, good, and *El Membrillo*. **Cheap**: *Ave Cesár*, P Montt 1776. Fast food, good. *Bambú*, Pudeto 450, Mon-Sat 1000-1800, vegetarian. *El Dominó*, Cumming 67. Traditional, serves *empanadas*, *chorillanas* etc. *Gioco*, Molina 586-B. Vegetarian set lunches with fruit juices. *La Puerta del Sol*, Montt 2033. Traditional Chilean dishes, great chips served outside.*Marco Polo*, Pedro Montt 2199. Delicious cakes, good Italian, good value *almuerzo*. *Sancho Panza*, Yungay 2250. Local specialities, popular. There are many supercheap restaurants on Pedro Montt and behind the bus station. Also on the second floor of the market (off Plaza Echaurren), where the portions are large (closed in the evenings). In the market, *Calagualá* restaurant is a cut above the rest. *Empanadas Famosas's de Adali*, S Donoso 1379-81. Best *empanadas* in Valparaíso.

Cafés Cerros Alegre and Concepción *Color Café*, Papudo 526, Co Concepción. Cosy arty café with a wide selection of teas and real coffee, fresh juice, good cakes, snacks and all-day breakfasts, regular live music, art exhibits, local art and craft for sale. *Pan de Magia*, Almte Montt 738 y Templemann, Co Alegre. Artesanal bakery selling cakes, cookies, and by far the best wholemeal bread in town. *Lavanda Café*, Almte Montt 454. Enjoy an expresso while having your clothes washed! Several café/bars (see below). **El Plan** *Bogarín*, Plaza Victoria. Great juices, sandwiches. *Café do Brasil*, Condell 1342. Excellent coffee, juices, sandwiches. *Chocolata*, Esmeralda. Good coffee and cakes. *Hespería*, Victoria 2250. Classic old-time coffee emporium, the internet annex makes a strange contrast. *Riquet*, Plaza Aníbal Pinto. Comfortable, expensive, good coffee and breakfast. Recommended.

Bars Cerros Alegre and Concepción *Brighton* (see Sleeping). Great views at night. *Café Vinilo*, Almte Montt 450. Lively café with international feel, art displays, good place to meet people. *Gremio*, Pasaje Gálvez, off C Papudo. Ultra modern café/bar. As a general rule

Eating
● *on map*
Many restaurants are closed Sun evening

Chile

there are 3 main sectors for nightlife in **El Plan**: **Errázuriz** is for live music/dancing, mixed crowd, slightly more classy than the rest; **between Plaza Sotomayor and Plaza Echauren** are young/studenty pubs, some with live music; and **Subida Ecuador** is loud and lairy, full of boozed-up young lads (single women beware!). *La Piedra Feliz*, Errázuriz 1054. Every type of music depending on the evening, large pub, live music area, and dance floor, entrance US$5. *Axe Havana*, next door. Salsa and Cuban music. *Bar Playa*, Cochrane, by Plaza Sotomayor. Old English-style bar, live music, student crowd. C Ecuador has dozens of bars, of varying quality, *El Coyote Quemado* is probably the most civilized; some can be rough, eg *El Muro*.

Festivals   **New Year** is celebrated by a spectacular firework display launched from the harbour and naval ships, which is best seen from the Cerros. The display is televised nationally and about a million visitors come to the city at this time. Book well in advance; accommodation doubles or trebles in price for the night, but it's well worth it: dinner with a view US$50-170).

Shopping   **Bookshop**: *CHAOS*, on Pedro Montt by the bus terminal. Excellent new and second-hand bookshop. *Librería Ivens*, on Plaza Aníbal Pinto. Good general bookshop. Many others. **Market**: Large antiques market on Plaza O'Higgins every Sun. Very good selection, especially old shipping items. Along Av Argentina there is a huge, colourful fruit and vegetable market on Wed and Sat and a crowded flea market on Sun. Good locally made handicrafts on Cerros Alegre and Concepción. **Department stores**: *Ripley* and *Falabella*, both on Plaza Victoria.

Transport   **Local Buses**: US$0.25 within El Plan, US$0.35 to Cerros, US$0.45 to Viña del Mar from C

Green bus 'Verde Mar' (O) from Av Argentina near the bus terminal to Plaza Aduana gives fine panoramic views of the city and bay

Errázuriz. **Ascensores**: US$0.10-0.20, slightly more expensive going up than down. **Taxis**: are more expensive than Santiago: a short run under 1 km costs US$1. Taxi colectivos, slightly more expensive than buses, carry sign on roof indicating route, very convenient.

Long distance Buses: Terminal is on Pedro Montt 2800 block, corner of Rawson, 1 block from Av Argentina; plenty of buses between terminal and Plaza Sotomayor. To **Santiago**, 1½ hrs, US$3-4, shop around, frequent (book on Sat to return to the capital on Sun). To **Concepción**, 11 hrs, US$12. To **Puerto Montt**, 17 hrs, US$18. To **La Serena**, 7 hrs, US$10. To **Calama**, US$35. To **Arica**, US$40, *Fénix salón cama* service, US$50. To Argentina: to **Mendoza** 4 companies, 6-7 hrs, US$15-30.

Trains: Regular service on Merval, the Valparaíso metropolitan line between Valparaíso, **Viña del Mar** (US$0.35-0.40), **Quilpué** and **Limache** (US$0.60-0.75); to Viña del Mar every 30 mins. Trains are 70 years old, made by FIAT, but are being replaced by a new fleet. Work on a new tunnel through Viña means slight delays (2003).

Directory   **Airline offices** LanChile, Esmeralda 1048, T251441. **Banks** Banks open 0900 to 1400, but closed on Sat. Many *Redbanc* ATMs on Blanco and Prat, and also one in the bus terminal. *Casas de Cambio*: Many on Esmeralda; also *Exprinter*, Prat 887 (the building with the clocktower at junction with Cochrane). Good rates, no commission on TCs, open Mon-Fri 0930-1400, 1600-1830. *New York*, Prat 659. Best rates for US$ cash on 3rd floor of stock exchange, Urriola y Prat. **Communications** Internet: average price US$1 per hr. Many places in El Plan. *@rob' Art Café*, Edwards 625, cheaper for students. *Café Bell@vista*, Bellavista 463, loc 201. *Internet*, Carampangue y Blanco. *Prat*, Condell 1443, of 24. Post office: Pedro Montt entre San Ignacio y Bolívar. Also above *Café Riquet* in Plaza Aníbal Pinto. **Telephone:** Lots of cheap call centres in El Plan, shop around. **Cultural centres** Instituto Chileno-Norteamericano, Esmeralda 1069. Library, free internet for members, regular cinema nights. **Embassies and consulates** Argentina, Blanco 890, of 204, T213691. Germany, Blanco 1215, of 1102, T256749. Peru, Errázuriz 1178, of 71, T253403. Spain, Brasil 1589, p 2, T214466. Sweden, Casilla 416-V, T256507. UK, Blanco 1190, p 5, T/F213063. **Tourist offices** In the Municipalidad building, Condell 1490, Oficina 102. Mon-Fri 0830-1400, 1530-1730. Municipal Tourist kiosk at bus terminal to the left of the public toilets (good map available), helpful. 0900-1300, 1530-1930 (closed Thu, Mar-Nov). At Muelle Prat, Nov-Mar 1030-1430, 1600-2000. **Note**: there is a well-displayed private kiosk at the bus terminal which gives details on, and transport to, selected hotels. If you want impartial advice, go to the municiapl kiosk.

Parque   This 8,000-ha park includes Cerro La Campana (1,828 m) which Darwin climbed in
Nacional La   1836 and Cerro El Roble (2,200 m). Some of the best views in Chile can be seen from
Campana   the top. Near Ocoa there are areas of Chilean palms (*kankán* – which give edible,

Chile

walnut-sized coconuts in March-April), now found in its natural state in only two locations in Chile. ■ *US$2. There are 3 entrances: at Granizos (from which the hill is climbed), reached by paved road from Olmué, 5 km east; at Cajón Grande (with natural bathing pools), reached by unpaved road which turns off the Olmué-Granizos road; at Palmar de Ocoa to the north reached by unpaved road (10 km) leading off the Pan-American Highway at Km 100 between Hijuelas and Llaillay. Euro Express micros from C Errázuriz in Valparaíso and 1 Norte in Viña del Mar go to within 1 km of Granizos and Cajón Grande, US$1, 1½ hrs, or take the train to Limache, and a micro from there to Ocoa, no transport from there. Get a taxi or colectivo from La Calera.*

Viña del Mar

Northeast of Valparaíso via Avenida España which runs along a narrow belt between the shore and precipitous cliffs is one of South America's leading seaside resorts. The older part is situated on the banks of a lagoon, the Marga Marga, which is crossed by bridges. Around Plaza Vergara and the smaller Plaza Sucre to its south are the **Teatro Municipal** (1930) and the exclusive **Club de Viña**, built in 1910. The municipally owned **Quinta Vergara**, formerly the residence of the shipping entrepreneur Francisco Alvarez, lies two blocks south. The **Palacio Vergara**, in the gardens, houses the **Museo de Bellas Artes** and the Academia de Bellas Artes ■ *Museum hours Tue-Sun 1000-1400, 1500-1800, US$0.50, T680618.* Part of the grounds is a playground, and there is an outdoor auditorium where concerts are performed in the summer, and in February an international song festival, one of the premier music events is held. (Tickets from the Municipal theatre, or *Ticketmaster.*) El Roto festival is on 20 January, in homage to the workers and peasants of Chile.

On a headland overlooking the sea is **Cerro Castillo**, the summer palace of the President of the Republic; its gardens can be visited. Just north, on the other side of

Phone code: 032
Colour map 8, grid B1
Population: 304,203

Chile

Viña del Mar

Not to scale

■ Sleeping		● Eating	
1 Andalué	5 Res Remanso	1 Africa	5 Casino Chico
2 Caribe	6 Res Tajamar	2 Alster	6 El Encuentro
3 Offenbacher Hof	7 Res Villarrica	3 Armandita	7 Samoiedo
4 Res Capric	8 San Martín	4 Cap Ducal	

the lagoon is the **Casino**, built in the 1930s and set in beautiful gardens, US$5 to enter, jacket and tie for men required (open all year). It now includes a new 5-star hotel, **LL-L** *Hotel Casino de Viña*.

The main beaches, Acapulco and Mirasol are located to the north, but south of Cerro Castillo is Caleta Abarca, also popular. One of the most popular places in town is **La Grúa**, a converted cargo crane on the beach (you can't miss it), now full of bars and clubs. At sunset it gives beautiful views of Valparaíso. The coastal route north to Reñaca provides lovely views over the sea. East of the centre is the **Valparaíso Sporting Club** with a racecourse (meetings every Friday) and playing fields. North of here in the hills are the Granadilla Golf Club and a large artificial lake, the **Laguna Sausalito**, adjacent to which is the Estadio Sausalito (home to Everton soccer team, among many other sporting facilities). It possesses an excellent tourist complex with swimming pools, boating, tennis courts, sandy beaches, water skiing, restaurants, etc. ■ *US$2.50, children under 11, US$1.75. Take colectivo No 19 from C Viana.*

Museo de la Cultura del Mar, in the Castillo Wolff, on the coast near Cerro Castillo, contains a collection on the life and work of the novelist and maritime historian, Salvador Reyes. ■ *Tue-Sat 1000-1300, 1430-1800, Sun 1000-1400, T625427.* **Palacio Rioja**, Quillota 214, was built in 1906 by a prominent local family and now used for official municipal receptions, ground floor preserved in its original state. ■ *Tue-Sun, open to visitors 1000-1400, 1500-1730, US$0.40. Recommended.* **Museo Sociedad Fonk**, C 4 Norte 784, is an archaeological museum, with objects from Easter Island and the Chilean mainland, including Mapuche silver. ■ *Tue-Fri 1000-1800, Sat-Sun 1000-1400, US$1. Recommended.*

The **Jardín Botánico Nacional**, formerly the estate of the nitrate baron Pascual Baburizza, now administered by Conaf, lies 8 km southeast of the city. Covering 405 ha, it contains over 3,000 species from all over the world and a collection of Chilean cacti, but the species are not labelled. ■ *US$1. Take bus 20 from Plaza Vergara.*

Sleeping
■ *on map*
There are many more places to stay including private accommodation (E-F pp; ask at tourist office). Out of season agencies rent furnished apartments. In season it's cheaper to stay in Valparaíso. Av Valparaíso, especially near Von Schroeders, is unsafe at night

Many in **L-A** range, some with beach. **L-AL** *Gala*, Arlegui 273, loc 10, T686688, galahotel@ webhost.cl All mod-cons. **AL** *Alcázar*, Alvarez 646, T685112, hotelalcazar@ chile.ia.cl 4-star, good restaurant. **AL** *Cap Ducal*, Marina 51, T626655, F665471. Old mansion charm, restaurant. **A** *Genross*, Paseo Monterrey 18, T661711, genrosshotel@hotmail.com Beautiful mansion, airy rooms, garden patio and sitting room, informative, English spoken. **B** *Andalué*, 6 Poniente 124, T684147, F684148. With breakfast, central. Recommended. **B** *Hoffenbacher Hof*, Balmaceda 102, T621483, F662432. **B** *Quinta Vergara*, Errázuriz 690, T685073, hotelquinta@hotmail.com Large rooms, beautiful gardens. **C-D** *Res Capric*, von Schroeders 39, T978295. Dark rooms, with breakfast (special rates for HI card holders). **C-D** *Res Victoria*, Valparaíso 40, T977370. Without bath, with breakfast, central. **D** pp *Julia Toro Córtez*, Toro Herrera 273, T621083, T09-885 8307 (mob), julia_toro_cortez@hotmail.com Family house, breakfast included. **D** *Res de Casia*, von Schroeders 151, T971861. Safe. **D** *Res Tajamar*, Alvarez 884, T882134, opposite railway station. Central. **D** *Res Villarica*, Arlegui 172, T881484, F942807. Shared bath, good. **F** pp *Res Blanchart*, Valparaíso 82, T974949. With breakfast, good service. **Youth hostels** **F** pp *Asturias*, Valparaíso 299. Has double rooms with bath, internet. See also *Res Capric* above.

Eating
■ *on map*
Many good bars and restaurants on and around San Martín between 2 and 8 Norte Cheap bars and restaurants around Calle Valparaíso and Von Schroeders. Not too safe at night

Expensive: *Alster*, Valparaíso 225. Smart. *Flavia*, 6 Poniente 121, good Italian food, service, desserts and wine selection. **Mid-range**: *Africa*, Valparaíso 324. Extraordinary façade, very good, has vegetarian. Next door is *Tropical*, fresh juices, sandwiches, vegetarian food. *Armandita*, San Martín 501. *Parrilla*, large portions, good service. *El Encuentro*, San Martín y 6 Norte. Fish, very good. *Kumei*, Valparaíso entre Von Schroeders y Ecuador. Good set lunches, wide selection. *Machitún Ruca*, San Martín 529. Excellent. *Pizzería Mama Mía*, San Martín 435. Good. *Raul*, Valparaíso 533. Live music. *Samoiedo*, Valparaíso 637, Confitería, grill and restaurant. **Cheap**: *Café Big Ben*, Valparaíso 469. Good coffee, good food. *Café Journal*, Alvarez near Von Schroeders. Great set lunch, good beer, student favourite at night. Recommended. *Casino Chico*, Valparaíso y von Schroeders. Fish, seafood.

Bars: *Barlovento*, 2 Norte y 5 Poniente. *The* designer bar in Viña, on 3 floors with a lovely roof terrace, serves great pizzas.

Buses Terminal at Av Valparaíso y Quilpué. To **Santiago**, US$3, 2 hrs, frequent, many companies, heavily booked in advance for travel on Sun afternoons, at other times some buses pick up passengers opposite the train station. To **La Serena**, 6 daily, 8 hrs, US$10. To **Antofagasta**, 20 hrs, US$35. **Trains** Services on the Valparaíso Metropolitan line (Merval) stop at Viña (details under Valparaíso). Trains will be disrupted by works on the line until 2005 or so.

Transport
Beware pickpockets around shops in the terminal

Banks Many *Redbanc* ATMs on Libertad near 7 y 8 Norte; also on C Valparaíso (but this is not a safe area at night). Many *casas de cambio* on Arlegui. **Communications** Internet: *Etnia Com*, Valparaíso 323, T711841. Inexpensive. *Rue Valparaíso*, Valparaíso 286, T/F710140, www.multimania.com/ruevalparaiso Cybercafé with net phone. **Telephone:** *CTC*, Valparaíso 628. *Global Telecommunications/Entel*, 15 Norte 961. **Cultural centres** *Centro Cultural*, Libertad 250, holds regular exhibitions. **Tourist offices** *Sernatur*, Valparaíso 507, of 303, T882285. Municipal office on Plaza Vergara.

Directory

North of Viña del Mar the coast road runs through Las Salinas, a popular beach between two towering crags, Reñaca (long beach, upmarket, good restaurants) and Cochoa, where there is a sealion colony 100 m offshore, to Concón (18 km). There is a much faster inland road, between Viña del Mar and **Concón**, on the southern shore of a bay at the mouth of the Río Aconcagua. It has six beaches and is famous for its seafood restaurants. Horses can be hired here. **Quintero** (*Population*: 16,000) 23 km north of Concón, is a fishing town situated on a rocky peninsula with lots of small beaches (hotels and *residenciales*).

Resorts north of Viña del Mar

    Horcón (also known locally as Horcones) is set back in a cove surrounded by cliffs, a pleasant small village, mainly of wooden houses. On the beach young travellers sell cheap and unusual jewellery and trinkets, while horses drag the small fishing boats out of the sea. Vegetation is tropical with many cacti on the cliff tops. Packed out in January-February, the rest of the year it is a charming place, populated by fishermen and artists. A new condominium by Caucau beach is set to change the atmosphere of the town. Further north is well-to-do **Maitencillo** (*Population*: 1,200), with a wonderful long beach and 14 km beyond is **Zapallar** (*Population*: 2,200) a fashionable resort. A hint of its former glory is given by a number of fine mansions along Avenida Zapallar. At Cachagua, 3 km south, a colony of penguins may be viewed from the northern end of the beach. **Papudo** (*Phone code*: 033 *Population*: 2,500), 10 km further north, was the site of a naval battle in November 1865 in which the Chilean vessel *Esmeralda* captured the Spanish ship *Covadonga*. Following the arrival of the railway Papudo rivalled Viña del Mar as a fashionable resort in the 1920s but it has long since declined. With its lovely beach and fishing port, it is an idyllic spot.

Beware if cycling from Valparaíso, the road is very bad with lots of traffic

Sleeping and eating Concón A *Hostería Edelweiss*, Borgoño 19200, T811040, F903666. Modern cabins, comfortable, sea views, includes breakfast, excellent food in attached restaurant, German spoken. Highly recommended. Several other *cabañas* and motels. Good seafood *empanadas* at bars. Excellent seafood restaurants at Caleta Higuerilla, Av Borgoño, and at La Boca; cheaper *picadas* in Alto Higuerillas. **Horcón C** *Arancibia*, **E** without bath, T796169, pleasant gardens, good food. **E** *Juan Esteban*, Pasaje Miramar, Casa 2, T796056, www.geocities.com/jestebanc Also **F** pp, English, Portuguese, Italian spoken, nice terrace with view, fully equipped cabañas, **B** for 4 people. Recommended. Lots of *cabañas* in Horcón, generally **B-C** for 4 people, shop around. *El Ancla*, *cabañas* and restaurant. Recommended. *El Roti Schop*. Famous for its excellent *empanadas*. **Papudo B** *Carande*, Chorrillos 89, T791105. Best, quiet. **B** *De Peppino*, Concha 609, T791108. Many more. *La Maison des Fous*, Blanco 151, restaurant/piano bar, unusual, good food. **C** *Moderno*, Concha 150, T711496.

Transport Buses from Valparaíso and Viña del Mar: To **Concón** several, eg bus 1, 111 or 10 (from Av Libertad in Viña, or Errázuriz in Valparaíso), US$0.50; to **Quintero** and **Horcón**, *Sol del Pacífico*, every 30 mins, US$1, 2 hrs; to **Zapallar** and **Papudo**, *Sol del Pacífico*, 4 a day (2 before 0800, 2 after 1600), US$3.

Chile

Chile

Resorts south near the mouth of the Río Maipo

San Antonio is a commercial centre for this part of the coast. It is a container and fishing port and is the terminal for the export of copper brought by rail from El Teniente mine, near Rancagua. To the south are the resorts of Llolleo and Rocas de Santo Domingo. **Cartagena**, 8 km north of San Antonio, is the biggest resort on this part of the coast. The centre is around the hilltop Plaza de Armas. To the south is the picturesque Playa Chica, overlooked by many of the older hotels and restaurants; to the north is the Playa Larga. Between the two a promenade runs below the cliffs; high above hang old houses, some in disrepair but offering spectacular views. Cartagena is very popular in summer, but out of season it is a good centre for visiting nearby resorts of Las Cruces, El Tabo and El Quisco. There are many hotels and bus connections are good. For more information on Cartagena, look at www.cartagena-chile.cl

North of Cartagena in the village of **Isla Negra** is the beautifully-restored **Museo-Casa Pablo Neruda**. Bought by Neruda in 1939, this house, overlooking the sea, was his writing retreat in his later years. It contains artefacts gathered by Neruda from all over the world. Neruda and his last wife, Mathilde, are buried here; the touching gravestone is beside the house. ■ *T035-461284 for opening hrs or to book English guide (see also his house, La Chascona, under Santiago Sights, and La Sebastiana, under Valparaíso Sights), US$4. It is open for guided tours in Spanish, English or French (last 2 only after 1500), Tue-Sun 1000-2000 in summer, rest of year Tue-Fri 1000-1400, 1500-1800. It has a good café specializing in Neruda's own recipes. Tours from Santiago, departing at 0900 from Plaza de Armas (Compañía y Ahumada), US$20 and include seaside resorts, T232 2574.*

Sleeping San Antonio A *Rocas de Santo Domingo*, La Ronda 130, T444356, F444494. Generally good, including breakfast, but staff unfriendly, restaurant, 20 minutes to sea. **Cartagena D** *Violeta*, Condell 140, T450372. Swimming pool, good views. **F** pp *Res Carmona*, Playa Chica, T450485. Small rooms, basic, good value. **F** pp *Residencial Paty's*, Alacalde Cartagena 295, T450569. Nice spot, good value. **Isla Negra F** pp *Hostal Casa Azul*, Av Santa Luisa s/n, T035-461154. Shared bath, hot showers, garden, kitchen and laundry facilities, breakfast included, helpful. Highly recommended

Transport From San Antonio: buses to Valparaíso, *Pullman Bus*, every 45 mins until 2000, US$2; to Santiago, Pullman Bus, every 10 mins, 0600-2200, US$2. **Isla Negra** Pullman *or* Bahía Azul *bus from Santiago, 1½ hrs, US$2.80, from Valparaíso 1 hr, US$2.50.*

Santiago

North of Santiago

Along the coast is a string of fishing villages, deserted beaches and resorts, while inland the scenery is wonderfully dramatic. The land becomes less fertile as you go further north. The largest resort is La Serena, from where access can be made to the pisco-producing Elqui Valley and to one of the world's major astronomical centres.

From the Río Aconcagua to the Río Elqui is a transitional zone between the fertile heartland and the northern deserts. The first stretch of the Pan-American Highway from Santiago is inland through green valleys with rich blue clover and wild artichokes. North of La Ligua, the Highway mainly follows the coastline, passing many beautiful coves, alternately rocky and sandy, with good surf, though the water is very cold. The valleys of the main rivers, the Choapa, Limarí and Elqui, are intensively farmed using irrigation to produce fruit and vegetables. There is a striking contrast between these lush valley floors and the arid mountains with their dry scrub and cactus. In some areas, condensation off the sea provides sufficient moisture for woods to grow. Rainfall is rare and occurs only in winter. On the coast the average temperature is 15° C in winter, 23° in summer; the interior is dry, with temperatures reaching 33° in summer, but it is cooler in winter and very cold at night.

Ovalle and around

This town lies inland in the valley of the Río Limarí, a fruit-growing and mining district. Market days are Monday, Wednesday, Friday and Saturday, till 1600; the market (*feria modelo*) is off Benavente (east of the centre). The town is famous for its *talabarterías* (saddleries), products made of locally mined lapis lazuli, goats cheese and dried fruits. **Museo del Limarí**, in the old railway station, Covarrubias y Antofagasta, has displays of petroglyphs and a good collection of Diaguita ceramics and other artefacts. ■ *Tue-Fri 0900-1300, 1500-1900, Sat-Sun 1000-1300, US$1, free on Sun.* Unofficial tourist information kiosk on the Plaza de Armas.

Phone code: 053
Colour map 8, grid A1
Population: 53,000
Altitude: 200 m
412 km N of Santiago

The **Monumento Nacional Valle del Encanto**, about 22 km southwest of Ovalle, is a most important archaeological site. Artefacts from hunting peoples from over 2,000 years ago have been found but the most visible remains date from the Molle culture (AD 700). There are over 30 petroglyphs as well as great boulders, distributed in six sites. Camping facilities. ■ *0800-1800, US$0.50. Getting there: no local bus service; you must take a southbound long distance bus and ask to be dropped off – 5 km walk to the valley; flag down a bus to return. Alternatively, use a tour operator like Tres Valles, Libertad 496, T629650.***Termas de Socos**, 35 km southwest of Ovalle on the Pan-American Highway, has a swimming pool and individual tubs fed by thermal springs, as well as sauna, jacuzzi and water massage (entrance US$5, very popular). It also boasts a reasonable hotel (**L**, T 02-681692, Casilla 323, full board) and a campsite (**F** per tent, but bargain) nearby. ■ *Bus US$2.* **Monumento Nacional Pichasca**, 47 km northeast of Ovalle, is reached by an unpaved and largely winding road. It contains petrified tree trunks, archaeological remains, including a vast cave with vestiges of ancient roof paintings, and views of rock formations on the surrounding mountains. ■ *0800-1800, US$2.20. Daily buses from Ovalle to San Pedro pass the turn off about 42 km from the city. From here it is 3 km to the park and about 2 km more to sites of interest.*

Parque Nacional Fray Jorge, 90 km west of Ovalle and 110 km south of La Serena at the mouth of the Río Limarí, the Park is reached by a dirt road leading off the Pan-American Highway. It contains original forests which contrast with the otherwise barren surroundings. Receiving no more than 113 mm of rain a year, the forests survive because of the almost constant covering of fog. ■ *Sat, Sun and public holidays only, entry 0900-1600, last departure 1800, US$2.50. Visits closely controlled owing to risk of fire.* Two campsites, one in the desert and one at the admin area, both with hot showers; also rooms available at an old hacienda, **F** pp, and a *cabaña*, **B**. Camping costs US$16 pp including park entry. Waterproof clothing essential. ■ *Round trip in taxi from Ovalle, US$30, Abel Olivares Rivera, T Ovalle 620352, recommended.*

B *Gran Hotel*, Vicuña Mackenna 210 (entrance through Galería Yagnam), T621084, yagnam@terra.cl Decent rooms, negotiate. **B** *Turismo*, Victorio 295, T623258, F623536. Parking, modern, overpriced. **D** *Roxy*, Libertad 155, T620080. Constant hot water, big rooms, patio, slightly rundown. Recommended. **F** pp *Res Socos*, Socos 22, T629856. Breakfast extra, lots of other extras. **F** pp *Venecia*, Libertad 261, T09-7635928 (mob). Safe. Recommended. *Bavaria*, V MacKenna 161. Maindishes and sandwiches, overpriced. *Club Social Arabe*, Arauco 255. Spacious glass-domed premises, limited selection of Arab dishes, not cheap. *La Bocca*, Benavente 110. Specializes in shellfish. *Club Comercial*, Aguirre 244 (on plaza), open Sun. *El Quijote*, Arauco 294. Good seafood, inexpensive. Good value *almuerzos* at *Casino La Bomba*, Aguirre 364, run by fire brigade. *Yum Yum*, V MacKenna 21. Good, cheap, lively.

Sleeping & eating

Ovalle has 3 bus terminals, 2 rural and 1 long distance. Buses to Santiago, several, 6½ hrs, US$7; to Valparaíso, 6 hrs, US$8; to La Serena, 20 a day, 1¼ hrs, US$2.50; to Antofagasta, 14 hrs, US$16; to Arica, 24 hrs, US$21.

Transport

The good inland road between Ovalle and La Serena makes an interesting contrast to Ruta 5 (Panamericana), with a fine pass and occasional views of the Andes across cacti-covered plains and semi-desert mountain ranges. North of Ovalle 61 km a side

There are no hotels, but some pensiones

Chile

road runs 44 km southeast (last 20 km very bad) to **Andacollo** (*Population*: 10,216. *Altitude*: 1,050 m). This old town, in an area of alluvial gold washing and manganese and copper mining, is one of the great pilgrimage sites in Chile. In the enormous **Basilica** (1893), 45 m high and with a capacity of 10,000, is the Virgen del Rosario de Andacollo. The Fiesta Grande from 23-27 December attracts 150,000 pilgrims. The ritual dances date from a pre-Spanish past. Colectivos run to the festival from Benavente, near Colocolo, in La Serena, but 'purists' walk (torch and good walking shoes essential). There is also a smaller festival, the Fiesta Chica on the first Sunday of October. *Colectivo* to Ovalle, US$2; bus, US$1.40. The tourist office on the Plaza arranges tours to the Basilica and to mining operations.

Coquimbo

Phone code: 051
Colour map 8, grid A1
Population: 106,000
84 km N of Ovalle
A tourist kiosk in Plaza de Armas is open in the summer only

On the same bay as La Serena is this important port, with one of the best harbours on the coast and major fish-processing plants. The city is strung along the north shore of a peninsula. On the south shore lies the suburb of Guayacán, with an iron-ore loading port, a steel church designed by Eiffel, an English cemetery and a 83-m high cross to mark the Millennium (US$1.50 to climb it). In 1981 heavy rain uncovered 39 ancient burials of humans and llamas which had been sacrificed; they are exhibited in a small museum in the Plaza Gabriela Mistral. Tours of nearby islands with sealions go from beside the fish market, can be cold and rough but boats have blankets and life vests (US$2). Nearby is **La Herradura**, 2½ km from Coquimbo, slightly more upmarket and with the best beaches. Resorts further south, Totoralillo (12 km), Guanaqueros (37 km) and Tongoy (50 km), have good beaches and can be reached by rural buses or colectivos.

Generally accommodation is much cheaper than in La Serena and the seafood is better

Sleeping and eating D *Iberia*, Lastra 400, T312141. Recommended. D *Prat*, Bilbao y Aldunate, T311845. Comfortable, pleasant. E *Vegamar*, Las Heras 403, T311773. Several hotels in La Herradura. **Camping** *Camping La Herradura*, T263867, mac-food@ ctcinternet.cl F for up to 5 people. Recommended restaurants: *Sal y Pimienta del Capitán Denny*, Aldunate 769, one of the best, pleasant, old fashioned. *La Picada*, Costanera near statue of O'Higgins. Good *pebre*. *Mai Lai Fan*, Av Ossandón 1. Good Chinese. *La Bahía*, Pinto 1465. Good value. *La Barca*, Ríos y Varela. Modest. *La Bahía*, Pinto 1465. Good value.

Festivals Coquimbo hosts *La Pampilla*, by far the biggest independence day celebrations in Chile. Between 200-300,000 people come from all over the country for the fiesta, which lasts for a week from **14-21 Sep**. It costs a nominal US$1.50 to enter the main dancing area (*peñas* cost extra); plenty of typical Chilean food and drink.

Transport Bus terminal at Varela y Garriga. To **La Serena**, US$0.30.

La Serena

Phone code: 051
Colour map 8, grid A1
Population: 120,000
473 km N of Santiago

La Serena, built on a hillside 2 km inland from Bahía de Coquimbo, is an attractive city and tourist centre, 11 km north of Coquimbo and is the capital of IV Región (Coquimbo). The city was founded by Juan de Bohón, aide to Pedro de Valdivia, in 1544, destroyed by Diaguita Indians in 1546 and rebuilt by Francisco de Aguirre in 1549. The city was sacked by the English pirate Sharpe in 1680. In the colonial period the city was the main staging-post on the route north to Peru. In the 19th century the city grew prosperous from copper-mining. While retaining colonial architecture and churches, the present-day layout and style have their origins in the 'Plan Serena' drawn up in 1948 on the orders of Gabriel González Videla, a native of the city.

Sights

There are 29 other churches, several of which have unusual towers

Around the attractive Plaza de Armas are most of the official buildings, including the Post Office, the **Cathedral** (built in 1844 and featuring a carillon which plays every hour) and the **Museo Histórico Casa González Videla**, which includes several rooms on the man's life. ■ *Tue-Sat 0900-1300, 1600-1900, Sun 1000-1300, US$0.80.* Ticket also valid for **Museo Arqueológico**, Cordovez y Cienfuegos, outstanding collection of Diaguita and Molle Indian exhibits, especially of attractively decorated pottery, also Easter Island exhibits. ■ *Tue-Sat 0900-1300, 1600-1900, Sun 1000-1300, US$0.80*. **La Recova**, the craft market, at Cienfuegos y Cantournet, includes a large display of handicrafts and, upstairs, several good restaurants. One block west of the Plaza de Armas is the **Parque Pedro de Valdivia**, near which is the delightful Parque Japonés, "El Jardín del Corazón". ■ *Daily 1000-2000, US$1.25*.

Avenida Francisco de Aguirre, a pleasant boulevard lined with statues and known as the **Alameda**, runs from the centre to the coast, terminating at the **Faro Monumental**, a small, neo-colonial mock-castle and lighthouse, now a pub. ■ *US$0.45*. A series of beaches stretch from here to Peñuelas, 6 km south, linked by the Av del Mar. Many apartment blocks, hotels, *cabañas* and restaurants have been built along this part of the bay. Most activity is around the middle of the beach, where swimming is safest. If you don't like crowds, head for the northern or southern extremes.

There are no buses along Av del Mar, but it is only ½ km off Route 5. The tourist office in the bus terminal has accommodation information, helpful. Do not be pressurised at the bus station into choosing rooms. There is much more choice than touts would have you believe. **A** *Pucará*, Balmaceda 319, T211966, F211933. With breakfast, modern, helpful, quiet. **A** *Francisco de Aguirre*, Córdovez 210, T222991, www.chile-hotels.com/faguirre With breakfast, good rooms, reasonable restaurant. **A** *Mediterráneo*, Cienfuegos 509, Casilla 212, T/F225837.

Sleeping
■ *on map*
Route 5 from La Serena to Coquimbo is lined with cheap accommodation

Chile

La Serena

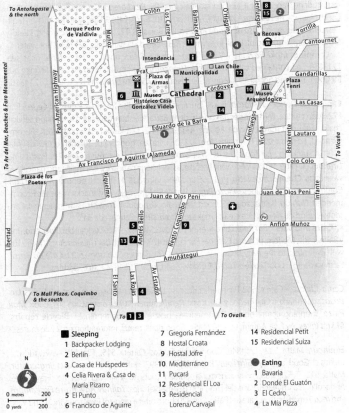

■ **Sleeping**
1 Backpacker Lodging
2 Berlín
3 Casa de Huéspedes
4 Celia Rivera & Casa de María Pizarro
5 El Punto
6 Francisco de Aguirre

7 Gregoria Fernández
8 Hostal Croata
9 Hostal Jofre
10 Mediterráneo
11 Pucará
12 Residencial El Loa
13 Residencial Lorena/Carvajal

14 Residencial Petit
15 Residencial Suiza

● **Eating**
1 Bavaria
2 Donde El Guatón
3 El Cedro
4 La Mía Pizza

0 metres 200
0 yards 200

Includes good breakfast. Recommended. **B** *Berlín*, Córdovez 535, T222927, F223575. Safe, efficient, good value. **C** *El Punto*, Andrés Bello 979, T228474, www.punto.de **F** pp without bath, with breakfast, recently refurbished, tasteful, comfortable, café, laundry, parking, English and German spoken. Recommended. **C** *Res Suiza*, Cienfuegos 250, T216092. With breakfast, good beds, excellent value. Highly recommended. **C-D** *Hostal Croata* Cienfuegos 248, T/F224997. **E** without bath, with breakfast, laundry facilities, cable TV, patio, hospitable. Recommended. **E** *Edith González*, Los Carrera 889, T221941/224978. **F** without bath, cooking and laundry facilities, meets passengers at bus terminal. Recommended. **E** *Hostal Jofre*, Rgto Coquimbo 964 (entre Pení y Amunátegui), T222335, hostaljofre@hotmail.com With breakfast, good beds, garden, free internet, discount for teachers, cheaper Apr-Oct, near bus terminal. **E** *Rosa Canto*, Cantournet 976, T213954. Kitchen, comfortable, family run, good value.

All **F-G** pp: *Amunátegui 315*. Kitchen facilities, patio, good beds. Recommended. *Backpacker Lodging*, El Santo 1058, T227580. Kitchen facilities, central, camping. *Casa de Huéspedes*, El Santo 1410, T213557. Convenient for bus terminal, including breakfast, hot water, cable TV. Recommended. *Celia Rivera*, Las Rojas 21, T215838. Near terminal, use of kitchen. *Gladys*, Alberto Coddou 1360, T09-540 3636 (mob). Includes breakfast, cable TV, hot water, kitchen facilities, helpful, Gladys works at tourist information in bus terminal (15 mins away). *Gregoria Fernández*, Andrés Bello 1067, T224400, gregoria_fernandez@hotmail.com Very helpful, good beds, with and without bath, close to terminal, excellent breakfast, garden, good local information; if full she will divert you to her mother's house, also good but less convenient for the bus station. Highly recommended. *Res El Loa*, O'Higgins 362, T210304. Without bath, with breakfast, good inexpensive home cooking, good value. *Lodging for Tourists*, Mauricio Betrios y Mary Rosas, San Juan de Dios Pení 636, T211407. Hot shower, includes breakfast, student place, helpful, kitchen facilities, laundry. *Res Lorena*, Cantournet 850, T223330. Quiet, pleasant. *Res Lorena/Carvajal*, Av El Santo 1056,T/F224059. Family home, kitchen facilities, central camping. *Casa de María Pizarro*, Las Rojas 18, T229282. Very welcoming, laundry facilities, camping, helpful. Book in advance. *Res Petit*, de la Barra 586, T212536. Hot water.

Camping *Maki Payi*, 153 Vegas Norte, about 5 km north of La Serena, near sea, T213628. Self-contained cabins available. *Hipocampo*, 4 km south on Av del Mar (take bus for Coquimbo and get off at Colegio Adventista, US$7.50 site by Playa El Pescador), T214316.

Eating
● on map
Most restaurants close off season on Sun. For good fish lunches (middle range/cheap) try the restaurants on the upper floor of the Recova market

Expensive: *Donde El Guatón*, Brasil 750. *Parrillada*, paradise for meat eaters. *El Cedro*, Prat 572. Arab cuisine. **Mid-range**: *Bavaria*, E de la Barra 489. International menu, good service, chain restaurant. *Ciro's*, Av de Aguirre 431, T213482. Old-fashioned, good lunch. Recommended. *La Mía Pizza*, O'Higgins 360, T215063. Italian, good value (branch on Av del Mar 2100 in summer). *La Tabla*, Av del Mar 3200. For seafood, extensive wine list. *Pastissima Limitado*, O'Higgins 663. Wide variety of pizzas, delicious pancakes, live music and dancing at weekends. **Cheap**: *Diavoletto*, Prat 565 and O'Higgins 531. Fast food, popular. *Mai Lai Fan*, Cordóvez 740. Good Chinese. *Plaza Royal*, Prat 465. Light meals and snacks, pleasant. Recommended. *Qahlúa*, Balmaceda 655. Good fish, seafood, popular. *Taiwan*, Cantournet 844. Cantonese, good quality. For ice cream, make for *Bravissimo*, Balmaceda 545.

Cafés and bars *Bar Real*, Los Carrera y Cordóvez, at Plaza. Nice cocktail bar. *Bocaccio*, Prat y Balmaceda. Modern, popular. *Café del Patio*, Prat 470. Café with bar (*Tijuana Blues*) from 2100 with live music to the early hours. On Sat, offers *The Beatles Club* from 2300. *Café do Brasil*, Balmaceda 461. Good coffee. *Tahiti*, Córdovez 540, local 113. Real coffee, pastries.

Shopping *Cema-Chile*, Los Carrera 562. For handicrafts. Also *La Recova* handicraft market, see Sights. *Las Brisas* supermarket, Cienfuegos y Cordóvez. *Rendic* supermarket, Balmaceda 561, good. *Mall Plaza*, shopping centre on the Panamericana next to the bus terminal. **Bicycle repairs**: *Mike's Bikes*, Av F de Aguirre 004, T224454. Good parts, rental, information on cycle routes.

Tour operators *Elquitour*, Matta 522, T214846. Good. *Friends*, Los Carrera 515, T215517, www.turismo friends.cl Good agency. *GiraTour*, Prat 689, T221992, giratour@ctcinternet.cl *Ingservitur*, Matta 611, T/F220165, www.ingsvtur.cl Guided tours to Valle del Encanto, Fray Jorge, Andacollo, Isla Chañaral, Valle del Elqui and to observatories. *Talinay Adventure Expeditions* and *Inca Travel*, both at Café del Patio, Prat 470, both offer a range of local tours including Valle del Elqui, Mamalluca, Reserva Nacional Pingüino de Humboldt, also trekking and climbing. Approximate tour prices: Valle del Elqui US$20, Parque Nacional Fray Jorge US$28, Tongoy US$24, Isla Damas US$35, observatory US$16, city tour US$9.

Local Buses: City buses US$0.25. **Car hire**: *Daire*, Balmaceda 3812, T293140, recommended, good service; **La Florida** at airport, T271947. Cheapest is *Gala*, Balmaceda 1785, T221400. **Taxis**: US$0.75 + US$0.20 per every 200 m. Colectivos with fixed rates, destination on roof; also to Coquimbo from Aguirre y Balmaceda, and Ovalle and Vicuña from Domeyko y Balmaceda.

   Long distance Air Aeropuerto Gabriela Mistral, 5 km east of the city. To **Santiago**, *LanChile/Lan Express*; also to destinations in northern Chile. **Buses** Bus terminal, El Santo y Amunátegui (about 8 blocks south of the centre). Buses daily to **Santiago**, several companies, 7-8 hrs, US$8 (classic), US$10 (*semi-cama*)-13 (*salón-cama*). To **Valparaíso**, 7 hrs, US$10. To **Caldera**, 6 hrs, US$7. To **Calama**, US$20, 15 hrs. To **Antofagasta**, 12-13 hrs, several companies, US$15, and to **Iquique**, 18 hrs, US$20. To **Arica**, US$20. To **Vicuña** and **Pisco Elqui**, see below. To **Coquimbo**, bus No 8 from Av Aguirre y Cienfuegos, US$0.30, every few minutes. *TurBus* office, Balmaceda entre Prat y Cordovez.

Transport

Airline offices *LanChile*, Prat y Balmaceda, T225981, also an office in the Mall Plaza. **Banks** ATMs at most banks and outside *Las Brisas* supermarket. *Corp Banca*, O'Higgins 529, Visa. *Casas de cambio*: *Cambio Caracol*, Balmaceda 460, in the basement, building closed 1400-1600. *Cambio Intercam*, De la Barra 435B. *La Portada*, Prat 515, open all day Sat. If heading north note that La Serena is the last place to change TCs before Antofagasta. **Communications Internet**: Cyber Cafe at *Ingservtur*, Matta 611. *Cyber-Bazaar 2000*, Av F de Aguirre 343-A. *Net Café*, Cordovez 285, T212187, also bar. *Shalom*, Av F de Aguirre 343. **Telephone**: *CTC*, Cordovez 446. *Entel*, Balmaceda 896 and Prat 571. **Cultural centres** *Instituto Chileno Francés de Cultura*, Cienfuegos 632, T224993. Library, films, etc. *Centro Latino-Americano de Arte y Cultura*, Balmaceda 824, T229344. Dance workshops, art gallery, *artesanía*. **Tourist offices** Main *Sernatur* office in Edificio de Servicios Públicos (next to the Post Office on the Plaza de Armas), T225199. Mon-Fri 0845-1830 (2030 in summer), Sat-Sun 1000-1400 (1000-1400, 1600-2000 in summer). Kiosks at bus terminal (summer only) and Balmaceda y Prat, helpful. Open in theory Mon-Sat 1100-1400, 1600-1900. There is also a private kiosk at the bus terminal; do not confuse with *Sernatur*.

Directory

Chile

The Elqui Valley, east of La Serena, is one of the main astronomical centres of the world, with three important observatories. Tour operators in La Serena and Coquimbo (including *Ingservtur* and *GiraTour*), receive tickets from the observatories and arrange tours to Tololo and La Silla (to Tololo US$22 pp). See also under Tour operators, Antofagasta.

Observatories
Book tours up to 3-4 months ahead in holiday times

   El Tololo at 2,200 m, 89 km southeast of La Serena in the Elqui Valley, 51 km south of Vicuña, belongs to Aura, an association of US and Chilean universities. It possesses one of the largest telescopes in the southern hemisphere (4-m diameter), seven others and a radio telescope. ■ *It is open to visitors by permit only every Sat 0900-1200, 1300-1600; for permits (free) write to Casilla 603, La Serena, T051-205200, F205212, then pick your permit up before 1200 on the day before (the office is at Colina Los Pinos, on a hill behind the new University – personal applications can be made here for all three observatories). They will insist that you have private transport; you can hire a taxi, US$35 for the whole day, but you will require the registration number when you book.* **La Silla** at 2,240 m, 150 km northeast of La Serena, belongs to ESO (European Southern Observatory), and comprises 14 telescopes. ■ *Every Sat, 1430-1730; registration in advance in Santiago essential (Alonso de Córdoba 3107, Santiago, T228 5006/698 8757) or write to Casilla 567, La Serena, T224527, www.eso.org Getting there: from La Serena it is 114 km north along Route 5 to the turn-off (D Posada La Frontera, cabañas), then another 36 km.* **Las Campanas** at 2,510 m, 156 km northeast of La Serena, 30 km north of La Silla, belongs to the Carnegie Institute, has four telescopes and is a smaller facility than the other two. ■ *It is open with permission every Sat 1430-1730, T224680, or write to Casilla 601, La Serena. Getting there: follow Route 5 to the same junction as for La Silla, take the turning for La Silla and then turn north after 14 km. La Silla and Las Campanas can be reached without private transport by taking any bus towards Vallenar 2 hrs, US$3.25) getting out at the junction (desvío) and hitch from there.*

The Elqui Valley

The valley of the Río Elqui is one of the most attractive oases in this part of northern Chile. There are orchards, orange groves, vineyards and mines set against the imposing, arid mountains. Elqui is also well-known as a centre of mystical energy. The road up the valley is paved as far as Pisco Elqui, 37 km beyond Vicuña, the valley's capital. Except for Vicuña, most of the tiny towns have but a single street. The Elqui Valley is the centre of *pisco* production with nine distilleries, the largest being Capel in Vicuña. Huancara, a fortified wine introduced by the Jesuits, is also produced in the valley.

Vicuña
Phone code: 051
Colour map 8, grid A1
Population: 7,716
66 km east of
La Serena

This small, friendly town was founded in 1821. On the west side of the plaza are the municipal chambers, built in 1826 and topped in 1905 by a medieval-German-style tower, the Torre Bauer, imported by the German-born mayor of the time. The tourist office is on Plaza de Armas. There are good views from Cerro La Virgen, north of town. The *Capel Pisco* distillery is 1½ km east of Vicuña, to the right of the main road. ■ *Guided tours (in Spanish) are offered Dec-Feb, daily 1000-1800, free. No booking required.* **Museo Gabriela Mistral**, Gabriela Mistral 759, containing manuscripts, books, awards and many other details of the poet's life. ■ *Mon-Sat 1000-1900, Sun 1000-1800, US$1.* Next door is the house where the poet was born. **Observatorio Astronómico Comunal de Vicuña**, on Cerro **Mamalluca**, 10 km from Vicuña, 1500 m above sea level, offers tours to the public at 2100, 2300, 0100 in summer, 1800, 2000, 2200 in winter. ■ *Gabriela Mistral 260, T411352, F411255, www.mamalluca.org* Price is US$5.50 for tour, including talk and viewing through telescope, plus US$2 for transport, guides in Spanish and English for groups of 5 or more. Book in advance.

Sleeping and eating **B** *Hostería Vicuña*, Sgto Aldea 101, T411301, F411144. Swimming pool, tennis court, restaurant. **D** *La Elquina*, O' Higgins 65, T411317. Lovely garden, laundry and kitchen facilities. **On Gabriela Mistral** **D** *Valle Hermoso*, No 706, T411206. Comfortable, parking. **E** *Sol del Valle*, No 743. Including breakfast, swimming pool, vineyard, restaurant. **Camping** *Camping y Piscina Las Tinajas*, east end of Chacabuco. Swimming pool, restaurant. Eating places are mainly on G Mistral *Club Social de Elqui*, No 435. Very good, good value *almuerzo. Michel*, No 180. Popular, good value *almuerzo. Halley*, at No 404. Good meat dishes, also *chopería*, swimming pool (US$5 pp). *Yo Y Soledad*, No 364. Inexpensive, good value.

From Vicuña a 46-km road runs south through the Andes to the village of **Río Hurtado**, a secluded, picturesque place in a spectacular valley. Beyond the village the old trading route from Argentina, known as the Inka Trail, leads to Vado Morrillas, 3 km west of Hurtado. Along the trail are rock paintings, old Indian campsites and aqueducts.

Sleeping **AL-A** *Hacienda Los Andes*, Vado Morillas, T053-691822, www.haciendalosandes.com German-Austian management, bed & breakfast, colonial-style, English spoken,

horse riding and outdoor activities, starting from US$80 for 1 day. Access from Vicuña or Ovalle via Monumento Nacional Pichasca.

Transport Buses to **La Serena**, about 10 a day (more in summer), most by *Vía Elqui/Megal Bus*, first 0800, last 1930, 1 hr, US$1.50, colectivo from Plaza de Armas US$2.50. To **Pisco Elqui**, 10 a day, *Vía Elqui*, 1 hr, US$1.50.

From Vicuña the road runs through Paihuano (camping) to Monte Grande, where the schoolhouse where **Gabriela Mistral** lived and was educated by her sister is now a museum. ■ *US$0.50*. The poet's tomb is at the edge of town, opposite the *Artesanos de Cochiguaz* pisco distillery, which is open to the public. (Buses from the plaza in Vicuña.) Here the road forks, one branch leading to the **Cochiguaz** valley. There is no public transport. Along this road are several new age settlements; it is said that the valley is an important energy centre. There are several campsites. At night, there is no better place on earth to star gaze. When the moon is new, or below the horizon, the stars seem to be hanging in the air; spectacular shooting stars can be seen every couple of seconds, as can satellites crossing the night sky. The other branch leads to **Pisco Elqui**, an attractive village with the newly restored church of Nuestra Señora del Rosario on a shady plaza. It's also famous for its night skies and beautiful scenery. Here there is the *Tres Erres* pisco plant (open for visits). Horses can be hired, with or without guide, US$4 per hour with guide, recommended – ask at the *Hotel Elqui*. Pisco Elqui is also a new age centre, where all sorts of alternative therapies and massages are available. Buses to La Serena, US$2.50, via Vicuña.

> **Pisco Elqui**

> Chile

Sleeping and eating **AL** *Misterios de Elqui*, C Prat, T1982544, www.misteriosdeelqui.cl Plush *cabañas*, sleep 4, swimming pool, good expensive restaurant. **A** *Los Datiles*, Prat s/n, T1982540. *Cabañas* sleep 5, swimming pool, good restaurant. **A-B** *El Tesoro del Elqui*, T/F1982609. *Cabañas* (sleep 3), café, pool, German spoken. **E** *Elqui*, O'Higgins s/n by the plaza. T1982523. Hot shower, good restaurant. Recommended. **F** pp *Casa Valentina*, Rodríguez s/n, fampintz@hotmail.com With breakfast, helpful, informative, English and German spoken. Recommended. **F** pp *Hostería de Don Juan*, old wooden house, with breakfast, fine views, not always open. **G** pp *Hospedaje*, Prat 12. Cheapest, friendly, fleas. **F** *Camping El Olivo*, small restaurant, pool, excellent facilities, closed in winter. There is a juice bar and pancake restaurant on the plaza. Well-stocked supermarket 1 block from the plaza.

> *Prices are much lower outside Jan-Feb*

Paso Agua Negra (4,775 m) is reached by unpaved road from Rivadavia. Chilean immigration and customs at Juntas, 84 km west of the border, 88 km east of Vicuña. Border open 0800-1700; Jan-Apr only, check rest of year. No public transport beyond Rivadavia.

> **Border: Paso Agua Negra**

North of La Serena

Santiago

North of the Río Elqui, the transitional zone continues to the mining and agro-industrial centre of Copiapó. Thereafter begins the desert, which is of little interest, except after rain. Then it is covered with a succession of flowers, insects and frogs, in one of the world's most spectacular wildlife events. Rain, however, is rare: there is none in summer; in winter it is light and lasts only a short time. Annual precipitation at Copiapó is about 115 mm. Drivers must beware of high winds and blowing sand north of Copiapó.

The Huasco valley is an oasis of olive groves and vineyards. It is rugged and spectacular, dividing at Alto del Carmen, 30 km east of Vallenar, into the Carmen and Tránsito valleys. There are pisco distilleries at Alto del Carmen and San Félix. A sweet wine known as Pajarete is also produced.

Vallenar

Phone code: 051
Colour map 8, grid A1
Population: 42,725
Altitude: 380 m
194 km N of La Serena

This is the chief town of the Huasco valley. At the mouth of the river, 56 km west, is the pleasant port of **Huasco** (cheap seafood restaurants near the harbour). The **Humboldt Penguin Natural Reserve** is on Islas Chañaral, Choros and Damas, where, besides penguins, there are seals, sea lions, a great variety of seabirds and, off-shore, a colony of grey dolphin. Isla Damas has interesting flora, too. No public transport to Punta de Choros (42 km from Panamericana; C Cabañas Los Delfines, T09-639 6678 (mob)); tours from La Serena, 0830-1800. Permission to land on Isla Damas (US$2.50) from *Conaf* in Punta de Choros, T051-272798.

Listed hotels and
restaurants all
recommended
Cheap eating places
along south end
of Av Brasil

Sleeping and eating A *Hostería Vallenar*, Ercilla 848, T614379, hotval@ctc.cl Excellent, pool, restaurant. **B** *Cecil*, Prat 1059, T614071. Hot water, pool, modern. **C** *Hostal Camino del Rey*, Merced 943, T/F613184. Cheaper without bath, good value. **D** *Vall*, Aconcagua 455, T613380. With breakfast, good value. **E** *Viña del Mar*, Serrano 611, T611478. Nice rooms, *comedor*. For eating, try *Bavaria*, Serrano 802. Good all round. *Pizza Il Boccato*, Plaza O'Higgins y Prat. Good coffee, good food, popular. *La Pica*, Brasil y Faez. Good for cheap meals, seafood, cocktails.

For tourist information
the staff at the
Municipalidad on
Plaza de Armas are
helpful

Tour operators and Transport *Agencia de Viajes Irazu*, Prat 1121A, T/F619807. They do not organize excursions, but will organize flights. If it rains (usually Sep-Oct) a guided tour of the desert in flower can be done with *Roberto Alegría*, T613865. **Bus offices** Each bus company has its own terminal: *TurBus*, Merced 561; *Pullman*, opposite (the most frequent buses going north); *Tas Choapa*, next door.

Copiapó

Phone code: 052
Colour map 6, grid C2
Population: 100,000
Altitude: 400 m
144 km N of Vallenar

The valley of the Río Copiapó, generally regarded as the southern limit of the Atacama desert, is an oasis of farms, vineyards and orchards about 150 km long. Copiapó is an important mining centre. Founded in 1744, Copiapó became a pros-perous town after the discovery in 1832 of the third largest silver deposits in South America at Chañarcillo (the mine was closed in 1875). The discoverer, Juan Godoy, a mule-driver, is commemorated at Matta y O'Higgins. Fiesta de la Candelaria, first Sunday in February. **Museo Mineralógico**, Colipí y Rodríguez, one block east from Plaza Prat, is the best of its type in Chile. Many ores shown are found only in the Atacama desert. ■ *Mon-Fri 1000-1300, 1530-1900, Sat 1000-1300, US$0.80.* The museum at the **railway station** opens irregularly, but the Norris Brothers steam locomotive and carriages used in the inaugural journey between Copiapó and Caldera in 1851 (the first railway in South America) can be seen at the Universidad de Atacama about 2 km north of the centre on Avenida R Freire.

Sleeping

AL *Diego de Almeida*, O'Higgins 656, Plaza Prat, T/F212075, dalmeida@tnet.cl TV, fridge, good restaurant, bar pool. **AL** *Hostería Las Pircas*, Av Copayapu 095, T213220, hosteria.laspirca@chilnet.cl Bungalows, pool, good restaurant. **B** *San Francisco de la Selva*, Los Carrera 525, T217013, hosanco@entelchile.net TV, café-bar, garage, modern. **B-C** *Montecatini*, Atacama 374, T211516. Good, modern, quiet, breakfast. **B-C** *Palace*, Atacama 741, T212852. Comfortable, good breakfast, nice patio. **D** *Res Chacabuco*, O'Higgins 921, T213428. **F** shared bath, quiet, near bus terminal. **D** *Res Rocío*, Yerbas Buenas 581, T215360. **E** without bath, good value, attractive patio. **E** *Res Nuevo Chañarcillo*, Rodríguez 540, T212368. Without bath (more with), comfortable. Recommended. **E** *Res Torres*, Atacama 230, T240727. Shared bath, hot water, quiet, good value.

Eating

Mid-range *Bavaria*, Chacabuco 487 (Plaza Prat) and round corner on Los Carrera. Good variety on offer. *El Corsario*, Atacama 245. Good food, value and atmosphere. **Cheap** *Benbow*, Rodríguez 543. Good value *almuerzo*, extensive menu. *Don Elias*, Los Carrera e Yerbas Buenas. Excellent seafood. *Chifa Hao Hwa*, Colipi 340 and Yerbas Buenas 334. Good Chinese. *La Pizza de Tito*, Infante y Chacabuco. Pizzas, sandwiches and *almuerzos*.

Air Airport 12 km north of town. *LanChile/Lan Express*, Colipi 484, T213512, daily to/from Santiago, also to northern destinations. **Buses** Terminal 3 blocks from centre on Freire y Chacabuco. To **Santiago** US$15, 12 hrs. To **La Serena** US$7.50, 5 hrs. To **Caldera**, US$1-2, 1 hr. **Bicycle repairs**: *Biman*, Los Carrera 998A, T/F217391, excellent.

Transport

Banks *Redbanc* ATMs at central banks and in *Plaza Real* shopping mall. **Communications** Internet: *Zona Virtual*, Rodríguez y Colipi, T240308, www.zonavirtual.cl *Terra*, Chacabuco 3280, US$1.80 per hr. **Post Office**: O'Higgins 531. **Telephone**: *CTC*, O'Higgins 531; *Entel*, Colipi 484. **Cultural centres** *Casa de la Cultura*, O'Higgins 610, Plaza Prat. Wide range of arts, workshops, *artesanía* shops, good café *El Bramador*. **Tourist office** Los Carrera 691, north side of Plaza Prat, T212838, helpful.

Directory

Paso San Francisco is reached either by poor unpaved road northeast from Copiapó, via the Salar de Maricunga and Laguna Verde or by an unpaved road southeast from El Salvador: the two roads join near the Salar de Maricunga, 96 km west of Paso San Francisco. On the Argentine side a paved road continues to Tinogasta. Chilean immigration and customs are near the Salar de Maricunga, 100 km west of the border, open 0900-1900; US$2 per vehicle charge for crossing Saturday, Sunday and holidays. Always take spare fuel.

Border with Argentina: Paso San Francisco
This crossing is liable to closure in winter T052-238032 for road reports

This is a port and terminal for the loading of iron ore. **Iglesia de San Vicente** (1862) on the Plaza de Armas was built by English carpenters working for the railway company. **Bahía Inglesa**, 6 km south of Caldera, 6 km west of the Highway, is popular for its beautiful white sandy beaches and unpolluted sea (very expensive and can get crowded January-February and at weekends). It was originally known as Puerto del Inglés after the visit in 1687 of the English 'corsario', Edward Davis.

Caldera
Phone code: 052
Colour map 6, grid C2
Population: 12,000
73 km W of Copiapó

Sleeping and eating Caldera B *Hostería Puerta del Sol*, Wheelwright 750, T315205. Includes tax, cabins with kitchen, view over bay. **B** *Portal del Inca*, Carvallo 945, T315252. Cabins with kitchen, English spoken, restaurant not bad, order breakfast on previous night. **C** *Costanera*, Wheelwright 543, T316007. Takes credit cards, simple rooms. **E** pp *Res Millaray*, Cousiño 331, Plaza de Armas. Good value, basic. *Miramar*, Gana 090. At pier, good seafood. *El Pirón de Oro*, Cousiño 218. Good but not cheap. **Bahía Inglesa B** *Los Jardines de Bahía Inglesa*, Av Copiapó, *cabañas*, T315359. Open all year, good beds, comfortable. *Camping Bahía Inglesa*, Playa Las Machas, T315424. **C** tent site, fully equipped *cabañas* for up to 5 persons, **B**. *El Coral* restaurant has some cabins **C**, T315331, Av El Morro, overlooking sea, good seafood, groups welcome, open all year.

Cheaper to stay in Caldera than Bahía Inglesa in summer

Transport Buses to **Copiapó** and **Santiago**, several daily. To **Antofagasta**, US$11, 7 hrs. Buses on the Panamericana do not go into Caldera, but stop at Cruce Caldera, outside town (*Restaurante Hospedaje Mastique*, Km 880, is a good place to eat and stay, **D**). To travel north, it may be better to take a bus to **Chañaral** (Inca-bus US$2), then change. Between Bahía Inglesa and Caldera colectivos charge US$1 all year; frequent bus service Jan-Feb US$0.30.

The valley of the Río Salado, 130 km in length, less fertile or prosperous than the Copiapó or Huasco valleys, is the last oasis south of Antofagasta. **Chañaral**, a town with old wooden houses perched on the hillside at the mouth of the Salado, is 93 km north of Caldera. In its heyday it was the processing centre for ore from the nearby copper mines of El Salado and Las Animas. Now it is a base for visits to beaches and the Parque Nacional Pan de Azúcar. There is a tourist information kiosk on the Pan-American Highway at the south end of town (closed winter). If it is closed, go to the Municipalidad.

Chañaral
Phone code: 052
Colour map 6, grid C2
Population: 12,000
968 km N of Santiago

Sleeping and eating B *Hostería Chañaral*, Miller 268, T480055. Excellent restaurant. **C** *Nuria*, Costanera 302, T480903. Good. **E** *Jiménez*, Merino Jarpa 551, T480328. Without bath, patio with lots of birds, restaurant good value. Recommended. **F** *La Marina*, Merino Jarpa 562. Basic, patio, good value. Eating: *Rincón Porteño*, Merino Jarpa 567. Good and inexpensive.

Chile

Transport Bus terminal Merino Jarpa 854. Frequent services to Antofagasta US$10, 5 hrs, and Santiago.

Parque
Nacional Pan
de Azúcar
There are heavy fines
for driving in 'restricted
areas' of the park

The park, north of Chañaral, consists of the Isla Pan de Azúcar on which Humboldt penguins and other sea-birds live, and some 43,754 ha of coastal hills rising to 800 m. There are fine beaches (popular at weekends in summer). Fishermen near the *Conaf* office offer boat trips round Isla Pan de Azúcar to see the penguins, US$5 pp. Vegetation is mainly cacti, of which there are 26 species, nourished by frequent sea mists (*camanchaca*). The park is home to 103 species of birds as well as guanaco and foxes. There are two entrances: north by good secondary road from Chañaral, 28 km to Caleta Pan de Azúcar; from the Pan-American Highway 45 km north of Chañaral, along a side road 20 km (road in parts deep sand and very rough, 4WD essential). A taxi costs US$25 from Chañaral, or hitch a lift from fishermen at sunrise. There is a *Conaf* office in Caleta Pan de Azúcar, 0830-1800 daily, maps available. Park entry is US$4. **Camping E** per site, no showers, take all food and drinking water; also 2 *cabañas*, T213404. **Tour operator** *Subsole Atacama Adventure* (Sergio Molina), Merino Jarpa s/n, Chañaral, T09-523 6549, kekomoli@123mail.cl Specializes on tours in the park, enthusiastic.

Taltal
Phone code: 055
Colour map 6, grid C2
Population: 9,000
146 km N of Chañaral

This is the only town between Chañaral and Antofagasta, a distance of 420 km. Along Avenida Prat are several wooden buildings dating from the late 19th century, when Taltal prospered as a mineral port of 20,000 people. It is now a fishing port with a mineral processing plant. North 72 km is the Quebrada El Médano, a gorge with ancient rock-paintings along the upper valley walls.

Sleeping and eating C *Hostal de Mar*, Carrera 250, T611612. Comfortable, modern. C *Hostería Taltal*, Esmeralda 671, T611625. Excellent restaurant, good value *almuerzo*. C *Verdy*, Ramírez 345, T611105. **E** pp without bath, spacious, restaurant. Recommended. Opposite is **E** *Taltal City*, without bath. **E** *San Martín*, Martínez 279, T611088. Without bath, good *almuerzo*. *Caverna*, Martínez 247. Good seafood. *Club Social Taltal*, Torreblanca 162. The old British club (see the ballroom and poker room), excellent, good value.

Transport Buses to Santiago: 2 a day; to Antofagasta, *TurBus* and *Ramos*, US$5. Many buses bypass Taltal: to reach the Panamericana take a taxi, US$8.

Antofagasta

Phone code: 055
Colour map 6, grid C2
Population: 225,316
1,367 km N of
Santiago

The largest city in Northern Chile, Antofagasta is the capital of the Second Region and is a major port for the export of copper from La Escondida and Chuquicamata. It is also a major commercial centre and home of two universities. While not especially attractive in itself, its setting beside the ocean and in view of tall mountains is dramatic. Despite this being the driest region, the climate is delightful. Temperature varies from 16° C in June/July to 24° C January/February, never falling below 10° C at night.

Sights In the main square, **Plaza Colón**, is a clock tower donated by the British community in 1910 to commemorate 100 years of Chilean independence. It is a replica of Big Ben in London. **Calle A Prat**, which runs southeast from Plaza Colón, is the main shopping street. Two blocks north of Plaza Colón, at the old port, is the **former Aduana**, built as the Bolivian customs house in Mejillones and moved to its current site after the War of the Pacific. It houses the **Museo Histórico Regional**, which has fascinating visual displays (explanations in Spanish only) on life on land and in the oceans, development of civilization in South America, minerals, human artefacts, recommended. ■ *Tue-Sat 1000-1300, 1530-1830, Sun 1100-1400, US$1, children half-price; museoanto@terra.cl* Opposite are the former **Capitanía del Puerto** (now the administrative offices and library of the Museo Regional) and the **former Resguardo Marítimo** (now housing Digader, the regional coordinating centre for sport and recreation).

East of the port are the buildings of the **Antofagasta and Bolivia Railway Company** (FCAB) dating from the 1890s and beautifully restored, but still in use. **Museo del Ferrocarril a Bolivia** at Bolívar 255 has an interesting museum of the history of the Antofagasta-Bolivia railway, with photographs, maps, instruments and furniture. Reservations must be made 48 hours in advance, T206311, jlyons@fcab.cl **Museo Geológico** of the Universidad Católica del Norte, Av Angamos 0610, inside the university campus. ■ *Mon-Fri, 0900-1200, 1500-1800, free, Gchong@socompa.ucn Colectivo 3 or 33 from town centre.* Tours of the port by boat leave from *La Cabaña de Mario*, C Aníbal Pinto s/n between the Museo Regional and the Terminal de Pescadores. ■ *30 mins, US$3.50.*

The fantastic cliff formations and symbol of the Second Region at **La Portada** are 16 km north, reached by any bus for Mejillones from the Terminal Centro (or ask at a travel agency). Taxis charge US$11 (for a small extra fee, taxis from the airport will drive past La Portada). Hitching is easy. From the main road it is 2 km to the beach which, though beautiful, is too dangerous for swimming; there is an excellent seafood restaurant (*La Portada*) and café (open lunch-time only). A number of bathing beaches are also within easy reach.

Juan López, 38 km north of Antofagasta, is a windsurfers' paradise (**A** *Hotel La Rinconada*, T261139; **C** *Hostería Sandokan*, T692031). Buses at weekends in summer only, also minibuses daily in summer from Latorre y Sucre. For those with their own transport, follow the road out of Juan López to the beautiful cove at Conchilla. Keep on the track to the end at Bolsico. The sea is alive with birds, especially opposite Isla Santa María.

Mejillones (*Population*: 5,500), a little fishing port 60 km north of Antofagasta, stands on a good natural harbour protected from westerly gales by high hills. Until 1948 it was a major terminal for the export of tin and other metals from Bolivia: remnants of that past include a number of fine wooden buildings: the Intendencia Municipal, the Casa Cultural (built in 1866) and the church (1906), as well as the Capitanía del Puerto.

Sleeping
■ *on map*

AL *Antofagasta*, Balmaceda 2575, T/F228811. Garage, pool, lovely view of port and city, good but expensive restaurant (bar serves cheaper snacks), with breakfast, beach, but rooms facing the city are noisy due to all night copper trains. **A** *Plaza*, Baquedano 461, T269046, F266803, hplaza@chilesat.net TV, salon de té, pool and sports, parking. Recommended, also has apartments. **B** *Ancla Inn*, Baquedano 508, T224814, www.ancla.inn@entelchile.net Salón de té, also has 4 self-contained apartments. Recommended. **B** *Colón*, San Martín 2434, T261851, F260872. With breakfast, comfortable, hot water, quiet, cash only. **B** *Marsal*, Prat 867, T268063, F221733, marsalhotel@terra.cl Modern, very comfortable, Catalan owner. Recommended. **B** *Parina*, Maipú, T223354, F266396. Modern, comfortable, restaurant, conference centre, good value. **B** *Sol del Horizonte*, Latorre 2450, T/F221886, hotelsoldelhorizonte@123click.cl Cable TV, bar, pleasant, good value. Recommended. **C** *Dakota*, Latorre 2425, T251649. With breakfast and cable TV, popular, good value. Recommended. **C** *San Martín*, San Martín 2781, T263503, F268159. TV, parking, safe.

D *Ciudad de Avila*, Condell 2840, T/F221040. TV, restaurant, OK. **D** *Hostal Frontera*, Bolívar 558, T281219. Good hot shower, good beds, TV, convenient for TurBus and Pullman. **D** *Maykin*, Condell 3130, T/F259400. Modern, helpful, good value. Recommended, but takes in short-stay guests. **D** *Hostal del Norte*, Latorre 3162, T251265, F267161. Without bath, comfortable, quiet. **D** *Valdivia*, Ossa 2642, T265911. Recommended. **E** pp *Res El Cobre*, Prat 749, T225162. Without bath, clean, but unattractive. **E** pp *Res La Riojanita*, Baquedano 464, T226313. Basic, very helpful, noisy but recommended.

Camping To the south on the road to Coloso are: *Las Garumas*, Km 6, T247763 ext 42, **E** per site (bargain for lower price out of season), **C** for cabins, cold showers and beach (reservations Av Angamos 601, casilla 606). *Rucamóvil*, Km 11, T223929 and 7 *cabañas*. Both open year-round, expensive.

Chile

Eating

● *on map*
Above the market are several good places selling cheap seafood almuerzos and supercheap set lunches Many bars and restaurants are closed on Sun

Expensive: *Club de la Unión*, Prat 474, p 2. Open to non-members, excellent *almuerzo*, good service. **Mid-range**: *Chifa Pekín*, Ossa 2135. Chinese, smart. *D'Alfredo*, Condell 2539. Pizzas, good. *El Arriero*, Condell 2644. Good service, cheaper set lunch, popular, live music. *Panda*, Condell y Baguedano. Self-service, eat all you can for US$8. *Pizzante*, Carrera 1857. Good pasta and seafood. *Tío Jacinto*, Uribe 922. Good seafood. **Cheap**: *Casa Vecchia*, O'Higgins 1456. Good value. *Chicken's House Center*, Latorre 2660. Chicken, beef and daily specials, open till 2400. *Oliver Café Plaza*, Plaza Colón. Self-service, modern. Recommended. Good fish restaurants in *Terminal Pesquero Centro* and at *Caleta Coloso*, 8 km south.

Cafés It is difficult to find coffee or breakfast before 0900. For real coffee: *Café Bahía*, Prat 474, and *Café Caribe*, Prat 482. Open 0900. *Café Haiti*, in Galería at Prat 482. *Cafetería* of *Hotel Nadine*, Baquedano 519, real coffee, pastries, ice cream. Recommended. Good **panaderías**: *Chez Niko's*, Ossa 1951. *La Palmera*, Ossa 2297. *Panadería El Sol*, Baquedano 785. Ice cream at *Heladería Latorre*, Baquedano y Latorre.

Bars & clubs

Bars: *Bar Picadillo*, Av Grecia 1000. Lively atmosphere, also good food. *Castillo Pub*, Pasaje Carrera 884. Live music, good food with good value *almuerzo*, good fun. *Wally's Pub*, Toro 982. British expat-style with darts and beer, closed Sun. **Clubs**: The most popular are south of the town in Balneario El Huascar.

Antofagasta

0 metres 100
0 yards 100

Chile

Teatro Municipal, Sucre y San Martín, T264919. Modern, state-of-the art theatre. *Teatro* **Entertainment**
Pedro de la Barra, Condell 2495. Thatre run by University of Antofagasta, regular
programme of plays, reviews, concerts etc, high standard, details in press.

29 Jun, *San Pedro*, patron saint of the fishermen: the saint's image is taken out by launch to **Festivals**
the breakwater to bless the first catch of the day. On the **last weekend of Oct**, the foreign
communities put on a joint festival on the seafront, with national foods, dancing and music.

Bookshops *Librería Andrés Bello*, Condell 2421. Good selection. *Librería Universitaria*, **Shopping**
Latorre 2515. Owner Germana Fernández knowledgeable on local history. Opposite is
Multilibro, very good selection of Chilean and English-language authors. **Market** Munici-
pal market, Matta y Uribe. *Feria Modelo O'Higgins* (next to fish market on Av Pinto). Excel-
lent fruit and veg, also restaurants. **Supermarkets** *Las Brisas*, Baquedano 750. *Korlaert*, on
Ossa 2400-2500 block. *Líder* on road to La Portada.

Many including *Turismo Corssa*, San Martín 2769, T/F227675. Recommended. *Intitour,* **Tour**
Baquedano 460, T266185, F260882, intitour@entelchile.net   *Maerz* (Joseph Valenzuela **operators**
Thompson), PO Box 55, T243322, F259132, maerz@entelchile.net For tours in German.
Tatio Travel, Washington 2513, T/F263532.English spoken, tours arranged for groups or
individuals. Highly recommended. *Terra Expedition Tour*, Balmaceda 2575, *Hotel
Antofagasta*, T/F223324. To Salar de Atacama, etc.

Local Car hire: *First*, Bolívar 623, T225777. *Iqsa*, Latorre 3033, T264675. **Transport**

Long distance Air: Cerro Moreno Airport, 22 km north. Taxi to airport US$10, but cheaper if
ordered from hotel. Bus US$4 or less, *Aerobus* (T221047), *Tur Bus* and others. *LanChile, Lan*
Express fly daily to Santiago, Iquique and Calama; also to other northern airports. *Sky* daily to
Santiago and Iquique.

  Buses: No main terminal; each company has its own office in town (some quite a distance
from the centre). Buses for **Mejillones** and **Tocopilla** depart from the Terminal Centro at
Riquelme 513. Minibuses to Mejillones leave from Latorre 2730. Bus company offices:
Flota Barrios, Condell 2682, T268559; *Géminis*, Latorre 3055, T251796; *Pullman Bus*,
Latorre 2805, T262591; *TurBus*, Latorre 2751, T264487. To **Santiago**, 20 hrs (*Flota Barrios*,
US$50, *cama* includes drinks and meals); many companies: fares US$35-40, book 2 days in
advance. If all seats to the capital are booked, catch a bus to **La Serena** (11 hrs, US$15, or
US$25 *cama* service), or **Ovalle**, US$18, and re-book. To **Valparaíso**, US$30. Frequent buses
to **Iquique**, US$9, 8 hrs. To **Arica**, US$10, 13½ hrs. To **Chuquicamata**, US$5, frequent, 3 hrs.
To **Calama**, several companies, US$4, 3 hrs; to **San Pedro de Atacama**, *TurBus* at 0630,
US$9.50, or via Calama. Direct to **Copiapó**, *TurBus* daily, 7 hrs, US$14.

  To Salta, Argentina *Géminis*, Wed, Sun, via Calama, San Pedro de Atacama, Paso de
Jama and Jujuy, US$43, 18 hrs.

Airline offices *LanChile*, Paseo Prat, T265151. *LAB*, San Martín 2395, T260618. **Banks** *Corp Banca,* **Directory**
Plaza Colón for Visa. ATMs at major banks around Plaza Colón, *Hotel Antofagasta*, and *Las Brisas* and *Impossible to change*
Tricot supermarkets. *Casas de Cambio are mainly on Baquedano, such as Ancla*, No 524, Mon-Fri *TCs south of*
0900-1400, 1600-1900 (at weekends try ice cream shop next door) and shopping centre at No 482-98. *Antofagasta until you*
Communications Internet: *Intitour*, see tour operator above, US$0.60 per hr. Cybercafé, Maipú y *reach La Serena*
Latorre, US$1.30 per hr. Sucre 671, US$0.80 per hr. **Post Office**: on Plaza Colón. 0830-1900, Sat
0900-1300. Also at Washington 2613. **Telephone**: *CTC*, Condell 2529 and 2750 (open Sun). *Entel Chile*,
Condell 2451. **Cultural centres** Instituto Chileno Norteamericano, Carrera 1445, T263520.
Instituto Chileno Alemán, Bolívar 769, T225946. Centro Cultural Nueva Acrópolis, Condell 2679,
T222144, lots of activities, talks, discussions. **Consulates** Argentina, Blanco Encalada 1933, T220440.
Bolivia, Washington 2675, p 13, T225010. France and Belgium, Baquedano 299, T268669. Germany,
Pérez Zujovic 4940, T251691. Italy, Matta 1945, of 808, T227791. Netherlands, Washington 2679, of
902, T266252. Spain, Rendic 4946, T269596. **Tourist offices** Prat 384, T451818. Mon-Fri 0930-1200,
1400-1700, very helpful. There is also a kiosk on Balmaceda, Mon-Fri 0930-1300, 1530-1930, Sat-Sun
0930-1300; kiosk at airport (open summer only). *Conaf*, Argentina y Baquedano.

Chile

Tocopilla
Phone code: 055
Colour map 6, grid B2
Population: 24,600

Tocopilla is 187 km north of Antofagasta via the coastal road and 365 km via the Pan-American Highway. It has one of the most dramatic settings of any Chilean town, sheltering at the foot of 500-m high mountains that loom inland. There are some interesting early 20th century buildings with wooden balustrades and façades. The port facilities are used to unload coal and to export nitrates and iodine from María Elena and Pedro de Valdivia. There are two good beaches: Punta Blanca (12 km south) and Balneario Covadonga, with a swimming pool.

There is a good range of eating places in town

Sleeping C *Bolívar*, Bolívar 1332, T812783. **F** pp without bath, modern, helpful. Opposite is *Sucre*, same ownership, same price. **C** *Vucina*, 21 de Mayo 2069, T/F813088. Modern, good restaurant. **E** pp *Casablanca*, 21 de Mayo 2054, T813187. Helpful, good restaurant, good value. **F** pp *Res Royal*, T/F 811488, 21 de Mayo 1988. Helpful, basic, without breakfast or bath. Several others.

Bus company offices are on 21 de Mayo

Transport Buses to **Antofagasta** many daily, US$3, 2½ hrs. To **Iquique**, along coastal road, 3 hrs, US$4, frequent. To **Chuquicamata** and **Calama**, 2 a day, 3 hrs, US$5.

Quillagua is officially the driest place in the world

East of Tocopilla a good paved road runs up the narrow valley 72 km to the Pan-American Highway. From here the paved road continues east to Chuquicamata. North of the crossroads 81 km is **Quillagua** (customs post, all vehicles and buses are searched) and 111 km further is the first of three sections of the **Reserva Nacional del Tamarugal**. In this part are the **Geoglyphs of Cerro Pintados**, some 400 figures (humans, animals, geometric shapes) on the hillside (3 km west of the highway). The second part of Tamarugal is near La Tirana (see page 648), the third 60 km north of Pozo Almonte.

The coastal road from Tocopilla north to Iquique is now a very good paved road, 244 km, offering fantastic views of the rugged coastline and tiny fishing communities. The customs post at Chipana-Río Loa (90 km north) searches all southbound vehicles for duty-free goods; 30 minutes delay. Basic accommodation is available at San Marcos, a fishing village, 131 km north. At Chanaballita, 184 km north there is a hotel, *cabañas*, camping, restaurant, shops. There are also campsites at Guanillos, Km 126, Playa Peruana, Km 129 and Playa El Aguila, Km 160.

Calama

Phone code: 055
Colour map 6, grid B2
Population: 106,970
Altitude: 2,265 m
202 km N of
Antofagasta

Calama lies in the oasis of the Río Loa. Initially a staging post on the silver route between Potosí and Cobija, it is now an expensive, unprepossessing modern city, serving the nearby mines of Chuquicamata and Radomiro Tomic. Calama can be reached from the north by Route 24 via Chuquicamata or, from the south, by a paved road leaving the Pan-American Highway 98 km north of Antofagasta at Carmen Alto (petrol and food). This road passes many abandoned nitrate mines (*oficinas*).

Two kilometres from the centre on Av B O'Higgins is the **Parque El Loa**, which contains a reconstruction of a typical colonial village built around a reduced-scale reproduction of Chiu Chiu church. ■ *Daily 1000-1800*. Nearby in the park is the **Museo Arqueológico y Etnológico**, with an exhibition of pre-hispanic cultural history. ■ *Tue-Sun 1000-1300, 1540-1930*. Also the new **Museo de Historia Natural**, with an interesting collection on the *oficinas* and on the region's ecology and palaeontology. ■ *Wed-Sun, 1000-1300, 1430-2000, US$0.65*.

Sleeping **L** *Lican Antai*, Ramírez 1937, T341621, hotellicanantai@terra.cl With breakfast, central, good service and good restaurant, TV. Recommended. **L-AL** *Hostería Calama*, Latorre 1521, T341511, hcalama@directo.cl Comfortable, good food and service. **AL** *Park*, Camino Aeropuerto 1392, T319900, F319901 (Santiago T233-8509). First class, pool, bar and restaurant. Recommended. **A** *El Mirador*, Sotomayor 2064, T/F340329, hotelelmirador@hotmail.com With bath, good atmosphere, clean, helpful. Recommended. **C** *Casablanca*, Sotomayor 2160, on plaza. Quiet, safe, with breakfast. **C** *Génesis*, Granaderos 2148, T342841.

Cheaper double rooms, **D**, near Geminis bus terminal. Recommended. **D** *Hostal Splendid*, Ramirez 1960, T341841. Central, clean, friendly, hot water, often full, good. **E** pp *San Sebastián*, Pinto 1902, T343810. Good beds, meals available, decent choice, family run, rooms with bath and TV in annex across the street. **F** pp *Casa de Huéspedes*, Sotomayor 2079. Poor beds, basic but reasonable, pleasant courtyard, hot shower. **F** pp *Cavour*, Sotomayor 1841, T317392. Simple, basic, hospitable. **F** pp *Claris Loa*, Granaderos 1631, T319079. Quiet, good value, central.

Mid-range: *Bavaria*, Sotomayor 2095. Good restaurant with cafetería downstairs, real coffee, open 0800, very popular, also at Latorre 1935. *Los Adobes de Balmaceda*, Balmaceda 1504. Excellent meat. *Los Braseros de Hans Tur*, Sotomayor 2030. Good ambience, good food. *Mariscal JP*, Félix Hoyos 2127. Best seafood. *México*, Latorre 1986. Genuine Mexican cuisine, live music at weekends. **Cheap**: Best Chinese is *Nueva Chong Hua*, Abaroa 2006. Several places on Abaroa on Plaza 23 de Marzo: *Club Croata*, excellent value 4-course *almuerzo*, good service; *D'Alfredo Pizzería* and *Di Giorgio* (poor service) for pizzas, etc; *Plaza*, good *almuerzos*, opens early, good service. *Lascar*, Ramírez 1917. Good value *almuerzo*. *Pukará*, Abaroa 2054B. Typical local food, excellent, very cheap.

Eating

Market on Antofagasta between Latorre and Vivar, selling fruit juices and crafts. Craft stalls on Latorre 1600 block. **Supermarkets** *Económico*, Grecia 2314, *El Cobre*, Vargas 2148.

Shopping

Several agencies run 1-day and longer tours to the Atacama region, including San Pedro; these are usually more expensive than tours from San Pedro and require a minimum number for the tour to go ahead. Operators with positive recommendations include: *Azimut 360*, T/F333040, www.azimut.cl Tours to the Atacama desert, mountaineering expeditions. *Turismo Buenaventura*, T/F341882, buenventur@entelchile.net *Colque Tours*, C Caracoles, T851109, colquetours@terra.cl 4WD tours of Andes and salt plains into Bolivia. *Turismo El Sol*, V. Mackenna 1812, T340152. Main office in San Pedro de Atacama. *Turismo Tujina*, Ramirez 2222, T/F342261.

Tour operators

Local Car hire A 4WD jeep (necessary for the desert) costs US$80 a day, a car US$63. All offices close Sat 1300 till Mon morning. Airport offices only open when flights arrive. *IQSA*, O'Higgins 877, T310281. If intending to drive in the border area, visit the police in San Pedro to get maps of which areas may have landmines. See Essentials, page 52 for agency web addresses.

Transport
Remember that between Oct and Mar, Chilean time is 1 hr later than Bolivian.
A hired car shared between several people is an economic alternative for visiting the Atacama region.

Long distance Air *LanChile/Lan Express* (T341394), daily, to **Santiago**, via Antofagasta; *Sky* 6 days a week. Taxi to town US$6 (courtesy vans from Hotels *Calama*, *Alfa* and *Lican Antai*). Also buses into town. Recommended service with *Alberto Molina*, T324834; he'll pick you up at your hotel, US$3.

Trains To **Uyuni** (Bolivia), weekly service, Wed 2300, though often doesn't leave till early next morning. If on time the train arrives in **Ollagüe** at 0830. The Chilean engine returns to Calama and you have to wait up to 7 hrs for the Bolivian engine. You have to disembark at the border for customs and immigration. Interpol is in a modern building 400 m east of the station. Through fare to Uyuni is US$13.45. Book seats (passport essential) after 1500 on day of travel from the *Ferrocarril* office in Calama (closed 1300-1500 for lunch), or a local travel agency. Catch the train as early as possible: although seats are assigned, the designated carriages may not arrive; passengers try to occupy several seats to sleep on, but will move if you show your ticket. Sleeping bag and/or blanket essential. Restaurant car operates to the border, cheap. There is no food or water at Ollagüe. If you haven't brought any with you, you'll suffer as you wait for the Bolivian engine to turn up. Money can be changed on the train once in Bolivia, but beware forged notes.

A very uncomfortable journey with many delays, and no heating or toilets (improvise in the space between the carriage and the dining car)

Buses No main terminal, buses leave from company offices: *Frontera*, Antofagasta 2041, T318543; *Kenny Bus*, Vivar 1954; *Flota Barrios*, Ramírez 2298. To **Santiago** 23 hrs, US$25 (*salón cama*, US$40). To **Valparaíso/Viña del Mar**, US$25. To **La Serena**, usually with delay in Antofagasta, 15 hrs, US$20. To **Antofagasta**, 3 hrs, several companies, US$4. To **Iquique**, 6 hrs, via Chuquicamata and Tocopilla, US$7, most overnight, but *Tur Bus* have one early morning and one mid-afternoon service. To **Arica**, usually overnight, US$9, 12 hrs, or

Thieves operate at the bus stations

▶ *The slow train to Uyuni*

The line between Calama and Oruro in Bolivia is the only section of the old Antofagasta and Bolivia Railway line still open to passenger trains. It is a long, slow journey but well worthwhile for the scenery. The journey is very cold, both during the day and at night (-15°C). From Calama the line climbs to reach its highest point at Ascotán (3,960 m); it then descends to 3,735 m at Cebollar, skirting the Salar de Ascotán.

Chilean customs are at Ollagüe and the train is searched at Bolivian customs at Avaroa. From the border the line runs northeast to Uyuni, 204 km (six hours), crossing the Salar de Chiguana and running at an almost uniform height of 3,660 m. Uyuni is the junction with the line south to the Argentine frontier at Villazón. Río Mulato is the junction for Potosí, but it is much quicker to travel by bus from Uyuni.

change in Antofagasta. To **Chuquicamata** (see below). For services to **San Pedro de Atacama** and Toconao, see below. **To Argentina** *Géminis* on Wed and Sun, US$35 (leaving from *Pullman* terminal), 22 hrs. **To Bolivia** *Buses Manchego* leave for Uyuni at midnight, Wed and Sun, US$10.50, also serving Ollagüe, US$5.25, T318466.

Directory **Banks** Exchange rates are generally poor especially for TCs. Many *Redbanc* ATMs on Latorre and Sotomayor. *Casas de Cambio*: *Moon Valley*, Sotomayor 1960. Another at No 1837. **Communications** Internet: At Calle Vargas 2014, p 2, And 2054, both US$1.50 per hr. *Cybercafé Machi*, Vivar 1944. **Post Office**: Granaderos y V Mackenna. 0830-1300, 1530-1830, Sat 0900-1230, will not send parcels over 1 kg. **Telephone**: *CTC*, Sotomayor 1825. *Entel*, Sotomayor 2027. **Consulates** **Bolivia**, Vicuña Mackenna 1984, T344413, apply for visas before 1500, helpful. **Tourist office** Latorre 1689, T345345, map, city tours, helpful. Mon-Fri 0900-1300, 1430-1900.

Chuquicamata

Phone code: 055
Colour map 6, grid B2

Altitude: 2,800 m
The town surrounding the mine will close in 2003 and the families will be moved to Calama

North of Calama 16 km is the site of the world's largest open-cast copper mine, employing 8,000 workers and operated by Codelco (the state copper corporation). Everything about Chuquicamata is huge: the pit from which the ore is extracted is four km long, two km wide and 730 m deep; the giant trucks, with wheels over 3½m high, carry 310 ton loads and work 24 hours a day; in other parts of the plant 60,000 tons of ore are processed a day. ■ *Guided tours, by bus, in Spanish (also in English if enough people) leave from the office of Chuqui Ayuda (a local children's charity) near the entrance at the top end of the plaza, Mon-Fri 0945 and 1400 (less frequently in low season – tourist office in Calama has details), 1 hr, US$2.25 requested as a donation to the charity; register at the office 30 mins in advance; passport number essential. Filming permitted in certain areas. In order to get on the tour, the tourist office in Calama recommends that you catch a colectivo from Calama at 0800. From Calama: yellow colectivo taxis (marked 'Chuqui') from the corner of the main plaza, US$1.50.*

The desert to the eastern side of the road is extensively covered by minefields. There is no petrol between Calama and Uyuni in Bolivia. If really short try buying from the carabineros at Ollagüe or Ascotán, the military at Conchi or the mining camp at Buenaventura (5 km from Ollagüe)

From Calama it is 273 km north to Ollagüe, on the Bolivian border. The road follows the Río Loa, passing **Chiu Chiu** (33 km), one of the earliest Spanish settlements in the area. Just beyond this oasis, a small turning branches off the main road to the hamlet of **Lasana**, 8 km north of Chiu Chiu. Petroglyphs are clearly visible on the right-hand side of the road. There are striking ruins of a pre-Inca *pukará*, a national monument; drinks are on sale. If arranged in advance, Línea 80 *colectivos* will continue to Lasana for an extra charge Pre-book the return trip, or walk back to Chiu Chiu. At **Conchi**, 25 km north of Lasana, the road crosses the Río Loa via a bridge dating from 1890 (it's a military zone, so no photographs of the view are allowed). Beyond Chiu Chiu the road deteriorates, with deep potholes, and, north of Ascotán (*carabinero* checkpoint at 3,900 m), it becomes even worse (ask about the conditions on the Salares at Ascotán or Ollagüe before setting out, especially in December/January or August). There are many llama flocks along this road and flamingoes on the salares.

Ollagüe

Colour map 6, grid B2
Altitude: 3,690 m

This village, on the dry floor of the Salar de Ollagüe, is surrounded by a dozen volcanic peaks of over 5,000 m. The border with Bolivia is open 0800-2100; US$2 per vehicle charge for crossings 1300-1500, 1850-2100. A bad unmade road from Ollagüe runs into Bolivia. Police and border officials will help find lodging. There are few services and no public toilets. At this altitude the days are warm and sunny, nights cold (minimum temperature -20° C). There are only 50 mm of rain a year, and water is very scarce. Ollagüe can be reached by taking the Calama-Uyuni train or by *Manchego* bus (see above). If you stop off, hitching is the only way out.

Between Chiu Chiu and El Tatio (see below), **Caspana** (*Population*: 400; *altitude* 3,305 m) is beautifully set among hills with a tiny church dating from 1641 and a museum with interesting displays on Atacameño culture. Basic accommodation is available. A poor road runs north and east through valleys of pampas grass with llama herds to **Toconce**, which has extensive prehispanic terraces set among interesting rock formations. A community tourism project has been set up, designed to help stem the flow of people moving to Calama. Three rooms are available, accommodation for up to 12 people, with full board, **B**. There are archaeological sites nearby and the area is ideal for hiking. Further information from the tourist office in Calama, who may also help with arranging transport, or T321828, toconce@mixmail.com

San Pedro de Atacama

San Pedro de Atacama is a small town, more Spanish-Indian looking than is usual in Chile. Long before the arrival of the Spanish, the area was the centre of the Atacameño culture. There is a definite sense of history in the shady streets and the crumbling ancient walls, which drift away from the town into the fields, and then into the dust. Owing to the clear atmosphere and isolation, there are wonderful views of the night sky. Lunar landscapes, blistering geysers and salt flats are all close by. Now famous among visitors as the centre for excursions in this part of the Atacama, San Pedro can be overrun with tourists in summer. The **Iglesia de San Pedro**, dating from the 17th century, has been heavily restored (the tower was added in 1964). The roof is made of cactus. Nearby, on the Plaza, is the **Casa Incaica**, the oldest building in San Pedro.

Museo Arqueológico, the collection of Padre Gustave Paige, a Belgian missionary who lived in San Pedro between 1955 and 1980, is now under the care of the Universidad Católica del Norte. It is a fascinating repository of artefacts, well organized to trace the development of prehispanic Atacameño society. Labels are in Spanish are good, and there is a comprehensive booklet in Spanish and English. ■ *Mon-Fri, 0900-1300, 1500-1900; Sat-Sun, 1000-1200, 1500-1800, US$1.50, museospa@entelchile.net*

Phone code: 055
Colour map 6, grid B2
Population: 2,824
Altitude: 2,436 m
103 km SE of Calama
(paved; no fuel,
food or water)

Main tourist season
Oct-end Feb, with high
prices and pressure
on resources

Sleeping
■ *on map*
There is electricity,
but take a torch
(flashlight) for walking
at night. Residenciales
supply candles, but
better to buy them in
Calama beforehand.
Accommodation is
scarce in Jan/Feb
and expensive

L *Explora*. Luxury full-board and excursion programme, advance booking only (Av Américo Vespucio Sur 80, p 5, Santiago, T206 6060, F228 4655, explora@entelchile.net). Recommended. **L** *Hostería San Pedro*, Solcor, T851011, hsanpedro@chilesat.net Pool (residents only), petrol station, tents for hire, cabins, hot water, has own generator, restaurant (good *almuerzo*), bar, takes Amex but no TCs. **L** *Tulor*, Atienza, T/F851248, tulor@chilesat.net Good service, pool, heating, laundry, excellent restaurant. Recommended. **AL** *Kimal*, Atienza y Caracoles, T851159, kimal@entelchile.net Comfortable, excellent restaurant. **A** *El Tatio*, Caracoles, T851263, hoteleltatio@usa.net Comfortable, small rooms, bargain off season, English spoken. **AL** *La Casa de Don Tomás*, Tocopilla, T851055, dontomas@rdc.cl Very pleasant, quiet, pool. Recommended, book in advance. **B** *Casa Corvatsch*, Le Paige, T/F851101, corvatsch@entelchile.net Cheaper rooms **F** pp, pleasant views, English/German spoken, usually recommended, but some mixed reports. **B** *Hostal Takha-Takha*, Caracoles, T851038. **F** pp for cheaper rooms, lovely garden, nice rooms, camping **G** pp, laundry facilities. **B** *Tambillo*, Le Paige, T/F851078. Pretty, comfortable, 24-hr electricity and hot water, good value. **B** *Res Licancábur*, Toconao, T851007, **C** off-season, cheaper rooms **E-F** pp, nicely furnished, with character. **C** *Katarpe*, Atienza, T851033, katarpe@galeon.com Comfortable, quiet, nice patio, good value. Recommended. **C** *Res Juanita*, on the plaza, T851039, 09-491 7663 (Mob), newgeston@hotmail.com **E** without bath, hot water, run-down, restaurant. **D** *La Quinta Adela*, Toconao, T851272, qtadela@cvmail.cl Hot water, no breakfast, good. **D** pp *Res*

Sonchek, Calama 370, T851112. Pleasant but strict, shared bath, also dormitory, no towels, laundry facilities, use of kitchen, garden, restaurant, French and English spoken, mixed reports. **D** *Hostal Vilacoya*, Tocopilla. Set around courtyard, comfortable beds, hot water, helpful, well-equipped kitchen, luggage store, free internet. **E** pp *Hostal Casa Adobe*, Atienza 582, T851249. Shared hot shower, laundry facilities, hospitable. **E** pp *Casa de Nora*, Tocopilla, T851114. Family accommodation, simple rooms, lovely patio. Recommended. **E** pp *Hostal Edén Atacameño*, Toconao, T851154. Renovated, rooms with and without bath, hot water, laundry, parking, also camping with laundry and cooking facilities, **F. E** pp *Res Chiloé*, Atienza, T851017. Hot water, sunny veranda, good beds and bathrooms, good meals, laundry facilities, luggage store, good value. **F** pp *Res Florida*, Tocopilla, T851021. Without bath, basic, quiet patio, hot water evenings only, laundry facilities, no singles. From **F** pp *Sumaj-Jallpa*, Volcán El Tatio 703, on edge of town, T851416. Swiss-Chilean owned, spaceous, kitchen, pool table, prices vary, new.

Camping *Kunza*, Antofagasta y Atienza, T851183, **F** pp, but nighclub next door at weekends.

Eating
● on maps
Price codes:
see inside front cover
Few places are open
before 1000

Mid-range: *Adobe*, Caracoles. Open fire, good atmosphere and meeting place, loud music, internet. *Café Etnico*, Tocopilla 423, cafeetnico@hotmail.com Good food, cosy, book exchange, internet. *Café Export*, Toconao y Caracoles. Nice décor, vegetarian options, real coffee, English spoken, loud music. *Casa Piedra*, Caracoles. Open fire, also has a cheap menu, many of the waiters are musicians, good food and cocktails. Recommended. *La Casona*, Caracoles. Good food, vegetarian options, cheap *almuerzo*, large portions, popular. Recommended. **Cheap**: *Café Tierra Todo Natural*, Caracoles. Excellent fruit juices, "the best bread in the Atacama", real coffee, yoghurt, best for breakfast, opens earliest. *Café El Viaje*, Tocopilla in the Casa de la Arte. Nice patio, good for vegetarians, travel information, internet. *Quitor*, Licancábur y Domingo Atienza. Good, basic food. *Tahira*, Tocopilla. Excellent value *almuerzo*, local dishes. **Bars**: *La Estaka*, Caracoles. Lively after 2300, also good cuisine and service. Recommended.

Chile

San Pedro de Atacama

■ Sleeping
1 Casa Corvatsch
2 El Tatio
3 Hostal Edén Atacameño
4 Hostal Takha-Takha
5 Hostal Vilacoyo
6 Hostería San Pedro
7 Katarpe
8 Kimal
9 Kunza Camping
10 La Casa de Don Tomás
11 Residencial Chiloé
12 Residencial Florida
13 Residencial Juanita
14 Residencial Licancábur
15 Residencial Sonchek
16 Tambillo
17 Tulor

● Eating
1 Adobe & Casa Piedra
2 Café El Viaje
3 Café Etnico
4 Café Export
5 Café Tierra Todo Natural
6 La Casona

● Bars & clubs
7 La Estaka

0 metres 50
0 yards 50

Mountain biking: bicycles for hire all over town, by the hour or full day. Tracks in the desert can be really rough, so check the bike's condition and carry a torch if riding after dark. *Pangea*, Tocopilla, T851111. English spoken, US$2 per hr, US$15 per day. Recommended. **Mountaineering**: Some climbs go to very high altitude – be acclimatized. *Campamento Base*, Toconao 544, T851451, basecamp@mail.com A bit more expensive than others (US$80-100 a day), but offers full insurance, for all levels of ability, good breakfast, good guides, English and German spoken (Stephan will give 5% discount to *Footprint* owners). Also offers rock climbing and has a good vegetarian café. Highly recommended. **Sand boarding**: *Desert Sports*, Toconao 447A/B, T851373, cabanasports@hotmail.com Good value, tuition, pizzería, also rents mountain bikes. Recommended. **Swimming Pool**: *Piscina Oasis*, at Pozo Tres, only 3 km southeast but walking there is tough and not recommended. Open all year daily (except Mon) 0500-1730, US$1.50 to swim, sometimes empty. Camping US$3 and picnic facilities, very popular at weekends.

Sport & activities

Usual tour rates (may rise in high season): to Valle de la Luna, US$4.50. To the Salar de Atacama US$7, plus US$3.50 entry to Los Flamencos national park and US$1 to enter Toconao. The Salar and Toconao are also included in an Altiplano lakes tour, 0700-1800, US$25-30. To El Tatio (begin at 0400) US$14 (take swimming costume and warm clothing). *Cordillera Traveller*, Toconao 447B, T851111, ctraveler@123mail.cl Good value. *Cosmo Andino Expediciones*, Caracoles s/n, T/F851069, cosmoandina@ entelchile.net Very professional and experienced. several languages spoken, owner Martin Beeris (Martín El Holandés). Recommended. Opposite are *Desert Adventure*, Caracoles s/n, T/F851067, desertsp@ctcinternet.cl Recommended. *Atacama Inca Tour*, Toconao s/n, Frente a la Plaza, T581034, F851062. Private and group tours. Recommended as knowledgeable and environmentally aware. *Labra*, Caracoles s/n, T851137. Expert guide Mario Banchon, English and German spoken. Recommended. *Rancho Cactus*, Toconao, T851108, F851052. Offers horseriding with good guides to Valle de la Luna and other sites (Farolo and Valerie – speaks French and English). *Expediciones Corvatsch/Florida*, Tocopilla s/n, T851087, F851052. Group discounts. *Turismo El Sol*, Tocopilla 432-A, T851230, turismoelsol@hotmail.com Internet access as well as tours. *Southern Cross Adventure*, Toconao 544 (see under Santiago, Tour operators). *Turismo Colque*, Caracoles, T851109, www.colquetours.com runs tours to Laguna Verde, Laguna Colorado, Uyuni and other sites in Bolivia. 3 days, changing vehicles at the border as the Bolivian authorities refuse permits for Chilean tour vehicles, US$85 pp (75 low season), basic accommodation, take food and especially water (1-day tour to Laguna Verde possible), entrance to Eduardo Avaroa Reserve in Bolivia is included. Passports are stamped en route (check if you need a visa for Bolivia in advance – consulate is in Calama). Recommended. Other companies offer this trip, eg *Pamela*, Toconao 522, T09-877 0495 (Mob). Beware of altitude sickness. Bolivian company *Andean Summits* also has a local office here for cross-border expeditions, www.andeansummits.com

Tour operators

Beware of tours to Valle de la Luna leaving too late to catch sunset – leave before 1600

Before taking a tour, check that the agency has dependable vehicles, suitable equipment (eg oxygen for El Tatio), a guide who speaks English if so advertised, and that the company is well-established Report any complaints to the municipality or Sernatur

Buses From Calama: *Tur Bus* daily 0950, *Atacama 2000* 3 a day from Abaroa y Antofagasta, *Frontera* 9 a day from Antofagasta 2142, last bus 2030, US$1.50, 1½ hrs. *Transfer Licancábur* direct from Calama airport to San Pedro, US$7, reserve in advance, T09-942 5978, F055-334194. To Calama, *Tur Bus*, 1800 (continues to Antofagasta); *Frontera* first 0900, last 1900. *TurBus* to *Arica*, 2030, US$15. Frequencies vary with more departures in Jan-Feb and some weekends. Book in advance to return from San Pedro on Sun afternoon. **To Argentina**: *Géminis*, Wed and Sun, to *Salta*, US$35, reserve in advance and book Salta hotel as bus arrives 0100-0200 (schedules change often). Tour operators offer transport to Salta for US$50, take food and drink.

Transport

Banks There is no bank or ATM, so take plenty of pesos: only place that changes TCs is *cambio* on Toconao, 1030-1800 daily. Some agencies and hotels change dollars. **Communications** Internet: several places in town (see Eating, above), shop around for best prices. **Post Office**: G Paige s/n, opposite museum. Mon-Fri 0830-1230, 1400-1800, Sat morning only. **Telephone**: *CTC*, Caracoles y Toconao, 0900-1300, 1800-2000, public fax 851052. *Entel* on the plaza, Mon-Fri 0900-2200, Sat 0930-2200, Sun 0930-2100. **Tourist office** On the plaza, with little information, rarely open, www.sanpedroatacama.com

Directory

Around San Pedro de Atacama

Although sunset is the best time to visit, it is also the most crowded with visitors

Do not leave any rubbish behind on desert excursions-the dry climate preserves it perfectly

The **Valle de la Luna** with fantastic landscapes caused by the erosion of salt mountains, is a nature reserve 12 km west of San Pedro. It is crossed by the old San Pedro-Calama road. Although buses on the new Calama-San Pedro road will stop to let you off where the old road branches off 13 km northwest of San Pedro (signposted to Peine), it is far better to travel from San Pedro on the old road, either on foot (allow three hours there, three hours back; no lifts), by bicycle (only for the fit and difficult after sunset) or by car (a 20-km round trip is possible). The Valle is best seen at sunset (if the sky is clear). Take water, hat, camera and torch. Camping is forbidden.

North of San Pedro along the river is the **Pukará de Quitor**, a pre-Inca fortress restored in 1981. The fortress, which stands on the west bank of the river, was stormed by the Spanish under Pedro de Valdivia. A further 4 km up the river there are Inca ruins at Catarpe. At **Tulor**, 12 km southwest of San Pedro, there is an archaeological site where parts of a stone-age village (dated 800 BC-500 AD) have been excavated; can be visited on foot, or take a tour, US$5 pp. Nearby are the ruins of a 17th century village, abandoned in the 18th century because of lack of water.

El Tatio

Warning: People have been killed or seriously injured by falling into the geysers, or through the thin crust of the mud. Do not stand too close as the geysers can erupt unexpectedly Altitude: 4,500 m

El Tatio, the site of geysers, is a popular attraction. From San Pedro it is reached by a maintained road which runs northeast. The geysers are at their best 0630-0830, though the spectacle varies: locals say the performance is best when weather conditions are stable. A swimming pool has been built nearby (take costume and towel). There is a workers' camp which is empty apart from one guard, who will let you sleep in a bed in one of the huts, **F**, take food and sleeping bag. From here you can hike to surrounding volcanoes if acclimatized to altitude. There is no public transport and hitching is impossible. If going in a hired car, make sure the engine is suitable for very high altitudes and is protected with antifreeze; four-wheel drive is advisable. If driving in the dark it is almost impossible to find your way: the sign for El Tatio is north of the turn off (follow a tour bus). Tours arranged by agencies in San Pedro and Calama.

Toconao

*Colour map 6, grid B2
Population: 500
37 km S of San Pedro de Atacama*

Toconao is on the eastern shore of the Salar de Atacama. All houses are built of bricks of white volcanic stone, which gives the village a very characteristic appearance totally different from San Pedro. The 18th century church and bell tower are also built of volcanic stone. East of the village is a beautifully green gorge called the Quebrada de Jérez, filled with fruit trees and grazing cattle (entry US$1). Worth visiting are the vineyards which produce a unique sweet wine. The quarry where the stone (*sillar*) is worked can be visited, about 1½ km east (the stones sound like bells when struck). There are basic *residenciales* (**F** pp), eg *Residencial Valle deToconao*, on Láscar, nice and quiet. ■ Frontera *bus from San Pedro, 4 a day, US$0.80.*

The 3rd largest expanse of salt flats in the world

South of Toconao is one of the main entrances to the **Salar de Atacama**, a vast 300,000-ha salt lake that's home to the pink flamingo and other birds (though most of the flamingos have moved to lakes higher in the Andes and numbers depend on breeding times). The air is so dry that you can usually see right across the Salar. A huge lake half a metre below the surface contributes to a slight haze in the air. The area is also rich in minerals. ■ *Entry is controlled by* Conaf *in Toconao, US$3.50.* Three areas of the Salar form part of the **Reserva Nacional de los Flamencos**, which is in seven sectors totalling 73,986 ha and administered by *Conaf* in San Pedro.

From Toconao the road heads south through scenic villages to the mine at Laco (one poor stretch below the mine), before proceeding to Laguna Sico (4,079 m), and Paso Sico to Argentina.

Hito Cajón for the border with Bolivia is reached by road 45 km east of San Pedro. The first 35 km are the paved road to Paso de Jama (see below), then it's poor to Hito Cajón. From the border it is 7 km north to Laguna Verde. Chilean immigration and customs are in San Pedro, open 0900-1200, 1400-1600. For the Bolivian consulate, see under Calama. ■ *Bolivian immigration only gives 1 month entry here.*

For Argentina, the **Paso de Jama** (4,200 m) is reached by paved road, which continues unpaved on the Argentine side to Susques and Jujuy. This is more popular than the **Paso Sico** route, which is mainly used by heavy traffic (paved on the Chilean side, about 40 % paved in Argentina to San Antonio de los Cobres). Chilean immigration and customs are in San Pedro. When crossing by private vehicle, check the road conditions before setting out as Paso de Jama can be closed by heavy rain in summer and blocked by snow in winter.

Border with Bolivia & Argentina
At all border crossings, incoming vehicles and passengers are searched for fruit, vegetables and dairy produce, which may not be brought into Chile

The Far North

Santiago

Chile

The Atacama Desert extends over most of the Far North to the Peruvian border. The main cities are Iquique and Arica; between them are old mineral workings and geoglyphs. Large areas of the Andean highland have been set aside as national parks.

The Cordillera de la Costa slowly loses height north of Iquique, terminating at the Morro at Arica: from Iquique north it drops directly to the sea and as a result there are few beaches along this coast. Inland the central depression (pampa) 1,000-1,200 m is arid and punctuated by salt-flats south of Iquique. Between Iquique and Arica it is crossed from east to west by four gorges. East of this depression lies the sierra, the western branch of the Andes, beyond which is a high plateau, the altiplano (3,500-4,500 m) from which rise volcanic peaks. In the altiplano there are a number of lakes, the largest of which, Lago Chungará, is one of the highest in the world. The coastal strip and the pampa are rainless; on the coast temperatures are moderated by the Pacific, but in the pampa variations of temperature between day and night are extreme, ranging from 30° C to 0° C. The altiplano is much colder.

Iquique

The name of the capital of I Región (Tarapacá) and one of the main northern ports, is derived from the Aymara word *ique-ique*, meaning place of 'rest and tranquillity'. The city is situated on a rocky peninsula at the foot of the high Atacama pampa, sheltered by the headlands of Punta Gruesa and Cavancha. The city, which was partly destroyed by earthquake in 1877, became the centre of the nitrate trade after its transfer from Peru to Chile at the end of the War of the Pacific. A short distance north of town along Amunátegui is the Free Zone (Zofri), a giant shopping centre selling all manner of imported items, including electronic goods: it is worth a visit (much better value than Punta Arenas), good for cheap camera film (Fuji slide film available). ■ *Mon-Sat 0800-2100. Limit on tax free purchases US$650 for foreigners, US$500 for Chileans. Colectivo from the centre US$0.50.*

Phone code: 057
Colour map 6, grid B2
Population: 145,139
492 km N of Antofagasta
47 km W of the Pan-American Highway

The beaches at Cavancha just south of the town centre are good; those at Huaiquique are reasonable, November-March. There are restaurants at Cavancha. Piscina Godoy is a fresh water swimming pool on Av Costanera at Aníbal Pinto and Riquelme, open in the afternoon, US$1 There are several hills where you can paraglide, good for beginners.

Iquique has some of the best surfing in Chile, not for beginners

In the centre of the old town is the unfortunately-named **Plaza Prat**. On the northeast corner of the Plaza is the **Centro Español**, built in Moorish style by the local Spanish community in 1904; the ground floor is a restaurant, on the upper floors are paintings of scenes from Don Quijote and from Spanish history. Three blocks north

Sights

of the Plaza is the old **Aduana** (customs house) built in 1871; in 1891 it was the scene of an important battle in the Civil War between supporters of President Balmaceda and congressional forces. Part of it is now the **Museo Naval**, focusing on the Battle of Iquique, 1879. Along Calle Baquedano, which runs south from Plaza Prat, are the attractive former mansions of the 'nitrate barons', dating from between 1880 and 1903. The finest of these is the **Palacio Astoreca**, Baquedano y O'Higgins, built in 1903, subsequently the Intendencia and now a museum of fine late 19th century furniture and shells. ■ *Tue-Fri 1000-1400, 1500-1900, Sat-Sun 1000-1300, US$1*. **Museo Regional**, Baquedano 951, contains an archaeological section tracing the development of prehispanic civilizations in the region; an ethnographical collection of the Isluga culture of the Altiplano (AD 400), and of contemporary Aymara culture; also a section devoted to the nitrate era which includes a model of a nitrate office and the collection of the nitrate entrepreneur, Santiago Humberstone. ■ *Mon-Fri 0800-1300, 1500-1850, Sat 1030-1300, Sun (in summer) 1000-1300, 1600-2000*. Sea lions and pelicans can be seen from the harbour. There are cruises from the passenger pier. ■ *US$2.50, 45 mins, minimum 10-15 people*.

Excursions
Many other sites around Iquique, including the Giant of the Atacama (see page 638), are difficult to visit without a vehicle

To **Humberstone**, a large nitrate town, now abandoned, at the junction of the Pan-American Highway and the road to Iquique. Though closed since 1961, you can see the church, theatre, *pulpería* (company stores) and the swimming pool (built of metal plating from ships' hulls). ■ *Entry by 'donation', US$1.50, guided tours Sat-Sun, leaflets available. Colectivo from Iquique US$2; phone near site for booking return*. Nearby are the ruins of other mining towns including Santa Laura. Local tour companies run trips to the area, including Humberstone, Santa Laura, Pisagua and **Pozo Almonte**, 52 km east (population about 5,400). This town was the chief service provider of the nitrate companies until their closure in 1960. The **Museo Histórico Salitrero**, on the tree-shaded plaza, displays artefacts and photographs of the nitrate era. ■ *Mon-Fri 0830-1300 and 1600-1900*. To Cerro Pintados (see page 638) take any bus south, US$2.50, and walk from the Pan-American Highway then hitch back or flag down a bus.

Sleeping
Accommodation is scarce in the weeks before Christmas as many Chileans visit Iquique to shop in the Zofri. All hotels in list recommended

AL-A *Arturo Prat*, Plaza Prat, T411067, hap@entelchile.net 4-star, pool, health suite, expensive restaurant, tours arranged. **A-B** *Barros Arana*, Barros Arana 1330, T412840, hba@ctcreuna.cl Modern, pool, good value. **B** *Atenas*, Los Rieles 738, T431075. Pleasant, personal, good value, good service and food. **B** *Cano*, Ramírez 996, T416597, hotelcano@hotmail.com Big rooms, nice atmosphere, good value. **C** *Caiti*, Gorostiaga 483, T/F423038. Pleasant, with breakfast and all mod cons. **C** *Inti-Llanka*, Obispo Labbé 825, T311104, F311105. Nice rooms, helpful, good value. **D** *Danino*, Serrano 897, T417301, F443079. With breakfast, free local phone calls, modern, good value. **D** *Hostal América*, Rodríguez 550, near beach, T427524. Shared bath, no breakfast, motorcycle parking, good value. **D** pp *Hostal Jean IV*, Esmeralda 938, T/F510855, mespina@entelchile.net With breakfast, nice lounge and patio, convenient for buses to Bolivia, excellent value. **E** pp *Hostal Cuneo*, Baquedano 1175, T428654. Modern, nice rooms, shared bath, helpful, pleasant, good value. **E** pp *Oregon* (also called *Durana*), San Martín 294, T410959. Central, hot water, breakfast included. E pp *Res Nan-King*, Thompson 752, T423311. Small but nice rooms. **F** pp *Casa de Huéspedes Profesores*, Ramirez 839, T314692, inostrozaflores@entelchile.net With breakfast, helpful, old building with lots of character. **F** pp *Hostal Li Ming*, Barros Arana 705, T421912, F422707. Simple, good value, small rooms.

Eating
The restaurants on the wharf on the opposite side of Av Costanera from the bus terminal are poor value

Expensive: *Bavaria*, Pinto 926. Expensive restaurant, reasonably priced café serving real coffee, snacks and *almuerzo*. *Casino Español*, good meals well served in beautiful building, and *Club de la Unión*, roof terrace with panoramic views, open lunchtimes only, both on Plaza Prat. *Otelo*, Valenzuela 775. Italian specialities, seafood. **Mid-range**: *El Barril del Fraile*, Ramírez 1181. Good seafood, nice atmosphere. *Boulevard*, Baquedano 790. Good, French, English and French spoken. *Colonial*, Plaza Prat. Fish and seafood, popular, good value. *Sciaraffia*, Sgto Aldea 803 (Mercado Centenario). Open 24 hrs, good value, large choice.

Cheap: *Bolivia*, Serrano 751. *Humitas* and *salteñas*. Recommended. *Compañía Italiana de Bomberos*, Serrano 520. Authentic Italian cuisine, excellent value *almuerzo*, otherwise more expensive. *La Picada Curicana*, Pinto y Zegers. Good local cuisine, good value *menu de la casa*. Many *chifas* including **Win Li**, San Martin 439, and *Sol Oriental*, Martínez 2030 and 6 cheaper ones on Tarapacá 800/900 blocks. There are several good, cheap seafood restaurants on the 2nd floor of the central market, Barros Arana y Latorre.

Cafés *Cioccolata*, Pinto 487 (another branch in the Zofri). Very good. **Splendid**, Vivar 795. Good *onces*, inexpensive. **Salon de Té Ricotta**, Vivar y Latorre. Very popular for *onces*, quite expensive. For juices, snacks: *Tropical*, Baquedano y Thompson; *Via Pontony*, Baquedano y Zegers; *Jugos Tarapacá*, Tarapacá 380.

Bars *Santa Fé*, Mall Las Américas, locales 10-11-193. Mexican, live music, great atmosphere, very popular. *Taberna Barracuda*, Gorostiaga 601. For late night food, drink, video entertainment, dancing, nice décor, nice atmosphere.

Altazor Skysports, Serrano 145, of 702, T431328, altazor@entelchile.net *Empresas Turísticas*, Baquedano 958, T/F416600. Good tours, student discount, ask for guide Jaime Vega González. *Iquitour*, Lynch 563, T/F412415. Tour to Pintados, La Tirana, Humberstone, Pica, etc, day tours start at US$20. *Viatours*, Baquedano 736, T/F417197, viatours@entelchile.net

Tour operators
The tourist office maintains a full list

Local Car hire: *Iqsa*, Labbé 1089, T/F417068. *Procar*, Serrano 796, T/F413470.

Transport

Long distance Air: Diego Aracena international airport, 35 km south at Chucumata. Taxi US$9.50; airport transfer, T310800, US$3.20 for 3 or more passengers, unreliable. *LanChile/Lan Express* and *Sky* fly to *Arica, Antofagasta* and *Santiago*. *Lan Express* flies to **La Serena**. See Getting there, Essentials, for international flights.

Buses: Terminal at north end of Patricio Lynch (not all buses leave from here); bus company offices are near the market on Sgto Aldea and B Arana. *Tur Bus*, Ramírez y Esmeralda, with *Redbanc* ATM and luggage store. Southbound buses are searched for duty-free goods, at Quillagua on the Pan-American Highway and at Chipana on the coastal Route 1. To **Arica**, buses and colectivos, US$5, 4½ hrs. To **Antofagasta**, US$9, 8 hrs. To **Calama**, 4 hrs, US$7. To **Tocopilla** along the coastal road, buses and minibuses, several companies, 4 hrs, US$4. To **La Serena**, 18 hrs, US$20. To **Santiago**, 28 hrs, several companies, US$30 (US$50 *salón cama*).

International buses: to Bolivia *Litoral*, T423670, daily to **Oruro**, US$8, and **La Paz**, US$12. *Bernal, Paraíso, Salvador*, and others from Esmeralda near Juan Martínez around 2100-2300, US$8-13 (may have a cold wait for customs to open at 0800).

Airline offices *LanChile*, Tarapacá 465, T427600, and in Mall Las Américas. **Banks** Numerous *Redbanc* ATMs in the centre and the Zofri. *Cambios: Afex*, Serrano 396, for TCs. *Money Exchange*, Lynch 548, loc 1-2. Best rates for TCs and cash at *casas de cambio* in the Zofri, eg *Wall Street* (sells and cashes Amex TCs). **Communications** Internet: *Fassher Internet*, Vivar 1497, p 2. US$0.80 per hr. Same price is *PC@NET Computación*, Vivar 1373. More central is *Obispo Labbé y Serrano*, US$1.50 per hr. **Post Office**: *Correo Central*, Bolívar 485. **Telephone**: *CTC*, Serrano 620. *Entel*, Tarapacá 476. **NB** Correos and phone companies all have offices in the Plaza de Servicios in the Zofri. **Consulates** Bolivia, Gorostiaga 215, Departamento E, T421777. Mon-Fri 0930-1200. Italy, Serrano 447, T421588. **Netherlands**, Manzana 11, Galpón 2, Zofri, T426074. **Peru**, Zegers 570, T411466. **Spain**, Manzana 2, Sitio 5 y 9, Zofri, T422330. **Language schools** *Academia de Idiomas del Norte*, Ramírez 1345, T411827, F429343, idiomas@chilesat.net Swiss run, Spanish classes and accommodation for students. **Tourist offices** Serrano 145, of 303, T427686, sernatur_iquiq@entelchile.net Masses of information, helpful, Mon-Fri, 0830-1630.

Directory

From Pozo Almonte 74 km (paved), **Mamiña** (*Population*: about 600. *Altitude*: 2,750 m) has abundant thermal springs and a mud spring (Baño Los Chinos; open 0930-1300). The therapeutic properties of the waters and mud are Mamiña's main claim to fame. Mineral water from the spring is sold throughout northern Chile. There are ruins of a pre-hispanic *pukará* (fortress) and a church, built in 1632, the only colonial Andean church in Chile with two towers. An Aymara cultural centre, *Kaspi-kala*, has an *artesanía* workshop and outlet.

Around Iquique

Chile

La Tirana (Population: 550. Altitude: 995 m) is famous for a religious festival to the Virgen del Carmen, held from 10 to 16 July, which attracts some 80,000 pilgrims. Over 100 groups dance night and day, starting on 12 July. All the dances take place in the main plaza in front of the church; no alcohol is served. Accommodation is impossible to find, other than in organized camp sites (take tent) which have basic toilets and showers. It is 10 km east of the Pan-American Highway (70 km east of Iquique), turn-off 9 km south of Pozo Almonte.

Try the local alfajores, delicious cakes filled with cream and mango honey

Pica (*Population*: 1,767. *Altitude*: 1,325 m), 42 km from La Tirana, was the most important centre of early Spanish settlement in the area. Most older buildings date from the nitrate period when it became a popular resort. The town is famous for its pleasant climate, citrus groves and two natural springs, the best of which is Cocha Resbaladero. ■ *0700-2000 all year, US$2, snack bar, changing rooms, beautiful pool. Tourist office.*

Sleeping and eating Mamiña There are several hotels and *residenciales* offering rooms with bath fed by the springs and full board. They include **B** pp *Los Cardenales*, T438182, T09-545 1091 (mob). Beautifully designed, comfortable, superb food, English and German spoken, pool. **B** pp *Refugio del Salitre*, T751203, T420330. Secluded, nice rooms, pool. **C** pp *Termal La Coruña*, T09-543 0360. Good, Spanish cuisine, horse riding, nice views. **C** pp *Llama Inn*, T Iquique 419893. Room only, good meals extra (including vegetarian on request), comfortable, pool, English spoken. **Pica C** *Suizo*, Ibáñez 210, T741551. Austrian-Danish owners, with shower, TV, modern, comfortable, parking, excellent food in café. **D** *Los Emilios*, Cochrane 213, T741126. Pool, with breakfast. **D** *San Andrés*, Balmaceda 197, T741319. With breakfast, basic, good restaurant. **D** *El Tambo*, Ibáñez 68, T741041. House dates from nitrate era, shared bath, hot water, good value, *cabañas* for rent. Under same ownership is **D** *O'Higgins*, Balmaceda 6. Modern, well furnished. Campsite at *Camping Miraflores*, near terminal, T741338, also rents *cabañas* as do 3 other places. *El Edén*, Riquelme 12. 1st class local food in delightful surroundings. On Balmaceda, *La Palmera*, No 115, and *La Mía Pappa*, both good. *La Viña*, Ibáñez 70. Good cheap *almuerzo*.

Transport Mamiña Transportes Tamarugal, Barros Arana 897, Iquique, daily 0800, 1600, return 1800, 0800, 2½ hrs, US$4, good service. Also Mamiña, Latorre 779, daily. **Pica** Minibus Iquique-Pica: San Andrés, Sgto Aldea y B Arana, Iquique, daily 0930, return 1800; Pullman Chacón, Barros Arana y Latorre, many daily; Santa Rosa, Barros Arana 777, daily 0830, 0930, return 1700, 1800. US$2.50 one-way, 2 hrs.

From Iquique to the Bolivian Border At **Huara** (population 450), 33 km north of Pozo Almonte, a road turns off the Pan-American Highway to **Colchane**. At 13 km east of Huara are the huge geoglyphs of **Cerro Unitas**, with the giant humanoid figure of the Gigante del Atacama and a sun with 24 rays, on the sides of two hills (best seen from a distance). This road is in a terrible state, with long-term roadworks and a diversion heavily damaged by lorries. Some buses from Iquique to La Paz and Oruro pass through, or La Paloma at 2300 from Esmeralda y Juan Martínez. 173 km northeast is the Bolivian border at Pisiga (open daily 0800-1300, 1500-1800).

Some of the best volcanic scenery in northern Chile

Northwest of Colchane, the **Parque Nacional Volcán Isluga** covers 174,744 ha at altitudes above 2,100 m. The village of **Isluga**, near the park entrance, 6 km northwest of Colchane, has an 18th century Andean walled church and bell tower. Wildlife varies according to altitude but includes guanacos, vicuñas, llamas, alpacas, vizcachas, condors and flamingoes. ■ *Park Administration at Enquelga, 10 km north of the entrance, but guardaparques are seldom there. Phone Arica 58-250570 for details of hospedaje at the guardería (D pp).*

At Zapiga, 80 km north of Pozo Almonte, there is a crossroads: east through **Camiña** (*Population*: 500. *Altitude*: 2,400 m), a picturesque village in an oasis, 67 km east of Zapiga along a poor road. Thence mountain roads lead across the Parque Nacional Volcán Isluga to Colchane. The westerly branch runs 41 km to **Pisagua** (*Population*: 200), formerly an important nitrate port, now a fishing village. Several old wooden buildings are National Monuments. The fish restaurants make a pleasant stop for a meal. Mass graves dating from just after the 1973 military coup were discovered near here in 1990. At Km 57 north of Huara there is a British cemetery at Tiliviche dating from 1825. The **Geoglyphs of Tiliviche** representing a group of llamas (signposted, to left, and easily accessible), Km 127, can be seen from the highway.

North towards Arica
The Pan-American Highway runs across the Atacama desert at an altitude of around 1,000 m, with several steep hills which are best tackled in daylight (at night, sea mist, camanchaca, can reduce visibility)

Arica

Chile's most northerly city, 20 km south of the Peruvian border, is built at the foot of the Morro headland, fringed by sand dunes. The Andes can be clearly seen from the anchorage. Arica used to be the principal route for travellers going overland to Bolivia, via the Parque Nacional Lauca. Now there is competition from the San Pedro de Atacama-Uyuni route, so new routes are being considered to link this part of the coast with San Pedro, via the high altitude national parks. This is an important port and route-centre. The road route to La Paz via Tambo Colorado is now paved and Arica is frequented for sea-bathing by Bolivians, as well as the locals. A 63-km railway runs north to Tacna in Peru. Regrettably, Arica is also becoming a key link in the international drugs trade.

Phone code: 058
Colour map 6, grid A1
Population: 174,064

The **Morro**, with a good view from the park on top (10 minutes' walk by footpath from the southern end of Colón), was the scene of a great victory by Chile over Peru in the War of the Pacific on 7 June 1880. **Museo Histórico y de Armas**, on the summit of the Morro, contains weapons and uniforms from the War of the Pacific. ■ *Daily 0830-2000 (2200 Jan-Feb), US$0.60.*

Sights

At the foot of the Morro is the Plaza Colón with the cathedral of **San Marcos**, built in iron by Eiffel. Though small it is beautifully proportioned and attractively painted. It was brought to Arica from Ilo (Peru) in the 19th century, before Peru lost Arica to Chile, as an emergency measure after a tidal wave swept over Arica and destroyed all its churches. Eiffel also designed the nearby **Aduana** (customs house) which is now the Casa de la Cultura. ■ *Mon-Fri 0830-2100.* Just north of the Aduana is the La Paz railway station; outside is an old steam locomotive (made in Germany in 1924) once used on this line. In the station is a memorial to John Roberts Jones, builder of the Arica portion of the railway. The **Casa Bolognesi**, Colón y Yungay, is a fine old building painted blue and white. It holds temporary exhibitions.

Worthwhile sights outside Arica include the **Museo Arqueológico de San Miguel** at Km 13 on the road east to the Azapa valley. Built around an olive press, it contains a fine collection of pre-Columbian weaving, pottery, wood carving and basketwork from the coast and valleys, and also seven mummified humans from the Chinchorro culture (8000-1000 BC), the most ancient mummies yet discovered. Explanations in several languages are loaned free at the entrance. ■ *Daily Jan-Feb 0900-2000, Mar-Dec 1000-1800, US$2. T224248, www.uta.cl/masma/ Take a yellow colectivo from P Lynch y Chacabuco and 600 block of P Lynch, US$1.* In the forecourt of the museum are several boulders with pre-Columbian petroglyphs. In San Miguel itself is an old cemetery and several typical restaurants. On the road between Arica and San Miguel there are several groups of geoglyphs of humans and llamas ('stone mosaics') south of the road (signed to Cerro Sagrado, Cerro Sombrero – an Azapa Archaeological Circuit is advertised). North of Arica along Route 11, between Km 14 and Km 16, is the **Lluta valley** where you can see along the hillsides four groups of geoglyphs, representing llamas, and eagle and human giants. The road continues through the Parque Nacional Lauca and on to Bolivia. Take a bus from Mackenna y Chacabuco.

Chile

Chile

Sleeping

■ on map
In Jan-Feb the municipality supplies cheap basic accommodation, ask at the tourist office. Cheap residenciales on Prat 500 block, Velázquez 700 block, P Lynch 600 block. Others opposite bus terminal

L *Arica*, San Martín 599, T254540, F231133, about 2 km along shore (frequent micros and colectivos). Best, price depends on season, good value, good and reasonable restaurant, tennis court, pool, lava beach (not safe for swimming), American breakfast. **L** *El Paso*, Gen Velásquez 1109, T231965. Bungalow style, pleasant gardens, swimming pool, with breakfast, good restaurant *Araksaya*. **A** *Savona*, Yungay 380, T232319, F231606. Comfortable, quiet. Highly recommended. **A** *Volapuk*, 21 de Mayo 425, T252575, volapuk@ctcreuna.cl Good service, nicely decorated, with breakfast, hot water, TV, a/c. **B** *Diego de Almagro*, Sotomayor 490, T224444, F221248. Helpful, comfortable, parking, stores luggage. Recommended (but ask for a room without a balcony as these are not secure). **B** *Plaza Colón*, San Marcos 261, T/F231244, hotel_plaza_colon@entelchile.net With breakfast, comfortable, convenient. **C** *Hotel D'Marie-Jeanne y David*, Velásquez 792, T/F258231. With breakfast, TV, laundry, parking, snacks in café, French spoken. **C** *Sotomayor*, Sotomayor 367, T232149, reservas@hotelsotomayor.cl Comfortable, helpful, restaurant, parking, cheaper if paying in dollars. **D** *Hostal Jardín del Sol*, Sotomayor 848, T232795, F231462. With breakfast, safe, laundry. Recommended. **D** *Hostal Venecia*, Baquedano 741, T255937, F252877. Spotless, small rooms. Recommended. **D** *Res América*, Sotomayor 430, T254148. **F** pp without bath, hot water, hospitable, breakfast included if staying more than 1 day. **D** *Res Las Condes*, Vicuña Mackenna 628, T251583. Helpful, hot showers, kitchen, motorcycle parking. **D** *Res Nilda*, Raúl del Canto 947, T222743. Very nice *casa de familia*, kitchen facilities, laundry, near bus terminal and Playa Chinchorro.

E *Hostal Chez Charlie*, Paseo Thompson 236, T/F250007, latinor@entelchile.net Central, comfortable, shared bath, hot water, good value, French and English spoken (same owner as *La Ciboulette* and *Latinorizons*). **E** *Hostal Ecuador*, Juan Noé 989, T/F251934. With breakfast, very helpful, kitchen, laundry. **E** pp *Mar Azul*, Colón 665, T256272, www.hotelmarazul.cl Small rooms and family rooms, fan, TV, restaurant, small pool, sauna. **E** *Res Las Vegas*, Baquedano 120, T231355. Basic, dark rooms, safe, central. **E** *Stagnaro*, Arturo Gallo 294, T231254. With breakfast, good value. Recommended. **E** pp *Tarapacá*, Maipú 455, T252680. New, with breakfast, helpful, laundry. **F** pp *Res Blanquita*, Maipú 472, T232064. Breakfast extra, laundry and kitchen facilities. **F** pp *Res Caracas*, Sotomayor 867, T253688. Breakfast included. **F** *Res Chillán*, Velásquez 747, T251677. Hot shower, laundry, nice garden. **F** pp *Res El Sur*, Maipú 516, T252457. Small rooms, shared bath, basic. Better value is **F** pp *Res Pepe*, next door, Frente Comercial Parina, T253996. Attentive owner. **F** *Sunny Days*, Tomás Aravena 161 (a little over half way along P de Valdivia, 800 m from bus terminal), T241038, sunnydaysarica@ hotmail.com All-you-can-eat breakfast, hot water, kitchen, laundry facilities, videos, book exchange, bikes and body boards for rent, nice atmosphere, lots of information.

Camping *El Refugio de Azapa*, Valle de Azapa, Km 1.5, T227545.

Eating

■ on map
Many good places on 21 de Mayo and offering meals, drinks, real coffee, juices and outdoor seating

Mid-range: *Bavaria*, Colón 613, upstairs. Good restaurant, coffee and cakes. *Chin Huang Tao*, Lynch 224. Excellent Chinese. *D'Aurelio*, Baquedano 369. Italian specialities, good pasta, seafood. *Don Floro*, V MacKenna 847. Good seafood and steaks, good service. Highly recommended. *El Rey del Marisco*, Colón 565, upstairs. Excellent seafood. *Los Aleros del 21*, 21 de Mayo 736. Recommended for seafood and service. *Maracuyá*, San Martín 0321. Seafood, splendid location on the coast. **Cheap**: *Acuario*, Muelle Turístico. Good food in fishy environment, good value *menu de casa*. *La Bomba*, Colón 357, at fire station. Good value *almuerzo*, friendly service. *La Ciboulette*, Paseo Thompson 238. Good food, pleasant atmosphere. Recommended. *La Jaula*, 21 de Mayo 293. Snacks, meals, good. *Papagallo*, Colón 639. Lunches, juices, extensive menu. *Yuri*, Maipú y Lynch. Good service, cheap lunches. Recommended. Cheaper Chinese restaurants include *Kau Chea*, 18 de Septiembre y Prat, good value, and *Shaolin*, Sotomayor 275. There are many cheap restaurants on Baquedano 600/700 blocks including *San Fernando*, corner with Maipú. Simple breakfast, good value *almuerzo*.

Entertainment *Teatro Municipal de Arica*, Baquedano 234. Wide variety of theatrical and musical events, exhibitions. Recommended.

Festivals **24-26 Jan**, folk music and dance carnival. **Late Feb**, *Ginga Carnaval*, annual group dance competition, 3 nights. **29 Jun**, *San Pedro*, religious service at fishing wharf and boat parades. **First weekend of Oct**, *Virgen de las Peñas*, pilgrimage to the site of the Virgin, 4-5 hrs inland.

Poblado Artesanal, Plaza Las Gredas, Hualles 2825 (take bus 2, 3 or 7). Expensive but especially good for musical instruments, open Tue-Sun 0930-1300, 1530-1930, *peña* Fri and Sat 2130. *Mercado Central*, Sotomayor y Sangra, between Colón and Baquedano. Mostly fruit and vegetables. Smaller fruit and veg market, with food stalls, on Colón between 18 de Septiembre and Maipú. *Feria Turística Dominical*, Sun market, along Chacabuco between Valásquez and Mackenna. Good prices for llama sweaters. **Bookshop** *Andrés Bello*, Sotomayor 363, wide selection.

Shopping *Many shopping galerías in the centre, also pharmacies, electrical appliances and clothes shops Ferias for clothes on Velázquez*

Swimming Olympic pool in Parque Centenario, Tue-Sun, US$0.50. Take No 5A bus from 18 de Septiembre. The best beach for swimming is Playa Chinchorro, north of town. Buses 7 and 8 run to beaches south of town – the first two beaches, La Lisera and El Laucho, are both small and mainly for sunbathing. Playa Brava is popular for sunbathing but not swimming (dangerous currents). **Surfing** Strong currents at Playa Las Machas which is popular with surfers. Good surfing on La Isleta near Club de Yates and on Playa Chinchorro.

Sport & activities

Globo Tour, 21 de Mayo 260, T/F231085. Very helpful for international flights. *Latinorizons*, Bolognesi 449, T/F250007, latinor@entelchile.net Specializes in tours to Parque Nacional Lauca, small groups in four-wheel drive Landcruiser; also bike rental. Recommended. Several others. Agencies charge similar prices for tours: Valle de Azapa US$12; city tour US$10; Parque Nacional Lauca, see page 654.

Tour operators

Local Bus buses run from 18 de Septiembre at Bolognesi, US$0.25. Colectivos on fixed routes within city limit line up on Maipú entre Velásquez y Colón (all are numbered), US$0.50 pp (more after 2000). Taxis are black and yellow and are scarce; hire a colectivo instead, US$1.20-1.50. **Car hire** *American*, Gen Lagos 559, T252234, servturi@entelchile.net *Cactus*, Baquedano 635, T257430, cactusrent@latinmail.com *Ghama*, Diego Portaqles 840, of 161, T225158. *Hertz*, Av Andrés Bello 1469 and at airport, has been recommended for good service. Several others and at Chacalluta airport. Rates start at US$26 per day, up to US$50-60 for 4WD. Antifreeze is essential for Parque Nacional Lauca, 4WD if going off paved roads. **Automóvil Club de Chile**: Chacabuco 460, T252878, F232780.

Transport

Chile

Long distance Air: Airport 18 km north of city at Chacalluta, T222831. Taxi to town US$9, colectivo US$4-5 per person. Flights to **La Paz**, *LanChile*; to **Santiago**, *LanChile*, *Lan Express* and *Sky* via Iquique and, less frequently, Antofagasta. *LanChile* also to **Copiapó**. To **Lima**, from Tacna (Peru), enquire at travel agencies in Arica.

   Buses: Bus terminal at Av Portales y Santa María, T241390, many buses and colectivos (eg No 8) pass (US$0.25, or US$0.50); terminal tax US$0.15. All luggage is carefully searched for fruit 30 mins prior to boarding and at two stops heading south. Bus company offices at bus terminal. Local services: *Flota Paco (La Paloma)*, Germán Riesco 2071 (bus U from centre).

   To **Iquique**, frequent, US$5, 4½ hrs, also collective taxis, several companies, all in the terminal. To **Antofagasta**, US$10, 10 hrs. To **Calama** and **Chuquicamata**, 12 hrs, US$9, several companies, all between 2000 and 2200. To **San Pedro de Atacama**, 2200, 11½ hrs, US$15. To **La Serena**, 18 hrs, US$14-20. To **Santiago**, 28 hrs, a number of companies, eg *Carmelita*, *Ramos Cholele*, *Fénix* and *Flota Barrios* US$22-26, also *salón cama* services, run by *Fichtur*, *Flota Barrios*, *Fénix* and others, US$34 (most serve meals of a kind, somewhat better on the more expensive services; student discounts available). To **Viña del Mar** and **Valparaíso**, US$26, also *salón cama* services.

   International buses: to **La Paz**, Bolivia, at least 6 companies from terminal, US$10-12, most via **Putre** and **Chungará** (some daily); for Visviri/Charaña route, see below. *Géminis*, T241647, to **Jujuy** and **Salta**, Argentina, Tue and Sat.

Airline offices *LanChile*, 21 de Mayo 345, T255941 (closes 1330 on Sat). **Banks** Many *Redbanc* ATMs on 21 de Mayo and by Plaza Colón. Money changers on 21 de Mayo and its junction with Colón, some accept TCs. *Cambio*, in Cosmo Center, Colón 600, cash and TCs, reasonable rates. **Communications** Internet: Plenty of *locutorios* with internet and cyber cafés in the centre, eg on 21 de Mayo or Bolognesi, average price US$0.75-1 per hr. *Virtual Home*, Velázquez 650, p 1, lots of

Directory

Arica

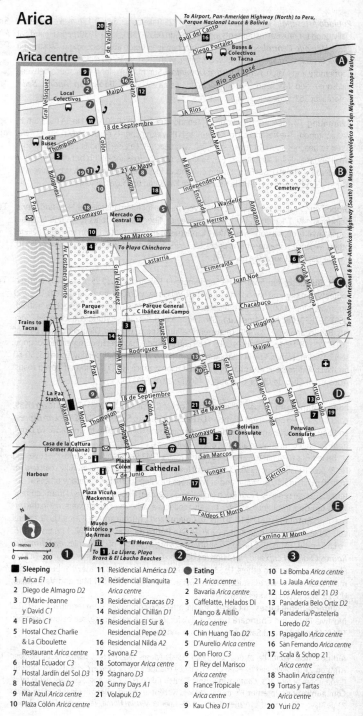

Arica centre

To Airport, Pan-American Highway (North) to Peru,
Parque Nacional Lauca & Bolivia

Sleeping

1 Arica *E1*
2 Diego de Almagro *D2*
3 D'Marie-Jeanne
   y David *C1*
4 El Paso *C1*
5 Hostal Chez Charlie
   & La Ciboulette
   Restaurant *Arica centre*
6 Hostal Ecuador *C3*
7 Hostal Jardín del Sol *D3*
8 Hostal Venecia *D2*
9 Mar Azul *Arica centre*
10 Plaza Colón *Arica centre*
11 Residencial América *D2*
12 Residencial Blanquita
   Arica centre
13 Residencial Caracas *D3*
14 Residencial Chillán *D1*
15 Residencial El Sur &
   Residencial Pepe *D2*
16 Residencial Nilda *A2*
17 Savona *E2*
18 Sotomayor *Arica centre*
19 Stagnaro *D3*
20 Sunny Days *A1*
21 Volapuk *D2*

Eating

1 21 *Arica centre*
2 Bavaria *Arica centre*
3 Caffelatte, Helados Di
   Mango & Altillo
   Arica centre
4 Chin Huang Tao *D2*
5 D'Aurelio *Arica centre*
6 Don Floro *C3*
7 El Rey del Marisco
   Arica centre
8 France Tropicale
   Arica centre
9 Kau Chea *D1*
10 La Bomba *Arica centre*
11 La Jaula *Arica centre*
12 Los Aleros del 21 *D3*
13 Panadería Belo Ortiz *D2*
14 Panadería/Pastelería
   Loredo *D2*
15 Papagallo *Arica centre*
16 San Fernando *Arica centre*
17 Scala & Schop 21
   Arica centre
18 Shaolin *Arica centre*
19 Tortas y Tartas
   Arica centre
20 Yuri *D2*

machines, quick. **Post Office:** Prat 375, down pedestrian walkway. Mon-Fri 0830-1330, 1500-1900, Sat 0900- 1230. To send parcels abroad, contents must be shown to Aduana (first floor of post office) on Mon-Fri 0800-1200. Your parcel will be wrapped, but take your own carton. *DHL*, Colón 351.**Telephone:** *Entel-Chile*, 21 de Mayo 345. Open 0900-2200. *CTC*, Colón 430 and at 21 de Mayo 211.Many other phone offices. **Consulates** Bolivia, P Lynch 298, T231030. **Peru**, San Martín 235, T231020. **Cultural centres** Instituto Chileno-Británico de Cultura (library open Mon-Fri 0900-1200, 1600-2100), Baquedano 351, T232399, Casilla 653. **Tourist office** *Sernatur*, San Marcos 101, T252054, a kiosk next to the Casa de la Cultura. Very helpful, English spoken, good map, list of tour companies. Mon-Fri 0830-1330, 1500-1900. Head office is at Prat 305, p 2,T232101, sernatur_arica@entelchile.net Municipal kiosk also on San Marcos, opposite Sernatur, opens at 0830. **Useful addresses** Conaf, Av Vicuña MacKenna 820, T250570. Mon-Fri 0830-1300, 1430-1630 (take Colectivo 1). Aug-Nov is best season for mountain climbing; permits needed for summits near borders. Write, fax or visit **Dirección Nacional de Fronteras y Límites del Estado** (DIFROL) Bandera 52, p 5, Santiago, F56-2-697 1909.

By road to Bolivia

1) Via **Chungará** (Chile) and **Tambo Quemado** (Bolivia). This, the most widely used route, begins by heading north from Arica on the Pan-American Highway (Route 5) for 12 km before turning right (east towards the cordillera) on Route 11 towards Chungará via Putre and Parque Nacional Lauca. This road is now paved to La Paz, estimated driving time 6 hrs. 2) Via **Visviri** (Chile) and **Charaña** (Bolivia), following the La Paz-Arica railway line. This route should not be attempted in wet weather.

Border with Peru: Chacalluta-Tacna
Between Oct-Mar Chilean time is 1 hr later than Peruvian, 2 hrs later Oct-Feb/ Mar, varies annually

Immigration is open 0800-2400; a fairly uncomplicated crossing. For Peruvian immigration. When crossing by private vehicle, US$2 per vehicle is charged between 1300-1500, 1850-2400 and on Saturday, Sunday, holidays. Drivers entering Chile are required to file a form, *Relaciones de Pasajeros*, giving details of passengers, obtained from a stationery store in Tacna, or at the border in a booth near Customs. You must also present the original registration document for your car from its country of registration. The first checkpoints outside Arica on the road to Santiago also require the *Relaciones de Pasajeros* form. If you can't buy the form, details on a piece of paper will suffice or you can get them at service stations. The form is *not* required when travelling south of Antofagasta. There are exchange facilities at the border.

Transport Colectivos: run from the international bus terminal on Diego Portales to Tacna, US$3 pp, 1½ hrs. There are many companies and you will be besieged by drivers. For quickest service take a Peruvian colectivo heading back to Peru. Give your passport to the colectivo office where your papers will be filled. After that, drivers take care of all the paperwork. *Chile Lintur*,T225038; *San Andrés*, T260167; *San Remo*, T260509; *El Morro*, T262477; *Perú Express*, T249970. Colectivos will pick you up from hotel. Also buses from the same terminal, US$1.50, 2½ hrs. For Arequipa it is best to go to Tacna and catch an onward bus there. **Train**: Station is at the end of Chacabuco, Arica-Tacna and vice versa 0500 and1600, US$1; service is frequently cancelled.

Border with Bolivia: Visviri

Immigration is open 0800-2400. Chilean formalities at Visviri, Bolivian formalities at Charaña, 10 km east. When crossing with a private vehicle, US$2 per vehicle is charged between 1300-1500, 1850-2100 and Saturday, Sunday and holidays.

Transport Buses from Arica to Visviri, *Humire*, T220198/260164, Tue and Fri, 1030, US$7, also Sun 0830 en route to La Paz; *Martínez*, Tue and Fri 2230 en route to La Paz, both from terminal. Colectivos from Arica US$10. In Visviri take a jeep across the border to Charaña. Buses from Charaña to La Paz, leave before 1000, US$11, 7 hrs. Trucks leave afternoon.

Parque Nacional Lauca

176 km E of Arica.
Access is easy as the
main Arica-La Paz
road runs through the
park and is paved.
During the rainy
season (Jan-Feb)
roads in the park
may be impassable;
check in advance
with Conaf in Arica.
It can be foggy as
well as wet
in Jan-Mar

The Parque Nacional Lauca, stretching to the border with Bolivia, is one of the most spectacular national parks in Chile. On the way is a zone of giant candelabra cactus, between 2,300-2,800 m. At Km 90 there is a pre-Inca *pukará* (fortress) above the village of Copaquilla and, a few kilometres further, there is an Inca *tambo* (inn) at Zapahuira. Situated at elevations from 3,200 m to 6,340 m (beware of soroche unless you are coming from Bolivia), the park covers 137,883 ha and includes numerous snowy volcanoes including three peaks of over 6,000 m. At the foot of Volcán Parinacota and its twin, Pomerape (in Bolivia – they are known collectively as Payachatas), is a series of lakes among a jumble of rocks, called Cotacotani. Black lava flows can be seen above Cotacotani. **Lago Chungará** (4,517 m, 7 km by 3 km) is southeast of Payachatas, a must for its views of the Parinacota, Sajama and Guallatire volcanoes and for its varied wildlife. At the far end of the lake is the Chile/Bolivia border. The park contains over 140 species of bird, resident or migrant, as well as cameloids, vizcacha and puma. A good base for exploring the park and for acclimatization is **Putre** (*population*: 4,400; *altitude*: 3,500 m), a scenic village, 15 km before the entrance with a church dating from 1670 and surrounded by terracing dating from pre-Inca times, now used for cultivating alfalfa and oregano. From here paths provide easy walking and great views. Festivals: *Pacahayame*, last Sunday in October, festival of the potato: religious celebration and traditional dancing. *Feria de la Voz Andina*, November (check dates and reserve room and transport in advance), with dancing, foods, handicrafts, very popular.

At **Parinacota** (4,392 m), at the foot of Payachatas, there is an interesting 17th century church – rebuilt 1789 – with 18th-century frescoes and the skulls of past priests (ask for the man with the key). Local residents knit alpaca sweaters, US$26 approximately; weavings of wildlife scenes also available. Weavings are sold from stalls outside the church. It's a walk of about one hour from the village to Cotacotani. From here an unpaved road runs north to the Bolivian border at Visviri (see above). You can climb Guane Guane, 5,097 m, in two to three hours, ask at the *Conaf refugio*. Lago Chungará is 20 km southeast of Parinacota.

Tours One-day tours are offered by most tour operators (see next page) and some hotels in Arica, daily in season, according to demand at other times, US$17-20 pp with breakfast and light lunch; but some find the minibuses cramped and dusty. You spend all day in the bus (0730-2030) and you will almost certainly suffer from soroche. You can leave the tour and continue on another day as long as you ensure that the company will collect you when you want (tour companies try to charge double for this). Much better are 1½-day tours, 1400-1800 next day (eg *Latinorizons*), which include overnight in Putre and a stop on the ascent at the Aymara village of Socorama, US$56. For 5 or more, the most economical proposition is to hire a vehicle. Full-day tours of the National Park starting at 0830, arranged in Putre, cost US$45, covering all aspects of Lauca.

Sleeping **Putre** **AL** *Hostería Las Vicuñas*, T/F228564. Bungalow-style, helpful, heating, restaurant,

If arriving from Bolivia,
remember that no
fresh produce may be
brought across the
border into Chile, so
plan accordingly if
using a Conaf refugio

does not accept TCs or credit cards. **B** *Casa Birding Alto Andino*, see below. 2 bedroom house, heating, cooking facilities, naturalist library. **C** *Res La Paloma*, O'Higgins. **D** with shared bath, hot showers after 0800 unless requested, no heating but lots of blankets, good food in large, warm restaurant, indoor parking; supermarket opposite. **D** *Hostal Cali*, Baquedano. **E** with shared bath, pleasant, no heating, hot water, good restaurant, supermarket. *Res Rosamel*, Latorre y Carrera, on plaza, T300051. Hot water, pleasant, good restaurant. **Camping** Sra Clementina Cáceres, blue door on C Lynch, allows camping in her garden. Several eating places. *Bar Kuchamarka*, Baquedano between La Paloma supermarket and *Hostal Cali*. Popular, good, food available. Accommodation available in **Parinacota** with various families, ask at the food and *artesanía* stands. There are 3 *Conaf* refuges **in the park**, but check in advance with Conaf in Arica that they are open: at **Parinacota** (also camping US$6

Chile

per tent), at **Lago Chungará**, and at **Las Cuevas** (emergencies only, no tourist facilities). The first two have cooking facilities, hot showers, **E** pp, sleeping bag essential, take your own food, candles and matches. Advance booking recommended. A map of the park is available from *Sernatur* in Arica. Maps are also available from the *Instituto Geográfico Militar*.

Putre has several stores, 2 bakeries and several private houses selling fresh produce. Petrol is more expensive than in Arica but available in cans in Putre from the *Cali* and *Paloma* super-markets and from *ECA*, a government subsidized market on the plaza (cheapest). Other than a small shop with limited supplies in Parinacota, no food is available outside Putre. Take drinking water with you as water in the park is not safe. **Shopping**

Alto Andino Nature Tours, Baquedano 299 (Correo Putre) T058-300013 (voice mail), F058-222735, www.birdingaltoandino.com Allow a week for reply to email. Run general tours and specialist bird-watching tours to remote areas of the park, to the Salar de Surire and Parque Nacional Isluga and to low-level parts of Atacama; English spoken, owner is an Alaskan biologist. *Freddy Torrejón and Eva Mamami*, Valle de Surunche, Putre, T058-253361, F225685, www2.gratisweb.com/losandeschileno/ Run tours to local sites and offer accommodation and meals. *Turismo Taki*, is located in Copaquila, about 45 km west of Putre, 100 km east of Arica. Restaurant, camping site and excursions to nearby *pucarás*, Inca *tambo* and cemetery, good local food, English and Italian spoken. **Tour operators**

Buses *La Paloma* buses leave Germán Riesco 2071, Arica for **Putre** daily at 0630, 4 hrs, US$2.50, returning from La Paloma supermarket 1300 (book in advance); *Jurasi* collective taxi leaves Arica daily at 0700, picks up at hotels, T222813, US$6.50. If you take an Arica-La Paz bus for Putre, it is about 4 km from the crossroads to the town at some 4,000 m, tough if you've come straight up from sea level. *Martínez* and *Humire* buses run to **Parinacota** Tue and Fri. *Hostal Cali* runs buses to Bolivia. Bus to La Paz from Putre crossroads or Lago Chungará can be arranged in Arica (same fare as from Arica). **Transport**

Hitchhiking Hitching back to Arica is not difficult; you may be able to bargain on one of the tour buses. Trucks from Arica to La Paz sometimes give lifts, a good place to try is at the Poconchile control point, 37 km from Arica.

Banks Bank in Putre changes dollars but commission on TCs is very high. **Tourist office** On main plaza, helpful, English spoken, organizes tours. **Directory**

South of Lauca is the beautiful **Reserva Nacional Las Vicuñas**, at an average altitude of 4,300 m, covering 209,131 ha of altiplano. Many of these beautiful creatures can be seen as well as, with luck, condors, rheas and other birds. A high clearance vehicle is essential and, in the summer wet season, 4WD vehicle: take extra fuel. Administration is at **Guallatiri**, reached by turning off the Arica-La Paz road onto the A147 2 km after Las Cuevas, where there is also a *Conaf* office. ■ *Mar-Nov.* The same road leads into the **Monumento Natural Salar de Surire**, which is open for the same months and for which the same conditions apply. The Salar, also at 4,300 m, is a drying salt lake of 17,500 ha. It has a year-round population of 12,000-15,000 flamingos (Chilean, Andean and James). Administration is in **Surire**, 45 km south of Guallatiri and 129 km south of Putre. At Surire there is a *Conaf refugio*, four beds, very clean, prior appli-cation to Conaf in Arica essential. There is also a campsite at Polloquere, 16 km south of Surire, no facilities. There is no public transport to these wildlife reserves, but tours can be arranged in Putre or Arica. Operators such as *Latinorizons* are developing routes through these parks from Arica to San Pedro de Atacama. *Altitude: 4,300-6,060 m Be prepared for cold, skin burns from sun and wind*

Immigration is open 0800-2100; US$2 per vehicle crossing 1300-1500, 1850-2100 and Saturday, Sunday and holidays. ■ *For details of through buses between Arica and La Paz see above under Arica.* **Border with Bolivia: Chungará**

Chile

South of Santiago

Santiago

One of the world's most fecund and beautiful landscapes, with snowclad peaks of the Andes to the east and the Cordillera de la Costa to the west, the Central Valley contains most of Chile's population. A region of small towns, farms and vineyards, it has several protected areas of natural beauty. To the south are the major city of Concepción, the port of Talcahuano and the main coal-mining area. Five major rivers cross the Central Valley, cutting through the Coastal Range to the Pacific: from north to south these are the Rapel, Mataquito, Maule, Itata and Biobío, one of the three longest rivers in Chile.

Rancagua
Phone code: 072
Colour map 8, grid B1
Population: 167,000
82 km S of Santiago

The capital of VI Región (Libertador Gen Bernardo O'Higgins) lies on the Río Cachapoal. Founded in 1743, it is a service and market centre. At the heart of the city is an attractive tree-lined plaza, the **Plaza de los Héroes**, and several streets of single-storey colonial-style houses. In the centre of the plaza is an equestrian statue of O'Higgins. The main commercial area lies along Avenida Independencia, which runs west from the plaza towards the bus and rail terminals. The National Rodeo Championships are held at the end of March, with plenty of opportunities for purchasing cowboy items.

Sleeping and eating AL *Camino del Rey*, Estado 275, T239765, F232314. 4-star, best. **A-B** *Rancagua*, San Martín 85, T232663, F241155. Quiet, secure parking. Recommended. **C** *España*, San Martín 367, T230141. Cheaper without bath, central, pleasant. *Bravissimo*, Astorga 307, for ice cream. *Lasagna*, west end of Plaza, for bread and *empanadas*.

Train station, T230361

Transport Trains Main line services between Santiago and Concepción and Chillán stop here. Also regular services to/from **Santiago** on Metrotren, 1¼ hrs, 10-13 a day, US$2.65. **Buses** Main terminal at Doctor Salinas y Calvo; local and Santaigo buses leave from the Terminal de Buses Regionales on Ocarrol, just north of the market. Frequent services to **Santiago**, US$3, 1¼ hrs.

Curicó
Phone code: 075
Colour map 8, grid B1
Population: 103,919
Altitude: 200 m
192 km from Santiago

Situated between the Ríos Lontué and Teno, Curicó is the only town of any size in the Mataquito Valley. It was founded in 1744. In mid-March is the Fiesta de la Vendimia with displays on traditional wine-making. In the **Plaza de Armas** there are fountains and a monument to the Mapuche warrior, Lautaro, carved from the trunk of an ancient beech tree. There is a steel bandstand, built in New Orleans in 1904, which is a national monument. The church of **San Francisco** (1732), also a national monument, partly ruined, contains the 17th century Virgen de Velilla, brought from Spain. Overlooking the city, the surrounding countryside and with views to the distant Andean peaks is **Cerro Condell** (100 m); it is an easy climb to the summit from where there are a number of walks. Some 5 km south of the city is the **Torres wine bodega** take a bus for Molina from the local terminal or outside the railway station and get off at Km 195 on the Pan-American Highway. ■ *0900-1230, 1500-1730, no organized tour, Spanish only, worthwhile, T310455. For information on the vineyards of Curicó, see the Ruta del Vino de Curicó, www.rvvc.cl*

Sleeping and eating AL *Comercio*, Yungay 730, T310014, F317001. Cheaper without bath. Recommended. **D** *Res Rahue*, Peña 410, T312194. Basic, meals, annex rooms have no ventilation. **E** *Prat*, Peña 427, T311069. Pleasant patio, laundry facilities. **E** *Res Colonial*, Rodríguez 461, T314103. Good, **F** without bath. *Club de la Unión*, Plaza de Armas. Good. *American Bar*, Yungay 647. Real coffee, small pizzas, good sandwiches, pleasant atmosphere, open early morning to late afternoon including weekends. Recommended. *El Fogón Chileno*, M Montt 399. Good for meat and wines. *Café-Bar Maxim*, Prat 617. Light meals, beer and wine. *Centro Italiano Club Social*, Estado 531. Good, cheap meals.

Transport Trains Station is at the end of Prat, 4 blocks west of Plaza de Armas, T310028. To/from **Santiago**, 4 a day, 2½ hrs, US$5 *salon*, US$4.15 *turista*. To/from **Chillán**, 4 a day, 3 hrs, US$7 *salon*, US$5 *turista*. **Buses** Long distance terminal at Prat y Maipú. Local buses, including to coastal towns, as well as some long distance services, from Terminal Rural, Prat y Maipú. *Pullman del Sur* terminal, Henríquez y Carmen. Many southbound buses bypass Curicó, but can be caught by waiting outside town. To **Santiago** US$5, 2½ hrs, *Pullman del Sur*, frequent. To **Temuco**, *LIT* and *TurBus*, US$7.

The park is in two parts, one at Radal, 65 km east of Curicó, the other at Parque Inglés, 9 km further on. At Radal, the Río Claro flows through a series of seven rock bowls (*siete tazas*) each with a pool emptying into the next by a waterfall. The river goes through a canyon, 15 m deep but only 1½m wide, ending abruptly in a cliff and a beautiful waterfall. ■ *Oct-Mar. Administration is in Parque Inglés. Dirty campsites near entrance. Getting there: buses from Molina, 26 km south of Curicó to within 7 km of Park, on Tue and Thu 1700, returning Wed and Fri 0800; impossible to hitch the rest of the way. Daily bus from Curicó in summer, 1545, 4½ hrs, returns 0745 (Sun 0700, returns 1900). Access by car is best as the road through the park is paved.*

Area de Protección Radal Siete Tazas

At 56 km south of Curicó, this is the most important city between Santiago and Concepción. It is a major manufacturing centre and the capital of VII Región (Maule). Founded in 1692, Talca was destroyed by earthquakes in 1742 and 1928. Just off the Plaza de Armas at 1 Norte y 2 Oriente is the **Museo O'Higginiano** in a colonial mansion in which Bernardo O'Higgins lived as a child. The house was later the headquarters of O'Higgins' Patriot Government in 1813-14 (before his defeat at Rancagua). In 1818 O'Higgins signed the declaration of Chilean independence here: the room (Sala Independencia) is decorated and furnished in period style. The museum also has a collection of regional art. ■ *Tue-Fri 1030-1300, 1430-1845, Sat-Sun 1000-1300.* The Maule valley is another wine producing region, with vineyards that can be visited.

Talca
Phone code: 071
Colour map 8,
grid B1
Population: 160,000
258 km from Santiago
via dual carriageway

Sleeping **A** *Cabañas Entre Ríos*, Panamericana Sur Km 250, 8 km north, T223336, F220477 (Santiago: San Antonio 486, of 132, T633 3750, F632 4791). Very good value, excellent breakfast, pool, very helpful owner. Highly recommended. **B** *Cordillera*, 2 Sur 1360, T22187, F233028. **C** without bath, good breakfast. **B** *Hostal del Puente*, 1 sur 407, T220930, F225448. Large breakfast extra, family-owned, parking in central courtyard. Recommended for atmosphere, price and surroundings. **B-D** *Amalfi*, 2 Sur 1265, T225703. With breakfast, old-fashioned, central. **D** *Casa Chueca*, 5 mins from Talca by the Río Lircay, Casilla 143, T197 0096, T09-419 0625 (mob), F197 0097, www.trekkingchile.com Free pick up from Taxutal terminal (phone hostal from bus terminal then take Taxutal A micro in direction of San Valentín; get off at last stop where hostal will pick you up), or taxi US$5.20. With breakfast, very good vegetarian food (US$6), Austrian and German owners, many languages spoken, lovely setting, swimming pool, good tours (including climbing) arranged. Enthusiastically recommended. **D** pp *Hostal Victoria*, 1 Sur 1737, T212074. Good. Cheap hotels between Nos 1740 and 1790 of 3 Sur, near 11 Oriente. At **Pelarco**, 18 km northwest, **E** *Hosp Santa Margarita*, T/F09-335 9051, www.backpackersbest.cl Swiss run, with breakfast, reservations advised (Casilla 1104, Talca).

Transport Buses: terminal at 12 Oriente y 2 Sur. To **Chillán**, frequent, US$2. To **Puerto Montt**, US$15, 12 hrs. **Train**: station at 2 Sur y 11 Oriente, T226254. To **Santiago**, 5 a day, US$3.85.

Directory Banks: *Edificio Caracol*, Oficina 15, 1 Sur 898, for US$ cash. **Communications** Internet: at 1 Poniente 1282 and 2 Sur 1661 (free, reserve in advance). **Post Office:** 1 Oriente s/n. **Telephone:** *CTC*, 1 Sur 1156 and 1 Sur 835. **Tourist office** 1 Poniente 1281, T233669. Mon-Fri 0830-1930 (1730 winter).

At the mouth of the Río Maule, 89 km from San Javier on the Panamericana (south of Talca), **Constitución** is an important port and seaside resort. The coast, especially to the north, is beautiful, while south a paved road runs through thick forest to the small towns of **Chanco**, **Pelluhue** (several places to stay, including **E** pp *Res Hostería Las*

Constitución and the coast

Palmeras, Condell 837, T09-579 2431, in an old, tatty house, great atmosphere, meals extra) and **Curanipe**. There are black sand beaches and dunes in this little visited part of Chile. For information, tours and lodging in this area, contact Alejandro of *Ruta Verde*, T744 8224, www.rutaverde.cl Speaks English, good fun. Recommended.

Vilches
63 km E of Talca

This is the starting point for the climb to the volcanoes Quizapu (3,050 m) and Descabezado (3,850 m). For walks on Descabezado Grande and Cerro Azul (ice axe and crampons needed) contact recommended guide Carlos Verdugo Bravo, Probación Brilla El Sol, Pasaje El Nickel 257, Talca (Spanish only). ■ *5 buses a day, US$1.50, 2-2½ hrs.* The **Reserva Nacional Altos del Lircay** 2 km from Vilches, covers 12,163 ha and includes three peaks, several small lakes and the Piedras Tacitas, a stone construction supposedly made by the aboriginal inhabitants of the region. There are two good hikes: Laguna del Alto, 8 hours, and El Enladrillado, 12 hours. A visitors' centre and administration are near the entrance.

To the border with Argentina: Paso Pehuenche

A road south of Talca, paved for the first 65 km, runs southeast from the Panamericana along **Lago Colbún** and up the valley of the Río Maule, passing through mountain scenery to reach the Argentine border at Paso Pehuenche. At the western end of the lake is the town of Colbún, from where a road goes to Linares on the Panamericana. Thermal springs 5 km south of Colbún at Panimávida, and 12 km, Quinamávida. Campsites on south shore. **C** pp *Ecological Reserve Posada Campesina*, at Rabones on the road Linares/Panimávida, T09-752 0510, full board, *estancia* offering forest trails, trekking and horseback expeditions, English spoken, highly recommended. Paso Pehuenche (2,553 m) is reached by unpaved road southeast from Lago Colbún. Chilean customs is at La Mina, 106 km from Talca, 60 km from the border (*Camping La Querencia*, 4 km west of La Mina). On the Argentine side the road continues to Malargüe and San Rafael. The border is open December-March 0800-2100, April-November 0800-1900.

Chillán

Phone code: 042
Colour map 8, grid B1
Population: 146,000
Altitude: 118 m
150 km S of Talca

Chillán is capital of Ñuble province and a service centre for this agricultural area. Following an earthquake in 1833, the site was moved slightly to the northwest, though the older site, Chillán Viejo, is still occupied. Further earthquakes in 1939 and 1960 ensured that few old buildings have survived. Chillán was the birthplace of Bernardo O'Higgins (Arturo Prat, Chile's naval hero, was born 50 km away at Ninhue). The Fiesta de la Vendimia is an annual wine festival held in the third week in March.

Sights

The centre of the city is Plaza O'Higgins, on which stands the modern **Cathedral** designed to resist earthquakes. Northwest of the Plaza O'Higgins, on the Plaza Héroes de Iquique, is the **Escuela México**, donated to the city after the 1939 earthquake. In its library are murals by the great Mexican artists David Alvaro Siqueiros and Xavier Guerrero which present allegories of Chilean and Mexican history. ■ *Daily 1000-1300, 1500-1830.* The **Mercado y Feria Municipal** (covered and open markets at Riquelme y Maipón) sell regional arts and crafts and have many cheap, good restaurants, serving regional dishes; open daily, Sunday until 1300. Three blocks further south is the **Museo Naval El Chinchorro**, Collin y I Riquelme, contains naval artefacts and models of Chilean vessels. ■ *Tue-Fri 0930-1200, 1500-1730.* In **Chillán Viejo** (southwest of the centre) there is a monument and park at O'Higgins' birthplace; it has a 60 m long mural depicting his life (an impressive, but sadly faded, mosaic of various native stones), and a **Centro Histórico y Cultural**, with a gallery of contemporary paintings by regional artists. ■ *The park is open 0830-2000.*

Quinchamalí is 27 km southwest of Chillán, a little village famous for the origiality of its craftsmen in textiles, basketwork, black ceramics, guitars and primitive paintings (all on sale in Chillán market). Handicraft fair, second week of February.

A *Cordillera*, Arauco 619, on Plaza de Armas, T215211, F211198. 3-star, small, all rooms with heating, good. A *Rucamanqui*, Herminda Martín 590 (off Plaza de Armas), T222704. Spartan, but OK. B *Quinchamalí*, El Roble 634, T223381, F227365. Central, quiet, hot water. C *Floresta*, 18 de Septiembre 278, T222253. Quiet, old fashioned. C *Libertador*, Libertad 85, T223255. Large rooms, without breakfast, parking, good, a few minutes' walk from the railway station. D *Claris*, 18 de Septiembre 357, T221980. Welcoming, hot water, but run down, E pp without bath. D *Cañada*, Libertad 269, T234515. Without bath or breakfast, good beds. F pp *Hosp Sonia Segui*, Itata 288, T214879. Good, especially breakfast, helpful, but bathroom dirty.

Sleeping
■ *on map*
Lots of cheap hospedajes on Constitución 1-300

Mid-range: *Arcoiris*, El Roble 525. Vegetarian. *La Cosa Nostra*, Libertad 398. Mainly Italian homemade food, top quality, excellent wine and cocktails, nice atmosphere, German and Italian spoken. *Café París*, Arauco 666. Fine restaurant upstairs. *Fuente Alemana*, Arauco 661. For real coffee. In Chillán Viejo, *Los Adobes*, on Parque O'Higgins. Good food and service. **Cheap**: *Club Comercial*, Arauco 745. Popular at lunchtime, good value *almuerzo*,

Eating
● *on map*
The Chillán area is well-known for its pipeño wine and longanizas (sausages)

Chillán

To Talca & Santiago via Pan-American Highway (north)

To Chillán Viejo, Concepción & Los Angeles via Pan-American Highway (south)

Sleeping		
1	Cañada	
2	Claris	
3	Cordillera	
4	Floresta	
5	Hospedaje Sonia Segui	
6	Libertador	
7	Quinchamalí	
8	Rucamanqui	

Eating		
1	Arcoiris	
2	Café Europa	
3	Café París	
4	Fuente Alemana	
5	Jai Yang	
6	La Casa Nostra	
7	La Masc'a	

0 metres 200
0 yards 200

Chile

popular bar at night. *Jai Yang*, Libertad 250. Good Chinese. *La Copucha*, 18 de Septiembre y Constitución. Inexpensive meals and sandwiches. *La Masc'a*, 5 de Abril 544. Excellent meals, *empanadas de queso*, drinks.

Transport **Trains** Station, T222424. To **Santiago**, 2 daily, 4½ hrs, *salón* US$7.50. **Buses** 2 long-distance terminals: Central, Brasil y Constitución (*TurBus, Línea Azul, Tas Choapa, LIT*); Northern, Ecuador y O'Higgins for other companies. Local buses leave from Maipón y Sgto Aldea. To **Santiago**, 5½ hrs, US$7-11. To **Concepción**, every 30 mins, 1¼ hrs, US$3. To **Curicó** or 2 a day, US$5. To **Temuco**, 4½ hrs, US$5.

Directory **Banks** Better rates than banks at *Casa de Cambio*, Constitución 550, or *Café de París* (ask for Enrique Schuler). **Communications** Internet: *Gateway*, Libertad 360. *Planet*, Arauco 683, p 2. **Post office:** in Gobernación on Plaza de Armas. **Telephone:** *Entel*, 18 de Septiembre 746. *CTC*, Arauco 625. **Tourist office** 18 de Septiembre 455, at the side of Gobernación, T223272; street map of city, leaflets on skiing, Termas de Chillán, etc.

Termas de Chillán East of Chillán 82 km by good road (paved for the first 50 km), 1,850 m up in the Cordillera, are thermal baths and, above, the largest ski resort in southern Chile. There are two open-air thermal pools (officially for hotel guests only) and a health spa with jacuzzis, sauna, mud baths etc. Suitable for families and beginners and cheaper than centres nearer Santiago, the ski resort has 28 runs, nine lifts, snowboarding and other activities. It also has two hotels (the 5-star *Gran Hotel*, and the 3-star *Pirigallo*) and condominium apartments. Season: middle December to the end of March. Lift pass US$30 per day, US$20 per half-day. Information and reservations from Termas de Chillán, Avenida Libertad 1042, Chillán, T223887, F223576, or Santiago, Avenida Providencia 2237, oficina P 41, T02-233 1313, F02-231 5963, www.termaschillan.com Equipment hire about US$25 pp.

Sleeping At Termas de Chillán. At Las Trancas on the road to the Termas, Km 70-76 from Chillán are **AL** *Parador Jamón*, *Pan y Vino*, Casilla 618, Chillán, T373872, F220018, arranges recommended horse riding expeditions, and **B** pp *Hotel Los Pirineos*, T293839. There are many other *cabañas* in the village and *Galería de Arte de Luis Guzmán Molina*, a painter from Chillán, Entrada por Los Pretiles Km 68.5. **Camping** 2 km from the slopes.

Transport Ski buses run from **Libertador** 1042 at 0800 and from Chillán Ski Centre, subject to demand, US$30 (includes lift pass). Summer bus service (Jan-mid-Mar), from Anja, 5 de Abril 594, Thu, Sat, Sun only, 0730, US$5 return, book in advance. Taxi US$30 one way, 1½ hrs. At busy periods hitching may be possible from Chillán Ski Centre.

Concepción

Phone code: 041
Colour map 8, grid B1
Population: 210,000
516 km from Santiago

The third biggest city in Chile, and the most important city in southern Chile, is also a major industrial centres. Capital of VIII Región (Biobío), Concepción is 15 km up the Biobío River. Founded in 1550, Concepción became a frontier stronghold in the war against the Mapuche after 1600. Destroyed by an earthquake in 1751, it was moved to its present site in 1764. The climate is very agreeable in summer, but from April to September the rains are heavy; the annual average rainfall, nearly all of which falls in those six months, is from 1,250 mm to 1,500 mm.

Sights In the attractive Plaza de Armas at the centre are the **Intendencia** and the **Cathedral**. It was here that Bernardo O'Higgins proclaimed the independence of Chile on 1 January 1818. **Cerro Caracol** can easily be reached on foot starting from the statue of Don Juan Martínez de Rozas in the Parque Ecuador, arriving at the Mirador Chileno after 15 minutes. From here it is another 20 minutes' climb to **Cerro Alemán**. The Biobío and its valley running down to the sea lie below. On the far side of the river you see lagoons, the largest of which, **San Pedro**, is a watersport centre.

Chile

The **Galería de la Historia**, Lincoyán y V Lamas by Parque Ecuador, is a depiction of the history of Concepción and the region; upstairs is a collection of Chilean painting. ■ *Mon 1500-1830, Tue-Fri 1000-1330, 1500-1830, Sat-Sun 1000-1400, 1500-1930, free.* The **Casa del Arte**, Roosevelt y Larenas, contains the University art collection; the entrance hall is dominated by *La Presencia de América Latina*, by the Mexican Jorge González Camerena (1965), a mural depicting Latin American history. ■ *Tue-Fri 1000-1800, Sat 1000-1600, Sun 1000-1300, free. Free explanations by University Art students.*

Concepción

Sleeping		Eating
1 Alborada	7 Residencial Central	1 Big Joe Saloon
2 Cecil	8 Residencial Colo Colo	2 Casino de Bomberos
3 Concepción	9 Residencial O'Higgins	3 Chung Hwa
4 El Dorado	10 Silvia Uslar	4 El Rancho de Julio
5 Manquehue		5 Le Château
6 Residencial Antuco		6 Mar y Tierra
& Residencial		7 Piazza
San Sebastián		8 Yiet-Xiu

N

0 metres 300
0 yards 300

Chile

The **Museo y Parque Hualpen**, a house built around 1885 (a national monument) and its gardens; contains beautiful pieces from all over the world, two hour visit, recommended. ■ *Tue-Sun 1000-1300, 1400-1900, free.* The park also contains Playa Rocoto, at the mouth of the Río Biobío. Take a city bus to Hualpencillo from Freire, ask the driver to let you out then walk 40 minutes, or hitch. Go along Avenida Las Golondrinas to the Enap oil refinery, turn left, then right (it is signed).

Sleeping
● *on map*
Good budget accommodation is hard to find

A *Alborada*, Barros Arana 457, Casilla 176, T/F242144. Good. **A** *Concepción*, Serrano 512, T228851, F230948. Central, comfortable, heating, English spoken. Recommended. **A-B** *El Dorado*, Barros Arana 348, T229400, F231018. Comfortable, central, cafeteria, parking. **B** *Manquehue*, Barros Arana 790, p 8, T238350. Highly recommended. **C** *Cecil*, Barros Arana 9, T230667, near railway station. With breakfast, quiet. Highly recommended. **C-D** *Res Antuco*, Barros Arana 741, flats 31-33, T235485. Recommended. **C** *Res San Sebastián*, Barros Arana 741, flat 35, T242710, F243412. Reductions for HI (both of these are entered via the Galería Martínez). Recommended. **D** *Res Central*, Rengo 673, T227309. With breakfast, large rooms, a bit run down. **D** *Res Colo Colo*, Colo Colo 743, T227118. With breakfast. **E** *Res O'Higgins*, O'Higgins 457, T228303. With breakfast, comfortable. **E** *Silvia Uslar*, Edmundo Larenas 202, T227449 (not signed). Excellent, good breakfast, quiet, comfortable.

Eating
● *on map*

Expensive *Le Château* Colo Colo 340. French, seafood and meat, closed Sun. **Mid-range** *Big Joe Saloon*, O'Higgins 808, just off plaza. Popular at lunchtime, open Sun evening, good breakfasts, vegetarian meals, snacks and pizzas. *El Rancho de Julio*, O'Higgins 36. Argentine *parrillada*. *Piazza*, 631, p 2r. Good pizzas. **Cheap** *Casino de Bomberos*, O'Higgins y Orompello. Good value lunches. *Mar y Tierra*, Colo Colo 1182, Seafood. *Yiet-Xiu*, Angol 515. Good, cheap Oriental cuisine. *Chung Hwa*, Barros Arana 262.

Cafés & bars

Several *fuentes de soda* and cafés on Caupolicán near the Plaza de Armas including: *Café El Dom*, No 415, *Café Haiti*, No 515, both open Sun morning, good coffee; *Fuente Alemana*, No 654. Recommended. *Treinta y Tantos*, Prat 356. Nice bar, good music, wide selection of *empanadas*, good breakfasts and lunches. Recommended. *La Capilla*, Vicuña MacKenna 769, good *ponches*, popular. *Nuria*, Barros Arana 736. Very good breakfasts and lunches, good value. *QuickBiss*, O'Higgins between Tuscapel and Castellón. Salads, real coffee, good service, good lunches. *Saaya 1*, Barros Arana 899. Excellent *panadería/pastelería/rotisería*.

Shopping
Main shopping area is N of Plaza de Armas

Feria Artesanal, Freire 757. *Galería Internacional*, Caupolicán y Barros Arana is worth a visit. *Las Brisas* supermarket, Freire y Lincoyán. *Supermercado Unimarc*, Chacabuco 70. *Plaza del Trébol* mall with multiscreen cinemas north of the city off the road to Talcahuano (near the airport). Take any bus for Talcahuano.

Tour operators

Alta Luz, San Martín 586, p 2, T217727. Tours to national parks. *Chile Indomito Adventure*, Serrano 551, of 3, T221618, Trekking in Reserva Nacional Ralco. *South Expeditions*, O'Higgins 680, p 2, of 218D, T/F232290. Rafting and trekking expeditions, 1 and 2-day programmes.

Transport

Long distance Air Airport north of the city, off the main road to Talcahuano. Flights daily to and from **Santiago** (*LanChile/Lan Express*); less frequent to **Valdivia**, **Temuco** and **Puerto Montt**. *Lan* run bus services to the airport from their office, leaving 1 hr before flight, US$2.50, also meet flights. Taxi US$8.

Trains Station at Prat y Barros Arana, T226925. Regular nightly train to/from **Santiago**, 9 hrs; *salón* US$10, *turista* US$8. Also suburban services from Talcahuano to Chiguayante. Booking offices at the station and at Galería Plaza, local 13, T225286.

Buses Main long distance terminal, known as Terminal Collao, is 2 km east, on Av Gen Bonilla, next to athletics stadium. (To the city centre take a bus marked 'Hualpencillo' from outside the terminal and get off in Freire, US$0.40, taxi US$4.) *TurBus*, *Línea Azul* and *Buses Bío Bío* services leave from Terminal Camilo Henríquez 2 km northeast of main terminal on J M García, reached by buses from Av Maipú in centre. To **Santiago**, 8½ hrs, US$12. To **Valparaíso**, 9 hrs, US$12 (most via Santiago). To **Los Angeles**, US$3. To **Loncoche**, 7 hrs,

US$6.50. To **Pucón**, 8 hrs, US$8. To **Valdivia**, US$10. To **Puerto Montt** several companies, US$15, about 12 hrs. Best direct bus to **Chillán** is *Línea Azul*, 2 hrs, US$2. For a longer and more scenic route, take the *Costa Azul* bus which follows the old railway line, through Tomé, Coelemu and Ñipas on to Chillán (part dirt-track, takes 5½ hrs). Services to **Lota**, **Lebu**, **Cañete** and **Contulmo** are run by *J Ewert* (terminal at Carrera y Tucapel) and *Los Alerces* (terminal at Prat y Maipú). To **Talcahuano** frequent service from Plaza de Armas (bus marked 'Base Naval'), US$0.30, 1 hr, express US$0.50, 30 mins.

Airline offices *LanChile*, Barros Arana 560, T248824. **Banks** ATMs at banks, most of which are on O'Higgins. Several *cambios* in Galería Internacional, entrances at Barros Arana 565 and Caupolicán 521. **Communications** Internet: *Barros Arana 541* and *Caupolicán 567*. **Post Office:** O'Higgins y Colo Colo. **Telephone:** *CTC*, Colo Colo 487, Angol 483. *Entel*, Barros Arana 541, Caupolicán 567, p 2. **Cultural centres** Alliance Française, Colo Colo y Lamas. Library, concerts, films, cultural events. **Chilean-British Cultural Institute**, San Martín 531. British newspapers, library. **Chilean-North American Institute**, Caupolicán 301 y San Martín. Library. **Consulates** Argentina, San Martín 472, of 52, T230257. **Tourist office** Aníbal Pinto 460 on Plaza, T227976, has information on the more expensive hotels and *residenciales*. *Automóvil Club de Chile*, O'Higgins 630, Of 303, T245884, for information and car hire (T222070). *Codeff* (Comité Nacional pro Defensa de la Fauna y Flora), Caupolicán 346, oficina E, p 4, T226649.

Directory

Situated at the neck of a peninsula, **Talcahuano** has the best harbour in Chile. It is Chile's main naval station and an important commercial and fishing port. Two good roads run from Concepción. The **Huáscar**, a relic of the War of the Pacific, is in the naval base and can be visited. ■ *Tue-Sun 0900-1230, 1330-1730, US$1.50; surrender passport at main gate.* On Península Tumbes is **Parque Tumbes**, owned by Codeff: paths lead along the coast, no services, no admission charge (details from Codeff office in Concepción). *Benotecas*, on the seafront, has a row of four restaurants sharing one window facing the harbour, superb fish and seafood in each one, reasonable prices, recommended. *La Aguada*, Colón 912, shellfish dishes. *Domingo Lara*, Aníbal Pinto 450, seafood specialities, excellent.

Talcahuano
Population: 244,000
Fine seafood at low prices in the market

Chile

South of Concepción

South of the Biobío is the Costa del Carbón, the main coal producing area of Chile, linked with Concepción by road and two bridges over the Biobío. **Lota** (*Population*: 52,000; 42 km south of Concepción) was, until its closure in 1997, the site of the most important coalmine in Chile. ■ *Guided tours by former miners, 1000-1700, US$5, T870682.* In the church on the main plaza you can see a virgin made of coal. The **Parque de Lota**, covering 14 ha on a promontory to the west of the town, was the life's work of Isadora Cousiño, whose family owned the mine. Laid out by English landscape architects in the last century, it contains plants from all over the world, ornaments imported from Europe, romantic paths and shady nooks offering views over the sea, and peafowl and pheasants roaming freely. ■ *Daily1000-1800, till 2000 in summer, US$2.50, no picnicking.* **South of Lota** the road runs past the seaside resort of **Laraquete** where there are miles of golden sands. Buses from Concepción-Lota, 1½ hrs, US$0.50. Many buses by-pass the centre: catch them from the main road.

Costa del Carbón

Some 149 km south of Concepcíon, Lebu is a fishing port and coal washing centre. It lies at the mouth of the Río Lebu and is the capital of Arauco province. Enormous beaches to north and south are popular on summer weekends: 3 km north at Playa Millaneco are caves with steep hills offering good walks and majestic views.

Lebu
Phone code: 041
Population: 20,000

Sleeping **A** *Hostería Millaneco*, at Playa Millaneco, T/F511540. *Cabañas* sleep 7, good restaurant. Recommended. **D** pp *Central*, Pérez 183, T/F511904. **E** without bath, parking. Recommended. **D** *Gran*, Pérez 309, T511939. **E** without bath, old fashioned, *comedor*. **E** *Res Alcázar*, Alcázar 144. With breakfast, cold water.

Cañete

Phone code: 041
Colour map 8, grid C1
Population: 15,642
There is nowhere to change dollars in town

A small town on the site of Fort Tucapel where Pedro de Valdivia and 52 of his men were killed by Mapuche warriors in 1553. **Museo Mapuche**, 1 km south on the road to Contulmo, is housed in a modern building inspired by the traditional Mapuche *ruca*; includes Mapuche ceramics and textiles. ■ *0930-1230, 1400-1830, daily in summer, closed Mon in winter, US$1.50.*

Sleeping and eating **C** *Nahuelbuta*, Villagrán 644, T611073. Cheaper without bath, pleasant. **D** *Derby*, Mariñan y Condell, T611960. Without bath, basic, restaurant. **E** *Comercio*, 7° de la Línea, T611218. Very pleasant. Recommended. **E** *Gajardo*, 7° de la Línea 817 (1 block from plaza). Without bath, old fashioned, pleasant. Real coffee at *Café Nahuel*, off the plaza. A very good eating place recommended by the locals is *Don Juanito*, Riquelme 151.

Transport Buses leave from 2 diifferent terminals: J Ewert, *Inter Sur* and *Thiele* from Riquelme y 7° de la Línea, *Jeldres*, *Erbuc* and other companies from the Terminal Municipal, Serrano y Villagrán. To **Santiago**, *Inter Sur*, daily, 12 hrs. To **Concepción**, 3 hrs, US$3.50. To **Lebu** US$1.50. To **Angol** US$3.50.

Contulmo

Population: 2,000

A road runs south from Cañete along the north side of Lago Lanalhue to **Contulmo**, a sleepy village at the foot of the Cordillera. It hosts a Semana Musical (music week) in January. The wooden **Grollmus House and Mill** are 3 km northwest along the south side of the lake. The house, dating from 1918, has a fine collection of every colour of *copihue* (the national flower) in a splendid garden. The mill, built in 1928, contains the original wooden machinery. From here the track runs a further 9 km north to the *Posada Campesina Alemana*, an old German-style hotel in a fantastic spot at the water's edge (open December – March, details from Millaray 135, Contulmo). The **Monumento Natural Contulmo**, 8 km south and administered by *Conaf*, covers 82 ha of native forest.

Sleeping **In Contulmo** **C** *Contulmo*, Millaray 116, T894903. **E** pp without bath, hospitable. Recommended. **D** *Central*, Millaray 131, T618089. Without bath, no sign, very hospitable. **On the lake**: **B** pp *Hostal Licahue*, 4 km north towards Cañete (Casilla 644, Correo Contulmo) T09-870 2822 (mob). With breakfast, also full board, attractively set overlooking lake, pool. Highly recommended. **Camping at Playa Blanca, 10 km north of Contulmo** *Elicura*, clean, US$6. Recommended. *Playa Blanca*, clean. *Camping Huilquehue*, 15 km south of Cañete on lakeside.

Transport Buses to Concepción, Thiele, *US$4.50, 4 hrs; to Temuco*, Thiele *and* Erbuc, *US$4; to* Cañete, frequent, US$1.

Los Angeles and around

Phone code: 043
Colour map 8, grid C1
Population: 114,000

Situated on the Pan-American Highway, Los Angeles is 110 km south of Chillán. It is the capital of Biobío province. Founded in 1739 as a fort, it was destroyed several times by the Mapuche. It has a large Plaza de Armas and a good daily market. Some 25 km north of Los Angeles is the spectacular Salto El Laja where the Río Laja plunges 47 m over the rocks. Free entry out of season – swimming in some of the cool natural pools, popular with local teenagers. Buses (Bío-Bío) from Los Angeles, US$1, 30 minutes.

Sleeping **A** *Gran Hotel Müso*, Valdivia 230 (Plaza de Armas), T313183, F312768. Good restaurant open to non-residents. **C** *Res Santa María*, Plaza de Armas, and **C** *Winser*, Rengo 138, are both overpriced but otherwise OK. Private house at Caupolicán 651, **E**, large breakfast, good value. Opposite, also No 651, basic, cheaper. **E** pp *Res Winser*, Colo Colo 335, T323782. Small rooms. **Outside town**: recommended are: **D** pp *Antukelen*, Camino Los Angeles-Santa Bárbara-Ralco, 62.7 km southeast on the Alto Biobío, reservations Siegfried Haberl, Casilla 1278, Los Angeles, T09-450 0210. Camping US$15 per site, *cabañas*, showers, German, English and

French spoken, vegetarian food, Spanish classes, natural therapy centre and excursions.**D** pp *El Rincón*, Panamericana Sur Km 494 (20 km north of LA), exit El Olivo (Cruce La Mona) 2 km east/south, T09-441 5019, F043-317168, elrincon@cvmail.cl Beautiful property beside a small river, restful, South American and European cuisine, includes vegetarian (**B** pp full board), Spanish classes, tours arranged, English, French, German and Spanish spoken. At Salto El Laja are: **A-B** *Hostería Salto del Laja* (Casilla 562, Los Angeles, T321706, F313996), with good rooms but overpriced restaurant, two swimming pools (dirty), on an island overlooking the falls; and **B** *Complejo Turístico Los Manantiales*, T/F314275, with camping.

El Arriero, Colo Colo 235. Good *parrillas* and international dishes. *Bavaria*, Colón 357. Good. *Rancho de Julio*, Colón 720. Excellent *parrilla*. *D'Leone*, Av Alemania 686. Good lasagne. *Julio's Pizzas*, Colón 542. Cheap, good. **Eating**

For local excursions, car rental or air tickets, contact *Interbruna Turismo*, Caupolicán 350, T313812, interbruna@hotmail.com The local **tourist office** is also a good source of information and arranges trips, at Lautaro 267, T321700, www.ccla.cl/ **Tour operators**

Long distance bus terminal on northeast outskirts of town, local terminal at Villagrán y Rengo in centre. To **Santiago**, 9 hrs, US$12. To **Viña del Mar** and **Valparaíso**, 10 hrs, US$14. Every 30 mins to **Concepción**, US$3, 2¼ hrs. To **Temuco**, US$5, hourly. To **Curacautín**, daily at 0600, 3 hrs, US$4. **Transport**

Banks ATMs at banks and at supermarket at Av Alemania 686. *Agencia Interbruna*, Caupolicán 350, T313812, F325925, best rates. **Tour operators** , *Agencia Interbruna*, address above, interbruna@hotmail.com, offers local and national tours. *Los Angeles*, Lautaro 267, T321700, www.ccla.cl **Tourist office** Caupolicán, close to the Post Office. *Conaf*, Ercilla 936, 0900-1300. **Directory**

East of Los Angeles by 93 km via a road which runs past the impressive rapids of the Río Laja, this park is dominated by the Antuco volcano (2,985 m), which is still active, and the glacier-covered Sierra Velluda. The Laguna is surrounded by stark scenery of scrub and lava. There are 46 species of birds including condors and the rare Andean gull. ■ ERS *Bus from Los Angeles (Villagrán 507) to Abanico, 20 km past Antuco (US$1.50), then 4 km to park entrance. Or bus to Antuco, 2 hrs, weekdays 5 daily, 2 on Sun and festivals, last return 1730, then hitch last 24 km. Details from Conaf in Los Angeles (see above).* **Parque Nacional Laguna de Laja**

Sleeping *Cabañas y Camping Lagunillas*, T321086 (or Caupolicán 332, of 2, Los Angeles T231066) 50 m from the river, 2 km from park entrance. Open all year, restaurant, poor campsite US$2.50 pp. Camping not permitted on lake shore. 21 km from the lake is the *Refugio Chacay* offering food, drink and bed (**B**, T Los Angeles 222651, closed in summer). 2 other *refugios*: *Digeder*, **E**, and *Universidad de Concepción*, both on slopes of Volcán Antuco, for

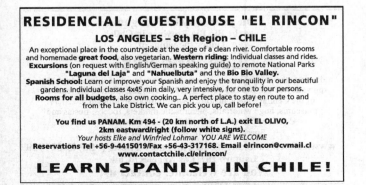

both T Concepción 229054, office O'Higgins 740. Nearby is the Club de Esquí de los Angeles with 2 ski-lifts, giving a combined run of 4 km on the Antuco volcano (season, May-Aug). **Abanico: E** pp *Hostería del Bosque*, restaurant, also good campsite.

Angol
Phone code: 045
Colour map 8, grid C1
Population: 39,000

Capital of the Province of Malleco, **Angol** is reached by paved roads from Collipulli and Los Angeles. Founded by Valdivia in 1552, it was seven times destroyed by the Indians and rebuilt. The church and convent of **San Beneventura**, northwest of the attractive Plaza de Armas, built in 1863, became the centre for missionary work among the Mapuche. **El Vergel**, founded in 1880 as an experimental fruit-growing nursery, now includes an attractive park and the **Museo Dillman Bullock** with pre-Columbian Indian artefacts. ■ *Mon-Fri 0900-1900, Sat-Sun 1000-1900, US$1. 5 km from town, colectivo No 2.* There is an excellent tourist office on O'Higgins s/n, across bridge from bus terminal, T711255. *Conaf*, Prat 191, p 2, T711870.

Sleeping Several in town. **D** pp *La Posada*, at El Vergel, T712103. Full board. **D** *Res Olimpia*, Caupolicán 625, T711162. Good. **E** *Casa de Huéspedes*, Dieciocho 465. With breakfast.

Transport Bus to **Santiago** US$6.50, **Los Angeles**, US$1.20. To **Temuco**, *Trans Bío-Bío*, frequent, US$2.50.

Parque Nacional Nahuelbuta
Rough maps are available at the park entrance for US$0.25

Situated in the coastal mountain range at an altitude of 800-1,550 m, this beautiful park covers 6,832 ha of forest and offers views over both the sea and the Andes. Although the forest includes many species of trees, the monkey puzzle (*araucaria*) is most striking; some are over 2,000 years old, 50 m high and 3 min diameter. There are also 16 species of orchids as well as pudu deer, Chiloé foxes, pumas, black

woodpeckers and parrots. There is a Visitors' Centre at Pehuenco, 5 km from the entrance, open summer only 0800-1300, 1400-2000. Camping is near the Visitors' Centre, US$9 – there are many free campsites along the road from *El Cruce* to the entrance. ■ *Open all year (snow Jun-Sep).*

Transport Bus to **Vegas Blancas** (27 km from Angol) 0700 and 1600 daily, return 0900 and 1600, 1½ hrs, US$1.20, get off at *El Cruce*, from where it is a pleasant 7 km walk to park entrance (entry US$4.50).

The Lake District

Santiago

Chile

The Lake District, stretching southwards from Temuco to Puerto Montt, is one of Chile's most beautiful regions. There are some 12 great lakes of varying sizes, as well as imposing waterfalls and snowcapped volcanoes. There are a number of good bases for exploring. Out of season many facilities are closed, in season (from mid-December to mid-March), prices are higher and it is best to book well in advance, particularly for transport. About 20,000 Mapuches live in the area, more particularly around Temuco. Although Mapudungun is becoming less prevalent, there are possibly 100,000 more of mixed descent who speak the Indian tongue, nearly all of them bilingual.

Temuco

Founded in 1881 after the final treaty with the Mapuches and the arrival of the railway, this city is the capital of IX Región (Araucanía). Although at first sight rather grey and imposing, it is a lively university city and one of the fastest growing commercial centres in the south. The city centre is the Plaza Aníbal Pinto, around which are the main public buildings including the cathedral and the Municipalidad. Very little of the old city remains; practically every wooden building burned down following the 1960 earthquake. Temuco is the Mapuches' market town and you may see some, particularly women, in their typical costumes in the huge produce market, the **Feria** (Lautaro y Pinto). Mapuche textiles, pottery, woodcarving, jewellery etc are also sold inside and around the **municipal market**, Aldunate y Diego Portales (it also sells fish, meat and dairy produce), but these are increasingly touristy and poor quality. There is a handicraft fair every February in the main plaza. The **Casa de la Mujer Mapuche**, Prat 283, sells many crafts, including textiles made by a Mapuche weavers' co-operative, all with traditional designs (Monday-Friday 0900-1300, 1500-1900). **Museo de la Araucanía**, Alemania 84, is devoted to the history and traditions of the Mapuche nation, with a section on German settlement. ■ *Mon-Fri 0900-1700, Sat 1100-1645, Sun 1100-1300, US$1 (free Sun). Take bus 1 from the centre.* For information on visits to Mapuche settlements, eg Chol Chol, go to the *Sernatur* office in the Plaza. There are views of Temuco from **Cerro Ñielol**, a park with a fine collection of native plants in the natural state, including the national flower, the *copihue rojo*. This is a good site for a picnic. At the top of the hill there is a restaurant (T214336, open 1200-2400). On Cerro Ñielol is also La Patagua, the tree under which the final peace was signed with the Mapuches in 1881. ■ *Entry US$1, 0830-2030. Bicycles are only allowed in before 1100.*

Phone code: 045
Colour map 8, grid C1
Population: 225,000
Altitude: 107 m
679 km S of Santiago

L *Terraverde*, Prat 0220, T239999. 5-star, best in town. **AL** *Nuevo Hotel de la Frontera*, Bulnes 726, T200400, F200401. With breakfast, excellent. **A-B** *Bayern*, Prat 146, T276000, F212291. 3-star. Small rooms, clean, helpful. **A-B** *C'est Bayonne*, Vicuña MacKenna 361, T235510, netchile@entelchile.net With breakfast, small, modern, German and Italian spoken. **A** *Don Eduardo*, Bello 755, T214133, deduardo@ctcinternet.cl Parking, suites with kitchen. Recommended. **B-C** *Continental*, Varas 708, T238973, continental@ifrance.com Popular with business travellers, old fashioned building, large rooms,

Sleeping
■ *on map*
Accommodation in private houses, category E-F, can be arranged by tourist office

excellent restaurant, popular bar, cheaper rooms without bath. Recommended. **C** *Espelette*, Claro Solar 492, T/F234805. Helpful, quiet. **C** *La Casa de Juanita*, Carrera 735, T213203. Cheaper without bath, breakfast, hot water, laundry, heating, parking, very helpful. Recommended. **D** *Bulnes 1006 y O'Higgins*. Good double rooms, hot water, above drugstore, ask for house key otherwise access limited to shop hours. **D**Chapelco, Cruz 401, T952736, F952734. Cable TV, laundry, good service, Spanish owned, great chef.Recommended. **D** *Flor Acoca*, Lautaro 591. Hot water, breakfast. **D** *Hostal Argentina*, Aldunate 864. With breakfast, hot water. **D** *Oriente*, M Rodríguez 1146, T/F233232. Recommended. **D** *Rupangue*, Barros Arana 182. Hot shower, helpful, good value. **E** *Hosp Aldunate*, Aldunate 187, T213548. Cooking facilities, also **F** pp dormitory accommodation. **F** pp *Casa Blanca*, Montt 1306 y Zenteno, T272667, F212740. Slightly run down, but cheap alternative for room with private bath. **F** pp *Hospedaje 525*, Zenteno 525, T233982. Without breakfast, new section has small rooms with bath, good value, older part has poor beds but also good value.**F** pp *Maggi Alvarado*, Recreo 209, T263215. Small rooms, helpful, student place, nice atmosphere. **F** pp *Hosp Millaray*, Claro Solar 471. T645720. Simple, basic. Other private houses on this street. **F** pp *Blanco 1078*, T272926, T09-566 7542 (mob). Use of kitchen, good breakfast.

Camping *Camping Metrenco*, on Pan-American Highway, Km 12.

Eating
● *on map*
Many good restaurants around Av Alemania and Mall Mirage, about 10 blocks west of centre The market has several restaurants

Mid-range: *Caletas*, in the Mercado Municipal. Fish/seafood. *Centro Español*, Bulnes 483. *D'Angelo*, San Martín 1199. Good food, pleasant. *La Parrilla de Miguel*, Montt 1095, good for meat and wine. **Cheap**: Make for the produce market or the rural bus terminal, where there are countless restaurants serving very cheap set meals at lunch.*Artemesa*, Aldunate 620, p 8. Vegetarian with views. *Ñam-Ñam*, Portales 802. Sandwiches etc, good. *Pront Rapa*, Aldunate 421. For take-away lunches and snacks. *Quick Biss*, Varas 765. Self-service, including salad bar, good. *Restaurante del Sur*, Portales 921. Open 24hrs. *Temedors*, San Martín 827. Good value lunch. **Cafés**: for real coffee: *Marriet*, Prat 451, loc 21, and *Ripley*, Prat y Varas.

Shopping

Crafts Best choice in the indoor municipal market at Aldunate y Portales. **Fishing equipment** *Jabalí*, Montt 1047. **Supermarket** *Las Brisas*, Caupolicán y Montt, and Rodríguez 1100 block. There is a modern shopping mall north of city; buses 2 or 7. *Frutería Las Vegas*, Matta 274, dried fruit (useful for climbing/trekking).

Tour operators *Turismo Gira*, Montt 1027, of 204. Good. *Turismo Ñielol*, Claro Solar 633, T/F239497. To Parque Nacional Conguillio US$34; to Villarrica volcano US$60.

Transport

Local Car hire: *Automóvil Club de Chile*, Varas 687, T248903 for car hire and at airport. *Euro*, MacKenna 426, T210311, helpful, good value. *Christopher Car*, Varas 522, T215988, recommended. *Full Famas*, at airport and in centre T215420, highly recommended. **Motor mechanic**: *ServiTren*, Edgardo Schneider Reinike and Peter Fischer (peocito@yahoo.de),Matta 0545 y Ruta 5, T/F212775, for cars and motorcycles, German spoken **Bicycle repairs**: on Balmaceda, *Don Cheyo*, No 1266, another at No 1294, *Monsalves*, No 1448, opposite rural bus terminal. Several others on Portales eg *Oxford*, *Bianchi*.

Long distance Air: Manquehue Airport 6 km southwest of the city. *LanChile, Lan Express* to **Santiago, Osorno, Valdivia** and **Puerto Montt**. Sky to Santiago and Puerto Montt. There is an airport transfer service to hotels in Villarrica and Pucón, US$12 (may not run out of season). Taxis charge US$4.50. There is no public bus.

Trains: Station at Barros Arana y Lautaro Navarro, T233416. To **Santiago**: at 2030, 12 hrs: fares *turista* US$12.45, *salón* US$15, *cama* US$31, cabin (sleeps 2) US$70, restaurant car mid-price (or take your own food). Ticket office at Bulnes 582, T233522, open Mon-Fri 0900-1300, 1430-1800, Sun 0900-1300 as well as at station. No train service south of Temuco.

Buses: New long-distance bus terminal north of city at Pérez Rosales y Caupolicán, city bus 2 or 10; taxi US$2.50. *JAC* has its own efficient terminal at Balmaceda y Aldunate, 7 blocks north of the Plaza. *NarBus* and *Igi-Llaima* are opposite. Buses to **Santiago**, overnight, 9 hrs, US$8 (*salón-cama* US$22). To **Concepción**, **Bío Bío** (Lautaro entre Prat y Bulnes), US$5, 4½ hrs. To **Chillán**, 4 hrs, US$5. *Cruz del Sur*, 3 a day to **Castro**, 10 a day to **Puerto Montt** (US$6,

Chile

5½ hrs), to **Valdivia** US$3, 2½ hrs. To **Osorno** US$4, 4 hrs. To **Villarrica** and **Pucón**, *JAC*, many between 0705 and 2045, 1¾ hrs, US$3, and 2 hrs, US$4. Buses to neighbouring towns leave from Terminal Rural, Pinto y Balmaceda. To **Coñaripe**, 3 hrs, and **Lican Ray**, 2 hrs. To **Panguipulli**, *Power* and *Pangui Sur* 3 hrs, US$3. *Pangui Sur* to **Loncoche**, US$1.50, **Los Lagos**, US$2.50, **Mehuin** in summer only. To **Curacautín** via Lautaro, *Erbuc*, US$2, 4 daily, 2½ hrs. To **Lonquimay**, *Erbuc*, 4 daily, 3½ hrs, US$3. To **Contulmo**, US$4, 2 hrs, **Cañete**, US$4 and **Lebu**, *Erbuc* and *Thiele*.

Buses to Argentina: *Igi Llaima* 4 days a week and *San Martín* 3 a week to **Junín de los Andes**, US$15. *Ruta Sur* (Miraflores 1151) to **Zapala**, 10-12 hrs (US$25), 3 a week. To **Neuquén**, 7 companies, 16 hrs (US$27), via Paso Pino Hachado. To **Bariloche** you have to change bus in Osorno, US$23.

Airline offices *LanChile*, Bulnes 699, T272138. **Banks** Many ATMs at banks on Plaza Aníbal Pinto. **Directory** Also at the *JAC* bus terminal (Visa). Many *cambios* around the plaza, all deal in dollars and Argentine pesos. Good rates at *Germaniotour*, M Montt 942, after 1100. **Communications** Internet: Many on Prat and Mackenna, south of the Plaza, US$0.50-0.65 per hr. *Araucanet*, A Varas 924, Plaza de Armas,

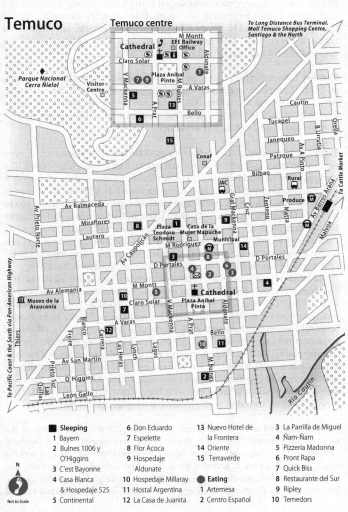

■ Sleeping
1 Bayern
2 Bulnes 1006 y O'Higgins
3 C'est Bayonne
4 Casa Blanca & Hospedaje 525
5 Continental
6 Don Eduardo
7 Espelette
8 Flor Acoca
9 Hospedaje Aldunate
10 Hospedaje Millaray
11 Hostal Argentina
12 La Casa de Juanita
13 Nuevo Hotel de la Frontera
14 Oriente
15 Terraverde

● Eating
1 Artemesa
2 Centro Español
3 La Parrilla de Miguel
4 Ñam-Ñam
5 Pizzería Madonna
6 Pront Rapa
7 Quick Biss
8 Restaurante del Sur
9 Ripley
10 Temedors

below street level, T406090. Email, fax, photocopying and other telecommunications services. Also at M Montt 334, near Las Heras, T402680, open until 2030. **Post Office:** Portales 839. **Telephone:** *CTC*, A Prat just off Claro Solar and plaza. *Entel*, Bulnes 303. **Consulates Netherlands**, España 494, Honorary Consul, Germán Nicklas, is friendly and helpful. **Medical services Hospital**, Manuel Montt 115. **Tourist offices** *Sernatur*, Bulnes 586, on main plaza, T211969. Good leaflets in English. Daily in summer 0830-2030, Mon-Fri 0900-1200, 1500-1700 in winter. Also in the municipal market. *Conaf* is at Bilbao 931, T234420. *Sernap* for fishing permits, Miraflores 965.

East of Temuco

This region has many national parks, native forests, microclimates and flora and fauna found nowhere else. It is great for hiking, or touring by car or even mountain bike. There are also various skiing opportunities.

Curacautín
Population: 12,737
Altitude: 400 m

Curacautín is a small town situated 84 km northeast of Temuco (road paved) and 56 km southeast of Victoria by paved road. Deprived by new, stricter controls of its traditional forestry industry (there were several sawmills), Curacautín is trying to recreate itself as a centre for tourism. It is a useful base for visiting the nearby national parks and hot springs. There is no ATM in town; best exchange rate at *Banco del Estado*. ■ *Bus terminal on the main road, by the plaza. Buses to/from Temuco, Los Angeles and Santiago. Taxi from Temuco airport US$35.*

Sleeping C *Plaza*, Yungay 157 (main plaza), T881256. Restaurant good but pricey, accommodation overpriced. **E** *Hostal Las Espigas*, Miraflores 315, T881138, rivaseugenia@hotmail.com Good rooms, kitchen, breakfast, dinner available on request. **E** *Turismo*, Tarapacá 140, T881116. Good food, comfortable, good value. **E** Rodríguez 705 (corner of plaza), with breakfast, kitchen facilities.

Termas de Manzanar, are indoor hot springs, 17 km east of Curacautín (US$5, open all year, run down, overpriced) are reached by bus from Temuco and Victoria. The road passes the Salto del Indio (Km 71 from Victoria; *cabañas* US$1), and Salto de la Princesa, 3 km beyond Manzanar (*hostería*, camping). **L-A** *Termas de Manzanar*, T/F045-881200, termasmanzanar@ indecom.cl Overpriced, but also simple rooms with bath. **C** *Hostería Abarzúa*, T045-870011, simple, **E** without bath. **D-F** pp *Anden Rose*, 5 km west of Manzanar, Casilla 123, Curacautín, T056-9-869 1700, andenrose@gmx.net With breakfast, double rooms and dormitory, camping **G**, restaurant, bike, horse, kayak rental, tours arranged, German run. Many *cabañas* nearby. *La Rotonda del Cautín*, T1971478, mid-price restaurant, good food, friendly.

The beautiful pine-surrounded **Termas de Tolhuaca** are 35 km to the northeast of Curacautín by unpaved road, or 82 km by rough, unpaved road from just north of Victoria (high clearance four-wheel drive vehicle essential). ■ *US$2.50-5, open all year. Taxi from Curacautín US$21.* And 2 km north of the Termas is the **Parque Nacional Tolhuaca**, including waterfalls, two lakes, superb scenery and good views of volcanoes from Cerro Amarillo. Park administration is near Laguna Malleco, with a campsite nearby. Much of the park, together with the neighbouring Reserva Nacional Malleco, was severely damaged by forest fires in early 2002. It will take several decades fully to recover. ■ *Dec-Apr. Taxi from Curacautín US$17.* **AL** *Termas de Tolhuaca*, with full board, including use of baths and horse riding, very good, T045-881164, www.termasdetolhuaca.cl **E** pp *Res Roja*, food, camping near the river, good.

Reserva Nacional Nalcas Malalcahuello

Situated northeast of Curacautín, this 31,305 ha park is on the slopes of the **Lonquimay volcano**. It is much less crowded than nearby Parque Nacional Conguillío. The volcano began erupting on Christmas Day 1988; the new crater is called Navidad. To see it, access is made from Malalcahuello, 15 km south and half-way between Curacautín and Lonquimay town. In the park, which is one of the best areas for seeing unspoilt araucaria forest, Conaf has opened several marked trails, from one hour to two days in length. There is a municipal *refugio* at the foot of the volcano. The teacher at Malalcahuello school, José Córdoba, organizes tours and horse riding for groups. Sra Naomi Saavedra at *Res Los Sauces* arranges transport.

The Lake District

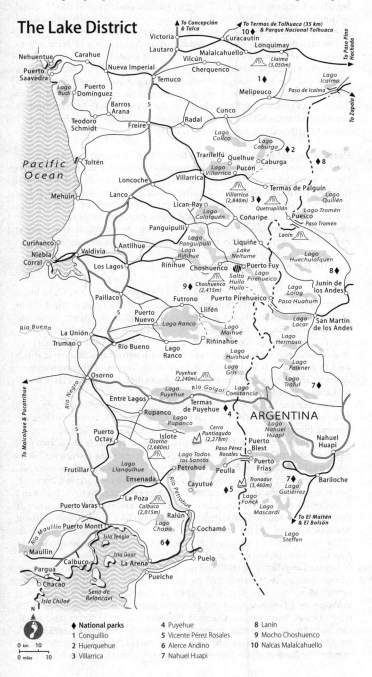

♦ **National parks**

1 Conguillio	4 Puyehue	8 Lanín
2 Huerquehue	5 Vicente Pérez Rosales	9 Mocho Choshuenco
3 Villarrica	6 Alerce Andino	10 Nalcas Malalcahuello
	7 Nahuel Huapi	

0 km   10
0 miles   10

From Malalcahuello it is a one-day hike to the Sierra Nevada mountain, or a two-day hike to Conguillio national park (with equipment and experience, otherwise use a guide). ■ *Bus* Erbuc *from Temuco via Lautaro, US$2 to Malalcahuello, 4 a day, 2½ hrs, 3½ to Lonquimay town, US$3. Taxi Curacautín-Malalcahuello US$12.* Conaf *office on main road in Malalcahuello gives information, as does* La Suizandina, *which gives good access to treks and the ascent of the volcano, see below.*

Los Arenales ski resort is at Las Raices Pass on the road from Malalcahuello to Lonquimay town. Four lifts go up to 2,500 m with great views. It is a good, small resort with a nice restaurant. ■ *Season Jun-Sep. Taxi from Curacautín US$17. In winter access from Lonquimay town side only.* Also in winter, the main route from Malalcahuello to Lonquimay town, goes through the ex-railway tunnel of Las Raices. At 4.8 km it was, until recently, the longest tunnel in South America. Now it's in poor condition, unlit and has constant filtration. There is talk of repair, but it's unwise to go through by bicycle. ■ *Toll US$1.50.*

Sleeping *Res Los Sauces*, in Malalcahuello, **D** pp full board, or **E** pp with use of kitchen, hot water, good value. Accommodation is also available at the Centro de Ski Lonquimay, 10 km from the bus stop, **B** pp with breakfast, full board also available, open only in season, ski pass US$17. **E-F** pp *La Suizandina*, Km 83 Carretera Internacional a Argentina, T045-1973735 or 09-884 9541, www.suizandina.com Hostel 3 km before Malalcahuello (*Erbuc* bus from Temuco 2½ hrs), with a range of rooms (**A** in private room with heating and breakfast), camping US$5, laundry, book exchange, bike and ski rental, horse riding, travel and trekking information, German and English spoken, good meals available. Recommended.

Parque Nacional Conguillio

East of Temuco by 80 km, this is one of the most popular parks in Chile, but is deserted outside January/February and weekends. In the centre is the 3,125 m **Llaima volcano**, which is active. There are two large lakes, Laguna Verde and Laguna Conguillio, and two smaller ones, Laguna Arco Iris and Laguna Captrén. North of Laguna Conguillio rises the snow covered Sierra Nevada, the highest peak of which reaches 2,554 m. This is the best place in Chile to see araucaria forest, which used to cover an extensive area in this part of the country. Other trees include cypresses, lenga and winter's bark. Birdlife includes the condor and the black woodpecker and there are foxes and pumas.

Crampons and ice-axe are essential for climbing Llaima, as well as experience or a guide. Climb south from *Guardería Captrén*. Allow 5 hours to ascend, two hours to descend. Information on the climb is available from *Guardería Captrén*. There is a range of walking trails, from 1 km to 22 km in length. Details are available from park administration or *Conaf* in Temuco. **Llaima** ski resort, one of the prettiest in Chile, is reached by poor road from Cherquenco, 30 km west (high clearance vehicle essential).

There are three entrances: From Curacautín, north of the park: see Transport below; from **Melipeuco**, 13 km south of the southern entrance at Truful-Truful; and from Cherquenco to the west entrance near the Llaima ski resort. It is then a two or three day hike around Volcán Llaima to Laguna Conguillio, which is dusty, but with beautiful views of Laguna Quepe, then on to the Laguna Captrén *guardería*. ■ *Dec-Mar, US$4.Information on all 3 roads into the park and administration by Lago Conguillio. There is a Visitors' Centre at Laguna Captrén.*

Sleeping
& eating
Buy supplies in Temuco, Curacautín or Melipeuco: much cheaper than the shop in the park

At **Laguna Conguillio** campsite (US$15 per tent, hot water, showers, firewood), cheaper campsite (*camping de mochileros*, US$5 pp, plus US$1 pp for shower, US$2 for firewood), *cabañas* (**A** summer only, sleep 6, no sheets or blankets, gas stove, and café/shop). **In Melipeuco E** *Germania*, Aguirre 399. Basic, good food. **E** *Hospedaje Icalma*, Aguirre 729. More spacious. Recommended. **C** *Hostería Hue-Telén*, Aguirre 15, Casilla 40, T581005. *Cabañas* for 4 people, good restaurant, free municipal campsite. Also *Camping Los Pioneros*, 1 km out of town on road to the park, hot water. *Restaurant Los Troncos*, Aguirre 352. Recommended. Also *Ruminot*, on same street. In the park, 3 km south of Laguna Verde is *La Baita*, cabins (**AL-A**) with electricity, hot water, kitchen and wood stoves, T730138, on-line bookings at www.labaitaconguillio.cl Charming, lots of information, Italian/Chilean owned.

To the northern entrance: taxi from Curacautín to Laguna Captrén, US$21 one way. To the western entrance: Daily buses from Temuco to Cherquenco, from where there is no public transport to the park. Transport can be arranged from Melipeuco into the park (ask in grocery stores and *hospedajes*, US$20 one way). Private transport is the best way to see the area.

Transport
*For touring, hire a
4WD vehicle
in Temuco*

Paso Pino Hachado (1,884 m) can be reached either by mostly paved road, 77 km southeast from Lonquimay, or by unpaved road 103 east from Melipeuco. On the Argentine side this road continues to Zapala. Chilean immigration and customs are in Liucura, 22 km west of the border, open December-March 0800-2000, April-November 0800-1800. Very thorough searches and 2-3 hour delays reported. Buses from Temuco to Zapala and Neuquén use this crossing: see under Temuco. **Paso de Icalma** (1,298 m) is reached by unpaved road, 53 km from Melipeuco, a good crossing for those with their own transport. On the Argentine side this road continues to Zapala. Chilean immigration is open December-March 0800-2100, April-November 0800-1900.

**Border with
Argentina**

Villarrica

Wooded Lago Villarrica, 21 km long and about 7 km wide, is one of the most beautiful in the region, with the active, snow-capped Villarrica volcano (2,840 m) to the southeast. The town of Villarrica, pleasantly set at the extreme southwest corner of the lake, can be reached by a 63-km paved road southeast from Freire (24 km south of Temuco on the Pan-American Highway), or from Loncoche, 54 km south of Freire, also paved. Founded in 1552, the town was besieged by the Mapuche in the uprising of 1599: after three years the surviving Spanish settlers, 11 men and 13 women, surrendered. The town was refounded in 1882. At Pedro de Valdivia y Zegers is the **Muestra Cultural Mapuche** featuring a Mapuche *ruca* and handicraft stalls. ■ *Open all summer. Livestock market every Mon about 1400; riding equipment for sale.* In January and February Villarrica has a summer programme with many cultural and sporting events and on 18-19 September the *Gran Fiesta Campestre de Villarrica* is held in the indoor riding arena of the **Parque Natural Dos Ríos**, with typical foods, music, dancing, competitions and shows. Dos Ríos is 13 km west of Villarrica between the Ríos Voipir and Toltén, a private nature park with bed-and-breakfast accommodation, lots of sports, especially riding, fishing, boating, birdwatching: www.dosrios.de

*Phone code: 045
Colour map 8, grid C1
Population: 36,000
Altitude: 227 m
Much qieter than
Pucón*

Chile

LL *Villarrica Park Lake*, Km 13 on the road to Pucón, T450000, www.villarrica.com/parklake 5-star. **AL** *Hostería la Colina*, Ríos 1177, overlooking town, T411503, www.hosteriadela colina.com With breakfast, large gardens, good service, good restaurant. Recommended. **A** *El Ciervo*, Koerner 241, T411215, www.villaricanet.com/elciervo German spoken, beautiful location, pool. Recommended. **A** *Hotel y Cabañas El Parque*, 3 km east on Pucón road, T411120, www.hotelparque.cl Lakeside with beach, tennis courts, with breakfast, good restaurant set meals. Recommended. **A** *Hotel Yachting Kiel*, Koerner 153, T411631, www.villarricanet.com/yachting **B** off season, lakeside, good. **A-B** *Bungalowlandia*, Prat 749, T/F411635, bungalowlandia@villarrica.net. *Cabañas* for 2, dining room, good facilities. **B** *Hostería Bilbao*, Henríquez 43, T411186, www.7lagos.com/bilbao Small rooms, pretty patio, good restaurant. **C** *Kolping*, Riquelme 399, T/F411388. Good breakfast. Recommended. **C** *Rayhuen*, Pedro Montt 668, T411571. Lovely garden. Recommended. **D** Vicente Reyes 854, T414457. Good breakfast, good bathrooms but only one for 4-5 rooms, use of kitchen, camping in garden. **F** pp *La Torre Suiza*, Bilbao 969, T/F411213, www.torresuiza.com Kitchen facilities, camping, cycle rental, book exchange, smallbreakfast, reserve in advance. Recommended. **F** pp *Hostería Las Rosas del Lago*, Julio Zegers 897, T411463. Helpful and clean. **F** pp *Maravillas del Sur*, Bilbao 821, T411444. With bath and breakfast, good value, parking. Several private homes on Bilbao, eg *Eliana Castillo*, No 537. Also Urrutia 407, large breakfast, kitchen. Matta 469, cooking

Sleeping
*Private homes in
D range on Muñoz
400 and 500 blocks,
Koerner 300 block
and O'Higgins 700
and 800 blocks*

facilities. **Youth hostel** E pp *Res San Francisco*, Julio Zegers 646. Shared rooms. **Camping** Many sites east of town on Pucón road, open in season only: nearest is **E** *Los Castaños*, T412330, up to 6 people.

Eating *El Tabor*, S Epulef 1187. Excellent but pricey. **Mid-range**: *Rapa Nui*, V Reyes 678. Good, closed Sun. *El Rey de Mariscos*, Letelier 1030. Good seafood. *Treffpunkt*, P de Valdivia 640. *The Travellers*, Letelier 753. Varied menu including vegetarian, Asian food, good bar, English spoken. **Cheap**: *Alternativa*, V Reyes 739. Good *almuerzo*. *Café 2001*, Henríquez 379. Coffee and ice cream, good. *Dinner's*, Vicente Reyes 781, and *Chito Fuentes*, Reyes 665. Chilean fast food.

Transport **Bus** terminal at Pedro de Valdivia y Muñoz. *JAC* at Bilbao 610, T411447, and opposite for Pucón and Lican-Ray. Terminal Rural for other local services at Matta y Vicente Reyes. To **Santiago**, 10 hrs, US$20, several companies. To **Pucón**, with *Vipu-Ray* (main terminal) and *JAC*, in summer every 15 mins, 40 mins' journey, US$0.50; same companies to **Lican-Ray**, US$1. To **Valdivia**, *JAC*, US$3.50, 3 a day, 2½ hrs. To **Coñaripe** (US$1.60) and **Liquiñe** at 1600 Mon-Sat, 1000 Sun. To **Temuco**, *JAC*, US$3. To **Loncoche** (Ruta 5 junction for hitching), US$1.50. To **Panguipulli**, go via Lican-Ray, occasional direct buses. To **Junín de los Andes (Argentina)** *San Martín* (Muñoz 604) 3 a week and *Igi-Llaima*, Valdivia 611, T412733, 4 a week, US$25, 6 hrs, but if the Tromén pass is blocked by snow buses go via Panguipulli instead of Pucón.

Directory **Banks** ATMs at banks on Pedro de Valdivia between Montt and Alderete. *Carlos Huerta*, A Muñoz 417, *Central de Repuestos*, A Muñoz 415 (good rates), *Turcamb*, Henríquez 576, and *Cristopher Exchange*, Valdivia 1061, all change TCs and cash. **Bicycle shops** *Mora Bicicletas*, G Korner 760, helpful. **Communications** Internet: At the *Central de Llamadas*, Henríquez 567, 2nd floor. *Cybercafé Salmon*, Letelier y Henríquez. **Post Office:** A Muñoz 315. Open 0900-1300, 1430-1800 (Mon-Fri), 0900-1300 (Sat). **Telephone:** *Entel*, Henríquez 440 and 575. *CTC*, Henríquez 544. *Chilesat*, Henríquez 473, best rates. **Tourist offices** On Gral Urrutia, Plaza de Armas. Offers aommodation.

Pucón

Phone code: 045
Colour map 8, grid C1
Population: 13,000
Altitude: 227 m

Pucón, on the southeastern shore of Lago Villarrica, 26 km east of Villarrica, is the major tourist centre on the lake. The black sand beach is very popular for swimming and watersports. Between New Year to end-February it is very crowded and expensive; off season it is very pleasant. Apart from the lake, other attractions nearby include whitewater rafting and winter sports (see Skiing below). There is a pleasant walk to **La Península** for fine views of the lake and volcano, pony rides, golf, etc (private land owned by an Apart-Hotel, ask permission first). There is another pleasant *paseo*, the **Otto Gudenschwager**, which starts at the lake end of Ansorena (beside *Gran Hotel Pucón*, Holzapfel 190, T441001) and goes along the shore. Launch excursions from the landing stage at La Poza at the end of O'Higgins, US$4 for two hours.

Walk 2 km north along the beach to the mouth of the Río Trancura (also called Río Pucón), with views of the volcanoes Villarrica, Quetrupillán and Lanín. To cross the Río Pucón: head east out of Pucón along the main road, then turn north on an unmade road leading to a new bridge; from here there are pleasant walks along the north shore of the lake to Quelhue and Trarilelfú, or northeast towards Caburga (see page 699), or up into the hills through farms and agricultural land, with views of three volcanoes and, higher up, of the lake. The journey to Caburga (see below) is a perfect mountain bike day trip.

Sleeping
In summer (Dec-Feb) rooms may be hard to find. Plenty of alternatives (usually cheaper) in Villarrica

Prices below are Jan-Feb. Off-season rates are 20-40% lower and it is often possible to negotiate. **LL** *Antumalal*, luxury class, 2 km west, T441011, www.antumalal.com Very small, picturesque chalet-type, magnificent views of the lake (breakfast and lunch on terrace), gardens, with meals, open year round, pool. **L** *Interlaken*, Colombia y Caupolicán, T441276, F441242. Chalets, open Nov-Apr, water skiing, pool, TCs changed, no restaurant. **AL** *Hostería El Principito*, Urrutia 291, T441200. Good breakfast. **A** *Gudenschwager*, Pedro de Valdivia 12, T441156, gudens@cepri.cl Classic Bavarian type, views over lake, volcano and mountains, attentive staff, comfortable, excellent restaurant (open in summer only). **A** *La Posada*, Valdivia 191, T441088, laposada@unete.com Cheaper without bath, full board available, also spacious cabins (**C** low season), small breakfast. **A** *Los Maitenes*, Fresia 354, T441820. Light and airy, comfortable, homely, breakfast, TV. **A** *Munich*, Alderete 275, T/F442293. Modern, spacious, German and English spoken. **B** *Gerónimo*, Alderete 665, T/F443762, www.geronimo. bizhosting.com Quiet, bar, restaurant, open all year. **B** *Hostería Millarrahue*, O'Higgins 460, T411610. Good, inexpensive restaurant. **C-D** *Hosp La Casita*, Palguín 555, T441712, lacasita@entelchile.net Laundry and kitchen facilities, English and German spoken, large breakfast, garden, motorcycle parking, ski trips, Spanish classes, **D** off season. Recommended. **C-D** *La Tetera*, Urrutia 580, T/F441462, www.tetera.cl 6 rooms, some with bath, with breakfast, German and English spoken, book swap, information centre, good Spanish classes, agency for *Navimag* ferries, book in advance. Recommended. **C** *Hosp El Montañés*, O'Higgins 472, T441267. Good value, TV, central, restaurant, next to JAC buses. **D** *Res Lincoyán*, Av Lincoyán, T441144, www.lincoyan.cl Cheaper without bath, comfortable. **D** pp *Hostería ¡école!*, Urrutia 592, T/F441675, trek@ecole.cl With breakfast, no singles, also dormitory accommodation, **E** pp (sleeping bag essential), good vegetarian and fish restaurant, ecological shop, forest treks, rafting, biking, information, language classes, massage, youth hostelling discount, best to reserve in advance. **E** *Hostal Backpackers*, Palguín 695, T441373, hostal@politur.com With or without bath, quiet, next to JAC buses, internet, 10% discount on *Politur* activities, Navimag reservations, tourist information, new. **E-F** pp *Casa de Campo Kila-Leufu*, about 20 km east on road to Curarrehue, T09-711 8064, margotex@yahoo.com Rooms on the Martínez family farm, contact daughter Margot in advance, English spoken, price includes breakfast and dinner, home-grown food, horseriding, boat tours, treks. **E** pp *Donde Germán*, Brasil 640, T442444, dondegerman@latinmail.com Fun, organizes tours, internet, book in advance.

Recommended accommodation in private houses, all **F** pp unless stated: **On Palguín** *Familia Acuña*, No 223 (ask at *peluquería* next door). Without breakfast, kitchen and laundry facilities. *María del Pilar García*, No 361, no sign, above saddlery. English spoken, quiet, use of kitchen. **On Lincoyán** **D** *Hosp El Refugio*, No 348, T441347. With breakfast, good. *Hosp Sonia*, No 485, T441269. Use of kitchen, meals. *Hosp Irma Torres*, No 545. Cooking facilities. *Hosp Lucía*, No 565, T441721, luciahostal@ hotmail.com Safe, quiet, cooking facilities. *Casa Eliana*, Pasaje Chile 225, T441851. Kitchen facilities. Adriana Molina, No 312. With breakfast, helpful. No 630, T441043. Kitchen facilities, good value. **F** *Casa de María*, Urrutia 560, T443264. Use of kitchen, good location. *Hosp Graciela*, Pasaje Rolando Matus 521 (off Av Brasil). Comfortable, good food. Irma Villena, Arauco 460. Use of kitchen, very hospitable. **G** pp *Roberto y Alicia Abreque*, Perú 170. Basic, noisy, popular, kitchen and laundry facilities, information on excursions. **G** pp *Casa Richard*, Paraguay 140. Cooking facilities. **G** *Tr@vel Pucón*, Blanco Encalada 190, T444093, Pucontravel@terra.cl Garden, tours, kitchen, Spanish classes, near *Turbus* terminal.

Many families offer rooms, look for the signs or ask in bars/restaurants

Camping There are many camping and cabin establishments: those close to Pucón include *La Poza*, Costanera Geis 769, T441435, **F** pp, hot showers, good kitchen. Recommended. West along Lago Villarrica: **A-B** *Huimpalay-Tray*, Km 12, T450079 (Santiago 231 4248). Gorgeous location on lake, well-equipped. Recommended all round. *Saint John*, Km 7, T441165/92, Casilla 154, open Dec-Mar, also *hostería*. Several sites en route to the volcano, including *L'Etoile*, Km 2, T442188, in attractive forest, **C** per site; *Mahuida*, Km 6. Cheaper sites en route to Caburga. **Camping equipment** *Eltit supermarket*, O'Higgins y Fresia. *Outdoors & Travel*, Lincoyán 361, clothing, equipment, maps.

Expensive: *Ana María*, O'Higgins 865. Classic Chilean food. *En Alta Mar*, Urrutia y Fresia. For seafood and fish. *Puerto Pucón*, Fresia 251. Spanish, stylish. **Mid-range**: *Brasil*, Fresia 477. Chilean food. *El Fogón*, O'Higgins 480. Very good. *El Palet*, Fresia 295. Genuine local food, good value. Recommended. *El Refugio*, Lincoyán 348. Some vegetarian dishes, expensive wine. *La Buonatesta*, Fresia 243. Good pizzería. *La Maga*, Fresia 125. Uruguayan grill, good, if pricey. *Nau Kana*, Fresia. Oriental food. **Cafés and bars** *Fresia Strasse*, Fresia 161. Good coffee and cakes. *Holzapfel Backerei*, Holzapfel 524. German cafe. Recommended. *La Tetera*, Urrutia 580, teas, coffee, snacks. *Pub La For You*, Ansorena 370, English-style pub, runs minibuses in high season to its club 1 km from town. *Vagabundo*, Fresia 135. Also serves good value meals.

Eating
See Sleeping for recommendations

Chile

Sport & activities

Pucón and Villarrica are celebrated as centres for fishing on Lake Villarrica and in the beautiful Lincura, Trancura and Toltén rivers. In high season, sports shops open, especially for biking and watersports

Fishing: Local tourist office will supply details on licences and open seasons etc. **Horse riding**: enquire at *La Tetera* for Hans Bacher (Austrian), or *Rancho de Caballos* (German run, see Termas de Palguín, below). Day excursions US$55, also half-day US$35. *Centro de Turismo Ecuestre Huepil Malal*, T09-643 2673, Rodolfo Coombs and Carolina Pumpin, PO Box 16, Pucón, 40 mins from town. Highly recommended. **Hydrospeeding**: *Fabrice Pini*, Colo Colo 830, US$55 for 30 mins. **Mountain biking**: Bike hire from US$1.50 per hr to US$10 per day from several travel agencies on O'Higgins. **Watersports**: water-skiing, sailing, windsurfing at Playa Grande beach by *Gran Hotel* and La Poza beach end of O'Higgins (more expensive than Playa Grande, not recommended). Playa Grande: waterskiing US$10 for 15 mins, Laser sailing US$11 per hr, sailboards US$10 per hr, rowing boats US$4 per hr. **Whitewater rafting**: is very popular on the Río Trancura. Many agencies offer trips (see below), Trancura Bajo (grade 3), US$10-15; Trancura Alto (grade 4), US$25.

Tour operators

All arrange trips to thermal baths, trekking to volcanoes, whitewater rafting, etc. For falls, lakes and termas it is cheaper, if in a group, to flag down a taxi and bargain

Many agencies, so shop around: prices vary at times, quality of guides and equipment variable. In high season, when lots of groups are going up together, individual attention may be lacking. Prices for climbing Villarrica are given below. Tours to Termas de Huife, US$20 including entry. *Aguaventura*, Palguín 336, T444246, www.aguaventura.com On O'Higgins: *Anden Sport*, No, T441048, F441236. Agency specializing in skiing, rafting, trips to springs, hiking tours. Good contact for travellers. *Florencia*, No 480, T443026. *Politur*, No 635, T/F441373, www.politur.com *Rayenco* No 524, T449506, aventur_ rayenco@latinmail.com Tours, fishing, accommodation (**E**), internet. *Roncotrack*, O'Higgins y Arauco. Quadbike excursions. *Sol y Nieve* (esq Lincoyán), T/F444098, www.solynieve.cl Well established.

Transport

Local Car hire: Prices start at US$25 for a car. *Christopher Car*, O'Higgins 335, T/F449013. *Pucón Rent A Car*, Camino Internacional 1395, T441922, kernayel@cepri.cl *Sierra Nevada*, Palguín y O'Higgins. **Taxis**: *Co-operative*, T441009.

Long distance Air Airport 2 km on Caburga road. *Lan Express*, 4 flights a week to **Santiago** in summer. **Buses** No municipal terminal: each company has its own terminal: *JAC*, Uruguay y Palguín; *TurBus*, O'Higgins, 1180, east of town; *Igi Llaima* and *Cóndor*, Colo Colo y O'Higgins. *JAC* to **Villarrica** (US$0.50), **Temuco** (frequent, US$3, 2 hrs, *rápido* US$3.50, 1¾ hr) and **Valdivia** (US$5). *TurBus* at 1030 direct to **Valdivia, Osorno** and **Puerto Montt**, 6 hrs, US$6, daily in summer, 3 a week off season. To **Santiago**, 10 hrs, US$12, many companies, early morning and late evening; *semi cama* service by *TurBus* and *JAC*, US$40. Colectivos to **Villarrica** from O'Higgins y Palguín. **Buses to Argentina**: Buses from Temuco to **Junín** pass through Pucón, fares are the same as from Temuco.

Directory

Airline offices *LanChile*, Urrutia y Costanera, daily 1000-1400, 1800-2200. **Banks** ATMs in *Banco Santander*, O'Higgins y Fresia, *Eltit*, supermarket, O'Higgins, *Banco BCI*, Fresia y Alderete, and in casino. Several *casas de cambio* on O'Higgins. *Eltit*, also changes TCs, but rates for TCs in Pucón are poor. **Communications** Internet: Several sites on O'Higgins, US$2 per hr. Also at Palguín y O'Higgins. **Post Office**: Fresia 183. **Telephone**: CTC, Gen Urrutia 472. *Entel*, Ansorena 299. **Tourist offices** In the municipal building, O'Higgins 483, T441125/443238, sells fishing licences (US$1 per month), www.pucon.com Do not confuse with the Chamber of Tourism at the entrance to Pucón from Villarrica. *Conaf*, O'Higgins 669, very helpful.

Parque Nacional Villarrica

The park has three sectors: **Volcán Villarrica**, **Volcán Quetrupillán** and the **Puesco sector** which includes the slopes of the Volcán Lanín on the Argentine border. Each sector has its own entrance and ranger station. A campsite with drinking water and toilets is below the refuge, 4 km inside the park. The **Villarrica** volcano, 2,840 m, 8 km south of Pucón (entry US$6) can be climbed up and down in eight to nine hours, good boots, ice axe and crampons, sunglasses, plenty of water, chocolate and sun block essential. Beware of sulphur fumes at the top – good agencies provide gas masks, otherwise take a cloth mask moistened with lemon juice – but you can see into the crater with lava bubbling at 1,250°.

Entry to Volcán Villarrica is permitted only to groups with a guide and to individuals who can show proof of membership of a mountaineering club in their own country. Several agencies take excursions, US$30-40, including park entry, guide, transport to park entrance and hire of equipment (no reduction for those with their own equipment); at the park entrance equipment is checked. Entry is refused if the weather is poor. Travel agencies will not start out if the weather is bad: establish in advance what terms apply in the event of cancellation and be prepared to wait a few days. Many **guides**, all with equipment; ask for recommendations at the tourist office. For US$4 you can take the ski lift for the first part of the ascent, saves 400 m climbing.

Skiing The Pucón resort, owned by the *Gran Hotel Pucón*, is on the eastern slopes of the volcano, reached by a track, 35 minutes. The centre offers equipment rental (US$15 per day, US$82 per week), ski instruction, first aid, restaurant and bar as well as wonderful views from the terrace. Lift ticket US$15-25 full day, to restaurant only US$5; high season is July to November. Information on snow and ski-lifts (and, perhaps, transport) from tourist office or *Gran Hotel Pucón*. Good for beginners; more advanced skiers can try the steeper areas.

Skiing trips to the summit are very tough going and only for the fit

Lago Caburga (spelt locally Caburgua), a very pretty lake in a wild setting 25 km northeast of Pucón, is unusual for its beautiful white sand beach (it also has a black sand beach - other beaches in the area are of black volcanic sand). The west and much of the shores of the lake are inaccessible to vehicles. The north shore can be reached by a road from Cunco via the north shore of **Lago Colico**, a more remote lake north of Lago Villarrica. The village of Caburga, at the southern end is reached by a turning off the main road 8 km east of Pucón. **D** *Hostería Los Robles*, near the lake shore, T236989, lovely views, good restaurant, campsite, closed out of season. The southern end of the lake and around Caburga is lined with campsites. There is a supermarket in Caburga. Rowing boats may be hired US$2 per hour. Just off the road from Pucón, Km 15, are the **Ojos de Caburga**, beautiful pools fed from underground, particularly attractive after rain (entry US$0.30; ask bus driver to let you off). Alternatively, take a mountain bike from Pucón via the Puente Quelhue. East of the lake is **B** *Landhaus San Sebastián*, F443057, with bath and breakfast, good meals, laundry facilities, English and German spoken, Spanish classes.

Lagos Caburga & Colico

Transport To **Caburga**: taxi day trips from Pucón, US$25 return. *JAC* bus departs regularly for Caburga (US$1 single), and there are colectivos from Ansorena y Uruguay or you can try hitching. If walking or cycling, turn left 3 km east of Pucón (sign to Puente Quelhue) and follow the track (very rough) for 18 km through beautiful scenery. Recommended.

East of Lago Caburga, the park includes steep hills and at least 20 lakes, some of them very small. Entrance and administration are near **Lago Tinguilco**, the largest lake, on the western edge of the park. From the entrance there is a well-signed track north to three beautiful lakes, Lagos Verde, Chico and Toro (private car park, US$1.50, 1½ km along the track). The track zig-zags up (sign says 5 km, but worth it) to Lago Chico, then splits left to Verde, right to Toro. From Toro you can continue to Lago Huerquehue and Laguna los Patos (camping). ■ *The park entrance is 7 km (3 km uphill, 3 km down, one along Lago Tinquilco) from Paillaco, which is reached by an all-weather road which turns off 3 km before Caburga, US$3.25. The park is open officially only Dec-Mar, but you can get in at other times. The warden is very helpful; people in the park rent horses and boats. Take your own food. Take JAC bus from Pucón, daily in summer, 3 times a week otherwise, early.*

Parque Nacional Huerquehue
Good walking here, to see if you're fit enough for Villarrica volcano

Sleeping *Refugio Tinquilco*, 3½ km from park entrance, where forest trail leads to lakes Verde and Toro, T02-777 7673, T09-822 7153 (mob), patriciolanfranco@entelchile.net **B** with bath to **E** for bed and no sheets, meals extra, heating, hot water, electricity sunset to midnight, cooking facilities, very good. Recommended. **D** *Hospedaje Carlos Alfredo Richard*, southwest shore of the lake, 2 km from park entrance, parque_huerquehue@

hotmail.com Large rooms with bath, hot water, breakfast included, restaurant, rowing boats for hire (also at Arauco 171 in Pucón, shared rooms, use of kitchen, internet access). Camping only at the park entrance, 2 sites, US$8. 1½ km before the park entrance, 2 German speaking families, the Braatz and Soldans, offer accommodation, **E** pp, no electricity, food and camping (US$6); they also rent rowing boats on the lake. **E** pp Nidia Carrasco Godoy runs a *hospedaje* in the park, T09-443 2725 (mob). With breakfast, hot water, camping.

Transport *JAC* bus from Pucón to Paillaco, 1½ hrs, US$1, Mon-Fri 0700, 1230, 1700, Sat-Sun 0700, 1600, returns immediately – last at 1800.

South of the Huerquehue Park on a turning from the Pucón-Caburga road there are **Termas de Quimey-Co**, about 29 km from Pucón, campsite, two cabins and hotel (*Termas de Quimey-Co*, T045-441903), new, less ostentatious or expensive than **Termas de Huife** (*Hostería Termas de Huife*, T441222, PO Box 18, Pucón), Km 33, US$12 high season (US$9 low), including use of one pool, modern, pleasant (hotel offers daily shuttle from/to Pucón, or taxi from Pucón, US$23 return with taxi waiting, US$16 one way). Beyond Huife are the hot springs of **Los Pozones**, Km 35, set in natural rock pools, US$5, US$7 at night.

Reserva Forestal Cañi, south of Parque Nacional Huerquehue and covering 500 ha, is a private nature reserve. It contains 17 small lakes and is covered by ancient native forests of coihue, lenga and some of the oldest araucaria trees in Chile. From its highest peak, El Mirador, five volcanoes can be seen. There is a self-guided trail; for tours with guide, contact *Fundación Lahuén*, Urrutia 477, T/F441660, Pucón, lahuen@interaccess.cl US$17 pp plus transport, or *Hostería ¡école!*

The route to Argentina From Pucón a road runs southeast via Curarrehue to the Argentine border. At Km 18 there is a turning south to the **Termas de Palguín**. There are many beautiful waterfalls within hiking distance: for example, Salto China (entry US$0.60, restaurant, camping); Salto del Puma (US$0.60) and Salto del León (US$1.25), both 800 m from the Termas. **D** *Rancho de Caballos* (Casilla 142, Pucón), T441575, restaurant with vegetarian dishes, laundry and kitchen facilities; also, *cabañas* and camping, horse riding, self-guided trails, English and German spoken. From Pucón take Bus Regional Villarrica from Palguín y O'Higgins at 1100 to the junction (10 km from Termas); last bus from junction to the Termas at 1500, so you may have to hitch back. Taxi from Pucón, US$17.

Near Palguín is the entrance to the **Quetrupillán** section of the Parque Nacional Villarrica (high clearance vehicle necessary, horses best), free camping, wonderful views over Villarrica Volcano and six other peaks. Ask rangers for the route to the other entrance.

The road from Pucón to Argentina passes turnings north at Km 23 to **Termas de San Luis** and Km 35 to **Termas de Pangui** (15 km from main road), both with hotels, the latter with teepees (T045-411388 and 045-442039 respectively). It continues to Curarrehue, from where it turns south to Puesco and climbs via **Lago Quellelhue**, a tiny gem set between mountains at 1,196 m to reach the border at the Mamuil Malal or Tromén Pass. To the south of the pass rises the graceful cone of Lanín volcano. On the Argentine side the road runs south to Junín de los Andes, San Martín de los Andes and Bariloche.

Chilean immigration and customs is at **Puesco**, open December-March 0800-2100, April-November 0800-1900, US$2 per vehicle at other times. There are free Conaf campsites with no facilities at Puesco and 5 km from the border near Lago Tromén. Daily bus from Pucón, 1800, 2 hours, US$2.

Lago Calafquén

Dotted with small islands, Lago Calafquén is a popular tourist destination. **Lican-Ray** 25 km south of Villarrica on a peninsula on the north shore, is the major resort on the lake. There are two fine beaches each side of the rocky peninsula. Boats can be hired (US$2 per hour) and there are catamaran trips (US$3; trips to islands US$11 per hour). Although very crowded in season, most facilities close by the end of March and, out of season, Lican-Ray feels like a ghost town. The tourist office on the plaza is open daily in summer, Monday to Friday off season. 6 km to the east is the river of lava formed when the Villarrica volcano erupted in 1971.

Colour map 8, grid C1
Population: 1,700
Altitude: 207 m

On Playa Grande B *Hostería Inaltulafquen*, Casilla 681, T431115, F410028. With breakfast, English spoken, comfortable. **On Playa Chica** C *Hosp Los Nietos*, Manquel 125, T431078. Without breakfast. **D** *Res Temuco*, G Mistral 515, T431130. Without bath, with breakfast, good. **Camping** *Floresta*, T211954, **B** for 6 people, ½ km east of town. 6 sites to west and many along north shore towards Coñaripe. *Café Ñaños*, Urrutia 105. Very good, reasonable prices, helpful owner. *Restaurant-Bar Guido's*, Urrutia 405. Good value.

Sleeping & eating

Buses leave from offices around plaza. To **Villarrica**, 1 hr, US$1, *JAC* frequent in summer. In summer, there are direct buses from **Santiago** (*TurBus* US$12, 10 hrs, *salón-cama* US$25) and **Temuco** (US$3). To **Panguipulli**, Mon-Sat 0730.

Transport

Coñaripe (*Population*: 1,253), 21 km southeast of Lican-Ray at the eastern end of Lago Calafquén, is another popular tourist spot. Its setting, with a 3-km black sand beach surrounded by mountains, is very beautiful. From here a road (mostly *ripio*) around the lake's southern shore leads to Lago Panguipulli (see below) and offers superb views over Villarrica volcano, which can be climbed from here. Most services are on the Calle Principal. **A** *Hotel Entre Montañas*, on plaza, T408300. **D** *Antulafquen*, T317298, homely. **F** pp *Hospedaje Chumay*, on Plaza, T317287, turismochumay@hotmail.com With restaurant, internet, tours, some English spoken, good. Campsites on beach charge US$20, but if you walk ½-¾ km from town you can camp on the beach free. Cold municipal showers on beach, US$0.35. Tours: hiking to Villarrica Volcano with Leo Barrios at *Hospedaje Chumay*, who also organizes trips to various thermal springs, as does tourist office in summer (on plaza, open 15 November – 15 April daily, otherwise weekends only). **Termas Vergara** are 14 km northeast of Coñaripe by a steep *ripio* road which continues to Palguín, nice pools, campsite, minimarket ■ *Buses to Panguipulli, 7 a day (4 off season), US$1.80 and 16 daily to Villarrica, US$1. Nightly bus direct to Santiago, Turbus and JAC.*

From Coñaripe a road runs southeast over the steep Cuesta Los Añiques offering views of tiny **Lago Pellaifa**. The **Termas de Coñaripe** (T411407), excellent hotel (**A** pp) with four pools, good restaurant, cycles and horses for hire, are at Km 16. Further south at Km 32 are the **Termas de Liquiñe** (hotel, T063-317377, **A** pp full board, cabins, restaurant, hot pool, small native forest; accommodation in private houses, **E**; **F** *Hosp La Casona*, T045-412085, Camino Internacional, hot shower, good food, comfortable; tours from Lican-Ray in summer, US$17, 0830-1830 with lunch). Opposite Liquiñe are the new *Termas Río de Liquiñe*, good heated *cabañas*, good food, personal spa bath, large outdoor thermal pool. From there you can walk up to the thermal source, US$0.25 to cross river by boat, one hour excursion. ■ *There are 8 different thermal centres at Liquiñe, entrance from US$4 to US$7 pp.* There is a road north to Pucón through Villarrica National Park, high-clearance vehicle essential.

The border with Argentina, **Paso Carirriñe**, is reached by unpaved road from Termas de Liquiñe. It is open 15 October-31 August. On the Argentine side the road continues to San Martín de los Andes.

Chile

Lago Panguipulli

Phone code: 063
Colour map 8, grid C1
Population: 8,326
Altitude: 136 m

Rates of exchange
poor for cash, TCs not
accepted anywhere

The lake is reached by paved road from Lanco on the Pan-American Highway or unpaved roads from Lago Calafquén. A road leads along the beautiful north shore, wooded with sandy beaches and cliffs. Most of the south shore is inaccessible by road. **Panguipulli**, at the northwest corner of the lake in a beautiful setting, is the largest town in the area. The streets are planted with roses: it is claimed that there are over 14,000, sadly competing with weeds in 2003. The **Iglesia San Sebastián**, is in Swiss style, with twin towers; its belltower contains three bells from Germany. Fishing excursions on the lake are recommended. Boat hire US$3. There are also good rafting opportunities on rivers in the area. In the last week of January is Semana de Rosas, with dancing and sports competitions. The tourist office is on the plaza. ■ *Dec-Feb only.*

Sleeping
& eating

B *Hostería Quetropillán*, Etchegaray 381, T311348. Comfortable. **D** *Central*, Valdivia 115, T311331. Good breakfast. Recommended. **D** *Olga Berrocal*, JM Carrera 834. Small rooms. **D** *Eva Halabi*, Los Ulmos 62, T311483. Good breakfast. **F** pp Hostal Orillas del Lago, M de Rosas 265, T311710 (or 312499 if no reply, friends have key). From plaza walk towards lake, last house on left, 8 blocks from terminal. Good views, kitchen, backpacker place. **Camping** *El Bosque*, P Sigifredo 241, T311489, US$7.50 per site. "Small but perfect", hot water. Also 3 sites at Chauquén, 6 km southeast on lakeside. *Café Central*, M de Rosas 750. Fixed menu all day. *El Chapulín*, M de Rosas 639. Good food and value. Several cheap restaurants in O'Higgins 700 block.

Transport

Bus terminal at Gabriela Mistral y Portales. To **Santiago** daily, US$20. To **Valdivia**, frequent (Sun only 4), several lines, 2 hrs, US$3. To **Temuco** frequent, *Power* and *Pangui Sur*, US$2, 3 hrs. To **Puerto Montt**, US$7. To **Choshuenco**, Neltume and Puerto Fuy, 3 daily, 3 hrs. To **Coñaripe** (with connections for Lican-Ray and Villarrica), 7 daily Mon-Fri, 4 Sat, 1½ hrs, US$2.

Choshuenco (*Population*: 622) lies 23 km east of Panguipulli at the eastern tip of the lake. Various *hosterías*, including **D** *Hostería Rayen Trai* (former yacht club), María Alvarado y O'Higgins. Good food, open all year. Recommended. *Restaurant Rucapillán* lets out rooms. To the south is the **Reserva Nacional Mocho Choshuenco** (7,536 ha) which includes two volcanoes: Choshuenco (2,415 m) and Mocho (2,422 m). On the slopes of Choshuenco the Club Andino de Valdivia has ski-slopes and three *refugios*. This can be reached by a turning from the road which goes south from Choshuenco to Enco at the east end of Lago Riñihue (see page 681). East of Choshuenco a road leads to Lago Pirehueico, via the impressive waterfalls of **Huilo Huilo**, where the river channels its way through volcanic rock before thundering down into a natural basin. The falls are three hours' walk from Choshuenco, or take the Puerto Fuy bus and get off at *Alojamiento Huilo Huilo*, Km 9 (1 km before Neltume) from where it is a five-minute walk to the falls. **E** pp *Alojamiento Huilo Huilo*, basic but comfortable and well situated for walks, good food.

East of Choshuenco is **Lago Pirehueico**, a long, narrow and deep lake, surrounded by virgin *lingue* forest. It is totally unspoilt except for some logging activity. There are no roads along the shores of the lake, but two ports. **Puerto Fuy** (*Population*: 300) is at the north end 21 km from Choshuenco, 7 from Neltume, with **F** pp at *Restaurant Puerto Fuy*, hot water, good food. Accommodation is also in private houses (eg **E** *Hostal Kaykaen*, meals, use of kitchen, bike rental). A campsite is on the beach (take your own food). **Puerto Pirehueico** is at the south end, with **E** pp in *Hospedaje Pirehueico*. There is accommodation in private houses. A ferry runs from Puerto Fuy to Puerto Pirehueico, then a road to the Argentine border crossing at Paso Huahum.

Transport Buses Daily *Puerto Fuy* to Panguipulli, 2 daily, 2 hrs, US$3. **Ferries** The *Mariela* sails from Puerto Fuy to Puerto Pirehueico, 2-3 hrs, US$1.50, cars US$16, bikes $3. A beautiful crossing (to take vehicles reserve in advance at the *Hotel Quetropillán* in Panguipulli). Schedule: twice daily each way. In summer there is a daily bus service to Argentina.

The border with Argentina, **Paso Huahum** (659 m), is a four hour walk from Puerto Pirehueico. On the Argentine side the road leads to San Martín de los Andes and Junín de los Andes. Chilean immigration is open summer 0800-2100, winter 0800-2000.

Valdivia

Valdivia was one of the most important centres of Spanish colonial control over Chile. Founded in 1552 by Pedro de Valdivia, it was abandoned as a result of the Mapuche insurrection of 1599 and the area was briefly occupied by Dutch pirates. In 1645 it was refounded as a walled city, the only Spanish mainland settlement south of the Río Biobío. The coastal fortifications at the mouth of the river also date from the 17th century. They were greatly strengthened after 1760 owing to fears that Valdivia might be seized by the British, but were of little avail during the Wars of Independence: overnight on 2 February 1820 the Chilean naval squadron under Lord Cochrane seized San Carlos, Amargos and Corral and turned their guns on Niebla and Mancera, which surrendered the following morning. From independence until the 1880s Valdivia was an outpost of Chilean rule, reached only by sea or by a coastal route through Mapuche territory. From 1849 to 1875 Valdivia was a centre for German colonization of the Lake District.

Phone code: 063
Colour map 8, grid C1
Population: 110,000
839 km S of Santiago

Situated at the confluence of two rivers, the Calle Calle and Cruces which form the Río Valdivia, the capital of Valdivia province is set in rich agricultural land receiving some 2,300 mm of rain a year. To the north of the city is a large island, Isla Teja, where the Universidad Austral de Chile is situated.

The city centre is the tree-lined, shady **Plaza de la República**. A pleasant walk is along **Avenida Prat** (or **Costanera**), which follows the bend in the river, from the bus station to the bridge to Isla Teja, the **Muelle Fluvial** (boat dock) and the riverside market. Boats can be hired at the bend for US$2.50 per hour. Sealions lounge around the dock. On **Isla Teja**, near the library in the University, are a **botanic

Sights

Valdivia

Sleeping
1 Hospedaje Andwandter
2 Hospedaje Elsa Martínez
3 Hospedaje Internacional
7 Hostal Casa Grande
8 Hostal Centro Torreón
9 Hostal Esmeralda
10 Melillanca
11 Palace
12 Pedro de Valdivia
13 Prat
14 Residencial Germania

Eating
1 Café Haussmann
2 Dino
3 Entrelagos
4 New Orleans
5 Palace

garden and **arboretum** with trees from all over the world. On boat trips round the island you can see lots of waterfowl. **Lago de los Lotos** in Parque Saval on the island has beautiful blooms in November, entry US$0.50. Also on Isla Teja is the **Museo Histórico y Antropológico**, run by the University, which contains archaeology, ethnography and history of German settlement. ■ *Tue-Sun, 1000-1300, 1400-1800, US$2.* Next door is the **Museo de Arte Moderno**. ■ *Tue-Fri 1000-1300, 1400-1800, Sat-Sun 1000-1300, 1500-1900, US$0.60.*

Excursions The district has lovely countryside of woods, beaches, lakes and rivers. The various rivers are navigable and there are pleasant journeys by rented motor boat on the Ríos Futa and Tornagaleanes around the Isla del Rey. Boat tours go to the **Santuario de la Naturaleza Río Cruces**, flooded as result of the 1960 earthquake, where lots of bird species are visible. ■ *Isla del Río, daily 1415, 6 hrs, US$15 pp.* In summer there is a regular steam train service to **Antilhue** (20 km), where there are places to eat, picnic and walk. This is the only steam train in Chile, good.■ *US$4. Ecuador 2000, T214972, depart 1000 every Sun Jan-Feb, other weekends and holidays throughout the year, phone to check. 1½-hr trip, return 2 hrs later.*

Sleeping
■ *on map*

AL *Pedro de Valdivia*, Carampangue 190, T/F212931. Good. **AL** *Puerta del Sur*, Los Lingües 950, Isla Teja T224500. 5 star, the best. **A** *Melillanca*, Alemania 675, T212509, F222740. Recommended. **B** *Hostal Centro Torreón*, P Rosales 783, T212622. With breakfast, without bath, old German villa, nice atmosphere, car parking. **B** *Palace*, Chacabuco y Henríquez, T213319, F219133. Good, comfortable. **C** *Prat*, Prat 595, T222020. With good breakfast, TV. **D** *Hostal Esmeralda*, Esmeralda 651, T215659. **E** without bath, a bit rundown, big rooms, breakfast, also *cabañas*, parking. **E** *Donde Marcelo*, Janequero 355, T/F205295. Quiet, fresh bread for breakfast, helpful. Recommended. **E** *Hosp Elsa Martínez*, Picarte 737, T212587. Highly recommended. **F** Henríquez 749, Casa 6, T222574, F204313. Charming old house, large rooms, kitchen, laundry, English spoken. Highly recommended.

Around the bus terminal E *Res Germania*, Picarte 873, T212405. With breakfast, poor beds, German spoken, HI reductions. **On A Muñoz, outside terminal F** pp No 345. With breakfast. **F** pp No 353. Breakfast. Recommended. **On C Anwandter E** *Hostal Casa Grande*, No 880, T202035. With bath, TV, attractive old house, laundry facilities. Highly recommended. **F** pp *Hosp Andwandter*, No 482. With bath, breakfast, hot water. **F** pp *Hospedaje Ana María*, José Martí 11, 3 mins from terminal, T222468. With breakfast, shared bath, use of kitchen, good value, also *cabañas*.

Other, cheaper accommodation F pp, Gen Lagos 874, T215946. With breakfast, old German house, pleasant family atmosphere. Recommended. **F** pp Riquelme 15, T218909. With breakfast, good value. **F** pp *Hosp Internacional*, García Reyes 660, T212015. With breakfast, helpful, English and German spoken, use of kitchen. Recommended. **F** pp Sra Paredes, García Reyes 244. With breakfast. Recommended. **G** *Albergue Juvenil*, García Reyes s/n, off Picarte, Jan/Feb only.

Campsite *Camping Centenario*, in Rowing Club on España. **E** per tent, overlooking river. *Isla Teja*, T213584, lovely views over river.

Eating
■ *on map*
Several restaurants on the Costanera facing the boat dock, good food and atmosphere. Others upstairs in the municipal market

Mid-range: *La Calesa*, Yungay 735. Peruvian and international, music, art gallery, pier. Highly recommended. *La Cava del Buho*, Av Alemania 660. Very good food, service and interesting décor. *Palace*, Arauco y P Rosales. Popular, good atmosphere. *Selecta*, Picarte 1093. Pleasant, excellent fish and meat. *Shanghai*, Andwandter y Muñoz. Pleasant Chinese. **Cheap**: *Chester's*, Henríquez 314. Good, popular. *New Orleans*, Esmeralda 652. Large portions. **Cafés**: *Café Haussmann*, O'Higgins 394. Good tea and cakes. *Café Express*, Picarte 764. Real coffee. *Dino*, Maipú y Rosales. Good coffee. *Entrelagos*, Pérez Rosales 622. Ice cream and chocolates. **Bakery** *La Baguette*, Libertad y Yungay. French-style cakes, brown bread. Repeatedly recommended. *Cervecería Kunstmann*, Ruta T350, No 950, T292969, www.cerveza-kunstmann.cl On road to Niebla. Restaurant serving German/Chilean food, brewery with 5 types of beer, beautiful interior, museum. Recommended.

Semana Valdiviana, in **mid-Feb**, culminates in Noche Valdiviana on the Sat with a proces- **Festivals**
sion of elaboratedly decorated boats which sail past the Muelle Fluvial. Accommodation is
scarce during festival.

Bookshop/Cultural centre: *Librería/Centro Cultural 787*, Pérez Rosales 787. Old mansion, **Shopping**
with café and art exhibitions. **Supermarket**: *Hiper-Unico*, Arauco 697. There's a colourful
riverside market with livestock, fish etc.

Turismo Koller, José Martí 83, T/F255335, turismokoller@koller.cl *Paraty Club*, Indepen- **Tour operators**
dencia 640, T215585. *OutDoorsChile*, Quineo 636, T253377, www.OutDoorsChile.com Has *To Corral and Niebla,*
information on the web in English and German. *try the kiosks along*
the Muelle Fluvial

Air *LanChile/Lan Express* to/from **Santiago** every day via Temuco, or Concepción. **Transport**
Buses Terminal at Muñoz y Prat, by the river. To **Santiago**: several companies, 11 hrs,
most services overnight, US$12, *salón cama* US$30. Half-hourly buses to **Osorno**, US$3,
several companies, US$3-5. To **Panguipulli**, US$3, *Empresa Pirehueico*, about every 30
mins, US$3. Many daily to **Puerto Montt**, US$5, 3 hrs. To **Puerto Varas**, 2¾ hrs, US$4. To
Frutillar, US$4, 2½ hrs. To **Villarrica**, by *JAC*, 6 a day, 2½ hrs, US$3.50, continuing to
Pucón, US$4.50, 3 hrs. Frequent daily service to Riñihue via Paillaco and Los Lagos. **To**
Argentina: to Bariloche via Osorno, 7 hrs, *Bus Norte*, US$14; to **Junín de los Andes**,
Igi-Llaima, 4 times a week, *San Martín*, 3, US$18.

Airline offices *LanChile*, Maipú 271, T218841/258840. **Banks** *Redbanc* ATM at *Supermercado* **Directory**
Hiper-Unico (see above). Good rates for cash at *Banco Santander*, P Rosales 585, *Corp Banca* (Visa),
Picarte 370, will change cash and TCs. *Banco Santiago*, Arauco e Independencia, MasterCard. *Casa de*
Cambio at Carampangue 325, T213305. *Turismo Austral*, Arauco y Henríquez, Galería Arauco, accepts
TCs. **Communications** Internet: *Café Phonet*, Libertad 127. *Centro Internet Libertad*, Libertad 7. **Post**
Office: O'Higgins y Maipú. **Tourist offices** Av Prat 555, by the dock, T215396. Good map of region and
local rivers, list of hotel prices and examples of local crafts with artisans' addresses. Open daily in summer,
weekends only in winter. There is a helpful kiosk in the bus terminal, mainly bus information. *Conaf*,
Ismael Valdéz 431, T218822. *Automóvil Club de Chile*, García Reyes 49075, T250376, also for car hire.

At the mouth of the Río Valdivia there are attractive villages which can be visited by **Coastal resorts**
land or river boat. The two main centres are Niebla on the north bank and Corral **near Valdivia**
opposite on the south bank. **Niebla**, 18 km from Valdivia, is a resort with seafood restaurants and accommodation (also plenty of *cabañas* and campsites on the road from
Valdivia). To the west of the resort is the Fuerte de la Pura y Limpia Concepción de
Monfort de Lemus, on a promontory. Partially restored in 1992, it has an interesting
museum on Chilean naval history. ■ *Daily in summer 1000-1900, closed Mon in winter, US$1, Wed free. Tourist information and telephone office nearby.*

Sleeping *Cabañas Fischers*, T282007. **C** per cabin, 2 campsites. **D** pp *Villa Santa Clara*,
T282018 (Casilla 52, Valdivia). With breakfast, kitchen and laundry, also *cabañas*.
Las Delicias, T213566. With restaurant with 'a view that would be worth the money even if
the food wasn't good'. Also *cabañas* and camping.

Corral, a fishing port with several good restaurants is 62 km from Valdivia by road
(unsuitable for cars without four-wheel drive or high clearance). The Castillo de San
Sebastián, with 3 m wide walls was defended by a battery of 21 guns. It has a museum
and offers a view upriver. In summer 18th-century battles are re-enacted. Entry
US$4 January-February, US$1 rest of the year. North along the coast are the remains
of Castillo San Luis de Alba de Amargos (three km) Castillo de San Carlos, with
pleasant beaches (4 km). The coastal walks west and south of Corral are splendid.

In midstream, between Niebla and Corral is **Isla Mancera** a small island, fortified
by the Castillo de San Pedro de Alcántara, which has the most standing buildings.
The island is a pleasant place to stopover on the boat trips, but it can get crowded

Chile

when an excursion boat arrives. (**C** *Hostería Mancera*, T/F216296, open December-March, depending on weather, no singles, phone first: water not drinkable.)

Sleeping D *Hostería Los Alamos*. A delightful hideout for those seeking a quiet life. **E** *Residencial Mariel*, Tarapacá 36, T471290. Modern, good value.

Transport The tourist boats to **Isla Mancera** and **Corral** offer a guided half-day tour (US$20 with meals – cheaper without) from the Muelle Fluvial, Valdivia (behind the tourist office on Av Prat 555), 1330 daily. The river trip is beautiful, but you can also take a bus to Niebla from the north end of the wharf, next to the bridge in Valdivia, roughly every 20 mins between 0730 and 2100, 30 mins, US$0.75 (bus continues to Los Molinos), then cross to Corral by boat, hourly, US$0.75. There are occasional buses from Valdivia to Corral.

Osorno

Phone code: 064
Colour map 8, grid C1
Population: 114,000
921 km from Santiago
105 km N of
Puerto Montt

Founded in 1553, abandoned in 1604 and refounded in 1796, Osorno later became one of the centres of German immigration. On the large **Plaza de Armas** stands the modern cathedral, while to the east of the plaza along MacKenna are a number of late 19th century mansions built by German immigrants, now National Monuments. **Museo Histórico Municipal**, Matta 809, includes displays on natural history, Mapuche culture, refounding of the city and German colonization. ■ *Mon-Sun 1100-1900 in summer; winter Mon-Fri 0930-1730, Sat 1500-1800, US$1, entrance in Casa de Cultura.*

Sleeping and eating AL *Del Prado*, Cochrane 1162, T235020. Pool, garden, good meals, well-located, charming. **A** *Waeger*, Cochrane 816, T233721, PO Box 802, F237080. 4-star, restaurant, comfortable. Recommended. **B-C** *Eduviges*, Eduviges 856, T/F235023. Spacious, quiet, attractive, gardens, also *cabañas*. Recommended. **C** *Res Riga*, Amthauer 1058, T232945. Pleasant. Highly recommended but heavily booked in season. **C** *Res Hein*, Cochrane 843, T234116. **D** without bath, old-fashioned, spacious, family atmosphere. **Near bus terminal** (all **F** pp): Amunátegui 520. Good. *Res Sánchez*, Los Carrera 1595, T232560, crisxi@telsur.cl Family-owned, with breakfast, shared bath, use of kitchen, basic, like stepping back 50 years. *Res San Diego*, Los Carrera 1575. With breakfast. Private houses at Germán Hube, pasaje 1, casa 22, población Villa Dama, use of kitchen. Recommended. **Camping** Municipal site off Ruta 5 near south entrance to city, open Jan-Feb only, good facilities, US$5 per site, swimming pool. **Mid-range eating**: *Dino's*, Ramírez 898, on the plaza. Restaurant upstairs, bar/cafeteria downstairs, good. *Peter's Kneipe*, M Rodríguez 1039. Excellent German restaurant. **Cheap**: *Waldis*, on Plaza de Armas. Real coffee. *Travels* in bus terminal for cheap snacks. Bakery at Ramírez 977 has good wholemeal bread.

Transport Air: *Lan Express*, Matta 862, T314900, daily flights Osorno-Santiago, via Temuco. **Buses**: Main terminal 4 blocks from Plaza de Armas at Errázuriz 1400. Left luggage open 0730-2030. Bus from centre, US$0.30. To **Santiago**, frequent, US$13, *salón cama* US$30, 11½ hrs. To **Concepción**, US$10. To **Temuco**, US$4. To **Pucón** and **Villarrica**, *TurBus*, frequent, US$6. To **Valdivia**, frequent, 3 hrs, US$3-5. To **Frutillar**, US$1.50, **Llanquihue, Puerto Varas** and **Puerto Montt** (US$3) services every 30 mins. To **Puerto Octay**, US$2, *Vía Octay* 6 daily Mon-Sat, 5 on Sun (4 return buses). To **Bariloche**, 5 hrs, US$14. Local buses to **Entre Lagos, Puyehue** and **Aguas Calientes** leave from the Mercado Municipal terminal, 1 block west of the main terminal. To **Entre Lagos** frequent services in summer, *Expreso Lago Puyehue* and *Buses Puyehue*, 1 hr, US$1.20, reduced service off-season. Some buses by both companies continue to **Aguas Calientes** (off-season according to demand) 2 hrs, US$2.

Directory Banks: ATMs at *Bancos BCI*, MacKenna 801, and *Santiago*, MacKenna 787 (Visa). For good rates try *Cambio Tur*, MacKenna 1010, T234846. *Turismo Frontera*, Ramírez 949, local 11 (Galería Catedral). **Communications**: Internet: 3 internet places in the mall at Freire 542. *Chat-Mail-MP3*, P Lynch 1334, near Colón. **Tourist offices**: *Sernatur* in provincial government office, Plaza de Armas, O'Higgins s/n, p 1, T234104. Municipal office in the bus terminal and kiosk on the Plaza de Armas. Both open Dec-Feb. Contact *Club Andino*, O'Higgins 1073, for advice on skiing.

Chile

About 47 km east of Osorno, Lago Puyehue is surrounded by relatively flat country-side. At the western end is **Entre Lagos** (*Population*: 3,358) and the **Termas de Puyehue** is at the eastern end. ■ *Entry US$15 pp, 0900-2000*.

Sleeping and eating E *Hospedaje Miraflores*, E Ramirez 480, T371275. Quiet. Recommended. **E** pp *Hosp Millarey*. Ramírez 333, T371251. With breakfast, excellent. *Restaurant Jardín del Turista*. Very good. *Pub del Campo*, reasonable prices. Highly recommended. **On the south lakeshore** *Chalet Suisse*, Ruta 215, Km 55 (Casilla 910, Osorno, T Puyehue 647208, Osorno 064-234073). *Hostería*, restaurant with excellent food. **B** *Hostería Isla Fresia*, located on own island, T236951, Casilla 49, Entre Lagos, transport provided. **At the Termas L** pp *Hotel Termas de Puyehue*, T232157/371272 (cheaper May to mid-Dec). 2 thermal swimming pools (one indoors, very clean), well maintained, meals expensive, in beautiful scenery, heavily booked Jan-Feb (postal address Casilla 27-0, Puyehue, or T Santiago 231 3417, F283 1010), reception can be inexperienced. Accommodation also in private house nearby, **E** pp full board. **Camping** *Camping No Me Olvides*, Km 56, US$10, also *cabañas*. *Playa Los Copihues*, Km 56.5 (hot showers, good), all on south shore of Lake Puyehue.

Transport Bus 2½ hrs, schedule under Osorno. Buses do not stop at the lake (unless you want to get off at *Hotel Termas de Puyehue* and clamber down), but continue to Aguas Calientes.

The Park, east of Lago Puyehue, stretches to the Argentine border. On the east side are several lakes and two volcanic peaks: **Volcán Puyehue** (2,240 m) in the north (access via private road US$2.50) and **Volcán Casablanca** (also called Antillanca, 1,900 m). Park administration is at Aguas Calientes, 4 km south of the Termas de Puyehue. There is a ranger station at Anticura. Leaflets on attractions are available.

At **Aguas Calientes** there is an open-air pool with very hot thermal water beside the Río Chanleufú (open 0830-1900, US$2), and a very hot indoor pool (open Monday-Friday in season only, 0830-1230, 1400-1800, Saturday, Sunday and holidays all year, 0830-2030, US$6, children US$3).

From Aguas Calientes the road continues 18 km southeast to **Antillanca** on the slopes of Volcán Casablanca, past three small lakes and through forests. This is particularly beautiful, especially at sunrise, with the snow-clad cones of Osorno, Puntiagudo and Puyehue forming a semicircle. The tree-line on Casablanca is one of the few in the world made up of deciduous trees (southern beech). From Antillanca it is possible to climb Casablanca for even better views of the surrounding volcanoes and lakes, no path, seven hours return journey, information from Club Andino in Osorno. Attached to the *Hotel Antillanca* is one of the smallest ski resorts in Chile; there are three lifts, ski instruction and first aid available. Skiing quality depends on the weather: though rain is common it often does not turn to snow. See under Osorno for buses. No public transport from Aguas Calientes to Antillanca; try hitching – always difficult, but it is not a hard walk.

Sleeping A *Hotel Antillanca*, T235114. Includes free mountainbiking and parapenting, at foot of Volcán Casablanca, excellent restaurant/café, with pool, sauna, friendly club-like atmosphere. **Camping** *Chanleufú*, in Aguas Calientes. With hot water, US$4 pp, good *cabañas* (**A** in season, **C** off season) T236988, a poorly-stocked shop – better to take your own food, and an expensive café. *Los Derrumbes*, 1 km from Aguas Calientes, no electricity, US$20 per site. *Conaf refugio* on Volcán Puyehue, but check with *Conaf* in Anticura whether it is open.

Chilean immigration is open the second Saturday in October to 1 May 0800-2100, otherwise 0800-1900. The Chilean border post is at Pajaritos, 4 km east of **Anticura**, which is 22 km west of the border. For vehicles entering Chile, formalities are quick (about 15 minutes), but includes the spraying of tyres, and shoes have to be wiped on a mat. Pay US$2 to 'Sanidad' and US$1.25 at the documents counter. Passage will be much quicker if you already have Chilean pesos and don't wait to change at the border. This route is liable to closure after snow

Transport To Anticura, bus at 1620 from **Osorno**, 3 hrs. Several bus companies run daily services from **Puerto Montt** via Osorno to Bariloche along this route (see under Puerto Montt for details). Although less scenic than the ferry journey across Lake Todos Los Santos and Laguna Verde (see page 690) this crossing is far cheaper, more reliable and still a beautiful trip (best views from the right hand side of the bus).

Lago Llanquihue

The lake, covering 56,000 ha, is the second largest in Chile. Across the great blue sheet of water can be seen two snowcapped volcanoes: the perfect cone of Osorno (2,680 m) and the shattered cone of Calbuco (2,015 m), and, when the air is clear, the distant Tronador (3,460 m). The largest towns, Puerto Varas, Llanquihue and Frutillar are on the western shore, linked by the Pan-American Highway. There are roads around the rest of the lake: that from Puerto Octay east to Ensenada is very beautiful, but is narrow with lots of blind corners, necessitating speeds of 20-30 kph at best in places (see below).

Puerto Octay
Phone code: 064
Colour map 8, grid C1
Population: 2,500
56 km SE of Osorno

A small town at the north tip of the lake in a beautiful setting, Puerto Octay was founded by German settlers in 1851. The town enjoyed a boom in the late 19th century when it was the northern port for steamships on the lake. The church and the enormous German-style former convent survive from that period. **Museo el Colono**, Independencia 591, has displays on German colonization. Another part of the museum, housing agricultural implements and machinery for making chicha, is just outside town on the road to Centinela. ■ *Tue-Sun 1500-1900, Dec-Feb only*. 3 km south along an unpaved road is the Peninsula of **Centinela**, a beautiful spot with a launch dock and watersports. From the headland are fine views of the volcanoes and the Cordillera of the Andes; a very popular spot in good weather, good for picnics (taxi US$2.50 one way).

Sleeping and eating E pp *Hosp Raquel Mardorf*, Germán Wulf 712. Owners have *Restaurante La Cabaña* at No 713. F pp *Hosp La Naranja*, Independencia 361. Without bath, with breakfast, restaurant. E-F pp *Zapato Amarillo*, 35 mins' walk north of town, T/F391575, PO Box 87, Puerto Octay, www.zapatoamarillo.8k.com Excellent for backpackers and others (book in advance in high season), use of spotless kitchen, great breakfasts with homemade bread, German and English spoken, mountain bikes, canoes, tours (house has a grass roof). Highly recommended. *Restaurante Baviera*, Germán Wulf 582. Cheap and good. *Fogón de Anita*, 1 km out of town. Mid-price grill. **Camping** *El Molino*, beside lake, US$5 pp. Recommended. **Centinela** AL*Hotel Centinela*, T 391326, www.hotelcetinela.cl Newly restored, superb views, also has *cabañas*, excellent restaurant, bar, open all year. F pp *Hostería La Baja*, Casilla 116, T391269. Beautifully situated at the neck of the peninsula, with breakfast and bath. **Camping** Municipal site on lakeside, US$10 per site. *Cabañas* on the peninsula.

Transport Buses to **Osorno** 9 a day, US$2; to **Frutillar** (1 hr, US$0.90), **Puerto Varas** (2 hrs) and **Puerto Montt** (3 hrs, US$2) *Thaebus*, 5 a day. Around the east shore: to **Las Cascadas** (34 km; E *Hostería Irma*, very pleasant, good food; also farmhouse accommodation and camping) Mon-Fri 1730, return next day 0700.

Frutillar
Phone code: 065
Colour map 8, grid C1
Population: 5,000
Altitude: 70 m

About half-way along the west side of the lake, **Frutillar** is divided into Frutillar Alto, just off the main highway, and Frutillar Bajo beautifully situated on the lake, 4 km away. (Colectivos run between the two towns, five minutes, US$0.50.) Frutillar Bajo possibly the most attractive – and expensive – town on the lake. At the north end of the town is the **Reserva Forestal Edmundo Winckler**, run by the Universidad de Chile, 33 ha, with a guided trail through native woods. **Museo Colonial Alemán**, includes a watermill, replicas of two German colonial houses with furnishings and utensils of the period, a blacksmith's shop (personal engravings for US$5), and a *campanario* (circular barn with agricultural machinery and carriages inside), gardens and handi-craft shop. ■ *Daily 0930-1900 summer, Tue-Sun 0930-1400, 1530-1800 winter, US$2*. In late January to early February there is a highly-regarded classical music fes-tival and a new, state-of-the-art concert hall has been built for this on the lakefront (accommodation must be booked well in advance).

Sleeping North of Frutillar Bajo **L** *Salzburg*, T421589 or Santiago 206 1419. Excellent, restaurant, sauna, mountain bikes, arranges tours and fishing. **In Frutillar Bajo** On Av Philippi: **A** *Ayacara*, No 1215, T421550. Beautiful rooms with lake view, welcoming, have a *pisco sour* in the library in the evening. **C** *Hosp El Arroyo*, No 989, T421560. With breakfast. Highly recommended. **C** *Winkler*, No 1155, T421388. Cabins. Recommended. **C** No 451, T421204. Good breakfast. **C-D** *Hosp Costa Azul*, No 1175, T421388. Mainly for families, good breakfasts. **C-D** *Residenz/Café am See*, No 539. Good breakfast. **D** pp *Hosp Vivaldi*, No 851, T421382, Sra Edith Klesse. Quiet, comfortable, excellent breakfast and lodging, also family accommodation. Recommended. **D** *Hosp Trayén*, No 963, T421346. With bath, nice rooms, good breakfast. **C** *Casona del 32*, Caupolicán 28, Casilla 101, T421369. With breakfast, com-fortable old house, central heating, English and German spoken, excellent. **D** Pérez Rosales 590. Excellent breakfast.

In Frutillar Alto **D** *Faralito*, Winkler 245. Cooking facilities (owner can be contacted at shop at Winkler 167, T421440). Cheap accommodation in the school, sleeping bag required. *Several along Carlos Richter (main street)* **Camping** *Playa Maqui*, 7 km north of Frutillar, T339139. Fancy, expensive. *Los Ciruelillos*, 2 km south, T339123. Most services.

Eating *Club Alemán*, Av Philippi 747. Good but not cheap. *Casino de Bomberos*, Philippi 1060. Upstairs bar/restaurant, memorable painting caricaturing the firemen in action. *Guten Apetit*, Philippi 1285. Lunch/café, mid-range to cheap. Many German-style cafés and tea-rooms on C Philippi (the lakefront) eg *Salón de Te* Frutillar, No 775. *Der Volkladen*, O'Higgins y Philippi. Natural products, chocolates and cakes, natural cosmetics.

Transport Buses to **Puerto Varas** (US$0.75) and **Puerto Montt** (US$1.25), frequent, *Full Express*. To Osorno, *Turismosur* 1½ hrs, US$1.50. To **Puerto Octay**, *Thaebus*, 6 a day, US$0.90. Most buses leave from opposite the *Copec* station in Alto Frutillar.

Directory **Tourist office** On lakeside opposite *Club Alemán*, helpful.**Useful services** Toilet, showers and changing cabins for beach on O'Higgins. *Banco Santander*, on the lakeside, has *Redbanc* ATM.

Puerto Varas and around

This beauty spot was the southern port for shipping on the lake in the 19th century. The Catholic church, built by German Jesuits in 1918, is a copy of the church in Marieenkirche in the Black Forest. North and east of the **Gran Hotel Puerto Varas** (1934) are German style mansions dating from the early 20th century. **Parque Philippi**, on top of the hill, is pleasant; walk up to *Hotel Cabañas del Lago* on Klenner, cross the railway and the gate is on the right. The tourist office is atSan Francisco 441, T232402, F233315, helpful, finds cheap accommodation, also has an art gallery. ■ *0900-2100 in summer*. Puerto Varas is a good base for trips around the lake. On the south shore two of the best beaches are Playa Hermosa (Km 7) and Playa Niklitschek (entry fee charged). **La Poza**, at Km 16, is a little lake to the south of Lago Llanquihue reached through narrow channels overhung with vegetation. **Isla Loreley**, an island on La Poza, is very beautiful (frequent boat trips); a con-cealed channel leads to yet another lake, the Laguna Encantada.

Phone code: 065
Colour map 8, grid C1
Population: 16,000
20 km N of
Puerto Montt

L *Los Alerces*, Pérez Rosales 1281, T233039. 4-star hotel, with breakfast, cabin complex (price depends on season when rest of hotel is closed), attractive, helpful. **L** *Colonos del Sur*, Del Sal-vador 24, T233369, www.colonosdelsur.cl Good views, good restaurant, tea room. Also at

Sleeping
■ *on map*

Chile

Estación 505. **AL** *Antonio Varas*, Del Salvador 322, T232375, F232352. Very comfortable. **AL** *Cabañas del Lago*, Klenner 195, T232291, calago@entelchile.net On Phiippi hill overlooking lake, good breakfast, restaurant. Also self-catering cabins sleeping 5 (good value for groups), heating, sauna. **AL** *Licarayén*, San José 114, T232305, F232955. Overlooking lake, comfortable, book in season, **C** out of season. Enthusiastically recommended. **A** *Amancay*, Walker Martínez 564, T232201, c_bittner_amancay@chile.com *Cabañas* for 4, also has rooms, **D** with bath, **E** without, includes breakfast, good, German spoken. Recommended. **A** *Bellavista*, Pérez Rosales 60, T232011, F232013. Cheerful, restaurant, overlooking lake. Recommended. **B** *Loreley*, Maipo 911, T232226. Homely, quiet. Recommended. **C** *Las Dalias*, Santa Rosa 707, T233277. Quiet, cheaper with shared bath, central, good breakfast, parking, German spoken.

E pp *Hospedaje Amac*, San Bernardo 313, T234216. Apartment-style, comfortable, heating in lounge, TV, use of kitchen, hot water. **E** pp Andrés Bello 321. Nice atmosphere, good breakfast **E** pp *Outsider*, San Bernardo 318, T/F232910, outsider@telsur.cl With bath, real coffee, meals, also horse riding, rafting, sea kayaking, climbing, very popular, reserve in advance. **E** *Res Alemana*, San Bernardo 416, T232419. With breakfast, without bath. **E** *Hosp Imperial*, Imperial 653, T232451. Includes breakfast, central. Recommended. **E** *Hosp Ellenhaus*, Martínez 239, T233577. Laundry facilities, lounge, hospitable. **F** pp *Casa Azul*, Manzanal 66 y Rosario, T232904, www.casa azul.net Cosy rooms, good breakfast (US$4), kitchen facilities, German and English spoken. Highly recommended. Reserve in advance in high season, likewise **F** pp *Compas del Sur*, Klenner 467, T232044, mauro98@telsur.cl Chilean-Swedish run, kitchen facilities, internet, good breakfast, helpful, German, English, Swedish spoken. Highly recommended. **F** pp *Hosp Don Raúl*, Salvador 928, T234174. Laundry and cooking facilities, camping **F** pp. Recommended. **F** pp *Elmo & Ana Hernández Maldonado*, Itata 95. Breakfast or use of kitchen, helpful. Recommended. **F** pp *Colores del Sur*, Santa Rosa 318, T231850. Kitchen, hospitable, meeting place.

Camping Sites on south shore of Lago Llanquihue east of Puerto Varas: *Trauco*, Imperial 433. *Playa Hermosa*, Km 7, T252223, fancy, take own supplies, recommended. Km 8, *Playa Niklitschek*, T338352, full facilities; Km 20, *Playa Venado*, *Camping Municipal*; Km 49, *Conaf* site at Puerto Oscuro, beneath road to volcano, very good. *Campo Aventura* has 2 lodges with camping facilities, horse riding, fishing, birdwatching, Spanish classes and vegetarian food. Contact: San Bernardo 318, Puerto Varas, T/F232910, www.campo-aventura.com

Wild camping and use of barbecues is not allowed on the lake shore

Expensive: *Merlín*, Imperial 0605, on road out of town. Some rate it highly, others disappointed. **Mid-range**: *Mediterráneo*, Santa Rosa 068. Good. At the Puerto Chilo end of Pérez Rosales are *Dicaruzzo*, No 01071, recommended and *Ibis*, No 1117, warmly recommended. *Donde El Gordito*, downstairs in market. Large portions, mixed reports. *Espigas*, Martínez 417, local 3. Vegetarian. *La Olla*, V Pérez Rosales 1971, on lakefront, 1 km east of town. Good, popular for seafood, fish and meat. **Cheap**: *El Amigo*, San Bernardo 240. Large portions, good value. *Domino*, Del Salvador 450. Good. *Café Danés*, Del Salvador 441. Coffee and cakes. *Giorgio Café*, San Bernardo 318. Danish-run, good food. Recommended. *Terranova*, Santa Rosa 580. Pleasant, helpful café on main plaza.

Eating
● *on map*

Supermarkets: *Las Brisas*, Salvador 495. *Vyhmeister*, Gramado 565. Good selection.

Shopping

Cycling: *Turismo Biker*, in *Terranova Café*, www.turismobiker.com Touring and downhill as well as standard tours. Cycle hire:*Thomas Held Expeditions*, Martínez 239, T/F311889, US$20 per day. **Fishing** Licence US$2.50 a year, obtainable from Municipalidad. Expeditions organized by many operators. **Horse riding**: *Cabañas Puerto Decher*, Fundo Molino Viejo, 2 km north, T338033, guided tours, minimum 2 people, mixed reports. *Quinta del Lago*, Km 25 on road to Ensenada, T338275, www.quintadellago.com All levels catered for, US$7 per hr, also trips in ox cart and *cabañas*. See also *Campo Aventura*, above.

Sport & activities
The area around Puerto Varas is popular for fishing

Al Sur, Del Salvador 100, T232334, F232300, www.alsurexpeditions.com Rafting on Río Petrohué, good camping equipment, tours, trekking maps, English spoken, official tour operators to Parque Pumalin. *Andina del Sud*, Del Salvador 72, T232511. Operate 'lakes' trip to Bariloche, Argentina via Lago Todos los Santos, Peulla, Cerro Tronador (see under Puerto Montt, To Argentina), plus other excursions. *Aqua Motion*, C San Francisco, T/F232747, www.aquamotion.cl For trekking, rafting and climbing, German and English spoken, good equipment, also offers ethno-astronomical tours based in La Serena. *Kokayak*, San José 320, T346433. Kayaking and rafting trips. *Tranco Expeditions*, San Pedro 422, T311311. Trekking on volcano, rafting, fishing and more. Recommended. *Travel Art*, Imperial 0661, T232198, F234818, www.travelart.cl Biking and hiking tours. Several others. Most tours operate in season only (1 Sep-15 Apr).

Tour operators

Buses To **Santiago**, normal US$24, *semi cama* US$36, *cama* US$48, *TurBus*, 12 hrs. To **Puerto Montt**, 30 mins, *Thaebus* and *Full Express* every 15 mins, US$0.50. Same frequency to **Frutillar** (US$0.75, 30 mins) and **Osorno** (US$3, 1½ hrs). To **Valdivia** US$4. To **Bariloche**, *Andina del Sud*, by lakes route, see above. Buses, eg *Cruz del Sur*, *Tas Choapa*, daily, 7 hrs, US$12. Minibuses to **Ensenada** and leave from San Bernardo y Martínez, hourly. **Taxi** from Puerto Montt airport, US$16.

Transport

Banks *Redbanc* ATMs at several banks. *Turismo Los Lagos*, Del Salvador 257 (Galería Real, local 11). Daily 0830-1330, 1500-2100, Sun 0930-1330, accepts TCs, good rates. **Communications** Internet: *Ciber Service*, Salvador 264, loc 6-A. *George's*, San Ignacio 574. Av Gramado 560, p 2. San José 380, p 2. **Post Office**: San José y San Pedro. **Telephone**: 4 agencies in town. **Tourist office** San Fransisco 413 in Municipalidad, T321309, secturismo.puertovaras@munitel.cl Beware of places offering "tourist information", eg on pier. They may be only giving information about their paying members' services.

Directory

East of Puerto Varas by 47 km, Ensenada is at the southeast corner of Lake Llanquihue, which is the town's main attraction. A half-day trip is to Laguna Verde, about 10 minutes from *Hotel Ensenada*, along a beautiful circular trail, one-hour

Ensenada

long, behind the lake (take first fork to the right behind the information board), and then down the road to a campsite at Puerto Oscuro on Lago Llanquihue. The site is quiet and secluded, a good spot for a picnic. Ludwig Godsambassis, owner of *Ruedas Viejas*, who works for *Aqua Motion* in season, works independently as a guide out of season and is very knowledgeable. Minibuses run from Puerto Varas, frequent in summer (see above). Hitching from Puerto Varas is difficult.

Sleeping and eating AL *Cabañas Brisas del Lago*, T212012. Chalets for 6 on beach, good restaurant nearby, supermarket next door. Highly recommended for self-catering. **AL** *Hotel Ensenada*, Casilla 659, Puerto Montt, T338888. Olde-worlde, good food (closed in winter), good view of lake and Osorno Volcano, runs tours, hires mountain bikes (guests only). Also *hostal* in the grounds, cooking facilities, cheaper. **C** *Hosp Ensenada*, T338278. Excellent breakfast. **C** *Ruedas Viejas*, T/F212050, for room, or **D** in cabin, about 1 km west from Ensenada, HI reductions. Basic, damp, restaurant. **C** *Hosp Arena*, T212037. With breakfast. Recommended. **E** pp *Hospedaje* above *Toqui* grocery. Cheapest in town, basic, quiet, hot water, use of kitchen, beach in the backyard. Recommended. **Camping** *Montaña*, central Ensenada, **E** per site. Fully equipped, nice beach sites. Also at Playa Larga, 1 km further east, US$10 and at Puerto Oscuro, 2 km north, US$8. *Trauco*, 4 km west, T212033. Large site with shops, fully equipped, US$4-9 pp. *Canta Rana* is recommended for bread and *kuchen*. *Ruedas Viejas*, the cheapest eating place.

Most eating places close off season, there are a few pricey shops. Take your own provisions

Volcán Osorno North of Ensenada, can be reached either from Ensenada, or from a road branching off the Puerto Octay-Ensenada road at Puerto Klocker, 20 km southeast of Puerto Octay. Weather permitting, *Aqua Motion* (address under Puerto Varas) organize climbing expeditions with local guide, transport from Puerto Montt or Puerto Varas, food and equipment, US$150 pp payment in advance (minimum group of two, maximum of six with three guides) all year, setting out from the *refugio* at La Burbuja. They check weather conditions the day before and offer 50% refund if climb is abandoned because of bad weather. From La Burbuja it is six hours to the summit. *Conaf* do not allow climbing without a guide and insist on one guide to every two climbers. Only experienced climbers should attempt to climb right to the top, ice climbing equipment essential.

Sleeping The **Club Andino Osorno** (address under Osorno) has 3 *refugios*: north of the summit at La Picada (20 km east of Puerto Klocker) at 950 m; south of the summit: *La Burbuja*, 14 km north of Ensenada at 1,250 m; and, 15 km from Ensenada at 1,200 m *Refugio Teski Club*, **D** pp, bunk accommodation, restaurant and bar, sleeping bag useful, bleak site just below snow line; a good base for walking.

Parque Nacional Vicente Pérez Rosales

Lago Todos los Santos
The most beautiful of all the lakes in southern Chile

This long, irregularly shaped sheet of emerald-green water has deeply wooded shores and several small islands rising from its surface. In the waters are reflected the slopes of Volcán Osorno. Beyond the hilly shores to the east are several graceful snow-capped mountains, with the mighty Tronador in the distance. To the north is the sharp point of Cerro Puntiagudo, and at the northeastern end Cerro Techado rises cliff-like out of the water. The ports of **Petrohué** at its western and **Peulla** at its eastern ends are connected by boat. Trout and salmon fishing are excellent in several parts including Petrohué. ■ Conaf *office in Petrohué with a visitors' centre, small museum and 3D model of the park. There is a guardaparque office in Puella. Free entry.*

There are no roads round the lake and the only scheduled vessel is the *Andina del Sud* service with connections to Bariloche (Argentina), but private launches can be hired for trips (tickets for two-hour lake tours are sold on the Petrohué-Puella ferry). Isla Margarita, the largest island on the lake, with a lagoon in the middle, can be visited (in summer only) from Petrohué, boats by *Andina del Sud* leave 1500, US$30.

Petrohué, 16 km northwest of Ensenada, is a good base for walking. The **Salto de Petrohué** (entrance, US$1.50) is 6 km (unpaved) from Petrohué, 10 km (paved) from Ensenada (a much nicer walk from Petrohué). Near the falls is a snackbar; there are also two short trails, the Senderos de los Enamorados and Carileufú. **Peulla**, is a good starting point for hikes in the mountains. The Cascadas Los Novios, signposted above the *Hotel Peulla*, are stunning once you have climbed to them.

The park is infested by horseflies in Dec and Jan: cover up as much as possible with light-coloured clothes which may help a bit

On the south shore of Lago Todos Los Santos is the little village of **Cayutué**, reached by hiring a boat from Petrohué, US$30. From Cayutué it is a three hour walk to Laguna Cayutué, a jewel set between mountains and surrounded by forest. Good camping and swimming. From here it is a five-hour hike south to Ralún on the Reloncaví Estuary (see below). This is part of the old route used by missionaries in the colonial period to travel between Nahuel Huapi in Argentina and the island of Chiloé. It is now part of a logging road and is good for mountain bikes.

At Petrohué L *Fundo El Salto*, near Salto de Petrohué. Run by New Zealanders, mainly a fishing lodge, good home cooking, fishing trips arranged, Casilla 471, Puerto Varas. **E** pp *Familia Küschel* on other side of river (boat across). With breakfast, meals available, electricity only 3 hrs in afternoon, dirty, noisy, poor value, camping possible. Albergue in the school in summer. Conaf office can help find cheaper family accommodation. **At Peulla L** *Hotel Peulla*, PO Box 487, Puerto Montt, T258041 (including dinner and breakfast, direct personal reservations A3, PO Box 487, Puerto Montt, cheaper out of season). Beautiful setting by the lake and mountains, restaurant and bar, expensive meals (lunch poor), cold in winter, often full of tour groups (tiny shop at back of hotel). **D** pp *Res Palomita*, 50 m west of hotel. Half board, family-run, simple, comfortable but not spacious, separate shower, book ahead in season, lunches.

Sleeping & eating
There is a small shop in Andino del Sud building but best to take your own food

Camping At Petrohué on far side beside the lake, US$5 per site, no services, cold showers, locals around the site sell fresh bread (local fishermen will ferry you across, US$0.50). At Peulla, opposite *Conaf* office, US$1.50. Good campsite 1½ hrs' walk east of Peulla, take food.

Camping and picknicking is forbidden

Minibuses: from Puerto Varas to Ensenada continue to Petrohué (US$3), frequent in summer. Last bus to Ensenada at 1800. **Boat**: The boat between Petrohué and Peulla costs US$30 day return or one way (book in advance). It leaves Petrohué at 1100, Peulla at 0830 (not Sun, 1 hr 40 mins – most seating indoors, no cars carried, cycles free), commentaries in Spanish, English and German. This connects with the *Andina del Sud* tour bus between Puerto Montt and Bariloche (see under Puerto Montt). Local fishermen make the trip across the lake, but charge much more than the public service.

Transport
It is impossible to do this journey independently out of season as then there are buses only as far as Ensenada, there is little traffic for hitching and none of the ferries takes vehicles

For crossing the border with Argentina, **Paso Pérez Rosales**. Chilean immigration is in Peulla, 30 km west of the border, open summer 0800-2100, winter 0800-2000.

The Reloncaví estuary, the northernmost of Chile's glacial inlets, is recommended for its local colour, its sealions, dolphins and its peace. **Ralún**, a small village at the northern end of the estuary, is 31 km southeast from Ensenada by a poorly paved road along the wooded lower Petrohué valley. Roads continue, unpaved, along the east side of the estuary to Cochamó and Puelo and on the west side to Canutillar. In Ralún there is a village shop and post office. Lodging (**E** pp) is available at restaurants *El Refugio* and *Navarrito* and *posadas Campesino* (**F** pp) and *El Encuentro* (**E** pp). *Cabañas Ralún*, T Santiago 632 1675 or Puerto Varas 278286, at south end of the village, has cabins, **A** for 6. Just outside the village there are thermal springs, reached by boat, US$2.50 pp. ■ *Bus from Puerto Montt via Ensenada, 7 a day,* Bohle and Fierro, *between 1000 and 1930, 6 on Sat, return 0700-1830, US$2.* Fierro *buses also go to Canutillar via Ensenada and Ralún.*

Reloncaví Estuary

Cochamó, 17 km south of Ralún on the east shore of the estuary, is a pretty village, with a fine wooden church similar to those on Chiloé, in a striking setting, with the estuary and volcano behind. **E** *Cochamó*, T216212, basic but clean, often full with salmon farm workers, good meals. Recommended. **E** *Hosp Maura*, JJ Molina 12,

Chile

beautiful location overlooking the estuary, excellent food, good for kids, highly recommended. Also a large number of *pensiones* (just ask), *cabañas*, a campsite and a few eating places. ■ *Bus* Fierro *to Ralún, Ensenada, Puerto Varas and Puerto Montt, 3 daily; to Puelo 2 daily.*

Campo Aventura (San Bernadino 318, Puerto Varas) T/F065-232910, www.campo-aventura.com In Valle Río Cochamó, offers accommodation 4 km south of Cochamó (E pp, kitchen, sauna, camping) and at their other base in the valley of La Junta. They specialize in horseback and trekking between the Reloncaví Estuary and the Argentine border, 2-10 days. *Sebastián Contreras* is a recommended independent guide who offers tours on horseback and hires out horses, C Morales, T216220.

Puelo, further south, on the south bank of the Río Puelo, is a most peaceful place (ferry crossing until bridge over Río Puelo is completed). Basic lodging is available at the restaurant or with families – try Roberto and Olivia Telles, no bath/shower, meals on request, or Ema Hernández Maldona; two restaurants. From here the road (very rough) continues to Puelche on the Carretera Austral. **Transport** *Buses Bohle* from Puerto Montt, Sun 0900 and 1500 (from Puerto Varas 30 minutes later). Daily buses from Cochamó Mon-Sat 0745 and 1645, Sun 1100 and 1500. In summer boats sail up the Estuary from Angelmó. Tours from Puerto Montt US$30. Off season the *Carmencita* sails once a week, leaving Puelo Sun 1000 and Angelmó Wed 0900 (advisable to take warm clothes, food and seasickness pills if it's windy).

Puerto Montt

Phone code: 065
Colour map 8, grid C1
Population: 110, 139
1,016 km S of Santiago

The capital of X Región (Los Lagos) was founded in 1853 as part of the German colonization of the area. Good views over the city and bay are offered from outside the Intendencia Regional on Avenida X Region. The port is used by fishing boats and coastal vessels, and is the departure point for vessels to Puerto Chacabuco, Laguna San Rafael and for the long haul south to Puerto Natales. A paved road runs 55 km southwest to Pargua, where there is a ferry service to Chiloé.

Puerto Montt

N
0 metres 200
0 yards 200

■ Sleeping	6 Casa Perla	12 Hospedaje Leticia	18 O'Grimm
1 Albergue	7 Club Presidente	13 Hospedaje Suizo	19 Residencial
2 Alda González	8 Colina	14 Hostal Pacífico	Central
3 Burg & Café Amsel	9 El Talquino	15 Le Mirage	20 Residencial El
4 Casa Gladis	10 Gamboa	16 Millahue	Turista
5 Casa Patricia	11 Hospedaje Erica	17 Montt	21 Residencial El Tata

Chile

The **Iglesia de los Jesuitas** on Gallardo, dating from 1872, has a fine blue-domed ceiling; behind it on a hill is the **campanario** (clock tower). **Museo Regional Juan Pablo II**, Portales 997 near the bus terminal, documents local history and has a fine collection of historic photos of the city; also memorabilia of the Pope's visit. ■ *Daily 1030-1800, US$1.* The fishing port of **Angelmó**, 2 km west, has become a tourist centre with seafood restaurants and handicraft shops (reached by Costanera bus along Portales and by collective taxi Nos 2, 3, 20 from the centre, US$0.30).

The wooded **Isla Tenglo**, reached by launch from Angelmó (US$0.50 each way), is a favourite place for picnics. Magnificent view from the summit. The island is famous for its *curantos*, served by restaurants in summer. ■ *Boat trips round the island from Angelmó, 30 mins, US$8.***Parque Provincial Lahuen Nadi** contains some ancient trees in swampland, more accessible than some of the remoter forests. Take the main road to the airport, which leads off Ruta 5. After 5 km, turn right (north) and follow the signs. West of Puerto Montt the Río Maullin, which drains Lago Llanquihue, has some attractive waterfalls and good fishing (salmon). At the mouth of the river is the little fishing village of **Maullin**, founded in 1602.

L *Vicente Pérez Rosales*, Varas 447, T252571. With breakfast, excellent restaurant, seafood. Recommended. **AL** *Viento Sur*, Ejército 200, T258701, F258700. Good restaurant, sauna, gym, excellent views. **AL** *Burg*, Pedro Montt y Portales, T253941. Modern, central heating, centrally located, good, interesting traditional food in restaurant. **AL** *Club Presidente*, Portales 664, T251666, F251669. 4-star, with breakfast, very comfortable, also suites. Recommended. **A** *Le Mirage*, Rancagua 350, T255125, F256302. With breakfast, small rooms. **A** *Hostal Pacífico*, J J Mira 1088, T256229. **B** without bath, with breakfast, cable TV, parking, comfortable. Recommended. **A** *Res Urmeneta*, Urmeneta 290, T253262. **B** without bath, comfortable, IYHA reductions. Recommended. **B** *Montt*, Varas y Quillota, T253651. **C** without bath, good value, good restaurant. **C** *Colina*, Talca 81, T253502. Spacious, good restaurant, bar, car hire. Recommended. **C** *Millahue*, Copiapó 64, T253829, F253817, and apartments at Benavente 959, T/F254592. With breakfast, modern, good restaurant. **D** *Res Embassy*, Valdivia 130, T253533. **E** pp without bath, stores luggage.

Near the bus terminal **E** *Res El Turista*, Ancud 91, T254767. With and without bath, with breakfast, comfortable, small rooms, heating. Recommended. The following are all **F-G** pp: *Casa Gladis*, Ancud 112 y Mira. Some double rooms, or dormitory style, kitchen and laundry facilities, crowded. *Res Central*, Lota 111, T257516. Use of kitchen, basic, popular with Chileans. *Vista Hermosa*, Miramar 1486, T/F268001. Cheaper in low season, with breakfast, very good, without bath, ask for front room (10 mins' walk from terminal). *El Talquino*, Pérez Rosales 114 esq JJ Mira, T253331. Includes breakfast, hot water, family-run, cosy. Recommended. *Hosp Leticia*, Lota 132, T256316. Hot showers, with breakfast, basic, safe, cooking facilities. Recommended. *Hosp El Valle*, Chorrillos 1358, T258464. Hot showers, internet. *Sra Victoria*, Goecke 347, T288954. Family-run, quiet.

Other cheaper accommodation All **F** pp unless otherwise stated: *Alda González*, Gallardo 552, T253334. With or without bath, with breakfast, cooking facilities, popular. Recommended. **G** pp *Res El*

Sleeping
■ *on map*
Accommodation is expensive in season, much cheaper off season. Check Tourist Office

Chile

22	Residencial Embassy
23	Residencial Emita
24	Residencial Urmeneta
25	Vicente Pérez Rosales
26	Viento Sur
27	Vista Hermosa

● **Eating**
1	Balzac
2	Café Real & Café Alemán
3	Centro Español
4	Club Alemán

To Pelluco, Chamiza & Camino Austral

Several lodgings in F pp range on C Huasco, east of the Plaza de Armas

Chile

Tata, Gallardo 621. Floor space, very basic, popular, packed in summer. **E** *Aníbal Pinto 328*. With breakfast, popular, laundry facilities, 10 mins' walk from centre. Recommended. *Casa Perla*, Trigal 312, T262104, casaperla@ hotmail.com With breakfast, French, English spoken, helpful, meals, Spanish classes offered off season. Recommended. **E** *Casa Patricia*, Trigal 361. Family run, welcoming. *Hosp Erica*, Trigal 309, T259923. Kitchen facilities, TV, big bathroom, good views. *Gamboa*, Pedro Montt 157, T252741. With breakfast, TV, comfortable, warm. *Res Emita*, Miraflores 1281. Includes breakfast with homemade bread, safe. *Hosp Suizo*, Independencia 231, T/F252640. With breakfast, painting and Spanish classes, German and Italian spoken, Spanish classes. *Hosp Rocco*, Pudeto 233, T/F272897, hospedajerocco@hotmail.com Without bath, with breakfast, real coffee, English spoken. *Albergue*, in school opposite bus station (2 Jan-15 Feb). Sleeping bag on floor (**G** pp), cold showers, kitchen and laundry facilities, no security.

Camping *Camping Municipal* at Chinquihue, 10 km west (bus service), open Oct-Apr, fully equipped with tables, seats, barbecue, toilets and showers. Small shop, no kerosene. *Camping Anderson*, 11 km west, American-run, hot showers, private beach, home-grown fruit, vegetables and milk products. *Camping Metri*, 30 km southeast on Carretera Austral, T251235, *Fierro* bus, US$2 per tent.

Eating

• *on map*

Local specialities include picoroco al vapor, a giant barnacle whose flesh looks and tastes like crab, and curanto

Expensive: *Balzac*, Urmeneta y Quillota. Very good. *Centro Español*, O'Higgins 233. Very good. *Club Alemán*, Varas 264. Old fashioned, good food and wine. *Club de Yates*, Costanera east of centre. Excellent seafood. **Mid-range**: *Café Amsel* (in *Hotel Burg*), Pedro Montt y Portales. Superb fish. *New Harbour Café*, San Martín 185 y Urmeneta. Good coffee and atmosphere (closed Sin lunchtime) **Cheap**: *Al Passo*, Varas y O'Higgins. Simple food, warm atmosphere. *Café Real*, Rancagua 137. For *empanadas*, *pichangas*, *congrío frito*, and lunches. *Costa de Reloncaví*, Portales 736. Good. *Dino*, Varas 550. Restaurant upstairs, snacks downstairs (try the lemon juice). *Rincón Sureña*, Talca 86. Excellent lunches, popular.Excellent and cheap food at **Rodoviaria** in bus terminal (all credit cards accepted). **Cafés** *Café Alemana*, Rancagua 117. Good, real coffee. *Café Plaza*, Urmeneta 326. Good location, pool table, nice atmosphere. *El Rinconcito*, Portales 1014, Galería Comercial España, a good bar.

In **Angelmó** There are several dozen small, seafood restaurants in the old fishing port, very popular, ask for *té blanco* (white wine – they are not legally allowed to serve wine). *Asturias*, Angelmó 2448. Often recommended. Check hygiene before eating in those seafood restaurants on stilts. *Puerto Café*, Angelmó 2456 (above Travellers). Vegetarian dishes, real coffee, English spoken. Recommended.

Other seafood restaurants in **Chinquihue**, west of Angelmó. In **Pelluco** (4 km east), many seafood restaurants, including *Pazos*, T252552. Best *curanto* in Puerto Montt. *Azurro*, good Italian restaurant and, around the corner, a great pub called *Taitao*, façade like a galleon.

Shopping

Woollen goods and Mapuche-designed rugs can be bought at roadside stalls in Angelmó and on Portales opposite the bus terminal. Prices are much the same as on Chiloé, but quality is often lower.

Supermarkets *Fullfresh*, opposite bus terminal, open 0900-2200 daily. *Fullfresh* also in the *Paseo del Mar* shopping mall, Talca y A Varas, and in the old railway station. *Santa Isabel*, Varas y Chillán. *Dimarse*, Varas y Chillán. Sells bulbs for Maglight torches/flashlights. *Libros*, Portales 580. Small selection of English novels, also maps.

Sport & activities

Rafting and watersports: *Alsur*, Varas 445, T/F287628. **Sailing**: 2 Yacht Clubs in Chinquihue: *Marina del Sur* (MDS), T/F251958. Modern, bar and restaurant, sailing courses, notice board for crew (*tripulante*) notices, *MDS Charters* office (also Santiago T/F231 8238) specializes in cruising the Patagonian channels. Charters US$2,200-8,500 per week depending on size of boat. *Club de Desportes Náuticas*, founded by British and Americans in 1940s, more oriented towards small boat sailing, windsurfing, watersports.

Tour operators

There are many tour operators. We have received good reports about: *Andina del Sud*, very close to central tourist kiosk, Varas 437-445, T257797/257686. Sells a daily tour at 0830 (not Sun) to Puerto Varas, Parque Nacional V Pérez Rosales, Petrohué, Lago Todos los Santos,

Peulla and back, and to other local sights, as well as skiing trips to the Osorno volcano (see below for trip to Bariloche). *Petrel Tours*, San Martín 167, of 403, T/F255558. *Travellers*, Av Angelmó 2456, PO Box/Casilla 854, T262099, F258555, www.travellers.cl Close to 2nd port entrance and *Navimag* office, open Mon-Fri 0900-1330, 1500-1830, Sat 0900-1400 for booking for *Navimag* ferry *Puerto Edén* to Puerto Natales, bespoke incoming tours, car hire, also runs computerized tourist information service, book swap ('best book swap south of Santiago'), map display, TV, real coffee, English-run. Most offer 1-day excursions to Chiloé (US$20) and to Puerto Varas, Isla Loreley, Laguna Verde, and the Petrohué falls: both these tours are much cheaper from bus company kiosks inside the bus terminal, eg Bohle, US$15 to Chiloé, US$11 to the lakes. Some companies, eg *Reloncaví*, also offer 2-day excursions along the Carretera Austral to Hornopirén, US$76 including food and accommodation.

Transport
See Essentials, page 52 for international agencies

Local Car hire: *Automotric Angelmó*, Talca 79. Cheap and helpful. **Automóvil Club de Chile**, Ensenada 70, T254776, and at airport (US$235 per week). *Autovald*, Portales 1330, T256355. Cheap rates. *Full Famas,* Portales 506, T258060 and at airport. Helpful, good value, has vehicles that can be taken to Argentina. **Cycle repairs**: *Kiefer*, Pedro Montt 129, T253079. 3 shops on Urmeneta, none very well stocked. **Motorcycle repairs**: *Miguel Schmuch*, Urmeneta 985, T/F258877.

El Tepual Airport is 13 km NW of town

Long distance Air: *ETM* bus from terminal 1½ hrs before departure, US$2; also meets incoming flights. *ETM* minibus service to/from hotels, US$4 pp, T294294. Taxi US$12. To **Santiago** and **Punta Arenas** many daily flights by *LanChile, Lan Express*. To **Temuco**, *LanChile/Lan Express* daily. *Sky* also flies to Santiago and Temuco daily. In Jan, Feb and Mar you may well be told that flights are booked up, but cancellations may be available from the airport. To **Balmaceda**, *Lan Express* daily. To **Chaitén**, *Aeromet* daily 1200, US$45.

Buses Terminal (very crowded, well-organized, but beware hotel touts) on sea front at Portales y Lota, has Telephone, restaurants, *casa de cambio* (left luggage, US$1.50 per item for 24 hrs). To **Puerto Varas** (US$0.50), **Llanquihue**, **Frutillar** (US$1.25), **Puerto Octay** (US$2) and **Osorno** (US$4) minibuses every few minutes, *Expreso Puerto Varas, Thaebus* and *Full Express*. To **Ensenada** and **Petrohué**, *Buses JM* at least 3 a day. To **Pucón**, US$6. To **Temuco** US$6, to **Valdivia**, US$5, 3½ hrs. **Concepción**, US$10. To **Santiago**, express 13 hrs, US$15, *cama* US$35, several companies including *TurBus*, very good, and *Tas Choapa Royal Class*. To **Punta Arenas**, *Austral* and *Ghisoni*, between 1 and 3 times a week, US$53-70 depending on company (bus goes through Argentina via Bariloche), 32-38 hrs. Take plenty of food for this "nightmare" trip. Book well in advance in Jan-Feb and check if you need a multiple-entry Chilean visa. Also book any return journey before setting out. For services to **Chiloé**, see page 699.

Buses to Argentina via Osorno and the Puyehue pass Daily services to Bariloche on this route via Osorno, US$14, 7 hrs, are run by *Cruz del Sur, Río de la Plata, Tas Choapa* and *Bus Norte*. Out of season, services are reduced. Buy tickets for international buses from the bus terminal, not through an agency. Book well in advance in Jan and Feb; ask for a seat on the right hand side for the best views. For the route to Argentina via Lago Todos Los Santos see below.

Shipping offices in Puerto Montt: *Catamaranes del Sur*, Av Diego Portales 510, T267533, and Km 13 Chinquihue, T482308 (Isadora Goyenechea 3250, of 802, Las Condes, Santiago, T333 7127), www.catamaranesdelsur.cl *Cruce de Lagos*, www.lakecrossing.cl, includes departures to **Puerto Varas** and **Bariloche**. *Navimag* (Naviera Magallanes SA), Terminal Transbordadores, Angelmó 2187, T432300, www.navimag.com *Skorpios Cruises*, Angelmó 1660 y Miraflores (Castilla 588), T252619, F258315, www.skorpios.cl *Transmarchilay Ltda*, Angelmó 2187, T270400, or 600-600 8687/88, www.tmc.cl

Directory
This is the last city with Visa ATM before Coyhaique

Airline offices *LanChile*, O'Higgins y Urmeneta, T253141. **Banks** For Visa *Corp Banca*, Pedro Montt y Urmeneta, good rates. For MasterCard ATM, *Banco de Santander*, A Varas 520. Many other ATMS in the city. Commission charges vary widely. *Afex*, Portales 516. *Turismo Los Lagos*, Varas 595, local 13. *La Moneda de Oro* at the bus terminal exchanges some Latin American currencies, not Argentine pesos (Mon-Sat 0930-1230, 1530-1800). Obtain Argentine pesos before leaving Chile. **Communications** Internet: *Latin Star*, Av Angelmó 1684, T310036. Interenet café, cheap phone rates, stamps, fax, English spoken, helpful. Others on Av Angelmó near *Navimag*. 3 internet cafés on San Martín (eg No 232). **Post Office:** Rancagua 126. Open 0830-1830 (Mon-Fri), 0830-1200 (Sat). **Telephone:** Pedro Montt 114 (has free internet access for 30 mins) and Chillán 98. *Entel*, Urmeneta y Pedro Montt. *Telefónica del Sur*, A Varas entre Talca y Pedro Montt. **Consulates** Argentina, Cauquenes 94, p 2, T253996, quick visa service. **Germany**, Varas y Gallardo, p 3, of 306. Tue-Wed 0930-1200. **Netherlands**, Chorillos 1582, T253003. **Spain**, Rancagua 113, T252557. **Tourist offices** *Sernatur* has two offices, in the Gobernación Provincial building on the Plaza de Armas. Daily in summer 0900-1300, 1500-1900, Mon-Fri in winter 0830-1300, 1400-1800. Also in the Intendencia Regional, Av Décima Región 480 (p 3), Casilla 297, T/F254580. 0830-1300, 1330-1730 Mon-Fri. For more information and town maps, go to the kiosk just southeast of the Plaza de Armas run by the municipality. Open till 1800 on Sat. *Telefónica del Sur* and *Sernatur* operate a phone information service (INTTUR), dial 142 (cost is the same as a local call). Dial 149 for chemist/pharmacy information, 148 for the weather, 143 for the news, etc. The service operates throughout the Tenth Region. *Conaf* is at Ochogavia 458, and Amunátegui 500 (off Gallardo) for information on national parks (in theory). *Automóvil Club de Chile*, Esmeralda 70, T252968.

To Argentina via Lago Todos Los Santos

This popular route to Bariloche, involving ferries across Lago Todos Los Santos, Lago Frías and Lago Nahuel Huapi is outstandingly beautiful whatever the season, though the mountains are often obscured by rain and heavy cloud. The route is via Puerto Varas, Ensenada and Petrohué falls (20 minutes stop) to Petrohué, where it connects with catamaran service across Lago Todos Los Santos to Peulla. Lunch stop in Peulla two hours (lunch not included in fare: *Hotel Peulla* is expensive, see page 691 for alternatives). Chilean customs in Peulla, followed by a 1½-hour bus ride through the Paso Pérez Rosales to Argentine customs in Puerto Frías, 20 minute boat trip across Lago Frías to Puerto Alegre and bus from Puerto Alegre to Puerto Blest. From Puerto Blest it is a beautiful ½ hour catamaran trip along Lago Nahuel Huapi to Puerto Pañuelo (Llao Llao), from where there is a 45-minute bus journey to Bariloche (bus drops passengers at hotels, camping sites or in town centre). From 1 May to 30 August this trip is done over two days with overnight stay in Peulla, add about US$90 to single fare for accommodation in *Hotel Peulla*. (Baggage is taken to *Hotel Peulla* automatically but for alternative accommodation see under Peulla.)

Transport The route is operated only by *Andina del Sud* see under Tour operators. Bus from company offices daily at 0800; the fare is a hefty US$140 one way. Note that the trip may be cancelled if the weather is poor; difficulty in obtaining a refunds or assistance have been reported. Try both Puerto Montt and Puerto Varas offices if you want to take the trip in sections.

Sea routes south of Puerto Montt

Taxi from centre to ferry terminal, US$2. All shipping services should be checked in advance; schedules change frequently

To Puerto Natales The dramatic 1,460 km journey first goes through Seno Reloncaví and Canal Moraleda. From Bahía Anna Pink along the coast and then across the Golfo de Penas to Bahía Tarn it is a 12-17 hours sea crossing, usually rough. The journey continues through Canal Messier, Angostura Inglesa, Paso del Indio and Canal Kirke (one of the narrowest routes for large shipping). *Navimag's* vessel *Magallanes* makes the journey. It calls at Puerto Chacabuco en route south and north, and stops off Puerto Edén on Isla Wellington (1 hour south of Angostura Inglesa). This is a fishing village with one *hospedaje* (20 beds), three shops, scant provisions, one off-licence, one café, but no camping, or running water. Population is 180, plus five *carabineros* and the few remaining Alacaluf Indians. It is the drop-off point for exploring Isla Wellington, which is largely untouched, with stunning mountains. If stopping, take food; maps (not very accurate) available in Santiago.

The *Magallanes* sails **to Puerto Natales** throughout the year on Mon respectively, taking 4 days and 3 nights. It returns on Fri (board the night before). Check-in closes 2 hrs before boarding, which is 2 hrs before sailing. Confirm times a day in advance. The fare, including meals, ranges from US$250 pp in C berth (sheets are extra, take your own or a sleeping bag), to US$345-398 in 4-bed cabins, to over US$1,000 in a private cabin (high season prices). 10% discount on international student cards in cabin class only. Cars are carried for US$280 (US$190 northbound), motorcycles US$56 and bicycles US$34. Payment by credit

It is cheaper to fly and quicker to go by bus via Argentina The route does not pass Laguna San Rafael

card or foreign currency is accepted in all *Navimag* offices. The vessel is a mixed cargo/passenger ferry which includes live animals in the cargo. Apart from videos, entertainment on board is limited. Some report good food, others terrible. Most passengers take their own food and alcohol. Standards of service and comfort vary, depending on the number of passengers and weather conditions. Take seasickness tablets. **Booking** Economy class can only be booked, with payment, through *Navimag* offices in Puerto Montt and Puerto Natales. Economy tickets are frequently sold just before departure. Cabin class can be booked in advance through *Travellers* in Puerto Montt (see Tour operators), through *Navimag* offices in Puerto Montt, Puerto Natales and Punta Arenas, or through *Cruceros Australis* (*Navimag* parent company) in Santiago, Av El Bosque Norte 0440, Las Condes, T442 3110, F203 5173. Book well in advance for departures between mid-Dec and mid-Mar especially for the voyage south (Puerto Natales to Puerto Montt is less heavily booked). It is well worth going to the port on the day of departure if you have no ticket. Departures are frequently delayed by weather conditions – or even advanced. For details and next season's fares: www.travellers.cl, or see *Navimag*'s website.

To Puerto Chacabuco *Navimag*'s ferry *Edén* sails twice weekly (Thu and Sun) to Puerto Chacabuco (80 km west of Coyhaique). The cruise to Puerto Chacabuco lasts about 24 hrs. The fares are US$25 for a reclining seat, US$66 for a bunk with shared bath, US$82 for a bunk in a cabin with private bath, US$100 pp in a double cabin with bath. There is a small canteen; long queues if the boat is full. Food is expensive so take your own. Off season this same vessel goes to Laguna San Rafael, on specific dates depending on the time of year. It is a 5-day, 4-night trip, with activities, all meals and a boat trip to the glacier. Accommodation ranges from cabins costing US$646 (pp in double suite), to bunks at US$354 (with bath) and US$328 (without bath), to reclining seats at US$208 pp.

To Chaitén *Navimag*'s *Alejandrina* sails on Fri, 10 hrs, US$23 for a chair. *Transmarchilay*'s *Pincoya* sails 3 times a week, 10 hrs, US$19 chair, US$39 bunk, US$10 for a bicycle. *Catamaranes del Sur*'s *Chaitén* also sails 3 times a week, taking 4½ hrs, US$40 for a reclining seat.

To Laguna San Rafael The m/n *Skorpios 1, 2* and *3* of *Skorpios Cruises* leave Puerto Montt (vessels *2* and *3*) or Puerto Chacabuco (*1*) for a luxury cruises with various itineraries. The fare varies according to season, type of cabin and number of occupants: a double ranges from US$410 (low) to US$620 (high) on *Skorpios 1*, from US$890 (low) to US$1,650 (high) on *Skorpios 2* and US$1,680 (low) to US$2,500 (high) on *Skorpios 3*. It has been reported that there is little room to sit indoors if it is raining on *Skorpios 1*, but generally service is excellent, the food superb, and at the glacier, you can chip ice off the face for your whisky. (After the visit to San Rafael the ships visit Quitralco Fjord where there are thermal pools and boat trips on the fjord.)

Patagonia Connection SA, Fidel Oteíza 1921, of 1006, Providencia, Santiago, T225 6489, F274 8111, www.patagoniaconnex.cl Operates *Patagonia Express*, a catamaran which runs from Puerto Chacabuco to Laguna San Rafael via Termas de Puyuhuapi, see page 710. Tours lasting 4 to 6 days start from Puerto Montt and include the catamaran service, the hotel at Termas de Puyuhuapi and the day excursion to Laguna San Rafael. High season 20 Dec-20 Mar, low season 11 Sep-19 Dec and 21 Mar-21 Apr. High season fares for a 6-day tour from US$1300-2100, all inclusive, highly recommended.

Catamaranes del Sur offers 3-day trips to the glacier for US$679, every 3 days in summer, every week in spring and autumn. Also 1-day trips from Puerto Chacabuco, which are much cheaper.

Raymond Weber, Av Chipana Pasaje 4 No 3435, Iquique, T09-885 8250/883 3685, www.chilecharter.com Runs charters on luxury sailing catamarans to Laguna San Rafael and Golfo de Ancud.

Other Routes See under Quellón and Chaitén for details of *Navimag*, *Transmarchilay* and other sailings between Chiloé and the mainland.

Chiloé

The culture of Chiloé has been strongly influenced by isolation from Spanish colonial currents, the mixture of early Spanish settlers and Mapuche indians and a dependence on the sea. Religious and secular architecture, customs and crafts, combined with delightful landscapes, all contribute to Chiloé's uniqueness.

Thick forests cover most of the western side of the island of Chiloé. The hillsides in summer are a patchwork quilt of wheat fields and dark green plots of potatoes. The population is 116,000 and most live on the sheltered eastern side. The west coast, exposed to strong Pacific winds, is wet for most of the year. The east coast and the offshore islands are drier, though frequently cloudy.

*Colour map 9, grid A1
The island is 250 km long, 50 km wide and covers 9,613 sq km. Marea Roja, the toxin that is potentially fatal in humans, was found here in mid-2002. Seek advice before eating any shellfish here*

Getting there Buses Puerto Montt to Pargua, frequent, US$2, 1 hr, though most buses go through to Ancud (3½-4 hrs) and Castro. Transport to the island is dominated by *Cruz del Sur*, who also own *Trans Chiloé* and *Regional Sur* and have their own ferries. *Cruz del Sur* run frequent services from Puerto Montt to Ancud and Castro, 6 a day to Chonchi and Quellón; their fares are highest but they are faster (their buses have priority over cars on *Cruz del Sur* ferries). Fares from Puerto Montt: to Ancud, *Cruz del Sur* US$4.50, *Regional Sur* US$4.50, **Queilén Bus** (independent company), US$4; to Castro, *Cruz del Sur* US$7.50, *Trans Chiloé* US$6 and *Queilén Bus*; to Chonchi, US$7, Quellón, US$9. There are direct bus services from Santiago, Osorno, Valdivia, Temuco and Los Angeles to Chiloé. Buses drive on to the ferry (passengers leave the bus). **Ferries** About 24 crossings daily, 30 min crossing, operated by several companies including *Transmarchilay* and *Cruz del Sur*; all ferries carry buses, private vehicles (cars US$10 one way, motorcycles US$6, bicycles US$3) and foot passsengers (US$1).

Ins & outs
Regular ferries cross the straits of Pargua between Pargua, 55 km SW of Puerto Montt on the mainland, and Chacao on Chiloé Dolpins, seals and birds can be seen

The original inhabitants of Chiloé were the Chonos, who were pushed south by the Mapuches invading from the north. The first Spanish sighting was by Francisco de Ulloa in 1553 and in 1567 Martín Ruiz de Gamboa took possession of the islands on behalf of Spain. The small Spanish settler population divided the indigenous population and their lands between them. The rising of the Mapuche after 1598 which drove the Spanish out of the mainland south of the Río Biobío left the Spanish community on Chiloé (some 200 settlers in 1600) isolated. During the 17th century, for instance, it was served by a single annual ship from Lima.

History

The islanders were the last supporters of the Spanish Crown in South America. When Chile rebelled the last of the Spanish Governors fled to the island and, in despair, offered it to Britain. Canning, the British Foreign Secretary, turned the offer down. The island finally surrendered in 1826.

The availability of wood and the lack of metals have left their mark on the island. Some of the earliest churches were built entirely of wood, using wooden pegs instead of nails. These early churches often displayed some German influence as a result of the missionary work of Bavarian Jesuits. Two features of local architecture often thought to be traditional are in fact late 19th century in origin. The replacement of thatch with thin tiles (*tejuelas*) made from alerce wood, which are nailed to the frame and roof in several distinctive patterns, and *palafitos* or wooden houses built on stilts over the water.

The island is also famous for its traditional handicrafts, notably woollens and basketware, which can be bought in the main towns and on some of the off-shore islands, as well as in Puerto Montt.

Although the traditional mainstays of the economy, fishing and agriculture, are still important, salmon farming has become a major source of employment. Seaweed is harvested for export to Japan. Tourism provides a seasonal income for a growing number of people. Nevertheless, the relatively high birth rate and the shortage of employment in Chiloé have led to regular emigration.

Ancud and around

Phone code: 065
Colour map 9, grid A1
Population: 23,148

Ancud lies on the north coast of Chiloé 30 km west of the Straits of Chacao at the mouth of a great bay, the Golfo de Quetalmahue. Founded in 1767 to guard the shipping route around Cape Horn, it was defended by two fortresses, the Fuerte San Antonio and Fuerte Ahui on the opposite side of the bay. The port is dominated by the **Fuerte San Antonio**, built in 1770, the site of the Spanish surrender of Chiloé to Chilean troops in 1826. Close to it are the ruins of the **Polvorín del Fuerte** (a couple of cannon and a few walls). A lovely 1 km walk north of the fort leads to the secluded beach, **Arena Gruesa**. 2 km east is a **Mirador** offering good views of the island and across to the mainland, even to the Andes on a clear day. Near the Plaza de Armas is the **Museo Regional**, with an interesting collection on the early history of Chiloé.

Chiloé

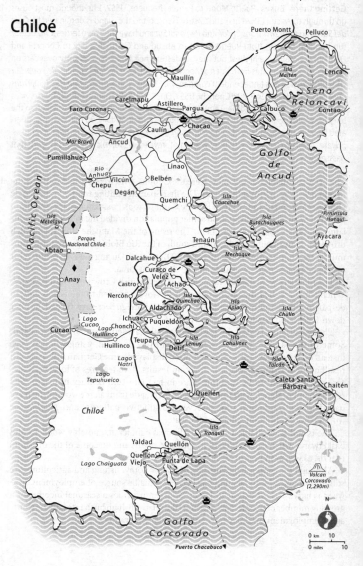

■ *Summer daily 1100-1900, winter Tue-Fri 0900-1300, 1430-1830, Sat 1000-1330, 1430-1800, US$1, reductions for students. Has good shops and café.*

To **Faro Corona**, the lighthouse on Punta Corona, 34 km west, along the beach, which offers good views with birdlife and dolphins. The duty officer may give a tour, recommended. To **Pumillahue**, 27 km southwest, where nearby there is a penguin colony (the birds are seen early morning or late afternoon): hire a fishing boat to see it, US$5.50 pp. ■ *Buses: Mon-Sat 0645, return 1730; no bus is suitable for seeing the birds.*

Chepu, on the coast southwest of Ancud (35 km) is famed for its seafishing and the drowned forest and environment of its river (a wide range of birds here). It is also the northern entry for the Parque Nacional Chiloé, see page 704.

Sleeping
In summer the school on Calle Chacabuco is used as an albergue

L *Hostería Ancud*, San Antonio 30, T622340, www.hosteriancud.com Overlooking bay, attractive, very comfortable, helpful, restaurant. **AL** *Lacuy*, Pudeto 219 near Plaza de Armas, T/F623019. With breakfast, restaurant. Recommended. **A** *Montserrat*, Baquedano 417, T/F622957. With breakfast, good views, attractive. **C** *Hostería Ahui*, Costanera 906, T622415. With breakfast, full of charm, good views. **C** *Polo Sur*, Costanera 630, T622200. Good seafood restaurant, not cheap, avoid rooms overlooking club next door. **C** *Res Germania*, Pudeto 357, T/F622214. **C** without bath, parking, comfortable. **C** *Hosp Alto Bellavista*, Bellavista 449, T622384. Very helpful, good breakfast, with sleeping bag on floor much cheaper. **D** *Hosp Alinar*, Ramírez 348. Hospitable. **D** *Hosp Santander*, Sgto Aldea 69. **E** without bath. Recommended. **D** *Lluhay*, Cochrane 458, T622656. Meals served. Recommended. **E** pp *Elena Bergmann*, Aníbal Pinto 382. Use of kitchen, parking. **E** pp Pudeto 331, T622535. Without bath, old fashioned, very nice. **E** pp *Hosp San José*, Pudeto 619. With breakfast, good family atmosphere, hot water, shared bath, use of kitchen, internet. Recommended (new house under construction, 2003). **E** pp *San Bernardo*, Errázuriz 395, T622657. Good dormitory accommodation. **E** *Hosp Sra Martha*, Lautaro 988. With breakfast, TV, kitchen facilities, good beds. Recommended. **F** pp *Hosp Su Casa*, Los Alerces 841, T623382. Excellent breakfast, hot shower, TV room. **F** *Familia Vallejos*, Aníbal Pinto 738, T622243. Very friendly, basic. Recommended.

Camping *Arena Gruesa* at north end of Baquedano, T623428. *Playa Gaviotas*, 5 km north, T09-653 8096 (mob). *Playa Larga Huicha*, 9 km north, **E** per site, bath, hot water, electricity.

Eating
Excellent cheap seafood restaurants in market area

Mid-range: *Coral*, Pudeto 346. Good. *Jardín*, Pudeto 263. Good local food. **Cheap**: *Carmen*, Pudeto 159. Chilean cooking, *pasteles*. *El Cangrejo*, Dieciocho 155. Seafood. Highly recommended. *Hamburguería*, Av Prat. Much better than name suggests, good seafood. *Lydia*, Pudeto 254. Chilean and international. *La Pincoya*, Prat 61, on waterfront. Good food, service and views. *El Trauco*, Blanco y Prat. Seafood excellent. Highly recommended.

Tour operators

Austral Adventures, Av Prat 176B, Casilla 432, T/F625977, www.australadventures.com Tours on land and sea. *Turismo Ancud*, Pudeto 219, Galería Yurie, T622235. *Paralelo 42*, Latorre 558, T622458. Recommended for tours to the Río Chepu area, including 2-day kayak trips, guide Carlos Oyarzun.

Transport

Buses Terminal on the east outskirts at Aníbal Pinto y Marcos Vera, reached by bus, or Pudeto colectivos. To **Castro**, US$2.50, frequent (see below), 1½ hrs. To **Puerto Montt**, frequent services by *Cruz del Sur, Regional Sur* and *Queilén Bus*. To **Quemchi** via the coast, 2 hrs, US$1.50.

Directory

Banks ATMs at *BCI*. **Communications Internet**: Phone office at Pudeto 219 has internet. **Post Office**: on corner of Plaza de Armas at Pudeto y Blanco Encalada. **Telephone**: Plaza de Armas. Mon-Sat 0700-2200. **Tourist offices** *Sernatur*, Libertad 665, T622665. Ask here about the Agro Turismo programme, staying with farming families. Mon-Fri 0900-1300, 1430-1730.

Ancud to Castro

There are two routes: direct along Route 5, the Pan-American Highway, crossing rolling hills, forest and agricultural land, or via the east coast along unpaved roads passing through small farming and fishing communities. The two main towns along the coastal route, **Quemchi** (*Population*: 2,000, basic accommodation) and Dalcahue, can also be reached by roads branching off Route 5.

Chile

Dalcahue (*Population*: 2,300), 74 km south of Ancud, is more easily reached from Castro, 30 km further south. It is one of the main ports for boats to the offshore islands, including Quinchao and Mechuque. The wooden church on the main plaza dates from the 19th century. The market is on Sunday, from 0700 to 1300; good quality. Tourist kiosk in season. There are various basic hotels (**D-E**) and a restaurant. Buses to Castro, hourly, 40 minutes, US$1. Also collective taxis.

Quinchao
Don't miss the oysters sold on the beach

The main settlement on this island is **Achao**, a quiet, pretty fishing village with a market. Its wooden church, built in 1730 and saved by a change of wind from a fire which destroyed much of the town in 1784, is a fine example of Chilote Jesuit architecture. The original construction was without use of nails. The tourist office at Serrano y Progreso is open between December and March only. There are various hotels (**D-E**) and restaurants. Ferry from Dalcahue, frequent, free for pedestrians and cyclists. *Arriagada* buses from Ancud, five a day. Frequent to Castro, US$1.50, *Achao Express.*

Castro

Phone code: 065
Colour map 9, grid A1
Population: 20,000
88 km S of Ancud

The capital of Chiloé lies on a fjord on the east coast. Founded in 1567, the centre is situated on a promontory, from which there is a steep drop to the port. On the Plaza de Armas is the large **Cathedral**, strikingly decorated in lilac and orange, with a splendid wood panelled interior, built by the Italian architect, Eduardo Provosoli in 1906. South of the Plaza on the waterfront is the **Feria**, or Mercado Municipal de Artesanía, where excellent local woollen articles (hats, sweaters, gloves) can be found (also imported goods). *Palafitos* can be seen on the northern side of town and by the bridge over the Río Gamboa. There are good views of the city from **Mirador La Virgen** on Millantuy hill above the cemetery. **Museo Regional** on Esmeralda, contains history, folklore, handicrafts and mythology of Chiloé and photos of the 1960 earthquake. ■ *Summer Mon-Sat 0930-2000, Sun 1030-1300; winter Mon-Sat 0930-1300, 1500-1830, Sun 1030-1300.* **Museo de Arte Moderno**, near the Río Gamboa, in the Parque Municipal, over 3 km northwest of the centre, reached by following Calle Galvarino Riveros up the hill west of town, take bus marked 'Al Parque'. ■ *1000-1900, T632787, F635454.*

Sleeping

AL *Hostería Castro*, Chacabuco 202, T632301, F635668. Attractive building, wonderful views. Recommended. **AL** *Gran Alerce*, O'Higgins 808, T632267. Heating, helpful, breakfast, also has *cabañas* and restaurant 4 km south of Castro. **AL** *Unicornio Azul*, Pedro Montt 228, T632359, F632808. Good views over bay, comfortable, restaurant. **A** *Cabañas Trayen*, 5 km south of Castro, T633633. **B** off season, lovely views. **B** *Casita Española*, Los Carrera 359, T635186. Heating, TV, parking. Recommended. **B** *Chilhue*, Blanco Encalada 278, T632956. Good.

On San Martín (convenient for bus terminals) **B-C** *Hostal Quelcún*, No 581, T632396. Cheaper without bath, some rooms small, heating, helpful. **E** pp *Hosp Chiloé*, No 739. Breakfast. Recommended. **E** pp *Pensión Victoria*, No 747. Small rooms, pretty. **E** pp *Res Capullito*, No 709. Quiet. **F** pp *Hospedaje Mansilla*, No 879-B. With big breakfast, central. Highly recommended. **F** pp *Lidia Low*, No 890. With good breakfast, warm showers, use of kitchen.

Several lodgings on Los Carrera 500-700 blocks, E range

Other Budget accommodation D *Hilton*, Ramírez 385. Good value, restaurant. **D** *Hosp Sotomayor*, Sotomayor 452, T632464. With breakfast, quiet, small beds. **E** pp *Hosp de Jessie Toro*, Las Delicias 287. Good breakfast, helpful, spacious, good bathrooms, also cabins. Warmly recommended. **E** pp *Res La Casona*, Serrano 488, above TV shop. With breakfast. Recommended. **E** *Hosp El Molo*, O'Higgins 486, T635026. Comfortable, safe, welcoming, internet. **E** pp Eyzaguirre 469. Comfortable. Recommended. **E** pp Freire 758. Breakfast, good value. **E** pp Chacabuco 449. Good beds, quiet, water only warm. **E** pp *Lodging El Mirador*, Barros Arana 127, T633795. Good breakfast, **C** with bath, cosy, relaxing, kitchen. Highly recommended. **F** pp *María Zuñiga*, Barros Arana 140, T635026. Includes breakfast, comfortable, cooking facilities, secure. Recommended. **F** *Hosp América*, Chacabuco 215,

T634364. With breakfast, shared bath, cable TV, very good food. **F** *Globetrotters*, Thompson 262. Kitchen, living room, cable TV, information, owner enjoys a party. **F** *Hosp Victoria*, Barros Arana 745. Warm water. Recommended. **F** pp *Hosp Polo Sur*, Barros Arana 169, T635212. Safe, cooking facilities, wonderful views. Basic accommodation Dec-Feb in the Gimnasio Fisical, Freire 610, T632766, **F** with breakfast.

Camping *Camping Pudú*, Ruta 5, 10 km north of Castro, T635109, cabins, showers with hot water, sites with light, water, children's games. Several sites on road to Chonchi.

Mid-range:*Donde Eladio*, Lillo 97.Meat and seafood specialities. **Cheap**: *Palafito* restaurants near the Feria Artesanía on the waterfront offer good food and good value, including *Rapa Nui*, *Mariela* and *La Amistad*. *Don Camilo*, Ramírez 566. Good food. Recommended. *Maucari*, Lillo 93. Good seafood. *Sacho*, Thompson 213. Good sea views, clean. **Cafés**: *La Brújula del Cuerpo*, Plaza de Armas. Good coffee, snacks. *Stop Inn Café*, Martín Ruiz shopping centre, Gamboa. Good coffee. In the market, try *milcaos*, fried potato cakes with meat stuffing. Also *licor de oro*, like Galliano.

Eating
Breakfast before 0900 is difficult to find

Cema-Chile outlet on Esmeralda. For books on Chiloé, *El Tren*, Thompson 229, *Anay*, Serrano 357, and *Libros Chiloé*, Blanco Encalada 204. Cassettes of typical Chilote music are widely available. **Supermarket** *Beckna*, O'Higgins y Aldea. Bakes good bread. The municipal market is on Yumbel, off Ulloa, uphill northwest of town: fish and vegetables.

Shopping

Turismo Isla Grande, Thompson 241, *Navimag* and *Transmarchilay* agents. *Pehuén Expediciones*, Blanco Encalada 299, T632361, pehuentr@entelchile.net *LanChile* agency, horse riding, trips to national park and islands.*Turismo Queilén*, Gamboa 502, T632776. Good tours to Chonchi and Chiloé National Park. Recommended. Local guide *Sergio Márquez*, Felipe Moniel 565, T632617, very knowledgeable, has transport. Tour prices: to Parque Nacional Chiloé US$25, to Isla Mechuque (east of Dalcahue) US$37.

Tour operators

Local buses: frequent services to Chonchi, choose between buses (*Cruz del Sur*, *Queilén Bus* and others), minibuses and colectivos (from Esmeralda y Chacabuco). *Arroyo* and *Ocean Bus* both run to Cucao, 6 a day in season, US$2.20 (1 a day off season, avoid Fri when school children are going home – much slower, lots of stops). To **Dalcahue** frequent services by *Gallardo* and *Arriagada*, also colectivos from San Martín 815. To **Achao** via Dalcahue and Curaco de Vélez, *Arriagada*, 4 daily, 3 on Sun, last return from Achao 1730, US$1.75. To **Puqueldón** on the island of Lemuy, *Gallardo*, Mon-Fri 1315, US$2. To **Quemchi**, 2 a day, 1½ hrs, US$2.50. To **Quellón**, *Regional Sur* and *Trans Chiloé*, frequent. To **Queilén**, *Queilén Bus*, 6 a day, US$2.50. **Long distance buses** Leave from 2 terminals: *Cruz del Sur*, T632389, *Trans Chiloé* and *Arriagada* from Cruz del Sur terminal on San Martín behind the cathedral. Other services leave from the Municipal Terminal, San Martín, 600 block (2 blocks further north). Frequent services to **Ancud** and **Puerto Montt** by *Cruz del Sur*, *Trans Chiloé* and *Queilén Bus*. *Cruz del Sur* also run to **Osorno**, **Valdivia**, **Temuco**, **Concepción** and **Santiago**. *Bus Norte* to Ancud, Puerto Montt, Osorno and Santiago daily. To **Punta Arenas**, *Queilén Bus*, Mon, 36 hrs, US$60. **Bicycle hire**: San Martín 581. **Ferries**: *Catamaranes del Sur* ferry *Chaitén* sails Castro-Chaitén, Tue, Thu 0900, US$25, returning same days at 1800, 2 hrs 40 mins. *Navimag's* *Alejandrina* sails from Chaitén to Castro on Wed, returning on Thu, 6-hr crossing, US$20 for a seat, US$16 standing. *Transmarchilay's* *Pincoya* does the same route 3 times a week, also 6 hrs.

Transport

Banks Many of the banks in the centre have ATMs for credit and bank cards (pesos only). *Banco de Chile* with ATM at Plaza de Armas, accepts TCs (at a poor rate). *BCI*, Plaza de Armas, MasterCard and Visa ATM. Better rates from *Julio Barrientos*, Chacabuco 286, cash and TCs. **Communications** Internet: *Cadesof Ltda*, Gamboa 447, p 2, entry from alley beside *Chilexpress*. O'Higgins 486, open 0900-1300, 1600-2200, US$7 per hr. *N@vegue*, San Martín 309. **Post Office**: on west side of Plaza de Armas. **Telephone**: Latorre 289. *Entel*: O'Higgins entre Gamboa y Sotomayor. **Tourist offices** Information kiosk on the Plaza de Armas opposite Cathedral. It has a list of accommodation and prices. *Conaf* is on Gamboa behind the Gobernación building.

Directory

Chile

Chonchi

Phone code: 065
Colour map 9, grid A1
Population: 3,000

Chonchi is a picturesque fishing village 25 km south of Castro. From the plaza Calle Centenario, with several attractive but sadly neglected wooden mansions, drops steeply to the harbour. Fishing boats bring in the early morning catch which is carried straight into the nearby market. The wooden church, on the plaza, was built in 1754, remodelled in neo-classical style in 1859 and 1897 (key from handicraft shop next door). Sadly, its steeple fell down in a storm in early 2002. There is another 18th century church at Vilopulli, 5 km north. A tourist information kiosk is open in the main plaza in summer.

Sleeping and eating **A** *Posada El Antiguo Chalet*, Gabriela Mistral, T671221. **B** in winter, charming, beautiful location, very good. **B** *Cabañas Amankay*, Centenario 421, T671367. Homely, kitchen facilities. **D** *Huildin*, Centenario 102, T671388. Without bath, old fashioned, good beds, also *cabañas* **A**, garden with superb views, parking. **D** *Hosp Mirador*, Alvarez 198. With breakfast. Recommended. **E** *Esmeralda By The Sea*, on waterfront 100 m south of market, T/F671328/954 (Casilla 79), gredycel@entelchile.net With breakfast, good beds, shared bath, attractive, welcoming, English spoken, boat trips offered, use of internet, bunkhouse for 8, cooking facilities, book exchange, rents bicycles. Highly recommended. **E** *Res Turismo*, Andrade 299, T671257. Without bath, with breakfast. **G** *Sra Fedima*, Aguirre Cerda 176. Own sleeping bag required, use of kitchen, good. **Camping**: *Los Manzanos*, Aguirre Cerda y Juan Guillermo, T671263. **E** per site. For eating, try *La Parada*, Centenario 133. Good selection of wines, erratic opening hours. Recommended. *El Alerce*, Aguirre Cerda 106. Good seafood, excellent value. *El Trébol*, Irrazával 187. Good food and good views.

Shopping Handicrafts from *Opdech* (Oficina Promotora del Desarrollo Chilote), on the waterfront, and from the *parroquia*, next to the church (open Oct-Mar only).

Transport **Buses** and taxis to **Castro**, frequent, US$1, from main plaza. Services to **Quellón** (US$3) and **Queilén** from Castro and Puerto Montt also call here.

Cucao

From Chonchi a road leads west to **Cucao**, 40 km, one of two settlements on the west coast of Chiloé. At Km 12 is Huillinco (road paved), a charming village on Lago Huillinco (**E** pp *Residencia*, good food, or stay at the Post Office). At Cucao there is an immense 15 km beach with thundering Pacific surf and dangerous undercurrents. **E** *Hosp El Arrayan*, T633040, ask for Erice or Ojede. Friendly, good food and restaurant. **E** pp *Hosp Paraíso*, T633040 (Sra Luz Vera), ask for Sra Edvina for horse-hire. **E** pp *Posada Cucao*, T633040, with breakfast, meals. **E** pp with full board or *demi-pension* at *Provisiones Pacífico* (friendly, good, candles provided, no hot water). **E** pp *Casa Blanca*, with breakfast. **E** *Chela*, close to beach and withing walking distance of park, helpful, use of kitchen, good breakfast. There are several campsites including *Parador Darwin*, which also has rooms (**F** pp), breakfast, vegetarian and other meals, real coffee, recommended. *Las Luminarias* sells excellent *empanadas de machas* (local shellfish). For buses from Castro see above; in season as many as four buses a day, last departure 1600, reduced service off-season; hitching is very difficult. Taxi from Chonchi US$4.50.

Parque Nacional Chiloé

The Park, which is in three sections, covers 43,057 ha. Much of the park is covered by evergreen forest. The northern sector, covering 7,800 ha, is reached by a path which runs south from Chepu (see page 701). The second section is a small island, Metalqui, off the coast of the north sector. The southern sector, 35,207 ha, is entered 1 km north of Cucao, where there is an administration centre (limited information), small museum and guest bungalow for use by visiting scientists (applications to Conaf via your embassy). Park entry US$2. No access by car. Maps of the park are available (**NB** *Refugios* are inaccurately located.)

A path runs 3 km north from the administration centre to Laguna Huelde (many camp sites) and then north a further 12 km to Cole Cole (*refugio*, free camping, dirty) offering great views, best done on horseback (return journey to/from Cucao nine hours by horse). The next *refugio* is at Anay, 9 km further north on the Río Anay. There are several other walks but signposting is limited. Many houses in Cucao rent horses at US$2.50 per hour, US$22 per day (check horses and equipment carefully). *Miguelangelo Allende* has been recommended. If you hire a guide you pay for his horse too. Horseflies are bad in summer (wear light coloured clothing).

There are pleasant beaches nearby at Quellón Viejo (with an old wooden church), Punta de Lapa and Yaldad. The launch *Puerto Bonito* sails three times daily in summer from the pier, US$12.50 to tour the bay passing Punta de Lapa, Isla Laitec and Quellón Viejo. A trip can also be made to Chaiguao, 11 km east, where there is a small Sunday morning market. Horses can be hired US$2.50 per hour. Also kayaks with a guide, US$2.50 per hour. Camping US$3.50. **Museo de Nuestros Pasados**, Ladrilleros 255, includes reconstructions of a traditional Chilote house and mill. Tourist kiosk on the Plaza de Armas, ask about *hospedajes* not listed in their information leaflet. ■ *Mid-Dec to mid-Mar.*

Quellón
Phone code: 065
Colour map 9, grid A1
Population: 18,700
92 km S of Castro
Amazing views of the mainland on a clear day

Sleeping and eating B *Melimoyu*, P Montt 375, T681250. Good beds, parking. **C-D** *Playa*, P Montt 427, T681278. Without breakfast or bath, not very clean. **E** pp *Hosp La Paz*, La Paz 370, T681207. With breakfast, hot water. **F** pp *Las Brisas*, P Montt 555, T681413. Without bath, basic. **F** pp *Club Deportes Turino*, La Paz 024. Floor space and camping, cold water, kitchen facilities, basic, open Dec-Feb only. *Albergue*, Ladrilleros, near Carrera Pinto, **F** pp, dormitory accommodation. *Rucantú* on P Montt. Good food, good value. *El Coral*, 22 de Mayo. Good, reasonably priced, superb views. *Fogón Las Quilas*, La Paz 053, T206. Famous for lobster. Recommended. *Los Suizos*, Ladrilleros 399. Swiss cuisine, good, slow service, internet.

Transport **Buses** To **Castro**, 2 hrs, frequent, *Cruz del Sur*, US$3; also services to **Ancud** and **Puerto Montt.Ferries** From Dec to early Mar, the *Navimag* vessel *Alejandrina* sails to **Chaitén** on the mainland, once a week, 5 hrs crossing, US$18 reclining seat, US$15 passenger. *Navimag*, Pedro Montt 457, Quellón, T682207, F682601, www.navimag.com

Directory **Banks** *Banco del Estado*, US$12 commission on TCs, no credit cards, no commission on US$ cash.

The Carretera Austral

Santiago

The Carretera Austral, or Southern Highway, has now been extended south from Puerto Montt to Villa O'Higgins, giving access to the spectacular virgin landscapes of this wet and wild region, with its mountains, fjords and islands, hitherto isolated communities, and picturesque ports. Puyuhuapi is the perfect place to break the journey, but the main town is Coyhaique, and from nearby Chacabuco, boats leave for the magnificent glacier of Parque Nacional Laguna San Rafael.

A third of Chile lies to the south of Puerto Montt, but until recently its inaccessible land and rainy climate meant that it was only sparsely populated and unvisited by tourism. This vast maze of islands separated from the coast by intricate fjord-like channels. Ships were the only means of access and remain important for exporting the timber grown here, and for bringing visitors; see page 697. There is great hiking at **Cerro Castillo** *and* **Ventisquero Colgante**, *white water rafting at* **Futaleufú**, *excellent fishing on the* **Río Baker**, *and thermal springs at* **Chaitén** *and* **Puyuhuapi**, *as well as the unspoilt national parks of* **Hornopirén**, **Queulat** *and* **Parque Pumalín**.

Portal for the Aisén region: www.patagonia chile.cl

Getting there and around This road can be divided into 3 major sections: Puerto Montt-Chaitén, Chaitén-Coyhaique, and Coyhaique-Villa O'Higgins. The road is paved only for about 150 km north and south of Coyhaique, expected to be complete by 2005. Currently, it's 'ripio' (loose stones) and many sections are extremely rough and difficult after rain.

Ins & outs
Buses run along the route three times a week in Jan and Feb, but fill up fast

Chile

Cyclists can't expect to make fast progress and motorists need to carry sufficient fuel and spares, especially if intending to detour from the highway itself, and protect windscreens and headlamps from stones. Unleaded fuel is available as far south as Cochrane. There is now a road between Puerto El Vagabundo and Caleta Tortel, and the Carretera Austral is connected by a free ferry between Puerto Yungay and Río Bravo, where it continues to Villa O'Higgins. So far, there is little infrastructure for transport or accommodation among the tiny rural hamlets, so allow plenty of time for bus connections, and bring cash, as there are few banking facilities along the whole route. Having your own transport here is definitely preferable. Camping will give you more freedom for accommodation, and there are many beautiful sites, though note that food supplies are limited and tend to be expensive.

Best time to visit The landscape throughout the region is lushly green because there is no real dry season. On the offshore islands and the western side of the Andes annual rainfall is over 2,000 mm, though inland on the steppe the climate is drier and colder. Westerly winds are strong, especially in summer, but there's plenty of sunshine too, especially around Lago General Carrera, which has a warm microclimate. Jan and Feb are probably the best months for a trip to this region.

Puerto Montt to Chaitén

This section of the Carretera Austral, 242 km, includes two, sometimes three ferry crossings. Before setting out, it is imperative to check when the ferries are running and, if driving, make a reservation: do this in Puerto Montt (not Santiago), at the *Transmarchilay* office, Angelmó 2187, T600-600 8687. The alternative to this section is by ferry from Puerto Montt or Quellón to Chaitén.

Ranger posts have little information; map available from Conaf in Puerto Montt. No camping within park boundaries

The road (Ruta 7) heads east out of Puerto Montt, through Pelluco and after an initial rough stretch follows the shore of the beautiful Seno Reloncaví. It passes the southern entrance of the **Parque Nacional Alerce Andino**, which contains one of the best surviving areas of alerce trees, some over 1,000 years old (the oldest is estimated at 4,200 years old). Wildlife includes pudú, pumas, vizcachas, condors and black woodpeckers. There are two entrances: 2½ km from Correntoso (35 km east of Puerto Montt) at the northern end of the park (with ranger station and campsite) and 7 km east of Lenca (40 km south of Puerto Montt) at the southern end. There are three other ranger posts, at Río Chaicas, Lago Chapo and Sargazo. ■ *US$5. To north entrance: take* Fierro *or* Río Pato *bus to Correntoso (or Lago Chapo bus which passes through Correntoso), several daily except Sun, then walk. To south entrance: take any* Fierro *bus to Chaicas, La Arena, Contau and Hornopirén, US$1.50, getting off at Lenca sawmill, then walk (signposted).*

Transport At 46 km from Puerto Montt (allow one hour), is the first ferry at **La Arena**, across the Reloncaví Estuary to Puelche. 30 mins, every 1½ hrs, US$10 for a car, US$5 for motorcycle, 0715-2045 daily. Arrive at least 30 mins early to guarantee a place; buses have priority. Roll-on roll-off type operating all year.

Hornopirén
Colour map 9, grid A1
Population: 1,100
58 km S of Puelche

Río Negro is now called **Hornopirén** after the volcano above it. From here you catch the second ferry, to Caleta Gonzalo, one of the centres for the Parque Pumalín (see below). At the mouth of the fjord is **Isla Llancahué**, good for hiking in the forests amid beautiful scenery. *Hotel Termas de Llancahué* charges **A** full board (excellent food), hot spring at the hotel. To get there, make arrangements by phoning T09-653 8345. The hotel will send an open boat for you; the one hour crossing affords views of dolphins and fur seals.

Electricity 1900-0100 **Sleeping and eating** (Electricity 1900-0100). **A** *Holiday Country*, O'Higgins 666, T263062, hot shower, restaurant. *Hornopirén*, Carrera Pinto 388, T255243, at the water's edge.

Transport Buses *Fierro* run daily 0800 and 1500 from **Puerto Montt**. **Ferries** Hornopirén to **Caleta Gonzalo**, *Transmarchilay*, daily 1600, 4 hrs (may be much longer if the ferry cannot dock in rough weather). Going north the ferry leaves Caleta Gonzalo at 0900, daily. Fare for cars US$80 (capacity 21), motorcycles US$16, passengers US$13(capacity 80), bicycles, US$9. Ferry operates Jan-Feb only and can be very busy; there can be a 2-day wait for vehicles to get on the ferry.

Caleta Gonzalo is the entry point for Parque Pumalin for visitors from the north. On the quay is a smart café serving excellent (and pricey) organic food, a visitor centre selling tasteful handicrafts, and cabañas for rent, tiny and perfectly designed, with lake views. The park, created by the US billionaire Douglas Tompkins, is a private reserve of 320,000 ha which has been given Nature Sanctuary status. Covering large areas of the western Andes, with virgin temperate rainforest, the park is spectacularly beautiful, and is seen by many as one of the most important conservation projects in the world. You can visit the model farm, a native tree nursery and an apiculture project, producing delicious honey, sold in the visitor centre. There are several self guided trails, showing examples of ancient alerce trees, rainforest and waterfalls, and exemplary campsites run on strict conservation lines, with well designed picnic shelters and good washing facilities (but no hot water). Cabañas (**AL**), sleep up to 4; meals extra. Camping at several sites US$8 per tent. Information centres: Buin 356, Puerto Montt, T(065) 250079; Fiordo Reñihué, Caleta Gonzalo, T(1712) 196-4151; O'Higgins 62, Chaitén, T(065) 731341. In USA T(415)229-9339, pumalin@earthlink.net

Parque Pumalin

South of Caleta Gonzalo the Carretera Austral winds through the park's beautiful unspoilt scenery, and there is a steep climb on the ripio road to Laguna Blanca, with panoramic views. At Caleta Santa Bárbara, 12 km from Chaitén, there's a wonderful sweeping black sand beach fringed with woodland and with views of the mighty Morro Vilcum, good for swimming and wild camping.

The capital of Palena province, **Chaitén** is rather a bland town and a port for ferries to Puerto Montt and Quellón. Its charms lie in the splendour of its setting, against thickly forested vertical mountains, the dramatic peak of volcano Michimahuida, and the broad open bay of Corcovada. There's great hiking nearby and it's a base for exploring Parque Pumalin. The rustic, open-air thermal pools, **Termas El Amarillo**, in the middle of the beautiful forest, are 25 km away. ■ *Open dawn to 2100, US$3pp, highly recommended, several cabañas nearby.* Despite the growth in adventure tourism, services are still generally poor, bus and boat services sporadic and there are no taxis in town. Most facilities are along the coast road, Av Corcovado, with good views of the bay. There is excellent fishing nearby, especially to the south in the Ríos Yelcho and Futaleufú and in Lagos Espolón and Yelcho (see below). Fishing licences are sold at the Municipalidad on the plaza.

Chaitén
Phone code: 065
Colour map 9, grid A1
Population: 3,258

Sleeping and eating A *Los Coihues*, Pedro Aguirre Cerda 398, T/F731461, coihues@ telsur.cl Spacious, attractive rooms in traditional house, good attention from the owners. Recommended. **A** *Mi Casa*, Av Norte 206, up on hill at end of Diego Portales, T731285, hmicasa@telsur.cl Small pleasant rooms, and fine views from the restaurant which serves good fish, but overpriced. **B** *Brisas del Mar*, Av Corcovada 278, T731266, cababrisas@ telsur.cl Pleasant *cabañas* for 4 to 6 facing sea, but no view, best restaurant in town. **B** *Schilling*, Corcovado 230, T731295. With breakfast, heating, restaurant. **C** *Cabañas Tranqueras del Monte*, Av Norte s/n (head for *Mi Casa* and turn left), T731379, tranquer@telsur.cl Splendid views over bay, well-equipped, comfortable *cabañas*, also **B** rooms, superb breakfasts, charming hosts Doria and Francisco, very knowledgeable, speak perfect English. Also offer a good package to explore the Carretera Austral. Highly recommended. **D** pp *Llanos*, Av Corcovdo 378, T731332. Small place facing the sea with kind owners and lovely rooms, dinner in restaurant (US$5 for 2 courses). Good mechanic next door. **D** pp *Corcovado*, Av Corcovado 408, T731221. Rather superior place, also facing sea, wood panelled rooms with comfortable beds, most with bath, restaurant (US$5 for 2 courses). *Cabañas* for 4 too. **E** pp *Hosp Rita*, Almte Riveros y A Prat, T731502. Warm, Rita runs a great place with comfy beds in whitewashed rooms, good atmosphere, use of kitchen. Recommended.

Chile

Camping *Los Arrayanes*, fabulous setting, right on the sea with great views of Volcán Corcovado, hot showers, and fire places.

Mid-range: *El Flamengo*, Corcovado 218. Family run, plain but good fish dishes, also serves meat. *El Quijote*, O'Higgins 42. More modest, also recommended. *El Triángulo* is cheapest in town, open all day Jan-Feb.

Tour operators Your first port of call in Chaitén should be *Chaitur*, O'Higgins 67, T731429, nchaitur@hotmail.com Run by Nicholas, a charming and helpful North American with information and booking for all buses and boats, and internet access. Excellent, personlised excursions to places far and near: Parque Pumalin, hiking at Ventisqueo Yelcho (astounding white glacier), Santa Bárbara beach, boat excursions, fishing, horses, trekking, mountain biking, very reasonable prices.

Transport Air Flights to **Puerto Montt** with *Aeromet*, daily 1200, 35 mins, US$45. T731844. Book through *Chaitur*. **Buses** Several companies operate minibuses along the Carretera Austral to Coyhaique from next to *Chaitur*, O'Higgins 67: in Jan-Feb up to 6 a week, in winter 2 a week with overnight stop in La Junta or Puyuhuapi. Even in summer, prepare to wait extra days. All details from *Chaitur*, T731429. To **La Junta** US$11, 4 hrs; to **Puyuhuapi** US$13, 5 hrs; to **Coyhaique** US$25, 11 hrs. Buses travel full, so are unable to pick up passengers en route. To **Futaleufú**, US$9, 5 hrs, *Ebenezer* or *Cordillera*, daily Jan-Feb, otherwise 3-4 a week. Ring *Chaitur* from Futaleufú to request. To **Caleta Gonzalo**, daily Jan-Feb 0700 to connect with boats. Hitching the whole route is slow, even in summer.

All boat services vary season to season: check with the local office Reduced service in winter

Ferries Port about 1 km north of town. To **Puerto Montt**, *Catamaranes del Sur*, Av J Todesco 180, T731199, 3 a week, US$40 one way (see under Castro for service to Chiloé). *Navimag*, Carrera Pinto 188, T731571, *Alejandrina* to Puerto Montt Fri 0900, 10 hrs, US$23; on Sat the same ship sails to **Quellón** (Chiloé), 1000, 5 hrs. *Transmarchilay*, Av Corcovado 266, T731272/3, *Pincoya* 3 times a week, to both Puerto Montt and **Castro** (Chiloé).

There is no other ATM between here and Coyhaique

Directory Banks There is one ATM on the plaza, for Maestro, Mastercard and Cirrus, not Visa. *Banco del Estado*, O'Higgins y Libertad, on plaza, changes dollars and TCs in working hours. **Communications** Internet: at the *Entel* office and *Chaitur*. **Tourist offices** In the Municipalidad on the plaza. Better information at *Chaitur*.

Chaitén to Coyhaique

Chileans are rightly proud of this almost virgin stretch of land Don't leave litter, take out all rubbish

This section of the Carretera Austral, runs 422 km though breathtaking and varied scenery, passing tiny villages, most notably the idyllic Puyuhuapi, where there are thermal pools, and good trekking in Parque Nacional Queulat. A road branches off east to the Argentine border, the picturesque Futaleufú, with excellent rafting, and west to Puerto Cisnes.

Puerto Cárdenas, 46 km south of Chaitén, is on the northern tip of **Lago Yelcho**, a beautiful lake on Río Futaleufú surrounded by hills, much loved by anglers for its salmon and trout. Further south at Km 60, a path leads to **Ventisquero Yelcho** (two hours' walk there), a dramatic glacier with high waterfalls. Sleeping at Lago Yelcho, T731337, www.yelcho.cl a smart fishing lodge on banks of the lake with comfortable rooms and *cabañas*, tastefully decorated with views straight to the lake (booked solid Jan-Feb); also attractive campsite, all facilities. Recommended.

At **Villa Santa Lucía**, an uninspiring modern settlement 87 km south of Chaitén, with basic food and accommodation, a road branches east to the Argentine border. There are two crossings: Futaleufú and Palena, both reached from **Puerto Ramírez** past the southern end of **Lago Yelcho**, 24 km east of Santa Lucia. Here the road divides: the north branch runs along the valley of the Río Futaleufú to Futaleufú and the southern one to Palena. The scenery is spectacular, but the road is hard going: single track *ripio*, climbing steeply in places (tough for bikes; allow plenty of time).

Sleeping At Villa Santa Lucía Several places on main street: ask at *Nachito*, the café where the bus stops, which serves good breakfasts. *San Antonio* and *El Trébol*, are basic, but the most recommendable. Another, opposite *Nachito*, is a last resort only. All **D** pp, none has hot water. **At Puerto Ramírez** *Hostería Río Malito*. Rooms, camping, fishing. Also *Hospedaje Las Casas*. Far better to stay in Futaleufú, if plans allow.

Futaleufú
Phone code: 065

This once tranquil border town, 8 km west of the border, is growing into a hugely popular tourist centre. The rickety houses, neatly slatted with *alerce* wood, and spruce vegetable gardens, nestle in a bowl amid steep mountains on the Río Espolón. There is good hiking and some of the most challenging white water rafting in the world on the Río Futaleufú. **Lago Espolón**, west of Futaleufú, reached by a turning 41 km northeast of Villa Santa Lucía, is a beautiful lake in an area enjoying a warm microclimate: 30° C in the day in summer, 5° at night, with excellent fishing at the lake's mouth. Several *cabañas* and campsites. *Banco del Estado* on the plaza has no ATM, but may change cash. Visit the fledgling **tourist office** at O'Higgins and Prat, T721370/721241 for accommodation and maps of walks. Futaleufú to Chaitén: *Transportes Cordillera*, T258633, and *Ebenezer* between them 3-4 times a week, daily January-February.

Sleeping and eating **AL** *El Barranco*, O'Higgins 172, T721314, www.elbarrancochile.com Elegant rustic rooms, luxurious, pool, good restaurant, and expert fishing guides, horses and bikes for hire. **AL** *Río Grande*, O'Higgins y Aldea, T721320, www.exchile.com Also upmarket but not such good value, spacious attractive rooms, international restaurant, popular with rafting groups. **B** pp *Antigua Casona*, Rodríguez y Cerda, T721311, pcoronadop@yahoo.es Very attractive old house, owners speak English and have a delightful country house *Posada Anchileufú*, T721311. **B** Cosy *cabañas* in secluded riverside setting at Río Espolón, T721216, follow Cerda to the end, also recommended parrilla. **D** pp *Hospedaje Adolfo*, O'Higgins 302, T721256, hospedajeadolfo@hotmail.com Best value in this range, very comfortable rooms in

Chile

family home. **F** pp *Continental*, Balmaceda 595, T721222. Oldest in town, without breakfast, basic but welcoming. There are lots of campsites, many beautifully situated on river bank. For fish meals go to rustic *Martín Pescador*, Balmaceda y Rodríguez, T721279. *El Encuentro*, O'Higgins 653, is cheaper and cheerful. *La Antigua Casona* is the best café and bar, cosy and stylish, serving delicious food and wines. *Futaleufú*, Cerda 407. Serves meat dishes and local foods. *El Copihue*, Cerda y Prat. For cheap pizza and pasta.

Tour operators *Centro Aventura Futaleufú* (at *Río Grande* hotel), O'Higgins 397, T721320, www.exchile.com *Austral Excursiones*, Hnos Carrera 500, T721239, www.australexcursiones.cl Both offer rafting, riding, mountain biking and canoeing or kayaking trips. The best horseriding is at *Rancho Las Ruedas*, Pilota Carmona s/n, T721294.

Border with Argentina
If entering from Argentina, no fresh produce may be brought into Chile

Chilean immigration is in Futaleufú. Straightforward crossing. The border is just west of the bridge over the Río Grande. For Argentina immigration, see page 208. Change money in Futaleufú; nowhere to change at the border but you can pay the bus fare to Esquel (Argentina) in US dollars. From west side of plaza in Futaleufú a *Jacobsen* bus runs to the border, three times a week, and daily January-February, US$3, 30 minutes, connecting with services to Trevelin and Esquel. Alternatively, cross into Argentina further south near **Palena**, which is 8 km west of the border and has a Chilean immigration office. *Expreso Yelcho* bus from Chaitén twice weekly in summer, US$12, 5½ hours.

La Junta
Phone code: 067
Population: 1,070

A drab village 151 km south of Chaitén; only stop if desperate to use the service station, where there's a minimarket (selling stove alcohol) and phone. **A** *Hostal Espacio y Tiempo*, T314141, www.espacio-y-tiempo.cl Restaurant, attractive gardens, fishing expeditions. **D** *Hostería Valdera*, Varas s/n, T314105. Includes breakfast, good value. **D** *Res Copihue*, Varas 611, T314184. Without bath, includes breakfast, meals. **D** *Café Res Patagonia*, Lynch 331, T314120. Good meals, small rooms, poor bathrooms. Buses to Coyhaique, six a week January-February, 7 hours, US$12, two a week in winter. To Chaitén, 4 hours, US$11. **Lago Rosselot**, surrounded by forest in the **Reserva Nacional Lago Rosselot**, 9 km east of La Junta, can be reached by a road which continues east, 74 km, to Lago Verde and the Argentine border. *Campo Aventura* have built an outback camp with a 6-km nature trail, all visitors get a free guidebook. Stefan Weidmann runs great 3-15 day sea kayaking trips with *Patagonian Waters*, T314300, see www.southernchilexp.com

Puyuhuapi
Phone code: 067
Population: 500

With the most idyllic setting along the whole Carretera Austral, Puyuhuapi lies in a tranquil bay at the northern end of the Puyuhuapi fjord, 45 km south of La Junta. The blissful thermal pools at **Termas de Puyuhuapi** are nearby. The village was founded by four German-speaking Sudeten families in 1935, and handwoven carpets are still made here by the Hopperditzel brothers, now world renowned. ■ *T325131, www.puyuhuapi.com open daily in summer 0830-1930, closed lunch. English spoken.* This is the best stopping point between Chaitén and Coyhaique with phone, fuel, several shops, but no banking facilities: hotel owners will change dollars. Buses to Coyhaique six times a week in summer, also private minibuses: ask at food shops.

South of Puyuguapi, 24 km, is the **Parque Nacional Queulat**, 154 hectares, most visited for the spectacular hanging glacier **Ventisquero Colgante**. 2.5 km off the road passing the *guardeparques'* house, you'll find parking and camping areas. Three walks begin from here: a short stroll through the woodland to a viewpoint of the Ventisquero, or cross the river where the path begins to Laguna Tempanos, where boats cross the lake in summer. The third, 3.25 km, takes 2½ hours to climb to a panoramic viewpoint of the Ventisquero, where you can watch the ice fall into huge waterfalls like sifted sugar. ■ *Open daily Dec-Mar 0830-2100, rest of year 0830-1830. Entrance US$3, camping US$11 per spot, Conaf campsite with cold showers. Luis Lepio, T325139, runs bus service to park daily if there's demand, Mon to Fri, 1030, also guide for fly fishing.*

Sleeping and eating AL *Hotel Termas de Puyuhuapi* Splendidly isolated on a nook in the sea fjord, the hotel owns the thermal baths: outdoors by the fjord so that you can dive in for a refreshing swim afterwards, or in the lovely indoor spa complex where there are jacuzzis of sea water, good for sufferers of arthritic and skin conditions, expert massage facilities. Good packages for de-stressing with all activities from riding, trekking, mountain biking, yoga and the thermals included. Room price includes use of baths, boat transfer to hotel, full board US$40 extra, excellent restaurant. Guests met at Balmaceda airport, or arrive by boat from Pto Chacabuco, taking in the San Rafael lake and glaciers (US$1000 for 2 for 4 nights, all included). Highly recommended. Reservations: *Patagonia Connection*, Santiago, T225 6489, F274 8111 or directly at the *Hotel Termas de Puyuhuapi*, T/F325103, www.patagonia-connection.com Boats leave frequently from a 2 hrs' walk from town, US$3 each way, 10 mins' crossing. **A** *Cabañas Aonikenk*, Hamburgo 16, T325208. Small cosy *cabañas* for 2-6, by waterfront, friendly owner also runs good little café. **A** *El Pangue*, 18 km north , T325128, www.elpangue.cl Luxurious *cabañas* in splendid rural setting, horseriding, restaurant, trekking, pool, great views, restful. Recommended. **B** *Hostería Alemana*, Otto Uebel 450, T325118, www.hosteria_ alemana@entelchile.net A large traditional wooden house on the water, very comfortable, lovely lake views and garden. Recommended. **B-C** *Casa Ludwig*, Otto Uebel s/n, T/F325220, www.contactchile.cl/casaludwig **C-D** low season. In a beautiful 4-storey house built by first German settlers, with wonderful views of bay, charming owner Luisa offers a range of rooms, including the snug attic with shared bath, good breakfast included, very comfortable; Luisa is knowledgeable about the area, speaks German and English. Highly recommended. **D** pp *Hostería Elizabeth*, Llantureo y Henríquez, T325106. Includes breakfast, homely place. **E** pp *Res Carretera Austral*, Otto Uebel s/n, T325119, F1984661. Economical and pleasant, food shop too. *Café Rossbach*. Run by the descendants of the original German settlers, an attractive place by the water for delicious salmon. The best café, also selling handicrafts is **Lluvia Marina**, next to *Casa Ludwig*, veronet@entelchile.net Superb food in relaxed atmosphere, a great place to just hang out, owner Veronica is very helpful.

At 59 km south of Puyuhuapi, a winding road branches west and follows the Río Cisnes 35 km to **Puerto Cisnes** (*Population*: 1,784), a quiet fishing village at the mouth of the river on Puyuhuapi fjord, set amongst steep mountains. The Río Cisnes, 160 km in length, is recommended for rafting or canoeing, with grand scenery and modest rapids except for the horrendous drop at Piedra del Gato. Good camping in the forest, and fuel is available in the village. **B** *Hostal Michay*, Mistral 112, T346462. **C** *Res El Gaucho*, Holmberg 140, T346514. With bath and breakfast, dinner available, welcoming. **D** *Hosp Bellavista*, Séptimo de Línea 112, T346408. Also various *cabañas*: *Brisas del Sur*, T346587, *Portal del Mar*, T346439, and *Cerro Gilberto*, T346440, all fine. To Coyhaique, *Transportes Terra Austral*, T346757, *Bus Norte*, T346440, run a daily (not Sun) service between them , US$14. **Puerto Cisnes**

At 89 km south of Puyuhuapi is **Villa Amengual** (**E** pp *Res El Encanto*, Fca Castro 33-A, T188-2-1964517). At Km 92 a road branches east, 104 km to La Tapera and to the Argentine border. Chilean immigration is 12 km west of the **border**, open daylight hours only. On the Argentine side the road continues to meet up with Ruta 40, a section with few services for fuel or food.

Coyhaique

A growing centre for tourism, Coyhaique is a busy small town perched on a hill between the Ríos Simpson and Coyhaique. It's good starting point for exploring the Carretera Austral and for trekking and fishing expeditions further afield, as well as booking San Rafael Glacier trips. The **Museo Regional de la Patagonia Central** in the Casa de Cultura traces local history through photos of the first pioneers. ■ *Tue-Sun winter 0830-1300 1430-1830, summer 0900-2100, US$1, Baquedano 310*. From the bridge over the Río Simpson look for the **Piedra del Indio**, a rock outcrop which looks like a face in profile. Just outside the town, the **Reserva Forestal Coihaique** has some beautiful trails for walking or biking, with several

Phone code: 067 *Colour map 9, grid A1* *Population: 43,297* *420 km S of Chaitén* *Get cash here as there are no banks along the Carretera Austral*

picnic grounds and a campsite on the river bank. A satisfying walk is up to Cerro Cinchao, and great views from Sendero Los Leñeros to Laguna Verde. Walk to laguna Verde and Laguna Venus particularly recommended. ■ *Follow Baquedano to the end, over bridge, and past the guardeparque's hut where all the trails begin. Well-marked walks between 20 mins and 5 hrs. Information from Conaf, address below.* Ski centre **El Fraile**, 29km from Coyhaique, is 1599 m above sea level, with 5 pistes, powder snow, in the middle of *ñire* and pine forests (1,000 people capacity).

Sleeping

■ *on map*
Plentiful accommodation is of a higher standard, and more expensive than elsewhere in southern Chile The tourist office has a list

A *Hostal Belisario Jara*, Bilbao 662, T/F234150, www.belisariojara.itgo.com Most distinctive and delightful, an elegant and welcoming small place, with TV and excellent breakfast. Recommended. **A** *El Reloj*, Baquedano 828, T231108, hotelreloj@patagoniachile.cl Tasteful, quiet place with a good restaurant, charming, comfortable wood panelled rooms. **A** *Los Ñires*, Baquedano 315, T232261, F233372. Bland but pleasant place with comfortable rooms, good restaurant. **A** *San Sebastián*, Baquedano 496, T/F233427. Modern, spacious rooms with great views over the Reserva, with breakfast, good value. Recommended. **B** *Hostal Bon*, Serrano 91, T231189. Simple but very welcoming place, with multilingual owner. They also have *cabañas* near Reserva Forestal 1km away. **B** *Cabañas Mirador*, Baquedano 848, T233191. Attractive, well-equipped *cabañas*, also **C** rooms in lovely gardens with panoramic views of the Reserva Forestal, and Río Coyhaique below, great value. Recommended. **D** pp *Hospedaje* at Baquedano 20, T232520, Patricio y Gedra Guzmán. Welcoming, well-maintained, lovely place, simple *cabañas*, with splendid views over the Reserva Forestal, very helpful hosts who speak English, space for camping, access to river, great value. Recommended. **D** *Albergue Las Salamandras*, Sector Los Pinos, 2 km south in attractive forest, T/F211865. Camping, kitchen facilities, winter sports and trekking (Jun-Oct). Recommended.

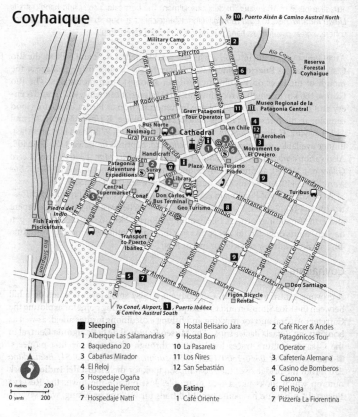

Coyhaique

■ Sleeping	8 Hostal Belisario Jara	2 Café Ricer & Andes
1 Alberque Las Salamandras	9 Hostal Bon	Patagónicos Tour
2 Baquedano 20	10 La Pasarela	Operator
3 Cabañas Mirador	11 Los Ñires	3 Cafetería Alemana
4 El Reloj	12 San Sebastián	4 Casino de Bomberos
5 Hospedaje Ogaña		5 Casona
6 Hospedaje Pierrot	● Eating	6 Piel Roja
7 Hospedaje Natti	1 Café Oriente	7 Pizzería La Fiorentina

0 metres 200
0 yards 200

E pp *Hosp Pierrot*, Baquedano 130, T231315. Hospitable, attractive place homemade bread, internet access. Recommended. **E** *Hosp Natti*, Av Simpson 417, T231047. Good, basic but clean little rooms, laundry next door. **F** pp *Hosp Ogana*, Av Ogana Pasaje 8, 185, T232353. Cooking facilities, with breakfast, helpful, also camping and *cabañas*. **F** *Don Santiago*, Errázuriz 1040, T231116. With parking and kitchen, good value. Many more *hospedajes* and private houses with rooms; ask tourist office for a list.

Cabañas. AL *Los Pinos*, Camino Teniente Vidal, Parcela 5, T234898. Fishing area, near river and beach and natural park. *Don Joaquin Cabañas*, Km 2 Camino Aerodromo, T21453, www.coyhaique.com Attractively built of wood, on banks of Río Simpson, well-equipped, for 4 to 8 people, with TV and full service. **B** *Río Simpson*, T/F232183, (09)8889535 (Mob), Km 3 road to Pto Aisén. Very reasonable for 6, fully equipped, horse hire, fishing. **B-C** *La Pasarela*, T234520, F231215, Km 1.5 Carretera a Aisén. Good atmosphere, *comedor*.

Camping There are many camping sites in Coyhaique and on the road between Coyhaique and Puerto Aisén, eg at Km 1, 2 (**Camping Alborada**, US$8.50 per site, T238868, hot shower), 24, 25, 35, 37, 41, 42 (**Camping Río Correntoso**, T232005, US$15 per site, showers, fishing, *Automobile Club* discount) and 43. Camping in Reserva Forestal, Km 1, towards Puerto Aisen. See above for access details.

Tourist office on plaza or Sernatur in Coyhaique have a full list of all sites in XI Región

Chile

Eating
● *on map*

Mid-range: *Casona*, Obispo Vielmo 77, T238894. Justly reputed as best in town, charming family restaurant serves excellent fish, *congrio* especially, but best known for grilled lamb. *Café Ricer*, Horn 48. Central, warm and cosy, handy meeting place, serving breakfast to dinner, with good vegetarian options. **Cheap**: *Casino de Bomberos* next to the fire station, Gral Parra 365, T231437. For great atmosphere and a filling lunch. Recommended. *Pizzería La Fiorentina*, Prat 230. Tasty pizzas, good service. Recommended. **Cafes and bars**: *Cafe Oriente*, Condell 201. Coyhaique's oldest, was moved on rollers several blocks to its present position, serves a good lunch and tasty cakes. Also recommended for tea and lunch is *Cafetería Alemana*, Condell 119. *Piel Roja*, Moraleda y Condell. Good music, drinking and dancing, popular with Europeans, open Wed, Fri, Sat 1000-0500 for dancing, pub other nights. Recommended.

Shopping

Feria de Artesanía on the plaza. *Artesanía Manos Azules*, Riquelme 435. Sells fine handicrafts. Supermarkets: *Multimas*, Lautaro 339, y Prat. *Central*, Magallanes y Bilbao, open daily till 2230 and at Lautaro y Cochrane. *Brautigam*, Horn 47. Stocks fishing and camping gear.

Tour operators
Tours only operate Dec to Mar

Andes Patagónicos, Horn 48, T/F216711, www.patagoniachile.cl/ap Open 0900-2300 through *Café Ricer*. Inspired and reasonably priced trips, including Caleta Tortel, English spoken, hire cars. Also do tours along Carretera Austral by road 5 day 4 nights, and from Puyuhuapi to an island where you can see *toninas*, little dolphins, staying in a secret place, all diving equipment provided. *Geo Turismo*, E Lillo 315, T237456, www.geoturismopatagonia.cl Impressive range of conventional tours and more specialized tours for photographers, fishing, kayaking, all equipment and expert guides included, horse riding and trekking, English spoken. San Rafael Glacier combined with other destinations, also goes to Caleta Tortel, taking boat from there to Steffens glacier, La Isla de los

Muertos and Jorge Montt glacier. Fly drive holidays from Chaitén or Coyhaique, allowing you to leave the car at the other end, car hire US$75 per day, plus 18% IVA . *Gran Patagonia*, Parra 97, T214770, www.granpatagonia.cl English spoken, can organize Laguna San Rafael by boat and 45 min flights, which leave daily in summer. Also conventional trips. *Patagonia Adventure Expeditions*, Dussen 357, T/F219894, www.adventurepatagonia.com Jonathan and Ian, both English speakers, organize professional adventure tourism, from half day trips to 22 day, multi-environment expeditions. Area of speciality is the Northern Patagonian ice cap, all extended adventures happen there. Also fishing. *Turismo Prado*, 21 de Mayo 417, T231271, www.turismopradopatagonia.cl Good travel agent for flights and excursions, changes money and TCs without commission. Trips to Laguna San Rafael by charter flight, US$200pp, unforgettable 4 hr round trip.

Transport

If renting a car, a high 4WD vehicle is recommended for Carretera Austral. Buy fuel in Coyhaique, several stations

Local Bicycle rental: *Figón*, Simpson y Colón, T234616, check condition first, also sells spares. **Repairs**: *Tomás Madrid Urrea*, Pasaje Foitzich y Libertad, F252132. Recommended. **Car hire**: *Automundo AVR*, Bilbao 510, T231621. *Aysén Tour*, Gral Parra 97, T/F217070. *Ricer Renta Car*, Horn 48, T232920. **Taxis**: US$5 to airport (US$1.65 if sharing). Fares in town US$2, 50% extra after 2100. Taxi colectivos (shared taxis) congregate at Prat y Bilbao, average fare US$0.50.

Long distance Air: Most flights from Balmaceda (see page 716), although Coyhaique has its own airport, Tte Vidal, about 5 km southwest of town. *Don Carlos*, to **Chile Chico** (daily, US$39), **Cochrane** (Mon, Fri, US$70) and **Villa O'Higgins** (Mon, Thu, US$104, recommended only for those who like flying, with strong stomachs, or in a hurry).

Terminal at Lautaro y Magallanes, but few buses use this. Most leave from their own bus company offices

Buses: *Bus Norte*, Gen Parra 337, T251003/232167; *Don Carlos*, Subteniente Cruz 63, T232981; *Suray*, A Prat 265, T238387; *Daniela*, Baquedano 1122, T231701; *Hernández*, 12 de Octubre 337, T254600; *Turibus*, Baquedano 1259, T231333. *Bus Sur*, José Menéndez 565, T241708. *Acuario 13*, Terminal, T232067/240990; *Los Ñadis*, Terminal, T211460. Full list of buses from tourist information.

To/from **Puerto Montt**, via Bariloche, all year, *Turibus*, Tue and Sat 1700, US$46, with connections to Osorno, Santiago and Castro, often heavily booked. *Queilen Bus*, T240760, goes to Puerto Montt, Osorno, Ancud, Castro, once a week. To **Punta Arenas** via Coyhaique Alto, *Bus Sur*, Mon and Thu 1030, US$40 . To **Puerto Aisén**, minibuses run every 45 mins, 1 hr *Suray* and *Don Carlos*, US$2, connections for **Puerto Chacabuco**. To **Puerto Ibáñez** on Lago Gen Carrera, several minibus companies (connect with ferry to Chile Chico) pick up 0530-0600 from your hotel, 3 hrs, book the day before (eg *Sr Parra*, T251073, *Don Tito*, T250280), US$7.

Minibuses along the Carretera Austral always full; book early. Bikes can be taken by arrangement

Buses on the **Carretera Austral** vary according to demand: north to **Chaitén**, *Bus Norte* and *Daniela* (T231701), between them 6 days a week, US$25 ; in winter these stop overnight in La Junta, only northbound buses stop at Pto Aisén. To **Puerto Cisnes**, *Terra Austral* (T254335), Mon-Fri, US$14. South to **Cochrane** daily in summer with either *Don Carlos*, *Acuario 13*, or *Los Ñadis*, US$20. All buses stop at **Cerro Castillo**. (US$5), **Bahía Murta** (US$10), **Puerto Tranquilo** (US$11) and **Puerto Bertrand** (US$15).

To Argentina: *Giobbi*, T232067, at Terminal Municipal, runs buses **Comodoro Rivadavia**, US$27, 0930, arrives 2000, passes Sarmiento 1830. Daily buses from Com Rivadavia to Bariloche. Other options are given under Balmaceda and Chile Chico. Many border posts close at weekends.

Shipping: *Navimag*, Ibáñez 347, T233306, F233386. *Skorpios*, Parra 21, T213755, www.skorpios.cl *Transmarchilay*, Parra 86, T231971.

Directory

Airline offices *LanChile*, Moraleda 402 y Parra, T231188. *Don Carlos*, Subteniente Cruz 63, T231981. *Aerohein*, Baquedano 500, T232772. **Banks** *Banco Santander*, Condell 100, MasterCard and Visa ATM. Best *casa de cambio*: Turismo Prado, see Tour operators. *Emperador*, Bilbao 222, T233727. **Communications** Internet: *Cyber Patagonia*, 21 de Mayo y Condell. Cheap, good. Another branch at Prat 360, p 2. Others in centre. Post Office: Cochrane 202. **Telephone**: *Entel*, Prat 340, also has internet access, US$1.35 per hr. **Language schools** *Baquedano International Language School*, Baquedano 20, at *Hospedaje* of Sr Guzmán (see Sleeping), T232520, www.patagoniachile.cl/com/bils US$300 per week course including lodging and all meals, 4 hrs a day one-to-one tuition, other activities organized at discount rates. **Tourist offices** In the bright green cabin in the plaza, helpful, with details on buses and accommodation. *Sernatur* office (less helpful), Bulnes 35, T231752 www.sernatur.cl, www.patagoniachile.cl, or email sernatur_coyhai@entelchile.*Mon-Fri 0830-2100, Sat & Sun 1100-2000. Conaf*, los Coigues s/n T212125, aysen@conaf.cl

A 43-km road runs east to this crossing. On the Argentine side the road leads through Río Mayo and Sarmiento to Comodoro Rivadavia. Chilean immigration is at Coyhaique Alto, 6 km west of the border, open May-August 0800-2100, September-April 0700-2300.

Border with Argentina: Coyhaique Alto

Puerto Aisén and Puerto Chacabuco

The paved road between Coyhaique and Puerto Aisén passes through **Reserva Nacional Río Simpson**, which has beautiful waterfalls, lovely views of the river and very good fly-fishing. Administration is at the entrance; campsite opposite the turning to Santuario San Sebastián, US$5.

Phone code: 067
Colour map 9, grid A1
Population: 13,050
426 km S of Chaitén

    Puerto Aisén is 65 km west of Coyhaique at the meeting of the rivers Aisén and Palos. Formerly the region's major port, it has been replaced by Puerto Chacabuco, 15 km to the west, and though it remains an important centre for services, there's little of interest to the visitor. It's also very wet. In summer, the *Apulcheu* sails regularly down the **Aisén Fjord** to **Termas de Chiconal**, a spectacular two hour trip by boat, US$30 – book in *Sernatur* (Gobernación, Esmeralda 810, T332562), or *Tursimo Rucaray*, Tte Merino 840, T332862.

    The longest suspension bridge in Chile and a paved road lead to **Puerto Chacabuco** 15km away; a regular bus service runs between the two. The harbour, rather a charmless place, is a short way from the town.

www.portchacabuco. cl, gives information on shipping movements

Sleeping in Puerto Aisén Most recommended place to stay is **B** *Caicahues*, Michimalonco 660, T335680. **C** *Hosp San Jorge*, Ramírez y Serrano Montaner, T333587. Also pleasant. **D** *Hosp Luisa*, Av Municipal 546, T332719. Good, welcoming. **D** *Res Serrano Montaner*, Montaner 471, T332574. Very pleasant and helpful. Recommended. **E** pp *Hosp Marclara*, Caupolicán 970, T333030. Good value. There are several places to eat along Tte Merino and Aldea. **In Puerto Chacabuco** **AL** *Hotel Loberías del Sur* , José Miguel Carrera 50, T351115. Comparatively luxurious, the restaurant serves the best food in the area (owned by *Catamaranes del Sur*, see Shipping, below). **A** *Cabañas El Mirador*, Fundo San Andrés en Circunvalación s/n, T353232. Cabins for 5, very comfortable and recommended. **D** pp *Hosp La Estrella*, José Miguel Carrera 412, T351127. Also pleasant, good value.

Sleeping & eating
Accommodation is hard to find, most is taken up by fishing companies in both ports

Buses To **Puerto Chacabuco**, *Don Carlos* and *Suray* every 30 mins to 1 hr, US$1. To **Coyhaique**, *Don Carlos* minibuses 8 daily, *Suray* minibuses hourly, both US$2, 1 hr journey. **Ferries** *Navimag's Edén* sails each Tue and Fri from Puerto Chacabuco to Puerto Montt, taking about 24 hrs (fares given under Sea routes south of Puerto Montt, page 697). It diverts from its schedule in summer to run a 5-day trip from Puerto Montt to Laguna San Rafael, calling at Puerto Chacabuco, fares US$252 double in cabin, US$168 for a seat. *Catamaranes del Sur* also have sailings to Laguna San Rafael, US$472-525 pp in double cabin, depending on season. **Shipping Offices:** *Agemar*, Tte Merino 909, T332716, Puerto Aisén. *Catamaranes del Sur*, J M Carrera 50, T351112, www.catamaranesdelsur.cl *Navimag*, Terminal de Transbordadores, Puerto Chacabuco, T351111, F351192. *Transmarchilay*, Av O'Higgins s/n, T351144, Puerto Chacabuco. It is best to make reservations in these companies' offices in Puerto Montt, Coyhaique or Santiago. For trips to Laguna San Rafael, see below (page 698).

Transport

Banks *Banco de Crédito*, Prat, for Visa. *Banco de Chile*, Plaza de Armas,changes cash, not TCs. **Communications** **Post Office:** on south side of bridge. **Telephone:** on south side of Plaza de Armas, next to *Café Rucaray*, which posts boat information and has internet. *Entel*, Aldea 1202. Internet access.

Directory for Puerto Aisén

Chile

South of Coyhaique

The southernmost section of the Carretera Austral, 443 km, ends at Villa O'Higgins and is the wildest and most dramatic, with beautiful unspoilt landscapes around Lago General Carrera. The fairy tale peaks of Cerro Castillo offer challenging trekking, and there's world class fishing in the turquoise waters of Río Baker. A road runs off to Puerto Ibañez for lake crossings to Chile Chico, a convenient border crossing to Argentina.

Balmaceda From Coyhaique, the Carretera Austral heads south past huge bluffs, through deforested pasture and farmsteads edged with *alamo* trees, before entering flatter plains and rolling hills. At around Km 41, a paved road runs east to **Balmaceda** on the Argentine border at Paso Huemules (no accommodation). Chilean immigration is open May-July 0800-2000, September-April 0730-2200.

Transport Air: Balmaceda airport is used by *Lan Chile* and *Sky* for flights from **Santiago** via **Puerto Montt** for Coyhaique, and once a week to Punta Arenas. *Don Carlos* flies to **Chile Chico** US$41. Airlines run connecting bus services to/from Coyhaique, US$2 (leave town 2 hrs before flight). Minibuses to/from hotels, US$4.50, several companies including Hernán Valencia T233030, Transfer AM T250119. Taxi from airport to Coyhaique, 1 hr, US$6. **Buses** Daily to Coyhaique, 0800, US$1.70.

Puerto Ibáñez The Carretera Austral starts to climb again, past the entrance to the Reserva Nacional Cerro Castillo (see below). It winds up through the attractive narrow gorge of Río Horqueta, to a pass between Cerro Castillo and its neighbours, before dropping down a 6-km slalom into the breathtaking valley of Rio Ibáñez. (This is currently the most southerly paved section and the road is safe and wide here). Here the road forks east to Puerto Ibáñez, a further 31 km away, for the ferry crossing of vast Lago General Carrera.

Puerto Ibáñez (*Population*: 828) is the principal port on the Chilean section of the lake, a nondescript place you'll probably just pass through to reach the ferry. There are various hotels (**D-E** eg **E** *Vientos del Sur*, Bertrán Dixon 282, T 423208, good; *Cabañas Shehan Aike*, Luis Risopatrón y Aiba Contreras, T(067)423284, 200 m from the beach, English and German spoken), also a campsite, but no other services. Fuel (sold in 5-litre containers) is available at Luis A Bolados 461 (house with 5 laburnum trees outside). Most shops and restaurants are closed on Sunday. There are some fine waterfalls, the Salto Río Ibañez, 6 km north.

Transport Minibus: to Coyhaique, 2½ hrs, US$7. There is a road to **Perito Moreno**, Argentina, but no public transport. **Ferries** The car ferry, *Chelenco*, sails from Puerto Ibañez to **Chile Chico**, daily in summer, 3 times a week otherwise, US$3 per adult, US$1.50 for bikes, cars US$45, uncomfortable 2½ hr crossing, take food and warm clothing, as the ferry is completely open. Passports required, reservations possible (*Sotramin*, Portales 99, Coyhaique, T233515). At the quay, *Café El Refugio* has toilets and sells sandwiches and snacks. Minibuses meet the ferry in Puerto Ibáñez for Coyhaique, and buses meet the ferry in Chile Chico for Los Antigos, see page 719.

Villa Cerro Castillo From the turning to Puerto Ibáñez the Carretera Austral goes through **Villa Cerro Castillo** (Km 8), a quiet village in a spectacular setting beneath the striking, jagged peaks of **Cerro Castillo**, overlooking the broad valley below. There's a petrol station, public phone, several food shops and a tiny **tourist information** kiosk by the road side (Jan Feb only), with details of guides offering trekking to the Cerro, among them Jorge Aguilar and Francisco Calderón.

The village is a good place to stop for a few days with two appealing attractions. There's a truly spectacular 4-day trek around the fairytale castle peaks of Cerro Castillo, in the **Reserva Nacional Cerro Castillo**, whose entrance is 64 km south of